MARKETING MANAGEMENT IN THE 21ST CENTURY

Noel Capon

Professor of Business
Graduate School of Business, Columbia University

James M. Hulbert

Kopf Professor of International Marketing
Graduate School of Business, Columbia University

Upper Saddle River, New Jersey 07458

Library of Congress Cataloging-in-Publication Data

Capon, Noel.
    Marketing management in the 21st Century / Noel Capon and James Mac Hulbert.
        p.   cm.
    Includes index.
    ISBN 0-13-915695-X
        1. Marketing—Management.   I. Title: Marketing management in the twenty-first
    century.   II. Hulbert, James M.

HF5415.13.C265 2000
658.8—dc21
                                                                        00-040643

Senior Editor: Whitney Blake
VP/Editorial Director: James Boyd
Assistant Editor: Anthony Palmiotto
Editorial Assistant: Melissa Pellerano
Senior Marketing Manager: Shannon Moore
Marketing Assistant: Kathleen Mulligan
Managing Editor (Production): John Roberts
Senior Production Editor: M.E. McCourt
Permissions Coordinator: Suzanne Grappi
Associate Director, Manufacturing: Vincent Salta
Production Manager: Arnold Vila
Manufacturing Buyer: Diane Peirano
Design Manager: Pat Smythe
Senior Designer: Cheryl Asherman
Interior Design: Jill Yutgowitz
Cover Design: Amanda Wilson
Illustrator (Interior): Electragraphics, Inc.
Manager, Print Production: Christy Mahon
Full-Service Project Management: Graphic World Publishing Services
Printer/Binder: Courier, Westford

Credits and acknowledgments borrowed from other sources and reproduced, with permission, in this textbook appear on the appropriate page within text.

Reprinted with corrections May, 2001.

10 9 8 7 6 5 4 3 2
ISBN 0-13-915695-X

To our mentors, the late Professors John Howard and Abraham Shuchman

Brief Contents

v

Contents

Preface

This book is about developing market strategy and managing the marketing process. One of the ways in which it differs from so many other introductory graduate-level marketing texts is that it focuses on what the prospective manager needs to know. It is unashamedly normative in emphasis, for marketing is an applied field, and we focus on the manager, not just the marketer. It is the responsibility of text writers to provide the guidance necessary for good practice. For those of you committed to a career in marketing, and we hope there are many, this book will form a solid foundation as you continue your marketing studies. However, the vast majority of you will not work in marketing departments; in many cases you have aspirations to be general managers and CEOs. We write for you also, because an appreciation and understanding of marketing is central to virtually every important decision that managers make.

Marketing activity is at the core of managing a business; it provides the focus for interfacing with customers and is the source of intelligence about customers, competitors, and the business environment in general. Marketing is concerned with the long-term relationships of the firm with its customers as well as short-term sales activity. In this era of such managerial concerns as quality management, downsizing, reengineering, and outsourcing, marketing has become a major organizational thrust rather than just a task assigned to a single functional department. This book emphasizes the role of marketing in creating value for customers. Successful creation of customer value in turn leads to the creation of value for other firm stakeholders, including shareholders and employees.

OUR CUSTOMERS: STUDENTS

For student readers, this book provides an introduction to the role of marketing in the modern corporation, both at the level of the firm and the marketing function. The book focuses on providing a set of concepts and ideas for approaching marketing decisions, on providing a common language with which to think about marketing issues, and on the structuring and analysis of managerial problems in marketing. It prepares future general managers and CEOs to deal with core marketing issues by providing a way of thinking strategically about the firms' products, services, and markets and represents what the general manager must know about marketing.

At the conclusion of this book, students should have developed frameworks for analyzing markets, customers, competitors, and complementers, and for approaching marketing problems. They should be able to develop market strategy and implementation programs comprising the 4Ps and an S (also termed the *marketing mix*) of product, price, place, promotion and service, in a variety of contexts—domestic/international, products/services, industrial/consumer, private/public sector, and not-for-profit.

As students work through this book they are expected to develop a high tolerance for ambiguity, a quality of all successful general managers. You will learn that there are no right or wrong answers to marketing problems, just some that are better than others. There are no simple (or even complex) formulae in which to plug a set of numbers and secure the "right" answer. Instead, students learn to approach complex and unstructured marketing problems in a creative and measured way.

OUR CUSTOMERS: MARKETING FACULTY

For marketing faculty, this book offers a contemporary perspective on marketing in the modern corporation. It also includes material that is not typically covered in marketing texts, such as an emphasis on the real "bottom line" of marketing activities, shareholder value. By understanding and acting upon the principles developed in this book, students will avoid the many pitfalls of competing in an increasingly global, complex, and competitive environment and be able to enhance shareholder value for their organizations, large and small, even though their work may involve marketing in many different countries around the world. These, after all, should be the goals for which marketing educators strive.

The book achieves its purpose by stating a set of behaviorally based learning objectives for each chapter, and then providing material to achieve those objectives. In addition, the device of contrasting "old way versus new way" is employed to provide a sense of the changing role of marketing in the modern corporation. Each chapter concludes with a set of provocative questions designed to make students think about marketing rather than view marketing as a cut and dried topic.

Learning how to think in the appropriate way to deal with marketing problems requires a considerable degree of effort from both faculty and students. In order to provide students with the opportunity to develop skills in marketing problem solving we recommend that this book be used in conjunction with a set of case studies chosen by each instructor. In addition, with this book, faculty are provided access to an Instructors Manual and a set of overhead transparencies.

WHAT MAKES THIS BOOK UNIQUE

In this section we present the Capon and Hulbert "top ten" list, highlighting those areas in which the book differs from other offerings.

One: As noted above, the book has a normative focus. As such, it takes a position on what should, and what should not, be appropriate courses of action. We believe that readers should know where we stand and what we believe is right.

Two: We emphasize the important link between product markets and capital markets. We make the product/market–capital/market relationship explicit and show how world-class marketing decision making must always consider capital market implications.

Three: The book attempts to reflect the structural realities of the modern economy. For example, we are conscious of the fact that in advanced economies, services account for upwards of 70% of GNP, and that advances in telecommunications and computers are changing the nature of the marketing function for many organizations. This reality is reflected in the text; we discuss the Internet throughout, as well as devoting Chapter 21 to the topic.

Four: We treat the marketing mix as we feel it should be treated, as the means to implement the product/market strategy. We believe that other critical questions must necessarily precede decisions about marketing mix elements. Among them: What is the essential role of marketing in the corporation? What is the appropriate role of marketing for increasing shareholder value? What is a market strategy, and how do you know if your market strategy is complete? Why are brands important and what are the key issues involved in developing a branding strategy? Only after such questions have been resolved should marketing implementation decisions be made.

Five: The book introduces what we believe are a number of genuinely new ideas drawn from our most recent research and writings, which directly address the dramatic and rapid changes that are taking place in marketing today.

Six: We tend to avoid descriptive data about the institutions that conduct marketing activities. It is not that we believe it is unimportant for students to understand the institutional framework within which marketing activity is conducted. Rather, because the environment is changing so quickly, students should understand that marketing institutions are themselves a variable, certainly changing in the medium and long run (and possibly in the short run also). In addition, marketing institutions vary from country to country around the world. In writing for students who will be competing in a global marketplace, we have chosen to focus on ways of thinking about marketing issues that are enduring and that transcend institutional differences.

Seven: Although consumer marketing is a critically important area, we balance our discussion of consumers as targets for marketing effort with considerable emphasis on organizations, for example, firms and governments, as customers. Indeed, some of the more interesting developments in marketing practice today are concerned with organizational marketing.

Eight: We have not included chapters on International Marketing, Marketing Research or Marketing Information Systems; rather, this material has been integrated throughout the text. Regarding international marketing, we believe strongly that the fundamental underpinnings of marketing are consistent regardless of country setting and, consequently, throughout the book, have made a concerted attempt to be global in outlook. Many leading firms are now developing product and branding strategies on a global basis and are scrapping their geographic-based organizational structures and processes in favor of truly global organizations. Furthermore, the Internet is breaking down national barriers.

Nine: Our intention is to give you only what you really need, when you need it, by taking care of some of the sorting tasks and saving you time and effort.

Ten: We firmly believe that graduate study in marketing should include significant student experience in facing marketing problems via case-method or simulation approaches. However, we also believe that instructors should feel free to search the many case libraries, rather than be constrained to a set of cases included with the text. Our goal has been to write a world-class marketing textbook.

The focus of our efforts is aimed squarely at the challenges facing managers in for-profit business organizations. However, we also believe this book will prove useful to those interested in not-for-profit and public sector marketing. We believe that the vast majority of the concepts we discuss are readily transferable to these other sectors; the major difference concerns organizational objectives. In the for-profit sector, objectives are unambiguously concerned with profit and shareholder value; in the not-for-profit and public sectors, organizational objective setting is often a complex undertaking.

AUTHORS

The authors are long-time tenured faculty at one of the world's leading Graduate Schools of Business, at Columbia University. Individually, they have won excellence in teaching awards from Columbia University and the Graduate School of Management,

UCLA and, in addition to teaching in the United States, have taught or held visiting faculty positions in Australia (Monash University), Brazil (Fundacao Joao Pinheiro), England (Bradford Management Centre, Henley Management College, London Business School), France (INSEAD, University of Grenoble), Greece (The Athens Laboratory of Business Administration), Hong Kong (The Hong Kong University of Science and Technology), Iran (The Industrial Management Institute), the People's Republic of China (China European International Business School) and Wales (Cardiff Business School).

Both authors are frequently called on by major corporations around the world for consultation and educational assignments. For over 20 years, Mac Hulbert has been director of Columbia's Marketing Management Program. Noel Capon, a former associate director of this program, is currently director of Columbia's Competitive Marketing Strategy, Key Account Management, Sales Management, and Senior Sales Executive programs.

ACKNOWLEDGMENTS

We thank our colleagues at the Graduate School of Business, Columbia University, for providing the stimulating environment that helped us develop and test many of the ideas presented in this book. In particular, we thank Professors Michel Pham and Bernd Schmitt for providing insightful feedback on drafts of the book and acknowledge the roles played by the late Abe Shuchman, who emphasized the importance of educating practicing managers, and the late John A. Howard, who for many years provided leadership in marketing and created an environment within which a variety of ideas and philosophies could flourish. Second, we thank our many students who, over the years, have challenged us to refine and sharpen our ideas. In addition to MBA and Executive MBA students, we include participants in both open enrollment and in-company executive programs. As our own work with companies has shifted from education *qua* education to the very real challenges of organizational change, these students, including many CEOs, have involved us in attempting to resolve key marketing issues vital to effective corporate functioning. Third, we wish to acknowledge our many friends in industry whose ideas have, in their different ways, made valuable contributions to our thinking. These include William K. Brandt, Robert Christian and Bob Pratt. In addition, Jefferson Freeman, Gwen Ortmeyer, and Hastings Read read the entire manuscript and provided valuable feedback. Fourth, we wish to thank several of our Columbia colleagues who gave freely of their time to comment on individual chapters: Andrew Gershoff—Chapter 17, Sunil Gupta—Chapter 6, Kamel Jedidi—Chapter 13, Gita Johar—Chapters 4 and 14, Don Lehmann—Chapter 12, Francoise Simon—Chapter 11 and John Zhang—Chapter 18. In addition, Tony Carter—Chapter 15 and Liam Fahey—Chapter 5 were extremely helpful. Another helpful colleague was Enrique Arzac. Ellen Capon read the book from cover to cover and provided valuable customer-oriented feedback from the perspective of an entering MBA student. Fifth, we acknowledge our colleagues Pierre Berthon, Professor of Marketing at the University of Bath, Great Britain, and Leyland Pitt, Curtin University, Australia, who provided the basis for Chapter 21, on the Internet. Finally, we should like to thank those Prentice Hall staff who have supported and encouraged us along the way, including Kate Moore, Sales Representative; Whitney Blake, editor; Mary Ellen McCourt, production editor; Shannon Moore, marketing manager; and Anthony Palmiotto, assistant editor.

We would also like to thank the following reviewers: Sandy Becker, Rutgers University; Jim Murrow, Drury University; Bill Gray, Keller Graduate School of Management; Ron Lennon, Barry University; Andrew Yap, Florida International University; and Paul McDevitt, University of Illinois, Springfield.

Finally, we acknowledge a debt to our respective spouses who, as active professionals, know full well the commitment necessary to complete a major writing assignment such as this.

Noel Capon
Professor of Business
Chair of Marketing Division
Graduate School of Business
Columbia University

James M. Hulbert
Kopf Professor of International Marketing
Graduate School of Business
Columbia University

CHAPTER

1

INTRODUCTION TO MARKETING MANAGEMENT

LEARNING OBJECTIVES

When you have completed this chapter, you will understand

- the purpose and organization of this book

- why marketing is so important to the future of business organizations

- the relationship between success in product markets and success in capital markets

- the critical role that the objective of enhancing shareholder value plays in marketing decision making

- the various meanings that can be applied to the term *marketing*

- the constant evolution of the practice of marketing

- the six tasks of strategic marketing

- the four principles for developing marketing strategy

INTRODUCTION

This chapter presents the case for why marketing is needed, taking pains to link success in capital markets with success in product markets. It examines the various meanings of marketing and explores why marketing must change and why traditional approaches no longer suffice. The six tasks of strategic marketing are then presented. These are the jobs that must be completed effectively for the firm to deliver value to the appropriate set of customers and hence optimize shareholder value. This chapter concludes by identifying a set of four principles for developing and implementing market strategy. Finally, it explains the chapter organization of the book, much of which centers around the six strategic marketing tasks.

WHY MARKETING?

"Why marketing?" is a simple but important question. Economics, the social science that studies resource allocation under scarcity, can be used to answer theoretical questions. A variety of applied fields, including logistics, finance, operations management, and sales, can handle the practicalities of supplying goods and services to customers. Thus it is certainly legitimate to ask why we need marketing. The answer lies in the profound structural changes that increasingly characterize the world economy. Simply put, the widespread economic success from the 1950s forward has driven increasing numbers of country economies from scarcity of supply to scarcity of demand. As affluence rises and an increasing portion of consumer spending becomes discretionary, it becomes a correspondingly greater challenge to induce consumers to purchase. Furthermore, whereas in low-level economies the scope of competition for the consumer dollar is limited, competition expands dramatically as more purchases become discretionary. Selecting between a new computer and a European vacation may seem a rather absurd notion, but in high-level economies, inter-sectoral choices are a reality for more and more consumers and corporations. Finally, as competition among sellers becomes more intense, customer focus moves from being desirable to being absolutely necessary. Customers, consumer and organization, are inexorably taking center stage in the organization of business activities, and increasing numbers of articles concerning customer-based re-organizations are appearing in the business press.[1]

Marketing and the Profit Motive

When teaching groups of executives we sometimes ask the question: "What are you in business for?" After the initial silence that greets such a fundamental and seemingly irrelevant question, the responses typically center on profit and profitability. Leaving aside the issues of profit measurement and time horizon that so often bedevil the translation of this goal into reality, the almost universal focus on profit raises two other critical questions: First, why is securing profits important? Second, what is the basic prerequisite for earning profits?

The reasons for securing profits often depend on who is answering the question: owner/managers, independent shareholders, or non-owner/managers. For example, for most corporate managers owning little or no stock in the company, the ultimate organizational goals are typically growth and survival as an independent entity.[2] Organizational survival increases the probability of their individual economic well-being, while growth may both increase the chances of firm survival and provide opportunities for career advancement.[3] By contrast, independent shareholders are most likely concerned with the production of economic value; after all, economic value enhances shareholder wealth.[4] In the near term, however, for both independent shareholders and owner/managers, organizational survival may be the critical objective. Certainly, for the over 100,000 business entities (mostly owner-managed) that fail each year in the U.S., and the many more that fail around the world, survival must be ensured before increasing shareholder value becomes a meaningful objective.[5]

A critical conflict between organizational survival and growth, and economic value, arises for owner/managers when greater value can be secured by having the firm cease to operate as an independent entity. Allowing the firm to be acquired may produce greater immediate value than continued independent operations over the long run.[6] The conflict between corporate managers and independent shareholders is often most evident when hostile takeover bids are contemplated. Managers, especially those who own few shares in the firm, are more inclined to value organizational survival whereas independent shareholders favor immediate value production.[7] In capitalist systems, owners' rights are generally regarded as primary among the various stakeholders; as a result, the owners' interests usually prevail.[8]

Capital Markets and Product Markets

The foregoing discussion should have clarified the principle that generating value for shareholders is a key requirement for firms capitalized in the financial markets. These markets are remorselessly competitive, for capital is the ultimate fungible resource, flowing at the touch of a button from one instrument, or even country, to another. Managers facing competitive pressures in product markets sometimes forget that unless senior management ensures that the firm remains competitive financially, its very survival will be jeopardized.

Shareholder value is, to a large extent, driven by expectations of future profit performance. All things being equal, if the capital markets anticipate high future profits, shareholder value increases; conversely, if low future profits are anticipated, shareholder value decreases. Of course, anticipation of future profit performance is based on many factors. From time to time, some firms, especially those in the high technology sector, enjoy significant shareholder value without ever making a profit. Perhaps, however, the most widely employed indicator of future profits is the consistency of past and current profits.

Achieving consistently high profit levels clearly increases the chances of firm survival over the long term. This does, however, leave unanswered a more fundamental question: "What is the basic prerequisite for making profits?" Asked another way:

- What must be done to produce the profits necessary to ensure organizational survival, growth, and enhanced shareholder value?
- What key assets must be present to generate these profits?

To answer these questions, attention must be shifted from capital markets to product markets.

The most obvious place to search for these critical assets is on the firm's balance sheet: cash, accounts receivable, inventory, land, plant and equipment, and so forth. Each of these assets may play a role in helping to produce profits, but quite frequently the asset *per se* may not be essential for this purpose. For example, accounts receivable are of little value if the customer cannot pay; nor is inventory (finished goods, raw materials, work in process) of use if there is no market for the products; nor is plant and equipment for making these unwanted products. In fact, the situation may be more serious inasmuch as balance sheet assets may function as strategic liabilities. If a firm with significant investment in plant and equipment to make products for a particular market is faced with a sudden shift in demand, management may be best advised immediately to write off its "investment" and address some new and more promising opportunity. Too often, however, the prior investment acts as an inertial force, binding the firm to an historic strategy and slowing its market response. By contrast, a new entrant unburdened by such asset baggage may be able to move faster and secure significant advantage over its better-established but slower-moving rival.

Example: During the 1980s, many executives around the word viewed IBM as the best-managed company in the world. However, the computer market leader consistently under-funded its entry into personal computers, preferring to devote its major efforts to mainframes, where it had major capital, human, and market investments. This strategic decision not only resulted in Microsoft securing a stranglehold on operating system software, but also allowed the extensive growth of such PC start-ups as Compaq, Dell, Gateway, and Packard Bell. From 1982 to 1990, only once were IBM's profits below $4 billion; profits were over $6 billion three times, including 1990. In 1991, 1992, and 1993, IBM's losses were, respectively, $2.8 billion, $5.0 billion, and $8.1 billion! By contrast, shortly after Netscape's entry into Internet browser software, Microsoft wrote off a $100 million investment in software development as it sought to catch up to and surpass its new rival. More recently, the assets of many "bricks and mortar" companies have caused them difficulties in competing with Internet start-ups. Interestingly, many of these start-ups that enjoy high shareholder value, such as Yahoo! and Amazon.com, have little in the way of fixed assets.

The only asset the firm really needs over the long run is paying customers. Customers are the sole source of sales revenues; all firm activities are costs. Viewed a little differently, it is the ability of the accounting "assets" to contribute to revenue generation that makes them assets, not their historical acquisition cost less cumulative depreciation. Thus, if the firm has customers, it has revenues; if revenues exceed costs, it makes profits. It is the presence of customers that allows the firm to secure whatever operating assets it requires to produce goods and services. If the firm has current customers (or good potential prospects), it can typically obtain the capital, real estate, data-processing equipment, people, and so forth, necessary to produce (or otherwise secure), finance, and deliver the goods and services. From this perspective, customers are a necessary condition for the production of profits, and are therefore the most important identifiable "asset".[9]

The vital implication of this reasoning is that creating and retaining customers is not only a necessary condition for current and future profits, but is also critical for organizational survival and growth, and for creating shareholder value. To the extent that the firm's value-creating potential is measured by its market value, market value represents the firm's perceived ability to attract and retain customers over the long run. This is the central job that management must accomplish successfully. If management performs its job well, profits result.[10] Hence profits become not only a means of enhancing survival prospects, but also a measure of how well management is performing its most basic task. Current and potential profits provide the crucial link between performance in product markets and performance in capital markets. Using this logic, the difference between the firm's market value and the book value of its assets is a measure of management's value added.

Of course, this does not mean that the firm should indiscriminately accept all those who wish to become its customers. Some customers may be costly to maintain; others may fall outside the firm's business scope, and others may not be able to pay. Better to invest resources in selecting customers who will pay than engage in sophisticated bad debt management! As explored later, selecting groups of potential customers (targeting) is one of the key elements in strategic marketing and a hallmark of firms that practice marketing well.

Unfortunately, the individual firm is not alone in attempting to secure customers. Competitors seek these same customer assets and each firm must continually struggle to target, attract, and retain (create and recreate) the right customers. Correspondingly, the firm should attempt to ensure that competitors acquire only those customers the firm finds less desirable. The firm succeeds in its task only to the extent that it delivers greater overall value to customers than its competitors.

This rationale does not mean that profits necessarily result from success in attracting and retaining customers. If the costs of this activity are excessive (and intense competition is one factor that may make it so), there will be no economic profit. Thus, although attracting and retaining customers are the key tasks to be accomplished by the organization, they are best viewed as necessary but not sufficient alone to achieve profits, survive, grow, and enhance shareholder value. Notwithstanding this caveat on customer selection, the nature of business activity may be visually depicted in a general manner as shown in Figure 1.1.[11]

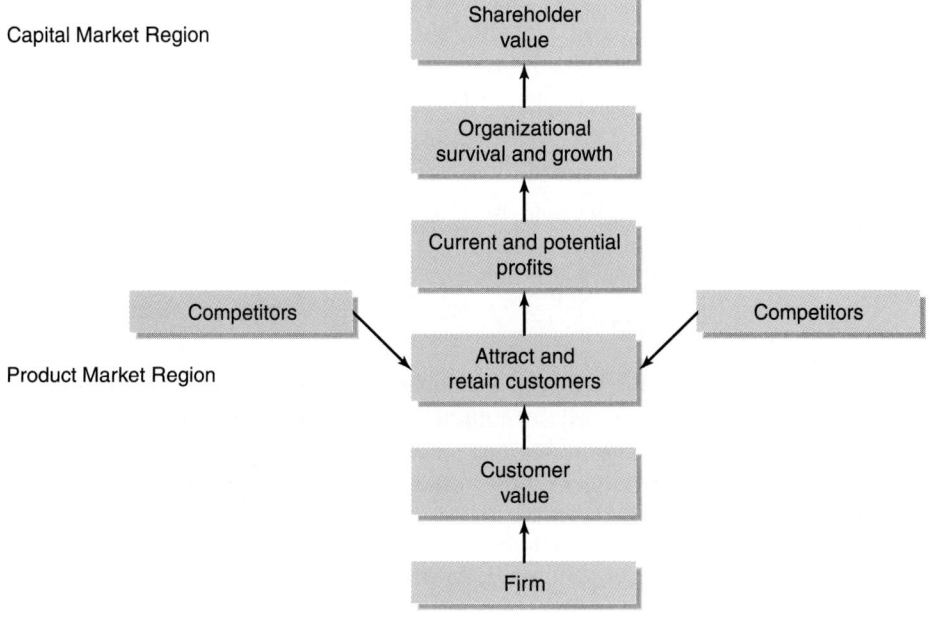

Capital Market Region

Product Market Region

FIGURE 1.1

A Hierarchy of Objectives

In conclusion, the case for marketing is twofold. First, increasingly customers do not need to purchase in order to sustain themselves; they choose to purchase. This fundamental change from a seller's market to a buyer's market puts the customer in the catbird seat and makes customer focus essential. Second, attracting and retaining customers is the major task to be accomplished by the firm and, therefore, constitutes the central job description for the firm, its managers, and its employees.

WHAT IS MARKETING?

Significant confusion exists in many organizations regarding the nature of marketing. For many firms, marketing is synonymous with advertising. For others, it means giving away T-shirts, event tickets, and related gifts to good (or potential) customers. For still others, marketing is support materials for the salesforce or what the consumer does at the supermarket on a Saturday morning! This book takes a hard line on the definition of marketing. The foregoing examples may describe aspects of marketing, but they do not describe the essence of marketing.

A good place to start understanding marketing is with the eminent management theorist, Peter Drucker. Drucker rightly receives considerable credit as a progenitor of the customer orientation and modern marketing. However, it is too often forgotten that Drucker focused on the business as a whole, and embraced far more than the idea of marketing as a functional department. The following excerpt makes his position very clear:

> If we want to know what a business is we have to start with its *purpose*. There is only one valid definition of business purpose: *to create a customer.* It is the customer who determines what a business is. For it is the customer, and he alone, who through being willing to pay for a good or service, converts economic resources into wealth, things into goods. What the business thinks it produces is not of first importance—especially not to the future of the business

and its success. What the customer thinks he is buying, what he considers "value" is decisive . . . Because it is [the purpose of a business] to create a customer, [the] business enterprise has two—and only these two—basic functions: *marketing* and *innovation* (emphasis added).[12]

Drucker also makes clear that, when discussing a function, he uses the term much more broadly than a functional department. Consider the following:

"Marketing is so basic that it cannot be considered a separate function (i.e., a separate skill or work) within the business . . . it is, first, a central dimension of the entire business. It is the whole business . . . seen from the customer's point of view. Concern and responsibility for marketing must, therefore, permeate all areas of the enterprise."[13]

Drucker conceives of marketing as a guiding corporate philosophy for the organization as a whole. This was, in fact, the original exposition of marketing as a concept,[14] even though it remained neglected for many years. Drucker's ideas can be expanded to define this meaning of marketing as the task of securing and retaining customers, a task requiring the commitment of all who work for the firm. Because this task concerns the entire organization, this level of marketing is everybody's business, a concern of every function. In the broadest interpretation, it encompasses the manner in which the firm interfaces with its various environments, notably its customers and competitors. The danger, of course, is that this view of marketing is so broad it might become nobody's business. This book devotes considerable space to this interpretation of marketing because, as noted earlier, increased competition requires a corporate/business level commitment to marketing, a challenge that will require senior management to play a leadership role. Firms that ignore this level of marketing and suggest that marketing is solely an issue for the marketing function or department are making a fundamental error.[15]

Drucker's concept of marketing as philosophy is valid, but that philosophy still must be operationalized. To create customers and defeat competitors, the firm must undertake a set of activities or tasks most often performed by persons with marketing or product management titles. The second part of this chapter develops six tasks; their elaboration constitutes the majority of the book. These tasks are traditionally viewed as responsibilities of the marketing department, but they are not necessarily performed in that department. This might occur by design but probably more often occurs by default. These tasks constitute the second important meaning of marketing. It should be noted, however, that the definition of marketing as a set of tasks is significantly different from Drucker's original concept of marketing. Failure to understand this distinction is common and often leads to serious problems.[16]

As noted earlier, the field of marketing is in continuous change. In a powerful earlier incarnation lodged firmly in the marketing department, marketing essentially referred to the "marketing mix," the set of implementation programs that the firm would develop to address a particular market or market segment. Later, in the era of "strategic marketing," it became clear that the choice of markets and market segments, and the manner in which the firm would position its offerings in those markets and segments, were logically decisions that had to be made prior to designing the marketing mix. However, the locus of these decisions has never been clear-cut. Depending on the organization, it has typically floated between business managers and senior marketing executives. This book's perspective not only embraces these prior incarnations but also includes the critical issue of orienting the firm as a whole to the changing customer, competitor, and general environments. To successfully orient the firm, senior corporate management must play a leadership role in ensuring that the entire organization develops an external rather than an internal orientation. For this reason this book addresses marketing at both the marketing department and corporate/business levels.

MARKETING: THE NEED FOR CHANGE

In a recently published book, Stephan Haeckel, Director of IBM's Advanced Business Institute, opined that "marketing's future is not as *a* function of business, but as *the* function of business."[17] Haeckel's comments reflect the perspective of an astute, insightful practitioner charged with thinking ahead about the way in which IBM and other companies are going to have to change themselves. Intense competition, faced by virtually every firm in the global economy, requires no less than a total re-evaluation of how the firm competes. Customers are increasingly intolerant of even the smallest departures from their expectations of absolute satisfaction. As choice increases, customers can impose their will on all but a small minority of suppliers by taking their business elsewhere. Achieving the degree of inter-functional or inter-business cooperation required to meet these high goals is a formidable challenge to management. Recent history attests to the surprisingly high customer attrition rate among even large businesses; that attrition is likely to increase rather than decline.

This book advocates both an outward orientation that embraces far more than the customer, and redirection of the efforts of the firm as a whole to the competitive challenge. Achievement of such an integrated approach to marketing requires that marketing, as a philosophy, move out of the department and into the business. Such a paradigm shift requires the kind of zeal that accompanied the growth of marketing departments in the 1950s and 1960s, or the onslaught of total quality management (TQM) in the 1980s. It will also require significant changes in attitude from those who may have taken the customer for granted, or mistakenly placed other enterprise stakeholders on inappropriate pedestals. The process will unalterably change the very nature of marketing and cause companies to redefine the role of marketing.

The meaning of marketing will continue to evolve, and so will its practice. For example, direct marketing is revolutionizing the relationship of supplier to customer. The classic distinctions between retailing, wholesaling, and manufacturing are breaking down, and the product/service distinction is becoming meaningless as former purchasers increasingly lease or rent. The advent of large-scale customer databases is changing marketing in fundamental ways as companies secure information on the final customers for their products, customers who, only a few years ago, were anonymous in a mass market. Furthermore, the arrival of the Internet and the World Wide Web promises even greater changes as the process of marketing communication shifts from active sender/passive receiver into an interactive process. Today, we can explore the Web for information on products and services prior to purchase, and interactively communicate with suppliers, favored or otherwise. In the future, intelligent agents will "shop" for us, while the increasingly widespread access to information on suppliers' offers and prices presage ever-intensifying competition.

The sections ahead challenge and equip you with the concepts and tools to enable you to manage marketing efforts in the twenty-first century, and to achieve success in the fastest-changing, most competitive marketplace environment ever experienced. No one has the ability to forecast all the implications of these changes. This book, however, encourages you to think about them. Each chapter includes a section called "The Changing View" that contrasts the "Old Way" with the "New Way." By incorporating cutting-edge ideas, you can acquire a competitive advantage. To start on your journey, the six key tasks of strategic marketing, followed by four principles upon which the development and implementation of marketing strategy should be based, are presented.

THE TASKS OF STRATEGIC MARKETING

If a comprehensive survey were conducted of marketing departments across various countries and industries, the results would no doubt show personnel engaged in an enormous number of marketing-related activities. These might include gathering information on

INTRODUCTION TO
MARKETING
MANAGEMENT

customers and competitors, developing advertising and direct-mail brochures, interacting with research and development (R&D) on new products, and preparing advice for the sales force. Most likely, all or many of these activities add value to the firm's marketplace activities. However, certain questions must be asked: Which of these activities are critical? What are the core elements of strategic marketing? What are the tasks that must be performed to ensure that the true strategic function of marketing in the organization is being accomplished?

Certainly, if a marketing department were created in an organization where previously there was none, its members would find things to do. The pressures of organizational life deriving from the expectations of those in other parts of the organization alone are typically sufficient to keep people busy. But being busy is no substitute for spending effort on those activities that make a real difference. Of course, in some organizations, certain marketing tasks can be performed outside the marketing department. The critical issue for the firm is less where the tasks are performed than whether they are performed appropriately and effectively. This section identifies specific strategic marketing tasks that must be tackled:

> Task 1: Determine and Recommend which Markets to Address
> Task 2: Identify and Target Market Segments
> Task 3: Set Strategic Direction
> Task 4: Design the Marketing Offer
> Task 5: Secure Support from Other Functions
> Task 6: Monitor and Control Execution and Performance

Task 1: Determine and Recommend Which Markets to Address

It is perhaps a truism to say that leading firms have little to fear if environmental change is minimal. Under such circumstances, doing things the "same old way" is likely sufficient to continue a historic profit stream and maintain market leadership. However, this is not the situation most corporations face today. Indeed, as we move into the twenty-first century, the pace of change seems to be increasing. Regardless of the particular type of change (or combination of changes) the firm faces at any time (for example, customer, competitor, economic, technological, social or legal/regulatory), change *per se* poses significant threats to current business.

Although they may have been profitable in the past, businesses are unlikely to remain profitable unless they take major new strategic initiatives. By the same token, significant change opens up a host of opportunities for new businesses. In recent years, a variety of new markets and new industries have been created, seemingly from scratch. In the face of such environmental turbulence, organizations must make critical choices about where to invest the firm's scarce resources, for it is likely that pressures to enhance shareholder value will lead to faster rates of change in firms' business portfolios in the years ahead.

> **Example:** In 1998, Westinghouse finally shed its remaining industrial businesses. Long a manufacturer of electrically related products, the company's leadership decided to focus on the entertainment industry. Westinghouse purchased CBS and changed its corporate name from Westinghouse to CBS.[18]

At the broadest and most general level, the firm must make choices of industry and market. These are critical investment decisions and are typically strategic for the corporation as a whole, or for individual divisions or business units. Choice of market certainly ranks along with choice of technologies and products as one of a firm's most important decisions. Given the choice of "owning" a market or owning a factory, most senior managers would rather own a market. Furthermore, the recent trend toward outsourcing emphasizes the importance of markets over facilities, although owning a market is, of course, much more difficult than owning a factory.

Organizations must answer the following questions regarding the portfolio of businesses that should comprise the set of product markets in which the firm will compete:

- Which new businesses should be added?
- Which of the current businesses should continue to receive investment (and how much)?
- From which businesses should the firm withdraw?

For each of these decisions to be made sensibly, input about the market opportunity is vital. However, because these decisions should be made by senior management, the marketing contribution to Task 1 is advisory. Marketing has two key roles to play in these types of decisions: opportunity identification and advice to corporate management on proposed strategic actions.

IDENTIFICATION OF OPPORTUNITIES Marketing is the sole corporate function charged with explicit responsibility to focus attention outside the organization. Marketing should scan the environment to identify new areas of opportunity, collect and analyze appropriate data, and bring these opportunities to the attention of top management for go/no go decisions. Clearly, it is simply impossible to scan all possible markets with the depth necessary for sound strategy development. It is here where the scope of the business as defined by senior management plays a key role.[19]

ADVICE ON PROPOSED STRATEGIC ACTIONS In addition to its role in identifying opportunities, marketing has a critical advisory role to play in many proposed corporate-level strategic decisions such as those regarding acquisitions, strategic alliances, new distribution systems, divestitures, and market withdrawal. Unfortunately, these decisions are frequently made for financial reasons with at best superficial concern for marketing issues. In part this occurs because although all organizations have a chief financial officer, few have a chief marketing officer. When marketing issues are ignored or just not explored, the impact can be costly.

> **Example:** In 1996, AT&T finally gave up on its disastrous acquisition of computer manufacturer NCR, which once again became independent. Purchased in 1991 for $7.84 billion, under AT&T's ownership NCR lost roughly half of its value, not including over $2 billion in operating losses. A not insignificant element in this debacle concerned Teradata, a firm that made special database computers that were becoming popular with major retailers. Teradata threatened to cancel an arrangement that allowed NCR to use Teradata technology because it feared its then-biggest customer, AT&T, would switch to NCR. To maintain the technology, AT&T had to buy Teradata for over $500 million.[20] Perhaps in-depth (or even cursory) marketing analysis would have identified this problem!

> **Example:** In 1999, AT&T completed its sale of Language Lines, a service that provided language interpretation via multilingual operators and customer service representatives. AT&T business salespeople expressed confusion and concern about this action, because Language Lines was an important element in offering prospective customers a comprehensive telecommunications package.

Indeed, providing advice on prospective acquisitions is a critical matter in many organizations. Recent research has demonstrated that most large acquisitions (over $100 million) lead to reductions in shareholder value for acquiring firms![21] A concern for shareholder value argues that CEOs contemplating acquisitions should receive better advice. The decisions will be made anyway; they might as well be based on good marketing information and analysis. Clearly, marketing has a critical role to play in the decision process, although not all critical advice will necessarily be well received.[22] Hambrick and Hayward have shown that acquisition decisions are often driven less by objective reality than by CEO hubris.[23]

In summary, the thrust of this first marketing task is to ensure that good advice, based on sound marketing principles, is offered when firms make these crucial decisions.

Task 2: Identify and Target Market Segments

Whereas marketing's role regarding modifications to the firm's business portfolio must necessarily be advisory, within the scope of the business portfolio designed by top management, marketing's explicit responsibility is to identify those customers the firm should attempt to serve. The critical concept is market segmentation.[24]

The fundamental underpinning of market segmentation is the notion that in any product market, customers have a diverse set of needs. Although a marketing offer directed at the market as a whole satisfies customer needs to some extent, such an "average" approach leaves many customers unsatisfied and receptive to alternative offers that are more precisely directed at their specific needs.

Market segmentation is the process of grouping together actual and potential customers in a market for the purpose of forming *market segments.* Each of the market segments so formed is comprised of customers seeking similar sets of benefits with similar levels of priority. However, from market segment to market segment, customers have different sets of needs, and seek different sets of benefits.

Whereas the market segmentation process results in the formation of several market segments, the process *per se* offers little information regarding what action the firm should take. Management must determine where it can most effectively use the firm's strengths and exploit competitor weaknesses in forming the closest possible match between customer needs and the firm's offer. It must identify the most attractive segments for the firm to address, and the extent to which the firm can bring to bear the appropriate resources in order to be successful.

Once top management has decided that the firm should address a particular market, the quality of the market segmentation and targeting process is arguably the most critical of all marketing tasks. Successful segmentation and targeting is the basis for profitable operations. By the same token, ineffective segmentation and targeting decisions can lead to serious consequences.

> **Example:** Boeing, world leader in large passenger jet aircraft, made a disastrous eight-year foray into under–20- to 90-seat aircraft with its 1986 purchase of De Havilland (DH). DH's products sold to a different set of customers than those traditionally served by Boeing. By 1992, when it was sold to Bombardier, DH had lost nearly $1 billion building Dash-8 turboprops. In contrast, by 1996, the Dash-8 family had tripled its share of the turbo-prop market to 35%, accounting for two-thirds of regional planes sold worldwide. Bombardier, which focused only on small aircraft, had increased market share from 10% in 1992 to 42%.[25]

Task 3: Set Strategic Direction

Whereas the quality of the market segmentation process and the choice of target segments are critical, several important strategic decisions about how to compete in these segments must also be made. Thus the firm must formulate its objectives for each targeted segment and conceptualize the basic rationale for why customers in each segment will purchase from the firm rather than from competitors. In what is often termed the *positioning decisions,* the firm must develop an approach to each market segment that forms an overarching framework for the design of its various marketing offers.

But this task is not performed just once. As the environment changes and the product category in which the firm competes evolves, the firm faces a variety of scenarios related to growth of the market and market segments, and its competitive position. For each relevant scenario, the firm must decide, for example, whether to take an aggressive or a defensive posture, and whether to optimize performance in market share, profit, or cash flow.

Finally, since most firms address more than one market segment and more than one market, important decisions concerning strategic integration across market segments and markets must be made. A crucial element here is the *branding decision,* the means by which customers recognize the firm's offers. In recent years, brands have become major corporate assets, and branding has become a critical marketing function. Serious marketing decisions must be made regarding the development and use of the firm's brand assets.

Task 4: Design the Marketing Offer

Whereas Task 3 focused on broad resource allocation issues, Task 4 is concerned with the design of marketing offers so that selected customer targets behave in the manner desired by the firm. Although purchase of the firm's products and services is typically the ultimate goal, behaviors such as active selling, holding inventories, or making strong purchase recommendations can also be crucial. In some cases, multiple behaviors are required, for example, purchase then referral to other potential customers. Before the process of marketing offer design commences, the firm must be clear both about customer targets and the customer behaviors it seeks.

The overall design of the marketing offer comprises a total benefit package. The tools available to perform this design task have traditionally been equated with the marketing mix elements of product, place, promotion, and price, now typically enhanced with service.[26]

- Product benefits are delivered to satisfy customer needs. They are designed into the product, package, and so forth. The greater the benefits (relative to the price paid), the better the chance that customers will exhibit the required behavior.
- Place (or location) benefits concern the time and place convenience of securing the product/service.
- Promotion, embracing both personal and impersonal communications, is the means by which the firm informs and persuades customers that product, service, and location benefits are being offered. However, for branded products, communication adds value in and of itself since the reassurance, imagery, status, and related customer satisfaction delivered by communications is integral to what the customer buys.[27]
- Price is the net monetary outlay that, relative to customers' perceptions of the benefits received, determines the net value received for behaving in the desired manner.
- Services included in the offer are often key elements distinguishing the firm from its competitors. Services may be provided by the manufacturer, an intermediary, or some combination. They may be received before purchase or after purchase.

These design elements comprise many interrelationships. The greater the perceived product, service, and location benefits, the greater can be the price. In addition, price itself may carry information about the benefits being offered: High prices may imply high value, whereas low prices may imply low value. Of course, if the benefits do not offer high customer value compared to competitive offers and price is high, market share will decline.

A second set of interrelationships concerns different customer targets. For example, intermediaries are typically concerned with such benefits as profit margin and inventory turnover. However, they should also be assured that the product will truly deliver benefits to satisfy a final customer's needs (and so provide the volume to assure inventory turnover). Furthermore, the intermediary customer target may play a key role in communicating with final customers and persuading them to purchase the product.

This design task is complicated if the firm is creating multiple offers for several customer targets in several market segments. Since resources are limited, the marketing manager must weigh such strategic considerations as the degree of effort on each market segment and the likely sales and profit response of different marketing mix options. Since the potential number of marketing mix permutations for just one market segment is infinite, only lack of imagination and capability can be blamed for offers that are identical or near-identical to those of competitors, unless the firm decides on an imitation strategy. The major corollary, of course, is that if marketing is doing its job, "commodity" products need not exist. Indeed, several companies have banned the word, arguing that its mere usage encourages unimaginative marketing approaches.

Although people in marketing positions are typically responsible for orchestrating elements of the marketing mix to create offers that appeal to target customers, in virtually all companies they do not possess commensurate authority. Designing and delivering an offer demands an extraordinary degree of cooperation among the firm's different functions and this underscores the need for integrated marketing and teamwork.

The disconnect between responsibility and authority has important implications for the skills required to effectively manage marketing. To do so one must encourage and stimulate cooperation across multiple functions, typically relying heavily upon interpersonal skills. Difficulties created by mismatches of responsibility and authority are an important reason why more companies are embracing a broader perspective of marketing that views some strategic marketing tasks as responsibilities better discharged by general or business management.

Whereas this marketing task focuses on design, it is useful to think of execution largely as a task for other organizational functions.[28] However, the interface between design and execution may be a source of significant coordination problems between marketing and (for example) engineering, operations, or the sales force. The focus of strategic marketing should be on benefit design—what the customer would like to receive; by contrast, engineering (product development) and operations generally focus more on features, the product/service characteristics required to deliver the benefit package. Unfortunately, in consumer-goods companies, marketing managers often have little technical expertise, and the technical gap is only closed by goodwill. In industrial companies, the opposite is often the case—managers are technically strong but short on marketing expertise.

Task 5: Secure Support from Other Functions

Whereas the first four tasks were strategic in nature, Tasks 5 and 6 are primarily concerned with marketing's operating responsibilities. In many organizations, marketing executives view Task 5 as one of ensuring that other organizational functions commit to supporting the offer designed by marketing. However, the world is not that simple, and here we run into a fundamental paradox related to the traditional view of marketing.

Marketing requires two very different types of support—support for design and support for implementation. Support for design is conditioned by considerations of technical, operational, and economic feasibility whereas support for implementation assumes that the design has been fixed. However, whereas marketing's conclusions regarding what is necessary and desirable to serve customer's needs may not be feasible in the short run, a key marketing responsibility is nonetheless to keep the organization focused on what targeted customers desire, regardless of current feasibility. Here is the paradox: Once marketing abdicates its missionary role and adopts the view of what is possible based on the firm's current capabilities and competencies, it ceases to perform one its most important roles, pushing the firm to evolve to deliver future competitive advantage.[29] While this role clearly reflects a longer-term task, short-term pressure frequently leads to long-term capitulation and competitive vulnerability.

Performing the marketing task in the face of this paradox requires extraordinary strength. For this reason, good marketing managers periodically need intellectual and emotional renewal. It also helps explain why good operational marketing managers may not be difficult to find, but good strategic managers are relatively rare.

The second type of support is required for successful implementation. This support is often described as internal marketing, or "getting buy-in." As noted earlier, in functional organizations, marketing typically has responsibility for offer design but rarely has line authority over the various organizational functions responsible for implementation. However, commitment of other functions and departments to the offer is crucial, for the strategy chain is only as strong as its weakest link. If a key function does not play its part in implementation, the effort expended by all other functions may be in vain.

For many years, management research has demonstrated the importance of participation in gaining commitment to important decisions. What is not always realized is that a properly orchestrated group process can actually improve the quality of strategy. Marketing must embrace this broader perspective since the requirement to integrate and focus all the firm's resources has been enhanced by increasing competitive pressure.[30] It is reputed that Japanese firms are better at achieving such coordination, and that this helps them compete with Western firms. Certainly, interdepartmental strife and rivalry driven by "silo thinking" has hampered far too many European and U.S. corporations. As a result, precious management time is mistakenly redirected away from dealing with external opportunities and threats, and toward ending destructive internal conflict.

Recent organizational moves to process management have helped some firms develop cross-functional team approaches to solving these problems, although the potential for barriers between process teams remains inasmuch as any form of organizational specialization breeds some level of differentiation.[31] Regardless of the specific organizational structure chosen, reaching across formal reporting lines is inevitably required for effective implementation; structural solutions alone do not solve coordination problems.

> **Example:** Faced with a new competitive threat, a major health care company decided that three of its business units should jointly develop strategy to fully satisfy the needs of personnel in hospital operating rooms. Despite agreement on this rationale, senior management in the three units could not agree on a coherent strategy and the attempt was dropped.

Implementation of market strategy is often a complex undertaking, particularly for new product launches. Functions requiring coordination range from "boundary-spanning" elements related to the customer environment to functions more internal to the firm. Boundary-spanning functions may include the sales force, advertising department (and agency), customer service, credit control, and market research; internal functions are likely to include operations, logistics, product development, information systems, and human resources. In recent years, the complexity level has increased as increasing numbers of hitherto internal functions have been outsourced. Team-based approaches generally ameliorate coordination problems but they do not obviate the need for careful planning. Traditional network planning techniques such as PERT and Gantt charts have much to offer firms engaged in complex coordination tasks.

Implementation poses special problems in organizations with poor internal working relationships or systems problems. Out-of-kilter planning systems are surprisingly common. The key elements of market strategy must be in place before coordinated sales, advertising, promotion, or distribution plans are developed. Yet in many firms, these activities are either unplanned, planned out of sequence, or developed independently. In such cases, even the possibility of successful implementation is jeopardized, and achievement of an integrated offer is virtually impossible.

> **Example:** A major money center bank developed and extensively advertised several new consumer-loan products. Demand approximated marketing's forecasts, but the large number of applications totally overwhelmed the bank's antiquated credit-approval system.

Perhaps the major difference between strategy and implementation is that whereas strategy is often generated by a small group of people, implementation involves many organizational members ranging from those with customer-contact responsibilities, (for example, salespeople and customer service) to others whose work lives are deeper in the corporation. As a result, human-resource issues play an important role in marketing. Obviously, the firm is unlikely to be successful without a well-developed marketing offer; it should be equally clear that a brilliantly conceived offer is worthless if poorly implemented.

Task 6: Monitor and Control Execution and Performance

Whereas Task 5 has an internal focus, Task 6 is concerned with how to monitor and control firm activities and performance in the marketplace. Although such groups as the field salesforce, promotion experts, and advertising agencies implement the marketing offer, overall responsibility for modifying and evolving the offer lies with marketing, which must ensure that sensitive market feedback systems are in place.

Essentially, marketing should ask three questions:

- Are the various elements of the offer design being implemented as planned?
- Is the firm's market and financial performance reaching planned objectives?
- Have there been significant changes in the environment that necessitate reconsidering the objectives and strategies?

If marketing identifies an implementation problem, the required steps are fairly straightforward. Unfortunately, all too often, antiquated or inappropriate management systems create difficult but avoidable implementation problems. Systems such as planning, objective setting, and compensation can have a dramatic effect. For example poorly-set objectives may lead to suboptimal allocation of effort and an unfavorable motivational impact on employees.

Salesforce compensation systems based on sales volumes provide a classic example. Frequently, these systems have a built-in ratchet such that success in one year leads automatically to higher targets in succeeding years. These quota-setting systems may work well in growth markets, but often generate great dissatisfaction and low motivation in mature and declining markets. Furthermore, since sales volume per unit of selling effort is typically more easily achieved with established products, new products are often undersupported at launch. We believe that many new products fail because the *de facto* effort is less than the planned effort.

Performance under plan may require further data gathering and analysis, as well as appropriate "course correction" actions via fine-tuning the strategy, modifying tactics and, where necessary, adjusting objectives. Alternatively, should key environmental assumptions be violated, major changes in objectives and strategies may be required.

THE PRINCIPLES OF STRATEGIC MARKETING

The tasks of marketing management are obviously important to an understanding of the role of marketing within the firm. Of more interest to the strategist, however, is how managers should go about executing those responsibilities. Four principles are fundamental to successful execution of the marketing job. These are the Principle of Selectivity and Concentration, the Principle of Customer Value, the Principle of Differential Advantage, and the Principle of Integration.

The Principle of Selectivity and Concentration

As noted above, providing advice on the selection of markets and decisions regarding which market segments to target is among marketing's primary responsibilities. However, at the heart of the decision process is a basic principle of market strategy: *The Principle of Selectivity and Concentration.* Of course, this principle is not confined to the development of market strategy, but to strategy in general. Indeed, military literature abounds with support for this principle. Napoleon said that the secret of strategy was the concentration of firepower on the right battlefield, Von Clausewitz opined that the heart of all strategy was the concentration of strength, and Liddell-Hart emphasized concentration of strength against enemy weakness.[32]

In the marketing arena, two aspects comprise the principle of Selectivity and Concentration. First, the marketing manager must carefully choose the market target (selectivity); second, resources should be concentrated toward that target (concentration).

Of course, selectivity is widely preached by marketers, but is less often practiced, because the drive for sales volume too often overwhelms sound strategic judgment.

The Principle of Selectivity and Concentration focuses on one key issue—the danger of attempting too much and dissipating the impact of limited resources by spreading them over too many alternatives. No organization, no matter how large or how successful, has infinite resources. Some countries, like Japan, have always been conscious of resource limitations; this consciousness is embedded in its culture and lifestyle. Others, like the U.S. and Australia, have historically been resource rich and are, perhaps, less culturally attuned to making selective resource allocation decisions.[33]

The best-known marketing manifestation of selectivity is market segmentation, discussed in Task 2. Unfortunately, although segmentation has occupied a venerable position in the marketing literature for many years, most writing focuses on segmentation methods. These studies are important, because they focus on what analyses to conduct on market information once gathered, and they also provide better descriptive understanding of markets. However, they only *permit* better strategy decisions; they by no means *guarantee* them. The central strategy issue concerns not just developing a segmentation approach, but acting upon the results by selecting segments and concentrating resources (targeting), to the exclusion of alternatives.[34] The firm will be much less vulnerable to competitive imitation to the extent that it identifies opportunities to leverage its distinctive competencies, those areas where it possesses an inherent advantage over competition.[35]

In addition to securing competitive advantage, practicing concentration may allow the firm to probe its segments in greater depth and uncover hidden opportunities. Indeed, many large firms frequently experience their most difficult competitive problems with smaller firms that focus resources on a particular market segment. This concentration enables the "small fry" to attain greater leverage with slender resources than larger competitors that spread resources too thinly. Unfortunately, too often the herd instinct prevails in business and, rather than leverage distinctive competence, imitation leads to the opposite situation: Followers compete on the basis determined by previous entrants which, if the latter are smart, favors them.

Of course, a concentration policy involves risks. Concentration of finite resources on some opportunities means that others must be forgone. Some options that might have proved attractive will be rejected, others will be mistakenly chosen. However, hedging bets by allocating small amounts of resources to all feasible options will certainly fail; in competitive markets, failure is often guaranteed. For this reason, some experts have labeled this principle *Concentration and Concession,* to emphasize that not only must resources be concentrated in some segments, other segments should be conceded to competitors.[36]

The Principle of Customer Value

The *Principle of Customer Value* very simply states that success in targeted market segments is directly related to the firm's ability to provide perceived value to customers. This principle is central to understanding the job of the marketing manager, and drives marketing research activity that seeks to probe deeply into customer needs, wants, priorities, and experiences. A corollary of this principle is that although firms develop, produce, and deliver products and services, customers perceive value only in the benefits that these products and services provide.

It follows, therefore, that customer values should drive product and investment decisions, and that the firm's ability to deliver value to customers should be a critical basis for evaluating firm performance. Understanding the customer should form the basis for the overarching strategic framework within which the marketing offer is designed and constructed, and the offer design *per se.* However, choice of customers will always be an issue; so is the underlying assumption that customers know their needs and wants. In recent years there has been a welcome questioning of both these critical issues. First, there is increased understanding that, for new product technologies at least, too much focus on current customers may distract the firm from significant opportunities with new customers.[37] Second, even if the correct target customers are identified, because of the extreme uncertainty with new technologies, their expressed needs and wants may be misleading. Nonetheless, to adapt a famous expression from United States Presidential politics in the early 1990s, "It's the customer, stupid."

Finally, customer values are not static but rather constitute a moving target. As the environment changes and customers accumulate life (or organizational) experience, their needs change. As a result, the values they seek change as well. World-class companies invest extensively to identify these developing customer needs and wants, and continually feed these results into product and service decisions. If completed effectively, market offers are continually modified and enhanced so that customers remain highly satisfied, if not delighted, with the values they receive. The failure to observe this simple lesson led some of the most successful retailers in the United States and United Kingdom—Sears, K-Mart, Sainsbury's, and Marks and Spencer—into crisis in the late 20th century.

The Principle of Differential Advantage

The *Principle of Differential Advantage,* closely related to the Principle of Customer Value, is loosely equivalent to what is sometimes called competitive advantage, unique selling proposition (USP), or "edge," and lies at the heart of every successful marketing strategy. This principle states that the firm must not only deliver value to customers, but must do so better than competitors. In simple terms, this principle asserts that the way to make high profits is to offer customers something they want but cannot get elsewhere.

More formally, a differential advantage is a net benefit or cluster of benefits, offered to a sizable group of customers, which they value and are willing to pay for, but cannot get, or believe they cannot get, elsewhere. In other words, the firm should design an offer, using the levers of the marketing mix, that provides an economically justified group of customers with the benefits they seek but which are not provided by competitors. If the firm can achieve a differential advantage, it should be able to secure improved prices.[38]

Several implications flow from this basic concept. First, it emphasizes the competitive nature of business. Simply attempting to offer value by meeting customer needs is insufficient, because competitive parity is the likely ultimate result. For long-term gain, the firm must develop an offer that is better or different, *in ways important to the customer.*

> **Example:** A classic case of securing differential advantage was Frank Perdue's success in the United States' East Coast chicken market, previously a commodity business. Armed with data demonstrating that consumers' most severe problem with chicken was quality variability (unobservable until the opaque cellophane wrapper was opened at home), he developed and implemented an optimal feeding schedule for chicken, then strongly advertised a consistency benefit at a price 30% higher than the commodity price. He was very successful!

Second, some "differentials" are better than others because they are more difficult to copy. For this reason, many manufacturers favor differentials based on product. However, other marketing mix elements such as long-term relationships, better product availability, communication messages, and service may be less liable to competitive matching.[39] Furthermore, competitive advantage based on a manufacturing process may be more sustainable than one based on product, and one based on an organizational process such as a parts delivery system may be even better. Finally, competitive advantage based on people and people processes, such as customer relations, qualified technicians, and a willingness-to-serve culture, may be even more sustainable.[40]

Third, no matter how secure a differential advantage may appear, competitive activity will eventually erode it away.[41] Consequently, the marketing manager must recognize that maintenance of differential advantage is a continuing challenge and the search for rejuvenation must be constant and ongoing. To manage the market strategically, the manager should plan ahead by funding a series of development programs to sustain the advantage over time. Ideally, the firm should retain a potential differential advantage "on the shelf," ready to trump the competitor's ace when required.[42] Indeed, the firm's true differential advantage may exist not in specific marketplace actions that put it ahead of competition for a period of time, but in the meta-level ability to create, over time, a series of differential advantages using the variety of tools available to the marketing manager.[43]

Fourth, to actively pursue the creation and recreation of differential advantage requires a constant willingness for the firm to outdate its own offering. Cannibalization is the price of sustained market leadership. Unfortunately, many large firms have a poor track record here because the political constituencies for current offerings are so strong. "If it ain't broke don't fix it" is so often a strongly expressed sentiment. One McKinsey consultant believes the initiative passes to the challenger by default.[44]

Finally, not all differences result in advantage; the business world is littered with efforts that were truly different, but that failed. Differences in the offer must create benefits that target customers truly value before one can say with confidence that differential advantage has been achieved.[45]

The Principle of Integration

The *Principle of Integration* governs the success or failure of all efforts discussed thus far. It states that to assure success, all elements in design and execution must be carefully integrated and coordinated. As noted earlier, the chain analogy is a powerful metaphor for marketing management. For example, poor advertising can ruin an otherwise excellent product, delayed promotional materials can doom a product launch to failure, and improper pricing can cause havoc with sales forecasts.

> **Example:** In 1998, *New York Magazine* planned a promotion to offer consumers the magazine free for six weeks; then they would be invited to become paying subscribers. Unfortunately, the request for subscription arrived *before* the first week of free magazines.

Whereas most executives would agree in principle with the need for a carefully integrated plan and strategy, achieving such integration in practice is difficult. Problems typically stem from different functions or departments squabbling over priorities, and the receipt of ambiguous messages from senior management. The result is a mishmash of an offer, or one so diluted by the politics of coalitions spanning many years that an integrated benefit package does not result. A senior division manager in a well-known multinational corporation described the situation to his incoming superior by stating, "There have been too many years of business units versus corporate, too many years of control versus trust, too many years of operating in silos, too many years of manipulating the facts to serve personal interests, and too many years of defending internal turf at the expense of market share and position."

> **Example:** During a seminar at a major U.S. computer company, one of the authors identified a sales forecasting department reporting to the production director. When asked about this somewhat unusual organizational location, in particular why the sales forecasting group was not in the sales or marketing department, the production director replied, "Oh yes, they've got one too. But we can't believe a word they say, so we have to have our own for production scheduling!"

> **Example:** A business unit of a major foreign importer of electronic equipment shared the sales force of a larger sister unit for part of its product line. Management of the sister unit refused to allow the shared salespeople and sales management to attend the business unit's annual strategy conference!

Integration is most likely secured in those organizations with a corporate-wide external perspective. Shared values incorporating a common belief that the firm must focus on serving customers better than competitors can promote the common sense of purpose required in a hyper-competitive world. Achieving integration requires agreement on priorities and the development of close and cooperative working relationships among all those involved in designing and implementing the offer. These agreements are much more easily achieved with shared values. For firms that are functionally organized, organizational innovation may be required to promote coordination among the various functions.[46] A military analogy is useful, but not encouraging. One of the better-known U.S. strategy analysts has argued that there can be no such thing as strategy for one branch of the armed forces.[47] However, it was not until the Gulf War that, for the very first time in a major campaign, the various branches came under a unified command structure. This innovation in integration permitted operations that sped the war to a swift conclusion.

Market strategy design must be completed under strict constraints; once agreement is reached on the key elements of selectivity and concentration, customer value, and differential advantage, many aspects of the offer should fall into line within fairly narrow limits. Indeed, from the customer's perspective, it is typically essential that this integration take place to ensure the creation and delivery of value. Once the design is completed, the firm must make certain that management systems (especially, but not exclusively, planning systems), organization structure, and action plans are in place to ensure successful implementation of the integrated design. A tremendous amount of detailed planning must be conducted to ensure marketplace success; this planning sets the direction and timing of marketing actions that, in the final analysis, are the only concrete manifestation of marketing strategies and plans.

CHAPTER ORGANIZATION

To address rigorously the theme of *Marketing Management in the 21st Century,* the presentation is organized into four sections: I. "Marketing and the Firm," II. "Fundamentals for Strategic Marketing," III. "The Tasks of Marketing," and IV. "Future Directions." In addition to this introductory chapter, the "Marketing and the Firm" section includes chapters on environmental change and its implications, and the externally oriented firm.

Chapter 2, "The Environmental Imperative," discusses the impact of environmental change on the firm as whole and the marketing job in particular. This discussion of factors that affect the relationship between companies and their customers leads logically to making the case for an organizational shift toward a company that is much more outward focused, in which management concentrates its efforts externally rather than internally. This case is developed in Chapter 3, "The Externally Oriented Firm."

The second section of the book, "Fundamentals for Strategic Marketing," lays the foundation for developing market strategy. Chapter 4, "Customers," and Chapter 5, Competitors and Complementers, focus on the four Cs: customer, competitor, complementer and company. Chapter 4 focuses mainly on customers, both consumers and organizations. The chapter commences by discussing a series of issues in identifying customers, then shifts to the customer decision process, focusing specifically on customer value and customer purchase behavior. Chapter 5 discusses the various types of competition faced by the firm and reviews the basic components that drive strategic analysis of competitors as compared to the company, and the understanding of market structures. This chapter also introduces a little-discussed entity—complementers, those organizations whose sales may positively impact the firm's sales.

The third and longest section of the book, The Tasks of Marketing, is organized around the six tasks of marketing introduced earlier in this chapter. Chapter 6, "Identifying Opportunities for Creating Shareholder Value," focuses on Task 1, Determine and Recommend which Markets to Address. It discusses two critical elements for creating shareholder value: securing profitable growth and increasing margins. The chapter also develops frameworks for developing a growth strategy, setting criteria for evaluating growth opportunities, and selecting implementation methods. In addition, it identifies a set of options for improving margins in current businesses. Task 2, Identify and Target Market

Segments, is addressed in Chapter 7, "Market Segmentation and Targeting." Three basic topics are covered: methods of grouping customers into market segments (the fundamental unit for developing market strategy); the characteristics of meaningful segments; and the targeting process by which the firm decides which segments to address.

Task 3, Set Strategic Direction, comprises four separate chapters. Chapter 8, "Market Strategy: The Integrator," advances the concept of strategy as a fundamental integrating force that drives implementation not only of the marketing mix but of other functional activity programs. Chapter 8 also develops the critical elements of a product/market strategy in some depth. Chapters 9 and 10 focus on the competitive aspects of strategy by adopting a scenario approach to strategic options available to the firm in different competitive situations. Chapter 9, "Competitive Market Strategies in Introduction and Growth," focuses on the introductory and growth stages of the product life cycle, and Chapter 10, "Competitive Market Strategies in Maturity and Decline," focuses on maturity and decline. Chapter 11, "Managing Brands," deals with the increasingly important subject of developing and managing brand equity, as well as examining the newer, but possibly more important, subject of customer equity.

Design the Marketing Offer, Task 4, is addressed in seven chapters and focuses on what are frequently termed the 4 Ps and an S (product, place, price, promotion and service.) This is also termed the marketing mix and must be integrated to support and deliver the benefits promised to customers. Chapter 12, "Managing the Product Line," focuses on managing the composition of the product line, leaning heavily on strategic portfolio frameworks as a counterbalance to traditional methods of financial analysis. Issues addressed include product line breadth (including trade-offs between product proliferation and product line simplification), extending product life, product cannibalization, product replacement, secondary markets, and legal and ethical issues including product safety and packaging, and product disposal. Chapter 13, "Developing New Products," discusses success factors for innovative companies, the relationship between marketing and innovation, and different ways for firms to approach the innovation challenge. The chapter concludes by describing the classic new product development process and indicating the ways in which it is changing.

Chapter 14, "Integrated Marketing Communications," lays out a framework for integrated communications, then focuses on impersonal communication, particularly advertising. Chapter 15, "Directing and Managing the Field Sales Effort," deals with personal selling efforts. This chapter both develops the elements of a sales strategy and discusses a set of organizational issues that must be addressed so that the sales strategy can be implemented as planned. In Chapter 16, "Distribution Decisions," the focus shifts to providing customers with products and services when and where they want them. This chapter focuses on choosing and managing marketing-channel relationships, an area where substantial innovation is occurring.

In recent years, as product quality has improved across the board, customer service before and after the sale has become an increasingly important competitive weapon and a powerful means of differentiating the firm's offer from the offers of competitors. This topic is addressed in Chapter 17, "Managing Services and Customer Service," where the importance of customer service in retaining and delighting customers and the negative consequences that occur when service encounters are poorly managed are examined. This chapter concludes with views on why a service advantage may often endure longer than a technological advantage. Finally, Chapter 18, "Managing Price and Value," focuses on pricing, an implementation area that has tremendous leverage for revenues and profits. Issues of pricing strategy and tactics of implementing pricing decisions are addressed.

Task 5, Secure Support from Other Functions, is addressed in Chapter 19, "Ensuring the Marketing Offer Is Implemented as Planned." This chapter first explores the contrast between marketing as a function and marketing as a philosophy, then develops an assessment, diagnosis, prescription, and implementation system for ensuring that the firm becomes truly externally oriented and customer focused. Formal and informal organizational forms currently being developed to replace the longstanding approaches to organizing marketing are discussed.

The discussion of the tasks of marketing concludes with Chapter 20, "Monitor and Control Execution and Performance," which focuses on the identically named Task 6. This chapter discusses ways of ensuring that the marketing effort is implemented as planned and that the desired results are achieved.

Section IV, Future Directions, is comprised of one chapter and a postscript. Chapter 21, "Marketing and the Internet," discusses the manner in which the Internet is affecting the current marketing paradigm. Finally, the Postscript briefly explores a variety of directions in which marketing practice may develop.

At the conclusion of each chapter, a chapter appendix lists the Web addresses of companies and brands noted in the chapter.[48] The Book Appendix provides material on financial analysis for marketing decisions. This material is fundamental for any serious student of marketing and should certainly be thoroughly digested before reading Chapter 18, "Managing Price and Value."

SUMMARY

These four sections, 21 chapters, postscript, and appendix set out a comprehensive framework for 21st century marketing. While they encompass tried and true frameworks, they also synthesize the new developments that are changing the landscape of marketing practice. In an era in which attracting and retaining customers is ever more important yet ever more difficult, and in which competitive challenges are increasing in depth and scope, firms will only survive, flourish, and deliver value to shareholders to the extent that they change significantly their philosophies and practices of marketing.

Chapter 1 laid out six key tasks for marketing, and four principles upon which marketing strategy should be based. To the extent that marketing practitioners have a solid understanding of these tasks and principles, and a commitment to put them into practice, they improve the chances that their organizations will survive and grow, and that shareholder value will be enhanced.

By learning about marketing with the help of this material, you will be well equipped to survive and prosper in your careers as marketers, general managers, and CEOs.

THE CHANGING VIEW

As discussed previously, each chapter will present an "Old Way" versus "New Way" distinction as a means of capturing some of the major issues discussed in the chapter.

Old Way	New Way
Organizational survival is major firm objective	Shareholder value is major firm objective
Marketing as only a function	Marketing as a philosophy as well as a function
Accounting profit	Shareholder value
Manage the status quo	Manage change
Seller power	Customer power
Non-discretionary purchasing power	Discretionary purchasing power
Owner/manager separation	Owner/manager convergence
Product markets pre-eminent	Capital markets pre-eminent
Customers as "necessary"	Customers as key assets
Accept all orders	Select customers
A department markets	The firm markets
Marketing as a one-way process	Marketing as an interactive process
Supplier chooses options	Customer chooses options

QUESTIONS FOR STUDY AND DISCUSSION

1. Explain the relationship between firm performance in product markets and in capital markets.

2. Do you agree that the practice of marketing is going to have to change? Why or why not?

3. The authors draw on Peter Drucker's writings to support their view of marketing's role in the firm. Can you identify other management gurus who take a similar (or different) position?

4. Explain the structural changes in advanced economies that have created the economic case for marketing.

5. Discuss the distinction between marketing as a philosophy and marketing as a functional department.

6. What are the organizational implications of treating marketing as a philosophy rather than as a functional department?

7. Why might a firm turn down an order?

8. Explain in financial terms the concept of customers as assets.

9. What challenges will be posed for managers by marketing becoming an interactive process?

10. Why do the interests of managers and shareholders sometimes diverge? What impact might this divergence have on the firm's customers?

11. Discuss the implications of the statement, "The firm markets, not the department."

12. Identify three examples of companies where you believe the firm markets, and three where the department markets.

13. Provide documentary evidence of a shift from seller power to buyer power in three product markets with which you are familiar.

14. Argue the case for why superior marketing performance will produce superior returns for shareholders.

15. Explain why selling is different from marketing.

16. How would you approach the task of identifying the impact of the Internet on marketing practice?

END NOTES

1. See, for example, "Shadowing Industry Trends, Morgan Stanley Creates Two Big Divisions," *The New York Times,* January 17, 1997, or "P&G, Seeing Shoppers Were Being Confused, Overhauls Marketing," *The Wall Street Journal,* January 15, 1997.

2. Concerns over the ability of managers to direct very large enterprises and the inability of investors fully to understand highly diversified businesses has led to a questioning of the value of size and growth *per se.* As a result, increasing numbers of large corporations are being broken up into more manageable units. Examples include Imperial Chemical Industries (ICI) and the Hanson Trust in the UK and ITT in the US.

3. Organizational downsizing may be a necessary short-term action for long-run survival.

4. The production of economic value by organizations is the engine of economic growth for individual nation states.

5. A key distinction between Communist and Capitalistic systems is the role of organizational failure. To a large extent, firms in Communist systems are not allowed to fail. (Witness the apparent determination of the PRC government to maintain loss-ridden state-owned enterprises in China.)

6. Sometimes it is necessary to sell all or part of the firm to secure the capital and managerial talent to allow it to function at all.

7. This conflict is one manifestation of the so-called principal/agent problem in economics. In the U.S., the Securities and Exchange Commission (SEC) has consistently encouraged share ownership by managers as a means to ameliorate this problem.

8. Even in continental Europe and Japan where, traditionally, companies were viewed as having a variety of stakeholders with legitimate claims on the firm, the primacy of shareholders is gaining ground. In Germany, significant corporate restructing is being driven by a desire to improve shareholder value, *Financial Times,* September 28, 1999; in Japan such leading firms as Sony and NEC have embraced a shareholder value philosophy.

9. Taking a similar overarching perspective, Srivastava, Shervani and Fahey identify two types of non–balance-sheet assets. *Relational* market-based assets are "outcomes of relationships between the firm and key external stakeholders including distributors, retailers, end customers, other strategic partners, community groups and even governmental agencies." *Intellectual* market-based assets comprise the knowledge the firm possesses about the environment including market conditions and such entities as customers, competitors, channels, suppliers, and social and political interest groups. R.K. Srivastava, T.A. Shervani, and L. Fahey, "Market-Based Assets and Shareholder Value: A Framework for Analysis," *Journal of Marketing,* 62 (January 1998), pp. 2–18.

10. If this job is performed poorly, the firm's survival is at risk. A dramatic example of this occurred in the United States in the 1980s and early 1990s. Of the 500 firms in the *Fortune* 500 in 1981, only 271 remained as independent entities in 1992! Most of the missing 229 were merged out of existence.

11. Some firms have extended the link between customer satisfaction and shareholder value to embrace employees. For example, Nortel asserts that "The link between employee satisfaction and customer satisfaction that delivers shareholder value has been clearly established," *Fortune,* March 30, 1988. Richard Branson of Virgin says, "I am convinced that companies should put their staff first, customers second and shareholders third–ultimately that's in the best interests of customers and shareholders," interviewed in D. Sheff, "The Virgin Billionaire," *Playboy,* February, 1995. A senior Citibank executive said, describing his firm's relationship managers: "Our critical assets walk in the door at 9:00 a.m. and walk out of the door at 6:00 p.m."

12. P.F. Drucker, *The Practice of Management,* New York, Harper and Row, 1954, pp. 37–38. (Emphasis added)

13. P.F. Drucker, *Management: Tasks, Responsibilities, Practices,* New York, Harper and Row, 1973, p. 63.

14. P.F. Drucker, *The Practice of Management,* New York: Harper and Row, 1954, p. 37

15. J.M. Hulbert and L.F. Pitt, "Exit Left Center Stage? The Future of Functional Marketing," *European Management Journal,* 14 (February 1996), pp. 47–60.

16. These two levels are still the subject of ongoing debate and tension. See W. Fletcher, "Expanding Marketing," *The Financial Times,* January 20, 1997.

17. S.H. Haeckel, Preface, in D.R. Lehmann and K.E. Jocz (eds.), *Reflections on the Future of Marketing,* Cambridge, MA: Marketing Science Institute, 1997.

18. In May 2000, the Federal Communications Commission (FCC) approved the acquisition of CBS by Viacom, one of the biggest mergers in the history of the media industry.

19. Of course, some opportunities that fall outside the firm's current business scope may be worth pursuing.

20. *The Economist,* March 23–29, 1996.

21. M. Bradley, A. Desai and E.H., Kim, "Synergistic Gains from Acquisitions and Their Division between the Stockholders of Target and Acquiring Firms," *Journal of Financial Economics,* 21 (1988), pp. 3–40; E. Berkovitch and M.P. Narayanan, "Motives for Takeovers: An Empirical Investigation," *Journal of Financial and Quantitative Analysis,* 28 (1993), pp. 347–362.

22. Michael Dell argues that Compaq's acquisition of DEC was a poor move. He believes that the firms winning in PCs and networking are not the broad, diversified companies like IBM, but fast, flexible firms like Cisco, Compaq, and Dell, that teamed up with independent service firms like Andersen Consulting, EDS, and KMPG. The firing of Edward Pfeiffer, Compaq's CEO, in April 1999 suggests that Dell's argument should be taken seriously.

23. M.L.A. Hayward and D.C. Hambrick, "Explaining the Premiums Paid for Large Acquisitions: Evidence of CEO Hubris, *Administrative Science Quarterly,* 42 (1997), pp. 103–127.

24. Market segmentation is addressed in much greater depth in Chapter 7.

25. *Business Week,* March 3, 1997.

26. Previously, the marketing mix was known as the 4 Ps, nowadays as the 4 Ps and an S.

27. That communications value is a vitally important issue is well known by many consumer goods companies. However, far too many company executives see only the expenses involved in marketing communications. This point is examined in Chapter 14.

28. A useful metaphor for the relationship between marketing and sales (for example) is that of, respectively, architect and builder.

29. See K. Simmonds, "Removing the Chains from Product Strategy," *Journal of Management Studies,* 5 (1968), pp. 29–40.

30. Hulbert and Pitt, *op. cit.*

31. P.R. Lawrence and J. Lorsch, *Organization and Environment: Managing Differentiation and Integration,* Cambridge, MA: Harvard University Press, 1967.

32. Important examples of this principle in action were the Inchon landings orchestrated by General MacArthur in the Korean War and Allied use of air power and mobility in the Gulf War.

33. As the twenty-first century unfolds, resource constraints are almost universally recognized. They are, of course, fundamental to microeconomics, the social science concerned with problems of scarce resource allocation.

34. Other dimensions of selectivity concern product portfolio choices; which level(s) in the distribution system to address; whether to focus on non-users, current customers or competitors' customers; and which members of the decision-making group to target.

35. Note that a focus on distinctive competence should not be construed as a straitjacket. Market opportunities should not be discarded merely because the firm currently does not possess the required competencies.

36. J.B. Quinn, *Strategies for Change: Logical Incrementation,* Homewood, IL: Irwin, 1980.

37. See C.M. Christensen, *The Innovator's Dilemma: When New Technologies Cause Great Firms to Fail,* Boston, MA: Harvard Business School Press, 1997.

38. Relating this principle to microeconomics, differential advantage is akin to the notion of monopolistic competition, the economic state in which participants earn greater than the going interest rate.

39. Service is an increasingly used method of securing differential advantage but it may not necessarily be directly related to the product under consideration. For example, provision of inventory control services, luxury boxes at major sporting events, and willingness to take payment in products subsequently to be bartered are examples of non-directly related services.

40. H. Simon, *Hidden Champions: Lessons from 500 of the Worlds Best Unknown Companies,* Boston, MA: Harvard Business School Press, 1996. See also, J.R. Williams, "How Sustainable is Your Competitive Advantage," *California Management Review,* 34 (Spring 1992), pp. 29–52; P. Ghemawat, "Sustainable Advantage," *Harvard Business Review,* 64 (Sept./Oct. 1986), pp. 53–94.

41. For further discussion, see R. D'Aveni, *Hypercompetition,* New York: The Free Press, 1994.

42. Procter and Gamble's Tide has been the leading detergent for around 50 years; however, in that time period it has had more than 50 product/packaging changes.

43. For alternative approaches to developing differential advantage, see G. Stalk, P. Evans and L.E. Shulman, "Competing on Capabilities: The New Rules of Corporate Strategy," *Harvard Business Review,* 70 (March/April) 1992, pp. 57–69 and D.J. Collis and C.A. Montgomery, "Competing on Resources: Strategy in the 1990s," *Harvard Business Review,* 73 (July/August) 1995, pp. 118–128. For the role of knowledge assets in securing competitive advantage, see D.J. Tecce, "Capturing Value from Knowledge Assets," *California Management Review,* 40 (Spring 1998), pp. 55–78.

44. See R.L. Foster, *Innovation: The Attacker's Advantage,* New York: Summit, 1986.

45. However, some recent research suggests that any difference may be better than none. See G.S. Carpenter, R. Glazer and K. Nakamoto, *Readings on Market-Driving Strategies: Towards a New Theory of Competitive Advantage,* New York: Addison Wesley Longman, 1997.

46. For example, leading package goods companies have developed category-planning teams that may include representatives of such functions as marketing, finance, market research, innovation, development, sales, and supply chain management. In addition, working groups for individual segments may include these functions plus purchasing, supply chain planning, logistics, customer service, and engineering.

47. E.N. Luttwak, *Strategy: The Logic of War and Peace,* Cambridge MA: Belknap Press, 1987.

48. To the extent possible, when a company no longer exists as an independent entity, the Web address of the surviving organization is provided.

WEB RESOURCES

Amazon.com	www.amazon.com
America Online	www.aol.com
AT&T	www.att.com
Boeing	www.boeing.com
Bombardier	www.bombardier.com
CBS	www.cbs.com
Compaq	www.compaq.com
De Havilland	www.bombardier.com
Dell	www.dell.com
Gateway	www.gateway.com
IBM	www.ibm.com
Microsoft	www.microsoft.com
NCR	www.ncr.com
Netscape	www.netscape.com
New York Magazine	www.newyorkmag.com
Packard Bell	www.packardbell.com
Teradata	www.att.com
Viacom	www.viacom.com
Westinghouse	www.westinghouse.com
Yahoo!	www.yahoo.com

2

THE ENVIRONMENTAL IMPERATIVE

LEARNING OBJECTIVES

When you have completed this chapter, you will understand

- the importance of environmental forces in affecting the nexus of firm, suppliers, customers, and competitors

- the importance of predicting, responding to, and shaping the future environment

- how to develop a framework for examining the environment that will better position you to deal with future uncertainty

- what some futures experts believe are important trends that managers need to consider

INTRODUCTION

Chapter 1 emphasized that for the firm to achieve its objectives of survival, growth, and improved shareholder value, the critical task is to win the competitive battle of creating and recreating customers in the face of competitive threats. This statement raises the question of which customers the firm should seek to create and recreate, and what competitive threats it faces in attempting to do so. Later chapters discuss these issues in depth, but first the following questions should be asked:

- What environmental factors can affect the relationships among the firm, its customers, competitors, and suppliers?
- What factors influence the firm's suppliers, and what impact can they have on the firm's ability to attract customers and defeat competitors?
- What factors influence the types of customers the firm wants to serve and what factors influence their purchasing decisions?
- What factors affect the types of competitors the firm faces and the manner in which they compete?

We often take for granted the set of circumstances in which we find ourselves and base our individual, family, and organizational decisions on the reality of the here and now. However, if we step back a little, we realize that our situation today is very different from a few years or even a few months ago. The fact that our circumstances today differ markedly from those of a short while ago should teach us to expect tomorrow to be very different from today.

For the marketing strategist, acknowledging this future difference is critical, for it implies that the set of assumptions that guide decisions taken today will most likely not be valid for decisions that must be made tomorrow. To raise the probability that tomorrow's actions are indeed based on valid assumptions, the strategist must attempt to predict, be ready to respond to, and sometimes influence the future environment. The purpose of this chapter is to provide a broad view of the firm's environment and to sensitize the reader to the nature of environmental change. In doing so, the chapter provides some frameworks for thinking about the future that may be useful regardless of the particular product market under consideration.

This chapter is divided into four sections. The first section highlights a series of changes that have taken place in the past few years in order to illustrate the scope of change in today's world. The second describes the firm's business environment and identifies elements of both the firm's general business environment and its task environment. The third section focuses on approaches to addressing environmental change and highlights notable failures in this area. Finally, the chapter describes innovative actions taken by companies to address customer needs and defeat competitors, and presents some predictions of futurist gurus as a way of encouraging you to think more broadly and less conventionally about threats and opportunities.

RECENT ENVIRONMENTAL CHANGES

This section focuses on an arbitrary point in time and identifies a series of changes and/or events that have affected the world of business. These changes and events are not an exhaustive list; indeed, the first question at the end of this chapter asks you to identify other important changes since the selected date, January 1, 1990.

A decade has passed since the beginning of the 1990s. Such a time period is beyond the scope of most marketing plans, but less than the time horizon of some corporate plans. The following set of changes and events illustrates the scope of change and the difficulty of predicting the future.

- In 1990, a large tract of Asia and part of Europe was governed by the USSR under a centralized communist system. In 1991, the Soviet empire collapsed, leading to the emergence of many independent countries.[1] Many of these countries moved to develop western-style democratic institutions and the trappings of capitalist systems, including public share ownership of corporations and stock markets. These changes were not confined to the former Soviet Union; former Eastern bloc countries such as Poland, Hungary, and Bulgaria also shed their communist systems. The changes had a major impact on defense contractors in the West and created opportunities for business-to-business and consumer marketers.

- In 1990, Yugoslavia was a single independent country. In the new millennium, it was reduced to a shadow of its former self, comprising only the former provinces of Serbia and Montenegro. From the remainder of the country, several independent nations had formed, including Slovenia, Croatia, and Bosnia. Bosnia had suffered a bitter civil war involving substantial "ethnic cleansing" and was host to an international peacekeeping force. In addition, the Serbian province of Kosovo was virtually independent following an extensive bombing campaign by NATO.

- Following the breakup of the USSR, Germany was reunified. The Federal Republic of Germany (West Germany) was joined with The German Democratic Republic (East Germany). Although the merger prompted a construction boom in the newly enlarged Germany, the ensuing financial crisis raised German unemployment to high levels.

- In 1990, a few university researchers communicated with each other online using the *Bitnet* system. In the new millennium, millions of people around the world were communicating by e-mail. The Internet had become a part of the world's daily life, and "surfing the Web" was becoming a hobby-like experience. Increasingly, the Internet was becoming an important engine of commerce, and many companies were earning millions of dollars in revenue each year through their Web sites.

- In 1990, Princess Diana of Britain was unhappily married to Prince Charles. By 1997, she had been separated from her husband for several years. When she was killed in an automobile accident in Paris in August, 1997, the world was fascinated by the story of her life for weeks afterward.

- In 1990, it was common for U.S. executives to wear a suit and tie to work every day. In the new millennium, not only was "casual Friday" becoming the norm in most of American industry, many companies, including such financial powerhouses as Morgan Stanley and Goldman Sachs, were allowing casual dress every day.

- In 1990, persons wanting to make telephone calls had to find a telephone. In the new millennium, this search was no longer necessary, as personal cellular phones had become the communication vehicles of choice for many people.

- In 1990, South Africa was ruled by a government formed by the minority white race. Just a few years later, apartheid had been dealt a fatal blow, the electoral franchise was universal, and the government was comprised mainly of those of black skin color. As a result, economic sanctions of many years' standing were lifted.

- In 1990, ski slopes around the world were populated almost exclusively by skiers. In the new millennium, skiers were in the minority on many slopes, as young people turned to the increasingly popular sport of snowboarding. Snowboarders gained a measure of respectability (that not all desired) as the 1998 Winter Olympics in Nagano, Japan, included snowboarding competition for the first time. In addition to snowboarding, one observer estimated 20 million people in the United States alone were participating in so-called extreme sports.[2]

- In 1990, and for many subsequent years, California enjoyed its expected mild weather climate. However the winter of 1998 brought severe storms created by a weather condition known as *El Niño*.

- By the start of the new millennium, rainforest destruction, contributing to global warming, was reaching alarming proportions in such countries as Brazil and Indonesia. Additionally, scientists were reporting continuing destruction of the earth's ozone layer.

- In 1990, a group of countries known as "Asian Tigers" (Hong Kong, Indonesia, Malaysia, Thailand, The Philippines, and Singapore) were enjoying strong current and predicted economic growth. In 1997, currency collapses occurred all over Southeast Asia. From mid-September 1997 to end-January 1998, selected currency losses were 194% in Indonesia, 44% in Malaysia, 51% in Thailand, and 27% in The Philippines. By early 2000, many of these economies had substantially recovered.
- In 1990, a broad coalition of countries participated in the Gulf War to evict Iraqi forces from Kuwait. Throughout most of the 1990s, United Nations weapons inspectors sought to identify and eliminate Iraq's weapons of mass destruction. In 1998, in the face of Iraqi intransigence, new attacks were initiated.
- Since the dawn of space travel, an underlying assumption has been that astronauts should be young. In 1998, former astronaut John Glenn returned to space at age 77.

As you examine these examples of changes and events from around the world, you will realize several things. Some changes, such as rainforest destruction, may have been predictable; others, such as Germany's reunification and the Asian currency collapse, were largely unpredictable. For at least some of the examples, such as the Asian currency collapse, marketplace implications are readily foreseeable; for others, such as rainforest destruction and California's climate change, the implications are less clear. For some changes and events, such as the death of Princess Diana, the implications may be fairly well contained[3]; for others, such as the breakup of the USSR and global warming, they can be expected to be widespread. In the remainder of this chapter, frameworks and approaches are presented that will enable you to better deal with environmental changes and events that you will face in the future.

THE FIRM'S BUSINESS ENVIRONMENT

The firm's environment[4] comprises both the general business environment and its task environment. The firm's general business environment includes a set of governmental, economic, technological, physical, cultural, and managerial process forces that impact not only the firm itself, but also its customers, competitors, and suppliers. The firm's customers, competitors, and suppliers, termed the *task environment,* are discussed in the next section.

Dimensions of the Firm's General Business Environment

Key elements of the firm's general business environment are highlighted in Figure 2.1. This section identifies specific examples of changes that have occurred in recent years, and to the extent possible, makes some predictions. However, prediction is not the primary purpose of this chapter.

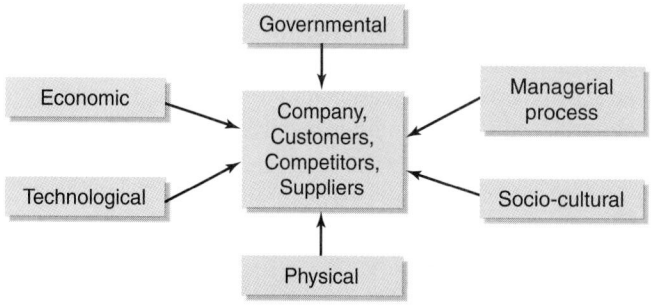

FIGURE 2.1

Environmental Forces Affecting the Firm, Customers, Competitors, and Suppliers

GOVERNMENTAL INFLUENCES   Governments set the rules of the business game and sometimes also play the game. Historically, they have intervened in national economies to pursue political ends and to redress the perceived failure of market mechanisms to achieve consumer welfare goals. In some countries, such as the United States, this "interference" included extensive government regulation of such areas as competitive entry, product performance, price setting, distribution, and advertising. In other countries, such as Great Britain after the second World War, state-ownership of business corporations was vigorously pursued. In still others, such as India and Japan, state-driven mercantilism to increase exports and reduce imports has been the pattern. Since World War I, increased government involvement has been the norm around the world.

However, since the oil crisis of the early 1970s, the pendulum has shifted from government involvement to a reliance on free markets. Around the world, regulatory barriers are coming down in such previously protected industries as airlines, banking, railroads, insurance, telecommunications, and trucking, as governments realize that regulations designed in an earlier era to protect consumers or competitors are no longer beneficial. Far too often, regulation locked in competitive structures, restricted competitive entry and innovation, and denied customers the benefits that competition could bring.[5]

In many countries, government-owned organizations are joining the private sector as governments adopt the view that private enterprise is more effective than government in promoting consumer welfare, even in such previously unlikely countries as the People's Republic of China (PRC). This trend has been aided by political change in many countries, such as the collapse of communism in the USSR and Eastern Europe, and the displacing of military dictatorships in Latin America.[6]

Historically, most governmental influence was an intra-national activity, either at the national or local level. However, agreements between nations, effected through supra-national bodies such as the World Trade Organization (formerly GATT), the International Monetary Fund, the North American Free Trade Association (NAFTA),[7] Mercosur,[8] and the European Union, are taking on increasing importance as individual nations are subject to regulations laid down by these bodies.[9] However, these organizations have less power than institutions within individual nations, and their enforcement abilities may be sorely tested as individual nations become concerned about national sovereignty issues.

Regulation and state ownership are typically enacted through legislation in the political process. Where regulation is concerned, regulatory bodies such as (in the United States) the Environmental Protection Agency (EPA), Federal Communications Commission (FCC), Federal Trade Commission (FTC), National Transportation Safety Board (NTSB), and their equivalents in other countries, typically enact rules embodying the legislation. The judicial system acts as arbiter when some believe that the rules are either unfair or are not being followed appropriately.[10]

Typically, business organizations can effect political and regulatory action in several ways, depending on the specific country. For example, in the United States, contributions may be made to political campaigns, lobbyists can attempt to influence both legislation and the rule-making process, and lawsuits may be brought to advance firm interests. Sometimes industry bodies such as trade associations more effectively undertake these actions.

> **Example:** In early 2000, four U.S. property and casualty insurance companies— Chubb, Hartford, Kemper, and Liberty Mutual—approached the U.S. Congress to complain about an income-tax loophole being used by Bermuda-based firms that, they believed, disadvantaged insurance companies based in the United States.[11]

ECONOMIC INFLUENCES   Essentially, the economic environment portrays the economic well-being of nations, geographic regions within nations, and groups of nations. Many measures of economic well-being are available, but critical metrics include per capita income, spending and savings/investment patterns, inflation, and unemployment rates. All things being equal, the greater the level and growth of per capita income and the lower inflation and unemployment levels, the greater the level of economic activity, as individuals, households, and organizations engage in commerce as buyers and sellers.

The health of product and service markets is closely related to the state of the financial markets. If interest rates are high and rising, stock prices are falling, and the currency value (against a stable benchmark) is low and falling, the economy is likely to be unhealthy. In general, unhealthy economies and the actions necessary for their stabilization and improvement lead to higher prices and increased unemployment. In some countries with underdeveloped financial markets, international transactions have shifted away from the money economy to various forms of barter.

From the early 1990s onward, many aspects of the world economy were extremely positive; during the Clinton administration, the U.S. economic environment was sufficiently strong to protect the President from allegations made in the 1998 "sexgate" scandal. By contrast, having enjoyed strong economic growth for many years in the late 1990s, several of the "Asian Tigers" suffered from unstable financial markets and enormous shocks to their economies. Furthermore, many countries continue to have largely underdeveloped economic systems with several, especially in Africa, being largely subsistence economies.

In recent years it has become clear that the implications of an economic downturn in one country are no longer confined to that country. The greater interconnectedness of countries in the global economy means that economic problems in one area reverberate around the world. Thus, the impact of South Korea's economic collapse and Japan's 1998 slip into recession were felt not only by neighboring countries, but also by Europe and the Americas.

Concerns regarding economic activity in individual countries have led to a growth in regional trading blocs, such as Mercosur and the Andean Pact[12] in South America, NAFTA, the Caribbean Free Trade Area,[13] and the Association of South East Asian Nations (ASEAN).[14] The most advanced grouping, the European Union, has a major political component and has introduced a single currency, the Euro. Furthermore, the presence of such cartels as OPEC (for oil) should not be forgotten, for the dependence of many industrialized countries on Middle Eastern oil remains a strategic vulnerability.[15]

TECHNOLOGICAL INFLUENCES   Virtually all observers of the business scene agree that the pace of technological change is accelerating. The first section of this chapter noted some broad-brush environmental changes that have occurred since 1990, but touched only cursorily on technological change. Tracking technological change since the end of World War II, however, would reveal that many of the products and services we take for granted today have been developed since that time. A partial list would include color television, copier machines, synthetic fibers and almost all plastics, cellular telephones, computers, integrated circuits, microwave ovens, passenger jet aircraft, communication satellites, virtually all antibiotics and numerous other life-saving drugs, ATMs, video and audio tape recorders, compact discs, and many other innovations. Today, new technology in the form of the Internet is changing the way firms in entire industries compete, and is offering customer benefits that were unimaginable just a few years ago.

Many of these innovations have fundamentally changed (and are changing) individual, household, and organizational life. Frequently, new products and services have improved the human experience and have played major roles in driving economic growth through job creation. On the other hand, these new technologies have often displaced older technologies whose benefit/cost ratio was no match for the new entrant. Examples include ATMs for bank tellers, jet aircraft for propeller aircraft, copy machines for carbon paper, and compact discs for long-playing records. In the U.S. credit reporting industry, the introduction of computers shrunk the 2,000 or so manual (mainly local) credit bureaus to three.

The engines driving these innovations have been human ingenuity and corporate investment in research and development. However, by no means do major corporations develop all major technological change. One need only consider those of today's major corporations that were started by entrepreneurs in the postwar period, such as Acer, Apple, Compaq, Intel, Microsoft, Polaroid, Texas Instruments, Sony, Xerox, and others to realize that technological change, and the products and services it spawns, can arise from many different sources. Furthermore, some inventors are extremely prolific—Jerome Murray, who held 75 patents, invented such diverse products as the electric carving knife, the audible pressure cooker, the passenger aircraft boarding ramp, and a pump that made open-heart surgery possible.[16]

History is replete with examples of major companies that turned down inventors who approached them with inventions that were ultimately successful. Chester Carlson, inventor of xerography, was turned down by IBM, Kodak, and 3M before Edward Wilson, CEO of a relatively small Rochester company, Haloid Corporation, had the courage to bet the future of his company on Carlson's invention.[17] More recently, all major appliance manufacturers turned down James Dyson, inventor of the bagless vacuum cleaner. He eventually started his own company that in 1998 enjoyed over 30% of the British market.[18] Trevor Baylis, inventor of the clockwork radio that is having a dramatic impact in the world's poorer regions where batteries are too expensive, had exactly the same experience. Consider also the experience of Apple Computer founder Steve Jobs during his attempts to raise interest in his and Steve Wozniak's personal computer:

> **Example:** "So we went to Atari and said, 'Hey, we've got this amazing thing, even built it with some of your parts, and what do you think about funding us? Or we'll give it to you. We just want to do it. Pay our salary, we'll come work for you.' And they said 'No.' So then we went to Hewlett Packard, and they said 'Hey, we don't need you. You haven't gone through college yet.'"

Two important implications follow from these examples. First, successful companies may develop an unhealthy focus on their own current activities unless they make strenuous efforts to avoid doing so. Second, the vital role played by risk capital in establishing new businesses and even industries must be recognized. Some allege that the economic success of Silicon Valley is as dependent on venture capital firms as it is on the abilities of entrepreneurs and inventors. Certainly, many European businessmen, particularly in countries like France, bemoan the absence of favorable attitudes and infrastructures in their countries. Some of them have left for Great Britain's more hospitable business climate.[19]

PHYSICAL INFLUENCES The physical environment, roughly viewed as comprising the natural and manmade environment, is all around us; changes large and small affect our daily lives and the functioning of our organizations. Natural and manmade forces coexist in an uneasy equilibrium, but whereas some natural forces seem independent of human action, others are profoundly affected by it.

For example, man seemingly has little or no control over such natural phenomena as asteroids hitting the earth, monsoons, hurricanes and tornadoes, everyday weather patterns (including *El Niño*), and the development of many viruses and other diseases. On the other hand, large-scale changes such as the destruction of rainforests, global warming, retreating coastlines, pollution, raw material shortages, and loss of the ozone layer are typically attributable to human action.

The ability to identify the business implications of changes in the physical environment is critical for management. At a basic level, change in climate has an important impact on product demand in many categories, such as beer, soft drinks, and umbrellas. More fundamental physical changes may have a variety of consequences. For example, heightened awareness of the damage to the natural environment caused by pollution has given rise to new industries such as pollution control and renewable energy. In some countries, such as France and Germany, pollution has become an important political issue, and legislators are elected as members of "green" parties. Indeed, in many countries, the strength of the environmental movement has led to strong legislation affecting firms' production systems, products, and packaging. In Germany, for example, firms are responsible for the disposal of the packaging in which their products are shipped.[20]

SOCIO-CULTURAL INFLUENCES Culture can be defined as "the distinctive customs, achievements, products, outlook, etc., of a society or group; the way of life of a society or group."[21] The society or group may be the inhabitants of a nation, such as the French, a geographic region within a nation, such as the South or the Midwest in the United States, a geographic region encompassing multiple nations, such as Latin America, or a people without regard to geographic location, such as the Armenian, Jewish, and Chinese Diaspora. Furthermore, an individual may belong to multiple groups that each have different cultures, such as Turkish immigrants in Germany.

Cultures differ from one another on many different levels, such as language, religion, values and attitudes, education, social organization, technical and material culture, politics, law, and aesthetics (Table 2.1). Cultures also change over time. Within any individual cultural group, subcultures develop that may reflect not only broad group culture, but also specific subcultural elements, such as baby boomers and Generations X and Y.[22]

> **Example:** Among the baby boomers in the United States, increasing lifespans have led to a shift in concern from dying too early to having insufficient savings for old age. Related product implications include a reduction in demand for life insurance and increased demand for mutual funds.

Other examples abound. The "dress-down" movement in many U.S. corporations has major implications for fiber, garment, detergent, and washing machine manufacturers. In addition, purchasing in club stores affects manufacturers; they are unable to secure the breadth of customer data available from supermarkets.

To a large extent people do not notice culture in their everyday lives, but it becomes evident when they encounter a different culture. This is a special issue as firms move

TABLE 2.1   The Cultural Environment

Language	Spoken, written, official, linguistic pluralism, hierarchy, international, mass media
Religion	Sacred objects, philosophical systems, beliefs and norms, prayer, taboos, holidays, rituals
Values and attitudes	Time, achievement, work, wealth, change, scientific method, risk-taking
Education	Formal, vocational, primary, secondary, higher, literacy, human resources planning
Social organization	Kinship, institutions, authority structures, interest groups, mobility, stratification, status systems
Technical and material	Transportation, energy systems, tools and objects, communications, urbanization, science, invention
Politics	Nationalism, sovereignty, imperialism, power, national interests, ideologies, political risk
Law	Common, code, foreign, home country antitrust policy, international, regulation
Aesthetics	Beauty, good taste, color, music, brand names, architecture

Taken in part from V. Terpstra, *The Cultural Environment of International Business,* Cincinnati, OH: Southwestern Publishing, 1978, Figure 1. See also V. Terpstra and K. David, *The Cultural Environment of International Business,* 3rd edition, Cincinnati, OH: Southwestern Publishing, 1991.

out of their domestic markets and into foreign markets. Here the issue is less one of cultural change than of attempting to understand a culture that is different. Indeed, a company acting in an ethnocentric manner may ruin an otherwise successful strategy implementation.[23]

Example: A U.S. technology firm was well placed to win a major contract from a Chinese company. However, at a banquet given by the Chinese company, the senior person on the U.S. team started eating before the host, a cultural no-no. The contract was finally given to a French firm whose technology was inferior, but with which the Chinese felt more comfortable.[24]

These issues have sometimes compromised companies' international expansions. In the United States, Japanese companies have been found guilty of discrimination against both women and Americans, while the U.S. head of the Scandinavian pharmaceutical firm Astra was fired for sexual harassment. However, casual observation suggests that practices considered sexual harassment in the United States are regarded as quite normal in some other countries.

An important contemporary cultural issue is the tension between localism and globalism. On the one hand, individual groups seek their own identities and also act out their group membership in various ways. Important bases for group membership include religion and nationalism. Thus the growth of Muslim and Hindu fundamentalism are important factors in the Middle East/North African region and India, respectively, and in recent years the number of independent countries in the world has increased markedly.[25]

By contrast, the development of multinational governmental organizations such as the United Nations, the World Trade Organization, and UNESCO, as well as the ready availability of communications via television and motion pictures, enhance globalism. Thus it is difficult to overstate the benefit that Philip Morris' *Marlboro* brand received from the scores of cowboy movies distributed around the world for more than half a century. In fact, concern has been raised in many countries about American influence, particularly from Hollywood and TV shows such as *Dallas* and MTV. Indeed, the French government is fighting a rearguard action against what it views as an American cultural invasion in general and an anglicizing of the French language in particular. However, concern is not limited to language:

Example: In late 1999, protests in many European countries against genetically altered foods led to rejections and bans on products such as Monsanto's *Roundup Ready* soybean seeds. Similarly, in August 1999, several McDonald's franchises in Belgium and France were badly damaged or destroyed by protesters angry about the "globalization of food."

Another important issue in today's globalizing environment is the extent to which new cultural groups are being developed across national lines. Many observers have commented on the growth of a group of well-traveled, internationally oriented, upscale, sophisticated businesspersons developing a cultural identity that crosses national and ethnic borders.[26]

MANAGERIAL PROCESS INFLUENCES The managerial process environment encompasses the received wisdom on how to lead and manage organizations. Received wisdom changes over time as new knowledge is developed through research efforts at schools of business and management, the culling of experience by consultants, and feedback received by managers on their actions. However, it is subject to the same processes of innovation diffusion as other ideas and patterns in a society.[27]

We identify two important examples of changes in managerial thought in recent years—corporate strategy and the structure of business organizations. In the late 1960s, a major thrust in many corporations in the United States and other countries was conglomeration. The conglomerate was an organization comprised of disparate business units—for example, ITT, Gulf & Western and Litton Industries in the United States, and

THE ENVIRONMENTAL
IMPERATIVE

Slater Walker and The Hanson Trust in Great Britain. The rationale for conglomeration was diversifying risk as in a financial portfolio. To a large extent, this rationale has fallen into disrepute, as investors are better able to diversify their own risks by investing in multiple corporations.[28] In its place, the watchword has become *focus:* Corporations are urged to "stick to their knitting" and base strategies on core competencies. As a result, many firms are divesting business units unrelated to a common strength or purpose.

> **Example:** Pacific Dunlop (revenues A\$3 billion [Australian dollars]), formerly one of Australia's most diverse companies, is slimming down to concentrate on its more profitable businesses with growth potential. Beginning in late 1995, it discarded several operations with sales over A\$100 million. These included its food group Petersville Sleigh (A\$1.06 billion), several plastics and polystyrene businesses (A\$107 million), Cochlear bionic ear business (A\$125 million), Pasta House (US\$100 million), Telectronics (A\$166 million), and GNB Technologies (value about A\$1 billion).[29]

A second example concerns organizational structure. Dating from the 1950s, corporations were urged to structure their divisions as independent profit centers. Today, divisions and profit centers have largely been discarded in favor of strategic business units (SBUs), entities with well-defined customers, competitors, and technology, formed on the basis of external strategic considerations rather than on internal rationales.[30] In addition, strategic planning concepts that were virtually unknown until the late 1960s have become permanent elements of many organizations' lexicons and are embedded in this book. Such concepts as the experience curve, portfolio models and policy matrices, strategic objectives, and market share/profitability relationships are all part of today's managerial kit bag.[31] Some more recent developments are likely to become similarly enshrined in practice: Total quality management (TQM), reengineering, and shareholder value have arguably already graduated to this status.

This is not to suggest that each new buzzword has value for the individual manager. Indeed, one of the problems managers face is distinguishing fads with little long-run potential for improving organizational effectiveness from those concepts that may have fundamental impact. All too often, a consultant or academic interested in profit or vainglory dresses up an old idea in new clothes. Among other responsibilities, managers must become fully conversant with developing knowledge on leading and managing organizations, have the capability and confidence to sort wheat from chaff, and learn how to apply important and useful knowledge in their firms. The ability to create organizations that effectively master and deploy knowledge, and are capable of staying abreast of knowledge development, is the focus of much work by academics and firms.[32] Knowledge is increasingly seen as a critical source of competitive advantage, and the creation of effective learning organizations has become a Nirvana to be sought. As we look toward the future, those managers who can identify and assimilate new knowledge, separate the important from the unimportant or incorrect, and adopt and implement the new managerial wisdom, will secure advantage over their competitors.

INTERACTIONS AMONG DIMENSIONS OF THE GENERAL BUSINESS ENVIRONMENT Although these six environmental forces—governmental, economic, technological, physical, socio-cultural, and managerial process—were discussed independently, in reality, each environmental domain interacts with its sister dimensions. For example, a new multinational and multicultural group of well-traveled, internationally oriented, upscale, sophisticated businesspersons was discussed earlier. However, the emergence of such a group is directly related to several factors: a positive economic environment that makes it profitable to travel and offers increasing global business opportunities, a governmental environment that permits capital flows, a technological environment that makes international travel and communications a matter of course, and a managerial process environment that looks favorably on international business.

Several writers argue that the interconnectedness of the environment is increasing even as the rate of change increases and it becomes more turbulent.[33] The challenge for the firm is to identify changes in the environmental dimensions *per se*, their interactions, and the implications of each on the firm's current and future business opportunities. Clearly, the greater the changes in these environmental variables and the greater the interaction among them, the greater the degree of turbulence faced by the firm in dealing with its customers, competitors, and suppliers.

The purpose for addressing these characteristics of the broader environment is twofold: First, the following chapter develops the idea of being externally oriented. However, the current purpose is to gain greater insight into the forces that influence change among the firm's suppliers, customers, and competitors, and hence have implications for the firm. In a global environment, good coordination of the firm's intelligence can often create competitive advantage, for ideas and practices typically diffuse from one part of the environment or country to another. Although many insights gained are industry specific, these examples illustrate environmental change leaders:

- Germany is often viewed as a leader in environmental legislation and related political activism, and many believe that actions in Germany presage change elsewhere.
- California is still the geographic area most closely watched for youth-oriented trends, but in U.S. male fashion, young African-American males are viewed as a leading influence.
- In computers, telecommunications, medicine, and biotechnology, leading companies keep close tabs on university programs at Stanford, MIT, and Cambridge.
- In the 1980s, as denationalization and privatization swept the globe, many countries sent deputations to talk to Britain's radical Thatcher government that was busily dismantling over forty years of socialist dogma. Today, these activities often progress beyond intelligence gathering. For example, at the turn of the millennium, seven of ten British electricity distribution companies were owned by North American utilities eager to experience the impact of competitive supply markets prior to the arrival of similar conditions domestically.

The basic supposition underlying the discussion to this point is that by spending a little time thinking about the future, firms may deal with it better. However, unlike the efforts that occur in so many firms, it is prudent to look beyond the obvious in an attempt to better understand the broad and fundamental forces that reshape industries and firms globally. The most important factors changing an industry and the players within it typically emanate from outside the industry itself—hence the importance of an external orientation.

The Firm's Task Environment: Customers, Competitors, and Suppliers

This section focuses on the firm's task environment. It commences with a discussion of customers—individual/household customers first, followed by organizations—and then moves to a discussion of competitors and suppliers.

CUSTOMERS: INDIVIDUAL CONSUMERS/HOUSEHOLDS   Using the nation as the organizing framework, we look first at the diverse and changing demographics characterizing world markets.

- **Population size**: Population sizes differ significantly across countries around the world. Growth rates differ also; the growth rate in many Western countries is scarcely sufficient to sustain the population, while in many less-developed countries it is extraordinarily high.[34] The combination of total population and wealth distribution impacts the size of many consumer markets. Marketers in the United States and, to some extent, in Europe, tend to view their home regions as the major sources of opportunity. But as economic development spreads throughout the world, these traditional markets often represent declining percentages of global market potential.

- **Age distribution**: The population's age distribution has an important impact on customer needs and hence required goods and services. In Western countries, populations are generally aging (with median ages often in excess of 30 years) as birth rates slow, family size decreases, and life expectancy increases. The market of affluent "empty-nesters" presents a significant opportunity and challenge to marketers who have traditionally targeted the youth market hoping to build lifetime loyalty. By contrast, in many emerging markets (Mexico, Brazil, and Indonesia, for example), median ages are still low (often less than 20 years).

- **Population mix**: Changes in many countries' population mix may open up significant ethnic and language segments. Immigration into such countries as the United States, Germany, and Australia, and cross-border travel in search of work are good examples. In particular, the potential for population shifts in Europe has increased as a result of the formation of the European Union. In addition, differential birth rates across subgroups within nations will, in time, substantially change their demographic landscapes.

- **Wealth and wealth distribution**: In the post-World-War II period, it was common to divide the world into three wealth categories—the United States, Western European countries, and less-developed countries (LDCs). More recently, countries such as Sweden, Singapore, and Japan have rivaled the United States in per capita income. Furthermore, prior to the 1997 Asian crisis, many countries that had been classified as LDCs (such as South Korea and Thailand) were growing at rates that, if continued, would have enabled them to catch up with developed Western countries within a few years. Not only has absolute wealth increased in many countries, but the distribution of per capita income has also been evening out, compared to many poor LDCs in which a small elite, often related to the governing politicians, maintains a stranglehold on the country's wealth.

- **Geographic population shifts**: Notwithstanding population shifts caused by transitory labor, many within-country population shifts occur worldwide. For example, as country wealth is enhanced, urbanization increases as people leave rural areas, and cities become overcrowded. In many Western countries, suburban growth is followed by city regeneration. A more recent trend, supported by improvements in information and telecommunications technology, is "exurban" growth, a return to rural communities. More specifically, population shifts in the United States seem to follow the sun, and the Southeast's and Southwest's gains are the Northeast's loss. Similarly, many Northern Europeans move to Spain, Portugal, and the Tuscany region of Italy.

These factors are just some of the more important dimensions on which a marketing analyst would want to collect data. Other variables of interest are marriage (rate and age), family size, births in and out of wedlock, infant mortality, divorce, remarriage, mortality rates, and work force composition. In most cases, good predictions can be made about these sorts of variables. If current data is collected on birth and infant mortality rates, future family formation predictions can be made with a fair degree of certainty.

In addition to these demographic factors, several other trends have widespread importance:

- **Increased consumer knowledge**: Many firms report that consumers are becoming more sophisticated in making their purchasing decisions. In part this results from increased educational opportunities, government action to require greater consumer access to information, and increasing levels of competition. In many product categories, consumers learn more about products being offered and are making more intelligent decisions. Better-educated consumers are typically more willing to innovate, a factor that is related to reduced levels of brand loyalty experienced by some firms.

- **Comfort with technology**: Personal computers and the Internet will cause major changes in the ways that consumers make purchase decisions. Direct marketing has already made significant inroads in store traffic in many countries, and immediate access to choice alternatives via new information systems may revolutionize the way consumers shop. Not only has the reduction in trade barriers under the World Trade Organization (WTO) and its predecessor organizations led to greater electronic access to global markets, but entry barriers are reduced for firms willing to use this channel to reach customers. This trend is expected to increase as the more technologically literate parts of the population—the young—age.

Historically, organizations have developed strategies on national or even narrower bases. However, major corporations are increasingly concerned with multinational, regional, or global strategies. As a result, their concerns may focus less on specific data from an individual country than on data combined across several countries.

CUSTOMERS: ORGANIZATIONS   Firms in consumer products or service businesses require significant information on consumers and families. Firms that sell to other organizations may also need to follow these sorts of variables as the customers of their customers may in turn be consumers. Regardless, they certainly must be familiar with trends affecting their organizational customers. Several are evident, such as globalization, the basis of economic activity, and increasing account concentration.

- **Globalization**: One of the more important trends affecting corporations is a changing mindset from national, regional (multinational), or even international, to global. In particular, many large companies have shifted from serving mainly domestic markets from domestic plants to serving multiple markets from multinational plants. Even traditionally domestic industries like retailing are globalizing quickly, as retailers like Ikea (Sweden), Carrefour (France), Wal-Mart (United States), Marks and Spencer (Great Britain), and Royal Ahold (Holland) move into overseas markets. Similarly, whereas the terminal form of economic structure reached in many industries is domestic oligopoly (in which a few major competitors together comprise high market share), industries now seem to be driving toward global oligopoly (examples include the automobile tire and telecommunication switch industries), or global duopoly (as in large passenger aircraft). This trend has encouraged cross-border mergers and acquisitions in such industries as pharmaceuticals and investment banking, and partnership arrangements, as in the passenger airline industry.
- **The basis of economic activity**: The industrial revolution was based in manufacturing; today, advanced Western economies are increasingly based in services. In addition, in the United States and many other countries, new business start-ups have demonstrated remarkable growth rates since the early 1980s and are responsible for significant employment growth.
- **Increasing account concentration**: Many separate environmental forces have led to a trend for firm sales to be concentrated, with fewer but more powerful direct customers. Sales to customers in mature industries are affected by a generalized trend toward oligopolistic market structures as weaker competitors either exit or are acquired by stronger competitors.[35] In 1997, a record $1 trillion in mergers occurred involving U.S. companies, including 156 over $1 billion (compared to 97 in 1996). Indeed, from 1995 to 1997, 27,600 companies joined together, more than in the entire 1980s. (Table 2.2 provides selected industry data.)[36] Worldwide, acquisition value from 1990 to 1993 averaged $400 billion; in 1998 alone, acquisition value exceeded $2.4 trillion.[37]

TABLE 2.2 The Pace of Mergers and Acquisitions: Selected Industries, 1992–1997

Industry	Number of Deals	Total Value
Commercial Banks	2,492	>$200 billion
Radio and Television	1,435	$162 billion
Insurance	5,114	$110 billion
Health Services	NA	$107 billion
Investment Brokers	NA	$104 billion
Oil and Gas Refining	NA	$96 billion
Hotels and Casinos	NA	$84 billion

Driven by competitive pressure, customer power, scale-driven buying advantages, and the huge capital requirements of competing globally, many different industries are witnessing concentration among existing players. In the U.S. retail industry, such "category killer" stores as Home Depot, Sports Authority, and Circuit City have decimated competition. Indeed, sometimes the acquired was a former star company and the acquirer a younger, more agile company.

Example: In 1998, PC manufacturer Compaq acquired Digital Equipment (DEC). DEC, the glamour computer company of the 1970s based on minicomputers, had a difficult time adjusting to the PC revolution. Also in 1998, telecommunications giant MCI was taken over by Internet provider WorldCom. Previously successful MCI had been unable to cope with the rapidly changing telecommunications environment.

International regionalization and globalization, noted above, have accelerated this trend in many industries. For example, in 1993, the percentage of industry sales accounted for by the top four global producers in various industries was 98% in civil aviation, 51% in automotive, 40% in information processing, and 35% in telecommunications equipment. Profitability appears related to degree of concentration (Figure 2.2).

Finally, in many markets, buying groups have developed as countervailing forces to the power of suppliers.

COMPETITORS The nature and intensity of competition is changing quite dramatically in many different industries. The environmental forces discussed earlier are a major influence on this change.

- **Technology**: Technology has vastly increased the alternatives available to solve customer problems.

Example: Consider a relatively simple product like fruit juice. Today, in many countries, it can be bought in a variety of packaging forms: glass bottles, Tetra-Pak containers, cans (aluminum and tinplate), foil packs, and plastic containers of various types.

Whether the customer need is home entertainment, food and drink, or leisure activity, the choices are staggering. Nor are the alternatives limited to the product or service *per se,* for entrepreneurial activity often combines with innovations in distribution strategy to provide radically new alternatives, as with Amazon.com, the successful Internet-based retailer. Of course, choice passes power to customers, for without choice the customer has no power. As the following chapter discusses, the arguments for an external orientation are based on hard economics, not merely on values.

- **Government**: It was noted earlier in this chapter that government policy in many countries is fostering increased competition through such actions as deregulation and privatization. When Federal Express commenced operations in 1971, it was the

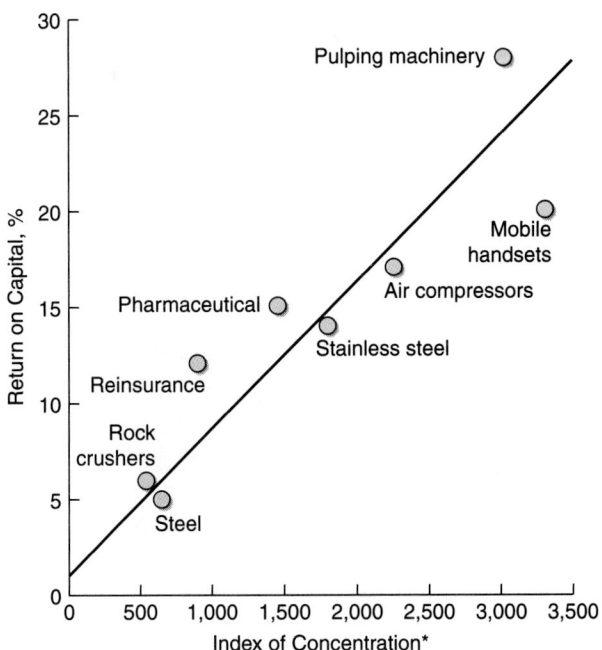

FIGURE 2.2

Industry Profitablilty Versus Global Concentration

The Economist, Jan. 23, 1999.

first new airline in the United States in over 30 years! Since the heavy hand of airline regulation was lifted in the late 1970s, a succession of new airlines have been launched, though most, unlike the brilliantly successful Southwest Airlines, have failed to survive as independent entities.

- **Globalization**: The third major influence on the intensity of competition has been globalization, a phenomenon fostered by intergovernmental agreements to reduce trade barriers, but greatly facilitated by technological advances in transportation and communications. In the 1950s, 1960s and even 1970s, many industries were characterized by a pattern of regional dominance. Companies were powerful in their domestic markets or home regions and participated to a much more modest extent in other markets. Of course, there were exceptions. Companies from previously imperial countries like Britain and France typically had established far-flung operations, often under the protection of trade preferences. Firms in some industries, notably oil and automobiles, had led the way in internationalizing their operations, often primarily to avoid prohibitive import tariffs. And a few outstanding companies like Gillette and Hoover had pioneered the concept of a multinational corporation.

  However, by the 1980s, the quest for growth overwhelmed old arrangements in all but a few industries. Previously local firms began to jockey for global dominance in many industries, leading to dramatic transformation of company portfolios. Much of this change was accomplished via mergers and acquisitions as intensifying competition placed ever-greater pressure on weaker players no longer sheltered behind trade protection walls. As noted earlier, this trend has led to a high degree of global concentration in several industries. The 21st century will witness the emergence of strengthened international institutions for dealing with the challenges posed by global monopoly and oligopoly and the consequent threat to global consumer welfare.

- **Implications**: The marketing philosophy argues that satisfied customers are much more likely to re-purchase in the future. However, if the seller is a monopolist, customers are forced to re-purchase even when intensely dissatisfied. Conversely, as markets become more competitive, ever-higher levels of performance are required to retain customers; stated colloquially; "the bar is always rising." As is explained later in the book, this process has dramatic impact on the search for competitive advantage.

Rising competitive intensity mandates that firms achieve much higher competency levels in marketing. This is one of the major reasons you are taking this course and reading this book! Later chapters focus on the challenge of competitive market strategy, and devote considerable space to the challenge of outwitting competitors in the quest for targeted customers' loyalty.

SUPPLIERS   Several forces have combined to lead to increasing concentration among suppliers:

- **Changes in the procurement process**: In recent years, companies have realized the critical importance of the procurement (purchasing) function to long-term corporate health. Since significant labor inputs have been replaced by capital in many industries, expenditures on capital equipment, raw materials, and supplies now represent increasing portions of firm costs. As a result, procurement decisions have become more consequential, leading to increased proficiency in purchasing, involvement of multiple management levels, and greater centralization of decision making. This process has also been affected by organizational downsizing, implementation of TQM, vertical alliances, and development of flatter organization structures. In particular, rapid advances in transportation, telecommunications and computer technology have aided centralization of decision making. Whereas historically, various corporate units may have operated independently for procurement purposes, the increasing capability of the center to gather data from disparate units has led to a shift in procurement practices. For example, in many retail chains, the corporate office is now heavily involved in procurement decisions for individual stores, whereas in previous years these stores would have operated more autonomously.
- **Affirmative reductions in numbers of suppliers**: In recent years, many firms have made affirmative decisions to decrease their numbers of suppliers. In part, these decisions have been driven by TQM and a desire to secure tighter control over raw material inputs. Adoption of *Kaizen*,[38] a concern to reduce working capital, and an overall focus on improving efficiency in the resource conversion process have led to reduction in the number of supplier relationships. The term *virtual integration* is sometimes used to describe the very close relationships that have evolved in vertical partnerships among suppliers, their customers and even their customers' customers. In some cases it appears that newer forms of competition will be among whole supply chains rather than among individual firms themselves. As firms have looked to their suppliers to provide more complex and tailored mixes of products and services, sometimes involving multiple technologies and customized service, increased effectiveness and efficiency in procurement becomes essential. Increasingly, this is acheived by forging close relationships with fewer suppliers leading to significant profit enhancements.[39] The outsourcing movement that has led many firms to seek closer relationships with suppliers has reinforced this trend. These changes are examined at greater length later in the book.

Intense competition and increased customer power have also played roles in changing supplier–customer relationships. Increased competitive intensity requires much more efficient supply chains, because a large portion of total cost to the final customer has traditionally come from various costs incurred in distribution. In some cases, the quest for this increased efficiency has led to industry-wide cooperation. Perhaps the best-known example is the Efficient Consumer Response (ECR) initiative in the U.S. grocery trade, jointly sponsored by manufacturers and retailers (large supermarket chains). This initiative is designed to eliminate billions of dollars of inventory from the grocery channel by shifting from supplier-push distribution to a consumer-pull system. Motivated by the pioneering best-practice example of cooperation between Procter & Gamble (and its suppliers) and Wal-Mart, this initiative would have been infeasible without the huge advances in information technology that have occurred in recent years.[40]

IMPLICATIONS   Rapid change characterizes every aspect of the task environment. Marketers have always aimed at moving targets, but today the targets are moving ever faster and traditional thinking about customers is likely to be quickly outdated. As global concentration increases in traditional industries, firms find themselves dealing with organizations that are not just customers, but are sometimes competitors and even suppliers. In the chemical industry, such relationship webs have existed for many years, but for other industries this is a new development. As supermarkets introduce high-quality store-branded products, many brand manufacturers have been rethinking their strategy; as airlines begin to cooperate in worldwide partnerships like the Star Alliance, the rules of the game have changed there also. The increased competitive intensity previously discussed requires that firms pay closer attention to their customers in a world where the rules of the competitive game are changing rapidly. Business today poses daunting intellectual challenges, for unprecedented problems and opportunities are created by radical change. However, the global rewards for mastering these changes are also unprecedented.

ADDRESSING ENVIRONMENTAL CHANGE

The foregoing indicates that, for the sake of its future health, the firm must confront the significant challenge of dealing with changes in both its general business and task environments. For those changes that are at least partially predictable, it should engage in a three-stage sequence.

- Attempt to predict the future change or event
- Identify the set of implications (if any) that this change or event may have for the firm
- Decide what action to take when the change or event actually occurs

In deciding where to place efforts, it is useful to classify potential environmental changes using the simple framework in Figure 2.3. Potential changes in both low-impact cells B and D should probably be monitored, but if the potential impact is truly low, it should not consume a great deal of management effort.

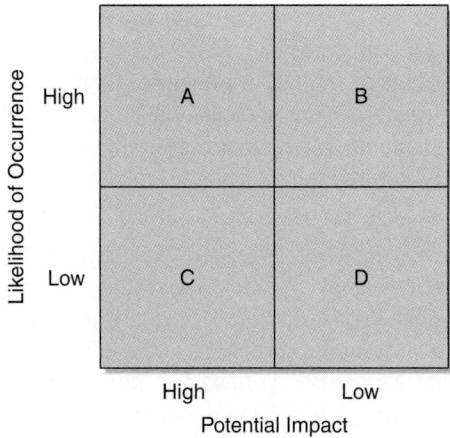

FIGURE 2.3

Assessing the Importance of Environmental Change

Contingency Planning

The high probability/high impact cell A is clearly critical; management should put in place plans to deal with such changes should they occur. The firm should then be able to move swiftly and confidently if and when the change or event actually takes place. This approach is known as *contingency planning,* and is widely practiced by emergency services in most countries. Indeed, any reader who has participated in a fire drill in a large building has experienced the impact of contingency planning. The most difficult changes to deal with are those in cell C, high impact but low probability of occurrence. Here again, the best response is to develop contingency plans, for should the low-probability event occur without prior consideration of firm action, the effects could be devastating.

Scenario Analysis

In cases where the possible outcomes are limited but the consequences are important, such as fire or no fire, contingency planning may be sufficient. In other cases, the possible outcomes may be more numerous, but the implications still significant. In such cases, it may be worthwhile to engage in scenario analysis in which a set of most-likely outcomes is identified. It is rarely possible to develop a contingency plan for each possibility, but strategies can often be pre-tested against these scenarios. The goal is to identify strategies that are robust, meaning that they produce good results regardless of which particular scenario ultimately materializes. Perhaps the best known exponents of scenario analysis are the Departments of Defense of the U.S. and other countries, for construction of scenarios is a key technique for designing the mix and deployment of weapons and personnel to protect national security.[41] Firms that engage in such exercises often claim that the process of thinking through the options is in itself valuable, for it sensitizes managers and employees to the idea of possible futures and encourages flexibility. Another possible outcome is that managers may recognize the opportunity to influence the firm's environment so as to mitigate its risks. The insurance industry's effort to educate its customers to manage risk effectively is an excellent example.[42]

Crisis Management

In some cases, however, the events that occur are largely unpredictable and time and effort spent in forecasting may be wasted. As the environment changes ever more rapidly, managers should increasingly focus on developing a rapid response capability. Such capability requires effectively surfacing the relevant issues, identifying their implications, and developing action steps. Many companies have taken their senior executives through exercises in crisis management after witnessing the enormous differences in how firms have dealt with crises.

> **Example:** The contrast between Johnson & Johnson's handling of the Tylenol poisoning crisis in the mid-1980s and Exxon's mismanagement of the 1989 Exxon Valdez oil spill (for which the cleanup cost $3 billion) was so marked that only the most incompetent of CEOs could have failed to take note! Johnson & Johnson immediately recalled all *Tylenol* capsules and only relaunched when a new packaging system was developed. By contrast, despite considerable evidence that the captain of the Exxon Valdez was an alcoholic, Exxon sued Sperry Marine Inc., claiming that a steering system it designed malfunctioned and caused, or helped cause, the tanker to run aground!

The *Tylenol* case illustrates the important principle that negative occurrences need not have negative outcomes. Because of its highly effective and well-regarded response to the situation, *Tylenol* emerged from the crisis stronger than ever, and Johnson & Johnson received an enormous boost in consumer approval. Furthermore, environmental occurrences that affect one organization negatively may open opportunities for others. Thus, in 1998, with the potential impeachment of President Clinton gathering momentum and dire predictions being made for the economy, many Washington area law firms posted increased business, and *Domino's Pizza* vastly increased its volume as lawyers worked late into the night.

No one believes that predicting the future is easy. However, too many firms are prepared to relinquish their responsibility to think about their future environments and rely upon "experts." This approach is not foolproof, as shown in a few examples of how "experts" have fallen flat in their predictions.[43]

- *We don't like their sound, and guitar music is on the way out.*—Decca Recording Company, in rejecting the Beatles (1962)
- *Stocks have reached what looks like a permanently high plateau.*—Irving Fisher, Professor of Economics, Yale University; *A severe depression like that of 1920–21 is outside the range of probability.*—Harvard Economic Society (November 16, 1929)
- *I think there is a world market for maybe five computers.*—Thomas Watson, IBM Chairman (1943); *There is no reason for any individual to have a computer in their home.*—Ken Olsen, Chairman and Founder of Digital Electronic Corporation (1977)
- *This "telephone" has too many shortcomings to be seriously considered as a means of communication. The device is inherently of no value to us.*—Western Union internal memo (1876)
- *The wireless music box has no imaginable commercial value. Who would pay for a message sent to nobody in particular?*—David Sarnoff's associates responding to his urging to invest in radio in the 1920s
- *The Edsel is here to stay.*—Henry Ford II to Ford dealers (1957)
- *The concept is interesting and well-formed, but in order to earn better than a "C," the idea must be feasible.*—Yale University Professor responding to Fred Smith's (later founder and CEO of Federal Express) term paper proposing reliable overnight delivery service.

The message from these examples is that predicting the future is fraught with peril. Nonetheless, managers must address the future. The approaches discussed in this section may enable better decision making in the face of environmental uncertainty and change.

WHERE ARE WE GOING NOW?

The purpose of this section is to stimulate thinking about change. The section provides examples of some innovative strategies that have enabled some firms to prosper, but have made the environment difficult for others, before turning to the ideas of well-known futurists.

Examples of Innovative Strategies

The strategies discussed here have enabled their creators to prosper while other firms have suffered. The pressures created by these innovations and the accompanying changes in the nature and intensity of the competitive environment are important factors in the drive to create learning organizations. In competitive markets, standing still is suicidal. Consider the following examples.

- In recent years, direct marketers have pioneered the concept of data-based marketing, transforming markets from a series of anonymous transactions into relationship marketing via customer identification and transaction tracking. The associated ability to collect, store, and mine customer-oriented data in a data warehouse, combined with mass customization, suggests the emergence of a powerful competitive force that has had significant impact on traditional competitors.
- Vertical marketers act simultaneously as retailers, wholesalers, and manufacturers, in effect disintermediating product markets. Dell Computer provides one example discussed later in the book; others include Ben and Jerry's, McDonald's, Starbucks, and The Body Shop. These firms can influence the complete ambiance in which their products are purchased and/or consumed. This ability may well engender branding advantages via a process, that two of our colleagues have labeled "synesthesia."[44]
- As competition intensifies and the weak succumb, the survivors are correspondingly smarter and more sophisticated. Increasingly, therefore, the overall ability of

firms to practice the principles of classical marketing will increase; however, since all survivors possess these capabilities, deriving competitive advantage from such practices will grow more difficult. Increasingly, firms will have to develop innovative ways of getting closer to customers so as to identify, in the words of the Spice Girls, "what (they) really, really want." This imperative is leading to a postmodern shift to ethnographic approaches in market research, for only deep customer insights are likely to lead to competitive advantage in the 21st. century.[45]

- Required core competencies are changing rapidly in a wide variety of industries; the revolution in information technology is a major driver. For example, mastery of this technology by Tesco, the British supermarket chain, demonstrates it has achieved a core competence in the supermarket sector. Launched in 1995, Tesco's loyalty card (paying a 1% quarterly rebate based on cumulative purchases) has 14 million memberships (9 million cards used every week). Tesco analyzes data from over 500 million shopping baskets per annum and provides tailored rewards and incentives to 37,000 consumer groups via 36 million personalized mailings each year. This database was the foundation for Tesco's entry into financial services, where a sophisticated targeted direct mail effort is providing customers with innovative banking products.[46] As another example, overseas expansion and manufacturing strategies of Japanese auto companies have forced component suppliers around the world to master TQM, JIT, and a variety of new skills to remain competitive. Finally, pharmaceutical companies have been affected by the growth of biotechnology. Many have been forced to acquire positions in emerging companies to ensure that they possess competencies increasingly seen as vital to their futures.

- Market efficiency is heavily affected by information availability. Historically, information acquisition was difficult and expensive; today, the electronic revolution is transforming the situation rapidly. This process has already occurred in financial markets where real-time information is available virtually everywhere. Similarly, the World Wide Web is providing a low-cost means of accessing information in product markets. As inefficiency is driven out of product markets, the only sustainable price differences will be those reflecting differences in customer perceived value; those due to lack of information will disappear. Indeed, information technology will lower search costs by permitting it to take place vicariously; it will also increasingly permit buyer/seller matching via intelligent search engines. Disintermediation will certainly increase as a result as, for example, with Dell's highly successful Internet site.

- The Internet will transform the process of marketing communication. Historically, in consumer markets, information has been primarily sent one way in undifferentiated one-to-many mass communication. The Internet allows consumers to be addressed relatively cheaply as individuals; they can easily communicate with suppliers and also with other consumers through such vehicles as America Online.

- The product/service distinction is being clarified. The distinction has puzzled marketers and other pundits for far too long, and is essentially arbitrary as offers purchased by the majority of buyers comprise a mixture of tangibles and intangibles. Indeed, structural changes in the economy and company strategies transform products into services and vice versa. For example, an activity conducted in-house by a manufacturer is typically counted as value-added in the product sector; that same activity (unless it is manufacturing), conducted by an out-sourcing supplier, is counted in the service sector. Furthermore, since McDonald's operates restaurants, the government classifies it as a service business; however, its strategy of growing take-home sales (local "manufacturing" of products for later consumption) has been so successful that in the United States, 60% of revenues are earned from product removed from the premises before being eaten.

Durable goods manufacturers provide some of the most interesting examples. Commercial jet engine manufacturers traditionally made little profit on engine sales; profit was made on spares and maintenance. However, as engine quality and performance have improved, the revenue yield from these activities is declining; industry players are actively discussing pricing by hour of operating life. Furthermore, products as diverse as automobiles, railroad cars and locomotives, computers and copiers, light bulbs, and furniture are now offered as "services" to market segments comprising customers who prefer to avoid the initial capital outlay by renting or leasing.

- The Internet has reduced entry barriers in many industries. Constructing a low-cost virtual presence is possible for entrepreneurs anywhere in the world; however, lack of name recognition may still be a serious problem. Managing and eliminating customer risk will be important to the success of new Internet-based businesses and is providing opportunity for branded intermediaries. Perhaps information-based businesses and services will gain most from the Internet revolution, since physical products (particularly if they require direct experience) may continue to require some form of conventional distribution system.[47]

- As competition intensifies, sources of advantage will become more fleeting. Technologies will move from the empirical and inductive to the predictive and deductive, increasing the ease of emulation. For example, pharmaceutical companies are shifting away from "trial and error" to the design of molecules, and the mathematics of engineering has advanced to the point that prototypes do not have to be tested destructively. Firms will have to move faster to gain first-mover advantages,[48] and more-educated and better-informed customers will be more willing to try new products, including those from new producers.

    Some authors have argued that no advantage is truly sustainable and that increasingly, advantage will be arbitraged away even more quickly in "hyper-competition."[49] In this world, it will no longer be sufficient for firms to secure competitive advantage. Rather, as noted in the previous chapter, competitive advantage in a product market must become the result of a process for developing competitive advantage. In the future, the successful competitive advantage process will become the true differentiator of the successful company.

Environmental turbulence and non-traditional competition often lead to the birth of new markets or market segments, identified and served initially by innovative competitors. Several have emerged in recent years. In financial services, small to mid-size companies were traditionally unable to fund potential growth with loans from commercial banks; either interest rates were exceedingly high or covenants were extremely restrictive. Recognition of this need, and the willingness of a substantial group of investors to invest in small high-risk companies in exchange for a high interest rate, led to development of the junk bond market.[50]

In very different fields, Calyx and Corolla revolutionized the retail flower business by delivering flowers direct from growers via Federal Express[51]; Barnes and Noble shifted book retailing from buying books to providing customers with an in-store shopping experience; and Amazon.com is providing consumers with a convenient way to purchase books through the Internet.

The implications for corporations are clear: environmental change alters historic market realities. Effort placed on identifying the market implications of environmental change opens opportunities. Firms that grasp these opportunities will reap significant rewards.

The Future Gurus

Some writers make a living attempting to predict the future. We should not believe all that they tell us, but we should not ignore it either. Indeed, it is a worthwhile exercise to assume that their predictions are on target and identify the consequent implications for the firm, the process we earlier called *scenario analysis*.

TABLE 2.3 Megatrends

10 Megatrends for the 1980s	10 Megatrends for the 1990s
Industrial society to information society	The booming global economy of the 1990s
Forced technology to high tech/high touch	The renaissance of the arts
National economy to world economy	The emergence of free-market socialism
Short term to long term	Global lifestyles and cultural nationalism
Centralization to decentralization	The privatization of the welfare state
Institutional help to self help	The rise of the Pacific Rim
Representative democracy to participatory democracy	The decade of women in leadership
Hierarchies to networking	The age of biology
North to South	The religious revival of the new millennium
Either/or to multiple option	The triumph of the individual

This section highlights two well-known futurists, John Naisbitt and Faith Popcorn. Naisbitt focuses on what he calls *megatrends*—large social, economic, political, and technological changes that are slow to form, but once in place, influence us for seven to ten years or longer. In 1982, he identified ten megatrends for the 1980s.[52]; in 1992, he identified ten megatrends for the 1990s (Table 2.3).[53] Readers should make their own judgments regarding both the extent to which the 1980s trends came to fruition and the extent to which the 1990s trends have relevance to the new millennium.

Popcorn, by contrast, focuses more on culturally based trends. In the mid-1990s, she identified 16 major trends "driving America and the rest of the consumer world" (Table 2.4).[54]

TABLE 2.4 Popcorn's Cultural Trends

Cocooning	Stay at home trend
Clanning	Inclination to join groups
Fantasy adventure	Excitement in risk-free escape from the daily routine
Pleasure revenge	Bacchanals of forbidden fruit
Small indulgences	Need for emotional fixes to counter everyday stress
Anchoring	Comfort from the past to anchor the future
Egonomics	New ways to make personal statements
Female think	Marketing consciousness of caring, sharing, and family
Emancipation	Freedom for men to be individuals
99 lives	Assuming multiple roles
Cashing out	Personal fulfillment in a simpler way of living
Being alive	"Wellness" adding generous years of good health
Down-aging	Sense of acting and feeling younger than one's age
Vigilante	Consumer: market manipulation through pressure, protest, and politics
Icon toppling	Rejection of monuments of business/government and "pillars of society"
Save our society	Social consciousness based on ethics, passion, and compassion

F. Popcorn and L. Marigold, *Clicking: 16 Trends to Future Fit Your Life, Your Work, and Your Business,* New York: HarperCollins, 1996.

TABLE 2.5 "The Future Ain't What It Used To Be": A Selection of Ten Cultural Trends

Passion Point	Selected Cultural Trend
Mind	Altered States: Seeking to change one's emotional or psychological state
Body	Biomorphing: The ability to shapeshift any part of one's anatomy
Spirit	Soul Searching: Finding contentment with yourself, God, soulmates
Experience	Vice Versing: Accepting that hedonism in moderation is natural
Identity	Artisan: Renaissance of arts and crafts
Society	We the People: Growth of grass-roots politics
Nature	Outer Limits: Growing fascination with unexplainable phenomena
Relationships	Kid Quake: Kids reshaping family and social dynamics
Fear	Detox: Rising sensitivity to chemicals and pollutants
Technology	Virtuality: Technological blurring of reality and imagination

V. Abrahamson, M. Meehan, and L. Samuel, *The Future Ain't What It Used To Be: The 40 Cultural Trends Transforming Your Job, Your Life, Your World,* New York: Riverhead Books, 1998.

Finally, in the framework of America's 10 "passion points"—mind, body, spirit, experience, identity, society, nature, relationships, fear, and technology—a group of more recent futurists, asserting that "The Future Ain't What It Used To Be," have identified 40 cultural trends. Table 2.5 presents a single trend from each of the passion points.

No one can reliably predict the future. However, as noted earlier, the process of contemplating alternate future scenarios and their implications for the firm, its customers, competitors, and suppliers is a valuable process in its own right, and a key tool for fostering an external orientation, the subject of the next chapter.

SUMMARY

This chapter makes the case that corporations are dealing with a vastly different world today than they faced a few years ago, and that the pace of change shows no sign of slacking. Major changes have occurred, are occurring, and will continue to occur in the firm's supplier, customer, and competitor task environment, and in the variety of general environmental domains that influence relationships among the firm and its customers, competitors, and suppliers.

Just as placid, unchanging environments permit established competitors to reap long-run profits with little requirement for innovation, the turbulent environments facing corporations today threaten established competitors. Firms that operate in traditional ways will not achieve their objectives. Unless, in the face of significant environmental change, they develop new and innovative approaches and have the resources, confidence, and guts to invest in them, they face a sure death from those competitors that compete in different ways, with different assumptions about the world.

But just as environmental turbulence is the enemy of established, tradition-bound bureaucracies, it is also the vehicle by which new, small, flexible organizations are able to upset the established order. For these firms, today's environmental turbulence offers immense opportunities. However, for these firms, just as for those that have been and currently are successful, the price of success must be eternal vigilance.

Chapter 3 commences the task of explaining how to achieve long-run success in the face of these environmental imperatives. In particular, the chapter makes the key distinction between internal and external perspectives, and identifies the telling differences between these two polar approaches to leading and managing business organizations.

THE CHANGING VIEW

Old Way	New Way
Change is evolutionary	Change is revolutionary
Slowly evolving competency shifts	Faster-changing competency shifts
The future is predictable, all we need is good forecasting	The future is not completely predictable; flexibility is required
Reactive to environmental change	Proactively influencing environment
Economic growth driven by manufacturing	Economic growth driven by services
Individual national economies	Integrated global economy
Change is a problem	Change is an opportunity
Ill-informed buyers	Better-informed buyers
Marketing focus on the young	Worldwide aging of population
Clear product–service distinctions	Blurring of product–service distinctions
Competitive advantages long lasting	Competitive advantages quickly dissipated
Transactional focus	Relationship focus
Independent firms	Networked firms

QUESTIONS FOR REVIEW AND DISCUSSION

1. In addition to those noted in the first section of the chapter, identify three major environmental changes that have occurred since 1990. What are the general implications of these changes for business?

2. Identify three major environmental changes that will impact the organization you will work for when you graduate. What are the implications of these changes for the firm, its suppliers, customers, and competitors?

3. American managers often appear ethnocentric to their competitors outside the United States. Explain how you will avoid becoming one of these managers. List the personal steps you will take to ensure this.

4. Education for management is a multibillion dollar industry. How do you expect globalization to change this industry in the next 25 years?

5. Discuss the major demographic changes that will take place in your country in your working lifetime. What are the managerial implications of these changes?

6. Identify the three major cultural changes that will affect consumer markets in your country in the next 10 years.

7. How will technological changes in computers and the Internet impact the industry in which you expect to commence your career?

8. How do you assess the potential impact of: a) The World Trade Organization, b) The European Union, c) The International Monetary Fund on the industry in which you expect to commence your career?

9. What major regulatory changes might occur in your country in the next 10 years? Pick an industry. How do you expect these firms to be affected?

10. What are the critical cultural differences between the country in which you live and that of a country in a different continent? (Pick your own country.)

11. It was noted that many corporations have made determined efforts to restrict the scope of their activities by redefining and narrowing their missions. Yet, around the world we find exceptions: For example, one of the United States' most prof-

itable companies is the widely diversified General Electric, and in Asia, many successful family-owned businesses are broadly diversified. How do you account for this apparent paradox?

12. Select a company you would like to work for and three trends developed by the Future Gurus. Identify the implications of these trends for your chosen firm.

13. Select a foreign country in which you are interested in working. Identify critical differences from your home country across the cultural dimensions of language, education, law and politics, religion, technical and material culture, values and attitudes (e.g., towards time, work, achievement, wealth, love, risk-taking, change), aesthetics, and social organization.

14. In 1996, *Fortune* published a long article entitled "Asia Stinks."[55] Identify a company with operations in Asia. What implications do Asia's environmental problems have for its future?

15. Identify a firm in an industry in which you are interested in working and examine how the required competencies have changed in the last 10 years. How might they have to change in the next 10 years?

16. Select a firm and identify both high- and low-probability, high-impact changes that might affect it.

END NOTES

1. For example, in Europe, Belarus, Georgia, Estonia, Latvia, Lithuania, and Ukraine; in Asia, Kazakstan, Kirgizstan, Tajikistan, Turkmenistan, and Uzbekistan.

2. These sports, sometimes called *alternative sports,* are too many to enumerate in full, but in addition to snowboarding include skateboarding, roller-blading, free climbing, speed climbing, freestyle skiing, sky surfing, and BMX competition.

3. One industry affected by Princess Diana's death was diamonds. The engagement ring she received from Prince Charles had a sapphire stone rather than a diamond. This spawned a fad of non-diamond engagement rings that was rekindled on her death.

4. See N. Capon and J.M. Hulbert, "The Integration of Forecasting and Strategic Planning," *International Journal of Forecasting,* 1 (Fall 1985), pp. 123–133, for an analysis of environmental forces. See also L.G. Cooper, "Strategic Marketing Planning for Radically New Products," *Journal of Marketing,* 64 (Jan. 2000), pp. 1–16.

5. Government action around the world continues to impact commercial organizations. For example, in the U.S., the Private Securities Litigation Reform Act of 1995 limited lawsuits filed by individual stockholders and made those filed more difficult to prosecute. Law firms specializing in this type of litigation were severely affected.

6. For a thoughtful discussion of the shift from government control to market mechanisms, see D. Yergin and J. Stanislaw, *The Commanding Heights,* New York: Simon and Schuster, 1998.

7. Member countries are Canada, Mexico, and the United States.

8. Member countries are Argentina, Brazil, Paraguay, and Uruguay.

9. The European Union is deregulating a variety of industries, including air travel, energy, postal services, publishing, and telecommunications (*Business Week,* February 2, 1998).

10. The U.S. Justice Department's antitrust suit against Microsoft is an important contemporary example.

11. *The New York Times,* March 9, 2000.

12. Members are Bolivia, Colombia, Ecuador, Peru, and Venezuela.

13. Members include Antigua and Barbuda, Barbados, Belize, Jamaica, Montserrat, St. Lucia, Trinidad and Tobago.

14. Members are Brunei Darussalam, Indonesia, Laos, Malaysia, Myanmar, The Philippines, Singapore, Thailand, and Vietnam.

15. See P.F. Drucker, "The Changed World Economy," *Foreign Affairs,* 64 (Spring 1986), pp. 768–791.

16. *The New York Times,* February 11, 1998.

17. See J.H. Dessauer, *My Years with Xerox: The Billions Nobody Wanted,* Garden City, NJ: Doubleday, 1971.

18. See "Doing a Dyson (A), (B), (C), *European Case Clearing House,* 599-051-1BW. Most major vacuum cleaner manufacturers have since copied Dyson's invention; Dyson is suing Hoover for patent infringement.

19. See "Once Upon a Time, Bill Gates Came to France," *Business Week,* February 10, 1997. In early 1998, *The New York Times* reported that upwards of 200,000 French citizens were living and working in Britain (*The New York Times,* March 29, 1998).

20. For one firm's struggles to address environmental issues in Germany, see "Procter & Gamble Company: Lenor Refill Package," *Harvard Business School* 9-592-016.

21. *The New Shorter Oxford English Dictionary,* Oxford: Clarendon, 1993.

22. Generation X comprises 17 million persons born after the post World War II baby boom; Generation Y (echo boomers, the millennium generation), born between 1979 and 1994, comprises 60 million persons (versus 72 million baby boomers), *Business Week,* February 15, 1999.

23. See E. Hall, *The Silent Language,* Garden City, NY: Anchor, 1973.

24. R. Stanat, quoted in *Australian Financial Review,* March 27, 1998.

25. At the end of the 1940s, the United Nations had 59 members; at the end of the 1960s, 126; in early 2000, with the addition of Kiribati (pop. 82,000), Nauru (pop. 11,000), Tonga (pop. 98,000), and Tuvalu (pop. 10,000), membership reached 189.

26. See for example a study of 35,000 consumers in 35 countries by Roper Starch Worldwide cited in *The Economist,* February 28, 1998.

27. N. Capon, J.U. Farley, and J. Hulbert, "International Diffusion of Corporate and Strategic Planning Processes," *Columbia Journal of World Business,* 15 (Fall 1980), pp. 5–13.

28. Paradoxically, many would consider one of the world's most successful companies, General Electric, a conglomerate.

29. *The Age,* March 20, 1998. In March 1998, US$1 = A$1.53.

30. Even SBUs have come under attack. Prahalad and Hamel, in making the case for leveraging corporate competencies, argue that the costs of this form of decentralization outweigh the benefits. G. Hamel and C.K. Prahalad, *Competing for the Future,* Boston, MA: Harvard Business School Press, 1994, pp. 32–34.

31. See N. Capon, J.U. Farley, and J.M. Hulbert, *Corporate Strategic Planning,* New York: Columbia University Press, 1987.

32. See I. Nonaka and H. Takeuchi, *The Knowledge-Creating Company,* New York: Oxford University Press, 1995.

33. R.S. Achrol, "Evolution of the Marketing Organization: New Forms for Turbulent Environments," *Journal of Marketing,* 55 (October 1991), pp. 77–93.

34. See "Social Marketing Company in Bangladesh," in N. Capon and W. Van Honacker, *The Asian Marketing Case Book,* Singapore: Prentice Hall, 1999, for an example of a successful population control program based on packaged goods marketing techniques.

35. As noted earlier, of the *Fortune* 500 in 1981, only 271 were independent entities in 1992.

36. *The New York Times,* January 19, 1998.

37. Securities Data Company, 1999.

38. *Kaizen,* developed at Toyota, focuses on continuous improvement through just-in-time delivery throughout the production process and rigorous problem solving to eliminate process abnormalities and problems.

39. Supply chain management has become an increasingly important issue in recent years.

40. For a description, see G. Stalk, P. Evans, and L.E. Shulman, "Competing on Capabilities: The New Rules of Corporate Strategy," *Harvard Business Review,* 70 (March/April 1992), pp. 57–69.

41. See *The Economist,* March 21, 1998, for an example of scenario analysis in attempting to understand the future for Japan.

42. The reader's university or college is likely to have a "wellness" program designed to reduce claims against a group health policy.

43. Some examples from *Business Week,* July 15, 1996.

44. *Synesthesia* is defined as the stimulation of one sense by another as in the association of colors with music. (B. Schmitt and A. Simonson, *Marketing Aesthetics,* New York: The Free Press, 1997.)

45. See F.J. Gouillart and F.D. Sturdivant, "Spend a Day in the Life of One of Your Customers," *Harvard Business Review,* 72 (Jan./Feb. 1994), pp. 116–125.

46. See "TESCO PLC: Getting to the Top . . . Staying at the Top? *European Case Clearing House,* 599-037-1BW. Recently, Tesco has relaunched its loyalty card into gold, silver, and bronze tiers, reflective of customer profitability. Many observers believe that decisions by U.S. chains to allow Nielsen and IRI to become scanner intermediaries is a major contributor to their poor margins, rendering them vulnerable to suitors. (In mid-1999, 25% of the U.S. supermarket industry was foreign-owned; some industry experts believe the percentage will rise to 50%.)

47. L. Pitt, P. Berthon, and R.T. Watson, "Cyberservice: Taming Service Marketing Problems with the World Wide Web," *Business Horizons,* 42 (Jan./Feb. 1999), pp. 11–18.

48. See Chapter 6.

49. R. D'Aveni, *Hypercompetition: Managing the Dynamics of Strategic Maneuvering,* New York: The Free Press, 1994.

50. In this view, Mike Millken was not a "finance" person; he was a "marketing" person.

51. For more detail on Calyx and Corolla's innovative strategy, see "Calyx and Corolla," *Harvard Business School,* 9-592-035.

52. J. Naisbitt, *Megatrends: Ten New Directions Transforming Our Lives,* New York: Warner Books, 1984.

53. J. Naisbitt, *Megatrends 2000: New Directions for Tomorrow,* New York: William Morrow, 1990.

54. F. Popcorn and L. Marigold, *Clicking: 16 Trends to Future Fit Your Life, Your Work, and Your Business,* New York: HarperCollins, 1996.

55. *Fortune,* December 9, 1996.

WEB RESOURCES

3M	www.3m.com
Astra	www.astrazeneca.com
Barnes and Noble	www.bn.com
Ben and Jerry's	www.benjerry.com
Calyx and Corolla	www.calyxandcorolla.com
Dell Computer	www.dell.com
Fedex	www.fedex.com
Ford	www.ford.com
Fortune	www.fortune.com
General Electric	www.ge.com
Gillette	www.gillette.com
Gulf & Western	www.gulf-western.com
Haloid	www.xerox.com
Hewlett Packard	www.hp.com
Home Depot	www.homedepot.com
Hoover	www.hoover.com
IBM	www.ibm.com
Ikea	www.ikea.com
Intel	www.intel.com
ITT	www.itt.com
Johnson & Johnson	www.johnsonandjohnson.com

WEB RESOURCES *(continued)*

JP Morgan	www.jpmorgan.com
Kodak	www.kodak.com
Litton	www.litton.com
Marks and Spencer	www.marks-and-spencer.co.uk
McDonald's	www.mcdonalds.com
Microsoft	www.microsoft.com
Monsanto	www.monsanto.com
New York Times	www.nytimes.com
Pacific Dunlop	www.pacdun.com
Philip Morris	www.philipmorris.com
Polaroid	www.polaroid.com
Procter and Gamble	www.pg.com
Royal Ahold	www.ahold.com
Sony	www.sony.com
Southwest Airlines	www.southwest.com
Sperry.Marine	www.sperry-marine.com
Sports Authority	www.thesportsauthority.com
Star Alliance	www.star-alliance.com
Starbucks	www.starbucks.com
Tesco	www.tesco.co.uk
Texas Instruments	www.ti.com
The Body Shop	www.the-body-shop.com
Tie Rack	www.tie-rack.com
Union Pacific	www.uprr.com
Wal-Mart	www.walmart.com
Warner Brothers	www.warnerbros.com
WorldCom	www.wcom.com
Xerox	www.xerox.com

3

THE EXTERNALLY ORIENTED FIRM

LEARNING OBJECTIVES

When you have completed this chapter, you will understand

- the different perspectives or orientations a firm can exhibit

- that a firm can possess a variety of internally oriented perspectives, but that each has deficiencies for long-run corporate health

- that developing an external perspective[1] is the only way for the firm to be ready to deal with its increasingly turbulent environment and so prepare for the future

- that firms face a variety of impediments to developing an external perspective

- that externally oriented firms, in addition to measuring product profitability, develop and act on measures of customer profitability

- that customer retention is a critical variable in driving firm profitability

- that firms may have other reasons, in addition to lack of profit, for turning potential customers away.

INTRODUCTION

This chapter focuses on marketing at the organizational level. The purpose of the firm may be viewed from many different perspectives, and this chapter includes discussion on the nature of these perspectives. Only one of these perspectives, an external orientation, is compatible with identifying and selecting those opportunities that will drive profit, organizational growth, and survival over the long run, and hence enhance shareholder value.

Customers sit at the centerpiece of the external orientation. As discussed in Chapter 1, unless the firm is able to win customers in the face of efforts by competitors, it will not secure profits, ensure organizational growth and survival, and enhance shareholder value. However, customers must be profitable to serve. The firm should be very clear about which customers are profitable for the firm and which are not, and understand the critical role of customer retention in enhancing firm profits. Management should be aware of reasons other than lack of profit that might lead it to turn away potential customers.

INTERNAL PERSPECTIVES

In the simplest organization, all functions are carried out by a sole proprietor, who seeks and serves customers, arranges financing, performs operational functions, manages the payroll, and so forth. As a result, the proprietor has intimate contact with all aspects of the business. Often such proprietors, who are of course the key decision makers in their enterprises, are leaders in treating their customers as important assets. Many of us can recount occasions when owners of a local garage, dry cleaner, hardware store, or other business have gone out of their way to serve us and treat us as important and valuable assets.[2,3]

As organizations grow, they typically develop specializations to secure greater levels of efficiency. Departments, management systems, and business philosophies are developed for operations, sales, product design, finance, legal, technology, and so forth, and managerial responsibility and authority are awarded to each of these functions. In order to ensure that the required tasks and activities are properly carried out, managers are frequently motivated, measured, and rewarded for the extent to which they meet the objectives set for their particular functions. Researchers as diverse as biologists and management theorists have noted that specialization creates differentiation; thus, a second-order result of organizational growth is that many key decision makers are organizationally far removed from the firm's customers.

Difficult situations occur when organizations engage in merger or acquisition. Frequently, individual departments have their own methods of operation and fight fiercely to retain their own systems. For example, in some recent bank mergers, systems conversions were difficult to carry out because competing departments fought for their own systems, rather than focusing on implementing the most appropriate system for serving customers.

In most firms, each organizational function has a particular mission and method of operating. For example, the job of most sales departments is to increase sales; for most operations departments, the key task is to produce acceptable-quality products at the lowest cost. Major problems arise when these individual functional operating philosophies and related sub-goals are internally inconsistent or are incongruent with environmental demands and customer requirements.[4] To the extent that the environment is stable and customers' needs persist with little change, these operating philosophies and competently set functional subgoals can endure over the short and medium run. However, when the environment and customers' needs change, especially when they change quickly, functional operating philosophies and goals set at one time are unlikely to be appropriate at another.

A particular problem occurs when a single functional operating philosophy becomes dominant and results in organizational behavior that runs counter to environmental demands. For example, consider the following functional philosophies:

Operations: "Our job is to reduce unit costs."

Obviously there is nothing inherently wrong with cutting costs; lower costs present the potential for lowering prices or improving profit margins. However, if a cost-cutting philosophy becomes so dominant that it outweighs other considerations, then actions taken to put the philosophy into practice might interfere with the goal of securing and retaining customers. For example, typical actions to reduce costs include product line pruning, short-cuts in design, avoiding new products, cuts in research and development, reduced service, reduced promotional spending, lengthened delivery times, pressuring suppliers for price reductions, and so forth. Firms that pursue unbridled cost reduction philosophies are frequently described as having an *operations orientation*.

> **Example:** In the late 1980s, operations personnel at the Union Pacific Railroad met operating budgets by canceling cargo pickups and sending out trains with insufficient locomotive power!

Of course, there are many occasions when cost-cutting actions are absolutely appropriate. For example, layers of bureaucratic fat might need to be removed, or the firm's strategy might be focused narrowly on a particular set of customers for whom price is the critical decision variable. However, a cost-cutting philosophy may be totally inappropriate at, for example, the start of a product life cycle, when new products, a broadened product line, high promotional expenses, and short delivery times are often crucial for the firm to secure customers and achieve market position. Because of the inappropriateness of a single-minded devotion to cost reduction, we have great concern that the current focus in American firms on downsizing (rightsizing) and reengineering might go too far. The result will be low-cost organizations that are unable to provide to the market products and services that customers truly need or desire.

A particularly insidious version of the operations orientation is found in those multi-national companies whose "cultural imperialism" results in the transfer of their domestic strategies wholesale into foreign markets without considering that the customer environment might be different!

> **Example:** Nabisco corporate policy dictated that products produced around the world should be identical to those in the United States, including recipes, raw materials, process control, and quality standards. In China, the combination of lack of focus on customer needs, imported raw materials (leading to high prices), overly optimistic forecasts, and excess capacity resulted in significant losses. Said a spokesperson from French competitor Danone, "I'm grateful to Nabisco's marketing department; their actions have strengthened our position!"

Sales: "Our job is to increase sales."

Again, who could argue that increasing sales is not a worthy objective for a business organization? The problem is with the associated managerial actions. What tends to accompany this operating philosophy is a short-term focus on sales volume (often without regard for profitability), insufficient market research, little marketing planning, indiscriminate targeting of customers, and product lines that are far too broad. Other problems include excessive inventory levels, prices and discounts (and credit terms) that are too favorable to customers, excessive focus on sales-force efforts to have the customer buy what the company offers (versus what the customer might truly desire), and a reliance on budgets. Firms that pursue sales goals indiscriminately, with insufficient attention to *profitable* sales, are frequently described as having a *sales orientation*.

Of course there are many circumstances when it is appropriate to focus major resources on developing new products, carrying an extensive inventory, cutting prices, and engaging in heavy promotional and sales-force efforts. Typically these occasions occur when the firm's goal is market penetration (for instance, early in the product life cycle or upon entry into a new geographic arena). Such behavior, however, may be inappropriate at other times when, perhaps, the firm's market position is more stable and earning profits in the short run takes on more significance.

THE EXTERNALLY
ORIENTED FIRM

Example: Today Taiwan-based Chi Mei is one of the world's largest plastic producers. Early in its corporate life, Chairman Wu found the warehouse full of acrylic sheet inventory, dozens of sheets of different dimensions to meet different customer requirements. Wu decided that Chi Mei should focus on the four sheet types that represented 70 percent of the market. Production and inventory costs were lowered, prices were reduced on those four types, and customers requiring special dimension sheets paid a premium.

Finance: "We must increase return on investment."

Too heavy a focus on near-term profit can mortgage the organization's future. Firms that are "managed by the numbers" typically eschew expenditures with long-term payoff in favor of actions that increase profits today. Budgeting and forecasting frequently preempt business planning, and a heavy focus on short-term profit leads to insufficient capital investment; reductions in advertising, marketing research, and other marketing expenditures; and pricing decisions that focus on short-term profit rather than long-term market considerations. Firms with an excessive orientation towards short-run profits are described as having a *financial orientation*.[5]

Naturally under certain circumstances, it may be appropriate to focus singlemindedly on short-term profits or cash flows, especially for individual business areas that have been performing poorly or for areas from which the firm is contemplating exit, and in turn-around situations. However, if a financial orientation dominates the organization as a whole, the firm is likely to become competitively vulnerable in its product markets and will eventually be unable to sustain viable market positions.[6,7]

Technology: "Customers will want our products because of our leading technology."

Firms operating with a *technological orientation* focus their attention on research, development, and engineering, with little recognition of economic considerations. Market criteria and marketing influence in product planning to guide research and development are inadequate or nonexistent because the product is considered the responsibility of the technical organization. There is a tendency to over-engineer products beyond what the customer needs or is willing to pay for, and development, product, and facility decisions are often made by engineering and manufacturing management, without marketing participation.[8]

Again, there is nothing wrong with producing first-class products, but only if customers truly desire the features built into them and are willing to pay the price. If the customers are other engineers, this approach can work reasonably well. Certainly in high-tech industries, it is important that marketing personnel have sufficient technical expertise to play useful roles. However, since the industrial revolution, the new product graveyard has been continually replenished by the efforts of countless firms that drove product development without sufficient consideration of market requirements.[9]

GENERAL CHARACTERISTICS OF INTERNAL AND EXTERNAL PERSPECTIVES

The preceding discussion adopted the position that although individual functional perspectives are important, and might be crucial for firm success, too heavy a focus on one or another can lead to inappropriate decision making. Furthermore, each perspective has various implied time horizons (for example, technological: medium/long term; sales: short term) and differing investment priorities that can put one perspective in conflict with another.

The tip-off for a firm operating with one or another dominant internal perspectives is the statement, "This is the way we do things around here." This is a clear message that the firm is internally driven and that, regardless of environmental change, it is intent on continuing a set pattern of behavior. The focus of these internally oriented firms is on their own activities—products, processes, costs and internal performance criteria—rather than on external considerations.

The external perspective stands in sharp contrast to these internal perspectives. Rather than emphasize internal functions of the organization, the firm with an external perspective continually looks outward to the environment. It focuses its attention and efforts on customers, competitors, and broader environmental variables that may lead to behavioral change, rather than on its products and internal processes. Furthermore, it recognizes that to secure customers against competitive attack over the long run, it must invest in its markets.

Example: Soft drink manufacturers Pepsi, Coca-Cola, and Dr. Pepper are signing school districts to multi-year exclusive distribution arrangements. In one instance, Pepsi paid Jefferson County, Colorado (88,000 pupils) $2.1 million for a seven-year contract.[10]

The firm operating with an external perspective understands that, although the products now produced and the processes currently in place may be the key reasons for its past and even current success, if the environment is changing, its products and processes will also have to change. Indeed, the firm with an external perspective realizes that change is inevitable and rather than fear change, welcomes it as a challenge. It understands that threats to current business brought about by change are accompanied by new opportunities that become the "lifeblood" of the organization. In contrast to the differing functional views on time horizons and resource allocation priorities that attend internal perspectives, the externally driven firm is typically very clear about its desire for long-run customer relationships so as to position itself for the future. Consequently, it has a long-run view of profit performance.

Example: In 1986 when Johnson and Johnson's Tylenol brand was beset with difficulties about capsules laced with cyanide, the company took a $250 million write-off as a long-term investment in its customers. As noted, the brand survived the poisoning scare and continues as a profitable contributor to Johnson and Johnson's shareholders' value

The externally oriented firm is able to avoid the tyranny of the quarterly earnings statement and believes, as does John Medlin (former CEO of Wachovia Bank), "You've got to expect a down quarter from time to time."[11] See Table 3.1 for a summary of the differences between internal and external orientations.

Implicit in the foregoing discussion is the notion that the responsibility for developing an external perspective throughout the firm does not reside solely in the marketing department. Certainly marketing has a key role to play in identifying critical

Table 3.1 General Characteristics of Internal and External Orientations

	Internal	External
Focus	Products	Markets
Know-how	Inherent in patents, machinery	Inherent in people, processes
Process	Mass production	Mass customization
Communications	Mass media	Tailored
Priorities	Efficiency and productivity	Flexibility and responsiveness
Measurement	Profit, margin, volume	Value, satisfaction, retention
Customer perspective	Transactional	Relational
Organizational philosophy	Bureaucracy	Adhocracy

Adapted from S.H. Haeckel, "Adaptive Enterprise Design: The Sense-and-Respond Model," *Planning Review*, (May/June 1995), pp. 7–13, 42.

environmental contingencies. Indeed, acting as the organization's "point person,"[12] marketing, more than every other function, has the responsibility to look outward into the environment to understand and interpret the many changes.

However, the key responsibility for developing an external perspective must be placed at the top of the organization. Only the power vested in senior management positions can make the adoption of an external perspective an overarching thrust that constrains and embraces individual functional perspectives. In some quarters, top-level corporate officers have recognized that the organization-wide adoption of an external perspective, or the building of a "marketing culture," is a critical corporate priority. In a study conducted at INSEAD a few years ago, over 100 CEOs and board-level European executives rated "creating a marketing culture throughout the organization" as the third most important strategic marketing issue they faced.[13]

The term *external orientation* is used here rather than *marketing culture, customer orientation, market focus,* or any of the myriad of permutations that appear in company lexicons or the business press. There are several reasons for this: First, for 30 years or more "marketing" has been associated with a functional department; the realities of organizational politics are such that mere use of the term might constitute a significant impediment to change by precipitating unnecessary opposition from other functions. Second, for too many people, the term *marketing* has become identified with customer focus or even customer service, a serious misrepresentation because an external orientation encompasses competitors as well as customers. In addition, it also admits an understanding of the broader general environment within which the firm and its suppliers, customers, and competitors take action.[14] Finally, Philip Kotler has pointed out that a firm may be customer oriented but not market oriented. A market-oriented firm does a good job of selecting markets to compete, but may do a poor job serving customers in those markets; a customer-oriented firm may do the reverse. Both of these options are clearly suboptimal. The term *external orientation* is designed to subsume both good selection of markets and excellence in meeting the needs and wants of customers in those markets—both expressed and latent—the subject matter of most of the book.

> **Example:** Among modern companies that have been highly successful by identifying and serving customer needs are *Home Depot, Toyota, Barnes and Noble* (bricks and mortar retail activities), *Amazon.com, Starbucks, The Body Shop* and *Nokia*.[15,16]

HOW THE DIFFERING PERSPECTIVES TREAT KEY MANAGEMENT ISSUES

Thus far the notion of organizational perspectives has been addressed at a somewhat abstract level. Tom Peters, in pointing out that managers should "walk the talk," was underlining a hypocrisy that destroys leadership credibility in many firms. So often, company materials, such as annual reports, employee handbooks, and even training courses, embrace the principles of an external orientation. Too many times, however, managerial behavior, particularly the way in which decisions are made, strays from these principles. It is therefore appropriate to question what people say and observe how particular decisions are made. This point is illustrated by several examples; these may serve as the basis for an investigation with previous and potential employers or other organizations with which you have an affiliation.

Examples are organized in several categories: the planning system, defining the market arena, treatment of customers, marketing spending, product-line decisions, cost to the customer, and business organization. Figure 3.1 presents a questionnaire based on these categories, which you may use as a diagnostic tool to evaluate an organization's degree of external versus internal orientation. In the Chapter Appendix we reproduce one of the best-known publicly available instruments designed to assess organizational culture or orientation.[17]

In completing the following questions, please focus on your business unit rather than the company as a whole. For each pair of questions, select a number on the scale between 1 and 7.

A. The Planning System

1. Objective setting

We maintain a strong external focus in setting objectives	1—2—3—4—5—6—7	Our objectives are set with a predominately internal focus

2. Planning and budgeting

Our plans comprise largely numerical budgets	1—2—3—4—5—6—7	Our plans are expressed largely in words

3. Gathering market information

We pay little attention to customer/ competitor data gathering and analysis	1—2—3—4—5—6—7	We put major efforts into customer/competitor data gathering and analysis

4. Forecasting

We do a good job of forecasting sales volume	1—2—3—4—5—6—7	We do a terrible job of forecasting sales volume

5. Information systems

We develop information systems to reduce costs and increase operating efficiency	1—2—3—4—5—6—7	We develop information systems so we can be more effective in the marketplace

B. Defining the Market Arena

1. Attitude toward the "rules of the game"

We actively work to make legal and regulatory rulings in our favor	1—2—3—4—5—6—7	We accept the rulings made by various legal and regulatory bodies

2. Attitude toward regulation

We have a fine-tuned sense of those regulations that are good for the firm	1—2—3—4—5—6—7	We actively dislike all forms of regulation

C. Treatment of Customers

1. Attitude toward customer service

Having to deliver customer service is a necessary evil	1—2—3—4—5—6—7	We believe that customer service is a crucial means of securing differential advantage

2. Attitude toward product/service defects

We go out of our way to avoid any type of product defect	1—2—3—4—5—6—7	We believe in "buyer beware"

3. Allocation under scarcity

When we have supply shortages, we use standard allocation formulae to allocate our capacity	1—2—3—4—5—6—7	When we have supply shortages, we make strategic allocation decisions

D. Marketing Spending

1. Attitude toward marketing expenditures

When profits are under pressure, marketing budgets are the first to be cut	1—2—3—4—5—6—7	We regard our marketing budgets as investments in the business

2. Response to shortfalls

Under financial pressure, we make strategically focused budgeting decisions	1—2—3—4—5—6—7	Under financial pressure, we cut budgets by the same percent across the board

3. Response to recession

In recessionary times, we tend to increase or hold firm our marketing budgets	1—2—3—4—5—6—7	In recessionary times, we cut our marketing budgets

E. Product Line Decisions

1. Approach to product development

We have a haphazard approach to new product development	1—2—3—4—5—6—7	Our new product development procedures are clearly established and communicated

2. Product line breadth

We make careful product line choices to avoid too broad or too narrow a product line	1—2—3—4—5—6—7	Our product line is misbalanced (too narrow or too broad)

F. Cost the Customer Pays

1. Approach to setting prices

We set prices based on customer value	1—2—3—4—5—6—7	We set prices on a cost-plus or target-return basis

2. Credit extension

Our credit policy is rigidly applied regardless of customer	1—2—3—4—5—6—7	Our credit policy is informed by the strategic realities we face

G. Business Organization

We place high value on cross-functional integration	1—2—3—4—5—6—7	Our organizational structure is characterized by functional silos

FIGURE 3.1

A Diagnostic Instrument for Assessing an External versus Internal Orientation

Note: To put all scores on a comparable basis, questions A2, A3, A5, C1, C3, D1, E1, and F2 should be reverse coded by subtracting the indicated number from 8. (Example, if you gave the item a rating of 2, it should be 8–2 5 6)

The Planning System

OBJECTIVE SETTING   In part because of the functionalization problem discussed above, many internally focused companies place significant emphasis on achieving functional goals, such as cost reduction targets and sales volume. By contrast, externally oriented firms place more emphasis on externally focused goals more closely related to the performance of the business as a whole, such as shareholder value, market share, customer satisfaction, brand health, long-run profit, or market occupancy ratio.[18] Measuring performance in customer-related terms and making comparisons with competitors is an important underlying philosophy.

PLANNING AND BUDGETING   Many internally oriented companies do not properly comprehend the purpose or process of planning and budgeting. In many such firms, marketing plans do not exist, and even the distinction between plans and budgets is not well understood. The firm may believe it has a plan when all that exists is a budget. (A necessary, though not sufficient, distinction between the two is that the former is expressed largely in words, the latter solely in numbers!) In addition, many companies seem to believe that the purpose of planning is to develop budgets for control purposes. By failing to consider other purposes of planning, they compromise the potential for high performance.

Planning and budgeting are interrelated activities. The primary purpose of planning is to make better decisions that drive the business toward higher performance on the objectives sought by management. Budgeting, where the financial implications of alternative strategies and courses of action, in terms of revenues, costs, and profits are explored, is derivative of the plan. Planning is a creative strategy development exercise; budgeting is an analytic exercise, profoundly different in purpose and even employing different brain modalities![19]

A specific example of an internal approach to planning and budgeting concerns development of the advertising budget. The budget-setting process is often treated as a simple arithmetic exercise using an agreed-upon advertising-to-sales ratio, where the denominator may be either last year's sales or next year's projected sales. The critical problem with this approach is that it "puts the cart before the horse." The direction of causality is inappropriate: sales should result from advertising, not the other way around. (Indeed, if the sales forecast is independent of the advertising budget, does the firm need a marketing department?) By contrast, the external perspective for developing the advertising budget starts from the market. In the planning process, the firm assesses the market situation and its own and competitors' positions, and develops strategic objectives and overall firm strategy. Advertising objectives are an important output of this process, and exploration of the ability of several possible advertising budgets to achieve these objectives leads to selection of the advertising budget.

GATHERING MARKETING INFORMATION   Internally oriented firms are typically unwilling to spend sufficiently on market information gathering, such as conventional customer research and competitive intelligence. For example, for most manufacturers, budgets for technological R&D are several orders of magnitude greater than for market information, despite the fact that new product failure research suggests, time after time, that inadequate market analysis and customer and competitive response forecasts are often key reasons for failure.[20] We should note, however, that when we emphasize the externally orientated firm's focus on marketing information, we are concerned with an openness towards, and a willingness to gather, external market information, rather than with the formality of a full-fledged marketing research department. Externally focused firms truly understand the potential benefits of marketing information, think far beyond collection and analysis costs, and may be delighted to identify customer problems, for therein lies opportunity.

Externally oriented firms know the value of securing information on customers, both their own and those of competitors, and understand well the many uses for customer databases. Specifically, they seek information that can be used in future marketing programs and activities. By contrast, internally oriented firms fail to understand the enormous marketing value of properly collected customer data. For example, many banks and insurance companies collect customer data for administrative reasons (sometimes legally mandated), such as initiating the relationship; rarely do marketing considerations enter these data-gathering efforts.

Regarding competitor information, in our experience, few companies do a first-rate job of data collection; even those internally oriented firms that collect and analyze some level of customer data often bypass competitive data altogether. By contrast, the externally oriented firm understands that the "business game" requires it to secure customers in the face of actions by competitors. As a result, the ability to identify, describe, analyze, predict, and manage competitor actions is crucial, not just for today's direct and indirect competitors, but also those the firm may face tomorrow.

FORECASTING   Many internally oriented firms are hampered by chronic errors in forecasting sales volume. Unwillingness to invest in market information leads to a superficial understanding of demand dynamics and volume forecasts that are notoriously poor. Despite resulting operational problems that lead to increased costs from excessive inventories or lost revenues from missed delivery dates, these firms are often amazingly reluctant to invest the time and effort necessary to solve the problem. (For example, between 1995 and 1996, insufficient raw material supplies caused by inadequate forecasting, plagued Apple Computer.) By contrast, as a consequence of superior marketplace knowledge, externally oriented firms are distinguished by better sales forecasts and objectives that are more often met.

INFORMATION SYSTEMS   Nowadays many firms spend large amounts of money on information system development, frequently as the result of decisions to automate work processes. Typically, the information system development driver is a concern to reduce costs and improve operating efficiency. The inward-oriented firm stops there; the externally focused firm asks how the information system can enable it to be more effective in the marketplace.[21]

For example, over the years, many financial institutions have automated various internal processes associated with different product lines: checking accounts, savings accounts, automobile loans, and so forth. In each case, efficiency gains were achieved, but because these upgrades occurred sequentially, each new system was more advanced but frequently incompatible with systems introduced earlier. Thus, the financial institution is typically unable to ascertain easily whether, for example, the checking account customer also has an automobile loan. The externally focused institution develops these operating information systems with customers in mind, and enables a single account officer to access all relationships with an individual customer at the touch of a button.[22]

> Example: Many people have multiple insurance policies with a single company. Often these policies were initiated on different dates with the result that multiple annual insurance premiums must be paid during the year. Although many consumers might want to avoid this inconvenience and write a single check once a year, most insurance companies cannot accommodate this request.

Defining the Market Arena
ATTITUDE TOWARD THE "RULES OF THE GAME"   Firms operate according to a set of rules laid down by various, mostly national (but some international) governmental and regulatory bodies. The firm with an internal perspective passively accepts these various regulatory and legal imperatives, views them as written in stone, and operates in a

THE EXTERNALLY
ORIENTED FIRM

manner consistent with those rules.[23] By contrast, the externally oriented firm views such legal and regulatory imperatives as made by men and women and inherently flexible. It seeks to change the rules so that it is more favorably treated.

> **Example:** In the 1970s, Bankers Trust lost a significant amount of corporate loan business to commercial paper, underwritten by investment banks.[24] Because the Glass-Steagall Act (1933) explicitly prohibited commercial banks from underwriting securities, most commercial banks were resigned to this loss of business. In contrast, Bankers Trust commenced issuing commercial paper itself, thus inviting legal action from securities firms. Ultimately the Supreme Court upheld Bankers Trust's position, signaling a change in the rules of the game.

> **Example:** In the late 1980s, Canadian life insurance companies successfully lobbied regulators to permit only full-time agents to sell life insurance. This action was directly targeted at the imminent market entry by A.L. Williams (now part of CitiGroup), an aggressive firm relying mainly on part-time agents.

ATTITUDE TOWARD REGULATION Many executives have a knee-jerk (internal) reaction to certain issues rather than a thoughtful (external) approach that examines the issue in detail in a dispassionate manner. For example, ask most American executives what they think about government regulation, and they will be highly negative. But if the firm has had experience in dealing with regulators, the presence of regulation might provide the firm with significant competitive advantage.[25]

> **Example:** Compared to many sectors of the U.S. economy, until recently the insurance industry had seen relatively little direct entry by foreign competitors. One contributing factor is the state-by-state regulation system that requires, for example, new policies be approved in each state. Regulatory expertise, therefore, serves as a barrier to entry for potential new competitors.

Treatment of Customers

ATTITUDE TOWARD CUSTOMER SERVICE Companies operating with internal orientations frequently fail to recognize the strategic importance of customer service, a broad term embracing many different activities. Too often an internal perspective means that once the sale is made, customers are on their own, and sellers have little interest in anticipating the difficulties customers might find in using the firm's products and services.

> **Example:** Once the leader in performance ticketing, Ticketron lost the Los Angeles Forum business by ignoring client requests for system changes. Then, despite a 60-day cancellation clause, it ceased operations at the Forum after 10 days. These actions set the stage for a substantial decline in Ticketron's business.

> **Example:** A few years ago, a major life insurance company discontinued its toll-free number service for policy holders because it was getting too many information requests!

Manufacturers often schedule the manufacture of spare parts at their convenience, resulting in long delivery delays and costly downtime for customers.[26] In other cases, the customer service organization is a stepchild, perhaps reporting to manufacturing or purchasing rather than to marketing or general management. As a result, service positions are not staffed by the most competent people, field service representatives are often poorly educated and trained, and the whole activity is often underbudgeted and the first to be cut in a crisis.

By contrast, firms with an external perspective recognize that their ability to win repeat customers depends on ensuring that customers remain at least satisfied with prior purchases. They recognize that service is a source of potential competitive advantage, not a "necessary evil." They place great emphasis on the delivery of prompt, high-quality service and are sensitive to its importance to customers. Of course, delivering excellent customer service is a critical issue for service firms, but it is also increasingly important for goods manufacturers as a means to differentiate their products from those of competitors.

A particularly fine example of a customer service organization is the GE Answer Center.

> **Example:** Not only does a simple phone call allow GE to provide customers with information on GE products (ranging from washing machines to jet engines), over half the calls received by the Answer Center relate to imminent purchasing decisions. Thus the Answer Center is also a highly effective sales promotion device.

> **Example:** In the late 1980s, before fax machines were widespread, Taiwan-based plastics producer Chi Mei provided hundreds of free fax machines to key customers so that inter-firm contact might be more convenient and orders processed more conveniently.

ATTITUDE TOWARD PRODUCT/SERVICE DEFECTS   The accepting attitude toward product defects, manifest in many internally oriented firms, arises from a belief that reductions in defect rates come at significant cost. In recent years, this "received wisdom" has been affected, to some extent, by the success of the quality movement and a generalized belief that much of the success enjoyed by Japanese companies has resulted from superior product quality. Rather than accepting product defects as "coming with the territory," the externally oriented firm strives to avoid product defects.[27] It believes that getting it right the first time is not only a superior way to treat customers, but that it also is cheaper.[28] Indeed, evidence from the PIMS program shows that low quality is the high-cost way to operate, a phenomenon that the Japanese label the *Taguchi effect*.[29]

Regardless of how hard the firm attempts to reduce defects, from time to time inferior products may be sold to customers. These situations provide an acid test of a company's true orientation. Internally oriented firms typically cite *caveat emptor* (buyer beware) and might deny that a problem exists, often resorting to legal maneuvering in attempts to minimize potential negative short-term financial consequences. Several well-publicized cases in recent years have demonstrated the extent to which firms with product problems can find themselves in significant, life-threatening difficulty by failing to put the customer first, facing up to the possibility of a problem, and vigorously attempting to make things right.

> **Example:** Despite significant evidence that the tread separated from the fabric carcass, Firestone consistently refused to acknowledge any problem with its *Firestone 500* tire. The negative publicity led to loss of market share and eventual acquisition by Japanese producer Bridgestone. (In Summer 2000, Bridgestone–Firestone faced yet another tire quality crisis.) Similarly, in 1994, Dow Corning lost a major lawsuit related to breast implants and entered bankruptcy in 1995.

By contrast, externally oriented firms put the customer first. Thus in 1980, Procter and Gamble (P&G) withdrew *Rely* tampons as soon as it became aware of toxic shock syndrome. P&G allowed the importance of long-term relationships with consumers to outweigh any concerns of short-term profit. Clearly, ethical issues are involved in these decisions, but here we aren't describing ethics, just good business sense.

ALLOCATION UNDER SCARCITY   When a product is in short supply, the firm is faced with the decision of either raising the price or administering an allocation or rationing mechanism. When shortages are temporary, many firms prefer to allocate rather than raise prices. Internally oriented firms frequently supply products to customers generating the highest gross margins and cut others off, or cut back all customers by an equal proportion of their historic orders, sufficient to match the total shortfall.

Both of these approaches are unacceptable to externally oriented firms. The former method fails to consider the long-term profit potential of customer relationships; the latter treats customers unselectively. The externally oriented firm recognizes the strategic importance of decisions about which commitments to fulfill and makes its allocation decisions based on long-term customer development objectives. As a result, large current customers may be less favorably treated than high-potential new customers.

Marketing Spending

ATTITUDE TOWARD MARKETING EXPENDITURES   As noted above, in firms with an internal perspective, marketing expenditures are frequently treated as an expense, even as a necessary evil, to be avoided if at all possible. Advertising, sales, and customer-service expenditures are often minimized and are the first to be cut when crises threaten and budgetary pressures rise. Although many firms are content to allocate resources to technological development or hard assets, such as plant and equipment, where the results of their investment can easily be observed, they are often far less willing to place resources into those intangible marketing expenditures where measuring the effect is much more difficult.

> **Example:** Several years ago, a Columbia MBA was charged with the task of developing a launch plan for a new consumer product for which the firm believed it had one year's lead time. She believed that the current sales force would be unable to handle the new responsibility. As a result, she built into her plan a temporary pioneer sales force to secure distribution; later, the regular sales force would fulfill the maintenance function. Unfortunately, the accountants were unhappy with the early profit projections and removed the pioneer sales force, leaving the regular sales force to perform the introduction task. As the MBA believed, the sales force was overloaded and the new product did not receive the attention it required. In six months the firm had one competitor, in one year three competitors, and in three years it was out of the market. Question: Was the pioneer sales force being treated as an expense or an investment?

Firms with an external perspective treat marketing expenditures as investments, specifically in customer and market development. Rather than conceiving advertising and sales expenditures as unnecessary and excessive costs of doing business, firms with an external perspective truly believe that such expenditures made in the short run will provide benefits in the medium and long run. Thus rather than viewing them as expenses, the externally oriented firm proceeds on the basis that these expenditures are truly investments, as important to the future of the firm as investments in its productive capacity. Citibank's drive to dominance in New York City retail banking in the late 1970s was based on first-mover advantages secured largely by excessive investment in ATMs. Furthermore, although its fund performance track record was solid for many years, Fidelity only clearly became America's pre-eminent direct marketer of mutual funds in the mid- to late-1980s. At that time, it made large investments in advertising and promotion under the simple rationale that "share of spend" (share of voice) should be positively related to "share of market."[30]

RESPONSE TO SHORTFALLS   Many companies respond to financial pressures with across-the-board budget reductions: for example, "In order to spread the pain evenly, each department's budget will be cut by 10 percent." Although there is some value in making all managers conscious of the importance of controlling costs, such edicts, issued from a consummate internal perspective, are rarely optimal.

The externally oriented firm starts from the external reality, diagnoses the situation, and responds on the merits. Depending on this reality, if budget cutting is in order, perhaps some budgets should be cut by 20%, and others by far less. The important factor is the particular set of firm objectives and the strategic contingencies it faces. Budget cutting judgments should be based on these objectives and contingencies, and made according to deliberate strategic thrusts.

RESPONSE TO RECESSION   Recession is an excellent time to build market position and secure long-term relationships with customers. To achieve its goals, the firm must have sufficient resources to withstand the downturns, but even so, internally oriented firms frequently fail to grasp the opportunities because they are preoccupied with immediate financial results and are insensitive to competitive market opportunities. In too many companies, the gut reaction is to cut back on soft expenditures, such as advertising and promotion, before cutting hard investments, such as plant and equipment, a seemingly paradoxical reaction when the major problem is lack of orders!

Externally oriented firms recognize that recession may provide an opportunity to secure strategic advantage, and they are more likely to persevere with current marketing efforts, or at least cut back less than competitors. By contrast, internally oriented firms are more likely to ascribe their losses to the recession *per se* rather than to their competitors' growing market share. Since they may not fully comprehend the competitive threat, their cut backs may be excessive and therefore worsen their positions.

Product-Line Decisions

APPROACH TO PRODUCT DEVELOPMENT   We saw earlier how differing internal perspectives can lead to either an avoidance of new products (operations orientation) or a proliferation of new products (sales orientation). Regardless, firms with internally driven perspectives often have no organized process for new product development. Lacking a mechanism for identifying, screening, and selecting development possibilities often forces such companies into patterns of imitative responses to the initiatives of others, leading to declining margins. In addition, as noted earlier, technically sophisticated firms often fall into the trap of building into their products features for which customers have little use.

By contrast, in firms with an external perspective, new product development procedures are clearly established and communicated, and the organizational responsibilities for new product development are likewise unambiguous. Moreover, the externally oriented firm performs its market research homework thoroughly and only develops products that have sufficiently broad appeal for a defined set of customers. It carefully manages product line breadth so that those responsible for the selling effort fully understand, and are competent to sell, their assigned products.

Whereas they recognize the danger of bloated product lines, new product development efforts are central to the functioning of externally oriented firms; in addition, they are likely to take place in parallel (several at the same time) rather than in sequence (one after the other). Concurrently, measurement systems, such as those that require a defined percent of revenues to be generated by products introduced within the last four or five years, may stimulate new product development.

> **Example:** Alfred Zeien, Gillette's CEO and the manager who led its turnaround, has stated that he would like to see 50 percent of sales coming from products introduced within the last five years.[31] For over 30 years, 3M, one of the world's most innovative large companies, has targeted 30 percent of revenues from products added in the previous five years!

PRODUCT LINE BREADTH   Many internally oriented companies run a great danger of offering an inappropriate breadth of product line, too narrow or too broad. Operations-oriented firms frequently offer narrow product lines that, in the face of diverse customer needs, lead to worsening market performance. Ford's Model T is the classic example of the narrow product line and rigidity that often accompany an operations orientation. Manufacturing economics are typically improved by long runs of limited product variety and at times may represent as viable a strategy today as it did in the 1910s and 1920s when it led Ford to take 55 percent of the American automobile market by 1924. (The

THE EXTERNALLY
ORIENTED FIRM

advent of flexible production systems has tempered this relationship somewhat.) However, when customer needs change and become more varied, a rigid operations focus can spell disaster.[32]

On the other hand, sales-oriented and technologically oriented companies, for different reasons, often offer product lines that are too broad. Sales-oriented firms tend to proliferate products because of an unwillingness to turn down customer requests and an overwhelming desire for sales volume. In technologically oriented firms, managers' engineering interests may entice them into solving a wider and wider variety of customer application problems, with consequent product line growth.

Externally oriented firms recognize they cannot meet the needs of all possible customers today while simultaneously generating the profits necessary to serve customers in the future! They learn to be selective about both choice of customer targets and the set of needs the firm will attempt to satisfy. By carefully managing product line breadth, they are able to shrink marketing costs and improve margins.

> **Example:** In the early 1990s, major consumer goods company Procter and Gamble significantly reduced the items in its product line. By 1995 it had reduced the number of items in its product line by one third. For example, in hair care, the number of items was reduced almost by half, yet market share increased by five points.[33]

Of course, some variety is not only necessary, but also desirable. "You can have any color you want as long as it's black" doesn't make it in today's competitive and sophisticated markets.

Cost to the Customer

APPROACH TO SETTING PRICES   The internally oriented firm approaches the price-setting task from a cost-plus or target-return perspective. This approach has the advantage of simplicity, for if the firm can identify its costs, prices are determined by adding on a desired profit margin, a simple arithmetic exercise. But there are problems. First, identifying the relevant costs is typically a difficult job; firms using this approach frequently make educated guesses at costs and these guesses typically range widely in quality.[34] Second, price determination requires a calculation of cost per unit that must be based on an assumption of volume so that fixed costs can be allocated. However, because price itself affects volume through demand-curve mechanisms, these price-setting processes are clearly indeterminate.

The external perspective starts with the customer and seeks to quantify perceived value delivered by the product or service. It tempers this value with competitive factors and the firm's own strategic objectives before arriving at the actual price. As a result, the relationship of price to cost is not direct: price attempts to capture value to the customer, whereas cost is an internal issue in which (typically) the customer has no direct interest. Of course cost enters the decision inasmuch as it is required to develop the profit schedule—the profit obtained at different prices (and consequently different volumes and costs)—and as a floor below which price should not drop. Furthermore, inwardly oriented firms typically use full cost allocation systems; by contrast, outwardly oriented firms work with direct costing systems that permit better business decisions.[35]

The sharp difference between internal and external perspectives is the importance that externally oriented firms place on the customer, seeking first to understand marketplace impact. These firms treat cost as an arithmetic entity in a profit schedule rather than as the price driver.

CREDIT EXTENSION   Most classic arguments about credit policy reflect disagreement over the degree of conservatism versus liberality with which credit is extended. Sales departments typically argue for loose guidelines to facilitate sales volume; controllers and financial officers, wary of collection problems, often err on the conservative side. Our concern is less with the policy regarding overall credit risk than with its application. In internally oriented firms, the credit policy is rigorously and rigidly applied. By contrast, credit extension in a truly externally oriented firm is often selective; more generous terms are granted to those customers upon whom the firm's long-term goals are focused.

Business Organization

The business units (or divisions) in most corporations are organized by function. At the apex sits a general manager to whom report functional VPs of R&D, Operations, Finance, Marketing, Sales, Logistics and the like. Typically, each functional area has its own budget and develops functional strategies aimed at achieving the business unit's objectives. The problem, of course, is that unswerving dedication to achieving functional objectives may be the cause of many of the internally focused decisions we have just discussed.

By contrast, externally oriented organizations strive to break down these internally focused "functional silos." They place high value on cross-functional integration and often shift from an individual- to team-based organization where customer needs are placed first and the full weight of various functions is applied to satisfying and delighting customers.[36] In addition, democratic processes are favored over autocratic processes; knowledge rather than position determines power; and the culture is open and learning oriented, rather than closed, focused, and driven by tradition.

IMPEDIMENTS TO DEVELOPING AN EXTERNAL PERSPECTIVE

The arguments presented thus far in this chapter should make a compelling argument for the adoption of an external perspective. Doing so is not easy, for many organizations fall too close to the internal end of the internal–external perspective scale on the dimensions we discussed.[37]

Among the major reasons for internal perspectives are

- **Fixed investment in plant and equipment:** Firms are frequently unwilling to scrap in-the-ground assets when the market shifts against them and, as a result, fail to satisfy evolving customer needs. Faced with the prospect of writing off a perfectly serviceable plant, many firms opt to continue with the status quo. Management either attempts to persuade customers that their current products and services are optimal, or may even convince itself that market signals suggesting changed requirements are not to be believed.
- **Rigidities in the line organization:** Although task specialization makes bureaucracy an efficient organizational means for completing repetitive tasks, it acts like a dead weight when markets change and the firm must also. As corporations grow, the bureaucratic model leads to functional specialization; rules and behaviors become embedded, often reinforced by day-to-day work pressures. Although specialization is typically necessary to develop the expertise required to perform effectively, all too frequently the organizational differentiation necessary to achieve the benefits of specialization is not accompanied by mechanisms that encourage lateral communication and cooperation. As a result, the various differentiated organizational units operate as functional "silos."
- **Short-term pressures for efficiency, cost reduction, and profit maximization:** Specialization brings with it expectations regarding the efficiency of organizational subunits. For example, manufacturing strives to reduce unit costs; sales attempts to maximize sales. Unfortunately, a single-minded drive for efficiency by individual

subunits rarely results in behavior that is effective for the organization as a whole. More likely, it generates destructive conflict, resolved by internally focused compromise to the benefit of competitors. These pressures are exacerbated by ineffective goal-setting or reward systems.

- **Presence of a dominant culture:** All organizations have cultures that guide the everyday patterns of behavior of their members. Frequently cultures develop over long periods and may be highly resistant to change. Very often one or more functional areas dominates organizational decision making. For example, a culture in which operations personnel are dominant is likely to favor actions that improve operating efficiency;[38] a culture in which CEOs consistently are selected from the sales force is likely to follow actions favoring a sales orientation.[39]

Example: In early 1999, Procter and Gamble's (P&G) CEO Durk I. Jager, was attempting to break the "Proctoid" mentality and change P&G's 160-year corporate culture of secrecy and discipline in favor of a more open culture that would permit a better response to changing market demands.[40]

- **Social fabric of institutions:** Individuals in organizations know, and interact with, each other on a day-by-day basis, year in and year out. Customers, competitors, and suppliers are occasional intruders to be dealt with before the real business of the workday resumes! This factor is especially prevalent among front-line employees in service organizations, as captured by the following quotation developed by a business owner concerned with this issue.

> "The customer is the most important in our business. The customer is not dependent on us; we are dependent on him. The customer is not an interruption of our work; he is the purpose of it. A customer does us a favor when he comes to see us; we aren't doing him a favor by waiting on him. A customer is part of our business, not an outsider. He is not just money in the cash register; he is a human being with feelings like our own. He comes to us with his needs and wants; it's our job to fill them. A customer deserves the most courtesy we can give him. He is the life-blood of this and every business. He pays your salary. Without him we would have to close our doors. Don't ever forget it."[41]

- **Reward systems:** People in organizations do what is "inspected" rather than what is "expected." In other words, they tend to behave in ways that produce results that are rewarded. If goal setting and reward systems reinforce internal perspectives, behavior consistent with those perspectives is likely to follow. For example, operations managers rewarded for driving down costs are likely to resist broadening the product line by adding new products. Conversely, sales managers rewarded for sales volume are unlikely to take kindly to trimming the product line. And engineers anxious to produce new products are unlikely to wait for market research or to be overly concerned with the firm's ability to produce their designs at reasonable cost.

- **Generalized resistance to change:** Most large organizations need a modicum of predictability to function effectively. This requirement sometimes results in rigidity via programmed "standard operating procedures," and creates an entrenched preference for the status quo that is a powerful barrier to change.[42] Furthermore, many managers prefer "a quiet life"; they are much happier continuing current practices than following an external perspective that often implies new and different behavior. Indeed, organizational change may be viewed as a drama in which the dramatic tension is created by conflict between the natural human desire for stability and the apprehension created by change.[43] This tension may be destructive[44]; resolving the tension created by the need to change is, we believe, one of the hallmarks of a successful leader.

- **Accounting systems:** Many firms' systems do not produce data in a form that supports the taking of an external perspective (see the following section).

As we noted, shifting from an internal to an external orientation, especially in a large organization, is not a simple task; it requires significant consistent and visible leadership, typically from the top of the organization.[45] Increasing depth of customer contact to encourage organizational learning about customer needs must be backed by extensive and timely information on customers by systematic and periodic customer satisfaction surveys.[46]

Organizational processes can aid this switch. For example, financial compensation may be tied to customer satisfaction as measured by survey instruments (conducted by independent third parties); R&D personnel may be required to write embryonic marketing plans before securing funding for research projects; job descriptions may be written that somehow relate tasks to "customers"; cross-functional teams may be constructed to address specific customer-related issues. Other typical actions include hiring marketing professionals,[47] hiring customers to work for the firm, in-depth, cross-functional marketing education,[48] implementation of a rigorous marketing planning system and, especially for service organizations, "excessive" training at lower organizational levels.[49] These issues are addressed in greater depth in Chapter 19.

IMPLICATIONS FOR SELECTING CUSTOMERS

In the previous sections, we both argued for an organizational approach to business focused on an external orientation and discussed some of the inhibitors to putting this into practice. Many indicators of an external orientation focus on customers; indeed, the critical marketing function is to secure and retain customers. However, management should not accept willy-nilly all those that wish to become its customers. Not only may they be unprofitable to serve, there may be other reasons why potential customers should be turned away. We commence this section with a discussion of customer profitability, then make the case that customer retention is a key to enhancing firm profitability. We conclude by identifying several legitimate reasons, some of which are fairly obvious, why the firm might not want to engage in seller/customer transactions.

Customer Profitability

Most business organizations have systems in place to measure product profitability. Indeed, managerial accounting processes are designed to help managers make product line decisions and answer such questions as, Are our current products profitable? Should we add the new product to the product line? In recent years, the very best systems have incorporated activity based costing (ABC) methods to help the firm secure more precise answers to these sorts of questions. Unfortunately, few firms have the very best systems, and those in place vary markedly in quality; in many cases, they cause the firm to make incorrect product-line and other decisions. In the book's Appendix, we make some observations about typical financially oriented accounting systems and introduce contribution-based systems that are far more appropriate for making marketing decisions.

The purpose of this section is different. Here we focus not on *product* profitability but on *customer* profitability. As we have already made abundantly clear, firms secure profits first and foremost by securing customers; products are merely a means to that end. Thus, an understanding of product profitability, while important, is insufficient; the firm must fully grasp customer profitability. A simple example will illustrate the point:

Suppose the firm sells one product (1) to two groups of customers. Figure 3.2 demonstrates that although the product is profitable overall (Figure 3.2A), when the costs are broken out by customer, group A customers are profitable, but group B customers are not (Figure 3.2B). (Note that some costs are directly associated with each customer group;

A: Overall Product Profitability

Sales	$10.0 million
Costs	$ 8.5 million
Profit	$ 1.5 million

B: Customer Profitability

	Product I	Customers A	Customers B
Sales	$10.0 million	$7.0 million	$3.0 million
Direct Costs	$ 7.5 million	$4.0 million	$3.5 million
Profit Contribution	$ 2.5 million	$3.0 million	($0.5 million)
Other Costs	$ 1.0 million		
Profit	$ 1.5 million		

C: Customers A Only

Sales		$7.0 million
Direct Costs	$4.0 million	
Other Costs	$1.0 million	
Total Costs		$5.0 million
Profit		$2.0 million

FIGURE 3.2

A Simple Example of Customer Profitability

other costs cannot be attributed to either group and so are considered separately. If the firm were to stop selling to either customer group A or B, these other costs [sometimes called indirect costs] would remain.) If the firm sold only to customer group A, it would increase its profits (Figure 3.2C).

Figure 3.2 demonstrates that measuring profitability by customer is very important. Unfortunately, few firms are readily able to complete this sort of calculation for their own customers. This is an impediment to securing overall firm profitability: "If you can't measure it; you can't manage it."

Some firms do examine revenues and profits by customer. These examinations have revealed some interesting findings, in particular the presence of the 80:20 rule: 80% of the firm's revenues come from 20% of its customers.[50] As a result of this finding, many firms have instituted some form of key account management to address these most important customers. However, equally important is the 20:80 rule, the logically consistent analogue of the former rule: 20% of the firm's revenues come from 80% of its customers. Question: what does it cost to serve this 80% of customers, and is it profitable to do so? Many firms find that the answers to these two questions are, respectively, "a lot," and "no." Indeed, especially in those cases where customers have traditionally been the responsibility of an on-the-road sales force, firms are paring down these customer bases by introducing telemarketing, assigning customers to distributors, using Web-based methodologies, or just ceasing to do business with them.

Serious decisions must be made not only about small customers, however, because customer profitability is not necessarily related to customer size. Indeed, many companies find that customer profitability follows an inverted U function in which the smallest and largest customers are unprofitable (Figure 3.3). Small customer profitability is typically driven by the cost of doing business; large customer profitability is often related to buyer power and excessively low prices.[51]

MARKETING
AND THE FIRM

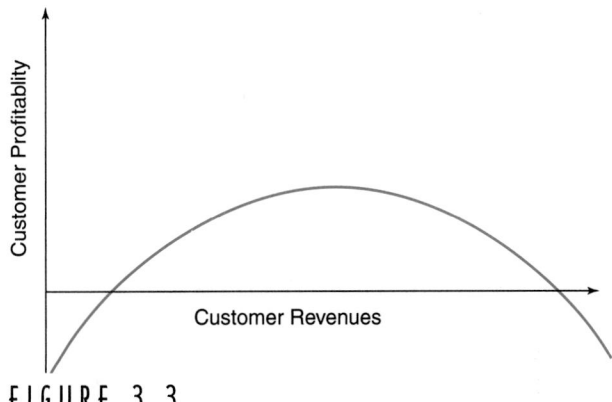

FIGURE 3.3

An Often-Found Relationship Between Customer Revenues and Net Customer Profitability

Nonetheless, the firm should be careful not to make precipitous decisions; today's small customers may one day become large customers. Furthermore, although a large customer may be unprofitable according to the firm's accounting methodology, it may carry a large portion of the firm's overhead burden that would have to be reassigned to other customers if the customer relationship were to cease.[52]

Of course size is not the only basis upon which customers may be classified. An important task for marketing managers is to explore different means of classifying the firm's customers in order to identify individual groups that are especially profitable or unprofitable. Once management identifies individual customer groups by profitability, it is ready to make some decisions. For example, since the high-profit group is unlikely to be homogeneous, management may identify smaller groupings or segments each with its own profile of needs and wants. Specific actions might include selling additional products or improving products and services for individual segments to bind these customers more closely to the firm.

Example: A study in the insurance industry found that after ten years, 75% of multiple product customers were still policy holders, compared to 45% of single product customers.[53]

In addition, the firm may target new customers with similar profiles. The firm might also decide to disengage from certain customers by reducing service, raising prices, or simply ceasing to do business with them. See the following example for a financial services firm that reclassified its customer base:

Example: A financial services institution traditionally classified its customers into four groups based on a combination of account balances and demographic characteristics: *upscale* (over 45 years, balances over $60K), *prime* (over 45 years), *emergent* (less than $60K, under 45 years), and *small business*. Using this classification scheme, each of the four groups appeared to be profitable (Figure 3.4A).

Reclassification on a different basis also produced four groups: *heavy hitters* (long-term customers, high balances, high activity), *comfortables* (long-term customers, high balances), *growers* (newer customers, high activity), and *movers* (newer customers, high activity). The profitability pattern of the four new groups was markedly different; indeed, one group showed losses (Figure 3.4B).

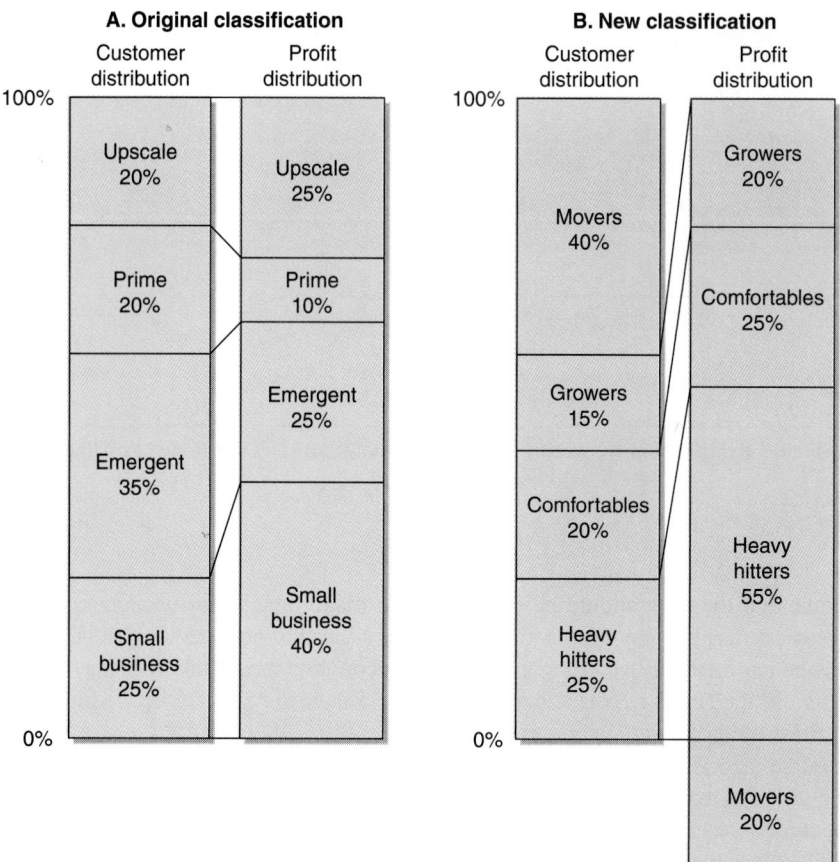

A. Original classification

B. New classification

FIGURE 3.4

Example of Customer Classification

As a result of this analysis, the firm raised prices for products purchased largely by *movers*. Its goal was to reduce the number of high-activity customers and make those that remained more profitable. At the same time, it developed a new targeting scheme to identify *heavy hitters*.

For management to make these sorts of decisions, it must collect and organize its accounting data such that it is able to separate out revenues and costs by customer. Of course the firm might want to develop a customer database for many different reasons: for example, good information on current customers not only gives management confidence in launching new products for these prime prospects, it may reach them at a cost lower than for new customers. A well-developed customer database will also allow management to examine the profitability of customers over time and address the critical importance of customer retention.

Customer Retention

As indicated above, management should be cautious in making decisions based on customer profitability data without fully understanding the dynamics of customer relationships. A particularly important issue concerns customer retention and the profit impact of long-term customer relationships where

Customer Retention Rate =

$$\frac{\text{Number of Customers on December 31 Who Were Customers on January 1}}{\text{Number of Customers on January 1}}$$

FIGURE 3.5

Company Profitability by Retention Rate in the Insurance Brokerage Industry

Sources: Annual reports, Bain estimates.
Note: U.S. operations only.

First, the ability to achieve any revenue and growth objective is strongly conditioned on the firm's customer retention rate. For example, if the firm's goal is 15% growth, a 95% retention rate implies that, on average, its customer acquisition rate must be 20%; a retention rate of 80% implies that its customer acquisition rate must be 35%![54]

Second, empirical research conducted at Bain and Company demonstrates that, in many industries, customer retention is strongly related to customer profitability.[55] A typical example is shown in Figure 3.5.

These two factors demonstrate the critical importance of customer retention to firm profitability. Indeed, Reicheld has demonstrated that small increases in customer retention can improve profitability dramatically in many industries (Figure 3.6).

EXPLANATION OF CUSTOMER RETENTION/PROFITABILITY EFFECT Several reasons may account for improvement in profitability resulting from increases in customer retention. For example:

- Customer acquisition typically requires considerable investment; this cost should only be incurred once.[56]
- Assuming a well-run organization, customers will provide a base level of profit.
- Over time, customers may increase purchases.
- Firm operating costs for dealing with customers may decrease.
- Satisfied customers may provide referrals to other customers.[57]
- Firms may extract price premia from long-term satisfied customers.

Of course not all of these reasons will be effective in each situation.

The second "duration" effect relates in part to the relationship between customer longevity and retention rate. Thus, if the retention rate improves from 50 percent to 75 percent, average customer longevity increases from two to four years; however, if the retention rate improves from 90 percent to 95 percent, average customer longevity increases from 10 to 20 years! Furthermore, the retention/defection rate is not constant across all levels of customer longevity; long-term customers are likely to defect at slower rates than more recently acquired customers, a factor that works in favor of increased profitability for firms with high retention rates.

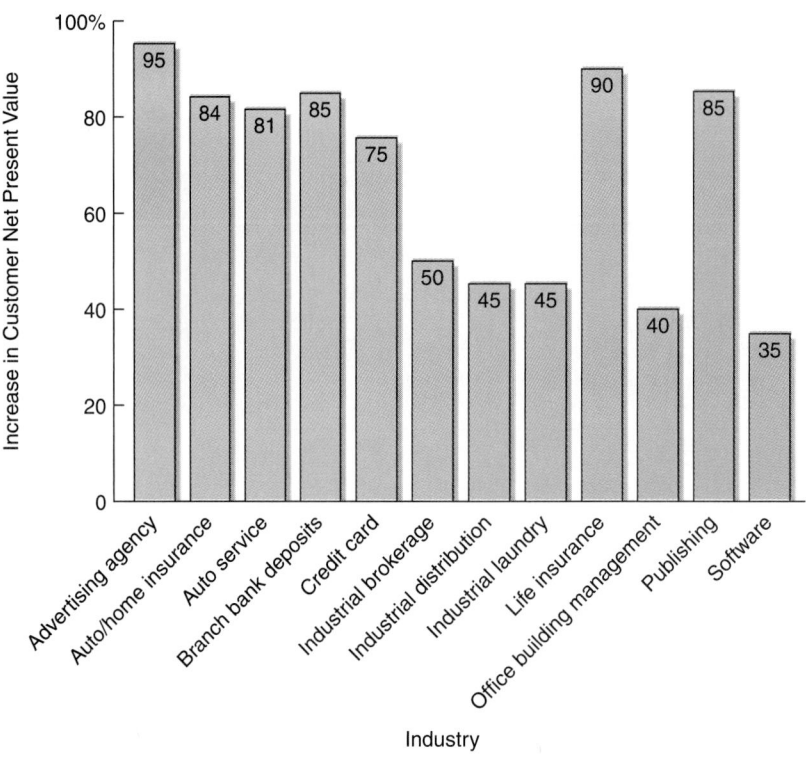

FIGURE 3.6

Improving Customer Retention by 5% in Selected Industries

The combination of these two effects is well illustrated in data secured from the credit card industry, where annual profit is shown by length of the relationship (Figure 3.7).[58]

To the extent that this effect is widespread, it has important implications for allocating promotional expenditures. In particular, many companies spend extensively to secure new customers, but allocate relatively few resources to retain existing customers. These data suggest that under-spending on current customers can have severe profitability implications.[59]

CUSTOMER SATISFACTION   As we discuss later, achieving high levels of customer satisfaction is a critical goal for firms that want to achieve high retention rates. However, in large part because of increasing competition, customer satisfaction is no guarantee of high rates of customer retention. Indeed, satisfied customers increasingly are defecting.[60] The critical message is that the firm must strive not only to satisfy, but also to "delight" its customers. This notion is captured in Figure 3.8.

Figure 3-8 depicts the change from uncompetitive (AA′) to competitive (BB′) markets.[61] Along the AA′ line, customer loyalty rises quickly even though customer satisfaction remains low; the absence of alternatives prohibits customers from readily switching suppliers. As competition increases (represented by the arrow) to a curve BB′, a different situation is depicted. At low customer satisfaction there is little customer loyalty; however, when satisfaction rises, loyalty still remains low. The reason: customers have many alternatives and will switch from "good" suppliers if a better deal is offered. Nonetheless, very high levels of satisfaction pay off in high loyalty.

Example: Military officers have been perceived to be poor risks by auto insurance companies. They moved frequently and on each occasion had to initiate a new policy with a new agent. Since a critical variable for assessing risk was "time at

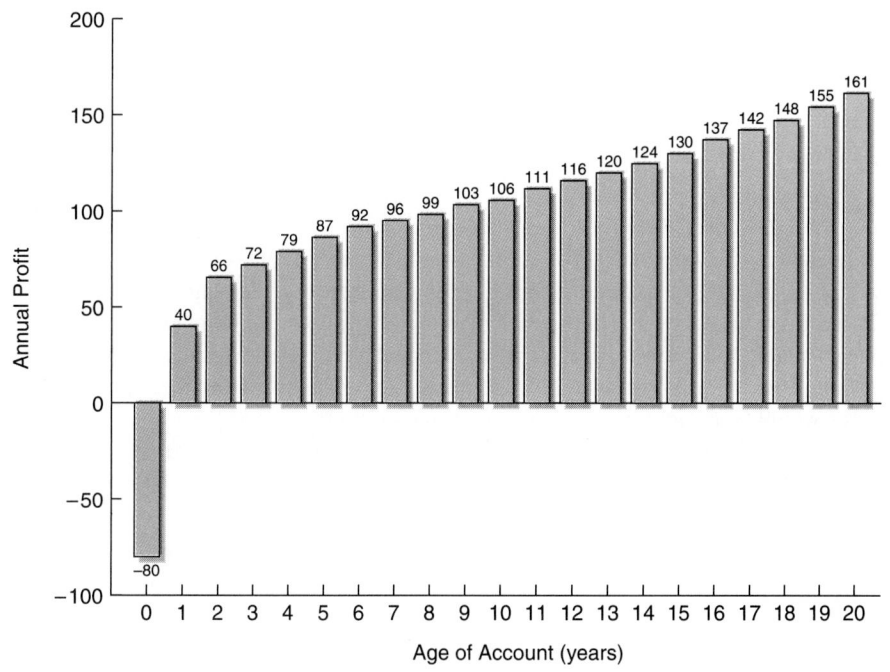

FIGURE 3.7

Profitability in the Credit Card Industry by Length of Customer Relationship

current address," insurance was difficult to secure and expensive. USAA's innovation was a nationwide distribution system that could be accessed by mail or telephone and a single policy that stayed in force when they moved. Satisfying the basic need and excellent customer service had led to an extremely loyal customer base of highly transient customers. Less than 2 percent of USAA's customers defect voluntarily each year.[62]

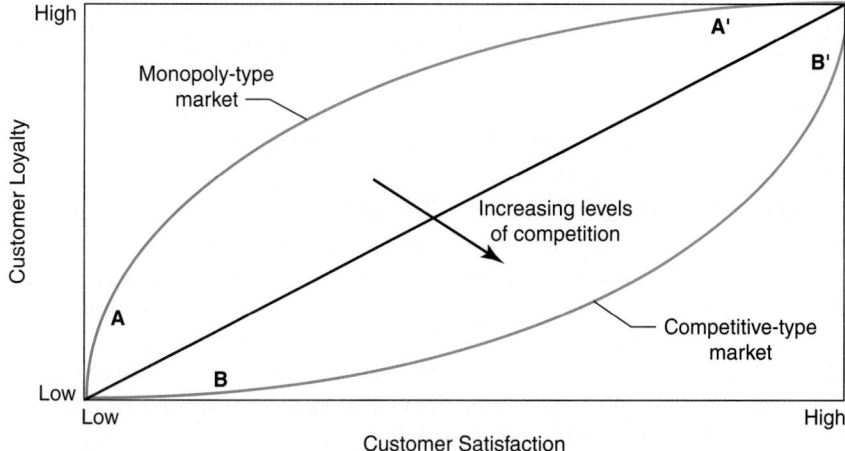

FIGURE 3.8

A Customer Satisfaction/Loyalty Chart

THE EXTERNALLY
ORIENTED FIRM

Turning Away Potential Customers

As a general rule, companies do not want to transact unprofitable business with customers. However, in addition, several other reasons may cause the firm to turn away potential customers.

- **Competition**: The customer is a current or potential competitor. To sell the firm's product would provide the competitor with marketplace advantage, for example, by allowing it to reverse engineer the firm's products.
- **Non-payers**: Customers receive products and services, perhaps intending to pay, but either do not pay or put the firm to enormous cost in collecting on the debt.
- **Potential costs**: Doing business with a potential customer might open the firm to unacceptable future costs. For example, management might conclude that the firm is unable to provide servicing through its current organization and that service costs would be prohibitive.
- **Foreclosing options**: Business on the customer's terms forecloses other options for the firm. For example, an advertising agency for one of Procter and Gamble's brands is unlikely to be able to do work for Colgate Palmolive or Lever Brothers.[63]
- **Impact on firm reputation**: The firm might conclude that a potential customer would use its product inappropriately, leading to failure. Publicizing this failure would negatively impact the firm's reputation.
- **Impact on the offer**: For service businesses, such as restaurants, airlines and business schools, fellow customers are often integral to the firm's offer. For example, to serve a group of rowdy sports fans at an expensive restaurant would doubtless affect the ambiance, and result in the loss of business from other customers. Furthermore, in part the role of admissions departments at universities and colleges is to maintain and improve their institutions' reputation and educational experience by selecting the "right" students. Specific types of customers that firms should attempt to avoid are
    Thieves: They use their customer status to rob other customers (or the firm).
    Belligerents: They verbally abuse service personnel.
    Family feuders: They make scenes at service delivery points.
    Vandals: They destroy equipment.
    Rule breakers: Like unruly airline passengers, these customers may pose a physical danger to others, impact the service experience for fellow customers, and raise costs for the firm.[64]
- **Mismatched to the offer**: This more subtle issue is concerned with the match between the customer's true needs and the firm's offer. If, despite a mismatch, the customer purchases the product and is dissatisfied, serious negative word of mouth can ensue.[65]

SUMMARY

As environmental turbulence and the pace of change increase and competitive challenges grow in depth and scope, more and more firms will have to manage their own metamorphoses in active ways. The gentler pace of change that permitted incremental evolution to suffice will no longer prevail. Of several organizational perspectives or orientations, only the external perspective is compatible with meeting critical environmental challenges. By contrast, firms driven by one of several forms of internal orientation will be unable to make the changes necessary to survive in the new environmental reality. Those firms, whose ways of doing things are set in concrete, will not survive.

Across a host of dimensions, internal perspectives lead to inertia and lack of responsiveness. By contrast, an external orientation, shared by all functions of the firm, unshackles the organization. Such firms prepare for the future by recognizing critical environmental imperatives and by being prepared to make the complex and tough decisions necessary to keep the firm headed in the right direction.

It is one thing to understand the perils of an internal orientation; it is quite another to develop an organization that is truly externally oriented. Because developing and maintaining such an organization is a highly complex undertaking, we identified some drivers of an internal orientation and suggested some practical means for introducing an external orientation.

Customers are the centerpiece of an external orientation. However, since firms should only accept customers that are profitable in the long run, systems must be put in place to measure customer profitability. Management should also be clear about the role of customer retention in driving firm profitability and understand that reasons other than potential profit may lead to potential customers being turned away.

THE CHANGING VIEW

Old Way	New Way
Internal orientation	External orientation
Marketing is done by the marketing department	Marketing is done by the firm as a whole
"Tried and true" is the safest way to get ahead	Questioning the status quo is essential in a fast-moving world
Marketing expenditures are costs to be minimized	Marketing expenditures may be some of the most important investments the firm makes
The purpose of planning is to come up with a budget	The purpose of planning is to make better decisions
Innovate when necessary	Innovation is a prerequisite to long-term survival
Specialization and functionalization	Multi-skilling and flexibility
Multiple often-conflicting performance measures	Shareholder and customer-value-based measures
Mass markets	One-to-One
Customer knowledge paid lip service	Customer insight recognized as crucial
Measure product profitability	Measure customer profitability

QUESTIONS FOR STUDY AND DISCUSSION

1. Complete the market orientation scale for your educational institution. What actions would you take to increase its external orientation? Be prepared to defend your position in class.

2. Explain the relationship between functional performance measures and internal orientations.

3. Many managers view planning activity as a complete waste of time. Why do they feel this way and how could the perception and reality be changed?

4. Give three examples of companies that have changed the rules of an industry and have succeeded.

5. Give three examples of firms that you believe tried to change rules and failed. Why did they fail?

6. Pick a company with which you are familiar and telephone them with a service problem. Record the response and be prepared to play excerpts in class. (Check first that recording your own telephone conversation is legal in your state or

country.) Do you believe the response you received indicates whether this company is internally or externally oriented?

7. Consider two companies: Company 1, customer retention rate is 95 percent; Company 2, customer retention rate is 90 percent. Assume that each company's acquisition rate for new customers is 15 percent p.a. How long will it take each company to double its customer base?

8. The following three matrices represent customer transition rates for Companies A and B from time 1 to time 2. (Matrix I: In time 2, Company A retains 80 percent of the customers it had in time 1; in addition, it secures 20 percent of Company B's customers.)

	I			II			III	
	Time 2			Time 2			Time 2	
Time 1	A	B	Time 1	A	B	Time 1	A	B
A	0.8	0.2	A	0.9	0.1	A	0.95	0.05
B	0.2	0.8	B	0.2	0.8	B	0.2	0.8

What will be the long-run market share of Company A in each scenario? (Hint: assume that each company starts with 50 customers.)

9. Pick a company with which you are familiar and ask the relevant executive whether systems are in place to measure a) product profitability, b) customer profitability. If the answer is "Yes" to a) but "No" to b), probe the reasons for this state of affairs. Be prepared to discuss your findings in class.

10. "A crisis is usually required to produce a shift to an external orientation." Discuss.

11. Why do firms so often remain wedded to historical patterns of behavior even in the face of clear evidence calling for change?

12. Interview an executive and ask him to tell you of instances where the "functional silo" phenomenon has hurt the performance of a firm with which he or she is familiar.

13. From your own experience or that of someone you know, add three additional examples (to those in the book) of how inward-oriented firms treat key management issues.

14. Explain why the terms "customer focus" or a "customer service philosophy" do not embrace your text's concept of an external orientation.

15. How do these two objectives differ? a) creating shareholder value; b) reporting consistent increases in quarterly profits?

END NOTES

1. Several terms are used in common practice to convey approximately the same idea: outward orientation, market orientation, customer orientation, the marketing concept, market driven, and market focused. We discuss our own terminological choice later in this chapter.

2. Simon reports that in his successful small company sample, personnel in many functions displayed intensive interaction with customers in functions. H. Simon, *Hidden Champions: Lessons from 500 of the World's Best Unknown Companies*, Boston, MA: Harvard Business School Press, 1996.

3. An interesting example of not treating customers as valuable assets is provided by the life insurance industry. Policyholders whose originating agents have left the firm are often called, and treated as, "orphans"; left to languish with no attention paid to them by an agent.

4. The term "functional silo" is often used to capture the idea of independent behavior by individual functional areas.

5. This orientation was perhaps best exemplified at ITT under CEO Harold Geneen in the 1970s; see H. Geneen, *Managing*, Garden City, NY: Doubleday, 1984.

6. The long-term view attributed to many Japanese firms, compared to the short-term profit orientation of many American companies, has frequently been cited for the relatively strong international performance of Japanese firms. However, the Asian crisis in the second half of 1997 has led to significant re-thinking of this argument.

7. Privately held companies have the luxury of being less vulnerable to short-term profit pressures.

8. Of course, when really new products are being contemplated, customers may be unable to articulate their needs. Nonetheless, as the new product development process gains momentum, there is typically plenty of opportunity to secure customer feedback.

9. See also, E.S. McKay, *The Marketing Mystique*, New York: Amacom, 1979; revised by A.M. Rittenberg, Amacom, 1994. Some firms can be viewed as having a "legal" orientation in which they go out of their way to avoid any possibility of legal action rather than viewing legal decisions as falling within a broader business decision making framework. For this reason, some executives have dubbed their legal offices as the "sales prevention department." The strategic successes of Intel, however, demonstrate that appropriately aligned legal departments can play an important role in overall business strategy (see T. Jackson, *Inside Intel*, New York: Dutton, 1997).

10. *The Australian*, March 31, 1998.

11. See "Wachovia Bank and Trust Company" in N. Capon, *The Marketing of Financial Services*, Englewood Cliffs, NJ: Prentice Hall, 1992.

12. This term is taken from military usage.

13. The first two issues were coping with the increasing importance of product quality and greater service content and assessing changing customer characteristics.

14. This perspective is virtually identical to Narver and Slater. However, they retain the term *market orientation*, commonly employed by academics and practitioner-scholars at the Marketing Science Institute (MSI) (J.C. Narver and S.F. Slater, "The Effect of a Market Orientation on Business Profitability," *Journal of Marketing*, 54 [Oct. 1990], pp. 20–35). Kohli and Jaworski deal with the same concept, but place more emphasis on the firm's use of market intelligence and less on broader environmental understanding of the type we emphasized in Chapter 2. See A.K. Kohli and B.J. Jaworski, "Market Orientation: The Construct, Research Propositions and Management Implications," *Journal of Marketing*, 54 (Apr. 1990), pp. 1–18 and B.J. Jaworski and A.K. Kohli, "Market Orientation: Antecedents and Consequences," *Journal of Marketing*, 57 (July 1993), pp. 53–70. See also B. Shapiro, "What the Hell Is Market-Oriented," *Harvard Business Review*, 67 (Nov.–Dec. 1989), pp. 119–225 and R. Deshpandé, *Developing a Market Orientation*, Thousand Oaks, CA: Sage, 1999.

15. Slater and Narver emphasize the importance of differentiating between "expressed" needs, of which customers are aware, and "latent" needs that are not consciously understood. Their "market-oriented" firm seeks to satisfy both types of need, S.F. Slater and J.C. Narver, "Customer-led and market-oriented: Let's not confuse the two, *Strategic Management Journal*, 19 (1998), 1001-1006 and S.F. Slater and J.C. Narver, "Market-Oriented is More than being Customer-Led," *Strategic Management Journal*, 20 (1999), pp. 1165–1168.

16. For an interesting approach to identifying opportunities for satisfying customer needs, see, W.C. Kim and R. Mauborgne, "Creating New Market Space," *Harvard Business Review*, 77 (Jan./Feb. 1999), pp. 83–93.

17. See Kohli and Jaworski and Jaworski and Kohli, *op. cit*. We use such scales in our own research so are not opposed to them. However, we firmly believe that you should hone your observational skills to judge how well a particular organization conforms to the behavior we describe, hence Figure 3.1. We should emphasize that whereas the MARKOR scale has been tested for reliability and validity, no claims are made for the scaling properties of the questions in Figure 3.1.

18. The market occupancy ratio (MOR) is the number of customers served divided by total number of customers in the market. It is a particularly valuable measure in those cases in which the seller believes intra-customer penetration of sales potential is low and significant growth potential exists with these customers.

19. N. Herrmann, *The Whole Brain Business Book*, New York: McGraw-Hill, 1996.

20. See, for example, R. Cooper, "Dimensions of New Product Success and Failure," *Journal of Marketing*, 43 (Summer 1979), pp. 93–103.

21. See C. Wiseman, *Strategy and Computers: Information Systems as Competitive Weapons*, Homewood, IL: Dow Jones Irwin, 1985.

22. To give some idea of the scale of this problem, in 1997 a junior executive at a large American auto company admitted to one of the authors that a particular consumer's name might enter its databases in no less than 85 ways. However, management had just canceled a large-scale systems integration project to eliminate such redundancy (and generate a much more useful database) because it was too expensive!

23. One danger of an aggressive approach to regulation is to focus the firm's efforts entirely in this domain to the exclusion of a concern to deliver value to customers.

24. Underwriting is the process of raising money for corporations by issuing and distributing securities. Commercial paper is a short-term security (financial instrument) issued by corporations requiring funds and sold to other corporations with excess funds.

25. Consider the return to power by electoral process of communist governments in some Eastern European countries in the 1990s. By offering a degree of stability that immediate post-communist regimes were unable to provide, such governments have sometimes made their countries more hospitable to foreign investment.

26. Many service elements focus on time: for example, time to answer the telephone, time to process an insurance claim, or time to replace a lost credit card.

27. Many leading companies such as General Electric, Seagate Technology, Bombadier and AlliedSignal are now striving for "six sigma" quality, 3.4 defects per million, company wide, in products and processes.

28. In some cases, impressive improvements in quality were made when new management took over an existing facility; for example, the Motorola TV plant outside Chicago went from 164 errors per 100 sets to 3/4 per 100 a short time after being acquired by Matsushita.

29. The acronym PIMS stands for the **P**rofit **I**mpact of **M**arketing **S**trategy, a collaborative database and research project. Founded at GE under CEO Fred Borch, PIMS was later spun off so that the range of businesses encompassed by the database could be broadened. For a comprehensive description of the project and its results, see R.D. Buzzell and B.T. Gale, *The PIMS Principles: Linking Strategy to Performance*, New York: The Free Press, 1987. See also B.T. Gale, *Managing Customer Value*, New York: The Free Press, 1994.

30. "Share of spend" is the firm's advertising and promotion expenditures divided by total advertising and promotion expenditures from all competing firms; correspondingly, "share of market" is the firm's sales divided by total sales from all competing firms.

31. *Business Week*, January 19, 1998.

32. Ford failed to understand shifting customer needs and was caught flatfooted as General Motors, under Sloan, focused Chevrolet, Pontiac, Buick, Oldsmobile, and Cadillac automobiles on different market segments. By the early 1930s, Ford's market share was in the low 20s. See A.P. Sloan, *My Years with General Motors*, Garden City, NY: Doubleday, 1963.

33. *Business Week*, September 9, 1995.

34. Firms that adopt activity-based costing improve their ability to make more accurate cost determinations.

35. You will learn about these systems in your accounting classes. Briefly, full cost allocation requires that *all* costs incurred by the firm be allocated to individual products. By contrast, in direct costing systems, individual products only carry those costs related to their production and sales. Other costs must be covered by the contributions from all products in total. See, also, the Book Appendix.

36. See, for example, J.R. Hauser and D. Clausing, "The House of Quality," *Harvard Business Review*, 66 (May/June 1988), pp. 63–74.

37. Of course, a company may be at the internal end of the scale on some dimensions but at the external end on others.

38. For example, Chemical Bank (now Chase) used to have a 2,000-page branch manual; six pages were allotted to opening the front door!

39. One of our colleagues, Don Hambrick, has convincingly demonstrated the influence of the CEO background on his decisions. S. Finkelstein and D.C. Hambrick, *Strategy and Leadership: Top Executives and Their Effects on Organizations*, St. Paul, MN: West, 1996.

40. A mere 18 months later, Jager resigned in the face of P&G's worsening profit performance.

41. Reputedly developed by Mahatma Ghandi and hung in his law office in South Africa.

42. J.G. March and H.A. Simon, *Organizations*, New York: Wiley, 1958.

43. N. Tichy and M.A. Devanna, *The Transformational Leader*, New York: Wiley, 1990.

44. P. Senge, *The Fifth Discipline: the Art and Practice of the Learning Organization*, New York: Doubleday, 1990.

45. There is a significant literature on personality traits for leadership. However, one useful set for consideration is unity of person and purpose, single-mindedness, fearlessness, stamina and perseverance, and inspiring to others (Simon, *op. cit*).

46. Some organizations insist that senior management spend a fixed amount of time per month dealing with customer telephone calls; others give senior management a quota of on-the-road customer calls; and others have orchestrated meetings of their shipping personnel with key customers' receiving employees. Some highly successful small companies deliberately have no formal salesperson position so as to emphasize the importance of customer contact throughout the firm (Simon op. cit).

47. Among firms that have taken this route are Citibank, Chemical Bank, IBM, the U.S. Postal Service, and Midland Bank (UK).

48. SONY and Unilever are examples of companies the authors have worked with in this regard.

49. Airlines in particular have favored this approach: well-known examples are SAS, British Airways, and Singapore Airlines.

50. The 80/20 rule is just a rough guide. Each firm should examine its own customer profitability distribution. It may discover that this ratio is more like 90/10 or 95/5!

51. Sometimes mid-size customers are more profitable because, in addition to the products, they purchase related services. Large customers might conduct these activities in-house.

52. Overhead comprises those costs not directly assigned to individual products. It may include, for example, long-run R&D, corporate advertising, corporate legal, and government relations among others.

53. *National Underwriter*, September 7, 1998.

54. Customer "churn," the opposite of customer retention, is a critical issue in such industries as cable TV and long-distance telephone service. The annual churn rate is the percent of customers in Year 1 that were not customers in Year 2.

55. F.F. Reicheld, *The Loyalty Effect*, Boston, MA. Harvard Business School Press, 1996. See also B.J. Pine II, D. Peppers and M. Rogers, "Do You Want to Keep Your Customers Forever?" *Harvard Business Review*, 73 (March-April 1995), pp. 103–154 and R.C. Blattberg and J. Deighton, "Manage Marketing by the Customer Equity Test," *Harvard Business Review*, 74 (Jul./Aug. 1996), pp. 136–144.

56. As a simple example, a credit card company seeking new customers is lucky to achieve a response rate of 2 percent to 3 percent. To secure 1,000 applications it has to send 30,000 to 50,000 solicitations. When the costs of credit evaluation, card issuance, and entering customer data into the system are added in, it typically costs $50 to $100 for each new customer.

57. For example, Lexus reportedly secures more new customers from referrals than from any other source.

58. Technically, lifetime customer value (LCV) is given by:
$$LCV = m_0 + m_1 \times r_1/(1 + d) + m_2 \times r_1 r_2/(1 + d)^2 + m_3 \times r_1 r_2 r_3/(1 + d)^3 + \ldots\ldots - AC$$
where m = annual cash flow, r = year-to-year retention rate, d = discount rate, AC = acquisition cost

If annual cash flows and year-to-year retention rates are equivalent, it can be shown that:
$$LCV = m (1 + d)/(1 + d - r) - AC$$

59. Reicheld's work also demonstrates the importance of both employee and shareholder loyalty.

60. Research conducted by Ogilvy and Mather suggests that for automobiles, 85% report being satisfied but only 40% repurchase. In packaged goods, 2/3 of people identifying a "favorite" brand admit to having purchased another brand most recently. In business-to-business settings, 65% to 85% of defectors were satisfied or very satisfied with their former supplier.

61. See, J.L. Heskett, T.O. Jones, G.W. Loveman, W.E. Sasser Jr. and L. Schlesinger, "Putting the Service-Profit Chain to Work," *Harvard Business Review*, 72 (Mar./Apr. 1994), pp. 164–174 and T.O. Jones and W.E. Sasser, "Why Satisfied Customers Defect," *Harvard Business Review*, 73 (November-December 1995), pp. 88–99.

62. Term paper by Lisa Gray, MBA student, Columbia University, 1993; see also, Reicheld, *op. cit.*, p. 71.

63. One of the main reasons for Pepsico's 1997 divestment of its restaurant businesses—Kentucky Fried Chicken, Taco Bell, and Pizza Hut—was that Coca-Cola was able to persuade fast-food customers that selling Pepsi in its restaurants was aiding a competitor.

64. Lovelock and Wright term these five customer types and non-payers (deadbeats), Jaycustomers (C. Lovelock and L. Wright, *Principles of Service Marketing and Management*, Upper Saddle River, NJ: Prentice-Hall, 1999).

65. The ability of individuals to develop anti-firm Web sites is raising this concern to new levels.

66. A.K. Kohli and B.J. Jaworski and A. Kumar, "MARKOR: A Measure of Market Orientation," *Journal of Marketing Research*, 30 (Nov. 1993), pp. 467–477.

WEB RESOURCES

3M	www.3m.com
Apple Computer	www.apple.com
AT&T	www.att.com
Bain	www.bain.com
Bankers Trust	www.bankerstrust.com
Bridgestone	www.bridgestone.com
Chase	www.chase.com
Chi Mei	www.chimei.com
Citibank	www.citibank.com
Coke	www.cokecola.com
Colgate	www.colgate.com
Danone	www.danone.com
Dow Corning	www.dowcorning.com
Dr. Pepper	www.drpepper.com
Fidelity	www.fidelity.com
Firestone	www.firestone.com
Ford	www.ford.com
GE	www.ge.com
Gillette	www.gillette.com
Johnson and Johnson	www.johnsonandjohnson.com
Lever Brothers	www.unilever.com
Microsoft	www.microsoft.com
Nabisco	www.nabisco.com
NCR	www.ncr.com
Pepsi	www.pepsico.com
Procter and Gamble	www.pg.com
The Traveler's	www.travelers.com
USAA's	www.usaa.com
Wachovia Bank	www.wachovia.com

CHAPTER 3 APPENDIX

FORMAL MEASUREMENT OF THE DEGREE OF INTERNAL/EXTERNAL ORIENTATION

In recent years, marketing academics have sought to move beyond the notion of internal and external perspectives or orientations towards formal measurement of the degree of internal or external orientation exhibited by individual firms or by individual business units within firms. This Appendix presents a market orientation scale (MARKOR) comprising 20 individual items.[66] The scale is divided into three sections: *intelligence generation, intelligence dissemination* and *responsiveness*. We suggest that the reader apply this scale to his or her own organization as one way of diagnosing its degree of internal/external orientation.

THE MARKET ORIENTATION (MARKOR) SCALE

In completing the following questions, please focus on your business unit rather than the company as a whole. Please use the following scale:

I do not agree at all   1—2—3—4—5—6—7   I completely agree

1. In this business unit, we meet with customers at least once a year to find out what products or services they will need in the future.   _____

2. In this business unit we do a lot of in-house market research.   _____

3. We are slow to detect changes in our customers' product preferences.   _____

4. We poll end users at least once a year to assess the quality of our products and services.   _____

5. We are slow to detect fundamental shifts in our industry (for example, competition, technology, regulation).   _____

6. We periodically review the likely effects of changes in our business environment (for example, regulation) on customers.   _____

7. We have interdepartmental meetings at least once a quarter to discuss marketing trends and developments.   _____

8. Marketing personnel in our business unit spend time discussing customers' future needs with other functional departments.   _____

9. When something important happens to a major customer or market, the whole business unit knows about it within a short period.   _____

10. Data on customer satisfaction are disseminated at all levels in this business unit on a regular basis.   _____

11. When one department finds out something important about competitors, it is slow to alert other departments.   _____

12. It takes us forever to decide how to respond to our competitor's price changes.   _____

13. For one reason or another we tend to ignore changes in our customers' product or service needs.   _____

14. We periodically review our product development efforts to ensure that they are in line with what customers want.   _____

15. Several departments get together periodically to plan a response to changes taking place in our business environment.   _____

16. If a major competitor were to launch an intensive campaign targeted at our customers, we would implement a response immediately.   _____

17. The activities of the different departments in this business unit are well coordinated.   _____

18. Customer complaints fall on deaf ears in this business unit.   _____

19. Even if we came up with a great marketing plan, we probably would not be able to implement it in a timely fashion.   _____

20. When we find that customers would like to modify a product or service, the departments involved make concerted efforts to do so.   _____

MARKOR SCORING SHEET

1. Reverse code items 3, 5, 11, 12, 13, 18, 19 by subtracting the indicated number from 8: (Example: If you gave the item a rating of 2, it should be $8 - 2 = 6$.)

2. Add up the scores of items 1 through 6. The total is your

   INTELLIGENCE GENERATION SCORE: _____

   Divide the score by 6 to get a relative score: _____

3. Add up the scores of items 7 through 11. The total is your

   INTELLIGENCE DISSEMINATION SCORE: _____

   Divide the score by 5 to get a relative score: _____

4. Add up the scores of items 12 through 20. The total is your

   RESPONSIVENESS SCORE: _____

   Divide the score by 9 to get a relative score: _____

5. Examine the absolute and relative scores. Are you satisfied? Are there major differences between the relative intelligence generation, intelligence dissemination, and responsiveness scores? How could your business unit improve on areas with low ratings?

CHAPTER

4

CUSTOMERS

LEARNING OBJECTIVES

When you have completed this chapter, you will understand

- the many ramifications of defining the term *customer*

- the roles played by individuals in the purchasing decision process

- critical elements in the purchasing decision process, including problem recognition, information acquisition, evaluation of alternatives, choice, and post-purchase processes

- how to develop frameworks for analyzing customers' needs and wants, and benefits sought

- the ways in which customers make choices from a set of alternatives

- those factors that influence both consumer and organizational decision procedures

- how to classify customer purchases

- how to secure insight into customer needs as a prerequisite for creating customer and shareholder value

INTRODUCTION

Previous chapters emphasized that the firm's key operational objective is to attract and retain customers, thereby generating economic profit, improving the firm's prospects for survival and growth, and enhancing shareholder value. To achieve this goal, we must have a good understanding of customers and the customer decision-making process. This chapter considers customers individually; in Chapter 7, we discuss particular agglomerations of customers, or market segments—the fundamental unit for developing market strategy.

The chapter begins by defining customers. Without knowing who they are, it is impossible to understand them, let alone develop strategy to secure the desired purchase and/or recommendation behavior. The chapter addresses customers both at the macro level and at the micro level; an exploration of the various roles that individuals play in customer decision processes follows. This discussion leads to the customer decision process *per se*; our major focus is on problem recognition, evaluation of alternatives, and choice.

The problem recognition section incorporates an extensive discussion on customer needs and wants. This section introduces the distinction between features and benefits and develops a threefold category system that embraces functional, psychological, and economic benefits. It concludes with additional points on customer benefits. The Chapter Appendix highlights methods for gaining insight into customer needs and wants. The chapter next focuses on customers' evaluations of alternatives in making purchase decisions, including a discussion of several departures from rationality in purchase decision making. Having laid out the entire purchase decision process, the chapter presents a variety of influences on customer purchase decision making, first by consumers, then by organizations. It concludes by presenting three prototypical customer decision processes.

Although there are clear differences among customers considered as individuals, families, and organizations, they are treated similarly, because, at a general level, the same basic frameworks apply to each. Where appropriate, differences in decision making among particular customer entities are examined.

WHO ARE, OR SHOULD BE, OUR CUSTOMERS?

Yogi Berra, a famous baseball player and coach, is reputed to have said, "You can see a lot just by looking!" He might have added, "It's hard to find what you're looking for if you don't know what it is." This is literally the case in marketing, for the simple assumption that the customer is the entity that gives the firm money in exchange for goods and services is almost always inadequate! Targeting the right customer is often the key to successful marketing; conversely, misidentifying customers has serious consequences.

To define and identify a customer, one must begin by casting a broad net; targeting the "right" customer is a process that must begin with an open mind. Some compare the process with the detective's job; there are indeed parallels. Begin with a working definition of "customer":

> Any person or organization involved in the channel of distribution or decision (other than competitors) whose actions can affect the purchase of the firm's products and services.[1]

Several observations should be made about this definition:

- It encompasses both the firm's existing customers and those potential customers it seeks for the future.[2]
- It focuses on those persons or organizations that can influence the decision to purchase the firm's products and services. Thus the notion of customer is broadened far beyond the entity (person, family, or organization) that exchanges money (or goods and services) for the firm's products or services.

- In general usage, customers are usually thought of as existing at two different levels—macro and micro. At the macro level, the customer is an organizational unit, such as a business firm (including distribution entities such as wholesalers and retailers), government entity, or family. At the micro level, the customer is an individual with decision-making authority or influence in the organizational unit. Strictly speaking, however, from a marketing perspective, customers are always individuals. Organizations do not make decisions; people in organizations make decisions! Misidentifying micro-level customers may have serious consequences.

Example: Before its disastrous acquisition of computer firm NCR in 1991, AT&T largely failed in attempting to enter the computer industry. A critical element in this failure was AT&T's belief that its major customers, corporate telecom managers, with whom AT&T had good relationships, had significant influence with systems managers, responsible for computer purchases.[3] They did not.

Example: A prominent New York investment bank failed to secure the position as lead underwriter for an initial public offering (IPO) of stock. The bank focused its sales attention on the chief financial officer (CFO) and chief executive officer (CEO), but it neglected an individual who was not typically at the company when the investment bank came to call—the major shareholder!

Example: Monsanto has committed substantial resources to develop genetically modified crops. Although its products improve yields for its direct customers, the farmers, they offer no visible benefits for consumers. By failing to consider this customer group, in Europe, Monsanto has been at the center of a storm of criticism from various consumer and environmental groups.

- The firm has both direct customers (who exchange money or goods for the firm's products or services) and indirect customers (who receive the firm's products from intermediaries). Indirect customers may merit more attention than direct customers, even though the firm's product may have undergone a state change in a manufacturing process and be unrecognizable to the indirect consumer. As discussed later, emphasis on direct customers is typically referred to as "push" while emphasis on indirect customers is termed "pull."

Example: Traditionally, Intel Corporation placed primary promotional emphasis on its direct computer manufacturer customers via sales force effort. However, in the early 1990s, it launched the highly successful, multimillion dollar "Intel inside" advertising campaign. This campaign targeted indirect customers, channel members (distributors and retailers), and consumers. Although Intel products are ideally never seen by these customers, Intel nonetheless inserted the chip brand into their decision-making calculus.[4]

- Persons or organizations may be involved in a purchase decision in several different ways. Customers can be intermediaries and act as both purchasing customers (from the firm) and sellers (to other customers); or they can act as final consumers, purchasers, or users. Other persons or organizations, such as government, standards bodies, consultants, opinion leaders, or so-called "purchase pals," may be involved primarily as sources of influence (or standard setters) and play major roles in purchase/re-purchase decisions.[5]
- In addition to the purchase act, customers may take several behavioral actions that affect purchase. For example, they may influence purchase, take product delivery, or provide service to other customers.
- The definition implies that "purchasing" customers have the willingness and ability to pay. For various reasons (see Chapter 3), the firm might not want to do business with certain potential customers.

- There is not necessarily a direct relationship between a firm and its customers; the firm may not know, in an individual sense, who its customers are and, strange as it may seem, customers may not know who their supplier is.[6] Until recently, it was unusual for consumer goods companies to know the names of consumers of their products. Identifying these consumers so that they can be contacted directly is becoming increasingly important for these firms.[7] By contrast, in businesses such as financial services, because the nature of the service is an ongoing relationship, the firm must maintain detailed customer records for operational purposes. This data can also be used for marketing purposes.

WHAT ROLES DO CUSTOMERS PLAY IN THE PURCHASE PROCESS?

The discussion of customer definition noted that customers may be considered at both the macro and micro levels. Micro-level customers are present within organizations, such as households, business firms, and arms of governments; individual micro-level customers play various roles in purchase decisions. Developing an understanding of these role relationships in the decision-making unit (DMU) is crucial for the seller. Typical roles are:

- **Gatekeeper:** An individual who has the power to impede access to the decision maker and influencers. In many organizations, secretaries, administrative assistants, and purchasing agents play this role.
- **Influencer:** An individual whose opinion the decision maker values as he or she makes the decision. Individuals vary in the degree of influence they can bring to bear on a specific purchase decision. For an individual buyer, a friend or colleague may be an influencer; within a family, depending upon the product or service, an influencer might be the husband, wife, or children. In organizational purchases, many individuals from various functional areas may exercise influence. In addition, others who may play influencing roles include consumer associations, regulators, government officials, politicians, consultants, and "purchase pals."
- **Specifier:** A person exercising indirect influence on the purchase by virtue of his or her role in drawing up specifications, even though he or she might not otherwise be formally involved in the decision *per se*. For example, in a family housing decision, an architect might play this role; in an organization, it might be an engineer.
- **Decision maker:** The individual with the formal power to make the decision.
- **Buyer:** The individual with the formal power to consummate the purchasing act with a supplier. In Western families, for many products and services, the female head of household traditionally played this role; in rural Bangladesh, it is played by men. In organizations, purchasing agents are the "buyers."
- **User:** The individual who most directly receives the benefit of the product. Users often have little direct role in the purchase decision but, because they may effectively exercise veto power over the product's use, become powerful influencers. For example, young children are extremely powerful user/influencers for ready-to-eat cereal; in the factory, the worker who states, "I'm not going to work with that red stuff," has significant power, albeit mainly "nay" power.
- **Spoiler:** An individual who seeks to prevent the firm from making sales. Perhaps this is a disgruntled former employee, or a person whose brother-in-law works for the competition!
- **Champion:** A person who promotes the firm's interests in attempting to make sales. Such a person may previously have had a good experience with the selling firm or have a personal relationship with its personnel.
- **Information provider:** A person who keeps the selling firm advised of the purchasing organization's procurement processes, relationship quality (firm and competitor), and so forth.

TABLE 4.1 Examples of Roles in Organizational and Consumer Decision Making

Roles	Organizational	Consumer
Gatekeeper	Senior Human Resource (HR) personnel	Live-in housekeeper
Major Influencer	Senior line executives	Children
Specifier	Junior HR personnel who develop program content and process	Grandmother (has some basic requirements that must be met)
Decision Maker	CEO	Mother
Buyer	Purchasing department	Father
User	Middle managers	Mother, father, children, grandparents
Spoiler	Two senior line executives with MBAs from Harvard and Wharton	Daughter's boyfriend (has summer job at a family resort in the Caribbean)
Champion	Senior line executive committed to Columbia Business School after his marketing department was turned around	Second cousin (works for cruise line)
Information Provider	Bricker's (an authoritative publication on executive education)	Travel agent

Table 4.1 illustrates "actors" in these roles for two purchasing decisions. First is an organizational example: a leading multinational firm is deciding who should supply a series of middle management training programs; Columbia Business School is a potential supplier. Second, a consumer example: a family is trying to decide whether or not to take a cruise for the family vacation.[8]

QUESTIONS ABOUT ROLES The selling firm must understand how purchase decisions for its products are made, regardless of whether the customer is an individual, family, or organization. For example:

- Are they made by a single individual or by a group?
- If group decisions, what roles are relevant?
- Who are the key players?
- What are the power relationships among them?
- What coalitions of individuals form for purchase decisions, if any?
- Are these coalitions purchase-specific, or do they form and reform for different types of purchases?
- What mechanisms are used for conflict resolution?
- How may these differing characteristics be influenced in the selling firm's favor?

Regardless of the specific roles played by actors in the decision process, there remains the question of what motivates them to behave in the way that they do. This is a particularly important issue when the customer is an organization, since individual actors may seek benefits from one of two broad categories: organizational benefits and individual benefits. Suffice it to say that organizational benefits are those that accrue to the organization and help it achieve its business goals, while individual benefits are those that accrue to individuals. Marketers must be cognizant of each.

Example: In a classic study of the politics of organizational decision making, Andrew Pettigrew showed how internal politics played a major role in the decision by a major British mail order company to purchase a new computer system. "Because he sat at the junction of the communication channels between his subordinates, the manufacturers and the board (of directors), (the head of the Management Services department) was able to exert biases in favour of his own demands and at the same time feed the board negative information about the demands of his opponents."[9]

ROLE CHANGES No matter how well the firm understands the customer's social system, it must recognize that things change over time. In organizational buying, not only do specific individual actors occupying various roles move on as they are promoted or leave the organization, but the roles themselves may change over time as the customer organization evolves. In addition, significant organizational events, such as mergers and acquisitions, frequently lead to changes in the procurement process.

A similar pattern has occurred in family decision making where, generally speaking over time, the relative influence of both the mother and children has increased, and that of the father declined. This, in turn, has resulted in major changes in the way that many products—from automobiles to breakfast cereals—are marketed. Furthermore, significant family events, such as divorce, remarriage, and death, tend to change family decision-making patterns.

In taking a broad view of customers, it should be noted that in some industries and countries, employees often move from firm to firm. To the extent that these individuals are involved in decision making or influence roles in purchase decision processes in their new companies, from the supplier's perspective, a good prior customer relationship may be extremely valuable.

> **Example:** Some consulting organizations have human resource policies that anticipate employment time horizons of six to ten years for newly hired MBAs. These consultancies are willing to place their employees at high levels in client companies, as these placements can strengthen the consultancy client relationship and help cement future revenue streams.

HOW DO CUSTOMERS MAKE PURCHASE DECISIONS?

To address micro- and macro-level customers appropriately, the firm must understand the nature of the customer decision-making process (DMP). Clearly, the process ranges widely from a relatively simple decision, such as that of an individual's choice of mid-morning snack, to a decision by the U.S. government to purchase a new telecommunications system. Nonetheless, a simple model of the customer decision process (Figure 4.1) can encompass such widely different processes. It anticipates five distinct stages, some of which involve multiple subroutines and feedback loops among stages. These processes may be mapped for individuals, families, and organizations (in the same way that firms undertake process mapping as part of re-engineering efforts) so that managers in the supplier firm can identify particular points in the process where action on the firm's part can raise the probability of sales success.[10] Each of these stages are discussed in turn, the majority of the discussion focusing on problem recognition, evaluation of alternatives, and choice.

Problem Recognition

To create and recreate customers requires eliciting an appropriate behavioral response, typically purchase or influence leading to purchase.[11] There are many ways that organizations can make people behave in a manner consistent with their objectives, but some of these (such as force and threats of force) are not typically part of the marketer's arsenal.[12]

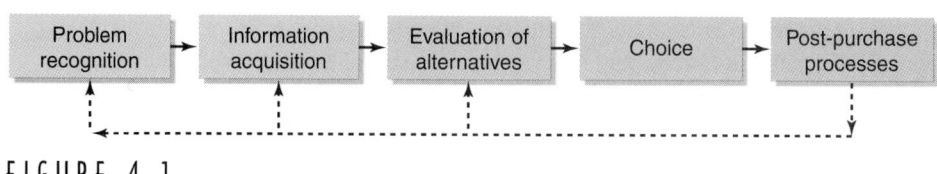

FUNDAMENTALS FOR
STRATEGIC
MARKETING

FIGURE 4.1

The Customer Purchase Decision Process

Indeed, marketing operates in a very narrow zone of behavioral inducement techniques, essentially involving two approaches: making offers to solve problems and satisfy customer needs, and communicating the value of those offers to customers.[13] Both of these approaches are necessary. No matter how well a firm's product or service satisfies customer needs or wants, it will not be purchased if customers don't know about it. Conversely, if the product or service is heavily communicated but does not solve a problem by satisfying customer needs or wants, it may be purchased once, but not again.[14]

Problem recognition occurs when the customer (individual, family unit, or organization) recognizes a need or want. These needs may vary in importance from critical inputs to keep the system functioning, such as food and drink for individuals, raw materials, and capital equipment for organizations, to those that are more discretionary. The problem may be recognized by the customer, may be pointed out by a potential supplier, or may be developed and refined as the purchase process proceeds.

The basic model is that customers' problems may be conceptualized as needs and wants. These needs and wants are satisfied by the provision of benefits; provision of benefits is made possible by product and service features or attributes. Of course, the seemingly infinite variety of products and services that currently are available to persons and organizations satisfy a plethora of customer needs and wants.

GENERALIZED NEED FRAMEWORKS   Individual needs have been subject to considerable study by psychologists, and a variety of general frameworks have been developed to understand them. Marketing scholars have attempted to apply these frameworks in a purchase decision context.

In one of the more popular frameworks, Abraham Maslow proposed a low-to-high need hierarchy comprising five major groups of needs:[15]

- physiological (food, drink, air, shelter, sex)
- safety and security (protection, order, stability)
- social (love, affection, friendship, belonging)
- ego (prestige, success, self-respect)
- self-actualization (self-fulfillment)

The manner in which this framework might have been employed by Folgers coffee is displayed in Figure 4.2. Note that some of these benefits are provided by the product while others are associated with Folgers' advertising. In general, it might be expected that customers would first satisfy their lower-level needs (such as physiological), before their higher-level needs (such as self-actualization). Furthermore, greater customer loyalty would result from satisfying higher-level needs than lower-level needs.

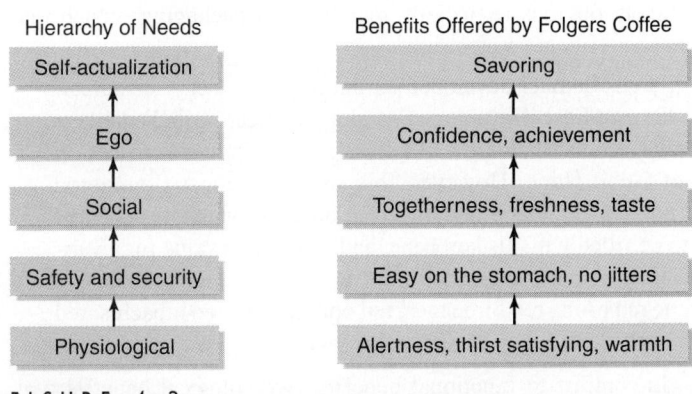

FIGURE 4.2

Maslow's Hierarchy of Needs and Folgers Coffee

A second popular framework developed by David McClelland identifies three major types of needs[16]:

- achievement: desire to achieve goals through one's own efforts
- affiliation: desire for acceptance by others
- power: desire to exert control over others' behavior

APPROACHES TO UNDERSTANDING CUSTOMER NEEDS   Customer needs can be satisfied by the provision of benefits. The following section distinguishes between benefits and features, then considers three types of needs and wants that may be satisfied by benefits delivered by a product or service: functional, psychological, and economic.[17]

Features versus Benefits   In marketing a product or service, it is often critical to distinguish between features/attributes and benefits. Firms produce and deliver products and services, but customers only perceive value in the benefits that these products and services provide. Some simple examples make this distinction clear. In its factories, Black and Decker manufactures electric drills whose features include color, drill speed, hardness of bit, drill bit gauge, drill weight, presence/absence of battery and battery life, capability to embrace other tools (such as a sander), and so forth. For the most part, customers have little interest in these features *per se*; what concerns customers are the benefits offered by the drill, notably the holes it can make and the ease of making them. A former president of competitor Stanley Works captured this notion when he said, "Last year we sold 40 million drill bits that nobody wanted." In a second example that captures the same feature/benefit distinction, Charles Revson, former chairman of Revlon, stated, "In the factories we make cosmetics; in the drug stores we sell hope!" Similarly, as already indicated, retailers and wholesalers may care little for the specific products they sell; they are more interested in benefits such as net profit, sales per linear foot, and return on investment.

A focus on benefits rather than features has the important additional value of broadening the view of competition. To return to the Black and Decker example, when the focus of attention is on features, key competitors are other electric drill manufacturers. When the focus of attention is on benefits, the firm necessarily considers all other methods of making holes: nails, explosives, woodpeckers (!), water drills, and lasers, an important broadening of the competitive scope that prepares the firm for new forms of competition.[18]

FUNCTIONAL, PSYCHOLOGICAL, AND ECONOMIC BENEFITS[19]

Functional Benefits   These benefits serve a particular purpose, typically by allowing the individual, family, or organization to do something that needs to be done. They are generally concerned with such dimensions as performance level, performance reliability, time and place availability, accuracy, and ease of use. For example, food fulfills the function of satisfying hunger needs; disc brakes enable the car to stop; and a word processing program reduces the author's labor in writing a book. However, the functional benefit provided by a product may not be intuitively obvious, especially regarding its packaging, which may offer unexpected functional benefits in its own right.

> **Example:** In 1892, Marcus Samuel developed an innovative strategy for defeating Standard Oil in the Far East. He planned to ship kerosene in bulk tankers through the Suez Canal versus Standard Oil's practice of shipping kerosene in cans via the Cape of Good Hope. However, this strategy almost floundered because Samuel had not realized that Standard's blue oil cans, which he expected consumers to bring to be filled with his kerosene, had significant value for a variety of functions. Quickly, he back-integrated into tin receptacle manufacture in the Far East and in time red roofs, red birdcages, red opium cups, red hibachis, red tea strainers, and red eggbeaters began to replace the blue.[20]

Psychological Benefits   In contrast to functional benefits, psychological benefits typically make people feel good in dimensions such as status, affiliation, reassurance, reduced risk by not changing suppliers, security, and scarcity.[21] These benefits may be associated

FUNDAMENTALS FOR
STRATEGIC
MARKETING

with functional benefits, but are different in kind. For example, in addition to the quality of the food, fine restaurants offer such benefits as perceived prestige and ambience. Certain models and brands of automobiles offer status in addition to functional comfort and transportation benefits. Laundry detergents offer cleaning, odor control, and comfort, but also satisfy such needs as the power to control washing problems, confidence in personal appearance, and caring for the family. And Steuben glassware offers gift buyers a risk reduction benefit and the near certainty that their gift will be appreciated. Recent neuroscience research suggests that affect is more important than cognition in human decision making (despite the fact that decision makers might disavow that this is the case).[22]

> **Example:** Sample advertising focused on these sorts of benefits includes "You're in good hands with Allstate," "Buy a Piece of the Rock (The Prudential)," and "Membership has its privileges (American Express)."

Another approach links self-concept theory with the notion of brand personality. Self-concept theory argues that people have a real self and an ideal self, and that they perceive products and brands in terms of the symbolic meaning to themselves and others. This symbolic meaning is captured in the concept of brand personality, a set of enduring and distinct human characteristics associated with a brand created largely by advertising. The greater the congruity between the ideal self and brand personality, the greater the preference for the brand. Table 4.2 presents the five brand personality dimensions identified in recent research, related descriptors, and prototypical products and brands that seem to exemplify these dimensions.

Economic Benefits   Here the focus is on economic aspects of the purchase, such as price, cost savings, credit terms, and profits. Some customers maintain that these are the only benefits that matter. For many intermediaries, such as wholesalers, distributors, and retailers, the core benefit from the purchase of goods for resale is the profit made on the spread between selling and buying prices.[23] For other types of customer, the economic aspect of the purchase is one of several benefits. In general, customers prefer to pay less rather than more for the functional and psychological benefits they receive because, as economists point out, this maximizes their utility. However, for some goods and services, customers may actually prefer higher prices, as these signal psychological benefits such as status and prestige. This would include perfume, designer brands, and Rolls Royce automobiles.

OTHER DIMENSIONS OF BENEFITS   Building on the threefold benefit classification, a series of related issues can be addressed—extra benefits, reduction of transaction costs, potential or actual benefits, and customers as benefits.

Extra Benefits   As indicated previously, a particular customer may seek functional, psychological, and economic benefits. However, as products move through their life cycles and competitive pressures increase, the competitive focus on functional and psychological benefits usually drifts toward economic benefits as customers seek the functional and psychological benefits they require at the lowest possible prices. It is the job of the marketing manager to probe customer needs for potential extra benefits so that the value the firm offers to its target customers exceeds that offered by competitors.

TABLE 4.2 A Brand Personality Framework

Brand Personality Dimensions (descriptors)	Prototype Brands
Sincerity (down-to-earth, honest, wholesome, cheerful)	Hallmark cards
Excitement (daring, spirited, imaginative, up-to-date)	MTV
Competence (reliable, intelligent, successful)	*The Wall Street Journal*
Sophistication (upper class, charming)	Guess jeans
Ruggedness (outdoorsy, tough)	L.L. Bean

J. Aker, "Dimensions of Brand Personality," *Journal of Marketing Research,* 34 (August 1997), pp. 334–356.

Example: Many consumer goods producers offer retailers systems for optimizing their shelf space in the form of "plan-o-grams" for individual product categories that specify the "best" arrangement of goods to maximize retail revenues.

Example: Lehmann Brothers private banking group provides money management seminars for the children of its high net-worth clients.

Example: A well-known, leading market share, computer-based supplier of information to professional firms found itself under considerable pressure from a competitor whose database increasingly approached the market leader in terms of comprehensiveness and ease of access. Anxious to gain market share, the competitor offered annual contracts at 30% of the market leader's price. Rather than compete on price, the market leader was able to leverage its corporate contacts to provide its clients insight about their current and potential customers. The value of this information far exceeded the 70% price differential and the market leader retained the business.

Similarly, when first introduced, a specific product may offer a set of benefits appropriate for one group of buyers or members of the buying unit. However, as competition increases and the product form develops, extra benefits may become available; also, cost reductions may lead to lower prices. Both developments are likely to attract new customers (see Chapter 9).

Reduction of Transaction Costs When customers purchase products and services, in addition to the price they pay, they may incur transaction costs. These costs fall into six categories[24]:

- **Search costs:** identifying the appropriate seller
- **Information costs:** learning about product characteristics, product availability, quality, and supplier reputation
- **Bargaining costs:** agreeing to terms of sale, including meetings, other forms of communication, legal expenses, and so forth
- **Decision costs:** evaluating competing sellers' terms, securing approval to purchase from organizational/household members
- **Policing costs:** ensuring that agreed terms are translated into actual goods and services; includes inspections and negotiations over delivery and payment
- **Enforcement costs:** ensuring that unsatisfactory arrangements are corrected; may include costs of lawsuits or arbitration

Firms can increase the value they offer customers by reducing these transaction costs. Of course, sellers also incur transaction costs. If they are able to reduce these costs, they may be able to reduce prices and thereby provide customers with additional economic benefits.

Potential versus Actual Benefits In most cases, customers make purchases because of the benefits those products and services deliver. However, just as MBA graduates worldwide may tell colleagues they are moving to New York City or London because of the theater and then rarely take advantage of the opportunities, so might customers purchase products and services because of potential rather than actual benefits.[25] For example, an industrial customer of a firm whose technological base is expanding may purchase products not because they are superior to competition today, but rather because the supplier/customer relationship will enable the firm to gain preferential access to new technology tomorrow.

Example: The American Express Platinum Card offers many functional benefits through its *Concierge* program, such as locating and arranging delivery of hard-to-find items or gifts, offering secretarial services in remote areas, and providing dining suggestions for a special occasion. Most Platinum cardholders rarely use these services.

Relatedly, at the point of purchase, a customer's motivation to buy a product may be driven by the offer of an extra benefit, such as a gift. However, if the customer has to take specific action to secure the gift, such as mailing in a coupon, the gift may never be requested or received. Clearly, the degree of use of these potential benefits has important economic implications for the firm.

Customers as Benefits   Typically, when thinking of customer benefits, the focus is on the particular set of products and services the firm and its competitors might offer. However, in a variety of cases, the critical customer benefit is another set of customers! For those companies wanting to purchase advertising space as a means of selling their own products and services, the benefit they seek from media companies is less the particular TV programs aired or news stories written than the number and type of viewers or readers. Similarly, advertisers on an Internet Web site are concerned less with the Web site *per se* than with the number and type of visitors.

Relatedly, in certain types of business transaction, the purchase price is driven almost entirely by the number and types of customers and potential customers. For example, the number and type of credit card customers typically determines the sale price of credit card portfolios, and the value of cable TV franchises is based on the number of current and potential customers (POPs) in the franchise area.

Organizations may be relatively unprofitable, yet have considerable shareholder value because of the extent of their customer bases. The basis for the several billion dollar market capitalizations of such Internet companies as Yahoo! and Amazon.com, whose profits are minimal or negative, is almost entirely based on their large numbers of customers.[26] In Amazon's case, customers add value to the shopping experience by providing book reviews for others.[27]

In some cases, the value that customers receive from other customers accelerates as new customers are added. Consider Ebay, the on-line auction company. Ebay's value to an individual customer increases with the customer base. For those with items to sell, more customers implies more potential buyers; for those wanting to buy, more customers implies greater product selection.

> **Example:** In June 1998, Israeli start-up Mirabilis Ltd. had 25 million users of its free ICQ (I Seek You) program that allowed instant message exchange over the Internet. Mirabilis was purchased by America Online for $287 million in cash, despite the fact that its revenues were zero![28]

As with ICQ, the shareholder value of America Online itself, and many other companies, is driven by the creation of these "communities of value." As customers are added, customer value improves for all customers.[29] As customer value increases, shareholder value also increases.

Customers also play an important role as a benefit in many service businesses where the service is "consumed" in the presence of other customers. Consider the reaction of the maitre d' at an expensive French restaurant faced with the prospect of serving a group of rowdy sports fans. Furthermore, a critical benefit each reader receives in graduate and executive education classes is fellow students. Consider your own experience in marketing class, assuming the same professor and same material, if all of your fellow students were a) graduate business students, b) senior marketing executives, or c) high school sophomores!

Because of the role customers play as benefits, many organizations set criteria for customer status. Many years ago, Rolls Royce set financial criteria for those wishing to purchase its automobiles, restaurants have dress codes, and universities and colleges have admission departments that select customers (students) from pools of applicants. Sometimes, enforcement of customer selection criteria can have unfortunate effects:

> **Example:** The New York Stock Exchange (NYSE) seeks major US (and increasingly global) companies for "listing" on the exchange. However, in the early 1980s, its listing requirements led it to refuse Microsoft! More recently, its

requirement of three consecutive years of positive net income has barred such Internet firms as Amazon, Yahoo!, Ebay and Priceline from an NYSE listing.

BEYOND BENEFITS   Some of the more recent work in consumer behavior focuses less on benefits received by customers than on consumption and consumers' need for experience. In a thoughtful exposition of this approach, our Columbia colleague Bernd Schmitt introduces the notion of experiential marketing, comprising five experience modules: sensory (sense), affective (feel), cognitive (think), physical (act), and social identity (relate)[30]:

- **Sense:** creates sensory experiences through sight, sound, touch, taste, and smell
- **Feel:** appeals to customer's inner feelings and emotions; attempts to create affective experiences ranging from mildly positive to strong emotions of joy and pride
- **Think:** appeals to the intellect with the objective of creating cognitive problem-solving experiences that engages customers creatively
- **Act:** enriches customers by showing them alternative ways of doing things, alternative lifestyles, and interactions
- **Relate:** contains aspects of the other four modules but reaches beyond the individual's personal, private feelings to something outside his/her private state

Information Acquisition

Once the initial problem is surfaced, information is acquired. The customer identifies available alternatives and determines their individual abilities to satisfy the various dimensions of needs and wants related to the problem by delivering appropriate benefits. Information may be acquired from externally available personal sources, such as friends, family members, colleagues, and salespeople, from impersonal sources such as advertising, the press, or the Internet, or from memory. As a result of this search process, the customer develops an "awareness set" of those alternatives that could possibly solve the problem.

Evaluation of Alternatives and Choice

The processes by which customers make purchase decisions among alternatives is a critical issue for marketers. Of all stages in the purchase decision process, evaluation of alternatives has probably received the most attention from marketing scholars. Evaluation of alternatives is based on information secured in the acquisition phase. Frequently, some number of alternatives is excluded from the "awareness set" with little evaluation, and the major evaluation stage is conducted on the "consideration set" (Figure 4.3).

THE RATIONAL MODEL   Assume that, in the problem definition and information acquisition stages, the customer has:

- identified a required set of benefits
- decided on the relative importance of those benefits in satisfying the underlying needs and wants, and
- formed a belief as to how well each alternative's attributes delivers those benefits

Awareness Set		Consideration Set
Mountain Dew	7-Up	Coke
Coke	Diet 7-Up	Mountain Dew
Diet Coke	Orange Slice	Sprite
Pepsi	Fanta	Root Beer
Diet Pepsi	Cherry Coke	Dr. Pepper
Root Beer	Cherry 7-Up	
Ginger Ale	Dr. Pepper	
Diet Ginger Ale	Diet Dr. Pepper	
Hi-C	Mr. Pibb	
Snapple	Caffeine-free Coke	
Sprite		

FIGURE 4.3

Illustration of Awareness and Consideration Sets for a Teenager's Choice of a Soft Drink[31]

TABLE 4.3 Illustration of a Business Traveler's Evaluation of Alternative Airline Choices for a London-New York Trip Using a Linear Compensatory Model

Benefits Offered	Relative Importance (A) (1–100)	British Airways		Continental Airlines		United Airlines	
		Belief (B) (1–10)	A × B	Belief (B) (1–10)	A × B	Belief (B) (1–10)	A × B
Schedule	20	8	160	5	100	6	120
Level of service	20	5	100	7	140	9	180
Probability of upgrade	10	2	20	3	30	7	70
Frequent flier program	30	9	270	2	60	8	240
Price	20	6	120	6	120	6	120
	100		670		450		730

With this information in hand, there are several ways in which customers' decisions might be described. In particular, they may use one or more of several different models—linear compensatory, lexicographic, conjunctive, or disjunctive.

Linear Compensatory Model   This model assumes that an alternative's overall desirability is based on a combination of the value offered by each benefit/attribute. In particular, poor performance on one attribute can be balanced by good performance on another attribute. This model can be stated formally as:

$$\text{Value of an alternative} = \sum_{i=1}^{i=n} A_i B_i$$

where, A_i = the importance of attribute i for the customer, and B_i = the customer's belief about the alternative's performance on attribute i and n = the number of salient attributes.

When the choice is made using a linear compensatory model, the alternative with the highest total value is selected. The process is illustrated in Table 4.3, in which United Airlines would be selected (730 >670 >450).

Lexicographic Model   In this model, each of the attributes is ranked in order of importance. The alternative with the best performance on the most important attribute is chosen. If several alternatives are tied on the most important attribute, the remaining alternative with the best performance on the second most important attribute is chosen. This process continues until a single alternative remains.

Pursuing the airline example, the most important attribute is "frequent flyer program." A decision using a lexicographic model would examine the relative ratings of the three alternatives on this attribute. In Table 4.3, British Airways (9) dominates both United Airlines (8) and Continental Airlines (2); thus, British Airways would be selected.

Conjunctive Model   For each attribute, the customer sets a performance cut-off value that must be met or exceeded. The selected alternative must meet or exceed each cut-off.[32] Imagine that a customer seeking an automobile identifies five critical attributes in the purchasing decision and sets cut-offs for those attributes as follows:

- Automobile fuel consumption: highway 25 mph
- Acceleration: 0–60 mph in <7 seconds
- Top speed: 130 mph
- Seating: seats four comfortably
- Speeds: minimum of 5 speeds

Any automobile that did not meet or exceed each cut-off would be eliminated; only an automobile that met or exceeded each cut-off would be chosen.

Disjunctive Model   For each attribute, the customer sets a performance cut-off value; the selected alternative must exceed the cut-off value for at least one attribute. The previous example of awareness and consideration sets was a teenager's decision to select a soft drink. Although the soft drinks in the awareness and consideration sets vary on several dimensions, in fact, the only attribute involved in the consideration set and choice decision was "taste." Hence, the decision was made using a disjunctive model.

These four choice models are pure cases; in practice, customers choose as if they are using combinations of these models. For example, for the conjunctive and disjunctive models, a secondary process might be necessary to resolve ties, or a customer might use a lexicographic model to reduce the set of alternatives then shift to a linear compensatory model to make the final choice.

> **Example:** Some university admission departments use a combination conjunctive/ disjunctive model to select students. They set minimum criteria for all potential acceptees, such as SAT scores and high school grades (conjunctive model), then accept students who excel in any area, such as writing poetry, athletics, or community service (disjunctive model).

Understanding the model(s) used by customers is an important aspect in the development of market strategy. If a customer employs a linear compensatory model, a variety of different actions may be appropriate:

- improve the firm's product on important attributes
- add new attributes, especially those that are important
- persuade the customer that the firm performs better on various attributes, especially those that are important
- persuade the customer that competitors perform worse on various attributes, especially those that are important
- persuade the customer that attributes on which the firm performs well are more important than they currently believe

Similar prescriptions may be developed for other evaluation models.[33]

DEVIATIONS FROM RATIONALITY   The foregoing discussion could indicate that customers have full information about all of their alternatives and well-defined criteria that lead to choice in a relatively straightforward manner. That would be an incorrect assumption, for the burgeoning research field of "behavioral decision theory" (BDT) has identified many purchase processes that do not seem to follow the "rational" model. Rather, in many cases, customers' preferences seem fuzzy and imprecise, and their choices affected by seemingly irrelevant factors. Although most research has been conducted on consumers, preliminary findings suggest that many of the effects also apply to organizational purchasing situations. Several key determinants of purchase decisions merit particular attention[34]:

- The set of alternatives being considered
- How the alternatives are evaluated
- Description of the alternatives
- Features of the alternatives

The set of alternatives being considered   Changing the set of alternatives, when all other factors remain constant can lead to major changes in purchase behavior. If two alternatives are offered, some percent of buyers will choose the lower-priced product (A) and some the higher-priced product (B). However, if a third higher-priced alternative (C) is offered, the percent of people selecting (attracted to) alternative B increases.

> **Example:** When customers were offered the choice between a low-priced microwave oven at $109.99 and a mid-range oven for $179.99, they chose the higher-priced oven 43% of the time. When a third oven at $199.99 was added to the choice set, the now mid-range oven was chosen 60% of the time.[35]

Next time you go to McDonalds, see how many sizes of soft drinks are offered!

How the alternatives are evaluated Many different factors can have an impact on the manner in which alternatives are evaluated. For example, when consumers' attention is focused on one of the alternatives by being asked such a seemingly innocuous question as, "How much more or less attractive to you is X," the probability of choosing X increases![36]

Furthermore, the manner in which alternatives are arranged can have a significant impact on the purchase decision. Building on the attraction effect (above), when products are organized by model (each display consists of several brands of comparable models) as opposed to being organized by brand (each display consists of several models of each brand), consumers are less likely to choose the lower-priced alternative.[37]

Description of the alternatives How alternatives are described has an important influence on choice. For example, ground beef labeled 75% lean was favored over identical ground beef labeled 25% fat, even after consumers tasted the product![38] This effect has been demonstrated in many different domains.[39]

Features of the alternatives When an unattractive option is added to an alternative, the alternative becomes less attractive.

> **Example:** Consumers were offered a choice between two brands of 35-mm film. When they were given the opportunity to purchase a golf umbrella for $8.29 (unattractive option) with one of the brands, its market share declined.[40]

Furthermore, if consumers are told of the choice made by another consumer and their "irrelevant" reason for choosing the alternative, they are less likely to choose that alternative.[41]

Post-Purchase Processes

Once the choice has been made, a number of post-purchase processes occur. These processes encompass the customers' feelings of consonance or dissonance about the purchase, satisfaction or dissatisfaction with the purchase, possible repurchase, communication to other customers or potential customers regarding the positive/negative experience, product disposal, and so forth.

> **Example:** As Internet access has increased, a growing phenomenon is the development of anti-firm Web sites such as Walmart-sucks.com, Chasemanhattansucks.com and dunkindonuts.org. These sites allow disgruntled customers to post their bad experiences.[42]

Whereas so many companies cease their customer-related efforts with purchase, it is clear that what happens after purchase can have an important impact on future business with the same or other customers.[43] By studying post-purchase processes, sometimes called total consumption systems analysis, the firm may find helpful new product or product modification ideas.

WHAT INFLUENCES THE CONSUMER PURCHASE DECISION PROCESS?

An earlier section examined the various roles that individual customers may play in the purchase decision process. The particular manner in which an individual behaves is conditioned by many factors. This section considers two major sets of influences—environmental and individual factors—each of which may impact one or more elements of the purchase decision process. This section focuses mainly on the consumer purchase decision.[44]

ENVIRONMENTAL INFLUENCES Environmental influences are typically classified from broad to narrow, in order, culture, social class, personal influence, family/organization, and situation.

Culture As noted in Chapter 2, when considering culture at the macro level, the society or group may be the inhabitants of a nation/state such as the French or Mexicans, or a geographic region within a nation/state such as the South or the Midwest in the United States.[45] Furthermore, the geographic region might encompass multiple nation states, such as Hispanic, or a people without regard to geographic location such as the Armenian, Jewish, and Chinese Diaspora. At a micro level, subcultures may reflect the macro culture but also comprise specific subcultural elements, such as African-Americans and baby boomers. Since culture is learned from the earliest stages of life, largely through organizational influence such as the family, schools, and religious institutions, individuals develop norms that are highly resistant to change.

Individuals' purchasing behavior is conditioned both by the norms of their own cultures and subcultures, but also by other cultures and subcultures that they want to emulate. In the United States, inner-city African-American youths have developed their own idiosyncratic styles of dress, yet these styles have also been adopted by middle-class suburban youths. As another example, notwithstanding such culturally driven behavior as consumption of raw fish, the Japanese are an attractive market for such American products as Levi's blue jeans, Marlboro cigarettes, and McDonald's.

Because cultural influences are so deep-seated, they are important for both consumer and business-to-business marketing. First, the values of individual cultures and subcultures, such as Asian-Americans, Hispanics, and Koreans, may allow them to be addressed specifically with marketing programs. Second, because cultures and subcultures have their own behavioral norms, corporations must be careful about cultural violations that could cost them business.

> **Example:** Giving gifts is a custom in most countries, but be careful in China: White, blue, and black gifts are associated with funerals while sharp objects (knives, scissors, letter openers) symbolize the cutting off of friendship.

> **Example:** In Germany, do not bring a dozen red roses to the wife of your largest customer. Presenting an even number of flowers is bad luck, and red roses suggest a strong romantic interest![46]

Social Class   All societies include hierarchically ordered groupings or social classes. Economic factors (wealth and income) are, perhaps, the dominant variables in deciding a person's social class, but occupation, residential location, education, and other variables also play a part. The various social classes are relatively homogenous regarding values and interests and, although individuals are born into a social class, they may move from one class to another during their lifetimes. Many related social class schemes have been developed; one of the more recent is shown in Table 4.4.

Because individuals have similar values and interests within social classes, purchasing behavior may also be similar across a broad variety of goods and services, such as clothing

TABLE 4.4   Social Class in America

Category	Description
Upper-Americans	
Upper-upper (0.3%)	Inherited wealth, aristocratic names
Lower-upper (1.2%)	Newer social elite, corporate leadership
Upper-middle (12.5%)	Managers and professionals
Middle-Americans	
Middle class (32%)	Average pay white-collar workers
Working class (38%)	Average pay blue-collar workers
Lower-Americans	
Lower (9%)	Working, living standards just above poverty
Real lower-lower (7%)	On welfare, poverty-stricken, usually out of work

A condensed version of the Coleman-Rainwater view (R.P. Coleman and L.P. Rainwater, with K.A. McClelland, *Social Standing in America: New Dimensions of Class,* New York: Basic Books, from Engel, Blackwell, and Miniard, *op. cit.*

and leisure activities. Furthermore, social class can also be important in business-to-business marketing as in matching salesperson to buyer.

Personal Influence Customers are subject to influence from other individuals, frequently members of reference groups that provide standards or values of behavior. Primary groups are those with which the individual has frequent face-to-face interaction, notably family members in consumer marketing and various organizational work groups in business-to-business marketing. Individuals have less direct contact with members of secondary groups, who might comprise fellow club or church members on the consumer side and professional organizations for business purchasing decisions. These may, nonetheless, have significant influence. Aspirational groups are those to which the individual aspires to belong; dissociative groups are those groups that the individual consciously avoids.

Influence can be transmitted via the existence of group norms and pressures for conformity, although acceptance of norms can also occur because of a psychological need for group membership. Much advertising seeks to generate purchase behavior based on these types of influence. Expertise is another major vehicle for securing influence and is seen most often in selling situations, particularly in business-to-business marketing where highly trained salespeople may secure high-value sales.

Word-of-mouth influence from opinion leaders often combines expertise influence based on experience with the product or service, together with some form of reference group membership. For example, regarding basketball sneakers, Michael Jordan is perceived to have significant expertise, yet he also belongs to a reference group (National Basketball Association players) to which many teenagers aspire.

Family A fourth environmental influence concerns the family. First, two main types of family exist: nuclear, the immediate group of father, mother and children; and the extended family, which includes grandparents, aunts, uncles, cousins, and in-laws. Depending on the specific culture, one of these two family types tends to predominate. In nuclear families, predominant in the West, family purchase decisions range among wife-dominant, husband-dominant, and syncratic (made by both husband and wife). (Of course, some purchase decisions are made by children.) Furthermore, these main categories may reflect all purchases or may vary from product type to product type; for example, husband makes major financial decisions, wife makes day-to-day supermarket/drug store purchases. Decision making in extended families tends to be even more complex.

In recent years, many cross currents have affected decision making in nuclear families. First, the increasing incidence of divorce has affected family structures and given rise to single parent and reconstructed families (such as second family for husband, first family for wife). Second, in many countries, marriage has been delayed, couples are deferring children and, as the Roman Catholic Church's influence declines, are more severely limiting family size. Third, women's roles are changing dramatically as they increasingly demand equality. These trends affect many societies, typically with some countries leading and others lagging.

Situational Factors Over and above the various environmental factors already described, critical influences on customer behavior are the situational conditions of purchase and use. Important dimensions of the purchase situation are the amount and presentation of information, time availability, aesthetics of the purchase location, and so forth. Although, as consumers, we come up against these factors daily, they are equally important in business-to-business marketing.

Example: A British supplier hosted a major Korean company that was contemplating Britain as a potential site for a new European factory. When the Korean delegation arrived at the supplier's offices, its members were surprised and gratified to see the Korean flag flying to welcome them. The thoughtfulness and attention to detail that this small gesture exemplified played a major role in their decision to build in Britain.

INDIVIDUAL INFLUENCE FACTORS   In addition to the environmental factors just discussed, several individual factors influence purchase decisions. Individual factors influencing organizational purchase behavior largely relate to the markets the firm has decided to target, the products and services it offers to those markets, and the degree to which a host of organizational activities are performed in-house or are outsourced to third-party suppliers.

Individual factors influencing consumer purchasing decisions include economic resources (including income and wealth) and access to credit, time availability, and cognitive resources.

- **Economic Resources:** Economic resources are a major factor in people's ability to buy. Around the world, economic growth has, on average, increased these resources yet these increases have been disproportionately higher in the developed countries. Nonetheless, significant increases have been achieved in some formerly less-developed countries (LDCs) such as South Korea, Malaysia, and Singapore, although many people around the world continue to live below the poverty level. In general, access to credit tends to parallel economic well being with sophisticated systems in the United States, less so in other countries.
- **Time Availability:** Time availability impacts customers' ability to search for and make decisions about purchases, but also influences the types of goods and services that they purchase. Thus, a general trend of reduced time for shopping played a major role in the growth of direct marketing that is now fueling the growth of Internet shopping. Lack of time availability for consumption affects the products people desire, such as fast-food restaurants, prepared meals, and in-home medical test kits.
- **Cognitive Resources:** Cognitive resources addresses people's ability to process information to make purchase decisions. Critical issues are the direction and intensity of attention; of course, without direction, there is no intensity. Direction is important because thousands of messages per day are available for customer attention; a critical issue for firms is to break through the "clutter" so that customers attend to their messages. Intensity refers to the extent to which customers process information that is received. Because of limited resources, customers often use cues to minimize cognitive effort; brand names play an important role in "chunking" information.

Our attention now turns to two summary constructs—life-cycle stage and lifestyles.

Life-Cycle Stage   Stage in the life cycle has an important influence on consumer purchasing behavior. Among the dimensions that comprise life-cycle stage are age, family size, single, or married (first, second, and so on) giving rise to the set of life stages in Figure 4.4. A related factor is occupation; this tends to change through life, in particular the role of women and whether they occupy solely a homemaker role or are also wage earners.

Lifestyles   Lifestyle embraces the way people live their lives and spend their time. The most influential VALS™ 2 framework recognizes two major lifestyle dimensions:

- **Self-orientation:** Self-orientation refers to the manner in which consumers pursue and acquire products, services and experiences to give "shape, substance, and character" to their identities. The VALS framework comprises three self-orientations:
  - Principle-orientation: guided by abstract idealized criteria
  - Status-orientation: guided by a desire for approval and opinions of others

Teenager, living at home, purchases from allowance, gifts, part-time jobs
Young, single, head of household, no children
Married, no children
Married, young children
Married, teenage children
Married, second family, young children
Married, no children, empty nesters
Single, widow/widower

FIGURE 4.4

Human Life-Cycle Stages

TABLE 4.5 The VALS™ 2 Lifestyle Framework

High Resources

• **Actualizers**	Successful, active, sophisticated, "take-charge" people with high self-esteem and abundant resources who seek to develop, explore, and express themselves in a variety of ways.

Moderately high resources

• **Fulfilleds** (principle-oriented)	Mature, satisfied, comfortable, well-educated, reflective people who value order, knowledge, and responsibility. They tend to base their decisions on strongly held principles, seem calm and self-assured, and focus their leisure activities on the home.
• **Achievers** (status-oriented)	Successful career and work-oriented people who feel in control of their lives. They value structure, predictability, and stability, and are deeply committed to their work and families. Their social life is structured around family, church, and business.
• **Experiencers** (action-oriented)	Young, vital, enthusiastic, impulsive, and rebellious. They seek variety and excitement, quickly become enthusiastic about new possibilities but are equally quick to cool. Their energy finds an outlet in exercise, outdoor recreation, sports, and social activities.

Moderately low resources

• **Believers** (principle-oriented)	Conservative, conventional people with concrete beliefs based on traditional established codes such as family, church, community, and nation. They follow established routines largely structured around homes, families, social, and religious organizations.
• **Strivers** (status-oriented)	Seek motivation, self-definition, and approval from the world around them. Unsure of themselves and low on economic, social, and psychological resources, strivers are deeply concerned with the opinions and approval of others.
• **Makers:** (action-oriented)	Practical people with constructive skills who value self-sufficiency. They live in a traditional context of family, practical work, and physical recreation, are unimpressed by material possessions other than those that have a practical purpose.

Low Resources

• **Strugglers**	Have limited economic, social, and emotional resources. They find the world pressing and difficult and focus on meeting the needs of the moment.

- Action-orientation: guided by a desire for social or physical activity and risk-taking
- **Resources:** Resources refers to the full range of psychological, physical, demographic, and material assets encompassing education, income, health, eagerness to buy, and energy level, ranging from minimal to abundant, upon which consumers may draw.

These two dimensions together give rise to eight lifestyles (Table 4.5).[47]

WHAT INFLUENCES THE ORGANIZATIONAL PURCHASE DECISION PROCESS?

There is significant value in discussing customer decision making in a general manner since, to a large extent, the similarities between consumer and organizational buying behavior outweigh the differences. Nonetheless, special features of organizational buying behavior suggest that we should focus attention on factors impacting this process:

- In general, formal organizational buying decisions involve greater amounts of money than household and individual decisions. As a result, the decision process is frequently more protracted, complex, and involves greater numbers of people. It is also much more likely to involve political considerations.[48]
- The role of personal selling is generally more important in those organizational buying decisions that involve significant microtailoring of the seller's offer. By contrast, advertising is often critical in the sale of consumer products, especially where the average purchase price is low.
- Organizational buying decisions are often subject to some type of process regulation imposed either by the buyer or an external authority.

Organizational purchasing is currently undergoing major changes. The following section examines three areas of change: increased corporate attention to procurement, changes in the procurement process, and affirmative reduction in numbers of suppliers.[49]

Increased Corporate Attention to Procurement

For many firms in many industries, vertical integration has been a way of increasing profits by capturing large amounts of value added in the conversion process from raw materials to finished goods. When the ratio of value added-to-revenue was high and, conversely, the procurement spend-to-revenue ratio low, the procurement function was perceived to be relatively unimportant. "Purchasing" was often viewed as a managerial backwater. Several factors have led to increases in the procurement spend-to-revenue ratio:

- Corporate downsizing and the increasing replacement of labor by capital has led to relatively greater expenditures on capital equipment, raw materials, and supplies rather than labor.
- Many companies have sought to increase flexibility through reduction in fixed cost levels via vertical disintegration (outsourcing).
- Company focus on core competence and the concomitant growth in outsourcing has increased the value of purchased goods and services for organizational use.
- The growth in importance of branding has led many firms to act as resellers for parts of their product lines, also raising the purchasing ratio.

In total, these changes can be quite dramatic. For example, from 1987 to 1997, the ratio of purchasing spend-to-revenue at IBM rose 57% from 28% to 44%.[50] The profitability implications of this shift have not been lost on corporate management. As procurement spend-to-revenue ratios have risen, procurement has taken on a more strategic role. Higher-quality managers have been assigned to purchasing with the explicit goal of reducing procurement costs. The results of increased focus on procurement are starting to come in. As an example, one $10 billion pharmaceutical company reduced its inbound supply costs by $1.5 billion!

Changes in the Procurement Process

As a result of the growing importance of procurement decisions, several changes are occurring in the procurement process:

- Centralization in procurement has been aided by rapid advances in telecommunications and computer technology. Whereas, historically, various corporate units may have operated independently for procurement purposes, the increasing ability of the center to gather data from its disparate units has led to a shift in the locus of procurement practice. More complete, accurate, and timely data on purchases from individual suppliers both provides buyers with greater leverage against individual suppliers and allows them to track purchasing performance against benchmark databases.
- Increasingly proficient procurement staffs have introduced new strategies to reduce costs, improve quality, and increase efficiencies. Specific procurement initiatives place great pressure on suppliers via such methods as "strategic sourcing" in which potential suppliers are invited to complete an extensive "Request for Information" (RFI) before responding to a very detailed "Request for Proposal" (RFP).[51,52] Procurement personnel, often using models of suppliers' cost structures, negotiate aggressively to select those suppliers best able to meet specifications at the lowest price. They have little or no regard for long-standing relationships (even if the supplier is an internal division), and may send their own consultants into suppliers' plants to help increase efficiency.
- In dealing with multibusiness firms, procurement personnel have begun to question whether it is really necessary to meet with salespersons from each of several individual firm divisions, rather than with a single supplier firm representative. This trend is fueling the development of key account management by supplier firms (see Chapter 15).

- Globalization is leading many firms to search more broadly for suppliers and to add global coverage as a critical choice criterion.
- B-to-B exchanges, made possible by the Internet, may have a significant impact on corporate procurement. In particular, reverse auctions, in which buyers specify their requirements and pre-vetted suppliers bid, are growing in popularity.

Affirmative Reductions in Numbers of Suppliers

Concurrent with changes in the procurement process, in recent years, many corporations have made affirmative decisions to forge closer relationships with fewer suppliers and only allow the "best" to compete for their business. These actions run directly counter to the traditional *modus operandi* of sending specifications to a large number of potential suppliers, then selecting a limited number based on such criteria as price and delivery, and increase the challenge for potential new suppliers. Several factors have led to these reductions: the quality movement and a desire by companies to secure tighter control over their raw material inputs; a desire to reduce input costs; the increased complexity of many purchases involving multiple technologies and customized service, and requirements for increased procurement effectiveness.[53]

> **Example:** Patrick Grace, president of Grace Logistics, claims that high volume purchasing for MRO (maintenance, repair, and operating supplies) can reduce outlays by 10% to 25%.[54]

In addition, the adoption of Kaizen and just-in-time inventory systems, a concern to reduce working capital, and an overall focus of improving efficiency and effectiveness in the resource conversion process via supply chain management, have all contributed to this trend. Finally, an organizational streamlining movement involving narrowing mission scopes and outsourcing has led many firms to seek closer relationships with suppliers in such matters as product development.

> **Examples:** Xerox cut its supplier base 90%, from 5,000 in 1980 to 300 in 1985. At Volkswagen in the mid-1990s, Jose Ignacio Lopez reduced the number of suppliers from 2,000 to 200 (some original suppliers became subcontractors), cutting the purchasing bill by DM1.7 billion (4%).[55]

Buyer-Seller Relationships

Buyers now seek several types of relationships with their suppliers (Figure 4.5). The options can be viewed on a "type of relationship" continuum running from vendor (buyer/seller of commodity items), through quality supplier (deliver superior value), to partnership (supplier firm makes significant contributions to the customer).[56]

VENDOR In this traditional adversarial type of buyer-seller relationship, the customer tends to have arms-length dealings with a large vendor base. Major characteristics are short-term contracts with frequent rebidding, suppliers chosen largely on the basis of price, and frequent supplier shifts for small price reductions, better delivery terms, and so forth. Dominant relationships are between sales and purchasing, and information flow is restricted since knowledge is perceived as eroding negotiating positions.

Vendor	Quality Supplier	Partnership
Commodity relationship	Deliver superior value products and services	Add organizational value

| Multiple supplier options | | Deeper customer/ supplier firm relationship |

FIGURE 4.5

The Supplier Firm/Key Account Relationship

QUALITY SUPPLIER   This relationship shifts from adversarial to one of mutual commitment. Both supplier firm and customer recognize significant value in a closer long-term relationship in which the two firms commit to each other. Each understands the importance of the interorganizational interface for producing high quality final products; each plans for continuous quality improvement; and the supplier firm secures differential advantage by delivering products and services that supply real customer value better than competitors.

PARTNER   This relationship moves beyond a concern for quality supplies to a long-run partnership in which the two firms share (or jointly develop) future strategies, technologies, and resources; both firms are concerned with decisions along the entire industry value chain. The supplier base is reduced considerably and critical buying decisions tend to be made on value rather than on price. Each firm is involved early in the other's product development cycles, and significant quantities of routine and sensitive information flow between the organizations as the supplier firm moves beyond its basic business to solve important problems for its customer. Partnership relationships involve multilevel interactions across the two organizations including joint quality control processes and bi-company project teams that share information and expertise to secure benefits for both parties. When the core rationale for serving the customer is broadened to embrace assisting the customer in achieving its objectives, many activities that would not be considered under narrower definitions of the customer relationship become possibilities.[57]

> **Examples:** Armstrong World Industries operates a management development program for its most important customers. This program is not a sales pitch for Armstrong's products and services; rather, the focus is to improve the skills of these customers' mid-level and senior managers. To the extent that management skill is improved, customers perform better and Armstrong's prospects or business are enhanced.[58]

> **Example:** A major manufacturer, noting that its key distributor frequently called for rush orders yet later "discovered" lost inventory, installed a new inventory control system for its customer.

HOW CAN CUSTOMER PURCHASE DECISION PROCESSES BE CLASSIFIED?

One way of understanding customer decision making is the threefold classification of routinized response behavior (straight rebuy), limited problem solving (modified rebuy), and extended problem solving (new buy).[59] In general, this classification corresponds to a dimension of low-involvement to high-involvement with the purchase.

Routinized Response Behavior

This type of decision making occurs when the customer has made a similar (if not identical) purchase many times before. Key characteristics of routinized response behavior are a well-defined set of purchase criteria and several familiar suppliers whose purchase offers are both well-known and only marginally distinguishable from each other. Since these decisions are relatively simple and require low involvement, they can be made fairly quickly. Examples include repetitive purchases of consumer package goods and corporate purchases of basic raw materials and supplies where financial and socio-psychological risk is limited. The key task for the supplier firm is to demonstrate superiority of its overall offer versus competition by promoting the "net competitive advantage."

Limited Problem Solving

This type of decision making occurs when there is some level of decision-making uncertainty. Buyers have well-established purchase criteria, but one or more alternatives is novel and performance on the purchase criteria is unknown or uncertain. Before a positive purchase decision can be made for one of these new alternatives, the customer has to engage in extensive information gathering (and testing). Limited problem solving purchases are exemplified whenever a new supplier must be considered by the buyer or where a new material might replace a traditional choice, such as substitution of plastics for metal, replacement of natural fibers by synthetic fibers, or replacement of traditional by genetically altered seeds. The selling task for the supplier firm is to make the customer comfortable with its new offer in the context of the customer's purchase criteria and to address specific concerns, typically including finding ways to reduce the buyer's perceived risk associated with the novel alternative.

Extended Problem Solving

This complex decision making is completely novel. Not only is the alternative (and frequently potential supplier) new to the customer, but criteria for making a purchasing decision have not been developed. Great uncertainty surrounds this purchase which, if consummated, may change the customer's behavioral patterns. Purchase of a first house for a consumer; for an organizational customer, outsourcing the work of an important department, or the first purchase of video conferencing facilities are examples. When organizations conduct extended problem solving, often their operational or management systems and several departments may be affected and, as a result, the breadth of personnel impacted may be quite extensive. Because many dimensions are new in extended problem solving, the customer may even lack a process to make the purchase decision. Thus, a key task for the potential supplier is to help the customer develop a purchase process and decision-making framework.[60]

Implications

Several important points should be made about this decision-making framework:

- For different customers, the purchase of a particular product or service may require different types of decision making. For example, purchase of video conferencing facilities may represent extended problem solving for an organization with no such experience; for a more experienced firm, this may approach routinized response behavior. A new house purchase may be routine for a family that has moved many times; for young newlyweds, it is likely to represent extended problem solving. Furthermore, for any particular customer, a product purchase that once represented extended problem solving typically shifts to limited problem solving and even routinized response behavior as experience with the product and purchase process accumulates.

- The individuals involved in the purchase decision typically vary by type of decision process. Extended problem solving decisions typically involve more, and more senior, individuals. Thus, in household buying decisions, extended problem solving typically involves the head of household, spouse, and possibly extended family members. For purchases by organizations, extended problem solving decisions are likely to involve many organizational members with the final decision taken at senior levels. By contrast, routinized response behavior decisions can often be programmed as a set of rules; in organizations, they are often made by mid- and low-level purchasing staff; in households, children alone may make these purchases.

- Organizations seeking to replace competitor suppliers often find it fruitful to try to shift decision making from routinized response behavior, which may favor an established supplier or suppliers, to limited or extended problem solving such that the whole decision nexus is re-evaluated. This can sometimes be achieved by re-framing a problem for the buyer. A purchasing agent may be instructed to buy at the lowest price, but if the seller can demonstrate that such purchases raise overall costs or lower profits, it may be more successful. This type of strategy frequently requires "selling up" to higher levels in the buying organization.

Example: Madden Graphics, a Chicago-based printer, earned thin margins selling printing services to customers' purchasing departments (routinized response behavior) in the face of tough competition. It discovered enormous waste and inefficiencies in one client's printed displays and other sales promotion materials targeted for grocery stores. As a result, Madden developed a direct-to-store printing and shipping program that integrated construction design, manufacturing, assembly, and distribution of point-of-sale materials requiring relationships with customer sales, marketing, and product promotion executives (extended problem solving). The result: 1990 revenues, $10 million; 1997 revenues, $120 million.[61]

SUMMARY

It was argued earlier that customers represent key organizational assets even more important than the hard assets found on the firm's balance sheet. In some industries, the customer base is a "real" asset in the sense of ongoing legal relationships, and can be sold, as when a financial services firm sells its "book of business." In fact, the only reason a buyer of any business should pay more than the disposal value of balance sheet assets is because of the expectation of a future profit stream, driven by the revenue stream contributed by current and future customers. It is therefore critical to develop insight into how customers buy and use products, as well as what motivates their behavior.

A customer may purchase not just one but several products from the same supplier. Such "loyal" customers have more value than a repeat customer for a single product or service. Not only is the level of business greater in any particular time period, but the set of relationships between the supplier firm and its customers binds them closer together and creates reciprocal dependency. Because they receive high value, not only are the customers' switching costs from one supplier to another increased, but they also can assist in recruiting other customers via positive word-of-mouth.

For these reasons, a clear understanding of what constitutes a customer and of customer roles in the decision-making unit (DMU) is critical. Furthermore, the firm needs to understand the decision-making processes (DMP), including the nature of customer needs and required benefits, the process of alternative evaluation and choice, together with the various factors that influence customer decision making. To the extent that the firm implements systems to secure greater understanding of customers than its competitors, it is better placed to serve them and gain the influence and purchase behavior critical to ongoing success. There is one important caveat: Regardless of how much effort the firm places on understanding its customers today, tomorrow's customers are likely to have different needs and make their decisions in different ways.

THE CHANGING VIEW

Old Way	New Way
Supplier power dominates	Customer power dominates
Focus on customers only	Focus on organizational stakeholders
Basic marketing concepts applied mainly in packaged consumer goods	Marketing concepts applied in many domains: product and service, public and nonprofit, nation states, politics, personal career
Customer wants and needs exogenous	Wants and needs may be endogenous
Domestic view of customers and markets	Global view of customers and markets
Customers passive	Customers pro-active and interactive
Customers uninformed and unsophisticated	Customers well-informed and increasingly sophisticated

Old Way	New Way
Basic understanding of customer may suffice	Sophisticated customer insights required
Marketing concepts applicable to consumers	Marketing concepts applicable to professional buyers
Cognitive bias in understanding the customer	Holistic view of customer behavior
Multiattribute models rule supreme	Eclectic modeling of buying decisions
Narrow view of customers, for example, direct customers only, or consumers only	Multitiered more complex view of customers

QUESTIONS FOR STUDY AND DISCUSSION

1. You are about to introduce a face powder for teenage Filipino girls. What benefits might you consider identifying in your advertising? What customers might you consider targeting?

2. Culture has an important impact on purchasing behavior. Work with a peer from another country and identify several types of purchase that are acceptable in your country but not in your colleague's country and vice versa.

3. Describe three purchase decisions you have made recently that fall into the categories of routinized response behavior, limited problem solving, and extended problem solving. Why do you categorize them in this manner?

4. What impact has the normative model of economic decision making had on denial behavior on the part of decision makers? What impact could this have on market research practice?

5. Describe a multiperson purchasing process with which you are familiar. Describe the roles of the different persons. As a marketer, how would you attempt to influence the process in your favor?

6. Develop a flow chart showing the consumption system for a familiar household product. Use the analysis to illustrate how you might develop new product concepts.

7. Select both a consumable and a durable good. Identify the transaction costs that you would incur by purchasing these products.

8. Explain one of your own buying decisions that was heavily influenced by emotion.

9. Why do marketers often create the opportunity for prospective customers to sample their products? Think of three new products you have tried in the last year. Explain how this happened.

10. How long have you used your current brand of toothpaste? Are you sure it is the best? Why or why not?

11. Despite the talk about "first-mover" advantages, pioneers often fail (consider the Apple Newton versus the Palm Pilot). Based on your understanding of buyer behavior, give three common reasons why later entrants might succeed.

12. Think of three examples where your own buying decision was unaffected by price. Why was this the case and what are the implications, if any, for marketers?

13. Can you expect traditional market research to give you good answers to why customers buy particular products? Why or why not?

14. Why do customers routinize some decisions?

15. The trend for corporations to reduce their numbers of suppliers was discussed in this chapter. However, some observers argue that, rather than be a permanent change, supplier reduction represents just a swing of the pendulum. Do you agree? Why might these observers take this position?

16. Give three examples of how the Internet has affected your purchasing, directly or indirectly.

END NOTES

1. In this chapter, the term *purchase* is used loosely, because in advanced Western societies, individual, family, and organizational customers are increasingly avoiding purchase, preferring to secure benefits from products by such methods as renting or leasing. The usage of "purchase" encompasses these methods.

2. Of course, the firm may decide that it wishes to discard some of its current customers.

3. *The Economist,* March 23–29, 1996.

4. Although not always clearly understood by marketers, this example illustrates why the branding concept and development of a relationship between buyer and seller is absolutely central to marketing. Without brand names, the product loses its identity; the seller can do no more than generic promotion. The buyer loses both a potential relationship and recourse in case of difficulty.

5. For example, specialized consultants play a major role in aircraft leasing decisions.

6. There has been an increasing trend to dissociate the company whose brand name is on the product from the actual product manufacturer (see Chapter 11).

7. In recent years, the field of database marketing has developed to aid companies seeking information on their final consumers, then use that data to engage in direct communications, make special offers, and so forth.

8. See M.H. Morris, P. Berthon, and L.F. Pitt, "Assessing the Structure of Industrial Buying Centers with Multivariate Tools," *Industrial Marketing Management,* 28 (1999), pp. 263–276 for an interesting study of role structure in an industrial buying situation.

9. A. Pettigrew, *Politics of Organizational Decision Making,* London: Tavistock, 1973, p. 266.

10. Other decision process models have been developed. For a particularly influential alternative, see J.A. Howard and J. Sheth, *The Theory of Buyer Behaviour,* New York: Wiley, 1969.

11. We do not intend to rule out special types of marketing that require other forms of behavioral response, such as voting (political marketing); we simply focus on mainstream marketing.

12. Some organizations, such as protection rackets, specialize in these techniques to encourage purchase of their services!

13. In addition to communicating the value of benefits to customers, advertising may create value *per se*.

14. This was essentially the reason that the U.S. auto industry lost so much market share in the 1970s and 1980s.

15. A. Maslow, *Motivation and Personality,* New York: Harper, 1954. This framework raises the question, discussed extensively by Freud, whether all needs are fully conscious.

16. D.C. McClelland, *Personality,* New York: William Sloane, 1951.

17. Another common classification comprises two categories, "rational," (subsuming functional and economic) and "emotional," (psychological). However, these are value-laden terms that may obscure the often vital importance of psychological benefits.

18. See G.S. Day and R. Wensley, "Assessing Advantage: A Framework for Diagnosing Competitive Superiority," *Journal of Marketing* 52 (April 1988), pp. 1–20, for a discussion of customer-based definitions of competition.

19. Another classification scheme distinguishes among search, use, and credence benefits. Search benefits are those about which customers can secure information, possibly from trial, prior to purchase and use, such as many consumer durable products. Use benefits cannot be examined prior to purchase and use, but are known after use, such as benefits associated with performances like a Rolling Stones concert. Even after purchase and use, the customer may not be able to tell whether the product has delivered credence benefits, such as a particular investment or medical procedure.

20. In addition, Samuel's cans, made locally, were not battered and chipped by the long ocean voyage. D. Yergin, *The Prize: The Epic Quest for Oil, Money, and Power,* New York: Simon & Schuster, 1991.

21. Some firms deliberately produce insufficient product to meet demand, specifically to create scarcity value.

22. See T. Ambler and T. Burne, "The Impact of Affect on Ad Memory," *Journal of Advertising Research,* 39 (Mar./Apr. 1999), pp. 25–34.

23. Of course, working capital related issues such as inventory turns and time to pay are also important.

24. From L. Downes and C. Mui, *Unleashing the Killer App: Digital strategies for market dominance,* Boston, MA: Harvard Business School Press, 1998; based on R.H. Coase, "The Nature of the Firm: Origin," *Economica,* 4 (1937), pp. 368–405.

25. In the movie *Wild Man Blues,* Woody Allen explains his love for New York City: he can always get duck wonton soup at 3:30 A.M., but would never want to!

26. Market capitalization is calculated by multiplying the share price by the number of shares outstanding.

27. Of course, the ability to provide a book review is an additional customer value.

28. Mirabilis chairman stated, "We're trying to aggregate as many eyeballs as possible," *Business Week,* June 15, 1998.

29. This phenomenon has been dubbed Metcalfe's law after the founder of 3Com corporation. Metcalfe's law states that the value of a network equals the square of the number of users. L. Downes and C. Mui, *op. cit.* See also J. Hagel III and A.G. Armstrong, *net.gain,* Boston, MA: Harvard Business School Press, 1997.

30. B. Schmitt, *Experiential Marketing: How to Get Customers to SENSE, FEEL, THINK, ACT and RELATE to your company and Brands:* New York: The Free Press, 1999. See also B.J. Pine II and J.H. Gilmore, "Welcome to the Experience Economy," *Harvard Business Review,* 76 (Jul./Aug. 1998), pp. 97–105.

31. Thanks to Paul and Peter Capon for their assistance with this illustration.

32. A particularly important use of a conjunctive model is in company qualification for the ISO 9000 standard.

33. For research on "cognitive algebra," see J.R. Bettman, N. Capon, and R.J. Lutz, "Multiattribute Measurement Models and Multiattribute Attitude Theory: A Test of Construct Validity," *Journal of Consumer Research,* 1 (March 1975), pp. 1–15; J.R. Bettman, N. Capon, and R.J. Lutz, "Cognitive Algebra in Multiattribute Attitude Models," *Journal of Marketing Research,* 12 (May 1975), pp. 151–164 and J.R. Bettman, N. Capon, and R.J. Lutz, "Information Processing in Attitude Formation and Change," *Communication Research,* 2 (Fall 1975), pp. 267–278.

34. This section relies heavily on I. Simonson, "Get Closer to Your Customers by Understanding How They Make Choices," *California Management Review,* (Summer 1993), pp. 74–84.

35. I. Simonson and A. Tversky, "Choice in Context: Tradeoff Contrast and Extremeness Aversion," *Journal of Marketing Research,* 29 (1992), pp. 281–295. See also G.E. Smith and T.T. Nagle, "Frames of Reference and Buyers' Perception of Price and Value," *California Management Review,* 38 (1995), pp. 98–116.

36. R. Dhar and I. Simonson, "The Effect of the Focus of Comparison on Consumer Preferences," *Journal of Marketing Research,* 29 (Nov. 1992), pp. 430–440.

37. I. Simonson, S. Nowlis, and K. Lemon, "The Effect of Local Consideration Sets on Global Choice between Lower Price and Higher Quality," *Marketing Science,* 12 (Fall 1993), pp. 357–377.

38. I.P. Levin and G.J. Gaeth, "How Consumers are Affected by the Framing of Attribute Information Before and After Consuming the Product," *Journal of Consumer Research,* 15 (1988), pp. 374–378.

39. In many cases this effect is trivial. For example, Kentucky Fried Chicken (KFC) would be unlikely to be more precise in labeling its core product. HDC for "hot dead chicken" somehow doesn't cut it.

40. I. Simonson, Z. Carmon, and S. O'Curry, "Empirical Evidence on the Negative Effect of Product Features and Sales Promotions on Brand Choice," *Marketing Science,* 13 (Winter 1994) pp. 23–40.

41. G.S. Carpenter, R. Glazer, and K. Nakamoto, "Meaningful Brands from Meaningless Differentation: The Dependence on Irrelevant Attributes," *Journal of Marketing Research,* 31 (August 1994), pp. 339–350. See, also, C.L. Brown and G.S. Carpenter, "Why Is the Trivial Important? A Reasons-Based Account for the Effects of Trivial Attributes on Choice," *Journal of Consumer Research,* 26 (March 2000), pp. 372–385.

42. Thus far, company response has been various. Some firms ignore the sites; others attempt to address customers' concerns or buy the sites; others build sites to refute the charges; others supply information to sponsors

of competitor hate sites and still others attempt to register such sites as IhatefirmX.com or FirmXsucks.com. *Business Week,* April 9, 1999. In February 2000, a competitor of Callaway Golf Co. agreed to place an apology on Yahoo! admitting to posting 163 disparaging messages under 27 different pen names.

43. See T. Levitt, "After the Sale is Over," *Harvard Business Review,* 61 (Sept./Oct. 1983), pp. 87–93.

44. For readers who want to explore psychological processes in consumer behavior in more depth, see J.F. Engel, R.D. Blackwell, and P.W. Miniard, *Consumer Behavior* (6th edition), Dryden: Hinsdale, IL, 1990, on which this section is based.

45. An interesting study classified North America into nine subcultures, J. Garreau, *The Nine Nations of North America,* Boston, MA: Houghton-Mifflin, 1981.

46. For tips on dealing with different cultures, see R.E. Axtell (ed.), *Do's and Taboos around the World,* New York: Wiley, 1993.

47. The figure is a summary of VALS™ descriptions developed by SRI International, Menlo Park, CA.

48. For a useful discussion of the role of politics in organizations, see P. Bloch, *The Empowered Manager: Positive Political Skills at Work:* San Francisco, CA: Jossey Bass, 1991.

49. The remainder of this section is heavily based on N. Capon, *Key Account Management and Planning.* New York: The Free Press, forthcoming, 2001.

50. J. Howard, IBM UK Ltd., "Changes in Global Purchasing Strategy," presentation to conference on Global Account Management: Best Practice, Cranfield School of Management, Great Britain, January 30, 1998.

51. The importance of reducing input costs can be seen in the allegation that when Jose Ignacio Lopez departed General Motors for Volkswagen, he took with him a 3,350-page printout listing 60,000 parts and suppliers for GM Europe, exact prices, and delivery schedules, *Fortune,* April 14, 1997.

52. Marriott Corporation has developed such sophisticated sourcing systems and high levels of procurement expertise that 60% of Marriott's purchasing and distribution activities are performed for non-Marriott clients, *NAMA Journal,* 32 (Fall 1996).

53. In Volkswagen's new plant in Brazil, component suppliers operate various areas of the plant.

54. See *Fortune,* February 20, 1995, "Purchasing's new muscle," that documents examples of reductions in numbers of suppliers.

55. See *The Economist,* December 7, 1996. In this process, some suppliers were forced to accept price cuts of up to 30%.

56. Xerox employs a fivefold scheme, termed the customer relationship triangle, embracing, in order: supplier, authorized supplier, preferred supplier, sole supplier, and quality partner.

57. See J.D. Burdett, "A Model for Customer-Supplier Alliances," *Logistics Information Management,* 5 (1992), pp. 25–31, for discussion on contrasting approaches to buyer/seller relationships.

58. To qualify for this program, the customer has to place a specified proportion of its business with Armstrong.

59. Note that this classification draws upon work by both Howard and Sheth, *op. cit.,* at Columbia Business School, and Robinson, Faris, and Wind at Wharton: P.J. Robinson, C.W. Faris, and Y. Wind, *Industrial Buying and Creative Marketing,* Boston, MA: Allyn and Bacon, 1967.

60. For further discussion of these decision process types and their implications for sellers, see J.M. Hulbert and J. Binkley, "Selling Strategy and Air Freight Decisions," *Transportation Journal,* 16 (Summer 1977), pp. 61–69.

61. A.J. Slywotzky and D.J. Morrison, *The Profit Zone,* New York: Times Business, 1997.

62. Focusing on customer needs has even entered the art world. Two Russian conceptual artists polled 1,001 adult Americans to identify their preferences in a painting: curves or angles? brushstrokes or smooth surfaces? "realistic" or "different" looks? famous or ordinary people? The result was V. Komar and A. Melamid, *Painting by Numbers: Komar and Melamid's Scientific Guide to Art,* New York: Farrar, Strauss, 1997.

63. F.J. Gouillart and F.D. Sturdivant, "A Day in the Life of Your Customers," *Harvard Business Review,* 72 (Jan./Feb. 1994), pp. 116–125.

64. M. Hammer and S.A. Stanton, "The Power of Reflection," *Fortune,* Nov. 24, 1997.

65. *The New York Times,* June 28, 1998.

66. *The New York Times,* Sunday, January 24, 1999.

67. Data collected in these manners can be analyzed by a variety of quantitative marketing research techniques.

68. Example provided by The Michael Allen Company.

WEB RESOURCES

7-Up	www.7up.com
Allstate	www.allstate.com
Amazon	www.amazon.com
America Online	www.aol.com
American Express	www.americanexpress.com
Armstrong	www.armstrong.com
Black and Decker	www.blackanddecker.com
British Airways	www.british-airways.com
Coca-Cola	www.cocacola.com
Continental Airlines	www.continental.com
Corning	www.corning.com
Diet 7-UP	www.7up.com
Diet Coke	www.cocacola.com
Diet Pepsi	www.pepsico.com
Dr. Pepper	www.drpepper.com
Dunkin Donuts	www.dunkindonuts.com
Ebay	www.ebay.com
Fanta	www.cocacola.com
Folgers	www.folgers.com
Guess jeans	www.guess.com
Hallmark	www.hallmark.com
Hi-C	www.cocacola.com
IBM	www.ibm.com
ICQ	www.aol.com
Intel	www.intel.com
Kellogg	www.kellogg.com
Kodak	www.kodak.com
L.L. Bean	www.llbean.com
Lehman Bros	www.lehman.com
Levi's jeans	www.levi.com
MTV	www.mtv.com
Marlboro	www.philipmorris.com
McDonald's	www.mcdonalds.com
Mirabilis Ltd.	www.aol.com
Mountain Dew	www.pepsico.com
Mr. Pibb	www.customer.coke.com
NBA	www.nba.com
Palm Pilot	www.palm.com
Pepsi Cola	www.pepsico.com
Prudential	www.prudential.com
Revlon	www.revlon.com
Slice	www.cocacola.com
Snapple	www.snapple.com
Sprite	www.cocacola.com
Stanley Works	www.stanleyworks.com

The Wall Street Journal	www.wsj.com
United Airlines	www.ual.com
Volkswagen	www.vw.com
Wal-Mart	www.walmart.com
Xerox	www.xerox.com
Yahoo!	www.yahoo.com

Chapter 4 Appendix: Identifying and Measuring Customer Needs

Identifying customer needs is a job for marketing research. Since many excellent works on marketing research are available, we shall not take scarce space for a detailed discussion of marketing research methodology. However, it is important to make some general observations. First, it is critical that firms expend considerable effort to identify customer needs. As competition increases, the ability to secure detailed knowledge of customer requirements will be a competence critical to gaining competitive advantage.[62] Frequently, the responses firms receive from such efforts are quite different from their before-the-fact expectations. World-class companies invest heavily for maximal understanding and feed the results of their studies into product and service development decisions. For example, in advance of its introduction of the new Advantix photographic system, Kodak conducted 22,000 interviews in 11 countries around the world.

Corporations typically use one or more of four basic approaches to identify customer needs. This section discusses one-on-one interviews, focus groups, anthropological methods, and surveys, together with conjoint analysis, a widely used method for identifying the importance of various product attributes in a purchase decision.

One-on-one interviews   Trained market researchers conduct in-depth interviews with individuals.

Focus groups   Groups of eight to 12 decision makers in the relevant product category are brought together under the guidance of a trained facilitator to discuss the product category and their needs and experiences with various products.

Anthropological methods   These newer methods involve observing customers interacting with products in their private or organizational lives. Many researchers believe these research methods provide greater insight than more conventional approaches.[63]

> **Example:** Tom Katzen, a merchandiser responsible for marketing Levi's jeans to teenagers, used to spend Saturday mornings at San Francisco's Fillmore auditorium. He would talk to the teens as they lined up for concert tickets about what they were looking for in jeans and observe their own customization efforts.[64]

> **Example:** Some companies hire "cool hunters" to observe people in their natural settings. These settings might be inner-city basketball courts or fashionable nightclubs, where patrons' tastes may eventually be adapted by the general population.[65]

> **Example:** Carlos Gutierrez, CEO of Kellogg, used to spend an hour each Sunday morning watching consumers buy cereal in a supermarket.[66]

Insight from these methods, followed by survey research to confirm/deny expectations, may provide excellent data on which to develop marketing strategies. Although these methods are appropriate for identifying customer needs, they are less valuable for measuring the importance or strength of individual needs. Measurement is usually best secured by some form of survey methodology.

Surveys Surveys are typically conducted by having customers respond to sets of questions, often by making checkmarks on scales. Survey questionnaires range from those with just a few questions that can be completed in a short time to others that might take an hour or more to complete. Such data may be collected by mail, telephone, face-to-face, or on-line.[67]

Most surveys ask direct questions about the importance of needs/benefits on simple rating scales. The underlying assumption is that customers are capable of making such determinations. This assumption may be valid, particularly for product solutions in established problem areas. However, when these conditions do not pertain, such as with radically new supplier-invented technology, the problem is more difficult.

Furthermore, customers have a tendency to say that they want the most of everything, but when social risk is involved they may avoid giving honest and open answers. As a result, preferences may be better revealed by direct observation of customer behavior.

> **Example:** In the early 1990s, Pepsi-supplied restaurants surveyed 7,000 restaurant owners/managers and determined that price was the critical decision variable because it was consistently rated as the most important. However, a study of 800 customers that had switched from Coke to Pepsi (or vice versa) showed that four service variables had higher correlations with switching behavior than price—poor delivery service, unreliable equipment, emergency service, and poor equipment maintenance.[68]

Relatedly, customers do not buy individual benefits; rather, they buy particular benefits embedded in the form of various offers. Thus, while focusing on individual benefits provides useful insights, it does not indicate how customers make trade-offs among benefits. More successful measurement approaches, therefore, tend to rely on methods requiring respondents to make choices (among real or simulated offers); the importance of different benefits (or product attributes) is inferred from their various choices. The most popular of these techniques is conjoint analysis.

Conjoint analysis Conjoint analysis is a widely used marketing research technique in which customers implicitly make those trade-offs in a task that typically requires making comparative judgments among different potential offers. The language of conjoint analysis is sometimes a little confusing at first, for alternatives are described in terms of "attributes" and "levels." Attributes are the product characteristics management is interested in exploring, such as color; levels are the color alternatives (red, blue, green).

> **Example:** A well-known battery manufacturer was contemplating launching a replacement automobile battery under its own name; it identified several attributes as critical to the purchase decision. These attributes were brand name (three existing brands plus the firm), built-in charge meter (yes/no), environmental safety (yes/no), rapid recharge (yes/no), 50% longer life (yes/no), price (current, +25%, +50%). These attributes and their associated levels, together with price, produced 192 combinations ($4 \times 2 \times 2 \times 2 \times 2 \times 3$), but only 16 were needed to capture fully the main effects of the various attributes.

Consumers were presented with each of the 16 alternatives described on an index card, such as brand B; charge meter, yes; environmental safety, no; rapid recharge, yes; 50% longer life, no; price, 50% above current. Each consumer was asked if they would purchase the battery described, then asked to rate batteries they would consider on a 1 to 100 preference intensity scale.

From this data, the researchers were able to calculate the value placed by consumers overall on the various attributes (Table 4A.1). They were also able to show that this value differed across different groups of consumers (segments).

Table 4A.1 shows that the strongest values are for price; as expected, these are increasingly negative as price increases (-252, -542). However, price is differentially valued by

TABLE 4A.1 Consumer Value for Battery Attributes in a Conjoint Analysis Study

Attributes	All Consumers	Segment A (32%)	Segment B (20%)	Segment C (28%)	Segment D (20%)
Brand B	+37	−14	+109	+79	+16
Brand C	−31	−18	+90	+16	−141
Brand D	+97	+39	+242	+118	+76
Price +25%	−252	−367	−463	−140	−81
Price +50%	−542	−783	−677	−320	−352
Built-in meter	+152	+60	+232	+188	+174
Environmentally safe	+153	+112	+208	+202	+101
Rapid charge	+120	+45	+122	+168	+140
Longer life	+204	+93	+267	+310	+179

From K. Jedidi, R. Kohli and W.S. DeSarbo, "Consideration/Choice Sets in Conjoint Analysis: A Latent Structure Approach," Working Paper, Columbia University, January 1998. Entries in the table are regression coefficients × 100 in equations predicting intention to purchase.

segment; segments A and B seem more concerned about price than segments C and D. Across all segments, longer life (+204) has greater value than the other three product design attributes (+152, +153, +120), but this is not consistent across segments. Segment A most values environmental safety (+112) but, in general, product design attributes are more valued by segments B and C than by A and D. Finally, brand name seems to be important although it matters much more for segment B than the other segments. Fairly consistently, brand D is the most preferred. (Note that the value for brand A is set at zero.)

CONCLUSION   Regardless of how much marketing research is conducted prior to product launch, in many cases, the ability of the product to truly satisfy customer needs can only be ascertained after customers have use experience. Of course, some customers are easier to please than others; in the short run, the firm may have an easier time focusing on those that are less demanding. However, to develop into a world-class competitor, the firm should consider seeking out really demanding customers (individuals, families, or organizations) so that its own performance is continually upgraded.

> Example: One German company has a policy of introducing all new products in Japan. It has found that Japanese customers are the most demanding in the world. Such demanding customers keep the firm on its toes and help it become a truly world-class competitor.

FUNDAMENTALS FOR
STRATEGIC
MARKETING

5

COMPETITORS AND COMPLEMENTERS

LEARNING OBJECTIVES

When you have completed this chapter, you will understand

- the importance of gaining insight about competitors

- how to develop a framework for competitor analysis and strategy

- how to identify competitors—actual and potential

- how to describe and evaluate competitors

- how to project competitors' future actions and manage their behavior

- how to secure insight on competition

- the importance of complementers in developing an integrated approach to the market

- the various forms of complementarity

INTRODUCTION

The increased intensity of competition in today's world was discussed in previous chapters. Of course, competition is not a new phenomenon for most companies, but for firms in previously highly-regulated industries now undergoing deregulation, for many state-owned monopoly enterprises now being privatized, and for firms accustomed to operating behind protective national tariff and quota barriers, exposure to competition is a severe shock. What is new for all, however, is the change in the type and level of competitive activity. Not only have these increased for firms in many sectors of the economy, most observers of the business scene anticipate that this increase will continue. Notwithstanding the major changes of the previous ten to 20 years, even more dramatic changes can be expected in the years ahead. To attract and retain targeted customers in this environment, managers must work ever harder to develop differential advantages. An in-depth understanding of competitors is necessary in order to achieve such advantages.

Despite growing management awareness of increased competition, there is often little emphasis on understanding competitors. Even when companies commit resources to competitive data gathering and analysis, most often this effort goes no further than basic description. These initiatives pale in comparison with resources spent attempting to understand customers. Do not misunderstand this position: It is of great importance to direct significant resources toward understanding customers, but recall that the firm will only reach its objectives by doing a better job than its competitors in securing customers. Both customers and competitors must be understood in depth.

In inward-oriented companies, the costs of collecting and analyzing market information, including customer and competitive data, are often cited as reasons for inactivity. What such companies fail to see, however, are the costs and risks of inaction. In benign, slow-changing environments, these costs and risks are typically low. In today's fast-changing competitive environment, however, the opposite is generally the case. Arguments for competitive data gathering, analysis, pre-emptive strategy development, and market-place action are stronger now than ever.

Figure 5.1 presents a framework for competitive analysis and strategy. A critical implication of this figure is that mere descriptive understanding of competitors does not suffice. Insights generated by competitor analysis must affect managers' decisions, or the efforts used to generate them will be wasted.

COMPETITORS

Identification: Who Are Our Competitors? Who Will They Be in the Future?

The term "competitor" can be defined as any organization whose products and services provide, or may in the future provide, similar (or superior) levels of customer benefit. Earlier, it was argued that a broad view of customers was appropriate so the firm neither misses market opportunities, nor fails to identify critical members of the decision-making unit. The same general argument is made for competitors. To the extent that the firm's managers take too narrow a view of its competition, they will fail to identify threats and react too late. What competes is what the customer decides competes. One of the most common mistakes that managers make in competitor identification is, implicitly, to take a supplier perspective rather than a customer perspective.

By contrast, to the extent that the firm understands the scope of competition, it can assemble resources to develop an appropriate competitive strategy, whether that response involves conflict, cooperation, or some other alternative.

Figure 5.2 is a schematic of the different types of competitive forces facing the firm.[1] The center of the figure shows the firm as competing in an existing competitive environment with a traditional set of competitors, the competitive status quo. However,

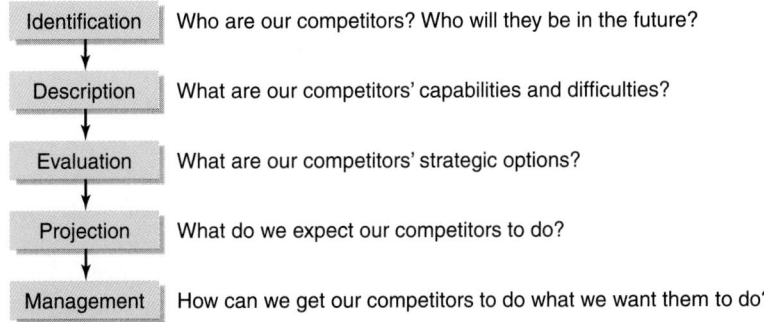

Identification	Who are our competitors? Who will they be in the future?
Description	What are our competitors' capabilities and difficulties?
Evaluation	What are our competitors' strategic options?
Projection	What do we expect our competitors to do?
Management	How can we get our competitors to do what we want them to do?

FIGURE 5.1

A Framework for Competitive Analysis and Strategy

in addition to traditional competitors, there are several other competitive forces that shape the firm's new competitive reality.

COMPETITIVE STATUS QUO   The firm's traditional rivalry with established competitors constitutes the competitive status quo. Typically, managers of rival firms know their traditional competitors well. Over time they observe the actions, performance results, successes, and failures of these competitors, and have a reasonably good idea of their strengths, weaknesses, likely future strategic moves, and so forth. It is not at all unlikely that firm managers have frequently worked for their key competitors, and vice versa.

Among traditional competitors, there may be "established rules of the game," even tacit collusion regarding which customers or customer types "belong" to each rival. Over time, one rival may outperform another for a period, then lose position in a constant ongoing tussle. Rarely does one firm gain significant advantage quickly over its traditional rivals. Typically, strong market positions are gained only as a result of long-run sustained effort. Examples of traditional rivalry include General Motors, Ford, and Chrysler in the U.S. automobile industry, Citicorp and Chase Manhattan in U.S. domestic banking, AT&T, MCI, and Sprint in telecommunications, Sony, Matsushita, and Philips in consumer electronics, and Boeing and Airbus in large passenger aircraft. A critical issue regarding direct competitors is the presence/absence of exit barriers. At times, competitors would like to

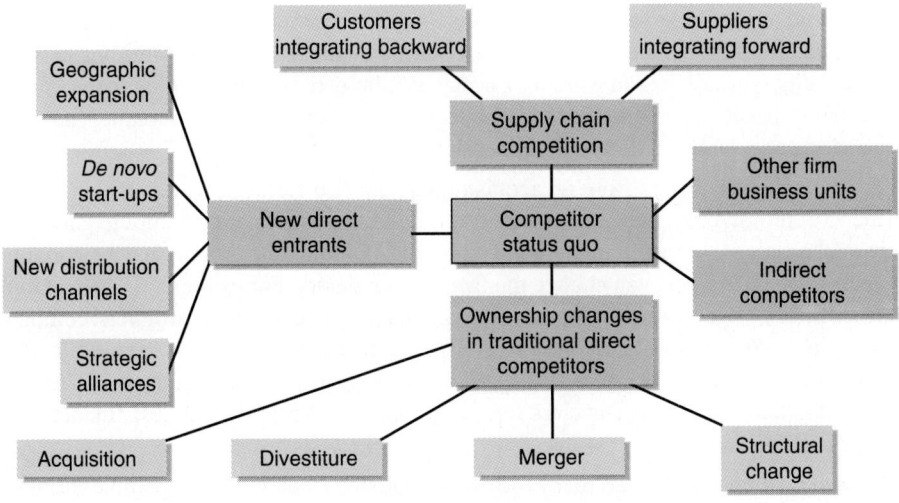

FIGURE 5.2

The Changing Competitive Reality

exit a market but are unable to do so for such reasons as long-term supply contracts and threatened law suits. From time to time, a firm may encourage a competitor to leave the market by helping make exit a more viable option.

OWNERSHIP CHANGES IN TRADITIONAL DIRECT COMPETITORS

Acquisition   Acquisition is a popular method adopted by firms seeking rapid growth, both within individual countries and as a means for expansion into foreign markets. For the firm competing with an acquired business unit, the key reality is that, regardless of whether or not a name change occurs or significant managerial changes are made, it has to compete with a different organizational entity. The acquirer made the acquisition presumably for a purpose, and this purpose will likely be worked out through the goals, strategies, and implementation plans of the acquirer. The purpose and mission of the competitor entity post-acquisition is likely to be different from its purpose pre-acquisition. Furthermore, the acquirer's degree of involvement in the acquiree's strategy making and operations may range from extremely deep (total integration into the acquirer's operations) to a more "hands-off" approach (a passive investor).

In most cases, the acquirer's management intends to assume control of the acquired entity, but the acquired firm's executives can also assume the most powerful positions.[2] For example, although Phibro Corporation, the commodities trading firm, acquired Salomon Brothers, a large investment banker, in 1981, former Salomon Brothers' executives ultimately rose to key decision-making positions, including CEO.

Nor should we assume that acquisitions are necessarily successful; the general record is not particularly positive. However, if the acquirer is experienced in making acquisitions, success is more likely and the competitive threat more significant. The key managerial implication is that the acquiree is unlikely to represent the same level and type of competition post-acquisition as it did before. Thus, the firm's assumptions for the competitive status quo must be fundamentally re-examined.

Divestiture   Ownership change also occurs when a business unit of an organization is released from the corporate family to become an independent entity. Lacking corporate resources, it may struggle; alternatively, unfettered by the corporate organization, perhaps no longer denied access to capital and other resources for growth, a smaller more nimble business may become a much tougher competitor. Recent spin-off examples include Ciba Specialty Chemical (Ciba Geigy), Cytec Industries (American Home Products), Clariant International (Sandoz), Lucent Technologies and NCR, (AT&T), Praxair (Union Carbide), Rhodia (Rhone Poulenc), Solutia (Monsanto) and Zeneca (ICI), some of which have prospered more than their original parents.[3] A special case concerns leveraged buyouts (LBOs) of business units or whole companies. After the LBO, although nominally the same organization, the new entity typically has an extremely heavy debt burden. Not only can its scope of business activity change radically as units or product lines are shed to reduce this burden, but operational decisions can be made to optimize cash flow.

Merger   A merger differs from an acquisition as the two former entities join as "equal" partners. In prototypical mergers, two firms pool their strengths and attempt to cancel out their weaknesses. As a result, the new entity is typically much larger and may be a tougher competitor. Such mergers can change the face of an industry. For example, in 1997, Grand Metropolitan merged with Guinness to form the major consumer products company, Diageo; in 1996, Sandoz and Ciba Geigy's pharmaceutical businesses merged to form Novartis that, in early 1999, was the world's largest pharmaceutical company. The 1998 merger of Citicorp and The Travelers formed CitiGroup, the world's largest financial services organization.

Structural Change   Although many forms of ownership exist, most competitive entities in advanced economies are public and private corporations. Transitions from other forms into the corporate organization can bring about fundamental shifts in the nature of competition. Among the various changes that fall into this category are so-called corporatization of state-owned organizations, privatization of state-owned enterprises, demutualization of "mutual" organizations,[4] and a shift from family-owned business or partnership to a corporate form.

> **Example:** In the early 1970s, most Wall Street firms were private partnerships. By the turn of the millenium, most firms had either been merged with, or acquired by, peer institutions. The only major firm that remained a partnership was Goldman Sachs. But in 1999, even Goldman Sachs ultimately decided to adopt a corporate ownership structure.

Whenever an enterprise undertakes such a shift in status, associated strategic issues are likely involved. Typically, a set of environmental pressures has led to a belief that a change in status will improve the organization's competitive position. Thus, the shift from partnership to corporation is often associated with a desire for access to capital; demutualization may be driven by both capital requirements and a desire to attract talented executives through the offer of stock options.

Changes in perspective may accompany such status changes. For example, whereas in mutual organizations management is theoretically responsible to the policy/account holders, in practice it is frequently responsible to no one. By contrast, demutualized corporate managers must be concerned with stockholder expectations. The increased access to resources that frequently accompanies these changes, and the heightened degree of scrutiny, typically has an important impact on the firm's objectives and strategies. As a result, it represents a vastly different competitive challenge.

NEW DIRECT ENTRANTS New direct entrants are competitors that offer basically similar products and services, but were not previously competitors; a critical issue for such competitors is the presence/absence of entry barriers. The most vivid examples of new direct entrants are geographic expansion by existing firms, *de novo* industry entry, new distribution channels, and strategic alliances.

Geographic Expansion New competitors with significant experience in similar products and services can be extremely tough competitors and can place significant pressure on those firms whose traditional markets they enter. Geographic expansion can occur at several levels: a within-country regional firm expanding into other country regions; a national firm expanding within a multicountry trading block; or a national or multicountry regional firm becoming global.

This type of competition can be extremely difficult to counteract if the expanding firm is a well-capitalized successful entity with significant business strengths and cost advantages resulting from profitable base business in its traditional markets. A superior cost position may represent an especially potent competitive weapon if marginal cost pricing is employed as a means of achieving market share.[5] The 1980s saw the decimation of several industries in advanced Western countries (such as consumer electronics) as Far Eastern firms entered their markets with high-quality, low-price products. Notwithstanding their considerable strengths, such entrants typically suffer from lack of market knowledge and established customer relationships, although these may be buttressed by local hiring or partnership arrangements.

***De Novo* Start-Ups** *De novo* start-ups can represent potent competition for existing players. They may represent substantial threats simply because they are new. They are unencumbered by old facilities and technology, established organizations, personnel set in their ways, and so forth. Newness provides them with a flexibility of action that established competitors might be unable to match.

> **Example:** In the computer industry, *de novo* start-ups, such as Compaq, Dell, and Gateway have been, and still are, significant competitive threats to IBM, the former dominant player.

New Distribution Channels In many markets, firms compete within an existing distribution channel structure. The development of new distribution channels for essentially similar products may pose fierce competition for incumbents.

Example: Direct marketers, such as L.L. Bean and Lands' End, offer competition to department stores. Furthermore, the Internet is offering an alternative distribution system for many manufacturers. Firms with in-place distribution systems are suffering severe competition from these new approaches exemplified by Amazon.com and others.

Strategic Alliances This form of competition often occurs when a firm wants to enter a new business area but lacks the requisite assets, such as capital, skills, technology, and market access, or is unwilling to assume the risk and full entry costs itself; it then seeks an alliance with a partner firm. The competitive threat results from pooling the strengths of two (or more) partners; a stronger organization is formed than could have existed independently.[6]

Example: General Mills, a large U.S. producer of breakfast cereals, lacked export distribution. Swiss-based Nestlé, one of the world's largest food companies, had excellent European distribution but did not carry breakfast cereals. The two companies allied to form Cereal Partners, now a major competitor in Europe.

Although the immediate impact of such alliance announcements may appear devastating, problems often occur when the partners' alliance objectives or ability to provide needed resources diverge over time.

Some of the more important alliances are vertical partnerships where the competitor forms close linkages with its suppliers.[7] In some cases, these partnerships result from mutual interests and are often positive-sum games (win-win situations) creating formidable supply chain advantages. In other cases, "partnership" may be forced on the weaker firm by the relative market power of the other and be no more than a somewhat unpalatable way of forestalling supply-chain competition. Although vertical alliances can be viewed as extensions of relationship marketing, they are perhaps more appropriately considered as distribution variants.[8]

INDIRECT COMPETITORS Indirect competitors are those firms offering similar benefits to the firm's products but in a significantly different way. In other words, they fulfill the same functions for customers and are often termed "functional substitutes" by economists. Such competition may take the form of different product or process technology. For example, Xerox copying machines compete with computers, fax machines, computer fax modems, and video conferencing. The New York Knicks compete for spectators/TV viewers with the New Jersey Nets and other pro-basketball teams—direct competition; the Knicks also compete indirectly with the New York Rangers (ice hockey), the New York Jets (football), and the New York Yankees (baseball). Furthermore, cruise lines, car companies, and clothing manufacturers may all compete for consumers' discretionary spending. Alternatively, the product form may be similar but the marketing approach novel, such as pyramid-structured sales forces like Amway (consumer goods) and A.L. Williams (life insurance), direct-selling organizations, or competitors operating through the Internet.[9]

Indirect competitors frequently operate in different industry sectors. Because of this difference, they often behave in ways unanticipated by traditional, and even new direct, competitors whose sector they enter. Furthermore, because of internal forces committed to existing ways of doing business, incumbents often dismiss indirect competitors as "not in our business" or "not understanding our market." As a result, the threat is typically more difficult to recognize because of its source, and is often dismissed, even if identified. This narrow perspective can be an immense competitive advantage to the indirect competitor. In certain industries, companies are prohibited by regulations from responding to competition by adding indirectly competitive products to their own product lines.

Example: For many years, U.S. commercial banks were unable to offer money market accounts and mutual fund products as a defense against mutual fund companies, such as Fidelity and Dreyfus, that competed directly for retail deposits.[10]

OTHER FIRM BUSINESS UNITS   A special case of competition arises when the firm provides multiple offers that satisfy the same basic set of customer needs. This situation may be either planned or unplanned.

In some corporations, the business scopes of individual business units, divisions, or products are designed to minimize duplication of resources.[11] In these firms, the organization structure is designed so that any given potential market opportunity is the responsibility of a single business unit or division. By contrast, other corporations deliberately build their organization structures to accept, and even encourage, inter-divisional and inter-product competition. These companies believe that the inevitable resource duplication will be more than balanced by the entrepreneurial successes of the individual business units. By competing amongst themselves, these firm divisions will be better prepared to compete against other corporations.

This form of competition is endemic when firms develop multiple products for a particular market. Although the firm may target individual offerings for specific market segments, it is inevitable that its products compete among themselves, in addition to competing with products from other firms. Furthermore, in some markets, customer loyalty may be low and product switching a frequent occurrence. In these situations, offering multiple competing brands into markets is far from irrational. A special case concerns product introduction where the firm currently has product entries, and new product sales will cannibalize sales of existing products.

Similarly, the firm might sanction parallel product development efforts as a way to improve time-to-market.

> **Example:** To support customers involved in foreign trade, Citibank embarked on several initiatives in the mid-1980s to develop electronic letters of credit. The Asia-Pacific Group was particularly innovative and was the first within Citibank to offer a functioning system to its customers. Having successfully implemented its system in the Far East, a sales team from Asia-Pacific began selling to Citibank customers in North America at the same time that the North American group was still trying to develop its own system![12]

Unplanned internal competition may arise from several sources and is typically destructive. Such competition usually occurs as the result of environmental change and product line evolution.

> **Example:** In the 1980s, the Steel Division of BHP, a large Australian resources company, benchmarked steel usage internationally by market sector. It discovered that the proportion of high-rise buildings using structural steel construction was lower in Australia than in any other industrialized country. Compared to foreign builders, Australian builders tended disproportionately to favor reinforced concrete.[13] Funded by three different product groups in BHP, a newly-formed, market-focused, structural steel development group (SSDG) was successful in changing the situation. However, soon after SSDG got off the ground, one of the three product groups discovered that usage of its products, reinforcing materials, was much lower in structural steel than in reinforced concrete construction. It withdrew financial support from SSDG and was instrumental, with the reinforcing industry, in forming an industry group to support reinforced concrete technology.

Situations can occur in which no centralized organizational unit has effective authority over individual organizational units, and inter-divisional competition grows out of control. A contemporary example concerns Andersen Consulting, a partnership and a major player in the consulting industry. Andersen Consulting was born out of Arthur Andersen's accounting business and quickly became not only a major consulting firm, but an increasingly profitable part of the Andersen organization. Its successful growth led to a major deadlock on partnership issues within the entire Arthur Andersen organization. One result of its internicene dispute was that the accounting group started seeking consulting business, often in competition with Andersen Consulting!

SUPPLY CHAIN COMPETITION A severe competitive threat can occur when existing supplier/firm/customer relationships in distribution channels break down. Two types of breakdown can cause significant competitive difficulties; in both cases, actions have the result of shortening the supply chain. The difference simply relates to the instigator of the action: customers integrating backwards, or suppliers integrating forwards.[14]

Customers Integrating Backwards This competitive threat occurs when the firm's *customer* decides to incorporate functions that the firm currently performs into its own operations. This backward integration generally occurs when the customer believes that it has the competence to fulfill the supplier function, and that potential for additional profit margin is sufficiently attractive.

> **Example:** A major distributor of farming products purchased its fertilizer farm-ready in bags from Monsanto. The distributor planned to back-integrate by erecting a small bagging plant on its premises and asked Monsanto to supply fertilizer in bulk. Unwilling to lose profit margin on the bagging operation, Monsanto refused. The distributor secured bulk supplies from another fertilizer manufacturer.

Backward integration competition is especially difficult to deal with because the firm that is back-integrating frequently has access to the ultimate customer. (In the previous example, the distributor had relationships with farmers.) Supplier firms often have little experience and expertise in responding to such competition by reaching forward and dealing further down the supply chain. (In the example, Monsanto had much weaker relationships with farmers.)

Suppliers Integrating Forwards This competitive threat occurs when the firm's *supplier* decides to incorporate functions that the firm currently performs into its own operations. Forward integration generally occurs when the supplier believes that it has the competence to fulfill the functions currently carried out by its customer firm, and that the potential for additional profit margin is sufficiently attractive.

> **Example:** In recent years, many U.S. companies have subcontracted production to indigenous firms in low labor cost parts of the world. In some industries, these foreign producers are starting to sell products in advanced Western countries. For example, local diamond manufacturing firms in India are now selling settings in the United States.

The main difference between forward and backward integration is that in forward integration the active party, the supplier, typically has no contractual relationship with the firm's customer. However, it may have frequent contact as a result of actions to stimulate demand for its products or to provide service, and may be encouraged into forward integration by the final customer.

Some firms go to considerable lengths to inhibit this type of competition, in particular by drawing a firm line regarding information provided to customers. Simon cites several examples: One firm relabels and repaints components secured from suppliers to prevent customers from recognizing their origin while another deepens its product line through vertical integration and creates incompatibility with component suppliers to reduce customer choice.[15] These actions are scarcely "customer-oriented," but may be highly pragmatic.[16]

AN ALTERNATIVE COMPETITIVE FRAMEWORK An alternative framework that classifies competitive threats as direct or indirect, current or potential, (Figure 5.3) can be helpful in deciding which competitor represents the most serious threats and against which the firm's resources should be deployed. Many firms are tempted to focus on actual/direct competitors (cell A); these are the competitors the firm encounters daily. However, as already noted, actual/indirect competitors (cell B) may represent an even more serious threat. We should note that firms face differing types of indirect competition that may be closer or further away from their current business (Figure 5.4).

FUNDAMENTALS FOR
STRATEGIC
MARKETING

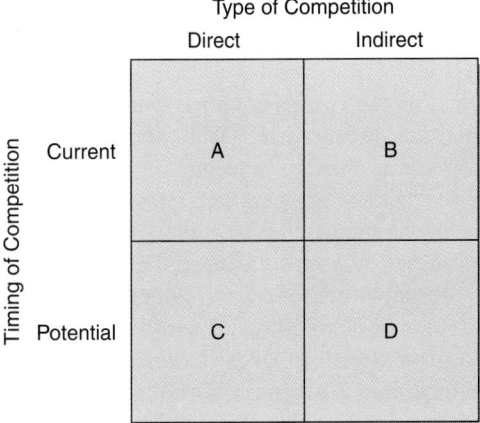

Type of Competition

FIGURE 5.3

A Framework for Competitive Threats

Looking to the future, the firm should consider potential competitors. These may be difficult to spot, especially potential/indirect competitors (cell D), but can become critical market players. Note also the interesting paradox that the more successful the company, the more likely it is to attract competition. Thus, the most important competitive targets for successful firms should be potential competitors, direct or indirect. Pre-emptive strategies are often the most effective in these situations.

In practice, the returns that lure entrants do not typically serve to motivate incumbents to enhance their competitiveness. Rather, too often, they seem lulled into a false sense of security. In truth, technology, deregulation, and globalization today form a vicious triumvirate where competitor threat identification is concerned and the task is now more difficult than ever. Firms tend to strategize more effectively against high probability threats, even where potential impact may be low, than with low probability, high impact threats—the typical combination for indirect competitors.

COMPETITIVE DYNAMICS One danger of a structural view of competition is that competitive dynamics may be understated. Microeconomics tells us that the incentive for new entry rises if incumbents earn economic profits. If entry barriers can be overcome, then good profitability becomes a leading indicator of future competitive intensity. As competition becomes compressed in both space and time, dramatic changes can occur. Local or regional competitors become national, previously national competitors become multinational, and the heightened level of global competition requires more immediate responses.

Whereas traditional competitors typically gain on one another by small increments, the new ways of competing, because they are often of a depth and scope quite different from any previously faced, may be truly life threatening. However, the level of

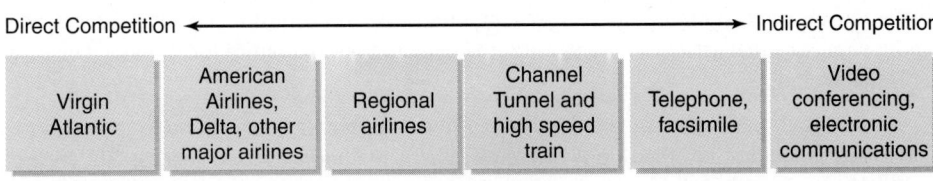

FIGURE 5.4

British Airways—A Spectrum of Direct/Indirect Competition

Prepared by Françoise Simon, SDC Group. Reproduced by permission.

danger is a function not only of the strength of the competitive thrusts, but also of the firm's ability (or lack thereof) to cast off traditional ways of doing business and respond appropriately.

Good strategic management should mean that the firm is not a passive entity waiting to deal reactively with whatever competitive threats arise. Over time, successful firms should expect increased competitive threats as changes in technology, regulation, and globalization lead other companies to seek new customers and expand into new markets. However, in the same way that firms can choose the customers they want to target to sell their products and services, so they may actively choose the competitors with which they want to compete. These two decisions are, of course, interdependent; if management wants to avoid a certain competitor or competitors, it can do so through choice of customer. The firm must make a prior decision: Does it want competition at all? A range of options may be available, including acquisition, forming an alliance, or vertically integrating, any of which can enable the firm to avoid head-to-head competition.

Competitors as Positive Factors

Although in the short run, the firm may enjoy greater earnings from monopoly or monopoly-like situations, such lack of competition may not be beneficial for the long run. Monopolies have a tendency to bureaucracy, rigidity, and sloth that make them ill-prepared to face the competition that eventually emerges when the environment changes, whether from globalization, technological discontinuities, or some other change.

> **Example:** In the 1960s and 1970s, Xerox, with a strong monopoly in dry copying, was one of the U.S.'s glamor companies, posting year-over-year sales and profits improvements for many years. However, this stellar performance masked serious problems of cost control and product quality. Around 1980, Xerox was surprised to discover that Japanese companies had a 40% to 50% cost advantage in copiers and were selling machines for almost what it cost Xerox to produce them. In addition, Xerox's quality rankings were decidedly inferior.[17]

Responding to the potential for this sort of problem, some organizations deliberately seek competitive situations to keep the firm "in fighting trim." Similarly, Porter showed that for many product categories, a country's leading world market share was associated with fierce domestic competition.[18]

A second example of viewing competition positively occurs early in the product life cycle when competitors may play a positive role in opening up a market. Sometimes this is related to standard setting where absence of agreed-upon standards among potential suppliers can impede progress in market development. Alternatively, it may occur when the relationship among competitors is complementary. For example, when color television became a technological possibility, it could not be commercially acceptable unless both consumers purchased color television sets and the television networks produced color television programs (which would not be worth doing unless consumers purchased television sets). This "chicken and egg" situation caused RCA to "invite" competitors to share the market development effort.[19]

Notwithstanding these situations in which competitive presence is viewed positively, firms mostly want to minimize competitive threats. As a result, they may consider developing strategies that affirmatively attempt to keep competitors out of the market. The possibilities include:

- **Political**: Seek governmental aid to restrict foreign entry through the imposition of tariffs, quotas, or other kinds of controls. This method was used successfully by Harley Davidson in the 1980s when the U.S. government imposed temporary high tariffs on large motorcycles to protect the "U.S. large bike industry." (The sole remaining U.S. manufacturer was Harley Davidson!)

- **Legal**: File lawsuits to impede entry. Braniff used this method in the early 1970s in an attempt to stop Southwest Airlines from competing in intrastate routes in Texas. Similarly, the Securities Industry Association attempted to stop commercial banks from underwriting commercial paper.
- **Regulatory**: Make life difficult for competitors by advocating regulatory changes that inhibit competitive entry or force competitors to expend resources. Such actions were taken in the U.S. municipal bond industry (mid-1980s) by Financial Guaranty Insurance Company (FGIC).[20]

Firms should note that such actions, although they may provide positive short-term results, may have long-term negative consequences. In the early 1980s, U.S. automobile manufacturers were successful in lobbying the U.S. government to press for "voluntary" quotas on imported, then primarily small, Japanese cars; the immediate effect was to slow the increasing competitive threat. The long-term effects were Japanese introduction of competitive medium- and large-size models (high margin products for U.S. manufacturers) and the commencing of domestic U.S. manufacture by major Japanese automobile manufacturers. These competitive actions arguably set the stage for extensive penetration of the U.S. market by Japanese competitors. In the FGIC case, competitor MBIA had to endure the pain and cost of changing its organizational form. As a result, however, it became a much tougher competitor.

Despite the possible negative consequences of these types of action, firms can succeed in keeping competitors out of the market or, at least, delaying entry to better prepare themselves for the competitive incursion.

Description: What Are Our Competitors' Capabilities and Difficulties?

When the firm has identified its most serious competitor threats and starts thinking about developing competitive strategy, it should ask questions about these competitors to identify clearly what the firm is up against. Among these questions are:

- What should cause us to fear them? This question seeks to understand competitors' major strengths, the basis on which they compete, and the key resources that can be brought to bear against the firm; answering this question reveals the true nature of the competitive threat. In particular, the firm might identify competitors' capabilities (or otherwise) to design, produce, market, finance, and manage specific product/markets.
- What are their vulnerabilities? Just as the firm has both strengths and weaknesses, so do competitors. Whereas the firm must defend against competitor strengths, weaknesses may provide an opportunity for attack.
- What strategies have competitors employed in the past? How successful have they been? What strategies are they employing now? Could they employ them in the future? An understanding of competitor history may provide clues to likely future behavior. To the extent that competitors have previously taken actions that proved successful, they are likely to take similar actions in the future. Equally, they are less likely to take similar actions to those that resulted in failure.

A Framework for Describing Competitors

Figure 5.5 presents a framework for competitive data gathering and description whose elements are the fundamental building blocks for competitor analysis.[21] The definitions of the various terms in the framework are:

Competitor's Organization

- **Infrastructure**: The line organization that sets out the basic responsibilities and reporting relationships.
- **Processes**: The competitor's information, control, and reward systems and processes.
- **Culture**: The behaviors, norms, beliefs, and values that together describe what the competitor stands for and how its members operate and behave.

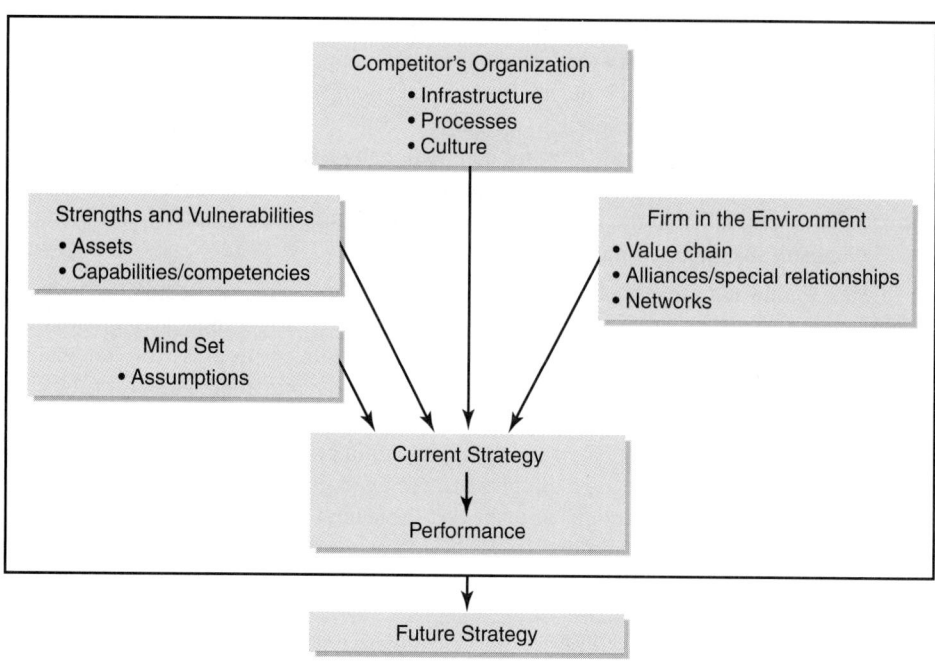

FIGURE 5.5

A Framework for Describing Competitors

Strengths and Vulnerabilities[22]
- **Assets**: The set of financial, physical, organizational, human, political, knowledge, and perceptual (e.g., how the competitor is perceived by customers and suppliers) assets. Competitor liabilities should also be included.
- **Capabilities/competencies**: The sets of activities that the firm does well, including both "local" expertise and broad scale organizational abilities. Also included are those activities that the competitor does not do well.

Firm in the Environment
- **Value chain**: The set of major work activities conducted by the competitor and the manner in which these are connected to external entities such as suppliers and customers. (Use of the value chain for assessing the firm versus competitors is discussed extensively in Chapter 6.)
- **Alliances/special relationships**: Alliances are formal economic relationships between the competitor and other entities (for example, supplier, customer, distribution channel). Special relationships are characterized by informality and, in addition to suppliers and customers, may embrace such organizations as government agencies, political parties, and public interest groups.
- **Networks**: Networks are interconnected sets of alliances and relationships in which each party fulfills a unique role. Rather than compete with a single rival, the firm may be part of a network competing with other networks.

Mind Set
- **Assumptions**: What the competitor takes for granted or as a "given"; assumptions are the outcomes of the analysts' judgment and are always inferred.

Current Strategy and Performance
- **Strategy**: The firm can observe the competitor's actions in the marketplace.
- **Performance**: Broadly speaking, performance measures are either financially based or market-oriented in nature. Financial measures range from stock price to product line profitability; market measures include market share and customer satisfaction.

TABLE 5.1 Competitive Assessment Analysis

Customer Needs/Required Benefits	Importance Rank	Required Capabilities/Resources				
		Efficient Manufacturing System	Good Distribution System	Just-in-time Delivery System	Well-funded R&D	Access to Low Cost Raw Materials
Easy Product Availability	1		*YYY			
Low Prices	2	*YN				*YN
Low Inventories	3			*YN		
Access to Cutting-Edge Technology	4				*YYN	
				etc.		

It is important to understand that competitor analysis may be conducted at several different levels. Depending on the level, different data are needed and different analysis methods are appropriate. For example, analysis at the product/market level requires detailed information on the competitor's strategy market segment by market segment, and in-depth understanding of its marketplace actions. At the business level, less detailed information is required on individual market segments, but more generalized information on the business as a whole. At the corporate level, less information is required on individual businesses as the focus shifts to the entire set of competitor businesses and their inter-relationships.

Evaluation: What Are Competitors' Strategic Options?

Evaluation involves using analysis to generate options for competitors, and exploring what patterns would be likely to evolve, should competitors avail themselves of any of these options. Three questions should guide the evaluation process:

- What options are available to the competitor?
- What would the competitor have to do to avail itself of each of these options?
- Is the competitor capable of making the changes necessary to implement a particular option?

A variety of analyses may be helpful in answering these questions, but three specific approaches are addressed in this section—competitor assessment analysis, game theory approaches, and decision trees. The firm might also secure insight from value chain and portfolio analysis.

COMPETITIVE ASSESSMENT ANALYSIS   The power of this framework is that it maps customer needs/required benefits for a specific market segment directly into the corporate resources required to satisfy the needs and deliver the benefits (Table 5.1).

In the left column of Table 5.1, the customer needs/required benefits are listed in order of importance. Along the top is the set of capabilities/resources that any firm would have to have to satisfy the customer needs and deliver the required benefits. Several questions must be asked of this matrix. First:

- What capabilities/resources are required for each need/benefit? Mark each cell with an asterisk "*". Typically, the resulting matrix is sparse, indicating that some capabilities/resources are irrelevant for satisfying specific customer needs.

For each matrix cell where capabilities/resources match with a need/benefit, three questions should be asked:

- Does the firm have the capabilities/resources to satisfy the need/deliver the benefit? If yes, enter Y; if no, enter N;

- For each cell with a Y, are the firm's capabilities/resources superior to the competitor? If yes, enter Y; if no, enter N;
- For each cell with a YY, would it be difficult for competitors to match the required capabilities/resources? If yes, enter Y; if no, enter N.

The resulting matrix may contain the entries: N, YN, YYN and YYY. An N entry implies a significant weakness for the firm, especially if a similar matrix performed from the perspective of an individual competitor contains an equivalent YYY. By contrast, a YYY entry for the firm implies significant and sustainable advantage over the competitor. The higher up in the matrix a particular entry appears, the more serious the implications, because the firm is advantaged or disadvantaged on a more important customer benefit.

The process of developing the matrix, and subsequent analysis of the completed matrix, can provide powerful insight into competitor capabilities and difficulties. Note that this assessment analysis can be used to compare the firm to individual competitors one at a time, or to an entire set of competitors.

When the analyses are completed and all questions have been answered, the company must make use of its findings. Too often, managers collect descriptive information about competitors, usually because the company's planning system requires it, then make little or no subsequent use of the data. Competitive intelligence efforts can be justified only if the data secured affect firm decisions. The first place this data should be used is to identify competitors' strategic options.

THE "PRISONER'S DILEMMA"   The Prisoner's Dilemma (so named because of its original application involving potential incarceration) is a game-theory approach that provides a useful framework for thinking through the effects of competitive actions. An illustration of the dilemma is shown in Figure 5.6 where the firm and its competitor each face a pricing decision.[23]

In Figure 5.6, the firm has to decide whether to hold or cut price; the competitor must make the same decision. The financial result for each depends on the actions of both parties. If the firm and the competitor both hold price (cell A), each makes moderate profit. However, if the firm holds price and the competitor cuts price (cell B), the competitor makes high profit but the firm loses money. Conversely, if the firm cuts price and the competitor holds price (cell C), the firm makes high profit but the competitor loses money. Finally, if the firm and competitor both cut price (cell D), each makes low profits.

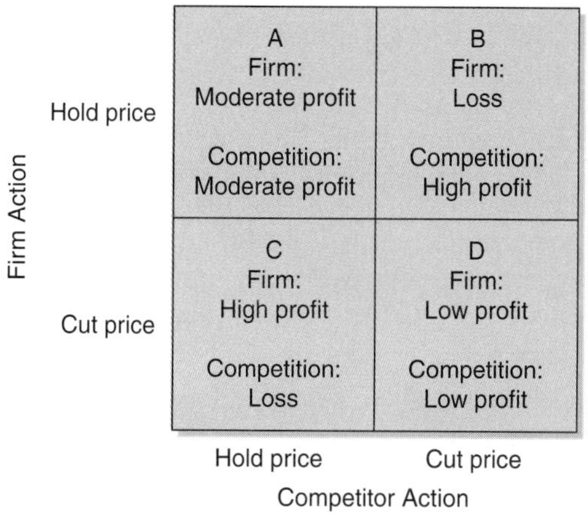

FIGURE 5.6

Illustration of the Prisoner's Dilemma

FUNDAMENTALS FOR STRATEGIC MARKETING

The problem for both firm and competitor is that neither knows what decision the other party will make. In making its decision, the firm has to weigh questions such as what is the likelihood that the competitor will cut price? Conversely, what is the likelihood that the competitor will hold price? If the firm cuts price, what is the likelihood that the competitor will be willing and able to match the price cut? The competitor is likely asking similar questions regarding the firm.

If the firm believes that the competitor would match any price cut, it might decide that a conclusion in cell A would be most advantageous. If this were the case, it might signal that the firm would hold its own price if the competitor refrained from price competition.[24]

DECISION TREES   An alternative means to analyze a competitive situation is via a decision tree. By attaching estimated payoffs and outcome probabilities to individual branches of the tree, the resulting expected values serve as a guide to choice.[25] However, criteria other than expected value may also be used to make choices (Figure 5.7). The situation modeled involves a decision of whether or not to introduce a new product in a setting where one of two competitive decisions may occur—rapid imitation, or no action.[26]

Even in the absence of quantitative estimates, useful insights can be gained. Assuming introduction costs are modest, the *launch now—A* branch dominates. First, one of the outcomes (payoffs) is as good as the best of the *do not launch* branch ($A_1 = B_1$). Second, A_2 dominates both B_2 and B_3. A_1 and A_2 are the best outcomes for the firm and fit the MAXIMAX decision criterion (choose the best of the best possible alternatives). Finally, B_2 is the worst possible outcome for the firm. By launching now, the firm avoids this outcome, thus fitting the MINIMAX decision criterion (choose the alternative that minimizes chances of maximum possible loss).

Obviously, the decision tree can be made more complex—and more realistic—by introducing the possibilities of lead times, first-mover advantage, and more innovative, competitive responses than mere imitation. Nonetheless, this simple example serves to illustrate the analytic process.

Projection: What Do We Expect Our Competitors to Do?

To answer this question, the firm must, in effect, put probabilities on the various options generated under competitor evaluation. In particular, management must estimate the likelihood that a competitor will continue its current strategy rather than make some significant change. A good starting point for projecting competitor action is attempting to understand what the competitor is trying to achieve. For example:

- What are the competitor's objectives in this market? Understanding objectives is a good starting point for predicting likely resource allocations.
- What market segments will the competitor address in the future, and on what bases will it seek to secure its objectives, for example, price leadership, operational excellence, product leadership, or distribution strength?
- What is the competitor's staying power in this market? Over and above a projection of likely competitor strategies is the question of determination to stay in the market. Is the competitor in the market for the long run, or can the firm expect a withdrawal if the going gets tough, either in the focal market or in other businesses? (It should not be assumed that competitor withdrawal is necessarily in the firm's best interest. A parent company may not strongly support a division competitive with the firm but, if released via an LBO or acquisition by a more committed organization, this competitive division may become a much stronger and more difficult competitor.)[27]

A more thorough approach is for the firm to develop several competitive scenarios.

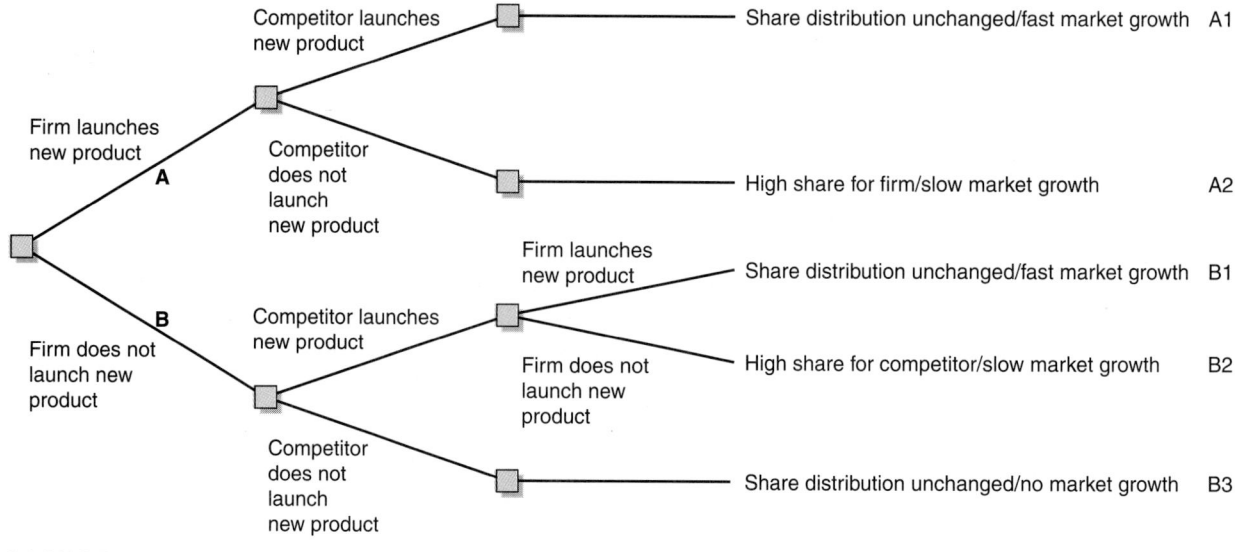

FIGURE 5.7

Illustration of a Decision Tree

The decision tree in the figure shows:

- Firm launches new product (A)
  - Competitor launches new product → Share distribution unchanged/fast market growth — A1
  - Competitor does not launch new product → High share for firm/slow market growth — A2
- Firm does not launch new product (B)
  - Competitor launches new product
    - Firm launches new product → Share distribution unchanged/fast market growth — B1
    - Firm does not launch new product → High share for competitor/slow market growth — B2
  - Competitor does not launch new product → Share distribution unchanged/no market growth — B3

SCENARIOS Scenarios are a valuable approach to projecting future competitor actions.[28] They are descriptive narratives of plausible alternative projections of how some future will evolve. Alternative scenarios allow the firm to compare and contrast how the competitor's actions might unfold under various conditions and assumptions, and suggest implications for the firm's own actions.

Scenarios have several important attributes:

- **Articulated plot and logics**: The "story" comprises a set of events and rationales that an individual can follow.
- **Internal consistency**: The logic must be internally consistent.
- **Specified time frame**: A time frame must be specified for key events, actions, and results.
- **Decision/action oriented**: Implications for the firm's current and future decisions must be derived and demonstrated.

Scenarios incorporate:

- **An end state**: An outcome at some point in the future.
- **A plot**: What the competitor must do to get to the end state.
- **Driving forces**: The conditions, trends, events, and other circumstances that shape or drive the story described in a particular plot.
- **Logics**: The evidence and rationale for the end state and the plot.

Scenarios can be of three major types:

- **Emergent scenarios**: Start with the competitor's current strategy and consider what might emerge.
- **Unconstrained what-if scenarios**: Based on open-end "what if" questions that suggest possible end states.
- **Constrained what-if scenarios**: Ask what the competitor might do under different sets of market or industry conditions.

A good example of a scenario is shown in Figure 5.8.

If the firm wants to make a prediction about what the competitor will actually do, it can select the most likely course of action from a set of alternative competitor scenarios.

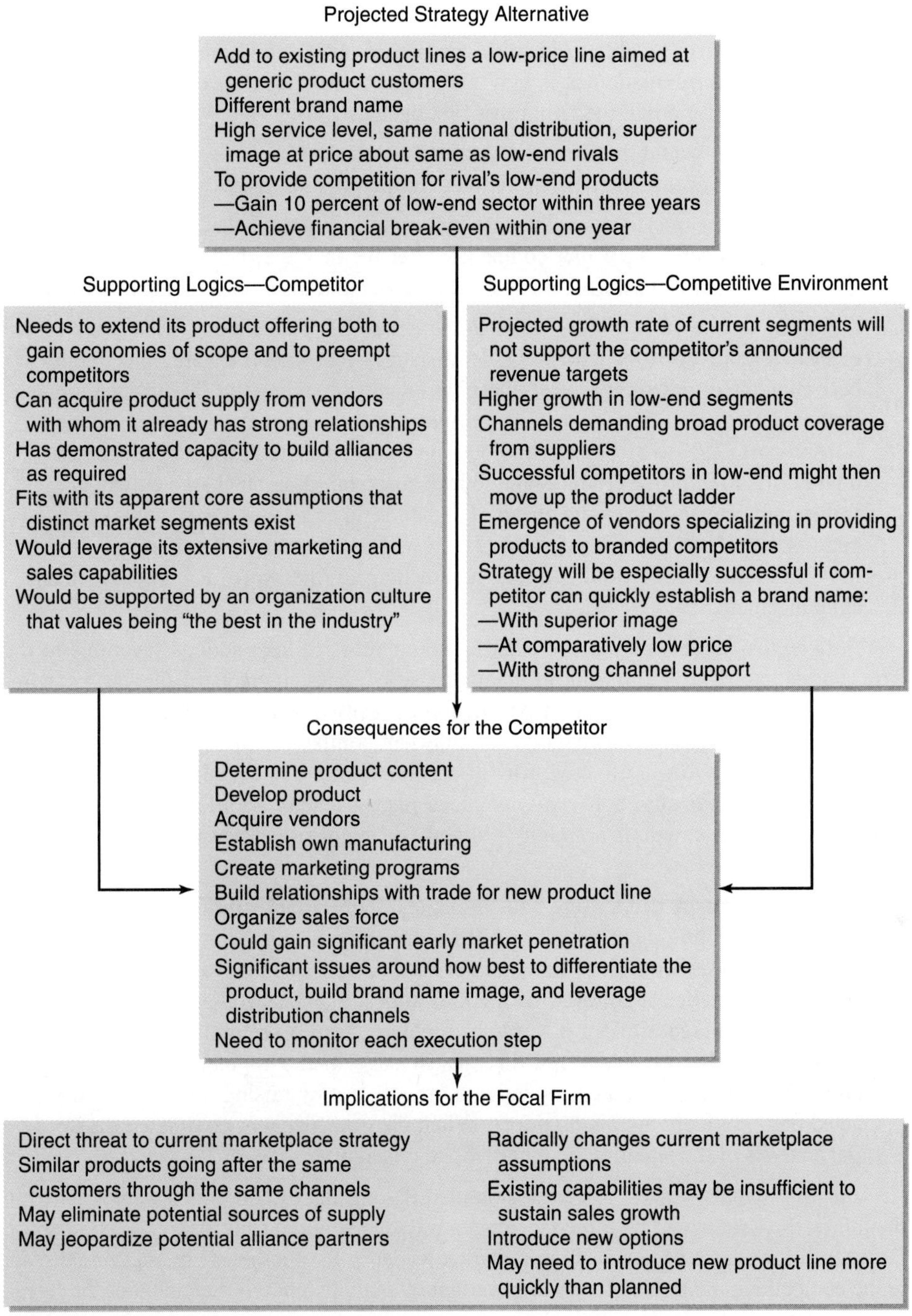

Projected Strategy Alternative

Add to existing product lines a low-price line aimed at generic product customers
Different brand name
High service level, same national distribution, superior image at price about same as low-end rivals
To provide competition for rival's low-end products
—Gain 10 percent of low-end sector within three years
—Achieve financial break-even within one year

Supporting Logics—Competitor

Needs to extend its product offering both to gain economies of scope and to preempt competitors
Can acquire product supply from vendors with whom it already has strong relationships
Has demonstrated capacity to build alliances as required
Fits with its apparent core assumptions that distinct market segments exist
Would leverage its extensive marketing and sales capabilities
Would be supported by an organization culture that values being "the best in the industry"

Supporting Logics—Competitive Environment

Projected growth rate of current segments will not support the competitor's announced revenue targets
Higher growth in low-end segments
Channels demanding broad product coverage from suppliers
Successful competitors in low-end might then move up the product ladder
Emergence of vendors specializing in providing products to branded competitors
Strategy will be especially successful if competitor can quickly establish a brand name:
—With superior image
—At comparatively low price
—With strong channel support

Consequences for the Competitor

Determine product content
Develop product
Acquire vendors
Establish own manufacturing
Create marketing programs
Build relationships with trade for new product line
Organize sales force
Could gain significant early market penetration
Significant issues around how best to differentiate the product, build brand name image, and leverage distribution channels
Need to monitor each execution step

Implications for the Focal Firm

Direct threat to current marketplace strategy
Similar products going after the same customers through the same channels
May eliminate potential sources of supply
May jeopardize potential alliance partners

Radically changes current marketplace assumptions
Existing capabilities may be insufficient to sustain sales growth
Introduce new options
May need to introduce new product line more quickly than planned

FIGURE 5.8

Scenario for a Yogurt Competitor: Low-Price Market Entry

Reproduced from Fahey, *op. cit.*, Table 16.3, p. 458, by permission.

Management: How Can We Get Our Competitors to Do What We Want Them to Do?

Not only may the firm be able to identify competitor options and predict future strategy, but under certain circumstances it may also be able to shape a competitor's actions. However, as a starting point, the firm must first decide:

- What actions would the firm like competitors to take?
- What actions would the firm prefer that competitors not take?

Answers to these questions lead to decisions regarding actions that the firm might take, or signals it might send, such that competitors behave in ways that are beneficial to the firm.[29] Perhaps the most powerful are *deterrent* signals that discourage competitive entry.

> **Example:** In the early 1970s, Texas Instruments (TI) published a strategy statement in a report to stockholders. Under a sharply focused corporate objective of becoming the dominant producer in each product field it entered, TI outlined four elements of this strategy: aggressive pricing to follow experience curve reductions in cost (25% to 30% for each doubling of accumulated production); continuing efforts to improve products and reduce costs; building on shared experience; and keeping capacity growing ahead of demand.[30] The message to potential competitors was clear. Enter if you want, but it will be a very tough game played by our set of rules! No doubt, many would-be entrants were deterred by this announcement.[31]

Pre-emptive signals may cause existing competitors to take actions favorable to the firm. For example, at equilibrium in many industries, market shares of the various competitors approximate their shares of production capacity. As a result, discouraging competitor plant capacity additions may be an important competitive objective; plant capacity announcements may be an effective way of accomplishing this end. In industries such as chemicals, the relationship between announced plant capacity additions and actual plant capacity coming on stream is not high. A slightly different signal was sent to a firm in the Far East:

> **Example:** Firms A and B were both strategically important subsidiaries of major U.S. multinational chemical companies competing in the Asia-Pacific region. Essentially these firms shared the market but, whereas firm A was the profitable market share leader, it believed firm B was at best a break-even operation. When the general manager of firm B was to be replaced, firm A secured information on his successor. It was discovered that this manager had a reputation as a "turn-around" manager, earned not by volume growth, but by raising margins. Firm A acted pre-emptively by raising prices. When the new manager completed his initial analysis of the situation he inherited, he raised prices, also!

Warning signals suggest to competitors that if some set of conditions were reached in the future, the firm would be forced to act in a way that would disadvantage the competitor. For example, a senior executive from a market leader in the toothpaste market might react to the competitive incursion of a product variant by making a public statement of the form:

> **Example:** We believe there is a place in the market for a natural toothpaste, but if market share reached 3%, that could be a real problem for us and we would necessarily have to protect our market position!

"Tit-for-tat" strategies are ways of bringing competitors into line. In executing these strategies, the firm avoids making unilateral gains; it matches, but does not exceed, competitor actions. It responds immediately to competitive moves, focuses on its own results, and attempts to allow competitors to forecast firm responses.

> **Example:** A strong, incumbent U.S. firm was facing sharp price competition from a new Japanese entrant. Rather than respond directly, U.S. management

instructed the firm's Japanese subsidiary to cut prices sharply. The Japanese firm stopped competing on price in the United States!

How to Secure Insight on Competitors

To answer the questions asked in the preceding sections requires a significant amount of competitive information.[32] We discuss both types and sources of competitive data.

TYPES OF COMPETITIVE DATA   The sorts of information the firm should collect should span the corporate, business unit, market, and market segment levels. It should be both qualitative, such as quality of management and anticipated strategic thrusts, and quantitative, such as profitability and market shares. It should also be comprehensive, including not only data on marketing and marketing-related issues, but also from areas such as operations, finance, cost and transfer pricing systems, logistics, and R&D.[33]

SOURCES OF COMPETITIVE DATA   The firm should attempt to develop multiple sources for obtaining particularly important data. For individual competitor analyses, data is sometimes present within the firm; the critical issue is to develop a process that brings this data to the appropriate part of the organization where it can be analyzed. In other cases, competitor data must be gathered from outside the firm.

In general, competitor data can be considered as primary, or secondary. Primary data implies a focused effort to secure information. Secondary data implies that the information is already available, but needs to be collected, sorted, and given meaning in the context of the questions management wants to answer.

PRIMARY DATA   Primary data sources include the firm's executives, salesforce, and other employees, such as R&D personnel who come into direct or indirect contact with competitors via professional activities essential to their work. Other important sources are the competitor's suppliers, distributors, and customers (who may overlap with the firm); trade associations; and industry specialists, such as consultants, investment bankers, and stock market analysts.

SECONDARY DATA   Sources of secondary data include several types of competitor communications. Examples include those required of a corporate entity (annual reports, 10Ks), marketing communications (advertising, promotional literature), and other periodic communications such as news releases, articles in the business press or local newspapers where the competitor is headquartered or has a facility, and patent filings. Communications from the competitor's customers may provide useful information, but perhaps the fastest growing source of competitive information is the Internet. In addition to the competitor's Web site, search engines such as *Yahoo!* and *Excite* can guide the analyst to multiple sources of competitive information. Other commonly available services will deliver competitive data automatically to preset criteria and information overload can be avoided using filtering technology.[34] See Table 5.2 for alternative data sources for various competitive concerns.

It is of course important not just to collect competitive data but to understand what the data means. In the previous section on managing competitors, several deliberate signals were noted that one competitor might send to another—deterrent, pre-emptive, warning, and "tit-for-tat." However, in addition to these types of signal, the firm may make important inferences about the competitor from information that was not intended as a competitive signal (Table 5.3)

Of course, the firm should always be aware that competitors might deliberately spread misinformation as a way of throwing the competition off the scent.

Example: In the late 1980s, Square D's competitors read in an industry trade journal that it planned to shrink the delivery time of its circuit boards and other customized components used in commercial buildings from ten to 12 weeks down

Table 5.2 Posture: Sample Internal and External Data Sources

Generic Modes of Competition	Sample Internal Sources	Sample External Sources
Product line	Marketing, sales and other personnel Industry studies conducted by the firm's own personnel	Competitors' product catalogs Industry trade associations Industry specialist consulting data firms Trade industry press

Features	Sales, marketing, engineering personnel
	Product observation
	Various product analyses conducted by a range of internal personnel
	    Product tear-downs
	    Product trials/comparisons
	    Sales force analysis
		Industry trade publication product reviews
		Competitors' promotion material
		Consultants' product review
		Specialist product assessment groups
		Customer-oriented publications

Functionality	Reverse engineering Manufacturing sales and other personnel assessments Product comparison studies	Customers' reports Retailer comments Distributors Specialist trade/industry observers Competitors' sales literature
Service	Service personnel comparisons Special studies conducted across multiple types of customers	Assessments of end-customers and channel members Competitors' sales and marketing materials Third-party assessments
Availability	Distribution and logistics personnel Sales force reports	Customers' survey Reports of channels Competitors' statements Studies by industry specialists and other third parties
Image and reputation	Marketing, sales, and advertising personnel Special tracking studies of competitor's individual promotions and advertisements	Competitors' advertising and promotion content Perception of end-customers and channels Research and surveys by others
Selling and relationships	Sales force reports Assessment by executives and others after visiting customers and channels	Interviews with selected end-customers and channel members
Price	Marketing, sales, and service personnel Sales force reports Interviews with customers and channels.	Competitors' price lists Retail and channel price lists and actual prices Interviews with end-customers

Reproduced from Fahey, *op.cit.*, Table 5.3, p. 133, by permission.

to one week. To its competitors, this plan, which required holding larger inventories and getting its employees to work overtime, seemed ridiculous in an industry that demanded customization and skilled labor.

In fact, Square D had discovered that customers would pay a substantial premium for faster delivery and had devised a new system for order taking, product design, and assembly to satisfy the unmet demand. However, it needed time to switch to new methods and find distributors that could implement the new approach. The story in the industry journal was false, but convincing competitors it was going in the wrong direction provided Square D with the head start it needed.[35]

Table 5.3 A Competitor Enhancing Its Customer Service

Indicators	Inferences
Hired new "customer service manager"	Alerts analyst that competitor is going to upgrade and renovate the quality of its service to customers
Reorganized customer support and service unit (CSSU)	Initial confirmation of alerting signal
CSSU now reports to VP of marketing (rather than sales)	Signals increased importance of service by the competitor
Initiating new training programs for sales force	Service is to be enhanced for all key customer segments
Emphasizes customer service in advertising	Service is of value in attracting and retaining customers
Comment of president: "Customers expect quality in services as well as in the product"	Service is becoming part of the competitor's mind-set—it will be institutionalized
Customer to our salesperson: "ABC is now doing things for us they never did before"	Confirms that service is being institutionalized and leveraged

Reproduced from Fahey, *op. cit.*, Table 4.1, p. 90, by permission.

PROCESSES FOR SECURING COMPETITIVE DATA Several specific processes are available for firms to structure their data gathering efforts:

- Formation of a competitive intelligence department responsible for collecting, analyzing, and distributing competitive information[36];
- Development of a competitive intelligence system whereby all firm employees that secure data on a particular competitor forward that information to a centralized site that checks, sorts, digests, and sends out the information to those who need it;
- Institutionalization of a shadow system in which individual executives or teams are given the responsibility to "shadow" specific competitors, and are charged with being able to answer the sorts of questions indicated previously;
- Formal review of business lost and business gained;
- Formal development of strategic plans for the competitor as part of the firm's strategic planning process;
- Gaming with multifunctional teams in which groups of executives are placed in the role of competitors in a competitive situation and asked to develop action plans.

In competitor analysis, there should always be a concern with the ethics and legality of collecting data on competitors. Clearly, there are a variety of illegal methods available for gaining information on competitors, including theft, wiretaps, and the placing of "moles" in competitors' organizations.[37] Other methods, though not necessarily illegal, may be considered unethical, such as pumping competitor employees for information on their employer in job interviews, especially if the firm has no intention of making job offers.

There is no need for, nor wisdom in, engaging in illegal or unethical behavior. Good competitive information can be secured by perfectly legal means. Organizations are inherently leaky; the lack of good, competitive information is normally attributable to unfocused data gathering efforts or allocation of insufficient resources.

COMPLEMENTERS

A broad definition of complementer would include any organization (except customers) whose activities positively impact the firm's sales. This section concentrates primarily on horizontally equivalent firms in the channel system.[38] The discussion is divided into three parts, based on the type of complementary firm: independent organizations, the firm itself, and competitors.[39]

Independent Organizations as Complementers

Perhaps the most obvious examples of complementarity are those found in economics, such as bread and butter, and coffee and cream. Other examples include laboratory equipment and laboratory chemicals hardware and software, and printers and toners. Suppliers can also be important complementers, an idea embedded in the TQM (total quality management) philosophy of forming partnerships with suppliers.

> **Example:** Demand for PCs made with Intel chips is dependent on the availability of software from Microsoft and others needing higher capacity machines. Correspondingly, Microsoft's software sales are highly dependent on the sales of personal computers, particularly on the continuing advances in chip design made by Intel.
>
> Telephone manufacturers are complements of network system providers. Customers will not be able to use Caller ID unless it is both provided by network suppliers and built into the circuitry of the telephone.
>
> Similarly, Sony and Tivo have agreed that Sony will manufacture the next generation of video recorders that save television programming to a hard disk (rather than a videotape), based on Tivo's design.[40]

Another example concerns home laundry. Design changes in clothes washers and dryers have major implications for detergent manufacturers. Furthermore, fabric design for clothes has important implications for both machine and detergent manufacturers. To the extent that clothes designers innovate with respect to fiber content and fabric design, the ability to clean clothes in the home may be affected.

These examples indicate that it may well be in the interest of complementers to interface with each other. In-home laundry example, there is significant value for machine and detergent manufacturers, fabric designers, and synthetic fiber manufacturers to collaborate on innovation to ensure that advances in one sector are aligned with complementary sectors.

The previously noted examples concern what might be termed as *strong* complementarity. A good example of *weak* complementarity is shopping malls. The sheer diversity of offerings from multiple stores provides consumers with a broad choice and acts as a magnet to draw them from large distances.[41]

The Firm as Complementer

Sometimes it is advantageous for the firm to develop relationships with complementary suppliers; on other occasions, it may be beneficial to offer the complementary product under its own name. For example, in France, in addition to passenger tires, Michelin sells the Michelin Guide book; the more people travel, the more they experience tire wear, and tire sales increase! A second example concerns financing organizations. Early in the twentieth century, General Electric formed the General Electric Credit Corporation (GECC) as a vehicle to offer financing for consumers to purchase its electrical home appliances; General Motors (GM), Ford, and Chrysler formed similar organizations to assist in the sales of their automobiles.

A particularly difficult issue is whether or not the firm should make a complementary product for a competitor. In its pre-Lexmark existence, IBM refused to make and sell supplies for competitive typewriters and printers, despite the fact that these were high margin items. Another example concerns General Motors Acceptance Corporation (GMAC): a long-running question for GM has been whether or not to allow GMAC to offer financing for non-GM vehicles, a dilemma exacerbated by the growth of multifranchise dealerships. This particular issue has taken on added importance during lean years in the automobile industry when much of GM's total profit has been generated by GMAC.

Another difficult issue occurs when a customer purchases products from several of the firm's business units. If the customer is satisfied with each of these relationships, everything is fine. But if dissatisfaction occurs with the product from one unit, sales from the other may be jeopardized. Relatedly, the manner in which the firm deals with one customer may affect its relationships with other customers.

> **Example:** When a major bank's leasing customer experienced financial difficulties and missed a payment, the leasing department placed a lien on certain customer assets to protect the bank's investment. Because other bank customers had independent relationships with the leasing customer, the lien caused them significant problems and negatively affected their own relationships with the bank.

Competitors as Complementers

Competitors act as complementers in a number of ways. For example, several competitors may be developing technology to meet a market need. Since customers face the uncertainty of which technology will ultimately be successful, and the risk that the product they purchase will be rendered obsolete by another technology, sales may be held back. In such situations, formal agreements among competitors to set standards may help grow the market. By collaborating with competitors the firm may be better off trading a dominant position in a small market for a less strong position in a much larger market.

> **Example:** In the consumer videotape market, Sony was first to enter with its Betamax format. One contributing reason for its failure was that JVC offered its VHS format to competitors. These competitors helped expand the market for VHS and ultimately led to Betamax's market demise.

> **Example:** For similar reasons, Intel allowed competitors AMD and Cyrix access to its MMX technology that enables chips to handle graphics and video better.[42]

At least one reason for the troubles at Apple Computer was Apple's refusal to allow other firms to manufacture computers based on Macintosh technology. As a result, virtually all other manufacturers settled on the PC format. A recent example of avoiding this problem is the agreement between Toshiba, Matsushita, Philips, and Sony on the format for DVDs.

A related example embraces bankcards for use at ATMs. For many years, innovator Citibank was successful in operating its own proprietary system. However, as national and international networks grew, customer value offered through networks exceeded that available from Citibank, and eventually it joined these network systems. A somewhat subtler example concerns the emerging biotechnology industry where commercialization success by an individual firm such as Monsanto or DuPont increases acceptance of products from this industry for all producers.

A different type of complementarity concerns the impact of competitor firms on suppliers. Dell and Compaq are fierce competitors, but they are also complementers. To the extent that each firm is successful in computer sales, chip volume is higher than for each firm individually. Resulting scale economies in chip manufacture should reduce chip costs and prices, ultimately leading to lower PC prices and increased sales volume for each firm. In a similar fashion, competitors frequently join together in trade associations that can lobby governments for favorable treatment, or engage in advertising and promotional activities to enhance sales for all.

Yet another type of complementarity with competitors concerns the front office versus back office distinction. In many industries, firms compete fiercely with competitors in one aspect of a product/market, yet complement and collaborate with those same organizations in another. For example, retail brokerage houses compete for retail investors, yet in clearing their trades, they rely on a high degree of collaboration with competitors. Investment banks compete for lead underwriting positions when corporations issue equity and debt, yet the losing banks frequently collaborate in forming syndicates to distribute the issues.

Other examples abound. Competitive Italian tile manufacturers join together to purchase freight to ship their goods around the world, and competitive U.S. paper makers routinely swap products at list price to save freight costs. The airlines, which compete for passenger traffic, collaborate in interline arrangements designed to ensure that passenger luggage moves efficiently from airline to airline.[43]

Sometimes complementarity may lead to difficulties if one organization does not want to be the complementer of the other:

> **Example:** Callaway Golf has been very successful with its oversize *Big Bertha* golf clubs. Golf ball manufacturer, Spalding, advertised its *Top-Flite/Club System C* balls, stating that they help improve play with *Big Bertha* clubs. Despite disclaimers that the balls had no connection with Callaway golf, Callaway sued for trademark infringement, false advertising, and unfair competition (ultimately settled out of court). Later, Callaway launched its line of *Callaway Rule 35* premium golf balls.

SUMMARY

Chapter 4 discussed customers; this chapter focused mainly on competitors. It presented a framework for identifying, describing, and evaluating competitors, and projecting and managing their actions. It also offered a variety of methods of gaining competitive insight. In addition, the chapter introduced complementers and described several types of complementarity. However, as the business environment changes ever faster and becomes more complex, managers will increasingly be unable to see other organizations simply as customers, competitors, or complementers. Rather, they may expect the firm's relationships with individual organizations to be multifaceted, possibly as customer, competitor, complementer, and supplier simultaneously. The complexity of dealing with an individual organization in so many roles will stretch the firm's managerial capabilities. However, as discussed earlier, a true external orientation at least endows the firm with the right perspective in asking the tough questions.

THE CHANGING VIEW

Old Way	New Way
Limited attention to competitor analysis	Much increased emphasis on competitor analysis
Focus only on direct competitors	Focus on broad competitor set, including both indirect and supply chain competitors, actual and potential
Competitor description only	Analysis/projection widespread
Competitive analysis of concern to sales and marketing only	Multifunctional involvement
Suppliers supply raw materials	By forward integration, suppliers are potential competitors
Customers purchase the firm's products	By backward integration, customers are potential competitors
Industry structure given	Industry structure a variable
Competitive consolidation nationally	Competitive consolidation (rationalization) globally
Independence assumed	Interdependence recognized, sometimes nurtured
Competitive strategy low priority	Competitive strategy high priority
Passive/reactive competitive strategy	Active/proactive competitive strategy
Local/regional/national competitive focus	Multicountry, regional/multinational/global competitive focus

Old Way	New Way
Focus on product-market level	Multilevel focus (corporate/SBU/product-market)
Cooperative options ignored	Cooperative options (alliances) considered
Competition among firms	Competition among networks
Conflict-based views of competition only	Collaborative arrangements more common
Ethical considerations often ignored	Ethical considerations becoming more salient

QUESTIONS FOR STUDY AND DISCUSSION

1. Indirect competition is always more difficult to confront than direct competition. Discuss.

2. Focus on a firm in an industry of interest to you. Identify its suppliers, customers, competitors and complementers. How do they interact?

3. Low probability/high impact threats can be devastating if they materialize. On the other hand, a successfully externally oriented firm may be able to identify an enormous number of potential competitive threats to its future. How would you go about setting up a system to choose which low-probability threats might be worthy of further investigation and analysis?

4. Some managers believe they are ethically justified in using any tactics that a particular competitor has deployed against them. Do you agree with this view? Why or why not?

5. Discuss the importance of counterintelligence in today's competitive environment.

6. What do you expect will be the impact of global competition on ethical standards in corporations? As CEO of your own corporation, how would you address the issues raised by your answer?

7. On April 21, 1999, leading computer company Compaq ran a full-page advertisement in *The New York Times* shortly after Eckhard Pfeiffer "resigned" as CEO. The advertisement, in the form of a letter from acting CEO Ben Rosen, "To the people of Compaq," indicated that while searching for a new CEO, Compaq, which had acquired Digital Equipment Company (DEC) a year or so earlier, would be run by a three-man office of the Chief Executive. The letter focused on Compaq's strengths, in particular its human resources, and the need to accelerate the pace of change. As a competitor of Compaq, what signals would you extract from this letter?

8. In May 1999, one month before a planned initial public offering (IPO) by Barnesandnoble.com, Amazon.com started offering 50% off all bestsellers, effectively selling these products at cost. How do you interpret Amazon's action?

9. Attempting to identify potential competitors is wasted time and effort. Better to gear your firm for a fast reaction to a new threat after it materializes. Discuss.

10. Some evidence suggests that large companies are much more inclined to dismiss competitive threats as insubstantial. Do you believe this to be true? Why or why not? How would you attempt to ensure that a successful large company retains a competitive outlook?

11. Many strategists argue that pre-emptive competitive strategy is most successful. Managers are inclined to view this approach as expensive. How would you make an economic case for pre-emption? (Hint: A well-developed decision tree might help.)

12. The structural model is of limited use in projecting competitive behavior. Discuss.

13. Interdependent networks of firms make the task of competitive analysis more difficult. Do you agree with this statement? Why or why not?

14. Do you believe that the process of global consolidation in existing industries will simplify the generation of competitive strategy?

15. Most firms show little imagination or insight in strategy formulation. Thus, for most companies, the term competitive strategy is an oxymoron. Discuss.

16. Vertical competitive threats from suppliers or customers have been much increased by new technology. Discuss.

17. The history of cartelization strongly suggests the superiority of the conflict, rather than collaborative, model of competition. Discuss.

18. What are the advantages and disadvantages of using the Internet as a tool of competitor analysis?

19. Companies that are enjoying considerable success run the risk of losing their competitive edge. How would you use the ideas presented earlier to prevent this from happening?

20. Choose a competitive situation with which you are familiar and analyze two of the competitors using one of the analyses presented here. What insights can you generate? What did you learn about the advantages and disadvantages of the analytic method you chose?

21. Are there legal or ethical issues raised by complementer relationships? Use the Microsoft/Intel (or other examples with which you are familiar) as a sample case to help you answer this question.

22. The U.S. Department of Defense is so named because its job is to defend the security of the United States. It does so by identifying potential targets and addressing them to remove the incentive for a would-be aggressor to attack. Are these principles applicable in the business world? How would you go about applying them?

23. Some graduate students were asked by their previous employers to play the role of researcher or potential customer at a trade show to gather competitor information surreptitiously. Would you hire students for this purpose? Discuss the ethical issues involved.

24. Merger and acquisition screening, as well as corporate-level competitor analysis, have become the same under the influence of inter-industry competition. Discuss.

ENDNOTES

1. This model was developed from Porter's (1980) general formulation of competitive forces, M. Porter, *Competitor Strategy: Techniques for Analyzing Industries and Competitors*, New York: The Free Press, 1980.

2. In some instances, a key goal of the acquisition is to secure management talent to direct and manage the acquiring firm.

3. See "New Life Through Chemistry," *The New York Times*, February 11, 1998.

4. The *mutual* form of organization, such as ownership by policyholders (insurance) or account holders (savings organizations) is relatively common in the financial services industry and has a long history. De-mutualization is occurring in many countries; among major entities that have de-mutualized are The Equitable (now AXA), The Prudential, and the British building society, The Halifax.

5. The essence of marginal cost pricing is to set prices based on direct product costs without any allocation for overhead costs. Sales gained in this manner provide a positive contribution but will not in total offset all overhead costs. If all fixed costs are covered by domestic sales, very competitive export prices may result, leading to allegations of "dumping" by existing competitors in affected importing countries.

6. Strategic alliances may offer either direct or indirect competition.

7. The firm itself may also form partnerships with its suppliers.

8. For an excellent treatise on partnerships, see J.D. Lewis, *Partnerships for Profit: Structuring and Managing Strategic Alliances*, New York: The Free Press, 1990.

9. In pyramid-structured sales forces, in addition to earning commissions from direct sales of products, salespeople earn overrides on the sales of products made by salespeople that they recruit, and so on, typically for several levels.

10. If the indirect competitive threat is too great, forces may build that cause governments to remove or amend the offending regulations.

11. An alternative term for business scope is *mission,* discussed in Chapter 19.

12. See Citibank N.A., in N. Capon, *The Marketing of Financial Services: A Book of Cases*, Englewood Cliffs, NJ: Prentice Hall, 1992.

13. For the Steel Division as a whole, structural steel was a more profitable building technology than reinforced concrete, although the latter used a considerable amount of steel.

14. See K. Harrigan, *Strategies for Vertical Integration*, Lexington, MA: Lexington Books, 1983.

15. H. Simon, *Hidden Champions: Lessons from 500 of the World's Best Unknown Companies*, Boston, MA: Harvard Business School Press, 1996.

16. This issue is addressed in more detail in N. Capon, *Key Account Management and Planning*. New York: The Free Press, forthcoming, 2001.

17. Xerox Corporation: The Customer Satisfaction Program, *Harvard Business School*, 9-591-055.

18. M. Porter, *The Competitive Advantage of Nations*, New York: Free Press, 1990. The highly competitive National Basketball Association (NBA) and the dominance of the United States in Olympic basketball is an interesting example of this principle in action.

19. Sharing technology with competitors is one manifestation of the increased complexity in interorganizational relationships.

20. See "Financial Guaranty Insurance Company," in N. Capon, *op. cit.*

21. Based on a competitor analysis framework in L. Fahey, *Outwitting, Outmaneuvering and Outperforming Competitors*, New York: Wiley, 1999.

22. Ideally this analysis should be conducted in the context of a more general objective, systematic analysis in which the firm assesses itself versus competition via an analysis such as SWOT—strengths, weaknesses, opportunities, and threats.

23. In marketing usage, the prisoner's dilemma is typically exemplified in a pricing format. However, the managerial decision could involve other marketing variables, such as new product introduction, service delivery, or advertising.

24. In several jurisdictions around the world, such "signalling" may lead to price fixing allegations.

25. The "expected value" of an outcome to the firm is the value of that outcome multiplied by the probability of its occurrence.

26. Figure 5.8 contains an implicit assumption that the market is elastic to innovation or marketing effort.

27. Consider organizations competing with the Discover card issued by Sears Roebuck's one-time subsidiary, Dean Witter. Faced with poor profitability in its core store operations, Sears spun off Dean Witter. Now joined with Morgan Stanley, Dean Witter in general, and Discover in particular, are much stronger competitors.

28. This section is based on Fahey, *op. cit.*, Chapter 16.

29. For an excellent discussion of signalling, see Fahey, *op. cit.*, Chapter 4.

30. April 18, 1973 report to stockholders. Paraphrased in D.F. Abell and J.S. Hammond, *Strategic Marketing Planning: Problems and Analytic Approaches*, Englewood Cliffs, NJ: Prentice Hall, 1979. Interestingly, while it may have deterred competitors, TI's espoused strategy was not highly profitable. For a full discussion of the experience curve, see Chapter 9 Appendix.

31. Some managers assert that competitive signalling should focus on the FUD factor: spread fear, uncertainty, and doubt.

COMPETITORS AND
COMPLEMENTERS

32. For a good source on securing competitive information, see L.M. Fuld, *Competitor Intelligence: How to Get It—How to Use It*, New York: John Wiley, 1985.

33. See D.R. Lehmann and R.S. Winer, *Marketing Planning*, Homewood, IL: Richard D. Irwin, 1996

34. Conversely, firms can develop software to identify which of their own Web pages are searched by competitors.

35. *The Economist*, January 24 1998.

36. In general, competitive analysis should be conducted close to the market but, in multibusiness firms, a corporate department focused on competitive data gathering and analysis may allow some economies to be achieved.

37. In 1997, *Business Week* reported that industrial espionage was rising in the United States, often driven by foreign governments; in particular, France, Israel, China, Russia, Iran, and Cuba were cited as the most aggressive. In 1996, the FBI reported 800 pending probes of thefts by foreign companies and governments, double the total for 1994! (*Business Week*, July 14, 1997). However, other countries were also targeted. For example, also in 1997, France requested the removal of several U.S. diplomats for allegedly spying on French preparations for the World Trade Organization (WTO) agreements.

38. A broad definition of complementarity would also include relationships with firms to secure resources it does not currently possess, either in type or in insufficient quantity. For example, it may enter into formal agreements to gain access to resources including formal joint ventures, R&D partnerships and supply, joint production, joint marketing, joint distribution and co-branding agreements.

39. Based in part on A. Brandenburger and B.J. Nalebuff, *Co-opetition*, New York, Doubleday, 1996.

40. *The New York Times*, Sept. 9, 1999.

41. In the early days of marketing as an academic subject, the power of stores to draw consumers was formalized as Reilly's law of retail gravitation.

42. *Fortune*, July 7, 1997.

43. One major exception is the highly profitable Southwest Airlines, which is not a part of interline agreements for transferring baggage across carriers.

WEB RESOURCES

A. L. Williams	www.travelersla.com
Amazon	www.amazon.com
Amway	www.amway.com
Airbus	www.airbus.com
AMD	www.amd.com
American Home Products	www.ahp.com
Anderson Consulting	www.ac.com
Apple Computer	www.apple.com
Arthur Andersen	www.arthurandersen.com
AT&T	www.att.com
AXA	www.axa.com
Barnes and Noble	www.bn.com
BHP	www.bhp.com.au
Boeing	www.boeing.com
Braniff	www.braniffinternational.org
Callaway	www.callaway.com
Canon	www.canon.com
Chase	www.chase.com
Chrysler	www.chrysler.com *or* www.daimlerchrysler.com
Ciba Geigy	www.novartis.com
Ciba Specialty Chemicals	www.cibasc.com
Citibank	www.citibank.com
Citicorp	www.citicorp.com
CitiGroup	www.citi.com

Clariant International	www.clariant.com
Compaq	www.compaq.com
Cyrix	www.viatech.com
Cytec	www.cytec.com
Dell Computer	www.dell.com
Diageo	www.diageo.com
Dell	www.dell.com
Digital	www.digital.com
Dreyfus	www.dreyfus.com
Du Pont	www.dupont.com
The Equitable	www.equitable.com
Excite	www.excite.com
Fidelity	www.fidelity.com
Financial Guaranty Insurance Company	www.fgic.com
Ford	www.ford.com
Fortune Magazine	www.fortune.com
Fuji	www.fujifilm.com
Gateway	www.gateway.com
General Electric	www.ge.com
General Motors	www.generalmotors.com
GMAC	www.gmacfc.com
Goldman Sachs	www.gs.com
Grand Metropolitan	www.diageo.com
Guinness	www.guiness.com
The Halifax	www.halifa.co.uk
Intel	www.intel.com
JVC	www.jvc.victor.co.jp/english/index-e.html
Kodak	www.kodak.com
L.L. Bean	www.llbean.com
Lands' End	www.landsend.com
Lucent Technologies	www.lucent.com
Matsushita	www.panasonic.com
MBIA	www.mbia.com
MCI	www.wcom.com
Michelin	www.michelin.com
Microsoft	www.microsoft.com
Minolta	www.minolta.com
Monsanto	www.monsanto.com
Morgan Stanley Dean Witter	www.msdw.com
National Basketball Association	www.nba.com
New Jersey Nets	www.nba.com/nets
New York Jets	www.newyorkjets.com
New York Rangers	www.newyorkrangers.com
New York Times	www.nytimes.com
New York Yankees	www.yankees.com
Nikon	www.nikon.com
Novartis	www.novartis.com
Philips	www.philips.com
Praxair	www.praxair.com
Rhodia	www.rhodia.com
Rhone Poulenc	www.rp-rorer.com
Salomon Brothers	www.salomonsmithbarney.com
Sandoz	www.novartis.com

Solutia	www.solutia.com
Sony	www.sony.com
Southwest Airlines	www.southwest.com
Spaulding	www.spaulding.com
Sprint	www.sprint.com
Square D	www.squard.com
SSDG	www.ssdg.com
Texas Instruments	www.ti.com
The Travelers	www.travelers.com
Tivo	www.tivo.com
Toshiba	www.toshiba.com
Union Carbide	www.unioncarbide.com
World Trade Organization	www.wto.com
Xerox	www.xerox.com
Yahoo!	www.yahoo.com
Zeneca	www.astrazeneca.com

CHAPTER

6

IDENTIFYING OPPORTUNITIES FOR CREATING SHAREHOLDER VALUE

LEARNING OBJECTIVES

When you have completed this chapter, you will understand

- the relationship between shareholder value, customer value, and total quality management

- the critical elements for creating increased shareholder value—profitable growth and improved profit margins

- the fundamental elements comprising a growth strategy, the nature of the criteria for evaluating individual growth options, and alternative implementation methods

- key methods of raising profit margins

- why marketing managers must be aware of these methods

INTRODUCTION

This chapter focuses on approaches to completing marketing *Task 1: Determine and Recommend Which Markets to Address.* Earlier, we emphasized the importance of attracting and retaining customers as the key underpinning for making profits, ensuring firm survival and growth, and enhancing shareholder value. This chapter begins by discussing the rise of the shareholder value philosophy and develops the relationship between delivery of value to shareholders and delivery of value to customers. We close a virtuous circle by relating these ideas to the evolution of total quality management (TQM). Then the two basic drivers of shareholder value are introduced: *profitable growth* by expanding and/or diversifying away from current business, and *improving profit margins* on current business. Most of the discussion focuses on the various options for both securing profitable growth and increasing profit margins.

SHAREHOLDER VALUE, CUSTOMER VALUE, AND TOTAL QUALITY MANAGEMENT

In many capitalist countries, particularly the United States, the shareholder value philosophy is deeply rooted; management's job is to maximize returns to shareholders.[1] Most large public companies in countries such as the United States, Great Britain, and Australia are financed in reasonably well-regulated but extremely competitive capital markets in which managerial underperformance is likely to provoke active opposition from shareholders, if not unfriendly takeover bids.[2] In other parts of the world, formal and informal regulation has generally tended to favor management rather than shareholders, providing it with many protections against unwelcome merger and acquisition advances from other companies or individuals. Some Asian companies and politicians have become ardent advocates of this form of capitalism, although, following the share and currency market crises that battered so many Asian countries in late 1997, these arguments seem significantly weaker. Certainly, the shareholder value philosophy is having a significant impact on the way in which nongovernmental continental European firms in France, Italy, The Netherlands, and Germany are managed. Even in Japan, such conservatively run companies as Matsushita, have instituted share repurchase plans, provided stock options for senior executives, and linked managers' salaries to share performance.[3]

The process of globalization and the consolidation that ensues suggest to us the inevitable spread of the shareholder value philosophy. As share ownership spreads in a country, whether directly or indirectly (via actively managed pension funds), the emerging political power of the shareholder will, assuming a modicum of democracy, ensure it continues. Thus, although management may occasionally talk of the firm's various stakeholders, the shareholder takes priority in the eyes of more and more senior managers.[4]

Rappaport notes several reasons for the rise of the shareholder value philosophy[5]:

- The threat of corporate takeover by those seeking undervalued, undermanaged assets
- Impressive endorsements by corporate leaders who have adopted the approach
- Growing recognition that traditional accounting measures such as earnings per share (EPS) and return on investment (ROI) are not reliably linked to the value of the company's shares[6]
- The reporting of shareholder returns and other financial measures in the business press
- A growing recognition that senior executives' long-term compensation should be tied more closely to shareholder returns[7]

Under the shareholder value concept, economic value is added and shareholder value increased when a firm not only makes a profit but makes sufficient profit to earn a return on its investment at least equal to its cost of capital.[8] Conversely, if the firm's ROI is less than its cost of capital, it is destroying both economic and shareholder value. Indeed, the estimated value of the firm's discounted future cash flows should be greater than the disposable value of its tangible and intangible assets to justify its continued existence.

We should also note that calculation of shareholder value is based primarily on estimates of future cash inflows and outflows and is grounded in economic rather than in accounting concepts, hence the EVA (economic value added) acronym.[9] Indeed, Rappaport, an accountant, spends an entire chapter (2) of his book pointing out the shortcomings of accounting data and explaining why they have led to incorrect managerial decisions. Perhaps the problems with accounting data are best exemplified in the debate over the "pooling" method, widely used to account for acquisitions. The Financial Accounting Standards Board (FASB) has proposed to bar "this disreputable form of accounting" because, as a veteran observer noted, "Pooling accounting is ridiculous because it allows companies to pretend that they paid much less for an acquisition than they did."[10]

Customers are the source of all cash inflows, with the exception of new investment or debt. Unless these customers see value in the products and services available, they will be unwilling to part with their resources, typically money, to acquire them. The basis of all markets is this exchange, wherein both buyers and sellers receive value. Buyers prefer the seller's products and services to their own resources; sellers prefer the buyer's resources to their products and services.

As discussed earlier, it is the firm's ability to attract and retain customers that creates its value. Within a competitive framework, we should ask why customers purchase from one supplier rather than from another. The answer is simple: because they believe, rightly or wrongly, that they will receive better value from one supplier than from the other. Customers assess this value by comparing the benefits they receive from one supplier for a certain price with the benefits they receive from a competitor supplier for a different price. This simple calculus, properly developed, provides an exceptionally valuable tool for understanding competitive positions in markets.[11]

Thus, the creation of customer value is at the crux of the creation of shareholder value. With striking parallelism, the same conclusion was reached by the quality movement, albeit after a long odyssey. Figure 6.1 vividly describes the painful evolution experienced by so many companies as they wrestled with the total quality concept.[12] The rewards from achieving stage 4 are evident. Although the comparisons are limited by the accounting data available in the PIMS database,[13] Figure 6.2 demonstrates the dramatic relationship between quality and return on sales (ROS).[14]

Additional evidence for the quality relationship is provided by *Business Week* (BW). For several years, BW tracked the share price of winners of the United States's Malcolm Baldridge National Quality Award versus the S&P 500 share price index.[15] BW found that the share price of this relatively small sample of firms consistently outperformed the index by a factor of 3:1; stockpickers take note![16]

As we have seen, the apparently straightforward concept of shareholder value raises more questions than it answers. This is often the case with financial theory, where the focus on capital markets too often assumes away the complexities of product markets and, in this case, the very real difficulty of forecasting future cash flows, let alone being responsible for creating them! (To give credit to Rappaport, he goes to some lengths to demonstrate these linkages.) Our perspective is perhaps best captured by paraphrasing George Day, who argued, there can be no shareholder value without customer value.[17]

Grounded in the critical importance of delivering customer value, a recently developed approach to viewing shareholder value focuses on the ratio of the firm's market value to sales revenue (Æ).[18] In this formulation, firms with Æs over 1.5 are creating value, firms with Æs under 1.0 are destroying value, and firms in which Æs are between 1.0 and 1.5 are in a stability zone. The trajectory of a selection of leading companies that have made serving customers the central focus of their strategies is quite instructive (Table 6.1).

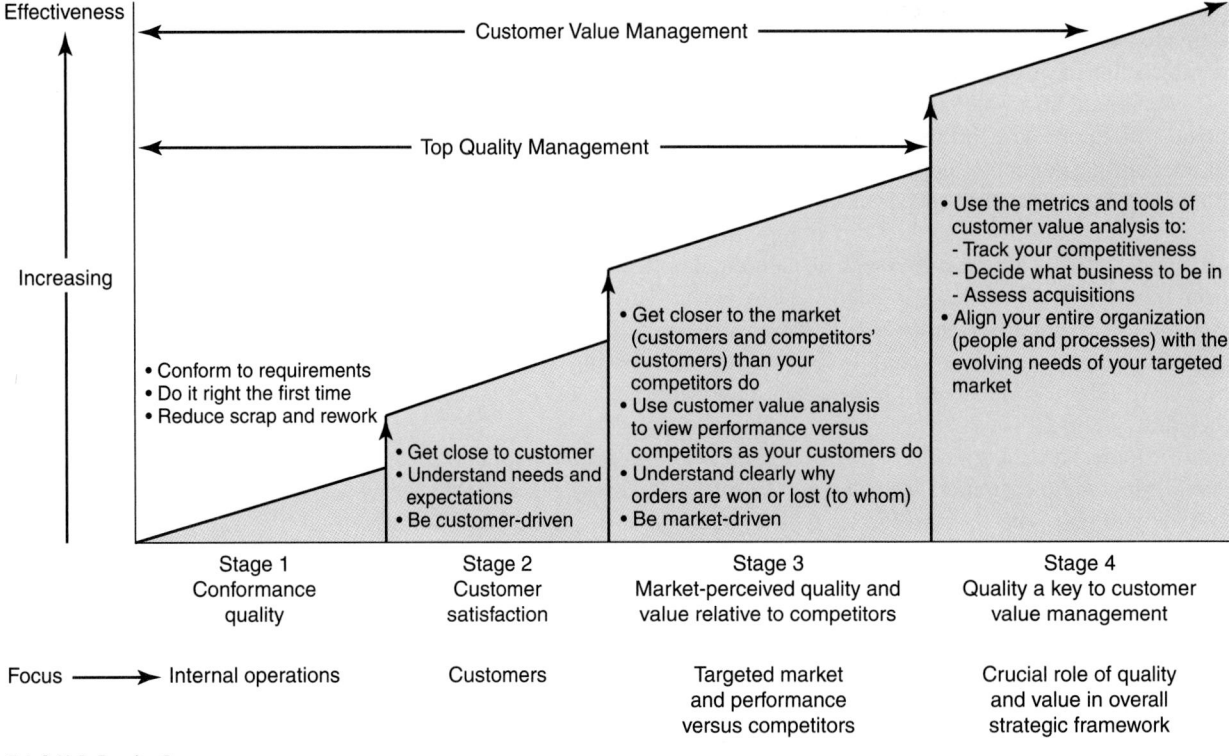

FIGURE 6.1

Total Quality Chart

IMPROVING SHAREHOLDER VALUE: OPTIONS FOR PROFITABLE GROWTH

This section focuses on **growth**, one of two major drivers for improving shareholder value. The next section addresses the second major driver, **profit margins**.

A strategy for growth must deal with three separate but interrelated matters. As with any strategy, it should (1) provide guidance in the selection of alternatives to be funded; (2) specify screening criteria with which to examine the generated alternatives; and (3) identify potential implementation methods.

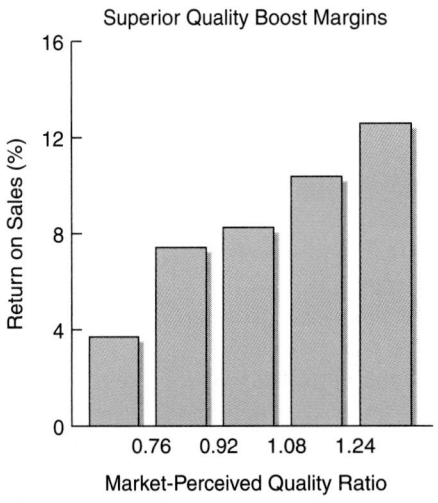

FIGURE 6.2

Relationship between Quality and Return on Sales

TABLE 6.1   Building Shareholder Value: Ratio of Market Value to Sales Revenues

Company	Early Period	Middle Period	Recent Period
General Electric	0.6 (1980)	1.0 (1987)	2.1 (1996)
SMH (Swatch)	0.4 (1987)	0.9 (1991)	1.9 (1996)
Charles Schwab	0.3 (1987)	1.1 (1992)	2.5 (1996)
Disney	1.2 (1984)	2.0 (1990)	2.3 (1996)
Thermo Electron	0.7 (1984)	1.3 (1990)	2.7 (1996)
Microsoft	6.4 (1989)	6.6 (1993)	8.3 (1996)
Intel	2.0 (1984)	3.1 (1992)	5.2 (1996)

Guidance for the Allocation of Resources

The framework presented here provides guidance for resource allocation across three dimensions: growth path, timing of entry, and compatability (or *fit*). First, however, the firm must be clear about its objectives.

OBJECTIVES   Long-run **growth** of sales revenues is critical for securing increased shareholder value. However, whether this sales growth is achieved from existing operations or from new ventures, investors seek higher returns from more risky investments.[19] Thus, any management strategy aimed at increasing shareholder value should consider the risks associated with specific ventures as well as the impact these ventures will have on the firm's overall business portfolio. Important dimensions of risk include the following:

- **Demand risk**: Is there a market?
- **Competitor risk**: Who will enter and what resources will they deploy?
- **Firm risk**: Does the firm have the competencies and resources to succeed?
- **Political risk**: How stable is the local government and will it (or its successor) take actions to make the market less attractive?
- **Physical environment risk**: Are natural disasters likely to affect the business?

As a consequence of these expectations, management may seek to achieve more **stable** returns, possibly trading profit quantity for profit quality, where high-quality profit is defined as a consistent stream of economic profit over time.

Example: A well-known ski resort was faced with a critical choice. One option was to develop ski trails on a neighboring hill. A second option was to invest in facilities such as mountain slides and outdoor staging for the local symphony orchestra that would make the resort more attractive to summer visitors. It elected to develop the summer facilities because of a desire to even out revenue and profit streams throughout the year.

Example: Schneider Electric Mexico focuses on markets that it can serve through its distribution channels rather than attempting to secure large business from major electricity generation projects that would lead to highly fluctuating sales revenues.

If management is to pay attention to the risk profile of the firm's portfolio of businesses, it must have a means of incorporating the underlying risk inherent in a venture or portfolio of ventures into its analysis. Such a tool is introduced in the following section when growth path and venture portfolio are discussed.

Yet, even a conscientious assessment procedure cannot protect against the unforeseeable. As discussed, the pace of change today is so fast that forecasting the future, especially the technological future, is fraught with peril. To deal with this problem, the firm needs

IDENTIFYING
OPPORTUNITIES FOR
CREATING
SHAREHOLDER VALUE

"insurance policies" to provide the necessary **flexibility**. Several types of "insurance" are available. For example, assuming the research and development (R&D) investment barrier is not too high, the firm may choose to investigate several competing technologies for solving particular problems. However, when the required investment increases, some form of technology-sharing agreement with other firms may provide insurance. This agreement may take the form of providing venture capital to startup companies with an option to buy, or taking equity stakes in new companies, as with major drug companies and new biotechnology firms. Alternatively, joint technology-development agreements with other firms, such as those promoted by MITI in Japan for many years, may be feasible. A specific example occurs in the resources industry, particularly oil exploration, where even large corporations such as Shell, Exxon, and BP often participate jointly in exploration activities to pool risk.

In summary, volume growth is critical in creating shareholder value. However, unmitigated revenue growth can ultimately destroy shareholder value. All too often, initially successful companies overextend themselves. Another way to frame this issue, however, is to say that they failed to recognize the risks associated with their strategies and that, without the flexibility to deal with the crisis, the resulting instability led to failure.

GROWTH PATH Although, in theory, a firm can pursue an infinite variety of growth options, in practice individual options seem more or less attractive based on the firm's core competencies, embraced in its current portfolio of businesses, technologies, products, and markets. Within the direction and constraints of where to seek business provided by the organizational mission (corporate or business),[20] the firm should approach its search for alternative growth opportunities by considering the interrelationships between specific opportunities and the firm's current competencies.

One way to array these alternatives is in terms of a product/technology dimension (existing, related, new), and a market dimension (existing, related, new), thereby developing the nine-cell matrix shown in Figure 6.3.[21] Used appropriately, this growth path matrix can assist the manager in being explicit about the degree of risk associated with various categories of options so that return/risk trade-offs can be intelligently made.[22]

Although nine cells are depicted in this matrix, four archetypal approaches for growth are embedded.

Market Penetration Growth focuses on the firm's existing set of products and markets. A firm using this growth strategy invests in its current businesses; it neither seeks new

Market \ Products/Technologies	Existing	Related	New
Existing	Market penetration	Product extension	Product expansion
Related	Market extension	Business extension	Business expansion, Concentric markets
New	Market expansion	Busines expansion, Concentric products	Conglomeration

FIGURE 6.3

The Growth Path Matrix

markets nor develops new product forms. Growth is secured via market penetration, selling existing or slightly modified products to its existing markets of current customers, competitors' customers, and nonusers. Inasmuch as this form of growth is consonant with the firm's core competencies, the market penetration option has the least knowledge risk. (Of course, such a strategy may involve significant risk if strong competitors are attacking its current market positions.)

Product Growth The matrix framework distinguishes two types of product growth strategy, extension and expansion, based on the closeness to, or distance from, the firm's current business on a product/technological dimension. In both cases, the new products are offered to the firm's existing markets. All things equal, because product expansion is more distant from the firm's technological base than product extension, it is more risky.[23]

> Example: For a bank skilled in making corporate loans, lock-box services might be considered a product extension; a product expansion might be complex derivative products that require significant new technological expertise. Ski resorts that expand their range of offerings beyond skiing to include ice-skating, downhill sledding, dog-sledding, snowmobiling, and tubing are practicing product extension.

Market Growth Again, two types of market growth strategy are identified, extension and expansion, based on closeness to, or distance from, the firm's current business on a market dimension. In neither case does the set of products offered change substantially.

> Example: For a bank skilled at making corporate loans, loans to public or non-profit enterprises might be considered a market extension; making loans to individual consumers might be a market expansion. Alternatively, for a domestically based firm in the English-speaking world, entry into another English-speaking country might be considered a market extension; entry into a non–English-speaking country might be considered a market expansion.

As with the two product strategy options, the more different the new markets from those currently targeted by the firm, the greater the risk.

> Example: Banc One, a consumer-oriented bank in Ohio, was an early licensee of Visa (formerly Bank Americard); it developed a processing capability for credit card slips. Management realized that as other banks became licensees, an opportunity existed to become a third-party processor for banks nationwide. Banc One entered this business, and for many years, profits from its processing activities were greater than those from its traditional banking business! (In 1998, Banc One merged with First Chicago NBD Company to form Bank One.)

> Example: Porsche is on the cutting edge of automobile technology. In addition to making and selling its own automobiles, it has developed a highly profitable "rent-an-engineer" business for such projects as Opel Zafira, DaimlerChrysler's A-Class, Smart Micro-car, Linde forklifts, the Airbus cockpit, and Harley Davidson big bikes. Initially conceived as a way to keep its engineering team intact during downturns, 1999 revenues from its contracting business were just short of $500 million (15% of total).[24]

Product and Market (Business) Diversification The four cells in the bottom-right corner of the matrix differ greatly from those previously discussed. Whereas in each of the previously discussed strategies a change is made on no more than a single dimension, for these strategies, change occurs on each of the two key dimensions, market and product/technology. Business extension requires moderate change (extension) on both the market and product/technology dimensions; the three other strategies require greater change. The greatest change is for conglomeration where both the market and product/-technology are new; for this double expansion strategy (conglomeration), the level of risk is clearly greatest.

Example: Good examples of failure from attempting this type of diversification, discussed elsewhere, were the acquisitions of computer company NCR by AT&T, and Snapple by Quaker.

Using the Growth Path   The growth path matrix can be used as a cross-sectional device to aid in managing a portfolio of ventures. If the venture portfolio for a firm or business unit were heavily laden with bottom-right corner alternatives, management and investors alike might have reason to be concerned about the overall high-risk profile. Such a portfolio might be appropriate for a venture capital firm but not for the typical corporation or business unit.[25] Conversely, complete firm/business unit attention on market penetration to the exclusion of other growth paths might suggest that the management team is ineffective in taking risks and exploring new opportunities.

A second issue concerns whether management should adopt a growth strategy focused on *product* growth or on *market* growth. The trade-off here is between market opportunity and organizational competence. If the sets of product-centered and market-centered opportunities are essentially equivalent, the firm's competence should dictate the choice. Thus, firms with high levels of technical expertise might be better off pursuing a *product*-growth strategy; conversely, firms whose strengths relate more to developing markets might prefer a *market*-growth approach. However, when management is unable to identify sufficient opportunities to exploit the firm's capabilities and resources or when its capabilities and resources do not match attractive opportunities, management should consider enhancing the firm's competence base to allow it to pursue these opportunities.[26]

To be used effectively, the firm/business unit should develop criteria so that individual opportunities may be placed in the various matrix cells. Furthermore, it might set differential rate of return cut-offs based on the risk profiles of these various kinds of alternative opportunities (Figure 6.4).[27]

A more longitudinal application reflects growth dynamics. At a particular point in time, an individual firm may succeed with many different growth strategies, related to available opportunities, organizational competencies, and the associated potential returns and risks. Indeed, management fashions change, and the conglomerate form that was much favored in the United States in the late 1960s and early 1970s has given way to a more focused approach, exemplified by the use of phrases such as "back to basics" and "stick to the knitting." Nonetheless, Rumelt's classic research suggests that companies that grow by

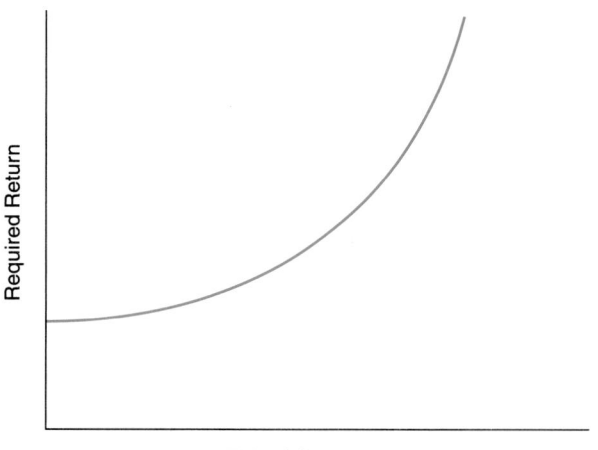

Risk of Opportunity

FIGURE 6.4

Required Rates of Return

maintaining some degree of "relatedness" in their businesses, for example, products/technologies or markets/customers, are more profitable than those diversifying in unrelated manners.[28]

Such gradual or evolutionary diversification typically implies lower risk because the firm uses more of its existing strengths, while simultaneously reducing transition costs by imposing lower stress on existing resources and competencies. Thus, the firm may secure some portfolio benefits of risk diversification yet still capitalize on the strengths and capabilities deriving from specialization. Furthermore, with experience, management may learn that the firm's risk profile differs for new products/technologies versus new markets; for example, a new product/technology growth path may, in general, be less risky than one involving new markets. Firms that move out from existing product/markets gradually (related-growth strategies) commit to evolutionary learning strategies. Over time, the existing product/market scope expands, becoming a growing absorbing state as the previously unknown moves closer to the known.

However, it would be a mistake to assume that firms should necessarily prefer opportunities with low risk to those with higher risk. Risk is only one of two key dimensions to be considered in the growth strategy decision; the other is potential return. Although all product/markets may converge to general equilibrium in the long run, at any point in time, some markets offer higher returns because of market imperfections driven by factors such as barriers to entry and government regulations; others are more competitive and afford only low margins. Indeed, if forecast profits in the firm's current product/markets are low, diversification away from this current business may be the only way for the organization to meaningfully improve shareholder returns. The growth path matrix should be viewed as a tool facilitating better management of risk, not as a means to quash all really new initiatives.

> **Example:** In the early 1980s, an analysis of American Can (AC) revealed that its businesses had significant excess capacity, were highly investment intensive, and operated in slow-growth markets in which buyers were oligopsonistic (few and strong). Anxious to increase ROI, CEO Woodside sold all of AC's businesses and engineered its transition into a financial services company, Primerica, where investment was low and distribution was a critical success factor.[29]

This example demonstrates the complexity of developing a growth strategy, especially when we consider the various implementation options. For example, conglomeration and business expansions generally are risky strategies. However, a *de novo* entry based on the firm's own R&D efforts may be more risky than acquisition of a successful ongoing operation. Regardless, it is clear that the firm's growth path across product/market cell boundaries is an extremely important matter.

TIMING OF ENTRY   For growth paths that involve some degree of newness in products/technologies and/or markets, the growth path framework addresses neither conditions in the market to be entered nor the capabilities and competencies needed for successful entry. Critical conditions concern market growth and size, future market potential, nature and level of competition, and so forth. In later chapters, we discuss strategic options at different phases of market development organized around a life cycle framework. In this section, we focus on market entry and the organizational resources required for entry at different phases of market development. We distinguish among two broad market types, undeveloped and developed markets, noting two possible entry strategies for each market type (Table 6.2).[30]

Undeveloped Markets—Pioneer   *Pioneers* do not enter existing markets; they create new ones. The products and services they bring to these markets typically result from consistent and extensive R&D spending. Some companies develop an overall strategic thrust and a risk-taking internal corporate culture that accepts the inevitable failures but, nonetheless, enables them consistently to be successful pioneers. Such companies must develop R&D

TABLE 6.2 Timing of Market Entry

Market Type	Market Entry Strategy
Undeveloped	Pioneer
Undeveloped	Follow-the-leader
Developed	Segmenter
Developed	Me-too

skills that enable them to develop new products and services, as well as a set of marketing skills so they can introduce the products into the uncharted waters of new markets. Typically, such companies require a degree of "organizational slack" so that they can commit the required human and hardware resources when the new markets they develop require them. In addition to these skill sets, they need the financial resources to support both heavy and consistent R&D expenditures and the costs of market development that often rival the hard R&D expenses![31] Companies that commonly pioneer new products include DuPont, 3M, Sony, and major pharmaceutical firms.

Successful pioneers may be able to secure limited monopolies (e.g., patents) on their discoveries and enjoy the high margins resulting from these positions. To secure this advantage, many pioneers employ armies of patent lawyers intent on protecting the firm's intellectual property.

> **Example:** In 1998, Ballard, the Vancouver-based firm pioneering fuel cell technology as a replacement for the internal combustion engine in automobiles, held more than 300 patents.[32]

Even when monopoly positions cannot be achieved, firms that successfully pioneer new markets may enjoy first-mover advantages, a set of benefits that accrue simply because the pioneer was the first entrant. This notion is discussed in more detail later, but suffice it to say, these advantages may last for many years. The more successful the pioneer in developing these advantages, the more difficult the competitive challenge for follower firms.

> **Example:** In the early 1980s, Merrill Lynch pioneered the Cash Management Account (CMA), which offered check-writing privileges, a credit card, and a margin account. Over 20 years later, Merrill Lynch still maintains the lead market share in this product form.

Christensen makes an interesting distinction between sustaining and disruptive technologies: *sustaining* technologies (either incremental or radical) are responsive to the needs of current customers, whereas, initially at least, *disruptive* technologies satisfy the needs of a different customer group.[33] He finds that current suppliers largely pioneer sustaining innovations, whereas new entrants often pioneer disruptive technologies. This behavior results from three related factors. Initially, the disruptive technology has inferior performance on the critical attributes required by customers of the then-current technology. Second, initial expectations of volume and profit margin in the disruptive technology are less attractive than investment to serve the needs of current customers. Third, following from the first two points, resource allocation processes within current suppliers underfund R&D in the new technology.

Unfortunately for incumbent firms, as volume builds in the disruptive technology, incremental improvements eventually make it competitive in the original application and may ultimately put those suppliers out of business. To escape this trap, Christensen advocates pursuing development in a very different organizational context, either by setting up an independent unit within the firm or by taking an equity stake in a corporation set up to exploit the new technology.

Example: In the disk-drive product class, 14-inch Winchester and 2.5-inch drives, sustaining innovations for mainframe and laptop computers, respectively, were by and large pioneered by current disk-drive suppliers. By contrast, 8.5- 5.25- 3.5- and 1.8-inch drives, each disruptive technologies initially satisfying the needs of different customer groups—manufacturers of minicomputers, desktop personal computers, laptop computers, and portable heart-monitoring devices, respectively—were largely manufactured by different firms. In addition, flash memory, a further disruptive technology used for handheld PDAs (personal digital assistants), electronic clipboards, cash registers, electronic cameras, and so forth was pioneered by new entrants.[34]

Undeveloped Markets—Follow-the-Leader Whereas the pioneer places extensive effort in producing new-to-the-world products and services via high investment in research, *follow-the-leader* firms focus attention on development. Theodore Levitt captured the notion of this strategic approach in the phrase, "used apple" policy: Let someone else take first bite of the apple—if it looks okay, go ahead; if not, stop![35]

Follow-the-leader firms allow pioneers to spend the research investment needed to develop new products and services, then follow as soon as possible with a focus on developmental R&D. Critical to this strategy is an ability to move fast when it becomes clear that the pioneer has developed a potentially successful product or service. Important resource needs are good competitive intelligence so that developmental work can begin as soon as possible, good developmental engineers who can develop products based on the pioneer's R&D efforts, and "can do" patent lawyers to find weak spots in the pioneer's patent filings. In addition, such firms need the financial ability both to maintain high levels of development spending for as long as necessary to match/overtake the pioneer in customer benefits, and to invest in a market in which the pioneer has started to develop first-mover advantages. Examples of companies that tend to use follow-the-leader strategies are J.C. Victor, which successfully followed Sony into the home videotape market, and the Ethicon division of Johnson & Johnson, which has consistently and successfully followed U.S. Surgical's medical device innovations some 18 months later with lower prices.

Example: In 1995, Netscape was first to market in an area that Microsoft was not seriously addressing. When it became clear to Microsoft that the Internet would play a major role in the computer and telecommunications industry, it refused to be dominated by stranded (sunk) costs. Rather, Microsoft wrote off more than $100 million in R&D investment in other products, refocusing its efforts in a determined effort to surpass Netscape.

Developed Markets—Segmenter The segmenter strategy can be extremely effective when the market is fairly well developed. At this stage, customers typically have substantial experience with the product, and as they learn more about it, their preferences evolve, often becoming more specific. Under these conditions, through market research efforts, a *segmenter* may be able to conceptualize the market in a different manner from current competitors and offer products and services that truly satisfy the needs of one or more customer groups (segments). Because the market has now grown significantly, these segments can be very large.

Executing a segmenter strategy successfully requires a skill set that differs markedly from those for the two undeveloped market entry strategies. At this stage, technological expertise is no longer the driving force; rather, marketing research to understand customers and identify potential market segments, as well as the ability to successfully address narrow market niches, are the major skills required. In addition, a modular design philosophy and flexible operating systems that allow the firm to address several segments simultaneously (but at low cost) are important supporting elements of a segmenter strategy.

Example: Chrysler successfully introduced the minivan into the mature automobile market, a "segmenter" innovation copied by all major automobile manufacturers. Mazda similarly opened up a whole new segment with the much-imitated *Miata (MX-5)*.

Developed Markets—Me-Too The segmenter entry strategy relies on adding customer value by carving the marketing pie ever more finely. By contrast, the *me-too* entry strategy depends on the attraction of low prices offered to customers uninterested in the extra benefits offered by high-value segmentation strategies. To create shareholder value, me-too strategies require a low-cost position. Attention is therefore focused on reducing costs through value engineering, efficient high-volume production, low overhead, and aggressive procurement. Me-too companies typically have limited product lines and are leaders in process innovation. Their strategies can play havoc in segmented markets where several competitors make value-added offers.

Example: Emachines began business in the summer of 1998. Using slightly older technology components, for example, Intel's *Celeron* chip ($60) versus the *Pentium III* ($450), its PCs were priced under $600 (without monitor), substantially lower than competition. Emachines outsourced manufacturing, set lower gross margin targets than competitors (10% versus 15%), and had only 20 employees. Half its sales were to first-time buyers; the other half were extra PCs for families. By February 1999, Emachines had secured 9.9% of the U.S. home PC market. Faced with such fierce competition, former low-price leader NEC Packard Bell was forced to lay off 15,000 employees and Compaq was under severe profit pressure.[36]

Implications If we review the capabilities required to pursue any of these strategies it soon becomes evident that they are in potential conflict. A successful pioneer, for example, must spend heavily on R&D and market development—a major contrast with the demands placed on a me-too entrant. If an early entrant is determined to remain in a market in which such strategies emerge, substantial changes may be required. Failure to manage these transitions lies behind the demise of quite a few businesses. These issues are developed more fully later but for present purposes, we argue simply that management should formulate an entry policy for any operating business. Only then can the appropriate competencies be nurtured.[37]

Screening Criteria

Each firm, and possibly individual business units within a firm, typically have different views of the risk–return trade-off. Firms with more conservative managements (and investors) may accept only low-risk opportunities and consequently are prepared to accept lower potential returns; other managements (and investors) may be prepared to accept higher risks for higher potential returns.[38]

Regardless of management's view of the risk–return trade-off, the criteria used to evaluate alternative opportunities may be similar; just the acceptable levels on those criteria may differ.

QUANTITATIVE CRITERIA Quantitative criteria include the standard financial manager's tool kit involving such measures as shareholder value creation, cash flow, payback, ROI, profit margin, net present value, and internal rate of return. In addition, they concern measures that help predict the sales revenues on which the financial measures are based; these include current and potential market size, market growth rate, number of competitors, and forecast sales/market share at maturity.

QUALITATIVE CRITERIA An important criterion is the concept of **compatibility (or fit).** Related to growth path, fit addresses the question of whether the firm has the appropriate set of resources and experience to support successfully the proposed new product/

market entry. The concept of fit embraces three subconstructs: product–market fit, product–company fit, and company–market fit.

Product–market fit addresses the question of whether the product is appropriate for the market. This type of fit should be assessed through market research and market testing. Simply stated, does the product satisfy the needs of customers in the targeted market segments in such a way that it offers advantage over competitors?

Regardless of whether the firm assesses a good product–market fit, it may not have good **product–company fit**, the skills and resources required both to engage in continual product upgrading and to market the product successfully. Indeed, potential competitive response may be such that, despite the possibility of a successful entry, the firm does not have the depth of financial, human and other resources to be successful over the long run.

> **Example:** In the late 1960s/early 1970s, Godfrey Hounsfield, a brilliant scientist working for the British company EMI, developed the technology for the first CAT scanner. Although best known for recorded music (the Beatles were launched on the EMI label), EMI successfully introduced the first CAT scanner in the United States. However, severe competitive pressure from major players such as GE, Hitachi, and Technicare ultimately forced EMI's withdrawal from the market. The losses incurred in this venture were largely responsible for EMI's subsequent merger with Thorn PLC.[39]

In many markets, distribution strength is critical to getting the product to customers. If the firm's access to distributors is curtailed and it has no other way to reach these customers, regardless of the degree of product–market fit, there may be little sense in pursuing the opportunity directly. Many independent inventors find themselves in situations of good product–market fit yet poor product–company fit because they have little ability to have their products well distributed.

> **Example:** *Un-du*, a product that removes oil-based stickers, was developed by independent inventor Charles Foley and manufactured by Doumar Products Inc. It had extensive difficulty securing distribution despite winning the "best new product" award at the Business Product Industry Association show in 1996. While Doumar was still seeking distribution outlets, its competitor, Magic American, with $30 million in sales and well-established distribution capacity, introduced "Sticker Lifter" under its GooGone brand name.[40]

Even if product–market fit and product–company fit are acceptable, the decision to launch may not be made because of poor **company–market fit**. Such situations often occur in potential geographic expansions. For example, the firm may be skilled at manufacturing, promoting, and distributing the product in its home market and may ascertain through market research that a foreign market seems attractive. The problem is that the firm has no presence in, and little knowledge of, the foreign market. Thus, poor company–market fit may lead to a no-go decision.

> **Example:** In the early 1990s, Citibank launched credit cards in several Asian countries. Because it had operated in these countries for many years, it was well connected and had good company–market fit. By contrast, if its strong domestic U.S. competitor First USA attempted such an entry, despite strong product–company fit, it would be hampered considerably by its poor company–market fit.

Relationships Among the Three Forms of Fit One significant difference separates product–company and company–market fit from product–market fit. If the product is not appropriate for the market, under no circumstances should the firm pursue the opportunity because, by definition, the product does not sufficiently satisfy customer needs. However, if product–market fit is good but the problem rests with either of the two other forms of fit, various options are available.

For example, although the product may not fit the company that developed it, it may fit another company. Sale of the technology to a company better suited to manufacture and distribute the product or formation of a distribution agreement with a strategic alliance partner are alternatives for securing profitable returns on the firm's technological asset.[41] Similarly, with company–market fit, if good product–market and product–company fit are present, the skills required for achieving good company–market fit may be secured by forming strategic alliances with companies well positioned in the market.

DISTINCTIVE COMPETENCE   The criterion of distinctive competence addresses the question of whether the firm "brings anything to the party." That is, does this particular opportunity use the firm's core competencies? And/or, will pursuing this opportunity allow the company to develop new core competencies? If the answer to both of these questions is no, then regardless of how attractive the opportunity may appear when examined from a superficial financial perspective, the firm should probably not pursue it.

If the firm would not use any of its distinctive competencies in pursuing a particular opportunity, two possible situations follow. First, it is likely that some other firm will pursue this opportunity and, using its own distinctive competencies, will be a more successful competitor. Second, other opportunities probably exist where the firm, using its competencies, would be more likely to succeed.

SYNERGY   Positive synergy reflects the notion that $2 + 2 = 5$; in other words, the combination of resources that the firm brings to the opportunity allows it to secure greater returns than if resources had to be provided independently. For example, the firm may secure distribution synergy from a new product by selling it through existing distribution channels, or it may secure manufacturing synergy by producing the product with spare capacity. Lack of positive synergy is not a reason not to pursue an opportunity, but its presence may allow the firm to secure handsome returns.

Negative synergy embraces the notion that $2 + 2 = 3$. Negative synergy occurs when pursuing a new opportunity would cause revenues and profits from existing products to be reduced. For example, a new product is launched into a product category in which the firm is currently competing. From a financial perspective, the net revenues and profits (losses) from both the old and new products would have to be considered in evaluating the new opportunity.

However, the reality is more complex because the appropriate financial criteria are not *historical* revenues and profits, but rather *forecast* revenues and profits in the absence of the new entry. Although the firm's new entry may "cannibalize" sales from existing products, if the opportunity were not pursued, sales might be lost to a competitor anyway. Better that the firm retain those sales even if its margins are lower!

> **Example:** More than a quarter of a century ago, the major U.S. automobile manufacturers General Motors, Ford, and Chrysler were reluctant to introduce small cars because they were inherently less profitable and might cannibalize sales of their large, profitable automobiles. As a result, first Volkswagen and later Toyota, Nissan, Honda, and other Japanese companies were able to secure footholds in the U.S. market with small cars. Having learned about the U.S. market and built a distribution system to sell these small cars, the Japanese companies were well placed to introduce their higher-priced models. The original U.S. decision may have avoided some level of short-term cannibalization (negative synergy) but had a major negative strategic impact in the long term.[42]

Implementing a Strategy for Growth

Until the late 1960s, perhaps the predominant method for implementing a growth strategy was internal development. Major U.S. corporations such as DuPont, Kodak, and General Electric tended to place significant investment in R&D, then launch new products into whatever markets seemed appropriate. This era was exemplified by the widespread "not invented here" (NIH) syndrome in which products/technologies emanating from other corporations were believed to be inferior.

Since then, a variety of other means of implementing growth strategies has become more widely accepted, including acquisition, strategic alliance, licensing and technology purchase, and equity investment. Of course, these alternatives are not mutually exclusive, and a corporation that seeks the profitable growth mode of improving shareholder returns may implement a technology strategy comprising elements of several implementation methods. On the other hand, considerable advantages in experience may be gained by focusing mainly on one or more implementation modes.[43]

INTERNAL DEVELOPMENT   The internal development method of achieving growth is perhaps the most widespread among major corporations. Product-technology-driven growth mostly results from extensive R&D spending that leads to new product and service introductions. Indeed, the evidence suggests a strong positive correlation between R&D spending and corporate profitability.[44] This implementation method can apply to any cell in the growth path matrix. Even for market penetration, minor product/service modifications may be an important route to growth.

Internal development has several advantages over alternative growth modes. First, and most important, everything is done in house. As such, the firm has total control over the entire growth process. Required resources are purchased or leased by the firm, and the firm makes its own decisions about interorganizational relationships such as those with suppliers and distributors; in addition, shortfalls in human resources are dealt with by hiring to requirements and acculturating newcomers to the firm's way of doing business.[45] Second, to the extent that alternative means of securing product/market access are available (e.g., by acquisition), internal development may be less expensive.

The major disadvantages of internal development are resource access and timing. At the limit, some required resources may just be unavailable to the firm, or may be too expensive and/or too risky for the firm to develop or acquire on its own. Furthermore, internal development takes time. In an era in which market windows are shortening, in-house development may be a luxury the firm cannot always afford.[46]

Because of these problems, some firms are modifying the internal development process by developing mechanisms to cut through the corporate bureaucracy and tap the creative potential of the entire employee base. To generate ideas, those employees whose ideas turn into successful products are often rewarded with stock options or "phantom stock."

> **Example:** In 1997, Procter & Gamble (P&G) formed a Corporate New Ventures (CNV) group, funded with $250 million seed money, reporting only to top management. Using a corporate collaboration network, *My Idea*, employees throughout the firm funnel ideas to an innovation panel. Go-ahead projects may tap into P&G's entire global resource base. By late 1999, 58 new products had been launched. A new cleaning product, *Swiffer*, was launched in 10 months, half the normal time.[47]

ACQUISITION   Acquisition has become a favored method of growth for many companies.[48] The major advantage of this form of growth is speed. An acquisition brings immediate access to a new market with an in-place set of products, operational capabilities, organizational processes, and so forth.

> **Example:** In early 1999, major drug company Warner-Lambert purchased Agouron Pharmaceuticals, a small biotechnology company, for $2.1 billion in stock. Analysts said that the purchase enabled Warner-Lambert to bolster its

IDENTIFYING
OPPORTUNITIES FOR
CREATING
SHAREHOLDER VALUE

product line in the anticancer and antiviral areas, where it had expertise but few marketable products.[49]

In the late 1990s, AT&T made several acquisitions of Internet (Teleport, IBM Global Network) and cable (TCI, MediaOne) businesses to position itself for delivering multiple products into the home. Between 1993 and late 1999, Cisco Systems made 42 acquisitions.[50]

However, if the acquired entity is currently successful, a major disadvantage of the acquisition route is that a high acquisition price may dilute the acquiring firm's shareholder's interests. A second problem concerns cultural fit of the acquired organization with the acquiring firm. Far too often, it proves impossible to marry the cultures of the two entities, leading to internecine warfare and/or divorce.

Example: In 1984, in its first acquisition in 25 years, IBM entered the telecommunications business by purchasing Rolm. Five years later IBM sold Rolm to Siemens A.G. Observers commented that the immense culture difference between conservative IBM and free-wheeling Rolm was one of several reasons for the divestiture.

Of course, during the period of integrating the acquisition into the firm, close competitors are unlikely to be passive. For example, when Quaker acquired Snapple, Coca-Cola expanded its *Fruitopia* line and matched Snapple's advertising budget. Furthermore, the opportunity for poaching key executive talent is likely to be enhanced.

Several business leaders and scholars have spoken out against acquisitions. For example, George Bull (former CEO of Diageo) has asserted that organic growth (internal development) is value-creating for shareholders but that acquisition is value-destroying. Several studies have demonstrated that acquisitions tend to dilute value for acquiring firm stockholders[51]; Hayward and Hambrick showed that for acquisitions over $100 million in value, CEO hubris drove these unfortunate decisions.[52]

Example: In mid-1997, drug company Eli Lilly reduced the accounting (book) value of its drug distribution arm, McKesson, by $2.4 billion, over half the $4.1 billion acquisition price, a stark admission that it had overpaid.[53]

Nonetheless, it is important to distinguish broadly between two very different types of acquisition. On one hand are the large (often-unrelated) acquisitions that make the headlines and are the sort of acquisition studied by Hayward and Hambrick. On the other are the more modest acquisitions that may be part of an ongoing pattern or strategy.

Example: 3M is one of the United States's most diversified and innovative companies. Despite extensive internal R&D, from time to time in its history, 3M has made small acquisitions to "fill in" its technology portfolio. These acquisitions include roofing granules (1930s); gummed paper- and fluoro-products (1940s); electric splicing and insulation, ceramics, and extruded plastics (1950s); film manufacturing, photo equipment, and pharmaceuticals (1960s); and digital image systems, disk-drive systems, and computer printers (1970s).[54]

An acquisition may be of an entire corporate entity or of an individual business unit from a corporation that may be rationalizing its business portfolio and shedding unwanted businesses.

Example: In 1984, Black & Decker, a successful producer of power hand tools, was seeking to expand into the home. It purchased the small appliance business from GE, which, in turn, was seeking to rationalize its portfolio of electric appliances used in the home.

It is often alleged that big acquisitions are more difficult to implement than smaller ones. Furthermore, some research evidence suggests that a strategy of many small acquisitions may provide higher returns than one of a few large acquisitions. Growth strategies involving many small acquisitions may not make headlines but may be quite effective. For example, Microsoft, an organization with significant commitment to internal development, is nonetheless an active acquirer.

One reason for the apparent success of many small acquisitions may be that the firm gains considerable expertise in this type of growth strategy. As such, it may develop an acquisition system that lowers acquisition costs and improves acquisition effectiveness. Furthermore, market imperfections are common in the market for small acquisitions. Large acquisitions are usually highly publicized, and the acquiring firm is much more likely to pay a proportionately higher price.

> **Example:** Starting in the 1970s, Banc One pursued an acquisition strategy called the "uncommon partnership." Acquired banks maintained considerable autonomy, but several activities were centralized in Columbus, Ohio. As interstate banking rules were relaxed, the acquisition rate increased, and in the mid-1980s, Banc One was acquiring a small- or medium-sized bank every eight weeks! As a result, Banc One developed considerable expertise in identifying potential acquisition targets, concluding acquisitions, and integrating the acquired banks into Banc One. Between 1975 and 1997, Banc One's assets grew from $1.5 billion to $116 billion and its net income grew from $16.8 million to $1.3 billion.[55]

STRATEGIC ALLIANCES   In the compatibility (or *fit*) section of *Screening Criteria* we noted that even though product–market fit was acceptable, the firm might be dissuaded from pursuing an attractive opportunity because of poor product–company and/or company–market fit. In each case, the firm lacks some type or level of resource that would enable it to pursue market entry with confidence.

One way to secure these lacking resources is by forming a strategic alliance. In general, the selection process for a strategic alliance partner involves matching strengths and weaknesses to provide the combined entity with a competitive advantage greater than either firm acting alone. For maximum pay-off, it is important that the partners complement each other's strengths (or compensate for liabilities) and do not merely duplicate resources or abilities. Prototypical strategic alliances are between small, innovative firms with new technology, and large firms with strong marketing capability, good reputations with customers, and financial resources. In some fields, the anticipated investment in potential new technology is so large and the risks so great that firms joining together is the only feasible way to pursue the opportunity.

In an increasingly turbulent environment in which knowledge of both specialized technologies and markets is essential for success, firms of widely different sizes and backgrounds should consider strategic alliances as one alternative method of implementing a growth strategy. However, although strategic alliances provide an attractive means of securing access to resources and reducing both risk and required investment, they are no panacea for firms implementing growth strategies. Many strategic alliances fail for reasons ranging from incompatible organizational cultures to a shift in focus at one of the partners, leading to a lessened interest in the strategic alliance.[56]

LICENSING AND TECHNOLOGY PURCHASE   Licensing and technology purchase are alternative methods of securing access to technology developed by other organizations. They differ both in terms of payment and in the extent of rights to use the technology. Typically, a licensing agreement specifies both a minimum royalty payment (fixed payment regardless of degree of use) and an earned royalty rate based on some measure of volume, for example, units or dollars, or profits. Technology purchases typically are arranged for a fixed sum. In both types of agreement, the firm secures access to the technology, but licensing agreements may constrain its use by the buyer. For example, the licensor may restrict the licensee to certain markets, thus prohibiting access to other markets.[57]

The main advantage of these two forms of implementing a growth strategy is that the acquiring firm avoids the risks and expense of the R&D effort that developed the technology. The disadvantage is that it may have to pay a high price for a successful technology. Firms that adopt these practices for implementing growth strategy should develop rigorous search processes to identify potential technologies that may justify commercialization. Often, licensees are companies with excellent market access; licensors are often small, focused technology companies that lack such access.

EQUITY INVESTMENT Many major corporations have augmented their own R&D efforts by corporate venturing, the taking of ownership positions in start-up companies. Here, again, the firm avoids direct R&D costs but has an equity position that it may be able to increase if the start-up company is successful. The most successful ventures are those that have a strong strategic rationale where, for example, the technologies being investigated relate to the firm's own technology portfolio.[58]

> **Example:** Xerox Technology Ventures (XTV) was formed in the aftermath of Xerox's inability to capitalize on several innovations developed by its Palo Alto Research Center (PARC).[59] From 1988 to 1996, XTV invested in more than a dozen companies focused on Xerox-related technologies such as electronic publishing, document processing, electronic imaging, workstation and computer peripherals, and software and office automation. A conservative estimate of Xerox's success, ignoring various ancillary benefits such as collateral investment in other projects, is capital gains of $219 million from a $30 million fund, a net internal rate of return of 56%![60]

> **Example:** UPS invested in Video Networks, a firm whose product avoided the necessity of physically delivering videotapes by digitally transmitting television content, only after the marketing group concluded that it logically extended UPS's digital document delivery service.

PROFIT-MARGIN–RAISING OPTIONS FOR IMPROVING SHAREHOLDER VALUE

Just as growth path and timing of market entry frameworks play a valuable role in laying out a series of potential directions for seeking growth opportunities, the firm's value chain (also termed *business system*) provides a framework for generating opportunities for raising profit margins in current businesses. This section describes the value chain concept, identifies five alternative ways to increase margins within the context of the value chain, and introduces a framework for making related managerial decisions. Then, the discussion moves outside the value chain to identify further alternatives for raising margins and enhancing shareholder value. Finally, key reasons why marketing managers should be informed about these issues, some of which may not, on first glance, seem to be directly marketing related are identified.

The Value Chain

The business firm is an organizational device for converting raw materials into products for sale (inputs into outputs). The firm's value chain (Figure 6.5) is a conceptual device for identifying the many activities involved in this process. Individual firms may identify a smaller or greater number of activities, each of which adds value in the conversion process. In addition to the value-adding activities noted in Figure 6.5, several support activities (e.g., legal, public relations, accounting, personnel, regulatory affairs, maintenance, basic research, quality assurance, finance) must also be conducted.

Typically, a diversified firm made up of several business units has several value chains. Depending on the interrelationships among these business units, an individual

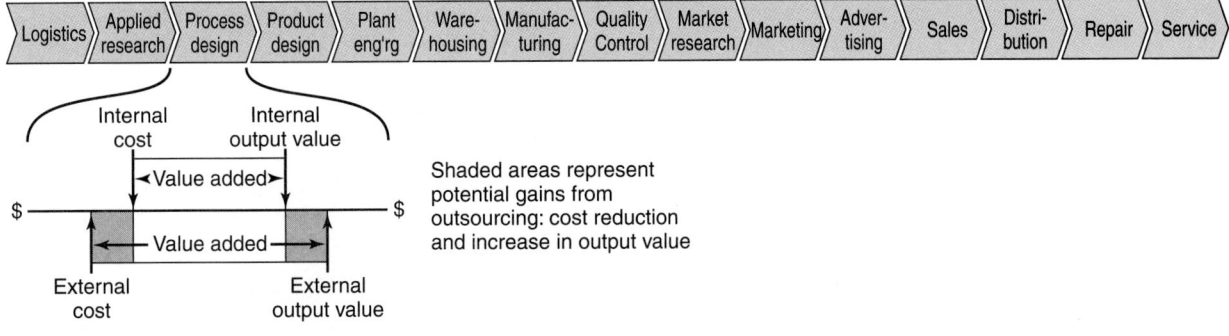

Logistics | Applied research | Process design | Product design | Plant eng'rg | Ware-housing | Manufac-turing | Quality Control | Market research | Marketing | Adver-tising | Sales | Distri-bution | Repair | Service

Internal cost

Internal output value

◄—Value added►

$ ———————————————————————————— $

—Value added—

External cost

External output value

Shaded areas represent potential gains from outsourcing: cost reduction and increase in output value

FIGURE 6.5

The Firm's Value Chain[65]

J. B. Quinn, *The Intelligent Enterprise: A New Paradigm*, New York: The Free Press, 1992.

business unit may or may not share individual value chain elements or provide inputs and/or receive outputs from sister business units. At any point in time, each of these value-adding and support activities is conducted in a more or less efficient manner. The challenge of margin raising is to see whether the costs of receiving value from conducting these activities can be reduced without sacrificing (and possibly increasing) the value provided. We consider five approaches: capturing value from customers, cost reduction, reengineering, outsourcing, and insourcing.[61]

CAPTURING VALUE FROM CUSTOMERS   Capturing value requires the firm to price its products such that it is appropriately paid for the value it delivers to customers. If the firm believes its products are underpriced, it may be able to improve margins simply by raising prices. The critical issue here is to truly understand customers' perceptions of the value the firm is currently delivering. In addition, if the firm adds value to its offer, it should be able to increase prices. The firm's value chain provides a framework for identifying those areas in which the application of increased investment and other resources may produce value for customers in excess of cost increases. Because we devote considerable attention to pricing later, we defer a detailed discussion.

COST REDUCTION   Cost reduction implies that the firm should examine its various value-adding and support activities and attempt to cut costs.[62] The focus of this option is to identify those activities where cost can be removed without affecting (and perhaps even enhancing) the delivery of customer value.

The areas that should be investigated and questions that should be asked concern the following:

- **Necessity**: Is this particular activity necessary? Can we do with less of it or without it altogether? Particular areas for investigation are marketing and administrative transaction costs that firms incur in dealing with current and potential customers.
- **Human resources**: Can we conduct the activity with fewer people (downsize, rightsize)? Can people whose wage levels are lower conduct the activity?
- **Raw materials and supplies**: Can the activity be conducted with fewer inputs? Can we use lower cost inputs? Companies often overbuild products; detailed analysis of customer needs may allow them to use fewer and/or lower-quality raw materials.
- **Capital**: Do we need all of our assets? Can we sell or lease assets without reducing our competitiveness? Can we conduct the activity with less expensive capital equipment? Can we increase use of existing assets, for example, by multishift versus

single-shift working? Can we develop methods for reducing working capital, for example, by reducing inventory, shortening accounts receivable, or lengthening accounts payable?[63]

- **Capital/labor ratios**: Would it be less expensive to substitute capital for labor (by using machines rather than people) or to substitute labor for capital?

Example: In the 1960s and 1970s, manufacture of many textile products left the United States for low-wage countries. By the 1990s, some of these were returning to the United States because newer technologies required less labor.

- **Geographic location**: Could we conduct our operations in a different country or region where operating costs (e.g., human resource, utilities, transportation, taxes) are lower? Where might this be?[64]
- **Customers**: Can we reorganize the firm's value chain such that customers undertake some of the cost-incurring steps currently completed by the firm? Examples include securing cash from banks by using ATM machines rather than tellers, shopping clubs where floor help is minimal, self-service restaurants, and many activities with widespread applicability such as order entry and tracking, purchase order management, product configuration, and even product development. Properly designed, customers may perceive greater benefit in conducting activities themselves, enabling the firm to both reduce its costs and add value to its customers.

Example: Starting in the 1980s, Federal Express (FedEx) offered its customers' package tracking by calling an 800 number. In the mid-1990s, FedEx developed an Internet-based system that enables customers to track packages, schedule pick-ups, and generate and print airbills, complete with barcodes.[65]

Highly publicized cost reduction efforts by many firms, especially via widespread lay-offs, have proved extremely beneficial to shareholder value in some cases. Perhaps one of the best examples of a manager using these approaches to restore profitability is "Chainsaw" Al Dunlap.

Example: At Scott Paper, Dunlap laid off 35,000 people (11% of the workforce), sold $3.5 billion in assets, improved shareholder value threefold, then sold the firm to Kimberly-Clark (1995).

However, many observers have expressed considerable concerns that workforce reductions might become excessive and that critical human resources lost to the organization may lead to impaired performance.

Example: Dunlap began on a similar path at small appliance manufacturer Sunbeam, where he became CEO in 1996. However, by June 1998, he had encountered significant problems, and as the Sunbeam share price dropped precipitously, he was unceremoniously fired.[66]

REENGINEERING Whereas cost reduction *per se* assumes that, after changes are made, the activity is conducted in an essentially similar way, just less expensively, reengineering examines fundamental assumptions underlying the way in which the activity is being conducted and seeks alternative approaches. The reengineering perspective is that many of the processes conducted by firms were put in place years previously and that the rationale for conducting an activity in a particular manner may no longer be relevant. Furthermore, changes in knowledge, customer needs, firm requirements, available technologies, and so forth may allow for different, more effective processes to be developed. The reengineering approach is perhaps best clarified by Figure 6.6.

Example: Figure 6.6 is a schematic of the traditional process within IBM Credit for offering a leasing contract to a client.[67] The IBM sales representative secures agreement from a corporate client to purchase a major computer system (typically several million dollars), then seeks the financing business. The following steps

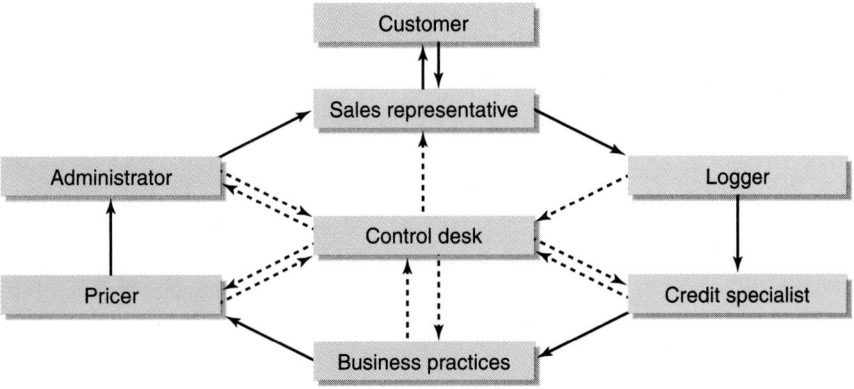

FIGURE 6.6

Reengineering—IBM Credit: Original System and First-Pass Solution

Note: The original system is designated by solid line arrows; the first-pass solution is designated by dotted line arrows.

occur: the salesperson provides information about the purchase and purchaser to the "logger," who takes down the information, creates a file, and routes it appropriately; a credit specialist conducts a credit check; a business practices person modifies the standard loan covenant to the customer's request; the pricer determines the appropriate interest rate; the administrator turns the information into a formal quote letter that is FedEx'ed to the sales representative for presentation to the client.

The basic problem with this system was that it took six days on average, but sometimes it took as long as two weeks. During this period, the customer might be anxious to complete the deal and/or the salesperson might be nervous that with the financing still undecided the customer might shift to a competitor. Furthermore, it was difficult for the salesperson to know where his or her deal was in the process. A call to the credit department might reveal that the credit analysis had been completed, yet the administrator might have no knowledge of the deal.

In an effort to solve the latter problem, IBM Credit installed a control desk. After each activity was conducted, the file was sent to the control desk for noting and forwarding. With one phone call, the salesperson could learn the status of the deal. The problem: Now the process averaged seven days.

At this stage, two IBM executives decided to identify the actual work time on a particular deal. They waited by the logger's desk for his or her work to be completed, then hand-carried the file to the credit specialist. The credit specialist was told to drop what he was doing and work on the new deal; this process was followed until the draft contract went back to the sales representative. Time to completion: 90 minutes.

IBM Credit determined that 90 percent of lease requests could be handled by a single individual, a "deal structurer," and that only 10 percent required specialized personnel (Figure 6.7). As a result of this process change, turnaround time dropped to four hours without additional headcount. (More recently, IBM Credit has developed an Internet-based system to further decrease the turnaround time.)

In this example, not only were costs reduced substantially, but customer value was significantly increased as customers received quotations more speedily and salespeople completed deals more expeditiously.[68] Furthermore, whereas we highlighted a reengineering project in marketing, opportunities for reengineering are ubiquitous and may be addressed in many value-added and support activities.

The Internet is a vehicle for reengineering business systems. In many supplier–customer relationships, purchase orders, invoices, shipping notices, telephone conversa-

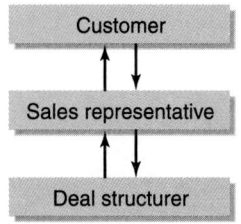

FIGURE 6.7

Reengineering Example— IBM Credit: Solution for 90 Percent of Requests

tions, and faxes have been superceded by Internet technology. In addition to direct cost reductions, companies often gain by inventory reductions.

Example: Sun MicroSystems's traditional cost for issuing a check for reimbursement was $35 per check. By moving to an Internet-based system for entering employee expenses and conducting the audit function in India (low-wage economy), Sun was able to reduce the check issuing cost to $2.95, an annual cost saving approaching $1 billion.

OUTSOURCING   The third method of margin raising involves outsourcing. Essentially, for each activity necessary to complete the input–output conversion process, the firm must make a make–buy decision. Should the firm conduct this activity in house with its own employees? Or should the activity be "outsourced" to a third-party organization? Recently, firms have rediscovered the make–buy decision, and an outsourcing trend for internal activities is well under way. Several advantages are claimed for outsourcing:

- Because the outsourcing supplier specializes in the activity, has a broad variety of customers, secures economies of scale, and develops a larger experience base, it may be less expensive. This is especially true if demand for the service is highly variable.
- If the outsourcing supplier provides the necessary capital equipment, it relieves pressure on the outsourcing firm's capital. This, in turn, enables the firm to variate costs that would otherwise be fixed, thus lowering its operating leverage. For capital-intensive firms in cyclical businesses, in which high fixed costs lead to lowered profits (or greater losses) in economic downturns, this can be a major benefit.
- The outsourcing supplier may be able to provide its employees with a more extensive career path, so they should be of higher quality and hence deliver superior performance.
- The outsourcing supplier is more likely to push the technology envelope and therefore provide the firm with access to world-class capabilities.[69]
- The inside department might operate like the monopoly supplier it is!

The main disadvantage of outsourcing is that the supplier may be less committed to providing superior service than an internal department. Furthermore, unless a "good" outsourcing contract is written, management could find itself contractually bound to a supplier who is providing inadequate service.[70] These concerns may be mitigated to the extent that the supplier operates in a competitive market and must strive for excellence to keep the business. Furthermore, the outsourcing firm may provide equipment to its supplier to secure some control of its operations.

Among areas that have seen significant outsourcing activity are support activities such as security services, payroll administration, mailroom, invoicing and bill paying, pension administration, inventory management, software development, data system management, and oversight of corporate assets such as vehicle fleets and industrial equipment.[71] However, many marketing activities, including developing advertising campaigns (to advertising agencies), selling activities (to agents and brokers), and customer service, may also be outsourced. Increasingly, major companies are outsourcing production activities.

Example: In 1997, Sara Lee Corporation a major producer of cakes (*Sara Lee*), handbags (*Coach*), sweatshirts (*Champion*), frankfurters (*Ball Park*), bras (*Wonderbra*), and panty hose (*L'Eggs*), decided to outsource virtually all of its manufacturing activities and become basically a manager of brand assets.

One underlying assumption in this business model is that the strength of Sara Lee's brand will inhibit finished product suppliers from attempting to sell products directly to end users. If this assumption does not hold, then somewhere in the future, the branded product seller may find it has a significant competitor to deal with.

Another far-reaching example of production outsourcing is Volkswagen's new Brazilian plant. Suppliers manufacture complete subassemblies on site, placing Volkswagen, whose workers are in a distinct minority, merely in the role of an assembler. Notwithstanding these examples, the firm should not outsource activities that represent core organizational competencies.

> **Example:** A previous Sara Lee attempt to outsource production ended in disaster. From 1969 to the early 1990s, the glove division grew from $6 million to $220 million (operating profit, $35 million) and *Aris-Isotoner* gloves had 75% of the U.S. department store market. In an outsourcing move, the firm's Manila plant was closed. However, the replacement low-cost producers cost 10 to 20 percent more, delivery time increased, and product quality dropped! By 1997, operating losses totaled $120 million and Sara Lee had invested more than $100 million to keep the firm afloat. In June 1997, *Aris-Isotoner* was "virtually given away" to Bain Capital. Clearly, Sara Lee did not understand that the Manila plant was *Aris-Isotoner's* critical core competence, its crown jewel.[72]

Notwithstanding such examples, to the extent that the firm's outsourcing strategy is well conceived, it should be able to devote greater intellectual and financial resources to activities that deliver customer value and secure competitive advantage in the medium and long run.

We may also approach outsourcing from a different perspective. As firms increasingly outsource to gain cost advantages, significant opportunities become available for suppliers of outsourced activities. For example, in the early 1990s, IBM UK identified four main features of activities that were central to its business: provide management and direction, maintain competence and control, differentiate IBM from its competitors, and sustain its uniqueness. All other activities represented outsourcing opportunities. From 1989 to 1993, IBM UK reduced its permanent headcount by one third and halved its contract staff.[73]

INSOURCING   Insourcing is the opposite of outsourcing. Insourcing is concerned with taking a purchased activity and conducting it in house. All of the various value-added activities noted in Figure 6.5 may be conducted either in house or out of house, and at any point in time, an individual firm has a distribution of in-house and out-of-house activities. A particularly interesting recent example of insourcing is the move of some major corporations to develop their own in-house financing operations, eliminating the need for investment banks to conduct debt and equity underwriting.

In our outsourcing discussion, we argued that prime candidates for outsourcing were activities that were not core organizational competencies. In other words, activities that were not central to producing customer value and securing long-term competitive advantage. These activities have to be conducted well, but even though outsourcing may reduce costs and increase value, long-term competitive advantage typically does not occur through these activities, in part because outsourcing suppliers often also sell to the firm's competitors.

By contrast, activities related to core organizational competencies should be conducted in house where they can be nurtured through internal investment. However, a firm's set of core competencies is not fixed; as noted earlier, it should evolve over time as the environment changes and strategies are developed to satisfy customer needs more effectively than competitors. For example, most corporations purchase telecommunications services from telecommunications suppliers. By contrast, for many years, Citibank believed that its internal global communications network afforded it competitive advantage in the battle for global customers.

Historically, most discussion of insourcing has concerned manufacturing and distribution activities where the terminology typically used is "vertical integration."[74] Firms have two vertical integration strategies available: forward integration (incorporating activities previously conducted by customers) and backward integration (incorporating activities previously conducted by suppliers).[75] Implementation of either strategy allows the firm to capture more of the overall value-added, thus providing opportunity for increased margins.[76] In addition to direct profit margin effects, backward integration may allow the firm to secure critical supply sources; forward integration may secure access to customers.

> **Example:** Historically, Coca-Cola's business focused on manufacturing the *syrup* and building the *Coca-Cola* brand via advertising to consumers. One of several reasons for the significant increase in Coke's shareholder value (1980, $4 billion; 1996, $130 billion) was due to forward integration to acquire its bottlers. As a result, Coke was better able to manage relationships with supermarket chains, fundamentally reengineer logistics, and directly capture value from its three major distribution channels, grocery, fountain, and vending.[77]

However, excessive vertical integration may have flexibility and secular disadvantages. Flexibility disadvantages relate to the firm's inability to shift direction when customer needs change. Relatedly, highly vertically integrated firms typically have high levels of fixed costs. As a result, although margins may be high when demand is strong, in economic downturns, they suffer severe margin pressures as sales volumes drop but costs remain high.

> **Example:** In the automobile industry, General Motors has historically been much more vertically integrated than Ford. As a result, in strong economy periods, General Motors historically made significantly higher profits than Ford. However, when automobile demand fell, Ford's profits held up better than General Motors's. Recently both GM and Ford have spun-off their parts subsidiaries to gain increased flexibility.

A recent insourcing trend adopted by some manufacturers is to provide value for customers by supplying extra services that were previously conducted by customers in-house.

> **Example:** In the early 1990s, faced with severe price pressures caused by deregulation of the electric utility industry, GE's Power Systems division reshaped its business by improving customer service. It reduced replacement time for old or damaged parts from 12 to 6 weeks and added value to the customer relationship via advice on conducting business in European and Asian countries. Furthermore, GE spurred labor cost savings by providing customers with maintenance staff for occasional equipment upgrades and moved 33% of engineers from new product development to new service development.[78]

A FRAMEWORK FOR USING THE FIRM'S VALUE CHAIN   In Figure 6.8, we join together value-added and relative cost in a 2 × 2 matrix as a means of gaining insight into where the various margin raising methods might be used.[79]

Each of the four cells suggests a different course of action for the firm:

- Activities in Cell A represent the core of the firm's value chain. The firm is delivering high customer value, yet incurring low relative costs. The goal here is to continue to add value with similar value–cost relationships.
- In Cell B, the firm delivers high customer value, but its costs are also high. The major goal for this cell is to reduce costs.

Activities in Cells C and D offer low customer value. If this value is unnecessary, the firm should contemplate ceasing the activity. However, if the value (although low) is necessary, different options should be considered.

- Cell C activities are strong candidates for outsourcing because the costs are high.
- Cell D activities could be continued at their current low costs unless ways are available to enhance the value customers receive. These activities need not be outsourced unless even lower cost options are available.

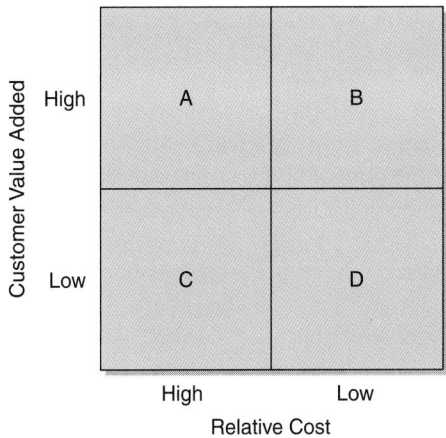

FIGURE 6.8

Value–Cost Analysis

Outside the Firm's Value Chain

This section discusses profit and shareholder value enhancement by moving outside the value chain. In particular, divestiture and organizational break-up, technology sale and licensing, and acquisition are discussed.

DIVESTITURE AND ORGANIZATIONAL BREAK-UP   The previously discussed options focused on raising margins in a particular business area; the divestiture option implies that the firm exit the business entirely. Numerous circumstances may lead corporations to consider divestiture of product lines within a business or of entire businesses.[80] First, the particular unit under consideration may not meet the firm's financial hurdles; it may be losing money, making low profits, or consuming excessive capital. Divesting the unit would raise average margins for the business unit or corporation as a whole.

> Example: Analysis of Clorox's businesses revealed that sales of appliances and frozen foods to restaurants and bottled water to offices accounted for 10% of sales, 26% of employment, and 0% of profits. Clorox exited all three areas.[81]

Second, the unit might be highly attractive to another corporation; selling the business might be an excellent way of increasing shareholder value in short order. Third, the business might not be a good fit with the firm's other businesses. Thus, regardless of current margins, the firm would be better positioned for growth and improving shareholder value by divesting the operation.

This latter situation is especially relevant for highly diversified companies. In some cases, investors find it difficult to assess the corporation's profit-generating capabilities, whereas in others, management may have run the business poorly. For these corporations, shares in a parent company often sell at a discount from the anticipated "break-up" value. By selling selected business units to new owners whom investors believe will use the assets better, value is created for the original shareholders; hence the investment community often speaks of "releasing value."[82] When top management decides to use this route for increasing shareholder value, marketing plays an important role in advising which units are best kept together.

A second order effect concerns the role of corporate size in driving shareholder value. CEOs of many companies seem to view size as the "Holy Grail" as they seek to develop larger companies.[83] Unfortunately, there is significant evidence that size is unrelated to profitability.[84]

TECHNOLOGY SALE AND LICENSING   A firm may increase profits by exploiting the value in its technology assets. The two major routes are to sell its technology outright to another firm or to license its use. Several reasons argue for technology sale. For example, the technology may not fit with the firm's other activities or otherwise meet its business criteria, or the firm may have insufficient capital and other resources to exploit its benefits. In any event, if the *certain* returns from sale are greater than the *risk-adjusted* returns from its own commercialization efforts, sale is the rational decision.

Licensing typically allows the firm to commercialize in some markets but provides licensees rights in other markets, typically defined by geography or field of use. Successful licensees can provide significant profits to the firm at minimal cost outlays. One caution with an aggressive licensing strategy is that when the agreements end, the firm may face well-financed competitors that it had previously put in business. For example, in the 1960s and 1970s, British chemical company ICI gained significant license fees from its polyester fiber patents, yet was ultimately less competitive than its former licensees and, in the mid-1990s, finally exited the business.

In addition to licensing technology, the firm may also contemplate leveraging its brand name into new product/markets by licensing. For example, in 1998, Coca-Cola had in excess of 240 licensees for more than 10,000 products; in 1997, more than 50 million product units were sold.[85]

ACQUISITION   Although acquisitions result in immediate growth for the acquiring entity, growth *per se* is not necessarily the immediate objective. The purpose of an acquisition may be to improve returns, either by reducing costs or by reducing capital employed. For example, the mid-1990s acquisition of American Cyanamid by American Home Products led to quick cost savings through merged operations and lay-offs. Furthermore, experts estimated that the aborted merger (1998) between British firms Glaxo and SmithKline Beecham would have saved nearly $2 billion over three years by reducing employment by 15,000 and consolidating operations.[86]

Relationship to Marketing

Persons with a narrow view of marketing might question the rationale for including the material in this section. After all, they might argue, don't many of the issues raised fall under the responsibility of some other functional area? The answer of course is yes! However, there are very good reasons why marketing managers should understand the material we have presented.

First, inasmuch as a considerable focus of this section was on cost reduction, marketing managers should be highly interested because action on costs constrains their pricing flexibility in the marketplace. As we shall see later, low costs do not necessarily imply that prices should be low, but they do afford marketing management the ability to make such a choice. High costs in general imply high prices unless losses are being planned! In addition to this generalized concern, marketing managers should examine their own organizations to see what cost-reduction initiatives might be undertaken.

Second, the reengineering discussion should encourage marketing managers to examine their own processes to see whether their costs may be reduced and/or the value from specific activities increased. For example, is the salesforce operating in the most effective manner? Would some customers served by "on-the-road" salespeople be better assigned to a telemarketing force? Is customer service being conducted efficiently and effectively? Does our brand management system make sense, or should we replace it with a focus on customer management?

Third, outsourcing not only may offer the firm considerable opportunities in general, it may offer specific advantages in marketing. For example, should market research be conducted in house or by a market research company? Would the firm be better off if its selling effort were conducted by independent agents rather than by an employee salesforce? Should the firm develop its direct mail campaigns in house or employ a specialized fulfillment organization?

Fourth, perhaps some marketing activities are ripe for insourcing, switched from external supply to being performed in house. For example, should the firm shift its distribution focus from third-party wholesalers to a direct-to-customer format? Is the advertising agency really providing value in its creative and advertising placement functions, or could this activity be conducted in house?[87] Is our service provider providing satisfactory service to our key accounts, or would they be better served by locating our own employees at major customers?

Finally, the "outside the value chain" discussion falls squarely within the responsibility of the first marketing task, Determine and Recommend Which Markets to Address.

SUMMARY

This chapter developed the link between customer value, TQM, and shareholder value. It also focused on the two basic directions for improving shareholder value: developing profitable growth and improving margins. Firms seeking profitable growth must be clear about their objectives, formulate a coherent strategy comprising decisions on growth path and timing of entry, and put in place quantitative and qualitative screening criteria to examine individual opportunities. Quantitative criteria should be financial and market based; qualitative criteria should embrace compatibility (or fit), distinctive competence, and synergy. Finally, the firm must decide how to implement its strategy using the various options of internal development, acquisition, strategic alliance, licensing, and technology purchase.

Methods of improving margins were mostly developed in the context of the value chain framework. In addition to price improvement as a major margin-raising option, we identified cost reduction, reengineering, outsourcing, and insourcing as important alternatives to consider for improving margins. Finally, we noted the role of divestiture and organizational break-up, technology sale and licensing, and acquisition in margin improvement. We concluded with a discussion of the importance for marketing managers of understanding the firm's margin-raising options.

THE CHANGING VIEW

Old Way	New Way
Profit	Shareholder value creation
Shareholder value considered separately from customer value	Customer value integral to shareholder value
Conglomeration is good	Conglomeration is bad
Reinvest in historically profitable businesses	Prudent selection of appropriate growth ventures
Insourcing	Outsourcing
Competencies fixed	Competencies variable
Growth always desirable	Demerger viable option
100% ownership	Strategic alliances, outsourcing
Organic growth by internally developed new products	Organic growth by expansion into global markets
Fixed industry boundaries	Permeable industry boundaries
Swift implementation of new opportunities desirable	Swift implementation of new opportunities critical
Portfolio emphasis on products and product/markets	Important to develop technology portfolios
Development effort focused on better long-term forecasting techniques	Development effort focused on reducing cycle times

QUESTIONS FOR STUDY AND DISCUSSION

1. Select a corporation with which you are familiar. Identify potential growth options for this firm in the various cells of the growth path matrix. Which do you think is more risky: product expansion or market expansion?

2. From your knowledge of the business world, identify examples of innovator, follow-the-leader, segmenter, and me-too entry strategies.

3. Many corporations have made determined efforts to restrict the scope of their activities. Yet, around the world we find exceptions: for example, one of the United States's most profitable companies is the widely diversified General Electric, and in Asia, many successful family-owned businesses are broadly diversified. How do you account for this apparent paradox?

4. Identify a business organization with which you are familiar. What opportunities can you identify that may allow it to reduce costs, reengineer, or outsource, or insource activities in its marketing operations.

5. Select a company with which you are familiar. Classify its various growth investments in the framework provided by the growth path matrix. How would you assess this venture portfolio in terms of prudent combinations of risk and return?

6. What considerations should corporate or business management review in deciding whether to invest in a particular growth option?

7. In the 1950s, a small company named Haloid decided to back an inventor named Chester Carlson. His dry-copy invention, dubbed xerography, changed the world. IBM, 3M, and Kodak all turned down the proposal. If, as a corporate executive you had used the concepts presented here, what decision would you have made? Why? (Without the wisdom of hindsight.)

8. In January 1998, Sara Lee Corporation announced the outsourcing of most of its production operations. What do you think motivated this decision? Do you believe it was soundly based?

9. As noted, Sir George Bull, chairman of Diageo, once opined, "acquisition destroys (shareholder) value; organic growth creates value." Discuss.

10. Strategic alliances have become a popular means of generating growth, especially in the global environment. Discuss the prospects for success of horizontal and vertical alliances.

11. Technology is our lifeblood; we must make every effort to commercialize products and services based on our technological investments. Discuss.

12. Engineers like to operate with high signal/noise ratio; in general, marketers operate with high noise/signal ratio. What are the implications of this disconnect?

13. Marketing is concerned with the imprecise application of the right principles; accounting is concerned with the precise application of the wrong principles. Discuss.

14. It is often argued that short-sighted shareholders have caused management to minimize R&D spending, thus jeopardizing the company's access to new products. Can you identify empirical evidence to support this proposition?

15. In mid-1998, *Virgin Cola* entered the U.S. market, directly challenging *Coke* and *Pepsi*. What strategy did *Virgin Cola* use? Was it successful? How did *Coke* and *Pepsi* respond?

16. The "give me a number" philosophy often leads firms to minimize or neglect the use of qualitative (hard to quantify) criteria in evaluating strategic options, despite their evident importance. How would you attempt to change this state of affairs?

END NOTES

1. Returns to shareholders are a combination of dividends and capital gains from increases in share price.

2. Sometimes, significant unrest occurs even when shareholder value has increased significantly. For example, toward the end of 1997, TIAA, a large institutional shareholder in Disney, openly argued for significant change in Disney's board membership. TIAA argued that too many outside board members were close personal acquaintances of CEO Michael Eisner.

3. *The New York Times*, March 25, 1998.

4. Of course, many forms of organization exist in addition to state-owned and publicly held corporations, including sole proprietorships, private corporations, and partnerships. In most cases, the goal of these organizations is to create wealth for the owners. However, for mutual organizations, typically owned by depositors (banking) or policy holders (insurance), ownership diffusion often means that the major wealth gainer is senior management.

5. A. Rappaport, *Creating Shareholder Value: The New Standard for Business Performance*, New York: The Free Press, 1986, p. 3; see also, A. Rappaport, *Creating Shareholder Value: A Guide for Managers and Investors*, New York: The Free Press, 1997.

6. EPS is calculated by dividing the firm's net profit by the number of shares outstanding; ROI is the firm's net profit divided by its investment.

7. A. Rappaport, *op. cit.*

8. Cost of capital is a combination of the firm's cost of equity and cost of debt. Note that if the firm is operating multiple businesses, then appropriate risk adjustments may result in different target rates of return for each business, see J. C. Van Horne, *Financial Management and Policy*, Englewood Cliffs, NJ: Prentice Hall, 1995, Chapter 8.

9. More precisely, EVA is operating net income on a cash basis (or operating net income excluding the amortization of goodwill and certain intangibles) less an explicit charge for capital. See G. B. Stewart III, "EVA[TM]: Fact, and Fantasy," *Journal of Applied Corporate Finance*, 7 (Summer 1994), 72–84. Simply speaking, there are three ways to increase EVA: increase profit without increasing capital, invest in projects expected to earn more than the cost of capital, and withdraw from projects earning unattractive returns. See also Appendix, Section 3.

10. F. Norris, "Can Regulators Keep Accountants from Writing Fiction?" *The New York Times*, Sept. 10, 1999.

11. This calculus is further developed in Chapter 18.

12. See B. T. Gale, *Managing Customer Value,* New York: The Free Press, 1994, Exhibit 1-1, p. 9.

13. The PIMS program is briefly described in Chapter 3.

14. See B. T. Gale, 1994, *op. cit.* Exhibit 1-3, p. 16.

15. The Standard and Poor's (S&P) 500 firm index is a broader measure of stockmarket performance than the Dow Jones average, based on 30 firms, but less broad than the Wilshire 5,000.

16. *Business Week*, March 16, 1998.

17. See G. S. Day, *Market-Driven Strategy*, New York: The Free Press, 1990.

18. A. J. Slywotzky and D. J. Morrison, *Value Migration*, New York: Times Business, 1996; and *The Profit Zone*, Times Business: New York, 1998.

19. These expectations are reflected in a stock's beta coefficient. Beta measures an individual stock's variability compared with a market portfolio. See Rappaport, *op. cit.* for more detail.

20. Issues of mission are discussed in Chapter 19.

21. For the origins of this approach, see J. M. Brion, *Corporate Marketing Planning*, New York: John Wiley, 1967, pp. 155–156. For a simpler version, see H. I. Ansoff, *Corporate Strategy*, New York: McGraw-Hill, 1965, p. 109. The four cells in Ansoff's 2×2 matrix are labeled *market penetration, market development, product development,* and *diversification.*

22. The growth path does not directly incorporate all possible types of risk, for example, political risk and physical environment risk, although these risks are partially addressed in the market dimension.

23. Note that we are taking the producer's position in this discussion. Although retailers incur some risk from product line extension and expansion, their knowledge of consumers and the limitation of their investment largely to working capital typically mitigates their risk.

24. *Business Week*, December 27, 1999.

25. We note that, of course, many entrepreneurial start-up companies begin life with little if any organizational competence.

26. We examine these issues in more detail later.

27. For more discussion on required returns and types of opportunities, see T. Kuczmarski, *Managing New Products*, Englewood Cliffs, NJ: Prentice Hall, 1988.

28. Richard P. Rumelt, *Strategy, Structure, and Economic Performance*, Cambridge, MA: Harvard University Press, 1974; see also Richard P. Rumelt, "Diversification and the Market Share Effect," *Strategic Management Journal*, 3 (Oct./Dec. 1982), 359–369; and C. H. Christensen and C. A. Montgomery, "Corporate Economic Performance: Diversification Strategy versus Market Structure," *Strategic Management Journal*, (Oct./Dec. 1981), 327–343.

29. For more detail of American Can's transition into Primerica, see Primerica Corporation, in N. Capon, *The Marketing of Financial Services*, Englewood Cliffs, NJ: Prentice Hall, 1992. In 1993, Primerica CEO Sandy Weill engineered a take-over of The Travelers, then a major insurance company, and adopted its name; in early 1998, The Travelers and Citibank merged to form the world's largest financial services institution, CitiGroup, with $700 billion in assets.

30. This section is based in part on H. I. Ansoff and J. M. Stewart, "Strategies for a Technologically-Based Business," *Harvard Business Review*, 45 (Nov./Dec. 1967), 71–83.

31. In some circles, the received wisdom holds that R&D spending is critical for success in developing new products. However, in many cases of successful new products, for example, color television, required market development spending outstripped R&D.

32. *The Economist*, October 31, 1998.

33. C. M. Christensen, *The Innovator's Dilemma: When New Technologies Cause Great Firms to Fail*, Boston, MA: Harvard Business School Press, 1997.

34. Other examples of the damage wrought by disruptive technologies on incumbents are handheld calculators on slide rule manufacturers, overnight package delivery (e.g., Federal Express) on freight forwarders, TV on radio, CDs on long-playing records, jet aircraft on turbo-props and ocean liners.

35. T. Levitt, *Managing for Business Growth*, New York: McGraw-Hill, 1974.

36. *Business Week*, April 5, 1999. More recently, PC prices have dropped even further.

37. For those who believe that competencies are corporate-level rather than business-level properties, it can be argued that all businesses under corporate ownership should share such policies.

38. The implicit assumption that risk will be accurately assessed and priced requires perfect capital markets. The goal of astute management is to seek imperfections where high returns are available at low risk. Because, as we have seen, assessment of both risk and return is qualitative and subjective, such opportunities are likely to exist. For a firm that accurately assesses both its own competencies and those required to capitalize on opportunities, much better risk management is feasible. Obviously, risk is much lower for a firm possessing the required competencies than for one that does not.

39. EMI and the CT Scanner (A) and (B), *Harvard Business School*, 9-383-194/195. Hounsfield was later awarded a Nobel prize for his contribution. (In the mid-1990s, Thorn divested EMI.)

40. *The New York Times*, January 18, 1998.

41. See F. Webster, "The Changing Role of Marketing," *Journal of Marketing* 56 (1992), 1–17.

42. As discussed earlier, other strategic errors were made in the early 1980s.

43. For more detail, see N. Capon and R. Glazer, "Marketing and Technology: A Strategic Co-Alignment," *Journal of Marketing*, 51 (July 1987), 1–14.

44. See, for example, N. Capon, J. U. Farley, and J. Hulbert, *Corporate Strategic Planning*, New York: Columbia University Press, 1988; and N. Capon, J. U. Farley, and S. Hoenig, *Toward an Integrative Explanation of Corporate Financial Performance*, Norwell, MA: Kluwer Academic Publishers, 1997.

45. This acculturation process is best exemplified by those Japanese companies whose employees wear firm uniforms, sing corporate songs, learn corporate mantras, and so forth.

46. Notwithstanding these problems, aggregate R&D spending by US firms is increasing, from $97.1 to $166 billion (1994 to 1999). Spending on "blue-sky" projects (potential products 10 years in the future) increased from $6.1 to $10.9 billion. Large spenders were life and information science companies, for example, R&D spending at Microsoft is 17% of sales. Source: Industrial Research Institute, from *The New York Times*, December 26, 1999.

47. *Business Week E. Biz.*, December 18, 1999.

48. In 1998, *The New York Times* reported that mergers and acquisitions among US companies were proceeding at an extremely high level and changing the face of American business, *The New York Times*, January 18, 1998; *The New York Times*, March 4, 1998. Mergers and acquisitions are also getting larger. At the time of writing, the five largest agree-upon, in increasing order, were acquirer/acquiree—Travelers Group/Citicorp $73 billion (April 1998), Pfizer/Warner-Lambert $90 billion (January 2000), Exxon/Mobil $86 billion (December 1998), MCI-Worldcom/Sprint $127 billion (October 1999), Vodafone/Mannesmann $140 billion (February 2000) and America Online/Time Warner $165 billion (January 2000). (The initially hostile Pfizer bid followed a proposed friendly takeover of Warner-Lambert by American Home Products.)

49. *The New York Times*, January 27, 1999.

50. *Fortune*, November 8, 1999.

51. Historical U.S.-based research suggests that acquisitions are dilutive for the acquirer about 70% of the time. Financial theory suggests a 50% figure but, in the "heat of the chase" it appears that acquirers typically overpay! See, for example, M. Bradley, A. Desai and E. H. Kim, "Synergistic Gains from Acquisitions and Their Division between the Stockholders of Target and Acquiring Firms," *Journal of Financial Economics*, 21 (1988), 3–40; E. Berkovitch and M. P. Narayanan, "Motives for Take-overs: An Empirical Investigation," *Journal of Financial and Quantitative Analysis*, 28 (1993), 347–362, M. L. Sirower, *The Synergy Trap: How Companies Lose the Acquisition Game*, 1997.

52. See, for example, M. A. Hayward and D. C. Hambrick, "Explaining the Premiums Paid for Large Acquisitions: Evidence of CEO Hubris, *Administrative Science Quarterly*, 42 (1997) 103–127.

53. *The New York Times,* June 24, 1997.

54. Example modified from J. B. Quinn, *The Intelligent Enterprise: A New Paradigm,* New York: The Free Press, 1992.

55. For more detail of Banc One's strategy, see Banc One, in N. Capon, *The Marketing of Financial Services*, *op. cit.*

56. See, for example, W. H. Bergquist, *Building Strategic Relationships: How to Extend Your Organization's Reach through Partnerships, Alliances and Joint Ventures*, San Francisco, CA: Jossey Bass, 1995.

57. For a series of case studies that exemplify issues in licensing, see Amicon Corporation (A,B,C,D), *Harvard Business School*, 9-574-093/4/5/6.

58. *Fortune*, December 21, 1998.

59. Among the inventions that Xerox pioneered at PARC were the Ethernet, the graphical user interface (the basis of the MacIntosh), the mouse, and Alto, an early personal computer.

60. P. A. Gompers and J. Lerner, "Can Corporate Venture Capital Work," Working Paper, Harvard Business School, 1998.

61. Value chain analysis of both the firm and its competitors plays an important role in competitor analysis by focusing on the following set of questions:
   • Where in the value chain does the competitor have a cost advantage?
   • Where in the value chain is the competitor at a cost disadvantage?
   • Where in the value chain does the competitor have a value advantage?
   • Where in the value chain is the competitor at a value disadvantage?
For those firms whose customers are organizations, a customer value chain analysis may prove a useful tool for understanding how and where its customers make profits. Armed with this information, the firm is better placed to develop strategies that deliver value to customers.

62. For a framework in which to consider cost reduction, see the discussion on the *Experience Curve*, Chapter 9 Appendix.

63. One reason for the success of Internet bookseller Amazon.com is its negative working capital: It maintains little inventory (turnover 26 times p.a.), receives cash from sales charged to customer's credit cards within one day, yet pays suppliers on average in 46 days, *The New York Times*, July 19, 1998.

64. To the extent that capital to labor ratios rise, labor cost issues may reduce in significance and location close to the market may overshadow the advantages of countries with low labor costs.

65. L. Downes and C. Mui, *Unleashing the Killer App: Digital Strategies for Market Dominance*, Boston: Harvard Business School Press, 1998.

66. See J. A. Byrne, *Chainsaw: The Notorious Career of Al Dunlap in the Era of Profit-at-Any-Price*, New York: Harper Business, 1999.

67. Modified from M. Hammer and J. Champy, *Reengineering the Corporation: A Manifesto for Business Revolution*, New York: Harper Business, 1994.

68. Reengineering is based on studying business processes; these often cut across many existing functional departments. As a result, the internal "political opposition" to change may be widespread, contributing to the failure of many well-intended reengineering projects.

69. Cost savings many be highly significant. For example, in the mid-1990s, AT&T (now Lucent technologies) claimed the Pentagon would save $1.5 billion by outsourcing the building of a new telephone system rather than developing it in house.

70. R. Peisch, "When Outsourcing Goes Awry," *Harvard Business Review*, 73 (May/June 1995), 24–37.

71. In some cases, outsourcing has moved into more strategic functions. For example, in the spring of 1996, Computer Software Associates, a major software developer, made an agreement for Digital Equipment's 22,000 computer-services engineers to support its products.

72. *Forbes*, October 20, 1997.

73. J. Gillett, "The cost-benefit of outsourcing: assessing the true cost of your outsourcing strategy," *European Journal of Purchasing and Supply*, 1 (1994), 45–47.

74. Vertical integration was one of the core corporate strategies identified by Alfred Chandler in his path-breaking book, A.D. Chandler, *Strategy and Structure: Chapters in the History of the Industrial Enterprise*, Cambridge, MA: MIT Press, 1962.

75. As discussed in Chapter 5, the firm faces a difficult competitive situation when either its supplier forward integrates or its customer back integrates.

76. Slywotzky and Morrison, *op. cit.*, argue that within an industry, the profitable areas shift over time in a process they term *value migration*. They argue that astute managers should actively seek the "profit zones" in their industries. See also R. Wise and P. Baumgartner, "Go Downstream: The New Profit Imperative in Manufacturing, *Harvard Business Review* 77 (Sept./Oct. 1999), 133–141.

77. By placing its bottling operations in a 49% owned subsidiary, Coca-Cola was able to escape the negative consequences of carrying bottling operations assets on its balance sheet.

78. *Fortune*, March 16, 1998.

79. Based on K. Ohmae, *The Mind of the Strategist*, New York: McGraw-Hill, 1982.

80. Of course, outright sale of the entire corporation may be the best way of enhancing shareholder wealth.

81. *Business Week*, June 16, 1997.

82. Some companies make a practice of offering a portion of subsidiary company shares to the public as a means of securing an external appraisal of their worth. In such cases, the aggregate value of the constituent businesses may be demonstrably greater than of the parent company as a whole.

83. Some cynics point to the positive relationship between company size and CEO compensation as an explanation for this behavior.

84. See, for example, N. Capon, J. U. Farley, and S. Hoenig, *Toward an Integrative Explanation of Corporate Financial Performance, op. cit.*

85. Note that the rationale for this type of licensing is very different from the near-free licenses to standardize a new technology.

86. *Business Week*, February 16, 1998. Interestingly, however, *Business Week* reported a study demonstrating that virtually every drug company formed by a major merger in the previous 30 years had less market share than previously held by the two firms combined!

87. Note that, in acquisitions and divestitures, where investment banks have typically played a major role, some movement to insourcing has occurred. Perhaps, the advertising arena is ripe for reconceptualizing the relationship between firm and advertising agency.

WEB RESOURCES

3M	www.3m.com
Administrative Science Quarterly	www.gsm.cornell.edu/ASQ/asq.html
Agouron	www.agouron.com
Airbus	www.airbus.com
America Online	www.aol.com
American Home Products	www.ahp.com
AOL	www.aol.com
AT&T	www.att.com
Ballard	www.ballard.com
Bank One	www.bankone.com
Black & Decker	www.blackanddecker.com
BP/Amoco	www.bpamoco.com
Business Product Industry Association	www.bpia.com
Business Week	www.businessweek.com
Charles Schwab	www.schwab.com
Chrysler	www.chrysler.com
Cisco Systems	www.cisco.com
Citibank	www.citibank.com
Clorox	www.clorox.com
Coca-Cola	www.cocacola.com
Computer Associates	www.cai.com
Compaq	www.compaq.com
Cyanamid	www.cyanamid.com
DaimlerChrysler	www.daimlerchrysler.com
Disney	www.disney.com
Dow Jones	www.dowjones.com
Dupont	www.dupont.com
EMI	www.emichrysalis.co.uk
Exxon	www.exxon.com
Exxon/Mobil	www.exxon.mobil.com
Federal Express	www.fedex.com
First USA	www.firstusa.com
Ford	www.ford.com
General Electric	www.ge.com
General Motors	www.gm.com
Glaxo-Wellcome	www.glaxowellcome.com
Harley Davidson	www.harley-davidson.com
Hitachi	www.hitachi.com
Honda	www.honda.com
IBM	www.ibm.com
IBM UK	www.uk.ibm.com
ICI	www.ici.com
Intel	www.intel.com
Johnson & Johnson	www.johnsonandjohnson.com
Journal of Applied Corporate Finance	www.sternstewart.com
Journal of Financial and Quantitative Analysis	www.depts.washington.edu/jfqa
Journal of Financial Economics	www.ssb.rochester.edu/fac/jfe
Kimberly-Clark	www.kimberly-clark.com
Kodak	www.kodak.com

Mannesman	www.mannesmann.com
Matsushita	www.panasonic.com
Mazda	www.mazda.com
MCI-Worldcom	www.wcom.com
MediaOne	www.mediaone.com
Merril Lynch	www.ml.com
Microsoft	www.microsoft.com
Mobil	www.mobil.com
NCR	www.ncr.com
NEC	www.nec.com
Netscape	www.netscape.com
The New York Times	www.nytimes.com
Nissan	www.nissan.com
Opel	www.opel.com
PepsiCo	www.pepsico.com
Pfizer	www.pfizer.com
Porsche	www.porsche.com
Primerica	www.pfsnet.com
Procter & Gamble	www.pg.com
Quaker	www.quakeroats.com
Sara Lee	www.saralee.com
Schneider Electric	www.schneider-electric.com
Scott Paper	www.kimberly-clark.com
Shell	www.shell.com
SMH (Swatch)	www.swatchgroup.com
SmithKline Beecham	www.sb.com
Snapple	www.snapple.com
Sony	www.sony.com
Sprint	www.sprint.com
Standard and Poor's	www.standardpoor.com
Strategic Management Journal	www.journals.wiley.com
Sun MicroSystems	www.sun.com
TCI	www.tci.com
Teleport	www.teleport.com
Thermo Electron	www.thermo.com
TIAA	www.tiaa-cref.org
Time Warner	www.timewarner.com
Toyota	www.toyota.com
Travelers Group/Citicorp	www.citi.com
Un-du	www.un-du.com
United Parcel Service	www.ups.com
U.S. Surgical	www.ussurg.com
Vodafone	www.vodafone.com
Volkswagen	www.vw.com
Warner-Lambert	www.warner-lambert.com
Worldcom	www.wcom.com
Xerox	www.xerox.com

CHAPTER

MARKET SEGMENTATION AND TARGETING

7

LEARNING OBJECTIVES

When you have completed this chapter, you will understand

- two important marketing concepts—segmentation and targeting

- how to form market segments

- several bases on which market segments can be developed

- criteria for forming market segments

- how to make difficult choices regarding the number of segments to develop

- segments-of-one

- how to choose which market segments to target for firm effort

- perceptual maps

INTRODUCTION

This chapter addresses the approach to completing marketing **Task 2: Identify and Target Market Segments** by building on earlier discussions of customers, competitors, and complementers. This chapter discusses the market segmentation process, highlighting both appropriate and inappropriate methods of forming segments. It also addresses the nature of market segments and provides criteria for forming acceptable segments; and presents alternative approaches to the targeting decision, the firm's selection of which market segments and customers to address. The important topic of positioning is deferred to Chapter 8.[1]

As a result of proper segmentation and targeting, the firm should be able to:

- determine how best to organize a market into readily-distinguishable groups of customers;
- identify the unique needs, wants, and preferences common to customers in each segment grouping;
- appraise the viability of, and select, a preferred segmentation scheme;
- decide which segments to address;
- determine the emphasis it wants to give each targeted segment in pursuit of business and market objectives.

MARKET SEGMENTATION

Market segmentation is the conceptual process of grouping together actual and potential customers in a market for the purpose of selecting targets for effort and for designing marketing programs. Several motives drive corporations to expend considerable effort on market segmentation. First, the process improves understanding of the market, in particular the nature and diversity of customer needs. Second, this improved understanding of customer needs leads to greater customer satisfaction through a clearer focus for the firm's market strategies. This fosters superior product and offer design, and better-targeted communication programs. Third, the combination of improved customer satisfaction and more efficient resource allocation leads to greater competitive advantage and superior profitability.

The end result of the market segmentation process is the identification of a number of market segments. Each of these segments comprises a group of current or potential customers that seek similar sets of benefits with similar levels of priority. In a sense, market segmentation leads to a compromise between mass marketing (one size fits all) and customization (unique offer for everyone). The formation of several market segments paves the way for the targeting decision, the selection of the market segment (or segments) that the firm decides to address.

The firm's market and financial performance is highly dependent on the quality of the process employed to develop market segments. To the extent that the market segmentation process is well managed and the targeting decision appropriately made, the firm secures the closest possible match between customer needs, wants, and priorities, and its offer. As a result, customer satisfaction is maximized, competitive advantage is created, and unit volume or profit margin improvements lead to enhanced shareholder value. Once the firm has decided to address a particular market (Marketing Task 1), the quality of the segmentation and targeting process is arguably the most critical of all marketing tasks.

To use a military analogy, the market segmentation and targeting process involves understanding the field of battle and deciding how to deploy one's forces. Disaster befalls the general whose incomplete understanding of the terrain, and of the strength and location of enemy forces, leads him to send inappropriately trained troops and the wrong type of materiel to the wrong part of the battlefield. In a similar manner, faulty market segmentation and targeting can lead marketing managers into the no-profit zone.

The Market Segmentation Process

The various approaches to market segmentation can be partitioned into externally and internally focused methods. In practice, though, the only valid approach to segmentation is external.

THE EXTERNALLY FOCUSED APPROACH The starting point for approaching the market segmentation process is a recognition that for any particular product market, the needs and wants of current and potential customers are typically heterogeneous. In other words, customers do not all seek identical benefits; rather, they seek a variety of different benefits, based on their differing needs and wants. Even customers who seek similar benefits may seek them with different orders of priority.

A proper market segmentation perspective assumes heterogeneity of needs and wants for all product markets.[2] When customers have heterogeneous needs and wants, a single marketing offer implies that many customers would find their needs and wants unsatisfied and therefore be vulnerable to a competitor that better tailors its offer. The marketing task is to develop segments of customers that have relatively homogeneous needs and wants from the group of actual and potential customers. However, the sets of needs and wants are different from segment to segment.

The development of market segments is a judgmental task requiring a high degree of conceptual skill. The process demands both creative insight and knowledge of existing and potential customers, typically acquired from data collected through marketing research efforts. In large-scale segmentation studies where significant amounts of survey data are collected, a variety of multivariate statistical techniques are available to supplement managerial judgment and the more rudimentary cross-tabulation analyses still widely employed. For example, regression, discriminant, and cluster analysis can each play an important role in identifying several homogeneous sets of needs and wants, as well as identifying related groups of customers.[3]

Once groups of customers with homogeneous needs and wants (market segments) have been identified, the focus turns to the targeting decision, the choice of which segments to select for effort. Firms typically do not have the resources to address all segments in a market and must make choices. Ultimately, marketing offers must be developed for the targeted market segments. These offers will necessarily be more precisely tailored to the needs and wants of customers (individuals and organizations) in these market segments than would a single marketing offer developed for actual and potential customers in general. The better matching that results from this effort drives up the value delivered to customers, increases customer satisfaction, and decreases competitive vulnerability.

When customers are organizations, such as in industrial markets and for consumer goods at the trade level, and where a high degree of customer concentration exists, the segmentation problem is often straightforward, reducing to segments of one for individual key accounts. However, when customer numbers are large, managers frequently work with sample statistics and significant volumes of data. As the costs of data storage and manipulation reduce, and firms become increasingly competent at data mining and warehousing, the market segmentation process can quickly become highly data-intensive.[4] Regardless, to do a good job it is typically insufficient to restrict the problem simply to data that exists on current customers; potential customers should also be included.

The development of market segments can be approached from two directions:

- Groups of customers with homogeneous needs and wants are formed; these groups are then described in terms of distinguishing characteristics for communications purposes.

Example: AT&T's data system organization identified three market segments based on the complexity of their communications needs. Customers in the Tier 1 segment had common, basic requirements and could be served with "off the shelf" products; Tier 2 customers required "off the shelf" products plus some options; for Tier 3 customers, tailored solutions were needed.

- Candidate descriptor or distinguishing characteristics are chosen. These "segmentation variables" typically fall into one of four categories—geographic, demographic, behavioral, or socio-psychological. The groups so formed are explored for homogeneous needs and wants within groups, heterogeneous needs and wants across groups.

These alternative processes give rise to two potential problems:

- Groups of customers with homogeneous subsets of needs and wants may be formed, but distinguishing group characteristics cannot be identified.
- More commonly, groups of customers are identified, but there is little evidence of intra-group homogeneity and inter-group heterogeneity of needs and wants.

In both cases, however, so long as analysts and managers have a clear understanding of the distinction between cause and correlation, less difficulty is encountered. Good segmentation should be preoccupied with finding the factors that cause differences in behavior, for these drive the customer search process. Descriptor or segmentation variables are, therefore, correlational, though vitally important in enabling marketers to communicate with, and distribute products to, targeted segments with reasonable efficiency.

In practice, the market segmentation process typically starts from both directions and converges somewhere in the middle:

- Attempts are made to first develop homogeneous subsets of needs and wants, then to identify distinguishing group characteristics;

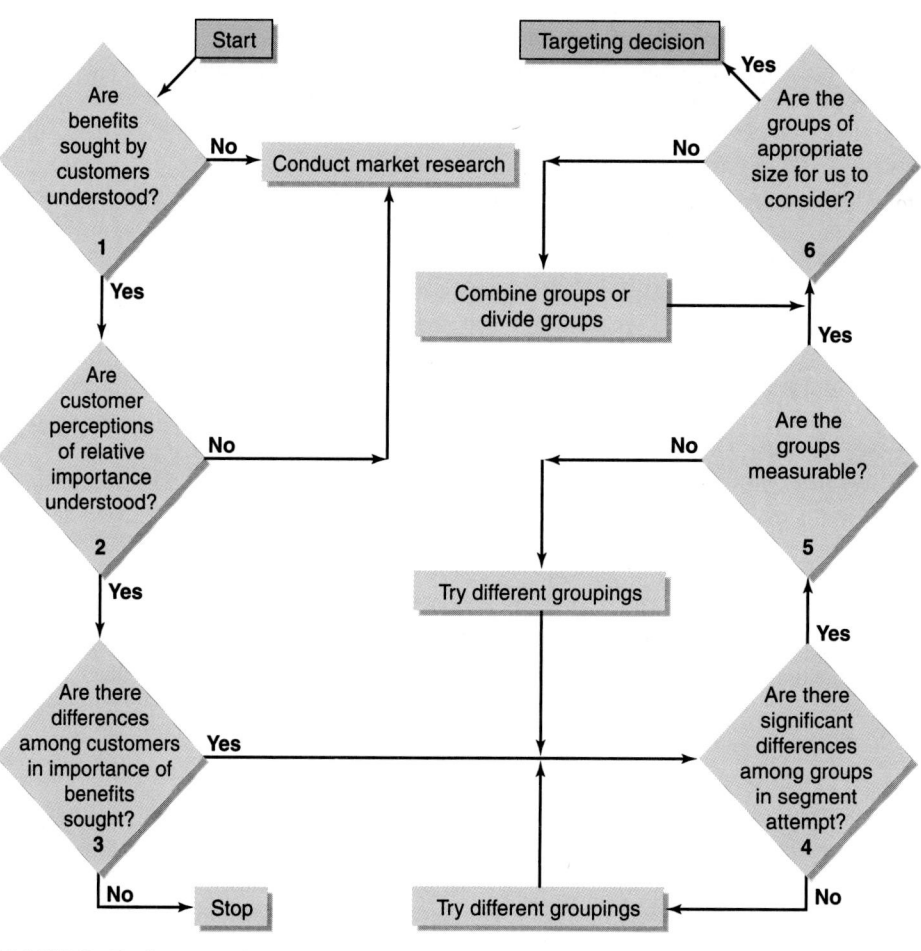

FIGURE 7.1

The Segmentation Approach

TABLE 7.1 Illustration of Market Segments in the Female Skin Care Market: Rank Order Importance by Segment

Customer Need/ Required Benefits	Definition of Market Segments Based on Age					
	14-18	19-29	30-39	40-49	50-64	65 and over
Beauty	5	4	1	2	2	3
Confidence	2	2	3	3	3	4
Economy	4	5	7	7	6	5
Health	6	6	4	4	4	2
Sexual Allure	3	1	2	5	5	6
Status	1	3	6	6	7	7
Youthfulness	7	7	5	1	1	1

- Groups of customers are identified by distinguishing characteristics, then needs and wants examined for intra-group homogeneity and inter-group heterogeneity.

Through an iterative process (Figure 7.1), the market is broken down into a number of market segments. See Table 7.1 for a typical market segmentation matrix.[5]

The core issue for market segmentation is to link the fundamental differences relating to customer needs and wants with the appropriate descriptor/segmentation variables. These fundamental differences ultimately drive the design of market offers. However, in addition to needs and wants, it may also be important to identify other differences, such as usage rate (heavy or light users), propensity to innovate (especially for new product launches), and loyalty status.

In general, grouping on these other variables precedes grouping based on needs and wants. For example, a firm such as McDonald's might decide to group its potential customers on the basis of heavy versus light users, then focus its efforts on heavy users. When it examines heavy users it might discover that one group of heavy users is families with young children, but that another heavy user group comprises single males in blue collar jobs. Clearly, marketing offers addressing each group would be quite different.[6]

INTERNALLY FOCUSED METHODS We reject internally focused approaches to market segmentation but, nonetheless, present several commonly found approaches as warnings to our readers. Oftentimes, firms understand that market segmentation has a critical role to play in the formulation of market strategy, but approach the process as a ritual, seemingly without a clear conviction of its strategic importance. For example:

- **"That's the way we've always done it"**: This internally focused method ignores the impact of changes in the environment, customers, and competitors. Clearly, a segmentation method that may have been appropriate in the past could now be outdated in a changing marketplace.
- **"That's the way the data are available"**: This passive method assumes (sometimes incorrectly) that independent data-gatherers had the firm's market segmentation problem as their prime goal when devising data collection instruments. When this method is used, it commonly involves government or trade association data used by several competitors in the same industry. In such cases, it is particularly insidious as it decreases the possibility that the firm can secure competitive advantage by its choice of segmentation scheme.[7]

- **"That's the way we're organized"**: This method implies that strategic direction is driven by current organization design (strategy follows structure), rather than organization being constructed based on a strategic response to environmental imperatives (structure follows strategy). This method tends to produce rigidity, a particular problem in a changing marketplace.
- **"That's the way competitors do it"**: This method accepts equivalence with competitors and ignores the potential for innovative market segmentation to redefine the market and secure superior market position. It renders a company's moves much more visible in the competitor's information system, and may well result in the firm competing on terms favorable to the competitor. Given a choice, the competitor would presumably segment a market in a way best suited to its capabilities and strengths.

Market Segments

In this section we introduce sets of segmentation variables and discuss the manner in which these variables, singly or in combination, can be used to form market segments. Criteria for acceptability of market segments are then presented, followed by a segmentation example. This section concludes with a discussion of standardized segments and the changing nature of market segments.

SEGMENTATION VARIABLES   Four categories of variables are typically suggested as possibilities among which distinguishing characteristics might be found:

- **Geographic** characteristics include country, region, county size, city or SMSA size,[8] population density, and climate.
- **Demographic** characteristics are physical descriptors of customers. For consumers, these include variables such as age, gender, education, family size, social class, language, race, nationality, religion, wealth, income, and occupation. For organizations, they include industry (SIC code), firm size, growth, profitability, balance sheet items, legal entity, number of years in business, and length of time at location.
- **Behavioral** variables include use occasion, decision-making practices, user situation, composition of the decision-making unit, and type of purchase decision. Specific variables for organizations include power structure (such as engineering dominated, financially dominated) and organization of the procurement function (such as centralized or decentralized).
- **Social/psychological** variables include personality, attitudes, sexual orientation, life stage, social class, and life style characteristics such as activities, interests, and opinions. Corresponding variables for organizations include organizational climate and culture, and inward/outward orientation.

FORMING SEGMENTS   Each characteristic gives rise to several customer groupings. For example, typical segments developed from the consumer demographic characteristic, education, are grade school or less, some high school, high school graduate, some college, and college graduate. Segments developed from the life stage variable might include single, just married, married with children, divorced with children, empty nester couple, empty nesters with grandchildren, and widow/widower. Similarly, for the organization demographic characteristic, firm size, *Fortune* 500, *Fortune* 501 to 1000, firms with sales greater than $100 million, firms with sales from $50 to $100 million, and firms with sales under $50 million. Sometimes marketers combine characteristics; Figure 7.2 illustrates two characteristics, but more may be used.

ACCEPTABILITY OF CUSTOMER GROUPINGS AS MARKET SEGMENTS   Clearly, there are many ways to group customers. However, before a grouping can be considered as a viable market segment, several criteria should be satisfied. In particular, segments should be measurable, differentiated, identifiable, appropriate size (revenue potential), and actionable.

Consumer Markets

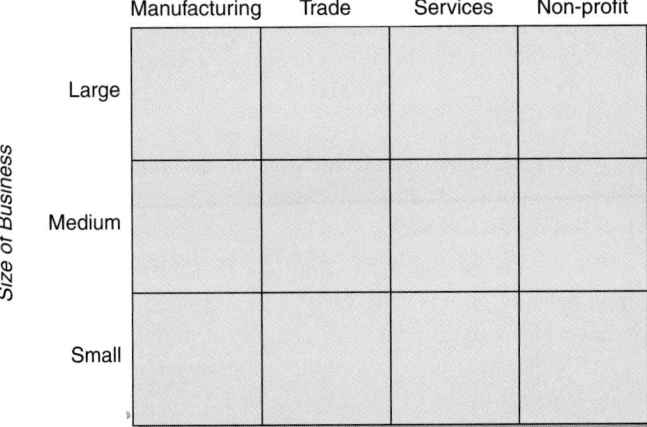

Employment Type

	White collar professional	Blue collar professional	Clerical	Labor	Student	Retired, housewife
Young, no children						
Young family						
Older family						
Older, no children						

Stage of Life Cycle

Business Markets

Type of Business

	Manufacturing	Trade	Services	Non-profit
Large				
Medium				
Small				

Size of Business

FIGURE 7.2

Matrix Methods for Segmenting Consumer and Business Markets

- **Measurable**: The firm is able to measure the number of members and propensity to purchase of each segment.
- **Differentiated**: People or organizations in the different segments have different needs and wants, causing them to respond differently to different marketing offers.
- **Identifiable**: Demographic and other characteristics of the segments can be identified for the purpose of reaching them with marketing offers.
- **Appropriate Size**: Neither too small for a large company (too costly), nor too large for a small company (potentially severe competition).

Example: In summer 2000, the magazine *Mirabella* ceased publication. In reporting the closure decision by Hachette Filipacchi Magazines, *The New York Times* noted that *Mirabella* was aimed at "women who are no longer 24 years old who care passionately about literary criticism and serious articles about, say, contemporary philosophers—and equally as passionately about where to buy those just adorable hot-pink leather pants."[9] Perhaps this was too small a segment for viability!

- **Actionable**: A strategy can be developed for each segment that the firm desires to target.

The important point that must be remembered about market segments is that they are not in any sense real, correct or incorrect or, indeed, immutable. What they are, however, are the products of the marketing manager's creative insight, and the fundamental units for developing market strategy.

A SEGMENTATION EXAMPLE   Experiencing significant price pressure, Mobil Corporation conducted a segmentation study of the gasoline market. This study identified five segments of gasoline buyers[10]:

- **Road Warriors** (16% of buyers): Generally higher-income, middle-aged men, drive 25,000 to 50,000 miles per year, buy premium gas with a credit card, purchase sandwiches and drinks from the convenience store, sometimes wash their cars at the car wash.
- **True Blues** (16%): Usually men and women with moderate to high incomes, loyal to a brand and sometimes a particular station, frequently buy premium gasoline and pay in cash.
- **Generation F3 (food, fuel, fast)** (27%): Upwardly-mobile men and women, half under 25, constantly on the go, drive a lot, and snack heavily from the convenience store.
- **Homebodies** (21%): Usually housewives who shuttle children around during the day, and use whatever gasoline station is based in town or along their travel route.
- **Price Shoppers** (20%): Generally neither loyal to a brand nor a station, rarely buy premium, frequently on tight budgets, efforts to woo have been basis of marketing strategies for years.

Mobil decided to target two of these segments—Road Warriors and Generation F3. It took two related actions—placed a major effort into convenience stores, and reduced time at the pump by introducing the Mobil *Speed Pass.*

STANDARDIZED SEGMENTS   Thus far the discussion has focused on developing market segments for individual product markets. However, some organizations develop standardized segments that have the potential for use in many product markets. For example, Claritas/NPDC's PRIZM lifestyle cluster system comprises 15 social groups containing 62 clusters in total—*Elite Suburbs* [5], *Urban Uptown* [5], *2nd City Society* [3], *Landed Gentry* [4], *The Affluentials* [5], *Inner Suburbs* [4], *Urban Midscale* [5], *2nd City Centers* [5], *ExUrban Blues* [4], *Country Families* [4], *Urban Cores* [3], *2nd City Blues* [4], *Working Towns* [4], *Heartlanders* [2] and *Rustic Living* [5].[11] The social group, *Country Families*, contains four ethnically white clusters—owners of single-family homes: *Big Sky Families, New Eco-topia, River City, USA,* and *Shotguns & Pickups.* These clusters are characterized as:

- **Big Sky Families**: Mid-scale couples, kids and farmland, 1.48% of U.S. households. Predominately under 18 and 35–64, high school and some college education, employed in blue-collar and farming jobs. Lifestyle preferences—rodeo fans, cat owners, pension plan, watch Fox Family Channel, read *Soap Opera Digest* and listen to variety radio.
- **New Eco-topia**: Rural white/blue-collar/farm families, 0.9% of U.S. households. Predominately over 45, high school, some college education and college graduates, employed in white- and blue-collar and farming jobs. Life style preferences—cross-country skiing, dog owners, have a *Keogh* account, watch *Jeopardy!* and read *Prevention.*
- **River City, USA**: Middle class, rural families, 1.78% of U.S. households. Predominately under 18 and 45–54, high school education, employed in blue-collar

and farming jobs. Lifestyle preferences—target shooting, bought paint at a hardware store, bought medical insurance from an agent, watch *Live with Regis and Kathy Lee* and read *Country Living*.

- **Shotguns & Pickups**: Rural blue-collar workers and families, 1.91% of U.S. households. Mixed age group, high school education. Life style preferences— fresh-water fishing, travel by car with camping equipment, have <$50,000 homeowner's insurance, watch *ESPN2* and read *Motor Trend*.

A national wholesale distributor of magazines used such a classification.

Example: The distributor, carrying several thousand magazines, had the problem of deciding what assortments of magazines to offer in the diverse geographic areas that it served. It first identified the set of magazines that appealed to each of the standardized segments. Then, for each geographic area, it identified the prevalence of the various segments and selected the magazines for distribution on that basis.

Consistent with increased globalization, based on interviews about core values with 1,000 people in each of 35 countries, Roper Starch Worldwide identified six global consumer segments residing, to varying degrees, in each country:

- **Strivers**: Place more emphasis on material and professional goals than other groups
- **Devouts**: Tradition and duty are very important
- **Altruists**: Interested in social issues and society welfare
- **Intimates**: Value close personal family
- **Fun Seekers**: Frequent restaurants, bars, and movies
- **Creatives**: Strong interest in education, knowledge, and technology

Although there was some overlap, Roper found that people in different segments generally pursued different activities, bought different products, and used different media.[12]

THE CHANGING NATURE OF MARKET SEGMENTS The importance of the market segmentation process and its centrality to marketing management cannot be overstated. Imagine one firm develops a conceptual perspective about a market that is superior to competitors. This firm is able to define segments such that the degree of heterogeneity in needs and wants across segments is superior to competition. Assuming that all competitors have equivalent competence in developing and executing marketing offers, the former firm should be more successful. Its marketing offers will be more precisely tailored to the needs and wants of customers in the marketplace than will those of competitors.

However, because customer needs and wants (and their priority orders) are constantly changing, the most appropriate market segmentation scheme changes over time. Two separate processes are at work here. First, when a new product market is developed early products typically provide functional benefits that satisfy some set of needs unmet by existing products. Later, competitive advantage is achieved by identifying customers with finer-grained sets of needs and satisfying them by delivering appropriate benefits. Some of these later benefits, such as availability and status, may be little related to the functional benefits that led customers to adopt the product in the first place.

Second, later in the life cycles of many products, customers assume competitive equivalence on the basic functional benefits that define the category. Thus the core functional benefits may be irrelevant to the purchase decision and should not be included in the segmentation process. Rather, segmentation should be based on new benefits, even though they may be far removed from the product's core.[13]

Example: Business persons deciding which airline to fly on a particular route typically identify such benefits as best on-time record, most convenient scheduling, best frequent flyer program, best meals, and most leg room. Typically, safety is not mentioned, yet safety is clearly the most important benefit sought by most customers. The reason for this omission is that safety has been taken out of the decision since consumers believe that, among a set of airline competitors, each is equivalent in delivering this benefit (since they are flying identical aircraft), regardless of whether this happens to be objectively true.[14]

ISSUES FOR MARKET SEGMENTS

Several topics often arise regarding market segments: how many market segments should be formed, segments-of-one, and how the firm should deal with aging market segments.

HOW MANY MARKET SEGMENTS?   Larger numbers of market segments imply a greater degree of homogeneity of customer needs and wants within market segments, and require more precisely tailored market offers to selected segments. If the firm is able to identify and tailor its offers to these segments, overall customer satisfaction should increase. On the other hand, as the number of market segments expands, product development costs are likely to increase, potential scale economies in advertising and promotion may be lost, and complexity is increased for equivalent market coverage. An important trade-off must be made between better satisfaction of customer needs and wants, achieved by identifying larger numbers of market segments, and the increased costs of serving them. The market segmentation process must include a step in which the number of identified market segments is rationalized; if segments developed in the segmentation process are not sufficiently different to merit separate offers, they should be collapsed.

One method of serving greater numbers of market segments, yet holding down design and production costs, is modularity, the use of individual components in multiple products serving multiple segments.

> **Example:** The fuselage design for the Boeing 707 was inherited by the 727, 737, and appeared yet again in the 757. The 737 and 757 are still in production in many different versions, meeting different customer requirements at significant cost savings for Boeing. Airbus has also used modularity in developing its successful product families.

Information technology is having an enormous impact on the cost of variety. For example, it allows companies such as L.L. Bean and Land's End to assemble a multitude of product basket orders of less than $100 and ship direct to consumers profitably.

In recent years, technological advances have increased design and production flexibility, and many firms have placed significant investment in reducing set-up times. As a result, product variations can increasingly be made at a reasonable cost and the "optimal" number of segments increased. This process is likely to be accelerated by global integration of marketing efforts that, by encouraging across country aggregation, may well permit within-country segments of previously sub-minimal scale to be profitably served.

SEGMENTS-OF-ONE   An interesting new segmentation thrust is for those consumers who want personally-designed products. Artisans have historically served this type of segment, such as bespoke tailors, but recent technological advances have made it possible to integrate personally-designed products with flexible mass production techniques.[15] One of the first examples of mass customization was the Japanese bicycle manufacturer, Panasonic:

> **Example:** Retail bicycle customers are measured for their bicycles, just as a person might be measured for a suit. Measurements are then faxed to the factory and the custom-made bicycle delivered to the store within a few days.

Levi Strauss offers custom-made jeans using a similar system. The advantages of this process are two fold. First, customer satisfaction is improved since precisely-tailored products are produced. Second, finished-goods inventory is reduced throughout the production and distribution system. Callaway, the golf club manufacturer, provides an extension of this idea:

> **Example:** Callaway is opening "performance centers" in which golfers will receive computer analyses of their swings and clubs. In the New York center, they will then be able to select custom designed clubs and, possibly, watch their assembly.[16]

Companies selling through the Internet are quickly developing "choiceboard" models.[17] At Dell Computer, customers design their own PCs; Mattell customers can design their own Barbie dolls; and Ford and Microsoft have announced a joint venture for customers to design their own automobiles.[18]

In addition, many Internet companies are personalizing their product offerings. For example, Hallmark will store your important anniversaries in their database and e-mail you at the appropriate time to select and send your greeting; Amazon.com will advise you of books that meet your preferences, based on your historic purchasing patterns.

An alternative way of viewing the segment-of-one phenomenon is that in several product categories, a segment of customers places a high value on personally-designed products.

AGING MARKET SEGMENTS   As discussed earlier, it is less expensive for the firm to promote and sell its products to current customers than to new customers. As a result, many firms have refocused their marketing efforts to secure increasing loyalty from current customers. However, a particular problem relates to the aging process.

> **Example:** The former Richardson Vicks product, *Old Spice*, was originally used by 18- to 25-year-old men. Promotion continued to target this group as it aged and although relatively successful, sales stagnated since use of *Old Spice* was less frequent with older men. Only when acquired by Procter & Gamble was effort placed on returning to the original age-defined segment now, of course, populated by potential new customers.
>
> Similarly, automobile firms place significant effort on first-time buyers, hoping to build lifetime loyalty.[19]

Targeting one age segment while attempting to secure sales from another is a tricky business. Spirits companies, such as Seagram, are faced with this problem as the customer base for brown spirits, such as whiskey and scotch, ages. An even more dramatic example is Readers Digest. In the mid-1990s, the median age of U.S. subscribers was 69 years. Literally, its customers were dying!

TARGETING MARKET SEGMENTS

When the market segmentation process is completed and several market segments have been formed, management must then decide how many and which segments to target. Targeting is simply the decision to allocate marketing effort at one or more market segments. Typically, firms have neither the resources nor the abilities to target all segments in a market. Rather, choices must be made as firms identify those segments that they believe will earn them profits. In making the targeting decision, the firm should be highly conscious of the *Principle of Selectivity and Concentration*.

Whereas marketing's role is advisory regarding which markets the firm should address Task 1, within the scope of those selected markets marketing's explicit responsibility is to identify those customers the firm should serve, selecting market segments, customer types and roles, and in some cases individual customers. These decisions may be strategic for the business unit, and are leading to a blurring of the traditional distinctions between marketing and sales.[20] As the use of sophisticated information technology, direct marketing (in its various forms), and key account management in the sales force grow, increasing internal change and re-definition of marketing and sales roles can be expected.

Targeting and Company Size

In general, targeting requires tough choices, although larger companies have greater resources and can afford to target multiple segments:

> **Examples:** In the hotel business, industry leader Marriott targets several market segments with different brands, such as *Marriott, Courtyard, Fairfield Inn, TownePlace Suites, Residence Inn*, and *Renaissance Hotels Resorts.*
>
> In the Internet service provider business, America Online (AOL) offers its flagship *AOL* service to customers willing to pay premium prices. For value shoppers, it offers the low-price oriented *Compuserve* service.

Smaller companies with fewer resources typically target fewer segments; these firms enjoy potential advantage in segment selection as their more limited resources lead to achievement of focus by default.[21] Many larger companies with greater resources have found to their peril that, spread too thin over several segments, they are uncompetitive compared to more focused adversaries.

> **Example:** In early 1999, AccessAir (Des Moines), Frontier Airlines (Denver), Pro Air (Detroit), Spirit Airlines (Melbourne, FL and Atlantic City) and Vanguard Airlines (Kansas City) were holding their own against such entrenched major competitors as American, United, Delta, and Northwest.[22]

Large companies typically achieve market and segment focus only with significant difficulty, since the various options tend to have supporting internal constituencies (frequently related to organization structure). As a result, the decision-making process is protracted and, if not handled skillfully, can be detrimental to the firm's success.

However, successful small focused companies also face dangers:

- They do not understand that a major reason for their success is a high degree of focus. As a result, they expend resources on expanding into segments where resource-rich competitors are stronger;
- Demand in their single segment may diminish drastically, and the firm has no other segments to cushion the impact. For example, if a firm targets a single industry, an industry recession may lead to dramatic reductions in demand for the firm's products and services;
- The small firm is so successful in growing its targeted segment that a large firm with significant resources attacks it directly. Examples of this problem abound, frequently in the maturity phase of the product life cycle where a smaller, innovative firm identifies a market niche and proceeds to serve it so well that it attracts the attention of major players.[23]

> **Example:** From 1989 to 1994, start-up Guiltless Gourmet (GG) grew its line of baked low-fat tortilla chips into a $23 million enterprise. However, snack giant Frito-Lay entered the market and by 1996, GG's revenues had dropped precipitously.[24]

- Addressing a small segment may lead to a high cost position that cannot be offset by high prices, for as the overall market develops, increased product quality and lower prices result from intense competition among rivals in the broader market.

Useful Data for Targeting

During the targeting process, managers may find it helpful to collect data, including:

- **Customers**: What will customers want in the future? How many of them will there be? What will be their purchasing power, willingness to buy?
- **Competitors**: Who will be competing for serving these customers' needs? What will they be offering? What performance results will they be seeking in return for meeting these needs?
- **Technology**: What kinds of products/services/technologies will be capable of meeting (or substituting for) these needs? What will be the timing of key technological developments? Who is sponsoring them? What is the future cost competi-

tiveness of relevant systems? What are the implications for our products/services and technologies?

- **Government**: What is the expected future course of government regulation in this market? How will it affect us? How might it change the nature of competition in this industry?
- **Resources**: What is the supply outlook for key resources? Is a monopsony or cartelization of supply likely?[25] Are competitors integrating backwards?

Selecting Target Market Segments: A Matrix Approach

This section presents a multifactor, analytic process that can be helpful in deciding which market segments to address. Conceptually, the choice of which market segments to target should be based on two dimensions—attractiveness of the market segment, and the strengths the firm can bring to bear upon the segment. All things being equal, if a market segment is attractive to the firm and it has the strengths to compete, it should target that segment. Conversely, if a market segment is not attractive and the firm does not have competitive strengths, the segment should be avoided. (This approach belongs to a family of approaches termed portfolio models, discussed more fully in Chapter 12.)[26] However, as with many managerial tools, it should be noted that although the results of the analysis have value *per se*, perhaps the greatest benefit is the insight gained when managers use this approach to organize their thoughts when engaging in conversation about target segments.

IDENTIFYING CRITERIA FOR TARGETING MARKET SEGMENTS   The crucial issue is to identify the appropriate factors for operationalizing these two dimensions. Sources for these variables include economic and marketing theory, and analysis of general databases, such as PIMS. In addition, empirical analysis of an individual firm's competitive history offers advantages of proprietary secrecy and reflects unique experiences and advantage. Many firms, however, use very general criteria. Table 7.2 highlights the sorts of factors typically considered as candidates for the two dimensions.

Market Segment Attractiveness Criteria   Since the firm is expected to use common market segment attractiveness criteria across a range of market segment choices, the selection of criteria is particularly crucial.[29] The factors in Table 7.2 should be viewed as representative, rather than comprehensive. Management should work diligently to identify those factors it finds most useful. In addition, it is insufficient to identify just the factor; the firm must also be concerned with directionality. For example, large market segment size or high market segment potential might be positive factors for a large firm with significant

Table 7.2   Candidate Market Segment Attractiveness and Business Strengths Criteria

Market Segment Attractiveness	Business Strengths
Market Segment Size	Market Segment Share
Market Segment Potential	Profitability Record
Market Segment Growth Rate	Liquidity
Ability to Use Available Resources	Financial Leverage
Potential Profit Margins[27]	Distribution Facilities
Likely Competitor Resources[28]	Consumer Marketing Skills
Technological Change	Production Capacity
Barriers to Entry	Technological Expertise
Barriers to Exit	Modernity of Plant and Equipment
Regulatory Constraints	Raw Materials Position
Social Factors	Government Relations
Degree of Vertical Integration	Sales Force

resources; by contrast, for a small firm with limited resources, small market segment size or small market segment potential might be more positive. After all, large firms often set minimum market segment size/potential cut-offs; too large a market segment might attract major players that otherwise would not enter.

> **Example:** Michael Steinbeis, CEO of Steinbeis Holding, the world leader in battery labels, has stated: "We want to be big in small markets. We may even pull out if a market becomes too large and, due to our size and resources, we can only be a small player."[30]

For many firms, high degrees of government regulation are anathema; yet, to firms experienced in dealing with regulatory bureaucracies, high regulation that poses an entry barrier for potential competitors without these skills might be highly positive. The crucial implication is that individualized selection criteria by firm tends to promote inherently healthy competitive diversity. Use of common criteria across firms promotes competitive convergence that, unless demand is highly elastic, tends to produce an unhealthy competitive climate.

Business Strengths Criteria In selecting business strengths for use in a multifactor analytic scheme, managerial objectivity can be a major issue. One means of avoiding an optimistic bias in identifying firm strengths is to choose an externally-oriented starting point. For example, the analysis might focus on the crucial factors for success in the segment under consideration. These can then be used as a template against which to assess the firm. Alternatively, if the firm chooses to start with a generalized list of business strengths, these might be reviewed by industry experts, ideally in a blind comparison, to ensure a sense of reality.

SELECTING MARKET SEGMENTS TO TARGET This section works through the process of assessing market segments. It commences with market segment attractiveness, then moves to business strengths. In each case, it develops an index number or factor score that represents, respectively, segment attractiveness and business strengths.

Market Attractiveness The process for developing a market segment attractiveness score comprises five stages. An illustration is shown in Table 7.3.

- **Stage 1: Factor Identification**. The firm seeks several factors (typically 6 to 10) according to the statement, "Given our history, objectives, culture, management style, successes, and failures, we like to be in market segments that offer:"
- **Stage 2: Factor Weighting**. Weight each factor by its importance to the firm: factor weights sum to 100.

Table 7.3 Market Segment Attractiveness Analysis

Factor	Weighting (for the firm or business)	Rating (1 to 10 scale) (for a specific segment)	Factor Score (weighting × rating)
High market growth	20	7	140
Large potential size	20	5	100
Little regulation	10	8	80
Weak competition	15	4	60
Easy access to customers	15	9	135
Ability to build new strengths	10	6	120
Use excess resources	10	2	20
	100		Total 655

Stages 1 and 2 only have to be completed once; the results are constant across the set of market segments being considered. The analysis now shifts to a particular individual market segment.

- **Stage 3: Market Segment Opportunity Rating**. Rate the particular market segment according to how well it measures up on each factor (1 = poor; 10 = excellent).
- **Stage 4: Develop Factor Scores**. For each factor, form a set of individual factor scores: weighting × rating.
- **Stage 5: Develop the Market Segment Attractiveness Score**. Sum the individual factor scores.

As a result of this process, the firm develops a market segment attractiveness score ranging between 100 and 1,000. The higher the number, the more attractive the market segment.[31]

Business Strengths The favored approach requires, as its starting point, selection of a series of factors relevant to the particular market segment being considered. The process for developing a business strengths score for market segments also involves five stages. An illustration is shown in Table 7.4.

- **Stage 1: Factor Identification**. The firm highlights several factors (typically 6 to 10) according to the statement, "To be successful in this market segment, any competitor must possess the following strengths:"
- **Stage 2: Factor Weighting**. Each of these factors is weighted by its importance for success in the market segment; factor weights sum to 100.

The analysis now shifts to the firm's possession of these critical strengths.

- **Stage 3: Firm Rating**. Rate the firm on its possession of these strengths (1 = poor; 10 = excellent).
- **Stage 4: Develop Factor Scores**. For each factor, form a series of individual factor scores: weighting and rating.
- **Stage 5: Develop the Business Strengths Score**. Sum the individual factor scores.

As a result of this process, the firm develops a business strengths score that ranges between 100 and 1,000. The higher the number, the stronger the firm's strengths for competing in this market segment.

COMPARING ALTERNATIVE MARKET SEGMENT OPPORTUNITIES Typically, management has to select its targets from a variety of market segments. The market segment attractiveness and business strengths analyses produce two index numbers for each market segment under consideration. The various potential target segments can thus be plotted on a two-dimensional matrix. This is shown in Figure 7.3, where both the market

Table 7.4 Business Strengths Analysis

Factor	Weighting (for a specific segment)	Rating (1 to 10 scale for the firm or business)	Factor Score (weighting × rating)
Good R&D	25	7	175
Well-trained sales force	15	9	135
Low-cost operations	10	4	40
High-quality service	15	6	90
Deep pockets	10	9	90
In-place distribution	20	5	100
Fast-moving organization	5	3	15
	$\Sigma = 100$		Total 645

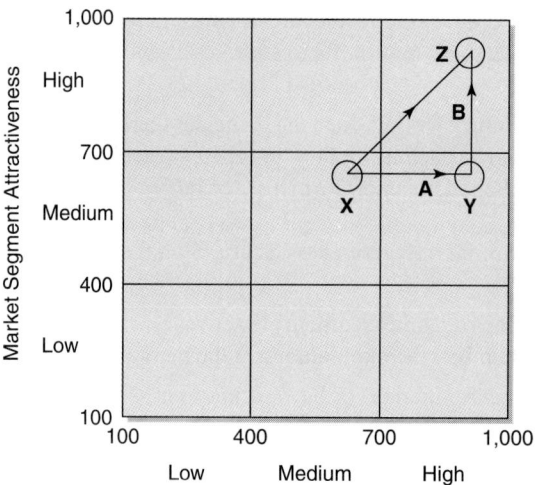

FIGURE 7.3

Market Segment Attractiveness/Business Strengths Matrix

segment attractiveness and business strengths dimensions have two cut points (400 and 700) to form a nine-cell matrix.

Placing Entries in the Matrix Placing the various market segments in the matrix provides guidance in the targeting decision. In general, market segments in the high/high, high/medium, and medium/high cells are good targeting candidates. Those in the low/low, low/medium, and medium/low cells are poor candidates. Entries on the diagonal—low/high, medium/medium, high/low—suggest that the firm should proceed with caution, or undertake further analysis. Notwithstanding these prescriptions, the relative positions of various segment opportunities may provide more valuable insights.

The matrix also provides specific insights on the dynamics of changing the position of a market segment. By decomposing scores on each dimension, management can understand the reason for its position and generate ideas about how to change. Consider, for example, market segment *X* from the illustration. To reach the desirable position *Z*, the segment must make two moves—one horizontal (A) to position *Y* and one vertical (B). The horizontal move focuses on improving business strengths, accomplished by returning to the business strengths analysis and identifying important success factors where room for improvement exists. Appropriate investment may shift the market segment to a medium/high market segment attractiveness/business strengths position.

The vertical move is somewhat more subtle. It requires deeper market analysis with a view to redefining the market segment so that it becomes more attractive to the firm. Perhaps a modified segmentation approach may identify individual segments for which the firm is better suited.

In this analysis, it is implicitly assumed that the market segments were independent, and that targeting one segment has no effect on targeting another. If the firm contemplates targeting more that one segment, it should consider potential synergies (positive and negative) that may derive from addressing multiple segments. It should also consider complexity problems resulting from the requirement to design and deliver different marketing offers to multiple market segments.

Selecting Target Market Segments: Perceptual Maps

A complementary approach for addressing the targeting issue is to develop a visual representation (map) of the market, such as that shown in Figure 7.4. In this illustration, two underlying dimensions describe required customer benefits. These are typically developed

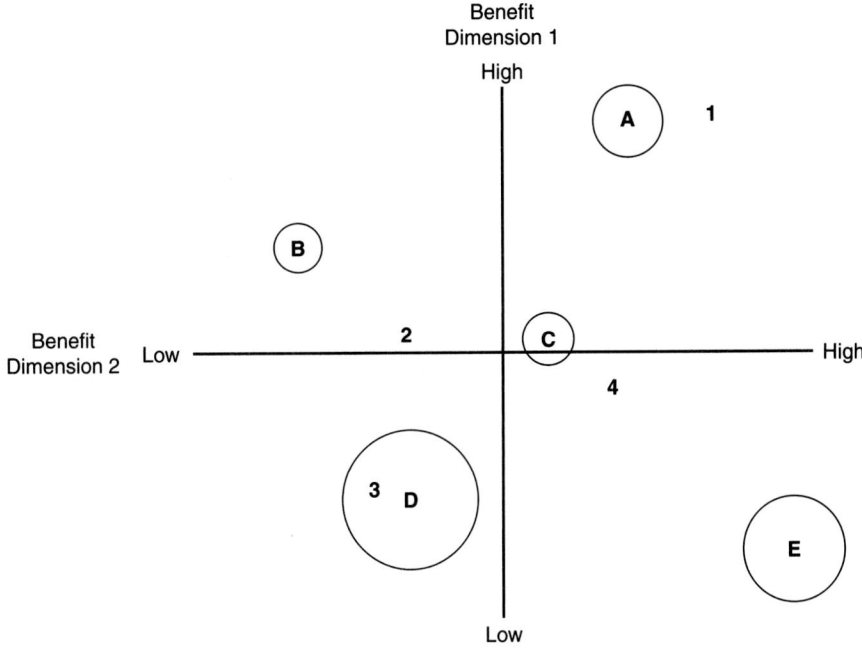

FIGURE 7.4

Visual Representation of Market Segments and Competitive Offers

from customer survey data and an analytic process such as multidimensional scaling.[32] The various market segments (A to E) are represented in terms of their ideal points, the ideal combination of benefits that each market segment requires.[33] The size of the circle representing each market segment is proportional to its size.

The various competitive offers (1 to 4) are represented in terms of customer perceptions of each offer's ability to deliver those benefits. The underlying assumption is that, *ceteris paribus*, an offer's market share of a market segment is directly related to its closeness to the market segment ideal point (the center of the circle).[34]

The perceptual map describes how well each competitive offer is serving current customer needs.[35]

- Segment A: Offer 1 should have the highest market segment share; however, it can improve its position by modifying the perception of its benefit mix by moving west on benefit dimension 2.
- Segment B: Offer 2 is closest to this segment's ideal point but does not serve it well. It can improve its position by moving its perceptions in a northwest direction.
- Segment C: Offer 2 probably secures some sales from Segment C, but probably less than Offer 4, which can improve its position in the segment by moving northwest.
- Segment D: This segment is well served by Offer 3. A new entry into this segment would face an entrenched competitor.
- Segment E: This segment is not well served by any offer; it represents an opportunity for a new market entry.

These observations demonstrate that the decision of which segment(s) to target is a function of both customers, as represented by the market segments, and competitors. For example, although it is the largest segment, and thus offers the greatest potential, Segment D is also the segment that is best served by a competitor, 3. A firm contemplating entry into this market might be better advised to target Segment E, which seems to be ignored by competitors.

The key objective for any competitive offer is to approach the ideal point of the targeted market segment. Although the perceptual map also suggests objectives for individual competitive offers, it does not, of itself, indicate what specific actions the firm should take. Thus, recalling that both the ideal points and the representations of competitive offers are customer perceptions, various forms of communication may move an offer closer to the ideal point of the targeted segment.[36] Alternatively, product development might be necessary to modify the offer's benefit mix. Or, especially in the case of addressing Segment E, a new market entry may be required.

SUMMARY

Market segmentation is fundamental to the development of market strategy. This chapter discussed the process of market segmentation that results in the development of a number of market segments. It also discussed a series of issues concerning market segments and developed two approaches for addressing the market segment targeting decision.

Market segment targeting represents the starting point for developing market strategy. For each market that the firm addresses, it must develop strategy for individually targeted segments. If more than one segment is targeted in a market, the firm must develop different strategies for the several market segments.

THE CHANGING VIEW

Old Way	New Way
Market segments based mainly on demographics	Market segments based on multiple types of variables
Crude segmentation	Precise segmentation
Segmentation primarily consumer focused	Extending beyond customers to organizational stakeholders
Intuition-driven segmentation	Analytically-driven segmentation
Basic marketing concepts applied mainly in consumer packaged goods	Marketing concepts applied in many domains: public and non-profit, nation/states, politics, personal career
Domestic view of customers and markets	Global view of customers and markets
Customers uninformed and unsophisticated	Customers well-informed and increasingly sophisticated
Databases poorly developed	Databases central to segmentation
Few large-market segments	Many small segments tending toward segments-of-one
Low levels of analytic expertise	Increasingly sophisticated analyses

QUESTIONS FOR STUDY AND DISCUSSION

1. Select a product market with which you are familiar. Develop a benefit segmentation matrix in which you identify the importance order of benefits for the various segments.

2. Many marketers make the mistake of confusing causal and correlational variables in developing market segments. Describe a product/market situation with which you are familiar and show how failure to understand this distinction could mislead marketers.

3. Explain the difference between product proliferation and market segmentation.

4. Finance has developed extremely sophisticated methods for evaluating resource allocation decisions. Why is it that the failure rate of new investments, in projects, markets and businesses remains so high?

5. How would you use the concepts discussed here to manage the firm's shareholder base?

6. Do politicians employ segmentation? Describe an example that you have witnessed, directly or indirectly.

7. Some people believe that market segmentation raises profound ethical issues of equity. Do you agree? Why or why not?

8. A major auto company recently realized that there were literally 85 ways in which a customer's name might enter into one of its databases, yet axed a proposal to develop a system that coded all data by customer on the grounds of expense. Using concepts discussed in this chapter, explain why this decision might decrease shareholder value while also creating major problems for customers.

9. Economists argue that segmentation promotes higher levels of utility (value) for customers. Marketers have observed that segmentation sometimes makes customers angry. How can you reconcile these points of view?

10. Why do marketers consider so many alternatives in trying to decide how to segment a market?

11. Too many segments are impossible to administer. Discuss.

12. It is unethical to apply marketing concepts, such as segmentation, in the political realm, for their use vitiates the entire concept of democracy. Discuss.

13. A global segmentation scheme is infeasible . . . people are too different. Discuss.

14. Most large companies cannot administer simple segmentation schemes, let alone complex ones. Do you agree? Why or why not?

15. Developing database management skills is a core competence for all firms in today's environment. Discuss.

ENDNOTES

1. Although this discussion is focused almost exclusively on customers, most of the approaches discussed can be usefully applied to other firm stakeholders such as shareholders and employees.

2. A possible exception is products at an early product life cycle stage where the technological benefit delivered by the pioneer may overshadow all other options. See, P. Berthon, J.M. Hulbert and L.F. Pitt, "Organizing for More than Markets: a Conceptual Model and Preliminary Empirical Application," paper presented at the February 1998 meetings of the American Management Association, Austin, TX.

3. For a well-organized summary on market segmentation, see G. Lillien and P. Kotler, *Marketing Decision Making: A Model Building Approach*, New York: Harper and Row, 1983. The classic work on market segmentation is R.E. Frank, W.F. Massy and Y. Wind, *Market Segmentation*, Englewood Cliffs, NJ: Prentice Hall, 1972. See J.H. Myers, *Segmentation and Positioning for Strategic Marketing Decisions*, Chicago, IL: American Marketing Association, 1996, for a more recent treatment.

4. M.J.A. Berry and G. Linoff, *Data Mining Techniques for Marketing, Sales and Customer Support*, New York, John Wiley, 1997

5. Table 7.1 shows one respondent's rank-order of customers' priorities with respect to benefits. Clearly, we would prefer better (more accurate) importance measures. These might be secured using a variety of marketing techniques.

6. Some heavy users in the single male segment visit fast food restaurants upwards of 20 times per month, spending in excess of $40 per day! *The Wall Street Journal*, January 12, 2000.

7. Of course, the firm may be able to gain competitive advantage by superior analysis of secondary data.

8. **S**tandard **M**etropolitan **S**tatistical **A**rea, a Bureau of the Census definition that covers urban agglomerations regardless of political boundaries; the latter tend to be arbitrary for marketing purposes.

9. *The New York Times*, April 28, 2000.

10. *The Wall Street Journal*, January 30, 1995.

11. An earlier *PRIZM* system comprised 40 clusters in 12 broader social groups. Other commercially available segmentation schemes include VALS™ 2 (see Chapter 4), ClusterPlus (Donnelly Marketing Information Services) and MicroVision (Equifax/National Decision Systems).

12. *Marketing News*: July 20, 1998.

13. In the consumer behavior literature, the terminology employed for those attributes critical in the purchase decision is *determinant* attributes.

14. This example may not hold for all airline routes. Furthermore, in the early 1980s, when questions were raised about the safety of the DC 10, this aspect re-entered consumers' decision processes. In the mid-1990s, the U.S. FAA was heavily criticized for its record in promoting safety, despite having forbidden some non-U.S. airlines from flying to the United States on safety grounds.

15. See B.J. Pine II, B. Victor, and A.C. Boyton, "Making Mass Customization Work," *Harvard Business Review*, 71 (Sept./Oct. 1993), pp. 108–119, and B.J. Pine II, D. Peppers and M. Rogers, "Do You Want to Keep Your Customers Forever?" *Harvard Business Review*, 73 (March/April 1995), pp. 103–114.

16. *The New York Times*, March 7, 1998.

17. A.J. Slywortzky, "The Age of the Choiceboard," *Harvard Business Review*, 78 (Jan/Feb. 2000), pp. 40–41.

18. *The New York Times*, September 21, 1999.

19. Of course, some firms target their products at specific age segments, such as magazines for teenagers, and have to replenish their customer bases continually.

20. Historically, marketing's concern has been with aggregates of customers or customer types and customer roles; by contrast, sales has focused on individual customers.

21. Stockbroker Edward D. Jones provides a nice example of a focused strategy; it largely concentrates offers for its brokerage services in rural areas and small towns.

22. *Business Week*, April 5, 1999.

23. The essence of a niche strategy lies in the firm's ability to defend its position in the niche. However, it is also possible that the large company may elect to acquire rather than fight; in such cases, small company owners may reap large financial rewards. This was the case for liquid soap innovator Minnetonka that was eventually purchased by Colgate Palmolive.

24. *Business Week*, April 24, 2000.

25. Monopsony means one seller. Cartelization of supply occurs when a group of suppliers attempts to manage the market, such as the oil producers in OPEC.

26. Financial analysis of opportunities in different segments might also be attempted. However, conventional financial analysis typically embeds assumptions about market conditions that portfolio models render explicit. At a minimum, systematic analysis of the type presented here should be used to complement any financial analysis.

27. This criterion is always important, but especially so in some areas of financial services. For example, automobile insurer Geico has earned high profits, in part, by focusing only on drivers with excellent records (a segmented approach).

28. Note that competitors may segment the market on different bases. As a result, segments targeted by two competitors may overlap in some areas but not in others.

29. Frequently, individual business units within the firm develop their own attractiveness criteria. However, if across-business-unit comparisons are to be made, standardization on a set of attractiveness criteria has many benefits.

30. Quoted in H. Simon, *Hidden Champions: Lessons from 500 of the Worlds Best Unknown Companies*, Boston, MA: Harvard Business School Press, 1996.

31. Readers schooled in modeling will note that we are using a linear compensatory model with correlated variables and scale properties that are, at best, interval (not ratio). In practice, however, these theoretical concerns seem to cause little difficulty. When parallel analyses are conducted, a high degree of convergence of relative positions is generally observed, although care must be taken not to attach too much importance to the absolute- as opposed to the relative-factor scores.

32. For further information on scaling procedures to develop perceptual maps, see any respectable marketing research text, such as D.R. Lehmann, J. Steckel and S. Gupta, *Marketing Research*, Reading, MA: Addison Wesley, 1997. Three-dimensional market representations can also be developed but, for most practical purposes, two-dimensional representations are most useful. If the market is best described by three dimensions (A, B, C), then three separate two dimensional representations can be developed (AB, AC, BC).

33. Note that "high" is not necessarily better than "low." The ideal point notion is counter to the major alternative, "more is better." Consider aero-engines for the manufacturer of a 50-seat aircraft. Very low power engines do not get the plane off the ground; very high power engines are too heavy and negatively affect other aerodynamic factors. Ideal power is somewhere between high and low.

34. Since market segments are rough groupings of customers in a market, ideal points are best viewed as "centers of gravity" of benefits required by customers in each segment, or the means of distributions of benefit requirements. Note that although this segmentation representation indicates segment size, it does not indicate other segment characteristics, such as growth or potential size, that may be important in deciding which segment to target.

35. Note that several of the various competitive offers may come from the same firm.

36. A more difficult task is to persuade customers in a market segment to shift their ideal points. However early entrants may have this opportunity as they learn customer preferences.

WEB RESOURCES

AccessAir	www.accessair.com
Airbus Industrie	www.airbus.com
Amazon.com	www.amazon.com
American Airlines	www.americanair.com
AOL	www.aol.com
Artisans	www.artisansgallery.com
AT&T	www.att.com
Boeing 707	www.boeing.com
Bureau of the Census	www.census.gov
Business Week	www.businessweek.com
Callaway	www.callawaygolf.com
Colgate Palmolive	www.colgate.com
Delta Airlines	www.delta-air.com
Edward D. Jones	www.edwardjones.com
Ford	www.ford.com
Fortune 500	www.fortune.com
Frito Lay	www.fritolay.com
Frontier Airlines	www.flyfrontier.com
Geico	www.geico.com
General Electric	www.ge.com
Hallmark	www.hallmark.com
Harvard Business Review	www.hbsp.harvard.edu/products/hbr
L.L. Bean	www.llbean.com
Land's End	www.landsend.com
Levi Strauss	www.levi.com
Marketing News	www.ama.org/pubs
Marriott	www.marriot.com
Microsoft	www.microsoft.com

WEB RESOURCES *(continued)*

Mobil Corporation	www.exxon.mobil.com
Northwest Airlines	www.nwa.com
OPEC	www.opec.org/DEFAULT.htm
Panasonic	www.panasonic.com
Pro Air	www.proair.com
Readers Digest	www.readersdigest.com
Richardson Vicks	www.pg.com
Roper Starch World-wide	www.roper.com
Seagram	www.seagram.com
Spirit Airlines	www.spiritair.com
The New York Times	www.nytimes.com
The Wall Street Journal	www.wsj.com
United Air	www.ual.com
Vanguard Airlines	www.flyvanguard.com

THE TASKS
OF MARKETING

CHAPTER

8

MARKET STRATEGY: THE INTEGRATOR

LEARNING OBJECTIVES

When you have completed this chapter, you will understand

- **the functions of a strategy**
- **how a strategy:**
  - **—provides direction**
  - **—guides the allocation of scarce resources**
  - **—helps secure competitive advantage**
  - **—assists in achieving interfunctional coordination**
- **the elements of a product/market segment strategy**
- **how to manage multisegment strategies**

INTRODUCTION

Strategy exists at several different levels in the firm, such as corporate, business-unit, and market strategy. This chapter focuses on the basic building block of a market strategy[1]—the market segment strategy. We explore the issues involved in designing strategy for a product or service in a market segment. Previous chapters defined a segment as a grouping of customers seeking similar benefits, different from the benefits sought by any other such grouping. As a result, the different requirements of each segment typically mandate different marketing approaches, even if the basic products/services offered to the various segments are similar. This chapter begins by introducing some basic definitions, followed by a general discussion on the functions of a strategy.

THE FUNCTIONS OF A STRATEGY

It is essential to have a clearly defined strategic vocabulary to avoid misunderstanding, as many terms are used loosely and disparately in the business world. Indeed, experience in working with corporations has shown that a poorly developed vocabulary poses a formidable barrier to good strategy development and implementation, particularly when a global perspective is being taken and coordination of strategies across geographies and cultures is required. This chapter defines three central concepts: objectives, strategies, and programs. The definitions used are drawn directly from their original usage in military vocabulary, and have the advantage of being simple and straightforward.

- **Objectives** are the desired results from the operation of the business.
- **Strategies** describe, in a general way, the anticipated allocation of resources (deployment of capabilities) to achieve these objectives.
- **Programs** describe the specific actions taken to implement a chosen strategy.

Why Have a Strategy?

Strategies do not always exist before the fact. Frequently, as illustrated by the phrase that "success has many authors," a firm achieves success, and after-the-fact examination of its actions reveals a pattern that someone designates a strategy. It is generally not possible for a researcher to know whether or not such a pattern existed as an idea or concept before the fact, and the issue is often regarded as moot.[2] This chapter, however, argues for the superiority of a properly thought-out strategy, while acknowledging that such forethought typically demands significant insight into how a market is likely to change and, specifically, how it will react to the firm's actions and those of competitors. It also acknowledges the effect of changes in the business environment on the role of strategy. In the absence of change, traditionally successful patterns of behavior will suffice. However, as the environment becomes ever more complex and fast-changing, although strategy development becomes more difficult, it also becomes more essential.[3]

A well-developed strategy should perform several functions: provide direction, guide the allocation of scarce resources, secure competitive advantage, and achieve coordination.

PROVIDE DIRECTION   The fundamental function of any strategy is to provide managers with direction on how to manage their businesses during some future time period. A corporate strategy is concerned with the enterprise as a whole, a business unit strategy with a business, and market and market segment strategies with markets and market segments, respectively.[4] Depending on the strategy type and the environment faced by the firm, the time scale for the strategy will be longer or shorter. In general, the more broad-based the strategy, the longer the time horizon; the time horizon for corporate strategy is likely to be longer than for a product/market segment strategy. Similarly, the content of strategy varies with level, but the purpose remains the same. By coordinating efforts in a common direction, the firm should make better use of its resources and capabilities, and thereby generate more value for shareholders.

GUIDE THE ALLOCATION OF SCARCE RESOURCES   Because company resources are limited at all organizational levels and in all functional areas, strategy must define in a clear yet general way how those scarce resources should be allocated to provide the direction discussed previously. Some individual resources, such as capital, manufacturing capacity, sales force time, shelf space, or technology, are more limiting than others. These limitations are felt most acutely when resources are shared among different organization units, such as manufacturing capacity with another business unit. These problems are typically greater at lower levels of strategy development. Strategy is absolutely essential at the market level, where critical decisions must be made on allocation of resources, both externally and internally. Externally, the firm must allocate resources across market segments; within market segments, it must decide which customers to target and how to compete with rivals. Internally, it must allocate resources across activities such as product development, advertising spending, and sales force effort.

Simply to acknowledge the resource allocation purpose of a strategy does not explain how to do the job. Indeed, the criteria by which the quality of resource allocation should be judged vary with the type of strategy. However, for market and market segment strategies, the main criterion is straightforward and relates to a further purpose of strategy: The resource allocation process should do the best possible job of assuring that the firm achieves advantage over its competitors.

SECURE COMPETITIVE ADVANTAGE   To achieve competitive advantage, a well-developed market or segment strategy should make clear why customers should buy from the firm rather than from competitors. Unfortunately, firm strategies do not always meet this test. Far too often, marketing managers behave as though they had little or no competition. Sometimes, strategy statements read as if competitors will not only ignore firm actions, but are expected to leave the market when the firm enters.[5]

In any competitive game, understanding the competitor's options is crucial. For example, a chess player must think several moves ahead to defeat an opponent; world-class players often attempt to think through an entire game from initial move to final checkmate. Chess players know that, by moving a piece to a certain square, the competitor has a discrete number of possible moves, many of them predictable. Subsequent moves attempt to reduce the competitor's options; and if these moves are skillfully chosen, the options are so constrained that eventually the opponent must capitulate. In other comparable arenas, such as professional sports and the military, tremendous efforts are expended to study and analyze competitors. Since most firms compete in oligopolies, the analogy is sound— although in the interests of fairness it should be noted that two-person games are easier to understand than n-person games.

Firms do not typically seek the capitulation or annihilation of competitors, but rather attempt to reduce their options, particularly those that pose major threats. Although the number of options open to competitors is far greater than in chess, firm strategies should consider likely competitor responses. Any strategy that cannot withstand reasonably probable competitor responses should be rejected. Those strategies that will enable the firm to beat competitors are worthy of further consideration. This process may involve developing contingent responses to alternative competitive scenarios and laying out potential subsequent moves. Not all of these options will end up in formal contingency plans, but the thought process should lead to both higher quality strategies and the ability to act pre-emptively.

To make the competitive advantage more operational, any strategy the firm develops should possess at least one of four attributes, listed in descending order of preference[6]:

- **Non-duplicable**: If possible, the strategy should commit the firm to actions that competitors *cannot* duplicate. A competitor lacking a key resource or ability that the firm is leveraging will be unable to duplicate its strategy. For example, there may be financial or technological limitations, lack of plant capacity, poor distribution coverage, or a less-established reputation.

- **Duplicable but unselectable**: Somewhat less desirable is a strategy that competitors could match, but which the firm is assured they will not. To be confident of such a judgment requires considerable insight into competitor resources and management. Perhaps previous experience has convinced the firm that competitors will not choose this option, resources are being placed behind other products and markets, or cash flow considerations make a price reduction out of the question.
- **Competitor relatively disadvantaged**: In this case, the firm predicts that competitors will duplicate its strategic moves, but believes this action will negatively affect them. For example, in a price-inelastic market, price reductions may be a key strategic action for the low market-share competitor. However, should the high market-share market leader follow the across-the-board price cut, its high volume will lead to significant opportunity loss, at least in the short term. Conversely, when a large competitor increases fixed-cost expenditures, such as R&D, market coverage, advertising, technical service, or product line breadth, small competitors attempting to match these actions generally suffer since the larger competitor can spread its fixed costs over greater volume.[7]
- **All competitors benefit**: In this case, the firm's strategic action is matched by competitors; not only does the firm benefit, but so do the competitors. For example, in an unprofitable industry, a price increase followed by immediate competitor matching may benefit all industry members. Other actions such as advertising reductions or service increases that competitors follow may also yield advantage to all firms. The general principle is to seek those actions that yield the greatest relative advantage to the firm.

ACHIEVING COORDINATION   The final purpose of a strategy is to ensure that managers from various organizational units are coordinated so they are all pulling in the same direction. A good strategy should integrate the various functions that provide resources for strategy implementation. Because the requirements of each market and market segment are unique, this integration must be achieved at the product/market level. The following example illustrates this point.

Imagine that a division general manager has asked the sales director what steps to take to improve profits. While some sales managers might respond that they wanted to reduce expenses, many more would suggest some combination of the following:

- A larger sales force
- Higher sales commissions
- More advertising support
- Better quality products
- New products
- Faster delivery
- Better distributor incentives
- More flexible credit policies
- Flexible pricing systems (especially downwards)

Next the manufacturing director is asked what steps might be taken to improve profits. He might offer the following advice:

- Fewer products (to facilitate longer production runs)
- Flexible delivery schedules (to accommodate manufacturing schedules)
- Moratorium on new products (these typically cause manufacturing problems during start-up)
- Relaxed quality control standards
- Better sales forecasting
- More working capital for raw material inventory
- New plant and equipment

The R&D director would likely respond that more time was needed to develop a product far superior to any currently on the market, and that increased budget was necessary to complete the development. The human resource director would probably want to hire better people, increase the training budget for current employees, and improve compensation and benefits packages. As "guardian of the firm's bottom line," the finance director would probably focus on ways to increase return on investment (ROI). Favored actions are to increase profits, such as by increasing prices, or reducing expenses, or decreasing the level of fixed investment and working capital via reduced inventories and tighter credit terms.

In most organizations, there is significant potential for severe conflict and discord among key functional managers. These managers act in ways appropriate for their organizational positions, consistent with existing reward structures, and based on their individual backgrounds and training. Thus the sales director suggests actions to increase sales, the manufacturing director wants to reduce costs, R&D wants to develop the best possible products, human resources wants to improve people quality, and finance wants to increase ROI. In other words, the individually required actions are totally consistent with individual functional managers doing their jobs as traditionally defined.

However, for the firm to develop a strategic direction, these conflicts must be resolved. In many companies, this is achieved through compromise where each functional area gives up a little to secure an agreement that all can accept. Alternative conflict resolution methods are for top management to make a decision, or for functional managers to exercise political power to secure an agreement most to their liking.

The problem with each of these decision-making methods is that they tend to be internally, rather than externally, focused. As a result, although one functional area may seem to gain advantage, the firm as a whole does not win. Instead, competitors win. Imagine the firm is developing strategy for a new product in a market where significant growth is expected in the short run, and the firm estimates its lead time over competitors to be six months. Decisions to cut back on advertising expenses, set high prices, and restrict working capital are likely to compromise the achievement of firm objectives. Other competitors, more sensitive to customer needs, will likely enter with offers better attuned to the market. When they succeed, the firm can take little consolation from the fact that it resolved its internal battles; the critical battle for customers was lost.

Although this example implies that each functional manager is being parochial or short-sighted by focusing exclusively (or at least largely) on their specific function, the harsh reality is that organizations worldwide often evaluate and reward managers for behaving as depicted. Sales managers are driven to reach sales quotas, manufacturing directors to run efficient plants, research directors to design better products, human resource directors to upgrade personnel quality, and finance directors to improve profitability (particularly by limiting investment). It must be recognized that performance standards and criteria (especially traditional measures that have experienced little change over the years) may be out of kilter with what is necessary today to win customers and beat competitors.

The key is to achieve integration by building a genuine consensus around the direction embodied in the strategy, and to ensure that the reward system and evaluation criteria are congruent with that direction. It is difficult to achieve coordinated execution of a strategy that is not accepted, is poorly articulated, or is not well understood; a well-articulated strategy is a necessary, if not sufficient, condition. However, developing a consensus requires a great deal of skill. The strategy development process has an important role in educating functional managers that seemingly reasonable actions may be inappropriate for the strategic direction the firm wants to take. Conversely, other functional managers should articulate clearly the very real resource trade-offs that must be made in developing alternative strategic thrusts.

Good strategy can be developed only when all functional managers take a holistic view of the business. To achieve this result requires significant skill in relationship building, managing group processes, and coordination activities. In the strategy development process, creativity should be valued, and conflict and contention seen to be both natural and healthy. However, once consensus has been achieved, the action shifts to program planning and execution. At this point, strategy resembles a yoke or harness. Just as the yoke keeps the oxen pulling as a team, so the strategy acts as a yoke or collar around the necks of managers to keep them from pulling in opposite directions. Strategy ensures that all important functions necessary to executing the product/market strategy are moving in the same "agreed" direction.

In summary, an important purpose in formulating market strategy is to encourage managers to begin the process by looking outward to the environment and focusing attention on external issues rather than succumb to insidious yet ubiquitous internal perspectives. In a well-run strategic planning process, managers gather a variety of external data and conduct numerous externally focused analyses. They should also see competitors—rather than compatriots—as the enemy, and avoid the inward approach of focusing attention on a lowest common denominator (LCD) compromise with sister functional areas. This increased sensitivity to its environment should lead the firm to be more attuned to external changes and their implications. A more proactive, rather than reactive, entity should result.

ELEMENTS OF THE PRODUCT/MARKET SEGMENT STRATEGY

This section describes the elements of an individual product/market segment strategy. The strategy framework developed can be viewed at a minimum as a template against which marketing and product managers can test their own strategies for completeness. It can also be viewed as a model to guide strategy development, one that is lacking in many companies. A product/market segment strategy contains four major elements and several subelements:

- **performance objectives**
  - strategic objectives
  - operational objectives
- **selection of strategic alternatives**
- **positioning**
  - choice of customer targets
  - choice of competitor targets
  - selection of core strategy/key buying incentive/value proposition
- **implementation**
  - description of supporting marketing mix programs
  - description of supporting functional programs

The first two major elements—performance objectives (strategic and operational) and selection of strategic alternatives—establish the broad direction of the product/market segment strategy. The third main element, made up of customer targets, competitor targets, and core strategy (sometimes known as the three Cs of market strategy), determines the product's positioning in the target market segment.[8] The final element, the marketing mix and functional support requirements, deals with the planning and integration of the programs (or tactics) necessary to implement the strategy successfully.

Objectives, strategic alternatives, and positioning are conceptual devices. The responsibility for their development lies with those charged with planning, typically possessing such titles as product or brand manager, or marketing or business director. Implementation, however, only occurs through the actions of many people throughout the organization. As indicated earlier, only if the conceptual development is agreed upon and well articulated can it provide the coordinating and integrating theme governing individuals' actions so that appropriate implementation occurs and the objectives are achieved. One of the best ways to assure this integration is to encourage as wide a participation as possible in the strategy development process. Coincidentally, the quality of strategy that emerges from such a process is often higher than if developed in a more restricted manner.

Setting Performance Objectives

CHOOSING STRATEGIC OBJECTIVES   Choice of strategic objectives is one of the most fundamental decisions for any product/market segment. It establishes, in a qualitative and directional sense, the results the firm wants to attain during the planning period. Typically, strategic objectives are grouped into three broad categories: profitability, cash flow, and growth. Although improvement in each of these objectives may be desired, trade-offs normally exist. Since significant growth typically requires increased spending, both expenses and capital (fixed and working) are likely to rise, with consequential short-term falls in cash flow and, sometimes, net profit. The impact of the interrelationships is dependent on both the rate of growth and investment intensity of the business. Nonetheless, to achieve maximum profits, cash flow, and market share all at the same time, while a neat trick, is rarely possible in the real world. As a result, before the strategy development process can proceed, it is essential that management determine which of these three broad categories of objectives is of greatest concern over the planning period. The basic task is to set priorities as to whether growth (sales volume or market share) is of greater concern than cash flow or profit, or vice versa. These strategic trade-offs must be addressed for each market segment the firm decides to target.[9]

Typically, one or two general directions is more important than the other. Thus in addition to a primary strategic objective, a secondary strategic objective should also be selected. Strategic objectives are usually stated qualitatively, but should unambiguously set a direction for the business in the segment. A typical statement might take the following form:

- Our primary objective in the young-family-with-children segment is to increase profits from sales of our "*Cold Chunks*" brand of ready-to-eat cereal. Our secondary objective is to maintain market share.

GUIDANCE IN CHOOSING STRATEGIC OBJECTIVES   Deciding on priorities among differing objectives is not an easy task. Nonetheless, it should be easier to attain the firm's objectives by concentrating efforts in markets and segments that are attractive, and where competitive advantage is considerable. The matrix analysis by market segment (Chapter 7) provides important guidance in setting these priorities, as do over-arching corporate and business unit objectives.

A useful device for thinking about the relationship of past to future is the notion of performance gaps. The firm might be viewed as having some set of performance measures that function as objectives. The typical large firm is established in several businesses and product/market segments. To the extent it continues to operate in these segments, much as previously, it anticipates some level of future performance—the momentum line (see Figure 8.1). If the objective line is greater than the anticipated performance, we can say there is a performance gap. In stable environments, anticipated performance is likely to mirror the

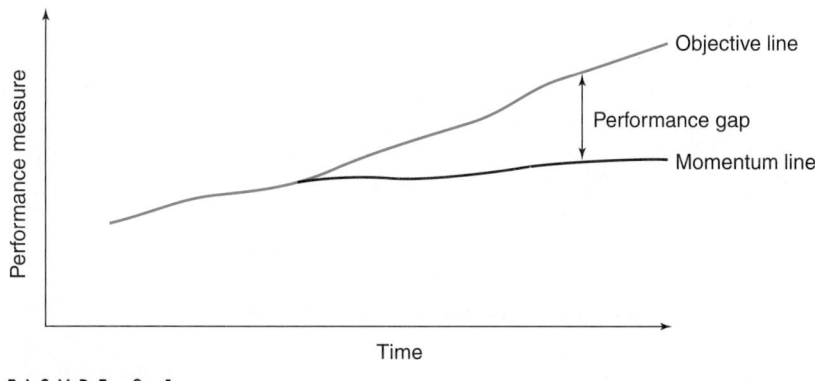

FIGURE 8.1

Performance Gaps

objectives over time, leading to small performance gaps. However, as the environment becomes more turbulent, the greater the likelihood that performance gaps will increase.

It was noted earlier that both the turbulence and rate of environmental change are increasing. The greater the extent of these changes, and consequent changes in customer requirements and competitive actions, the less likely that unchanged objectives and strategy in the firm's established product/market segments will lead to successful firm performance in the future. In other words, business as usual is likely to lead to increasing performance gaps. As a result, for those product/market segments that the firm decides to target, objective setting should proceed via more thoughtful processes.

Empirical evidence provides some guidance in considering priorities among objectives. It is especially useful to examine the manner in which the primary strategic objective might change across the product life cycle (see Figure 8.2). In the early stages (introduction and early growth), firms often set objectives of growing at, or faster than, the market growth rate. As market growth slows (late growth stage or when market share is considered sufficient), firms might choose to improve profit margins or ROI. During the maturity stage, and especially when decline appears imminent, cash flow concerns are likely to predominate. These guidelines are not meant as cast-iron prescriptions for choice of primary strategic objective (indeed, setting primary strategic objectives contrary to the received wisdom can often be an effective destabilizing competitive move). Rather, they reflect the behavior of many companies if it is assumed that, on average, business results are reflective of objectives. For example, results from the PIMS study show that sales growth and market share are high in early life cycle stages, and lower in late life cycle stages. By contrast, ROI and cash flow are negative in the start-up stage, and become positive later (Table 8.1).[10]

Whichever trade-off is chosen, the choice of strategic objective is central to all decisions that follow. Because it is such a critical choice, top management and business unit (or division) managers typically exert significant influence at the market level, although this influence may be somewhat less in setting strategic objectives for individual market segments. As discussed earlier, it is vital that those managers primarily concerned with the product/market area (typically market or product managers) be closely involved in the objective setting process, and that these decisions be based on a thorough analysis of customers, complementers, and competitors.

Inevitably, the process of setting strategic objectives frequently involves conflicting forces based on tension between characteristics of the product/market opportunity and capital market pressures for short-term profits. Trained to focus on the marketplace when set-

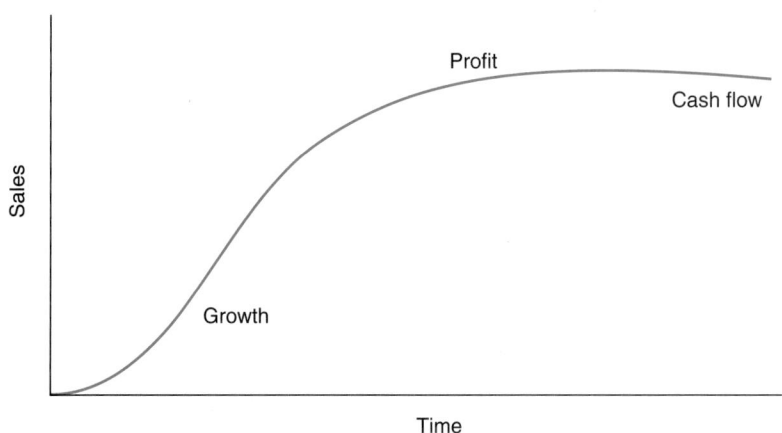

FIGURE 8.2

Evolution of Strategic Objectives

Table 8.1   Operating Results of PIMS Businesses

Category	Measure	Life Cycle Stage			
		Start-up	Growth	Early Maturity	Late Maturity
Market Performance	Sales Growth (%)	74	23	11	6
	Market Share (%)	8	25	24	24
Budget Levels	R&D/Sales (%)	10	3	2	1
	Marketing/Sales (%)	26	11	9	8
Financial Performance	ROI (%)	−19	25	22	17
	Net Income Growth (%)	7	20	15	11
	Investment Growth (%)	38	19	9	3
	Cash Flow/Investment (%)	−46	1	6	9

Data are four-year average percents, except growth rates; these are annual rates (current dollars); data in the "start-up" column are medians. Figures (except net income growth) secured from The Strategic Planning Institute, Cambridge, MA, June 1998.

ting strategic objectives, marketing and product managers typically concentrate most heavily on dimensions such as market growth, market size, competitive strength, and current market position. This focus must, however, be tempered by consideration of the firm's competitiveness in the capital markets. In too many cases, shareholder value takes second place to arbitrary and, too often, unthoughtful actions of managers, driven by a budgeting process that might not have taken into consideration the true interests of shareholders.

For example, suppose the firm is well positioned in a particular market segment, segment growth rate is high, and competitors are weak but likely to grow stronger over the planning horizon. Many marketing managers would counsel high investment in the short run to grow the business, gain market position, and preempt the increasingly strong competitive threat.[11] Although the apparently attractive opportunity seems to argue for growth, funds may be unavailable to support the achievement of these objectives, and profit (or even cash flow) may be set as the primary strategic objective. Such a decision may occur as a result of a sensible analysis of shareholder interests, or as the consequence of an arbitrary management decision.

In situations such as these where marketing is, in effect, overruled, it nonetheless has a key responsibility to articulate the options clearly and dispassionately so that senior management makes its decisions with the fullest possible information. This typically does not occur often enough, and the result is a failure to serve shareholders' interests because of blind conformity to senior management requests.

CHOOSING OPERATIONAL OBJECTIVES   Strategic and operational objectives differ in specificity. Whereas in a qualitative manner, strategic objectives establish the general direction the firm wants to take, operational objectives are quantitative, providing the numbers that tell how much is required and by when. Thus, the operational objective should specify the amount of sales volume (or market share), profit (or profit margin), or cash flow to be produced over each year of the planning period. To continue with the last example, a complete objective statement may appear as shown in Table 8.2.

Operational objectives provide a specific goal (or end result) to be achieved and offer a means of evaluating performance. Objectives should be challenging to the managerial team, but should also be realistic.[12] Objectives beyond the reach of managers are likely to act as disincentives (or demotivators), rather than as a positive force for better performance. The key word is operational; management is providing both standards for evaluation and concrete measurable targets toward which efforts should be directed. It is important to note that in the process of strategy development, at this stage, operational objectives

MARKET STRATEGY:
THE INTEGRATOR

Table 8.2 Segment: Young Family with Children

	Strategic Objectives	Operational Objectives*
Primary	Increase profits from sales of "Cold Chunks" brand of ready-to-eat cereal	from: $12 million in 200X to: $15 million in 200X + 1 $20 million in 200X + 2 $25 million in 200X + 3
Secondary	While maintaining market share	at 25% from 200X through 200X + 3

*Whereas operational objectives are typically set per annum in the strategic marketing plan, in the annual marketing plan they are typically calendarized by quarter or by month.

must be viewed as tentative. Only when the strategy and programs have been developed, and the revenues and costs projected, can the feasibility or otherwise of operational objectives be assessed.

A FINAL NOTE   As noted earlier, the objective setting process is critical as decisions about objectives frame the entire strategy. This notion is particularly important for it is found that many companies do not seem to ask the most basic question about objectives. All too frequently, top management states objectives in terms of dollar profits required over the planning period: "Over the next three years, $45 million must be delivered to the firm's bottom line!" The problem with such an objective is that the most basic question may not have been answered, such as, "How might the achievement of this objective affect performance on other important dimensions?" If these profits are achieved, but the ongoing value of the business is destroyed by running down assets (tangible or intangible), it is likely that shareholders' interests will not have been served. Likewise, if profits are achieved but market share reduced significantly, the consequences are likely to be similar.[13] Clearly, there is nothing wrong with an aggressive $45 million profit target if profit is the primary strategic objective. However, if the primary strategic objective is growth or market share, such an aggressive profit target may lead the firm to curtail just those expenses, such as new product development, advertising, or sales incentives, that are vital to achieving market dominance. A sensible assessment of the stage of development of the firm's business in a segment, the relative strength of competition, the capabilities of the firm and the available strategic options (Chapters 9 and 10) are the chief criteria to guide the selection of priorities in objectives. Senior management must address such trade-off issues.

Selection of Strategic Alternatives

Strategy for a market segment consists of two major elements: selection of strategic alternatives and developing a positioning strategy. Choice of strategic alternative is the starting point for strategy development, and may be thought of as the broad road map that must be followed to achieve strategic objectives. Strategic objectives constrain the alternatives that the firm is willing to consider. Without clear strategic objectives, the "tree" of strategy alternatives has almost an infinite variety of branches; a clear definition of objectives "prunes" the tree to a manageable size. An enormous amount of work still remains to flesh out the strategy, but the problem is significantly simpler.

Starting with the assumption that, for most managers, improving profits is the most important long-term goal for any product/market segment, a means-ends chain can be developed that suggests alternative ways of realizing the goal. One method in this development is to expand upon the revenue and cost components that comprise the profit equation. A variation is to increase sales volume, or become more productive, as the pathways to achieve the goal. For each of these broad pathways, more specific alternatives are available (Figure 8.3).

INCREASE UNIT SALES VOLUME   Four broad, strategic alternatives are available to increase unit sales volume; two focus on existing customers, two on new customers. The most profitable way to grow almost all business is to focus on the existing customer base.

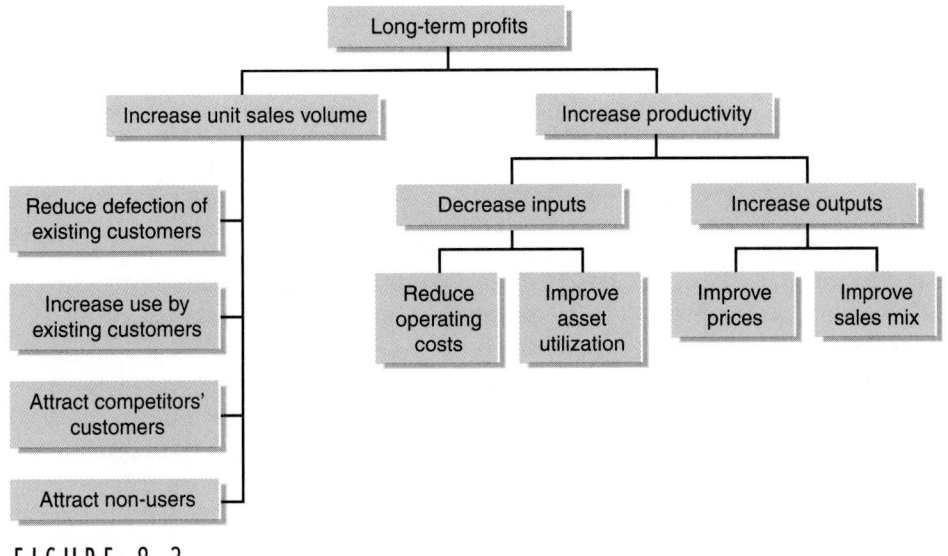

FIGURE 8.3

Developing Strategic Alternatives

The firm could reduce the rate at which it loses customers to competitors, or it could increase usage by existing customers. For these two options, as well as attracting competitors' customers, the customer has already purchased this type of product. By contrast, attracting non-users in the market segment implies a prior lack of product use. This distinction is important. Knowledge of basic product benefits can be assumed for the first three alternatives and implies a customer decision process dominated by routinized response behavior or limited problem solving. By contrast, if non-users are being attracted, the firm cannot assume any familiarity with the benefits; purchase decision-making is most likely to occur via limited and extended problem solving. Since the customer decision process may be quite different for each alternative, each clearly requires different actions by the firm.

Reduce Defection of Existing Customers The customer list of any business is a little like a leaky bucket. If the firm can plug some of the holes by reducing the defection rate, the business will grow faster.[14] Such thinking is integral to the idea of customer management and so-called relationship management; indeed, some organizations employ retention managers. For example, retention managers at NASDAQ attempt to halt successful companies' defection to the New York Stock Exchange. Other firms introduce customer loyalty programs designed to reward repeat business. Airline "frequent flyer" programs are, perhaps, the most well-known of these, but even small organizations can benefit from such initiatives. For example, in Hong Kong, many retail stores have formed loyalty clubs, typically based on a loyalty card that is "chopped" (nicked) with each purchase.[15] In addition to direct sales increases, these clubs gain valuable information on their customers. Improved customer service is one of the most effective ways of reducing defection; at some companies, customer retention is viewed as a major goal of the customer service function.

> **Example:** When customers return to Amazon.com, they find recommendations of books and CDs to purchase based on their previous purchase patterns.

Increase Use by Existing Customers Similar to the previous alternative, the firm has a relationship with its customers. Various tactics might encourage increased usage: enlarge the unit of purchase,[16] increase the rate of product obsolescence,[17] find new uses for the product,[18] and provide price incentives to purchase larger quantities.[19] For firms involved in business-to-business marketing, an effective approach is to help customers grow at the expense of their competitors. Examples of such strategies include distributor training programs, joint promotion strategies (often seen in retail outlets), providing advertising and promotion allowances, or "spiff" monies earned by retailer and distributor salespeople. Some of the best known examples, however, involve customers incorporating the seller's brand on their products in return for the seller advertising direct to final consumers; synthetic fiber manufacturers, such as DuPont and Rhone-Poulenc, are especially adept at this approach.

> **Example:** In the late 1980s, Australia's BHP, then the world's most profitable steel company, launched its "Strengthening Australia" television campaign to support manufacturers that co-branded the use of its steel. This highly successful campaign was re-introduced in 1999.

In recent years, the goal of securing increased usage by current customers has been aided by the application of advanced technology to explore the firm's customer database for opportunities, often extending across product categories. Financial services companies have been in the vanguard of such efforts, which range from targeted selling and marketing efforts, to such simple examples as that provided by Fidelity, the mutual fund giant. Fidelity has made it extremely easy for customers to transfer funds from one Fidelity fund to another.[20]

> **Examples:** The Royal Bank of Canada's (RBC) creation of a comprehensive customer database available on-line to all branches and offices not only speeded up many transactions, but revealed that its nine million customers purchased, on average, just three financial services from RBC, but over 14 services from other sources. Marketing efforts were refocused on existing customers, and profits soared.
>
> Vons, the West Coast supermarket chain, was one of the first to install scanners at the checkout counter. When it realized that it could capture the identity of customers and what they were buying, it began to target its promotions and coupons.[21]

Attract Competitors' Customers   This alternative is the predominant option (implicit or explicit) in most market strategies. It assumes that the firm and its direct competitors that fighting for the same customers, and that the competitor's product is currently being used. In some cases, users of competitors' products include the firm's own past customers, that the firm may find it difficult to re-attract. It is likely, of course, that the particular marketing actions that may enable the firm to regain a previously lost customer are quite different from those necessary to attract a customer with whom the firm has never done business.

Of all the strategic alternatives, attracting competitors' customers is the one most likely to lead to competitor retaliation, but when few non-users are available for targeting, such as credit card holders, it may be the only way to increase unit sales. Of course, rarely is the situation as clear cut as assumed above, with all the customer's business earned by either the firm or its competitor. In many cases, customers split business among several suppliers. The task then becomes one of increasing share of the customer's business (so-called "share-of-wallet" in credit cards) rather than seeking a total switch from the competitor to the firm. One potential danger of this focus is that firms over-rely on price as the tactic to induce customers to switch. Firms considering this approach should only develop their strategies after asking the basic question, "Why does this customer prefer to buy from the competitor?"

Attract Non-users in the Market Segment   As noted above, converting non-users in existing segments is a different task from those just discussed. Both the firm and its direct competitors may have been trying to sell to these potential customers, but for one reason or another they have not purchased any product variant. The task in selling to these customers is twofold: first, they have to be convinced to purchase the product type rather than another technology with which they may be comfortable, then to purchase the firm's offering, rather than those of competitors. In new markets, most customers are, by definition, non-users, hence the heavy costs of new market development.

Selecting the Route for Unit Growth The predominance of one or another of these alternatives is closely related to the stage in the product life cycle and the firm's competitive position (Chapters 9 and 10). By definition, early in the life cycle, few customers have ever tried the new product; as a result, most sales have to come from non-users. However, as the product moves from introduction, through growth, and into maturity, the emphasis shifts; the proportion of non-users decreases as more and more customers purchase the product. As a result, the focus of effort turns to current or competitors' customers, depending on the firm's competitive position. A leader with high market share typically focuses mainly on current customers, simply because they represent the bulk of the market; for similar reasons, firms with smaller shares in their market segments focus on competitors' customers.

However, even late in maturity, opportunities may be available to sell to non-users. For example, in the United States, some farmers refuse to use agricultural herbicides, preferring to rely on non-chemical methods; many small businesses prefer tried and true manual bookkeeping systems, rather than the more modern computer-based systems; and many faculty prefer to use chalk boards rather than more modern presentation methods. In each case, targeted efforts at non-users may bring positive results.

New Market Segments Whereas the four strategic alternatives discussed previously focus on increasing unit volume within the market segment, a further growth alternative is to broaden the firm's horizons to focus on new markets or market segments. Generically, these might include options such as geographic expansion, or seeking new customer groups based on demographics or socioeconomics. Examples include the Japanese firm Sunstar trying to sell its oral hygiene products in Europe, or Johnson & Johnson selling baby powder for cosmetic use to teenage girls in the Philippines. Because our focus is on developing strategy within a product/market segment, this alternative was not included in Figure 8.3. In fact, this growth option requires its own strategy, complete with strategic and operational objectives, strategic alternatives, positioning, and implementation.

INCREASING PRODUCTIVITY In Figure 8.3, productivity was defined (like an engineer) as the ratio of outputs to inputs. Increased productivity (or efficiency) can result either from increased outputs for a given input, or reduced inputs for a given output. For this purpose, output is defined as sales revenue; inputs are costs and assets. (We assume that unit sales volume is held constant.)

Increasing Outputs (inputs constant) Two strategic alternatives are available to increase sales revenues while holding unit sales volume constant. The most straightforward method is to improve prices. This alternative can be executed in a variety of ways, such as increasing list price, reducing discounts, or reducing trade allowances.[22] A second way is to improve the sales mix by selling higher volumes of more profitable product variants, and reduced volumes of less profitable product variants; the customer mix may also be modified to de-emphasize less-profitable customers. Many means are available to execute each of these alternatives.

Decreasing Inputs (outputs constant) The reduction of inputs to increase efficiency is the more obvious of the two alternatives. Cost reduction possibilities may be widespread in both marketing-related areas, such as advertising, sales force, and distribution, and more broadly in the firm, such as in operations, administration, and training. Many opportunities typically exist to cut elements of both fixed and variable costs. In a general sense, this particular route to profit improvement has received a lot of attention in recent years via such methods as downsizing (rightsizing), reengineering, and outsourcing.[23,24]

The second alternative is to improve asset utilization by cutting the financial costs of doing business. Clearly, assets are employed throughout the firm, but marketing managers are typically involved with, at most, just two forms of controllable assets—inventories and accounts receivable. When current assets are slimmed down, both cash investment and interest costs are reduced. Some organizations have focused so heavily on these assets that working capital (accounts receivable + cash + inventories − accounts payable) has turned negative. Insisting on faster payment from customers can reduce accounts receivable; inventory reduction possibilities form part of the growing field of supply chain management. One feature of these systems is that the supplying firm is linked directly to data on the sale of products further down the distribution system. As a result, its production operations are closely tied to ultimate demand and it is able to reduce raw material, work in process and finished goods inventories. In addition, improved distribution techniques may reduce the amount of inventory in the pipeline from supplier to final customer.

Summary of Increasing Productivity   The foregoing demonstrates that several strategic alternatives are available to increase productivity or efficiency in a product/market segment. One important way of viewing these alternatives is to examine their joint impact on return on investment (ROI). Take the basic definition of ROI and add "sales" to both the top and bottom of the equation. ROI is now a function of both profit margin and investment turnover.

$$\text{Return on Investment (ROI)} = \frac{\text{Profits}}{\text{Investment}} = \frac{\text{Profits}}{\text{Sales}} \times \frac{\text{Sales}}{\text{Investment}}$$

$$= \text{Profit Margin} \times \text{Investment Turnover}$$

The first three alternatives—improving price, improving sales mix, and cost reduction—relate directly to increasing profit margins. The final strategic alternative, improving asset utilization, results from an increase in asset turnover. Profitability can be improved through either means. Some firms, such as retail institutions, have relatively low profit margins but may enjoy high levels of ROI through high investment turnover via efficient inventory management.[25] By contrast, highly capital-intensive businesses may have a low investment turnover (annually or less) but should aim to enjoy correspondingly higher profit margins.

Positioning

Positioning is sometimes called the heart of the product/market strategy. Unfortunately, many consumer marketers who talk of positioning products such as soap and toothpaste use the term "positioning" quite loosely. Many also use the terms market segmentation and positioning almost interchangeably, treating positioning almost as a choice of market segment.

In contrast, developing strategy for a product/market segment implies that choice of market segment has already been made. Developing positioning for a product/market segment involves key decisions "within" the segment regarding customers, competitors, and benefits to be offered. The purpose of positioning is to create a unique and favorable image in the minds of target customers. To create this image, the firm must make decisions with respect to:

- customer targets
- competitor targets
- core strategy, key buying incentive, or value proposition for the customer

These three decisions are highly interrelated and must be made via an iterative process.

CHOICE OF CUSTOMER TARGETS   This decision has three basic dimensions:

- choice of manufacturing/distribution system by which the firm's product reaches the ultimate consumer;
- choice of level or levels in the manufacturing/distribution system at which the bulk of the firm's marketing effort is targeted, such as manufacturer, distributor, retailer, or consumer;
- choice of specific decision influences at each distribution level targeted, for example the manufacturer-purchasing agent, engineer, or production manager.

Choice of manufacturing/distribution system   Regardless of whether the firm makes a completed product/service or a component/raw material for some other product, several different types of entities may be involved before the final product reaches the ultimate consumer.[26] Thus a component manufacturer may sell products to finished goods manufacturers (or to subassembly manufacturers that, in turn, sell to finished goods manufacturers); finished products may then pass through distributors, wholesalers, and retailers before reaching end users. By contrast, finished goods manufacturers are not concerned with other manufacturers; rather, they reach final consumers via such entities as distributors, wholesalers, and retailers.

Although well-established channels may exist in many industries, competitive advantage is frequently secured by innovative channel decisions.

> **Example:** In the mid-1980s, Michael Dell realized that, as the personal computer market matured, experienced computer buyers no longer needed the reassurance and information provided by salespeople in traditional retail outlets. Dell bypassed the traditional distribution system and has been highly successful marketing directly to final consumers.

Furthermore, even if a conventional distribution system is employed, choices must be made about the specific members chosen.

> **Example:** Having developed a functioning system of automobile dealers for its Civic and Accord automobiles in the United States, one of its key markets, Honda chose not to sell its new Legend model through the same dealer system. Rather, since the market segment target for the new range was very different, Honda took the bold decision to establish a new brand name, Acura, and a new dealer system.[27]

Distribution issues are examined more fully in Chapter 16. For the remainder of this chapter, we assume that the channel decision has been made.

Choice of effort level   In addition to specifying the channel or channels of physical distribution and influence, choices must be made regarding the appropriate targets for effort. For example, should a firm selling finished consumer products place most effort on working with retailers (a push strategy), or on persuading consumers to purchase (a pull strategy)? Should a component/raw material manufacturer place major efforts on the manufacturer that converts its offerings into completed products, or on consumers that may purchase those completed products? Intel's *intel inside* campaign (Chapter 4) reflected the fact that key decision makers in the PC market were no longer solely data-processing professionals, but a broader class including line executives, users broadly defined, and, increasingly, consumers.

A similar situation occurred a few years ago when a Tasmanian copy paper manufacturer, distributing to Australian firms through a conventional paper distributor system, switched focus, developed a brand name, and successfully targeted Australian secretaries; distributors were relatively unconcerned. Consider, also, the strategic targeting decision faced by Okidata a few years ago:

> **Example:** Okidata's U.S. subsidiary has a small number of geographically focused distributors; distributors sell Okidata's products to dealers that, in turn, sell to corporate accounts. Since resource constraints prevent Okidata from allocating comparable effort at each level in the channel, it must make critical decisions about where and how much sales and service effort to place among these three entity types—distributors, dealers, and corporate accounts.

In general, the firm can rarely afford to apply equally high effort at all levels, nor is this necessarily wise. It should clearly designate the level receiving the largest effort (primary customer target) and others receiving less effort (secondary targets).

Choice of specific decision influences   Having decided the specific channel and channel level to be targeted, the firm must identify the specific buying influences to be addressed. For example, if the consumer household is to be targeted, should the focus be on the husband, wife, children, grandparents, or some other member of the extended family? College Savings Bank, offering certificates of deposit indexed to college cost inflation as a means of saving for college education, targets both parents and grandparents[28]; conversely, for many children's products, children themselves are targeted.

> **Example:** McDonald's choice of key customer target is evident from the Happy Meals for kids, the playgrounds, the choice of a clown as an icon, and even in its charity. Note that, at most, young children are influencers and their parents the "decision makers" (and payers).[29]

Analogous decisions must be made when the target of effort is an organization. For example, a well-known floor covering manufacturer decided to target efforts at retailers, rather than distributors or consumers; however, rather than offer greater retail margins to the store, it provided direct cash incentives ("spiffs") to retail store salespeople. Similarly, in selling to a factory, the firm must allocate effort among organizational positions such as production manager, chief engineer, other engineers, purchasing agent, and general manager.

Choice of customer target is one of the most crucial market strategy decisions; however, the obvious choice may be an ineffective option. Those unskilled in marketing practice often believe the appropriate target is the one who has the money; paradoxically, a better choice may be the one who doesn't! Others argue for choosing the heavy user; again, this may not be the most effective. Thus according to *Business Week*, McDonald's heavy users are those twenty-something blue-collar males who eat at McDonald's two or three times a week. Nonetheless, McDonald's key customer target remains young children; this choice is integral to its success.

Furthermore, the obvious choice may be ineffectual, precisely because it is obvious; for example, perhaps it is the competitors' target. It is often the case that contrarianism in developing market strategy can pay great dividends. For example, a critical element in Federal Express' drive to leadership in U.S. overnight package delivery was its early decision to target the harried and time-pressed professional, rather than the mailroom, or the logistics manager.

Several important considerations should guide the choice of target. First, the prospective target should be seeking the values built into the firm's offer. Obviously, if the firm designed its offer with a target customer in mind, this matching should be ensured. But in the real world, this does not always occur. Sometimes target customers are not easy to reach, and significant creativity may be required. In many institutional buying situations, the procurement system is typically designed to confront sellers with individuals, typically purchasing professionals, whose major interest is short-term cost minimization. The marketing and sales challenge is to overcome these obstacles, often by targeting designers, engineers, senior managers, sales and marketing managers, and operations managers, who are more likely to be value-responsive.[30]

Second, although selected targets should be influential in the overall buying process, they need not necessarily be decision makers. Too often in business-to-business marketing, a decision maker's subordinates may be neglected by over-eager sellers, possibly with fatal results. Three reasons explain why such targeting may be shortsighted:

- These individuals frequently determine which suppliers enter the buyer's consideration set. Membership is a necessary, though not sufficient, requirement for would-be sellers.
- Although less senior individuals, from executive to shop floor user, may not have "yea" power in a decision, they frequently have "nay" power. Thus the firm should cast a broad net, at least for marketing communications.
- Eventually, senior executives move on and may be replaced by their subordinates. The firm may build significant obstacles for itself by failing to treat these subordinates appropriately, especially if competitors have been more prescient.

Example: Unable to gain access to critical decision makers at a major retailer, the national account manager for an office supply company assiduously called on lower-level personnel who were correspondingly neglected by the incumbent supplier. Eventually, when these junior executives were promoted to senior positions, the relationships built up over many years paid handsome dividends.

The final criterion for choosing customer targets is an ideal, one that has little interest in the price; in particular, a person that will benefit in a personal way from a purchase decision but does not personally carry the cost. Examples include:

- Children as a means of influencing parental decisions[31];
- Business travelers, whose companies pay for services provided by airlines and hotels;
- Architects, interior designers, product designers;[32]
- Accountants, financial advisors, and lawyers for customers with investable funds;
- Politicians and regulators who, of course, want the best for the public but whose decisions are always paid for by the taxpayer!

Clearly, ethical issues may be involved in such targeting. Some may view targeting intermediaries in the arms business, such as those with family or political links to government buyers, ethically challenging; others may be concerned with advertising to children. Regardless, customer targeting is one area where a marriage of analysis and creativity can pay major dividends.

CHOICE OF COMPETITOR TARGETS   The term competitor is used broadly to include both current and future-potential competitors that are both direct (similar products and technologies) and indirect (meeting the same customer needs but with different products or technologies). Note that by choosing a market segment to target, the firm has already defined the competitive set—those organizations that currently (and in the future will) seek to meet the needs of the same customers that the firm has chosen to target. Typically, these competitors are a subset of the total number of competitors, since not all competitors address the same market segment. Further, it is unlikely that perfect overlap exists among the various market segment definitions used by competitors.

Choice of competitor target depends, in part, on the firm's strength in the market segment. For example, the largest and strongest firms can probably be less delicate in competitive positioning; thus Coca-Cola may have more leeway in the soft drink market than Pepsi, 7-Up, Schweppes, or RC. For other competitors, however, competitor targeting is very important, and for smaller competitors, it is vital. One useful way to help frame the competitor targeting decision is to divide competitors into two categories: those with which the firm would like to compete and those with which it does not want to compete. This partitioning should be helpful in both devising the core strategy/key buying incentive/value proposition and providing valuable assistance to the sales force to develop the sales strategy.[33]

The choice of competitive targets is affected not only by their relative strength, but also by the firm's perception of available opportunities. It may also be fundamental in shaping a target customer's perception of seller's offer. A simple example from the soft drink category (Table 8.3) illustrates these distinctions. There is no doubt that positioning creativity, particularly regarding competitors, may have dramatic impact on sales.

Examples: Honda repositioned the motorcycle from primary use (transportation) to secondary use (leisure) and transformed an industry. Its competitor targets changed dramatically.

Guinness took a drink (Guinness Stout) with a limited, traditional market, and vastly expanded usage by its positioning as a friendly beverage for younger consumers. It leveraged the brand's heritage via the experiential aspect of over 2,000 Irish pubs spread worldwide.

Table 8.3   Positioning Alternatives

Claim	Type	Opportunity Implications	Customer Implications
"7-Up tastes better than Sprite"[34]	Comparison with individual direct competitor	One lemon-lime soda must substitute for another	Compare us
"7-Up, the best-tasting lemon-lime soda"	Subcategory superiority	The whole lemon-lime subcategory	The best choice when drinking lemon-lime
"7-Up, the Uncola"	Out of category	The cola category	The alternative to drinking cola
"7-Up, the real thing, the only one," etc.	Implied or claimed uniqueness	All beverages?	There's no other drink quite like it

CORE STRATEGY/KEY BUYING INCENTIVE/VALUE PROPOSITION   The final positioning element goes by several names, such as core strategy, key buying incentive, unique selling proposition, and value proposition. It describes how the firm plans to compete for its targeted customers. It must provide a convincing answer to a deceptively simple question, "Why should the targeted customer buy from (or recommend) the firm's offer rather than that of the targeted competitors?" The firm must decide where it will place its efforts in terms of benefits offered in addressing targeted customers.

To develop a successful market segment strategy, the firm should:

- focus on satisfying important customer needs;
- attempt to meet these needs better than competitors; and, where possible,
- offer benefits that are difficult for competitors to imitate.

Other actions are likely to offer only temporary advantage. In designing the core strategy, the firm makes the Principles of Customer Value and Differential Advantage operational in a particular product/market segment.

> **Examples:** Federal Express delivers on time ("when it absolutely, positively has to get there overnight"); Apple's MacIntosh computers are easy to use; telephone calls made with Sprint are exceptionally clear ("you can hear a pin drop").

Other terms sometimes used to describe the core strategy concept, including key buying incentive, unique selling proposition and the value proposition, come close to representing the critical concept, but none captures it as well as core strategy.[35] Externally, core strategy is the firm's key competitive weapon in attempting to capture the customers it seeks. Internally, it defines the task for the firm's implementation programs—the marketing mix, and supporting functions. From the customer's perspective, it defines why benefits offered by the firm are superior to competition. It also provides the framework to both organize the many marketing mix activities, such as selling approach, advertising copy, and sales promotion, and to ensure that other functional areas are committed to delivering the promised benefits.

Following the discussion on customer targets, it is vital to recognize that if the firm selects more than one target, more than one positioning is required. For example, many consumer goods manufacturers target both retail distributors and consumers. Thus the core strategy for consumers typically revolves around a specific set of end-user benefits. Detergent manufacturers, such as Lever Brothers and Procter & Gamble, may offer consumer targets such functional benefits as clean clothes, stain removal, and "whiter whites," or such psychological benefits as reinforcing their caring for the family and being a good parent. By contrast, the positioning for retail distributors is likely to focus on potential profits, promotional support, ease of doing business, product delivery, and so forth.

Notice that for manufacturers of branded products, the consumer has always been the key customer target. In designing a core strategy for consumers, constraints are necessarily imposed on the possibilities for alternative targets. Thus because establishing the brand with consumers typically involves heavy spending on advertising and promotion, the firm is limited in its ability to offer retailers the margins they desire. By contrast, manufacturers of private brands have selected retailers as their key target. Because they must price low to create retailer margin opportunity, their advertising and promotion possibilities are significantly limited.[36]

In summary, whereas firms may design positioning statements for more than one customer in a market segment, they typically select a key target for the core strategy design and so, out of necessity, limit their options with other targets. In some cases, firms elect to develop positions for only one of several customer types in a market segment. Thus component and raw material manufacturers frequently develop core strategies for only their manufacturing customers, and small consumer goods manufacturers may place exclusive focus on retailers. Although this latter group are finished goods manufacturers that, of course, design products for end users, all other efforts targeted at consumers are undertaken by the retailers.

DEVELOPING POSITIONING STATEMENTS   This process is probably the most laborious and difficult element of product/market segment strategy development. Although the process has been described in a linear, sequential manner (forced by written communication), it is a complex, creative, and highly interactive process, often involving many cut-and-try attempts and simulated testing before a satisfactory combination is achieved. In those cases where the firm chooses a market segment in which it has a strong advantage, the core strategy may dictate the choice of customer or competitor targets. More typically, it follows a complex process beginning with a preliminary choice of customer target, then working through a series of consistency checks to arrive at well-integrated positioning (Figure 8.4). Ries and Trout capture the complexity of developing positioning when they state that, "Positioning is not what you do to a product—positioning is what you do to the mind of the prospect."[37]

In developing positioning strategy, we also recommend developing a common framework for use across the firm. One such framework requires statements that implicitly or explicitly distinguish the firm's offer from competitors and that fit the following format[38]: Convince [customer target] that they will receive [these benefits: core strategy] because we have [these capabilities/features].

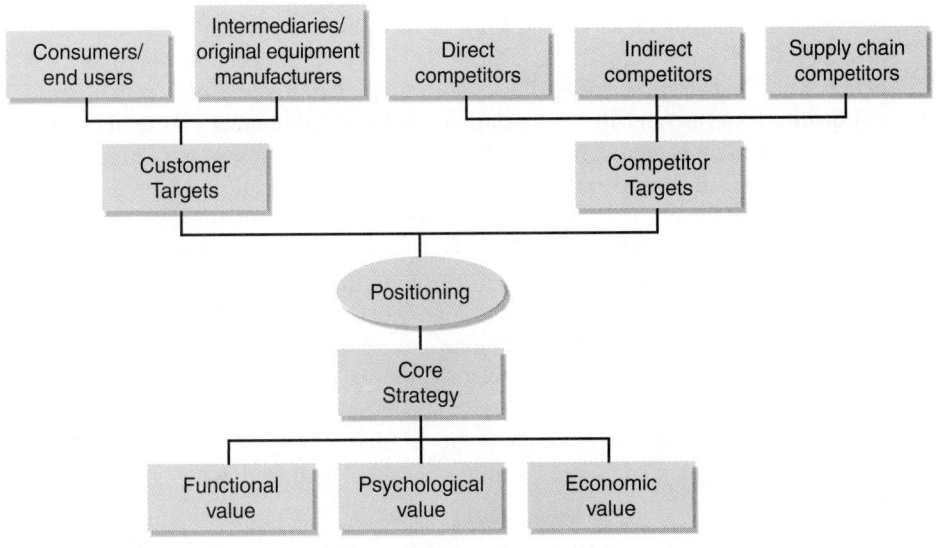

FIGURE 8.4

Developing Positioning in the Market Segment

Clear positioning statements have major value. For example, one of the most common complaints advertising agencies make about their clients is that they have not clarified their strategies. Although positioning statements are not advertising messages, they provide excellent guidance for the firm's advertising agency. Indeed, without such guidance, the agency's creative personnel have enormous difficulty.[39]

Positioning statements play a vital role in helping to guide and coordinate the firm's efforts in the marketplace; they are perhaps even more crucial internally, the subject to which the discussion now turns.

Implementation

Many marketing managers fail at the task of securing support from other parts of the firm. Because other senior functional executives, and even general managers, frequently understand so little of the external orientation and its implications, far too often the internal task remains undone. The marketing group may do a superb job of analyzing the external environment, setting performance targets, selecting strategic alternatives, and developing positioning statements. However, unless the actions of others are coordinated to support and actually deliver the benefits specified in the core strategy, the prospects for success are limited. This section deals first with the marketing mix, then with other functions.

SUPPORTING MARKETING MIX PROGRAMS   Almost every basic marketing book advocates the need to "integrate" the marketing mix, the implementation elements comprising product, promotion, distribution, service, and price. However, most books then neglect the concept in favor of "disintegration" by structuring their content around a separate discussion of each element. Integration, of course, should not be conducted in a vacuum; rather, the marketing mix should be integrated about the core strategy.

> Example: Suppose the firm bases its core strategy on the benefits that flow from superb product quality. Other elements of the marketing mix should be focused to support this theme.[40] We examine the implications of the core strategy for each element.
>
> Since the product must be of high quality, such as performance and durability, its appearance and brand name should further reinforce the quality concept. Likewise, if the firm advertises, the copy should focus on quality, and choice of media and format should be supportive. Sales promotional materials, such as brochures and display racks, should likewise be of high quality and, to the extent possible, the firm should try to ensure that only "appropriate" publicity is obtained. Selling strategies should also be carefully tailored to focus on the central quality benefits, and if distribution is involved, the number and quality of approved distributors should be carefully scrutinized. If quality were so high that an exclusive positioning were sought, then just a few distributors of the highest possible caliber should be used. If the firm offers truly high-quality products, the need for service should be minimal, but when needed, it should be superb. Finally, high product quality allows considerable pricing discretion. Depending on the firm's customer and competitor targets (and its strategic objectives), price can range from very high (specialty positioning), to competitive levels (more aggressive) or even lower. However, low prices should only be chosen with care. First, too low a price may render quality claims unbelievable to many customers[41]; second, although the production of high-quality products does not necessarily imply high costs, very high quality almost always does such that setting low prices may be foolhardy.

Had some other core strategy been selected, for example, the benefits of low price and widespread availability, a completely different set of marketing mix implications would have prevailed, for the core strategy provides the parameters within which the individual marketing mix strategies are developed. However, since many different individuals and departments may be involved in this process, such as advertising agencies, sales department, sales promotion experts, public relations department, and market research suppliers, managing the coordination process is not a simple task.

Furthermore, the firm should continually be on the lookout to ensure that its programs are, in fact, implementing the product/market segment strategy. For example, in the early 1990s, Goodyear eliminated commissions paid to technicians for auto parts and service at over 900 company outlets. Said a company spokesperson, "We believe by eliminating sales commissions, a perceived obstacle to customer trust, Goodyear will set higher standards on customer satisfaction."

SUPPORTING FUNCTIONAL PROGRAMS Finally, the firm must establish the various types and levels of support required from other functional areas to implement the proposed strategy. Of course, if one or more functional areas cannot meet these requirements, the core strategy must be revisited and reworked.

> **Example:** For a firm offering customer benefits that flow from superb product quality, several fairly obvious implications stand out. For engineering, product and process design; for manufacturing, process control and scheduling; for purchasing, procurement policies; for finance, providing necessary funds; for technical service, providing superb backup service; for customer service, billing, shipping, and follow-through; for transportation, scheduling and loss/breakage control, and so forth.

A genuine consensus must be built to commit functional areas, their managers, and employees to meeting these requirements, or the product/market segment strategy is bound to fail. Customers do not care which department or individual is at fault. If they fail to receive the benefits they anticipate, they rightly believe that it is the supplier's job to deal with such issues. The failure to integrate successfully across organizational elements to delight the customer is epitomized in phrases familiar to millions of consumers, "That's not my job," "You'll have to speak to my supervisor," "I can't do anything about that," "I'm sorry, but you'll just have to wait," and "We've tried to get it changed but they won't listen." These responses and their ilk have passed into the lexicon of marketing failure, testimony to the wide gaps that so often separate the high ideals of a strategy from its successful implementation.

MANAGING MULTISEGMENT STRATEGIES

In many cases, management wants to address multiple segments in a given market; as a result, marketing offers must be developed for each of the targeted segments. Because customers in each segment have homogeneous sets of needs that differ from customers in other segments, to a large extent, individual segment offers should be developed independently of one another. The end result of developing these several offers may lead to three different situations: The offers are basically independent, the offers produce positive synergy, or the offers produce negative synergy.

Positive synergy may result in many ways, such as by addressing the various segments through the same sales force, using similar distribution channels, and enjoying brand equity from the same brand. By contrast, the bases for negative synergy may be salesforce confusion, a single brand with negative brand equity in one or more segments, and the development of gray markets.[42]

> **Examples:** Good examples of positive and negative synergy in branding are GE and Gallo. Because the *GE* brand is so well and widely respected, new product market entries gain enormously from the GE name (positive synergy). *Gallo* is an

Table 8.4 Illustration of Multisegment Strategic Issues

Marketing Mix	Potential Problem	Possible Solution
Product	Increased production costs, delivery delays, increased inventory carrying costs	Modular design, just-in-time (JIT) assembly
Advertising	Exposure to different appeals	Ensure that appeals, while different, do not conflict
Salesforce	Salespeople ineffective in multiple segments	Extra training or develop specialized salesforces
Pricing	Trans-shipment (diversion)	Management of price differentials, consider differentiating such areas as brand and package
Distribution	Alienation of existing intermediaries	Secure financial/service package for existing intermediaries; consider different brand, package
Service	Alienation of customers not receiving premium service package	Try to ensure perceived equity, physical separation where possible

immensely strong brand in popularly-priced wine segments. However, placing the *Gallo* name on a $100 bottle of wine would probably have a negative effect on sales (negative synergy).

Management must orchestrate these independently-developed market segment strategies into a coherent multiple segment strategy for the market as a whole. Some of the issues to be considered are modular product design in situations where the product must be varied, and considerations of multiple distribution systems. The expense of brand development tends to predispose managers to work with an existing brand, extending and stretching to new segments but, as noted above, there may be complications. Table 8.4 summarizes some of the immediate implications to be considered when elements of the offer are varied across segments. The example is illustrative, but at a minimum conveys some of the challenges of operating in segmented markets. Such heterogeneity is typical of today's markets, and dealing with these problems involves some of the most intriguing and challenging issues of market strategy and tactics. In general, this problem area is a classic illustration of where multifunctional teams are invaluable, for by working together creatively, problems that might arise are surfaced and addressed effectively.

SUMMARY

This chapter reviewed the functions (or purposes) of market and product/market segment strategies in some detail. It was noted that strategy is often poorly understood, yet market strategy at the segment level is the guts of the firm's marketing effort and key to its overall success. This chapter discussed the role of objectives, (strategic and operational) strategic alternatives, positioning (customer targets, competitor targets, core strategy), and implementation programs (marketing mix, supporting functional programs) in developing the product/market segment strategy.

The importance of internal consistency across many areas was emphasized, such as consistency of performance objectives and strategy, consistency of positioning elements (customer targets, competitor targets, core strategy), and consistency between the strategy and implementation programs. Finally, it was emphasized that consistency must be sought across functions and departments; these organizational units must work together to deliver the benefits of the core strategy to customers. Without full integration, this entire strategy development effort will be insufficient in the competitive markets of today and tomorrow.

THE CHANGING VIEW

Old Way	New Way
All customers are good customers	Customer selection critical
Targeting *en masse*	Targeting with individual precision
Uniform objectives across products and markets	Differentiated objectives across products and markets
Marketers focus on volume and share	Marketers concerned with shareholder value creation (economic profit)
Functional programs poorly coordinated	Functional programs driven by integrated strategy
Strategy is the marketing mix	Marketing mix is driven by strategy
Internal, budgetary focus in strategy development	External, strategic focus in strategy development
Competitor considerations ignored or demeaned	Competitor considerations play major role in strategizing
Strategy development the province of marketing and general management	Cross-functional teamwork in strategy development
Compromise common, core strategy fuzzy	Clarity emphasized, core strategy clearly specified
Positioning concepts understood poorly or not at all	Positioning recognized as critical strategic element
Integration limited to marketing mix	Integration spans all functions

QUESTIONS FOR STUDY AND DISCUSSION

1. Explain the notion of trading off objectives.

2. Select a firm and product market with which you are familiar. Lay out what you perceive to be the firm's product/market strategy.

3. The material on market strategy contains a means/end chain for developing strategic alternatives. This particular chain is not the only possible device. Develop an alternative that fulfills the same function.

4. Many executives complain that their competitors' attempts to attack them rely almost exclusively on low selling prices. Based on the strategic principles discussed so far, how would you recommend attracting competitors' customers?

5. Shareholder value and cash flow analysis will increasingly require better financial justification for their recommended strategies. How would you set up a system to satisfy these requirements?

6. Many marketers believe that strategy in marketing revolves around two decisions—targeting and positioning. In this chapter, you have been exposed to a broader conception. Discuss the pros and cons of each approach.

7. Positioning maps (Chapter 7) are useful descriptive tools, although they are of limited assistance in strategy development. Discuss.

8. Show how the product/market strategy discussed in this chapter is related to the Tasks and Principles of Marketing.

9. Discuss the pros and cons of in- versus out-of-category positioning strategies.

10. Select a multiperson decision process with which you are familiar, and show your recommended customer targeting. Explain the reasons for your recommendations.

11. The material on market strategy contains examples illustrating how the choice of customer target or core strategy constrains subsequent options available to the marketer. Develop your own example of this constraint issue.

12. Why is the integration of the marketing mix around the core strategy insufficient to achieve marketplace success in the twenty-first century?

13. Using the concepts explained in the chapter, analyze what you believe to be an example of an unsuccessful market strategy and explain why it failed.

14. Using the concepts explained in the chapter, analyze what you believe to be an example of a successful market strategy and explain why it succeeded.

15. Why do apparently successful strategies become ineffective over time? What are the implications for management?

16. Many firms now develop market strategies in cross-functional teams. What, in your opinion, are the advantages and disadvantages of this approach?

17. Technically-oriented firms typically emphasize product improvement as their primary strategy, but too often fail to appreciate the crucial importance of positioning. How would you attempt to convince them that, no matter how good their product, positioning to key customer targets should be a crucial part of their strategy?

18. Sometimes the interests and motives of different participants in a buying process are in direct conflict. Develop your own example to illustrate such conflict, and indicate how you would develop your strategy in this situation.

19. Identify three examples of innovative and creative positioning strategies. What evidence can you collect to evaluate their business success?

ENDNOTES

1. The term "market" strategy is used rather than "marketing" strategy to emphasize that the efforts of many functional areas, not just marketing, are required to help develop and implement the strategy.

2. See H. Mintzberg, *The Rise and Fall of Strategic Planning*, New York: Free Press, 1994. See also N. Capon, Review of *The Rise and Fall of Strategic Planning*, by Henry Mintzberg, *Academy of Management Review*, (Jan. 1996), pp. 298–301.

3. For an interesting perspective on strategy, see B.D. Henderson, "The Origin of Strategy," *Harvard Business Review*, 67 (November-December 1989), pp. 139–143.

4. As we see in the next section, strategy is concerned with allocating scarce resources. At the corporate level, the focus is on the various business units; at the business level, the focus is on its various products and markets. For example, Jack Welch, CEO of General Electric must decide what resources to invest in jet engines, entertainment (NBC), financial services (GE Capital), electricity generation, plastics, locomotives, home appliances, and other GE businesses. The head of the home appliance business must decide what resources to invest in refrigerators, freezers, clothes washers and dryers, dishwashers, and ranges, as well as the mix between U.S. and non-U.S. markets, and between commercial and consumer segments.

5. A simple device that may improve the chances that competition is seriously considered is to re-label the "Marketing Plan" as the "Competitive Marketing Plan."

6. For interesting perspectives, see J.R. Williams, "How Sustainable is Your Competitive Advantage," *California Management Review*, 34 (Spring 1992), pp. 29–52, P. Ghemawat, "Sustainable Advantage," *Harvard Business Review*, 64 (Sept./Oct. 1986), pp. 53–94 and M.E. Porter and V.E. Millar, "How Information Gives You Competitive Advantage," 63 (July/August 1985), pp. 149–159.

7. As volume increases, the implicit fixed cost per unit is reduced.

8. Although the notion of positioning strategy is typically more familiar to consumer marketers than industrial marketers, the same basic principles apply, especially the three Cs concept.

9. Many organizations confuse performance objectives and mission. As shown in Chapter 19, mission is a broad statement of where the firm will seek business; by contrast, performance objectives are statements of those results the firm seeks to achieve.

10. Figures in the table are averages of more than 1,000 businesses pooled across time periods and industries.

11. For a study of the effectiveness of this argument, see A.J. Slywotsky and B.P.. Shapiro, "Leveraging to Beat the Odds: The New Marketing Mind-Set," *Harvard Business Review*, 71 (Sept./Oct. 1993), pp. 97–107.

12. The acronym SMART is often used to describe well-formulated objectives: **S**pecific, **M**easurable, **A**chievable, **R**ealistic, **T**imely.

13. For an example of how some leading firms are dealing with this issue, see the discussion of "brand health" checks in Chapter 11.

14. Issues concerning customer retention were discussed at some length in Chapter 3.

15. *The New York Times*, January 31, 1999.

16. This approach, masterminded by John Sculley and involving offering large bottles of soft drinks, was used by Pepsi to take away Coca-Cola's advantage with its "hour glass" bottle in supermarket business. See J. Sculley with J.A. Byrne, *Odyssey: Pepsi to Apple . . . A Journey of Adventure, Ideas and the Future*, New York, Harper & Row, 1987.

17. This approach, traditionally used by automobile manufacturers, diminishes the value of already-purchased products. It has become central to the strategies of many software companies that periodically introduce product upgrades.

18. Perhaps the chief exemplar of this strategy is Church and Dwight, whose Arm and Hammer baking soda product has found its way into end uses as diverse as cat litter, toothpaste, detergent, and cattle feed.

19. Price promotions have been a major feature of supermarket products and automobile marketing in recent years. Unfortunately, these tactics often do little more than shift purchases forward in time without securing an enduring increase in usage. As a result, they often create havoc in the supply chain, and destroy shareholder value.

20. In certain businesses, the nature of the product or service, typically those that involve a direct customer relationship such as financial services, leads to firms having significant data on their customers; this data can be used to make specific offers. In other areas, especially for many consumer goods, a variety of marketing tactics may require that the firm specifically identify its customers.

21. *Fortune*, March 4, 1996, pp. 193–194.

22. These alternatives are developed in more detail in Chapter 18.

23. One of the more successful cost reduction attempts is General Electric's *Work-Out* program, in which employees suggest changes in procedures, share best practices, and use reengineering tools like process mapping.

24. See the discussion in Chapter 6.

25. For example, supermarkets frequently complain to suppliers that profit margins are too low. However, since efficient organizations can turn inventory at least 25 turns per year, a 1% profit margin translates into a 25% ROI on inventory investment.
ROI = Profit/Investment = profit/sales $\times$ sales/investment = ROS $\times$ Inventory turns = 1 $\times$ 25 = 25%.
Wal-Mart leads the world in supply chain efficiency with inventory turns as high as 40 or 50 in some categories. According to some reports, Wal-Mart is now turning *Pampers* (P&G's diapers) 365 times a year!

26. In this discussion, the consumer may be either an individual, a family, or a formal organization.

27. Note that in other countries in the world outside the United States, Honda sells all its vehicles under the Honda brand name.

28. College Savings Bank (A) and (B) in N. Capon, *The Marketing of Financial Services: A Book of Cases*, Englewood Cliffs, NJ: Prentice Hall, 1992.

29. This is not to imply that the role of user (consumer of the food) is unimportant, but as most parents can attest, it is usually easier to get a child into McDonald's than it is to get them to eat when they are there.

30. Note that the McDonald's child is also value-responsive; value is represented by the contents of the Happy Meal!

31. In addition to McDonald's, breakfast cereal, snowboarding equipment, teenage fashion, and many more categories could be added.

32. In the argot of industrial marketing, this targeting is known as the "specification sell;" the goal is to specify the attributes of the product/service so that the purchasing entity has little choice of supplier.

33. In general, the firm may wish to avoid head-to-head competition with stronger competitors (which may provoke a strong response) and rather concentrate efforts against weaker firms. However, notwithstanding this general prescription, as discussed in Chapter 5, to compete against a strong competitor in some markets may lead to development of a more adept organization that is better equipped to face competition elsewhere.

34. In the United States, such a claim (including naming a competitor directly) may be used as advertising, provided acceptable statistical data is provided to support the claim. The "Pepsi Challenge" was conducted on just such a basis.

35. For more detail on the "value proposition," see "Achieving Market Focus," Chapter 7 in F.J. Gouillart and J.N. Kelly, *Transforming the Organization*, New York: McGraw-Hill, 1996.

36. Such activities would not, in any case, be targeted at consumers with whom, by definition, they have no relationship.

37. A. Ries and J. Trout, *Positioning: The Battle for Your Mind*, New York, McGraw-Hill, 1993.

38. Developed by Robert Christian, formerly of the Impact Planning Group, Old Greenwich, CT.

39. Communication and advertising strategy is discussed in more detail in Chapter 14.

40. Of course, product quality has many dimensions, but they need not be explored for the purpose of this example.

41. The Japanese heavy equipment manufacturer Komatsu ran into this problem when it first entered the U.S. market.

42. Gray markets occur when the firm attempts to sell the same product at two different prices in two different markets. Distributors purchase in the low price market, then resell products in the high price market, undercutting the manufacturer.

WEB RESOURCES

7-UP	www.7up.com
Academy of Management Review	www.aom.pace.edu/amr
Airbus Industrie	www.airbus.com
Apple Computer	www.apple.com
BHP	www.bhp.com
Boeing	www.boeing.com
Bridgestone	www.bridgestone.co.jp
Business Week	www.businessweek.com
California Management Review	www.haas.berkeley.edu/news/cmr
Charles Schwab	www.schwab.com
Coca-Cola	www.cocacola.com
College Savings Bank	www.collegesavings.com
Dell Computer	www.dell.com
Dupont	www.dupont.com
Dye Magnet	www.dyemagnet.com
Federal Express	www.fedex.com
Fidelity	www.fidelity.com
Gallo	www.gallo.com
GE Capital	www.ge.com/capital
General Electric	www.ge.com
General Motors	www.gm.com
Goodyear	www.goodyear.com
Guinness	www.guinness.com
Harvard Business Review	www.hbrp.harvard.edu/products/hbr
Honda	www.honda.com

IBM	www.ibm.com
Impact Planning Group	www.impactplan.com
Intel	www.intel.com
Jeep	www.jeepunpaved.com
Johnson and Johnson	www.johnsonandjohnson.com
Komatsu	www.komatsu.com
Lever Brothers	www.unilever.com
McDonald's	www.mcdonalds.com
Merrill Lynch	www.ml.com
Michelin	www.michelin.com
NASDAQ	www.nasdaq.com
NBC	www.nbc.com
New York Stock Exchange	www.nyse.com
Okidata	www.okidata.com
Pepsi	www.pepsico.com
Procter & Gamble	www.pg.com
Rhone-Poulenc	www.rhone-poulenc.com
Royal Bank of Canada	www.royalbank.com
Schweppes	www.cardburyschweppes.com
Sprint	www.sprint.com
The Strategic Planning Institute	www.thespinet.org

CHAPTER

9

COMPETITIVE MARKET STRATEGIES IN INTRODUCTION AND GROWTH

LEARNING OBJECTIVES

When you have completed this chapter, you will understand

- **the critical importance of competitive strategy making**

- **different types of market and product life cycles**

- **the role that competitive life cycles and other models can play in providing strategy frameworks[1]**

- **the nature of competitive situations in the introduction as well as early and late growth stages of the product form life cycle**

- **business characteristics in introduction and growth as a function of scenarios based on life cycle stage and competitive position**

- **how to develop alternative strategic possibilities, based on potential future scenarios**

INTRODUCTION

It was asserted earlier that the increased pace of environmental change lessens the firm's ability to forecast the future. As a result, it was argued that strategic thinking should be conducted in the spirit of contingency planning, whereby the firm identifies several scenarios and develops strategy in the context of those potential futures. In that spirit, this chapter uses a life cycle perspective to create future scenarios and identify several strategic options at different life cycle stages. Although predicting the timing of transitions from one life cycle stage to another is often difficult, life cycle stages are more easily identifiable and generate useful insights for competitive strategizing.[2]

BASIC CONCEPTS

Life cycles are conceptual devices for understanding patterns of behavior through time. They are mostly presented as two-dimensional representations of the evolution of sales revenues at the product class (or category) and product form (or subcategory) levels. Although individual examples may vary widely, regardless of life cycle type, these graphs of product class or product form sales usually resemble classic S-shaped curves (Figure 9.1).

- Introduction: sales volume initially low
- Early growth: sales volume grows at an increasing rate
- Late growth: sales volume grows at a decreasing rate
- Maturity: sales volume averages GNP growth year-to-year
- Decline: sales volume eventually declines.

Notwithstanding the ubiquity of life-cycle curves in marketing text books, and given appropriate data, after-the-fact plotting of any product life cycle is a trivial exercise. What is far more critical, but also more difficult for competitive strategy making, is the ability to predict life cycles before the fact.[3] In reality, sales curves often depart significantly from the idealized pictures shown below. Indeed, in truly new markets, product and process technology is often evolving so fast that distinguishing market, product class, product form, and even product item from process technology cycles may prove extremely difficult. Note also that, by definition, product form life cycle curves are drawn only for successful products. Since the history of innovation is strewn with technical breakthroughs that failed the commercialization test, this distinction is vital when examining research

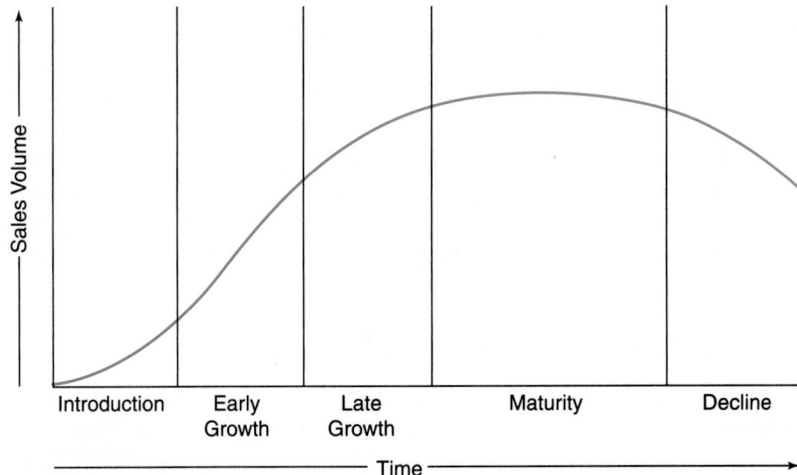

FIGURE 9.1

A Classic Life Cycle

underlying competitive strategy in early life cycle stages. However, it is important to emphasize that this interest in the life cycle concept is primarily as a tool, to help understand the evolution of competitive strategies in a market over time and assist managers in developing their own competitive strategies.

Types of Life Cycle

This section describes various types of life cycle.

THE MARKET LIFE CYCLE   The market life cycle focuses on markets defined in terms of a particular function or customer need requirement, and includes products from all competitors that satisfy the need.[4] For example, horse and carriage, bicycles, automobiles, rail, ships, and air travel all satisfy transportation needs. This simple need perspective provides the best insurance against the myopia that often leads to firms being "blindsided" by indirect competitors, and was the important message of Theodore Levitt's famous "Marketing Myopia" article.[5] It is sometimes difficult to define and gather data on markets, because functions or needs may be interpreted at different levels of specificity. Furthermore, needs are typically much less tangible than the products that satisfy those needs.

Functions or needs tend to be enduring, and to respond in reasonably predictable ways to delivered performance, regardless of product and process technology. They also reinforce an external perspective on customers and competitors that offsets the inward tendencies that tend to grow, if not dominate, company thinking over time. Peripheral vision is important for anticipating opportunities and threats[6]; one of the best ways to develop this vision is to focus on customer needs, including, of course, customer perception of the extent to which those needs are being met.[7]

Market life cycles have the broadest scope and longest duration of all life cycle types. However, within these function-based cycles, competing technologies, product classes, and product forms jostle for position. Customers may be indifferent to technology, product class, and product form, so long as they receive sufficient benefits to outweigh their costs. Of course, such costs may go well beyond the obvious overt financial costs for, as technology evolves, both learning requirements and adoption risks impose "cost" burdens that can impede transition.[8]

At the most aggregate level, market life cycles comprise several independent yet interacting product class and product form life cycles. Marketers' conventional approaches define product class and product form life cycles as follows:

THE PRODUCT CLASS LIFE CYCLE   This life cycle refers to all products from all competing manufacturers that, despite differences in appearance and performance, serve a set of functional needs in a roughly similar manner.[9] Typically, different product classes offer quite distinct customer benefits in satisfying the common underlying needs that form the basis of the market life cycle.

Of course, at any given point in time, the specific product classes comprising a market life cycle can be in various stages of evolution. For example, in the U.S. transportation market, horse and carriage is defunct, rail is in decline, automobiles are mature, and air transportation is in growth. Furthermore, individual market life cycles may be in different phases in different countries. For example, motorcycles and automobiles are in the growth stage in the People's Republic of China.

Just as a market life cycle comprises several product class life cycles, individual product class life cycles comprise several individual product form life cycles.

THE PRODUCT FORM LIFE CYCLE   This life cycle is a finer level of aggregation and comprises a homogeneous grouping of products from all competing producers. These products are more similar in perception and use by customers than items in a product class.[10] For example, product forms in the automobile product class include sports cars, luxury cars, compacts, subcompacts, and minivans. Servers, workstations, desktop personal computers, and laptop personal computers are product forms in the computer product class.

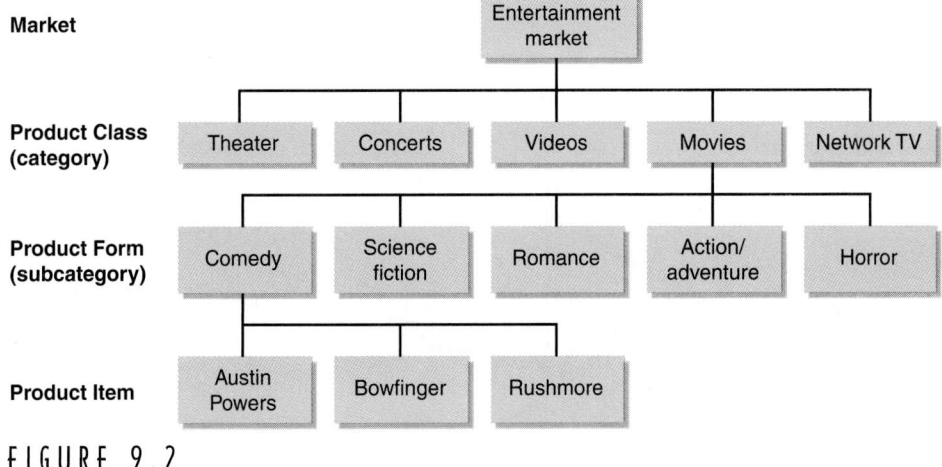

Market — Entertainment market

Product Class (category) — Theater | Concerts | Videos | Movies | Network TV

Product Form (subcategory) — Comedy | Science fiction | Romance | Action/adventure | Horror

Product Item — Austin Powers | Bowfinger | Rushmore

FIGURE 9.2

Illustration of a Market/Product Hierarchy

Figure 9.2 illustrates (incompletely) the hierarchical decomposition of the entertainment market into representative product classes and product forms. Decomposition is extended to the level of individual comedy movies, product items in this nomenclature.

In Figure 9.3, we depict the sales relationships for a typical product class that is well past the introduction stage. It illustrates the co-existence of various product form life cycles that together comprise the product class life cycle. (In turn, as noted earlier, the market life cycle comprises several product class life cycles.)

Example: In the late 1990s, Dye Magnet was introduced in the mature laundry market. The product, which consists of a treated piece of cotton cloth (close to the size of a washcloth), attracts dye and completely eliminates staining problems. Despite the presence of such giants as Procter & Gamble (P&G) and Lever Bros., Dye Magnet was introduced by an independent start-up.

Those who have attempted to define market or industry boundaries usually find that these distinctions are not easily made *ex ante*. Product technology, customer innovation, and regulatory decisions are rapidly changing these boundaries in many "industries." For

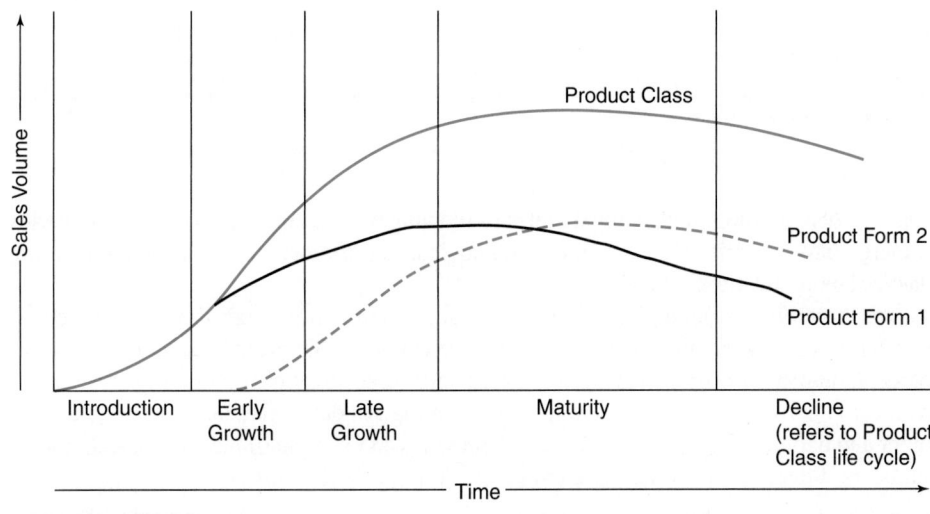

FIGURE 9.3

Product Form Life Cycles

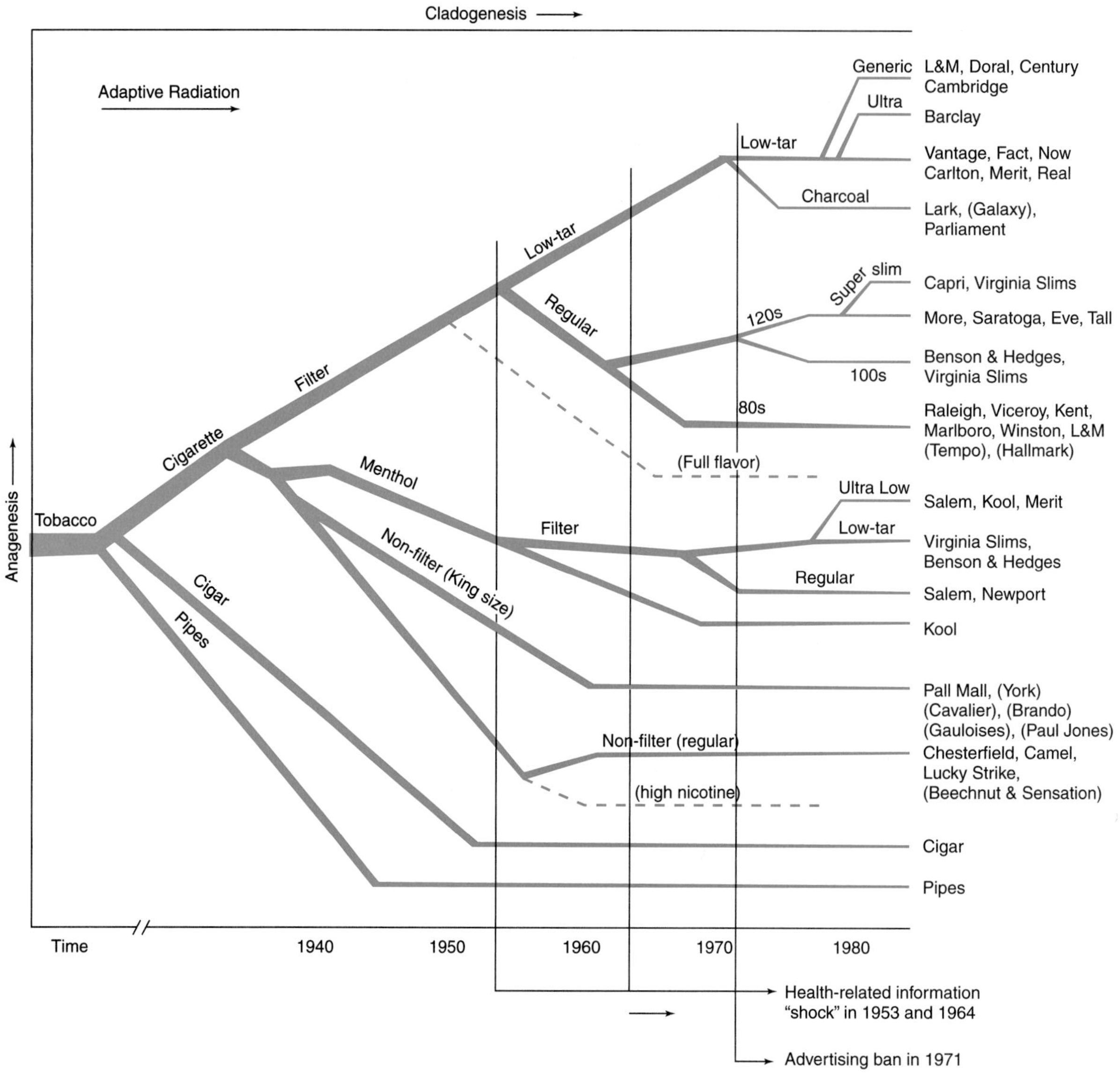

FIGURE 9.4

A Taxonomic Hierarchy for the Cigarette Industry

S.L. Holak and Y.E. Tang, "Advertising's Effect on the Product Evolutionary Cycle," *Journal of Marketing*, 54 (July 1990), pp. 16–29.

example, deregulation in the United States is allowing the banking and insurance industries to merge into financial services, and technological developments have made engineering plastics competitive with metals.

Furthermore, marketing researchers have suggested that biological models, based on an evolutionary framework, may provide a more complete picture of market development than competitive or product life cycles. These approaches explicitly recognize the roles of managerial activity and government mediation in market development, in addition to customer and competitor dynamics. Figure 9.4 provides an example of how biological models can be used to create a taxonomic hierarchy for the cigarette industry.

THE PRODUCT LINE/ITEM LIFE CYCLE The product line (or item) life cycle focuses on an individual firm's sales of a line of products or an individual product item.[11] Although these sales trajectories are critical for product and brand managers, they are not particularly useful for competitive strategy making as they provide little insight into market factors such as competitor entry and exit. Because individual producers make resource allocation decisions for specific models or brands, there can be many different shapes of product line/item sales curves. For example, a firm whose product has declining sales in a mature product form may increase advertising and reverse the decline.

IMPLICATIONS   The consistent life cycle patterns found for many products at both the product class and product form levels can provide important strategic insights. However, for the marketing strategist, scenario development at the product form level is usually the most valuable because marketing strategy is typically developed where product lines from individual firms compete for sales. For example, several investment bankers offer corporate debt financing, several automobile manufacturers offer minivans, and several computer manufacturers offer laptop computers. Indeed, for a firm contemplating entry into the laptop computer market, scenario development at the computer product class level may be of little value. By contrast, scenarios for laptop computers and other computer product forms would probably be more worthwhile.

The shortening of product form life cycles that firms are experiencing today not only makes scenario development more difficult, but it also has critical strategic implications.[12] First, under former longer life cycle conditions, firms could enter a market, fail, redevelop their products, and reenter; now, increasingly there is insufficient time to do so. Second, since the highest unit margins are often made during the early growth stage, the time to extract these high margins is diminished. Finally, since the time available to achieve dominant position is decreased, a premium is placed on good strategic thinking early in the product form life cycle. The life cycle analysis presented in this and the following chapter is specifically designed to improve the reader's ability to formulate good competitive strategies.

For the purposes of developing competitive scenarios, it is most useful to think in terms of market development for a significant innovation as represented by a new product form. For example, this might include markets for such major durables as laptop computers, cellular telephones, or DVD players.

DEVELOPING COMPETITIVE STRATEGIC OPTIONS: OVERVIEW

One approach to generating competitive strategic options is to use scenarios comprising two dimensions: life cycle stage and competitive position. We conceptualize the life cycle as comprising five stages: introduction, early growth, late growth, maturity, and decline; each stage is defined by a set of characteristics that distinguishes one from another. The combination of these life cycle stages with two competitive positions, leader and follower, results in ten strategic scenarios. However, we drop the leader/follower distinction for the introduction, late growth, and decline stages and focus on a reduced number of scenarios. In this chapter, we consider the introduction, early growth, and late growth stages; in Chapter 10 we address maturity and decline.

Each scenario follows a consistent process. Characteristics of the life cycle stage are described, then alternative objectives and strategic options for leader and follower are discussed. The discussion implicitly assumes the firm is a player in one of these scenarios; a separate but related issue is at what stage the firm should enter. Entry can be made in any life cycle stage. Following the discussion in Chapter 6, undeveloped markets correspond to the introduction and early growth stages of the product life cycle; developed markets correspond to the late growth, maturity, and decline stages. Chapter 10 addresses maturity and decline.

The power of the competitive life cycle approach is that significant commonalties in market conditions are present at similar life cycle stages across many different product types or technologies. These commonalties give rise to families of strategic options that operate as a starting point for developing strategy in individual cases. Of course, to suggest general marketing strategies for different strategic situations is a dangerous undertaking. Good marketing strategy development not only has a strong creative element, but in most cases the less the firm's actions are predictable to competitors, the better. Nonetheless, managers receive significant benefit from identifying broadly-defined strategic options and considering the issues they should contemplate in particular cases.

Alternative perspectives on competitive strategy are available. For example, Porter has identified the three generic strategies of low cost, focus, and differentiation that, he contends, should form the basis for competitive strategy making.[13] Although each strategic alternative has merit, these prescriptions are too simplistic for the complex, competitive, global environments faced by many firms today. In recent years, some strategy writers have shifted from a focus on externally-oriented notions, such as life cycles, to more internally-focused perspectives embracing core competencies and strategic resources.[14] Whereas competence is an important concept, the market environment should play a major role in strategy development. Not only can an overemphasis on core competence limit the firm's search for growth, we note that most successful entrepreneurial start-ups commence life with limited core competence, just the vision of a market opportunity.

As noted, this scenario approach assumes that the firm is an actor in the competitive life cycle. Far too often, firms may be very successful in one product form, but, for a variety of reasons, may not enter the new product form. The reasons are many, including a strong product focus that blinds management to the new product form, insufficient resources, and concerns with potential cannibalization of current sales.

> **Example:** The retail brokerage business encompasses three related product forms—full service brokerage, discount brokerage, and Internet trading. In the late 1990s, while industry leader Merrill Lynch continued to focus on full service brokerage, Charles Schwab, the leader in discount brokerage, fully embraced Internet trading and quickly developed a leadership position.[15]

Firms that are truly externally oriented recognize that customer needs must be the fundamental drivers of their actions, and that these needs may be satisfied by a number of different and evolving product forms, driven by a variety of technologies.

DEVELOPING COMPETITIVE STRATEGIC OPTIONS: INTRODUCTION STAGE

Product/Market Characteristics

The introduction stage often follows many years of R&D by one or more firms. Frequently, a single firm pioneers a product form, but competitors can enter prior to "take-off" during the introduction period, and jointly share the market development task. Introduction is a period of much uncertainty: customers may be fearful that the product will not perform adequately; producers may be unsure of the appropriate technology and the optimal market strategy. It is often unclear whether a market exists for the product, or whether insufficient customer acceptance will lead to product withdrawal and early termination of the life cycle.[16] Regardless of the amount and quality of market research, there may be considerable uncertainty regarding the particular benefits that will prove successful in persuading customers (first-time buyers) to purchase. Finally, there may also be considerable uncertainty regarding potential competition. Which firms will enter? For what objectives? With what strategies? And, which of several possibly competing technologies will prove to be most efficacious?

> **Example:** When home video was heralded as the new consumer home entertainment product, there was much uncertainty regarding the technology that would ultimately dominate. Would it be disc or tape? If disc, would it be the Philips non-contact laser system, or the RCA physical contact stylus? If tape, would it be Sony's *Betamax,* or VHS? Ultimately, tape dominated disc and VHS dominated *Betamax*, but in the interim, substantial investments were made in systems that did not secure major consumer acceptance.[17]

Typically, only a basic product design is available in introduction, as one or more entrants struggle to build profitable volume. Product quality may also be erratic as both product and process are in the shakedown stage. Price may not cover total costs in anticipation that volume will build, and that all costs, direct and indirect, will be covered later. Market development requires significant educational effort. Thus advertising may educate customers about the product form to stimulate primary demand, while personal selling informs customers and distributors about the use and value of the product as well as reducing uncertainties.

For competitors viewing the actions of the pioneers, it is important not to dismiss their attempts by falling into "the trap of the first version."[18] Early products are often characterized by both poor performance and poor quality. However, they may possess the seeds of important breakthroughs that become fulfilled as intellectual capital is expended and related technologies are involved in development.

The length of the introduction period may range from several months to many years. A major determining factor is the quantity and quality of marketing effort expended by entrants in the new and developing market. Characteristics of products with longer introduction stages are radical innovations requiring significant change in customer behavior, complexity, difficulty of demonstrating benefits, and high financial and technological risks of product use. Introduction may also be long if, despite substantial product benefits, the price is high relative to alternatives, and if the decision to adopt involves several people (as for industrial products) rather than a single individual. Other factors slowing introduction are distribution delays and economic changes affecting customer purchasing power. From the producers' perspective, technical problems with production processes, early product failure, or inability to expand capacity sufficiently to meet growing demand may also retard market development.[19]

Business Characteristics

The net financial position of the majority of products at the introduction stage is negative. Typically, pioneering firms incur large R&D and market research expenditures and invest significantly in plant, equipment, systems, and so forth to prepare for product launch. In many cases, revenues from the newly launched product are insufficient to cover ongoing variable operating costs. Even if revenues do cover operating costs, it is quite likely that the direct and indirect fixed costs associated with market entry, coupled with the need to develop a marketing infrastructure, will ensure that the product is initially unprofitable on a full-cost allocation basis. Together, the combination of capital expenditures and unprofitable operations is likely to lead to negative cash flows.

> **Example:** Gillette spent almost $1 billion on the development and initial marketing of its new *Mach3* razor. First year marketing spending was $300 million.[20]

Of course, different firms have different abilities to sustain these losses and negative cash flows in the short run. Large companies typically subsidize these entries from cash earned from other products that are dominant in their own markets and are at later stages in their life cycles.

> **Examples:** For many years, profits from *Tide* laundry detergent funded many of Procter & Gamble's new ventures; nylon 66 and polyester (*Dacron*) fibers served the same purpose for DuPont, as did mainframe computers for IBM.

However, even for established firms, the drive for short-term profit performance demanded of public companies often leads to insufficient risk-taking with new products. As a result, promising new businesses are not sustained. Small companies typically have fewer resources and frequently secure financial resources from venture capitalists although, if the value proposition is sufficiently compelling, the initial public offering market may be sufficiently strong to fund the growth.[21]

> **Examples:** In recent years, a large number of Internet firms have gone public. In many cases, such as Amazon.com, America Online, Netscape, Yahoo!, and Priceline, market capitalizations were extremely high despite these firms having made no profits.

Objectives

The pioneer's main objective should be to lay the foundation for market leadership. As the first (or, at most, one of very few) firms to offer a new set of benefits to customers, the pioneer is in a good position to plan market strategy for achieving leadership, hence profitable performance over the long run. The corollary of this strategic objective is that the pioneer should be prepared to accept losses in this start-up phase. A critical decision for the pioneer is how quickly to attempt to build the market.

Strategic Considerations

The ability of the pioneer to plan long-run strategy and achieve profit goals as the life cycle moves into early growth is directly related to attractiveness of the market and the number, strength, and entry time of competitors. The pioneer's challenge, therefore, is to develop the market by attempting to reduce uncertainty for customers, to build a marketing infrastructure, and to shape industry standards while simultaneously keeping ahead of competition. A key consideration for the pioneer is to forestall potential competition; to the extent that the pioneer is able to slow or reduce competitive entry, its options are enhanced.

Longitudinal empirical research suggests that successful early entrants may earn enduring advantage. This work, though, is often misinterpreted because of failure to recognize that the early entrant is defined *ex post*, and might more accurately be labeled "first survivor" rather than pioneer or prime mover. Nonetheless, there does seem to be a significant order of entry effect with significant market share penalties for later entrants.[22]

ENTRY BARRIERS   A critical issue in forestalling competition is entry barriers. High barriers make entry difficult for competitors; the challenge for the pioneer is to exploit existing barriers and, where possible, to create new barriers. Three types of barriers are considered: government-imposed, product/market-specific, and firm-driven.

Government-Imposed Barriers   The most common government-imposed barrier is a patent. Patents provide owners with legal monopolies for several years, and firms may seek assistance from the courts to enforce these barriers via patent infringement suits. For example, Merrill Lynch successfully used court action to slow competitor entry in Cash Management Accounts (CMAs) where, many years later, it remains market leader. Other impediments to competitors include trade barriers, preferential tax treatment, and outright subsidies that may advantage the pioneer. In some cases, the firm is the beneficiary of a barrier or barrier structure already in place. In other cases, it may lobby government for a particular provision that offers it differential benefit. Relatedly, firms may seek assistance from the courts or government to slow or eliminate competition.

> **Examples:** In the early 1970s, Braniff filed lawsuits in unsuccessful attempts to impede Southwest Airlines' entry into the intrastate Texas market. More recently, Sun Microsystems, Netscape Communications, and Novell encouraged the government to take action against Microsoft to slow its entry into various markets.

Product/Market-Specific Barriers   These types of barriers are related to the product form. They include access to capital, raw materials, human resources, and the necessity of a minimum scale of operation.[23]

Firm-Driven Barriers   These barriers comprise two broad types: a drive for low costs that allows low prices and may deter competitor entry, and the development and exploitation of first-mover advantages.

Drive for Low Costs   Low prices during introduction, typically termed penetration strategies, require significant effort to reduce costs continually, and management resolve to accept low margins for an extended period, despite large R&D expenditures that may have been necessary to bring the product to market. The intellectual underpinning of penetration pricing strategies is the "Experience Curve," the frequently documented, empirically derived relationship demonstrating that, in real terms, unit costs reduce in a predictable manner as

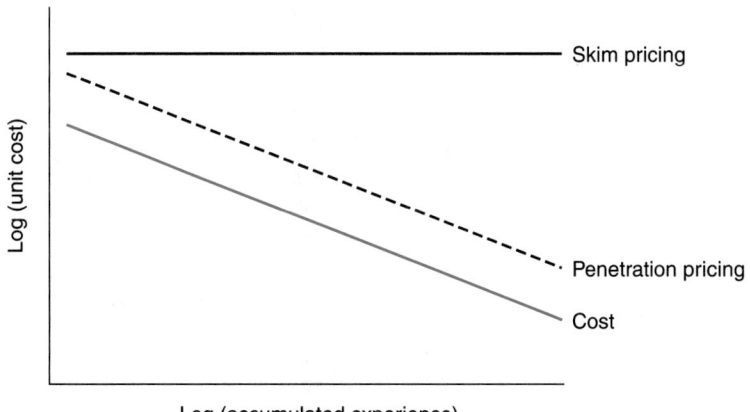

FIGURE 9.5

Penetration Pricing and Skim Pricing

accumulated volume increases (see chapter Appendix). Presence of the Experience Curve leads to two broad pricing options—penetration pricing and skim pricing (Figure 9.5).

Skim Pricing   In skim pricing, prices stay high as costs are reduced, and the firm earns high margins for limited fixed investment. However, high prices result in potentially slower market development and slower opening of distribution channels.[24] This strategy is viable if price-insensitive, early-adopting customers can be identified under conditions where government-imposed or product/market barriers are high, and the firm is either a monopolist or has few, but agreeable, competitors.[25]

> **Example:** During the introduction stage of polyacetyl plastic, both DuPont and American Celanese earned high net profit margins; prices were about ten times variable costs. Cutting prices was in neither firm's best interest; rather, much of the gross margin was invested in broadening the market by developing new applications.

If significant benefits are offered compared to alternative product forms, and if ongoing R&D is necessary to develop new benefits that take a long time to demonstrate, the market may well be price inelastic.[26] By contrast, if entry barriers are low and the market is price sensitive, skim pricing attempts are doomed to failure.

Notwithstanding the potential viability of skimming strategies under appropriate conditions, increasingly intense competition is speeding both innovation and imitation, and "skimming" windows may close more quickly. Many commentators believe that aggressive (penetration-type) launches are becoming a necessity in global competition; delay in multicountry launches merely permits competitors to steal successful innovation opportunities.[27] Evidence for the efficacy of heavily "front-ending" marketing expenditures, including penetration pricing, is growing.[28]

Stated differently, any skimming or niche-type entry depends on the defensibility of the niche for its medium- and long-term success. In ecological theory, the niche is that part of the environment in which any organism has an inherent competitive advantage over others.[29] Unless this condition pertains, pioneers who niche successfully can expect to be overwhelmed by later entrants wherever broader market potential exists. Thus firms that adopt skimming strategies must be ready to shift direction as market conditions change.

> **Example:** Early in the PC industry, Compaq built its success on a high-performance, high-price position, but in the early 1990s, as the market developed, it went through wrenching change to equip itself to compete on price in the PC market.

Penetration Pricing   In penetration pricing, the firm reduces prices to mirror ongoing cost reductions; as a result, the firm earns low margins. This pricing approach may be favored when the market is price elastic, entry barriers are low, and low price signals have the potential to deter competitive entry.[30] However, the firm must have deep pockets to finance a long period of low profits and negative cash flow. It must also be able to build capacity and grow quickly, and continually push costs down. The major disadvantage of penetration pricing is that huge bets must be made on the future under uncertain conditions. Few firms are prepared to forgo short-run profits, while simultaneously making large and continuing investments in the product.

Classic examples of penetration pricing in operation are Henry Ford's drive to put a Model T in every American garage and Texas Instruments' (TI) corporate strategy statement from the early 1970s, published in a letter to shareholders. As noted earlier, TI stated its commitment to aggressively price to follow learning curve reductions in cost, keep capacity growing ahead of demand, continue efforts to improve products, reduce costs, and build on shared experience. However, in hindsight, the limitations of these strategies have become clear. For example, as the automobile market developed, General Motors, led by Alfred Sloan, developed a market segmentation approach by relying on different models (Chevrolet, Pontiac, Buick, Oldsmobile, and Cadillac), allowing GM to sweep past Ford.

Notwithstanding these limitations, penetration pricing may be particularly beneficial if switching costs are high and there is a significant after-market. For example, software companies tend to price initial offerings low and upgrades high. Furthermore, firms that sell both durable goods and related consumables frequently price the durable low and the consumable high, such as cameras and film, or printers and toner.

First-Mover Advantages   The second method of forestalling competition is to build first-mover advantages. Being first provides the pioneer with several potential advantages, but these must be judiciously nourished or the pioneer will fall victim to a fast follower. In particular, the pioneer should be able to gain the greatest awareness as a product supplier and, if product quality is high, secure the leading reputation among both consumers and distribution channels, and develop strong brand equity.

Carpenter and Nakamoto suggest that first-in-the-mind may be the key to pioneering advantage. Building on work at MIT showing that the first brand in a product class was typically the best remembered, they demonstrated that preferences were also unduly influenced by the first brand to which the buyer was exposed. Left undisturbed, these preferences, possibly reinforced by usage and subsequent communication, could build a mountain of inelasticity as the first brand becomes the category prototype, the psychological standard against which subsequent entries are judged.[31]

> **Examples:** Generally accepted category prototypes include Jeep (in the United States) for four-wheel drive vehicles, Xerox for high-speed dry copying, Kleenex for paper tissue, Hoover for vacuum cleaners, and Cadillac for luxury automobiles.

Early presence in the market should afford the leader superior market knowledge. Given an ongoing commitment to innovation, this may translate into product and process technology leadership, and the ability to react quickly to advances made by others. Intel's extraordinary dominance of microprocessors provides a good recent example. Leadership may also provide the ability to both pre-empt scarce assets[32] and raise buyer switching costs, thus increasing the challenge for competitors that follow.

Companies in a variety of industries have earned long-run success from strategies built on first-mover advantages. Examples include DuPont's success with nylon, polyester, and aramid fibers; Citibank's long-time leadership in automatic teller machines (ATMs), Gillette with razors, Duracell with alkaline batteries, and 7-Eleven's success in the convenience store business, especially in Japan.[33]

On the other hand, failure to implement the appropriate strategies during introduction can lead to substantial market share and profit reductions.

Example: In 1994, Johnson & Johnson (J&J) introduced the "stent," a revolutionary device that virtually eliminated the "abrupt closure" problem associated with the widely-used balloon angioplasty technology for de-blocking coronary arteries; the long-term failure rate was cut by 50%. During the following three years, J&J achieved 90% market share, sales reached $1 billion, and margins were 80%. However, apparently relying on presumed patent protection, J&J failed to make product improvements. In addition, its rigid pricing and refusal to offer quantity discounts angered many cardiologists who welcomed competitive entry in 1997. Within 45 days, a new entrant, Guidant Corp., had gained 70% market share; by end 1998, J&J's share was less than 10%.[34]

An important decision for pioneering firms is whether to go it alone, or form a partnership or partnerships with other companies. Two of the major drivers to form partnerships or alliances in introduction are a need for skills or resources to complete the R&D necessary to bring the product to market, and the requirement for a common set of standards agreed among the various key potential suppliers. If neither of these conditions hold, a go-it-alone approach may be fine; if they do not, then partnering may offer a viable alternative.[35]

Example: To avoid a repeat of the VHS/Betamax battle in videotape, the Toshiba/Matsushita format for the digital video disc (DVD) was modified so that Sony and Philips (who had developed their own system) would join.[36]

Example: To improve the possibilities of success for the first new silver-based camera system in 50 years, Kodak joined with competitors Fuji, Canon, Minolta, and Nikon to develop a common set of standards for the Advanced Photo System (APS). Launched in early 1996, by 1999 APS film was approaching 10% market share.

DEVELOPING COMPETITIVE STRATEGIC OPTIONS: EARLY GROWTH STAGE

Product/Market Characteristics

Many products do not last beyond the introduction stage. However, survivors enter the early growth stage, characterized by both growth in sales and an increasing rate of growth of sales. The profitable margins that often accompany increasing sales growth tend to attract competitors; they continue to enter during early growth and, by their efforts, help increase the overall market growth rate. Frequently, supply shortages caused by the pioneer's inability to satisfy market demand ease entry for newcomers. In addition, new entrants may have a core of loyal customers from other product forms who would like to purchase the new product from their current suppliers.

In early growth, as new competitors struggle for market position, new distribution channels are opened and promotional activity remains high. Advertising emphasis shifts to brand differentiation and selective demand creation, and prices tend to fall as economies of scale permit price to be used as a competitive weapon. However, competition in early growth is not as intense as later in the life cycle. Many firms can increase sales, not at competitors' expense, but rather from the growth of the market as new customers enter. The corollary is that a firm's sales can increase while its market share decreases.

Competitive Position—Leader

BUSINESS CHARACTERISTICS   The leader has strong market position, and is typically the pioneer that held leadership position when the market started to grow rapidly. Although overall market acceptance of the product form now seems assured, key concerns relate to the entry of competitors, enticed by the attractiveness of the market. Rapid capacity expansion may deter competitors but, in practice, few firms are prepared to act preemptively and many followers are incapable of reading such signals. Firms and investors seem sucked into the "feeding frenzy" that sometimes accompanies rapid growth.[37]

By this stage, the product should be profitable for the leader. As the bugs associated with new product introduction are worked out, unit costs should be under control and reducing, as volume builds and economies of scale take effect.[38] However, regardless of the profit picture, cash flows may still be negative since continuing investment is probably required to support the increasing volume.

OBJECTIVES AND STRATEGIC CONSIDERATIONS: LEADER   Several objectives can be identified for the market leader. At the most fundamental level, the leader can decide whether or not to seek continued leadership. Suboptions for continued leadership are either to enhance or maintain its leadership position; suboptions for giving up leadership are to retreat to a market segment or segments, or to leave the market entirely.

Enhance Leadership Position   Pursuing this objective implies an attempt to dominate the market by achieving the maximum possible market share, even up to a 100%. Leaders pursuing this objective should ready themselves for the competitive onslaught by developing differential advantages, rather than relying on generic advantages of the product form. They should attempt to broaden the market and block competitors by entering new and emerging market segments and new geographic areas, employing new distribution channels, and offering new product varieties.

> **Example:** Tylenol achieved leadership in the acetaminophen portion of the analgesic market, in part by offering many product varieties, such as Tylenol for children and the elderly, Tylenol Cold, extra strength Tylenol, and Tylenol PM, packaged in various forms such as tablets, capsules, caplets, and liquid.

The firm should build capacity ahead of demand and aggressively drive costs down. The leader's drive for superiority should embrace dominating the communication vehicles, such as advertising and sales force. It should also set industry standards, keep a technological lead by continuous R&D investment, tie up suppliers, and gradually shift the competitive focus from indirect competitors (aimed at market development) to direct competitors (aimed at market share). In short, seeking to enhance an already strong position requires a "full court press" on the market.

> **Example:** In addition to McNeil Labs' Tylenol, firms that have successfully achieved market dominance include IBM in mainframe computers, Hartz in pet accessories, and DuPont in nylon, polyester, and Kevlar fibers.

Maintain Leadership Position   Despite the attraction of market dominance and the potential for securing a monopoly or monopoly-like position with its attendant positive profit implications, a leader might want to settle for maintaining leadership in a more modest manner. For example, the leader may be concerned about potential political, legal, and regulatory actions that might occur if its market position were too dominant.[39] In addition, strong competitors may enter the market and, by making it very clear that they will not withdraw, make enhancing market position too expensive. Or, customers may demand a second source of supply, making the presence of competitors a positive, rather than a negative, factor.

> **Example:** Even though Merrill Lynch captured many new customers for its CMA account when it offered the only alternative, other retail brokerage houses later developed similar products and secured business from many of their own customers.

One compelling reason to pursue a maintain objective rather than an enhance objective is a concern about technological standards. If the leader (possibly with patent protection) develops and maintains its own standards, it stands to make high profits by excluding competition. However, this competitive exclusion means it must bear the market development burden alone and, as noted earlier, face the possibility that the exclusion may motivate potential competitors to invent around the patent or develop alternative standards. For example, Apple's early refusal to license its Macintosh operating system undoubtedly stimulated Microsoft to develop *Windows*, its own graphical user interface. The presence of multiple standards may lead to slower-than-potential market development, as uncertainty leads potential customers to postpone purchases. In general, customers prefer open to closed systems. Because customer power increases during the course of the life cycle, pressure for open systems usually rises.

In many ways, pursuing a maintenance strategy is more difficult than an out-and-out drive for market share dominance. It requires good competitive intelligence, careful selection of customer and competitor targets, thoughtful contingency planning, a very clear sense of the strategy to be followed, and a boldness to stick to the strategy despite temporary perturbations. Specific actions are drawn from those listed under the enhance option, but are moderated to correspond to the more limited market share goals.

The rationale for either type of leadership objective is that the market leader is the best positioned of all firms to ride the cycle through to maturity. Leadership in maturity is often very profitable. The market leader's ability to maintain its position is a function both of its resource commitment to the market, and to the resource commitments of its competitors. The key challenge for the leader is to exploit, as fully as possible, all available market, cost, and technological sources of pioneering advantage (discussed earlier).

Regardless of whether an enhance or maintain objective is pursued, the leader's market strategy must evolve from one that is focused on selling to non-users (often users of products developed from some pre-existing technology) to one that is focused on repeat users and competitors' customers. Concurrently, the firm should broaden its product line, add service elements, strengthen the salesforce effort, and build brand identity through advertising and promotion. A particularly crucial issue for long-term leadership is R&D investment for ongoing innovation. Having expended significant effort to develop the product for launch and put the corresponding operations in place, many firms succumb to the temptation of fixing on the product technology too early. As a result, the leader may become vulnerable to competitors that out-invest in new technology and are able to offer products with superior benefits. The key message for the leader is to continue to invest in product development, and use its advantage of superior market access to be responsive to customers' acceptance of new products, or product features offered by competitors.[40] The continued introduction of new versions of the *Palm Pilot* is an excellent example.

Retreat to a Market Segment   Despite its early leadership position, there are several reasons why a strong market share objective (enhance or maintain) might not be appropriate for the early market leader. Potential market development expenses and ongoing R&D to develop new products may be beyond its resource capabilities. Or, a well-financed, determined competitor may enter with clear goals and the capability to secure market leadership. If the current leader believes it unlikely that it can win an extended market share battle, or if its resources are better suited to specialization than broadening the market, identifying and targeting a specific market segment or segments may be the most judicious action.

Whereas, in the introductory stage, opportunities for market segmentation are limited, they typically begin to emerge in early growth. The leader's key decisions involve resource allocation choices among various market segments. Since the pioneer cannot sustain a cost leadership position in the face of the emerging leader's (follower) increasing strength, it should select segments where it adds sufficient value to overcome this disadvantage. Its chosen segments must be sufficiently price-inelastic to withstand potential price-cutting by the new leader, for sustainability is essential to the viability of a segment specialist strategy. The nature of customer needs and competitive activity in these segments determines the firm's resource allocations among product development, advertising and promotion, sales force, and so forth.

To successfully implement a market segment retreat strategy, the firm must build in sufficient organizational flexibility to identify and enter new and emerging market segments and new geographic areas. Such flexibility must enable it to recognize and act on specific opportunities more quickly than the follower (emerging leader) whose focus is on the broad market, possibly by innovating new products.

Leave the Market   The notion of leaving a market in which it was the pioneering market leader may seem like a defeatist option but, for several reasons, may be a prudent action. The argument for this option (at this and other life cycle stages) is that if, from a shareholder perspective, the value from selling the business today is greater than the discounted stream of profits from operating the business over time, the firm should sell. Any difference between these two values is, of course, a prime example of capital market imperfection, but it can be argued that management, because of its privileged "insider" status, should be best equipped to perform the arbitrage activity on behalf of the shareholders. Some research supports this view, since management buyouts (MBOs) have typically out-performed other leveraged buyouts (LBOs).[41]

> **Example:** After World War II, former Captain Reynolds, who together with Colonel Biro in U.S. Navy Research, developed an underwater writing instrument, entered the ball-point pen business on the East Coast of the United States. In 1947, with sales booming, he sold out and purchased a ranch in Mexico where he lived for the next 35 years![42]

Of the several conditions that may lead to this situation, the most compelling is a high value placed on the business. Since market leadership in the early growth stage is relatively rare, such scarcity may imply significant value and a high acquisition price. If the new product form is strategically important or has a better strategic fit for another firm, such as allows use of an existing distribution system, salesforce, or factory, it should be worth more than to the current owner. The sell option may be especially attractive if the new product is less than central to the firm's set of businesses, if the firm lacks the resources to execute one of the other options effectively, or expects fierce competitive entry.[43]

It is worth noting that technologically prolific firms are particularly in need of a systematic approach to making these kinds of decisions. Because the more basic kinds of R&D can lead to relatively unpredictable outcomes, these firms may invent new products that they are singularly ill-equipped to commercialize successfully. In many cases, they would be better advised to sell to firms that are better positioned for marketing the innovation.

Competitive Position—Follower

BUSINESS CHARACTERISTICS   The follower's position is typically inferior to the market leader in several respects. Most likely it is a recent entrant, attracted by increasing market growth and the leader's inferred profitability. However, the costs of entry, together with less volume and overall experience than the leader, will most likely lead to higher unit costs. Profits depend largely on the leader's pricing strategy, but are generally low or negative; because of growth requirements, cash flows are likely to be heavy and negative.

OBJECTIVES AND STRATEGIC CONSIDERATIONS: FOLLOWER   Followers in the early growth stage have four basic options, each of which may duplicate and interact with the market leader: secure leadership, settle for second place, target a market segment, and leave the market. However, because followers start from inferior positions relative to leaders, choosing among these options has a different tenor.

Secure Leadership   Two broad options are available for pursuing the leadership objective: imitation and innovation. An imitation strategy means that the firm copies the leader, but is more effective in execution. For a successful imitation strategy, the follower should develop products rapidly to enter the market as soon as possible after the leader. Such action requires good competitive intelligence and significant spending on catch-up product development. The follower must make a long-term commitment to secure market leadership and be prepared to outspend the leader in market development; specific actions are similar to those indicated previously for the leader's "enhance leadership" option. Note, however, that if the follower can leverage an existing market or distribution infrastructure, the absolute marketing spend may be lower than the leader's.

> **Example:** In the early 1980s, IBM's entry into personal computers was successful in the short run. The market was growing quickly under Apple's leadership, and the IBM development team was charged with developing a marketable product in 12 months. They were successful by breaking many IBM precedents, such as shifting from heavy emphasis on internal sourcing to outsourcing. Successful

product development, heavy advertising, and use of brand equity enabled IBM to secure leadership within a few months of market entry.

The leapfrog option essentially implies going one better than the leader by developing new, innovative, and superior products, or developing defensible new market segments in advance of the leader (possibly entering new geographies). This option also implies high levels of resource spending. In either case, the follower must have sufficient flexibility to move fast and enter as soon as possible after the pioneer.

Example: Both Nintendo and Sega leapfrogged Atari's original 1980s videogame launch with 16-bit machines. However, in 1994, the Sony Playstation leapfrogged both firms by offering 3-D graphics and techno soundtracks.

When followers pursue imitative strategies, points of difference ultimately focus on price. Perhaps this focus is inevitable for some product forms, but the rate of transition is certainly affected by the players' competitive strategies.

Example: Later in the PC market, standardization on Intel processors and Microsoft software led to the rapid evolution of price competition, causing severe difficulties for IBM, Compaq, and Apple. IBM and Compaq rebounded, but not before significant deterioration of shareholder wealth in the short term. Apple's recovery was postponed until Steve Jobs returned to the company as acting CEO. Other industries that illustrate the potentially harmful effects of competitive strategy failures for incumbents include the U.S. airline industry and global consumer electronics.

More effective follower options typically avoid head-to-head price competition. Instead, followers often gain advantage by being more astute in tracking and anticipating emerging customer needs, thus spotting new segment opportunities before leaders. They offer new benefits or combinations of benefits before leaders, and may even change the "rules" of industry competition.[44] Entries that afford true differential advantage significantly raise the odds of successful followership.

To a large extent, a follower's ability to secure leadership depends on the actions of the pioneer. If the pioneer has rested on its laurels by under-investing in market development and distribution growth, been slow to bring out improved products, or presented a price umbrella under which others have entered, the follower's entry prospects are improved. In any event, the follower should seek to diminish the pioneer's advantages by developing (or using) reputation and brand equity, and by seeking technological superiority or cost advantage.

The critical issues for either option of securing market leadership are the expense of executing the chosen strategy and funding the required long-term commitment. Far too often, firms initiate quests for market leadership that do not secure the desired result. They then retrench, possibly achieving a similar position to that which a more modest strategy might have realized.

Example: Imagine a market growth rate of 15% per annum compounded, a leader with 40% market share growing at the market growth rate, and a follower 25% the size of the market leader. The compound annual growth rate required for the follower to catch the leader in six years is 45% per annum compounded! Clearly, the resource commitment is enormous.

Settle for Second Place Because the resources required to secure market leadership may be substantial, a strategy of settling for second place may be quite reasonable.[45] This strategy is especially viable when the leader is inhibited from driving for market dominance, and is content to attempt to manage the market. For example, the political/legal/regulatory environment may be favorable to a more competitive market, customers may demand a second source of supply, and standards issues may cause the leader willingly to accept direct competitors. Finally, the firm may require a presence in the market for strategic reasons, such as serving existing customers. Resources to execute this option should be invested as appropriate to secure these more limited aims.

Retreat to a Segment This option may be selected if the follower has insufficient resources to compete with the leader or other followers, and if specific emerging market segments appear attractive.[46]

Leave the Market Exit may be a sensible option on the same grounds as for the leader, but the value of a follower's position is likely to be less. Nonetheless, because the follower's uncertainties are well-known to the firm but less well-known to potential purchasers, the business may have greater immediate value than the long-run, discounted profit stream.

DEVELOPING COMPETITIVE STRATEGIC OPTIONS: LATE GROWTH STAGE

Product/Market Characteristics

In the late growth stage, sales continue to increase but the growth rate slows significantly. Much uncertainly from early life cycle stages has been resolved and strong competitors initiate tough actions to maintain their own rates of growth, forcing weaker entrants to withdraw. Customers (now comprising many repeat users) and their demands become more specific and offer extensive opportunity for market segmentation and differentiation, in contrast to the imitative strategies often found in early growth. Minor but extensive product redesign occurs as competitors seek differential advantage; variations proliferate as competitors adapt products to specific customer requirements. A solid distribution infrastructure is in place, but slowing sales growth makes distribution outlets more selective about brands and individual items carried. Price becomes a major competitive weapon, and distributor margins are squeezed. Purchase terms and amount/length of credit available, warranties, and service policies become more favorable to customers. As weaker competitors fade, price cutting and promotional actions become more prevalent.

Business Characteristics

At this stage the value of early product leadership is minimal and basic product form benefits lose their competitive appeal. Competition is more likely to focus on attributes that, in an absolute sense, are less important. What were once determining attributes (the basis for the decision) now become qualifying.

> **Example:** Early in the life cycle for passenger air transportation, safety was a determining attribute. Nowadays, for many travelers, safety is no longer determining since they believe that many major airlines, flying similar airplanes, qualify for being equally safe. Rather, today's determining attributes include frequent flier miles, time convenience, direct or with stops, and so forth.

Objectives and Strategic Considerations

Objectives for both leaders and followers boil down to market commitment. With increased opportunities for segmentation, firms must decide whether to seek market leadership by addressing many segments, or to settle for a more limited market specialist position with few segment entries.

The key feature of the late growth stage is the potential for market segmentation that makes market research skills critical. Firms that are focused on securing good customer and competitor data are able to segment markets, and can appropriately address targeted segments with "rifle shot marketing" that may reap significant rewards. Good profit opportunities may be present even in small market segments, especially in a global marketplace, but the firm should make the market segment/cost trade-offs explicit. Increased segmentation typically implies better satisfaction of customer needs, but at an increased cost. However, parts standardization and introduction of flexible manufacturing systems, supported by advanced information technology, can mitigate cost penalties. Inflexible operational systems create enormous handicaps at this stage of market development.

> **Example:** As noted earlier, both Boeing and Airbus, the two surviving Western producers of commercial aircraft, make significant use of modular design, parts

standardization, and advanced information technology. For example, the fuselage sections of the Boeing 727, 737, and 757 are identical and date to the world's first commercially successful large commercial jet, the 707. Boeing's latest aircraft, the 777, was designed using advanced computer-aided design/computer-aided manufacturing (CAD/CAM) systems, and was the fastest commercial aircraft design to move from drawing-board to service.[47]

Regardless of how few or many segments the firm targets, it should monitor evolving market segments, be ready for competitive entry, and attempt to ensure that targeted segments are defensible. Tough choices will be required, but this effort will result in a far-superior outcome than attempting to be a Jack of all trades, master of none.

SUMMARY

This chapter reviewed strategic options during the introduction, early growth, and late growth stages of the product form life cycle. It began by distinguishing different types of life cycles. Then, using a framework that described market characteristics at each developmental stage, it examined objectives and strategic considerations for pioneers in introduction, for leaders and followers in early growth, and for all firms in late growth. Understanding the process by which markets for products develop provides a useful way to develop competitive strategies in an anticipatory manner.

THE CHANGING VIEW

Old Way	New Way
Life cycles are fixed and constrained	Life cycles dynamic and can be influenced
Passive management of life cycle changes	Active management of life cycle changes
Entry strategies uninformed	Entry strategies driven by sophisticated understanding of market development
Maturity preordained	Product form rejuvenation possible
Sequential product introductions worldwide	Simultaneous new product launches in multiple countries
Slow market development	Rapid market development
Evolutionary change of management approach	Proactively planned change of management approach
Pre-emptive strategies rare	Pre-emptive strategies commonplace
Customer learning patterns poorly understood	Customer learning regarded as crucial
Imitation common	Innovation favored
Ample time to recoup front-end investment	Peak profit margin period arrives sooner, disappears earlier
Domestic, regional cycles predominate	Regional, global cycles dominate

QUESTIONS FOR STUDY AND DISCUSSION

1. Select an underlying customer need or set of needs. Identify the various product forms that have been developed over the years to satisfy this need. What conclusions do you draw regarding these evolving product forms?

2. It has been argued that functions and needs will persist, but that products and services are merely the means by which companies compete and are therefore ephemeral. Discuss.

COMPETITIVE
MARKET STRATEGIES
IN INTRODUCTION
AND GROWTH

3. Products may have life cycles, but brands do not. Discuss.

4. "As each new product form develops in our industry, we must ensure that we act quickly to have an entry of our own." How do you assess this recommendation?

5. Since technological pioneers are usually the first to introduce new products and therefore achieve some level of first-mover advantage, why are they not always market leaders when growth slows?

6. Identify pioneers that were still market leaders when growth slowed. Identify pioneers that were no longer market leaders when growth slowed. How do you account for this differential performance?

7. Intel and Microsoft have aggressively used legal strategies to protect their market positions. Since the effect of these strategies is to deter or delay entry, what implications does this have for related product life cycles?

8. Fast followers gain undue advantage from the R&D expenditures of pioneers. Do you agree?

9. Empirical research has demonstrated that the elasticity of various marketing instruments varies dramatically over the course of the product form life cycle. What would you predict about elasticities in the introduction and growth stages? Identify examples to support your predictions.

10. A successful pioneer has to be a master of both R&D and marketing. Do you agree? Give your reasons.

11. Retreating to a segment is one of the strategies discussed in the chapter. Under what conditions can such a strategy be viable over the long term?

12. What do you believe are preferred strategies for later entry during the fast growth stage? Why?

13. Large companies argue that they prefer a wait and see posture towards developing life cycles. Do you believe this is a deliberate policy, or a smoke screen for risk aversion and inability to move quickly? Defend your point of view.

14. The true pioneers are typically lost in the dusty archives of industry history. Many companies alleged to be first movers are typically the earliest entrants to survive until the present day. Do you agree with this statement or not? If it were true, what are the implications for managers?

15. Some of the generalizations about first-mover advantage are based on a limited series of experiments with consumers, referenced in the text. Do you believe it is appropriate to bet shareholder resources on such evidence? Why or why not? If you feel it is inappropriate, how would you suggest building a case that would justify such expenditure?

ENDNOTES

1. The term *competitive life cycle* is used to embrace a family of life cycle models that may provide insight into competitive strategy making.

2. See V. Mahajan, E. Muller, and F. M. Bass, "New Product Diffusion Models in Marketing: A Review and Directions for Research," *Journal of Marketing*, 5 (January, 1990), pp. 1–28 for a review encompassing the seminal Bass model for durables and many other new product forecasting models. Over the years, the concept of product life cycles has been subject to much discussion and criticism. For a good overview of these issues, as well as a discussion of the evolutionary and ecological perspectives on market development, see J. Czepiel, *Competitive Marketing Strategy*, Englewood Cliffs, NJ, Prentice Hall, 1992, pp. 221–253.

3. Differences in trajectory typically relate to duration of the various stages and the sharpness of sales increases and declines.

4. This is a very broad definition of market. Later, the chapter (and the book) discusses markets for product classes, forms, and even individual products. In these contexts, the term "market" has narrower connotations.

5. Unfortunately, many companies misinterpreted this article and ill-advisedly redefined their search for opportunity with insufficient regard to their capabilities. T. Levitt, "Marketing Myopia," *Harvard Business Review*, 53 (Sept./Oct. 1975), p. 26 *et seq.*

6. G. Day, *Market Driven Strategy: Processes for Creating Value*, New York: Free Press, 1990.

7. R.K. Srivastava, M.I. Alpert, and A.D. Shocker, "A Customer Oriented Approach for Determining Market Structures," *Journal of Marketing*, 48 (Spring 1984), pp. 32–45.

8. See, E.M. Rogers, *Diffusion of Innovations*, New York: Free Press, 1962. This topic is addressed in more detail in Chapter 12.

9. Sometimes termed the product category life cycle.

10. Sometimes termed the product subcategory life cycle.

11. This topic is discussed extensively in Chapter 13.

12. Some analysts measure total time from birth to death; others focus on the period from take-off to the onset of maturity. The latter measure has the appeal of representing the critical strategic period during which long-run competitive position is frequently established. Well-supported products entering maturity with dominant positions already secured are often very difficult to dislodge.

13. M.E. Porter, *Competitive Advantage: Creating and Sustaining Superior Performance*, New York: Free Press, 1985.

14. G. Hamel and C.K. Prahahad, "The Core Competence of the Corporation," *Harvard Business Review*, 68 (May/June 1990), pp. 79–91.

15. Later, Merrill Lynch developed an Internet strategy.

16. Of course, there must be a distinction between successful and unsuccessful innovation, based not on "technical" achievement, even in the broadest sense, but upon commercial success.

17. Now, years later, DVD threatens to replace VHS.

18. In his autobiography, Andy Grove, former Intel CEO, recounts how initially he dismissed the Macintosh computer as a toy. He believed that the graphical interface was a nuisance and the absence of a hard disk a severe limitation. A.S. Grove, *Only the Paranoid Survive*, New York, Doubleday, 1996

19. See Rogers, *op. cit.*

20. *Business Week*, February 1, 1999.

21. Observers frequently associate the high levels of entrepreneurialism and new company development in the United States with the strong venture capital market.

22. G.L. Urban, T. Carter, S. Garskin, and Z. Mucho, "Market Share Rewards to Pioneering Brands: An Empirical Analysis and Strategic Implications," *Management Science*, 32 (June 1986), pp. 645–659.

23. It is important to remember that product/market specific barriers change over time. For example, early in the cycle of mainframe computers, high entry barriers included capital and trained human resources. By contrast, today, entry into the personal computer business is relatively straightforward. For a more contemporary example, Microsoft built high barriers in software; smaller companies could not afford teams to write the large programs, nor did they have Microsoft's distribution clout. However, Java and the Internet have lowered these barriers, since distribution on the Internet is essentially free. The growth of the Linux operating system is an excellent example of this change.

24. See J. Dean, "Pricing Policies for New Products," *Harvard Business Review*, 28 (Nov./Dec. 1950), pp. 28–36 for the seminal article on skim pricing.

25. The synthetic fibers, plastics, and drug industries are full of examples of skimming strategies, in large part because of patent protection.

26. In price elastic markets, volume increases when prices are decreased; in price inelastic markets, volume is relatively unresponsive to price changes. This topic is discussed in more detail in Chapter 18.

27. Of course, in the context of global markets, entry in one country market is equivalent to entry in a geographic market segment.

28. A.J. Slywotsky and B.P. Shapiro, "Leveraging to Beat the Odds: The New Marketing Mind-Set," *Harvard Business Review*, 71 (Sept./Oct. 1993), pp. 97–107.

29. See B.D. Henderson, *Henderson on Corporate Strategy*, New York: HarperBusiness, 1984.

30. Penetration pricing relies on three simple relationships: When demand is price elastic, lower prices should result in high volumes; higher volumes should allow unit costs to be reduced; lower costs permit further price reductions in a continuing downward spiral.

31. G.S. Carpenter and K. Nakamoto, "Consumer Preference Formation and Pioneering Advantage, *Journal of Marketing Research*, 26 (August 1989), pp. 285–298.

32. When Pepsi attacked Coca Cola by introducing large size plastic bottles, it aggressively tied up bottle producing capacity to deny *Coke* similar type containers.

33. A particularly interesting feature of 7-Eleven's success in Japan is that, as an early mover, it had both its pick of sites and handed out franchises to many former liquor stores whose liquor licenses add, on average, Y100,000 to a convenience store's daily revenues. As a result, in the mid-1990s, 7-Eleven's average daily sales was Y676,000 versus Y494,000 for its nearest rival (*The Economist*, January 25, 1997).

34. *The Wall Street Journal*, September 18, 1998.

35. In the 1960s, RCA licensed its patent for color TV to spread the "catch 22" market development burden. To develop demand for color TV sets was difficult in the absence of extensive color TV programs; spurring production of color TV programs was difficult in the absence of a large installed base of color TV sets!

36. Industry observers have suggested that one reason for Apple Computer's difficulties was its early decision not to license the Macintosh operating system.

37. The consequences can, of course be miserable, particularly if tax policy favors a particular market. The authors have witnessed many such examples including, oil, gas, and real estate partnerships (US, 1970s/1980s), avocados and yabbies (Australia, 1970s/1980s) and ostrich meat (UK 1990s).

38. The extent to which costs reduce with increasing volume is related to the cost structure. If the cost base contains high levels of fixed costs, increasing volume over which to spread these costs results in reduced unit costs. There may, in addition, be experience effects (see Chapter Appendix).

39. One explanation for IBM's less than wholehearted product development efforts in personal computers in the 1970s was top management's preoccupation with fending off Justice Department attempts at organizational dismemberment.

40. An example of not following this prescription is IBM's failure to pursue minicomputers aggressively in their formative years; rather, it allowed DEC to gain a two- or three-year headstart before it entered.

41. In a LBO, an investment group becomes the new owner; in a MBO, existing management is significantly represented in the new ownership. See F.R. Lichtenberg and D. Siegel, "The Effects of Leveraged Buyouts on Productivity and Related Aspects of Firm Behavior," *Journal of Financial Economics*, 27 (1990), pp. 165–194.

42. In Britain, ballpoint pens are still called "biros." A somewhat different but related history of ballpoint pens is presented by J. Mingo in *How the Cadillac Got its Fins*, New York: HarperBusiness, 1994.

43. This strategy seems to be followed by small, high-technology companies that sell out early to more established firms. For owners of these firms, the attraction of early retirement might be an additional motivating factor. However, in terms of earlier discussion, such a decision should merely be viewed as maximizing shareholder value.

44. R. Buaron, "New Game Strategies," *McKinsey Quarterly*, (Spring 1981), pp. 24–30.

45. For Jack Welch, CEO of General Electric, either a number 1 or 2 position in a market is viable; not number 3 or below!

46. For example, across a wide range of American industry, the U.S. market share leader firm is not the lead firm in other parts of the world: in automobiles, General Motors leads in the United States, Ford is stronger abroad; Campbell's is the domestic canned soup leader, Heinz is leader in Europe. These reversals result from faster geographic segment targeting by follower firms in early product life cycle stages.

47. This philosophy has become particularly important in the automobile industry where it is called "platform engineering."

48. The most detailed treatment of experience curves is Boston Consulting Group, *Perspectives on Experience*, Boston, MA: Boston Consulting Group, 1972.

49. Accumulated experience is simply derived by adding each period's volume to the accumulation of previous periods, starting with the first period. Because of inflation and currency fluctuations, unit costs are often stated in terms of "constant" currency units.

50. Douglas Aircraft first documented this effect in manufacture of the DC3 in the 1930s. See, W.J. Abernathy and K. Wayne, "Limits of the Learning Curve, *Harvard Business Review*, 52 (Sept./Oct. 1974), pp. 109–119. For a theoretical treatment, see W.I. Zangwill and P.B. Cantor, "Toward a Theory of Continuous Improvement and the Learning Curve," *Management Science*, 44 (July 1998-7), pp. 910–920.

51. *Examples* from C.W. Stern and G. Stalk, Jr., *Perspectives on Strategy from the Boston Consulting Group*, New York: John Wiley, 1998. In the examples, an 80% (75%) slope implies that a doubling of accumulated experience leads to a 20% (25%) reduction in prices.

WEB RESOURCES

3Com	www.3com.com
3M	www.3m.com
7-Eleven	www.7-eleven.com
Airbus Industrie	www.airbus.com
Amazon	www.amazon.com
American Celanese	www.michelin.com
American Economic Review	www.jstor.org/journals/00028282.html
America Online	www.aol.com
Apple Computer	www.apple.com
Atari	www.atari.com
Boeing	www.boeing.com
Braniff	www.braniffinternational.org
Cadillac	www.cadillac.com
Campbell's	www.campbellsoups.com
Canon	www.canon.co.jp
Charles Schwab	www.schwab.com
Citibank	www.citibank.com
Coca-Cola	www.cocacola.com
Compaq	www.compaq.com
DuPont	www.dupont.com
Duracell	www.duracell.com
Ford	www.ford.com
Fuji	www.Fuji.com
General Electric	www.ge.com
General Motors	www.gm.com
Gillette	www.gillette.com
Guidant Corporation	www.guidant.com
Hartz	www.hartz.com
Harvard Business Review	www.hbsp.harvard.edu/products/hbr
Heinz	www.heinz.com
Hoover	www.hoover.com
IBM	www.ibm.com
Intel	www.intel.com
JVC	www.jvc.victor.co.jp/english/index-e.html
Jeep	www.jeepunpaved.com
Johnson and Johnson	www.johnsonandjohnson.com
Journal of Marketing	www.ama.org/pubs/jm
Journal of Financial Economics	www.ssb.rochester.edu/fac/jfe/jfe.htm
Kleenex	www.kimberly-clark.com
Kodak	www.kodak.com

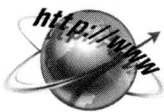
Lotus	www.lotus.com
Management Science	www.informs.org/pubs/mansci
McNeil Labs	www.tylenol.com
Merrill Lynch	www.ml.com
Microsoft	www.microsoft.com
Minolta	www.minolta.com
Netscape	www.netscape.com
Nikon	www.nikonusa.com
Nintendo	www.nintendo.com
Novell	www.novell.com
Panasonic	www.panasonic.com
Pepsi	www.pepsico.com
Philips	www.philips.com
Playstation	www.playstation.com
Priceline	www.priceline.com
Procter & Gamble	www.pg.com
Sega	www.sega.com
Sony	www.sony.com
Southwest Airlines	www.southwest.com
Sun Microsystems	www.sun.com
Texas Instruments	www.ti.com
Wall Street Journal	www.wsj.com
Xerox	www.xerox.com
Yahoo!	www.yahoo.com

CHAPTER 9 APPENDIX: THE EXPERIENCE CURVE

First identified in the late 1960s, the Experience Curve[48] holds that as a firm's accumulated volume in manufacturing and distributing a product increases, costs reduce in a predictable manner. This is revealed as a straight-line relationship when plotted as log (unit cost) versus log (accumulated experience).[49] This relationship has powerful implications for the product's cost trajectory over time, and hence the firm's marketing strategy; all things being equal, the lower the firm's costs, the greater its strategic options.

Of course, costs do not just decline over time; they are made to do so by tough-minded management forcing them down and, in recent years, via team-based efforts to seek sources of waste. These cost reduction efforts may be classified into several categories:

Learning   The Learning Curve, intellectual forebearer of the Experience Curve, captured the idea that individuals and organizations learn to complete specific tasks more quickly and efficiently. As a result, more tasks can be completed or products manufactured in a given time period, leading to lower costs.[50,51] Furthermore, the continual examination of organizational processes to isolate their value and improve methods of completing key tasks is fundamental to the growth of the reengineering discipline.

Scale Factors   Scale plays an important role in cost reduction as many classes of fixed costs can be spread over greater volume, leading to lower implied costs per unit. Unit costs, such as capital, R&D, administrative, distribution, and promotion, have the potential for being reduced as volume increases. In addition, increased volume may lead to greater bargaining power for lower raw material costs.

Process Technology Changes   Over time, improvements in production technology may enable cost reductions. In addition, manufacturing experience may allow plants to perform in excess of rated capacity, specialized maintenance may prolong plant life, and greater supply chain understanding may lead to inventory reductions in raw material, work in process, and finished goods.

Product Redesign   As the firm gains experience in manufacture and use, product redesign may lead to significant cost reductions. Reduction in product variety, materials substitution, increased standardization, technological development, and product simplification may reduce costs both directly and via inventory reductions. Furthermore, over time, lower cost components may become available, specifications may be relaxed as operating conditions are better understood, and experience with manufacture may lead to tighter design to specifications.

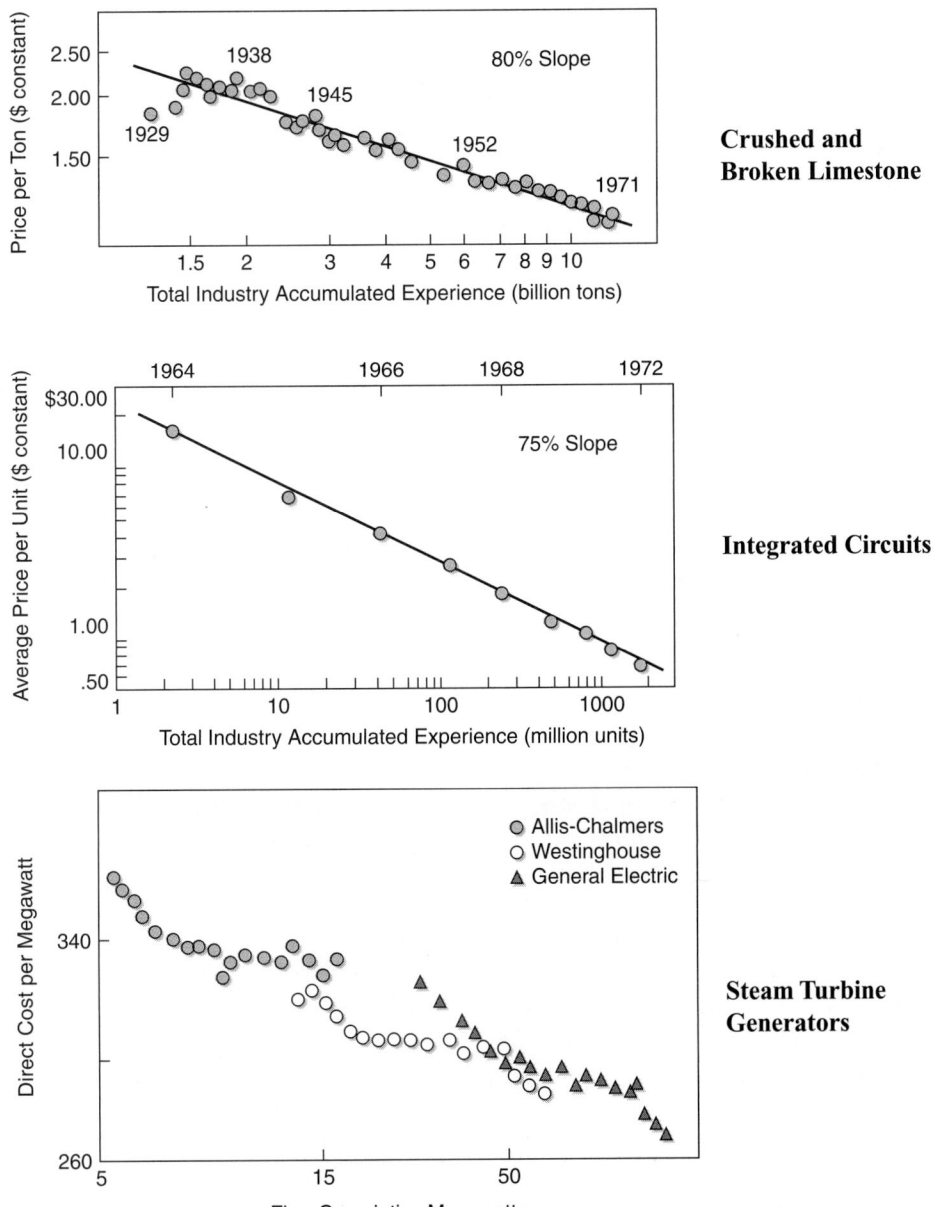

Crushed and
Broken Limestone

Integrated Circuits

Steam Turbine
Generators

FIGURE 9A.1

Experience Curve Examples

Substitution of Variable Costs for Fixed Costs and Vice Versa At a rudimentary level the firm's product costs are a combination of fixed and variable. Early in the product life cycle, when unit volume is increasing, the firm may shift from variable costs to fixed costs, such as by substituting capital for labor (using machines instead of people). This may lead to decreased unit costs as volume increases. By contrast, later in the life cycle when average volume grows at GNP rates subject to business cycle fluctuations, substitution of fixed costs by variable costs may prove advantageous, so that costs reduce as volume falls. As a related extension, an off-loading of certain activities via outsourcing may also lead to lower costs.

Of course, it is unlikely that product costs can be reduced on all dimensions simultaneously. Nonetheless, the Experience Curve provides an intellectual rationale for many firm cost-cutting activities in recent years. The specific activities embraced in downsizing, reengineering, outsourcing, and the like are consistent with the cost reductions implicit in the Experience Curve concept (Figure 9A.1).

> **Examples:** Three examples of experience curves are shown in Figure 9A.1.[51] Note that both the limestone and integrated circuit examples use log/log plots and are for prices rather than costs. The underlying assumption is that if prices are reducing, costs must also be reducing. By contrast, the steam turbine generator example plots year-by-year direct costs (each entry corresponds to a year) for three competitors.

COMPETITIVE MARKET STRATEGIES IN MATURITY AND DECLINE

LEARNING OBJECTIVES

When you have completed this chapter, you will understand

- **the nature of competitive situations in the maturity and decline stages of the product form life cycle**

- **that the competitive imperatives in maturity depend on the degree of industry concentration and fragmentation**

- **business characteristics in maturity and decline as a function of scenarios based on life cycle stage and competitive position**

- **how to construct sets of alternative strategic possibilities, based on potential future scenarios**

INTRODUCTION

This chapter continues the discussion started in Chapter 9 regarding a scenario approach to identifying alternative competitive strategic options. The focus here is on the maturity and decline stages of the product life cycle, stages that embrace the majority of the firm's products and services. Again, a series of life cycle stage/competitive position scenarios is used to develop sets of strategic options.

DETERMINING IF A MARKET IS REALLY "MATURE"

Before accepting the definition of a market as mature, it is important to consider whether or not there may be further growth potential. It is especially important in what are thought to be the later stages in the development of a market—maturity and decline—that managers think of life cycles as conditional sales forecasts. Examination of the conditions or assumptions upon which these forecasts rest is always warranted, lest they remain implicit and unrecognized. Indeed, in a recent article the authors assert, "There is no such thing as a mature business. There are only mature managers!"[1] There are several types of barriers to further growth in sales of a product form:

Technology

The technology on which a product form is based may limit both its performance and growth, such as vacuum tube technology's size and weight limitations that put radios in maturity. However, new technological innovations may obliterate these barriers. Transistor technology rejuvenated radios, improved microprocessors made personal computers (notebooks) portable, and advances in clockwork technology have produced wind-up radios, flashlights, a global positioning system (GPS) handset, and a landmine detector.[2]

Economic

Economic barriers are often linked to technology, but this is not always the case. For example, Monsanto discovered it had underestimated the price elasticity of demand for its Roundup herbicide when it came off patent in the Philippines, and it was forced to reduce price to meet generic competition.[3] Monsanto's sales, and those of its competitors, grew dramatically.

Behavioral

If an innovation requires significant behavioral change from customers, it is not unusual to experience barriers to growth. For example, since the early decision makers and users of personal computers tended to be "techies," operating systems like CPM and MS-DOS were acceptable. However, the inability of hardware and software makers to change the behavior of the mass of potential users almost mandated the development of more "Mac-like" graphical user interfaces, as seen in the succession of Windows releases by Microsoft.

Governmental Intervention

An important barrier to growth is the often-dead hand of government intervention. Explosions of growth can follow reduction or obliteration of regulations that impede competitive entry. This factor was recognized by Frederick Smith, founder and CEO of Federal Express, who moved quickly and effectively to expand his fleet in the wake of airfreight deregulation.

Insufficient Creativity

A major reason for lack of sales growth and ultimately decline is competition from new product forms that better serve customer needs, or even the disappearance of a need or want. Counterforces to this inter–product-form competition are attempts to remove barriers to growth via creativity and innovation.[4] Alternative approaches are increasing product use, developing new uses, entering new markets, repositioning and improving, or augmenting the product/service. Although these strategies may initially be pursued by only one producer, they are usually rapidly imitated if they are seen to be successful. Then a whole new cycle of growth may commence.

INCREASING PRODUCT USE   Increased use can be achieved by increasing the frequency of use or the quantity used per use occasion. Increasing frequency may be addressed by activities such as positioning the product for frequent use, sending reminder communications, making use easier, promoting different use occasions/locations, providing incentives, and reducing undesirable consequences of frequent use. Increased quantity per use occasion, such as dishwasher detergent, can be achieved through similar methods.[5]

> Examples: **Packaging**. Product use may increase by simply increasing packaging size (for example, 20 oz. rather than 12 oz. Pepsi).[6] In addition, packaging designed for dispensing ease may also encourage greater use, such as greater hole size for Tabasco hot sauce.
>
> **Obsolescence**. By introducing improved versions on a regular basis, management may be able to increase sales. Probably the best example is the fashion industry where clothing styles change with the season, but the automobile industry has used the annual model year in this manner for many years. A similar strategy is employed by software companies.
>
> **Expiry**. Manufacturers of several types of product now incorporate devices to indicate when the product should be discarded and hence repurchased. These devices range from open expiry dates on consumables, such as beer and cola drinks, to physical indicators on products such as razors, batteries, toothbrushes, and water filters.[7]
>
> **Convenience**. How product benefits are secured may have an important impact on volume. A good example is the pharmaceutical industry where a transition from injectables to daily tablets, to time-release capsules, and even long-lived patches eases consumers' burdens.

DEVELOPING NEW USES   New uses represent an alternative approach to increasing product volume. One of the more successful product form rejuvenations is Church and Dwight's success with Arm and Hammer baking soda.

> Example: In the 1970s, Arm and Hammer baking soda was the sole surviving branded sodium bicarbonate producer in a market that declined as its major applications—cake making and antacid—were superseded by new product forms. Following owner Church and Dwight's first new use attempt, removing refrigerator smells, uses of Arm and Hammer baking soda have spread to removing smells in sinks, swimming pool treatment, cat litter deodorizer, underarm deodorant, toothpaste, laundry detergent, and even as a productivity-enhancing antacid feed additive for dairy cattle!

ENTERING NEW MARKETS   New market entry can be an attractive way of reviving sales volume for products viewed as mature.

> Example: In the mid-1980s, FedEx's profitable business in the overnight delivery of documents came under threat from the use of fax machines. CEO Frederick Smith's response was to focus marketing effort on direct marketers shipping physical goods rather than documents. This successful effort supported the growth of the direct marketing industry. The logistical systems developed as part of this shift are playing a crucial role in the development of electronic commerce.

REPOSITIONING   New positioning by changing associations or adding new associations can sometimes have dramatic effects on volumes.

> Example: Honda's entry into the U.S. motorcycle market spawned huge market growth based on effective repositioning of motorcycling as an enjoyable leisure pursuit for the whole family—"You meet the nicest people on a Honda"[8]—rather than as just a niche activity for motorcycle fanatics.

PRODUCT/SERVICE IMPROVEMENT   Frequently, the cause of slowing sales is neglect coupled with a lack of concern to truly satisfy customer needs. If there is neither the managerial will to perform at a high level nor effective control systems to enforce appropriate behavior, product/service quality will decline, leading to loss in brand equity. These situations often appear in organizations with dominant market position. The remedy for this situation is fairly straightforward. Improve the offering!

> **Example:** In the late 1990s, many analysts foresaw the demise of Apple Computer. However, by mid-1999, following the launch of its G3 Powerbooks and the popular iMac, Apple returned to profitability. Over 25% of iMac buyers were new to computing, showing that Apple's innovations were contributing to growth in the overall market. In addition, over 10% had switched from the IBM platform, and Apple's retail market share once again exceeded 10%.

PRODUCT/SERVICE AUGMENTATION   Another effective option is adding services to the basic product offering. As product quality has improved in many manufacturing industries, product-based means of securing competitive advantage have become more remote. Firms are increasingly looking to services to rejuvenate brands and secure competitive advantage.

> **Example:** In the early 1990s, faced with disastrous financial results and a mandate to turn the company around, IBM CEO Lou Gerstner increased IBM's emphasis on services to its computer customers. In particular, rather than just sell hardware, IBM offered to operate customers' computer systems. This strategy has achieved noticeable success: IBM has announced that it operates information technology functions for such major U.S. companies as Kodak, Xerox, and DuPont.[9] Coincidentally, this shift of strategy has bolstered the prospects for IBM's mainframe business, still critically important to the firm.[10]

DEVELOPING COMPETITIVE STRATEGIC OPTIONS: MATURITY STAGE

Product/Market Characteristics

The maturity stage, characterized by slow-growing or constant year-to-year sales, is affected primarily by changes in basic macroeconomic factors and population growth. For many product forms, most sales are to repeat users. However, the implicit expectation that this stage may be long-lasting is not necessarily well-placed. A new substitute product form can cause rapid sales decline, as the compact disc did to vinyl records. Also, if any of the barriers to growth noted in the introduction to this chapter is surmounted, the market may be revived.

An important characteristic of maturity is that the competitive situation may vary from one approaching monopoly (or at least oligopoly) embracing few major competitors each with substantial market share, to one of many suppliers and a high degree of fragmentation.

In general, pricing tends to be competitive in concentrated markets, and attempts at market segmentation rely more on packaging and promotional strategies than on significant product differentiation. Industry structures stabilize in this period and market positions secured by early maturity may survive for many years as entry barriers rise over time, driven by such factors as increases in minimum scale, brand preferences, and distribution system domination.

> **Examples:** These include domination of mainframe computers by IBM, of steam turbine generators by General Electric, razors by Gillette, and silver-based image production by Kodak (at least in the United States).

Exceptions to this situation are likely to spring from process innovation. For example, Union Carbide's more efficient Unipol polyethylene process produced significant changes in that industry. Furthermore, by 1998, Nucor, producing steel exclusively by electric arc furnaces (so-called mini-mill technology) reached a sales volume comparable to

Bethlehem Steel, for many years the second largest steel manufacturer in the United States. The large U.S. steel producers, committed to traditional blast furnace technology, initially ignored the electric arc process.

Rapid imitation makes product-based differential advantages difficult to maintain. Producers may instead concentrate on retaining distribution outlets, since firms with broad product lines sold through common outlets have considerable advantages over more specialized producers. Consider, for example, Procter & Gamble's strength in supermarkets. Cost economies and market positions achieved by entrenched competitors often make for difficult entry in mature markets. However, incumbents sometimes create conditions that hasten their own demise. Accustomed to the high margins of early life cycle stages, when the most price-inelastic segments are being penetrated, they fail to broaden their approach to reach more price-elastic segments. Likewise, complacency can foster high costs, leading to high prices that lower-cost competitors can undercut, or failure to capitalize on the latest product or process technologies.

> **Example:** As noted earlier, in the early 1980s, Xerox, the original leader in xerography, was perilously close to failure. Having failed to develop small copiers, it found that the Japanese had a 40% to 50% cost advantage and that their prices approximated Xerox's manufacturing costs![11]

Each of these failures can enhance prospects for new entrants, often foreign, that would otherwise need even more significant resource spending to gain a competitive position. Successful late entrants often use advanced technology and target particular market segments.

Compared to the oligopolistic nature of concentrated markets, leaders in fragmented markets may command only a few market share points. Fragmentation can occur for several reasons: low barriers to entry and high barriers to exit, deregulation or regulation,[12] diverse market needs and, for products, insufficient experience curve effects to overcome high transportation costs.

Sometimes market fragmentation or concentration is in the eye of the beholder. For example, a British company may identify a few major competitors in its home market and consider it concentrated; if it examines the same industry in various European countries, it may similarly identify a high degree of concentration in each country. However, if it considered all markets together as a European market, it would no longer see a series of domestic oligopolies, but rather a single fragmented market. Starting from the smallest local perspective, as the view of the market becomes broader—local to intracountry regional; to national; to intercountry regional, such as the European Union; to global—what appears as an oligopoly at the lower level may seem fragmented at the next higher level.

Defining industry and market boundaries is rarely straightforward, but as shown later, the perspective taken by the firm in developing competitive strategy is a critical dimension in the maturity stage of the product life cycle.

CONCENTRATED MARKETS: COMPETITIVE POSITION—LEADER

Business Characteristics

All things being equal, market leaders in concentrated markets should have positive financial situations. Their high market share positions frequently lead to good relative cost positions, decent margins and, since demands for investment in plant and equipment are much less onerous than in the early growth stage, significant positive cash flow should be generated. As noted, poor management decisions can obviate these potential strengths.

Objectives and Strategic Considerations

For these products, the market leader has a choice of two major alternatives: seek to maintain leadership over the long run (sometimes called *milking*), or harvest the business.[13] Maintaining leadership usually involves incremental improvement of existing products and processes, focusing on increasing the frequency and amount of use, and developing new uses.

A particular concern for the various competitors at this stage of the life cycle should be the possibility of new product form innovations. These serve the same basic needs, perhaps better or less expensively, and therefore have the potential to obsolete the product form, as compact discs did to vinyl records. As noted, in some industries, process innovation may have a comparable effect as when electric arc mini-mills began to supersede integrated steel making.

LONG-RUN MARKET LEADERSHIP   The overarching strategic consideration for long-run leadership is cautious investment to maintain market position. Investment may be required in many areas, notably in process technology, to keep up with, or stay ahead of, developing methods for making the product more efficiently. Leaders should strive for continuous cost reductions,[14] seek the benefits of innovations in operations systems and product design, maintain tight working capital control, and manage the fixed/variable cost ratio carefully.[15]

Investment is also required in marketing activities, a point often misunderstood, especially by those who emphasize sales volumes rather than customers. When markets are not growing, most competing firms (leaders and followers) experience considerable turnover in their customer bases. As existing customers are lost, new customers are needed to replace them. Leaders may stay ahead, and follower firms may challenge leaders, by identifying new market segments and tailoring their marketing offers appropriately.

> **Example:** In the patented drug business, pharmaceutical firms with drugs coming off patent seek new segments by making over-the-counter versions, or by developing sustained release products offering advantages over pills that must be taken several times a day.

Minor product changes based on more subtle customer needs may also prove an avenue for increasing sales. Cereal manufacturers have enjoyed success with sweetened cereals, and Clorox, whose brands compete in mature markets, has used a similar approach to grow and improve its market share.

> **Example:** Customer research revealed that users of Clorox's Pine-Sol brand of household floor and wall cleaner did not actually like the smell of pine. Introduction of Lemon-Fresh Pine-Sol led to sales growth of over 25% per annum. Similarly, some consumers hated the smell of chlorine in Clorox bleach, the 60% market share leader. By adding a squirt of floral scent or a twist of lemon, it gained a full market share point from generic competitors. Finally, when it slightly modified countertop cleaner Formula 409 to eliminate streaking on glass, market share jumped from 17% to 20%.[16]

Advances in physical distribution may provide an avenue for securing differential advantage in a previously untapped market segment.

> **Example:** Historically, New York City restaurants secured fish from the Fulton Fish Market. Since fish caught off the Maine coast had previously been through the Portland and Boston fish auctions, it was typically several days before the fish was served to diners. Fish purveyor Rod Mitchell identified upscale New York City restaurants as a target segment and developed a system to deliver fish quickly. Fish off the boats is inspected at 6 A.M., purchased at 11:15 A.M., packed at 12:15 P.M., sent to New York, and unpacked at 9 A.M. the next day ready for lunch. The added customer value is reflected in the price received: $2 to $4 per pound versus $1 to $2 per pound for standard fish market cod.[17]

Two serious dangers for the leader are overinvestment and underinvestment. Overinvestment to improve market share in a slow growth market with entrenched competitors may not be worth the effort. Firms might be well-advised to seek more attractive investment opportunities elsewhere, such as in new product forms. Conversely, insufficient investment, often driven by top management's overly ambitious near-term profit expectations, may lead to severe loss in market position. These profit expectations can be met in the short run, but only by weakening the firm's competitive market position, such as by not keeping up with product and process development, or failing to address emerging segments, ultimately leading to market share loss.[18]

> **Example:** In 1985, 60% of the beer drunk in Japan was Kirin; Asahi had less than 10% market share. By 1997, Kirin's share was down to 43%, and Asahi's was up to 35%. According to *The Economist*, accustomed to dominance, Kirin's managers became overconfident and failed to act on most beer industry trends in the previous 20 years. They missed the distribution shift from small local shops, where they were strong, to supermarkets and discounters, and were late to invest in canning technology as cans replaced bottles. In addition, their advertising was a pale imitation of Asahi's, and too much resource was placed in new, small volume beers rather than supporting their core brands.[19]

A related example in the United States was Burlington Industry's failure to identify or act on the 1970s trend of women entering the workforce. Despite Burlington's position as a long-time leader in pantyhose with strong relationships to department store and specialty women's retailers, it was Hanes, then a marginal manufacturer, that specifically targeted working women. Hanes' improved product, together with a creative marketing plan built around the L'Eggs brand that involved distribution through supermarkets and drug stores, ultimately led to Burlington's demise. Or, again, both Carrier (air conditioning) and Otis (elevators) lost market position in the 1980s when parent United Technologies underinvested in these businesses.

A particular problem occurs when the firm is locked into a market position and finds it difficult to adjust as the market evolves. This problem is most acute when distribution entities are involved. For example, in the growth stage, a firm may decide to use entrenched distributors as a means to reach end users. Later, however, as some end users grow in size or expertise, they question the value offered by distributors and demand direct manufacturer-to-end user relationships as a means to secure lower prices and other benefits. The manufacturer is in a catch-22 situation: To retain its distributor focus, it risks losing sales at the end-user; to accede to the end user's request means upsetting a longstanding positive working relationship with the distributor.[20] "Old economy" firms face this challenge in adapting to the new realities of electronic commerce.

In addition to the sorts of actions discussed previously, the firm should position itself for protection against the potential erosion of market position from new product forms. It should assume a market-based rather than a product-based view of the world, and take the appropriate action to broaden its product line to meet evolving customer needs though approaches such as R&D, licensing, joint ventures, or acquisitions.[21]

HARVEST THE BUSINESS   Although the dominant objective for a market leader in maturity is long-run leadership, a harvest strategy, typically driven by some form of portfolio rationalization, may be more efficacious. Harvesting means emphasizing increases in short-term cash flow at the expense of maintaining market share or sales volume. The most extreme form of harvesting is to sell the business, but alternatives involve price increases and cost reductions, even though these may harm the business over the long run. Typical reasons for such a decision are:

- Obsolescence due to new technology: For example, DuPont, once the only rayon manufacturer in the United States, exited the rayon business in 1964 in anticipation of fast growth for nylon fiber.
- Government regulation restricting or eliminating future use of the product, as with some pesticides.
- Revision of corporate strategy, rendering the product less central to the firm. In recent years, many companies, often under pressure from the financial markets, have narrowed their search for opportunity as they "get back to basics" or "stick to their knitting."

- Future investment requirements are too high in comparison with alternatives, such as British Aerospace's decision to exit independent commercial jet aircraft production.
- Desire to avoid particular competitive conditions or competitors. A good example is Westinghouse's exit from its traditional markets where, over the years, it was frequently bested by General Electric. Westinghouse remade itself as the media company CBS, later acquired by Viacom.

Regardless of the motivation for harvesting, the firm may choose to harvest slowly or quickly. At one extreme, an outright sale of the business may be warranted; this option has the benefit of a quick, clean break and, frequently, the release of cash for investment elsewhere. However, if a large immediate cash infusion is not required, a slower, ongoing harvesting may be more appropriate. Action is required in three areas: investment, cost, and price. Future investment should be minimal, little more than is sufficient to operate the business. Costs should be pared by actions such as reducing the product line, rationalizing distribution, cutting advertising and promotion expenses, reducing service levels, and eliminating small or unprofitable customers. Finally, prices can be increased. In sum, these actions trade market share for profit and increased cash flow: The critical decision is the aggressiveness with which these actions are implemented.

CONCENTRATED MARKETS: COMPETITIVE POSITION—FOLLOWER

Business Characteristics
In general, market followers in concentrated markets have less favorable positions than leaders. Their financial situations tend to be less attractive as lower market share positions frequently lead to poor relative cost positions and less attractive margins. Of course, just as poor management decisions can obviate the strength of the leader, inspired management can overcome the inherently weaker position of a follower.

Objectives and Strategic Considerations
Broadly speaking, a follower has three possibilities: grow sales and improve market position, continue in the business for the long run, or harvest. Each of these three alternatives gives rise to a family of different options. Of course, the choice of option is not independent of the strength and actions of the market leader and other follower firms. Neither is it independent of the ownership structure as senior management in public companies is typically highly concerned about short-term profits, issues that, for private firms, may have less relevance than long-term shareholder wealth.[22]

GROWTH   The follower has three primary ways to pursue growth with the possible objective of ultimately dethroning the leader: market segmentation, kenneling, and direct attack.

Market Segmentation   Perhaps the dominant option for a follower seeking growth is segmentation and differentiation through innovation. As indicated in the previous chapter, segmentation possibilities generally commence in early growth and continue through late growth into maturity. The opportunities they offer the follower counteract the leader's advantages of strong market position and low costs that are too often associated with a lack of flexibility. The follower's strategy is basically disruption—to upset and disturb the market and force change, as Hanes did with its L'Eggs pantyhose brand. Creative market segmentation is a particularly powerful way of creating this disturbance.

> **Examples:** In the 1980s, Chrysler, the smallest of the "Big Three" U.S. automobile manufacturers, realized that consumers required a motor vehicle with greater room for families, hence its dazzling success with the minivan.
>
> Initially a relatively small player, MBNA's highly successful credit card strategy focuses exclusively on organizational affinities, such as universities, in effect using an innovative distribution channel to reach a special group of consumers.

A special form of segmentation is referred to as getting "back to basics." Typically, as products pass through their life cycles, producers add features to satisfy ever more fine-grained customer needs. As a result, prices rise throughout the industry. However, late in the life cycle, as Bic demonstrated for ballpoint pens and razors, a sizable group of customers may care little for these added features and simply prefer the basic functional benefits offered in the original version of the product form.

> **Example:** The Volkswagen Beetle (Germany), the Mini (Britain), and the 2CV (France) offered basic transportation in a recapitulation of Henry Ford's success with the Model T. More recently, European entrepreneurs have begun making extremely basic cars that can be driven without a license, capitalizing on legislation designed to protect mopeds—legislators forgot to specify the number of wheels.

Kenneling   This is a metaphor for gathering a set of "dog" products together under one roof. The concept that a follower company may acquire several unprofitable (or marginally profitable) low market share products from other firms and develop a strong competitor has intuitive appeal. Required actions for such a strategy include rationalizing operations, distribution, and marketing. The classic kenneling success is White Consolidated Industries. Before its acquisition by Electrolux, White successfully assembled a kennel of "white goods" (home appliances) comprising such brands as Bendix, Frigidaire, Kelvinator, and Westinghouse.[23] Also, for a period, Heileman was successful in assembling a group of local beer brands. It should be noted, however, that other attempts at kenneling have failed miserably.

Asea Brown Boveri (ABB) has implemented a combination of segmentation and kenneling strategies on a global scale:

> **Example:** ABB has acquired many smaller, heavy-equipment manufacturing firms worldwide. Post-integration, each affiliate produces products for a subset of its customers' needs, securing the remainder from its sister companies. In this manner, each affiliate specializes in the products it makes best, eliminating marginal and unprofitable activities; however, it continues to provide the localized attention and service required by customers on all products.[24]

A related strategy that may be effective in distribution-intensive industries focuses on strategic alliances. Much used in the international airline industry, strategic alliances are being used to develop global competitor groups that not only allow passengers to fly complex routes more easily, but afford revenue capturing opportunities from travelers that alliance members might otherwise lose to other airlines. The major grouping is the Star Alliance that is comprised of Air Canada, Lufthansa, SAS, Thai Airlines, United, Varig, Ansett, and Air New Zealand.

Direct Attack   The final growth alternative for the follower is a direct attack upon the leader's position. This option is especially viable if the leader has been lazy, over-milking the product via underinvestment, or arrogant in serving customers inadequately. The key to a successful attack strategy is to find the leader's weak spots and to invest accordingly.

> **Example:** In 1987, start-up Bloomberg went head-to-head with already established Dow Jones and Reuters by offering custom-made terminals with software, then unavailable from the two leaders. This action enabled subscribers to make their own analyses of financial information. By 1998, Bloomberg's service had grown the market; it had 90,000 clients worldwide versus 350,000 Reuters terminals.[25]

Relatedly, many small financial institutions have successfully offered low interest rate credit cards aimed at customers of major banks who pay high interest rates on credit balances.

Successfully capturing one market segment may provide a secure position from which to attack the leader in other market segments. This situation often occurs when success in the market segment is associated with building infrastructure, or when developing brand equity is relevant for addressing other market segments.

> **Example:** In the 1960s and 1970s, domestic U.S. automobile manufacturers built large horsepower vehicles and paid less attention to incipient demand for small cars. Although they could have imported small cars from European plants, large cars were more profitable. This omission opened a market window first for Volkswagen, then Japanese competitors, mainly Toyota, Nissan, and Honda. The Japanese firms successfully established distribution networks and secured viable market positions in the small car market, often the entry level for new buyers who then rewarded the brand owner with loyalty on new automobile purchases.
>
> In the early 1980s, actions by the U.S. auto companies spurred the foreign firms to further penetrate the U.S. market. Faced with a recessionary environment, increasing imports of Japanese cars, and under pressure from Detroit, the U.S. government arranged for a "voluntary" quota on Japanese imports. Faced with this impediment to continued profitable growth, the Japanese firms took two predictable actions. They began to import higher-priced cars that competed more directly with the U.S. firms, and began domestic U.S. manufacture.
>
> In the late 1940s, General Motors's share of the U.S. auto market was about 50%; in the late 1990s, it was struggling to retain 30% market share!

CONTINUE   The two "continue" options are to maintain position or rationalize.

Maintain   The maintain option implies holding market share roughly constant over the long run. This is a viable option if the firm holds a well-managed, profitable number two or three market position, or possesses specific strengths in one or more segments. Actions to maintain this position are similar to the long-run market leadership options.

Rationalize   However, if the product is basically unprofitable (a common situation for follower products in mature markets), a rationalizing option may be appropriate. Rationalizing requires a careful examination of all aspects of the business as well as tough decision making to cut costs wherever possible to turn a loss into at least a marginal profit. Although short-term considerations may suggest abandonment, there may be mitigating circumstances. For example, rationalizing may permit retention of a scarce yet skilled workforce, allow continued access to raw materials or technology, permit countervailing pressure on a competitor, or satisfy customers by offering a complete product line. Alternatively, high barriers may make it difficult for the firm to exit.

EXIT   The follower choosing this objective has two broad options: divest (sell to another organization) or liquidate (close down and sell the assets).

Divest   The divest choice requires that a marketing problem be solved: can the firm identify the right customer for this business? If so, the firm can exit financially intact.

Liquidate   If the product is making losses and no buyer can be found, the only reasonable action may be to liquidate. In liquidations, the issue of to whom the product (or indeed other asset) is sold is crucial. Sometimes firms are not even aware that they are disposing of assets.

> **Example:** In June 1997, British Airways' (BA) then increasingly beleaguered CEO, Robert Ayling, announced a change of livery for BA's aircraft. This involved eliminating the stylized Union flag (of the United Kingdom) from its planes' tailfins and replacing it with ethnic art as part of a £60 million branding program. BA claimed that the flag was an impediment to its goal of becoming a global airline. The following day, Richard Branson, founder and CEO of feisty Virgin Airways, announced he would add the flag to the tail of his aircraft. However, just two days later, Ayling announced that, faced with continuing negative reaction from British and foreign customers, the repainting program would cease, leaving BA's fleet with 180 ethnic logos and 160 Union flag designs. Ayling denied that his decision was influenced by Virgin's new livery featuring a prominent Union flag on a silver fuselage![26]

From time to time, management is unable or unwilling to make the tough decisions to exit from a product/market despite compelling economic and strategic arguments. For example, closing a plant in a small town may have such a devastating effect on the local economy that management is not prepared to act. Other barriers are emotional commitments.

Example: Former U.S. liquor importer, W.A. Taylor, operated mostly with extremely up-market brands, such as Benedictine and Brandy. However, also included in its product line was Old Smuggler, a whiskey brand that did not fit this positioning. The reason for its presence in the product line was that most of the firm's top managers at one time or another had been a brand manager for Old Smuggler. They could not bear to part with the brand![27]

Example: Ingersoll-Rand (IR) has a Rock-Drill business unit whose economic rationale is highly questionable. However, it was IR's original business when the firm was founded in the late 19th century!

FRAGMENTED MARKETS
Strategic Considerations

Since, by definition, no firm has a large market share in a fragmented market, the leader/follower distinction has little relevance.[28] The two major options, acquisition, and standardization and branding, each involve attempting to restructure the market. Some executives describe such strategies as organizing a previously fragmented market.

ACQUISITION Acquisition is an especially favored strategy when the basis of fragmentation is geographic. For example, as the European Union and globalization have become important forces, the French insurance company, AXA, has acquired several European insurance companies as well as The Equitable, a large U.S. insurer, in an attempt to gain strength in the fragmented global insurance industry. Sometimes, regulatory factors help companies pursue these strategies. For example, WMX (Waste Management) was assisted in its acquisition-led growth by tightening environmental regulation. Conversely, creeping deregulation in the U.S. banking industry allowed such acquisition-minded banks as Nations Bank and BancOne to become major national players. The implicit assumption of such strategies is that either scale economies have changed, or that a barrier to competition (such as regulation), previously protecting firms with high cost operations, no longer exists.

STANDARDIZATION AND BRANDING These strategies (frequently via franchising) have succeeded in industries whose entry barriers were initially very low. They have been used by organizations as diverse as Century 21, Holiday Inn, McDonald's, and Kampgrounds of America (KOA). These strategies often involve decoupling operations from marketing; decentralized operations are standardized and marketing reduces customer risk by developing strong brand identity through extensive advertising. Wayne Huizenga is attempting to achieve similar results in U.S. automotive retailing with Republic Industries.[29]

DIRECT ENTRY A third strategy involves direct entry in various parts of the fragmented market. For example, the Japanese zipper manufacturer YKK achieved global market leadership by aggressive pricing based on experience curve-based cost reductions.

DEVELOPING COMPETITIVE STRATEGIC OPTIONS: DECLINE STAGE
Product/Market Characteristics

Although the maturity stage may last many years, eventually sales turn downward, sometimes precipitously. Decline may be caused by growth of a substitute product, such as xerography replacing carbon paper, or by changing customer needs that render the product

COMPETITIVE
MARKET STRATEGIES
IN MATURITY
AND DECLINE

obsolete. When decline is swift, overcapacity often leads to fierce price competition. More stable firms may gain temporary respite as competitors drop out and leave their volume for the remaining players.

Sometimes the rate of decline is accentuated. Volume drops but fixed costs do not, leading to higher fixed costs per unit; firms raise prices to compensate, causing even lower volumes in a vicious cycle. In general, marketing expenditures drop and advertising may shift from mass to more specialized media to reduce advertising costs and target remaining customers more directly. Cost reductions are sought by pruning product lines to achieve greater scale economies. Later in decline, profitable opportunities may be available by selling to a core of loyal, relatively price-insensitive buyers.

Decline products sometimes have a resurgence, perhaps due to exogenous changes in customer tastes or inspired marketing. For example, though some may have ethical qualms, there is little doubt that the mid-1990s growth in U.S. cigar smoking was heavily influenced by creative marketing efforts.

Technology may also be a factor. For example, in 1990, the yo-yo toy was improved by introduction of the friction-reducing transaxle, making yo-yo tricks accessible to more players. In 1999, annual revenues from yo-yo sales had increased 2000% during the previous five years.

Business Characteristics

It has been shown that the generalized assumption of decline businesses as money losers is invalid. Table 10.1 measures the current return on investment (ROI) of a variety of decline businesses.

The table shows that only 8% of the sample registered a loss; another 13% were making no profit. However, overall, 72% of the sample was profitable; almost 40% earned 35% or more ROI. Of course, in the decline stage, investment in many products is largely written down, making the denominator in the ROI equation quite small. Nonetheless, the widespread belief that decline necessarily means losses is clearly wrong.[30]

Strategic Considerations

A useful way to conceptualize decline businesses is with the twin concepts of market hospitality and business strengths.[31] Several criteria suggest whether markets are hospitable or inhospitable to decline. (The conditions for inhospitable markets are presented here; hospitable markets have reverse characteristics.)

HOSPITABLE/INHOSPITABLE   A market may be viewed as inhospitable to decline if:

- the decline is rapid or uncertain
- the market is homogeneous and commodity-like or one comprising several price insensitive market segments
- the fixed/variable cost ratio is high, customer switching costs are low, and
- competitors are evenly balanced and perceive the market as strategically important.

Markets are particularly inhospitable if:

- competitor exit barriers are high: For example, assets cannot easily be redeployed to manufacture other products[32]
- strategic customers require the product, or long-term contracts are involved
- government or the community pressures competitors to stay in the business

TABLE 10.1 Profitability Distribution for Decline Businesses

Percent of Sample	8%	13%	38%	25%	5%	9%
Return on Investment (ROI)	−10%	0%	15%	35%	55%	60%

- competitors have emotional commitments to the product, or
- the product is part of a vertically integrated supply system.

BUSINESS STRENGTHS   Several characteristics identify firms with good business strengths. For example, they are well-positioned in attractive market segments, have low costs, good raw material contracts, and an ability to keep productive assets running even though they may have been in operation for many years.

THE DECLINE MATRIX   A combination of these two dimensions (Figure 10.1) produces one set of conditions, hospitable market and high business strengths, that suggests a strategy of seeking market leadership. Inhospitable markets imply harvest or immediate divestment strategies unless the firm is well-positioned in price insensitive market segments. Poor business strengths, even in hospitable markets, also suggest a harvest strategy.

- **Leadership**: The firm seeking leadership should increase market share in the near term by raising competitors' costs of competing, and improving their benefits of exit.[33] Fundamentally, the firm should demonstrate its commitment to the business by considering actions such as aggressive marketing. This can include broadening the product line, increasing promotion, and lowering prices (which may even reverse a decline).

   Example: After many years of declining subscriber bases under pressure from television, the Internet, and other communication vehicles, several major U.S. newspapers are starting to show modest sales increases. Their actions include door-to-door sales efforts, broader distribution (for example, *USA Today* is sold in corporate cafeterias, university dining halls, hospitals, hotel lobbies, and 1,100 Starbucks stores), improved product quality (such as color pages and later press deadlines), and earlier delivery.[34]

   In addition, they may consider increasing fixed investment, being prepared to buy competitors or their assets, clarifying the anticipated decline to competitors, and helping reduce competitors' exit barriers by actions such as offering long-term supply contracts and private label manufacture.

   Key operational goals are to satisfy customers, as always, but also to encourage competitors to leave. Whereas a pioneering firm may have few or no competitors early in the product life cycle, typically this condition is temporary as market growth attracts other entrants. However, at the other end of the life cycle, new entry is unlikely; the firm that continues to operate may eventually become the true monopolist and reap the full benefits of that position.

- **Segment, Harvest, Divest**: Pursuit of these options is similar to the previous description.

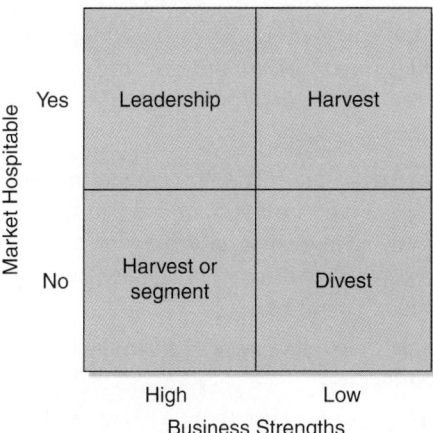

FIGURE 10.1

Strategic Options in Decline

SUMMARY

This chapter and Chapter 9 used the competitive life cycle framework combined with market position (leader/follower) to develop a series of scenarios with which to examine competitive strategy making. The family of options developed in this chapter form a useful set of options for the marketing manager, although perhaps the best strategies are contrarian in nature.

As discussed earlier, the firm's strategy should be strongly influenced by both the stage of the product life cycle and its competitive position. The specific actions it should take depend crucially upon customer needs, the strength of the firm and its competitors, and anticipated environmental considerations. Most critically, the firm should anticipate change and strive to influence change.

THE CHANGING VIEW

Old Way	New Way
Minimize investment in mature markets to maximize cash flow	Use innovation to rejuvenate market growth
Hide behind regulatory barriers	Aggressive government efforts to increase competition
Competition price-based	Competition value-based
Commoditization viewed as inevitable	Innovation a major strategic weapon
Tied to traditional distribution systems	Seek new ways of distribution to take advantage of new technologies to increase efficiencies and add value
Cut costs when times are bad	Cut costs continually
Industry structure viewed as fixed	Industry structure viewed as variable
Manufacturability ignored	Manufacturability vital
Sequential product development	Team-based concurrent product development
Decentralized purchasing	Centralized purchasing
Time ignored in operations systems	JIT becoming almost universal
Competition to the death	Merger and consolidation viewed as legitimate strategies in shareholders' interest
Accept low returns and cross-subsidize	Shareholder value discipline applied rigorously

QUESTIONS FOR STUDY AND DISCUSSION

1. "Since the product form where we have three entries has now reached maturity, investing heavily in basic R&D is the only way to assure our growth." Do you agree with this sentiment?

2. What is the difference between milking and harvesting?

3. In a business article, a leading professor suggested that U.S. companies over-milked their cash cows. In the 1997/98 Asian crisis, pundits argued that the so-called long-term view of Asian managers was no more than a justification for running unprofitable businesses supported by a corrupt or poorly regulated banking system. Can you resolve the apparent paradox? If so, how?

4. In some situations management may decide to exit a market. Explain the advantages and disadvantages of different exit strategies.

5. You have just been appointed the brand manager for First Class Mail at the U.S. Postal Service. How would you go about developing a strategy to maintain its viability given the enormous growth of e-mail?

6. Under what conditions might a firm consider retaining an unprofitable product in its product line?

7. Why do kenneling strategies so often fail?

8. Identify an example of a kenneling strategy. Explain why you believe it was adopted and what results it has produced.

9. Prepare a 20-year historic description of Church and Dwight's strategy for Arm and Hammer baking soda. What insights can you gain for developing strategy in mature and decline businesses?

10. If your goal is to maximize cash flow in a mature market, what principles should you use to develop competitive strategy?

11. Entrepreneurs have sometimes acquired fading products and brands in mature markets from their prior owners and made themselves lots of money. Why were they able to succeed whereas the large company that previously owned the product could not?

12. What are the biggest dangers of a milking strategy?

13. How important is efficiency in operations and distribution in maturing markets as opposed to growth markets? Explain your answer.

14. The shareholder value concept has had its greatest impact on the way maturing businesses are managed. Discuss.

15. Improvements in distribution efficiency are often the result of innovation by non-traditional competitors. Why is this the case?

ENDNOTES

1. G. Stalk, Jr., D.K. Pecaut, and B. Burnett, "Breaking Compromises, Breakaway Growth," *Harvard Business Review*, 74 (Sept./Oct. 1996), pp. 131–139.

2. *The Economist*, April 17, 1999.

3. Price elasticity of demand is the rate of percent change in quantity demanded relative to the percent change in price $= \partial Q/Q \div \partial P/P$.

4. A deep understanding of customer purchase and use behavior, their latent dissatisfactions, diseconomies in the industry value chain, analogous situations in other industries, and performance anomalies are some of the ways to identify creative opportunities, Stalk, Pecaut, and Burnett, *op. cit.*

5. An informal survey of plumbers found that less than 50% of manufacturers' recommended amounts were necessary to clean dishes.

6. Introduction of a large plastic bottle was an important element in Pepsi displacing Coke as the leading cola beverage in supermarkets, J. Sculley, *The Odyssey*, New York: Harper & Row, 1988.

7. *The New York Times*, April 24, 1998.

8. The successful tag line in Honda's original advertisements, developed by a UCLA student.

9. Ironically, it was IBM's refusal to enter this business many years earlier that led to Ross Perot's resignation and the founding of Electronic Data Systems (EDS).

10. See, W.C. Kim and R. Mauborgne, "Creating New Market Space," *Harvard Business Review*, 77 (Jan./Feb. 1999), pp. 83–93 for interesting approaches to securing growth in mature markets.

11. Xerox Corporation: The Customer Satisfaction Program, *Harvard Business School,* 9-591-055.

12. Although considerable restructuring of the U.S. banking industry has been occurring in recent years, in the mid-1990s, federal and state banking regulation had together led to a situation in which the United States had well over 10,000 commercial banks. By comparison, Britain, with about one fifth the population, to all intents and purposes, had four banks until recent deregulation increased the number somewhat.

13. Sometimes managers confuse milking with harvesting. Milking implies securing resources from the product for use elsewhere in the firm, but also emphasizes the necessity of feeding to ensure that the milk continues to flow. By contrast, harvesting implies a decision to exit the business over some period of time.

14. An interesting example of the drive for low costs was Toyota's designation of Thursday and Friday as the "weekend," to take advantage of low Saturday and Sunday utility rates.

15. As sales increase, firms frequently substitute variable costs with fixed costs; as a result, the implicit cost per unit falls. Conversely, in maturity, firms should consider variating their fixed costs so that, on the down side of the business cycle, costs do not remain high as sales volume falls.

16. *Business Week*, June 16, 1997.

17. *The New York Times,* March 4, 1998.

18. At this stage in the product life cycle, management must make sure that the appropriate financial measures are used inasmuch as much plant investment may be written off, and "sunk costs" are sunk. A focus on incremental avoidable costs versus potential return may be a better approach than relying on traditional accounting measures of performance.

19. *The Economist*, February 28, 1998.

20. This issue is discussed further in Chapter 16. For an excellent example of the problem, see Norton Company (A), *Harvard Business School*, 9-570-001.

21. For an excellent article on maintaining current business while simultaneously preparing for discontinuous change, see M.L. Tushman and C.A. O'Reilly, III, "Ambidextrous Organizations: Managing Evolutionary and Revolutionary Change," *California Management Review*, 28 (Summer 1996), pp. 8–30.

22. For example, billionaire Richard Branson, Chairman of the privately held Virgin Group, claims that Virgin Records, sold 20 years after its creation, did not show profits until its 15th year. Currently, Virgin is challenging Coke and Pepsi in soft drinks, British Airways and others in airline travel, and traditional British financial services firms with Virgin Direct. "Letters to the Editor," *The Economist*, March 7, 1998.

23. For example, in the 1980s, White purchased the Frigidaire division from General Motors for $500 million. One of its first actions was to close the plant.

24. Example from A.J. Slywotzky and D.J. Morrison, *The Profit Zone*, New York: Times Business, 1997. See also A.J. Slywotsky and B.P. Shapiro, "Leveraging to Beat the Odds: The New Marketing Mind-Set," *Harvard Business Review*, 71 (Sept./Oct. 1993), pp. 97–107.

25. *The Australian*, March 12, 1998.

26. *The Daily Telegraph*, June 7, 1999.

27. Personal communication from W.A. Taylor executive.

28. Of course, being the leader in one market arena, such as geographic, has advantages as a base for growth, but is not absolutely necessary. For example, GMAC assumed leadership in the U.S. mortgage banking business from zero position simply by acquiring two active firms.

29. The sale of automobiles over the Internet is another interesting development.

30. K. Harrigan, "Strategies for Declining Industries," *Journal of Business Strategy*, 1 (Fall 1980), pp. 20–34.

31. This section is based on K.R. Harrigan and M.E. Porter, "End-game Strategies for Declining Industries," *Harvard Business Review*, 61 (Jul./Aug. 1983), pp. 111–120.

32. A particularly serious exit barrier occurs if the competitor has poor financial management and is unaware that it is unprofitable.

33. Taking competitors out of the market may also occur in markets that are not in decline. In the mid-1990s, London-based Swire group was the majority owner of profitable Cathay Pacific Airways and a leading stockholder and manager of Dragonair (the airline of choice for business people flying to China). In 1996, in the run up to Hong Kong's return to China, China National Aviation Corporation (CNAC) (a shadowy group believed close to the People's Liberation Army) made an application to start an airline of its own in Hong Kong. To combat this threat, Swire rearranged its ownership structure to provide CNAC with the majority stake in Dragonair. Although some observers have characterized CNAC's actions as blackmail, others have noted that Dragonair should find it easier to secure landing rights in China and that CNAC will now be interested in using its influence to help preserve Cathay's and Dragonair's oligopoly. (*The Economist*, May 4, 1996)

34. *Fortune*, June 8, 1998.

2CV (France)	www.citroen.com
ABB	www.abb.com
Air Canada	www.aircanada.com
Air New Zealand	www.airnz.co.hz
Ansett	www.ansett.com.au
Apple Computer	www.apple.com
Arm and Hammer	www.armandhammer.com
Asahi	www.asahibeer.co.jp
AXA	www.axa.com
BancOne	www.bankone.com
Bayer	www.bayerus.com
Bethlehem Steel	www.bethsteel.com
Bic	www.bicworld.com
Bloomberg	www.bloomberg.com
British Aerospace	www.bae.co.uk
British Airways	www.british-airways.com
Burlington	www.burlington-ind.com
Carrier	www.carrier.com
Cathay Pacific Airways	www.cathay-usa.com
CBS	www.cbs.com
Chrysler	www.chrysler.com
Clorox	www.clorox.com
Coca-Cola	www.cocacola.com
Dow Jones	www.dowjones.com
Dragonair	www.dragonair.com
Dupont	www.dupont.com
Electrolux	www.electrolux.com
Electronic Data Systems	www.eds.com
Federal Express	www.fedex.com
General Electric	www.ge.com
General Motors	www.gm.com
Gillette	www.gillette.com
GMAC	www.gmacfs.com
Harvard Business Review	www.hbsp.harvard.edu/products/hbr
Hanes	www.hanes.com
Holiday Inn	www.holiday-inn.com
Honda	www.honda.com
IBM	www.ibm.com
Johnson and Johnson	www.johnsonandjohnson.com
Junghans	www.junghans.de
Kampgrounds of America	www.koa.com
Kirin	www.kirin.com
Kodak	www.kodak.com
L'Eggs	www.leggs.com
Lufthansa	www.lufthansa.com
MBNA	www.mbna.com
Microsoft	www.microsoft.com
Mini	www.mini.com
Monsanto	www.monsanto.com
Nations Bank	www.nationsbank.com
Nissan	www.nissan.com

Nucor	www.nucor.com
Otis	www.otis.com
Pepsi	www.pepsico.com
Procter & Gamble	www.pg.com
Republic Industries	www.michelin.com
Reuters	www.reuters.com
SAS	www.scandinavian.net
SEC	www.sec.gov
Star Alliance	www.star-alliance.com
Starbucks	www.starbucks.com
Tabasco	www.tabasco.com
Thai Airlines	www.thaiairway.com
Toyota	www.toyota.com
Union Carbide	www.unioncarbide.com
United	www.ual.com
United Technologies	www.utc.com
USA Today	www.usatoday.com
Varig	www.varig.com.br
Virgin Airways	www.flyvirgin.com
Volkswagen Beetle	www.vw.com
Westinghouse	www.westinghouse.com
White Consolidated Industries	www.wci.com
WXM (Waste Management)	www.wxm.com
Xerox	www.xerox.com
YKK	www.YKK.com

MANAGING BRANDS

LEARNING OBJECTIVES

When you have completed this chapter, you will understand

- the nature of brands and their functions for both buyers and sellers

- two different concepts of brand equity—organizational and customer—and approaches to measuring them

- checking brand health

- differences between umbrella- and multibranding

- how to revitalize struggling brands

- how organizational brand equity can be leveraged

- the role of brands in strategic alliances

- issues involved in global branding

INTRODUCTION

If this business were to be split up, I would be glad to take the brands, trademarks, and goodwill, and you could have all the bricks and mortar and I would fare better than you.[1]

—John Stuart, former Chairman of Quaker

In recent years, branding has become recognized as one of the more important decision areas for the firm. Once considered a minor matter of naming products or services, today brand equity considerations are among the most important drivers of change in contemporary marketing practice. For many companies around the world, the value of brands far outstrips the balance sheet value of its net assets. This realization is totally consistent with the externally-oriented marketing philosophy developed earlier, and is leading to a re-examination of the nature of firm assets. However, the subject of brand equity is complex, for it applies to organizations and their customers in different ways. This chapter explores this distinction, then proceeds to examine the myriad of branding decisions firms must make. Organizational issues are discussed in Chapter 19.

WHAT IS A BRAND?

Brands are a part of everyday life for both consumers and organizations. They are distinguishing names and symbols, such as logos, trademarks, package designs, and spokespersons. Brands are developed by sellers to identify their goods and services, to differentiate those goods and services from those of competitors, and to offer value to customers so that sellers secure marketplace and financial benefits.

Despite this straightforward definition, brands have a wide range of applicability. At the finest level, a brand refers to an individual product, such as Boxster (Porsche) or Corvette (Chevrolet). Brands are also applied to product lines comprising a group of closely related products serving a similar function. For example, the Ragu (family) brand is associated with several types of sauce including Pizza, Chunky Garden Style, Robust Blend Hearty, Light, Old World Style, and Cheese. More broadly still, a brand refers to a group of products or services that may fulfill many different functions. Often in these situations the brand is a corporate brand, such as CitiGroup, Marks and Spencer, IBM, Carrefour, GE, General Motors, or Yamaha (Figure 11.1).

Individual products or services are frequently identified by multiple brands. In some cases, single organizations use multiple brands, such as Toyota Corolla or Citibank Direct Access, to secure benefit from the family brand while, at the same time, develop recogni-

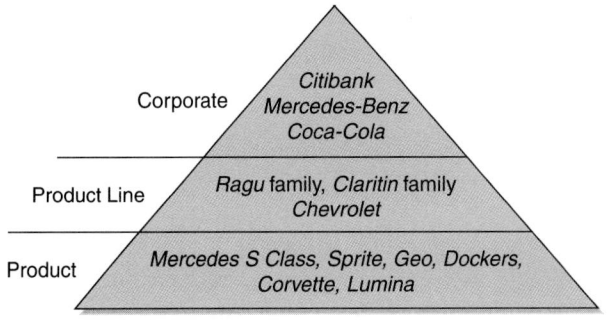

FIGURE 11.1

Branding at Multiple Levels

tion and preference for an individual product. In other cases, multiple organizations co-brand products for mutual benefit, such as Wells Fargo, MasterCard; Coca-Cola, NutraSweet; Hewlett Packard, intel inside, and Pentium. Sometimes brand names become synonymous with the product category, such as Band-Aid, Kleenex, Aspirin, Xerox, and Vaseline.

Although the focus is generally on brand names as the "signifiers of brands," other identifiers can be as, or more, important.[2] Examples include the color pink associated with such diverse products as the London-based Financial Times, and fiberglass batt insulation from Dow Corning (United States) and ACI (Australia). Other well-known identifiers are the shape of the bottles for Coca-Cola and Absolut vodka,[3] Betty Crocker, Wendy the "Snapple Lady," the Cadillac duck, the Taco Bell Chihuahua, the Nike swoosh, the Gerber baby, the Pillsbury doughboy, the Merrill Lynch bull, and the King of Spades for Raja condoms in Bangladesh.[4]

Today, there is no necessary relationship between a brand offered for sale by an organization and the production/operations necessary to deliver the products/service identified by the brand.[5] Most distribution companies, such as retailers, do not manufacture the private-label products they sell, but for manufacturing firms, the range of operations that might be conducted by the brand owner is very broad (Figure 11.2). They include:

- Totally integrated production facilities such as Ford's River Rouge plant to produce the Model T
- Assembly of subcomponents produced by other organizations, such as personal computers and contemporary automobiles
- Virtually no responsibility for production other than setting and monitoring adherence to quality control standards. Examples include Perdue chicken, Nintendo game cartridges, Nike sports shoes, and many designer products such as Ralph Lauren and Tommy Hilfiger

In some industries, contract manufacturing is a fast-growth phenomenon. For example, in 1999, over 10% of electronics hardware was contract manufactured (growth rate 20% p.a.) as traditional firms focused on marketing and innovation (R&D), viewing manufacturing as a service function.[6]

Example: A particularly interesting example of disconnecting the brand from the product is Yanni. A popular entertainment product, the Yanni name, the Yanni look (dark shag haircut, big droopy moustache, billowy shirts) and the "New Age" music he represents was developed through standard marketing techniques before a performer was ever hired. Early on, three different men were hired to tour simultaneously as Yanni. In January 1998, there were six Yannis on the 200-concert "Tribute" tour, including the Uzbeki Yanni who tours exclusively in the former Soviet Union.[7]

If the brand does not fulfill the function of identifying the producing organization, it is important to ask the question: What functions does a brand fulfill?

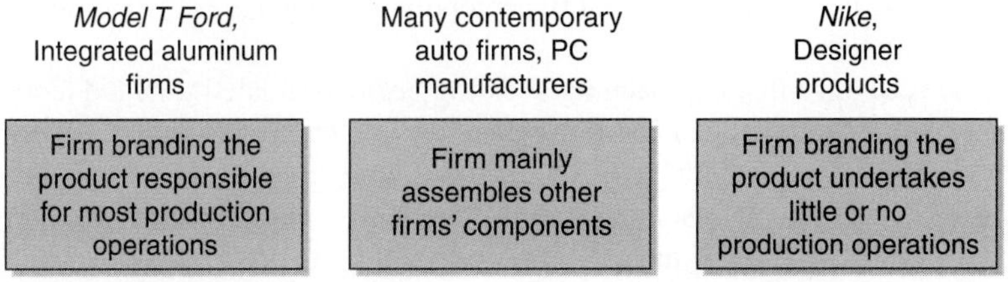

Model T Ford, Integrated aluminum firms	*Many contemporary* auto firms, PC manufacturers	*Nike,* Designer products
Firm branding the product responsible for most production operations	Firm mainly assembles other firms' components	Firm branding the product undertakes little or no production operations

FIGURE 11.2

Relationship between Production and Branding

THE FUNCTIONS OF BRANDS

Brands fulfill many functions for both sellers and buyers. For buyers, these functions may be summarized as follows: Positive brand associations, implying positive attitudes and intentions to purchase, may induce approaching behavior, such as trial or purchase. Conversely, negative associations, implying negative attitudes and intentions-to-not-purchase, may induce avoiding behavior and product rejection. Typically, sellers intend to induce positive attitudes and approaching behavior. However, brands may also create unintended consequences, such as negative attitudes and avoiding behavior.[8]

For Buyers

For buyers, brands fulfill functions that offer both prepurchase and postpurchase benefits. Prepurchase, the brand provides customers with information leading to either approaching or avoiding behavior. For example, because of information contained in brand names or other signifiers, positive or negative attitudes toward brand alternatives reduce search costs by identifying specific products within a product group. Such identification may lead directly to approaching or avoiding behavior.

An individually branded product or service may elicit either approaching or avoiding behavior, based on the buyer's expectations that functional, psychological, or economic benefits will, or will not, be forthcoming. Thus if potential customers concerned with functional benefits expect acceptable (or better) product/service quality from a brand, such as overnight delivery from Federal Express or high quality from Lexus automobiles, purchase risk is reduced, positive attitudes are induced, and approaching behavior will result. Alternatively, if they expect unacceptable quality, such as from Yugo automobiles, negative attitudes and avoiding behavior will be forthcoming. If a product is not branded, the supplier is not identifiable. In such cases, purchasers are not the supplier's customers; rather, they are customers of a commodity and the supplier is completely substitutable.

Customers may seek psychological benefits such as status and prestige from a brand. These include the American Express platinum card, Air Jordan sneakers, and most fashion products such as those from Dior, Gucci, and Armani. Furthermore, brand purchase may reduce the social and psychological risk of acquiring the "wrong" product for a gift, such as the famous Tiffany blue box or Steuben glassware, because of their prestige. In each case, positive attitudes and approaching behavior will likely result. Conversely, brands can generate negative attitudes and lead to avoiding behavior by offering buyers psychological liabilities, such as the U.S. regional airline, ValueJet, following its 1998 Florida crash.

Finally, for potential customers who seek economic benefits, positive attitudes and approaching behavior can result from a perception that the brand is associated with low prices; negative attitudes, and avoiding behavior, if the perception is converse. However, complications with this relationship may occur if there is a perception of positive price/quality relationships. Thus low price perception leading to positive attitudes and approaching behavior may be offset by low quality perception leading to negative attitudes and avoiding behavior, and vice versa.

It is important to recognize that approaching/avoiding behavior related to brand identification may be product-specific for an individual brand. For example, for many Americans, Tide detergent engenders positive attitudes and approaching behavior. However, because of Tide's strong association with detergents, negative attitudes and avoiding behavior would likely result if the products Tide toothpaste or Tide cookies were introduced.

Post-purchase, the brand offers psychological benefits, such as status, positive feelings associated with consumption, assurance that the product will continue to deliver functional benefits at expected ownership costs, and so forth. The brand has long-lasting importance over the buyer's ownership span, particularly if its use or possession is evident to others.

For Sellers

The basic function that the brand fulfills for sellers is the development of positive attitudes and encouragement of approaching behavior by buyers. Positive attitudes and approaching behavior may result from previous use, positive endorsement from other buyers, positive associations developed by seller communications, and so forth. The more positive customer attitudes and the greater the degree of approaching behavior, the greater firm sales and, providing brand costs are not excessive, profits. Indeed, brands are often a firm's most valuable assets[9]:

> **Example:** "Our biggest asset is four letters, S-o-n-y. It's not so much our buildings or our engineers or our factories, but our name."[10]

This potential for generating positive attitudes and approaching behavior follows the manner in which the brand is positioned in the market and the meaning the brand conveys to buyers. The brand's positioning in a market segment constrains the set of marketing implementation decisions. Thus positioning sets parameters on the level of product quality, the range of prices, distribution decisions, service levels, and the broad parameters of promotion strategy. Positive attitudes and approaching behavior are enhanced if there is both coherence between positioning and the set of implementation actions, as well as among the individual implementation actions. A brand positioned as high prestige would certainly lose credibility if product quality, service levels, and prices were all low. In addition, even if all these elements were consistent with the positioning but the product was distributed in low-class distribution outlets, a similar result would probably occur.

So-called vertical marketers such as Starbucks in the United States and Haagen Dazs in Europe understand the need for coherence between positioning and implementation, and use it to their advantage in operating their retail outlets. Auto companies, on the other hand, have historically had great difficulty in providing an equivalent brand-enhancing experience in their dealerships. Many models offered under General Motors' brands, such as Chevrolet, Pontiac, and Buick, seem remarkably undifferentiated.[11] Nonetheless, Saturn in the United States and Daewoo in Britain have begun to demonstrate the potential benefits of a coordinated approach, as both brands have focused on enhancing the point-of-sale experience by eliminating the haggling that some consumers find unpleasant, if not disturbing.

Specifically, successful branding leads to:

- positive attitudes and intentions to purchase
- product purchase
- repeat purchase of individual products
- purchase of other similarly branded items through cross-selling
- easier introduction of similarly branded new products inasmuch as customers are typically more willing to try a new product if the brand engenders positive attitudes and approaching behavior
- leverage in distribution channels and competitive barriers

A less often discussed function of brands for sellers is the role they play in aligning the firm to deliver some combination of functional, psychological, and economic value to customers in the marketplace. Not only should the brand offer a promise to customers, it should also serve as a motivational force to encourage employees and related third-party organizations, for example, advertising agencies, to undertake the necessary actions to deliver on that promise.[12]

THE CONCEPT OF BRAND EQUITY

Brand equity is a difficult concept to grasp, in part because of considerable definitional problems. The currently accepted definition of brand equity is:

> ". . . a set of brand assets and liabilities linked to a brand, its name and symbol, that add to (or subtract from) the value provided by a product or service to a firm and/or that firm's customers." (Aaker 1991)[13]

The assets and liabilities Aaker discusses include brand awareness, brand loyalty, perceived quality, brand associations and image (or brand personality), use satisfaction, and other proprietary assets such as patents, trademarks, and channel relationships.[14] This set can also include brand resilience, which is related to brand loyalty.

> **Example:** In the mid-1980s, although Tylenol market share plummeted to zero as the brand was withdrawn following a cyanide poisoning scare, it rebounded quickly when distribution and promotional activities recommenced. By contrast, Perrier, which suffered a similar problem related to benzene contamination several years later, has never recovered its pre-eminent position. Clearly, of the two brands, Tylenol demonstrated much greater resilience.

The basic problem with Aaker's pioneering definition of brand equity is that it confuses the beneficiary of the value of "the set of assets and liabilities" as it states that the value is provided "to a firm and/or," to "that firm's customers." It seems reasonable to question the usefulness of a definition of brand equity that envisages value that may be provided both to the firm *and* its customers, provided to the firm *but not* its customers, or provided to customers *but not* to the firm.

In addition, the listed set of assets and liabilities seems to represent disproportionately values for the firm rather than values for individual customers. For example, it is clearly valuable for the firm when a customer is brand loyal, for typically a lower ratio of marketing expense is necessary to support a given volume of sales. However, the value of brand loyalty to an individual customer is less clear. Positive value flows from the brand's ability to fulfill the functions discussed in the previous section, reduction of search cost, and expectations of securing functional, psychological, or economic benefits. However, brand loyalty may also have a negative aspect for customers to the extent that it impedes the search for other, more attractive options.

There is a clear delineation between brand equity as value to the organization and brand equity as value to the customer. Rather than focus on a single notion of brand equity, it is more useful to consider two related concepts: organizational brand equity and customer brand equity.

Organizational Brand Equity

Organizational brand equity is related to the brand's ability to attract customers, now and in the future; hence, the firm receives a series of cash flow streams.[15] Organizational brand equity is not constrained by current products, product lines, or by current customers. One of the major contributions of this equity concept is that it both admits and endorses the notion that the brand may have customer-attracting properties in its own right, over and above any particular product or set of products to which it is currently attached.

> **Examples:** In the mid-1990s, the brand name Pan Am, unattached to any aircraft, was sold for several million dollars.
>
> In 1997, Ralph Lauren's Polo brand raised roughly $767 million in an initial public offering (IPO), despite having negligible tangible assets.[16]
>
> In the late 1990s, the value of Amazon.com, the Internet bookseller also with few tangible assets, was several times that of Barnes and Noble, its long-established, conventional rival. This experience was replicated with other Internet companies, such as America Online and Yahoo!.

Relatedly, the organizational brand equity for the entire set of firm brands may be viewed as the difference between the firm's market value and its balance sheet book value.[17,18] A related perspective holds that organizational brand equity is a function of the difference between the price paid for the branded product and the price of an identical unbranded generic product.[19]

Organizational brand equity may also turn negative. Under such circumstances, the rational economic decision should be to cease the current mode of operations.

> **Example:** In the early 1990s, after Encyclopedia Britannica turned down a Microsoft approach to produce a digital version of its encyclopedia, Microsoft developed Encarta. Within 18 months, Encarta became the world's best selling encyclopedia. When Britannica approached Microsoft to reconsider the deal, it was informed that Microsoft research showed that Encyclopedia Britannica had negative brand equity and that it would have to pay Microsoft to use its name on a Microsoft product![20]

Customer Brand Equity

Customer brand equity is a separate and distinct, though related, concept to organizational brand equity. Customer brand equity is the value that an individual customer receives from a branded product or service, over and above the value received from an identical, unbranded (generic) product or service. This value may be greater than the price difference between the branded and generic product as individual customers may be willing to pay more than the asking price for the branded product.

The extent to which customer brand equity is positive for substantial numbers of customers is basically a reflection of the nurturing of trust between the brand owner and its customers, both current and newcomers. Anecdotal evidence suggests that, as with interpersonal trust, customer brand equity is generally built up slowly over time, but is fragile and can be quickly dissipated by negative information generated by managerial mishaps. Many companies in recent years were made acutely aware of the consequences of deterioration in customer's perceptions of these relationships. For example, Audi cars were alleged to have slipped into gear causing several deaths. Adverse side effects were reported from Dow Corning breast implants, and the Firestone 500 tire failed prematurely.[21] Intel's first Pentium chip made incorrect calculations, and Perrier water contained product impurities.

Yet, properly managed, the impact on organizational brand equity of properly nurtured customer brand equity can be extremely long-lasting, as shown in Table 11.1.

In the liquor industry, the 100 leading brands have an average age of over 100 years. The recognition that customer brand equity, often slow to build up, can endow long-term advantages to the brand owner raises serious and basic questions about such management practices as organization structure, job design, executive development, performance measurement, and promotion in many companies.

High customer brand equity does not just happen. Maintaining and building customer brand equity requires unswerving attention to customers, including building a customer-responsive culture that focuses specific attention on customer-contact personnel. In most cases, management carefully builds and nurtures its brands over a number of years, using a variety of brand-building activities such as advertising, public relations, product giveaways, increased service, product improvement, channel support, customer reward systems, and price maintenance.[22] However, as the pace of change increases, in some industries such as those related to the Internet, strong brands may be developed relatively quickly, such as AOL, Yahoo!, Java and Amazon.com.[23] Equally, such fast change can also cause brands to die quickly.

Just as some decisions can lead to enhanced customer brand equity, other decisions can exploit brand equity and cause it to decline. Activities that typically lead to reductions in customer brand equity are product proliferation, price-cutting, discounts and promotions,

TABLE 11.1 Leading US Brands, 1925 and 1999

Product	Leading Brand 1925	Position 2000
Batteries	Eveready	Leader
Biscuits	Nabisco	Leader
Breakfast cereal	Kellogg	Leader
Cameras	Kodak	Leader
Canned fruit	Del Monte	Leader
Chewing gum	Wrigley	Leader
Chocolates	Hershey	Leader
Flour	Medal	Leader
Paint	Sherwin-Williams	Leader
Razors	Gillette	Leader
Sewing machines	Singer	Leader
Shortening	Crisco	Leader
Soap	Ivory	Leader
Soft drink	Coca-Cola	Leader
Soup	Campbell	Leader
Tea	Lipton	Leader
Tires	Goodyear	Leader
Toothpaste	Colgate	Leader

T.S. Wurster, "The Leading Brands," *Perspectives*, Boston, MA: The Boston Consulting Group, and research by Ting Wu.

lower-price component substitution, channel downsizing and proliferation, and channel/supplier squeezing. In the quest for increases in volume, market share, and even profit, management may take actions that harm customer brand equity.[24]

> **Example:** In early 2000, sales of "cool" sportswear brand Tommy Hilfiger stalled. Observers attributed its problems to using the brand in too many product categories (including linens and infant clothes) and excessively broad distribution embracing over 10,000 department stores and discount outlets.[25]

> **Example:** In discussing IBM CEO Lou Gerstner's tenure as head of the charge card business at American Express, where a high premium was placed on customer brand equity, Shelly Lazarus of Ogilvy and Mather said: "I learned a big lesson from Lou. Once you've set a strategy, you never *ever* violate it. Nobody ever got a free card, a discounted card, bundled pricing. Lou would say: 'This is a violation of the brand, and we're not doing it.'"[26]

The Relationship between Organizational Brand Equity and Customer Brand Equity

Although there is no necessary direct relationship between high customer brand equity and high organizational brand equity, in general if customer brand equity is high for substantial numbers of customers, we would expect organizational brand equity to be high as well.

> **Example:** In 1983, Toyota and General Motors formed the Fremont, California, joint venture called New United Motor Manufacturing Inc. (NUMMI). From 1989 on, it manufactured two almost identical cars: Toyota Corolla and Geo Prism (GM). Over the next several years, the Toyota sold at a premium. It also depreciated more slowly so that after five years, its second-hand value was almost 18% more than the GM car.
>
> The effect of Toyota's brand strength on profit was substantial. From 1990–1994, both cars cost about the same to produce—$10,300. Toyota sales, priced to dealers at

$11,100, averaged 200,000 per annum; GM sales averaged 80,000 per annum at $10,700. As a result, Toyota made $128 million more operating profits from NUMMI than GM, and Toyota dealers made $107 million more than GM dealers.[27]

For customers to receive benefits from the brand, and for firms to reap the value of their brand equity, the brand must be available to customers. For example, in the late-1980s in Eastern Europe, Pepsi was the best-known cola brand, yet because local distribution was not in place, it secured little sales volume.

The distinction between customer and organizational brand equity was well illustrated in a simple Internet search experiment.[28] Internet sites for six brands of automobile (Ford, BMW, Lotus, Toyota, Morgan, Volvo) were identified and classified as either official (manufacturer, distributor, reseller) or enthusiast (clubs, individuals). The development of enthusiast sites may be viewed as a proxy for high customer brand equity.[29] Across the brands, Ford and Toyota had a high percentage of official sites; Lotus and Morgan had a high degree of enthusiast sites; Volvo and BMW fell in between. Clearly, the level of customer brand equity differs markedly across the automobile brands.

Whereas customer brand equity essentially focuses on the individual customer's willingness to pay a price more than some benchmark for the branded product, organizational brand equity is concerned also with the number of customers willing to pay that price. Thus in many product categories, one product may have high customer brand equity but low organizational brand equity, whereas another product may have low customer brand equity but high organizational brand equity. For example, a bottle of Lafitte Rothschild selling in the United States for over $100 per bottle can be said to have high customer brand equity for those customers willing to pay the high offering price, but low organizational brand equity because of relatively low volume. Conversely, Gallo wine has low customer brand equity, since consumers are unwilling to pay more than its relatively low price, but high organizational brand equity because of extremely high volume.

The distinction between organizational brand equity and customer brand equity was vividly demonstrated in the April 1993 Marlboro Friday incident, when Philip Morris dramatically cut prices on its cigarette brands by up to 20% in an effort to stem market share loss to generic cigarettes. Although previously many consumers were buying Philip Morris' brands, presumably believing they were receiving sufficient value (customer brand equity) for the prices they were paying, the loss of customers was reducing Philip Morris' organizational brand equity. When prices were reduced, sales increased substantially and the erosion of organizational brand equity was stemmed. KTNT Communications of Fort Worth, Texas, developed a strategy that clearly demonstrates the difference between organizational brand equity and customer brand equity:

> **Example:** In operated-assisted, long-distance calls, the caller is typically asked which long distance carrier they want to use. Most callers (97%) choose AT&T, Sprint, or MCI; the remaining 3% say something like: "just pick one," "I don't know," "I don't care," "you choose," or "whoever." KTNT registered over 40 of these apathetic expostulations and thus secured long-distance phone business despite the fact that, in Texas, KTNT's rates are two thirds higher than AT&T's. KTNT's many names have considerable brand equity for KTNT. However, since customers are not aware that they are selecting a branded service, there is zero or even negative customer brand equity.[30]

It was indicated earlier that brands with negative organizational brand equity should consider ceasing operations. However, brands may possess substantial negative customer brand equity for groups of consumers, yet still prove viable because of sufficient customers for which customer brand equity is positive.[31] For example, even before the tragedy of TWA Flight 800, many people associated TWA with negative customer brand equity and refused to fly the airline because of the age of its planes. Nonetheless, the airline continued operations because sufficient numbers of people associated TWA with positive customer brand equity.[32]

MEASURING BRAND EQUITY

Organizational Brand Equity

Measurement of organizational brand equity is necessary for several different reasons:[33]

- For acquisitions and divestitures of companies and organizational units, a numerical value of brand equity is very important.
- Firms developing strategies to manage their brand portfolios and improve the value of organizational brand equity need measurement methods to track performance over time.
- Advertising agencies want to demonstrate that reductions in advertising spending reduce brand equity.
- Recognizing the value of these most critical company assets is important for progressive accountants.

FINANCIAL-MARKET METHODS The market value, replacement cost, and earnings methods have the advantage of being congruent with a shareholder value perspective.

The Market Value method views organizational brand equity as the difference between market value, and balance sheet book value plus non-brand intangibles, such as patents, know-how, and human resources.[34]

> **Example:** In 1989 Ford paid $2.5 billion for the British car manufacturer Jaguar whose book value was $0.4 billion. The difference, $2.1 billion, placed on Ford's balance sheet as "goodwill," is mainly accounted for by Jaguar's organizational brand equity.

The Replacement Cost method focuses on the anticipated cost to replace the brand, factored by the probability of success.

Earnings Methods use earnings to develop measures of organizational brand equity.[35] For example, the Interbrand Group plc, London, employs two factors: annual after tax profits less expected earnings for an equivalent unbranded product averaged over time, factored by a proprietary developed multiple purporting to measure brand strength. Measures of brand strength are based on several factors:

- **Leadership**: ability to influence the market
- **Stability**: survival ability based on degree of customer loyalty
- **Market**: invulnerability to change of technology and fashion
- **Geography**: ability to cross geographic and cultural borders
- **Support**: consistency and effectiveness of brand support
- **Protection**: legal title

See Figure 11.3 for an illustration of this method for valuing the *Gillette* brand.

Other brands assessed by this method led to the values reported in Tables 11.2A and 11.2B.[37]

These values are of more than academic interest. Because of the problem of goodwill in acquisitions, several countries, including Great Britain, France, Australia, and New

Global sales	= $2.6 billion
Operating income	= $961 million
Estimated operating income from non-branded product line equivalent to Gillette	= $ 49 million
Earnings attributable to Gillette brand	= $912 million
Net income after 35% tax	= $575 million
Brand strength multiple = 17.9	
Estimated value of Gillette brand = $575 million × 17.9	= $10.3 billion

FIGURE 11.3

Illustration of the Interbrand Brand Valuation Method for Gillette[36]

Zealand, allowed companies to place values of acquired brands on their balance sheets as identifiable intangible assets.[38] In December 1997 the U.K. Accounting Standards Board issued FRS 10 on accounting for goodwill and intangible assets in acquisitions. FRS 10 allows that:

- intangible assets, including brands, be recognized separately from purchased goodwill;
- intangible assets believed to have long life, such as brands, do not need to be depreciated;
- the values of intangible assets must be reviewed for impairment at year end, based on economic value.[39]

However, because FRS 10 does not allow the capitalization of internally developed brands, a significant anomaly continues to exist.

Of course, as with any item of value for which a liquid market does not exist, brand valuations may be erroneous.

> **Example:** In 1994, Quaker Oats purchased the Snapple brand of fruit and tea soft drinks for $1.7 billion. Twenty-seven months later, it sold Snapple for $300 million, a loss of $1.4 million which, together with $160 million in operating losses in 1995/1996, amounted to roughly $2 million per day of Quaker's ownership. (Quaker's 1996 sales were $5.2 billion.)[40]

It seems that Snapple's organizational brand equity was not worth the $1.7 billion that Quaker paid.[41]

PRODUCT-MARKET METHODS These methods are based on the extra price commanded by a brand over a generic or unbranded equivalent. Unfortunately, this method has three problems:

- An unbranded equivalent may not exist to make the comparison;
- These methods ignore volume. Profits, after all, are a function of both price and volume, not price alone[42];
- No consideration is given to the potential for brand leveraging, or using the brand for a new product form or category.

Although the financial- and product-market methods provide interesting information, they are not very useful for day-to-day management of organizational brand equity. More appropriate measures relate to the components of brand equity noted earlier and discussed in the next section, and other proprietary assets such as patents, trademarks, and channel relationships. For most ongoing management purposes, changes in these measures are more important than their absolute values. This principle is reflected in the brand health checks (see below) that so many companies have recently put in place.

MANAGEMENT METHODS The basic approach to measurement is to use a "balanced scorecard"[43] approach, based on the components of organizational brand equity noted earlier of brand awareness, perceived quality, brand associations and image, customer satisfaction, and brand loyalty,

It should be clear that some of these components may be necessary, but not sufficient, conditions for high levels of organizational brand equity. Unless purchase is either currently occurring, or could occur at some point in the future, no organizational brand equity will be created. For example, many consumers have a high awareness of Rolls Royce automobiles, believe them to be of exceedingly high quality, have positive brand associations, and positive brand attitudes. Regrettably for Rolls Royce, not many automobile buyers are likely ever to buy or lease one.

Using these components, a series of operational measures of components of organizational brand equity can be constructed.[44]

TABLE 11.2A The Most Valuable Global Brands

Rank (1999)	Brand Name	Country of Origin	Industry	Organizational Brand Equity ($US B)	Brand Value as a Percentage of Market Capitalization
1	Coca-Cola	U.S.	Beverages	83.8	59%
2	Microsoft	U.S.	Software	56.7	21%
3	IBM	U.S.	Computers	43.8	28%
4	General Electric	U.S.	Diversified	33.5	10%
5	Ford	U.S.	Automobiles	33.2	58%
6	Disney	U.S.	Entertainment	32.3	61%
7	Intel	U.S.	Computers	30.0	21%
8	McDonald's	U.S.	Food	26.2	64%
9	AT&T	U.S.	Telecoms	24.2	24%
10	Marlboro	U.S.	Tobacco	21.1	19%
11	Nokia	Finland	Telecoms	20.7	44%
12	Mercedes	Germany	Automobiles	17.6	37%
13	Nescafe	Switzerland	Beverages	17.1	23%
14	Hewlett-Packard	U.S.	Computers	17.1	31%
15	Gillette	U.S.	Personal care	15.9	37%
16	Kodak	U.S.	Imaging	14.8	60%
17	Ericsson	Sweden	Telecoms	14.8	32%
18	Sony	Japan	Electronics	14.2	49%
19	Amex	U.S.	Financial services	12.6	35%
20	Toyota	Japan	Automobiles	12.3	14%
21	Heinz	U.S.	Food	11.8	64%
22	BMW	Germany	Automobiles	11.3	77%
23	Xerox	U.S.	Office equipment	11.3	40%
24	Honda	Japan	Automobiles	11.1	37%
25	Citibank	U.S.	Financial services	9.2	22%
26	Dell	U.S.	Computers	9.0	9%
27	Budweiser	U.S.	Alcohol	8.5	33%
28	Nike	U.S.	Sports goods	8.2	77%
29	Gap	U.S.	Apparel	7.9	39%
30	Kellogg's	U.S.	Food	7.1	52%
31	Volkswagen	Germany	Automobiles	6.6	30%
32	Pepsi-Cola	U.S.	Beverages	5.9	14%
33	Kleenex	U.S.	Personal care	4.6	21%
34	Wrigley's	U.S.	Food	4.4	50%
35	AOL	U.S.	Software	4.4	18%
36	Apple	U.S.	Computers	4.3	77%
37	LouisVuitton	France	Fashion	4.1	34%

THE TASKS
OF MARKETING

TABLE 11.2A (continued)

Rank (1999)	Brand Name	Country of Origin	Industry	Organizational Brand Equity ($US B)	Brand Value as a Percentage of Market Capitalization
38	Barbie	U.S.	Toys	3.8	46%
39	Motorola	U.S.	Telecoms	3.6	15%
40	Adidas	Germany	Sports goods	3.6	15%
41	Colgate	U.S.	Personal care	3.6	18%
42	Hertz	U.S.	Care hire	3.5	75%
43	IKEA	Sweden	Housewares	3.5	*
44	Chanel	France	Fashion	3.1	*
45	BP	U.K.	Oil	2.9	3%
46	Bacardi	Cuba	Alcohol	2.9	*
47	Burger King	U.S.	Food	2.9	8%
48	Moet & Chandon	France	Alcohol	2.8	23%
49	Shell	U.K.	Oil	2.7	2%
50	Rolex	Switzerland	Luxury	2.4	*
51	Smirnoff	Russia	Alcohol	2.3	7%
52	Heineken	Holland	Alcohol	2.2	15%
53	Yahoo!	U.S.	Software	1.8	14%
54	Ralph Lauren	U.S.	Fashion	1.6	66%
55	Johnnie Walker	U.K.	Alcohol	1.6	5%
56	Pampers	U.S.	Personal care	1.4	1%
57	Amazon.com	U.S.	Books	1.4	7%
58	Hilton	U.S.	Leisure	1.3	35%
59	Guinness	Ireland	Alcohol	1.3	4%
60	Marriott	U.S.	Leisure	1.2	52%

*Information not available.

TABLE 11.2B The Most Valuable Global Brand Portfolios

Rank (1999)	Brand Name	Country of Origin	Industry	Organizational Brand Equity ($US B)	Brand Value as a Percentage of Market Capitalization
1	Procter & Gamble	U.S.	Consumer goods	49	52%
2	Johnson & Johnson	U.S.	Consumer goods	48	45%
3	Nestlé	Switzerland	Consumer goods	39	50%
4	Unilever	U.K.	Consumer goods	34	50%
5	L'Oreal	France	Consumer goods	15	49%
6	Diageo	U.K.	Consumer goods	14	41%
7	Colgate-Palmolive	U.S.	Consumer goods	11	56%

Source: Interbrand Group plc.

Awareness   Awareness is important for identification and categorization. Brand awareness is most usefully conceptualized as comprising several levels of respondent behavior in brand recognition and brand recall tests, connoting increasing levels of awareness:

- unaware: no awareness when prompted ("never heard of it")
- recognition: recognition when presented with a list of brands
- aided recall: brand recalled when presented one at a time
- unaided recall: unprompted recall from memory
- top of mind recall: first brand in unprompted recall from memory
- recall dominance: only brand recalled from memory unprompted

Perceived quality   Product/service quality provides customers with functional benefits. Although it may provide the basis for premium pricing, increasing quality in many product categories has led to high quality becoming less a source of competitive advantage and more an entry ticket to the marketplace. Typical tools to measure perceived quality are surveys using high/medium/low quality questions. Because of the relative bluntness of quality measurements, Aaker advocates also using a leadership measure to tap into perceptions of leader, follower, and innovator.[45]

Brand associations   Brand associations are important for product positioning, differentiating products from competition, and extending brands to new product categories. Of course, management needs to know whether the associations that it desires, are, in fact, those held by customers. Typical tools for measuring brand associations are response latencies and surveys.

Customer satisfaction   High levels of customer satisfaction are important because they stimulate repeat purchase. However, even high levels of customer satisfaction may be insufficient to stop customers from switching to alternative suppliers. Customer satisfaction is most often measured by satisfaction/dissatisfaction questions in surveys and focus groups.

Loyalty   Loyalty is related to satisfaction and brings with it repeat business. This is particularly crucial as securing sales from current customers is typically less expensive than securing sales from new customers. Thus it is important to know the reasons for repeat purchase so that decisions can be made to increase loyalty: is it due to habit, obligation, lack of alternatives, attachment, or commitment? Typical tools for measuring brand loyalty are focus groups, surveys, and scanner data (for consumers). Brand loyalty may be conceptualized in a manner similar to awareness:

- negative advocate: strongly negative feelings lead to persuading others against use
- would never use: negative feelings leading to decisive action to use alternatives
- occasional user: occasional use
- brand switcher—not preferred: one of a number of brands purchased from time to time
- brand switcher—preferred: preferred brand but will use others if sufficient inducement
- truly loyal: will always purchase brand if available
- super loyal: will undertake significant search cost to find and purchase brand
- ultra loyal: will undertake significant search cost to find and purchase brand, and will actively suggest use to others

Note that value to the firm of buyers at different loyalty levels in a particular product class is closely related to frequency of purchase. For example, an infrequent ultra loyal buyer may have less value to the firm than a brand switcher—not preferred if the latter customer is a heavy user.

Customer Brand Equity

Customer brand equity is defined as the value an individual customer receives from a branded product or service over and above that received from an identical unbranded product or service. These values are best thought of as associations in the buyer's mind that represent differences between the branded product and its generic equivalent. These values can therefore only be assessed indirectly. One approach is to attempt to measure their economic worth. These methods attempt to identify the price premium an individual or group of individuals would pay for the brand. A second approach is the balanced scorecard. It attempts more inclusive and direct measurement of the value of the customer brand equity.

DOLLAR METRIC   In this direct method, customers are asked how much more they would be prepared to pay for the branded product versus an unbranded product. Similarly, the marginal customer brand equity of one brand over another can be secured by asking how much they would be prepared to pay for one brand or another.

CONJOINT ANALYSIS   In this indirect (trade-off) method, consumers are asked their relative preferences for various product/brand combinations at various prices. One output from such a study is a monetary value associated with each brand. (For an example and more detail on conjoint analysis, see Chapter 4.)

BALANCED SCORECARD   The balanced scorecard approach is much broader and more inclusive. It might include measures such as presence in the customer's consideration set, customer-based perceived quality, preference or satisfaction comparisons of the branded product with a similar generic product, brand associations, and the like.

Whereas measures of organizational brand equity must be conducted at the global level, customer brand equity measures are made at the individual level. As a result, customer brand equity can be developed for individuals, for groups of individuals (such as market segments), or for the market as a whole.

BRAND HEALTH

Although the absolute value of organizational brand equity is important in merger, acquisition, and divestiture activity, for most day-to-day managerial purposes, change in brand equity is a major consideration. A number of leading, fast-moving consumer goods (FMCG) companies have installed a system of brand health indicators to assess the direction of change, if any, in brand equity, and identify key issues that might otherwise pass unnoticed. These systems also help remedy a major defect in measuring brand manager performance, a focus solely on such results as profit, volume, or market share. Such a focus is rather like asking a corporation to show only an income statement. Brand equity is the balance sheet for the brand,[46] and provides assurance that good, short-term results have not been achieved at the expense of the brand's future.[47]

Brand health indicators typically consist of trend measures in areas such as customer purchase behavior, customer perception, marketing support, and profitability. In addition to historic trends, managers can also benchmark their brand's performance against competing brands. When the health of the entire brand portfolio is assessed using the same criteria, management gets a good overview of an entire business unit's or company's brand health. A typical set of brand health measures is displayed in Table 11.3.

A variety of methods is available for securing data to construct these measures. Some data, such as sales, advertising, and profitability, are derived from the firm's accounting system; typically, competitive sales, advertising, and distribution data can be secured from industry focused research suppliers. The perception measures are mostly secured by survey research.

Brand health checks are not a one-time event. The health of a firm's brands should be measured on a periodic basis, such as bi-annually or annually, and the results used to make appropriate changes in the firm's market strategy.

TABLE 11.3 Brand Health Check Measures

Type of Measure	Measure	
Purchasing	Market share	Brand sales versus total market sales (units and dollars)
	Market breadth	Number of customers purchasing the brand
	Market depth	Extent of repeat purchase
Perception	Awareness	Degree of awareness of the brand
	Uniqueness	Is the brand differentiated from competition?
	Quality	Perception of brand quality (actual quality in blind tests is also a useful measure)
	Value	Does the brand provide good value for money?
Marketing support	Advertising	Market share/advertising share
		Advertising/total marketing spend
	Distribution	Extent of distribution coverage in target outlets
		For retail goods, qualtity of display, especially in key accounts
	Relative price	Price compared to competitive brands
Profitability	Profit	Gross margin earned form the brand
		Economic value added (EVA) of the brand

CRITICAL ISSUES FOR THE MANAGEMENT OF BRANDS

The high potential for developing organizational brand equity and its role in determining the market value of corporations suggests that branding decisions should be given high priority by senior management. Management should consider carefully what should be branded and what relationships are desired between and among the corporate brand, product category brands, and individual product brands. Careful planning should be conducted for the evolving brand portfolio, including additions, deletions, and order of introduction. This is an emerging area of research and practice that is becoming known as brand architecture.

These decisions are particularly difficult because developing brand strategy may require dropping brand names that have developed considerable brand equity (both organizational and customer) over many years. In hindsight, one must often question whether management truly understood the value of the original brand. For example, the switch from MasterCharge to MasterCard coincided with a loss in marketshare to Visa, which changed its name from BankAmericard. Nissan squandered considerable equity in dropping its successful Datsun brand for the corporate Nissan brand.

> **Example:** In the mid-1990s, Federated Department Stores merged with R.H. Macy and Company. The newly-formed company combined Abraham and Strauss and Jordan Marsh units to form Macy's East and subsequently dropped both century-old names. Of the Jordan Marsh name change, Hal Kahn, chairman of Macy's East, was quoted as saying: "When a beautiful woman gets married, she takes a new name. And that's all Jordan Marsh is doing, taking the family name."[48]

Of course, many professional women now keep their family names when they marry! One is forced to ask what value Federated may have squandered by excising the Abraham and Strauss and Jordan Marsh brands.

A particularly critical issue in branding strategy is to decide what set of associations, such as personal, lifestyle, or customer type the firm wants to have for each of its various brands. In addition, should these associations be simple or complex? And how should the associations among different brands be integrated with, or differentiated from, each other? These choices are related to the positioning decision in the market strategy and implemented through marketing mix actions.

Just as the success of any strategy is only as good as its implementation, a host of detailed decisions must be appropriately made to execute the branding strategy. For example, brand names must be chosen based on criteria such as legal availability, length, memorability, pronounceability, types of associations, relationship to product features, and so forth. These decisions may take extensive research and can be especially complex if the brand is planned for use in countries with different language systems. Another key issue concerns the visuals used in advertising and packaging associated with the brand. Care must be taken with decisions such as choice of colors, shapes and materials, styles and themes, and the manner in which these are communicated. In the case of vertical marketers like Ben and Jerry's (ice cream), these decisions extend to the design and decor of retail facilities.

Other important issues to consider are strategic decisions about umbrella and multibranding strategies, brand revitalization, brand leveraging, strategic alliances, and global branding.

Umbrella or Multibranding Strategies

Although branding decisions encompass many different dimensions, one particularly important issue concerns the extent to which the firm pursues a multibranding or an umbrella-branding strategy. In a multibranding strategy, the firm selects an individual brand name or names for each of the various product categories in which it competes. As a result of this strategy, target customers may have a high recognition of the firm's various brands, but be relatively unaware of the firm itself. By contrast, a firm pursuing an umbrella branding strategy employs a single brand: either a corporate brand like IBM and Sony, or a family brand like Chevrolet and Plymouth for its various products.[49]

An example of a firm pursuing a multibranding strategy is Procter & Gamble (P&G). Among P&G's brands (product categories) are Sure (underarm deodorant), Crest (toothpaste), Tide (laundry detergent), Cascade (dishwasher detergent), Pringles (snack food), and many others. Furthermore, in a single product category, P&G may offer several brands. For example, in the United States, in addition to Tide, P&G offers seven other brands of laundry detergent—Cheer, Bold, Dreft, Ivory Snow, Gain, Era, and Oxydol. As a result of this multibranding strategy, P&G's brands are far better known to consumers than is P&G. Another example concerns Giant Food, Stop & Shop, BI-LO, Edwards Super Foods Stores and Tops Markets, all owned by Royal Ahold (Dutch), the fourth-largest food retailer in the United States.

Conversely, Yamaha pursues an umbrella-branding strategy. It sells a variety of electronic musical instruments, such as keyboards and guitars, traditional instruments, such as pianos, motorcycles, and even Grand Prix engines under its company name.

Arguments can be made for and against umbrella branding. In favor of umbrella branding, the firm may enjoy economies of scale in advertising and promotion for an individual brand. Furthermore, advertising for an individual product may bring benefits to similarly branded products in other categories. In addition, positive associations from a product in one category may transfer to another. For example, a consumer having a positive experience with a Yamaha piano might believe a Yamaha electric guitar would also be of high quality.

On the other hand, use of a single brand name may limit the firm's ability to target desired market segments and appropriately position its products. As a result, multibranding would be favored.

> **Example:** Both MCI and AT&T offer premium long-distance telephone service under their corporate names. To address the discount market segment, each widely advertises less expensive services: MCI offers 10-10-321 and 10-10-220 (as Telecom USA); AT&T offers Lucky Dog 10-10-345.[50]

In addition, if the product category relationships are too disparate, it might be a stretch to assume that the firm is able to perform equally well in two very different product categories. For example, a consumer may have little belief that Yamaha's strong performance in pianos has any relationship to the quality of its motorcycles.

A related issue is a concern with negative associations. For example, if a firm using an umbrella-branding strategy has a serious problem in one product category, negative associations might transfer to its other products.

> **Example:** In 1980, Procter & Gamble had a serious problem with its Rely brand of tampons. The ultra high absorbency led women to leave the tampon in place for an extended period of time, and many women contracted toxic shock syndrome. Several died. Rely was subsequently withdrawn from the market. Although the marketplace and financial impact on Procter & Gamble was severe, it might have been far worse had the firm employed an umbrella-branding strategy so that negative associations with tampons were transferred to other products.[51]

Brand Revitalization

The marketing landscape is littered with the corpses of once-valuable and famous brands that fell on hard times and disappeared. Of course, sometimes brands should be retired. However, since brands have value in and of themselves and are often major organizational assets, such decisions should be made consciously and not just as a result of managerial neglect.[52]

Most brands need never decline, yet many lose their value for a variety of different reasons—company neglect, affirmative actions to minimize investment and milk brand equity for profits and cash, mismatched positioning as the targeted market segment changes, overall market or market segment decline, and severe competitive pressure.

There is little doubt that as worldwide competitive intensity rises,[53] the economic viability of brands with weaker positions in individual markets, such as positions four and below, will diminish. In Europe today, some supermarkets feature only one or two manufacturer brands per category. Correspondingly, the space devoted to the retailers' own brands has been increasing.

A distinction should be made between revitalizing brands and strategies aimed at increasing sales. Many of the latter were presented in Chapter 10 (and reviewed in Table 11.4) where it was discussed whether or not a market should be viewed as mature.[54] These strategies may help revitalize a brand but, in most cases, brand revitalization is not the key objective. Rather, if it occurs, revitalization is a consequence of the successful pursuit of other objectives, typically sales growth. Of all these approaches, only repositioning is typically conducted with brand revitalization as the major objective.

TABLE 11.4 Summary of Strategies that Can Assist Brand Revitalization

Strategy	Examples
Increasing usage	Cascade dishwasher detergent
New uses	Arm & Hammer baking soda, Bayer aspirin
Enter new markets	Reader's Digest
Brand repositioning	Old Spice, Ovaltine, Burma Shave
Product/service improvement	Xerox, Macintosh computers
Product/service augmentation	IBM adding outsourced services
Obsolete current products	Windows software products
Brand extension	Smith Corona, Harley Davidson

BRAND REPOSITIONING   Repositioning may be achieved in three basic ways: reaching new and attractive market segments, changing associations or adding new associations, and altering the competitive target.

New Market Segments   Reaching out to new market segments is illustrated by the following examples:

> **Example:** A study of the Sears credit card database revealed that core customers were not the expected male hardware buyers, but instead 25- to 50-year-old women with children. In a highly successful repositioning, Sears expanded its offerings of clothing and cosmetics and reoriented its advertising towards women.[55]

A particularly critical situation occurs as consumers move through the life span. Often, the firm has two choices: follow its current customers as they age, or focus major efforts on a younger segment.

> **Example:** When Procter & Gamble acquired Richardson Vicks, Old Spice men's fragrance was a troubled brand. Originally introduced for young people, as they aged, Old Spice was increasingly targeted at an "empty nester" group of consumers; unfortunately, this group was comprised of less heavy users of the product category than young men. In a classic repositioning, Procter & Gamble relaunched Old Spice with a youthful advertising campaign, believing that it would not only attract a different and younger market segment, but that it would still retain many of its older habitual users. Market share improved.[56]

Colgate-Palmolive, Avon, and Reader's Digest have all been successful in reinvigorating their sales growth by increasing their efforts to reach new markets outside the United States.

New Associations   New associations are exemplified by numerous examples. Honda's repositioning of motorcycling, described in the previous chapter, is one noteworthy success, but there are more current illustrations available.

> **Examples:** The British Labor government announced a proposal to rebrand Great Britain. It's intent is to shift the tradition-based British brand from a focus on the past to one on the future by emphasizing an image of youthfulness, excitement, and opportunity.
>
>   Nostalgia marketing is an example of the opposite, wherein inherent brand values may allow a relaunch many years later, in part to appeal to memories and nostalgia. Ovaltine (powdered drink mix), Burma-Shave (shaving cream), and the Goodwood Revival Meeting (motor racing)[57] are recent examples.

Changing Competitive Targets   New competitive targets may reflect a fundamental change of mission or a simple realignment within a product class. Examples of a change of mission concern the indirect competitive threat discussed in previous chapters.

> **Example:** As the PC market has begun to mature in North America, Canadian PC manufacturer, IPC, advertises its PC, complete with large screen, speakers, and DVD player, as The Ultimate Home Entertainment Package.
>
>   Much of the sales growth of Bacardi light rum, the best-selling branded liquor in the world, has come from targeting other liquors, such as vodka or scotch, rather than other rums.

Repositioning is the prime means of brand revitalization. However, the best way to retain brand vitality is to continue to innovate. In particular, a rapid rate of new product introduction is a proven way to pre-empt the need for "revitalization." Intel provides a clear example of this principle in action and, whereas it historically pursued its strategy under the umbrella of the corporate brand name, more recently it has shown a similar commitment under the Pentium label.

Brand Extensions: Leveraging Customer Brand Equity

The determinants of customer brand equity are related to the functions fulfilled by the brand: reduction of search cost and expectations of securing various types of benefits. Marketers have traditionally espoused the idea that these functions can be extended within a product category via relatively minor product changes, such as color, flavor (Jello), size, shape, and physical form (Tylenol). These flankers may increase the branded product's sales and market share while fulfilling a valuable defensive role; sometimes, they are given a different brand name.

A much newer phenomenon has been the increasing number of attempts to place brands into product classes other than those with which they have been traditionally associated. This brand leveraging is of significantly greater scope than traditional flanking and, if successful, may contribute to brand revitalization. However, brand leveraging should not be confused with "umbrella branding," in which the entire branding strategy is based on a single umbrella brand.

Recent examples of brand leveraging are legion; they range from branding in related product categories, to branding in seemingly unrelated product categories. Examples of extending brands into related products are Flora, a well-known U.K. margarine brand extended into synthetic cheeses, dressings, and mayonnaise; and Smith Corona, a company most associated with typewriters, into cordless telephones, fax machines, and other communications products.[58] Examples of branding extensions into unrelated categories are Harley Davidson into restaurants, armchairs and toys, and Coca-Cola into products such as beach towels, boxer shorts, baby clothes, earrings, and fishing lures. In general, when the brand is extended into related product categories, the firm maintains control of the marketing effort; by contrast, branding extensions into unrelated categories are typically accomplished through licensing agreements in which the licensee has responsibility for all marketing efforts.

WHY LEVERAGE?   Two main factors drive brand leveraging: increased profits and the cost of developing new brands. The increased profits rationale occurs especially in unrelated product categories where the brand owner licenses use of the brand to another manufacturer, typically under quality control guidelines.[59] In addition to license fees, the brand owner may reap second-order benefits of increased brand awareness and the ability to address a different group of customers.

The second driver is often found in consumer products where the cost to launch a new brand in the United States now ranges from $50 to $100 million. Aaker uses similar estimates to point out that at $100 million per launch and success rates of around 25%, the expected cost of launching a successful newly-branded product is around $400 million! As these entry barriers have risen, marketers seeking to lower entry costs into new product categories have explored the possibility of extending brands from their traditional product categories into new category arenas.[60]

LEVERAGING: APPROACHES AND ISSUES   Brand extensions are likely to be successful to the extent that the new product secures instant awareness from the brand and that positive associations transfer to the new product inducing positive attitudes, intentions to buy, and product trial. Based on extensive study, Ed Tauber, a long-time student of branding, identified seven different approaches (Table 11.5).[61]

However, although leveraging an existing brand may appear to be an efficient method of entering new product categories, it may not be effective. The underlying problem is the relationship between the old and new product categories. Unless the set of associations between the brand and the two product categories is sufficiently strong, customer brand equity from the old category may not transfer to the new category sufficiently well to lead to successful launch.[62]

As discussed earlier, positive attitudes and an approaching relationship in one product category may even give rise to negative attitudes and avoiding behavior in the new product category. This can occur if customers believe the firm has insufficient expertise or is stretched too

TABLE 11.5 Approaches to Brand Extensions

Approach to Brand Extensions	Examples
Same product, different form	Ocean Spray cranberries to cranberry juice cocktail, Dole pineapples to pineapple sauce
Distinctive component/ingredient	Arm & Hammer cat litter, Philadelphia cream cheese salad dressing
Companion product	Kodak batteries for cameras, Aunt Jemima pancake syrup (formerly just pancake mix)
Customer franchise	Harley Davidson restaurants, Coca-Cola clothing
Expertise	Sony Discman (electronics), Bic disposable pens (low cost manufacturing)
Common benefit or attribute	Lysol for deodorizing the air, toilet bowl, tile; Ivory mildness in soap and shampoo
Designer/ethnic image	Ralph Lauren sunglasses, Ferrari watches

thin in its quest to produce quality or economic products. Furthermore, the psychological benefits received from the brand in one product category may lead to psychological liabilities for another product category as, for example, a Harley Davidson line of candies.[63]

Perhaps a more serious issue than failure of these new products is brand dilution, the potential for harming the equity of the brand and affecting sales of the original product by a series of failures of leveraged new product entries. This is an especially serious issue for companies that license their brand names to third party organizations for production and marketing branded products. Because of the potential for reducing the brand's asset value, companies such as AT&T have "brand police" organizations to protect their brands.

The strength of existing brand associations can be a serious issue when corporate acquisitions either do not include brand assets, or when the brand can be used for only a short time period. For example, the Philips/Lucent alliance for telephones was only able to use the AT&T brand for a few years. The difficulty of transferring positive associations from an existing brand to a new brand was highlighted several years ago in the well-publicized $300 million acquisition by Black & Decker (B&D) of the small appliance (housewares) business from General Electric (GE). In this case, the strength of existing associations made it difficult for new associations to take root.

Example: As part of the acquisition, B&D was able to use the GE brand name for five years, after which it would revert to General Electric. During that period, B&D spent over $100 million on advertising and promotion for the Black & Decker brand of home appliances. The result of this effort was that consumers still believed GE to be the housewares market leader. The associations of Black & Decker (male, outdoors) and GE (female, indoors), noted in Figure 11.4, provide an indication of why Black & Decker's task was so difficult.

Relatedly, when Enron was investigating entry into the U.S. retail electricity market, it sought information from consumers on various electricity suppliers. A consumer sample was asked the question, "If you had to select a supplier of electricity other than your current supplier, who would you choose?" Demonstrating the value of its brand, the firm most often chosen was General Electric; GE last produced electricity over 100 years ago![64]

The strength of some well-established brand associations has led whole companies to change their names to that of the better-known brand. In the U.K., United Scientific Holdings changed its name to Alvis (the automobile brand); in the U.S., Consolidated Foods became Sara Lee (packaged foods).

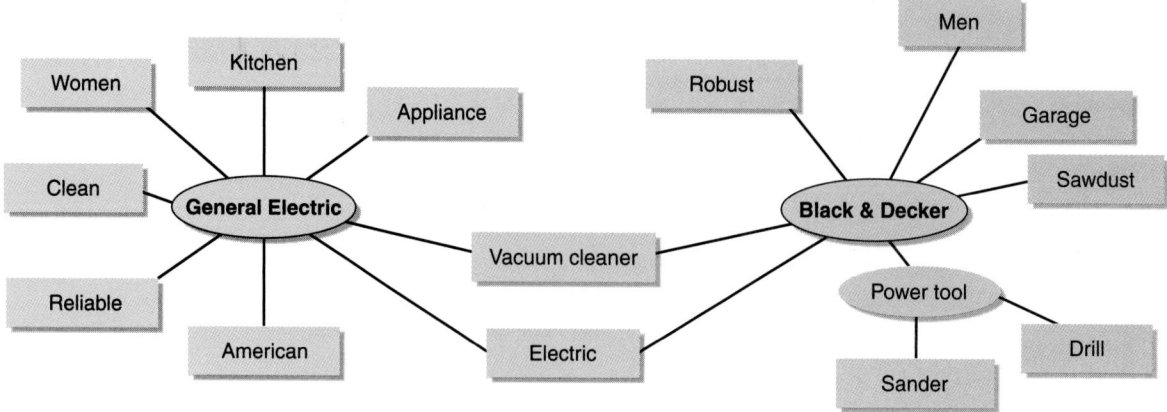

FIGURE 11.4

Example of Brand Associations

SHOULD THE FIRM LEVERAGE? At root, the decision of whether or not to attempt leveraging an existing brand for a new (to the firm) product category requires answers to several questions. Business environment and company-related factors determine whether an opportunity exists, regardless of branding issues. For example, is there sufficient potential demand? How strong is competition? Can the market be accessed through current distribution channels? Can the firm secure sufficient product supply (internal or outsourced)? Does the firm possess other required competencies? Consumer perceptions of the current and extension product categories, and the brand must also be considered:

- Do consumers perceive a fit between the core and extension product categories in terms of product features and concepts?
- What is the relationship between brand associations from the core product and potential associations from the extension?
- What is the reverse relationship between potential brand associations from the extension and brand associations from the core product?
- What, if any, is the role of the corporate brand in these various associations?

For brand extensions to be viable, the original brand must have a series of strong positive associations, and the difference between the brand and the extension should not be so extreme as to be incongruous. Brand extensions tend to fail when the association between the old and new product is not obvious, or when the original brand has a unique image. In other cases, a dominant brand already exists in the product category, or the quality of the new product is less than existing products with the same brand name.

However, it is quite possible for brand associations to be positive, for the brand to have high market share, for the proposed extension to be in the same product category, but for an extension to be inappropriate.

Example: Gallo is the largest selling American wine brand; however, research demonstrated that it was associated with inexpensive wines. As a result, to compete with Kendall-Jackson Vintner's Reserve Chardonnay, the fast-growing second-placed wine in the premium varietal market, it sought to distance itself from the Gallo name by introducing a totally new brand, Turning Leaf. Backed by extensive market research, and strong advertising and promotion, the new brand has been successful.

A particularly interesting case of brand leveraging is Virgin. Originally introduced as a brand of recorded music, Virgin Records, CEO Richard Branson initially extended the Virgin name to the airline business by launching Virgin Atlantic Airways. More recently,

Branson has launched a series of Virgin businesses, including Virgin Megastores (retail distribution), Virgin Direct (financial services), Virgin Publishing (books), Virgin Sound and Vision (educational computer software), and Virgin Hotel. Although the product categories contain few direct associations, the ability to use the Virgin name seems to be related to a higher-order sense of fun-loving, anti-establishment underdogness. In this regard, the attention given to Virgin's highly-publicized, successful legal battle against British Airlines as well as Branson's own activities, such as attempting an around-the-world balloon fight, have been highly supportive of these associations.[65]

However, some observers have criticized these extensions as random and capricious, noting that several new ventures have failed. Indeed, Virgin's entry into the British railroad business has brought complaints of poor punctuality which, if not addressed, could seriously impact Virgin's brand equity.[66]

Strategic Alliances

Strategic alliances range in type from informal or contractual working relationships, to the development of new organizations as legal joint ventures. Strategically, alliances are typically competency based, wherein the strengths of one party compensate for the weaknesses of the other, and vice versa. However, because the interests of the parties tend to diverge over time, the historical record of success of strategic alliances is not stellar.[67]

Obviously, the co-branding implications of strategic alliances are considerable. For example, Disney and McDonald's co-branded for the movie Hercules. In addition, they may be helpful for new businesses. The founder of Calyx and Corolla, a direct marketer of fresh flower delivery in the United States, stated bluntly that she would never have attempted to start her business without a firm delivery arrangement with Federal Express. She believed that leveraging the brand equity of Federal Express was essential to establishing the credibility of her start-up. Similarly, the agreement of many Intel PC-manufacturing customers to co-brand *intel inside* implicitly recognizes that their customers' brand associations are favorable, and lead to positive attitudes and approaching behavior.

Co-branding with customers is becoming more common as both suppliers and customers recognize its potential advantages. Co-branding by synthetic fiber manufacturers, such as Courtaulds, DuPont, ICI Fibres, Monsanto, and Rhone-Poulenc, with their customers for apparel, carpets, and other household textiles has been a standard practice for many years. Furthermore, two of the world's most profitable steel companies, BHP Steel and British Steel Corporation (BSC), have successfully co-branded with some of their customers.

Notwithstanding the positive benefits of co-branding, management should be concerned with the potential for customer confusion and loss in brand equity when disparate brands from different organizations are co-joined. The difficulties of brand leveraging were discussed previously at length, but at least in those cases all relevant decisions are under the firm's control. In co-branding situations, management has control over the associations linked to its own brand, but little or no control over the associations linked to its co-brand partner. The question arises, for example, how conservative bankers, whose credit cards are co-branded with Visa, react to Visa's strong attack advertisements directed at American Express.

A special case of co-branding occurs when the firm employs its own multiple brands on a single product. As indicated earlier, the basic goal is to secure for the product the benefit from a family or corporate brand. However, if the new product is positioned for a different segment than the family or corporate brand, this brand may detract from the new product.

Example: In the United States, Holiday Inn has dropped the Holiday Inn name from advertising for its upscale Crowne Plaza hotels. It found that this association was negatively impacting Crowne Plaza's positioning. However, in Asia, where the Crowne Plaza brand is less strong, it continues to associate Crowne Plaza with Holiday Inn.

Global Branding

Multinational companies should approach multinational branding decisions in a strategic manner, rather than as uncoordinated or incremental issues. Some issues in international branding are similar to the umbrella or multibranding decision discussed earlier, but globalization increases the potential for using similar branding elements worldwide.

Several arguments can be adduced in favor of developing global brands:

- Consumer tastes are becoming more homogeneous, driven by such visual media as film and television, and increased travel. Furthermore, many corporations are introducing global purchasing systems for which multiple brand names would be confusing.
- Efficiency in communications is enhanced as television stations, such as Star TV in Asia and CNN, are increasingly reaching multinational audiences.
- Economies of scale in advertising, promotional materials, and packaging can be secured. This is an especially important issue for high-cost visual media, such as television commercials where essentially the same advertisements can be used in different countries with voice-overs in different language translations.
- As individual travel continues to expand, sales volume from visiting consumers recognizing both their favorite brands and advertising for those brands is likely to increase.
- The brand may provide important national associations that have global appeal: examples are Rolls Royce (British upper crust), Marlboro (the American West), and Levis (hip, young Americans).

Regardless of these positive arguments, firms contemplating a shift to global branding must consider the transition costs to a global-brand strategy. In some cases, firms have to convert a multiple-brand strategy to global branding. In other cases, a single brand must be repositioned, such as British Airways' (BA) attempt to transform itself from a British Airline with global reach to a global airline based in Britain.[68] Increasingly, examples of successful global branding strategies are becoming evident. The following example is from the retailing industry, typically viewed as domestically oriented.

> **Example:** Hennes and Mauritz (HM), Sweden's fifth-largest company, operates 500 stores in 12 European countries. Sales outside Sweden are 80% of the total, and operating profits have grown by 22% per annum for the past decade. HM attributes its success to a global fashion trend driven by satellite television, movies, music, and the Internet.[69]

One major argument against global branding is the lessened ability to present a "local" appearance and thus tap deeply into individual geographic segments, especially if some degree of xenophobia is driving the purchase of local brands. In addition, if individual national markets are in different stages of development and different product associations would be required to be successful, then different brand names might be more sensible rather than confuse what the brand stands for. In addition, it may be difficult to represent a single brand appropriately in all cultures where the product will be sold. Naming is a particular problem, as the set of letters comprising a brand may have different meanings in various linguistic systems. See Table 11.6 for examples of unfortunate selections of brand names and slogans.[70]

Management must carefully weigh the pros and cons of global versus local branding. Even if global branding is judged appropriate, technical and legal restrictions may prohibit completely uniform implementation of a global brand strategy. In such cases, management should employ those implementation elements of the branding strategy that have global applicability, and make the necessary changes in those jurisdictions where this is not possible.[71]

Adoption of global branding does not imply global implementation of a branding strategy. Tastes may differ around the world leading to product design variations, pricing levels may reflect economic realities in various countries, and distribution and choice of promotion vehicles is frequently country specific. For this reason, many firms are guided by the simple adage, "Think global, act local."

TABLE 11.6 Unfortunate Translations in International Marketing

Company/Product	English	Translation
Chevrolet/car	Nova	"No va": doesn't go (Latin America)
Dairy Association/milk	"Got Milk?"	"Are you lactating?" (Mexico)
Coors/beer	"Turn It Loose"	"Suffer From Diarrhea" (Latin America)
Clairol/curling iron	"Mist Stick"	Mist is slang for manure (Germany)
Colgate/toothpaste	"Cue"	Sounds like "cull," slang for "ass" (France)
Pepsi/cola	"Come Alive With the Pepsi Generation"	"Pepsi Brings Your Ancestors Back From the Grave" (China)
Coca-Cola	Coca-Cola	"Kekoukela"; "Bite the wax tadpole," or "Female horse stuffed with wax" (China)
Perdue/chicken	"It takes a strong man to make a tender chicken"	"It takes an aroused man to make a chicken affectionate" (Latin America)
Parker/pens	"It won't leak in your pocket and embarrass you"	"It won't leak in your pocket and make you pregnant" (Mexico)
American Airlines	"Fly In Leather"	"Fly Naked" (Latin America)
Electrolux/vacuums	"Nothing sucks like an Electrolux" (American)	

Secured from the Internet.

For multinational, multiproduct, multimarket companies, a brand portfolio might be expected, comprising some global brands, some multicountry regional brands, and some national brands with responsibility for brand health placed at different levels in the organization. Furthermore, over time, brands might be expected to migrate in both directions as geographic scope is enhanced for some brands, and diminished for others.

Example: Coca-Cola has four global brands—Classic Coca-Cola/Coca-Cola, Diet Coke/Coke Light, Sprite and Fanta. It also has a variety of soft drink brands specific to regions, mostly supported by local bottlers and often outselling the corporate brands (Table 11.7).

TABLE 11.7 Coca-Cola Soft Drink Brands by Region

Americas	Europe, Middle East, Africa	Asia/Pacific
Cherry Coke	Cherry Coke	Lift
Kinley	Kinley	Ambasa
Kuat	Urge	Kin Cider
Tai	Lilt	Mello
Barq's	Schizan	Krest
Nordic Ginger Ale	Tab	Sarsi
Delaware Punch	Tab X-tra	Lemon & Paeroa
Manzana Lift	Mezzo Mix	
Fresca	Sensun	
Mello Yellow		
Minute Maid		
Mr. Pibb		
Surge		
Citra		
Quatro		

Example: Nestlé manages a four-level brand portfolio: 10 worldwide corporate brands, 45 worldwide strategic brands, 140 regional strategic brands, and 7,500 local brands (see the Nestlé branding tree, Figure 11.5). Individual brands may shift between levels. For example, in recent years, both Findus and Chambourcy have been redefined from worldwide strategic brands to regional strategic brands; conversely, a frozen food expansion into Eastern Europe is likely to be made under the German brand, Maggi.[72]

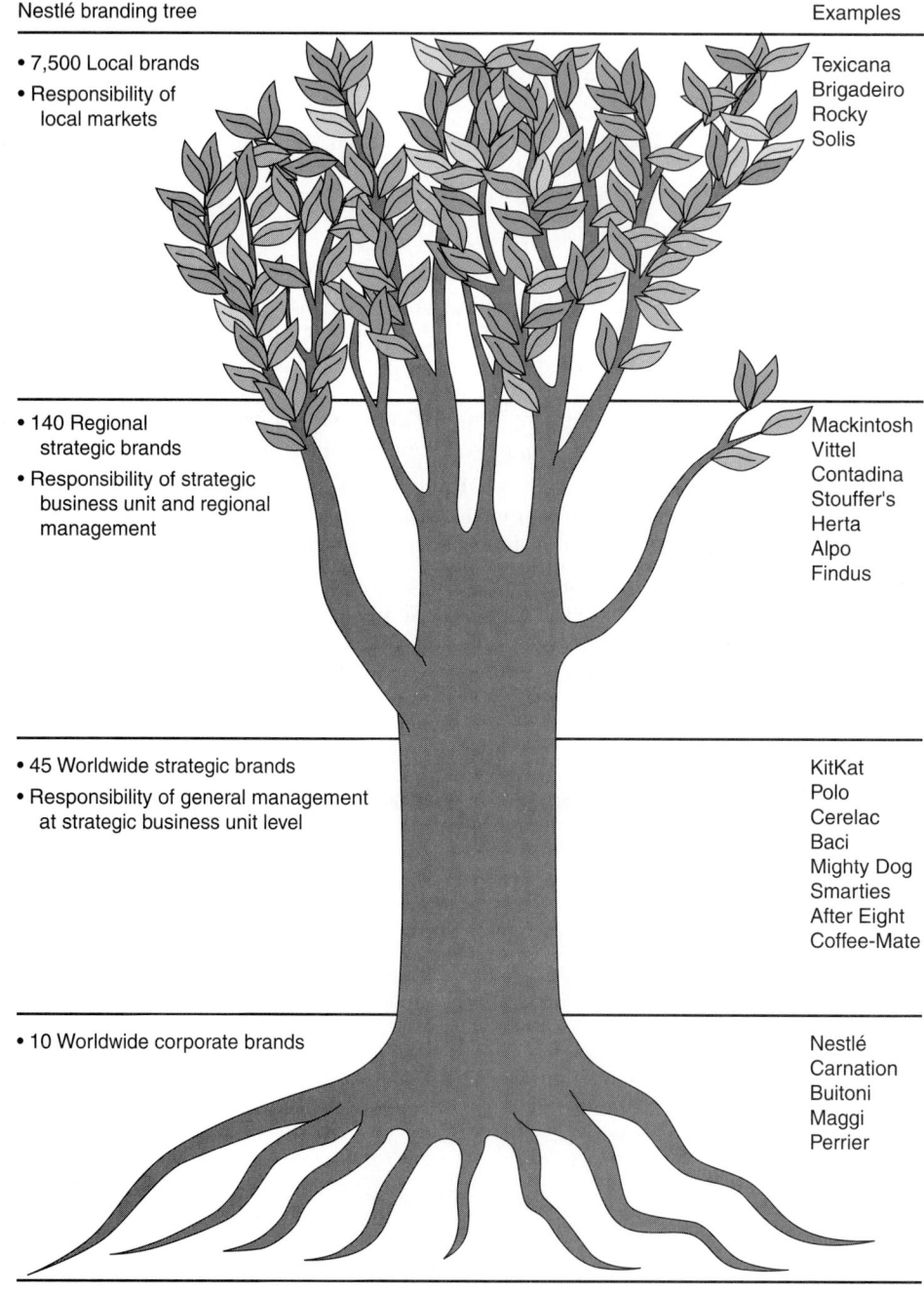

Nestlé branding tree   Examples

- 7,500 Local brands   Texicana
- Responsibility of   Brigadeiro
  local markets   Rocky
                                                        Solis

- 140 Regional   Mackintosh
  strategic brands   Vittel
- Responsibility of strategic   Contadina
  business unit and regional   Stouffer's
  management   Herta
                                                        Alpo
                                                        Findus

- 45 Worldwide strategic brands   KitKat
- Responsibility of general management   Polo
  at strategic business unit level   Cerelac
                                                        Baci
                                                        Mighty Dog
                                                        Smarties
                                                        After Eight
                                                        Coffee-Mate

- 10 Worldwide corporate brands   Nestlé
                                                        Carnation
                                                        Buitoni
                                                        Maggi
                                                        Perrier

FIGURE 11.5

The Nestlé Branding Tree

SUMMARY

This chapter emphasized the critical importance of managing brands for the value of the entire organization. Brands have long-term value, yet what may take many years to develop can be quickly lost through inappropriate managerial decisions. Whereas many organizations have historically focused their strategy making at the product/market or product/market segment level, this chapter's emphasis was on the critical requirement to develop an overarching and consistent brand strategy (sometimes called brand architecture). Such a strategy, targeted at customers and oriented against competitors, may have a significantly longer time horizon than strategies based on individual markets, segments, or products, and must deal with a set of issues that both embrace but also go beyond the product/market perspective.

Many of the examples were drawn from consumer products and services, in part because they are more recognizable to readers, but also because the focus of most research and practice on brands and brand equity has been in the consumer arena. This does not mean to imply, however, that branding issues are not relevant for business-to-business marketing. Companies such as Asco Systems, Brother, Canon, DuPont, Federal Express, IBM, Intel, Microsoft, Oracle, Sun Microsystems, TNT, Xerox, and many others are well aware of the issues raised in this chapter.

However, it is worth pointing out that in many of these companies, the language is different. Business-to-business firms may be more inclined to talk of customer trust and confidence, or the importance of being seen as risk-free and experienced with a track record and history in the market. Nonetheless, to all intents and purposes, these are some of the most critical components of brand equity in their milieu.

In addition, as technology companies executing business-to-business marketing strategies evolve, customer decision making may shift from technologists to individuals with little technical expertise. Hence the brand may become a more important decision-making variable than the technology itself! Furthermore, empirical evidence strongly suggests that a well-managed brand will outlast many changes in technology.[73]

Finally, anything can be branded—any product, any service, even yourselves![74] It was not so long ago that PC buyers were unconcerned with the chips that ran their PCs; today, as the result of Intel's actions, Pentium is a critical decision variable for many. Finally, take the world's most common substance, H_2O. Go to a store and compare the price of bottles of Perrier, Poland Spring, Evian, and other brands with similar sizes of Coca-Cola, milk, beer, and other products. What you will find is a vivid demonstration of the power of brands.

THE CHANGING VIEW

Old Way	New Way
Branding is a name	Branding is a multisensory experience
Brands tied to products/SKUs	Brands viewed as assets to be managed in their own right
Brand management a junior management responsibility	Brand management recognized as an important senior management responsibility
Corporate branding viewed as just a name	Corporate branding recognized as an important asset
Branding a major method of risk reduction for customers	Branding one of several ways for customers to reduce risk
Brand proliferation common	Brand rationalization common
New brands frequently considered	Brand extension preferred, if possible
Local and regional brands dominant	Global brands increasingly preeminent

Old Way	New Way
Brand owners require total control over their own brands	Brand owners willing to engage in cooperative strategies
Brands used only by brand owner	Brand licensing increasingly common
Brands added haphazardly	Brand architecture carefully considered
Co-branding rare	Co-branding an increasingly used strategy

QUESTIONS FOR STUDY AND DISCUSSION

1. Sara Lee Corporation has decided to outsource its manufacturing. Do you think this was a smart move from the perspective of improving shareholder value? Why? Why not?

2. Identify and summarize an example of a successful brand extension into a new product class. Why do you believe this extension was successful?

3. Identify and summarize an example of an unsuccessful brand extension into a new product class. Why do you believe this extension was unsuccessful?

4. In the late 1980s and early 1990s, many haphazard brand extensions were introduced in an apparent attempt to increase volume. What measurement systems tend to encourage this type of behavior?

5. Identify and summarize an example of a brand that is recognizable through multiple senses.

6. Identify an example, beyond those already described, of a totally integrated brand experience. Identify an example, beyond those already described, of a brand experience that was not well integrated.

7. Construct an argument for the Financial Accounting Standards Board (FASB) as to why companies should have the option to place brand values as intangible assets on their balance sheets. Construct a rebuttal to your argument.

8. Global branding has been aggressively marketed by several major advertising agencies as a panacea. Explain the circumstances under which global branding would be ill-advised for a multinational company.

9. Marketers are typically motivated to segment markets since they believe it improves volume potential. Is this notion inconsistent with global branding? Why? Why not?

10. The authors separate the concept of brand equity into two components— organizational brand equity and customer brand equity. Do you agree with this distinction? Why or why not?

11. Over the years Alberto Culver's VO5 hair care product line has been marketed worldwide. In most cases, individual country managers were given responsibility for sales and profits, but were offered little guidance from the head office regarding market strategy. As a result, the product line is positioned differently from one country to another. Now, top management has decided that VO5 should be a global brand. How would you approach this assignment?

12. The concept of goodwill in accounting is nothing more than a "fudge" factor. It bears no relationship to reality and the U.S. practice of amortizing goodwill makes no economic sense. Do you agree with these statements? Why? Why not? Feel free to discuss your answers with a financial accounting expert.

13. Some companies have an internally-oriented perspective on branding, failing to recognize that the value of a brand is totally dependent on its ability to attract existing or potential customers. Do you agree with this statement? Why or why not?

14. For brands to be treated as financial assets, there must be a foolproof way to assess their values. Do you agree with this statement? Regardless, how would you go about constructing a foolproof way to assess the value of a brand?

15. In the summer of 1999, Coca-Cola faced a crisis due to contamination of its products, and their full or partial withdrawal from stores in Belgium, France, and Holland. On the day of the announcement, Coke's stock price fell by over 10%. What does this suggest about shareholders' view of the crisis and of Coca-Cola management?

16. The crises that have affected major brands such as Tylenol, Pentium, Coca-Cola, and Rely are examples of some of the risks involved in brand ownership. What do you believe should be shareholders' expectations of prudent contingency management of major brands? Suppose you were appointed brand manager for such a brand and found there were no crisis contingency plans. How would you convince management that such a plan should be put in place?

17. The Internet will have a major impact on branding. Discuss.

ENDNOTES

1. Quoted in J. Sampson, "Brand Valuation: Today and Tomorrow," Ch. 20 in *Brand Valuation*, London: Premier Books, 1997.

2. Interestingly, companies are beginning to use the vernacular in naming brands; for example, Federal Express is now officially FedEx.

3. The importance of shape was also seen in Calvin Klein's lawsuit against Ralph Lauren for alleged infringement of its trademark by using a similar bottle shape for a fragrance product.

4. Referring to the examples of the "non-functional" pink color in fiberglass and the Financial Times (from a use perspective, although it may aid in identification), recent research has shown that such "irrelevant attributes" can have important differentiating properties; G.S. Carpenter, R. Glazer and K. Nakamoto, "Meaningful Brands from Meaningless Differentiation: The Dependence on Irrelevant Attributes," *Journal of Marketing Research*, 31 (August 1994), pp. 339–350.

5. This contrasts with an earlier era in which the artisan's mark or brand was critical in identifying the producer.

6. *The Economist*, February 12, 2000.

7. K. Andersen, "The Yanni Files," *The New York Times*, Op-ed, January 17, 1998.

8. See also P. Berthon, J.M. Hulbert, and L.F. Pitt, Brand Management Prognostications, *Sloan Management Review*, 40 (Winter 1999), pp. 53–65.

9. Brands may produce widespread positive attitudes and even serious intentions to purchase. But if a purchase does not occur, the brand has not fulfilled its critical function for sellers.

10. Ohga-san, Chairman and CEO, Sony, quoted in *Fortune*, June 12, 1995.

11. In 1995, General Motors began appointing 35 brand managers for its various models in an effort to develop individual brand identities.

12. We are indebted to colleague Bernd Schmitt for this insight.

13. David A. Aaker, *Managing Brand Equity*, New York: The Free Press, (1991), p.15. See also other books on branding by the same author: *Building Strong Brands*, New York: The Free Press, 1995; and *Brand Leadership* (with E. Joachimsthaler), New York: The Free Press, 2000.

14. Awareness is the *sine qua non* for brand equity; however, the cost to develop awareness can be staggering. For example, in 1996, Lucent Technologies (including Bell Laboratories), formerly a part of AT&T, spent $50 million to create awareness for the new company, *The New York Times*, June 3, 1996.

15. Organizational brand equity is sometimes termed *brand value*.

16. *The New York Times*, June 12, 1997.

17. When one organization is purchased by another, this amount is frequently carried on the balance sheet as goodwill.

18. Organizational brand equity can be thought of as representing the balance sheet for the brand.

19. In consumer package goods, a proximate measure of brand equity relates to the difference in price over a store brand. Of course, some store brands have considerable equity in their own right; for example, Bloomingdale's, Macy's, and Marks and Spencer.

20. From L. Downes and C. Mui, *Unleashing the Killer App: Digital Strategies for Market Dominance*," Boston, MA: Harvard Business School Press, 1998.

21. Failure of the Firestone 500 led directly to the Bridgestone takeover of Firestone. In August 2000, Bridgestone-Firestone recalled 6.5 million tires used on Ford sport utility vehicles following reports of tread separation that were believed to have led to numerous accidents and several deaths.

22. For a popular book on branding, see A. Ries and L. Ries, *The 22 Immutable Laws of Branding*, New York: HarperBusiness, 1998.

23. Fast building of customer brand equity may also occur with fads (such as Barney the dinosaur, the Pet Rock, and so forth).

24. Some observers explain the loss in market share of fast-moving consumer goods brands to store brands as a loss in brand equity due to excessive price promotions.

25. *Business Week*, April 24, 2000.

26. *Fortune*, April 14, 1997.

27. Source: Boston Consulting Group (John Lindquist) reported in *The Economist*, January 6, 1996.

28. P. Berthon, "Brand Functionality and Enactment: Evidence from the World Wide Web," Working Paper, Cardiff Business School, Wales, 1998. In summer 1999, there were 450 Anti-Divx Web sites for the home video format, *Divx*! *Fortune*, June 21, 1999.

29. Muniz and O'Guinn introduce the notion of brand community to demonstrate individuals' commitment to, and proselytising for, a brand, noting particularly MacIntosh computers and Saab automobiles, A. Muniz, Jr. and T.C. O'Guinn, "Brand Community," Working Paper, University of California, Berkeley and University of Illinois, 1998.

30. *The Economist*, April 26, 1997.

31. Negative brand equity for an individual customer implies that, all things equal, they would prefer an unbranded alternative to the brand under consideration.

32. Of course, a partial alternative explanation is that many customers in St. Louis (TWA's hub) had no alternative airline choices.

33. We thank our colleague Don Lehmann for providing insight into brand equity measurement. As long as similar methodologies are used across firms, rankings may be more useful than absolute measures of "brand value."

34. Of course, for accurate assessment, this method relies on an efficient market value for the brand. A recent study casts doubt on market efficiency. Thus, M.J. Cooper, O. Dimitrov, and P. Raghavendra, "A Rose.com by Any Other Name," www.mgmt.purdue.edu/mcooper/newpapers/dotcom.pdf, May 1999, showed that on average, the value of companies that change their names to include a web-orientation (.com, .net, or Internet) increased in value 125% more than comparable companies! This study was conducted before the Spring 2000 sell-off of Internet stocks.

35. The fundamental underpinning of this type of approach is to compare the revenues (price $\times$ volume) earned by the brand in a product category with the revenues (price $\times$ volume) earned (or estimated) by a generic product in the same category.

36. Brand Valuation Methodology: A Simple Example, *Harvard Business School*, 9-596-092. See also R. Perrier (Ed.), *Brand Valuation*, London: Premier, 1997. Note the Gillette example provides a 1996 value; the values in Table 11.2A are for 1999.

37. In 1996, *Business Week* reported results of a Harris Poll that placed Sony as the most recognized brand name in the United States, outranking McDonald's and Coke (May 27, 1996).

38. The problem of accounting for goodwill (the excess of acquisition price over net tangible assets) is that, in most countries, companies are penalized for good acquisitions by having to take significant amortization charges against income, or by writing off the amount against reserves.

39. See "Brand Valuation—A Practical Guide," *Accountant's Digest*, March 1999, Issue 405.

40. *The New York Times*, March 28, 1997.

41. This example demonstrates that the firm must keep in mind that brand equity is not unrelated to the brand's organizational context. For example, all too frequently, acquisitions lead to dilution of brand equity since the management attention that led to the original high valuation is frequently not sustained in the new organization.

42. A final method relates to royalty rates for those brands that are licensed; unfortunately, this information is typically highly confidential and difficult to secure.

43. It is worth noting that attempts to measure brand equity are congruent with other assaults on traditional performance measures. For example, in accounting, Kaplan and Norton have attacked traditional accounting measurement and called for a "balanced scorecard" approach embracing financial, customer, learning and growth, and internal business process measures, R.S. Kaplan and D.P. Norton, "Putting the Balanced Scorecard to Work," *Harvard Business Review*, 71 (Sept./Oct. 1993), pp. 134–147. See also "Using the Balanced Scorecard as a Strategic Management System," *Harvard Business Review*, 74 (Jan./Feb. 1996), pp. 75–85, by the same authors. In finance, an emphasis on cash flow and shareholder value has culminated in Economic Value Added (EVA), which avoids traditional arbitrary accounting driven definitions of investment and includes expenditures on marketing, training, R&D as investments.
44. See also, K.L. Keller, "Conceptualizing, Measuring, and Managing Customer-Based Brand Equity," *Journal of Marketing*, 57 (Jan. 1993), pp. 1–22, and K.L. Keller, "The Brand Report Card," *Harvard Business Review*, 78 (Jan./Feb. 2000), pp. 147–157.

45. David A. Aaker, "Measuring Brand Equity Across Products and Markets," *California Management Review*, 38 (Spring 1996), pp. 102–120.

46. We are indebted to our colleague Tim Ambler of London Business School for this insight.

47. For a discussion of some of the issues surrounding the brand management system, see P. Berthon, James M. Hulbert, and Leyland F. Pitt, "Brand Management Prognostications," *Sloan Management Review*, 40 (Winter 1999).

48. *The Boston Herald*, quoted in *The New York Times*.

49. A corporate brand uses the firm's name. The firm may also have a number of family brands, each comprising several different products.

50. Advertisements for 10-10-321 show direct price comparisons against AT&T, never against MCI, *Fortune*, June 22, 1998.

51. A related converse example is the potential damage to both Dow and Corning from litigation related to breast implants produced by their strategic alliance, Dow Corning.

52. See D. Desmet, L. Finskud, M. Glucksman, N.H. Marshall, M.J. Reyner, and K. Warren, "The End of Voodoo Brand Management," *The McKinsey Quarterly*, 2 (1998), pp. 107–117, for a model and interesting example of brand revitalization.

53. For example, in the 1970s there were 17 over-the-counter pain relievers, today 140; five hosiery brands, today 90. Jack Trout, quoted in *The New York Times*, February 10, 2000.

54. In his pathbreaking work, Aaker identifies seven different ways that brands might be revitalized—increasing usage, new uses, entering new markets, brand repositioning, product/service augmentation, obsoleting current products, and brand extension, Aaker, *op. cit.* Most of these were discussed in Chapter 10.

55. *Marketing News*, January 21, 1999.

56. In a similar move, General Motors executives decided that Oldsmobile should abandon its aging owner base and focus efforts on younger customers that typically buy imported automobile brands (*Fortune*, April 28, 1997).

57. For more details, see the case study *The Goodwood Conundrum* J.M. Hulbert and M.M. Lyman, Columbia Business School, 1999. See also www.goodwood.co.uk.

58. Smith Corona has outsourced production for its remaining sales of typewriters, supplies, and accessories, as well as all other products sold under the *Smith Corona* brand name, *The New York Times*, March 23, 1998.

59. In 1997, retail sales from corporate brand licensing in the United States and Canada were over $16 billion.

60. Corstjens and Carpenter make the interesting observation that whereas consumer package goods companies build and manage strong brand identities for the long run, pharmaceutical companies always give new products a new name, meaning that they must build a new brand for each new drug, a very expensive proposition, M. Corstjens and M. Carpenter, "From Managing Pills to Managing Brands," *Harvard Business Review*, 78 (Mar./Apr. 2000), pp. 20–21.

61. Tauber has reported that by the late 1980s, 80% of all new grocery products were attempts to extend or leverage existing brands, E. Tauber, "Brand Leverage: Strategy for Growth in a Cost Conscious World," *Journal of Advertising Research*, (Aug./Sept. 1988), pp. 26–30.

62. Furthermore, consumer goods retailers typically merchandise products by category rather than by brand; this may lead to high search costs for new products.

63. D.R. John, B. Loken, and C. Joiner, "The Negative Impact of Extensions: Can Flagship Products Be Diluted?" *Journal of Marketing*, 62 (Jan. 1998), pp. 19–32.

64. Personal communication from Jeff Skilling, President of Enron Corporation, June 1997.

65. *The New York Times*, Sunday, June 1, 1997.

66. *The Wall Street Journal*, March 4, 1998.

67. See K.R. Harrigan, *Strategies for Joint Ventures*, Lexington, MA: Lexington Books, 1985. In a comparative study of firm performance in Brazil, Brandt and Hulbert found that joint ventures had the worst performance of any grouping of firms, whether domestic or multinational, as measured by ROA, ROE, ROS, or growth in sales, W.K. Brandt and J.M. Hulbert, *A Empresa Multinacional No Brasil*, Rio de Janeiro: Editores Zahar, 1977.

68. *Fortune*, July 7, 1997.

69. *The Economist*, February 28, 1998.

70. For an excellent book on crossing cultures, see E. Hall, *The Silent Language*, Garden City, NY: Anchor, 1973.

71. In urging caution regarding global branding, Aaker and Joachimsthaler make an interesting distinction between "global branding" and "global brand leadership," D.A. Aaker and E. Joachimsthaler, "The Lure of Global Branding," *Harvard Business Review*, 77 (Nov./Dec. 1999), pp. 137–144.

72. A.J. Parsons, "Nestlé: The Visions of Local Managers," *The McKinsey Quarterly*, (1996-2), pp. 5–29. See also H. Riesenbeck and A. Freeling, "How Global Are Global Brands?" *The McKinsey Quarterly*, (1991-4), pp. 3–18 and B.V. Boze and C.R. Patton, "The Future of Consumer Branding as Seen from the Picture Today," *Journal of Consumer Marketing*, 12 (1995-4), pp. 20–41. As noted in Chapter 12, in 1999, Unilever decided to focus its marketing efforts on 400 global and regional brands.

73. *The Economist, op. cit.*

74. In 1997, as a promotional device, Sazerac Co., distributor of Dr. McGillicuddy's Schnapps, offered to brand municipalities as McGillicuddy City for a five-year period in exchange for a $100,000 donation, *Fortune*, February 15, 1999. Furthermore, several leading chefs are branding themselves and becoming spokepersons for kitchen equipment, tableware, food types, chef's attire, and so forth, *The New York Times*, April 10, 1999. In the Czech Republic, detergent manufacturer Dedra launched "Ordinary Laundry Detergent," similar in concept to Brand X products previously offered in the United States. Said CEO Cerny, "We're on television every night in commercials for Ariel and other similar products from multinational firms."

WEB RESOURCES

Air Jordan	www.nike.com
Alberto Culver	www.alberto.com
Alvis	www.alvis.com
Amazon	www.amazon.com
American Express	www.americanexpress.com
AOL	www.aol.com
Arm & Hammer	www.armandhammer.com
Armani	www.luxottica.it
AT&T	www.att.com
Audi	www.audi.com

Aunt Jemima	www.quakeroats.com
Avon	www.avon.com
Band-Aid	www.jnj.com
Bayer	www.bayer.com
Ben and Jerry	www.benjerry.com
BHP	www.bhp.com
Bic	www.bicworld.com
Black & Decker	www.blackanddecker.com
BMW	www.bmw.com
British Airways	www.britishairways.com
British Steel	www.britishsteel.com
Brother	www.brother.com
Budweiser	www.budweiser.com
Cadillac	www.cadillac.com
Calyx and Corolla	www.calyxandcorolla.com
Campbell	www.campbell.com
Canon	www.canon.co.jp
Cascade	www.cascadecomplete.com
Chevrolet	www.chevrolet.com
Citigroup	www.citi.com
Clairol	www.clairol.com
CNN	www.cnn.com
Coors	www.coorsandco.com
Courtaulds	www.courtaulds-textiles.com
Daewoo	www.daewoo.com
Dairy Association	www.dairy.com
Dior	www.dior.com
Disney	www.disney.com
Dockers	www.dockers.com
Dow Corning	www.dowcorning.com
DuPont	www.dupont.com
Electrolux	www.electrolux.com
Encyclopedia Britannica	www.eb.com
Enron	www.enron.com
Eveready	www.eveready.com
Evian	www.evian.fr
Financial Acounting Standards Board (FASB)	www.rutgers.odu/Accounting/raw/fasb
Federal Express	www.fedex.com
Ferrari Watches	www.ferrari.com
Financial Times	www.ft.com
Firestone	www.bridgestone-firestone.com
Ford	www.ford.com
Gallo	www.Gallo.com
General Electric	www.ge.com
General Motors	www.gm.com
Geo	www.geo.com
Gold Medal	www.general/mills.com
Gucci	www.gucci.com
Haagen Dazs	www.haagendaz.com
Harley Davidson	www.harley-davidson.com
Hennes and Mauritz	www.hm.com
Hershey	www.hershey.com

Hewlett Packard	www.hp.com
Holiday Inn	www.holiday-inn.com
Honda	www.honda.com
ICI	www.ici.com
IPC	www.ipc.com
Intel	www.intel.com
Ivory	www.ivory.com
Kendall-Jackson	www.kj.com
Kellogg's	www.kellogg.com
Kodak	www.kodak.com
Lexus	www.lexus.com
Life Savers	www.candystand.com
Lucent	www.lucent.com
Lysol	www.rfvsales.com
Microsoft	www.microsoft.com
Monsanto	www.monsanto.com
Nabisco	www.nabisco.com
Nestlé	www.nestle.com
Netscape	www.netscape.com
Ocean Spray	www.oceanspray.com
Old Spice	www.oldspice.com
Pan Am	www.panam.com
Parker Pens	www.parker.com
Perrier	www.perrier.com
Philadelphia Cream Cheese	www.kraftinternational.com
Philips	www.philips.com
Poland Spring	www.polandspringcamp.com
Pontiac	www.pontiac.com
Procter & Gamble	www.pg.com
Rhone-Poulenc	www.rp-rorer.com
Sara Lee	www.saralee.com
Saturn	www.saturn.com
Schlitz	www.pabst.com
Sears	www.sears.com
Sherwin-Williams	www.sherwin-williams.com
Smith Corona	www.smithcorona.com
Snapple	www.snapple.com
Sony	www.sony.com
Sprint	www.sprint.com
Starbucks	www.starbucks.com
Swift	www.swift.com
Taco Bell	www.tacobell.com
Tide	www.clothesline.com
Tiffany	www.tiffany.com
TNT	www.tnt-tv.com
Tommy Hilfiger	www.tommypr.com
Toyota	www.toyota.com
Tylenol	www.tylenol.com
Unilever	www.unilever.com
ValueJet	www.valuejet.com

Virgin	www.virgin.com
Visa	www.visa.com
Volvo	www.volvo.com
Wells Fargo	www.wellsfargo.com
Windows	www.microsoft.com
Wrigley	www.wrigley.com
Xerox	www.xerox.com
Yahoo!	www.yahoo.com
Yamaha	www.yamaha.com

CHAPTER

12

MANAGING THE PRODUCT LINE

LEARNING OBJECTIVES

When you have completed this chapter, you will understand

- **the importance of addressing the product line as a portfolio of products**

- **alternative approaches to product portfolio management**

- **interrelationships among products**

- **product line breadth and issues concerned with product proliferation and product line simplification**

- **issues surrounding extending product life, product cannibalization, product replacement, product quality, and secondary markets**

- **concerns regarding product safety and product and packaging disposal**

INTRODUCTION

Decisions about products and services typically feature prominently in any discussion of the firm's marketing mix, and rank along with choice of markets and segments in their implications for the firm as a whole. This chapter supports the concept of a total offer made to customers, but recognizes that the core product is central to the offer. Furthermore, most important decisions about products cross functional lines and, therefore, inevitably have broader manifestations for firm operations than other marketing mix decisions.

This chapter begins with an overview of the portfolio concept, examines the arguments for a balanced product portfolio, and discusses approaches to managing interrelationships among various portfolio elements. It then examines product line breadth, focusing on issues concerned with product proliferation and product simplification. The chapter concludes with discussion on extending product life, product cannibalization, product replacement, product quality, secondary markets, and legal and ethical issues, concentrating on product safety, and packaging and product disposal.

THE PRODUCT PORTFOLIO CONCEPT

The firm's product portfolio comprises the different product (and service) items offered to customers for which the firm receives revenues. This chapter takes the perspective of an individual business unit within the firm (comprising several product lines) and considers various product-related, resource-allocation issues relevant to managing that business. However, the approach is general and can also be used to consider the various business units in a corporate portfolio.

> **Example:** General Electric's (GE) corporate portfolio comprises businesses such as electric generators, locomotives, entertainment, financial services, jet engines, lighting, plastics, and home appliances. GE's CEO has to decide how to allocate resources across the various businesses.
>
> The product portfolio for the home appliances business unit includes individual products such as clothes washers and dryers, dishwashers, refrigerators, and stoves. The general manager of the home appliance business unit has to decide how to allocate resources across these various product lines.

The basic argument for a portfolio view of the business derives from the variety of objectives and associated resource requirements that may be appropriate for its various products. For example, during new product start-up and launch, significant resources are required for plant and equipment, R&D, promotion, and so forth so that products can meet their growth objectives.[1] Later, as growth slows and investment requirements diminish, older products should eventually become cash generators. Portfolio management requires a balance of products with different types of objectives and resource requirements.

If the firm has an imbalance in its product portfolio, shareholder interests are placed in significant danger. First, an overabundance of new products can often lead to liquidity concerns, a problem faced by many start-up companies, and most recently by many Internet-based firms.[2] Second, for firms with an excessive balance of mature products, excellent current results may mask a failure to reinvest at an adequate rate to maintain required investor returns. Since new product success is typically characterized by excellent rates of operating profit, a stream of successful innovations is an important contributor to long-term shareholder value creation. In either case, a severe imbalance can lead to acquisition by firms seeking, respectively, growth opportunities or cash flow.

The task for management is to treat its product line as a portfolio, set sensible objectives, and make appropriate resource allocations for its products as a function of their individual roles in the portfolio. Some portfolio elements should be set growth objectives, while others should have profit or profitability and cash flow objectives. Each product should receive those resources, such as financial and human, necessary to achieve its objectives.

Making Investment Decisions: Financial Analysis Methods

All too frequently, firms approach investment decisions from a purely financial perspective[3]; indeed, "capital budgeting" is treated as an important topic in most business school curricula. Since superior financial performance is a critical objective for management, analysis of potential investment returns is both important and proper.

Decades ago, historical accounting rates of return were in widespread use. Today virtually all companies use methods that take into account the time value of money. Some firms, however, still use forecast rate of return on investment (ROI) calculated by projecting future accounting data. Because this method considers the whole life of the investment, it is often considered superior to payback (the period of time required to pay back the original investment). However, since neither projected accounting returns nor payback distinguish returns earned in different time periods, such as year 1 or year 5, both are defective.[4] The most commonly used methods that consider time are internal rate of return (IRR) and net present value (NPV); more recently, the related concept of economic value added (EVA) has become popular.[5]

> Internal rate of return (IRR) and net present value (NPV) rely on discounted cash flow analyses, valuing returns (and expenditures) when they are earned (or paid out), discounting both future returns (cash inflows) and expenditures (cash outflows), to take into account when they are received/disbursed.[6] For IRR, the value of an opportunity is measured as that rate (%) which equalizes the inflows and outflows. For NPV, the value is measured as an amount, typically secured by discounting the cash flows at a "hurdle" rate.[7] EVA is simply NPV calculated using the firm's cost of capital, rather than an arbitrary hurdle rate.

All financial analysis methods have several points in common. The result of the analysis is a single figure, months/years for payback, a rate (typically a percent) for ROI and IRR, and an amount for NPV. Also, the methods are conceptually simple; given the set of inputs—investments, sales revenues, and costs—the analysis is straightforward, even though complex calculations may be required. The decision flowing from the analyses appears to be unambiguous: opportunities are ranked; those selected typically outrank or outperform the others on some criterion or hurdle rate that should be related to the firm's cost of capital. More complex techniques take into account the inherent riskiness of the project.

However, these methods suffer from two severe problems. Each relies on estimates of future sales revenues (sales units and prices), costs, and investments. As any manager knows, judging the short-term investment required for a well-defined project is difficult enough; predicting sales revenues several years into the future is a daunting task.[8] This task is also open to much organizational game playing. As most managers have observed in their careers, opportunity-champions may be tempted to "hockey stick" sales revenue estimates upwards and cost estimates downwards to turn marginal return projects into spectacular performers!

By contrast, hard-nosed financial managers are just as likely to make "realistic adjustments" to these forecasts (sales revenues down, cost and investment estimates up), and send potential returns plummeting. As a result, the decision of whether or not to invest too often reflects the political clout of various functional managers rather than the intrinsic value of the opportunity. Resolution of these conflicts, if not well-managed, leads to ill will and internecine conflict, producing polarization between a proposal's proponents and those, too easily seen as opponents, who judge it.

In addition financial analysis techniques are silent on strategic matters since their logic dictates that opportunities be pursued in order of estimated financial performance, regardless of other considerations. Thus a 22% return (assume IRR) opportunity will always be chosen over an 18% opportunity. However, the 18% opportunity may be central to the company's strategy, where the 22% opportunity may be peripheral. Strategically, the 18% opportunity should be chosen; financial analysis reaches the opposite conclusion.

A related problem is a vestige of the "every tub on its own bottom" philosophy. Whether for historical or political reasons, in some companies businesses allocate investment funds to individual products based on historical profitability. In this decision-making mode, mature (no growth) products tend to receive more investment than new products. By contrast, high-growth products are starved of funds since current profits are low. Even the EVA perspective (discussed earlier) is vulnerable to this kind of problem since new ventures, in their early stages, almost always appear to destroy rather than create shareholder value.

This danger of overinvesting in current products via incremental investments, and simultaneously starving newer products, is increased by the difficulty of forecasting several years in the future; forecasting errors are much greater for newer rather than more mature products. As a result, returns for new products are likely to be discounted to a greater extent than cost reduction projects for existing products. Thus management's quest (which may be misplaced) for more conservative, less-risky opportunities can easily lead to insufficient investment in potential new opportunities. This is a particularly serious concern when environmental imperatives require major shifts in products, markets, and businesses, for overuse of financial criteria can lead to insufficient investment in the future. It is these kinds of decision processes that often create advantage for the attacker, an unencumbered new entrant that competes with newer technology.[9]

To deal with these problems, some financial managers treat risk explicitly via risk analysis techniques or even full-blown simulations. However, these procedures have found less favor than originally anticipated and the *de facto* solution to the problem has been different.[10] Rather than focus on refinement of the numbers, the major thrust has been a closer and more explicit examination of the assumptions underlying the financial projections, such as the expected future growth rate of the market in which the products will be sold, and the targeted market share. Other questions arise: Against which companies will the firm be competing? What is the likely future market structure? How is technology expected to change? What is the role of government? These questions cannot be answered precisely. Rather, in the process of asking and attempting to answer such questions, management is explicitly addressing the validity of the assumptions underlying the financial projections. In the process, companies have typically shifted from an internally-oriented perspective on investment decisions to a more externally-oriented focus.

Making Investment Decisions: Portfolio Models

These same questions can be addressed more formally within portfolio analysis frameworks; such approaches are at the core of many firms' strategic planning systems. Portfolio analyses are probably best viewed as a set of additional tools for setting investment priorities, rather than as alternatives to financial analysis. They provide a systematic, organized, and easily communicated means of assembling, assessing, and integrating a variety of information. This information is helpful in establishing investment priorities and setting strategic direction for individual businesses by assisting management with allocation decisions among products or markets. In an analogous manner, product managers can apply the approach to setting priorities among different market segment opportunities.

Adoption of portfolio analysis typically has a dramatic impact on resource allocation processes in most companies, although research evidence suggests the impact is greatest when the commitment is thoroughgoing.[11] Table 12.1 notes the critical shift in perspective that accompanies the adoption of a portfolio-analytic approach, and highlights a set of issues typically not considered in purely financial approaches. As noted earlier, exclusive use of financial analysis techniques presents financial managers with enormous problems; similarly, this chapter does not advocate a focus on strategic factors to the exclusion of their financial implications. Rather, it is in the same camp as those forward-thinking finan-

TABLE 12.1 Investment Decisions and Strategic Direction

	Financial Analysis Techniques	Portfolio Analysis Techniques
Investment Decision Focus	Technologies/Facilities	Products/Markets/Customers/Applications
General Approach	Financial- and Budget-Oriented	Market- and Competitive-Oriented
Key Concerns	Derived Profit and Cash Flow Numbers	Analysis of Basic Market and Competitive Factors underlying the Numbers
Typical Measures	Return on Investment, Net Present Value, Internal Rate of Return	Market Size, Market Growth, Competitive Strengths, Market Potential
Tools	Capital Budgeting	Strategic Portfolio Analysis

cial managers who, far from being opposed to portfolio analysis, are eager to embrace approaches that improve the quality of critical investment decisions.

THE GROWTH-SHARE MATRIX   The original and most popular portfolio model is the growth-share matrix, introduced by the Boston Consulting Group (BCG). In this approach, the two matrix dimensions are forecast long-run growth rate and relative market share.[12] Typically, each dimension is bisected (high, low) to produce a four-cell classification (Figure 12.1). Each entry in the matrix represents a product or product line; typically, the size of each circle is proportional to the sales revenue or invested assets.

Long-run market growth rate (typically three or five years) is a straightforward construct to estimate, though reasonable managers' forecasts may differ.[13] There is a general tendency to forecast growth in physical units, such as pounds, meters, or tons, and these are generally adequate. However, if price competition is severe, unit growth may be associated with shrinking prices and revenue measures should be considered.

Relative market share (RMS) (of the market in which the firm's product competes) requires a little more explanation. For any firm, RMS is that firm's market share divided by the largest competitor's market share. This measure has the attractive property of indicating the dominant player directly, since it has a relative market share greater than 1.0. As a further advantage, it removes the effects of market structure and focuses directly on competitive strength. Thus absolute market share of, say, 50% in a two- or three-competitor market when the number two firm has 30% market share (RMS = 50/30 = 1.67) is competitively different from a ten-competitor market where the number two firm has 15% market share (RMS = 50/15 = 3.3). In the later case, the greater competitive strength is captured by the relative market share measure.[14]

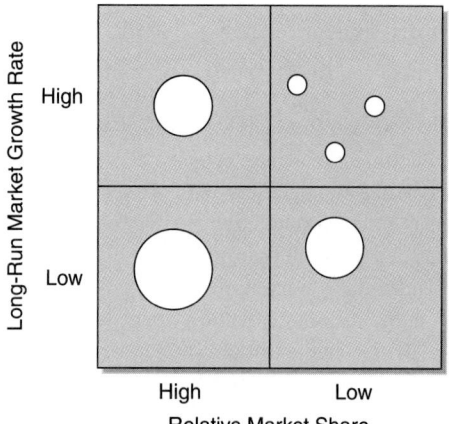

FIGURE 12.1

The Growth-Share Matrix

TABLE 12.2 Market Share/Profitability Relationships from the PIMS Study

Market Share	<10%	10–20%	20–30%	30–40%	>40%
ROI	14%	18%	23%	24%	33%

In application, considerable controversy frequently arises over where to place the cut point that divides high- and low-growth markets. Because the choice of cut point for continuous variables is, of course, completely arbitrary, many firms find it helpful to develop a choice rule. The critical issue is that external standards, such as GNP or GDP growth, should be used rather than such internal standards as current firm growth. For example, if a firm's overall growth rate were 1% per annum, an internally set cut point might be 4%; opportunities whose growth was in excess of 4% would appear attractive because they represent significantly higher growth than the firm currently enjoys. However, if the economy were growing at 8% per annum, such a standard would condemn the firm to shrinking, relative to the economy as a whole. A better cut point might be 8%, or even 10%.[15] The cut point for relative market share is typically placed at 1.0. As a result, products in market leadership positions fall to the left of the cut point; all others fall to the right.

The growth-share matrix places a strong emphasis on the relationship between entries in specific matrix cells and the financial characteristics of each entry. For example, products with high market shares are typically more profitable than those with low market shares; products whose volume is increasing quickly may require significant investment in fixed and working capital and market development, thereby reducing cash flow.[16] In general, these correlations are supported by experience curve arguments,[17] some of PIMS empirical research (Table 12.2),[18] and much anecdotal evidence (see Table 12.3).

As a result, typical inferences from a growth-share analysis suggest strong investment support for upper-left quadrant businesses (high growth/high share) using excess cash from lower-left quadrant businesses (low growth/high share). Investment in upper-right quadrant business (high growth/low share) should be carefully targeted, and lower-right quadrant businesses (low growth/low share) should be critically analyzed for divestment or retention. These prototypical prescriptions are developed further in Figure 12.2 by examining three separate issues: characteristics of businesses in the various matrix cells, investment considerations suggested by the analysis, and assumptions underlying the analysis. These should be considered only in conjunction with the discussion of growth-share matrix difficulties that follows.

Difficulties with the Growth-Share Matrix Figure 12.2 shows what many would regard as the classic strategic recommendations flowing from growth-share matrix analysis. However, these recommendations are potentially dangerous in application, simply because they are so widely advocated and applied. For example, high-growth markets are typically

TABLE 12.3 An Individual Firm Example: Distribution of Number of Products, Sales Revenues, Assets, and Profitability with Market Share

Market Share	<10%	10–20%	20–30%	30–40%	>40%
Number of Products (%)*	46.5	14.8	10.6	7.0	21.1
Sales Revenues (%)	27.5	15.8	7.9	17.6	31.2
Assets (%)	34.2	16.1	7.4	15.6	26.7
Profits (%)	4.0	8.2	9.2	22.7	56.7

*To be read as: 46.5% of the firm's products are in markets where it has <10% market share.

Low Market Growth/High Market Share (cash cows): Businesses in this matrix cell are typically highly profitable due to good cost position from economies of scale and experience curve effects, and because market leaders are frequently able to command premium prices. Since the market is mature (low growth), required reinvestment should be lower than before with consequential benefits for cash flow. If well-managed, and absent major environmental change, businesses in this cell can generate significant cash for many years, hence the term "cash cow." This cash can be invested in more attractive businesses.[20] Setting a cash generation priority typically translates into a hold market share objective. If significant environmental change occurs, such as a regulatory shift or radically new technology introduction, a deliberate harvesting strategy aimed at increasing short-term cash flow, at the expense of market share, may be implemented. Specific actions can include increasing price, reducing/eliminating service, or cutting advertising and promotional support.

A serious problem with these businesses is that management often desires long-run cash flow yet, faced with external requirements imposed by shareholders, unions, and even government, takes short-term action that severely harms long-term prospects.[21] In particular, in seeking earnings and cash flow in the short run, cash cows may be over-milked, receive insufficient investment, fail to keep up with advances in product and process technology, lose cost leadership, suffer deteriorating competitive position, and eventually run dry, unable to make profits and generate cash.[22] The experience of major U.S. and European automobile and steel companies is illustrative of this syndrome. Of course, overinvestment in mature products and businesses, driven by internally oriented financial investment criteria, is also a serious issue; diminishing returns can set in as competitive spending levels are needlessly and unprofitably escalated.

In summary, low growth/high share products should represent the firm's primary internal cash source. The bulk of cash should be invested to support growth elsewhere—in newer markets, products, and businesses. The twin dangers of over- and underinvestment demand a skillful balancing act from senior management.

Low Market Growth/Low Market Share (dogs): These businesses trail market leaders in low-growth markets. (Because a minority of markets are fast growing and only a single competitor can be dominant, it follows that these businesses are the most numerous in the economy.) If the dominant firm's business is well-managed, low market share business should have inferior cost position, lower prices, and consequently be less profitable than the leader. However, both because some businesses may be subject to negative scale effects, that is lower costs than the leader, and because follower firms may be better managed and have continually invested to force costs down, businesses with reasonably low relative market shares can be quite profitable.[23] However, if costs are bloated, or relative market shares are quite small, low or zero profitability is likely.

The typical objective for better-placed low-share businesses is appropriate investment for long-run cash flow maximization, just as with high-share businesses. However, poorly placed businesses might consider several different options: short-run cash maximization by liquidation,[24] divestiture, new segmentation approaches that provide market niche dominance, and a "kennel" strategy requiring acquisition of similarly placed businesses aimed at achieving viable scale.

High Market Growth/High Market Share (stars): These businesses are much-beloved, yet relatively rare; overall, few businesses are in dominant positions in high-growth markets. Typically, they are profitable, although not necessarily so at the very beginning of the life cycle, but investment in capacity expansion and increased working capital often means they are cash negative. Indeed, many new entrepreneurs with growing profitable operations find to their distress that profit and cash flow are not synonymous!

Growth markets typically evince considerable uncertainty with regard to ultimate market potential, evolution of customer needs, competitors, and technology. However, if market share position is sustained, both profitability and cash flows improve when market growth slows. If market dominance is maintained until maturity, "stars" cross the boundary to low market growth/high market share and should be highly cash generating; hence, they can support new growth businesses. As a result, the core recommendation for high share/high growth businesses is invest sufficiently to maintain or improve market position. The major danger is that management seeks profits too early, underinvests, and compromises market position to the point where the low-growth/high-share position is lost to a competitor and the business heads to the low-growth/low-share quadrant and poor performance.

As with low-growth/high-share businesses, management must be concerned with overinvestment and overly aggressive share gaining behavior. Since market leaders can rarely drive all competitors from markets without incurring enormous costs, some optimal market share level should be set as an operational objective.

High Market Growth/Low Market Share (problem children, lottery tickets, wildcats): Businesses in this position are typically viewed as the most risky because of the inherent uncertainty in high-growth markets and the weak market share position (compared to the leader). Often these businesses are marginally profitable, yet to continue to hold position and grow with the market they consume substantial cash for investment in fixed assets and working capital. Unfortunately, such investment does not guarantee future profits since businesses managed in this manner gravitate to the low-growth/low-share quadrant. As a result, the strategic investment decision for these businesses is often viewed as "double or quits." In other words, build market share and drive for dominance, ultimately seeking the low-growth/high-share cell via an intermediate high-growth/high-share position, or exit the business by gradual or more immediate means. Although the former strategy may be viable, largely depending on the actions of the market leader, very large investments are required for both market growth and market share gain. In many cases, a less risky, more modest approach is to identify one or more market segments and seek dominance by appropriate investment.

FIGURE 12.2

Prototypical Recommendations from Growth-Share Portfolio Analysis

viewed as attractive yet, if many competitors rush to enter and install too much capacity, prices may drop and all competitors may experience losses for considerable periods.

Good competitive strategy demands some element of contrarianism, particularly under the increasingly prevalent oligopolistic conditions in global markets. The major application of the growth-share matrix should be diagnostic, as a means of raising, and discussing, "what-if" questions.

Despite (or perhaps because of) its apparent simplicity, several technical problems are associated with the growth-share matrix. Any model to aid decision making rests on a number of basic assumptions, and its value in any particular situation is only as good as the applicability of these assumptions. The first assumption relates to the prior discussion; market attractiveness is measured exclusively by market growth rate. Because it is entirely possible to make significant losses in growth markets, market growth alone may not constitute a sufficiently robust market attractiveness measure.

A second core assumption is that strength of competitive position is captured by relative market share. In a static market, this proposition has some validity, but holding a lead market position without having access to critical inputs is not a position of strength. For example, competitors may destroy strong market positions through technological breakthroughs, or by securing scarce sources of supply. Indeed, some generalizations underlying the growth-share matrix have been shown as inaccurate. For example, using a large data sample from the PIMS project, Hambrick, MacMillan, and Day showed that the cash flow generalizations were flawed; PIMS own studies have produced similar results.[19]

The growth-share matrix makes two additional assumptions: the market share/profitability relationship and presence of downward-sloping cost experience curves. The results noted in Tables 12.2 and 12.3 both support the strong relationship between achieved market share and profitability, but this relationship may not hold universally.[25] Indeed, a critical choice in most portfolio analyses is market definition. Because of issues concerning the level of segmentation and geographic boundaries, market definition is typically not unambiguous, yet has a major impact on measures of both market growth and relative market share as well as placement of entries in the matrix.[26] Presence of downward-sloping cost experience curves, and comparable cost curves across competitors, is related to the market share/profitability relationship. This relationship might not always hold; for example, well-managed, small businesses frequently have better cost positions than major players, even though larger market share businesses might be relatively well managed.

THE MULTIFACTOR PORTFOLIO MODEL   In part because of difficulties with the growth-share matrix, several other portfolio approaches have been developed and widely disseminated. Perhaps the most widely used is the multifactor portfolio matrix, also known as the GE/McKinsey screen. In essence, this approach redefines the two axes of the growth-share matrix—long-run market growth rate and relative market share—as market attractiveness and business strength, respectively, then allows the user to identify a variety of factors to measure each dimension.[27] In its original formulation, this approach was called the stoplight matrix, a colored, two-dimensional (market attractiveness/business strengths) framework comprising three green/go (invest) cells, three red/stop (don't invest) cells, and three amber/be careful cells (Figure 12.3).[28]

COMPARISON OF GROWTH-SHARE AND MULTIFACTOR PORTFOLIO METHODS   An assessment of the value of the growth-share and multifactor portfolio approaches in choosing among investment opportunities proceeds best by comparison across a set of criteria (Table 12.4). The basic trade-off is captured in the first three items: criteria, measures, and realism. The major advantage of the growth-share matrix is the limited number of criteria and their unambiguous, objective nature. Since the basis for investment decisions is reduced to market growth and relative market share, the ability of managers to manipulate individual entries is limited. Although reasonable people may disagree about market growth forecasts, if agreement is formed on market definition, deriving relative market share is a measurement issue. Conversely, the limited number of criteria is a weakness because market growth and relative market share may not capture the full extent of critical issues and thus lead to a lack of realism.

By contrast, the number of criteria in the multifactor matrix can range within reasonable limits. This approach may embrace many factors that the growth-share matrix omits,

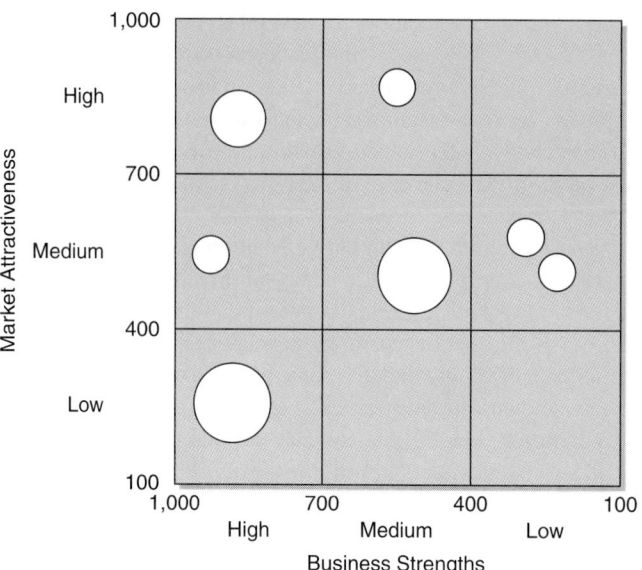

Market Attractiveness — High / Medium / Low (1,000 / 700 / 400 / 100)

Business Strengths — High / Medium / Low (1,000 / 700 / 400 / 100)

FIGURE 12.3

The Multifactor Portfolio Model[29]

and hence appear more realistic. However, specific criteria are subject to dispute among reasonable managers and the various weightings and ratings are typically subjective. As a result, political considerations and organizational power relationships can lead to manipulation of entries such that they enter the "required" cell. In the multifactor matrix, investment opportunities tend to gravitate toward the high/high corner (high market attractiveness/ high business strengths), possibly reflecting biased evaluations. By contrast, the majority of growth-share matrix entries, by definition, fall in the bottom right (low market growth/low relative market share).

Because of these factors, the growth-share matrix has the advantage in ease of implementation and communicability. Senior management can view an entire complex, diversified organization arrayed on a single sheet of paper. In addition, the matrix can be used to analyze the trajectory of businesses over time, to evaluate customers and suppliers, and to test the likely results from pursuing different strategic options. Overall, it is simpler to evaluate diverse businesses and market segments using the simple criteria from the growth-share matrix than to use the more complex multifactor matrix.

Conversely, whereas the multifactor matrix is useful both for assessing investment potential in current businesses and evaluating totally new opportunities, the growth-share matrix is only really useful for assessing existing businesses. Since, by definition, all proposed new opportunities, other than acquisitions, have zero relative market share, each such entry is a point on the right side of the matrix. Whereas risk can be explicitly built into the multifactor matrix, risk is not explicitly considered in the growth-share matrix. Furthermore, because of the market definition problem, fragmented markets are not dealt with well by the growth-share matrix, but are handled appropriately in the multifactor framework. Finally, although neither matrix deals well with marketplace dynamics, since neither explicitly assesses the costs of changing a position, the multifactor system makes explicit the business strength improvements required.

Perhaps the bottom line for both approaches to portfolio analysis is that they are aids, not substitutes, for strategy development. The value of the approaches is less in the specific numbers and entries in the matrix than in the discussion that leads to its formation. Especially for the multifactor matrix, the discussion of which criteria to employ and arguments about weightings and ratings are frequently at a very high level, and managers gain

TABLE 12.4 Comparison of Portfolio Approaches

Comparison criteria	Growth-share matrix	Multifactor matrix
Portfolio criteria	Limited but unambiguous	Unlimited but disputable
Measures	Basically objective	Highly subjective
Realism	May lack	May have more
Manipulate entries	Difficult	Easy
Grouping tendency of entries	Low market growth/low market share (bottom right)	High/high, high/medium, medium/high, medium/medium (top left)
Implementability	Easy	More difficult
Communicability	Easy	More difficult
Application across firm	Single set of criteria/measures	Multiple sets of criteria/measures
Accommodates new businesses	Not well	Yes
Explicit consideration of risk	No	Yes, if required
Appropriate for fragmented markets	No	Yes
Underlying focus	Cash flow	ROI
Sensitivity to market definition	Yes	Yes
Sensitivity to basic assumptions	Yes	Yes

significant insight about their choices. Anyone believing that these matrices represent some kind of strategy generating machine is extremely naive and is likely heading for a fall.

APPROACHES TO DEVELOPING PRODUCT PORTFOLIOS   Many firms use the growth-share matrix as the starting point for a portfolio approach to product line management. However, the generic problems of an overly-simplified approach, in particular the definition of relevant market, are particularly troublesome because of the behavior they may produce in marketing, product, and brand managers.

Such managers often like to demonstrate they have achieved or are maintaining a high share of served market, in part because products that show marketplace success in terms of high market shares tend to receive a disproportionate share of resources. One way to secure high market share is artificially to delineate narrow market boundaries. This behavior is a problem in dynamic market structures, and is accentuated by rote application of growth-share thinking to the resource allocation process.

In part because of this problem, firms should investigate alternative ways of displaying their product portfolios. The need for competitive differentiation is the strongest argument for using company-specific multiple factor analysis schemes. Some of the more revealing analyses directly relate market and financial performance. For example, Avon used portfolios based on sales growth and pretax return on assets (Figure 12.4) to develop objectives and strategy for its Mallinckrodt division.

In addition, firms could be more creative by developing portfolio displays that relate to other functional performance criteria. Plots of market attractiveness or such criteria as age of manufacturing plant, re-investment rate in facilities or other competency development area, such as human resources, or rate of spending on advertising and promotion could all yield useful insight.[30]

INTERRELATIONSHIPS AMONG PRODUCTS

A separate aspect of managing the product portfolio concerns interrelationships among products that may exist over and above those concerning resources. These interrelationships may require the firm to make serious product strategy decisions. It is useful to consider two types of interrelationships—those focused at the customer and those focused at the firm.

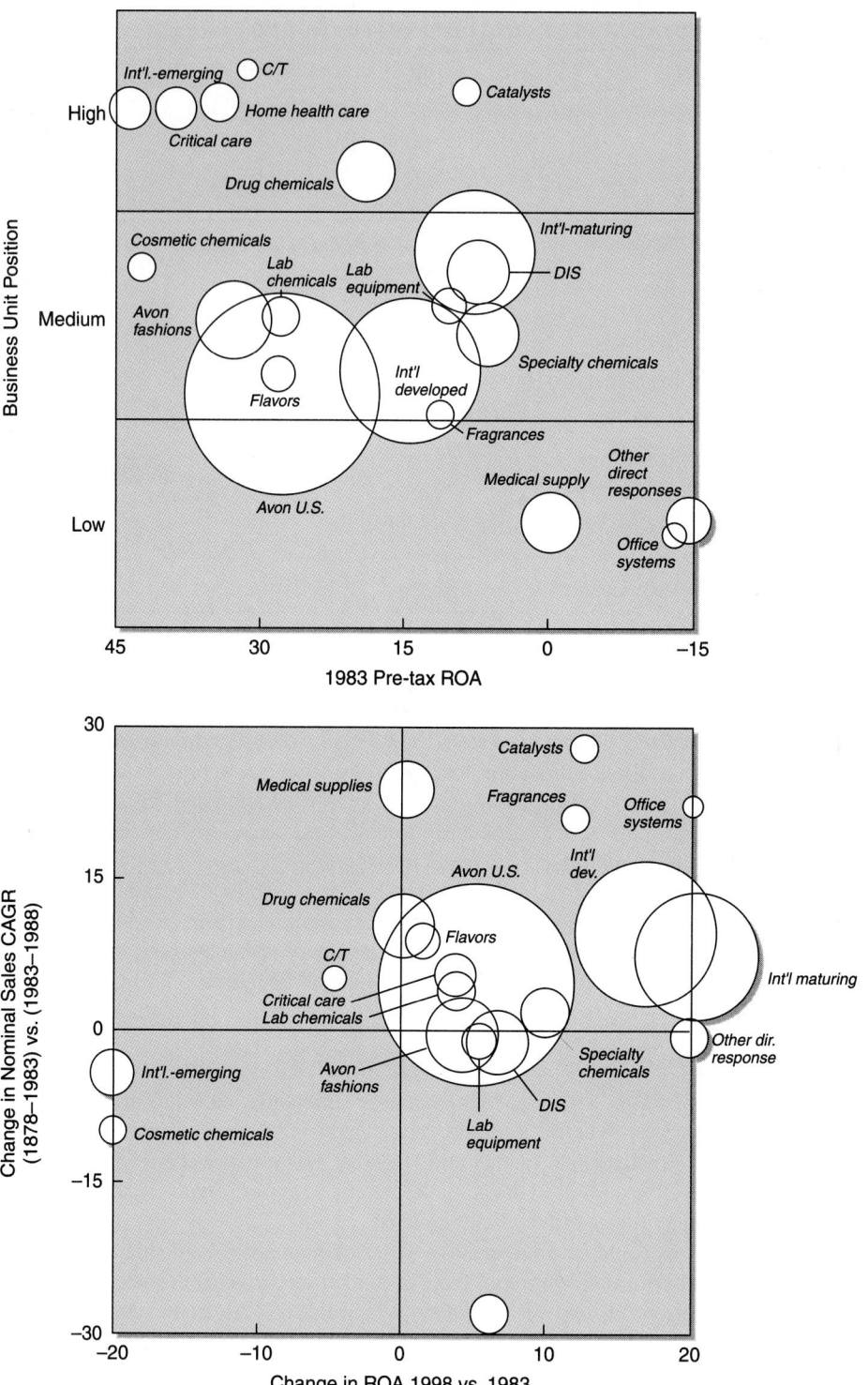

FIGURE 12.4

Historical and Projected Portfolios for Avon's Mallinckrodt Division

THE TASKS
OF MARKETING

Interrelationships at the Customer

Some products are direct complements, such as razors and razor blades, cameras and film, satellite dishes and program content. The nature of this complementarity is fairly straightforward and the firm might be successful offering either or both complementary products. If the firm offers both products, pricing issues are particularly crucial (see Chapter 18).

In other cases, the nature of the complementarity may be either positive or negative for the firm.

POSITIVE COMPLEMENTARITY   In many markets, the sequence of a customer's purchases over time is closely related to the initial purchase. This over-time complementarity results in the customer trading-up to higher-quality, higher-profit products from the same supplier. Thus, General Motors' historic product strategy was based on trading customers up from *Chevrolet* to *Pontiac*, *Buick*, and other higher value brands. More recently, Apple Computer has had success in securing loyalty to its Macintosh operating system as customers trade up to successive generations of Macintosh products. Similarly, many software customers buy successive versions of software products.

NEGATIVE COMPLEMENTARITY   The firm may lose sales as the result of customer dissatisfaction with its product strategy. This occurs when customers believe their interests are ill-served by the firm's actions. (Similar concerns occur with distributors when firms adopt alternate channels to reach end use customers.) Consider the following example:

> Example: The provision of research information by investment banks may affect their ability to sell investment banking services. In February 1999, Goldman Sachs issued a research report suggesting that Bangkok Bank was "the biggest risk factor in Thailand's banking system." As a result, the bank's share price dropped, angering both Thai government officials and many in the Thai financial industry that might be responsible for awarding future investment banking business.[31]

In some cases, customers may decide to cease doing business with the firm and seek alternative suppliers.

> Example: In the early 1980s, believing that the cola wars had reduced the potential for growth, PepsiCo acquired several restaurant chains, specifically Pizza Hut, Taco Bell, and Kentucky Fried Chicken, as new growth vehicles. These acquisitions also created guaranteed sales of Pepsi products. Archrival Coca-Cola was able to convince PepsiCo restaurant customers that by selling Pepsi, they were aiding a competitor. As a result, the No. 2 and 3 hamburger chains, Burger King and Wendy's, joined McDonald's in selling Coke exclusively.[32]

Interrelationships at the customer may also lead to regulatory problems:

> Example: In an effort to identify faster-growing opportunities than the audit business, major accounting firms have extended their product scopes to include consulting. However, because of the potential conflict of interest—failure to issue harsh audit opinions for current or potential consulting clients—the Securities and Exchange Commission (SEC) is concerned. In early 2000, Ernst and Young, one of the large accounting firms, sold its consulting business.

Interrelationships at the Firm

STRATEGIC ROLES   The previous section, especially Figure 12.2, discussed the various strategic objectives that might be set for different products in the product line. In addition, different products may have different strategic roles. A particularly interesting example is SMH's watchmaking business.

Example: SMH markets several brands of watches in three different price ranges: A class—Swatch, Flik Flak, Endura, and Lanco up to approximately Sfr. 100; B class—Tissot, Certina, Mido, Pierre Balmain, Hamilton, and Calvin Klein up to approximately Sfr. 1,000; and C class—Omega, Longlines, Rado, and Blancpain up to and exceeding Sfr. 1,000,000. Each brand class serves a different market segment but, in addition, fulfills a different role in the product portfolio. Thus most of SMH's profit emanates from the C class brands. A class brands, though profitable, mainly fulfill the function of acting as a firewall, preventing other companies from entering with low-priced watches and ultimately moving upmarket to compete with SMH's high profit brands.[33]

ORGANIZATIONAL UNITS   Another interrelationship issue concerns products offered by different units of the organization. In general, individual divisions or business units are tasked with pursuing separate product/markets, yet the ability to bring together required resources from different divisions may open up opportunities that neither is able to pursue separately. When divisions do not work together, significant opportunities may be lost.

Example: Multinational publisher, Bertelsmann, has a joint venture with AOL. Yet, its biggest magazine, *Stern*, placed a CD-ROM on its cover offering access to T-Online, Deutsche Telekom's Internet service, AOL's principal competitor. Said Bertelsmann's CEO, "It's as though Deutsche Telekom were to hand out AOL free with the German phone book."[34]

PRODUCT LINE BREADTH: PRODUCT PROLIFERATION VERSUS PRODUCT SIMPLIFICATION

Many companies face conflicting pressures on their product lines. On the one hand, the pressures of competition (in both product and capital markets) have unfavorably affected the economics of producing low-volume product variants.

Using the so-called DuPont formula, return on assets (ROA) can be expanded into two separate terms by adding "sales" as both a numerator and divisor:

$$\text{ROA} = \frac{\text{Profit}}{\text{Assets}} = \frac{\text{Profit}}{\text{Sales}} \times \frac{\text{Sales}}{\text{Assets}}$$

In the short term, the effect of more intense competition is to shrink net margins (Profit/Sales) such that only products with high sales volumes can generate sufficient asset turnover (Sales/Assets) to meet required ROA targets.

On the other hand compensating factors such as the integration of information technology into operations systems, product design, and manufacturing are lowering the cost of variety. In determining the number of products to offer, management will always have to trade off the conflicting pressures for broad versus narrow product lines.

Pressures for Product Proliferation

Many companies face strong pressures for product proliferation. Ideally, such pressures should be related to differences in customer requirements, driven by solid market analysis and robust market segmentation schemes, that might fill holes in the firm's product line.

Example: In recent years, Time Inc., long associated with such male-oriented publications as *Time, Sports Illustrated, Money* and *Fortune*, has broadened its product line by offering publications aimed at new audiences such as women, children, teenagers, and minorities. New publications included *Entertainment Weekly, In Style, People, People en Español, Teen People, Parenting, Sports Illustrated for Kids, Sunset, Baby Talk*, and *Martha Stewart Living*.[35]

Example: Faced with declining market share in its jeans business, Levi Strauss launched several new brands of jeans at multiple price points (Figure 12.5).

In other cases, the firm may offer virtually identical versions of the same product that tap into different customer needs and may be priced accordingly. Versions can be developed on such bases as time availability and product quality.[36]

TIME AVAILABILITY　　Various versions of the product are basically identical and differ only along a time dimension.

Examples: Package services, such as Federal Express, deliver before 10 A.M. but also later the same day.

Publishers offer hardcover books for enthusiasts and paperback books for those who can wait.

Airlines develop a variety of products for a single flight based on time of booking.

PRODUCT QUALITY　　Sometimes firms produce products that offer high value to customers who are willing to pay a high price. However, because other customers are more price sensitive, it is more economical for the producer to degrade the high-quality product to make a lower value version than it is to design a new product.[37]

Examples: Plastic producers sometimes sell high-quality plastics for rigorous uses (high price) and degraded product for less severe uses (lower price).

The IBM LaserPrinter Series E was identical to the standard LaserPrinter, but included a chip that slowed down its operation from 10 to 5 pages per minute.[38]

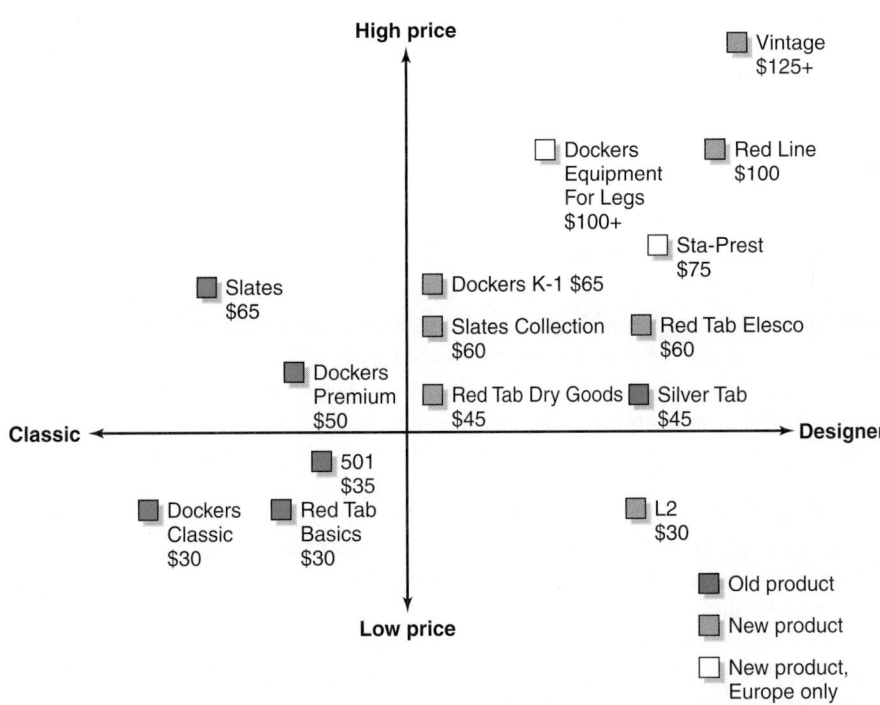

FIGURE 12.5

Levi's New Portfolio of Jeans

Fortune, April 12, 1999.

OTHER BASES In addition, different versions of information products can be developed on several bases. Included are user interface (simple for casual users, more complex for serious users), speed of operation (such as for mathematical programs), and flexibility of use (such as the ability to copy).

Some firms offer many product versions in an effort to dominate the product category, maximize display space in distribution, and exclude competition. Some of these so-called flankers may not be profitable in their own right, but their costs may be justifiable as a means of defending profitable products in the product line.

> **Example:** Procter and Gamble (P&G) has held the leading market share position in laundry detergents for many years. In the US, P&G offers eight different detergent brands, embracing 32 versions and a total of 96 stock keeping units (skus) (Table 12.5).

Finally, many consumer goods companies develop multiple offers by packaging individual products (such as batteries, razors, ballpoint pens) in multiple unit packs, either alone or in combination with other products.

Product Proliferation and Market Segmentation

Many students of marketing suffer genuine confusion about the concepts of market segmentation and product proliferation. Market segmentation relates to differences among customers that management finds useful in developing marketing strategy (Chapter 7). Market segmentation is a tool of convenience used by sellers as a compromise between the complexity of the "real world" and the limited ability of the firm to deal with this complexity. Product proliferation implies large numbers of product variations.

However, to address or target several market segments, multiple products are not necessarily required[39]; rather, the firm must develop multiple offers. Each offer comprises a combination of marketing mix elements. Several offers can be developed, based on an identical product but with variations in brand name, packaging, distribution, and so forth. Such an approach economizes on R&D expenditures.

> **Example:** Monsanto's Roundup herbicide is marketed to both hobby gardeners and commercial farmers. Although different packaging, distribution, and promotional programs are employed, the core product remains the same.

> **Example:** Merck produces the active pharmaceutical ingredient finasteride. This product is sold as a treatment both for hair loss (Propecia) and enlarged prostate (Proscar), but at different prices. Similarly, Glaxo Wellcome's bupropion hydrochloride is sold both as Wellbutrin for antidepression and as Zyban for smoking cessation.

However, this strategy is not always successful. Bausch and Lomb suffered significantly when it was revealed that the firm was selling identical products in the high-end contact lens market and in the disposable lens market. Furthermore, in consumer packaged goods, some private label or store brands are identical in composition to, and made on the same production equipment as, manufacturers' brands creating potential problems for the manufacturers' brands.

Conversely, broad product variety (product proliferation) is not necessarily evidence of market segmentation. For example, if several competitors were targeting a particular market segment that was attractive to the firm, management might decide to increase firm density in the segment by making several marketing offers incorporating multiple product variations. Such an approach might be especially valuable if customers in the segment have unstable need profiles or the segment is comprised of variety seekers.[40] In many cases, (such as jams and jellies, spices, fasteners, salad dressings, and cereals) customers may desire an assortment (ensemble) of products, in which case broad product variety is required.

> **Example:** MacNeil Labs offers many forms of Tylenol. It is available in capsules, caplets, and liquid, regular, and extra strength. Not all versions and sizes of the

TABLE 12.5 P&G's U.S. Offerings of Laundry Detergent (number of package sizes)

Tide	Cheer	Dreft	Gain	Bold	Ivory Snow	Oxydol	Era
Powder	**Powder***	**Powder**	**Powder**	**Powder**	**Powder**	**Powder**	**Powder**
• New Tide with Activated Hydrogen Peroxide (7)	• All Color Cheer (5)	• Dreft (1)	• Gain Original Scent (5)	• Bold Plain Powder (1)	• Ivory Snow Powder (1)	• Oxydol Powder (1)	NO PRODUCT ENTRY
• New Tide with Activated Hydrogen Peroxide and Mountain Spring (scented) (4)	• Cheer with Bleach (3)		• Gain with Bleach (3)				
• New Tide with Bleach (6)	• Cheer Free (1)		• Gain Gentle Breeze Scent (2)				
• New Tide with Bleach and Mountain Spring (scented) (3)							
• Tide Free (2)							
• Tide High Efficiency (1)							
Liquid	**Liquid**	**Liquid**	**Liquid**	**Liquid**	**Liquid**	**Liquid**	**Liquid**
• Tide Ultra (6)	• All Color Cheer (5)	• Dreft (2)	• Gain regular (4)	• Bold Ultra Liquid (1)	• Ivory Snow Liquid (1)	NO PRODUCT ENTRY	• Era Ultra (6)
• Tide Ultra with Mountain Spring (scented) (5)	• Cheer Complete (1)		• Gain with Bleach Alternative (3)				• Era Ultra with Bleach Alternative (2)
• Tide with Bleach Alternative (6)	• Cheer Free (3)						
• Tide with Bleach Alternative and Mountain Spring (scented) (1)							
• Tide Free (3)							
• Tide High Efficiency (1)							

*all products with fabric-protecting "Liquifiber."

brand are profitable but, as a whole, the Tylenol brand has been immensely lucrative for its owner, Johnson & Johnson (J&J).

Product Line Simplification

In recent years, product line rationalization has been largely driven by structural changes in the marketplace as consolidation has led to fewer, more powerful buyers emerging in many industries. For example, fast-moving consumer goods (packaged goods) companies in most European countries face, as customers, only four or five large supermarket chains, and these chains are increasingly looking at cross-border expansion and consolidation. Similarly, in the United States, significant customers comprise only about 20 supermarket chains, a few major warehouse groups, and three or four mass merchandisers; several of these retailers seem determined to become global players and are rapidly expanding into Asia and Latin America. As they grow larger, these buyers not only pressure seller margins, they also emphasize their own retail brands. The result is increased competition for shelf space that, together with the introduction of such initiatives as Efficient Consumer Response (ECR), Direct Product Profitability (DPP),[41] and shareholder value assessment has meant decreased space for named brands in many product categories. Faced with this pressure, firms have to decide whether it is more advantageous to maintain the number of brands and varieties, or to streamline their product and brand offerings.

Example: In 1999, Unilever announced that it would cut its brand portfolio by 1,000 of 1,600 brands and focus on a core group of 400 global and regional brands. These brands accounted for 90% of its $27 billion global revenues. The remaining national and local brands would be sold, lose marketing support, be withdrawn, or consolidated into stronger brands.[42]

The internal pressures that keep firms from making the tough product deletion decisions should not be underestimated.

Example: In his autobiography, Andy Grove, former CEO of Intel, describes the agonizing decision, in the face of intense competition, to exit the memory chip business on which the firm was founded and where it had once been the market leader, in favor of a concentrated effort on microprocessors.[43]

Less a function of external pressure but more of opportunity, globalizing firms are finding significant opportunities to rationalize their product lines. For example, in many cases, firms' subsidiary operations in foreign countries developed their product lines to meet local needs. Now that customers are becoming increasingly global in their requirements, some firms are taking the opportunity to simplify their product lines by turning multiple country specifications into a series of global specifications. Not only does such an approach often better meet customer requirements (especially in business-to-business marketing), it also allows for cost reductions.

Example: Faced with multinational customers requiring identical products worldwide, Betz Dearborn, a U.S.-based global manufacturer of boilers for industrial use, was able to cut the number of items in its product line by over 50% by rationalizing specifications across its various operating units.

Regardless of the rationale, product deletion decisions should be made thoughtfully. Rather than make these decisions in a knee-jerk reaction to immediate problems, they should plan for them carefully using a well-developed set of elimination criteria (Table 12.6).

TABLE 12.6 Potential Evaluation Criteria for Product Deletion Decisions[44]

Market potential	PEE* on other products (sales/profits)	PEE on capacity utilization
Substitute available	PEE on overhead recovery	Reallocation of exec./sales time
PEE on firm sales volume	Contribution to profit center	PEE on employee relationships
Availability of new product	PEE on working capital	Likely competitive reaction
Reallocation of resources	PEE on full-line policy	Component interchangeability
PEE on customer/distribution	PEE on firm image	PEE on fixed capital

*PEE = product elimination effect

Unfortunately, many firms develop significant profitability problems by pursuing mindless product deletion policies based on bottom-line results. They discover, to their dismay, that the high-volume (bottom-line loss) product they have dropped was carrying a large share of overhead. Elimination of this product means that the unit cost of the remaining products is now greater. (See Table 12.7 for a worked example.)

In this simple example, the firm is comprised of two products—A and B. To make this illustration more understandable, the traditional costing convention, embracing cost of goods sold (COGS), marketing and selling, and general and administrative costs (SG&A), has been rearranged to focus on three types of cost items:

- Variable costs, such as raw materials and direct labor, vary directly with sales volume. (Sales revenue less variable costs is variable or contribution margin.)
- Direct fixed costs are associated with the individual products, such as product managers, specialized production supervisors, and other technical personnel.
- Indirect fixed costs are not directly related to any product. They include corporate functions such as R&D, human resources, and shareholder relations. In this illustration, the indirect fixed costs are allocated to the two products on the basis of their share of sales revenues.

The firm makes a $500,000 profit for an unsatisfactory return on sales (ROS) of 1.4% on $35 million sales. Further investigation shows that the $500,000 profit is the combination of a $1.5 million profit on product B and a $1 million loss on product A. The seemingly logical action is to eliminate product A. However, as can be seen in the final column, the firm (now just product B) experiences a $1.5 million loss. The indirect fixed costs of $3 million that were formerly part of product A's income statement have not been eliminated. Product B now has to absorb these costs.[45]

Those companies simplifying their product lines by rationalizing their brand portfolios, such as Unilever in the earlier example, may have different problems. First, some of these brands have been starved of marketing support. Thus while short-run profits may be quite reasonable, it may be difficult to find companies willing to pay an acceptable purchase price, for they will realize that substantial investment may be required to rebuild the brand. Second, by selling a brand, the firm may be putting a competitor in business. Although the reason for selling the brand may be to focus the firm's effort, a determined competitor may upset its plans.[46]

TABLE 12.7 Simple Illustration of a Mindless Product Deletion Decision ($000s)

	Overall Firm	Product A	Product B	Firm Less Product A
Sales Revenues	$35,000	$15,000	$20,000	$20,000
Variable Costs	$19,500	$ 8,500	$11,000	$11,000
Variable Margin*	$15,500	$ 6,500	$ 9,000	$ 9,000
Direct Fixed Costs	$ 8,000	$ 4,500	$ 3,500	$ 3,500
Indirect Fixed Costs	$ 7,000	$ 3,000	$ 4,000	$ 7,000
Profit	$ 500	($ 1,000)	$ 1,500	($ 1,500)

*contribution margin

OTHER PRODUCT LINE ISSUES

Extending Product Life

In many cases, the firm may be able to undertake actions to extend the product's life rather than delete the product. This is a common practice in the pharmaceutical industry where prices tend to drop precipitously once a product comes off patent. The most common methods in that industry are:

- secure FDA[47] approval for other diseases
- new dosage formulations
- switch from prescription to over-the-counter
- different method of delivering the drug to the body

These methods can be generalized to other industries to extend individual product life cycles.

Product Cannibalization

One way to increase margins is to replace sales of low margin products with sales of higher margin products. To the extent that the firm can make such substitutions without losing volume, few would argue with the increased profits that such a strategy delivers.

> **Examples:** In mid-1998 Gillette introduced Mach3, the world's first triple-blade razor. Mach3 cartridges sell at a 50% premium over SensorExcel, Gillette's previously most expensive blade. By early 1999, Mach3 was the number one blade and razor. Colgate-Palmolive's Total toothpaste, priced 25% above mainstream brands, and Dr. Scholl's Dynastep, priced twice as much as older shoe inserts, have also become market leaders in their product forms.[48]

A more serious issue concerns the reverse case when the firm contemplates introducing a lower margin product that is expected to lead to reduced sales of a higher margin product. In such cases, pressures within the firm often build up against introduction; these generally take the form of demonstrating an overall profit reduction after introducing the new product, and may be sufficiently persuasive to inhibit product launch.

However, under certain circumstances, it can be shown that, despite revenue and volume reductions from current products, the new entry will cause overall revenues and profits to increase. For example, although the lower margin product may take some sales from the higher margin product, it may enable the firm to expand the market or to enter a market segment for which the previous product was not well suited.

> **Example:** Faced with growing price competition to its Pentium products from AMD and others, Intel introduced the Celeron microprocessor as a "fighting brand" to stem market share losses.

However, even if overall revenue and profit estimates are lower than they are currently, the new entry should not necessarily be abandoned. The critical comparison is less that of future profits versus current profits, but rather future profits with the new lower margin product versus future profits without the lower margin product. Thus, for example, the new product may allow the firm to retain market position in the face of current or anticipated future competition. If sales of the higher margin product are to be lost, better they are secured by the firm's lower margin product than by a competitor.

Unfortunately, management often makes the incorrect comparison, and although the firm may retain profits in the short run, the resulting competitive entry is allowed in what proves to be a long-run strategic error.

> **Example:** In the 1960s and 1970s, the U.S. automobile manufacturers allowed Volkswagen, Toyota, Datsun, and other foreign firms to gain a foothold in the United States by their entries in the small car market. Although the U.S. firms had the ability and, in many cases, products that could have been introduced (from

Europe), they hesitated to respond because of lower profit margins on small cars. This decision ultimately led to an overall long-run market share decline as the Japanese manufacturers later added higher quality models to compete with the high profit core of U.S. manufacturers' products.

Product Replacement Decisions

As noted earlier, the key to sustaining economic profit is to ensure that the firm continues to secure differential advantage. Successful new products spawn a cycle of imitation that mandates renewal of that advantage. The timing of these replacement decisions is critical to the maintenance of market position. In general, pre-emption is the most effective option for optimal management of these replacement decisions and is the key to long-term market ownership.

Product Quality

Historically, it was believed that there was a positive correlation between unit cost and quality—the higher the quality, the higher the cost. More recently, the quality movement has shown that this correlation is more likely to be negative—lower quality leads to higher costs—because of such factors as waste, rework, and repairs. In part because of this realization, quality has risen across the board and high product quality is increasingly a prerequisite for serious competition. However, in addition to important competitive factors, less-than-perfect product quality may leave a firm open to lawsuits.

> **Example:** In late 1999, Toshiba agreed to spend about $1 billion to settle a class action lawsuit based on an allegation by two customers who contended that Toshiba had sold five million defective laptop computers in the United States since 1987. The alleged defect which "is so inconsequential that the company itself could not duplicate the problem in the laboratory under normal operating conditions," concerned recording data onto floppy discs. Toshiba was believed to have agreed to such a large settlement because it was advised of the problem in 1987 by NEC, from whom Toshiba licensed the design, but did nothing to fix the problem.[49]

Secondary Markets

In some categories where customers purchase products with reasonable frequency, performance of the firm's products in secondary markets has important implications for sales of the firm's products in its primary markets.[50] First, in several consumer durables categories, customers consider the potential resale value of their products in making purchase decisions. As a result, it is in the firm's interest to keep the secondary market price high. In addition, higher resale prices imply lessened competition for the firm's products in its primary markets.

> **Example:** The resale price is particularly important in the automobile industry. Toyota, among other companies, has introduced a certification for previously-owned Toyota cars, designed to make them more attractive to buyers of second-hand vehicles.

Legal and Ethical Issues

The focus of this section is on product safety and disposal of products and packaging.

PRODUCT SAFETY In subsistence (premarket) economies, individuals and families are responsible for producing or acquiring products needed for their own sustenance; as such, they take personal responsibility for the products they consume. In market economies, individuals and families consume products often produced in distant places by individuals they do not know. These producers thus have a special responsibility to ensure that the products they offer to customers are not harmful to them.

In many jurisdictions, regulatory bodies, such as the Food and Drug Administration (FDA) and the Consumer Product Safety Commission in the United States, enforce laws protecting consumers from product hazards. Regardless, managers have an ethical responsibility to ensure that their products are not harmful to users. Unfortunately, some managers do not go as far as they should in protecting their customers.

> **Example:** In October 1996, production managers at the Odwalla Company apple juice plant ignored the requests of a quality supervisor to refuse a load of rotten apples. As a result, Odwalla sold apple juice tainted with E. coli bacteria, leading to one death and dozens of illnesses.[51]

Customers are sometimes harmed or killed from products that are inappropriately designed, produced, or used. Customer safety is not confined to products; ill-designed service establishments can also harm customers. Consider barrier collapses at sporting events, or subway design that permits passengers to be pushed on train tracks. In satisfying customer needs through product and service design, managers (marketing and otherwise) have a responsibility to make customer safety a pre-eminent consideration.

Of course, no matter how much effort firms devote to ensuring high product quality, problems will inevitably occur from time to time. How the firm deals with such errors can have an important impact on customers' perceptions and their future purchasing behavior. Consider the different manners in which firms reacted to major crises involving loss of life.

> **Example: General Motors**. In his book, *Unsafe at Any Speed*,[52] Ralph Nader asserted that the Corvair, GM's first rear-engine car, was unsafe and that several people had died when their cars went out of control. General Motors denied there was a problem and hired private detectives to investigate Mr. Nader's private life. Ultimately, Mr. Nader won a defamation suit against GM and the Corvair was withdrawn.

> **Example: Johnson and Johnson**. Several people died when capsules of Tylenol, manufactured by its McNeil Laboratories subsidiary, were laced with cyanide. Within a matter of days, Tylenol was totally withdrawn throughout the United States. When it was reintroduced several months later, Tylenol quickly regained its leading market position.

And, on a somewhat lighter note:

> **Example:** In the late 1990s, the British national newspaper, *The Guardian*, introduced a daily "Corrections and Clarifications" column in which it prominently presents its *mea culpas*. Such openness has received positive response. Furthermore, the satirical British weekly, *Private Eye*, said that, "The Grauniad's corrections are far, far more interesting than the original articles."[53]

DISPOSAL OF PRODUCTS AND PACKAGING   Products that customers purchase frequently arrive in some form of packaging. Packaging has a variety of functions, ranging from product protection (during transportation), customer use in its own right (such as receptacles), and communications (design and visuals). One feature that packaging shares with many products is the need for disposal.

Historically, manufacturers were little concerned with the disposal of products and packaging. However, increasingly, governmental jurisdictions concerned with the physical environment have passed laws concerning these matters. These movements are perhaps most active in Europe, with Germany at the forefront of environmental protection. Not only is there a social stigma attached to using large trash bins in some German communities, but federal law gives authorities the power to restrict or ban materials with problematic toxicity or waste volume, and some municipalities charge for garbage collection based on volume.[54]

Clearly, packaging and product disposal are not issues that all producers need necessarily be concerned with today, but they should be aware of the growing trend of environmental concern worldwide.

SUMMARY

Composing the product line is a major corporate challenge, but offers substantial opportunity to increase shareholder value. This chapter discussed the importance of managing the firm's products as a portfolio, and contrasted financial and strategic tools (portfolio analysis) as aids in fulfilling this managerial responsibility.

This chapter also discussed product interrelationships, issues of product line breadth, and the potential for intra-firm conflicts as the mix of products and businesses becomes more complex. As more firms adopt the economic value added (EVA) concept, many find that product line trimming leads to significant increases in shareholder value. In the past, firms added product offerings for internal rather than customer-related reasons. However, as competitive pressures increase, product line management will increasingly require that product additions add real customer value. As emphasized throughout this book, only by adding customer value can the firm increase shareholder value.

Relatedly, this chapter argued for a rigorous product deletion process comprising well-thought through criteria since short-sighted deletion can also lead to reduced profits. This chapter examined extending product life, product cannibalization, product replacement, product quality, and secondary markets, then concluded by introducing some legal and ethical issues, notably product safety, and packaging and product disposal.

THE CHANGING VIEW

Old Way	New Way
Products viewed independently	Products managed as a portfolio
Judgments made exclusively with financial criteria	Judgments based on market and financial criteria
Profit focus	Shareholder value focus
Product proliferation common, rationalization rare	Product line breadth carefully managed, rationalization common
Caveat emptor	Caveat vendor
Quality variable	Total Quality Management (TQM)
Ethical considerations relatively rare	Ethical considerations recognized as vital
Waste ignored	Environmental concerns important
Uniform business objectives by product	Business objectives tailored by product
Products and brands often treated similarly	Products and brands carefully discriminated
Reluctance to cannibalize products	Cannibalization managed strategically as part of product line renewal
Product profitability data rare	Product profitability data becoming ubiquitous
Product managers on pedestals	Product managers subject to executive control

QUESTIONS FOR STUDY AND DISCUSSION

1. Portfolio analysis is useful only when applied at the product level to inform resource allocation decisions among the various products of the business. Discuss.

2. The Boston Consulting Group developed the world's most popular version of strategic portfolio analysis, colloquially known as the growth-share matrix. Why have so many companies replaced (or augmented) it with multifactor matrices?

3. Much scientific evidence has documented that cigarette smoke, both inhaled directly and second-hand, causes cancer and heart disease. Imagine that you have been offered product manager jobs with both Philip Morris and

R.J. Reynolds, the world's leading cigarette manufacturers. Starting salaries are 20% higher than your other best offer. Will you accept either of these offers? Why or why not?

4. The traditional attitudes of sellers towards buyers can be summarized in the Latin phrase *caveat emptor*. Few companies espouse this philosophy today. Might economic forces explain this change? How?

5. The text discusses an example of a firewall brand used as part of a defensive market strategy. What, in your opinion, are the disadvantages of firewall brands?

6. Multifactor portfolio schemes often employ qualitative criteria in the rating system, thus introducing subjectivity into the analytic framework. Some executives object to this subjectivity. Are their views justified? Why or why not?

7. Some writers argue that the need for cash-flow balance in the corporate portfolio has been overstated since the firm typically has access to the capital markets. Do you agree with this argument? Defend your position.

8. The boom in Internet stocks has led to high market values for firms that are making significant losses and, sometimes, hemorrhaging cash. Obviously, investors may be universally optimistic. Can you think of any marketing-related reasons that might justify such high stock prices?

9. Why is it potentially dangerous to rely solely on financial analysis methods for evaluating possible product investments?

10. "By applying portfolio analysis only at the corporate level firms have made significant aggregation errors." Explain why finer-grained portfolio analysis is desirable.

11. Identify two situations where firms with high market share have performed poorly. What factors explain this? Are there any implications for the usual expectation of a positive market share/financial performance relationship?

12. Competition among product managers to demonstrate sales revenue increases has sometimes led to excessive product range extensions and a proliferation of product variants. What steps should management take to avoid this problem?

13. Select a firm with which you are familiar. Identify interrelationships among products in its product line.

14. The customer is responsible for product and packaging disposal. It is none of our business. Discuss.

15. When times are good (poor), the firm should add (delete) products. Discuss.

ENDNOTES

1. Chapters 9 and 10 discussed a variety of possible business objectives and strategies for individual product market entries enjoying differing competitive positions at different stages in the product form life cycle. Of course, the firm may launch a new product at various stages in the product form life cycle; alternative entry strategies are discussed in Chapter 6.

2. Having a balanced portfolio and choosing when to go to the capital markets is typically more desirable than being forced to go when liquidity is insufficient and the timing inopportune.

3. Joseph Bower's pioneering research demonstrated just how much the real world departed from academics' convenient, simplifying assumptions. J.L. Bower, *Managing the Resource Allocation Process*, Boston, MA: Harvard Business School Press, 1970.

4. Typically, the espoused goal of corporate management is to maximize return on shareholder equity (ROE). In most corporations, since composition of the investment dollar (debt or equity) is a matter for financial man-

agers, return-on-investment (ROI) is used as a proxy. Not only is ROI the measure used most frequently by major manufacturing firms for performance evaluation, it is also used to assess the worth of individual investments, see N. Capon, J.U. Farley and J. Hulbert, *Corporate Strategic Planning,* New York: Columbia University Press, 1988.

5. For a detailed treatment of these and other financial analysis techniques, see J.C. Van Horne, *Financial Management and Policy*, Englewood Cliffs, NJ: Prentice Hall, 1995.

6. In most firms, returns are earned from the sale of products; expenditures are for operating expenses (raw materials and labor) and for capital equipment. The principle underlying discounting is that the future value of one dollar is less that the value of that dollar today.

7. More precisely, IRR is that rate of return at which the NPV = 0; calculation of NPV assumes a discount rate. Furthermore, the IRR technique assumes reinvestment of surplus funds at the IRR, whereas NPV assumes reinvestment at the discount rate. See Van Horne, *op. cit.*, Chapter 6. The hurdle rate is the cut-off rate of return, below which investment proposals will not be funded.

8. Equity analysts do this continually but there is little comfort from their conclusions. If they were successful in this endeavor, managed funds would consistently out-perform index funds, which they do not. Further, the understanding of product/market strategy on the part of some of these analysts seems minimal. For example, *The Financial Times* (January 20, 1998) reported with astonishment that the financial community had discovered the contribution of R&D to companies' (long-term) profitability. Published research demonstrated this relationship very clearly over ten years earlier. Capon, Farley, and Hulbert *op. cit.*

9. R.L. Foster, *Innovation*: *The Attacker's Advantage*, New York: Summit, 1986.

10. W.K. Hall, "Why Risk Analysis Isn't Working," *Long Range Planning*, 8 (December 1975), pp. 25–29.

11. P. Haspeslagh, "Portfolio Planning: Uses and Limits," *Harvard Business Review*, 60 (Jan.-Feb. 1982), pp. 58–74.

12. Typically, portfolio models array (or map) the firm's various units (product/market segments or businesses, depending on level of analysis) or new investment opportunities into a two-dimensional graph (matrix). The visual appearance of the portfolio matrix structure, such as 2×2, 3×3 depends on the number of divisions made of each matrix dimension and is essentially arbitrary. From an examination of the placement of entries on the graph, management is able to assess potential return and risk [success probabilities], and gain insight into a variety of strategic options. It is the visual property of these matrices that provides much of their appeal; they allow senior managers to review current and potential businesses as entries on a single sheet of paper.

13. The iterative Delphi approach is a good method of seeking managerial agreement on this criterion. In this method, several individuals first make estimates. Each individual then receives information on the entire set of forecasts and is asked to reforecast. Typically, estimates converge.

14. As typically presented, the market growth dimension has a linear scale; the relative market share measure has a logarithmic scale. Note that in conventional presentations, relative market share is scaled high to low, rather than the more common x-axis scaling of low to high.

15. Of course, managers of businesses or products competing in slower growth markets typically seek lower cut points!

16. The economics of information products may differ substantially from these general statements.

17. See Chapter 9 Appendix.

18. Over many years, the relationship between market share, market growth, and profitability have been two of the more robust findings of the PIMS project.

19. D.C. Hambrick, I.C. MacMillan, and D.L. Day, "Strategic Attributes and Performance in the BCG Matrix-A PIMS-Based Analysis of Industrial Product Business, *Academy of Management Journal*, 25 (Sept. 1982), pp. 510–531; B.T. Gale and B. Branch, "Cash Flow Analysis: More Important than Ever," *Harvard Business Review*, 59 (Jul.-Aug. 1981), pp. 131–136.

20. Of course, for a variety of reasons, it is not necessarily the case that such businesses are cash generators.

21. Note that this framework does not address such questions as the firm's capital structure (extent of debt and equity) or dividend policy. Clearly, these decisions have a major impact on the firm's ability to secure cash from outside sources and its external cash requirements.

22. See R. Vernon, "Gone Are the Cash Cows of Yesteryear," *Harvard Business Review*, 58 (Nov./Dec. 1980), pp. 150–155.

23. In setting GE's strategy of being #1 or #2 in any business where it competes, CEO Jack Welch recognized that strong #2s could reach GE's demanding profit performance standards, but less competitively placed products could not.

24. For example, Anheuser Busch's closing of Eagle Snacks in 1996.

25. Of course, the relationship focuses on achieved market share; the process of securing market share may be unprofitable in the short run.

26. The general approach is to choose market boundaries that are strategically significant for the firm. Of course, since market boundaries change over time, this issue should be considered when analyses are repeated.

27. A derivative of this approach was used in the Chapter 7 discussion of Market Segment Targeting.

28. See also consultant Arthur D. Little's 20-cell matrix whose dimensions are stage of industry maturity (embryonic, growth, mature, aging) and competitive position (dominant, strong, favorable, tenable, weak); the Directional Policy Matrix from Shell Chemical, D.C. Hussey, "Portfolio Analysis: Practical Experience with the Directional Policy Matrix," *Long Range Planning* 11 (Aug. 1978), pp. 2–8; and a system developed by Mead Paper, C.W. Hofer and D.E. Schendel, *Strategy Formulation*: *Analytical Concepts*, St. Paul, MN: West, 1978. In each case, position in the matrix indicates (and sometimes dictates) investment strategy. In a sense, the various portfolio models are comparable to the several different financial analysis techniques for analyzing investment opportunities.

29. See also Figure 7.7.

30. For an extension of these ideas into the technology portfolio, embracing product, process and managerial technology, see N. Capon and R. Glazer, "Marketing and Technology: A Strategic Coalignment," *Journal of Marketing*, 51 (July 1987), pp. 1–14.

31. *The New York Times*, March 12, 1999. Other investment banking institutions have had similar problems, such as Morgan Stanley and HSBC in China.

32. More recently, PepsiCo has spun off its restaurant businesses into a separate company, leaving it once again able to compete with Coke in major accounts on an equal footing.

33. A.J. Slywotzky and D.J. Morrison, *The Profit Zone*, New York: Times Business, 1997.

34. *The Economist*, November 7, 1998.

35. *The New York Times*, January 8, 1998.

36. C. Shapiro and H.R. Varian, *Information Rules,* Boston, MA: Harvard Business School Press, 1999.

37. See also R. Denerke and P. McAfee, "Damaged Goods," *Journal of Economics and Management Strategy*, 5 (1996), pp. 149–174. Deliberate product degradation should not be confused with low product quality.

38. Shapiro and Varian, *op. cit.*, p. 59.

39. Should multiple products be required, the techniques of modular design (platform engineering) discussed in Chapter 9 may be applied.

40. J.A. Howard and J.N. Sheth, *The Theory of Buyer Behavior*, New York: Wiley, 1969.

41. ECR is a major supply chain initiative in the grocery trade. For more details, see Distribution Decisons, Chapter 15. DPP is a system for appraising the true profitability of a retail product item, pioneered by what is now Dayton-Hudson.

42. *The Wall Street Journal*, September 22, 1999. In 1991, Procter & Gamble eliminated 25% of the products in its product line. It sold off poorly performing products and reduced the numbers of varieties of others, such as from 30 to 15 for Head and Shoulders shampoo; *The Wall Street Journal*, January 15, 1997.

43. Grove believes that an emotional attachment to memories delayed Intel's exit, A.S. Grove, *Only the Paranoid Survive*, New York: Doubleday, 1996.

44. G.J. Avlonitis, "'Project Dropstrat': Product Elimination and the Product Life Cycle Concept," *European Journal of Marketing*, (September 1990), pp. 55–67. See also S.J. Hart, "Product Deletion and the Effects of Strategy," *European Journal of Marketing*, (October 1989), pp. 6–17; D.M. Lambert and J.U. Sterling, "The Product Abandonment Decision, *Management Accounting*, (August 1998), pp. 8–27 and Mark A. Mitchell, "Product Elimination Decisions: A Comparison of American and British Manufacturing Firms," *International Journal of Commerce & Management*, (1998), pp. 8–27. For classic articles in this area, see R.S. Alexander, "The Death and Burial of Sick Products," *Journal of Marketing*, (April 1964), pp. 1–7 and P. Kotler, "Phasing

Out Weak Products," *Harvard Business Review*, 43, (March/April 1965), pp. 108–118 and P.W. Hamelman and E.M. Mazze, "Improving Product Abandonment Decisions," *Journal of Marketing*, 36 (April 1972), pp. 20–26.

45. Those firms that cannot classify costs as variable and fixed run the real risk of unwittingly eliminating products that reduce overall profits. See the Book Appendix for more information on this form of financial analysis.

46. *Financial Times*, October 29, 1999.

47. **F**ood and **D**rug **A**dministration.

48. *Business Week*, February 1, 1999.

49. *The New York Times*, October 30, 1999. The two plaintiffs were each to receive $25,000; their lawyers' fees were expected to amount to $147.5 million!

50. Primary markets are those in which the firm sells its products; secondary markets are those where the product owner resells the product to another customer.

51. *The New York Times*, January 4, 1998.

52. R. Nader, *Unsafe at Any Speed: the Designed-In Dangers of the American Automobile*, New York: Pocket Books, 1966.

53. *The New York Times*, February 16, 1998.

54. The Procter & Gamble Company: Lenor Refill Package, *Harvard Business School*, 9-592-016.

WEB RESOURCES

AMD	www.amd.com
AOL	www.aol.com
Anheuser Busch	www.anheuser-busch.com
Arthur D. Little	www.arthurdlittle.com
Avon	www.avon.com
Baby Talk	www.pathfinder.com/parenttime/parenting/babytalk.html
Bangkok Bank	www.bbl.co.th
Bausch & Lomb	www.bausch.com
Bertelsmann	www.bertelsmann.de
Betz Dearborn	www.betzdearborn.com
Boston Consulting Group	www.bcg.com
Buick	www.buick.com
Burger King	www.burgerking.com
Cadillac	www.cadillac.com
Charles Schwab	www.schwab.com
Chevrolet	www.chevrolet.com
Coke	www.cocacola.com
Colgate	www.colgate.com
Consumer Product Safety Commission	www.cpsc.gov
Cutt Farms	www.ecoli.cas.psu.edu/fancy.htm
Datsun	www.nissan.com
Delphi	www.delphi.com
Dr. Scholl's	www.drscholls.com
DuPont	www.dupont.com
Entertainment Weekly	www.pathfinder.com/ew
Federal Express	www.fedex.com
Food and Drug Administration	www.fda.gov
Fortune	www.fortune.com
General Electric	www.ge.com

General Motors	www.gm.com
Gillette	www.gillette.com
Glaxo Wellcome	www.glaxowellcome.co.uk
Goldman Sachs	www.gs.com
Guardian	www.guardian.co.uk
Honda	www.honda.com
HSBC	www.hsbc.com
IBM	www.ibm.com
In Style	www.instylenetwork.com
Intel	www.intel.com
Johnson & Johnson	www.jnj.com
Kentucky Fried Chicken	www.kentuckyfriedchicken.com
Levi's	www.levi.com
Martha Stewart	www.marthastewart.com
McDonald's	www.mcdonalds.com
McKinsey	www.mckinsey.com
Merck	www.merck.com
Merrill Lynch	www.ml.com
Money	www.pathfinder.com/money
Monsanto	www.monsanto.com
Morgan Stanley Dean Witter	www.msdw.com
Odwalla	www.odwalla.com
Oldsmobile	www.oldsmobile.com
Parenting	www.pathfinder.com/parenttime
People	www.pathfinder.com/people
PepsiCo	www.pepsico.com
Philip Morris	www.philipmorris.com
Pizza Hut	www.pizzahut.com
Pontiac	www.pontiac.com
Private Eye	www.private-eye.co.uk
Procter & Gamble	www.pg.com
R.J. Reynolds	www.rjrt.com
SMH	www.theswatchgroup.com
Sports Illustrated	www.cnnsi.com
Sports Illustrated for Kids	www.sikids.com
Stern	www.stern.com
Sunset	www.sunsetmagazine.com
Taco Bell	www.tacobell.com
Teen	www.pathfinder.com/teenpeople
Time Inc.	www.time.com
T-Online	www.t-online.de
Toyota	www.toyota.com
Unilever	www.unilever.com
Volkswagen	www.vw.com
Wendy's	www.wendysintl.com

CHAPTER

13

DEVELOPING NEW PRODUCTS

LEARNING OBJECTIVES

When you have completed this chapter, you will understand

- the success factors used by innovative companies

- the relationship between marketing and innovation

- the different ways for firms to approach the innovation challenge

- the classic, new product development process

- the ways in which that process is changing to meet the challenges of today's competitive marketplace

INTRODUCTION

This chapter focuses on the critical issue of developing new products. It reviews how different companies and firms approach innovation, and presents the classic stage-gate new product development process, incorporating many of the new ideas that have radically changed this process in leading companies. This treatment also highlights the weaknesses that trammel the process in many firms.[1]

DEVELOPING NEW PRODUCTS

The firm has numerous means by which it can expand its product line. In addition to internal development, a comprehensive technology strategy might include acquisitions of business units or entire corporate entities, strategic alliances, equity investments in new ventures, as well as licensing and technology purchases as alternative or complementary means.[2]

Despite the important role other methods might play in developing the firm's product portfolio, internal development is usually at the center of ongoing evolution of the product line. To rely entirely on these other methods could be extremely risky as the firm would, in effect, be outsourcing its product line development.

New product development is becoming an increasingly crucial weapon as competition intensifies globally and the pressure on profit margins increases. In recent years, practitioners and academics alike have paid vastly increased attention to the ways in which companies innovate and manage the innovation process, as well as the issues involved in successfully bringing new products to market.[3]

INNOVATION AND INNOVATIVE COMPANIES

It is important to understand that innovation is not just about new products; firms can innovate in many ways. They can be innovative in their approach to the market, such as in the way they distribute (Dell Computer); in customer service (L.L. Bean, Virgin Airlines, or Nordstrom); even in the way they package their products (L'Eggs pantyhose with their original package) or advertise (Hamlet cigars).

Nonetheless, it would be foolish to underestimate the importance of new products. Because they are so visible and often require considerable resource commitments, much more attention has been focused, and knowledge generated, on this aspect of innovation.

However, in most industries, there is typically a wide variation in new product success rates. Some companies' performance with new products seems satisfactory—for example two thirds of Hewlett Packard's (HP) revenues are from products introduced in the previous two years—whereas others have dismal records. Researchers at Columbia Business School focused on product innovation as part of a larger study of corporate planning and strategy. In a fairly representative sample of the Fortune 500 manufacturing firms, it was found that about one third were product innovators; these firms typically secured among the highest rates of return on capital. The results suggest that successful product innovation is a consequence of several factors:

- Being positioned in high-growth markets provides significant stimulation to innovation; choice of markets is an important strategic decision and may have consequences for subsequent innovation.

Strategic and organizational variables also have a major influence:

- Companies that invest significantly and consistently in product R&D, especially with an applied focus, tend to be successful innovators.
- Innovative companies organize to foster their R&D efforts with formal structures that acknowledge the commitment to developing new products. Furthermore, their cultures are supportive of innovation.[4]

More generally, the factors in Figure 13.1 have been found to encourage innovation.[5]

Current thinking is leading to re-assessment of the relationship between good management practice and the management of innovation. For example, Christensen makes the distinction between "sustaining" and "disruptive" innovations. Sustaining innovations, which may be incremental or discontinuous, improve established products along existing performance dimensions that, historically, have been valued by major customers. By contrast, products developed from disruptive innovations offer very different value propositions and generally under-perform existing products. However, they have features that are valued by a few fringe customers, in part because they are typically cheaper, simpler, smaller, and more convenient to use. Examples include minicomputers (versus mainframes), personal desktop computers (versus mainframes and minis), small off-road motorcycles (versus powerful over-the-road bikes), transistors (versus vacuum tubes), and health maintenance organizations (HMOs) (versus conventional health insurers). Nonetheless, since their current customers do not want these initially inferior products, leading firms generally do not invest in disruptive technologies. As a result:

> ... good management was the most powerful reason they (leading firms) failed to stay atop their industries. Precisely because these firms listened to their customers, invested aggressively in new technologies that would provide their customers more and better products of the sort they wanted, and because they carefully studied market trends and systematically allocated investment capital to innovations that promised the best returns, they lost their positions of leadership.[6]

This may sound a little like heresy, but it also suggests that simplistic interpretations of marketing concepts are insufficient if not downright dangerous. Too many marketers, both academics and practitioners, operationalize the marketing concept as serving customers by listening to their needs and supplying them what they want. This widespread perspective can be faulty when it comes to managing innovation.

Revisiting the Purpose of a Business

Earlier, this book introduced Drucker's definition of business purpose—to create a customer and its two basic functions as marketing and innovation. Drucker was sufficiently perceptive to recognize that marketing alone was not sufficient:

> "Marketing alone does not make a business enterprise. . . . The second function of a business, therefore, is innovation—the provision of different economic satisfactions. . . . In the organization of the business enterprise, innovation can no more be considered a separate function than marketing. It is not confined to engineering or research, but extends across all parts of the business. . . . Innovation can be defined as the task of endowing human and material resources with new and greater wealth-producing capacity."[7]

Well-designed System	• Multiple new product development efforts • Continuous project evaluation • Measurement system rewards creativity and innovation • High importance to cross-functional communications
Right Type of Support	• Top management commitment • Selective top management involvement
Appropriate Personnel	• For idea generators, sponsors, coaches and mentors • Boundary spanners for internal/external boundaries • Product champions/internal entrepreneurs

FIGURE 13.1

Factors Found to Encourage Innovation

Thus, Drucker spoke of *creating* a customer, rather than *serving* a customer. Yet, as argued elsewhere,[8] many proponents of marketing have stressed serving rather than creating customers. For really new products, such as a new product form or class, the ability to create customers is essential for they do not pre-exist. There are only prospective customers. Serving customers may suffice in the short run, but innovation is essential over the longer run. Thus McKitterick, a second progenitor of modern marketing, has argued:

> "A company committed to the marketing concept focuses its major innovative effort on enlarging the size of the market in which it participates by introducing new generic products and services, by promoting new applications for existing products, and by seeking out new classes of customers who heretofore have not used the existing products. Only thinking of the customer and mere technical proficiency in marketing both turn out to be inferior hands when played against the company that couples its thought with action and actually comes to market with a successful innovation."[9]

It is instructive to note that perhaps the company most popularly viewed as the world's leading marketing company places tremendous emphasis on innovation. Indeed, 7% (7,000) of Procter & Gamble's (P&G) employees are scientists, operating in 17 different research centers around the world, filing almost 20,000 patent applications per annum. Said former P&G CEO Durk Jager, "Innovation is our game. People think of us as a marketing company, but we are really first and foremost a technology company. There are very few companies in the world that have the breadth and depth of technology capabilities that we do."[10]

The relationship between innovation and the customer may be considered as a two-way communication flow (Figure 13.2): The flow from the customer to innovation (B) usually comprises traditional market research, such as focus groups and surveys, and includes informal knowledge, observation, and more novel approaches to secure insight on customers being used by some firms.[11] The flow from innovation to the customer (A) refers to the way innovation changes customers' perceptions, expectations, and preferences. Innovation also shapes the way people live, the way society is structured, and the manner in which human beings conceptualize themselves.[12] There are many examples of innovations changing markets, such as the influence of the integrated circuit and microprocessor on countless consumer durables by improving convenience and functionality in ways consumers enjoy but still do not fully comprehend. Thus managers and their companies learn from customers; similarly, customers learn from products.[13]

Innovation/Customer Strategic Archetypes

This two-way innovation/customer flow is present for every product and service in every market. However, across businesses, the degree of focus on innovation or customers can vary substantially. By dichotomizing each of these dimensions, four strategic archetypes can be identified (Figure 13.3).

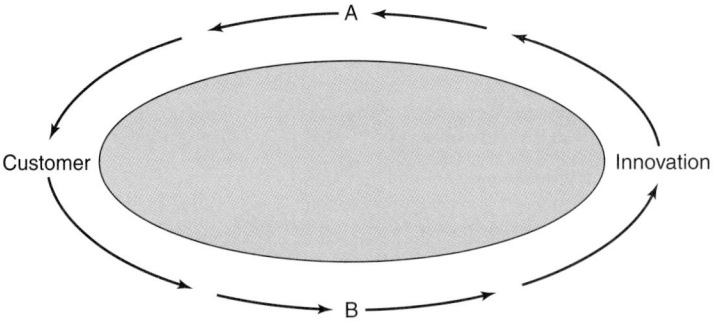

FIGURE 13.2

Communication Flows between Innovation and Customers

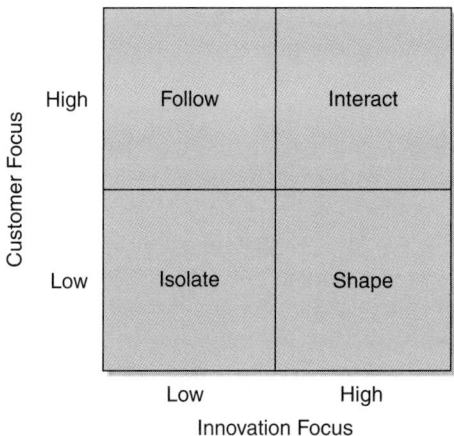

High ... Follow ... Interact

Customer Focus

Low ... Isolate ... Shape

Low ... High

Innovation Focus

FIGURE 13.3

Innovation/Customer Strategic Archetypes

ISOLATE (Low Customer Focus, Low Innovation Focus)   In these firms there is little or no communication between innovation and customers; the organization is the focus of its own attention.[14] Either little product development occurs, or what is done has little relationship to customer needs. Relatedly, market research is virtually nonexistent. Meaningful communication between product and market does not occur; they stagnate or evolve along separate paths. This mode characterized firms in the British motorcar and motorcycle industries in the late 1960s and 1970s, a period of limited product development that was often tangential to customer preferences. Most recent empirical research suggests that a large proportion of companies operate in this mode; 38% of an international sample of 130 managers.

FOLLOW (High Customer Focus, Low Innovation Focus)   In these firms, the customer drives innovation. The firm relies heavily on marketing research to identify customer requirements, establish parameters for product and service design, and drive development. The focus may be on entirely new products, or on modifying and refining existing products. A good new product example is the *Lexus* for which Toyota attempted to establish exactly what customers required in a luxury sedan before attempting development. A refinement example from the same industry is the M5 (or Miata) by Mazda, where engineers played a variety of engine sounds for potential customers so they could design the ideal sports car sound into the product.

SHAPE (Low Customer Focus, High Innovation Focus)   These firms focus on innovation rather than customers. Innovation shapes the market, and potential customers may not even be aware that they need or want the benefits derived from a particular innovation until they become available. Shaping occurs as the product defines the market by forming expectations and prototypical preferences. In the 1970s, Japanese manufacturers raised customer expectations by loading their cars with extras not normally available from competitors; customers asked why these extras were not otherwise available.

Examples of shaping preferences in the auto industry are Jeep (United States) and Land Rover (Great Britain) by defining the market for four wheel drive utility vehicles, and Chrysler by defining the market for minivans. These firms shaped customer category prototypes and disproportionately influenced the criteria against which later entrants were evaluated.[15] Sony has successfully pursued shaping strategies over the years with products such as the Walkman and Discman.

A great many shaping strategies fail, in part because of the high risks associated with the two large bets—innovation and customers.[16] Shaping also fails because technological pioneers often have a poor understanding of the market and customer learning processes.

INTERACT (High Customer Focus, High Innovation Focus)   In these firms a true dialogue is established between customers and innovation. The term dialogue is appropriate because it uses the speech metaphor to underpin the customer-innovation relationship, and provides a spectrum ranging from conversation to negotiation. Conversation implies a genteel two-way flow of information with ideas offered, modified, and evolved. By contrast, negotiation calls to mind a harder, power-play image between products and markets where trade-offs are made between customer values and product features. Many industrial markets operate in a negotiation-interact mode: The prospective customer issues an RFP[17] and invites potential suppliers to submit offers before moving forward with product/service development. By contrast, bespoke tailors involve their customers in conversational dialogues concerning the product that they will, in a very real sense, co-produce.

History provides many examples of the Interact mode. Many early high-end auto manufacturers, such as Bentley, Duesenberg, Alvis, and Bugatti, cooperated with independent coach builders to make cars to owners' specifications. Currently, Rolls Royce seems to be moving in this direction as a means of distinguishing itself from other high-quality car producers.[18] However, perhaps the best-known recent example is Boeing's successful inclusion of representatives from eight of its most important customers as members of the 777 design team.[19]

Successful Innovators

Followers, Interacters, and Shapers are likely to be innovators. However, each behaves in different ways since the orientations they represent tend to be deeply embedded in the firm's culture. In particular, successful firms of either type are skilled at dealing with uncertainty.[20] Following the precepts of Drucker and McKitterick, it seems that the best way to approach innovation is for the firm to operate in the Interact mode. Certainly, Followers and Shapers may be successful, but each can miss out on an important dimension: Followers can be insufficiently creative in developing new technology, and Shapers can suffer from a lack of understanding of market needs.

> **Example:** Operating in a Shaper mode, Sony pioneered home video with its Betamax system. Although the Betamax format offered superior picture quality to VHS, Sony underestimated the importance of recording time length and prerecorded movies. In part as a result of this oversight, Betamax was a failure in the consumer market and VHS became the dominant home video standard. Interestingly, Betamax is the current standard among video professionals.

By contrast, Interacters have both bases covered; they invest significantly in new technology, but also stay on top of evolving customer needs. Regardless, any firm that attempts product innovation on a continuous basis must follow a new product development process.

CRITICAL PARAMETERS IN THE NEW PRODUCT DEVELOPMENT PROCESS

The 1980s and 1990s witnessed great turmoil in the new product development process. As senior executives became more and more convinced of the vital importance of new products to their firms' long-term success, the pressure to perform increased, reinforced by rising competitive intensity. Many organizations benchmarked their product development efforts for the first time, seeking best practice on a global basis. Others totally re-engineered their approaches in attempts to speed the process while simultaneously improving new product development performance. Several major firms added bite to the importance of new products by including new product development measures in business managers' performance appraisals.

> **Example:** At 3M, a target of 25% of annual revenues from products not in the product line four years previously is set for each business. Correspondingly, 3M scientists are allowed to spend 15% of their time on independent innovation that is not an official 3M project.[21]

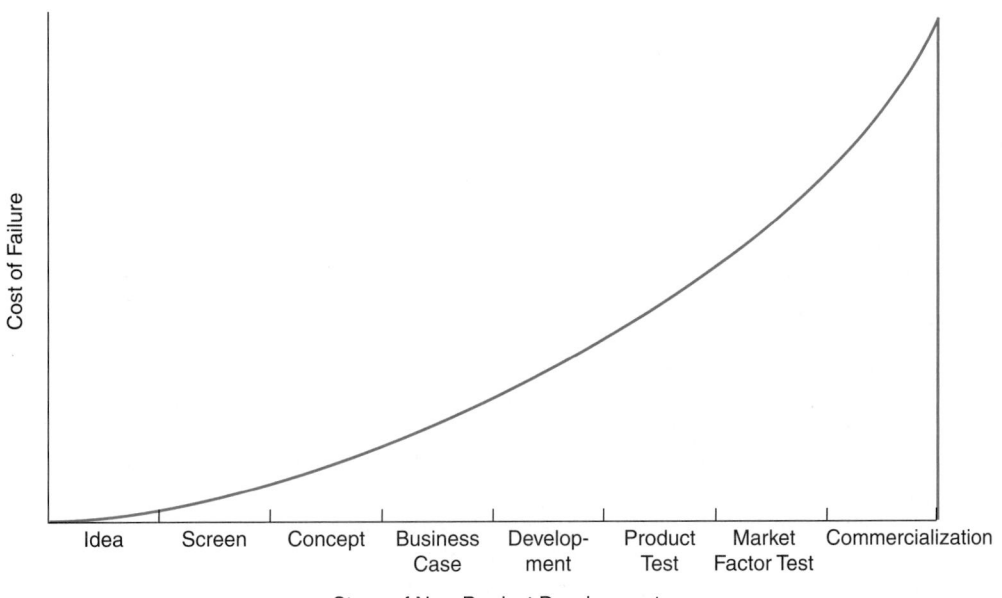

FIGURE 13.4
- -

Cost of Failure in New Product Development

Finally, new technologies have had a dramatic impact on the development process. Widespread application of CAD/CAM (computer-aided design/computer-aided manufacturing) systems, rapid prototype development, expansion of cross-functional teamwork, and use of techniques such as conjoint analysis (discussed earlier) and quality function deployment (QFD) have all played their role.[22]

Regardless, overall new product development success rates remain below aspiration levels in many firms. Although much has been learned about successful innovation management, competitive intensity has risen, the impetus to learn has increased, and the bar has risen as all competitors have improved together. Improvements in management technology (managerial systems and processes) tend to diffuse quickly through mechanisms such as workforce mobility, publications, trade associations, and conferences, such that many method or process-based innovations are arbitraged away, making enduring advantage difficult to attain.[23] Critical parameters in the new product development process are risk, financial return, and time.[24]

Risk

New product development is a risky business; it can be expensive, and certainly there is no guarantee of success. The best the firm can do is to raise its success probabilities, thereby reducing the odds of significant losses and wasted resources. Perhaps the most important approach the firm can take is to improve the quality and quantity of its new product ideas. Clearly, if the firm generates few ideas of marginal quality, success probabilities will be low, failure probabilities high. However, management should also understand that the further the firm goes through the process, from idea generation to commercialization, the greater its financial commitment and, hence, losses or wasted resources if the project ultimately fails (Figure 13.4). As a result, each stage should be seen as a kill point, at which the project may be stopped; moving beyond a kill point implies increasing the bet. Such decisions should not be taken lightly.[25] For each kill point, the firm should develop criteria that the developing project must satisfy before it moves to the next stage.

The corollary of the fact that many ideas, concepts, and so forth will be eliminated during the process is that the firm must have a large number of ideas to identify one that leads to a successful product. In many studies, the average ratio of new product ideas to successful products is about 100:1, but may be much larger in some industries. For example, in agricultural chemicals, the ratio of new chemical entities tested to successful products approaches 10,000:1.

Financial Return

The foregoing should not be taken to imply that the firm should not take risks; it must, of course, also consider potential financial return. If the potential return from a project is high, the firm may continue to advance through the process with lower success probabilities than if the potential return were much smaller. In fact, potential return from investing in new product development varies widely. At one extreme, the new product development process might be focused on the decision to add a new flavor of Jell-O to the product line; at the other, it might concern the development of plastic components as a replacement for silicon in microprocessors.

New product development can be conceptualized as comprising several different levels based on the scope of the effort. A fairly blunt approach identifies four.[26] These are illustrated with polyester plastic and super-conductivity.

- **Basic technology research**: Such efforts seek discontinuous innovation. For example, in the 1940s and 1950s, chemical company research focused on developing a plastic resin that might replace nylon in many applications; this research resulted in the discovery of polyester. The more recent original research on so-called high temperature super-conductivity also falls into this category.
- **Applied technology research**: One of the important application areas for polyester was in fibers; others were various types of plastic. Significant effort was devoted to securing fiber forms of polyester that could be processed on conventional spinning, weaving, and knitting equipment. In super-conductivity, the emphasis has now shifted to finding materials that still exhibit the property, but are sufficiently easy to make and use in application.
- **Market focused development**: Special polyester fibers were developed for specific end-use applications, such as industrial rubber goods, apparel, and household textiles. Work on electrical super-conductivity has not yet progressed to this point, but it is reasonable to predict that different types of super-conducting wires will be needed for specific applications.
- **Market tinkering**: Minor modifications made to current market entries.

The potential return and risk from these four types of effort is very different. Successful, basic technology research has broad applicability and may give rise to new products in many different applications. By contrast, success in market tinkering typically affects a much more limited area.[27] Current management thinking argues that different types of innovation must be managed differently. For example, Tushman and O'Reilly distinguish between incremental and discontinuous innovation; they suggest that the former can be accommodated within existing organizational arrangements, but that the latter should be separated.[28] Christensen's distinction between "sustaining" and "disruptive" innovations provides similar conclusions about organizational requirements.[29]

Time

The third critical parameter is time. Traversing the new product development process can be quite lengthy.

> **Example:** It took 21 years from Chester Carlson's first demonstration of the xerographic process for the first widely available commercial copiers to reach the market. Of course, this time period might have been shortened had firms that Carlson approached with the technology, such as IBM, General Electric, and Eastman Kodak recognized its potential and invested.[30]

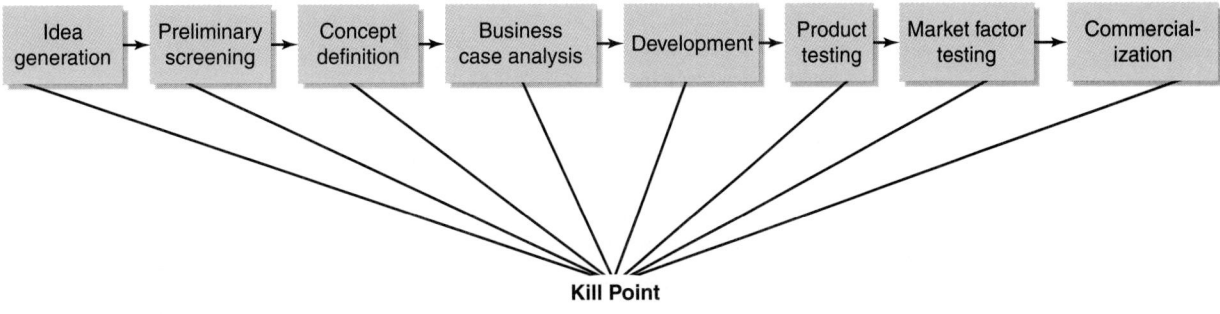

Kill Point

FIGURE 13.5

The New Product Development Process

Because of increased competitive intensity, time has become an increasingly important variable and firms are under great pressure to complete the development cycle faster, in part because first-mover advantage may be considerable. As a result, depending upon circumstances, it may be necessary for the firm to move quickly through, or even skip, certain stages of the process. However, this should be done only with full understanding of the pros and cons of such action. Regardless of time pressure, it is dangerous to move ahead without at least some degree of customer input.[31] Skipping a stage may allow the firm to make a fast response to competitive action or take advantage of a window of opportunity, but the costs of failure are high.

For each idea that enters into the process, at each kill point, management is in a position to make one of two types of error, type I and type II. A type I error occurs when management allows a project to proceed that ultimately fails; a type II error occurs when management kills a project that would have been successful had it been continued. The difficulty here, of course, is that the type I error is ultimately known, and the losses and resources consumed in pursing the failed development are visible and highly measurable. By contrast, type II errors are much more difficult to identify since the firm may never know that such an error was made; however, this characteristic does not make type II errors any less real.

Although this chapter discusses the new product development process in a stage-by-stage basis, and supports the kill point notion, it does not support a rigid linear system. The system should contain a myriad of feedback loops both within stages, for example, as the concept definition evolves, and between stages, such as between development and product testing. Indeed, despite attempts to reduce the time of the entire process, the firm that locks in a concept definition before development commences may risk producing an obsolete product. The firm must design into its system the flexibility to modify the concept even as development and testing continue so that the product that emerges is consonant with evolving market place realities.

STAGES IN THE NEW PRODUCT DEVELOPMENT PROCESS

This section presents the classic new product development process, comprising a stage-gate approach (Figure 13.5), incorporating new process innovations wherever appropriate. The firm's own process should be under continuous review in an effort to improve its effectiveness.

Idea Generation

Perhaps the most critical factor in raising success probabilities for the new product development process is to raise the quality of new product ideas. One of the mistaken myths held by non-marketers is that marketers believe the only good source of new product ideas is the customer.[32] Rather, the smart marketer seizes upon any possible source for a new product idea, yet realizes the immense gulf between a new product idea and a successful new product. Sources for new ideas include, but are not limited to, customers, suppliers (including advertising agencies and consultants), R&D, competitors, and conferences. Some companies run competitions among employees for the purpose of generating new product ideas.

The R&D department can be a significant source of new ideas but its success depends on many factors including budget, type of people hired and their motivations.

Example: Inaugurated in 1997, Kellogg's Institute for Food and Nutrition Research has invested heavily in food laboratories and restaurant quality kitchens. Researchers from 22 countries, who spend 15% of their time on their own ideas, have highly varied backgrounds. The results are impressive. In one month in 1999, the group generated 65 new product concepts and 94 new packaging ideas.[33]

Recent approaches involve offering seed capital to employees to pursue their ideas.

Example: In 1996, Shell's Exploration and Production division set up a GameChanger panel with the authority to allocate $20 million to unconventional business ideas from anywhere in the division. In three years, the process generated 300 ideas, some for entirely new businesses, most of which had never surfaced in the conventional management system.

Nonetheless, empirical research has established that, in several industries, most important innovations originate with customers.[34] A recent example concerns mail-order retailer L.L. Bean:

Example: A long-time customer wrote to L.L. Bean, complaining that its traditional lines of rugged outerwear were useful for weekends, but added, "there are only 52 weekends a year, and I need something to wear the rest of the time." The result was a new brand, Freeport Studio, offering low maintenance, style, and affordability.[35]

Many innovations developed by independent innovators were motivated by frustration with a common problem they experienced. The critical issue is the creative recognition that turns an observation into a new product idea.

Example: Independent inventor Carl Sontheimer developed the Cuisinart. In 1971, he spotted an ungainly but versatile machine designed to process food for restaurants at a French cookery show. He developed the Cuisinart for the home kitchen, based on the commercial machine.[36]

Example: In the winter of 1947, Kaye Draper, whose cat's sandbox had frozen, asked neighbor Edward Lowe for some sawdust from his father's sawdust business. On an inspiration, he offered her some kiln-dried (highly absorbent) granulated clay his father was selling to mop up grease spills. A few days later she came back for more and, thinking he might be onto something, filled some bags with 5 pounds of the material, marked them "Kitty Litter," and had a local pet shop offer them at 65 cents per bag (sand was one penny per pound). A business was born.[37]

Example: Swiss engineer George de Mistral saw a connection between burrs that stick on clothing and a new way of fastening that led to Velcro.

Example: In the early 1970s, Bill Bowermann, the University of Oregon track coach, developed a new outsole for running shoes by pouring rubber compound into his wife's waffle iron. This experiment led to the formation, with athlete Phil Knight, of Nike, now the world's leading athletic shoe manufacturer.

Sometimes market inefficiencies caused by regulations offer the conditions for new ideas that may build businesses. For example, in the international telephone market, leased lines, satellites, voice over the Internet, and automated callback systems have been used to circumvent local monopolies.

Example: In the mid-1990s, British Petroleum's German manager realized that gas station exemption from Germany's rigid shopping laws (stores closed at 6 P.M. on weekdays, 2 P.M. on Saturdays and all day Sunday) offered a business opportunity. He developed an electronic shopping kiosk where consumers used touch-sensitive screens to view short videos, secure advice, and select merchandise that could be collected or delivered the next day. Response from German consumers was highly enthusiastic.[38]

In addition to seemingly random idea generation, several schemes are available for the focused identification of new ideas, including individually focused activity, brainstorming (a group process where one person's idea may simulate another's), and combination individual/group processes.[39]

Among important considerations in raising the quality of new product ideas is the business unit's product/market scope. In general, focusing the firm's search for new ideas in areas covered by the product/market scope, where the firm has competence, is likely to be more productive than a generalized idea search.[40] However, product/market scopes evolve over time and too narrow a search may restrict potential opportunities.

Example: At the average ski resort, only 20% of the individual skier's (snowboarder) expenses are revenues to the hill, yet, at many hills, almost the entire emphasis is on skiing (snowboarding). By contrast, Vail Resorts (Colorado) manages six hotels, 72 restaurants, 40 shops, and over 13,000 condominiums. It earns so much money from these activities that it stops charging for its gondolas in the evenings. Although it had difficulties in the 1980s, the 1990s brought a broader view that has clearly been productive for Vail Resorts.[41]

Another approach is to examine the environmental imperatives upon which the firm's current product strategy is based, then attempt to identify changes that might open up new product opportunities. Among the environmental pressures discussed earlier were economic, governmental, regulatory, technological, physical, and sociocultural. Changes in any one of these dimensions might offer scope for new product ideas. Of course, new product ideas are sometimes developed serendipitously.

Example: Pfizer was testing a new drug, sildenafil citrate, as a treatment for angina when it identified the unexpected side effect of improved sexual performance. Pfizer quickly changed direction and developed the highly successful Viagra as a treatment for impotence.[42]

Finally, management should realize that ideas have their time, and what might have been a poor idea at one point in time might be attractive at another. For example, AT&T's video telephone failed in the post-World War II era, yet has been successfully relaunched as video conferencing in the 1990s. Developing an idea library and undertaking a systematic search process periodically may produce rich rewards.

Preliminary Screening

Preliminary screening is the first stage of cutting out new product ideas; ideas that make it through the preliminary screen move to concept definition, and then to business case analysis. Information requirements to screen appropriately depend upon the idea, but may take little more than a few phone calls to knowledgeable marketing, technical personnel, or friendly customers.

Among the criteria employed at this point are those related to fit with the business unit's strategy, its core competencies, and the potential of the idea to meet or exceed firm growth and profitability objectives. However, it would be a mistake for the firm to operate

DEVELOPING
NEW PRODUCTS

with a single set of criteria. It was indicated in the previous section that ideas vary drastically in scope, and have different return and risk profiles. Certainly, in the polyester (super-conductivity) example, it would be expected that criteria applied to developing the basic polyester plastic (super-conductivity material) should be quite different from criteria applied to market tinkering proposals.

Furthermore, the entire set of new product development opportunities should be viewed as a totality. Prudent new product management demands a sophisticated portfolio approach in which the firm maintains a balance among ideas that are low return versus high return, low risk versus high risk, and take a short versus long time to revenue generation.[43] Thus in addition to specific criteria that each idea should meet, each individual idea should be assessed on the basis of its position in the firm's development portfolio.

In conducting its preliminary screening, management should reflect on the number of major innovations that have been rejected by equally major companies as too low in market potential, or because they were a bad fit with the firm's existing strategy. It will never be known whether these innovations would have had a different history in the hands of others, but management would do well to consider the following:

- The telephone, rejected by Western Union
- The Beatles, rejected by Decca Recording Company
- Xerography, rejected by IBM, General Electric, and Eastman Kodak
- Cellular telephony, not exploited by AT&T
- The personal computer, rejected by Atari and Hewlett Packard

Screening decisions for ideas at the high end of the risk, return, and time dimensions are particularly difficult. Shaper or Interacter firms (both high-technology focus) contemplating basic technology research that might lead to "new to the world" discontinuous innovation may avoid the most egregious errors by considering the following rules:[44]

- Treat cautiously data secured by asking customers if they would like a product with which they have no experience, and which they may have difficulty conceptualizing.
- Use problem-focused research to determine whether customers view the need to be met by the proposed new product as serious, compared to others.
- Seek evidence that customers have devoted effort to solving the problem themselves. Such data is tangible evidence of real concern, avoiding the demand characteristics that often produce biased responses to problem-focused questions.[45]
- Do not underestimate the importance of market knowledge. Innovative firms, especially shapers, often overestimate the importance of technological novelty. If the technical problems are solvable, the extent to which the proposed new product fits with the firm's existing sales, distribution, and service competencies may well be a critical success factor.[46]
- Do not underestimate the amount of customer learning that might be required to adopt the innovation. New products with significant customer benefits often fail because this factor has been underestimated.

Screening rules such as those proposed should contribute to significant improvement in the firm's new product hit rate (low type I error), the proportion of new product ideas that ultimately prove to be successful. However, the goal of the new product development process is not to maximize the hit rate. High hit rates can be achieved simply by accepting only the most safe alternatives (high type II error); a firm following such a policy would never attempt anything new.[47]

Concept Definition

The next stage in new product development is to translate the new product idea into a sound definition of a product concept, for ideas alone are amenable neither to further development nor to any serious marketing research. Defining the concept is an iterative process that results either in concept approval or dropping the idea.

Consumer packaged goods companies seem especially sensitive to the importance of fixing on an appropriate expression of the new product idea. They recognize the importance of finding a product concept description that both appeals to consumers and provides suitable guidance for subsequent development. By contrast, technically oriented companies tend to focus immediately upon improving the product idea, and often accelerate the product development process. This trap is perhaps easier to fall into if the new product idea emerges from the firm's basic research program, rather than resulting from a market-driven process. In an attempt to deal with this problem, some industrial chemical companies are insisting that projects will be funded only if an embryonic marketing plan has been developed for the idea, thus forcing researchers to develop customer-focused concepts and make explicit the customer benefits likely to emanate from their projects.

The key point, however, is that the source of the new product idea is irrelevant; all that matters is whether or not it can be turned into a successfully commercialized new product. The central message that marketers must bring to the new product development process is that success can only be achieved if customer acceptance occurs. This is the critical issue, not the misleading and simplistic perspective imputed by marketing's critics, noted above, that suggests marketers believe new product ideas must emanate from customers. Whether or not the idea for the Sony Walkman would have emanated from consumers is irrelevant; what matters is that consumers purchased the product in sufficient quantity to generate economic profit for Sony.[48] Herein lies the importance of the product concept description; it is an important tool in helping to develop a product that will be sought after by target customers.

The crafting and testing of a concept description is greatly aided by understanding the needs and wants of customers, in particular their unmet needs and wants (or "problems" as we called them earlier). Such understanding may be secured from conventional market research techniques, for example, one-on-one interviews, focus groups and surveys, or from approaches such as conjoint analysis.

CONJOINT ANALYSIS Conjoint analysis (discussed in detail earlier) is probably the most popular market research technique for exploring alternative product concepts. Typically, target customers make choices among alternative product descriptions, but sometimes prototypes or mock-ups are used, especially for small and inexpensive products. The technique can be applied to the entire product, or just to its components, such as alternative package designs. Conjoint analysis allows marketers to deal with non-linear utility functions (customer value) as well as explore interaction effects between alternative combinations of attribute levels. Once the utility functions are estimated, they can be used to infer the acceptability of alternative product designs and even to estimate the potential impact of competitive responses through simulation models.

Although conjoint analysis and conventional marketing research techniques may afford significant insight, their use by so many companies may limit the competitive advantage gained.[49] As a result, some companies are employing more innovative approaches to marketing research to attain deeper customer insight. For example, ethnographic approaches that involve close observation of customers in everyday situations are being developed; and informed introspection is sought by firms that temporarily hire supplier personnel to market to their companies.

These market research methods should be viewed as a complement to, rather than as a substitute for, more conventional research. It should also be recognized that the assumptions underlying any market research technique designed to elicit customer needs and wants are, in some ways, quite restrictive. For example, researchers assume that customers are aware of, and willing to reveal (explicitly or implicitly), their needs and wants. This assumption may hold true for many well-established product classes, but is quite a stretch for new products involving discontinuous innovation.

A second implicit assumption is that customer preferences are stable. It would be very difficult to practice classical marketing if this were not the case most of the time, but it has become clear that, under certain conditions, not only are preferences unstable but they may also be influenced by marketers' efforts. The fashion industry provides ample anecdotal evidence to support preference instability, but experimental data now suggests that not only may buyers be influenced, they may be influenced to prefer seemingly irrelevant attributes.[50] Regardless of these reservations about market research, the probability that an average new product development will be successful is significantly enhanced by appropriate marketing research.

Business Case Analysis

Since the development phase of the product development process typically involves substantial funding, it is prudent to perform an analysis of the project's financial viability before proceeding further. A good business case analysis involves preparing a long-run marketing plan, comprised of a situation analysis and a strategy, based on the assumption that product development is successful and that the concept definition is realized through the process. Among the areas addressed in the situation analysis should be the market definition; an external analysis comprising environmental forces, industry structure, key success factors, competitors, and customers; an internal analysis comprising strengths and weaknesses, and previous strategies, actions, and results. The foregoing leads to a set of planning assumptions, market segment selection (targeting), strategy formulation, budgets, and forecasts.

The outputs of this exercise should include not only mean estimates of the various resource inputs and results, but also estimated variability as a measure of risk. It is worth noting that whereas risk concepts are well understood, and often well managed, in investment finance, this is not usually the situation in new product development.

In particular, management should develop estimates of revenues (volumes and prices), costs, investments, and consequent profits or losses. Although marketers have developed some fairly sophisticated models for forecasting sales trajectories based upon early sales data,[51] pre-market forecasting is much more difficult, even though it arguably has a greater potential payoff.[52] A particularly useful way of improving pre-market sales forecasts is by building a data bank to allow synthetic forecasts based on past experience. Regrettably, few large companies have been sufficiently committed to corporate learning to make such an investment, but the recent trend toward the appointment of "knowledge managers" in some companies is an encouraging step in the right direction.[53] Forecasting costs and investments is a specialized field that may require marketing inputs, but is typically performed by finance and accounting departments with inputs from functions such as purchasing and operations. The important point to recognize is that these inputs are also estimates, based on assumptions that should be made explicit rather than remain implicit.

All sensible methods of business case evaluation are based on estimates of future cash flow distributions over time. Based on these data and using discount rates appropriate to the project's risk, the analysis should produce both means and statistical distributions of returns. Sophisticated analyses would consider each project as one element in the venture portfolio and measure the project's contribution to the entire set of ventures.

Development

Once an acceptable and supportable concept description has been identified and the business case accepted, development commences. In industries where a high proportion of innovation is research based, firms now attempt to make a clear separation between the research and development phases. For example, in the pharmaceutical industry, many firms have high commitments to research into new chemical entities (NCEs); R&D budgets of 15% to 20% of sales are not uncommon. Whenever a promising NCE is identified, a cross-functional business team is usually formed to identify what needs (indications) it might meet. The focus of subsequent development effort is almost exclusively on whether or not the product meets a consumer need (helps an ill patient recover or move into remission) as well as ease of use by medical professionals (means and frequency of administration). Typically, the monies spent to satisfy the relevant professional and regulatory criteria are almost always far greater than those spent in the discovery process.[54] This provides a good example of the need for synthesis between research-based discovery and customer-sensitive development. It is precisely this balance that epitomizes the best practice of those companies that excel in managing innovation.

The firm's approach to development is strongly dependent upon the way in which costs are incurred after the project's business case has been approved. For example, for many frequently-purchased consumer goods, advertising, and promotion costs to introduce and sustain a new product can be far greater than development costs. Since much of the financial risk is related to whether or nor the product can be distributed and its benefits communicated to its target market, market factor testing (as discussed in the next section) consumes significant management attention and financial resources. By contrast, in major capital goods, such as commercial aircraft or consumer durables, most cost is incurred in the development process itself. Although customer acceptance is crucial in both cases, the differing risk patterns lead to very different budget allocations.

The development stage in the new product development process typically occurs deep in the organization where design and engineering initially focus on perfecting the product's functional performance. However, it is extremely important that other functions are involved in this process, otherwise development is driven solely by design considerations. For example, if manufacturing is not involved, the product may be difficult to manufacture. If service personnel and organizations are not involved, products designed to minimize assembly cost may place extraordinary burdens on service organizations and customers.[55]

In addition to various internal functions, major benefit in development can be derived from customer involvement.

> **Example:** One of the key lessons learned by Boeing was something management already knew at a general level: A combination of varying seasonal flight and class load factor patterns, as well as increasing unpredictability of demand meant that flexibility was becoming more and more important. This need led to development of 777, the world's most re-configurable aircraft. Airline participation meant that during the development process, design trade-off issues could be addressed promptly and thoroughly.[56]

In general, the arguments for both multifunctional development teams and customer involvement are similar: They help avoid the time-consuming, back and forth processes that slow linear, sequential development processes. Although achieving consensus among a diverse team is a skill not easily learned, it appears to pay significant dividends once it is acquired.

Notwithstanding the benefits of multifunctional team approaches to product development, at a broader level, excellent cross-functional coordination may lead to a loss of depth of functional knowledge as functional experts become disconnected from their specialties. The autonomy of individual project teams may lead to a loss in standardization across products. Toyota's process is designed to deal with such issues as these and avoids the extremes of chimney and committee (Figure 13.6).

Even customer involvement in development may be too narrow a perspective; perhaps complementary organizations should also be involved at the development stage. To pursue the Boeing 777 example one stage further:

> **Example:** Aircraft refuelers complained the refueling orifice of the aircraft was set 18 inches higher than any other aircraft, requiring rerigging of refueling equipment at every airport in the world where the aircraft would land.

Even where strong arguments can be made against limited customer involvement in development of the product's basic functional performance, the case for seeking customer input for the product's aesthetic, ergonomic, and use characteristics is overwhelming. Unfortunately, many product and service designers neither seek, nor take customer input into account preferring to emphasize their personal views of elegance, or trade appearance for practicality. In Figure 13.7, several examples are noted that refer not to any basic functional deficiency in the product, but which nonetheless resulted in considerable customer dissatisfaction. Companies committed to the modern concept of total quality management (TQM) should never make these kinds of mistakes.

The overall issues involved in these examples are the performance trade-offs that must be made across various product design attributes, and the concern to eliminate (or at least significantly minimize) negative side effects. To the extent that developers are highly customer-focused, this potential is minimized, although creative design approaches may be required if high-valued benefits are associated with less positive consequences.

Example: Sandoz developed Clozaril, an effective anti-schizophrenic drug for the small subset of refractory patients that did not respond to other medications. Unfortunately, 1% of patients receiving Clozaril suffered a potentially fatal drop in their white blood cell counts. To address this negative side effect, Sandoz designed a revolutionary, fail-safe system that involved a home health-care company visiting patients' homes to draw blood, a 24-hour blood testing service, and a database tracking system.[57]

CHIMNEY EXTREME	TOYOTA BALANCE	COMMITTEE EXTREME
Mutual Adjustment Little face-to-face contact.	Succinct written reports for most communication.	Reliance on meetings to accomplish tasks.
Predominantly written communication.	Meetings for intensive problem solving.	Predominantly oral communication.
Direct Supervision Close supervision of engineers by managers.	Technically astute functional supervisors who mentor, train, and develop their engineers.	Little supervision of engineers.
Large barriers between functions.	Strong functions that are evaluated based on overall system performance.	Weak functional expertise.
Integrative Leadership No system design leader.	Project leader as system designer, with limitations on authority.	System design dispersed among team members.
Standard Skills No rotation of engineers.	Rotation on intervals that are longer than the typical product cycle, and only to positions that complement the engineers' expertise.	Rotation at rapid and broad intervals.
Standard Work Procedures New development process with every vehicle.	Standard milestones—project leader decides timing, functions fill in details.	Lengthy, detailed, rigid development schedules.
Complex forms and bureaucratic procedures.	Standard forms and procedures that are simple, devised by the people who use them, and updated as needed.	Making up procedures on each project.
Design Standards Obsolete, rigid design standards.	Standards that are maintained by the people doing the work and that keep pace with current company capabilities.	No design standards.

FIGURE 13.6

How Toyota Avoids Extremes in Product Development

D.K. Sobek, II, J.K. Liker, and A.C. Ward, "Another Look at How Toyota Integrates Product Development," *Harvard Business Review*, 76 (July/Aug. 1998), pp. 36–49.

- Audio or video systems with controls (remote or otherwise) labeled in gold on a black casing that are virtually impossible to read in the low lighting conditions frequently preferred by consumers when using these products;
- Remote control devices for electronic products that lose their markings when subject to normal consumer usage;
- Airlines that ask passengers to arrive early for check-in, then reward such behavior with long lines; they also load early baggage first into the hold so it is last to be unloaded;
- The horn-push on American-made automobiles since airbags arrived. First placed on the steering wheel perimeter, then moved back to the center, they now require a harder push. Human factors experts know that moving controls around in this manner is a hazard;
- Incomprehensible messages from personal computer software after the machine has crashed, destroying the previous two hours work;
- An American sports car manufacturer that placed the emergency brake between the driver's seat and the door. As a result, a woman wearing a skirt could not enter or exit gracefully.[58]

FIGURE 13.7

Customer Dissatisfaction Experiences

QUALITY FUNCTION DEPLOYMENT (QFD)   Developed in Japan, QFD and its basic design tool, The House of Quality, have become important factors in mapping customer requirements into product design and facilitating communication between marketing and engineering. The House of Quality comprises several stages (Figure 13.8):[59]

- **Customer Requirements**. Customer requirements, including those of consumers, distributors, and regulators are collected in the form of customer attributes (CAs) (Item 1 in Figure 13.8). These CAs are organized into bundles of higher level requirements. For example, primary CAs for a car door included good operation and use and good appearance. Secondary CAs for good operation and use included easy to open and close door, isolation and armrest. Secondary CAs for easy to open and close door (tertiary CAs for good operation and use) included easy to close from outside, stays open on a hill, easy to open from outside. The relative importance of each CA is also measured.
- **Customer Attributes (CA)**. Both the relative importance of each CA is measured (importances sum to 100) (2A), as well as the firm's relative performance versus competing suppliers (2B). The firm can now see where important leverage can be gained for design effort.
- **Engineering Characteristics (EC)**. This stage comprises the critical translation from customer requirements to engineering characteristics necessary to produce them (3). At this stage, more CAs or redundant ECs may be identified. (The positive and negative signs refer to the direction of effect. For example, the negative sign on energy to close door means that the engineers hope to reduce the energy.) The entries in the sparse matrix (4) identify CA/EC relationships and their strengths. Of course, some engineering characteristics affect more than one CA; likewise, a single CA may be affected by more than one EC.
- **Objective Performance**. These measures (5) relate to current actual performance and are the basis for eventually establishing target levels.
- **Interaction of Engineering Characteristics**. The sparse matrix in the roof of the house identifies the relationships among the various ECs (6). Sometimes ECs have to be improved collaterally; sometimes engineering trade-offs must be made. For example, energy to close door is negatively related to door seal resistance and road noise reduction. This is the time for identifying creative engineering solutions.
- **Conclusion**. Identified in the basement are the conclusions of the analysis in terms of technical difficulty, imputed importance, estimated costs, and targets (7).

The design specifications developed through The House of Quality may be linked, in turn, to parts deployment, process planning, and production planning.

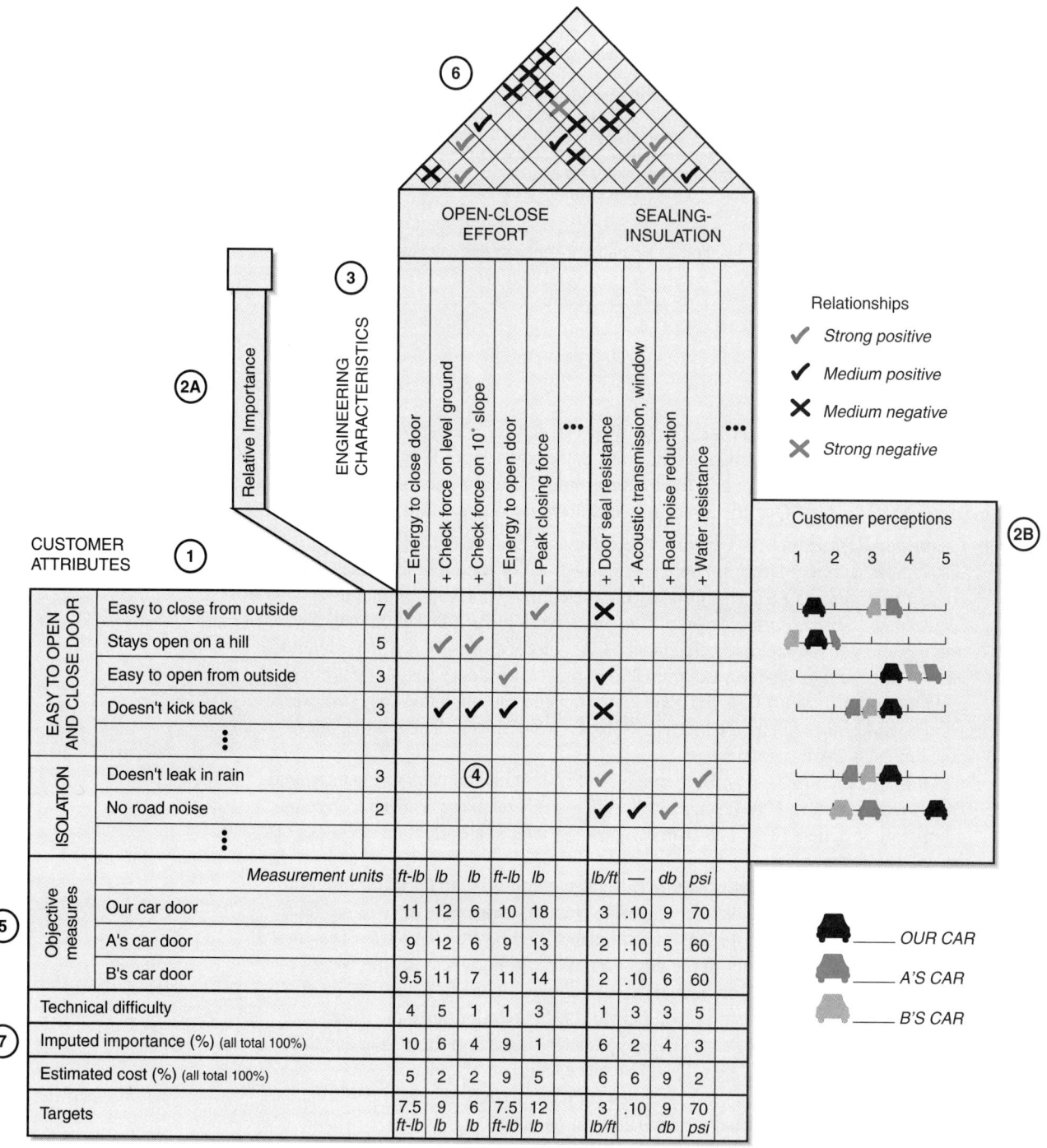

FIGURE 13.8

The House of Quality

Some elements of a design may be more fundamental as they form the platform on which other design elements must be based. However, whereas the firm must freeze on these elements early in the development process, others may remain flexible until later and so be designed based on evolving market data.[60]

Finally, since the development stage is typically the longest in calendar time, the firm should consider what steps it can take to speed up the process. Among the techniques the firm might consider are designing the development effort to process in parallel whenever possible and forming multiple teams that operate in series.

Example: In an effort to differentiate itself from competitors in the early 1990s, Intel commenced parallel chip development. Within the space of two years, it successively initiated development of its P5, P6, and P7 designs in three different locations.[61]

Example: Firms such as Bechtel, engaged in major construction projects, operate three teams working in different time zones around the world, such as London, U.S. Pacific, and Japan. Each team takes over from the other to provide continuous 24-hour development effort.

Product Testing

When the product comes out of development, it must be tested for the suitability of its functional, aesthetic, and other characteristics. There is not a single test, nor a single type of test; development typically proceeds via a series of development/testing/development feedback loops until the product is judged ready for market factor testing. A major distinction in the types of testing is between in-company (alpha) tests and customer (beta) tests, typically conducted in that order. Most products are subject to a battery of in-company tests. Sometimes these tests are run in parallel, in other cases they are run in series whereby success in one test makes the product eligible for a subsequent test. Typically, tests with customers are conducted only when the product has satisfied all in-company tests, but customers may conduct certain product feature tests before full development is completed. The increasingly popular beta tests are valued by customers since they permit an early look at the developing and soon-to-be introduced new product and may, if customers are other firms, have a significant impact on their own new product development efforts. In some cases, firms complete a series of beta tests as the product moves nearer to completion.

Example: Netscape introduced *Navigator 2.0* in January 1996 and immediately began work on *Navigator 3.0*. In developing *Navigator 3.0*, Netscape published a series of beta versions on the Web. Beta 0 (six weeks after the start of development) and beta 1 (two weeks later) were available only to Netscape employees, but four more versions followed, concluding with beta 6 (July), published about one month before launch.[62]

Inadequate testing can cause significant problems for the firm that may impact not only product profitability, but also company brand equity.

Example: In late 1997, Daimler Benz halted shipments of its first subcompact automobile, the new Mercedes A-Class, for three months. A Swedish motoring journalist tipped the car over while turning sharply at 38 mph in a moose-avoidance test. Mercedes' investment in the new car was estimated at $1.5 billion; cost estimates to solve the problem were $171 million.[63]

Market Factor Testing

As emphasized consistently in this book, market strategy is based on offers, not on products; thus far, this chapter has focused on products. Just as marginal products can sometimes be made successful by superior implementation of other marketing mix elements, so first-rate products may fail in the market from inferior implementation. Depending on the nature of the product and target market, the potential impact, expenditure, and risk attached to different elements of the marketing mix can vary dramatically.[64] Hence the extent and degree of testing should vary also. Depending on the circumstances, some market factor testing, which must occur with target customers, may proceed in parallel with ongoing product development.

SIMULATED ENVIRONMENTS   A variety of mechanisms is available. In consumer markets these include testing advertising messages via split cable TV or in movie houses, and testing packaging, pricing, and shelf placement in mock-up store displays in simulated shopping environments, often adjacent to shopping malls. (Frequently, advertising tests and simulated shopping experiences occur sequentially.) In some procedures, customers who select the test product are given a trial sample and asked to report their experience and repurchase intentions to the researchers. In other designs, salespeople visit customers in their homes and have them select products from brochures.

Critical measures are the percent of people who select the product for trial (cumulative trial) and the percent who become repeat users (cumulative repeat). Various analytic procedures are available to predict sales volumes and market share. Although these procedures may exhibit good internal validity, they suffer from the artificiality of the laboratory and so lack external validity. As a result, firms adopting these approaches are advised to use more than one approach to seek convergence. However, because of the external validity problem, many firms place new products in test markets.

TEST MARKETING   Test marketing is the most developed form of market factor testing. The firm selects a test market area and markets the product, including the full range of market implementation programs, just as it expects to proceed in the broad market. As firms increasingly look to global markets, they are considering simultaneous test marketing in multiple countries.

> **Example:** In 1999, Procter & Gamble test marketed a new dust mop, *Swiffer,* simultaneously in France and the United States. As a result, it decreased the time from launch to global distribution from five years to 18 months.[65]

Test marketing has its pros and cons. If properly implemented and not biased by excessive firm attention that could never be duplicated when the product was launched more broadly, it can provide invaluable data for fine-tuning the market launch. However, appropriate measurements must be taken, including input measures, such as advertising, training, and sales effort; intermediate measures, such as customer awareness and interest; and output measures, such as sales, profits, and customer satisfaction.[66] Since test marketing occurs under competitive conditions, less than stellar performance may lead to withdrawal, thus saving the costs of full-scale launch. In addition, firms can gain unexpected data from test marketing.

> **Example:** Despite the fact that Procter & Gamble's 1996 test market of *Febreze,* a laundry product designed to remove cigarette and other noxious odors from dry-clean-only fabrics, was largely a failure, about 10% of customers were extremely pleased. They found many other uses for the product, including odor removal from sofas, carpets, car interiors, and other household furnishings. Test marketed again with a broader positioning as an "odor neutralizer," *Febreze* was such a success that initial demand was 10 times forecast.

Notwithstanding these potential benefits, many firms avoid test marketing completely. Not only are test markets expensive, they take a long time to complete. As a result, they reduce the firm's time-to-market advantage and reveal intentions to competitors who may rush out with their own products. Rather than simply observe, competitors may also attempt to spoil a test market; if they are successful, the test has little predictive power. In addition, varying economic and political conditions, out-of-stocks, competitive advertising, and other changes can produce a low signal/noise ratio such that the test market effect is "drowned out."

VIRTUAL TESTING   The most recent addition to the researcher's arsenal is virtual shopping. The re-searcher recreates a shopping display and has customers shop as in a real store with all the distracting clutter. Displays can be modified quickly and results analyzed instantaneously.

> **Example:** Goodyear conducted a shopping study of 1,000 recent and potential purchasers of passenger tires. Respondents shopped in several virtual tire stores stocked with several brands and models offering various prices and warranty levels. Goodyear learned about its brand equity compared to competing brands, developed re-pricing ideas, and identified those competitors that were its greatest threat and those most vulnerable to attack.[67]

Commercialization

Provided the new product passes all the preceding stage-gates satisfactorily, product launch can proceed. At this stage, significant facilities investment may be required to scale up pilot plant production to commercial levels. The type of launch favored will, of course, depend on a myriad of factors including, but not limited to, target market size, company resources, likely lead time over competitors, expected degree of protection from competition due to proprietary knowledge or patents, and anticipated competitive intensity.

This section reviews some of the key issues in the launch phase. Although being first in the mind of prospective buyers is important for reaping first-mover advantage,[68] careful identification of prospective early buyers and developing persuasive communications remains a crucial task. Perhaps the most cited attempt to understand this process was by Everett Rogers.[69] Rogers identified a taxonomy of customers based on their adoption behavior for new products that appears to be applicable in a variety of markets; in consumer markets, early adopters were better-educated, younger, and advantaged socioeconomically. (Table 13.1).

There is also considerable evidence that word-of-mouth and personal influence are critical determinants of adoption. Risk reduction for prospective buyers is more easily accomplished by a trusted source, hence the widespread use of "respectable" spokespersons in advertisements, the targeting of leading specialist practitioners by the pharmaceutical and medical device industries, and the widespread use of trial installation and reference selling in business-to-business marketing. The widespread adoption of beta testing may have as much to do with word-of-mouth benefits for a successful innovation as it does with perfecting the product. Certainly Interacter firms would regard beta sites as opportunities to achieve the twin objectives of perfecting the product and favorably influencing prospective customers.

Not only do prospective buyers vary in their willingness to innovate, characteristics of new products have a major impact on adoption rates and the chances of successful commercialization. Rogers' work suggests five factors that affect speed of adoption (Table 13.2).

TABLE 13.1 Rogers' Adopter Groups

Group	Characteristics
Innovators	Venturesome, accept risk, not typically emulated
Early adopters	Adopt early and with care, typically opinion leaders
Early majority	Deliberate, ahead of most but not leaders
Late majority	Skeptical, like others to have tried
Laggards	Bound by tradition, suspicious of change

TABLE 13.2 Factors Affecting the Speed of Adoption

Factor (direction of effect)	Meaning
Relative advantage (increase)	The extent of benefits offered compared to existing alternatives
Compatibility (increase)	The relationship with past experience and current life style
Complexity (decrease)	Implies greater learning requirements
Divisibility (increase)[70]	Ability to try on a limited basis
Communicability (increase)[71]	The extent to which the benefits can be communicated

The use of Rogers' framework is illustrated by an example. Consider the successful introduction of the EZ Pass system on toll roads and bridges. The EZ Pass is a small device that attaches to a vehicle's windshield (windscreen). As the vehicle approaches the toll booth, an electronic signal recognizes the pass, allows passage, and deducts payment from an account that is automatically replenished by credit card when the balance falls below a preset level.

Relative advantage:	The vehicle passes through the toll booth more quickly; no need to worry about collecting and storing exact change
Compatibility:	The driver's behavior at the toll-booth is essentially unchanged; setting up the account is similar to common direct marketing transactions
Complexity:	Learning requirements are minimal; the driver attaches the device and drives through the toll booth
Divisibility:	If drivers do not like to use the device, they can easily switch back to paying cash
Communicability:	The benefits are easy to understand and to communicate

What is also clear, however, is that persons who are leaders in one product form or category may well be early/late majority or even laggards in another, suggesting the idea of category leaders or experts who are used by later adopters as a source of experience and expertise. These persons, once identified, are critically important communication targets, since they are a powerful influence on word-of-mouth communication.

Companies planning to introduce innovations should identify the likely innovators in the relevant product categories. For example, personnel at university teaching hospitals often play the roles of innovators and early adopters for pharmaceutical and medical device innovations; Avon keeps data on the innovators and early adopters of its cosmetic products and targets these consumers early when it launches new products.

It would be a major mistake to confuse successful completion of the development process with commercial success. First, despite extensive testing, previously unidentified problems may arise during the commercialization phase.

Example: In 1998, S.C. Johnson introduced the Allercare line, its first new product category since 1975. Allercare products were designed to remove dust mites, the leading cause of childhood asthma, from carpets and upholstery. They were developed over a ten-year period, tested in tens of thousands of homes, and promoted with a national TV campaign (Fall 1999) in excess of $10 million. Unfortunately, a small percent of consumers with severe allergies and asthma reported reactions to the level of fragrance. The products were withdrawn in January 2000.[72]

Second, all too often, firms assume that the best product will win the market; this is patently not the case. This discrepancy arises because of the different abilities of competitors to develop markets for their innovations.

SUMMARY

Successful new products are major contributors to shareholder wealth creation. This chapter examined the characteristics of successful innovative companies and developed four firm archetypes that differ considerably in their approach to innovation across the dimensions of market and technology focus: Isolate (low, low), Follow (high, low), Shaping (low, high), and Interact (high, high).

This chapter also examined the new product development process in some detail. A systematic process has the advantage that opportunities are thoroughly scoped out and careful evaluation of potential benefits, costs, and probabilities is conducted on a continuous basis. As a result, out-of-pocket losses are reduced since the probability that an ultimately unsuccessful product will slip through the system is minimized. However, short-circuiting the system may offer advantages as opportunities can be acted on swiftly if timing is important or unexpected competitive responses occur. Short-circuiting may also allow for greater intra-organizational competition and creativity, and may be acceptable when the cost of failure is low and products can be easily modified. Regardless, decisions to short-circuit should only be taken after a careful trade-off of the pros and cons of moving fast.

Unfortunately, in some companies, systematic approaches have resulted in overly bureaucratic and ponderous new product development processes that stifle creativity. These firms should either consider simplification, or separating innovation management into a completely new business area. Following Duncan's lead, Tushman and O'Reilly argued that discontinuous (radical) innovation can rarely be successfully accomplished within existing businesses.[74] They call for ambidextrous organizations, capable of both incremental innovation in existing businesses while fostering radical innovations in separate business units. These organizational issues are addressed later in the book, but there is little doubt that both the firm's formal and informal organization play major roles in its likely success with new products.

THE CHANGING VIEW

Old Way	New Way
Sequential processing	Parallel processing
Bureaucratic and slow	Entrepreneurial and fast
Functional orientation	Cross-functional teams
Financial criteria only	Market and financial criteria
Innovation viewed as of secondary importance	Innovation seen as primary
Innovation strategy unfocused	Innovation strategy clearly focused
Ideas discouraged	Ideas encouraged and nurtured
Not-invented-here (NIH) syndrome	Best-of-class benchmarking
Poor risk assessment	Risk profiles assessed
Poor design tools	Advanced design tools, such as quality function deployment (QFD), computer-aided design (CAD)

QUESTIONS FOR STUDY AND DISCUSSION

1. Select a company with which you are familiar and identify a major environmental change that affects it. Generate three potential new product ideas for your company related to this change.

2. Select a simple product with which you are familiar and develop a "House of Quality."

3. Competitors reacts so quickly, there is no time to go through a lengthy new product development process. Discuss.

4. The Internet will revolutionize test marketing. Discuss.

5. Under what conditions would you happily introduce a new product that you are sure will canibalize one of your existing products?

6. New product development teams should be led by a marketers. Discuss.

7. Many companies have benchmarked 3M and, as a result, have set a goal for a percent of sales to be generated by new products. Discuss the pros and cons of this approach.

8. Marketers overemphasize the customer and fail to understand or appreciate the importance of technology in new product development. Do you agree or disagree with this statement? Explain your response.

9. Attempting to develop formal approaches for new product development are preordained to fail because they drive out the freedom and initiative that are key to successful innovations. How, as a manager, would you deal with this commonly held viewpoint?

10. Why, in your opinion, have large companies turned down many inventors' ideas that have subsequently proved to be extremely successful? How should large companies act to prevent these opportunity losses?

11. Customer dissatisfaction, while it should be avoided where possible, affords a superb opportunity to learn. Can you recall examples when you were dissatisfied with a purchase experience? Did the company involved learn from your experience? Why or why not?

12. It is alleged that the Internet, by permitting customers to easily and conveniently "talk back" to firms, holds the potential for revolutionizing product development and improvement. Do you agree? Why or why not?

13. It is not unusual for a new product development program to be halted because the budget appropriation for the period in question has been used up. Is this good economic decision making from the shareholders' perspective? Why or why not?

14. Many innovations that might otherwise have succeeded fail because companies do not understand the market development process. How would you remedy this deficiency?

15. Software companies are often accused of launching products before they are ready and contain too many "bugs." Is this a wise business practice? What environmental changes might lead you to revise your opinion?

ENDNOTES

1. Parts of this chapter draw heavily on our work with other authors, to whom we have given credit wherever appropriate. However, we wish to acknowledge explicitly the influence and contribution of Professor Pierre Berthon of the University of Bath on our thinking on the relationship between marketing and technology.

2. See Chapter 6 and N. Capon and R. Glazer, "Marketing and Technology: A Strategic Co-Alignment," *Journal of Marketing*, 51 (July 1987), pp. 1–14.

3. For several years, The Marketing Science Institute has placed the marketing of really new products high on its list of research priorities.

4. See N. Capon, J.U. Farley, D.R. Lehmann, and J.M. Hulbert, "Profiles of Product Innovators Among Large U.S. Manufacturers," *Management Science*, 38 (Feb. 1992), pp. 157–169.

5. See also Synectics Corporation, "Succeeding at Innovation," Cambridge, MA, 1993.

6. C.M. Christensen, *The Innovator's Dilemma*, Boston, MA: Harvard Business School Press, 1997.

7. P.F. Drucker, *The Practice of Management,* New York: Harper and Row, 1956, pp. 65–67.

8. P. Berthon, J.M. Hulbert, and L. Pitt, "To Serve or Create? Strategic Orientations toward Customers and Innovation," *California Management Review*, 42 (Fall 1999), pp. 37–38.

9. J. A.B. McKitterick, "What is the Marketing Concept?" in Frank M. Bass (ed.) *The Frontiers of Marketing Thought and Science*, Chicago, IL.: The American Marketing Association, 1957, pp. 71–82.

10. Recently, P&G's innovation attempts have been criticized for being too risk averse, *The Economist*, June 12, 1999.

11. F.J. Gouillart and F.D. Sturdivant, "A Day in the Life of Your Customers," *Harvard Business Review*, 72 (Jan./Feb. 1994), pp. 116–125; J. Johanson and I. Nonaka, "Market Research the Japanese Way," *Harvard Business Review*, 65 (May-June 1987), pp. 29–32.

12. See N. Wiener, *The Human Use of Human Beings: Cybernetics and Society*, New York, Doubleday, 1954, and J. Mander, *In the Absence of the Sacred: The Failure of Technology and the Survival of the Indian Nations*, San Francisco: The Sierra Club, 1991.

13. See G.S. Carpenter and K. Nakamoto, "Consumer Preference Formation and Pioneering Advantage," *Journal of Marketing Research*, 26 (August 1989), pp. 285–298 and G.S. Carpenter, R. Glazer and K. Nakamoto, "Meaningful Brands from Meaningless Differentiation: The Dependence on Irrelevant Attributes," *Journal of Marketing Research*, 31 (August 1994), pp. 339–350.

14. See R.T. Woodruff, "Customer Value: The Next Source for Competitive Advantage," *Journal of the Academy of Marketing Science*, 25 (1997), p. 139.

15. Carpenter and Nakamoto, *op. cit.*

16. For further discussion on this issue, see J.B. Quinn, "Managing Innovation: Controlled Chaos," *Harvard Business Review*, 63 (May-June 1985), pp. 73–84.

17. **R**equest **F**or **P**roposal.

18. Rolls Royce recently announced that no two cars leaving its factory would be the same; each would be exactly tailored to the individual customer's specification, *Car*, 1997a, *The Times*, 1997.

19. "Tailor-Made Twinjet," *Flight International*, December 8, 1993.

20. H. Courtney, J. Kirkland, and P. Viguerie, "Strategy Under Uncertainty," *Harvard Business Review*, 75 (Nov./Dec. 1997), pp. 67–79.

21. The *Post-It Notes* innovation was developed by 3M scientist Art Fry in this 15% of time.

22. QFD is a set of planning and communication routines that focuses and coordinates organizational skills to design, manufacture, and market goods that customers will purchase and repurchase.

23. D.L. Liebermann and D.B. Montgomery, "First-Mover Advantages," *Strategic Management Journal*, 9 (1988), pp. 41–58.

24. For detailed discussion of the issues covered in the remainder of this chapter, see G.L. Urban and J.R. Hauser, *Design and Marketing of New Products*, Englewood Cliffs, NJ: Prentice Hall, 1993.

25. Implicit in this discussion is the notion that at any point in time, investment in the new product idea is a "sunk cost," and should not be considered in any decision of whether or not to proceed to a subsequent stage.

26. Booz Allen identifies six categories of new products: new to the world, new product lines (for the firm), additions to existing product lines, improvements/revisions of existing products, repositioning (existing products to new segments), and cost reductions.

27. Using this same framework in the pharmaceutical industry, *basic technology research* might refer to the identification of a new chemical entity; *applied technology research* to developing a drug for a particular indication; *market-focused development* to developing alternative delivery mechanisms for introducing the drug to the body, such as injection, oral; patch and *market tinkering* to developing different strength options or different alternatives for an individual delivery mechanism, such as oral liquid, spray, capsule, or caplet.

28. M. Tushman and C. O'Reilly, "Ambidextrous Organizations: Managing Evolutionary and Revolutionary Change," *California Management Review*, 38 (1996), pp. 8–30.

29. Christensen, *op. cit.*

30. *The New York Times*, November 30, 1998.

31. For example, in most cases, conducting a few focus groups can be accomplished fairly quickly at relatively low cost, yet may offer important insights.

32. Perhaps this myth has developed because so many marketing books are biased toward a consumer goods perspective or, more restrictively, non-durable consumer goods where research-based innovation is relatively rare.

33. *Financial Times*, September 28, 1999.

34. E. von Hippel, *The Sources of Innovation*, New York: Oxford University Press, 1988.

35. *The New York Times*, April 14, 1999.

36. *The New York Times*, March 26, 1998.

37. *The New York Times*, early 1996, Obituaries.

38. L. Downes and C. Mui, *Unleashing the Killer App: Digital Strategies for Market Dominance*, Boston, MA: Harvard Business School Press, 1998.

39. Several independent consulting organizations, such as Synectics, Cambridge, MA, have developed their own proprietary processes.

40. According to Booz-Allen and Hamilton, the past 20 years have witnessed a considerable improvement in efficiency in the early stages of the product development process. This change seems related to a heightened concern for building core businesses and focusing the innovation effort.

41. *The Economist*, January 31, 1998.

42. *Business Week*, May 11, 1998.

43. Kuczmarski's work on new products shows that, in general, "new-to-the-firm" products are riskier, as measured by failure rate, but they are also disproportionately important if successful. See Thomas D. Kuczmarski, *Managing New Products: Competing through Excellence*, Englewood Cliffs, N.J.: Prentice Hall, 1988.

44. The Marketing Science Institute recently initiated a major research effort focused on the marketing of "Really New Products." This effort marks both the significance attached to this area, but also the fairly low level of marketing knowledge.

45. For example, gas-phase chromatography was developed in a university environment long before instrument manufacturers realized that such a need existed. See also Von Hippel, *op. cit.*

46. Research conducted at Columbia Business School demonstrates that market-based synergies may be at least as important as technological synergy. See N. Capon, J.U. Farley, J. Hulbert, and L.E. Martin, "Corporate Diversity and Economic Performance: The Impact of Market Specialization," *Strategic Management Journal*, 9 (Jan./Feb. 1988), pp. 61–74.

47. For related discussion on screening for new ventures, see Chapter 6.

48. The idea for the Walkman emanated from Sony's honorary chairman Masaru Ibuka and was championed by then CEO Akio Morita, a remarkable and entrepreneurial executive. Not only were consumers not involved, but Sony's top management was opposed to the development. Mr. Morita insisted! Furthermore, the Walkman was not successful with its initial target, teenagers; initial sales came from Yuppies who used it for jogging and commuting, J. Mingo, *How the Cadillac got Its Fins*, Hew York: Harper Business, 1994.

49. Berthon, Hulbert, and Pitt, *op.cit.*

50. Carpenter, Glazer, and Nakamoto, *op. cit.*

51. For the classic model for non-durables see L.A. Fourt and J.N. Woodlock, "Early Prediction of Market Success for New Grocery Products," *Journal of Marketing*, 25 (Oct. 1960), pp. 31–38. For a review encompassing the seminal Bass model for durables and many other new product forecasting models, see V. Mahajan, E. Muller and F.M. Bass, "New Product Diffusion Models in Marketing: A Review and Directions for Research," *Journal of Marketing*, 54 (January, 1990), pp. 1–28.

52. The development of flow-based models appears to offer promise. See Glen L. Urban, John R. Hauser, and John H. Roberts, "Prelaunch Forecasting of New Automobiles," *Management Science*, 36, No. 4 (April, 1990), pp. 401–421.

53. The impetus for these appointments is that knowledge and human capital are being increasingly seen as the basis of competitive advantage. Unfortunately, few organizations have the systems and processes to assemble disaggregated knowledge in the corporation and bring it to bear on specific areas of need. Hence, the appointment of knowledge managers. In 1997, I. Nonaka was appointed Professor of Knowledge Management at the Haas School of Business, University of California, Berkeley, the first appointment in this field in a U.S. business school.

54. The use of a specific NCE for a particular indication is typically based on extensive clinical trials regulated by some government body, such as the Federal Drug Administration (FDA) in the United States.

55. William H. Davidow and Bro Uttal, *Total Customer Service: The Ultimate Weapon*, New York: Harper & Row, 1989.

56. The 777 is a favorite example of ours, not only because of the path-breaking design process, but because all Regional Directors on the project attended Columbia's executive course in Marketing Management, as had generations of Boeing executives before them. The 777 was one of few instances where Boeing was last to market; the MD-11 and Airbus 340 were already launched. Boeing made extensive use of CAD/CAM and virtual reality to bring the plane through the development process faster than any commercial jet aircraft in history.

57. Example from A.J. Slywotzky and D.J. Morrison, *The Profit Zone*, New York: Times Business, 1997.

58. Example from J.R. Hauser and D. Clausing, "The House of Quality," *Harvard Business Review*, (May-June 1988), pp. 63–73.

59. Based on J.R. Hauser and D. Clausing, *op. cit.*

60. See A. Ward, "The Second Toyota Paradox: How Delaying Decisions Can Make Better Cars Faster," *Sloan Management Review*, 36 (Spring 1995), pp. 43–61.

61. Example from A.J. Slywotzky and D.J. Morrison, *The Profit Zone*, New York: Times Business, 1997.

62. M. Iansiti and A. MacCormack, "Developing Products," *Harvard Business Review*, 75 (Sept.-Oct. 1997), pp. 108–117.

63. *The New York Times*, November 12, 1997.

64. For example, packaging, branding, advertising messages, sales presentations, reseller promotions and communication plans, service or warranty packages, display or trade show participation, and pricing.

65. This decreased roll-out time is being driven by pressure from increasingly global retail chains.

66. For consumer packaged goods, sales information is typically secured from point-of-sale scanner data and warehouse withdrawals; customer satisfaction and intermediate measures are secured from consumer panels or independent surveys. Use of supermarket "value shopping" cards also allows measures of repeat purchase.

67. R.R. Burke, "Virtual Shopping: Breakthrough in Marketing Research," *Harvard Business Review*, 74 (Mar.-Apr. 1996), pp. 120–131.

68. Carpenter, Glazer, and Nakamoto, 1989, *op. cit.*

69. E.M. Rogers, *Diffusion of Innovations*, New York: Free Press, 1962.

70. The firm may be able to increase divisibility by adapting its offer. For example, Airbus Industrie, Boeing's European competitor in commercial aircraft, was unable to break into the U.S. market until it offered a six-month free trial use of its planes. The offer was accepted by Eastern, at the time the financially weakest of the major airlines, not the typical profile for an early adopter.

71. This final characteristic is especially critical for new product class and product form innovations.

72. *Milwaukee Journal Sentinel*, January 15, 2000.

73. See R.B. Duncan (1976) The Ambidextrous Organization: Designing Dual Structures for Innovation, In *The Management of Organizational Design*, Vol. 1. Eds. R.H. Kilman, L.R. Pondy, and D.P Slevin, New York, NY: Elsevier, Tushman, and O'Reilly, *op. cit.*

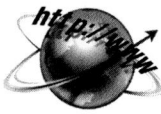

WEB RESOURCES

3M	www.3m.com
Airbus Industrie	www.airbus.com
Alvis	www.alvis.plc.uk
AT&T	www.att.com
Atari	www.atari.com
Bechtel	www.bechtel.com
Boeing	www.boeing.com
Booz Allen Hamilton	www.bah.com
British Petroleum	www.bpamoco.com
Bugatti	www.bugatti.cars.de
Chrysler	www.chrysler.com
Cuisinart	www.cuisinart.com
Daimler Benz	www.daimler-benz.com
Decca	www.decca.com
Dell	www.dell.com
Duesenberg	www.duesenbergmotors.com
Eastman Kodak	www.kodak.com
EZ Pass System	www.e-zpassny.com
General Electric	www.ge.com
Goodyear	www.goodyear.com
Hewlett Packard	www.hp.com
Hyatt	www.hyatt.com
IBM	www.ibm.com
Intel	www.intel.com
Jeep	www.jeep.com
L.L. Bean	www.llbean.com
Land Rover	www.landrover.com
Mazda	www.mazda.com
Netscape	www.netscape.com
Nordstrom	www.nordstrom.com
Pfizer	www.pfizer.com
Proctor & Gamble	www.pg.com
Rolls Royce	www.rollsroyceandbentley.co.uk
Sandoz	www.novartis.com
Shell	www.shell.com
Sony	www.sony.com
Toyota	www.toyota.com
Vail Resorts	www.vailresorts.com
Velcro	www.velcro.com
Virgin Airlines	www.fly.virgin.com
Western Union	www.westernunion.com
Zebco	www.zebco.com

CHAPTER

14

INTEGRATED MARKETING COMMUNICATIONS

LEARNING OBJECTIVES

When you have completed this chapter, you will understand

- **the need for an integrated communications strategy**

- **the elements that comprise a communications strategy**

- **the considerations involved in developing a communications strategy**

- **the firm's major non-personal communications options, including advertising, direct marketing, publicity and public relations, and sales promotion**

INTRODUCTION

The first part of this chapter addresses communications as a whole, discussing the firm's internal and external communications challenges and introducing the variety of available communications tools—including advertising, direct marketing, publicity and public relations, packaging, sales promotion, trade shows, and personal selling—that are available to management. The three critical questions that comprise the firm's communications strategy are presented, and the concept of integrated communications is addressed.

The chapter then focuses on non-personal communications, particularly advertising, arguably the most important topic in mass communications. The formulation of advertising strategy—including setting advertising objectives, issues in the development of both message and media strategy, and measurement of advertising effectiveness, are addressed. The chapter concludes with shorter discussions of direct marketing, publicity and public relations, and sales promotion that are playing an increasingly important role in many market strategies and often account for very large expenditures.

COMMUNICATIONS CHALLENGES

From a societal point of view, markets cannot function effectively without information.[1] Of course, firms are biased providers of information and are often criticized, especially for advertising. Nonetheless, marketer-provided information plays an important role in the operation of product markets and, in most reasonably well-ordered societies, legislation ensures at least minimum standards of truthfulness.

From the firm's perspective, marketing's overarching goal is to improve shareholder value. The driving force for securing this goal is for the firm to make profits by exchanging goods and services with customers, typically for monetary payment. Communication with customers by advertising, public relations, personal selling, or some other means is a vital contributor for securing desired customer behavior, typically purchase.

A major role of communications is to inform customers about issues such as the benefits inherent in the firm's product or service, its price, where it can be secured, and so forth. It must also be recognized that, whether through an emotional or inspirational advertisement, a clever public relations campaign, or a salesperson who does an outstanding job of interfacing with a customer, communications often create value in their own right.

Communications play a major role in marketing efforts by providing value to current and potential customers, and securing differential advantage. However, success in communications is not easily earned, for marketers frequently confront significant challenges, both inside and outside the firm.

Inside Challenges

In many firms, especially those that are technically oriented, marketers have to deal with a tendency to assume that the "best" product (usually defined by the firm's own engineers) is going to "win" in the marketplace. Managers in these firms often fail to recognize that, to be successful, the customer must believe the product is the best (in an overall value sense). Clearly communications play a major role in forming this belief. A related but more general problem is the widespread view of other functional managers that communications expenses are costs that should be minimized. As a result, in many firms, there is a tendency to under-fund communications efforts. Finally, the firm has multiple communications targets. In addition to current and potential customers, it must often address different entities, such as shareholders, current and potential employees, complementers, and suppliers with communications that are, at a minimum, not inconsistent. In most firms, responsibility for these different communications targets and the various communications tools is, unfortunately, widely diffused and consistency is difficult to achieve.

Outside Challenges

Externally, the firm's communications efforts do not occur in a vacuum; customer targets of the firm's communications efforts live in an information-rich environment. Indeed, the mind of any communications target is inevitably the target for a myriad of messages from other non-competing organizations. Although most information received by these targets has little direct relevance to customer needs, or the firm's products and services, its very ubiquity can affect receipt of the firm's communications. Somehow, the communications strategy must cut through this "noise" to have an effect.

Furthermore, these customer targets receive information daily about the firm and its products (and those of competitors) from a variety of sources, such as the media, government, intermediaries, and other customers. This information may treat the firm and its products positively, neutrally, or negatively. Some information of this type may have extremely powerful effects.

Example: In 1997, Apple Computer was reported in the press as rudderless, unprofitable, and experiencing market share declines. In the face of such news, many users of Macintosh computers shifted to PC technology and potential customers did not even consider a Mac purchase.

In contrast the media have often reported sympathetically on organizations such as Ben and Jerry's and The Body Shop, whose endorsement of social causes has held particular appeal for many journalists.

Most importantly, the firm must consider its competitors' communications. These entities may target the same customers as the firm and use a variety of communication devices in attempts to thwart the firm's efforts and secure purchase behavior for their own products and services. In addition, the firm may have to deal with third-party pressure groups, for example, environmentalists, attacking the firm. Regardless, the task for the firm is to devise communications strategies to ensure that its messages register more strongly with its communications targets.

COMMUNICATIONS TOOLS

To surmount these challenges, the firm has a variety of tools available to secure its communications objectives. These have traditionally been grouped into two major categories: personal communication and non-personal communication (Figure 14.1).

- **Personal communication** is direct interpersonal (face-to-face) contact with targeted individuals or groups.[2]
- **Non-personal communication** carries a message without interpersonal contact between sender and receiver.[3]

Note that, in general, non-personal communications, notably advertising, direct marketing, and packaging, are under greater firm control than personal communication that evolves during the interaction process.[4]

In addition, customers also interact with technical- and customer-service personnel. As relationship management has grown in importance, many firms have identified the crucial role played by customer service personnel in working with existing customers.[7] Finally, in those services businesses such as airlines and some restaurants where "manufacturing" occurs in the customer's presence, interaction may occur with operations personnel.

Other important dimensions are word-of-mouth and quasi-personal communication.

Word-of-Mouth Communication

Word-of-mouth communication occurs when customers advise one another of their experience with a particular product or service. Because customers have no commercial interest, they often have higher credibility than paid advertisers. In many cases, corporations have little control over word-of-mouth *per se*, as it derives from positive (or negative) experiences with the firm's products or services.

Non-personal Communication

Advertising is paid communication directed at a mass audience. It embraces many different modalities and media types. Included are visual-static (printed matter), such as newspapers, magazines, most billboards, signage, and point of purchase displays; visual-dynamic, such as TV and movies; and audio, such as radio.[6]

Direct marketing is communication directed at individuals. Although the bulk of direct marketing is still accounted for by printed direct mail, more sophisticated versions can be delivered via audio/video tapes, DVD, CD-ROMs, e-mail, and fax.

Packaging is simply the communication value of the package containing the product.

Publicity is communication that is not directly paid for, nor sponsored by, the firm involved. Typically, the firm provides information in the form of a story, press release, photograph, or video to a third-party transmitter, such as a news organization that incorporates the material in its own communications.

Public relations embraces publicity but is broader in scope. It includes other attempts to manage the company image and secure favorable customer response by sponsoring events, giving speeches, participating in community activities, donating money to charity, and other public activities.

Sales promotion embraces a set of activities that provide extra value to customers and are typically designed to lead to immediate sales. Consumer promotions include coupons, contests, games, rebates, premiums, samples, and point-of-purchase materials. Trade promotions include special price deals, merchandising allowances, and contests. Promotions have the advantage of bringing short-term sales benefits. However, they may also acculturate customers to promotions who will not purchase without them.

Trade shows are an important sales promotion device in several industries. Because many competing suppliers participate, trade shows tend to draw large numbers of current and potential customers. As a result, they offer suppliers the opportunity to display their new products at one time to a large audience.[7]

Personal Communication

Personal communications are mainly characterized by customer interactions with salespeople who may act individually or as part of a team effort. These individuals may operate at various customer locations, or in a fixed place, such as a retail store. In recent years, many firms have developed telemarketing forces to communicate with customers by telephone as a supplement to, or as a lower cost replacement for, the field sales force.

FIGURE 14.1

Traditional Definitions of Communication Tools

Nonetheless, companies may develop strategies to encourage positive word-of-mouth. The success of the movie, "The Blair Witch Project," was largely due to a word-of-mouth campaign, based on a highly original Internet site orchestrated by the distributors (Artisan Entertainment). In early 2000, Artisan was attempting to repeat its "virtual marketing" success with a new movie, "Cecil B. Demented."[8]

> **Example:** In January 2000, the producers of "The Big Tease," invited hundreds of hairdressers to watch previews in New York, Los Angeles, San Francisco, and London, hoping they would discuss the movie with their customers.

Quasi-Personal Communications

This form of communication, made possible by technological innovation, embraces interaction and feedback without human involvement, and supplements the traditional distinction between non-personal and personal communications. Although most of these interactions, based on artificial intelligence, are currently conducted via computer keypads and telephones, advances in voice recognition software suggest that customers may soon be able to conduct interactive voice dialogues with computer servers.

Nowhere is the development of quasi-personal communications seen as strongly as on the Internet where a sea-change of astounding proportions is being witnessed. Both the ability of firms and customers to communicate inexpensively on a one-to-one basis (and of customers to communicate with each other) is so changing traditional practice that it is difficult to foresee the ultimate outcome.[9]

Example: When repeat customers of Amazon.com sign on to its Web site, they receive book recommendations based on their prior purchases. If a previously purchased author writes a new book, customers receive an e-mail advising them of its availability.

DEVELOPING THE COMMUNICATIONS STRATEGY

In developing the firm's communications strategy, the three basic questions noted in Table 14.1 must be answered.[10]

Question 1: Who Are the Firm's Communications Targets?

The firm has two major types of communications targets. This chapter focuses on communications targets directly related to the firm's entry in various product/markets, notably on the various types of customer. Other communications targets not directly related to its product/market entries are briefly considered.

COMMUNICATIONS TARGETS IN THE FIRM'S PRODUCT MARKETS   Broadly speaking, the communications targets of most concern to marketing are specified in the positioning statement of the market strategy. The most important are current and potential customers, those persons or organizations in the channel of distribution or decision (other than competitors) whose actions can affect the purchase of the firm's products and services. For example, for a subcomponent manufacturer, the customer may be a component manufacturer, finished-goods manufacturer, distributor, retailer, or consumer. Customers can also include persons or entities not directly in the flow of goods and services, such as specifiers, standards agencies, and third-party advisors.

A useful way of thinking about communications targets is to distinguish between push and pull communications strategies.

- **Push strategy:** The focus of communications efforts is on direct customers. In the example in the previous paragraph, the subcomponent manufacturer would focus its major efforts on component manufacturers, leaving these firms to communicate with finished-goods manufacturers, and so on down the channel (Figure 14.2). Many industrial goods manufacturers use push strategies (via sales force efforts) to persuade direct customers to purchase their products.
- **Pull strategy:** The focus of communications efforts is on indirect customers further down the channel. The subcomponent manufacturer could focus its efforts on consumers, attempting to persuade them to purchase finished goods manufactured with

TABLE 14.1 Critical Questions for Developing a Communications Strategy

Basic Questions	Subsidiary Questions
1. Who are the firm's communications targets?	• Specifically, with what types of entity does the firm want to communicate?
2. What does the firm wish to accomplish with its communications efforts?	• How do its communications objectives vary by type of communications target?
3. What communications tools will the firm use to accomplish its communications objectives?	• What combination of advertising, direct marketing, publicity, public relations, packaging, sales promotion, trade shows, sales force effort, and other types of communications will it use?

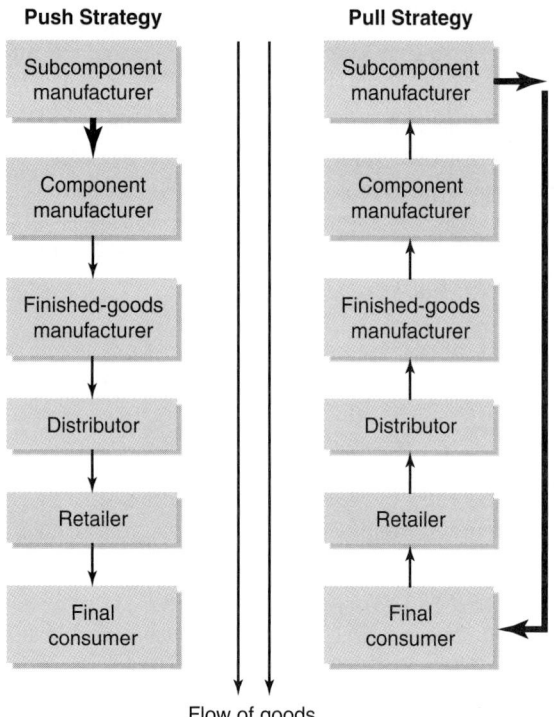

Push Strategy	Pull Strategy
Subcomponent manufacturer	Subcomponent manufacturer
Component manufacturer	Component manufacturer
Finished-goods manufacturer	Finished-goods manufacturer
Distributor	Distributor
Retailer	Retailer
Final consumer	Final consumer

Flow of goods

➤ Subcomponent manufacturer's communications effort

FIGURE 14.2

Communications Targets in Push and Pull Communication Strategies

its subcomponents from retailers (see Figure 14.2). Successful persuasion generates a pull effect in the channel, hence driving the firm's subcomponent sales. This process can be resultant—consumer demand generation is sufficiently strong for intermediaries to purchase—or anticipatory—the manufacturer uses media expenditure plans to convince intermediaries to purchase product for inventory because of the anticipated heavy consumer demand when the advertising is launched.

Although many companies use pure forms of push and pull strategies, it is perhaps more common to find combination strategies aimed at multiple communications targets. Many major, fast-moving consumer goods companies, such as Procter & Gamble and Lever Brothers, invest significant efforts in pull strategies via advertising efforts targeted at consumers. However, they also allocate significant push resources for interfacing with their retail (trade) customers. As the retail industry has become concentrated and its power grown at the expense of manufacturers, category management systems have developed, and correspondingly more push effort is now being directed at retailers.[11]

Nonetheless, in individual industries, sometimes either push or pull strategies tend to be favored by most competitors. However, great advantage can often be achieved by breaking the traditional mold.

Example: The synthetic fibers industry has traditionally placed extensive resources into consumer advertising to create downstream demand for its products. However, until DuPont launched Stainmaster carpet fiber, this had never occurred for carpets. DuPont does not manufacture carpets, yet the firm invested in extensive consumer advertising to convince consumers that carpets manufactured with its new fiber would be stain resistant. The advertising achieved great success.

Furthermore, communication targets change as the market strategy changes.

Example: The *intel inside* advertising campaign for the first time targeted consumers, and a recent change in Food and Drug Administration (FDA) guidelines on television advertising allowed pharmaceutical firms to augment their detailing activities at physicians with advertisements to consumers.[12]

Finally, in addition to customers, important product/market communications targets might include competitors and complementers. Although some forms of communication among competitors are illegal in many countries, firms nonetheless signal competitors, sometimes subtly, about the behavior they want them to exhibit.[13] Finally, since actions by the firm's complementers may be mutually reinforcing, these organizations may also be targets of communication.

OTHER COMMUNICATION TARGETS   Firms also have a variety of other communications targets not directly related to their product/markets. For example, factor input markets, such as for human resources and raw materials, may require communications efforts. Markets for capital provide a special case of factor inputs and firms (or their agents) employ communications in primary markets to secure debt and equity financing. They also use communications in secondary markets to influence the type of shareholder, such as short-term versus long-term investors,[14] and to help maintain the share price.

Example: In April 1999, following poor profit results and the firing of CEO Eckhard Pfeiffer, Compaq Chairman Ben Rosen published a full-page letter extolling Compaq's virtues to "valued customers, shareholders, and partners" on the back page of *The New York Times* Business Section.[15]

Finally, the firm can also identify communications targets in the general external environment, principally related to government where laws are drafted and regulations developed. Such targets may include political pressure groups that influence legislation.

Although executed for different purposes, communications to these targets may influence activities in product/markets. For example, help wanted advertisements for highly trained personnel may persuade customers that the firm is pushing the technological frontiers and that its products are worth buying. Or, if the firm is seen to be lobbying against environmentally friendly legislation, it might lose sales to "green" consumers.

Question 2: What Does the Firm Want to Accomplish with Its Communications Efforts?

In most cases the ultimate (if not the immediate) objective of marketing communications is to increase sales revenues. However, many other types of objective may be appropriate, depending on circumstances. A major consideration is the communications target:

- **Customers, competitors, or complementers**: Clearly the sort of communications objectives the firm sets for customer targets will be different from those it might set when its communications target are competitors or complementers. For example, communications objectives for customers will likely be directly or indirectly related to sales. However, for competitors and complementers, the firm may want to influence their marketplace actions.
- **Direct or indirect customers**: In the previous section, it was noted that a subcomponent manufacturer might have several different types of direct and indirect customers. Of course, it may decide not to communicate directly with each customer type, but should it do so, its objectives are likely to be very different across customers (Table 14.2).
- **Stage of customer development**: A major guide for setting specific communications objectives is provided by the four growth options in the strategic alternatives dimension of the market strategy:
  - Reduce customer defection rate
  - Increase use by current customers
  - Attract competitors' customers
  - Attract non-users in the market segment

TABLE 14.2 Illustration of Communications Objectives in the Marketing Channel

Type of Customer	Communications Objectives for Customers
Component manufacturer	• Learn how to assemble the firm's subcomponent into the customer's component
	• Purchase subcomponent for use in component
	• Inventory sufficient component quantities for demand by the finished-goods manufacturer
Finished-goods manufacturer	• Agree to purchase component (including firm's subcomponent) for finished product
	• Agree to use subcomponent brand on finished product
Distributor	• Have salespeople trained to sell the finished product to retailers
Retailer	• Agree to budget coop advertising funds for finished product
Consumer	• Purchase the finished product

Clearly, these different broad goals would likely translate into different communications objectives (Table 14.3).

Relatedly, the firm's communications objectives will likely depend upon the age and type of the business. For example, a new business will probably place substantial effort on identifying, qualifying, and selling to potential customers. Similar objectives can also be set in well-established businesses, such as life insurance where new customer development is a critical issue. Conversely, for well-established businesses focusing on customer retention and growth, management may place little effort on communications with potential customers, and set communications objectives in terms of sales, service, and justifying purchases for existing customers.

A critical issue in setting communications objectives relates to the fact that communications is only one area of marketing implementation. Whether or not the firm makes sales depends also on the quality of the market strategy and the other areas of marketing implementation, such as product, price, distribution, and service. Although sales is typically the ultimate goal of the entire marketing effort, the best possible communications strategy will not lead to sales if the product is ill-designed, of poor quality, priced too high, and distributed haphazardly. As a result, management should be wary of setting communications objectives in terms of sales.

Furthermore, an important role for objectives is comparison with actual results to provide managerial feedback. Knowing that sales targets have not been achieved may not be particularly useful in revising marketing communications.

TABLE 14.3 Illustration of Communications Objectives by Stage of Customer Development

Stage of Customer Development	Communications Objectives for Customers
Current customers: reduce defection rate	• Convince customers that their purchase was the best decision they could have made
Current customers: increase use	• Persuade to purchase and use in larger quantities
Competitors' customers	• Secure trial of the firm's product
Non-users of product form	• Secure new leads
	• Qualify potential customers

Question 3: What Communications Tools Will the Firm Use to Accomplish Its Communications Objectives?

As expected, the most appropriate communications tools are highly dependent on the particular communications objectives set for the various communications targets. For example, if the firm's communications goal is to secure widespread awareness of a new product among a broad consumer target group, advertising is likely to be more effective than sending salespeople door-to-door. On the other hand, if large industrial companies are target customers for sophisticated capital goods, elaborate personal selling activities are inevitably involved.

Figure 14.3 displays a chart to assist management in matching available communications tools to communications objectives at specific communications targets. In this illustration, the firm is targeting retailers to secure distribution and sale of a new product. The firm has decided to identify potential retailers via direct mail, qualify them by telemarketing, and then sell qualified retailers by personal selling effort. However, once retailers have decided to carry the firm's product, a sales and service team will be responsible for ongoing sales and service. Note that for this customer target, the firm has decided not to use advertising, publicity and public relations, trade shows, the Internet, or service personnel acting as individuals.

If the firm has also decided to target consumers, a similar chart for that type of customer would be developed, and for each other type of customer target.

An important issue is the differing financial implications of various combinations of communications tools and customer targets. For example, in the push and pull strategy dichotomy, pull strategies generally involve heavier fixed cost expenditures and significant cash outflows compared to push strategies. Plant investment and production are required to fill the distribution pipeline; then advertising and promotion expenditures are needed to generate the pull. Many companies address this problem by scaling-up via so-called "regional rollouts"; however, such strategies slow introduction and may open opportunity windows for competitors. In general, large companies find it easier to pursue pull strategies than small companies because they can cross-fund product introductions from other products in their portfolios. Indeed, the increased pace of new product introductions internationally is due, in part, to raised entry barriers because of these scale effects.

	Identify potential retailers	Qualify potential retailers	Sell qualified retailers	Sell and service retailer customers
Advertising	_____	_____	_____	_____
Direct mail	****	_____	_____	_____
Publicity and public relations	_____	_____	_____	_____
Trade shows	_____	_____	_____	_____
Internet	_____	_____	_____	_____
Telemarketing	_____	****	_____	_____
Personal selling	_____ _____		****	_____
Individual service	_____	_____	_____	_____
Sales and service teams	_____	_____	_____	****

FIGURE 14.3

Matching Communications Objectives and Tools

Example: In the early 1980s, Canon's bold shift to a pull approach brought it dominance of the U.S. 35mm SLR camera market, while its more push-oriented competitors foundered.

By contrast, push strategies generally involve higher variable costs since, to fulfill their promotional functions, intermediaries require incentives in the form of higher margins. Cash outflows are limited because the firm avoids the high costs of introductory advertising and promotion campaigns. As a result, smaller competitors are prone to favor push strategies.

INTEGRATING COMMUNICATIONS EFFORTS

Coordination and integration are vital to the successful execution of any strategy (Figure 14.4). Thus, market strategies must be consistent with corporate and business unit strategies (I), and market strategies themselves must coordinate and integrate a series of decisions in various marketing implementation areas, notably product, price, promotion/communications, distribution, and service (II). This section focuses solely on coordinating and integrating the firm's various marketing communications efforts (III).[16]

Integrated Communications

Integrated communications is concerned with using all of the various communications tools in an integrated manner to provide maximum impact in pursuit of the firm's goals. For communications focused on the firm's product/markets, integration must be achieved both horizontally among the various communications tools in an individual product/market strategy as well as across communications in multiple product/market strategies, and vertically between corporate and business level and product/market communications.

However, a higher level of integration involving all of the firm's communications targets should be considered, not just current and potential customers. Although having very different purposes, communications to different groups, such as customers, shareholders, and government entities, should, at a minimum, not be inconsistent, regardless of communication type. In particular, it must be recognized that individuals may be members of multiple groups and may thus be targets for several types of communications. For example, a government official can be a shareholder and a customer.

HORIZONTAL COMMUNICATIONS INTEGRATION: INDIVIDUAL PRODUCT/ MARKET STRATEGY In developing an integrated communications strategy for an individual product/market, marketers should consider three distinct issues:

- Do not send discrepant messages to individual communications targets. In developing a communications plan for a specific customer target, management can employ more than one communications tool. For example, it can supplement a direct mail campaign with mass advertising. Although having different purposes, messages from the two communications types should not be inconsistent, either in the messages or when they are received. Thus a mass advertising campaign designed to support the direct mail effort should not begin two weeks after the mailing is completed.
- Secure mutual reinforcement/synergy from different communication elements for individual communications targets. This is a higher purpose than avoiding discrepant messages. The challenge is to blend together the various elements of a communications strategy so that their differing contributions are mutually reinforcing, even synergistic. As product quality has increased recently in many domains, the importance of gaining differential advantage in communications has grown significantly.

Example: An electrical components manufacturer had marginal success with radio advertising. In 1996, it introduced an Internet site, but this also had little success. However, when it advertised its Internet site on drive-time radio, the results were spectacular, a real synergistic result.

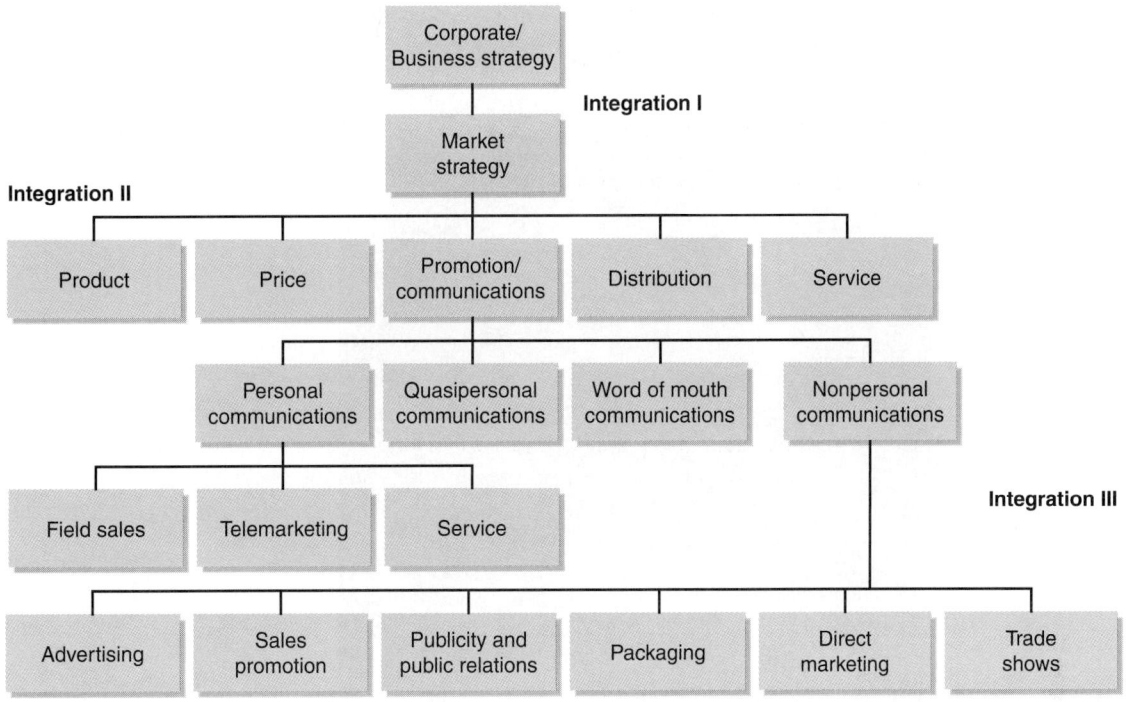

FIGURE 14.4
Coordinating and Integrating Strategic Elements

- Do not send discrepant messages to the various different communications targets. Although the communications purposes may be different for each target, management must avoid inconsistency in its communications. An even more difficult but important challenge is to ensure that the firm's own communications are consistent with communications from other entities in the distribution channel whose communications efforts impact sales of the firm's products.

Unfortunately, many companies fail to achieve the required levels of integration. In some cases, the culprit is organizational as companies often specialize their communications activities by splitting responsibility among various internal departments and outside groups, such as advertising agencies, intermediaries, and selling agents. Although individual advertising agencies may themselves house several communication specialties, each is typically managed separately, further accentuating communications fragmentation.[17]

HORIZONTAL COMMUNICATIONS INTEGRATION: MULTIPLE PRODUCT/ MARKET STRATEGIES   In addition to integrating communications for an individual product market, communications integration may also be required across different product markets. For example, if the strategic decision has been made to extend the brand across several products, product forms, or product categories, communications must be similarly integrated. However, as the financial value attached to successful brands has become better recognized, the locus of responsibility for guarding brand equity has risen higher in the managerial hierarchy and become more dissociated from the locus of responsibility for product/market related communications.

VERTICAL COMMUNICATIONS INTEGRATION   Even more serious integration challenges occur when the firm engages in corporate- or business-level communications. In these cases, it may be necessary to coordinate firm-level, business-level, and brand/product-level communications. At a minimum, consistency should be assured, but the goal should be

FIGURE 14.5

Example of an Advertisement Integrated with Personal Selling Communications

to attain synergistic benefits. One of the more famous business-to-business advertisements which ran for years, was for McGraw-Hill's business magazines (Figure 14.5). Examples of corporate-level advertising include "Better things for living through chemistry" (DuPont) and "GE brings good things to life."[18] Many argue that these campaigns act as helpful door openers for these firms' sales forces. In addition, to achieve vertical integration, advertising for GE refrigerators would have to be coordinated in content and, perhaps, timing with advertising for GE appliances in general and with the slogan "GE brings good things to life."

NON-PERSONAL COMMUNICATIONS: ADVERTISING

This section focuses on non-personal communications, specifically advertising. In many respects, advertising strategy represents a successive refinement of the basic ideas outlined earlier in the book for market strategy and in the previous section for communications strategies in general. However, in several industries, especially in fast-moving consumer goods (FMCG), advertising is a critical element in both the market and communications strategies to which firms devote immense resources in terms of thought, effort, and dollars. For this reason, a relatively fine-grained discussion of developing advertising strategy is presented.

The various elements of advertising strategy can be elaborated around a standard set of questions, similar in form to those in the previous section (Table 14.4). The nature of the linkages to market and communications strategies are indicated. Similar questions can be used to develop strategy for other forms of non-personal communication.

TABLE 14.4 Elements of the Advertising Strategy

Element	Question	Link to Market and Communications Strategies
Target audience	Who are we trying to influence?	Target market segments are identified in the market strategy
Advertising objectives	What are we trying to achieve?	Advertising objectives are directly related to strategic and operational objectives in the market strategy
Message content	What message do we want the target audience to receive?	Related to the core strategy (unique selling proposition) in the market strategy
Execution style	How shall we communicate the message?	The most effective means of communicating the message to target customers
Media selection and timing	Where shall we place our advertising? When will the message be sent?	Select media to reach target customers at the appropriate time
Advertising budget	How much shall we spend on advertising?	The advertising budget is one element of the entire communications budget
Program evaluation	How shall we evaluate our advertising?	Is the advertising program helping us achieve our market objectives?

Target Audience: Who Are We Trying to Influence?

The second task of marketing is to identify and target market segments. Because some market segments are typically more attractive than others, following market segment identification, management must decide which segments the firm should target and address with marketing effort. Products and services are designed and prices are set for these market segments, and distribution makes products available to these segments. Equally, if at the communications strategy level, advertising is selected as an appropriate communications medium, then these segments, including influencers and decision makers, should be the targets of the firm's advertising efforts. Segments must be sufficiently well-defined so that the appropriate media can be selected to reach them (see below).[19] The firm may also direct communications at various entities in the distribution channel.

Advertising Objectives: What Are We Trying to Achieve?

To set advertising objectives in a sensible manner, marketers should have some idea of the way in which advertising works.

HOW ADVERTISING WORKS Because of its critical importance as an implementation element for market strategy, perhaps more research effort has been expended on this topic than any other within marketing. The most commonly discussed approaches to understanding advertising effectiveness are termed hierarchy-of-effects models based on the presumption that the way in which advertising works is likely to differ across product type. As a result, two important classes of model have been developed—one for high-involvement products and one for low-involvement products (Figure 14.6).[20]

High involvement High-involvement products are those for which the buyer believes there is financial or psycho-social risk associated with purchase. Products such as an automobile or a ball gown for the consumer, or choice of an advertising agency for a corporate image campaign, are those for which the prospective customer typically engages in a learning process before making a purchase decision. The underlying idea in the

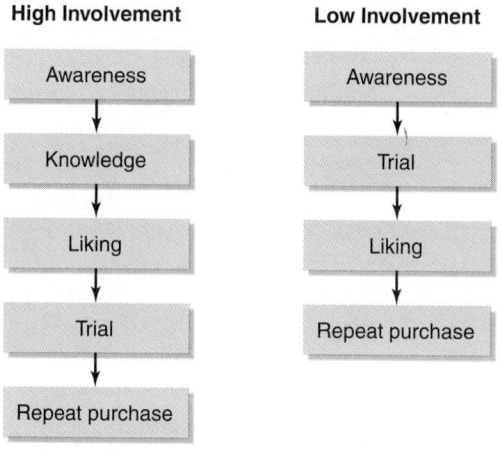

High Involvement

Awareness → Knowledge → Liking → Trial → Repeat purchase

Low Involvement

Awareness → Trial → Liking → Repeat purchase

FIGURE 14.6

Hierarchy-of-Effects Advertising Models

high-involvement hierarchy is that several stages must be traversed. Advertising creates product awareness that leads the customer through three critical sequential stages:

- Knowledge: learning about the product, its features and benefits
- Liking: developing positive feelings about the product
- Trial: purchasing the product

If the product experience is positive, the customer engages in repeat purchase, actions that can be reinforced by advertising.[21]

Low involvement Low-involvement products, such as many non-durables (for example, grocery items), where risk is low, require little understanding prior to purchase. Here, a different hierarchical process is proposed. The role of advertising is to create high awareness and induce trial.[22] Trial leads to liking, then repurchase which, again, can be reinforced by advertising.[23]

Although the validity of all hierarchy of effects models has been questioned, there is little doubt that knowledge, liking, and trial are critical intermediate variables between advertising and purchase.[24] However, in securing the crucial goal of repeat purchase, some intermediate variables are more important than others. The relative importance depends on product category, life cycle stage, brand, customer, time, and other factors.[25]

For market managers, the critical message is that they should focus on *knowledge, liking,* and *trial*, in addition to purchase, as critical variables that advertising might impact. However, they should not *assume* a particular sequential pattern but rather engage in marketing research activities to understand how advertising affects these variables in their particular market situation.

SETTING ADVERTISING OBJECTIVES When market objectives are discussed, a distinction must be made between strategic and operational objectives.[26] Strategic marketing objectives are qualitative and directional, whereas operational objectives include quantitative measures and time lines. The same basic framework is used for advertising objectives.

The strategic dimension of advertising objectives can be output or intermediary:

- **Output objectives** include dimensions such as sales, market share, and brand loyalty.
- **Intermediary objectives** relate to the hierarchy-of-effects models. Important dimensions include awareness, knowledge, liking, trial, purchase, repeat purchase, and purchase satisfaction.

As noted earlier, output objectives have the important characteristic of representing what the firm ultimately wants to achieve. The problem is that securing these objectives depends not only on advertising, but also on all other areas of marketing implementation. Thus a failure to achieve a particular output objective, such as sales, provides little in the way of feedback for modifying the advertising strategy.

By contrast, intermediary strategic objectives are typically much more directly related to advertising and provide excellent feedback information. The critical issue for management is to select the appropriate intermediary objective. For example, a pioneering firm introducing a radically new product must develop a market of non-users who, by definition, have to engage in extensive problem solving. If purchase and use of the product involves financial or social risk, a considerable educational task must be accomplished. High risk implies high involvement, and awareness may be the crucial strategic advertising objective.[27] As awareness levels rise, overall communication objectives will likely shift to trial and subsequently to encouraging loyalty and repeat purchase. Here, advertising may also play an important role.

Once management has agreed on the appropriate strategic dimensions of advertising objectives, the focus shifts to operational objectives. Critical issues are quantitative measures and time lines. The actual quantitative level depends in part on the product's current performance.

Examples of advertising objectives that include both strategic and operational dimensions are:

- To secure 90% awareness of Windows 2000 among business executives within one month of launch
- To increase repeat purchase of our new candy bar from 30% to 50% among 10-to 16-year-old boys by the end of the year

Message Content: What Message Do We Want the Target Audience to Receive?

A key characteristic of advertising is the limited time/space available to the advertiser—a limited life print advertisement in a newspaper or magazine, or a few seconds of television time.[28] As a result, the advertiser must be very clear about how to use its scarce resource. The focus of the advertising message should relate directly to the core strategy statement (unique selling proposition) in the market strategy. In a nutshell, why should a member of the target segment purchase (or recommend for purchase) the firm's product rather than that of a competitor? If the core strategy was well developed, the message should be based on benefits that are important to the target, and reflect either unique claims, or claims where the advertiser has significant differential advantage over its competitors. As with any element of the firm's communications, however, it is important to remember that promises embedded in these communications must be delivered, or the effects are likely to be negative.

Most major advertisers outsource the task of developing the specific message to an advertising agency, in particular to the creative department. It is the job of the creative department to take the core strategy statement and turn it into both a message to be communicated and its execution. The translation process from advertiser to agency frequently takes the form of a concept statement written by the advertiser that the advertising agency redevelops as a creative brief, setting the parameters for what the advertising has to accomplish.

In general, the message content should relate to the specific type of advertising objective. This is illustrated with Federal Express (Table 14.5).[29]

Execution Style: How Shall We Communicate the Message?

To turn the core message into an effective advertisement is a daunting and challenging task; here the creative aspects of advertising come into play. As Schmitt has put it: "Creation and production of creative output are the most visible part of advertising . . . Although judging creative output may be easy, the creative process seems to be an enigma, more art than science, mysterious and unexplainable. The essence of creativity seems to be a willingness to alternate between divergent and convergent thinking, between brainstorming and analytic reasoning, between pushing the limits and being reasonable and practical." The result, hopefully, ". . . culminates in an illumination—the Big Idea."[30] Perhaps one of the more successful and creative advertising campaigns in recent years has been for Absolut vodka.[31]

TABLE 14.5 Advertising Objective and Core Message—Federal Express

Year	Objective	Core Message	Slogan
1972	Awareness	Who are we? How do we work?	"Take away our planes and we'd be just like anybody else"
1978	Knowledge	How do we compare?	"When it absolutely, positively has to be there overnight"
1980–1987	Trial and Repeat Purchase	Try us! Don't switch	"Why fool around with anybody else"
1995	Repeat Purchase	Don't switch	"Don't be a dope"

Example: Between 1979 when the campaign was launched, and the late 1990s, Absolut's market share rose from 1% to greater than 60% among imported vodkas. The typical Absolut advertisement contains a two-word headline starting with Absolut, such as "Absolut Perfection," "Absolut Appeal," and "Absolut Original," and a picture of the distinctive Absolut bottle in a form related to the headline (Figure 14.7). The campaign has earned many awards and has set Absolut apart from its competitors.[32]

A major feature of the *Absolut* campaign is the variety of executions on a single theme, over 400 in total. In some cases, sheer variety may be important. For example, companies targeting the youth market may employ many advertising executions.

Example: Describing a change in strategy, a Unilever brand manager said: "PlayStation had 19 different advertising executions last year because Sony knows young consumers get bored easily. Three years ago we ran three Lynx executions a year—we raised this to 10, with more to come.[33]

As a means of framing the creative challenge, several distinct execution styles and ways of structuring the communication are available. These include humor, comparative advertising, virtual advertising, celebrity endorsements, fear, and issues of language.[34]

HUMOR Humor is widespread in advertising but should be used with some degree of care. In general, humor aids in creating awareness and sets a positive tone for the advertiser's message; on the other hand, it may distract from the product. The audience may remember the advertisement, but be unable to associate it with the product or, worse, associate the humor with a competitor's product, called mis-indexing. Furthermore, humor comes in many shapes and sizes, can become tedious if not varied, and what is humorous to one person may be totally unfunny to another.[35]

COMPARATIVE ADVERTISING In this type of advertising, the advertiser makes a direct comparison with competitors' products. Although banned in some countries, comparative advertising is often used by smaller market share products to enhance their chances of entering the consideration set of brands from which the customer will choose.[36] Well-known examples include the "We try harder" campaign from Avis and the Pepsi Challenge. Comparative advertising is found even in such unlikely areas as professional services.

Example: A Deloitte and Touche Consulting Group advertising campaign makes direct competitive comparisons, complete with references. For example: "Andersen Consulting: Number one in billings. Deloitte Consulting: Number one in overall customer satisfaction."

VIRTUAL ADVERTISING A new phenomenon, closely related to product placement is so-called "virtual advertising." Virtual advertising involves the electronic insertion of signs, logos and products into live and previously taped television programs (Figure 14.8).[37]

FIGURE 14.7

Examples of Absolut Advertisements

FIGURE 14.8

Virtual Advertising at a Televised Soccer Game

One significant benefit of this technique is allowing different advertisements to be inserted in different geographic areas. A second is their use in the program *per se*, rather than in a commercial break that viewers may either ignore (live transmission) or "fast forward" through (recorded program).

CELEBRITY ENDORSEMENT   Widely used, especially in TV advertising, well-known individuals endorse the use of the product. Celebrity endorsements are valuable for securing awareness, but can also add credibility to the product, so long as there is a reasonable match between the celebrity and the product being advertised. Of course, should the celebrity generate negative personal publicity, there is risk to the advertiser's brand. Problems can also arise if the celebrity endorses too many products, thereby endangering the very credibility the advertiser is seeking, or if attention is paid to the celebrity and not to the product. This is a special concern for those celebrities that endorse several products. One of the most sought-after celebrity endorsers is Michael Jordan, some of whose contracts are shown below (Table 14.6).[38]

In December 1999, celebrity endorsements reached a new level when former heavyweight champion, George Foreman, sold his name and image to grill manufacturer, Salton, for $137.5 million in cash and stock.

FEAR   The underlying rationale for fear appeals is to create anxiety; this anxiety can be removed by taking the action that the advertiser requires. Anxiety can relate to physical danger, social disapproval, monetary loss, and so forth. Fear appeals involving physical danger are common in advertising promoting seat-belt use, unprotected sex, and anti-drug and anti-cigarette use; personal hygiene products often use social disapproval appeals, while monetary loss is used in the security industry and for credit cards. However, developing fear appeals is not simple. Too-mild appeals might be ineffective; appeals that are too strong may be blocked out.[39]

LANGUAGE   Finally, an important issue is the language used in the advertising. Clearly, the language must be understandable to the audience, but management that puts in the extra effort to speak directly to its customers will gain an advantage. Many customer groups (organization or individual) have a language specific to the group. Bankers talk of "spreads" and "basis points," and African-American teenagers talk of "gangstas and y'all

TABLE 14.6 Michael Jordan's Contracts

Brand	1998 Value in Millions (est.)
Nike	$16
Gatorade	5
Bijan	5
MCI Worldcom	4
Hanes	2
Ball Park Franks	2
Rayovac	2
Oakley	2
Wilson Sporting Goods	2
Wheaties	2
AMF Bowling	1
CBS Sportsline	1
Chicagoland Chevrolet Dealer Assn.	1
Total	**$45**

wordupbra". Management wanting to serve its customers should learn their language. Firms seeking customers abroad must be clear about word meanings in the foreign country. A British firm whose product does a great job of "knocking you up" might be surprised at its reception in the United States.

Media Selection and Timing: Where Shall We Place Our Advertising? When Will the Message Be Sent?

Media selection decisions require the answers to four related questions:

- What does management want to accomplish with its media strategy?
- Which media classes should be used?
- Which media vehicles should be used?
- What media schedule should be implemented?

WHAT DOES MANAGEMENT WANT TO ACCOMPLISH WITH ITS MEDIA STRATEGY? Objectives for media strategy involve a basic trade-off between reach and frequency.

Reach and Frequency Reach and frequency are defined as follows:

- Reach is the number of targeted individuals exposed to the advertising at least once during the planning period.
- Frequency is the average number of times a targeted individual is exposed to the advertising. In general, high frequency is advocated when the message is complex, competes with multiple other messages, or the product is new.

These concepts lead to media objectives of the form:

Example: Reach 50% of the target audience five times in the next six months.

Many media buyers use the summary measure, gross rating points (GRP), to assist in their media buying decisions, where

$$GRP = reach \times frequency$$

Thus, the media objective noted above, to reach 50% of the target audience on average 5 times, requires 250 gross rating points (50% $\times$ 5 = 250).

Of course, GRPs alone may provide insufficient information for setting objectives. A GRP of 250 may be secured in various ways, such as 100% of the audience receiving, on average, 2.5 exposures; or 10% of the audience receiving, on average, 25 exposures.

As a result, management may set GRP objectives subject to minimum frequency requirements. On the other hand, excessive frequency can lead to wasted advertising spending because of diminishing returns.

When management uses more than one method of reaching its target audience, related media concepts are duplicated and unduplicated reach. For example, if two methods are used, duplicated reach is that portion of the target audience receiving both communications; unduplicated reach is that portion receiving just one communication. Depending upon its advertising objectives, management may want to enhance either type of reach.

In any event, the particular reach (duplicated and unduplicated), frequency, or GRP objectives sought from the media schedule should relate directly to the advertising objectives. Thus if the advertising objective were:

- To increase repeat purchase of our new candy bar from 30% to 50% among 10- to 16-year-old boys by the end of the year,

a corresponding media objective might be:

- To develop a media schedule that delivers 1,500 GRPs subject to a reach of at least 60%.

Impact Another aspect of the media decision is to consider what impact might be created. Although impact is also obviously affected by the advertisement itself, sometimes an innovative media strategy can make an enormous impact. This innovation may involve novel use of existing media, or first use of a new medium.

> **Example:** In the U.K., Häagen Dazs took the unusual step of launching its super-premium ice cream with black and white newspaper ads only. Although the copy was mainly responsible for the large amount of publicity, Haagen Daazs successfully launched a new brand and received a major advertising award for a first-year expenditure of only £375,000.

The media department is often regarded by agency creative people as boring and routine. Yet the best media executives bring considerable creativity to their work. This creativity brought advertising-supported bus shelters to the citizens of New York, and colorful, sponsored buses and taxis to the streets of many cities in the world. Whereas conventional media vehicles may be important in securing the required response to the advertiser's message, sometimes novelty can bring even greater rewards.

WHICH MEDIA CLASSES SHOULD BE USED? The term media class refers to the various types of medium that the firm might use, such as broadcast (television, radio), print (newspapers, magazines), outdoors (billboards), and so forth. Media classes differ across several dimensions: print advertisements can be read at leisure, but television and radio spots exist for short time-periods and are much more intrusive; outdoor advertisements have a longer presence than other media classes. Table 14.7 details the advantages/disadvantages of various media classes.[40]

When considering advertising, most people focus on print and broadcast media. However, firms are increasingly using less conventional options to avoid the clutter in these more widely-used media. A good example is outdoor advertising which, in addition to traditional billboards, includes buses, bus shelters, subway posters, street furniture, stadium displays, auto-racing cars, malls, and airport signs.[41] Technological improvements, low prices, and increased driving have made outdoor advertising a more attractive medium. In 1999, Ford placed the biggest ever billboard purchase, $50 million; indeed, some firms owe their successes to outdoor advertising.[42]

> **Example:** At the Taj Mahal in India is a sign that reads, "only 10,728 miles to Wall Drug," a $10 million per annum pharmacy in Wall, South Dakota (population 800). Purchased by Ted Hustead in 1931, the pharmacy's initial growth resulted from signs placed on nearby Route 16. Later, Wall Drug placed signs along every highway in South Dakota and neighboring states, indicating the distance from Wall Drug. Eventually, Wall Drug spent up to $300K per annum on a global billboard campaign that included London buses and every train station in Kenya. In addition to direct spending, Wall Drug benefited considerably from publicity generated by many newspaper and magazine articles, and from American GIs who placed their own "distance from Wall Drug" signs around the world.[43]

> **Example:** In Beijing, where billboards and television advertising are extremely expensive, the Ai Jia (love home) World Furniture Center, pays groups of 15 teenagers, wearing identical neon-yellow warm-up jackets bearing the Ai Jia name, and matching baseball caps, to ride in formation along set routes on Beijing streets.[44]

WHICH MEDIA VEHICLES SHOULD BE USED? The term media vehicle refers to a specific exemplar of the media class that management decides to use for its communication. Newspaper vehicles include *The New York Times*, *The Boston Globe*, and the *San Francisco Examiner*; magazine vehicles include *Time*, *Vanity Fair*, and *Good Housekeeping;* television vehicles are the actual programs during which the advertising runs, such as *60 Minutes*, the *Superbowl*, and *As the World Turns*.

Within a given media class, the various vehicles differ across several critical dimensions.

INTEGRATED
MARKETING
COMMUNICATIONS

TABLE 14.7 Media Characteristics

Media	Advantages	Disadvantages
Television	Mass coverage	Low selectivity
	High reach	Short message life
	Impact of sight, sound, and motion	High absolute cost
	High prestige	High production costs
	Low cost per exposure	Clutter
	Attention getting	
	Favorable image	
Radio	Local coverage	Audio only
	Low cost	Clutter
	High frequency	Low attention getting
	Flexible	Fleeting message
	Low production costs	
	Well-segmented audiences	
Magazines	Segmentation potential	Long lead time for ad placement
	Quality reproduction	Visual only
	High information content	Lack of flexibility
	Longevity	
	Multiple readers	
Newspapers	High coverage	Short life
	Low cost	Clutter
	Short lead time for placing ads	Low attention-getting capabilities
	Ads can be placed in interest sections	Poor reproduction quality
	Timely (current ads)	Selective reader exposure
	Reader controls exposure	
	Can be used for coupons	
Outdoor	Location specific	Short exposure time requires short ad
	High repetition	Poor image
	Easily noticed	Local restrictions
Direct Mail	High selectivity	High cost/contact
	Reader controls exposure	Poor image (junk mail)
	High information content	Clutter
	Opportunities for repeat exposures	

- **Audience type**: The extent to which the audience for the media vehicle is congruent with the firm's target audience. Some of the target audience may not be reached by the media vehicle; conversely, some of the media vehicle's audience may not be an advertising target and hence be wasted.
- **Audience size**: The number of readers/viewers/listeners for the vehicle. Note that for certain types of print media, circulation may bear little relationship to readership, for example, magazines in medical offices have multiple readership. Conversely, television viewers may mute the advertising, or record the program and fast-forward through the advertising during playback.
- **Cost**: Two costs are important. First is the absolute cost of advertising, such as one full page in *The New York Times*, or a 30-second commercial on *60 Minutes*. The

second is the cost per audience member. Different media classes use different measures so that informed comparisons can be made across media vehicle.[45] In print media, cost per thousand is very popular:

Cost per 1000 (CPM) = Absolute Cost of Advertising Space $\times$ 1000/Circulation[46]

- **Nature of the vehicle**: When the advertiser makes a media buy, it is, in effect, renting the eyes and ears of the audience for the media vehicle. Thus there is always a potential interaction between the advertisement and the media vehicle; this may have an important impact on vehicle choice. For example, if management were running a serious television advertisement, it might not want this to air during a comedy show, regardless of favorable cost and audience characteristics.

WHAT MEDIA SCHEDULE SHOULD BE IMPLEMENTED? Typically, management wants to optimize its media objectives—reach, frequency, gross rating points, and so forth—subject to a budget constraint. To secure the best media buy is a complex task even within one media class; advertising campaigns involving multiple media classes represent an even more difficult undertaking. For major advertisers, media schedules are developed mostly by advertising agencies using complex computer models typically modified by managerial judgment.

A second issue in media scheduling concerns the timing of the advertisements. At a gross level, two polar strategies are available:

- **Continuous**: a regular periodic pattern of advertising
- **Flighting**: repeated high levels of advertising followed by low, or no, advertising.
- **Pulsing**: a combination of continuous and flighting advertising. Pulsing may be employed within a single media vehicle or media class, but even more complex schedules involving advertising in multiple media classes and vehicles may also be developed.[47]

In general, continuous advertising is believed to be more effective for products that are purchased throughout the year whereas flighting and pulsing are more effective when demand is variable over time, for example, for such seasonal products as cruises and air travel.[48]

Advertising Budget: How Much Shall We Spend on Advertising?

The major difficulty in setting advertising budgets is uncertainty about the shape of the response function—the relationship between the level of advertising spending and the specific objectives that management wants to achieve. There are enormous differences in effectiveness across different advertising campaigns and different advertising executions. These differences may well be due to the creativity of the advertising—more effective advertising permits the required results to be secured with lower expenditures. Also, there are typically non-linearities in the advertising-response relationship; these may take a variety of forms. Suppose the objective is sales; Figure 14.9 presents two alternative advertising/sales response functions—concave downward (diminishing returns) (A) and S-shaped (B), each of which has some intuitive appeal and research support.[49] Management faces two problems. First, which is the appropriate shape of the response function for its market situation, A or B (or some other function)? Second, where on the response function is the firm currently operating? Certainly its actions at I or I′ would be quite different from those at II or II′.[50]

If management can deal with these problems, the budgeting decision reduces to a problem in marginal analysis—choosing that advertising budget where marginal revenue equals the marginal cost. Unfortunately, although this theoretical approach is useful for framing the budgeting problem, it is difficult to operationalize. Although, in practice, firms use several different approaches to setting the advertising budget, only the objective and task (build-up) method is grounded in this marginalist approach.

THE OBJECTIVE AND TASK METHOD FOR SETTING THE ADVERTISING BUDGET This method focuses on the advertising objectives to be achieved and the tasks that must be accomplished. Then, using a combination of logical deduction based on historical or experimental data, management estimates (builds up) the budget required to

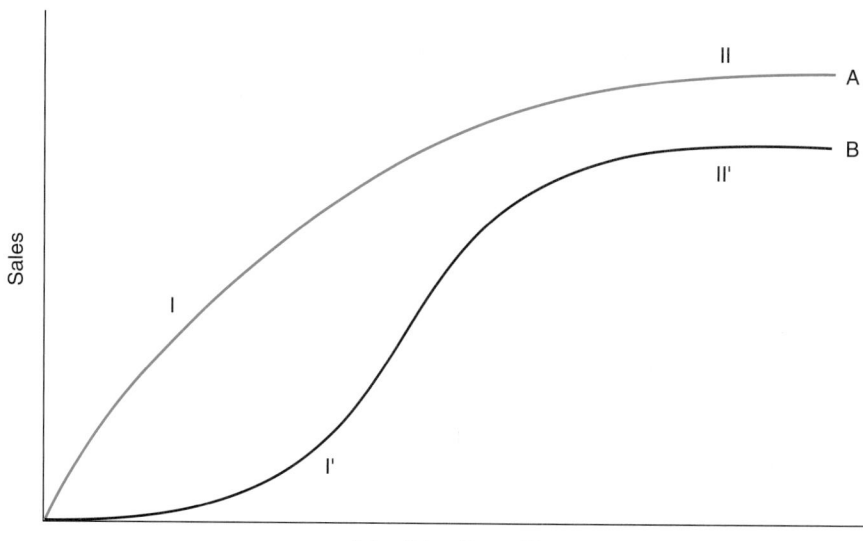

FIGURE 14.9

Alternative Advertising Response Functions

attain its objectives. This method requires feedback mechanisms for adjusting the budget based on success in reaching the objectives. From a planning perspective, the objective and task method has much appeal. However, the difficulty in linking advertising spending to attaining intermediate advertising objectives militates against its use in many firms. Nonetheless, there is little doubt that as companies increasingly embrace measures of economic profit, such as EVA, the pressure on managers to analyze and financially justify marketing and advertising expenditures will rise.[51] Management should strive to understand advertising spending-to-results relationships by investing in advertising research rather than use other less intellectually challenging, and ultimately self-defeating, rule-of-thumb approaches.

OTHER BUDGETING METHODS USED IN PRACTICE   In part because of the challenges involved in using the objective and task method, a variety of other budgeting methods are found in practice. Indeed, firms using objective and task methods sometimes calibrate their advertising budgets against these other methods. The main alternatives are two top-down methods—percent of sales and competitive parity.

- **Percent of Sales**. The budget is set as a percent of the firm's current sales, anticipated next year's sales, or some combination of the two.[52] While simple to implement, the method suffers from the logical inconsistency that sales determines advertising spending, rather than advertising leading to sales. Several problems result. First, management using this method is unlikely to make the large budget increases that may, at times, secure competitive advantage. Second, advertising is reduced in recessionary times when level or even increased spending might be appropriate. Third, this method offers no advice for new product introductions and militates against spending on growth products. Finally, managers are frequently seduced into making competitive comparisons based on advertising-to-sales ratios alone, relationships that are unrelated to absolute advertising spending or impact.
- **Competitive Parity**. Advertising spending is based on the actions of competitors. Either the firm matches competitor spending or uses competitor spending levels as a benchmark. For example, it may set the advertising budget such that its share of advertising is equivalent to its targeted market share. This method assumes that the firm and its competitors have similar objectives, that rivals have themselves made

good budgeting decisions, and that different campaigns are equivalently effective. None of these assumptions is likely to be true.

A final budgeting method found in practice—what the firm can afford—has nothing to recommend it.

Program Evaluation: How Shall We Evaluate Our Advertising?

Advertising can be tested in many different ways. Individual advertisements can be tested prior to use, different levels and types of advertising spending can be tested, or an entire advertising program can be evaluated.

EVALUATING INDIVIDUAL ADVERTISEMENTS   Advertisements can be tested in a laboratory setting prior to use or in an experimental field setting. A variety of experimental techniques are available; the particular testing methods depend upon the media class employed.

In the laboratory, print advertisements can be tested by showing subjects a group of advertisements, or by developing mock publications with advertising inserted and measuring recall of the test advertisements. Conceptually similar techniques can be used for broadcast media, such as inserting advertisements into a television program viewed by respondents in split cable systems,[53] or films viewed by respondents in a theater, shopping mall, or some other location.

These same techniques can be used in a real-world setting by using real publications and real television programs, yet sharply confining the geographic area involved. More complex methods involve developing two or more publications/television programs, differing only with respect to the advertising being tested, and exposing each to a different group of subjects.

Regardless of the experimental design, a variety of measures can be employed. For example:

- **Recognition**: Widely used for print advertising, subjects are taken through the publication and asked which advertisements they recognize[54]
- **Unaided recall**: Also widely used for broadcast advertisements, respondents are asked what advertisements they remember seeing during a particular program.[55]
- **Aided recall**: Widely used for broadcast advertisements, respondents are asked if they remember seeing an advertisement for a particular brand during a particular program.

TESTING LEVELS AND TYPES OF ADVERTISING SPENDING   To select the best advertising campaign, several alternative campaigns can be tested using experimental design procedures. Management selects its advertising objectives and puts a measurement system in place related to these objectives. In these experiments, each campaign is run in a separate geographic market area and the results compared using sophisticated models to identify the best campaign.

TESTING ADVERTISING PROGRAMS   The underlying basis for testing advertising programs relates to management's advertising objectives. Rather than take measurements at a single point in time, measurements are taken over time in tracking studies. Suppose for example, that management believes that the key advertising objectives should be set in terms of awareness, liking, trial, and repeat purchase, that it hypothesizes a hierarchical relationship, and that market research provides the results shown in Column I of Table 14.8.

- One critical problem is the low level of awareness. A successful campaign to improve awareness might lead to the result in Column II.
- Awareness may be fairly high, but liking is low. A successful campaign to improve liking might lead to the result in Column III.
- Liking has doubled, but trial and repeat purchase are still unsatisfactory. A further campaign may lead to the result in Column IV.

TABLE 14.8 Evaluation of an Advertising Program

Time Period	Percent of Target Audience			
	I	II	III	IV
Awareness	25	70	70	70
Liking	20	20	40	40
Trial	20	20	20	30
Repeat Purchase	15	15	15	25

In each time period, research provided the basis for deciding on the strategic advertising objective for the following period. Over time, management was able to track its performance and decide how to approach the succeeding period. The core message: For many companies, advertising costs are enormous. The time and effort spent on testing is typically well worthwhile.[56]

NON-PERSONAL COMMUNICATIONS: DIRECT MARKETING

Direct marketing is one of the fastest growing areas of communications.[57] Direct mail via brochures, catalogues, and statement inserts continues to represent a major portion of direct marketing practice. However, direct marketing is much broader, embracing multiple ways of requesting a direct response from customers, including traditional advertising methods, such as print or broadcast, packaging, package inserts, warranty cards, take-ones, fax, e-mail, and the Internet.

There are several critical differences between direct marketing and advertising:

- **Flexibility**: Certain forms of direct marketing, such as direct mail, can be developed more quickly than mass advertising, personalized, and avoid the waste inherent in mass advertising when it is received, in part, by an untargeted audience.
- **Desired customer response**: Whereas advertising objectives can be set on a variety of bases (such as awareness, knowledge, trial), direct marketing is more action-oriented and typically requests purchase.
- **Measuring program effectiveness**: Because the required customer response is frequently purchase, direct marketing enables firms to develop strong relationships between individual direct marketing programs and sales revenues. They are able to test the various elements of a program (such as message, mailing type, price, incentive) to identify those that have a significant impact on sales response.
- **Prediction**: The ability to track customer response means that management is able to make fairly accurate predictions of the results from individual direct marketing programs. The budgeting process is, therefore, less complex than for advertising.
- **Customer knowledge**: Direct marketing firms typically have much more information about customers than those that rely on advertising. In particular, they know precisely who has purchased their products, and may also be able to secure a variety of other types of customer-related data.
- **Offer development**: Knowing the products that their customers have purchased enables the direct marketer to tailor its messages and offers to individual customers.
- **New customer acquisition**: By relating their customer profiles to purchase patterns, direct marketers are able to identify high-quality prospects.

Several forces are driving the growth of direct marketing programs:

- Technological advances in computers and telecommunications allows firms to develop, manage, and mine customer databases;

- The growth of two-income families and generally increasing time-pressure, especially in advanced Western countries, have reduced the attractiveness of shopping trips for many people;
- Increasing quality of goods and services is reducing consumers' risk of buying unseen products;
- Growing professionalism of direct marketing organizations;
- Growth of the Internet.

The Internet has many of the same features as traditional direct marketing. Other mass communications or direct marketing efforts may lead a customer to a Web site, but once linked to that site, the Internet allows for a level of personalization and immediacy far greater than other methods, as in the Amazon.com example noted earlier.

Finally, the planning process for direct marketing is similar in spirit to that laid out for advertising. One of the major differences between direct marketing and advertising is that, in general, it is easier to test individual direct marketing campaigns than those for advertising which often do not seek a direct response. Nonetheless, refer to Table 14.4 and make the necessary translation to direct marketing.

NON-PERSONAL COMMUNICATIONS: PUBLICITY AND PUBLIC RELATIONS

As indicated in Figure 14.1, although publicity and public relations (P&PR) are closely related, public relations is somewhat broader in scope than publicity. Publicity is often viewed as a subset of P&PR. In general, publicity focuses on securing neutral or favorable short-term press coverage for some aspect of the firm's activities. Public relations is more concerned with long-term image-building via a myriad of activities, such as corporate publications, senior executive speeches, and financial support of worthy causes.

In using P&PR, management seeks to gain transmission of a message by an intermediary, typically the press, to its target audience. Ideally, the intermediary adds a positive element to the firm's message, but management must also be concerned that the press may adopt a negative perspective.

The major advantages of P&PR are twofold. First, the message sent by the intermediary organization is frequently viewed as impartial by the audience. Second, the firm does not pay for the communication. However, the drawbacks are significant. Management has no control over the intermediary's message so that its own message may be ignored, shortened, or modified in some other way. Also, whereas media planning is a critical feature of designing an advertising program, management cannot select the audience for receipt of a P&PR effort, except as it selects the intermediaries.

Important P&PR issues include proaction, responding to problems, and unintended consequences.

Proaction

Edward L. Bernays, the father of public relations, developed a simple formula:

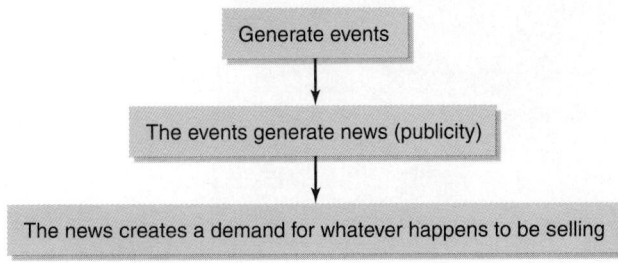

Perhaps the first modern example of public relations occurred in the 1920s.

Example: In the famous "Torches of Freedom" campaign, Bernays arranged for a small group of women to walk down Fifth Avenue in New York smoking cigarettes. This story was carried by newspapers nationwide and in the following weeks, women in many cities also took to the streets smoking cigarettes.[58]

Example: The well-known publicist, James Sterling Moran, staged numerous publicity stunts: hatching out an ostrich egg (over 19 days) to publicize *The Egg and I*, a best-selling book later made into a movie (Figure 14.10); opening an embassy for a mythical country in Washington to publicize a movie about a mythical country, "The Mouse that Roared," and rigging a taxi so that a chimpanzee appeared to be the driver to promote a Broadway show.[59]

Many firms have gained significantly from successful P&PR campaigns. Mutual fund company Vanguard does little advertising, but secures favorable press comment for its policy of providing low expense ratios. A financial services start-up gained significantly from P&PR efforts:

Example: In September 1987, College Saving's Bank launched its CollegeSure CD indexed to the average annual rate of college inflation. Its initial publicity and public relations efforts focused on news releases and press conferences. By the end of October, articles and editorials appeared in all major newspapers around the United States, in weekly news magazines (*Time, Newsweek, U.S. News and*

FIGURE 14.10

A Publicity Stunt for "The Egg and I"

World Report), major business magazines, and local newspapers. In total over 300 news stories were written or aired.[60]

Example: An obscure Canadian board game, *Trivial Pursuit*, achieved over $1 billion in sales from a PR campaign involving staged game playing events in parks, bars, restaurants and ski clubs, and giving away several hundred games.[61]

Of course, P&PR and advertising are alternative means of communicating with target customers. However, they may also be used synergistically to secure a more powerful impact than either could have achieved alone.

Example: In January 1999, Victoria's Secret (VS) spent $1.5 million on a 30-second television spot during the Super Bowl, and $4 million internationally to advertise its fashion show. This advertising led to extensive publicity and millions of visitors to VS's Web site, from around the world, to view the show.

Responding to Problems

In addition to focusing on the positive aspects of the firm's activities, P&PR can also be used to defuse difficult situations. Because the matter is already in the public eye, a great deal of skill is required. Well-developed P&PR campaigns can put the firm ahead; conversely, poor handling of a situation can have a significant negative effect.

Example: In the mid-1980s, Johnson & Johnson was widely praised for its handling of the Tylenol poisoning scare. In addition to its tangible actions of temporary product withdrawal and relaunch with enhanced packaging, senior executives, including J&J's CEO, were frequently seen on talk shows explaining the firm's actions and its commitment to customers.

By contrast:

Example: In 1999, Coca-Cola was involved in its worst ever health scare when around 200 people (including many children, some who were hospitalized) suffered nausea, headaches, and diarrhea after drinking Coke. Eventually attributed to bottling system failures, observers criticized Coke for ". . . forget(ing) the cardinal rule of crisis management—to act fast, tell the whole truth, and look as if you have nothing to hide." *The Economist* concluded that ". . . Coca-Cola has made a big mess of what should have been a small public-relations problem."[62]

Unintended Consequences

Because of its lack of control over the press and other communications intermediaries, management can never be sure about the outcome of its P&PR efforts. Of course, the press may react favorably to the firm's efforts, as in the Tylenol case, or unfavorably, as in the case of Coca-Cola.

The press may also develop a previously little-known issue, disadvantaging those who first brought it to the public's attention. An interesting example occurred in the publishing industry:

Example: In 1998, Canongate, a small British firm, published 12 paperback "Pocket Canons," biblical texts with introductions by celebrities such as Australian rock star Nick Cave (*Mark*) and feminist writer Doris Lessing (*Ecclesiastes*). Strongly worded protests against the publications by traditionalists only served to generate significant press coverage and create widespread interest in, and purchase of, the canons.

An interesting example of the perils and opportunities for P&PR occurred in the U.S. mouthwash market where Scope (Procter & Gamble [P&G]) and Listerine (Warner-Lambert) battle for dominance. The example demonstrates not only the unintended consequences of P&PR, but the use of creative P&PR to capitalize on a competitor's misstep.

Example: Unintended consequence: In an attempt to gain publicity for Scope, P&G released a kissing survey on Valentine's Day 1999, naming the most and least kissable celebrities in several TV categories. In particular, TV star Rosie O'Donnell was ranked the least-kissable talk show host. That morning, O'Donnell prominently displayed a bottle of Listerine on her show.

Example: Creative capitalization: Warner-Lambert reacted by running full-page Love-Letter-to Rosie ads in *The New York Times* and *USA Today*. Thousands of bottles of Cool Mint Listerine were sent to the show and given away by Rosie who kept a bottle of the mouthwash on her desk for the next several weeks. Starting March 11, Warner-Lambert agreed to donate $1,000 to O'Donnell's favorite charity for every kiss Rosie received from a celebrity guest. With each kiss, a Listerine bottle was shown and a banner displayed the running total of kisses. In addition to kissing Rosie, many guests gargled with, and endorsed, Listerine. Two months and 500 kisses later, Warner-Lambert presented Rosie with a $500,000 check. By comparison, a single 30-second commercial on the show cost $38,000.

The bottom line for P&PR is that creative strategies can secure highly successful results at a fraction of the cost of major advertising campaigns. However, P&PR must be used with care, for significant unintended consequences may result from poorly thought-through efforts.

NON-PERSONAL COMMUNICATIONS: SALES PROMOTION

Sales promotion comprises a potpourri of techniques used to satisfy several different marketing objectives. These techniques are mostly designed for short-term effects, but others have longer-run objectives. Sometimes sales promotions are directed at consumers (samples, deals, coupons, games, prizes, point-of-purchase, cash refunds, sports sponsorships, product placement in movies and television shows), sometimes at retailers (deals, prizes, co-op advertising allowances), and sometimes at organizational customers (literature, advertising allowances, trade shows, "spiffs"[63]). Of course, there is not a set number of techniques, rather new sales promotion devices are being developed all the time.

The critical issue in selecting a particular sales promotion device is to be clear about the firm's sales promotion objectives. If short-term sales are required, then "cents-off" coupons, cash refunds, point-of-purchase displays, and so forth may be appropriate, depending on the product class. On the other hand, if long-term image building is the goal, then sports sponsorships or naming buildings may have the desired result. Furthermore, individual sales promotion techniques may help achieve different objectives, depending how they are used. Consider the ubiquitous "cents-off" coupon (Table 14.9).

The planning process for sales promotion is similar in spirit to that laid out for advertising. Refer to Table 14.4 and make the necessary translation to sales promotion. Illustrative sales promotion techniques and related objectives are shown in Table 14.10.

Notwithstanding the necessity of developing a sales promotion plan, sales promotion should not be seen as a separate and distinct activity. Rather, whatever techniques are being considered, their use should be tightly integrated with other communications vehicles.

TABLE 14.9 Alternative Objectives and Actions for a "Cents-Off" Coupon

Objective	Action
Repeat purchase	Include coupon in product package
Consumer inventory-building	Include expiry date on the coupon
Induce trial among non-users	Distribute coupon in a magazine

TABLE 14.10 Illustration of Sales Promotion Techniques and Objectives

Sales Promotion Technique	Possible Objectives
Sampling	Trial (for new product)
Deals	Increase use; pre-emptive inventory building
Premiums	Trial, repeat purchase, increase use
Trade Shows	Awareness, interest, liking, intention-to-buy, trial, repurchase
Sports Sponsorship	Corporate image building, awareness
Point-of-Purchase Display	Knowledge, trial, increase use, repurchase
Literature	Interest, knowledge, increase use
Games	Trial, repeat purchase, increase use
"Spiff"	Customer salesperson effort, pull-through sales

Indeed, it is frequently necessary to communicate the availability of a sales promotion device to the target audience, such as by advertising the availability of cash rebates or money-back guarantees.

Although a variety of sales promotion programs can be underway at any point in time, in general they do not play the central role so often assumed by advertising or personal selling. Nonetheless, sales promotion often accounts for very large expenditures that may, on occasion, exceed advertising.

Example: Royal Philips Electronics paid $180 million to place its name on the home arena of the Atlanta Hawks baseball team and the Thrashers hockey club.[64] For Columbia Business School's new teaching building, Goldman Sachs, Merrill Lynch and Morgan Stanley Dean Witter each donated hundreds of thousands of dollars to have amphitheaters named for their companies.

Caveats

In recent years, consumer marketers have become concerned about the longer-term impact of short-term sales promotion devices, as promotions have accounted for increasingly large amounts of marketing budgets for consumer packaged goods.[65] The concern focuses on overexposure of consumers to short-term price decreases (via actual price reductions, coupons, and so forth) that may reduce brand equity and make them unwilling ever to pay the full product price.[66]

A related impact of periodic price decreases is the increased cost caused by fluctuating production schedules and inventory build-up. Developments in supply chain management have led manufacturers and their customers to seek lower total costs by smoothing out demand. As a result, many consumer goods companies have reduced their use of short-term incentives in favor of "everyday low pricing."

Finally, notwithstanding potential volume increases from using short-term sales promotion devices, the administrative burden of managing a large number of programs for many different products may be significant. Consider the P&G's experience:

Example: In the early 1990s, P&G conducted so many special promotions and price changes that one in four orders from retailers had errors. It had a 150-employee department to correct 27,000 orders per month—at a cost of $35–$75 per order.[67]

SUMMARY

This chapter began by noting the variety of communications challenges faced by the firm, but recognized that management has many different communication tools at its disposal. A set of questions was provided, whose answers, based on these tools, comprise the critical managerial challenge of developing an overall communications strategy. The issue of integrating communications efforts across a variety of dimensions was also addressed.

This chapter examined several non-personal communications tools. The main focus was the elements of an advertising strategy, again with a series of questions whose answers form the strategy. Finally, three increasingly important non-personal communications tools—direct marketing, publicity and public relations, and sales promotion—were briefly examined.

THE CHANGING VIEW

Old Way	New Way
Fragmented communications effort	Integrated communications effort
Faith/intuition	Measurement/tracking
Mass communication	One-to-one communication
Direct response methods rare	Direct response methods ubiquitous
Limited media/vehicle choices	Proliferating media/vehicle choices
Intermediaries usually involved	Movement to direct marketing
Passive audience	Active/interactive audience
Creativity desirable	Creativity becoming essential
Local/national advertising strategies	Regional/global advertising strategies
Short-term promotions common	Long-term brand equity a key concern
Customers are only communications target	Multiple communications targets, employees, shareholders, complementers, and so on

QUESTIONS FOR STUDY AND DISCUSSION

1. Social critics have attacked advertising at both the individual and aggregate level. How would you attempt to justify the legitimacy of this pervasive phenomenon?

2. It has been said that there are two places where all firms compete—in the capital markets and in customers' heads. How does this statement relate to the communications challenges faced by a firm?

3. Find two examples of advertising campaigns that are, in your opinion, directed at targets other than current or potential customers. (Exclude examples in the book or employment advertisements.)

4. Use the chart in Figure 14.3 to illustrate the communications mix for a campaign with which you are familiar.

5. Under what conditions might a firm heavily target communications at all levels in a distribution channel by combining a push and a pull strategy?

6. Enumerate the problems many companies face in developing integrated communications strategies. How would you recommend eliminating these problems?

7. Why is an understanding of the buying process in a particular market crucial to developing communications and advertising strategy?

8. Many advertisers use CPM (cost per thousand) as a decision criterion for choosing print media vehicles. Do you believe this is wise? What other considerations should enter into the choice?

9. Some critics argue that advertisers' heavy reliance on recall measurement is responsible for the intrusive and strident tone of some television commercials. Develop a counter-argument.

10. "Recall measurement is useless, since it bears no relationship to the product sales." Discuss.

11. Why, in your opinion, has direct marketing enjoyed robust growth, especially at a time when many traditional retailers are in difficulty?

12. Explain the pros and cons of using publicity and public relations as communications tools.

13. "Many sponsorship activities reflect the personal interests of senior executives, rather than enhancing shareholder value for the sponsor." Discuss this statement, using your own examples as illustrations.

14. Sales promotions are often thought to reduce brand equity. Can you think of three examples where promotional activities undoubtedly contributed to increased brand equity? What makes these promotions different?

15. Name three recent advertising campaigns that you believe are outstanding. If possible obtain copies of the advertisements to show to colleagues.

ENDNOTES

1. A widely-held view regarding the cause of the late 1990s Asian crisis was inadequate functioning of financial markets caused by a "lack of transparency" (lack of information) in corporate financial statements.

2. Telemarketing is included, although it is not strictly face-to-face.

3. G.E. Belch, M.A. Belch, and J. Pincus, *Advertising and Promotion: An Integrated Marketing and Communications Perspective*, Irwin: Homewood, IL, 1999.

4. An alternative classification is broadcast media, such as television, radio, and newspapers, and addressable media, such as email, direct mail, and the telephone. See "Note on Marketing and the World Wide Web," Boston, MA: Harvard Business School, 1996.

5. Sometimes called *retention marketing*.

6. J. Hulbert, and N. Capon, "Interpersonal Communication in Marketing: An Overview," *Journal of Marketing Research*, 9 (February 1972), pp. 27–34.

7. Trade shows are often considered as a type of sales promotion. For an interesting study of trade shows, see S. Gopalakrishna, G.L. Lilien, J.D. Williams, and I.K. Sequeira, "Do Trade Shows Pay Off," *Journal of Marketing*, 59 (July 1995), pp. 75–83.

8. "The Blair Witch Project" cost $31,000 to make; 1999 box office receipts were $142 million. *The Economist*, January 29, 2000.

9. D. Peppers and M. Rogers, *The One-to-One Future: Building Relationships One Customer at a Time*, NY: Currency Doubleday, 1993. In summer 1998, Procter & Gamble (P&G), one of America's largest advertisers, organized a conference of advertising and marketing executives to discuss what these changes implied for the practice of advertising in the future.

10. Other important issues concern the message and the budget. Budgeting for communications is less a matter for the communications strategy than for the market strategy. The market strategy is implemented by a series of marketing mix decisions concerning product, price, promotion/communications, distribution, and service. The parameters for spending in these various areas, in particular the level of resources allocated to communications, should be set at the market strategy level, preferably through some form of top down/bottom up process in which the trade-offs are clearly articulated.

11. Category management systems are discussed in Chapter 19. As an example, P&G vests responsibility for all laundry detergents in a single individual.

12. In most countries, various government bodies regulate advertising and other communications methods.

13. Issues of competitive signaling are addressed in Chapter 5.

14. In 1999, shares of Berkshire Hathaway, whose CEO is famed investor Warren Buffett, traded at over $70,000 per share, far in excess of the average share price on the New York Stock Exchange. Buffett believes that such a high price leads to a more stable group of shareholders and refuses to split the stock.

15. *The New York Times*, April 21, 1999.

16. It was indicated earlier that management must integrate all firm communications, regardless of target or purpose.

17. In 1999, Young & Rubicam (Y&R) developed a group incentive plan designed to forge closer inter-business relationships among its various units. Major clients (such as General Motors, Charles Schwab, and P&G) now pay fees based on such results as client sales, rather than commissions. *The Economist*, March 6, 1999.

18. Unfortunately, despite significant expenditures, the purpose of corporate advertising is not always clear. For example, is it to provide an umbrella for product/market activities, to persuade investors to become shareholders, or simply CEO self-aggrandizement?

19. For a full discussion of segmentation and targeting, see Chapter 7.

20. For an excellent discussion of the various hierarchy-of-effects models, see Belch, Belch, and Pincus *op. cit.*

21. Several individual high involvement models are based on a learning hierarchy, see Belch, Belch, and Pincus *op. cit.*

22. Note that with some categories giving sample product to customers (sampling) to induce trial is often more cost-effective than using persuasive communications.

23. Some use the terminology "think" for awareness and knowledge, "feel" for liking and "act" for trial. The two hierarchies then become high involvement—"think" → "feel" → "act"; low involvement—"think" → "act" → "feel."

24. D. Vakratsas and T. Ambler, "How Advertising Works: What Do We Really Know?" *Journal of Marketing*, 63 (Jan. 1999), pp. 26–43.

25. Note that in most cases the effects of advertising are believed to be short-term in nature, but long-term effects have been observed. See R.P. Leone, "Generalizing What Is Known about Temporal Aggregation and Advertising Carryover," *Marketing Science*, 14 (1995), G141–150; L.M. Lodish, M. Abraham, S. Kalmenson, J. Livelsberger, B. Lubetkin, B. Richardson, and M.E. Stevens, "How Advertising Works: A Meta-Analysis of 389 Real World Split Cable TV Advertising Experiments," *Journal of Marketing Research*, 32 (May 1995), pp. 125–139, and "A Summary of Fifty Five In-Market Experimental Estimates of the Long-Term Effects of Advertising, *Marketing Science*, 14 (1995), G133–140 by the same authors.

26. See Chapter 8.

27. In the January 2000 Super Bowl, companies were paying $3 million for a 30-second commercial.

28. An ongoing debate in advertising circles is the extent to which advertising in multiple countries should be standardized or adapted to individual countries. For a review of the arguments on this issue, see M. Agrawal, "Review of a 40-Year Debate in International Advertising: Practitioner and Academician Perspectives on the Standardization/Adaptation Issue," *International Marketing Review*, 12 (1995), pp. 26-48. Regardless, in moves designed to enhance the development of their global marketing and advertising strategies, many multinationals are putting all their business with a single advertising agency, such as Colgate Palmolive to Young and Rubicam, *The Economist*, December 6, 1996.

29. Thanks to Professor Gita Johar for this example.

30. B.H. Schmitt, "Advertising and Mass Communications," in N. Capon (Ed.), Section 7, *Marketing*, in *AMA Management Handbook* (3rd Edition), J. Hampton (Ed.), AMACOM, 1994, 2-108—2-115, p. 2-112.

31. Over the years many advertising campaigns have earned prizes for creativity, but have been unsuccessful in achieving their advertising objectives.

32. Schmitt, *op. cit.*

33. *Financial Times*, November 5, 1999.

34. In addition to these items, management must consider such issues of message structure as two-sided or one-sided messages, presentation order, and drawing conclusions that have been subject to extensive mass communications research. The interested reader is referred to any good advertising textbook.

35. For more insight on humor in advertising, see B. Sternthal and C.S. Craig, "Humor in Advertising," *Journal of Marketing*, 37 (Oct. 1973), pp. 12–18 and T.J. Madden and M.C. Weinberger, "Humor in Advertising: A Practitioner View," *Journal of Advertising Research*, 24 (Aug./Sept. 1984), pp. 23–26. For a taxonomy of humor in advertising, see P.S. Speck, The Humorous Message Taxonomy: A Framework for the Study of Humorous Ads," *Journal of Current Issues and Research in Advertising*, 22 (1993), pp. 1–44.

36. For a good review of the legal status of comparative advertising, see B. Buchanan and D. Goldman, "Us vs. Them: The Minefield of Comparative Ads," *Harvard Business Review*, 67 (May/June 1989), pp. 38–50. There is also an extensive literature on "deceptive advertising"; see G.T. Johar, "Consumer Involvement and Deception from Implied Advertising Claims," *Journal of Marketing Research*, 32 (August 1995), pp. 267–279.

37. *The New York Times*, October 1, 1999 D1.

38. *Business Week*, January 26, 1999.

39. See M.L. Ray and W.L. Wilkie, "Fear: The Potential of an Appeal Neglected by Marketing," *Journal of Marketing*, 34 (Jan. 1970), pp. 54–62 and B. Sternthal and C.S. Craig, "Fear Appeals Revisited and Revised," *Journal of Consumer Research*, 1 (Dec. 1974), pp. 12–18.

40. G.E. Belch and M.A. Belch, *Introduction to Advertising and Promotion Management*, Irwin: Homewood, IL, 1990, p. 311.

41. An important element in *Brut*'s 1999 advertising campaign was advertisements positioned at eye-level above urinals, mostly in bars. In total, 1999 revenues from out-of-home advertising approximated $5 billion, twice Internet advertising, 10% p.a. growth. In summer 2000, Siemens advertised a new line of cellular telephones by using 8000 special tabletops of cafés in France, *The New York Times,* August 15, 2000.

42. M. Gunther, "The Great Outdoors," *Fortune*, March 1, 1999.

43. *The New York Times*, January 17, 1999.

44. *The New York Times*, February 3, 2000. A 15-person team costs Ai Jia $1,200 per month, excluding uniforms and bicycles. By contrast, a one-time 15-second commercial at a local TV station costs $2,800 per month, and a large prominently located billboard costs $3,000 to $8,000 per month.

45. Clearly, the ability to certify the audience for various advertising vehicles, typically conducted by independent agencies, is critical to establishing good comparable cost data, such as Simmons Market Research Bureau (SMRB) and Mediamark Research, Inc. (MRI).

46. Note that cost per 1000 and other similar measures should ideally be based upon members of the target segment, not on the total audience.

47. For research on this issue, see the classic paper, H.A. Zielske, "The Remembering and Forgetting of Advertising," *Journal of Marketing*, 23 (Jan. 1959), pp. 239–243; see, also, J.A. Simon, "What Do Zielske's Real Data Show about Pulsing," *Journal of Marketing Research*, 23 (March 1979) pp. 415–420 and L.M. Lodish, Empirical Studies on Individual Responses to Exposure Patterns," *Journal of Marketing Research*, 8 (May 1971), pp. 214–216.

48. A related timing issue concerns competitive advertising.

49. J.A. Simon and J. Arndt, "The Shape of the Advertising, Response Function," *Journal of Advertising Research*, 20 (1980), pp. 11–28; P.B. Luchsinger, V.S. Mullen and P.T. Jannuzzo, "How Many Advertising Dollars are Enough," *Media Decisions*, 12 (1977), p. 59. See also D.A. Aaker and J.A. Carman, "Are You Overadvertising?," *Journal of Advertising Research*, 22 (1982), pp. 57–70 and C. Assmus, J.U. Farley, and D.R. Lehmann, "How Advertising Affects Sales: Meta Analysis of Econometric Results," *Journal of Marketing Research*, 21 (1984), pp. 65–74.

50. I or I′ increase spending; II or II′ hold or reduce spending.

51. For a discussion of these pressures, see J.N. Sheth and R.J. Sisodia, "Feeling The Heat," *Marketing Management* 4 (1995), 8-23. A significant advantage of direct marketing is its precision in measuring results.

52. Two-thirds of major firms use this method, Schmitt, *op. cit.*

53. Split cable systems feature identical programming in a confined geographic area with different advertisements appearing on each half of the cable system.

54. One of the more popular commercial measures of this type is the *Starch Readership Report*; in part, its popularity relates to the large database with which the results from a specific advertisement may be compared.

55. One of the more popular recall measures is the Burke day-after recall test.

56. For a full discussion of advertising testing, see Belch, Belch, and Pincus, *op. cit.*, Chapter 18.

57. For an excellent synopsis of direct marketing, see M. Kalter and E. Stearns, "Direct Marketing," in N. Capon (ed.), Section 2, Marketing, in *AMA Management Handbook* (3rd Edition), J. Hampton (ed.), New York: AMACOM, 1994, 2-116—2-121.

58. L. Tye, *The Father of Spin: Edward L. Bernays & the Birth of Public Relations*, New York: Random House, 1998.

59. *The New York Times*, October 24, 1999.

60. College Savings Bank (A) and (B) in N. Capon, *The Marketing of Financial Services: A Book of Cases*, Englewood Cliffs, NJ: Prentice Hall, 1992, pp. 93-121.

61. *The New York Times*, October 28, 1999.

62. *The Economist*, June 19, 1999, pp. 62–63. The problem was attributed to two unrelated causes: use of "bad" carbon dioxide at one plant and contamination from fungicide used to treat wooden pallets used to move packages of Coke cans.

63. A "spiff" is a direct payment from a firm to its customer's salesperson, contingent on salesperson performance.

64. Philips planned placement of 1,000 video monitors in the arena and creation of a retail showroom. For research on processes underlying sponsorship effectiveness, see G.V. Johar and M.T. Pham, "Relatedness, Prominence and Constructive Sponsor Identification," *Journal of Marketing Research*, 36 (Aug. 1999), pp. 299–312.

65. In the early 1990s, spending on trade (distributors and retailers) and consumer promotions accounted for 75% of marketing budgets for consumer packaged goods manufacturers, C.F. Mela, S. Gupta and D.R. Lehmann, "The Long-Term Impact of Promotion and Advertising on Consumer Brand Choice," *Journal of Marketing Research*, 34 (May 1997), pp. 248–261.

66. Mela, Gupta, and Lehmann, *op. cit.*

67. *The Wall Street Journal*, January 15, 1997.

WEB RESOURCES

Absolut	www.absolut.vodka.com
Amazon	www.amazon.com
AMF	www.amf.com
Apple	www.apple.com
Avis	www.avis.com
Ball Park Franks	www.ballparkfranks.com
Ben and Jerry's	www.benjerry.com
Berkshire Hathaway	www.berkshirehathaway.com
Bijan	www.bijan.com
Body Shop	www.the-body-shop.com
Boston Globe	www.boston.com
British Airways	www.british-airways.com
Canon	www.canon.com
Canongate	www.canongate.co.uk
CBS Sportsline	www.cbs.com
Charles Schwab	www.schwab.com
Coca-Cola	www.cocacola.com
Colgate	www.colgate.com
College Savings Bank	www.collegesavings.com
Compaq	www.compaq.com
Deloitte and Touche	www.deloitte.com
DuPont	www.dupont.com
Federal Express	www.fedex.com
Food and Drug	www.fda.gov
Gatorade	www.gatorade.com
General Electric	www.ge.com
General Motors	www.gm.com

Goldman Sashes	www.gs.com
Good Housekeeping	www.goodhousingkeeping.com
Häagen Dazs	www.haagen-dazs.com
Hanes	www.hanes.com
Intel	www.intel.com
Johnson and Johnson	www.jnj.com
Lever Brothers	www.unilever.com
McGraw-Hill	www.mcgraw-hill.com
MCI/Worldcom	www.wcom.com
Mediamark Research Inc.	www.mediamark.com
Merrill-Lynch	www.ml.com
Morgan Stanley Dean Witter	www.msdw.com
New York Times	www.nytimes.com
Newsweek	www.newsweek.com
Nike	www.nike.com
Oakley	www.oakley.com
Pepsi	www.pepsico.com
Procter & Gamble	www.pg.com
Rayovac	www.rayovac.com
Royal Dutch Philips	www.philips.com
San Francisco Examiner	www.examiner.com
Siemens	www.siemens.com
Simmons	www.smrb.com
Time	www.time.com
US News	www.usnews.com
USA Today	www.usatoday.com
Vanguard	www.vanguard.com
Vanity Fair	www.vanityfair.com
Victoria's Secret	www.victoriassecret.com
Volvo	www.volvo.com
Wall Drug	www.walldrug.com
Warner-Lambert	www.warner-lambert.com
Wheaties	www.wheaties.com
Wilson Sporting Goods	www.wilsonsports.com
Windows 95	www.microsoft.com
Young & Rubicam	www.yr.com

CHAPTER

15

DIRECTING AND MANAGING THE FIELD SALES EFFORT

LEARNING OBJECTIVES

When you have completed this chapter, you will understand

- **the purpose of a field sales strategy and its relationship to the market strategy**

- **the six tasks of sales management**

- **the relationship between marketing and sales**

- **how to lay out the key elements of a sales strategy including achieving sales objectives, determining and allocating sales force effort, and developing sales approaches**

- **important implementation issues, such as designing the sales organization and critical organizational processes, and securing and retaining the appropriate human resources for the selling effort**

INTRODUCTION

The previous chapter framed the firm's total communications efforts, discussing decisions involving customer targets, communication tasks and communication tools, then focused on impersonal communications. This chapter is concerned with personal communication, often the critical activity in securing implementation of marketing plans. The major distinguishing feature of most interpersonal communication is that the key actors, the field sales force, are usually outside of direct managerial supervision.

Although the importance of personal selling may be self-evident in business-to-business marketing, it is also vital in consumer marketing. Field sales force efforts are critical in achieving and maintaining distribution, setting up and servicing promotional displays, and serving trade customers. In some industries, resources spent on sales force effort are enormous and increasing. For example, several major U.S. life insurance firms each have in excess of 10,000 salespeople, and in 1999 the top 40 U.S. pharmaceutical firms employed almost 60,000 salespeople, up from 34,000 in 1994.

Unfortunately, in many companies, the critical interface between sales and marketing has been poorly managed. Marketing too often views the sales force as unable or unwilling to grasp the environmental complexities involved in developing market strategy. By contrast, the sales force views marketing as an "ivory tower" function far removed from, and unwilling or unable to assist in, the competitive battles fought by sales in the marketplace.

Yet for market strategy to be developed and implemented seamlessly, marketing and sales must work hand-in-hand. If this interface does not function smoothly, the sales force, the *only* function with specific responsibility to secure revenues, is forced to fight competition "with one hand tied behind its back." This underscores the importance of close coordination between market and sales strategies.

THE PURPOSE OF A FIELD SALES STRATEGY

Strategy involves the allocation of resources to achieve defined objectives. In this spirit, sales strategy seeks to achieve sales objectives by assessing the appropriate level of sales resources, then allocating those resources across various dimensions, such as products, market segments, as well as new and current customers. The specific actions required of the sales force are laid out in the sales program, typically comprising the sales action plans of individual sales representatives, sales supervisors, and sales managers.[1] Operationally, the basic purpose of sales strategy is to integrate product/market segment strategies and day-by-day selling effort.

If the firm sells a single product to a single market segment, sales force effort allocation by product or market segment is clearly not an issue.[2] More likely, however, the sales force has responsibility for multiple products sold to multiple market segments (Figure 15.1). In this example, the firm offers three products (or product groups) to three market segments; the seven checks represent targeted product/segment opportunities, and the two Xs represent unaddressed product/segments.

The sales strategy problem is deciding how much effort in total should be applied to its products and market segments and, assuming that the product/market segment distinction is strategic for the firm, how in the example the firm's selling effort should be allocated among the seven product/segments the firm wants to address. Sales effort allocation by product fails to consider market segments; equally, sales effort allocation by market segment does not consider products. To implement the product/market segment strategies appropriately, a complete sales strategy must address sales effort allocation by both product and market segment. Sales strategy allocates just one input—selling effort—to the selling process. What outputs (results) are achieved, such as sales, profit contribution, agreement to examine or test the product/service, or favorable customer attitudes, also depends on other elements of the firm's offer.

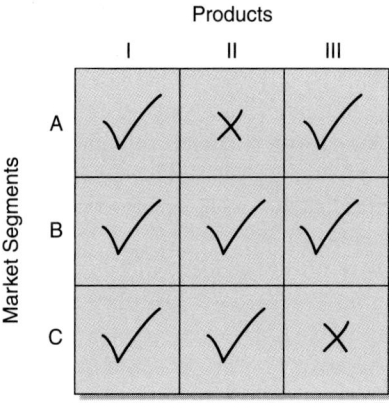

Products

	I	II	III
A	✓	✗	✓
B	✓	✓	✓
C	✓	✓	✗

Market Segments

FIGURE 15.1

Typical Sales Force Allocation Problem

Although the primary purpose of a sales strategy is to allocate selling effort, sales managers cannot directly control the level of effort. They attempt instead to determine how and why time is spent. Salespersons perform a variety of tasks, from traveling, intelligence-gathering, inventory-checking and customer service to training/education, participating in meetings, communicating, record-keeping, planning, merchandising, credit checking, and collections. The presence or importance of each of these activities varies from firm to firm, and depends on factors such as the type of business, line organization, and organizational processes. Sales managers must decide how the sales force should divide its time among these activities and, typically, seek ways to increase the proportion allocated to selling ("face time").

A second purpose of the sales strategy is to specify how to deal with customers and competitors. In particular, what specific customer and competitor targets should be chosen, and how the sales force should secure customer commitment to its products/services in the face of competitive challenges.

The final purpose of the sales strategy is to identify the specific requirements needed for implementation. Included are the appropriate organizational arrangements and processes that firms employ for directing and managing the selling effort, and the required human resources for sales force staffing.

THE FIELD SALES STRATEGY: RELATIONSHIP TO MARKET STRATEGY

At one level, since it should be integrated across products and markets, the field sales strategy has a much broader domain than the product/market segment strategy. However, at another level, the product/market segment strategy deals with sweeping and general resource allocation decisions, whereas the sales strategy is much more focused and specific.

As noted, an intimate and direct relationship should exist between market and sales strategies. Unfortunately, many organizations fail to ensure this close parallel and do not build in the interfaces developed in this chapter:

- The strategic and operational objectives developed in market strategy should be directly reflected in sales force objectives. This correspondence should be most direct for sales force business objectives; these must reflect the differentiated marketing objectives for the various product/market segments in which the sales force will operate.
- The choice of strategic alternatives in the market strategy (Chapter 8) should be related to the focus of the selling effort. For example, the sales force activity focus in new market development should be different from that in more mature markets.

- Product line focus is a key interrelationship for multiproduct sales forces. Crucial decisions, frequently involving significant conflict, concern balancing the selling effort for different products. A similar situation occurs for market segment focus.
- Positioning decisions in product/market segment strategies involving choice of customer and competitor targets and core strategy are reflected in the sales strategy's customer focus and sales approach, but are typically developed in greater detail.
- From the perspective of the product/market strategy, the sales strategy forms part of the supporting marketing mix. As such, it specifies the general parameters within which the sales strategy is developed. Implementation requirements in the sales strategy develop the necessary support activities and systems in greater detail and in a more focused manner.

Despite the logical relationships between market and sales strategy, it is a paradox that so many coordination problems arise at the marketing/sales interface. Some argue that achieving higher levels of coordination and cooperation have been hallmarks of Japanese corporate success.[3] By contrast, in the United States and Europe, close coordination between sales and marketing is frequently not achieved.

Several explanations have been advanced for this coordination problem: historical antipathy related to marketing's birth and development out of the sales force, inadequate interpersonal skills, poor conflict-resolution skills, discrepant time horizons (marketing—long, sales force—short), and general organizational problems. However, in too many companies, the planning system is to blame. Three related errors frequently occur:

- The finished marketing plan is delivered beyond end-of-period deadlines.
- The sales force must commence its planning process well into the operating cycle, and may finish before marketing plans are delivered.
- The sales force has no input into marketing objectives and strategies. As a result, the marketing plan is viewed as irrelevant to the day-to-day concerns of the sales force, leading to the view of marketing as an ivory tower department.

When insufficient coordination occurs, it is not unusual for sales management to discard objectives and strategies received from marketing as being out of touch with reality.

To develop sales objectives and strategies appropriately implies that marketing plans must be well developed, yet not completed, before the sales strategy development process commences. In the best processes there is considerable interaction between marketing and senior sales management as objectives and priorities are hammered out in a spirit of cooperation, rather than via political infighting or internecine conflict. This is especially critical when, as is frequently the case, a general sales force sells a variety of products to several market segments. Here, the field sales strategy and sales force activities play an essential integrating role. In some firms, marketing-sales coordinator positions have been developed to ensure that sales and marketing managers are present at the appropriate objective-setting and strategy-development meetings.

THE TASKS OF SALES MANAGEMENT

The six key tasks of sales management include:

- Task 1: Achieve sales objectives
- Task 2: Determine and allocate sales force effort
- Task 3: Develop sales approaches
- Task 4: Design the sales organization
- Task 5: Design critical organizational processes
- Task 6: Recruit, select, train, and retain salespeople

Task 1: Achieve Sales Objectives

Typically, sales forces undertake a variety of activities aimed at achieving different goals. They may be asked to secure information, collect payment, deliver goods, provide service, and entertain senior company management. Notwithstanding the importance of these different activities, one goal is ultimately crucial to the success of any sales organization—achieving sales objectives. The firm maximizes shareholder value, and survives and prospers, only when it receives revenues and makes profit from customers for the goods and services it offers. Sales is the only organizational function charged with this task.

STRATEGIC IMPORTANCE   Sales objectives can be developed on many bases, such as new products or existing products, new customers or existing customers, by market segment, by product group, and so forth. The critical issue for sales managers is to identify what basis for breakdown of objectives is strategic for the firm. If the firm is unconcerned whether sales and profits derive from one product group or another, then setting objectives by product group is a meaningless exercise. If it is unconcerned whether sales and profits derive from one market segment or another, or from existing or new customers, then setting objectives by market segment or by customer type is also meaningless. But if one of these dimensions is strategic for the firm, then this dimension should figure in the objective-setting process.

BUSINESS OBJECTIVES   Business objectives are financial or market measures of business performance, such as profits, sales volume, profitability, or expenses. Traditionally, sales objectives were set as gross volume based on units, or current or constant dollars (especially if inflation is high). More recently, management has set profitability objectives for the sales force. These objectives tend not to be based on bottom-line profits but rather are contribution-type measures.[4] The contribution measure is typically derived as sales revenues less direct costs (including sales force costs), but excludes those costs out of sales management control, such as head office and R&D burdens.

A critical feature of sales force business objectives is consistency with objectives developed in the business and product/market strategies. This is less difficult for sales forces specialized by product or market segment, but can be a major problem for unspecialized geographically based sales forces. Perhaps the most difficult situations are where the sales force sells several products to a variety of market segments.

Suppose, for example, the firm's products are the responsibility of individual product managers, each of whom has their own market and financial objectives. These objectives may involve growth, profitability, or cash flow maintenance; others may derive from plans for rapid decreases in sales, market share, and profits related to product phase-out or fast harvesting. Incorporating these differences in product/market objectives into business objectives for the sales force is a complex task, requiring a thoughtful translation. This translation is best achieved by the involvement of senior sales managers when marketing objectives are being set.

The example in Figure 15.1 assumes that sales by product/market segment are strategic for the firm, and the seven product/market segments addressed by the firm yield seven objectives (assumed in revenue dollars) (Figure 15.2).

However, these business objectives, developed for the sales force as a whole, must be decomposed for individual sales force control units, such as regions, districts, individual salespeople, or key accounts (Figure 15.3). A blanket division of general goals into subgoals is certain to be suboptimal since sales regions, districts, and territories vary in market and sales potentials, as well as workload characteristics, while salespeople similarly vary in capabilities and motivation. The best processes involve much discussion and negotiation, comprising both "top down" and "bottom up" characteristics. The "bottom up" element, comprised of information on territory sales potentials, and customer and competitor characteristics, is best developed in the context of a planning process whereby each salesperson prepares a sales action plan in consultation with their district manager (see Task 5).

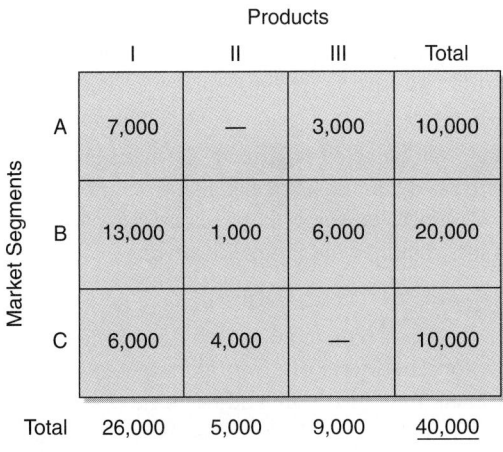

	Products			
	I	II	III	Total
A	7,000	—	3,000	10,000
B	13,000	1,000	6,000	20,000
C	6,000	4,000	—	10,000
Total	26,000	5,000	9,000	40,000

(Market Segments shown on vertical axis)

FIGURE 15.2

Product/Market Segment Objectives ($US 000s)

INPUT AND INTERMEDIATE OBJECTIVES   Input and intermediate objectives are based on actions that occur during the selling process.

- **Input objectives** focus on actions to be taken by the sales force, such as calls on potential customers, effort to sell certain products, or product training.
- **Intermediate objectives**, by contrast, focus on actions that the firm requires the customer to take. These actions may be necessary for reaching sales force business objectives, such as conducting factory trials or being awarded qualified supplier status.

As with business objectives, action objectives should be brief, specific, results-oriented, and time bound. In both cases, objectives set at the corporate (national) level must be decomposed for lower-level control units.

Intermediate objectives are particularly important in long-cycle sales processes where many months, or even several years, might pass between an initial customer contact and placement of an order. Many firms deliberately manage pipelines of selling situations by the achievement of sequential intermediate objectives, such as laboratory tests, factory trials, or tests by customers' customers. Pipeline management enables sales managers to forecast sales with greater accuracy and provide feedback to individual salespeople based on their performance versus intermediate objectives.

> **Example:** Jostens produces high school yearbooks. Although these are delivered to students in June, the selling cycle commences in the fall. In an effort to displace competitors, high school decision makers are asked to sign a card in early fall agreeing to allow the Jostens salesperson to make a presentation on its offer.

Units.   Sales objectives for Region I in fiscal 200X are 92,000 lbs. of Product A, 18,000 lbs. of Product B.

Current Dollars.   Sales objectives for Product A in Region II in fiscal 200Y are $1,365,000 to the electronics industry, $3,225,000 to the glass industry; sales objectives for Product B are $2,500,000 to the electronics industry, $1,250,000 to the food and beverage industry.

Contribution Margin.   Objectives for Region III in fiscal 200Z are to earn $750,000 contribution from Product A, $550,000 from Product B.

FIGURE 15.3

Examples of Sales Force Business Objectives Broken Down by Control Unit

Individual salespeople are set intermediate objectives based on the number of cards signed. Over time, Jostens has developed a predictive sales model based on the probability that it will make a sale if the salesperson makes a presentation.

From a management perspective, the crucial importance of these types of objectives is that gaps between objectives and performance can be acted on directly by management to influence the achievement of business objectives. By contrast, management cannot directly influence gaps in achievement of business objectives since these results have already occurred. (See Figure 15.4 for examples of intermediate and input objectives.)

Task 2: Determine and Allocate Sales Force Effort

Sales objectives—business, input, and intermediate—are achieved by sales force effort. Sales management must ensure that the appropriate levels of effort are targeted towards those products, market segments, and customers most likely to lead to meeting sales and profit objectives. To identify appropriate effort levels, careful analysis of all major customers and customer groups must be conducted to identify where the scarce resource of salesperson time will provide the best results. In this regard, a well-developed marketing plan should provide significant guidance.

Several related decisions concern the assessment and allocation of selling effort: sales force size, sales force activity focus, selling effort allocation, and customer focus.

DETERMINING SALES FORCE SIZE   To achieve sales objectives, the firm must have sufficient numbers of personnel, appropriately recruited, selected, trained, and motivated, to accomplish its tasks. In today's environment where managing headcount has become a critical human resource function, sales managers often have to fight difficult internal battles to secure sufficient salespeople. (See the Chapter Appendix for alternative methods of determining sales force size.) In addition to securing the necessary internal agreements on steady-state sales force size, sales management must plan for filling salesperson losses caused by attrition, promotion, and dismissal.[5]

SALES FORCE ACTIVITY FOCUS   Activity focus provides guidance for allocating sales force effort among different kinds of activities by setting priorities for the sales force as a whole. Typically, in mature markets, the overall activity balance varies little from planning period to planning period. By contrast, in fast-changing markets (growing or declining), significant changes in activity focus are likely. In new markets, salespeople typically spend significant effort making sales calls to potential new customers, forecasting volume requirements and desired product mix, gathering competitive intelligence, and training distribution system personnel. By contrast, in market decline, the focus shifts to consolidating distribution, facilitating liquidation, disposal or reassignment of inventory, and making collections.

Given limitations on sales force resources, sales managers must develop guidelines that specify how the sales force should divide its time among various potential activities.

Input Objectives
- Sales Calls: All salespeople conduct an average of five customer calls per day
- Training: All salespeople to have completed a selling skills refresher course by June 23, 200X
- Planning: All salesperson action plans to be completed and accepted by December 5, 200X
- Inventory: Checks of distributor inventories to be completed by October 1, 200X
- Call Reports: Call reports submitted by e-mail within 24 hours of call completion

Intermediate Objectives
By year end
- Conduct 10 factory trials of new product A
- Secure retailer agreements for $500,000 cooperative advertising
- Achieve qualified supplier status from 10 new customers
- Have 10 proposals accepted for evaluation by key account customers

FIGURE 15.4

Examples of Input and Intermediate Salesforce Objectives

These guidelines must be consistent with the sales objectives. A general activity classification comprising selling, servicing, traveling, and administration might yield the following set of activity focus guidelines:

Selling	Minimum	25%
Traveling	Maximum	30%
Servicing	Minimum	30%
Administration	Maximum	10%
Miscellaneous		5%
		100%

These guidelines should be established as overall targets for the entire sales force. Individual territories and salespeople may vary from the average, due to differences in sales potentials and workloads.

ALLOCATING SELLING EFFORT   As noted earlier, sales objectives can be broken out by dimensions such as new or existing products, new or existing customers, by market segment, by product group, and so forth. Since selling effort is the key determinant in achieving sales objectives, it must be allocated in a manner congruent with sales objectives. Thus if sales objectives are set separately for new and existing products, sales force effort should be allocated to new products and to existing products. If sales objectives are set separately for new and existing customers, sales force effort should be allocated to new customers and existing customers.

Sales objectives should not be expected to mirror the selling effort proportionately. For example, if sales volume objectives were set for existing and new products in an 80/20 ratio, the allocation of sales force effort would not be expected to be in the same ratio. Rather, proportionately less effort would probably be required to achieve the 80% sales of existing products and proportionately more effort for the 20% sales of new products; a 70/30 or 60/40 ratio might be appropriate. (The specific effort allocation is predicated upon assumptions about the sales response function [Chapter Appendix].)

Allocating Selling Effort by Product/Market Segment   Based on the example in Figure 15.2, sales management must achieve business objectives broken out by product and market segment. The sales strategy challenge is to allocate selling effort such that these objectives are achieved. The framework for selling effort allocation (Figure 15.5)

		Products			
		I	II	III	Total
Market Segments	A	20	—	15	35
	B	20	15	10	45
	C	10	10	—	20
	Total	50	25	25	100

FIGURE 15.5

Product/Market Segment: Sales Effort Allocation (%)

must be congruent with the framework for product/market segment objectives.[6] In this illustration, the firm has decided to place 20% of its entire effort selling product I to market segment A, 15% effort selling product III to market segment A, and so forth.

Suppose that across the sales force, 50,000 hours of selling time were available, an overall statement of sales effort allocation would take the form illustrated in Table 15.1.

Figure 15.5 and Table 15.1 represent the selling effort allocation that senior sales management believes will achieve the full set of product/market segment objectives. As with business objectives, these allocations must be decomposed for individual sales force control units, such as regions, districts, individual salespeople, or key accounts in a similar fashion to Figure 15.3.

Allocating Selling Effort by New versus Old Business Another important sales strategy dimension focuses on new versus old business. Figure 15.6 partitions sales opportunities into four categories based on whether or not products and customers are new to the firm.[7] Not only is this partition valuable for sales strategy development, it also reveals the enthusiasm likely to be engendered in the sales force for selling activity in each cell.

- **Cell A: Current Customers/Current Products—Highest Comfort**. Sales are achieved by deeper penetration of the current customer base with current products; they result from customer growth or increased share of customer business.
- **Cell B: Current Customers/New Products—Medium Comfort**. Sales are achieved through broadening the product range sold to current customers by introducing new products.
- **Cell C: New Customers/Current Products—Medium Comfort**. Sales are secured by selling current products to new customers.
- **Cell D: New Customers/New Products—Highest Discomfort**. This cell generally represents the most difficult sales opportunities, new products sold to new customers.[8]

As with the product/market segment approach, sales objectives and selling effort allocation can be developed across the four cells. Only cell A represents the continuation of current business; the other three cells represent different types of new business. Since new business frequently represents the firm's future, it is essential that the sales strategy be clear regarding the relative level of effort in these cells. However, it is one thing for management to prescribe sales force selling effort, it is quite another to ensure that this effort occurs as planned. In general, the higher the level of sales force discomfort in implementing a sales strategy, the greater management's role must be to ensure that the required effort actually occurs.[9]

TABLE 15.1 Illustration of Product/Market Segment: Sales Effort Allocation (hours)

Product	Selling Time	Market Segment	Selling Time	Product/Market Segment	Selling Time
I	25,000	A	17,500	IA	10,000
II	12,500	B	22,500	IB	10,000
III	12,500	C	10,000	IC	5,000
	50,000		50,000	IIB	7,500
				IIC	5,000
				IIIA	7,500
				IIIB	5,000
					50,000

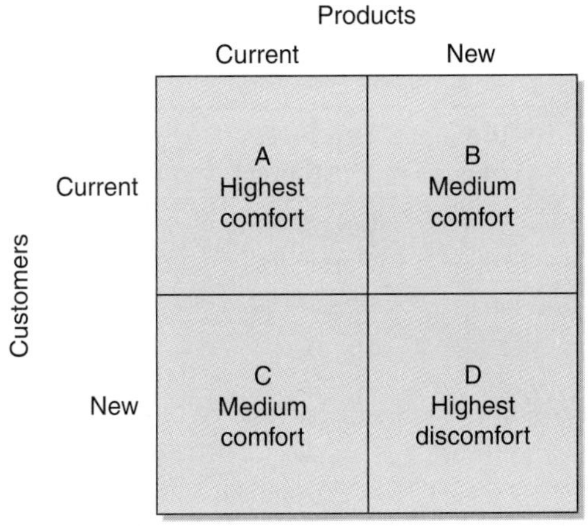

FIGURE 15.6

Sales Strategy Matrix for New versus Old Business

The distribution of sales objectives (and hence selling effort) across the four cells also relates to the firm's strategic situation. A firm in a mature industry is perhaps most likely to focus heavily in cell A. Conversely, a start-up company or a division with an expanding product line is likely to seek significant sales in cells B, C, and D; however, establishing priorities is likely to be difficult and demanding.

As with the product/market segment approach, both sales objectives and planned selling effort should be identified for each cell. It is unlikely that selling effort allocation by cell will mirror sales objectives (Figure 15.7). In a similar fashion as before, an overall statement for allocating 50,000 hours of selling time might take the form shown in Table 15.2.

Allocating Selling Effort by Customer Type In addition to decisions on sales force size, expected selling time as a proportion of total time available, and selling effort allocation by product/market segment and new versus old business, decisions must be made on selling effort allocation for different types of customers. Although norms may be set for individual customers (such as key accounts), they are usually established by customer type or class.

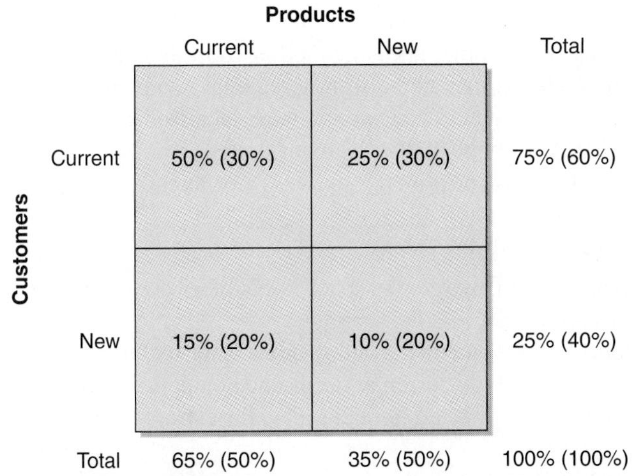

FIGURE 15.7

Illustration of Sales Strategy Matrix for New versus Old Business: Objectives (Selling Effort)(%)

TABLE 15.2 Illustration of New/Old Business: Sales Effort Allocation (hours)

Products	Selling Time	Customers	Selling Time	Products/ Customers	Selling Time
Current	25,000	Current	30,000	Current/Current	15,000
New	25,000	New	20,000	Current/New	10,000
	50,000		50,000	New/Current	15,000
				New/New	10,000
					50,000

Call norms are ideally based on a thoughtful appraisal of sales potential and expected response to given calling patterns.[10] A sample customer focus schedule is of the form:

Customer Type	Call Time	Call Frequency
A	1 hour	Twice per month
B	1 hour	Once per month
C	20 minutes	Once per quarter
D	10 minutes	Once per half year

As with the other allocation dimensions, these norms should not be thought of as rigid standards but rather as overall guidelines for allocating selling effort. Note that selling effort allocation does not deal with the issue of how selling effort is applied to customers. That question focuses on developing sales approaches.

Task 3: Develop Sales Approaches

Each product/market segment strategy should reflect a differential advantage: essentially, why targeted customers should buy (or recommend) the firm's offer rather than those of competitors. At the product/market segment level, these core strategy statements are relatively general. A critical task of sales management is to translate the generalized market segment offer into the specific message delivered by individual salespersons to individual customers.

This translation process may involve developing regional or other focused sales approaches. For example, in one region customer needs may differ from the market average, or the most severe competitive threats may come from a regional competitor rather than major national competitors. Such customer need variation and localized competition may not have been strongly considered when the market segment strategy was being developed.[11] However, for the regional sales force, positioning for these customers against local competitors may be crucial.

The translation process involves three distinct steps:

- Salespeople and sales managers must analyze the specific customer needs and competitive threats at their accounts.
- They must translate the core strategy statements into specific benefits for their accounts, dealing with both idiosyncratic customer needs and competitive offers. They must also be prepared to answer objections and sell against strong competitive offers.
- Since customer decision making units typically comprise several individuals or role positions, sales management must understand the differing perspectives each brings to the purchase decision and assist the sales force in orchestrating product and service benefits among these members.

The two major components of the sales approach are:

- The choice and substantiation of the critical benefits to motivate customers to buy the firm's products.
- The design of a process for communicating those benefits to customers.

CHOICE AND SUBSTANTIATION OF CRITICAL BENEFITS   Decisions must be made regarding the relative emphasis given to individual benefits and the choice of which individual customer roles, such as decision makers or influencers, to target for effort.[12] In any given customer organization, different benefits should probably be emphasized for different roles. For example, procurement personnel are more likely to be interested in price or total cost; engineers in product design; manufacturing personnel in operational efficiency.[13]

Example: A Fortune 500 company (competitor II) targeted an individual customer whose needs were identified and prioritized. Sales management's thought process illustrates the importance of the sales approach and the sharpening of competitive focus it provides. In Table 15.3, three competitors I, II, III, each sought the sale; competitor II identified four customer benefits in the purchase decision that declined in importance A>B>C>D.

Regarding the most important customer benefit, A, competitive superiority was ordered I>II>III. Only competitor II offered benefit B (such as a warranty). Benefit C was not offered by competitor I, but competitor II>III. Benefit D was not offered by competitor II, but competitor III>I. Firm II investigated the best sales approaches for each of the three competitors.

- For competitor I, a logical sales approach would be to focus on its offer of the best performance on A, the customer's most important benefit; it is, of course, vulnerable to the other benefits.
- Competitor II dominates III on benefits A, B, and C, and is only inferior on the customer's least important benefit, D; thus competitor I is its main competitive target. Competitor II's major problem is that competitor I ranks first on the customer's most important benefit, A. Possible sales approaches developed by competitor II are:
  - The competitor ranking on benefit A is incorrect; actually, competitor II>I;
  - Based on the customer's underlying needs, the criteria are incorrectly ordered; the correct order of benefits should be B>A>C>D. Competitor II now dominates I on the most important benefit;
  - The decision should be based on the benefit set rather than on individual benefits. Since competitor II offers A, B, and C, it is clearly superior to competitor I that only offers A, notwithstanding A's perceived superiority on this benefit.
- Competitor III was perceived to have little hope for securing the business. A sales approach focused on offering the best benefit D and the only offer of an A, C, and D combination might not carry much weight. A more important question for competitor III: why is it spending time selling to this customer if its benefits are so inferior to competition? Perhaps competitor III should focus on other customers where its particular benefits are better aligned with customer needs.

TABLE 15.3 Formulating Sales Approaches

Customer Benefits	Relative Importance	Competitor I		Competitor II		Competitor III	
		Benefit	Rank	Benefit	Rank	Benefit	Rank
A	1	A	1	A	2	A	3
B	2			B	1		
C	3			C	1	C	2
D	4	D	2			D	1

Since neither competitor offered all benefits sought by the customer, each was vulnerable to a new focused entrant with a better-matched offer. Thus Table 15.3 suggests directions for market research and product development. For example, if the customer's volume requirements were large, or if many customers had similar needs, developing an offer better matched to customer requirements might be well advised. Furthermore, since benefit rankings are rather crude measures of customer needs, more sophisticated research might yield better insight into the relative importance of different benefits, and clearly establish whether particular benefits are absolutely necessary or might be traded off against superior performance on others.

Finally, the expectation that few readers would probably be enthusiastic about accepting a salesperson position with competitor III highlights the central role of market strategy in providing the sales force with ammunition to perform its role.

COMMUNICATING BENEFITS TO CUSTOMERS Although most sales managers agree that establishing critical benefits to be communicated is necessary, they often shy away from designing a process by which these benefits should be communicated. Of course, complete standardization of the process is probably undesirable, yet in certain important areas sales management should at least offer guidance. For example:

- Establishing a process for generating call objectives, such as via pre-call planning: What should the salesperson attempt to achieve with individual customers at different stages of the buying process?
- Designing need elicitation procedures: What questions should the salesperson ask to establish customer needs and benefits sought?
- Determining the order of presenting benefits: What trade-offs should be made in using primacy and recency approaches?[14]
- Handling objections: What common customer objections might be anticipated, and how should these be dealt with?
- Setting the tone for sales interviews: How strident or aggressive should the salesperson be? With what time perspective should they be working?

The best approaches view selling as a system designed to facilitate the customer's buying process in which critical benefits are communicated to customers in the appropriate manner.

> **Example:** Bose Corporation is a leader in speakers. In its retail stores, potential customers, settled into a sofa, enjoy exquisite sound from a large TV and huge speakers. When the show is concluded, the salesperson executes "The Reveal," removing the "fake" speakers to show baseball-sized Bose speakers.[15]

Well-designed sales training programs, supplemented by coaching and counseling, are useful vehicles to provide guidance to individual salespeople.

Task 4: Design the Sales Organization

The field selling effort must be designed to implement the sales strategy so the appropriate types and levels of selling effort for specified products are applied against designated customer targets. The line sales organization should reflect the strategic realities faced by the sales force; the form chosen will affect the nature of the salesforce allocation decisions that must be made. Three critical issues should be considered:

- Should the selling effort be conducted by firm employees or outsourced to another organization (the make/buy decision)?
- How should an employee-based sales force be organized?
- How should the entire firm/customer organizational interface be managed?

EMPLOYEE-BASED OR OUTSOURCED SALES FORCE? Outsourcing has become an increasingly critical issue for many firms, deciding whether a particular organizational function should be conducted by the firm's employees, or outsourced to a third party.

Traditionally, these decisions concerned production operations, but more recently have included service functions such as legal, security, and computer systems. This issue is no less relevant in the sales force.

Where on-the-road personal sales effort is required, the firm can either develop its own sales organization or contract the selling function to third party agents, representatives, or brokers. Three major criteria are relevant to this outsourcing decision:

- **Control**: In general, the firm's ability to ensure that selling effort is applied as planned is greater when the firm's employees comprise the sales force, less when salespeople are independent agents, representatives, or brokers. However, if the firm compensates its in-house sales force largely by incentive compensation, it may likewise have little control.
- **Cost**: Since agents, representatives, and brokers are generally remunerated exclusively by incentive compensation, selling costs are frequently almost completely variable—no sales, no cost! Conversely, firms employing their own sales forces often incur substantial fixed costs embracing sales force overhead (including travel and entertainment expense) and the salary portion of sales force compensation that must be paid regardless of sales volumes achieved.
- **Modification**: For most firms, the choice of independent agents, representatives, and brokers versus a firm-employed sales force has an important flexibility component. Typically, agent, representative, and broker contracts are short-term in nature (often 30-day) and modifications can be made quickly. By contrast, major modifications in firm-employed sales forces typically take time and must be planned with care to avoid negative consequences. However, this may not always be the case.

Example: In 1998, Gerber, the U.S. baby food manufacturer, decided to shift from an in-house sales force to using brokers. Over 250 members of the sales force were summarily dismissed.

Although there is no right or wrong answer to this sales force issue, there may be conditions under which either an internal or outsourced sales force is more appropriate. For example, when the firm is engaged in new market entry but with unclear organizational commitment, in-place independent agents, representatives, or brokers may be preferable to building a new sales force organization. Conversely, employee-based selling efforts may be more appropriate when high market share in a mature market leads to predictable sales, or where long lead-times are involved.

ORGANIZING THE EMPLOYEE-BASED SELLING EFFORT Two essential questions characterize the organization of a sales force: should sales force effort be specialized? And, if so, how?[16] Two types of sales force are typically considered as unspecialized. First, those sales forces in which no geographic bounds are placed on an individual salesperson's search for opportunity; second, a geographic organization in which each salesperson is provided with a geographically-defined sales territory and represents the firm for all products, to all customers, for all applications, in that geographic area.

The major rationale for specialization is the increase in effectiveness that should follow from a more fine-grained focus. Specialized selling effort can be constructed in several different ways: product, maintenance or new business, distribution channel member, market segment or key account. Table 15.4 presents the pros and cons of various pure form organizations.

In practice, most firms use some combination of pure form organizations, in part because their sales forces are too small for the degree of specialization that might otherwise be warranted. For example, they might organize the selling effort by product in urban areas but have no specialization in those geographic areas where customer density is low (such as rural areas). Alternatively, product or market specialists might support a non-specialized sales force.

DIRECTING AND
MANAGING THE FIELD
SALES EFFORT

TABLE 15.4 Sales Force Organization

Organizational Form	Definition	Conditions
No Geographic Bounds	Salespeople free to make sales calls with no geographic constraints	• Difficult to identify customers • Relationships important (e.g., life insurance, stockbroking)
Geographic	Salesperson has total responsibility in a specific geographic area	• customer requirements and applications similar, product complexity low • sales force sometimes backed up by product specialists
Product	Different salespeople responsible for separate product lines	• product line large and heterogeneous and/or at different life cycle stages • products sold to different market segments • firm attempts to increase "face time" with critical customers
Maintenance/ New Business	Different salespeople responsible for: • finding new business • maintaining existing business	• significant new business opportunities available, especially for new products
Distribution Channel Member	Different salespeople responsible for different types of intermediaries and end-users	• products move through an extended channel structure • different selling activities required at each level
Market Segment	Different salespeople responsible for separate market segments (e.g., by industry, buying center, customer application)	• selling problems differ by market segment • specific "types" of salesperson likely to be successful in different market segments
Key Account*	Different salespeople responsible for the firm's most important customers	• small number of customers (current and/or potential) responsible for a high proportion of revenues (i.e., 80/20 rule)

*Technically a form of market segment organization; key account management may exist at several organization levels, for example, corporate, business and within a regional sales force. Typically, a single individual has responsibility for identifying opportunities and developing key account relationships. Key accounts may either be removed from regular salesforce resp accounts, or key account managers may be matrixed with the regular sales

Example: Wachovia Bank's account managers are supported by a variety of product specialists. However, to assure that account managers take full responsibility for understanding their products, the product specialist function is deliberately understaffed so that product expertise is only applied where absolutely necessary.[17]

Whenever some form of organizational specialization is employed, a major implication for individual geographic areas is that two or more salespeople may call on an individual customer. As a result, sales force specialization may lead to coordination problems.

Example: In the 1970s, IBM had one sales force for mainframe computers and one for minis. When this organization was introduced, mainframes and minis satisfied different customer needs. However, over time, product design evolution led

Pros	Cons
• No artificial barriers to salespersons' entrepreneurial drive	• Potential multiple calling on same customer • Little managerial control
• maximizes selling time • minimizes travel and administrative costs • close supervision • minimizes confusion for customer and salesperson	• salesperson may be unable to understand full complexity of customer requirements and the product line • salesperson must be "jack-of-all-trades," may be "master-of-none"
• sales force deployment decisions (for products) made at policy level • the sales force becomes product experts through close relationships with product-oriented personnel	• increased travel and administrative costs (vs. geographic sales force) • multiple calling on individual customers
• Optimizes use of more-difficult-to-find new business salespeople	• increased travel and administrative costs (vs. geographic sales force) • difficult handover from new business to maintenance sales force
• sales force deployment decisions (for intermediaries) made at policy level • clarity of focus for salesperson	• increased travel and administrative costs (vs. geographic sales force) • Potential for confusion between neighboring intermediaries
• sales force deployment decisions (for segments) made at policy level • greater flow of new product ideas from closer customer relationships • customer offered "best" solution • salespeople can be matched to market segments	• increased travel and administrative costs (vs. geographic sales force) • potential "feast or famine" with market segments
• focuses attention on those customers most critical to the firm's future • greater ability to identify opportunities for the firm	• increased travel and administrative costs (vs. geographic sales force) • difficulties interfacing with the regular sales force

force, which retains responsibility for day-by-day customer interaction. A recent trend has been the extension of national account management to global account management. For an in-depth treatment of key account management, see Noel Capon, *Key Account Management and Planning*, New York: The Free Press, forthcoming, 2001.

to smaller mainframes and larger minis such that either product might satisfy a particular customer need. Not infrequently, having made significant price concessions to a customer, an IBM salesperson might discover that their major competitor was IBM!

Example: In the early 1990s, British Aerospace Regional Aircraft (BARA) formed the Asset Management Division to dispose of second-hand planes, secured when several large customers entered bankruptcy. This division competes vigorously with the new plane sales division, frequently driving down prices.[18]

Other critical organizational design decisions relate to the degree of centralization/decentralization, number of management levels, and span of control. In recent years, as many corporations have downsized, sales forces have become more decentralized with fewer management levels and larger spans of control. A critical question is whether the sales management structure is robust enough to ensure that quality sales effort is directed at customers.

Securing Planned Selling Effort Sales force organization helps ensure that the sales force is appropriately specialized for the type of selling effort required. In addition, sales force specialization is a powerful means of securing the required level of selling effort. Once the specialization decision has been made, selling effort allocation is achieved by simply assigning the appropriate numbers of salespeople to the various specialized organizations. To pursue the example in Figure 15.5 and Table 15.1, if three market segment-based sales organizations (A, B, C) were formed, assuming away such issues as travel time and account concentration, the firm might staff the sales force in the ratio 35:45:20. This simple expedient ensures that planned selling effort allocation is achieved. (Equally, the firm might develop three product-based sales forces and assign salespeople in the ratio 50:25:25.)

Regardless of which organizational specialization is employed, sales effort implementation based on separate management processes is required for other dimensions. For example, if the sales force was organized by market segment, managerial processes would be necessary to secure appropriate allocation by product. Notwithstanding the particular organizational design selected, the particular geographic design for sales territories, districts, regions, and so forth should be based on an appropriate balance of workload and sales potential.

Modifying the Sales Force Organization Because of the problems exemplified by the IBM example, the salesforce organization should not be "locked in stone." Rather, management should anticipate that environmental change and developing market and sales strategy may require new forms of organization. We provide several examples:

Example: Historically, Stuart Dean sold cleaning services to apartment and office buildings in Manhattan through a four-person, geographically organized sales force. Building managers typically spent many years managing a single building, but in recent years they have become much more mobile and now shift buildings with relative frequency. Because of the importance of salesperson/building manager relationships in retaining and securing business, Stuart Dean has abandoned its geographic structure and each salesperson is now free to seek business throughout the city.[19]

Example: Major package goods manufacturers offer many product lines in several product categories, for example, detergents (clothes, dishes), dentifrice, deodorant, diapers (nappies) and/or cake mixes. Historically, in many companies, each product category was sold by its own salesforce. In recent years, because major supermarket chains have complained about the cost, in purchasing agent time, of interfacing with so many sales forces, packaged goods firms have consolidated selling efforts into a single key account manager directing a customer team responsible for all customer relationships.

Example: A foreign manufacturer targeting business firms with imported electronic goods set up a system of regional distributorships and local dealers served by a single geographically organized sales force. Analysis revealed not only that the functions of each of these entities were quite different, but also that selling effort was needed at business customers to "pull" product through the system. The firm decided to develop three types of salesperson: one focused on the distributors, a second on dealers, and a third on end users.

Sales force organization is a critical decision variable in ensuring that the required selling effort emerging from the sales strategy is applied appropriately. Whereas the line sales organization in many firms remains unchanged over the years, the increasingly turbulent environment and the necessary strategic changes require that the firm considers modifications on a periodic basis.

MANAGING THE ENTIRE FIRM/CUSTOMER ORGANIZATIONAL INTERFACE Individual salespeople are only one of several potential organizational interfaces with customers. Other types of relationships focus on organizational level and function. Regarding level, in many cases, more senior sales force personnel, such as district or regional sales manager, support individual salespeople by calling on individual customers. Furthermore, corporate executives, even CEOs, may be involved with important customers. Of course, when individual salespersons or account managers are charged with major responsibility for sales to the customer, they should play a major role in orchestrating these relationships.

Relationships based on function embrace a wide range of activities, including merchandising, commercial service, technical service, delivery of goods and services, research, and development. Typically, organizational units other than the sales force conduct these activities and, depending on circumstances, salespeople should be more or less closely involved with these relationships. Coordination problems may ensue when these organizational units act independently with their own priorities, or when salespeople are so driven to make sales that they disregard potential service problems and leave service personnel to fix messy situations. To avoid these problems, many companies are introducing team-based approaches, often coordinated by a key account manager.

When the customer base becomes concentrated, or where there are a few key customers among a much larger customer base, some firms are organizing multifunctional teams to interface in a coordinated manner with a variety of customer functions. In addition to sales and customer service personnel, such teams may include representatives from brand management, trade marketing, operations/logistics, market research, finance, and human resources. As vertical partnerships are forged within traditional distribution channel systems, and in customer-focused firms, teams may consciously become the dominant organizational form for managing key accounts. Multinational organizations are beginning to develop global account management systems whereby global account managers (often multilingual) develop global account strategies that are implemented by virtual teams located around the world.[20]

Task 5: Design Critical Organizational Processes

The major function of sales force organizational processes is to ensure that the required selling effort specified in the sales strategy is implemented. In this regard, organizational processes complement the sales force specialization decision. However, as any manager knows, it is one thing to plan resource allocations, but it is quite another to ensure that planned allocations are actually implemented in practice.

TOP DOWN/BOTTOM UP PLANNING Implementation of specified sales effort allocation is more likely if the sales force develops commitment by being involved in the process. The appropriate method is resolution of a top down/bottom up planning process. Top down, senior sales management decomposes overall sales objectives, pushes these down through the sales organization, and consults with lower-level management on how overall effort allocation should be refined for individual sales regions, districts, and territories. Bottom up, working with first line sales management and based on thorough territory analyses, individual salespeople develop territory-based sales objectives and sales action plans to achieve these objectives. These input, intermediate, and business objectives are aggregated across the sales organization and integrated with top down objectives during the planning process.

During the operating period, the managerial task emphasizes the role of the first-line sales supervisor to ensure that sales objectives are achieved and selling effort allocations are implemented as planned. If objectives are not met, or selling effort is not allocated as planned, corrective action should be taken. When effort is not allocated as planned, serious consequences may result.

Example: A start-up medical device company whose product assisted hemo-dialysis treatments[21] determined that sales effort should be focused on major teaching hospitals. A critical element in the sales strategy was that these potential customers should be heavily serviced to ensure that the device was appropriately used. Unfortunately, the salesperson in Germany was more concerned with expanding the number of customers quickly. This led to product misuse and a serious credibility problem for the firm.

Of course, sales management must be attuned to the fact that many factors, such as compensation systems, special product/market segment sales incentives, idiosyncratic salesperson behavior, unplanned opportunities, and so forth may lead salespeople astray from planned effort, and so interfere with the smooth transition of plan to action.[22]

REWARD SYSTEMS   Reward systems are powerful devices for ensuring that selling effort is implemented as planned and sales objectives are reached.

- **Promotions and Work Assignments**: Potential promotions, more interesting, or more responsible job possibilities may be highly motivating. However, sales management should not fall into the trap of believing that all salespeople want managerial responsibility. Some salespeople may not value this type of advancement, and they may not be competent in such roles. As the result of a faulty promotion, the firm may lose a star salesperson and gain a poor manager![23]
- **Financial Compensation**: Sales compensation systems can be a powerful method for securing the planned levels of sales force effort and achieving sales objectives. Sales compensation plans are essentially based on three elements:
  - salary—compensation paid regardless of sales performance (in the short run)
  - commission—variable compensation based on sales or profits
  - bonus—compensation based on attaining a level of sales or profits

In general, the greater the level of selling effort required to make the sale, the greater should be the percent of incentive compensation (commission and bonus). Incentive compensation can be used effectively to focus selling effort. For example, commission schemes that pay more highly for sales of new products, or bonuses paid for a given level of sales, will encourage appropriate effort.[24] Unfortunately, in many sales forces, the compensation scheme is not synchronized with sales objectives and planned effort allocation. Design problems are particularly acute if the compensation system is developed by human resource personnel with little or no sales management input. As a result, achieving desired sales effort can be difficult.

A particular problem is that, although sales strategies must continually adjust to environmental imperatives, sales compensation systems often lag the change in strategy. As a result, the system motivates behavior to implement an earlier sales strategy rather than the current sales strategy. Other motivation problems can occur when the incentive portion of compensation is low, when earnings are capped, when windfalls are poorly managed, or when the system is poorly administered.[25] Specific problems occur in systems where potential bonus amounts are uncertain, secret, and subjectively based. In the most efficiently run sales organizations, the planning process and the compensation system work in tandem to secure the appropriate effort allocations, and when compensation systems are modified, simulations predict the financial consequences of different types of sales results for both the firm and its salespeople.

Regardless of the overall compensation system, specific additional incentives may be desirable to support strategy implementation. Since overall compensation systems are not easily changed in the short term, providing first line sales managers with discretionary budgets is a useful way to focus resources. Such incentives may include special bonuses, prizes, evaluation points, stamp schemes, and training awards.

- **Recognition**: Recognition for superior sales performance is a relatively inexpensive yet powerful motivator. Creative sales management can develop a variety of recognition systems that motivate appropriate behavior throughout the sales force, such as highest level of sales, best sales growth, sales of most profitable products, most new accounts opened, or most lost accounts retrieved.[26]

Regardless of the type of reward, individual salespeople should be able to answer several important questions affirmatively before the reward system will motivate the required behavior and results:[27]

- Do I believe that I can achieve my objectives?
- Do I value the promised rewards contingent on my achieving these objectives?
- Do I believe that I will receive these rewards if I achieve my objectives?
- Is the reward system fair?

SUPPORT ACTIVITIES   In addition to the planning and reward systems, successful implementation of any field sales strategy depends on programming a myriad of supporting activities. These include technological aids, such as cell phones, laptop computers, voice mail and electronic mail, Web sites, design, printing, and distribution of sales literature, call report systems, systems for sharing best practices, working models, slide show presentations, reseller training or meetings, participation in trade shows, technical support, advertising coordination, and product knowledge training. Several of these requirements are developed by product or promotion managers and then integrated into a support program for the sales force.

Since salespeople are usually in constant customer contact, they are able to secure significant amounts of market intelligence on shifting customer needs and competitive activities, including data on business gained and lost. This information can be crucial to long-run corporate health, and sales management can play an important role in developing the appropriate systems to ensure its collection and use. However, in many organizations, salespeople are neither recognized nor rewarded for this information. Marketing and sales management should work closely together to develop information objectives and managerial processes that effectively tap this valuable resource.

Task 6: Recruit, Select, Train, and Retain Salespeople

People, salespeople, and sales managers, are the most important resource in the sales force. Before the process of securing top-rate salespeople can commence, sales management must be clear about the job criteria that salespeople must meet to be effective. These job criteria evolve from the sales strategy and are based on the knowledge, skills, and abilities necessary to carry out the mission of the sales job effectively.

To secure the right people, sales managers must work with four important variables:

- **Recruitment**: sizing and defining the pool from which salespeople will be selected
- **Selection**: using a set of criteria to choose salespeople from the recruitment pool
- **Training**: ensuring that those salespeople hired acquire the necessary knowledge, skills and abilities to make them effective
- **Retaining**: maintaining high performing salespeople in the sales force

Different organizations have different approaches to securing effective salespeople. Some firms search widely, have loose selection criteria, but train extensively. Other firms prefer to hire only experienced salespeople, have tight selection criteria, and offer little training. Most firms operate somewhere between these extremes. Note that the more narrow the firm's search, the more closely its selection criteria approach the job criteria.

Several trade-offs must be considered in this decision:

- **Time**: If salespeople are needed quickly, the firm may not have the luxury of a broad search and high levels of training. It may be forced to hire salespeople who can operate immediately in an effective manner.
- **Tolerance for failure**: For many firms, choosing the best possible salespeople is absolutely critical. Other firms operate with a sink-or-swim philosophy. Major life

insurance companies, whose agent forces number in the thousands, often expect to retain no more that 5% of their recruits after five years. As a result, they cast a wide net.

- **Company Philosophy**: Some firms refuse to hire salespeople that have previous selling experience. They believe it extremely important to train salespeople in their way of doing business.
- **Availability**: When competent salespeople are not available, such as in a new and growing industry, the firm must anticipate conducting significant training.

Regardless of the particular philosophy embraced for securing salespeople, a critical sales management responsibility is to ensure that the sales force is fully staffed at all times. Assuming that the sales territory design is well-developed based on workloads and sales potential, then a functioning salesperson should be in each territory at all times. Unfortunately, far too often, sales managers do not plan ahead for natural attrition and are forced to scramble when people move on. The key is to inventory salespeople. Salespeople may be inventoried internally by placing them in related roles, such as service representatives, prepared to move into a territory when it becomes available. External inventorying implies that sales managers must be continually interviewing and developing a short list of people to be offered a position when a vacancy occurs.

RECRUITMENT   The design of the recruitment pool is closely linked to the firm's philosophy for securing functioning salespeople. For example, firms embracing a philosophy requiring high degrees of training may merely require a college degree. At the other end of the spectrum, firms might follow the approach of a West Coast brokerage house, "We'll recruit anyone with more than five years experience at Merrill Lynch." The firm should always monitor its success with the current recruitment pool and be on the lookout for ways to upgrade its success rate.

> **Example:** In recruiting its drug detailing force, Merck historically recruited high-potential college graduates with majors in science, and focused its training largely on selling skills. More recently, Merck has abandoned this approach. It now recruits people with a demonstrated record of selling success, regardless of product or service, then provides them with science training.[28]

SELECTION   Because of the importance of the salesperson position in most organizations, firms should implement rigorous selection processes. These should involve multiple interviews, and focus on the roles and responsibilities of the salesperson and the required skill set. It is not unusual for firms to employ psychological testing instruments to aid in the selection process.

In making its sales force selection decisions, the firm must recognize that two errors are possible: hiring the salesperson who eventually fails (Type I), or not hiring the salesperson who would have succeeded (Type II). The first error is ultimately clear; the second error can only be detected by following up on rejected candidates. Although possibly time consuming, tracking both types of errors may enable the firm to sharpen its recruitment and selection policies.

TRAINING   The salesperson position is pivotal in the firm's dealings with its customers; for this reason, the firm should ensure that the personnel occupying these positions are well-trained. The purpose of training is to take the newly hired personnel appointed through the recruitment and selection process and mold them into effective salespeople. The specific sales force training required is in part a function of the firm and its customers, as well as a function of the knowledge, skills, abilities, and experience of the persons hired to be salespeople.

Some salespeople may require training in developing sales action plans; others may benefit from improving their selling, negotiation, and time-management skills. One approach to training is for the supplier firm's human resource department to prepare individualized sales training programs. An alternative approach is to develop a standardized training program that all new salespeople must complete. Of course, training should not be a one-time event, and periodic educational and training programs should be considered.

Sales management must understand that recruiting, selecting, training and retaining salespeople is a moving target. As the business environment evolves and the firm's strategy changes to match new realities, so too must the competencies and skills of the firm's sales force (salespeople and sales managers) also change. Indeed, even highly experienced salespeople may need training, though considerable sensitivity may be required from trainers. In some cases the new competencies can be achieved through training; in others, sales managers will have to make tough replacement decisions. Ongoing development of the sales force must be a critical and continuing sales management concern.

RETAINING   High performing salespeople are valuable firm assets. Under the best of circumstances, when such employees receive an internal assignment, succession planning is well developed and sufficient time is built in for a measured hand-over, still the personnel change may be fraught with difficulties. By contrast, when the salesperson leaves unexpectedly and succession planning is nonexistent, disaster may ensue.

Successful salespeople are vulnerable to poaching from competitors seeking to upgrade their own sales forces. Although individual salespeople may face significant switching costs and high risks in moving from known long-term employers to new organizations, firms that lag the market in rewarding salespeople will surely lose critical personnel. As a result, firms should maintain a database on the destination of departing employees so as to ascertain where a particular non-competitive situation exists.

Example: In the mid-1990s, Varityper, a $120 million manufacturer of desktop publishing equipment, lost several successful salespeople to new PC competitors offering higher salaries and commissions.

Firms must consider the full range of reward systems so as to preempt unexpected salesperson resignations. Leading sales forces are making sales force retention an important measurement criterion for sales managers.

SUMMARY

This chapter laid out the six key tasks of sales management. Together they form an integrated whole that defines, at a broad level, the job of sales management. As the job becomes tougher in the evolving business environment, the sales force must be managed strategically. Accomplishing the six tasks of sales management ensures that this will occur. The six sales management tasks differ from those of marketing. To a large extent, marketing management plays the role of designer; the sales force must make it happen. Nonetheless, the close integration between market and sales strategy development is absolutely crucial.

The first three sales management tasks focus on developing sales strategy.

- Task 1: Achieve sales objectives
- Task 2: Determine and allocate sales force effort
- Task 3: Develop sales approaches

Tasks four through six are concerned with sales strategy implementation.

- Task 4: Design the sales organization
- Task 5: Design critical organizational processes
- Task 6: Recruit, select, train, and retain salespeople

Even well-developed and implemented sales strategies do not guarantee success. Environmental conditions may change radically, firm operations may be weak, or the other marketing mix strategies may be ineffective. However, for most companies, better developed and implemented sales strategies can quickly and significantly improve the prospects for successful organizational performance.

THE CHANGING VIEW

Old Way	New Way
Salesperson the sole interface with customers	Salesperson manages many organizational personnel that interface with customers
Salespersons undervalued in the organization	Salespersons increasingly valued as the single organizational function responsible for revenue generation
Firms seek increased profits by cost reduction (such as downsizing, re-engineering)	Firms seek increased profits through revenue enhancement
Sales efforts managed on a domestic basis	Sales efforts for global customers managed on a global basis
Sales managers evaluated on sales volume	Sales managers evaluated on profit contribution
Salespeople operate by the seat of their pants	Salespeople carefully plan the use of their time in the context of an overarching sales strategy
Sales force organization and processes fixed for long periods of time	Sales force organization and processes continually modified to reflect environmental and strategic changes
Sales and marketing clearly separate	Sales and marketing increasingly intertwined
The sale as a focus	Building long-term, profitable customer relationships as a focus
Individualism emphasized	Increasingly part of multifunctional teams
Many low-powered sales personnel	Few high-powered sales personnel
Conflict	Cooperation
Sales push	Buyer pull
Salesperson skill requirements relatively low	Increasingly high skill requirements
Poor or loose service linkages	Closely linked to customer service

QUESTIONS FOR STUDY AND DISCUSSION

1. Despite its crucial importance, the sales/marketing interface is often characterized by schisms and even conflict. How would you recommend reducing these?

2. "Sales objectives too often emphasize outputs rather than inputs." Do you agree or disagree with this statement? Explain your reasoning.

3. Explain the difference between input and intermediate objectives. Why is this difference important?

4. Explain the concept of the sales response function. Why is the shape of this function important in allocating sales force effort? How, in practice, might the shape of this function be estimated?

5. Why might a single core strategy result in multiple sales approaches? Are there any lessons for marketers when sales management develops multiple approaches?

6. Give six disadvantages of outsourcing selling effort.

7. Explain the advantages and disadvantages of sales force specialization.

8. Why are some buyers and sellers forming vertical partnerships?

9. Account management appears to be in a process of evolution from a national to global basis. What economic forces would explain this shift?

10. Bureaucratic constraints often lead to sales force incentive schemes poorly matched to sales objectives and strategies. How would you avoid this problem?

11. If marketing is truly successful, selling is unnecessary. Do you agree? Explain your answer and justify the ongoing existence of sales forces.

12. Describe the sales organization for a firm with which you are familiar. Is this optimal? Why or why not?

13. The tasks of sales management discussed in this chapter suggest that sales managers need considerable analytic skills (for the planning and strategy part of the job) and, especially, considerable interpersonal skills (for the human resource aspects of the job). How easy is it to find people skilled in both areas? How do these skills compare with those commonly observed among salespeople?

ENDNOTES

1. Of course, large sales forces may have several levels of sales managers: for example, district sales managers who manage several salespeople, regional sales managers who manage several district sales managers, and a national sales manager who manages several regional sales managers.

2. Of course, allocation on other dimensions (e.g., role in the customer organization, new versus existing customers) may be required.

3. Others suggest that although the Japanese emphasis on "harmony and consensus" worked well in steady state environments, it has been less successful in dealing with discontinuities.

4. For a detailed discussion of contribution, see Book Appendix.

5. Since most sales forces have some degree of attrition, and since unfilled sales territories mean forgone sales, recruitment and selection should be an ongoing activity for sales managers.

6. Comparing Figures 15.2 and 15.5, note that each is a 3×3 matrix with the cells IIA and IIIC blank. Strictly speaking, however, the firm might set positive sales revenue objectives yet allocate zero sales force effort as, for example, with a declining product that maintained a core of loyal customers.

7. "New" refers to new to the company, not new to the world.

8. A more complex approach includes old/new applications as a further dimension for objectives and selling effort allocation.

9. Of course, some salespeople and sales forces thrive on seeking new opportunities. With the "comfort" dimension, we are speaking of general tendencies.

10. Several methods are available to assist with this type of allocation. One type, decision calculus models, uses managerial judgments of likely response and solves for the optimal allocation consistent with these assumptions. See, for example, L.M. Lodish, "CALLPLAN: An Interactive Salesman's Call Planning System," *Management Science*, 18, Part II. (Dec. 1971b), pp. 25–40.

11. Another way of thinking about this issue is to recognize that many segmentation schemes are unidimensional; here, for example, geography may have been omitted.

12. Note that this constitutes a key interface with the market strategy (Chapter 8).

13. A large volume of research suggests that much human information processing and decision making is based on relatively few criteria (e.g., G.A. Miller, "The Magical Number Seven, Plus or Minus Two," *Psychological Review*, 63 (Mar. 1956), pp. 81–97; J.M. Hulbert, "Information Processing Capacity and Attitude Management," *Journal of Marketing Research*, 12 (Feb. 1975), pp. 104–106). Thus incorporating too many benefits in a sales approach may confuse customers and/or create a credibility gap.

14. In other words, should the more powerful arguments come earlier or later in the sales call?

15. *The Economist*, January 15, 2000.

16. This discussion focuses on employee-based sales force effort, but with modification may also be appropriate for independent sales forces.

17. See *Wachovia Bank and Trust Company* in N. Capon, *The Marketing of Financial Services: A Book of Cases*, Englewood Cliffs, NJ: Prentice Hall, 1992.

18. N. Adams, J. Gillibrand, D. Treinish, K. Woodberry, and B. Zaldivar, "British Aerospace Regional Aircraft: Addressing the Need for Key Account Management," Term Paper for *Developing and Managing Strategic Customers, B8699-02*, New York: Graduate School of Business, Columbia University, Spring 2000.

19. As part of its reorganization, Stuart Dean instituted a process to avoid multiple calling on individual customers.

20. For the factors driving the growth of key account management, see Chapter 2; see also N. Capon *op. cit.*

21. Cleansing of blood to compensate for failed kidneys.

22. A particularly insidious problem occurs when individual product managers offer incentives for sales of their own products, in effect, bidding for salespeople's time.

23. Note that alternative career tracks involving increased responsibility, income, and recognition can be developed for career salespeople.

24. To avoid a narrow focus on easy-to-sell products, some firms employ product mix incentives.

25. "Caps" are maximum amounts salespeople may earn in a given period. "Windfalls" are sales that occur with little or no salesperson effort; management often exempts these sales from commission and/or bonus earnings.

26. These sorts of results may also be motivated by special incentives.

27. These questions are based on the expectancy/value model for securing motivated behavior.

28. Some companies are rewarding their current salespeople for recruiting new salespeople.

29. Of course, alternative sales response functions may be assumed; see the advertising response functions in Figure 14.9.

30. Lodish, *op. cit.*

WEB RESOURCES

Boze	www.boze.com
Gerber	www.gerber.com
IBM	www.ibm.com
Jostens	www.jostens.com
Merck	www.merck.de
Merrill Lynch	www.ml.com
Stuart Dean	www.stuartdean.com
The Economist	www.economist.com
Wachovia Bank	www.wachovia.com
Xerox	www.xerox.com

CHAPTER 15 APPENDIX: DETERMINING APPROPRIATE SALES FORCE SIZE

The underlying conceptual framework for deciding sales force size is the presumed sales response function in Figure 15A.1.[29] This curve suggests that at low levels of effort, few or no sales occur. But as sales effort increases, sales increase. Ultimately, regardless of the amount of effort, sales reach a maximum. Sales force size should be chosen such that the marginal return for adding (subtracting) a salesperson equals the marginal salesperson cost.[30]

Most people find this depiction intuitively reasonable; the problem is that sales managers typically have no idea where their sales force falls on the curve. Two broad approaches are available for approaching the sizing decision: experiment and analysis.

Experimental Methods

The experimental method basically requires sales managers to change the size of their sales force and see what happens. They should select a district or region as a trial area and then, to the extent that their hypothesis is supported, roll out the change to the entire sales force.

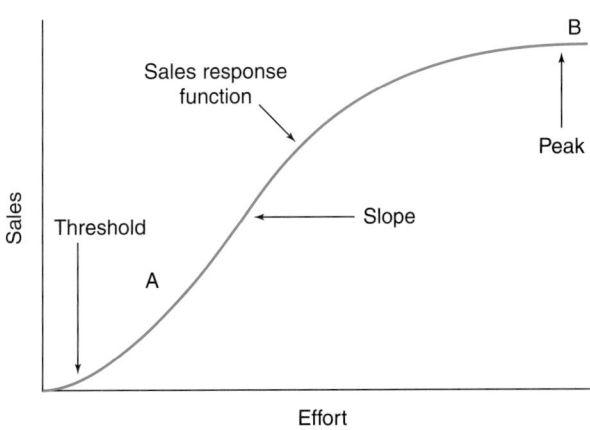

FIGURE 15A.1

Sizing the Sales Force

There are two broad hypotheses: The sales force is too small (perhaps at A) or the sales force is too large (perhaps at B). In the first case, additional salespeople should be added; in the second case, sales force size should be reduced. However, before experimenting, management should be clear about the criteria that would support or reject their hypotheses.

Analytic Methods

The broad analytic attack includes three steps:

- Identify the total number of hours required to sell to customers (A)
- Calculate the number of available selling hours per salesperson (B)
- Secure the required sales force size by dividing A by B

REQUIRED NUMBER OF HOURS   Two broad methods of approach are available—single factor models and portfolio models. In each case, the analytic goal is to identify the amount of selling time required for the sales force to reach its objectives. Once this is determined, sales force sizing becomes a fairly straightforward matter.

Single factor models   In the single factor model (Table 15A.1), customers are classified by value, such as A, B, C, and D accounts. Management identifies the number of customers in each category and judges the average number of hours of selling time needed per annum for accounts in each category. Simple multiplication provides the required number of hours of selling time, and addition across categories provides the total required hours across the entire customer base.

Portfolio models   The rationale for portfolio models is that simple partitioning of customers into a few categories is insufficient to capture the complexity of customers and potential customers. Portfolio models attempt to do this by using multiple dimensions.

TABLE 15A.1   Illustration of a Single Factor Model for Determining Required Selling Time

Account Type	Sales Potential/Sales	Number of Accounts	Hours/Account/ Annum	Required Hours/Annum
A	>$2M	100	100	10,000
B	$250K to $2M	250	50	12,500
C	$10K to $250K	800	12	9,600
D	<$10K	3000	4	12,000
		Total Required Hours/Annum		**44,100**

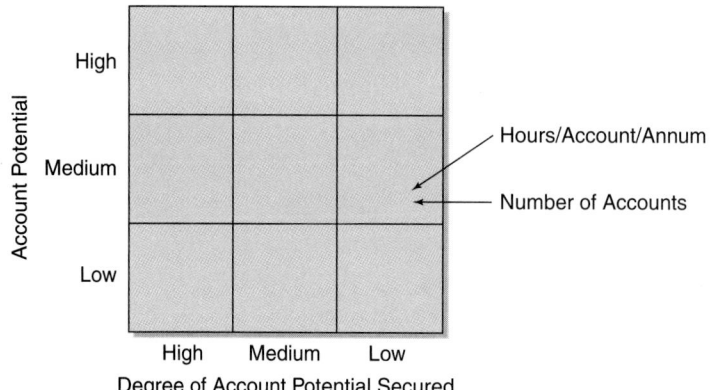

FIGURE 15A.2
Portfolio Model for Determining Required Selling Time

In this example (Figure 15A.2), account potential and degree of account potential secured (or market share at the account) are the two critical factors driving the allocation of selling effort; low, medium, and high levels on each factor are identified. Management identifies the number of customers in each cell and judges the average number of selling hours required per annum for customers in each cell. Multiplication of hours per annum by number of customers provides a total number of required hours per cell. Addition across cells provides the total number of selling hours required, as before.

AVAILABLE NUMBER OF HOURS   The number of available hours per salesperson is developed from an understanding of where salespeople spend their time, typically secured by a sales force audit. Suppose, for example, the following data are derived:

Customer contact time	30%
Administrative time: customer driven (such as follow up on customer issues)	35%
Administrative time: firm driven (such as sales district meetings, product training)	35%
Total	100%

CALCULATION OF SALES FORCE SIZE
We continue with the Table 15A.1 illustration (from this point, the calculation for portfolio models is identical):

- Maximum selling time per annum (hours) = (365 days less 104 [weekends] less 30 [holidays/vacations]) × 10 hours per day   = 2310 hours
- Actual selling time = Maximum selling time × 30% = 2310 × 30% =   693 hours
- Number of salespeople required = Total required hours/actual   = **44,100**/693
  selling time per salesperson (693 hours)   =   64

CHAPTER

16

DISTRIBUTION DECISIONS

LEARNING OBJECTIVES

When you have completed this chapter, you will understand

- the role of distribution channels in the economy
- the nature and function of distribution systems
- power and conflict in distribution systems
- critical elements of a distribution strategy
- trade-offs among alternative forms of direct and indirect distribution
- issues involved in on-going distribution management

INTRODUCTION

Although the focus of this chapter is on the set of distribution decisions made by the firm (micro level), we place these in context by first addressing the role of distribution in the economy as a whole (macro level). From one viewpoint, at least, the subject of distribution is so vast that it subsumes the entire economy. Although we can only scratch the surface, this material paves the way for discussing the nature and functions of distribution systems, and the pervasive characteristics of power and conflict.

The chapter addresses the development of distribution strategy, focusing on the major distribution decisions of distributor type, distribution channel depth and breadth, and questions of exclusivity. The relationship between distribution strategy and market strategy is explored, and the chapter concludes with observations about the ongoing management of distributors. Throughout the chapter, the roles of different distribution intermediaries are explored.

THE ROLE OF DISTRIBUTION CHANNELS IN THE ECONOMY

The products and services purchased by consumers and other end-customers typically derive from some set of raw materials, assemblies or subassemblies that have undergone changes in state, space, and time.[1] In its broadest view, distribution encompasses all of these changes. For example, a builder in Argentina purchases pre-fabricated steel beams to erect a new office tower. Activities that might occur prior to purchase include (Figure 16.1):

- raw materials, such as iron ore, coal, and limestone, were mined in Australia or Brazil, then shipped to an integrated steel manufacturer in Korea or Japan;
- the processing equipment for these raw materials was sourced in the United States or Germany;
- the capital necessary to finance the manufacture was secured from Japanese or Korean citizens through their bank accounts;
- the steel beams were manufactured;
- completed steel beams were shipped to a distributor in Argentina;
- the Argentine distributor completed minor finishing operations then delivered the beams to the building site.

Note that this view of distribution encompasses both a concentration phase and a dispersion phase—concentration of the various inputs in Korea or Japan, then dispersion

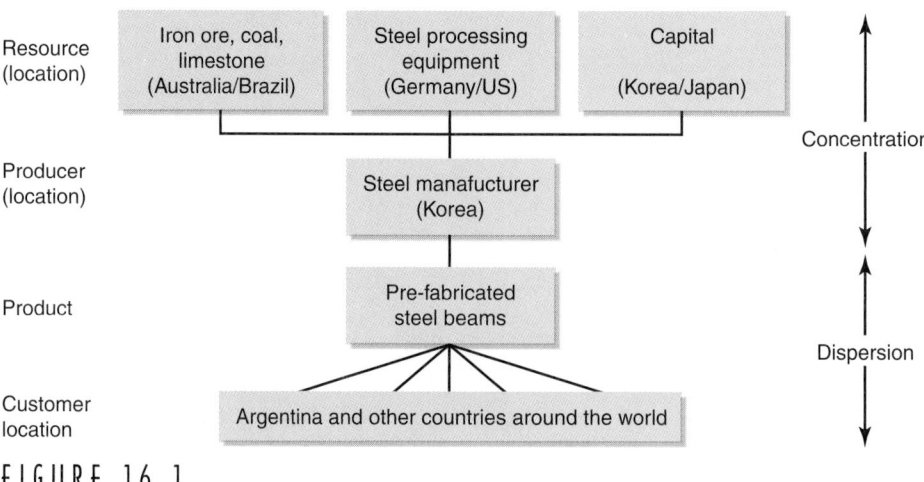

FIGURE 16.1

Illustration of Concentration and Dispersion in Distribution

of pre-fabricated steel beams to Argentina and other countries around the world. This framework also takes a broad, holistic view of distribution as encompassing three major changes: state (iron ore, coal, and limestone into prefabricated steel beams), physical location (Australia/Brazil and United States/Germany to Japan/Korea, then Argentina) and time.[2]

However, most marketers exclude changes of state from their discussion of distribution, preferring to confine the realm of distribution to changes in the time and place location of finished products (such as prefabricated steel beams). However, some state changes, such as final processing and repackaging, may well be conducted within the marketers' view of distribution. Furthermore, from the perspective of the steel manufacturer, securing raw material inputs (iron ore, coal, limestone, and capital equipment) is typically viewed as a matter for procurement; securing capital is a job for finance. Marketing is not involved in either case. Although these exclusions work tolerably well for physical goods, they are somewhat less meaningful for information-based products.

Nonetheless, distribution adds value. Most people readily understand that value is added when a change of state occurs (such as iron ore, coal, and limestone into prefabricated steel beams). The premise that value also resides in the location, in time and space, value added by distribution, is less readily accepted, but no less important.

THE NATURE AND FUNCTIONS OF DISTRIBUTION SYSTEMS

Distribution systems comprise a myriad of relationships between a great variety of enterprises. In many cases, producer and end-customer have a direct relationship and together fulfill many of the required distribution functions. More frequently, a variety of organizational types, including distributors, wholesalers, brokers, agents, manufacturers representatives, warehouse operators, shipping companies, retailers, banks, and finance companies, are involved in distributing a particular good or service to end-customers. Each of these entities fulfills a specific function or set of functions: for example, manufacturers representatives fulfill a selling function, banks and finance companies fulfill a financing function, and distributors may take title, sell, inventory, break bulk, and transport the product.[3]

At any point in time, the distribution network represents the collective view of what is necessary to complete the various distribution functions most effectively. However, although frequently inflexible in the short run, over time, customer needs, competitive action, and various environmental forces (Figure 16.2) place pressure upon the network. This leads to continual revisions in the set of distribution relationships which remain in a state of flux. Generalized indicators that a new approach to distribution may be warranted include unhappy end-customers, unexplored new channels, new technology, gaps in market coverage, deteriorating total system economics, complacent intermediaries, and dated systems interfaces.[4]

- Technological advances in capturing, transferring, and analyzing point-of-sale information, offering significant opportunities for increased efficiencies throughout the supply chain system;
- Greater organizational focus on supply chain management and reduction of working capital;
- The ability to use customer purchase data to gain significant insight into purchasing behavior, resulting in a power shift to retailers;
- Concentration in distribution systems and the emergence of powerful intermediaries;
- Advent of speedy, reliable, and increasingly inexpensive methods of transporting goods globally;
- Growth of direct marketing;
- Growth of purchasing via the Internet that will likely accelerate with broad-band access to the home. The increasing spread of Internet capability is leading to both disintermediation and direct-to-customer relationships, but also to re-intermediation;
- Vastly shortened product build times permitting widespread mass customization and the consequent ability to reduce inventory throughout the system.

FIGURE 16.2

Selected Environment Changes Impacting the Nature of Distribution Systems

Example: In the growth phase of the personal computer industry, retail distribution was essential so that salespeople could explain to potential customers the various technical features of alternative personal computers, and then help them make intelligent choices. By the late 1990s, the industry had evolved to the point that consumers were designing their own computers and placing orders directly with manufacturers. Retail distribution was much less important and successful manufacturers evolved their distribution strategies accordingly.

Just as management should continually assess the impact of environmental change on its current market offerings and scour the environment for new opportunities, so it should assess the impact of current and prospective changes on its existing distribution system. A distribution system that is appropriate for one point in time might be inappropriate for another; indeed, a shift in distribution strategy might offer an important way of securing differential advantage.

However, such changes are typically less easy to make than those involving other marketing mix elements. Price changes, promotion changes, and even product and service changes can typically be made in the near term; by contrast, for many firms, distribution arrangements may have been in place for many years and have a much greater "stickiness" associated with them. For example, the average tenure of Caterpillar's relationships with its 186 dealers worldwide exceeds 50 years![5]

Functions of Distribution

The overarching role of distribution systems for physical goods is to close the gaps in time and space between the manufacturer's finished product, consumers, and other end-customers. The functions must be performed by the supplier, a variety of potential intermediaries, or end-customers:

- **Transfer of title**: Legal ownership of the goods typically shifts from the producer to some other entity. Ultimately, this entity may be the end-customer, or a financing organization that holds title while the customer uses the product. Of course, title may also be transferred between channel intermediaries.
- **Promotion**: Different members of the system may contribute sales, advertising, public relations, and publicity efforts to enhance product movement through the channel.
- **Information provision**: Various types of information, in addition to promotion, flow back and forth among channel entities. These range from data about the customer marketplace, including customer requirements and competitor activities, and operational information concerning the availability and physical location of goods, inventory levels, change in title, state of financing arrangements, and so forth.
- **Physical movement**: The goods must be physically transferred (delivered) from the manufacturing site to the customer.
- **Inventory**: Not only must goods be transported, they may need to be inventoried.
- **Finance**: Once the product is produced, it must be financed until it reaches the customer and, if the customer does not purchase outright, while the customer has physical possession. Collection services may also be required.
- **Service**: Customers often require various types of service and support: pre-sale (product inspection and information about the product and its use), during the sale (help making the decision), and post-sale (installation, repair, maintenance, warranty). In addition, various managerial and consulting services may be required.
- **Quality assurance**: Both the final customer and channel intermediaries must be assured that the product reaches the agreed quality level.
- **Assorting**: Both the end-customer and channel intermediaries may require a variety of products and services to meet their needs. A wholesaler requires multiple products to serve its retailers. Retailers offer multiple products to consumers. This assorting or concentration function reduces customer search cost.
- **Bulk breaking**: Rarely does the final customer require the producer's complete output. Rather, the product volume manufactured must be disaggregated so that the

customer receives only the required amount. Other state changes, such as fitting, sizing, shaping, and finishing, may also be required (such as paint mixing, product assembly).

- **Risk**: Various types of risk may be incurred from product manufacture to customer possession. This risk can be shifted via insurance, warranties, and guarantees. The party assuming risk is an especially critical issue in financial services.
- **Impartiality**: In those situations where the purchase is complex, or where alternatives are difficult to identify or compare, impartiality may be a critical distribution function. The ability to fulfill this function is the *raison d'être* of many brokers, agents, and advisors in such financial services industries as insurance and financial advisory.
- **Buying experience**: Purchasing goods and services is an experience for the buyer. Experiences may range from a quick, easy, and technologically sophisticated purchase via the Internet to battling holiday crowds at a downtown department store on December 24. Increasingly, retailers are seeking to enhance the buying experience for customers.

Example: At the Forum shops in Las Vegas, Atlantis rises and falls on the hour. In Mall of America (Minneapolis, Minnesota) consumers are attracted to the 400 retail stores by Camp Snoopy, an indoor amusement park, and Underwater World, a walk-through aquarium. At Wizards stores, owned by toy manufacturer Hasbro Inc., about one third of the retail space is devoted to a game room.[6]

These functions are general; which specific entity performs each function is a separate question. The term distribution channel encompasses the various organizational entities that inhabit the space between producer and final customer. Furthermore, whereas much academic focus concerns the physical aspects of distribution such as movement, inventory, and transfer of title, these issues may be irrelevant for services (including information products) where promotion is often a major issue.

POWER AND CONFLICT IN DISTRIBUTION SYSTEMS

Distribution systems comprise many organizational entities that enjoy mutually beneficial relationships. Nonetheless, issues of power and conflict abound.

Power in Distribution Systems

Since the power distribution among distribution channel entities is typically asymmetric, the actions of some entities are more constrained than others. Table 16.1 identifies conditions for enhanced power in distribution systems.

The entity with the most power in a distribution system is called the channel captain. Broadly speaking, power may reside with manufacturers/brand owners, intermediaries, including distributor/wholesalers and retailers, or end-customers. When sellers are in a strong power relationship with intermediaries, they can typically impose restrictive conditions on re-sellers; conversely when intermediaries are the strong players, the reverse is true. Over time, power tends to shift from one set of entities to another.[7]

DISTRIBUTORS/WHOLESALERS In the early days of the industrial revolution, distributors/wholesalers were channel captains based on their abilities to link together and provide credit to distant manufacturers and retailers. To a large extent, economic changes and the growth in manufacturer and retailer power has diminished their once powerful role. Nonetheless, intermediaries continue to play a major role in many industries, and innovative positioning can be highly profitable:

Example: In the information technology industry, "value added resellers" (VARs) and "value added distributors" (VADs) combine physical products from several manufacturers and expertise from themselves and other firms to produce enhanced offerings for customers.

TABLE 16.1 Conditions for Enhanced Power in Distribution Systems

Upstream: Suppliers	Downstream: Distributors (End Customers)
demand greater than supply	supply greater than demand
supplier offers products important to the distributor's success	supplier's products unimportant to the distributor's success
supplier enjoys a monopoly-like position:	distributor enjoys a monopsony-like position:
technology is proprietary	products and services undifferentiated
few substitute products available	many suppliers available
few substitute suppliers available	few substitute distributors available
supplier poses a credible threat of forward integration	distributor poses a credible threat of backward integration[8]
distributor has high switching costs	distributor has few switching costs
individual distributors are unimportant to the supplier's success	distributor purchases a large percent of the supplier's output
supplier has extensive contact with end-customers	distributor has considerable end-customer information relative to the supplier

Example: The business insurance industry is dominated by insurance brokers who help identify and analyze corporate business risks, then seek appropriate coverage from insurance companies.

Example: In the United States in the 1980s and early 1990s, mutual funds became popular investment vehicles and their numbers increased significantly. However, a diversified investor had to engage in multiple interactions: multiple calls to purchase/sell individual funds and check fund balances, deposit/receive multiple checks and receive multiple statements. This administrative nightmare was mitigated in the early 1990s when Schwab introduced the *OneSource* account. By fulfilling the assortment function, Schwab allowed investors to conduct all their transactions with a single entity, vastly decreasing the administrative hassle and keeping their funds continuously invested.[9]

In these examples, the intermediary enhances customer value by fulfilling an assortment function. Essentially, the intermediary reduces the number of relationships required of the customer (and the supplier). Rather, each customer and supplier has a relationship with the intermediary.

The emergence of the Internet allows manufacturers to have direct relationships with end-customers and the potential to cut out intermediaries. Paradoxically, those firms enjoying the most success with Internet commerce are not manufacturers but intermediaries.[10]

Examples: Amazon.com offers an enormous selection of books, CDs, drugstore, and other consumer products. Through on-line auctions, both Amazon.com and Ebay link people with things to sell and people who want to buy. Priceline.com brokers sales of airline tickets and hotel rooms.[11]

In each of these examples, the intermediary sits at the concentration/dispersion nexus. The end-customer value they create is reflected in their high stock market valuations. Furthermore, a special feature of these high-traffic sites is the relative ease of adding product lines. Thus Amazon.com started as a bookseller; in early 1999, Dell Computer, the leader in PC sales over the Internet, added 30,000 outside products, including software, printers, and games, to its site.[12]

A special feature of a focus on intermediaries, especially in information products, is that the procurement/marketing model so prevalent when considering physical goods gives way to a marketing/marketing model as the firm essentially addresses different markets requiring different types of marketing expertise.

> **Example:** Investment banks seeking to underwrite securities must market their underwriting abilities to organizations wishing to raise capital. They must also market the securities to institutional and/or individual investors.

MANUFACTURERS/BRAND OWNERS In the early twentieth century, the growth of manufacturing organizations led to a gradual reduction in power of distributors/wholesalers. Combined with increasing brand power, manufacturers' roles were enhanced by their abilities to reduce costs and prices via mass production, and to design and manufacture products to end-customer specifications. Often driven by massive consumer advertising, brand leaders such as Coca-Cola, Pepsi, Kodak, Kellogg's, Budweiser, Gillette, Sony, Frito-Lay, Levi's, and Campbell's secured channel captaincy. Of course, brand owners are not necessarily manufacturers; for example, Nike, Polo, Calvin Klein, and many other brand owners have significant distribution power.

Furthermore, channel captaincy can be earned by manufacturers whose products are merely components of the products purchased by end-customers:

> **Example:** The *Nutrasweet* brand of aspartane artificial sweetener commands widespread distribution strength in soft drinks.[13]

It is the growth in manufacturers' power that has led many marketers to take a narrow view of distribution as focused on moving the manufacturer's finished product from the factory to end-customers.

RETAILERS The most recent trend across many areas of retailing has been the emergence of strong retail chains. For example, in supermarket retailing, enormous concentration has occurred: two chains (Tesco and Sainsbury) dominate the British market, and in the United States, warehouse clubs (such as Price Club, Cosco Wholesale Club, Sam's Wholesale Club) and operators such as Royal Ahold, Kroger, and Safeway, place significant pressure on manufacturers. Retailers like Carrefour (France), Marks and Spencer (GB), K-Mart, Sears, and Wal-Mart (United States) dominate in many areas, and category killers, such as Toys-Я-Us (toys) and Home Depot ("do-it-yourself"), virtually dictate the directions of their industries. In recent years major retail chains, slower than many industries to globalize, have expanded internationally with acquisitions in excess of $65 billion in 1995–1999, as opposed to $26 billion 1990–1994.[14]

These major retailers frequently become price leaders through enhanced buying power, efficient logistics systems, and powerful information technology enabling store offerings to suit local needs. Correspondingly, many manufacturers/brand owners have lost power as competition has emerged from strong retail store brands, and demands for "slotting allowances" to display manufacturers' products have increased.

> **Example:** In the 1995 Christmas season, to enhance its own highly profitable battery sales, Wal-Mart "persuaded" Kodak to stop supplying batteries with its cameras.

END-CUSTOMERS The generalized shift to greater industry concentration discussed in Chapter 2 has led to distribution strength for end-customers in many industries. Oligopsony situations offer great power to those few buyers since specialist industry suppliers simply have few customer options, such as large commercial aircraft (Boeing, Airbus) and passenger tires (Bridgestone, Goodyear, Michelin). As industry concentration increases, end-customers are likely to enjoy ever-greater channel power.

Strategic Conflict in Distribution Systems

At any point in time, a distribution system is best viewed as a set of organizational relationships in a meta-stable equilibrium. The system in place represents the collective organizational view of the most effective way to move products from producer to end-customers. However, as noted earlier, this system is subject to many environmental forces that can presage a realignment of organizational relationships. The realignments that occur are a function of these forces, power inequalities, and strategic conflict.

When organizations are engaged in multiple relationships, the potential for conflict is extremely high. However, a distinction must be drawn between operational conflict and strategic conflict. Operational conflict concerns daily matters, such as late shipments, invoicing errors, unfulfilled salesperson promises, unacceptable product quality, and so forth. While these conflicts are frustrating, annoying, and can lead to relationship disruption, most organizations work to minimize them.

By contrast, strategic conflict can change the nature of relationships among organizational entities in the distribution channel. Imagine a distribution channel comprised of a supplier, distributor, and end-customer (Figure 16.3). Strategic conflict can be initiated by downstream customers (distributors and end-customers), or by upstream supplier firms.

INITIATION BY DOWNSTREAM CUSTOMERS

- **End-customers grow and desire direct-to-supplier relationships**: Many new companies commence business by using distributors to reach customers, especially small end-customers. However, as end-customers grow, they may believe that the value provided by distributors is insufficient to compensate for their margins. These customers can request both a direct relationship with the supplier and lower prices. By acceding to this request, the supplier would abandon a distributor that has developed its business over many years. However, loyalty to the distributor may mean significant revenue loss to competitive suppliers who, without such historic ties, are prepared to deal direct.

  Example: The Norton company achieved market leadership in the grinding wheel industry through strong relationships with industrial distributors. However, whereas it enjoyed strong market share with small end-customers for which the distributors added considerable value, over-time market share with larger customers dropped precipitously as they preferred to deal directly with their grinding wheel suppliers.[15]

- **Distributors become large and change the power balance**: Increased scale through concentration and widespread availability of low-cost information technology providing significant data on end-customers shifts power to intermediaries. They make increasing demands on their suppliers.

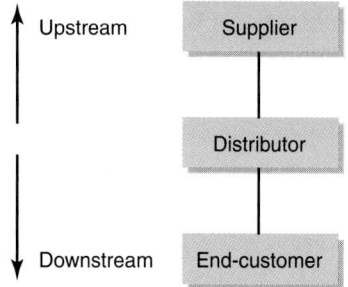

FIGURE 16.3

A Simple Distribution Channel

Example: Historically in the United States, automobile retailing was characterized by many small, single location retailers selling a single brand. Power resided with the major manufacturers—General Motors, Ford, and Chrysler. More recently, "mega-dealers" have emerged selling large volumes of multiple brands at multiple locations, shifting the power balance away from manufacturers.[16]

- **Distributors vertically integrate backwards**: Aggressive, innovative distributors may seek growth by back-integrating into the product supply system, disrupting established relationships.

Example: America's most profitable steel manufacturer, Nucor, was formed when a dissatisfied customer back-integrated into steel manufacture.

- **New buying influences introduced into the distribution channel**: As strong intermediaries develop, smaller intermediaries can be seriously disadvantaged, (particularly in securing attractive prices). New buying groups may develop modeled broadly after the long-standing Independent Grocers Association (IGA) and Tru Value hardware stores. These groups gain significant bargaining power and allow smaller distributors to compete on a more equal footing with their much larger rivals.

INITIATION BY UPSTREAM SUPPLIERS

- **To reach end users more efficiently, the supplier goes direct**: Such action leads to conflict with existing distributors.

Example: When Bass Ale piloted a home delivery service in Britain, cash-and-carry warehouses and convenience stores feared they would lose business. Nurdin and Peacock, a leading cash-and-carry operator, withdrew several Bass beers and encouraged customers to avoid Bass products. Bass abandoned the pilot.[17]

Furthermore, the increasingly widespread availability of the Internet has led many suppliers to face this potential conflict. If they refuse to sell direct over the Internet, they may miss out on a fast-growing distribution channel[18]; if they sell over the Internet, they risk the wrath of current distributors. In some cases, these potentially upset distributors are the firm's own employees.

Example: In the late 1990s, Merrill Lynch, the leading stockbroker in the United States, and many insurance companies, seemed paralyzed by the growth of the Internet. Although such firms as Schwab and E-trade provided on-line trading, and Quickquote and others offered term life insurance, many firms with large broker and agent forces made no significant move to offer products through this distribution system. By early 1999, Schwab's market value exceeded that of Merrill Lynch. Finally, in early 2000, Merrill Lynch began offering on-line brokerage services.

On the other hand, a limited direct strategy can offer considerable benefits to both the supplier and channel intermediary. For example, Nike's NikeTown flagship stores enhance brand awareness and prestige, and are now accepted by its athletics store distributors.[19]

- **To better penetrate the market, new types of distributors are added**: The supplier may add a new type of distributor to address what it perceives as a new market segment. The current distributor may view this addition as threatening.

Example: Hill's Science Diet pet food lost considerable support in pet shops and feed stores when it experimented with a "store within a store" pet shop concept in the competing grocery channel.[20]

Strategic Conflict and Power in Distribution Systems

The supplier should be concerned with the impact on the downstream customer of any strategic conflict that it might initiate, just as the downstream customer should be concerned with the impact on the supplier of strategic conflict that it might initiate.

In particular, each should be clear about the other's options, for although the impact may be severe, the entity's options may be limited.

> **Example:** In the example noted above, Norton saw significant market share erosion from large customers that dealt direct with competitive suppliers. Ultimately, Norton decided to sell direct even though it knew this action would severely affect some of its long-time distributors. However, in the absence of viable supply alternatives, Norton's distributors remained loyal.

> **Example:** In early 1999, Delta imposed a surcharge on any ticket not bought off its Web site, an announcement widely interpreted as increasing the pressure on travel agents whose commissions had already been cut.[21]

Regardless of the potential source of strategic conflict, in general, either party is better off if it improves its power position. A series of options for upstream suppliers (Table 16.2) and downstream customers (Table 16.3) is provided. Not only is enhanced power likely to reduce the probability of strategic conflict engendered by another entity, but should such conflict occur, the entity with more power will be better placed to respond.

A different option for the entity initiating strategic conflict is to mitigate the problem as viewed by the other. This situation occurs frequently when a currently important channel is in decline and the supplier wants to invest in its replacement.

> **Example:** When Goodyear began distributing through mass merchandisers, it kept independent dealers happy by introducing programs to drive share growth for replacement tires.[22]

TABLE 16.2 Illustrative Actions to Improve Supplier Power

Type of Action	Examples
Improve bargaining power	integrate disparate product lines[23]
Become central to the distributor's success	strongly support current products, especially in market downturns where such support may provide differentiation from competition
	develop value-added services, both directly and non-directly related to its own products
	innovate new products and, perhaps more importantly
	develop expectations of continuous innovation such that strong supplier relationships assure the distributor of early access to these innovations
Raise the distributor's switching costs	offer benefits to concentrate purchases with the supplier[24]
	develop customized products needing customized equipment and specialized training
	develop dedicated on-line access for simplified order placing and information provision
	increase the number of contact points within the distributor
	work to improve the firm's reputation by enhancing the quality of its relationships
	work to secure end user/testing agency qualification by brand rather than by the generic product
Broaden the scope of the supplier's options	develop an information base of, and demand preference from, end users
	broaden the distribution base
	both explore limited forward integration and demonstrate the folly of backward integration.[25]

TABLE 16.3 Illustrative Actions to Improve Distributor Power

Type of Action	Examples
Improve bargaining power	centralize purchasing operations
Action at end-customers	add value to end-customers
	build loyalty with end-customers
	introduce additional services
	consider branding service packages
Action with suppliers	persuade supplier to outsource activities to the distributor
	work to minimize supplier's costs
	increase number of contact points with supplier
Broaden the scope of the distributor's options	secure additional suppliers
	explore limited backward integration
	demonstrate disadvantages of forward integration

The Partnership Model

An increasingly popular alternative to the power/strategic conflict approach to distribution channel management is the partnership model. In this framework, significant cooperation and trust among various distribution channel entities enables all parties to benefit. In economic terms, this is a positive sum game.[26]

Partnerships in distribution frequently involve attempts to re-engineer the logistics system via supply chain management.[27] The thrust of re-engineering logistics systems is reduction of inventory from raw material in the supplier's factory to finished goods inventory on retail shelves, including both work-in-process and finished goods at the supplier firm, and product in transit and in warehouses. Simultaneously, stockouts should be reduced. The nature of the problem has been repeatedly demonstrated in simulations using "the beer game."[28]

The prototypical distribution partnership is between Procter & Gamble (P&G) and Wal-Mart.

Example: State-of-the-art information systems capture point-of-sale data for P&G products at Wal-Mart stores and are transmitted to P&G in real time. This data is combined with historic seasonal trends to improve manufacturing, purchasing, and packaging efficiencies to reduce internal inventory and cut costs. To reduce the volume of finished goods in transit, P&G products, coded by store destination, are placed directly onto Wal-Mart trucks at warehouse interchange points (cross-docking); full trucks leave at frequent intervals for store-to-store delivery. Thus once the product leaves the factory, the only inventory is on the supplier firm's truck, the retailer's store delivery truck, or on the retail shelves.[29] Additional partnering elements include paperless systems for receiving goods and managing accounts receivable and accounts payable.[30]

A second example of process re-engineering concerns Federated Department Stores:

Example: The traditional practice in garment distribution involved the following steps:

At the manufacturer: produce the garment, add a hang tag, press the garment, place the garment on a wire hanger, put polyethylene over the garment, put several garments in a box, and ship the box to a Federated facility.

At Federated: remove the garment from the box; remove the polyethylene, throw out the trash hanger, put the garment on a floor-ready hanger, put the garment in

TABLE 16.4 Source of Savings in the Food Industry

Cost item	Historic cost	Type of savings	New cost	Cost saving
Raw materials, manufacturing, packaging	43 cents	Smooth production planning: production facilities, purchasing, packaging	41 cents	2 cents
Marketing, selling, logistics, distribution, administration	27 cents	Re-engineer: logistics, transportation, warehousing, purchasing	22 cents	5 cents
Store operating expense	18 cents	More inventory turns, more space productivity, purchasing savings	16 cents	2 cents
Operating margin	12 cents	Lower fixed assets, lower inventory	10 cents	2 cents
			Total savings:	11 cents

new polyethylene, add a price tag, place the garment in a shipping container, ship to a Federated store. This activity took on average 20 minutes per box.

By providing garment manufacturers with floor-ready hangers and bar coding each item, Federated was able to streamline the process significantly from a 4.5-day post-production average to 2.5 days.

The major benefit from partnerships is a shift from the more typical adversarial relationship between supplier and distributor toward arrangements looking for win-win solutions. Thus better demand information allows retailers to offer more efficient store assortments and conduct more efficient promotion, leading to fewer sales at reduced prices. In addition, retailers receive value-added services from suppliers by off-loading the inventory control function. Suppliers gain from lower manufacturing and distribution costs and more effective use of promotional funds. Many firms are now acting under the rubric, "If it isn't moving, it isn't adding value," a radically different view from the more common approach that places finished goods in the warehouse and waits for customers to purchase.[31]

Industry-wide supply chain initiatives have emerged in several industries, in part in the face of competition from such dominant retailers as Wal-Mart, for example, Quick Response and Efficient Consumer Response in the textile and food industries respectively.[32] In the dry grocery goods area of the food industry, an estimated $10 billion has been saved on annual retail sales of $90 billion (11%) (Table 16.4).

DEVELOPING DISTRIBUTION STRATEGY

In the traditional perspective taken by marketers, the supplier is faced with the challenge of ensuring that its product/service reaches end-customers in the most effective manner. The particular method or methods employed must be consistent with the firm's market strategy and follow from a sensible consideration of the available channel options.

Suppliers' strategic decisions revolve around the key issues of distributor type, distribution channel depth and breadth, and exclusivity:

- Choice of distributor type concerns distributor characteristics, in particular the nature of their relationships with customers;
- Distribution channel depth concerns the number of intermediaries between the supplier and end-customer;
- Distribution channel breadth concerns the number of distribution entities at a particular level in the distribution system;
- Various types of exclusivity options are available for both intermediaries and suppliers.

Distributor Type

The selection of distributor type is closely related to the supplier's market strategy. It should select the distributor type most appropriate for the target market segment.[33] End-customers typically have preferences regarding the outlets through which they want to purchase products and services; these preferences should play a major role in selecting distributor types. For example, consumers do not expect to purchase bicycles in automobile dealerships, nor high fashion clothing in drug stores. Notwithstanding this caution, innovative selection of distribution outlets may be the route to securing differential advantage so long as the distribution type decision is informed by a well-thought through market segmentation and targeting process.

Example: The credit card industry is characterized by many participants addressing consumers via direct marketing. However, perhaps the most successful issuer, MBNA, has eschewed this approach in favor of seeking cardholders through intermediaries, various affinity groups such as Columbia University alumnae and Vietnam Veterans.

Furthermore, if the supplier wants to address two or more segments with essentially similar products, then it may be appropriate to use two different distribution systems.

Example: In the Pacific Northwest, similar products are sold to the marine industry through marine-supply distributors and to the forest-products industry through forest-products distributors. In each case, distributors carry many industry specific products and speak the language of their industries.

Example: Honda's initial entry into the U.S. automobile industry was with compact and subcompact cars, the Accord and Civic. An important element in its success was the development of a well-managed distribution system. However, when it came to introducing the higher priced Acura brand, aimed at a more upscale market segment, rather than leveraging its in-place distribution system, Honda developed a totally separate set of distributors.

Distribution Channel Depth

This section addresses direct and indirect options for reaching consumers, then discusses reaching organizational customers. The many supplier options for reaching consumers are displayed in Figure 16.4. The complexity of functions that must be performed leads, in practice, to a myriad of potential channel designs. Nonetheless, a critical distinction can be made between channel structures in which the major contact with end-customers is conducted by the supplier (direct), and those where one or more third-party organizations plays a major role (indirect).

REACHING CONSUMERS: DIRECT CHANNELS In direct channel designs, where the firm has significant direct contact with end-use customers, several models have had significant success and can be found in different sectors of the economies of various countries. In each case, direct methods combined with consumer database marketing skills offer powerful alternatives to indirect methods. Direct distribution has several forms:

- **Direct sales—face-to-face**: Salespeople sell (and deliver) products directly to customers on a face-to-face basis. The major advantage is direct customer contact leading to more intimate insight and knowledge of customer problems and unmet needs. Although the unfavorable economics of direct selling and distribution mitigate against its use for consumer goods in advanced economies, cosmetic firms Avon and Mary Kay, and Tupperware have built successful global businesses on this model.[34] Even automobiles and personal computers are sold in this manner.

Example: In Japan, salespeople traditionally visit consumers in an effort to sell automobiles. In the United States, Korean manufacturer Daewoo is recruiting U.S. college students to sell cars on commission to fellow students. In Britain,

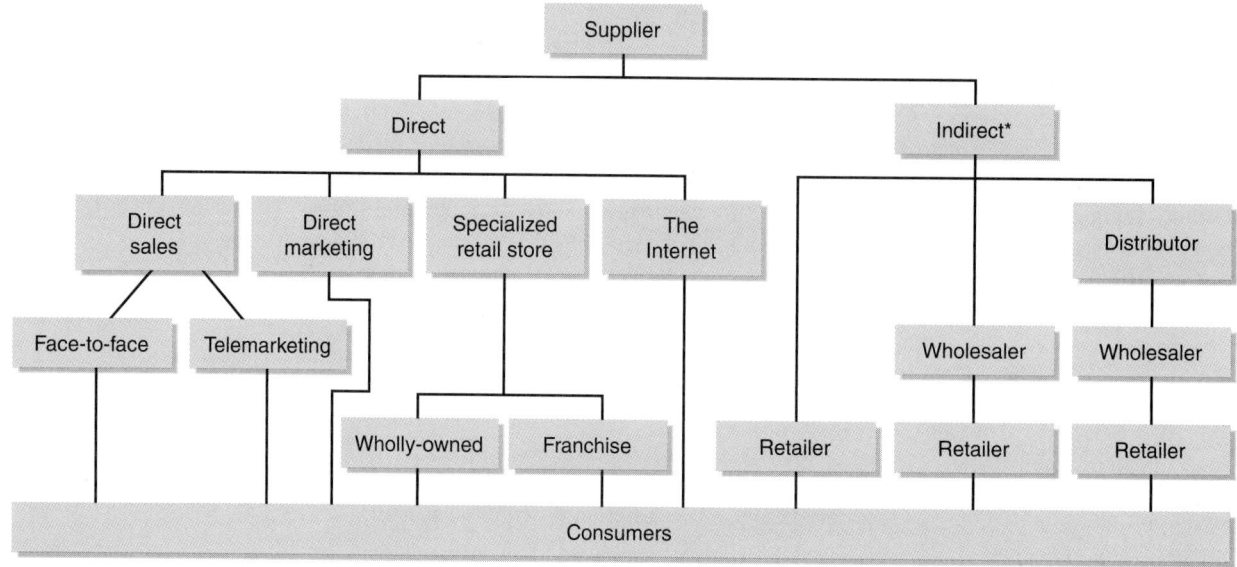

FIGURE 16.4

Reaching Consumers: Supplier Distribution Options (many simple and complex arrangements included)

Malaysian-based Proton is supplementing its car showroom strategy with relationship managers who visit current and potential customers at their homes with demonstration vehicles.[35] In the United States, Handtech.com sells personal computers through technology consultants who target friends, neighbors, and small businesses.[36]

In less-developed countries where incomes are much lower, direct distribution via personal selling may be more viable. For example, when Citibank launched its credit card in India, direct face-to-face sales was one of its more successful channels.[37]

- **Direct sales—telemarketing**: This variant of direct sales occurs when selling activity is conducted by telephone rather than by face-to-face salespeople. The growth of telemarketing, both outbound and inbound, is closely related to the effectiveness, yet high cost, of face-to-face selling. Major advantages are lower costs and, when managed from a central location, greater corporate control.
- **Direct marketing**: Impersonal communication is mostly sent from the firm to current and potential customers (outbound) by mail; products are delivered directly by a package delivery service from a remote location. In high-level economies, direct marketing growth (at the expense of local intermediaries) has been driven by low postal rates, ubiquitous credit card possession, and advances in telecommunications and computer technology. Leading firms, mostly wholesale goods suppliers such as Lillian Vernon, Lands' End, and L.L. Bean, develop demographic and product preference databases on customers and engage in data mining activities to fine-tune product development, assortments, and communications programs.
- **Specialized retail distribution**: Suppliers secure similar benefits to the direct face-to-face model with the additional advantage of full product display and inventory held close to the customer. In recent years, quality clothing firms and others have adopted this approach, often supplemented by factory outlet stores located in dedicated malls. U.S. firms using this approach for finished goods have been Sherwin Williams (paint), AT&T (telephone hardware), and IBM (personal computers).

Perhaps more common examples of specialized retail distribution are those where the firm's product offering undergoes a state change at the retail outlet. Common examples in the fast food industry include McDonalds, Kentucky Fried Chicken, Taco Bell, and Starbucks.[38]

This approach comes in two major versions, wholly owned and franchised. For the supplier, wholly owned retail distribution has the advantage of operational control and securing the entire retail margin, at the cost of significant investment and the risk of cash flow problems in the expansion phase. Franchising has the advantage of leveraging the firm's financial resources for faster growth and benefiting from franchisees' entrepreneurial drive. Frequently, firms employing specialized retail distribution have philosophies that support either ownership or franchising. However, many firms employ franchising for growth, and then purchase successful franchises. Alternatively, they use both methods, learning from the one to improve the other. Other examples of franchises include H&R Block (tax preparation), Kampgrounds of America (KOA) (campgrounds) and 7-11 (convenience stores). Although automobile firms in the United States have traditionally distributed their products through franchised dealerships, Ford purchased its franchises in Salt Lake City to develop the first Ford Superstore offering all the firm's brands—Ford, Lincoln, Mercury, Mazda, and Jaguar.[39]

Power and control are often important issues in franchising; some franchisers limit the number of outlets an individual franchisee may own in an attempt to maintain control. Unless managed appropriately, franchisee groups may place significant pressure on franchisers, especially in areas such as new products and advertising levies.

- **The Internet**: The fastest growing method of direct distribution, the Internet, shares credit card purchase, product delivery technology, and development of customer databases with direct marketing. However, direct marketing relies on outbound communications with customers where Internet sales result from affirmative action by customers to access the supplier's Internet site (inbound).

Although the Internet has the capability to "cut out" wholesale and retail intermediaries (disintermediation) in the physical world and spur direct supplier/end-customer relationships, in the corresponding information world, reduction of customers' search costs via the assorting/concentration function fulfilled by such portal sites as Yahoo!, AltaVista, and Excite and intermediaries such as amazon.com, ebay and Schwab is critical. One might argue that the potential for disintermediation in physical goods only occurs via effective assortment of information. Indeed, the high capital market valuations of Internet companies managing these sites underline the information value they provide to customers.

REACHING CONSUMERS: INDIRECT CHANNELS   Most consumer goods manufacturers distribute their products through indirect channels such as wholesalers and retailers. These options arise because some independent organizational entity/entities is either able to offer customers value added over and above the firm's independent efforts, or to fulfill one or more distribution functions at lower cost.

- **Customer value added**: Intermediaries may offer customers a variety of value-added benefits. For example, distributors, wholesalers, and retailers, including specialty stores, department stores, warehouse outlets, and "category killers," fulfill a critical assortment function by reducing customers' search costs. In IBM's Authorized Assembly Program, bare bones systems were shipped to distributors who agreed to use only IBM original parts. The distributors were more responsive to demand, and product quality improved. Intermediaries can also add value by the assurance that their brand equity provides the firm's product, such as Neiman-Marcus (United States) and Harrods (United Kingdom).

Of course, supplier success and brand equity growth may lead to reduced dependence on the intermediary's brand equity, possibly leading it to use alternative intermediaries.

- **Cost reduction**: Intermediaries have many ways to reduce the cost of fulfilling the various distribution functions. For example, market knowledge and customer relationships may provide market access benefits that otherwise would be extremely expensive or impossible for suppliers to secure. This issue is particularly critical in foreign environments where many direct entries founder on the rocks of inadequate market knowledge and insensitivity to local cultures and customers.

  By concentrating products from many manufacturers, intermediaries can achieve significant economies of scale. Agents, manufacturers' representatives, and brokers achieve economies in selling; package delivery and transportation companies achieve transportation economies; independent warehouses achieve inventory economies; banks and other financial institutions achieve economies in financing. Wholesalers and retailers can achieve economies in multiple functions, such as inventory, sales, and transportation. However, suppliers dealing with independent distributors may incur significant transaction costs embracing information collection, bargaining, adjusting agreements, and monitoring performance that are more expensive than if conducted in-house.[40]

Evolutionary changes in distribution typically occur when some organizational entity is able to improve the value added/cost trade-off. However, the nature of organizational relationships may lead to frictions within the distribution system such that higher value/lower cost options may be adopted only with some time delay. As noted above, although e-commerce allows manufacturers to secure inexpensive access to end-customers, many suppliers have been slow to sell over the Internet for fear of upsetting long-standing distribution relationships.

When using independent intermediaries, issues of power and control typically loom large. The more suppliers believe that the conditions of ultimate sale are important to its success, the more they attempt to influence the presentation, sales, and service of their products. The underlying problem for suppliers in many countries is that once title passes from manufacturer to intermediary, control is lost and the intermediary may make its own decisions with its products. Major brand name manufacturers, such as Levi's and Nike, are noteworthy for their efforts regarding this issue, sometimes taking legal action designed to protect their brand equity.

Although still found in some jurisdictions, manufacturers' power has been reduced in many countries by the abolition of resale price maintenance (RPM). Under RPM, the manufacturer was legally allowed to set the retail price of its products, thus giving it significant influence in the retail market place. Although many manufacturers have resorted to recommended retail prices where RPM is outlawed, these "recommendations" do not have the force of law.

A related problem for firms selling through distribution is keeping in touch with customer needs. All too frequently suppliers become disconnected from the market and lose touch with end-customers. There are several ways to address this issue. For example, the supplier can employ a sales or marketing force whose responsibilities focus on addressing end-customer needs and end-customer development. When sales opportunities arise, these are passed onto the relevant distributor. Alternatively, some suppliers own a token number of distributors.

REACHING ORGANIZATIONAL CUSTOMERS   Although the types of channel options available to firms selling to organizations are similar to those just discussed, the extent to which the various options are observed is very different. For example, relatively few suppliers operate specialized retail stores targeted at organizational customers, although many component suppliers do reach small businesses through retail stores or analogous outlets, often via independent distributors and wholesalers.

Compared to consumer products, many more suppliers sell to organizations via direct on-the-road sales forces, then ship products directly or through independent trucking firms. However, many suppliers use various types of industrial distributors to reach their targeted end-customers. Although suppliers should make their distribution decisions based on customer value added and low cost, the few simple rules in Table 16.5 can help identify products likely to be suitable for independent distributor distribution.[41]

However, these traditional discriminators between direct- and distributor-based distribution systems are coming under pressure from a combination of Internet purchases and efficient package delivery services that may improve the economics of direct distribution. As a result, forward-thinking industrial distributors are seeking to improve the value they offer end-customers.

Example: Marshall Industries, a $1.2 billion distributor of electronics components and systems for major manufacturers, traditionally served 30,000 retail customers through 37 sales offices. In the mid-1990s, Marshall opened an Internet channel that allowed customers to search its catalogue, place orders, and arrange shipments. Not only were customers able to check prices and inventory, they could also link directly to the manufacturers, potentially cutting out Marshall. However, Marshall changed its value proposition by offering product selection, configuration, and post-sales service including on-line seminars, video- and audio-training programs, a 24-hour "help" chat room, and a collaborative design lab. Although a risky move, Marshall believed that it was better to be a major player in a new distribution channel than focus on the past.[42]

Recent advances in working through industrial distributors relate to the key distributor function of providing the required product assortment to end-customers in a timely manner. The problem is that, although a large portion of product demand placed on distributors may be predictable, some product demand is unpredictable. Since holding sufficient inventory to satisfy both predictable and unpredictable demand is enormously expensive, distributors are frequently unable to provide customers with the products they need, when they need them.

To address this problem, suppliers are developing innovative solutions, for example, by setting up special warehouse systems.

Example: Volvo GM Heavy Truck Corporation sells commercial trucks and parts through regional warehouses and commercial truck dealers. In the mid-1990s, even though overall inventory levels were rising, dealers reported increasing stockouts. Volvo GM worked with FedEx Logistics to set up a warehouse in Memphis, Tennessee (FedEx' hub). Now, in response to a toll-free phone call, parts for emergency repair are shipped out immediately and can be picked up at the airport,

TABLE 16.5 Direct Supplier to End-customer Relationships or Industrial Distributors

Factors favoring direct supplier to end-customer relationships	Factors favoring use of industrial distributors
Small potential customer base	Large potential customer base
Custom-tailored products	Stockable items, manufactured in large quantities but sold in small quantities
Large quantity sales	Small quantity sales
Complex end-customer purchasing decision involving multiple functions and high-level executives	Simple end-customer purchasing decision, often by low-level purchasing agents
Delivery speed not critical	Rapid delivery and service

delivered to dealer offices, or even dropped off at the required site. Volvo's total inventory has been reduced by 15%, three warehouses were closed, and business lost by dealers to competitive part suppliers has been reduced significantly.[43]

An alternative approach is to develop systems that link together the inventories held by the supplier's distributors and allow products to move from one distributor to another.

Example: Okuma America, a machine tool builder, requires each of its 46 distributors to carry a minimal number of machine tools and selected repair parts in inventory. If a distributor receives an order for an out-of-stock item, it contacts Okumalink, a shared information technology system that keeps distributors informed about the location and availability of parts in Okuma warehouses. If the item is not available, the distributor can contact other distributors on-line to find the closest location and arrange for delivery direct to the customer's location.[44]

In other cases, distributors have formed alliances with other organizations in an effort to satisfy end-customer requirements, even those that fall outside the distributor's traditional assortment.

Example: Grainger Integrated Supply Operations (GISO) draws on three sources to serve the requirements of its end-customers: its traditional distribution business, a series of best-in-class specialty distributors that agree to provide complementary products,[45] and an internal sourcing group that scours the world to satisfy requests for unusual products and services.[46]

Making these new systems work requires a degree of interorganizational trust that is unusual for independently-minded distributors. Such trust requires equitable compensation arrangements that may need to be quite innovative.

Distribution Channel Breadth

Breadth of distribution is concerned with the number of entities at a particular level in the distribution system. Typically, marketers focus on retail distribution and concern themselves with the number of outlets at which products are made available to consumers. However, the breadth decision is important at all levels in the distribution system.

Example: Despite Dell's success pioneering a direct distribution channel for personal computers, market leader Compaq was seemingly locked into a distribution system involving multiple intermediaries.[47] In early 1999, Compaq CEO Pfeiffer was fired and acting CEO Rosen struggled to resolve Compaq's distribution problems. In May 1999, Compaq decided to shift its efforts from 40 distributors to four of its largest wholesalers. In addition, several leading distributors were able to co-locate assembly plants next to Compaq's manufacturing plants.[48]

Distribution breadth is typically conceptualized as being anchored by intensive and exclusive distribution; selective distribution represents an intermediate level of distribution breadth.

- **Intensive distribution**: When end-customers are unwilling to engage in search, the supplier attempts to have its products as widely distributed as possible, and stresses the goal of maximizing the number of outlets. Examples of products for which intensive distribution is sought include convenience goods such as soft drinks, cigarettes, and chewing gum.
- **Exclusive distribution**: The supplier is exceptionally careful in its selection of outlets, believing that the brand equity of the retailer transfers to its products; as a result, relatively few outlets are chosen. Examples of goods distributed exclusively include fine china and crystal, for which only high-class department stores such as Sachs Fifth Avenue, and specialty stores such as Tiffany's may be deemed appropriate. The supplier believes that the overall customer value offered is sufficient to compensate for consumers' search and travel costs.

- **Selective distribution**: At this midway point between intensive and exclusive distribution, the supplier applies a set of criteria to choose acceptable outlets, but is less restrictive than for exclusive distribution. An important issue concerns the density of retail stores that offer the supplier's product. A critical trade-off is between ready product availability for consumers, implying high retail density, and the absence of destructive competition among retail outlets, implying low density.[49]

The intensive, selective, or exclusive distribution decision should flow directly from the market strategy, more specifically from the choice of target market segment. The goal of distribution is not just to make the product available to target customers, for choice of distribution arrangements can also have significant impact on positioning.

Issues in Distribution Exclusivity

Three exclusivity issues are discussed—geographic exclusivity for distributors, product-line exclusivity for distributors, and exclusivity for the supplier.

GEOGRAPHIC EXCLUSIVITY FOR DISTRIBUTORS   A critical decision in developing a set of distribution intermediaries is whether or not to confer geographic exclusivity on individual distributors as, within limits, most manufacturers are able to enforce such restrictions. From the supplier's perspective, exclusivity provides distributors with a form of monopoly in their territories that can encourage investment in territory development.

> **Example:** J.E. Ekornes, a Norwegian furniture manufacturer distributing its products in France through 450 furniture dealers, believed over-distribution led to less than optimal dealer effort. In the mid-1990s, Ekornes cut its dealers to 150, gave them exclusive territories, and changed its salesperson compensation from commission to salary plus bonus based on level of retailer service. Dealers increased local advertising and dropped competing lines. Sales increased threefold.[50]

Conversely, monopoly can make exclusive distributors less than optimally aggressive in seeking business.

> **Example:** In early 1999, faced with declining market share, Canon USA removed geographic restrictions on its distributors in an effort to free up its strongest dealers to compete against Xerox.[51]

PRODUCT-LINE EXCLUSIVITY FOR DISTRIBUTORS   This dimension of exclusivity concerns products distributed through various channel systems. To reduce conflict among intermediaries, suppliers may consider offering different brands through different channel systems.

> **Example:** Black & Decker offers three different product ranges and brands for three different channels: Black & Decker through K-Mart and similar outlets, Quantum for serious enthusiasts at Home Depot, and DeWalt for professional contractors/builders through trade dealers.

EXCLUSIVITY FOR THE SUPPLIER   This dimension concerns the extent to which the supplier insists on exclusivity from its intermediaries. Three situations can be identified:

- The intermediary carries whatever products it wants, including products that compete with the supplier;
- The intermediary agrees it will not carry products that compete with the supplier;
- The intermediary agrees to carry only the supplier's products (exclusivity).

In most cases, suppliers would prefer that intermediaries not carry competing products. Such a position is infeasible for most retail distribution, but is frequently observed for channel intermediaries whose major function is sales and promotion. In those cases where strong supplier/intermediary partnership relationships exist, total exclusivity can be found. For example, many soft drink bottlers work with a single syrup producer and, increasingly, Coca-Cola and Pepsi are signing sole-source agreements with restaurant chains (such as

McDonalds with Coca-Cola) and several school districts. However, firms must be careful that their actions are not deemed anticompetitive:

> **Example:** On July 21, 1999, European Commission officials seized internal documents in dawn raids on Coca-Cola offices across Europe.[52] Shortly afterwards, a report by Italy's competition authority emerged alleging that Coca-Cola had designed a complicated system of exclusivity bonuses and discounts designed to "oust . . . Pepsi from the market." In addition, Coke was alleged to be offering rebates and volume discounts to retailers only if they regularly increased the shelf space for Coke products, and displayed in-store promotions and special offers.[53]

ILLUSTRATION OF DISTRIBUTION ARRANGEMENTS

Consider a small, U.S.-based candy manufacturer whose market strategy is developed on the basis of the domestic consumer middle market whose members purchase candy in retail stores. This firm does not use any form of direct distribution. It knows that not only do supermarkets and other retail stores offer consumers significant assortment benefits, selling, transportation, inventory, and financing are conducted much more cost efficiently by channel intermediaries.[54]

The candy manufacturer broadens its market strategy by targeting additional market segments. In addition to the domestic consumer middle market, it decides to address both major industrial corporations (for employee consumption) domestically and the Latin American market. As an illustration, it might employ the following distribution arrangements:

- **Consumer middle market (domestic)**: The firm reaches these customers through intermediaries. Consumers purchase candy from two major types of retail distribution—supermarkets and small stores. Supermarkets can be identified as majors—regional and national supermarket chains—others are identified as small regionals and locals.

   For major chains, the supplier's sales force sells directly; customer warehouses are supplied directly from the firm's own warehouse via third-party truckers. Accounts receivable, created by customer receipt of goods, are sold at a discount to a factoring organization.

   Small regional and local supermarket chains are reached through food brokers. Customer warehouses are served from geographically dispersed, independently owned warehouses supplied direct from the supplier's warehouse via third-party truckers. Financing is handled similarly to large chains.

   To reach small stores, the supplier uses a national distribution organization. This distributor purchases directly from the firm; the firm delivers product to the distributor's main warehouse in its own trucks and holds the accounts receivable until payment. The distributor makes its own arrangements to secure retail distribution.

- **Major corporations (domestic)**: The firm's sales force sells directly to corporate purchasing departments. For each customer, finished product is shipped to its various locations from geographically dispersed, independently owned warehouses supplied direct from the supplier's warehouse via third-party truckers, as for small regional and local supermarket chains. Similarly for financing, accounts receivable are sold at a discount to a factoring organization.

- **Latin American market**: The firm relies on an export agent with good contacts in various Latin American countries. The agent secures orders from local distributors that identify appropriate retail outlets and undertake various distribution functions in their own countries. The firm receives payment by letter of credit; its terms are f.o.b. the warehouse.[55] The export agent makes all administrative arrangements for a percent commission.

TABLE 16.6 A Step-by-Step Approach to Developing and Implementing Distribution Strategy

Step Number	Step Definition
1	Identify end-customer segments: should flow directly from the market strategy
2	Identify and prioritize segment requirements regarding channel functions: for example, type of assortment, applications engineering, credit terms based on data from key customers, and supplier executives
3	Benchmark supplier's and competitors' current channel capabilities and compare with customer requirements for each segment
4	A creative process to identify feasible channel options for each segment, fully considering switching costs and potential channel conflicts
5	Systematically evaluate the benefits and costs associated with each channel option for each market segment
6	Elaborate channel overlaps for multiproduct, multimarket businesses and make serious choices regarding all end-customer segments
7	Appoint a sufficient number of distributors to secure market coverage, yet minimize destructive distributor competition (distributor breadth decision)
8	Clearly assign distributor territories

This hypothetical illustration provides some insight into the complexity of distribution arrangements. If a small candy company's distribution is as complex as that described, companies with more extensive product lines targeted at greater numbers of market segments certainly have more complex arrangements.

A step-by-step method for developing distribution strategy is shown in Table 16.6.[56]

ONGOING DISTRIBUTION MANAGEMENT

It is one thing for the supplier to develop an appropriate distribution strategy, it is quite another to ensure that channel intermediaries behave in a manner that implements the strategy. Suppliers report a variety of common problems in dealing with these entities (including distributors, retailers, and other intermediaries (Table 16.7).

Other important concerns with intermediaries, especially distributors, are that:

- they are very independent
- they have inadequate succession plans
- they have too many resellers that compete with each other
- their objectives differ from the supplier's
- they compete with each other

Not every supplier faces each problem with a particular intermediary, but an accumulation of these problems can cause a supplier to reconsider its distribution strategy and, perhaps, choose to serve end-customers directly. Such a decision should not be made lightly, but if made, should be well planned to avoid negative consequences from unhappy former intermediaries. In particular, the supplier should first develop direct supplier-to-end-customer contact, possibly via a technical support force, then engage in limited direct distribution before moving entirely to direct distribution. The most recent thinking suggests that the best approach is to set up the alternative system independent of current distribution practice. The new system should have its own management, managerial practices, and incentives, possibly with a separate ownership structure that provides the firm significant options that can be exercised if the new approach is successful.

TABLE 16.7 Operating Problems with Resellers

Can't, or won't, meet supplier, set goals	Are overloaded with products from competing and non-competing suppliers
Carry insufficient inventory to serve customers rapidly	Do not allow supplier contact with the distributor's sales force
Are inadequately financed	Make ineffective use of the supplier's territory managers
Get very close to end-customers, will not provide end-customer data to the supplier	Do not use the supplier's promotional materials
Require fixed payments to carry the supplier's products	Primarily sell on price, not on value
"Cherry-pick" the supplier's product line	Do not follow the supplier's suggested pricing
Put insufficient effort with end-customers targeted by the supplier	Do not pass on supplier programs/rebates to end-customers
Do not stress the supplier's brand name (in the extreme, they push their own competitive private branded products)	Do an inadequate job of solving end-customer problems

More often than not, failed distribution strategies result from insufficient planning by suppliers and lack of shared understanding about the roles and responsibilities of both supplier and the various intermediaries. For example, during the selection process for distributors/dealers, the supplier should secure agreement on a number of policies. These policies can evolve over time, ideally through an ongoing dialogue between the supplier and distributor possibly via periodic meetings between supplier representatives and a council comprised of leading distributors.

Example: Honda faced a problem in major Pakistani cities where it had multiple retail dealers (Lahore-27, Karachi-16). Some dealers cut prices on various models, incurring the wrath of other dealers that may have invested significantly more in showroom and other assets. As a result, in each major city, Honda appointed committees comprised of two dealers and one Honda executive to monitor dealer compliance. Those dealers not complying with Honda's suggested retail prices were fined.[57]

The sorts of policy areas include:

- market segments to be addressed
- geographic coverage
- product range to be sold
- responsibility for large accounts
- treatment of distributor inventory when supplier reduces price
- sales to large accounts
- inventories and returns
- end-customer information[58]
- volume targets
- price levels

Since the compensation that distributors receive from suppliers is typically variable, the manner in which the commission system is designed has a critical impact on distributor behavior. Many problems that suppliers perceive with distributors occur because of standardized commissions applied indiscriminately across both product line and end-customers. More precisely developed compensation systems that provide variable commission rates based on sales by product mix, customer mix, new or old products, and new or old customers are more likely to secure the required distributor behavior to implement the supplier's strategy. In addition, compensation systems that address distributor inventory levels, quality of end-customer service, end-customer satisfaction, overall management of the supplier's business, and implementation of agreed-upon initiatives can be powerful motivators.

The more successful supplier-distributor relationships occur when the supplier thinks strategically about its distribution system and takes steps to ensure that its distributors are successful. In particular, the supplier seeks to provide distributors with value-added services such as training (including sales training for distributor salespeople), field technical support, field selling support (with distributor salespeople), inventory control systems, and product manuals.[59] In addition to interfacing with distributors via on-the-road salespeople, whose focus is on short-term results, the supplier assigns separate responsibility for distributor development. This individual, who should be a senior executive, takes a much more long-run view of the supplier's distributor relationships and, perhaps through a distributor council, plans for the long-run health of the firm's distribution system.

Notwithstanding its best efforts at distributor development, periodic clear-headed analysis by suppliers will reveal that some distributors consistently under-perform. The supplier should move swiftly to replace those distributors that prevent the supplier from reaching its own goals.

SUMMARY

This chapter focused on distribution, a critical area of market strategy implementation. It began by observing that, in the macro view, distribution subsumes much of the economy, then switched attention to the micro considerations of organizations involved in the distribution process. It was noted that many organizations play various roles in distribution systems, but that power is distributed asymmetrically in any given system. As a result, a variety of different types of organization, including manufacturers/brand owners, wholesalers/distributors, retailers, and end-customers, can play the role of channel captain.

This chapter used a power/strategic conflict model to develop alternative distribution scenarios, and to develop strategic options for supplier action in each scenario before addressing the more recent shift towards partnership relationships among organizations within the distribution system.

Distribution strategy was addressed and four major decision areas for suppliers were considered—type of distributor, depth of distribution, distribution breadth, and several exclusivity issues. This section concluded with an illustration of the relationship between market strategy and distribution strategy, and provided a step-by-step process for developing distribution strategy. Finally, some of the operational problems in supplier/distributor relationships were addressed and methods that would more tightly integrate the supplier's strategy and distributors' actions were suggested.

THE CHANGING VIEW

Old Way	New Way
Manufacturer as channel captain	Retail power increasing
Distribution arrangements fixed	Distribution arrangements variable
Conflict models dominate	Cooperative models ascendant
Push inventory systems (loading intermediaries common)	Pull inventory (efficient consumer response systems)
Direct marketing rare	Direct marketing common
Telecommunications infrequent	Telecommunications ubiquitous
Overnight distribution unavailable	Overnight distribution increasing
Fast delivery rare	Delivery speed highly valued
Information technology poorly used	Information technology essential

Old Way	New Way
Distribution local/regional	Distribution regional/national/global
Slow progression: exclusive → selective → intensive	Fast progression: exclusive → selective → intensive
Customers patient	Customers impatient

QUESTIONS FOR STUDY AND DISCUSSION

1. Figure 16.1 highlighted several environmental factors affecting the nature of distribution systems. Identify three additional forces leading to changes in distribution and indicate what types of change you expect as the result of these forces.

2. With recent advances in information and distribution technology, why do companies still use intermediaries?

3. So-called "vertical marketers" have become increasingly prominent in recent years. What, in your opinion, explains this phenomenon?

4. What is the relationship between customer targeting and breadth of distribution?

5. Whereas traditional models of supplier/distributor relationships focused on conflict, more recently cooperative models have become popular. Do you believe it is possible to cooperate when there are significant differences in bargaining power? Explain your answer.

6. How does the concentration/dispersion model apply in the information economy?

7. Distribution relationships create painful paradoxes for managers. On the one hand they are urged to build strong distributor relationships, yet on the other are told to be prepared to sever these relationships if end-customers' preferences change. How should this paradox be resolved? Give examples illustrating your answer.

8. Some pricing experts argue that intermediaries should be rewarded according to how well they perform the various tasks and functions expected of them. Despite this recommendation, rewards are typically restricted to volume discounts and advertising or promotional allowances. What factors mitigate against acting upon what seems to be a sensible recommendation?

9. In the nineteenth century, intermediaries were often the channel captains. Some commentators believe that the Internet will once again put intermediaries in the driver's seat of the economy. Give three reasons why this is likely to happen, and three reasons that suggest it is unlikely to occur.

10. As exemplified by the formation of such industry giants as Ford, GM, Alcoa, and US Steel, vertical integration was the key to success for major companies in the first part of the twentieth century. However, as the century draws to a close, most large, vertically integrated firms were engaged in vertical dis-integration. Why do you think this is occurring?

11. Your text describes the elements of distribution strategy as involving decisions about distributor type, depth, breadth, and exclusively, but does not include decisions about the functions or tasks to be performed by distributors. Do you agree or disagree with this model? Be prepared to defend your answer.

12. "Since giving exclusive rights to distributors is one of the few opportunities they have to create a differential advantage, a manufacturer that makes its products widely available cannot expect preferred distributor relationships." Do you agree with this statement? Why or why not?

13. In the view of some experts, the complexity of multibrand, multichannel relationships outweighs their advantages. What organizational and commercial problems might arise from such strategies?

14. How might manufacturers pre-empt backward integration moves by their large customers?

15. What environmental changes might tempt a manufacturer to forward integrate?

ENDNOTES

1. The term end-customer is used to identify the point at which the product loses its identity. Consumers are end-customers but so are organizations. Note, however, that promotional efforts by suppliers, such as consumer advertising, may push the end-customer further down the distribution channel. For example, whereas previously PC manufacturers were end-customers for microprocessers, the consumer-focused *intel inside* campaign introduced consumers as end-customers.

2. A related view holds that in nature resources are randomly distributed in meaningless heterogeneity but that since customers consume disparate bundles of resources, they typically require meaningful heterogeneity. Stated most broadly, the function of all distribution systems is to transform meaningless heterogeneity into meaningful heterogeneity, such as by bringing together California lettuce, Mexican tomatoes, and Arizona carrots into a delicious salad for a New York vegetarian.

3. The practice of defining the many different types of channel intermediary is deliberately avoided here; these are available from many sources.

4. C.B. Bucklin, S.P. DeFalco, J.R. DeVincentis, and J.P. Levis III, "Are You Tough Enough to Manage Your Channels," *The McKinsey Quarterly*, (1996), pp. 105–114.

5. D.V. Fites, "Make Your Dealers Your Partners," *Harvard Business Review*, 74 (Mar./Apr. 1996), pp. 84–95.

6. *Business Week*, December 20, 1999.

7. This section benefited from D. Ford, L.-E. Gadde, H. Hakansson, A. Lundgren, I. Snehota, P. Turnbull and D. Wilson, *Managing Business Relationships*, Chichester, GB.: Wiley, 1988

8. For example, Kroger, the large U.S. supermarket chain, owns several factories.

9. For mutual fund suppliers, Schwab vastly decreased their promotional costs, although they no longer had direct contact with investors in their funds. A. J. Slywotzky and D. J. Morrison, *The Profit Zone*, New York: Times Business, 1997.

10. See Chapter 21 and L. Pitt, P. Berthon, and J-P. Berthon, "Changing Channels: The Impact of the Internet on Distribution Strategy," *Business Horizons*, (Mar./Apr. 1999), pp. 19–28.

11. Interestingly, notwithstanding its direct relationship with consumers, Amazon.com works with tens of thousands of affiliates that direct consumer traffic to its Web site for a 15% commission on sales.

12. *Fortune*, March 29, 1999.

13. See also DuPont Stainmaster and *intel inside* examples discussed earlier.

14. *The Economist*, June 19, 1999.

15. Norton Company (A/B), *Harvard Business School*, 9-570-001/2.

16. From over 15,000 car dealerships a few years ago, the top 250 firms accounted for 35% of total industry volume by the late 1990s.

17. C.B. Bucklin, P.A. Thomas-Graham, and E.A. Webster, "Channel Conflict: When Is It Dangerous," *The McKinsey Quarterly*, (1997), pp. 36–43.

18. The Internet may also vastly increase the geographic scope of the supplier's customer base.

19. Bucklin, Thomas-Graham, and Webster, *op. cit*. Similarly, Avon has opened a Spa on New York's Fifth Avenue.

20. Bucklin, Thomas-Graham, and Webster, *op. cit*.

21. *The New York Times*, January 15, 1999.

22. Bucklin, Thomas-Graham, and Webster, *op. cit*.

23. In mid-1999, Heinz announced plans to combine its U.S. food, pet food, and food service divisions under one organizational unit to improve distribution and secure greater bargaining power with retail chains, *The New York Times*, October 5, 1999.

24. Armstrong World Industries offers significant educational benefits for distributors that place 100% of their business with Armstrong.

25. Limited forward integration can provide the supplier firm with important information regarding the challenges and opportunities faced by distributors. In addition to sending a message regarding the firm's broad options, actually running a distributor operation may allow the firm to serve its own distributors better. For example, faced with significant concentration in automobile distribution worldwide, manufacturers such as Ford and General Motors have both acquired equity stakes in, and secured complete ownership of, some distributors. Relatedly, in the mid-1990s, Merck acquired drug distributor Medco even though this action reduced Merck's return on equity by 50%. Finally, Claas, the leading manufacturer of harvesting combines, sells equipment through distributors that sell to farmers; however, it owns at least one retail outlet in each of its major countries, simply as a way of learning farmers' needs on the spot. These "exercise fields" allow employees in various internal functions to acquire first hand experience of farmers' problems and needs. H. Simon, *Hidden Champions: Lessons from 500 of the World's Best Unknown Companies*, Boston, MA: Harvard Business School Press, 1996.

26. For the role of trust in partnership relationships see J.C. Anderson and J.A. Narus, "A Model of Distributor Firm and Manufacturing Firm Working Partnerships," *Journal of Marketing*, 54 (Jan. 1990), pp. 42–58 and N. Kumar, "The Power of Trust in Manufacturer-Retailer Relationships," *Harvard Business Review*, 74 (Nov./Dec. 1996), pp. 92–106. See also J. Lewis, *Trusted Partners: How Companies Build Mutual Trust and Win Together*, New York: The Free Press, 1999.

27. M. Hammer and J. Champy, *Re-engineering the Corporation: A Manifesto for Business Revolution,* New York: Harper Business, 1994. A broad view of supply chain management encompasses not only product flow, but also customer relationship management, customer service management, demand management, order fulfillment, manufacturing flow management, procurement, product development, and commercialization and returns, M.C. Cooper, D.M. Lambert, J.D. Pagh, "Supply Chain Management: More than a New Name for Logistics," *The International Journal of Logistics Management*, 8 (1997), pp. 1–13.

28. J.D. Sterman, "Modeling Managerial Behavior: Misperceptions of Feedback is a Dynamic Decision Making Experiment," *Management Science*, 35 (March 1989), pp. 321–339.

29. This process is called the continuous manufacturer replenishment program (CMRP).

30. G. Stalk, P. Evans and L.E. Shulman, "Competing on Capabilities: The New Rules of Corporate Strategy," *Harvard Business Review*, 70 (March/April 1992), pp. 57–69.

31. See R.D. Buzzell and G. Ortmeyer, "Channel Partnerships Streamline Distribution," *Sloan Management Review* (Spring 1995), pp. 85–96.

32. The major characteristic of both programs is a switch from "supplier push," to "consumer pull." In supplier push, suppliers attempt to forecast required volumes in advance, produce products, then push to sell them to distributors/retailers. In consumer pull, suppliers cooperate with distributors/retailers to re-supply items that consumers are purchasing.

33. This discussion assumes that the firm has decided to reach end-customers via intermediaries. Direct-to-end-customer relationships are discussed in the next section.

34. Tupperware is sold only at Tupperware parties organized by Tupperware representatives. Both Tupperware and Avon have introduced kiosks in shopping malls as lead-generation devices, *The New York Times*, December 13, 1999.

35. *New Straits Times*, March 3, 1999.

36. *The New York Times*, August 8, 1999.

37. In many cases, such as Mary Kay, Amway, and Handtech.com, direct sales are conducted via a pyramid scheme in which salespeople receive commissions both on their product sales and the sales of salespeople they recruit, sometimes *ad infinitum*. For example, Handtech.com reps receive 10% commissions on the products they sell, half the $145 fee of salespeople they recruit, and 2%–5% of their recruit's sales. Note that a concern for the potential abuses of pyramid selling schemes has led to the banning of direct face-to-face consumer sales in China.

38. Interestingly, Lipton is attempting to emulate Starbucks' success with tea houses.

39. *Business Week*, June 8, 1998. General Motors and Chrysler already have experience with superstore retailing.

40. J.B. Heide, *Managing the Distribution System*, in N. Capon, (ed.), Section 3, *Sales and Distribution*, in *AMA Management Handbook* (3rd Edition*)*, J. Hampton, (ed.), New York: AMACOM, 1994, pp. 3-19–3-26.

41. J.D. Hlavacek and T.J. McCuistion, "Industrial Distributors—When, Who and How? *Harvard Business Review*, 61 (Mar./Apr. 1983), pp. 96–101.

42. Downes and Lui, *op. cit.*

43. J.A. Narus and J.C. Anderson, "Rethinking Distribution," *Harvard Business Review*, 74 (July/Aug. 1996), pp. 112–120.

44. Narus and Anderson, *op. cit.*

45. These distributors set their own prices and are paid by GISO upon delivery; GISO holds the accounts receivable. The specialty distributors pay an annual membership fee to participate and other small transaction-related fees, Narus and Anderson, *op. cit.*

46. Narus and Anderson, *op. cit*

47. In the early 1990s, Dell entered, then withdrew, from retail distribution, finding it incompatible with its direct model.

48. Compaq also commenced sales over the Internet, *The New York Times*, May 10, 1999.

49. This issue is also of critical concern to retail chains in deciding where to site their outlets.

50. Kumar, *op. cit.*

51. *The New York Times*, February 9, 1999.

52. *The Economist,* July 24, 1999.

53. Coke rejected allegations of abusive practices, *The Economist*, August 14, 1999.

54. However, the arrival of Internet commerce may allow this supplier to sell direct to consumers.

55. Free on board (f.o.b.) is the price paid by distributors for goods located at the firm's warehouse; the distributor is responsible for shipping the goods to its own country. The alternative arrangement, carriage, insurance and freight (cif) is the price paid for transported goods.

56. L.W. Stern and F.D. Sturdivant, "Customer-Driven Distribution Systems," *Harvard Business Review*, 65 (July/Aug. 1987), pp. 34–41; V.K. Rangan, A.J. Menzes, and E. Maier, "Channel Selection for New Industrial Products: A Framework, Method and Application," *Journal of Marketing*, 56 (July 1992), pp. 69–82; V.K. Rangan, *Designing Channels of Distribution*, Boston, MA: Harvard Business School, 1994, 9-594-116; J.M. Hulbert, *Marketing: A Strategic Perspective*, Katonah, NY: Impact Publishing, 1985.

57. See Atlas Honda Ltd.: Communication Plan 1993, N. Capon and W. Van Honacker, *The Asian Marketing Casebook,* Singapore: Prentice Hall, 1998. In many countries, such anti-competitive practices are illegal.

58. Some suppliers require distributors to report extensive information on each sale, such as by item, customer, and delivery and billing location.

59. For example, the "Merck Manual" comprises around 3,000 pages of disorders and suggested therapies; the "O-Ring Handbook" by Parker Hannifin Corporation helps design engineers specify solutions to prevent leakage in oil or air systems, Hlavacek and McCuistion, *op. cit.*

WEB RESOURCES

Airbus Industrie	www.airbus.com
Alcoa	www.alcoa.com
AltaVista	www.altavista.com
Amazon	www.amazon.com
Amway	www.amway.com
Armstrong World Industries	www.armstrong.com
AT&T	www.att.com
Avon	www.avon.com
Banana Republic	www.bananarepublic.com
Bass Ale	www.bass-brewers.com

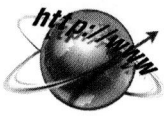
Black & Decker	www.blackanddecker.com
Boeing	www.boeing.com
Bridgestone	www.bridgestone.com
Budweiser	www.budweiser.com
Business Horizons	www.businesshorizons.org
Campbell's	www.campbellsoup.com
Camp Snoopy	www.campsnoopy.com
Canon USA	www.usa.canon.com
Carrefour	www.carrefour.com
Caterpillar	www.caterpillar.com
Charles Schwab	www.schwab.com
Chrysler	www.chrysler.com
Citibank	www.citibank.com
Claas	www.claas.com
Coca-Cola	www.cocacola.com
Columbia University	www.columbia.edu
Compaq	www.compaq.com
Cosco Wholesale Club	www.pricecostco.com
Daewoo	www.daewoo.com
Dell Computer	www.dell.com
Delta Airlines	www.delta-air.com
DeWalt	www.dewalt.com
Du Pont	www.dupont.com
Ebay	www.ebay.com
E-trade	www.etrade.com
Excite	www.excite.com
Federal Express	www.fedex.com
Federated Department Stores	www.federated-fds.com
Ford	www.ford.com
Frito-Lay	www.fritolay.com
Gap	www.gap.com
General Motors	www.gm.com
Gillette	www.gillette.com
Goodyear	www.goodyear.com
Grainger	www.grainger.com
H & R Block	www.handrblock.com
Handtech	www.handtech.com
Harrods	www.harrods.com
Hasbro	www.hasbro.com
Heinz	www.heinz.com
Hill's Science	www.hillspet.com
Home Depot	www.homedepot.com
Honda	www.honda.com
IBM	www.ibm.com
Independent Grocers Association	www.igainc.com
Intel	www.intel.com
Jaguar	www.jaguarcars.com
J.E. Ekornes	www.ekornes.fi
Kampgrounds of America	www.koa.com

Kellogg's	www.kelloggs.com
Kentucky Fried Chicken	www.kentuckyfriedchicken.com
K-Mart	www.kmart.com
Kodak	www.kodak.com
Kroger	www.kroger.com
L. L. Bean	www.llbean.com
Lands' End	www.landsend.com
Levi's	www.levi.com
Lillian Vernon	www.lillianvernon.com
Lincoln	www.lincolnvehicles.com
Lipton	www.lipton.com
MacDonalds	www.mcdonalds.com
Mall of America	www.mallofamerica.com
Marks and Spencer	www.marks-and-spencer.co.uk
Marshall Industries	www.marshall.com
Mary Kay	www.marykay.com
Mazda	www.mazda.com
MBNA	www.mbna.com
Merck	www.merck.com
Mercury	www.mercuryvehicles.com
Merck/Medco	www.merck-medco.com
Merrill Lynch	www.ml.com
Michelin	www.michelin.com
Neiman Marcus	www.neimanmarcus.com
Nike	www.nike.com
Norton	www.nortonco.com
Nucor	www.nucor.com
Nurdin and Peacock	www.nurdin-peacock.co.uk
Nutrasweet	www.nutrasweet.com
Okuma America	www.okumaamerica.com
Parker Hannifin Corporation	www.parker.com
Pepsi	www.pepsico.com
Price Club	www.pricecostco.com
Priceline	www.priceline.com
Procter & Gamble	www.pg.com
Proton	www.proton.com
Quantum	www.quantum.com
Quickquote	www.quickquote.com
Royal Ahold	www.ahold.nl
Safeway	www.safeway.com
Sainsburys	www.sainburys.co.uk
Sam's Wholesale Club	www.samsclub.com
Schwab	www.schwab.com
Sears	www.sears.com
Sherwin Williams	www.sherwin-williams.com
Sony	www.sony.com
Starbucks	www.starbucks.com
Taco Bell	www.tacobell.com
Tesco	www.tesco.de
Toys-Я-Us	www.toysrus.com
Tru Value	www.truvalue.com

WEB RESOURCES *(continued)*

Tupperware	www.tupperware.com
Underwater World	www.underwaterworld.com
US Steel	www.usx.com
Volvo GM Heavy Truck	www.volvotrucks.volvo.com
Wal-Mart	www.walmart.com
Yahoo!	www.yahoo.com

CHAPTER

17

MANAGING SERVICES AND CUSTOMER SERVICE

LEARNING OBJECTIVES

When you have completed this chapter, you will understand

- the distinction among products, service, and customer service

- why services are becoming more important

- the critical dimensions across which products differ from services

- how services differ from one another

- how to diagnose quality-related problems in the delivery of services

- the dimensions of customer service

- how to develop an effective customer service system

- the strategic role of customer service

INTRODUCTION

Although distinctions among products, services, and customer service are in general poorly understood, discrimination is important because of the increasing tendency of firms to seek competitive advantage through various service elements. Furthermore, managers must be very clear about the critical factors of intangibility, inseparability, variability, perishability, divisibility, acquisition, and the role of customers that distinguish physical products from services. They must also understand the implications of these distinctions for market strategy.

In many organizations, customer service is underfunded and poorly managed. Yet, if customer service, whether provided before or after purchase, is well designed and executed, the firm may reap significant competitive advantage. High-quality customer service may deliver significant benefits in terms of high levels of customer satisfaction, significant repurchase, and positive word-of-mouth. By using a diagnostic model to analyze their own service delivery systems, managers may be able to raise service quality in their firms.

DISTINGUISHING BETWEEN PRODUCTS, SERVICES, AND CUSTOMER SERVICE

Products and Services

One of the great confusions in marketing has been conceptual uncertainty regarding the distinction between products and services. A good way to approach this distinction and to be clear about customer service, is to recognize the implications of the oft-quoted statement addressed to companies, "Customers don't really want your products (services), they want the benefits that your products (services) offer." In some cases, benefits are provided by the acquisition of physical goods, such as house, car, washing machine, clothing, and food. In other cases, benefits are received without acquisition of physical objects, though physical objects may play a role in providing the benefits, such as haircut, travel, sports event, or medical procedure. This latter set of benefits is provided by services, classically defined as "any act or performance that one party can offer another that is essentially intangible and does not result in the ownership of anything."[1]

It should be recognized that although this definition of services includes the phrase "does not result in the ownership of anything," the acquisition of physical goods does not necessarily imply ownership. In principle, many physical objects from which an individual receives benefits can be owned by a third party, rather than by the individual receiving the benefits. Naturally, some people prefer ownership to renting/leasing, and certain product types may have no renting/leasing suppliers. Significant service businesses have been built up by separating product acquisition from ownership.

Products, Services, and Customer Service

The core product (or service) providing the central benefit required by customers can be distinguished from those elements of the marketing offer that surround it. Among these surrounding elements is customer service. At an implementation level, many marketing authors have expanded the traditional 4Ps (product, price, promotion, place) of the marketing mix to "4Ps plus an S" to recognize the critical service element of many implementation programs.

> **Example:** The Saturn division of General Motors has sought to distinguish itself from other automobile manufacturers by raising the level of service offered to its customers before and after selection of a Saturn.

In the Saturn example, the core is a physical product; however, the core may also be a service.

> **Example:** The core service offered by Federal Express is overnight transportation and delivery of packages. In addition to this core service, Federal Express also provides several surrounding, or ancillary, services including problem solving,

advice and information, billing statements, package tracing, documentation, pickup, supplies, and order taking.[2]

It should also be recognized that provision of customer service might involve other surrounding marketing mix elements. For example, information provided customers to assist them in making a purchase may be provided by media advertising or members of a sales force.

A particular definitional difficulty with customer service occurs when an organization refocuses its activities, and what has traditionally been defined as a surrounding customer service element becomes a core service in its own right.

> **Example:** For many years, General Electric (GE) has been a leading supplier of diagnostic equipment (X-Ray, CAT scanners, and NMR) to hospitals. As part of its marketing offer, GE provided after-sales customer service to ensure the machines continued to function as designed. In a strategic move beyond this level of service, GE offers to service any diagnostic machine regardless of manufacturer (such as Siemens and Hewlett Packard). For hospitals with multiple suppliers, this provided the significant advantage of a single servicing interface. In an even more radical shift, GE has suggested that hospitals outsource their entire diagnostic operations and allow GE to take over its management.[3]

The progressive shift from inclusion of after-sales service as a surrounding customer support element for the sale of diagnostic equipment to managing entire diagnostic operations represents a major change from providing "just" customer service to offering a new core service. For GE, managing a hospital's entire diagnostic operation represents an important new source of revenues and profit, in addition to placing it in a strong position to advocate purchase of its own diagnostic machines.[4]

This example is not unusual: Computer manufacturers Unisys and IBM are designing, installing and running other companies' computer operations, Xerox runs copy centers, and Pitney Bowes runs both copy centers and mail rooms. Ford has purchased an exhaust and brake chain (Europe), a scrapyard business (U.S.), Mazda's consumer finance arm, and will provide drivers with satellite-fed audio and other services for a monthly fee.[5] Finally, Boeing is placing more attention on financing, in part so that some of the financially weaker airlines can buy Boeing aircraft.[6]

The attraction of these service businesses is not hard to understand: margins are often higher on services than on products, require less capital outlay, and deliver significant ROI benefits.[7] The trend to outsourcing has facilitated these changes that, in effect, have turned durables and capital goods manufacturers into service suppliers. What was once a customer service has migrated into a core service in its own right.

GROWTH IN THE SERVICE SECTOR

The key rationale for focusing on product/service distinctions is that in advanced Western countries, services now account for upwards of 70% of both employment and GDP.[8] Not only are there substantial concentrations of services in the private sector, government and non-profit activities are comprised almost entirely of services.[9] In addition to rising incomes and age-related demographic shifts, several factors have led to growth in private sector services in recent years.[10]

Outsourcing

First, narrowing corporate strategies and the search for core competence has led companies to outsource various corporate services that were formerly provided internally, such as legal, security, payroll, and computer operations. Some firms have discovered that sets of activities performed in-house to support their regular businesses have value to other organizations, and so are packaged for sale.

Examples: GE, a world-class leader in manufacturing, offers consulting services to non-competitive manufacturers. Florida Light and Power, winner of Japan's prestigious Demming award, offers quality workshops for companies interested in improving their quality practices.

Other examples include Disney, Shell Oil, Xerox, and Scandinavian Airlines System (SAS). Disney offers executive programs in leadership and customer service; Shell offers accounting, information technology and other support services; Xerox consults on quality management and SAS trains flight crews from other airlines, maintains their planes, and helps other Swedish companies prepare employees for relocation.[11]

Such decisions are not always straightforward. For example, General Motors Acceptance Corporation (GMAC) was formed many years ago as a customer service for financing purchase of GM automobiles. For years it has struggled with the question of whether, and how much, to expand its scope to finance non-GM cars, an action urged by many of its dealers that sell competing vehicles but resented by GM product divisions.[12]

Franchising

In many arenas, such as restaurants, hotels/motels, and tax accounting, industry concentration has been accompanied by increases in franchising.[13] Franchising embraces standardization of service features and prices, introduction of brand names, symbols, uniforms, use of mass media for building awareness and brand preference, centralized marketing research, and strategic planning. In addition, the increase in franchising has led to new services aimed at managing franchising relationships.

Customer Behavior Changes

Changes in customer behavior (consumer and corporate) related to decreasing preference for outright purchase and ownership of goods have led to significant growth in financial services such as credit, rental, and leasing; major new areas of financial services, such as mutual funds, have resulted from bank disintermediation.

Deregulation

Deregulation in several industries, such as electricity, financial services, natural gas, transportation, and telecommunications, has led to easier market entry, freedom to compete on price, removal of geographic restrictions on service delivery, greater service differentiation, and increased use of mass media. A similar effect has occurred with the relaxation of professional association standards, such as for lawyers, architects, and accountants.[14]

Globalization

These and other trends have been fueled by globalization of many service industries, including travel, telecommunications, and financial services, and significant advances in computer and telecommunications technologies.

HOW SERVICES ARE DIFFERENT FROM PRODUCTS

Whether focused on the core service or surrounding customer service elements, there are several significant differences between services and products. These differences include the areas of intangibility, inseparability, variability, perishability, divisibility, acquisition, and the role of customers.

Intangibility

Physical goods are tangible. They can be touched, worn, kicked, or sat upon. Services cannot. Services are comprised of deeds, performances, or efforts focused on people, products, or information; they are intangible. Examples include:

- **People**: medical treatment, theater, restaurants, and education;[15]
- **Products**: retail distribution, car repair, house cleaning, and real estate;
- **Information**: marketing research, legal and financial services, and tax preparation.

Some offerings typically considered as services, such as restaurant meals or purchasing goods in a department store, have more elements of tangibility than others, but the core experience is still intangible. Perhaps the major implication of the tangibility/ intangibility difference between products and services is a greater subjectivity in customer response and evaluation for services than for most physical goods. As a result of this difficulty, customers use tangible elements of services to anticipate the experience and form their expectations. These tangible elements embrace service facilities, service equipment, and service personnel.[16] Some firms provide additional tangibility through service guarantees.

SERVICE FACILITIES   Service facilities can be conceptualized as comprising both an exterior and interior. The exterior fulfills the function of attracting customers, or providing information regarding the nature of the interior facilities where the service act is actually performed.

The interior comprises two types: off-stage, out of the customer's sight, and on-stage, where the deeds, performances, or efforts are experienced by the customer. The type and quality of the on stage facilities can have an important impact on how the service is perceived. Examples include experiencing a play at a small intimate theater as opposed to Radio City Music Hall in New York, or having one's car serviced in a clean, well-organized facility rather than one that is dirty and messy. In addition, services can be redefined by shifting an activity traditionally conducted off-stage to on-stage (or vice versa). For example, Benihana of Tokyo has been extremely successful by placing cooking, a typical off-stage activity for restaurants, on-stage for customers to experience.[17]

SERVICE EQUIPMENT   Service equipment (physical goods) is typically required to provide services. At a minimum, a haircut requires a pair of scissors and a mirror, and air travel requires an airplane. The service experience is often strongly influenced by the quality of the equipment. For example, many passengers feel differently about a long-distance flight when an airline's planes are relatively new (Singapore Airlines) than when they are relatively old (some U.S. airlines).

SERVICE PERSONNEL   Service personnel are frequently required for service delivery. This activity may occur off-stage or on-stage. The provision of airline service requires airplane mechanics and baggage handlers who do not generally interact with passengers, but who play critical roles in the service delivery process. The airline service also requires ticket agents and flight attendants who interact directly with customers. Customer experience of the service is influenced by how all service personnel (off-stage and on-stage) perform their functions as well as by the appearance, demeanor, and manner of on-stage personnel. Hence the attention given to uniform design and appearance in many people-intensive services. In addition, bringing personnel on-stage, whose roles are typically performed "off-stage," or vice versa, can modify the customer experience. To pursue the airline example, historically, passengers had little or no experience of pilots, certainly not the chief pilot; nowadays, pilots make frequent onboard announcements and often appear at deplaning time to converse with passengers.

On-stage activity is important because of the many interactions between the customer and service personnel fulfilling multiple functions, such as telephone operators, salespersons, repair persons, maintenance staff, or receptionists. Jan Carlzon, president of SAS, coined the phrase "moment of truth" to emphasize that each service provider/customer interaction was an opportunity for either customer satisfaction or dissatisfaction.[18] In addition to judgments made by customers about their own interactions with service personnel, they also make service supplier judgments based on interactions they observe between supplier personnel and other customers. A particular difficulty for many manufacturers is that most customer contact, and hence perception of service, occurs not with their own employees but with employees of other firms, such as distributors. Managing customer service is thus a major challenge, such as in automobile distribution.

Another problem faced by many service firms is the fact that the customer-employee relationship is often closer than the customer-firm relationship and, for services as diverse as investment banking, beauty salons, advertising agencies, and restaurants, when employees leave for another organization, they often take cusomers with them. The challenge for the services firm is to strengthen the bond between customer and the firm. Among techniques that can be employed include improving or increasing direct company communications with customers, and introducing different incentive systems for employees. For example, Merrill Lynch (ML) has progressively shifted retail broker compensation away from commission on trades to assets under management. ML believes that this shift affects broker behavior and enhances the relationship between ML and its customers.

SERVICE GUARANTEES   Because of the difficulties customers face in evaluating services, offering service guarantees may be an effective way of easing the purchase decision. Hart argues that a good service guarantee should be unconditional, easy and painless to invoke, and easy and quick to collect on.[19] In addition, it should be simple to understand, communicate, and meaningful in the context of the specific service for which the guarantee is offered (the punishment should fit the crime). Such a guarantee should build customer loyalty, sales, and market share in part from the customer's positive experience with the guarantee, post the experience that led to the guarantee being invoked, and from the guarantee's impact on service quality. Firms offering service guarantees are likely to improve quality since they:

- Set clear performance standards that typically boost employee performance and morale;
- Focus on the customer's definition of good service;
- Generate reliable data (through payouts) of where performance is poor;
- Examine the entire service delivery system for failure points.

Hart identifies several conditions under which service guarantees have maximum impact. These include when the price of the service is high, when the customer's ego is involved, when the customer has little experience with the service, and when the negative consequences of service failure are high. Other conditions include when the industry has a bad image for service quality, when the firm depends on frequent customer purchases, and when the firm's business is strongly affected by word of mouth.

Inseparability

For services, production and consumption are inseparable. Whereas physical goods are manufactured, shipped, stored and resold, a service is inexorably linked to its provider. This inseparability can create significant problems for providers and customers alike. For physical goods, the problems of accurately forecasting demand are solved by carrying inventory. In a real sense, inventory volume represents management's inability to forecast accurately.[20] Inseparability in the services domain makes carrying inventory an impossibility, thus placing a heavy burden of the firm's ability to forecast.

SUPPLY/DEMAND BALANCING   Supply/demand balancing is a critical challenge for managing service operations. It is conducted by increasing supply and decreasing demand, or by decreasing supply and increasing demand.

Modifying Supply   Long-run supply can be increased with appropriate capacity additions, but in the short/medium run, increases must be secured through devices such as stretching capacity (by increased hours or reduced downtime), renting/sharing extra facilities/equipment, and adding part-time workers.[21] A critical concern in service operations is that as capacity utilization increases, perceived service quality may be reduced unless managed carefully. Conversely, if supply exceeds demand, capacity may be temporarily decreased by scheduling equipment maintenance and cross-training employees so they can be used in other functions.

Modifying Demand   On the demand side, management must attempt to understand the patterns of demand and secure answers to questions such as:

- Does demand for the service follow a regular, predictable cycle?
- If so, what is the cycle length (for example, day [commuting], week, month or year)?
- What are the causes of cyclical demand fluctuations (such as work schedule, pay-day, school vacations, or climate)?
- What are the causes of seemingly random demand fluctuations (such as weather, births, or crime)?
- Can the use pattern of the service be disaggregated over time into different market segments, use patterns, or profitability)?

Once the use patterns are understood, management must decide which market segments to address. Then it may take various marketing actions to either increase or decrease demand as necessary.[22] For example, it may vary the service offering, modify the time, place or price of the service offering, implement communications strategies and store demand (by queues or reservation systems).[23]

> **Example:** The demand pattern for many resort hotels is comprised of an annual cycle often described as including peak, shoulder, and low seasons. In peak season, at standard prices, demand often outstrips supply; in low season, supply outstrips demand; in the shoulder seasons (before and after peak season) effective marketing can often bring supply and demand into balance. In peak season, typical strategies are to raise prices, attempt to switch customers to shoulder seasons, and be effective in scheduling to minimize room vacancies. In low season, marketing strategies may involve targeting non-traditional market segments with attractive offers, such as Miami Beach hotels seeking British tour groups in the summer months, and scheduling activities such as room painting and renovations. For shoulder seasons, effective communications and offering lower prices can often increase capacity utilization.[24]

Variability

Variability is a natural consequence of significant human involvement in many service delivery systems. Of course, variability is endemic in manufacturing processes; the major operational goal of quality initiatives is to reduce variability. However, factory conditions also allow for the implementation of many quality initiatives (including work teams and process control charts), close supervision, and tough quality control inspections that are difficult, if not impossible, to implement in many service businesses.

FOCUS ON HUMAN CAPITAL   The major method of dealing with service variability is appropriate attention to employee selection and training. In recent years, companies in many industries have sought to improve employee performance. Notable is the airline industry in which several carriers, including British Airways, Singapore Airlines, SAS, and Swiss Air have placed extensive resources into employee selection and training. The results have been most positive.

Whereas unplanned variability in the manufacturing process is almost always negative, the potential variability in services can be extremely positive as human service providers can tailor their behavior in a service act directly to the individual customer. Notwithstanding these benefits, this sort of behavior does not occur automatically. It must be planned for by appropriate employee recruitment, selection and training programs, by a reward system that encourages employees to go the extra mile to serve customers, yet does not penalize them for innovating (including breaking rules) in the quest for customer satisfaction.

SUBSTITUTION OF CAPITAL FOR LABOR   An alternative method of dealing with employee-caused quality variability problems in services is the removal of the human element by automation. Thus automatic car washes substitute machines for humans, and dispensing machines for various goods and services (including cash, sandwiches, and tickets for transportation and movies) remove or lessen human involvement. Many of

MANAGING SERVICES
AND CUSTOMER
SERVICE

these innovations are driven less by variability issues than by cost reduction via substitution of capital for labor, but the variability impact applies nonetheless. Of course, despite the presumed efficiency of automated service delivery, machines break down; in addition, some customers may have difficulty interfacing with machines, or may prefer human contact. For example, despite their efficiency, bank ATMs are not universally valued over human tellers.

Perishability

Perishability is tightly linked to inseparability and the inability to inventory services. The provision of services is strongly time-bound as capacity to produce services and the sale of those services must be tightly linked. The psychiatrist whose patient fails to arrive for an appointment or the airline whose plane leaves with empty seats loses the revenue opportunity forever.

Not only should management consider various demand/supply-balancing activities, it should also be exceptionally well informed of the financial issues surrounding the costs to secure and serve additional customers versus the revenue loss of service capacity unsold.

> **Example:** Many services companies operate with low variable costs and high fixed costs, such as airlines, theaters, and hotels. As a result, the contribution margin per customer is often very high. For example, on a trans-Atlantic flight for which a passenger might pay $600 in coach, given the plane is scheduled to fly, the only relevant marginal costs are for extra fuel (minimal), meals, and sundries (just a few dollars). Such economics suggest that the airline might spend a significant amount on advertising, since relatively few passengers would be needed to cover these extra costs, or reduce prices to specific market segments.[25]

Divisibility

Most products comprise a single entity. For example, an automobile is conceived of as a single unit rather than as a collection of components, such as engine, transmission, wheels, and seats. Conversely, many services (both core and surrounding) comprise a process or sequence of activities conducted over time. Figure 17.1 shows a sequence of activities required for attending an evening adult education course.[26]

This difference has important implications for service delivery design. The sequence of activities comprises a blueprint of the service that can function as a planning and diagnostic document for systematically identifying and preparing for dealing with service problems. The blueprint provides the basis for redesign as new means of increasing customer value and reducing costs are identified by either adding or subtracting customer service elements.[27]

Acquisition

Products are acquired (and frequently owned); services are not acquired in a physical sense (for example, theater and travel). Customers may experience the physical manifestation of a service, such as the car that runs more smoothly, the dashing haircut, or the department store purchase at home, but the service typically remains, at best, as a set of associations in memory. If positive, these associations can lead to repurchase intentions and positive word of mouth. Because of the potentially high salience of these service associations, service providers should attempt to build on these positive aspects for future sales.

The Role of Customers

The impact of fellow customers on the service experience is a crucial difference from products. Rarely are goods producers concerned that sales to certain customers (or customer types) negatively impact their offerings (although they may refuse sales because of post-purchase service considerations).[28] By contrast, this is a critical issue for many service providers that put in place systems, such as nightclub bouncers, admission departments of

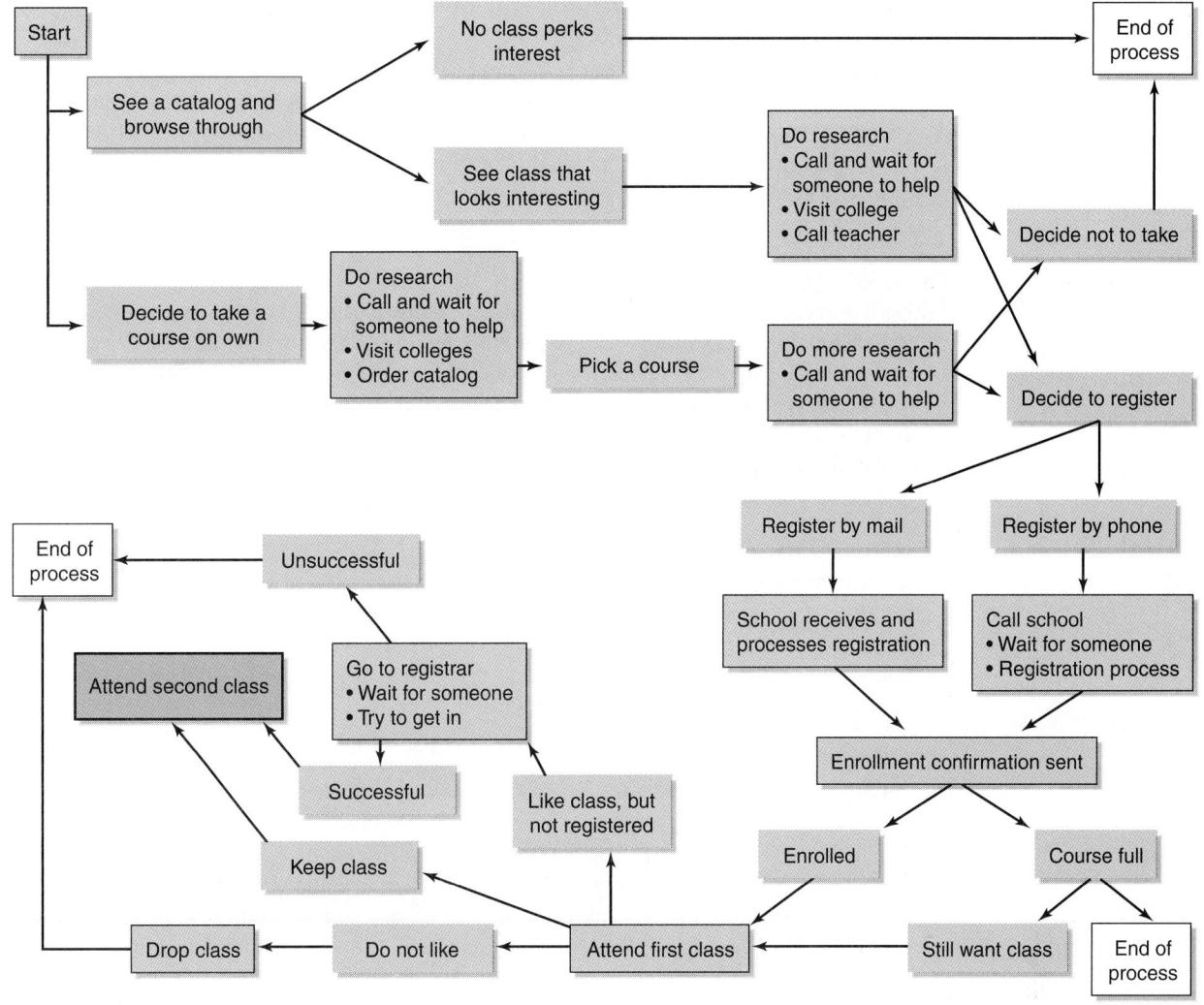

FIGURE 17.1

A Service Blueprint for an Evening Adult Education Course[27]

educational institutions, and maitre d's in restaurants, for affirmatively refusing to deal with customers who want to purchase their services.

Furthermore, despite the general prescription offered by marketing practitioners that "the customer is always right," in many settings, especially when other customers are present, service delivery personnel must be empowered to decide that this blanket prescription is in error. For example, the drunken airline passenger, the MBA student sleeping in a finance class, the baseball fan behind home plate shouting out pitches,[29] and the abusive or uncooperative customer may not only be dissatisfied with the service, they also reduce service value for all customers.

Since many services are experienced in group settings, the nature, dress, and behavior of fellow customers is a critical element in service perception. For example, for many passengers, the airline travel experience is closely correlated with the number of young children in close proximity. In business education, discussion of a complex marketing case is a different experience if the students are beginning undergraduates versus advanced graduate students.

INTRASERVICE DISTINCTIONS

In addition to distinguishing services from products, services can be classified in various ways that lead to important implications for market strategy development. Earlier, the chapter noted that services can process products, people, or information. Other important distinctions among services concern the location of the service act, the extent to which the customer needs to be present when the service is delivered, and whether or not the service is offered as part of a "membership" relationship.

Location of the Service Act

Certain products, such as factory maintenance, house cleaning, and gardening, must remain in location for receipt of service, but for other products, location is a variable. For example, customers can either drive to the garage for service or the garage can add extra value by picking the car up from home (and delivering a "loaner"). Families can watch a movie in the theater at the prescribed time, rent the video (some months later), or record it at home from TV while at work and watch it later. In many societies, medical services are delivered in hospitals and doctors' offices; in other societies, delivering them at home provides greater value.

Customer Presence

Services can be divided into those for which the customer must be present and where customer presence is unnecessary. For example, for many services based on processing products, such as house cleaning, car repair, and lawn care, customer presence is not required. However, customer presence may play a role in monitoring service quality. For other services, such as a haircut, travel, and educational services, customer presence is defined into the service.

Membership

For some services, the organization has a membership relationship with its customers. In a non-membership relationship, each purchase and use of the service requires an affirmative decision, such as most retail distribution and movies. By contrast, in a membership relationship, the "joining" decision is made at one point in time and service use occurs without an affirmative selection decision on each occasion. Some membership relationships involve continuous service delivery, such as checking accounts and automobile insurance; benefits are enjoyed unless affirmative action is taken to end the relationship or it expires naturally. Other membership relationships involve discrete transactions, such as long-distance telephone service and shopping clubs. An important implication for service organizations involved in non-membership relationships is that a shift to membership may enhance customer loyalty. For example, a theater may develop a subscription series, or a business school may develop a consortium of firms for executive education offerings.[30]

SERVICE QUALITY

The critical requirement for securing high repurchase levels and strong positive word-of-mouth is high levels of customer satisfaction related to service quality.

A Model of Service Quality

The most influential framework for diagnosing service quality issues was developed by Berry and his coworkers (Figure 17.2).[31] Essentially, the model identifies five "gaps." The critical gap driving customer satisfaction/dissatisfaction is Gap 5, the difference between perceived service and expected service.

It is important to note that, in this model, customer satisfaction is not related to any absolute service quality standard, but rather to expectations disconfirmation, the difference between perceived quality and expected quality. If expectations exceed perception, customer dissatisfaction occurs. If perception exceeds expectations, customer satisfaction or even customer delight is achieved. This framework has an interesting implication that

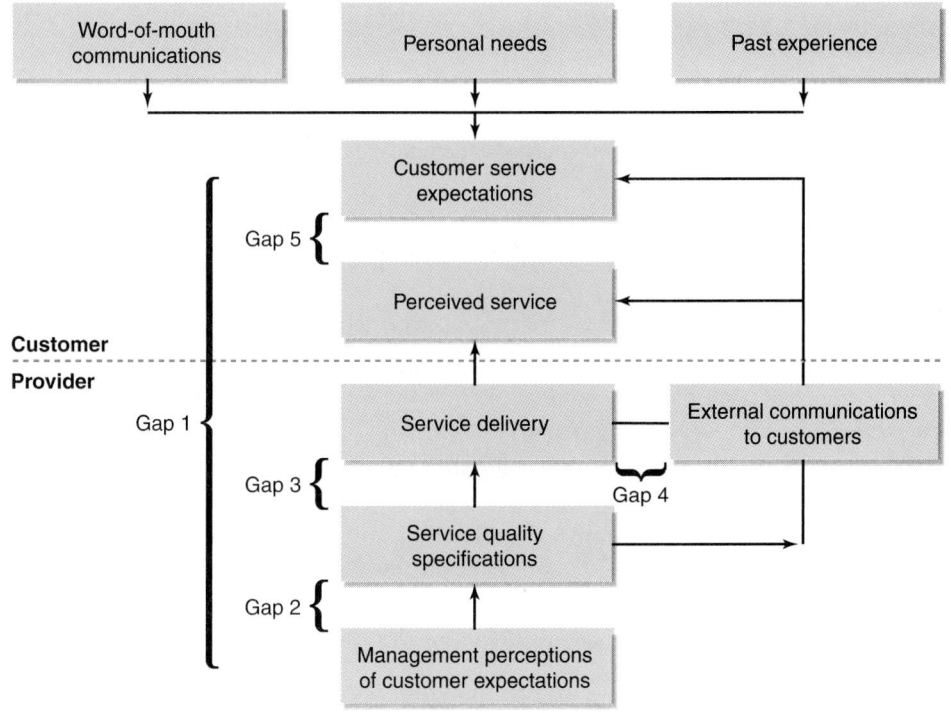

FIGURE 17.2

The SERVQUAL Model for Diagnosing Service Quality

places many service firms in a dilemma. To improve customer satisfaction, the firm should not only focus on improving service quality, it should also "manage" customer expectations to assure a positive service quality perception less expectations difference. However, if expectations are managed downwards too aggressively, customers will not purchase the service in the first place. Conversely, if a firm aggressively promotes its ability to offer service but fails to deliver on its promises, it may be worse off than a firm making more modest claims.

> **Example:** A major computer manufacturer, A, promised that a service visit would be made within four hours of the request being received. Its competitor, B, promised service visits within eight hours. In fact, company A averaged five and a half hours; company B averaged seven hours. Although company A's service performance was measurably better, company B received higher customer satisfaction ratings!

Perhaps the overarching issue for improving customer satisfaction is that increasingly tough competition is raising customer expectations such that achieving a positive service quality perception less expectations difference is becoming increasingly difficult.

The other gaps that cumulatively lead to Gap 5 are:

- **Gap 1**: Not understanding what the customer requires (management perceptions of customer expectations versus customer service expectations);
- **Gap 2**: Service quality standards do not match managerial beliefs regarding customer expectations (service quality specifications versus management perceptions of customer expectations);
- **Gap 3**: Service performance does not match service quality specifications (service delivery versus service quality specifications);
- **Gap 4**: Communications about service quality not matched by service delivery (external communication to customers versus service delivery).

Berry's research suggests that the key variables impacting perceived quality, in order, are:

- **Reliability**: Ability to perform the promised service dependably and accurately
- **Responsiveness**: Willingness to help customers and provide prompt service
- **Assurance**: Knowledge and courtesy of employees and ability to convey trust and confidence
- **Empathy**: Provision of caring, individualized attention to customers
- **Tangibles**: Appearance of physical facilities, equipment, personnel, and communication materials

Service Quality Issues

Several service quality issues are addressed—performance and information, improving the service offer, and service quality failures.

PERFORMANCE AND INFORMATION   An important feature of service quality is not only the service performance but accurate knowledge of when the service will be delivered. One method of supply/demand balancing is to employ queuing systems. For most people, queuing is a negative experience; setting customer expectations about queue length, then exceeding or delivering on those expectations can mitigate this experience.

> **Example:** Passengers for London's *Heathrow Express* are provided with accurate estimates of train departures.

IMPROVING THE SERVICE OFFER   In some cases, perception of service quality may be related to the addition of service elements. This is particularly the case in mature industries where it is difficult to secure a competitive advantage.

> **Example:** Bandag sells truck tire retreads, a commodity product comparable in price and quality to competitors, to over 500 dealer-installers around the United States. To develop a competitive advantage, it provides additional services by assisting dealers in filing and collecting on warranty claims from tire manufacturers.[32] Bandag offers comprehensive fleet management services to its largest national accounts and embeds computer chips in the rubber of newly retreaded tires to gauge pressure and temperature, and count revolutions. It can then advise customers of the optimal time to retread, reducing downtime caused by blowouts and so improve fleet operations.

In other cases, removal of service elements can lead to an increase in perceived quality.

> **Example:** Southwest Airlines has done away with ticket counters (passengers buy tickets on the plane), has no assigned seating, has eliminated interline (baggage transfer from one airline to another), meals, and other services, and it uses secondary airfields. However, Southwest is highly successful since it offers passengers low fares, frequent flights, and high on-time performance. It manages costs effectively, in part by minimizing airplane time on the ground.[33]

One particularly important method for enhancing perceived quality is customer participation in the service delivery process—sometimes termed customer co-production. Customer participation in services has a long history, dating at least to the introduction of supermarkets where customers replaced store clerks in securing merchandise from store shelves. Other examples include self-service restaurants and use of the Internet to work out travel plans and buy airline tickets.

> **Example:** Several years ago, Federal Express developed a tracking system that customers can access by telephoning customer service representatives. More recently, Federal Express has developed an on-line system that allows customers to check the status of packages themselves. This customer service element provides greater value to customers at lower cost to Federal Express.

In addition, several product companies have begun to involve customers in the design operation. For example, Anderson Windows uses a multimedia system called the "Window of Knowledge" to help customers design their own windows. Levi Strauss launched a service where women provide their own measurements and receive jeans tailored to their exact dimensions.

SERVICE QUALITY FAILURES   Even though good service management attempts to maximize service quality, errors will occur no matter how dedicated the company and its employees. Paradoxically, the drive for service efficiency often results in the development of inflexible systems unable to deal with idiosyncratic customer behavior.

> **Example:** A customer parked in a lot across the street from the bank. He was told that his parking would be validated if he did business at the bank. He cashed a check but the teller refused to validate the parking because he had not made a deposit. The customer explained that, although this was not his regular branch, he was a long-time bank customer and had millions of dollars in various accounts. Neither the teller nor the bank manager would budge from the refusal. The customer drove 40 blocks to his regular banker telling him that he would close all his accounts if he did not receive a phone call of apology by the end of the day. The phone call was never made![34]

How the firm deals with these situations is crucial, for not only can appropriate response minimize customer defections and turn a potentially unhappy customer into both a loyal customer and a company advocate, it can be a major vehicle for improving the firm's products, services, and customer service.[35] Findings that relatively few aggrieved customers complain[36] strongly suggests that firms should design systems that not only make complaint behavior easier, but also train personnel to ensure swift and aggressive follow-up on these complaints.

Increasingly, customers are going public with their complaints, especially on the Internet. Customers exasperated by poor service or unresponsive organizations can, with little effort, post the story on a bulletin board or set up a Web site. As a result, some firms have departments of "Web watchers" who monitor customer complaints and answer questions. However, some firms don't get it.

> **Example:** Sears considered establishing a Web answer line. It ran a test but "was swamped" with so many questions—a couple of hundred a day—that it could not answer them all and abandoned the proposal.[37]

THE DIMENSIONS OF CUSTOMER SERVICE

Customer service is an important element in the marketer's arsenal regardless of whether the firm is offering a product or a service. Although customer service shares many of the same attributes as services in general, a variety of special considerations concern customer service alone. Customer service can be defined as:

> Any act, performance, or information that one party offers, or arranges to have offered, that is essentially intangible, that enhances the value of a core product (or service), and promotes the relationship between the organization offering the core product (or service) and the customer.

Several elements of this definition bear scrutiny. Customer service is intangible, in a similar manner to services in general. Customer service "promotes the relationship between the organization . . . and the customer." Hence, it is intimately concerned with the subfield that has become known as "relationship marketing." Also, the organization may offer customer service directly, or arrange for it to be offered by a third party (for example, a distributor).

Two different approaches are useful for classifying customer service: the nature of the supplementary service element and the timing of service delivery.

Supplementary Service Elements

Customer service comprises several supplementary elements that support the core product or service. In his "flower of service," Lovelock identifies eight dimensions that embrace the extensive variety of these elements:

- **Information**: data provided in response to customers' questions and in anticipation of their needs
- **Consultation**: dialogue to probe customer requirements and develop a tailored solution
- **Order-taking**: accepting applications, orders, and reservations
- **Hospitality**: consideration and courtesy in attending to customer needs
- **Safekeeping**: looking after customers' possessions
- **Exceptions**: supplementary services that lie outside the routine of normal service delivery (such as special requests, special communications, problem solving, and restitution)
- **Billing**: requests for payment
- **Payment**: action taken to pay the bill

These dimensions provide a framework for identifying additional service elements to improve service quality.

Timing of Service Element

In some cases it may be helpful to categorize customer service as pre-purchase (or acquisition), and post-purchase.[38] Each phase has different customer requirements and, consequently, is associated with different types of customer service activities. However, since organizations typically seek repeat purchase behavior (customer retention), post-purchase activities should meld into pre-purchase activities for another purchase cycle.[39]

PRE-PURCHASE Pre-purchase customer service is conceptualized as those activities that help prepare the customer for the purchase decision. Among activities fulfilling this function are the various forms of advertising and promotion (including branding) designed to provide product and location information to the customer, and personal selling. New technology may be involved, as when a women's clothing store used advanced imaging technology to show a customer how she would look in a dress made from a particular fabric with a chosen style.

Other examples include:

Example: At Bass Pro Shops in Springfield, Mo. shoppers can cast into a test pool before buying a fly fishing rod. At The Musician's Planet, musicians can try out a guitar and make a demo tape. At REI, a Seattle-based outdoors store, consumers can engage in activities such as attempting a 64-foot climbing wall, testing a water pump in an indoor river, or entering a rainstorm to test a Gore-Tex jacket.[40]

POST-PURCHASE Post-purchase customer service helps the customer use the product and deals with any problems or complaints that may occur. Methods of delivering this sort of service include installation, spare parts availability and, traditional technical service departments in many manufacturing companies. They also include toll-free telephone numbers now available for over 80% of consumer products in the United States, backed up by customer service agents ready to offer advice and solve customer problems.[41] In recent years, the spread of telephone-based service methodologies has grown dramatically as business-to-business marketers have sought to cut costs incurred by on-the-road service personnel. Among one of the more successful endeavors is the GE Answer Service; it handles over four million calls per year for the entire range of GE products, from dishwashers to jet engines.

Another important feature of post-purchase customer service is its capability to act as an early warning system to detect product quality problems. Relatedly, well-delivered post-purchase customer service is often a key determinant of future purchases. These purchases derive from two sources: high levels of repurchase intention and high levels of positive word-of-mouth.

High Re-purchase Intention   Many companies have realized that regardless of the core product, the ability to offer excellent service to customers may be as (or even more) critical to repurchase than technical excellence of the core product. For example, one of the major reasons IBM came to dominate the mainframe computer business in the 1970s and 1980s was not so much superior product technology (which was first rate but not always the best) but rather its attention to customer service. This was captured in the epigram; "You never get fired for buying an IBM."

Word-of-Mouth   For many years, marketers have treated positive word-of-mouth as an important factor in the purchase of products and services. Its importance derives from its impartiality compared to all forms of advertising and personal selling, which are always partial. However, word-of-mouth is two-sided in its impact: positive word-of-mouth is helpful to the firm, negative word-of-mouth can be devastating. Recently, a Washington DC-based consultant, TARP, demonstrated what marketers have suspected for many years—negative word-of-mouth travels much further than positive word-of-mouth. In addition, research by Blockbuster, the video-store chain, revealed that customers who had a bad experience told 10 to 20 people.[42]

Excellent customer service offers four important word-of-mouth benefits:

- Provides non-users with persuasive information that may lead them to purchase;
- Provides current users with external validation of their own purchases;
- Avoids the potential for non-users not considering purchase of the product because of a customer's poor product experience;
- Avoids the potential for reducing the probability of repurchase by current users.

The importance of word-of-mouth promises to be even greater in the future as new methods of harnessing the power of customers are developed. Already, company-sponsored user clubs have had significant impact on efforts to increase sales by developing a strong product affinity and providing positive group experiences for customers, including validation of the purchase decision and easing product use. Examples include Apple Computer's Mac User Clubs and Harley Davidson's Harley Owners Group (HOG) Clubs. More recently, Internet Web sites enable users to exchange product/service experiences. These sites, which may be either company- or customer-sponsored, are powerful means for either supporting or, in the case of customer-sponsored sites, also detracting, from firm efforts.[43]

DEVELOPING AN EFFECTIVE CUSTOMER SERVICE SYSTEM

In their book on customer service, Davidow and Uttal develop a set of principles for delivering outstanding customer service related to six core elements: strategy, leadership, personnel, design, infrastructure, and measurement.[44]

Strategy

By strategy, Davidow and Uttal mean segmentation and positioning based on customers' service expectations rather than on their needs for the core product or service. They argue that several customer service segments can exist in one needs-based market segment; conversely, one customer service segment can cut across several needs-based segments. In the following example, Wells Fargo Bank does not seem to have understood this basic issue.

Example: In late 1995, San Francisco-based Wells Fargo Bank purchased First Interstate Bancorp in a hostile takeover. Whereas Wells Fargo's strategy was to focus on efficiently executing customer transactions using the most convenient low-cost method, First Interstate was a traditional bank where "customers could expect hand-holding and personalized service." Following the takeover, branch closings and personnel losses led to degraded service levels which, together with aggressive competitor actions,[45] brought significant customer defections: 1% per month (December 1996 to June 1997) of customers outside California![46]

To develop the customer service strategy, extensive data should be gathered on customers' service requirements and competitive offerings. On this basis, the firm should at least meet customers' required service levels and surpass those of competitors; ideally, it should set customer expectations slightly below what the firm can deliver.

Leadership

To deliver top-flight customer service, senior firm executives must foster a service-oriented culture in which customer-first actions are supported at every turn. Customer service must be everybody's business, and the bureaucracy that frequently stands in the way of putting the customer first should be dismantled. Davidow and Uttal cite Nordstrom fashion retail stores, well-known for exemplary customer service including accepting returned merchandise with no questions asked, and for its employees who go above and beyond reasonable expectations to serve customers. Nordstrom's fosters such a culture in part by inverting the traditional management pyramid and placing customers at the top. The typically low status retail store clerk is given high status as a "sales representative," right next to customers.

Personnel

Depending on the particular type of customer service being considered, the basic building blocks of facilities, equipment, and personnel will be differentially important in the customer's perception of service quality. However, compared to facilities and equipment, the behavior of human personnel in service delivery has the potential for being much more variable. As a result, service firms must pay special attention to the management of their human resources, especially the on-stage personnel that have contact with individual customers.

Reicheld has argued that long-term employees offer significant economic benefits to service firms.[47] Included are avoidance of hiring costs, reduction of training costs, training benefits from experienced personnel, greater personnel efficiency from experience, ability to seek out better customers, customer retention through personal relationships, customer referral, and referral of high quality job applicants.

RECRUITMENT AND SELECTION   The firm's charter or vision statement acts as a superstructure within which the firm can develop recruitment and selection policies to ensure that only employees with the appropriate set of knowledge, skills, and abilities enter the organization. These policies should be well-constructed and rigorously applied. Clearly, the specific set of required characteristics varies with the particular service requirements; Berry and Parasuraman have identified a general list including competence, courtesy, credibility, responsiveness, and commitment.[48]

TRAINING   In addition, the firm should develop training programs to ensure that each service employee knows both how to behave with customers and to fulfill their functions. For example, each year in Pakistan, senior Honda mechanics run "Mechanic Training Camps" to impart the latest knowledge in maintenance and repair to Pakistani mechanics. Rather than hire experienced personnel and train them in the firm's way of doing business, many service firms prefer to take raw recruits and develop them from scratch. Le Salon Orient and Rever, major hairdressing salons in Hong Kong, run their own schools from which they select the most promising candidates for their own organizations.

REWARD AND RECOGNITION   A variety of different reward programs can be developed to motivate service employees to serve customers. Advantage should be taken of the variability inherent in human behavior to encourage service personnel to "go the extra mile." Programs that identify "service heroes" can spur others to greater efforts.

Example: Five years after launch in 1989, TelPizza in Madrid, Spain had 185 stores and 40% market share, double that of Pizza Hut, by focusing on managing and rewarding its 4000+ delivery boys. Each "pizza ambassador" is given a small geographic area so they can find addresses easily and get to know their customers. Up to 20% of their time is spent in pre-sales customer service, handing out coupons and menus to build awareness. Every "pizza ambassador" is rewarded when business increases in the territory.[49]

Example: Alan Ho, founder of Vinataxi, the leading taxi service in Ho Chi Minh City, installed a rigorous selection program for taxi drivers such that only about 3% of applicants passed. Failed applicants that still want employment have the opportunity to take a two-week driving course and retake the test. Once hired, all taxi drivers take a personal grooming course. All on-duty drivers are required to wear a company-provided uniform: white T-shirt, yellow cap with Vinataxi's logo, dark trousers, and shoes. (Many Vietnamese wear sandals; Ho considers these dangerous for driving.) Drivers are placed in teams and team bonuses are awarded for high revenues.

In Ho's points system, each driver is awarded 20 points; points are subtracted/awarded for behavior on the job. For example, good deeds (returning wallets and personal belongings left in taxis) and customer testimonials (calling in appreciation of excellent service) earn extra points. Conversely, customer complaints and damages attributable to driver carelessness lead to point deductions. If points reduce below 10, the driver is fired; high levels of points lead to bonuses. Ho also monitors taxi driver behavior via "FBI motorcycle patrols"; he believes that the patrolmen (hired drivers waiting for taxis) who cruise the streets looking for passenger-carrying taxis with their meters not running both enforce Vinataxi policy and learn an important lesson about "stealing" from the company.

Design

Many products need to be serviced. In addition, when product components break down they need to be replaced. When products are manufactured without concern for servicing or component replacement, providing exemplary customer service is almost impossible as the difficulties are frustrating for both service personnel and customers.[50] The key is to involve service staff as design team equals early in the new product development process so that serviceability becomes a key design criterion. Regardless of how well designed the product, component failure is always possible. The firm should identify the likely breakdown points, taking due consideration of the use/abuse that customers may inflict on the product, and design firm responses to exceed customer expectations. Finally, involving customers in the process can both enhance customer value and reduce firm costs:

Example: Shouldice Hospital near Toronto specializes in straightforward hernia operations. It doesn't advertise, receives few referrals from private physicians, yet with prices around one third those in many U.S. hospitals, has a long waiting list of prospective patients from all over the United States and Canada. Shouldice's success, in addition to its highly focused strategy, is closely related to a service design system that includes ample customer participation. Patients fill out pre-registration forms, shave there own groins and abdomens, and conduct their own physical therapy by walking and climbing stairs (designed into the daily routine). Roommates are assigned based on background and interests, and frequent social activities (designed into the day), especially among post- and pre-operative patients, minimize anxiety. The experience is so positive that many past patients attend Shouldice alumni activities![51]

The specific design of the customer service function is shaped by many factors. Among those that should be considered are[52]:

- Presence or absence of intermediaries: Some customer-contact tasks are better performed by intermediaries. The firm relinquishes a degree of control over the interactions and must put systems in place to ensure high quality across organizational boundaries.
- High-contact or low-contact: The greater the number of customer contact points, especially those distant from managerial control, the greater the requirement that individual service personnel act responsibly without supervision.
- Institutional or individual purchases: When several individuals are involved in receipt of service, as with institutional customers, coordination requirements are increased.
- Duration of the service delivery process: The greater the time of service delivery, the greater the requirement for information on service delivery status.
- Capacity-constrained services: Reservation or queuing systems will be required.
- Frequency of use and repurchase: Systems should be put in place for remembering prior customers and treating them appropriately.
- Level of complexity: Differential levels of complexity imply differing levels of education and training for service personnel.
- Degree of risk: The greater the consequence of service failure for customers, the greater the necessity for more highly trained service personnel.

Infrastructure

Service infrastructure is the backbone of service delivery. No matter how committed the service personnel, unless the appropriate technological and organizational infrastructure is in place, it may be difficult for them to perform as required. Indeed, it is a paradox that the seemingly most people-intensive service systems have the highest infrastructure investment requirements. For example, the major airlines reservation and check-in systems are backed up by immense investments in computer hardware, software, and telecommunications. Infrastructure investment to meet and exceed customer expectations can have immense payoffs as competitive matching is often more difficult than producing products with equivalent performance and quality levels.

The demand for appropriate organizational infrastructure is focused on the nature of the interfaces between the organization and the customer. In general, most customers want simple interfaces—a single customer service representative to handle all the customer's issues. What customers find intensely annoying is being passed from one inappropriate customer service representative to another. The problem typically arises because organizations develop specialized functions. Specialization provides efficiencies by developing specialized knowledge, but search and coordination costs increase for customers. To fully satisfy customers' service requirements may require a total reengineering of the customer interface.

> **Example:** Historically, the Xerox customer interface included three separate organizations—sales, service, and business operations—each managed separately. In this system, commissioned salespeople strove to place machines with customers. If, after the sale, the customer had a question about the machine or wanted to switch to a slightly different product as their needs became better known, it would be difficult to find the salesperson because they were busy searching for the next commission opportunity. As a result, the customer service organization was left dealing with a host of problems created by the sales force.

Xerox addressed this problem by forming partnerships of sales, service, and business operations, the three functions that managed the field operation. District and regional levels operated as equal partners for managerial decisions and planning. District partnerships were given increased responsibility to resolve customer problems, take advantage of business opportunities, and focus advertising locally; reward systems were also brought into line.[53]

Some organizations seemingly strive to remove the customer interface altogether. How often has the customer been transferred to an extension that didn't answer, trapped in phone-mail with no exit, or in a tone-based enquiry system with seemingly infinite "do-" loops? How else to account for the behavior of a $5 billion New Jersey-based company when a 4:35PM weekday call elicits the response: "This is the World Headquarters of X Company. Our switchboard is open from 9:30AM to 4:30PM Eastern Standard Time. In an emergency, please contact security at xxx-yyyy." Compare this example to mutual fund manager Fidelity Investments that offers 24-hour, 7-day per week service to buy, sell, and transfer mutual funds.

An especially innovative approach to securing differential advantage via infrastructure improvement using the Internet was taken by a French distributor.

> **Example:** Supervox is a French distributor of electrical, sanitary, and gardening products serving about 10,000 mom-and-pop stores throughout Europe. Typically, an order placed by one of its customers would take a week to 10 days to be filled. Supervox purchased unsold IBM PCs that were "too primitive for schools" for about $200 each and installed them, complete with modems, Web browsers, and basic software, at customer locations. When the retailers go onto the Web, they find Supervox' catalog. Each order receives a confirming fax or e-mail, and Supervox achieves a promised 48-hour delivery 98% of the time.

Measurement

To achieve superior customer service, management must identify and measure the critical elements that drive customer satisfaction. Typically, overall customer satisfaction is based on some limited number of customer requirements. For each of these requirements, standards can be set for firm performance. Performance against these standards, which should be monitored and modified over time as customer expectations change, should be rigorously controlled. Reward programs should be targeted against these standards.

> **Example:** American Express believes that one important customer service measure is the length of time to answer the telephone. The company not only monitors this performance variable assiduously, the waiting time is prominently and continuously displayed for all customer service operators. In addition, supervisors listen in on customer/employee conversations to monitor employee behavior. Other measurement standards focus on time to replace lost cards and speed in customers' receipt of bills.

Although customer satisfaction is an important measure, customer defection may be more valuable. Many customer defectors are "satisfied" customers, and loyal customers are more profitable than new customers.[54] Identifying customer defectors, then engaging in root cause analysis may provide valuable information for improving service performance.

THE STRATEGIC ROLE OF CUSTOMER SERVICE

Superior customer service can play an important strategic role for the organization. As the quality movement continues to strengthen and become more widespread, firms are increasingly finding that competitive advantage cannot be secured through superior product quality. In looking elsewhere for competitive advantage, customer service is an obvious candidate. The focus here is on two related approaches for getting closer to customers—database marketing, and reward and recognition programs.

Database Marketing

Database marketing can play a critical role in securing improved customer retention (loyalty marketing), yet in many product and service areas there is rarely direct interaction between customer and organization. As a result, unless they proactively seek out customer information, many firms do not know who their customers are.[55] In addition, in those arenas where customer data is collected as an integral feature of the business relationship, such as bank accounts, insurance policies, and telephone service, service providers neither collect the full set of useful customer information nor use it fully for marketing purposes.

Our colleague Rashi Glazer has developed a customer information model potentially comprising data from several firm and external databases embracing:

- Customer characteristics: such as demographic data independent of any relationship with the firm
- Customer responses to firm decisions: such as perceptions and preferences, including marketing mix response data such as price sensitivity and information sources, the where, how, and why they buy
- Purchase history: data on products purchased and associated revenues, costs, and profits.

This matrix is at least three-dimensional as each entry is indexed in time when customers purchase products. With such information, firms are better able to manage and segment current customers, and discriminate among them on the basis of price sensitivity. They are better able to communicate on an individual basis, including making tailored offers, possibly related to critical life cycle or other situational needs. Finally, they can increasingly automate customer interactions, secure data on product and service problems that can be affirmatively addressed, and have increased confidence in, and reduce the cost of, introducing new products.[56,57]

A glimpse of the future:

Example: At 6:30 p.m., about to leave his office, Joe recalls it's his turn to prepare dinner; he surfs to a Web site maintained by Pillsbury. The computer recognizes the address—it's Joe again—flashes a query to the corporate database and analyzes the answer. He was here six days ago and two weeks before that. Both times he's requested data on meals he could prepare with a minimum of fuss from prepackaged goods. Bet he's back for the same thing.

The computer accesses another Pillsbury database and comes back with meals that, according to research, are popular with time-sensitive professional males. What's on the menu?—Garlic Pasta Chicken Salad? No! He had that last time and that was a Saturday. He's picked it the last three times he's been at the site. Something else in poultry then. Ah! There we go! Fiesta Chicken. Quick, simple to prepare, spicy—Joe's picked spicy meals every time he's downloaded a recipe—and popular with males in his age range.

By the time Joe has finished clicking on the "What's new in main dishes" button, an entire meal has been planned for him, including recipes, suggested side dishes, and even the wine. Joe looks at the Fiesta Chicken page, sees a lovely picture of the dish, recipe beside it.

Now, where is Joe located? Last time he was on the site he requested information on stores carrying the Green Giant brand along Route 128 near the intersection with Mainfair. A quick check of the MapInfo business-oriented geographic information system reveals a light industry area populated by R&D startups. Joe is probably at work and he's going to pick up what he needs for the chicken while driving home. A map flashes on the screen; here are the stores where he can most conveniently pick up the Green Giant products he needs for Fiesta Chicken and some Pillsbury baked goods for desert![58]

A customer database can distinguish between high and low value customers, and high and low loyalty customers (Figure 17.3). Each of the four cells suggests different courses of action:

- A: High value/high loyalty: objective—retention
  action—targeted loyalty/reward programs
- B: High value/low loyalty: objective—switch from competitors to high value/high loyalty group
  action—sampling and targeted sales promotion to gain trial then loyalty/reward programs
- C: Low value/high loyalty: objective—increase purchases
  action—cross sell other products
- D: Low value/low loyalty: no special effort

Despite the importance of high value, high loyalty customers, businesses sometimes offer better service to their lowest profit customers. For example, supermarkets with express checkouts for eight items or less might consider reducing waiting time for customers with extensive purchases.

Reward and Recognition Programs

Reward and recognition programs are an important element of post-sales service for many firms and embrace many potential customer benefits. Economic benefits, delivered in reward programs, can be used for the same or a similar product (such as airline frequent flier programs) or for something quite different, such as the opportunity to win a vacation package after signing up for a mortgage. Effective programs are those that deliver greater value to loyal customers and so bind them closer to the firm. The critical issue for these types of reward is that they should be perceived as valuable by customers, offering cash value, choice, aspirational value (benefits to aspire to), and convenience, and have redemption rules that are clearly understandable.[59]

Example: Smitty's Super Value, a $650 million Phoenix-based regional hypermarket chain comprised of 24 stores, offers a full range of grocery, clothing, electrical, and household goods in a highly competitive market. Smitty's Shoppers Passport, a magnetic card swiped at checkout every visit, has 750,000 members and 60% use in any six-week period. At any time, approximately 2,000 items are on instant discount promotion (100% supplier funded); a points scheme operates in selected stores for eight-week periods, and gifts are redeemable from an appeal-researched catalog.

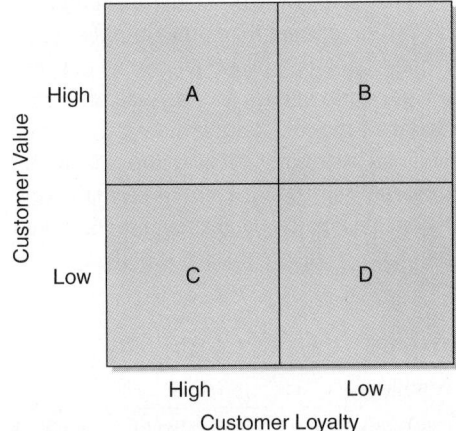

FIGURE 17.3

Customer Value and Loyalty

The customer database, maintained on transaction data, is used for selective mailing of coupons, magazines, and information; customers whose sales change or decline receive special mailings. For example, families with kids 12 and under are mailed coupons for toys, videos, clothes, cakes and so forth three weeks before the birthdays. The system, whose start-up costs were 20% of sales (now 1%), is fully integrated into the business and is the main vehicle for all marketing activity.

Smitty's results are spectacular: cardholders' purchase baskets are 50% higher than non-cardholders, cardholders account for 70% of sales, sales of participating products increased 200%, and customer data is sold to suppliers for $200,000 per annum. The challenge for Smitty's: keep customers interested and the scheme fresh.[60]

By contrast,

Example: Notwithstanding the apparent success of airline frequent flier programs, they have come under considerable criticism for the difficulty of redemption. All major airlines block out certain flights, often for weeks at a time, so that frequent flier redemption is not allowed. In addition, they often allocate so few seats on individual flights that it is impossible for a typical family to travel together on their reward![61]

Other customer service benefits comprise items such as special lounges (equipped for business travelers), free limousine service (airlines), valet parking (clubs and restaurants) and information on children's development (Kimberly Clark's program for Huggies Disposable Diapers).

SUMMARY

In many cases, services can satisfy all customer needs. In certain instances, customers prefer to purchase a product to deliver the service; at other times, it is more convenient to purchase the service. Regardless of whether the core benefit is delivered by a product or service, many customer service elements typically surround the core.

Services (core and surrounding elements) are different from products: In particular, they may be distinguished by their intangibility, inseparability, variability, perishability, divisibility, acquisition, and the role of customers, each of which leads to important marketing implications. Securing high service quality, defined as the difference between perceived and expected quality, is an important yet complex task that can be aided by a diagnostic model. Individual services can be distinguished in important ways—whether the focus is on products, people, information, location of the service act, presence of the customer, or membership in the service organization—that also have important marketing implications.

Customer service, frequently involving other marketing mix elements, can be conceptualized as pre- and post-purchase. Firms that do a good job in customer service reap benefits of high repurchase intentions and positive word-of-mouth. Quality delivery depends on many factors, including developing a customer service strategy, leadership, managing service personnel, service design, and constructing an organization focused on delivering customer service and an effective measurement system. Finally, database marketing, and reward and recognition programs play an important role in customer service delivery.

THE CHANGING VIEW

Old Way	New Way
Service an afterthought	Service recognized as key competitive weapon
Service separate from marketing	Service seen as crucial to customer retention
Narrow view of service	Broad view of service

Old Way	New Way
Most services provided internally	Outsourcing resulting in externalization of service provision
Low tech	High tech
Service performance unmeasured	Service performance carefully tracked
Peak demand management rare	Peak demand management ubiquitous
Relatively narrow range of services available	Explosive growth in service variety
Intuitive service management	Analytic service management
Customer databases non-existent	Customer databases often pivotal in service management
Zero or negative reward for customer loyalty	Loyalty incentives very common
Customer expectations ignored	Customer expectations seen as crucial for customer satisfaction

QUESTIONS FOR STUDY AND DISCUSSION

1. Why are many advanced economies overwhelmingly service dominated?

2. Why do some social critics think it's bad to work for McDonalds? Do you agree with their point of view?

3. Bring to class three examples of "high tech" services not mentioned in the chapter.

4. Apply the SERVQUAL model to an aspect of the operations of your educational institution. Did you find the application useful? Why or why not?

5. Some authors argue that the World Wide Web will change interpretation of some classic product/service distinctions. For example, technology will permit increasingly realistic emulation of human service providers and provide vicarious pre-purchase exploration of the service experience. Examine each of the distinctions discussed in the chapter. How might these be affected by broadband Internet access?

6. Some writers argue that service providers often miss opportunities to increase customer satisfaction and loyalty because they do not exert enough effort to "tangibilize" their services. Pick three frequently purchased services and illustrate how they might be better "tangibilized."

7. Customer targeting is a much more crucial issue for many service providers than it is for manufacturers. Do you agree with this statement? Why or why not?

8. Some service providers "bundle" all the elements of their offer together (such as single price admission to an amusement park with unlimited use of rides) while others "unbundle" (such as *a la carte* restaurant menus). As a consultant, what guidelines would you suggest to a service-provider client on the issue of "bundling" or "unbundling?"

9. In some situations, customers are comfortable with co-production of services; in other cases, they see their participation as undesirable. How might a service provider choose when to encourage co-production?

10. "Word-of-mouth is the priceless promotion." Do you agree with this statement? Why or why not?

11. Customer information management is increasingly important to good service delivery, yet many companies are unwilling to invest in upgrading relevant information systems. How would you go about making an economic case for such investment?

12. "Once customers become accustomed to a given service package, it is dangerous to change it, particularly if there is any perceived service diminution associated with the change." Do you agree with this statement? How would you minimize the risks associated with such a change?

13. Managing the delivery of a complete service experience is a demanding management challenge. What three principles should drive management decisions in such a situation?

14. In many service companies, the human interface with customers is a critical element in their success. Such companies often have the problem that customers follow employees when they leave the firm. How would you recommend minimizing these customer defections?

ENDNOTES

1. *The Economist* defines a service as "anything that cannot be dropped on your foot!"

2. C.H. Lovelock, Product Plus: How Product + Service = Competitive Advantage, New York: McGraw-Hill, 1994.

3. Philips Medical Systems has adopted in similar strategy in Europe. The customer pays a fixed charge per image from one of its diagnostic scanners. Philips manages the entire imaging facility, including responsibility both for maintenance of existing equipment, and replacement and upgrading as required.

4. In early 1997, GE purchased Greenwich Air Services in a move that doubled its share of the market for servicing jet engines, *The New York Times*, March 11, 1997.

5. *The Economist*, August 7, 1999.

6. *The New York Times*, October 5, 1999.

7. This shift by manufacturers to offer services often results in competition with independent consultants. Thus, companies like Andersen Consulting argue that manufacturers like IBM and Unisys cannot be impartial in their recommendations to clients; the manufacturers disagree, they say they must put the customer first, regardless of whose "product" is the best (C.H. Deutsch, *The New York Times*, January 7, 1997).

8. See C.H. Lovelock, *Services Marketing*, 4th Edition, Upper Saddle River, NJ: Prentice Hall, 2000.

9. Services and social behaviors dominate offerings of public and non-profit organizations. Several features distinguish public and non-profit marketing from marketing in the private sector. These include the dominance of non-financial objectives, the requirement to attract resources from various sources (customers, donations, volunteers, grants), multiple constituencies, the ability to secure free or inexpensive support, the tension between implementing the organization's strategy and customer satisfaction, public scrutiny, non-market pressures, and complex management problems embracing employees, volunteers, and trustees.

10. As economies advance, two situations occur: Totally new services are developed and consumers "outsource" services they previously performed themselves (meal preparation, gardening).

11. *The New York Times*, January 22, 1998.

12. See N. Capon, *The Marketing of Financial Services: A Book of Cases*, Englewood Cliffs, NJ: Prentice Hall, 1992.

13. In general, the franchiser develops the broad strategy; franchisees are entrepreneurs who implement the strategy and often supply capital.

14. For elaboration on trends in services, see Lovelock, 2000, *op. cit*.

15. Lovelock, 2000, *op. cit.* makes the further distinction between services directed at people's bodies (such as health care, transportation) and those directed at people's minds (such as education, radio, TV).

16. Some service scholars conceptualize service as comprising physical evidence (physical surroundings and all tangible cues), participants (all human actors in the service encounter including firm personnel and other customers), and process (procedures, mechanisms, and flow of activities), M.J. Bitner, "Evaluating Service Encounters: The Effects of Physical Surroundings and Employee Responses," *Journal of Marketing*, 54 (Apr. 1990) pp. 69–82.

17. In the financial services industry the on-stage, off-stage distinction is termed front office and back office. See E. Goffman, *The Presentation of Self in Everyday Life*, New York: Doubleday Anchor, 1959.

18. J. Carlzon, *Moments of Truth*, Cambridge, MA: Ballinger Publishing Company, 1987.

19. C.W.L. Hart, "The Power of Unconditional Service Guarantees," *Harvard Business Review*, 66 (July-August 1988), pp. 54–62.

20. Many manufacturing companies are seeking to improve their working capital positions by reducing product storage both in their own facilities (such as raw materials, work-in-process, finished goods) and in those of their customers (and distributors).

21. An interesting conceptual distinction is between optimum capacity utilization, the preferred level, and maximum capacity utilization, the level at which the firm can operate for short periods of time but which is not sustainable in the long run.

22. To affirmatively decrease demand is often termed "demarketing."

23. Queuing may reduce customer satisfaction.

24. See "The Mass Transit Railroad in Hong Kong," in N. Capon and W. Van Honacker, *The Asian Marketing Case Book*, Singapore: Prentice Hall, 1999, for an example of a supply/demand imbalance problem.

25. The trick in this example is to be able to separate the low price segment of passengers from those willing to pay a higher price. The airlines used to use the "standby" device for this purpose until they discovered that the Saturday night stopover more effectively separated business people willing to pay a higher price from the segment of lower price paying customers.

26. Developed by MBA student Cory Linton from R. Schachter and C.H. Lovelock, "The Boston Adult Education Center," in C.H. Lovelock, *Services Marketing*, 3rd. edition, Upper Saddle River, NJ: Prentice Hall, 1996, pp. 254–267.

27. See G.L. Shostack, "Service Positioning Through Structural Change," *Journal of Marketing*, 51 (January 1987), pp. 33–34.

28. Part of the folklore surrounding the British automobile company Rolls Royce is that in its early days, the firm positively vetted all prospective customers to assure itself they had the financial means for appropriate upkeep of the automobile.

29. *The New York Times*, June 10, 1997. In a game between the New York Mets and the Cincinnati Reds, a fan behind home plate called out the catcher's instructions to the Mets' pitcher. Despite his efforts, the Reds' batters were unable to take advantage and the Mets won 4-2. Some of the issues in this section were noted in Chapter 3.

30. Sometimes membership organizations are treated differently from non-member organizations in a legal sense. For example, in Taiwan, local restrictions prohibited the construction of hypermarkets in areas zoned for industrial use. Major hypermarket operators attempted to skirt this prohibition by requiring a membership fee and making their stores into "clubs."

31. A. Parasuraman, V.A. Zeithaml, and L.L Berry, "A Conceptual Model of Service Quality and Its Implications for Future Research," *Journal of Marketing*, (Fall 1985), pp. 41–50.

32. B.J. Pine II, D. Peppers and M. Rogers, "Do You Want to Keep Your Customers Forever," *Harvard Business Review*, 73 (March-April 1995), pp. 103–114.

33. To achieve ground efficiency, Southwest Airlines benchmarked Indy 500 pit crews.

34. From C.W.L. Hart, J.L. Heskett and W.E. Sasser Jr., "The Profitable Art of Service Recovery, *Harvard Business Review*, 68 (Jul./Aug. 1990), pp. 148–156.

35. Colin Marshall, CEO British Airways in *High Life*, British Airways in-flight magazine.

36. Technical Assistance Research Program (TARP), *Consumer Complaint Handling in America: An Update Study, Parts I and II*, Washington, DC: TARP and U.S. Office of Consumer Affairs, April 1986. The three primary reasons for not complaining were: not worth the time or effort, a belief that no one would be concerned or act upon the problem, lack of knowledge about where to go or what to do.

37. R. Furchgott, "Surfing for Satisfaction: Consumer Complaints Go on Line," *The New York Times*, Sunday June 8, 1997.

38. H. Takeuchi and J.A. Quelch, "Quality is More than Making a Good Product," *Harvard Business Review*, 61 (Jul./Aug. 1983), pp. 139–145.

39. For extended purchase decisions, it is sometimes useful to decompose pre-purchase customer service into finer-grained categories.

40. *The New York Times*, February 28, 1998.

41. An additional major purpose of these systems is to develop a customer database.

42. R. Furchgott, "Surfing for Satisfaction: Consumer Complaints Go on Line," *The New York Times*, Sunday June 8, 1997.

43. For example, Johnson & Johnson (J&J) (Japan) sponsors a site that enables its physician customers to exchange experiences in using J&J products. Companies such as United Airlines, America On-line, McDonald's, Gap, Chase Bank, Microsoft, and many others have to deal with detracting sites.

44. W.H. Davidow and B. Uttal, *Total Customer Service*, New York, NY: Harper & Row, 1989. See also J.L. Heskett, T.O. Jones, G.W. Loveman, W.E. Sasser Jr. and L.A. Schlesinger, "Putting the Service-Profit Chain to Work," *Harvard Business Review*, 72 (March-April 1994), pp. 164–174; R.T. Rust, A.J. Zahorik, and T.L. Keiningham, "Return on Quality (ROQ): Making Service Quality Financially Accountable," *Journal of Marketing*, 59 (April 1995), pp. 58–70.

45. For example, one competitor handed out business cards to customers waiting in line at Wells Fargo branches; another ran an advertisement urging customers to call 1-800-FED-UP to hear a message that began: "We have just bought your old bank. For a summary of the ways we will be jerking you around, press one. For a list of employees you like who have been fired, press two."

46. Material for this example from *Business Week*, June 7, 1997.

47. F.F. Reicheld, *The Loyalty Effect*, Boston, MA: Harvard Business School Press, 1996.

48. L.L. Berry and A. Parasuraman, *Marketing Services: Competing through Quality*, New York: Free Press, 1991, p. 16.

49. S. Rapp, *Direct* magazine. See Capon and Van Honacker, *op. cit.,* for the Honda and Vinataxi examples.

50. Davidow and Uttal, *op. cit.*, use the tragedy of the May 1979 DC10 crash, in which the pylon assembly holding the engine failed, to make this point. The National Transportation Safety Board report criticized McDonnell Douglas saying that it should have foreseen that the pylons would be removed for maintenance and should have designed the assembly "to eliminate, or at least minimize, vulnerability to damage . . . (since) . . . the maintenance operation, regardless of the procedure used, would be difficult to perform and would be particularly vulnerable to damage-producing errors."

51. Shouldice Hospital Ltd., *Harvard Business School*, 9-683-068.

52. Lovelock, 2000, *op. cit.*

53. Xerox Corporation: The Customer Satisfaction Program, *Harvard Business School*, 9-591-055.

54. F.F. Reicheld and W.E Sasser Jr., "Zero Defections: Quality Comes to Services," *Harvard Business Review*, 68 (Sept./Oct. 1990) pp. 105–111, T.O. Jones and W.E Sasser Jr., "Why Satisfied Customers Defect," *Harvard Business Review*, 73 (Nov./Dec. 1995) pp. 88–99 and F.F. Reicheld, "Learning from Customer Defections," *Harvard Business Review*, 68 (Mar./Apr. 1996) pp. 56–69.

55. Several devices are now used extensively including customer value cards, lead generation (TV, press, mail inserts, door drops), customer-get-customer campaigns, syndicated questionnaires, third-party lifestyle databases, telephone "help" lines, special events, and loyalty cards used in connection with purchase.

56. See R. Glazer, "Strategy and Structure in Information-Intensive Markets: the Relationship between Marketing and IT," *Journal of Market-Focused Management*, 2, (1997), pp. 65–81. Glazer further argues that key IT functions performed by the firm (i.e., information acquisition, information distribution, information interpretation, organizational memory) should be organized into "departments" within decision teams.

57. To be useful, data in the database should be: relevant, structured, current, consistent, accurate, accessible, complete, and secure.

58. Excerpted from M.J. Tucker, "Poppin' Fresh Dough," *Datamation*, (May 1997), pp. 50–58.

59. L. O'Brien and C. Jones, "Do Rewards Really Create Loyalty" *Harvard Business Review*, 63 (May/June 1995), pp. 75–82.

60. Excerpted from a presentation by M. Atkinson, Managing Director, Tequila Asia Pacific (Singapore) Pte. Ltd.

61. B.B. Buchholz, "You've Earned a Free Ticket. Just Try Getting It," *The New York Times*, June 1, 1997.

WEB RESOURCES

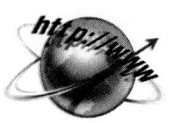

American Express	www.americanexpress.com
Anderson Windows	www.andersoncorp.com
Apple	www.apple.com
Bandag	www.bandag.com
Bass Pro Shops	www.basspro.com
Benihana of Tokyo	www.benihana.com
Blockbuster	www.blockbuster.com
British Airways	www.britishairways.com
Disney	www.disney.go.com
Federal Express	www.fedex.com
Florida Power and Light	www.fpl.com
General Electric	www.ge.com
General Motors	www.gm.com
General Motors Acceptance Corp.	www.gmacfs.com
Green Giant	www.greengiant.com
Harley Davidson	www.harley-davidson.com
Hewlett Packard	www.hp.com
Honda	www.honda.com
IBM	www.ibm.com
Kimberly Clark	www.kimberly-clark.com
Levi's	www.levi.com
McDonalds	www.mcdonalds.com
Merrill Lynch	www.ml.com
Nordstrom	www.nordstrom.com
Pillsbury	www.pillsbury.com
Pitney Bowes	www.pitneybowes.com
Pizza Hut	www.pizzahut.com
REI	www.rei.com
Scandinavian Airlines System	www.sas.se
Sears	www.sears.com
Shell Oil	www.shell.com
Shouldice	www.shouldice.com
Siemens	www.siemens.com
Singapore Airlines	www.singaporeair.com
Southwest Airlines	www.southwest.com
Supervox	www.supervox.fr
TARP	www.e-satisfy.com
The Musician's Planet	www.marsmusic.com
Unisys	www.unisys.com
Wells Fargo	www.wellsfargo.com
Xerox	www.xerox.com

18

MANAGING PRICE AND VALUE

LEARNING OBJECTIVES

When you have completed this chapter, you will understand

- **the critical importance of pricing decisions in generating shareholder value**

- **the difference between pricing strategy and pricing tactics**

- **the key role of price in capturing customer value**

- **the role of costs in pricing decisions**

- **how to incorporate competitors' objectives in setting prices**

- **the role of strategic objectives in setting prices**

- **the pricing toolkit and the price waterfall**

- **a series of tactical issues in setting actual prices**

INTRODUCTION

Pricing is a difficult yet increasingly important subject in many companies in the face of heightened competition. Pricing decisions are critically important to the creation of shareholder value, yet are often based on inaccurate or incomplete information. Furthermore, too many managers do not understand the appropriate role of costs in pricing decisions, and in some firms market considerations play virtually no role whatsoever. Yet, pricing is a critical variable for market strategy and is often pivotal in the following situations:

- Introducing new products
- Entering new markets
- Repositioning a brand or product in an existing market
- Undertaking a significant change in competitive position
- Contemplating a major change of strategic objectives
- Facing discontinuous market shifts such as major technological change or new entrants.

In many cases, problems arise because managers fail to appreciate that pricing strategy cannot exist independent of the market strategy. Yet, pricing is perhaps more intimately connected to market strategy and positioning than any other marketing mix element. Indeed, those who speak loosely of pricing as the means to gain market share or improve margins should be treated with suspicion. Improving share or margins may be appropriate strategic objectives for the strategy as a whole, secured through an agreed, integrated set of actions. Ascribing to price alone the ability to achieve these objectives usually demonstrates an incorrect view of the importance of price and a poor understanding of market strategy.

A further reason for firm difficulties with pricing decisions may be the critical importance of price to firm profitability. Pricing decisions have greater profit leverage than any other marketing implementation variable, so managers are often hesitant to make changes in pricing strategy.

Finally, pricing strategy is treated in a light and almost casual manner by many marketing scholars. Marketing texts often pay too much attention to generalized, descriptive approaches to price setting, in lieu of normative insights. There is clearly great utility in teaching how prices are set in practice, but more emphasis on the right way to set prices is sorely needed.[1,2]

THE IMPORTANCE OF PRICE

Price occupies a unique place among marketing mix elements as it affects both margin (price less cost) and volume (by virtue of demand elasticity). Since volume influences cost through economies of scale and experience curve effects, price also affects cost. Of all marketing mix variables, price has the most leverage in determining product profitability. Figure 18.1 illustrates the powerful effect of price on profitability, based on an empirical analysis of over 2,000 companies.[3]

To understand the mechanics of this relationship, examine the calculations in Table 18.1 that illustrate the impact of price change on profitability. An important underlying assumption in this numerical example is that unit volume stays constant as prices are increased. If the firm were able to achieve a 1% increase in price without loss of volume, then profit and ROI increase by 10%, and ROS by 9%. Each marketing manager should ask the question, "Can I find a way to realize 1% higher prices without losing significant volume?" If the answer is yes, the example demonstrates the type of profitability impact that might be expected. However, the upside potential is the good news; if price were reduced by 1%, the firm would suffer corresponding decreases in profits, ROS, and ROI if volume did not increase. (Note the importance of this illustration for those areas of the organization that, like the sales force, frequently press for price cuts to increase volume.) This high degree of

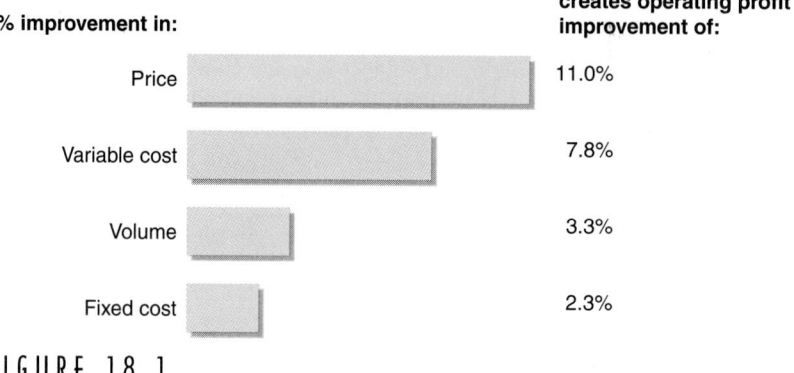

1% improvement in:	creates operating profit improvement of:
Price	11.0%
Variable cost	7.8%
Volume	3.3%
Fixed cost	2.3%

FIGURE 18.1

Illustration of Price Impact on Profit: Comparison of Profit Levers

leverage occurs because the change in revenue drops to the bottom line; no other elements of the income statement are affected by the price change.[4] Clearly, the firm's pricing strategy must be determined carefully. Four related variables should be considered: perceived customer value, costs, competitive offers, and the firm's strategic objectives (Figure 18.2).

CRITICAL ELEMENTS IN PRICING STRATEGY: PERCEIVED CUSTOMER VALUE

The increasing levels of competition faced by many firms often leads to requests for lower prices. Management is thus led to believe that it has a pricing problem. However, this view may be excessively narrow; perhaps the firm has a value problem or, more precisely, a perceived value problem.

Parties to economic transactions exchange value.[5] Individual products and services can be viewed as bundles of utilities (values or benefits) that may satisfy a variety of needs. Value to the customer can be enhanced by when and where (time and place utility) the product is made available, the ease of evaluating the product, and the provision of associated services. The exchange can be viewed as a balance between what the customer gets and what the customer has to give up. Although economics has traditionally focused on the dollar price the customer relinquishes, time, effort, and risk assumption are also typically involved in purchase decisions. Reduction of these elements can be viewed as additional benefits and Figure 18.3 shows these explicitly.[6]

TABLE 18.1 Illustration of Price Impact on Profit

Price Increase	Baseline	1%	2%	3%
Sales ($000)	1,000	1,010	1,020	1,030
Variable costs ($000)	500	500	500	500
Fixed costs ($000)	400	400	400	400
Profit (pre-tax) ($000)	100	110	120	130
Profit improvement (%)		10%	20%	30%
Return on sales (%)	10%	10.9%	11.8%	12.7%
ROS improvement (%)		9%	18%	27%
Total investment ($000) (assumed)	600	600	600	600
ROI (%)	16.7%	18.3%	20%	21.7%
ROI improvement (%)		10%	20%	30%

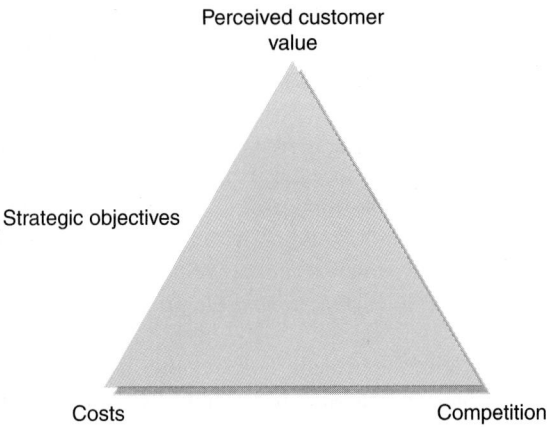

FIGURE 18.2

Critical Elements in Pricing Strategy

Creating Value

Perceived customer value is the net perceived benefit the customer receives from the product or service. It comprises the perception of the benefits received, less the perception of the costs incurred in securing those benefits. Customers can receive a variety of functional and psychological benefits from an individual product. These benefits may be subjective, but are typically measurable and are directly related to customers' perceptions of both the product's ability to satisfy their needs and wants, and of their overall importance. Value may be enhanced by such means as adding new benefits, clarifying/reducing uncertainty about promised benefits, and making the product/service easier to secure.

Perceived value is created primarily by the non-price elements in the marketing mix, including product, promotion, distribution, and service. Pricing may also create value as price provides information about product quality. The market strategy coordinates and integrates the marketing mix as well as the contributions of other functions to ensure that the designed benefits are delivered to customers. Unfortunately, some technical organizations confuse what they view as real value with perceived value. Management is particularly

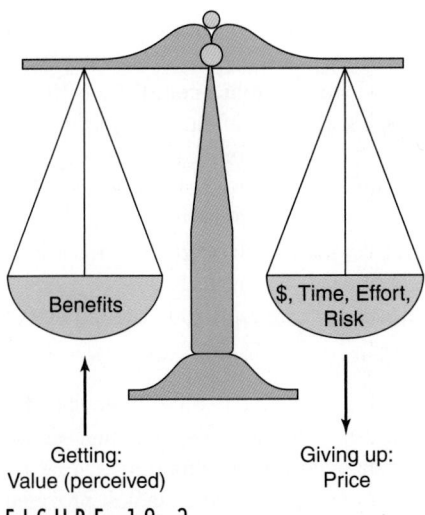

FIGURE 18.3

The Value Exchange Paradigm

unlikely to recognize the vital importance of marketing communications in creating value perception and makes the often-fatal assumption that the better product will win. More astute marketers recognize that customers will only purchase what they believe is the best value.

Costs incurred by the customer include price, the assumption of risk, and the time and effort necessary to secure the product. Firms that can reduce these elements should be able to realize higher dollar prices and higher profits, so long as excessive costs are not incurred. Conceptually, the maximum price customers should be willing to pay is equivalent to the total perceived benefit, less the total perceived cost (excluding price). The greater the difference between benefits provided to customers and the price charged, the greater the value delivered to customers.

Unless the firm is the low-cost producer and is confident it can retain that position, it is better off improving the value-price relationship by adding perceived value and accepting the cost penalty, rather than reducing prices. The firm may be able to segment the market and build a position in a segment from which dislodgment, particularly on the basis of price, is difficult. By contrast, advantage based on price and cost demands continuing vigilance in product and process technology, for one competitive breakthrough can destroy the foundations of the strategy.

Nagle and Holden identify ten critical areas and a series of related questions that seek to ascertain customer value attached to the firm's product[7]:

- **Perceived substitutes**: Of what alternatives and their prices are buyers aware? Can the firm influence buyers' price expectations by positioning its product relative to substitutes?
- **Unique value**: What attributes are important to buyers in selecting a supplier? Does the firm's product have unique attributes that distinguish it from the competition? How do customers value these attributes? What can be done to enhance the importance of these attributes and diminish the importance of comparable attributes offered by competitors?
- **Switching costs**: What investments have customers made in their suppliers that would be incurred again if they switched? For how long are they locked in?
- **Competitive comparison**: Is it difficult or easy for buyers to compare alternatives? Can they compare by observation or must they purchase and consume? Are experts required? How experienced are customers in using the firm's product and other alternatives. Are prices directly comparable or are calculations required?
- **Price/Quality**: Is there a positive price/quality relationship for this product?
- **Expenditure**: How significant is the absolute expenditure for this product, and as a percent of income/wealth?
- **End benefit**: What is the end benefit to which the firm's product contributes? How price sensitive are buyers of the end benefit? For what portion of the end-benefit cost does the price of firm's product account? Can the product be repositioned in customers' minds as related to an end benefit for which the buyer is price insensitive?
- **Shared cost**: Do buyers pay the full cost? If not, what portion do they pay?
- **Fairness**: How does the product's current price compare with people's experience with this sort of product? What do they expect to pay?
- **Inventory**: Do buyers hold inventory? Do they expect current prices to be temporary?

Measuring Value

While several methodologies are available for measuring perceived value, three specific methodologies are discussed: perceived value analysis, conjoint analysis, and value-in-use analysis. Each of these methods rely on data regarding customers' perceptions of value delivered by various individual benefits and market offers. In general, this data is best provided by customers (the firms', competitors', non-using potential customers) directly, but managerial judgment, although typically subject to bias, may provide a reasonable approximation.

TABLE 18.2 Illustration of Perceived Value Analysis

Benefits Required	Relative Importance Weighting	Competitor A Price = $500 Rate (1–10)	Total	Competitor B Price = $450 Rate (1–10)	Total	Competitor C Price = $300 Rate (1–10)	Total
Chair Design	20	5	100	7	140	6	120
Comfort	30	6	180	8	240	4	120
Fabric Quality	15	10	150	9	135	8	120
Fabric Design	15	5	75	7	105	4	60
Ease of Purchase	20	8	160	10	200	8	160
	100	Grand Total	665	Grand Total	820	Grand Total	580

PERCEIVED VALUE ANALYSIS Table 18.2 presents a simplified version of a perceived value analysis for the purchase of an easy chair. Basically, the analysis requires identification of the benefits the customer requires, the relative importance of those benefits, and the perceived ability of the various competitive offers to deliver the required benefits. In the analysis, the relative importance of several benefits is made to sum to 100 and each competitor is rated (1–10 scale) on its ability to provide each benefit. The importance weight is multiplied by the rate for each benefit, for each competitor, and the totals summed by competitor. The resulting grand totals are a measure of the perceived value offered by each competitor. Note that price does not enter into the analysis; however, it is important for interpretation.

In the example, competitor B offers the greatest perceived value, followed by competitors A and C, respectively. However, competitor A has the highest price, followed by competitors B and C, respectively. It appears that competitor C is appropriately the lowest priced competitor as it has the lowest perceived value, but that the prices of competitors A and B are misordered. Since it offers higher perceived value, competitor B could presumably raise its price. Alternatively, it should be gaining market share by offering greater value for a lower price. This relationship can be displayed pictorially by means of a "customer value map," as shown in Figure 18.4.[8,9]

CONJOINT ANALYSIS Conjoint analysis as a method for understanding the relative utilities placed by customers on different product attributes was introduced in Chapter 4. In Figure 4A.1, in addition to the attributes, three levels of price (current, +25%, +50%) were

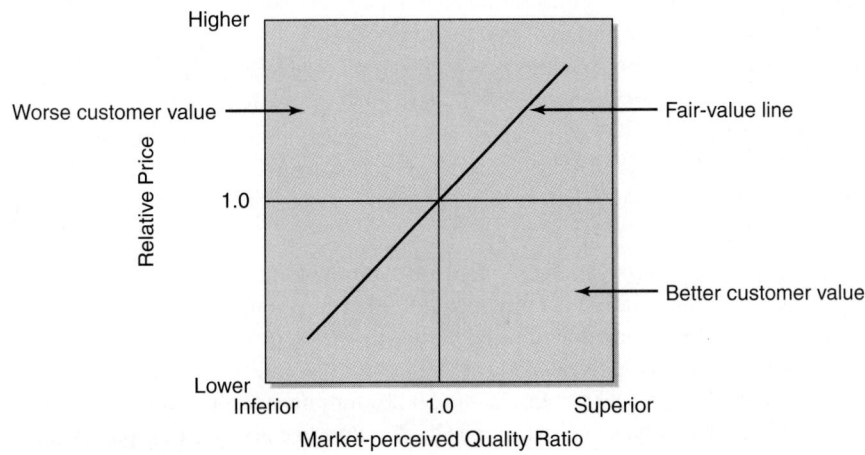

FIGURE 18.4

Customer Value Map

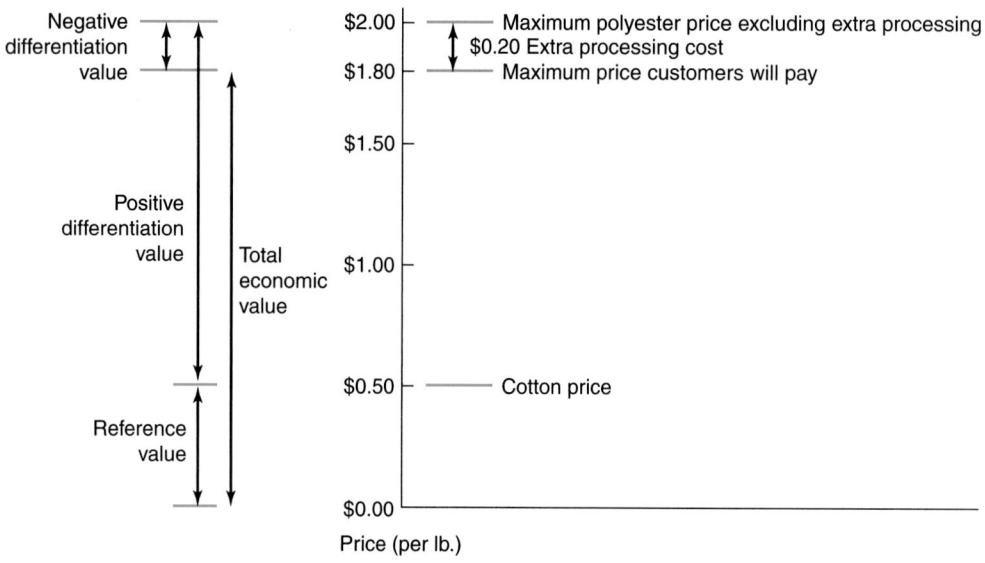

FIGURE 18.5

Illustration of Value-in-Use Analysis

included in the research design. From this type of analysis, both the perceived value (utility) of the various attributes could be identified together with the disutility of price.[10] Since conjoint analysis uses the judgments of customers themselves rather than managers, it is clearly preferable to perceived value analysis based solely on managerial input.

VALUE-IN-USE ANALYSIS Value-in-use analysis, also termed economic value to the customer (EVC) is a method of estimating the price equivalence of the firm's product as opposed to a competitive product.[11] It is frequently employed in industrial markets when a new product form is being introduced. The task is to identify the maximum price customers should be prepared to pay based on the enhanced customer value offered by the new product. Typically, the focus is on functional benefits, but psychological benefits could also be included. High maximum prices are the firm's reward for providing high levels of customer value; low maximum prices are the penalty for providing low value. The focus here is on the maximum price the firm can charge; the actual price charged is influenced by three other factors—costs, competitive offers, and the firm's strategic objectives. A simplified example can clarify the notion of maximum price:

> **Example:** The strength of the textile fiber is crucial for conveyor belt manufacture. Suppose the market price for cotton yarn to make conveyor belts is $0.50 per lb. In certain applications, polyester yarn, which is four times as strong as cotton, can be used as a replacement. However, the extra cost of processing polyester fiber is $0.20 per lb. What is the maximum price per lb. that customers would be willing to pay for polyester fiber?

In this example, customers can simply replace cotton with polyester. Since polyester is four times as strong as cotton, customers could either buy four pounds of cotton for $2.00 ($0.5 × 4 = $2.00) or one pound of polyester. However, processing polyester fiber costs an extra $0.20 per lb. of polyester. Customers should be indifferent between paying $0.50 per lb. for cotton and $1.80 per lb. ($2.00–$0.20) for polyester. The maximum price customers would pay for polyester is $1.80 per lb. At any price above $1.80 per lb., customers would be better off sticking with cotton (Figure 18.5).[12]

In most cases, the value-in-use calculation is more complex as costs other than the new product cost (price) are included, such as operating, maintenance, and financing costs

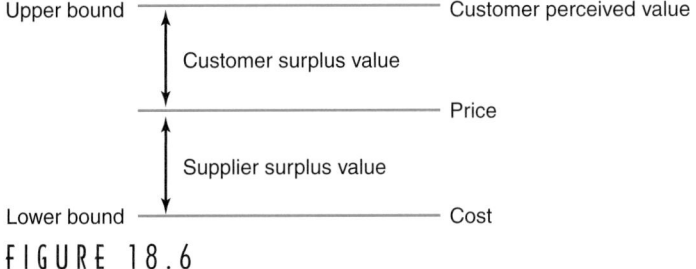

FIGURE 18.6
Pricing as Value-Sharing

(see the example in Figure 18.8). Value-in-use analysis is typically used when economic considerations are dominant and purchase involves substantial amounts of money. In addition, many business purchases must be justified on the basis of value-in-use analysis, even if the real reasons for purchase are quite different.

Capturing Value

When the firm has measured the amount of value it has created, it must decide how much of that value to provide to customers and how much to retain for itself. A low price transfers a large amount of net value to customers; conversely, a high price implies a large amount of net value retained by the firm. All things being equal, the more net value the firm is prepared to transfer to customers, the greater the number of customers it will attract.

In general, the firm would expect to pass greater net value along to customers if it were well positioned in a growth market and was pursuing growth and market share objectives, demand was price elastic, competitors were strong and aggressive, and entry from potential competitors was likely. Conversely, it would more likely keep value to itself if it were pursuing profit and cash flow objectives, the market was mature or declining, demand was price inelastic, competition was weak or lax, and threat of competitive entry was low.[13]

Figure 18.6 illustrates how the pricing decision can be viewed as an exercise in sharing value with customers.

A final issue concerns the point at which price enters into the design of the market offer. In most cases, firms develop products and services, then set prices based on factors such as customer value, competitive offers, and the firm's strategic objectives. However, some firms, such as Avon (the cosmetics firm), reverse the process. They identify the price at which they want a product to sell, then work backwards to develop a product design that delivers an appropriate level of customer value at a sufficiently low cost so they can make an adequate profit margin.[14]

CRITICAL ELEMENTS IN PRICING STRATEGY: COSTS

For many firms, costs play a major role in pricing.[15] Cost-plus is the most-used pricing method.[16]

Cost-Plus Pricing

In cost-plus methods, the product cost (current or anticipated future) is incremented upward by a margin (mark-up or mark-on) to establish the selling price. Table 18.3 shows the total costs for an item of capital equipment incremented upward by a standard mark-up.

ADVANTAGES OF COST-PLUS SYSTEMS Cost-plus pricing systems have three main advantages. First, they are legally aceptable and, in certain cases such as government contracting, may be required. Second, because the price developed in this manner is always above cost, if sales are made, they should be profitable. Third, assuming costs are known, the pricing task is quite simple, certainly far easier than systems that involve

TABLE 18.3
Example of Cost-Plus Pricing[17]

Variable Costs	$400,000
Direct Fixed Costs	$200,000
Indirect Fixed Costs	$100,000
Total Fixed Costs	$300,000
Total Costs	$700,000
Standard Mark-Up @ 15%	$105,000
Price	$805,000

calculating customer value. Cost-plus systems are often used in situations such as supermarket pricing where many different products must be priced.

DISADVANTAGES OF COST-PLUS SYSTEM Cost-plus pricing systems have three main disadvantages: implicit limits on growth and profit potential, arbitrary cost measurement, and prices that are not matched to market realities.

Implicit Limits to Growth and Profit Potential By definition, cost-plus systems are focused internally and do not take into account external market realities—neither customer perceptions nor competitive offers. Since they do not address the issue of what customers may be prepared to pay, two potential problems occur. First, the cost-plus formula may lead to a price lower than customers are prepared to pay. In Table 18.3, perhaps customers are prepared to pay $900,000 for the item. If so, then the firm forgoes $95,000 ($900,000–$805,000) in potential profit for each item sold. Conversely, the analysis may lead to a price greater than customers are prepared to pay. Perhaps some potential customers are only prepared to pay $750,000. They will not purchase the product at $805,000 and the firm will forgo $50,000 ($750,000 − $700,000) profit on each item it might have sold. By ignoring demand considerations, firms pricing in this manner jeopardize shareholders' interests by sacrificing both margin and growth, the two main operating drivers of shareholder value. Furthermore, strict adherence to a cost-plus pricing system leaves the firm highly vulnerable to competitive action, especially if competitors have a good understanding of the firm's costs.

Arbitrary Cost Measurement In most cases, the unit product cost can be viewed as comprising two elements—variable costs and fixed costs.[18]

Variable costs vary directly with the volume of sales and production, increasing as volume increases and decreasing as volume decreases. Variable cost per unit is the direct incremental cost of making and selling an extra unit of product. What costs are considered as variable depends on the specific product and technology but, for manufactured products, usually include raw materials, utilities to power production machines, direct labor, and sales commissions among others.

Fixed costs, by contrast, do not vary with the volume of sales or production. They include overhead items, such as managerial salaries, depreciation, and SG&A. Typically, some portion of fixed costs (direct) is related to the individual product. Another portion (indirect), such as corporate R&D, is shared among many products, and each product receives an allocation, frequently based on product volume.

Whereas it is relatively straightforward to identify an individual product's variable cost, the fixed cost per unit required to arrive at the total product cost for pricing purposes depends on the product's sales volume: fixed cost per unit = fixed costs/sales volume. Since volume varies with price, the sales volume is determined by the price. Thus cost-plus systems have the inherent problem that the output of the system, the price, is also an input to the determination of price as it drives the volume that produces the fixed cost per unit figure.

Mismatch with Market Realities   In cost-plus systems, as overall demand falls and lower prices might be in order, fixed costs must be spread over a smaller number of units. Higher unit costs lead directly to higher-than-optimal prices. When demand surges and higher prices might be in order, fixed costs are spread over a greater number of units, leading to lower unit costs and lower-than-optimal prices.

Unfortunately, the pricing infrastructure in many companies is geared to cost-plus systems. The problems indicated can be partially addressed by using varying percentage mark-ups for different products as a function of demand.

The Appropriate Roles for Costs

Despite their major role in the profit identity (profit = revenues − costs), costs should play a relatively minor role in pricing. In some cases, however, costs are important.

BIRTH CONTROL   This role of costs relates to the introduction of new products. As part of the process for evaluating new products, a full-scale financial analysis should be undertaken. If the estimated financial return from the new product exceeds a criterion, such as the firm's hurdle rate,[19] approval to go ahead is typically given subject to funds availability. The basis for such analyses is typically an estimate of future cash flows based on target prices, volumes, and costs. Costs clearly play an important role. The specific costs relevant for this decision are the full incremental costs associated with the new product.

A related approach is for marketing research to determine the range of prices that a new product would command. Based on the required financial return, the firm can then calculate the required product cost. This information is provided to engineering and manufacturing to develop a product that offers the appropriate level of customer benefits at the required product cost.[20] This approach is not only consistent with an external orientation but is basically identical to the strategy that enabled Henry Ford to dominate the world's automobile industry with the Model T.[21]

When considering new product introduction, the firm is making a go/no-go decision. In either approach, if the full cost estimates are such that the firm is unlikely to meet its financial goals, the project should be scrapped.

FLOOR   Costs also play an important role in the decision of whether to continue with, or drop, an existing product. If price does not exceed cost, the firm will not make a profit and should seriously consider a temporary or permanent cessation of activity. However, the relevant costs are different from the birth control costs. At least in the short run, the appropriate cost is the marginal cost of producing and selling the product, exclusive of overhead allocations.[22]

For example, suppose a product's marginal cost was $4 per unit and the fully-loaded cost (including all overhead allocations) was $6 per unit. At a price of $7 per unit, the firm makes a bottom-line profit (7 − 6 = 1). At prices less than $4 per unit the firm loses money on every item it makes and sells. Thus $4 is the floor price and, except under unusual circumstances, prices below $4 should invoke product withdrawal.[23] At $5 per unit the firm makes a bottom-line loss (5 − 6 = −1), but a positive contribution (5 − 4 = 1) to overhead and profits. It should maintain the product, at least in the short run. Obviously, the firm cannot price all products in this region over the long run, but for a limited time such pricing may be perfectly reasonable. In shareholder value terms, cash flow is the key economic consideration.

ARITHMETIC   Other than these two special cases, the major role played by costs is in profit planning. Table 18.4 shows various prices and estimated unit volumes. The volume estimates lead directly to estimated revenues and costs (related to volume), and hence to estimated profit. This information should be fed into the firm's decision calculus for price determination. If profit were the major objective, from the three options given, the price should be set at $12 per unit.

TABLE 18.4 The Arithmetic Role of Costs

Price	Volume Estimate	Revenues	Costs	Profit
$8	650	$5,200	$4,800	$400
$10	500	$5,000	$4,500	$500
$12	400	$4,800	$4,100	$700

The relationship between price and volume at the market level is shown by the demand curves of classic microeconomics. Individual product demand curves are related in part to the market demand curve, and in part to competitive offers. Three simple demand curves can be identified: elastic, inelastic, and positive sloping, as noted in Figure 18.7.

A price elastic demand curve occurs when volume increases significantly as price decreases (A). A price inelastic demand curve occurs when volume is relatively insensitive to changes in price (B). A positive sloping demand curve occurs when sales increase as price increases (C).

Across all products, relatively elastic demand curves are probably the model form. When inelastic demand curves occur, product sales are likely sensitive to other marketing mix elements, such as advertising and sales force effort. Positive sloping demand curves occur when product quality is difficult to assess and price is perceived to convey significant quality information, as with many fragrances and prestige cars.

Marketers are sometimes advised to set prices at what the market will bear, but as the foregoing demonstrates, the market will bear many prices. One of the most crucial decisions for marketers is how to position the offer or, said differently, what volume do they want to attempt to sell and what price?

CRITICAL ELEMENTS IN PRICING STRATEGY: COMPETITION

In general, when setting prices, firms have three considerations concerning competition. Given a set of existing competitive prices, what value does the firm want to offer customers? Simply setting prices at the competitor's level—competitive equivalence—does not address the relative value offered to customers by the firm and its competitors. What assessment can the firm make regarding competitive response once its prices are announced? And what response should the firm make to competitors' price actions?

Customer Value

The value that customers perceive in a firm's offer is not independent of other alternatives for satisfying the underlying set of needs. As illustrated in the value-in-use analysis, perceived customer value is determined in direct relation to the competitive product. The

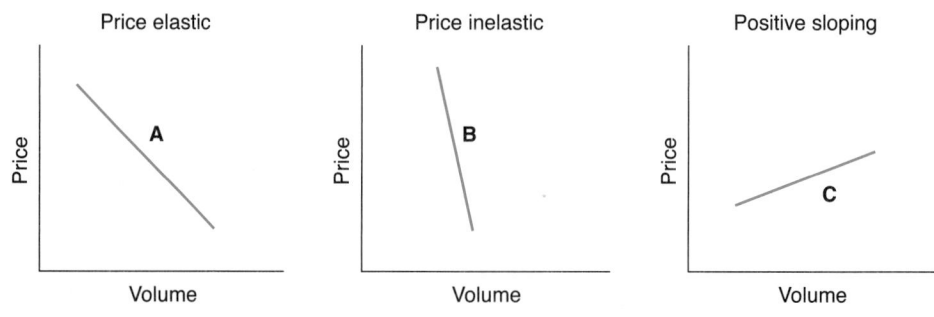

FIGURE 18.7

Market Demand Curves

perceived value analysis, Table 18.2, shows the role played by price in equilibrating the different offers providing differing levels of customer benefits.

Regardless of how much value a firm offers in some absolute sense, all things being equal, if two firms' offers are totally equivalent, customers will generally purchase the product with the lower price. Thus, competitive offers play a critical role in the pricing decision. The critical issue, however, is generally not price superiority; rather, it is offer superiority in which price plays a balancing role.

Competitive Response

When the firm's prices are announced, competitors have the option of holding their prices steady, making modifications in their pricing schedules, or taking other actions. In setting its prices, the firm should consider likely competitive responses, both price changes and other actions, such as increased advertising and greater service.

Regarding prices, the type of competitive response depends on several factors, such as whether the firm has raised or lowered prices, the comparability of the various competitive offers, the number of competitors and their market shares, and competitor profitability. For example, if competitor profitability is low and the firm is a major player and raises prices, it is likely that competitors will accept the firm's price leadership and also raise prices, particularly if market demand is inelastic. If the market offers are otherwise identical and the firm lowers prices, competitors are also likely to follow suit, as seen in the PC industry in recent years. On the other hand, if marketing offers are highly differentiated, competitors are profitable, and the firm raises prices, it is unlikely that competitors will follow. For example, when individual high-quality restaurants raise prices, a wholesale price movement is not generally observed.

PRICE LEADERSHIP   In oligopolistic markets where none of the players has significant differential advantage, destructive price competition is always a possibility. This is especially so when variable costs are low (fixed costs high) since the temptation to cut price and earn significant variable (contribution) margin for particular pieces of business is present for all competitors. In such circumstances, the firm may be able to assume a price leadership role in which all competitors view it as the price leader and follow its pricing moves.

Those firms attempting to exercise price leadership typically make their pricing strategy highly transparent.

Example: In early November 1999, Coca-Cola raised concentrate prices to its bottlers by 7%, twice the usual rate. A couple of weeks later, PepsiCo announced a 7% increase to its bottlers.[24]

Sometimes price leaders are prepared to "punish" competitors that don't fall into line.

Example: Several years ago in the low-growth, barely profitable British aluminum market, the British Aluminium Company (BACO) was engaged in tough oligopolistic competition with Alcoa and Alcan. BACO attempted to lead prices upwards by dividing the market into three regions: "ours"—long-term contract customers of British Aluminium; "theirs"—long-term contract customers of major competitors; and "up-for-grabs"—customers that purchased "spot" and frequently switched suppliers. BACO determined it would not lose business at any of its customers on price; furthermore, if a competitor attempted to secure business at this type of customer by offering a low price, BACO would immediately *punish* the competitor by making a low bid at one of their customers. Pricing decisions were placed at a senior level in the firm and for a period of time this tit-for-tat strategy was effectively executed as Alcoa and Alcan got the message.[25]

On the other hand, American Airlines' (AA) attempt to rationalize pricing in the U.S. domestic airline industry in 1992 ended in failure. Although competitors Delta, United, Continental, Northwest, USAir, and American West followed AA's lead within a few days, TWA, believing that what was good for American Airlines must be bad for TWA, undercut AA's prices by 10% to 20% and the price leadership attempt failed.[26]

Conditions under which price leadership is most likely to be successful are varied. They include relatively few competitors and high entry barriers, growth markets and differentiated products. Also relevant are the leader's power to retaliate and forego short-run profits, managers with long-run performance measures, low industry secrecy, and social relationships among key industry executives. All significant pricing decisions must be taken at high levels in the competing firms.

There are many combinations of the various factors relevant to assessing competitive response to a firm's pricing actions. Only by possessing good competitive information can the firm make reasoned judgments of likely competitive response to a variety of potential pricing actions and hence make sensible pricing decisions.

In addition to securing competitor information, the firm may want to announce intentions to competitors with the goal of influencing their actions. For example, pre-announced price increases enable the firm to gauge likely competitor response, and warning and other signals may preempt likely competitive moves.

Firm Response to Competitors

Although it is generally advantageous to make the first move, in many cases firms are forced to respond to price actions taken by competitors. Management should think through the long-run consequences of its pricing decisions. When pricing decisions are taken independently without the benefit of a pricing strategy framework, a once profitable market can be ruined by excessive price competition brought on by direct competitive matching. For a strong incumbent, cutting prices should generally be the last competitive action taken after all others have been exhausted. However, the more limited the firm's ability to offer sustainable differential advantage, the more likely it will be forced into responding in comparable terms. Ultimately, the delinquent marketer is forced into acting as a commodity competitor and using the only weapon available—a price cut.

At the risk of redundancy, such competitive actions are disastrous to all but the low-cost producer; the manner in which it uses its cost advantage determines whether or not its competitors survive. By not responding in kind, the firm stands a better chance of avoiding the vicious downward spiral until prices barely cover costs. However implemented, the firm should take pains to avoid price confrontation. The short-term goal is to avoid increasing the customer's bargaining power. In responding to competitors' pricing moves, it is a good idea to keep customers a little confused.

Suppose, for example, the firm has a dominant market share and is faced by severe price competition from a new or smaller player. How should the leader address this new pricing strategy? We discuss several types of potential responses classified as non-price and price actions:

NON-PRICE ACTIONS   Two major items fall into this category—clarify the firm's position and invest in fixed cost marketing expenditures.

Clarify the Firm's Position   If the firm holds the strongest position, letting competitors know its intentions and capabilities can be a highly valuable tactic. This is especially true if the firm has cost leadership, for it demonstrates to competitors that they will lose a price battle.

> **Example:** In several product areas, Sara Lee is the low-cost supplier. Rather than build market share via price competition, Sara Lee prefers to charge relatively high prices and compete by building brand equity. However, knowledge of its low cost position deters others from cutting prices.[27]

Invest in Fixed-Cost Marketing Expenditures   Even small price changes can have a major impact on profits. If the firm meets price competition from the new entrant across the board, it will suffer an immediate and significant reduction in profits. (Conversely, the new entrant has little to lose from upsetting the industry pricing structure.) Rather, it may be better off investing in a variety of fixed-cost marketing expenditures, such as advertising, improving product quality, service, or better delivery. As a large player it has the advantage that it can spread these fixed costs over a large volume. AT&T initially used this approach when confronted with price competition from Sprint and MCI although, ultimately, price reductions were necessary to achieve market share objectives.

> **Example:** When the financial crisis affected southeast Asia in 1997, many luxury hotels in Malaysia began competing on price. By contrast, the Ritz-Carlton increased service. The general manager greeted arriving flights with music, drinks, and a model room, and provided various extra services such as servicing laptops and other electronic devices. Occupany rates improved and the Ritz-Carlton enjoyed higher margins than competing hotels.[28]

PRICE ACTIONS   Items in this category include indirect price retaliation, changing the basis of competition, market segment focus and if all else fails, cut prices.

Indirect Price Retaliation   Direct reaction to price competition can lead to a price war. One approach is to identify markets where the smaller player is strong, then make identical price cuts in those markets. Hopefully, the competitor will get the message and cease its price discounting where the firm is strong.

Changing the Basis of Competition   Shifting the basis of competition by grouping several products together (bundling), or developing loyalty programs, can be effective strategies. Such actions take away the competitor's direct price advantage. For example, McDonald's bundled several products and introduced "value meals" in the face of price competition from other fast-food operators.

Market Segment Focus   If the firm believes that the competitor is determined to remain in the market (perhaps it has already built a plant), the firm might decide which market segments/customers it will cede to the new entrant. Then it takes steps to secure its position with targeted segments/customers by improving service and offering multiyear contracts, and directs its competitor to less desirable (from the firm's perspective) areas of the market. Alternatively, it might serve less desired market segments with functionally equivalent products offered under different brand names at low prices, for example, private label products.

Cut Prices   If none of these or other creative actions are successful and the firm must cut price, it should seek methods of cost reduction that allow it to retain margins. Several cost reduction methods were discussed in Chapter 6 and again in Chapter 9 when the experience curve concept was introduced. Of course, if a "fight-it-out" strategy is not successful, ultimately the firm may be forced to withdraw from the market.

CRITICAL ELEMENTS IN PRICING STRATEGIES: STRATEGIC OBJECTIVES

The final influencing factor on the firm's pricing decisions is its strategic objectives in the product/market segment.[29] Broadly speaking, major objectives the firm may seek include growth, market share, profits and cash flow. Since some of these objectives are mutually contradictory, the firm must make choices among objectives and pricing strategies. All things being equal, if the firm has set market share and growth objectives, it should price low and provide significant net value to customers. Related conditions for setting low prices include a price-elastic market, anticipated cost reductions, available capacity, deep pockets to absorb initially low profit margins, and a desire to deter competitors.

Profit objectives should lead to higher prices and greater net value retained by the firm. If the firm has set cash flow objectives, especially as a prelude to market withdrawal, the firm should price even higher. The sorts of conditions favoring higher prices include a mature or declining market, identification of price inelastic market segments, and weak and/or lazy competitors.

Chapter 9 introduced two polar opposite short-run strategic objectives for new products: high profits and high growth. Each objective required specific pricing strategies for implementation. To secure high profits, the firm engages in skim pricing; prices are kept at a high level and the firm retains significant value for itself from those relatively few customers that purchase. Over time, the firm can reduce prices periodically with the goal of persuading greater numbers of customers to purchase each time that prices are lowered. This pricing strategy is sometimes called sequential skimming.[30] In penetration pricing, the firm prices close to costs; such pricing should lead to high market share in the short run with profits delayed and ultimately secured from high volumes and low margins.

USING THE PRICING STRATEGY ELEMENTS TO SET PRICE FOR A NEW PRODUCT

To illustrate the four critical elements in pricing strategy consider the decision faced by a company introducing a new item of capital equipment. Assume that the firm believes its product offers superior value to the directly competitive product and that management has calculated or identified the following:

Price of the directly competitive product	$260,000
Economic Value to the Customer (EVC) (calculated from value-in-use analysis)	$360,000
Direct out-of-pocket manufacturing cost	$100,000
Fully loaded manufacturing cost	$160,000

How should the company price its new product?

The discussion in the previous section suggestes four major considerations in setting the price: customer value, costs, competition, and the firm's strategic objectives. The relevant figures are arrayed in the pricing chart (Figure 18.8).

Two approaches should be discarded right away.

Cost-plus pricing requires a mark-up based on cost. Since the pricing decision concerns a new product, the direct out-of-pocket cost of $100,000 is not relevant. What is more important is the fully loaded manufacturing cost, $160,000. If the firm's mark-up were 75%, cost-

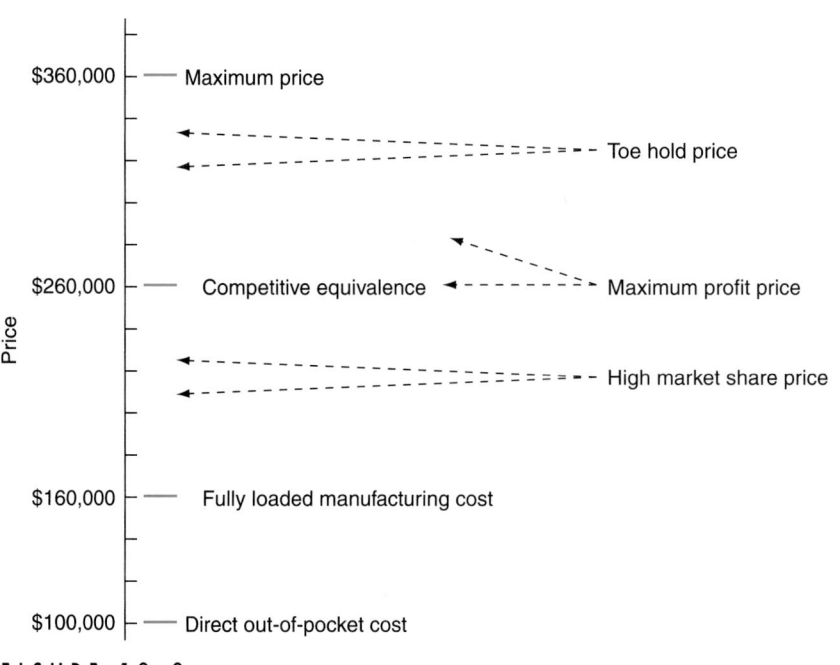

FIGURE 18.8

Pricing Analysis for a New Item of Capital Equipment

plus pricing would suggest a price of $280,000; if the mark-up were 50%, the suggested price would be $240,000. In one case the price is above the competitor's, in one case it is below. In neither case is customer value considered. Cost-plus pricing is not very helpful.

Competitive equivalence pricing suggests setting the price based on the competitor's price. The competitor's price is $260,000. At a price of $260,000 the firm would be supplying customers with considerable additional value. However, the critical question is: Would that be a correct sharing of surplus with customers? Also, just focusing on the competitor's price doesn't address the question of what the firm wants to achieve and how the competitor might respond.

The appropriate place to start the determination of price is to identify the pricing range.

The Pricing Range: Customer Value and Firm Costs

The appropriate place to start in deciding the price is with the value supplied to customers. The economic value to the customer is $360,000.[31] At that price, customers should be indifferent between the competitor's product and the firm's product. (Of course, because the firm's product is new, there may be less assurance that the firm's product will live up to its advertised performance characteristics.) The $360,000 figure represents a maximum price that could be set.

At the other extreme, the minimum price for a new product should be the fully loaded manufacturing cost of $160,000. Thus the actual price must fall between $160,000 and $360,000. The question now becomes where within this range is the appropriate price.

Strategic Objectives and Competitive Response

The actual price set by the firm is critically dependent on both the firm's strategic objectives and the likely competitive response. These two variables in turn are likely to be correlated. Take, for example, three possible strategic objectives: toe hold, short-term profit, and market share.

A toe-hold objective implies that the firm wants to have a market presence but little more than that. Perhaps it has identified a small segment it believes is willing to pay a high price, somewhere near the top of the range, say around $320,000. At such a high price (and very high margin), with a relatively low volume objective, the likelihood of significant competitive response is low.

A short-term profit objective implies significantly higher volume but lower margin. Pricing for this objective would more closely approach the competitor's price. Because, of the greater value in the firm's offer, it might set the price anywhere between $280,000 and $300,000. At these prices the firm is likely to earn volume at the expense of the competitor and might expect some level of competitive response. However, a price above the competitor's might signal a desire not to engage in price competition.

If market share is the major strategic objective, the firm might price below the competitor's $280,000 price. At a price of $220,000 to $240,000 the firm would still earn significant margin but might also sell high product volumes. At these prices, however, competitor response can be expected to be significant and the firm should have made plans for how to deal with the likely competitive action.

CONTEMPLATING PRICE CHANGES FOR AN EXISTING PRODUCT

To address the issue of changing prices for an existing product new concepts are introduced that build off the definitions of fixed and variable costs introduced earlier in this chapter. For ease of exposition, the simple illustration in Table 18.5 is used.[32] The traditional income statement has been restated so that costs are now partitioned into two categories—variable costs and fixed costs.[33] Note that the difference between sales revenues and variable costs is termed variable margin; it is also sometimes termed contribution margin (implying contribution to fixed costs).

TABLE 18.5 Example of Product Income Statement (000s)

Sales Revenues (SR) (40 million lbs. @ 50 cents/lb.)	$20,000
Variable Costs (VC)	12,000
Variable Margin (VM) (Contribution Margin)	8,000
Fixed Costs (FC)	6,600
Net Profit before Taxes (NP)	1,400

Recall that sales revenue (SR) less variable costs (VC) equals variable margin (VM):

$$SR - VC = VM, \text{ or restated, } SR = VC + VM.$$
$$20,000 - 12,000 = 8,000 \qquad 20,000 = 12,000 + 8,000$$

If these equations are divided by the number of units sold, the same equation on a per unit basis becomes:

$$SP - VCU = VMU \qquad SP = VCU + VMU, \text{ where:}$$
$$50c - 30c = 20c \qquad 50c = 30c + 20c$$

SP = Selling Price (Sales revenue divided by number of units):   20,000/40,000 = 50 cents

VCU = Variable Cost per Unit: 12,000/40,000 = 30 cents

VMU = Variable Margin per Unit (contribution margin per unit):   8,000/40,000 = 20 cents

The VMU is an extremely important concept. Because it is derived by subtracting variable costs from sales revenue, any financial calculations based on the VMU do not have to be concerned with variable costs. The only job that the VMU has to do is to cover fixed costs; any remainder is profit.

A related concept, variable margin rate (VMR) is simply defined as the fraction (percent) of sales revenue available for fixed costs and profit. The VMR is calculated by dividing the variable margin per unit by the selling price (VMR = VMU/SP). In the example,

$$VMR = VMU/SP$$
$$VMR = 20c/50c = 0.4 \text{ or} = \underline{40\%}$$

Similarly, for the variable cost rate

$$VCR = VCU/SP$$
$$VCR = 30c/50c = 0.6 = \underline{60\%}$$

Contemplating a Price Decrease

Assume that management is contemplating a 10% price decrease from 50 cents to 45 cents. The key calculation is to determine what sales volume would be necessary at the new price, 45 cents, for the firm to be indifferent from a profit perspective, between a 50 cent and 45 cent price.

The change in price directly affects the VMU. Recall that the previous section showed:

$$SP = VCU + VMU$$
$$50c = 30c + 20c$$

When the price is changed, the variable cost per unit does not change; what changes is the VMU. Thus:

$$@ SP = 45 \text{ cents; } 45c = 30c + 15c; VMU = 15 \text{ cents;}$$

The necessary sales volume to produce the same profit at a 45 cent price can be calculated in a similar fashion to previously:

$$\text{Target volume (units)} = \text{Target to Cover/VMU}$$

The target to cover is the sum of fixed costs, $6.6 million, plus the original profit, $1.4 million; in total, $8 million.

Target volume (units) = Target to Cover/VMU = $8 million/15 cents = 53.3 million lbs.

% Increase = (53.3 − 40)/40 = 32.5%

Target volume ($) = Target volume (units) × SP =

53.3 million lbs. × 45 cents = $24 million.

Contemplating a Price Increase

By contrast, if a price increase to 55 cents was being contemplated,

@ SP = 55 cents; 55c = 30c + 25c; VMU = 25 cents;

Target volume (units) = Target to Cover/VMU = $8 million/25 cents = 32 million lbs.

% Decrease = (32 − 40)/40 = 20%

Target volume ($) = Target volume (units) × SP =

32 million lbs. × 55 cents = $15.31 million.

These results are summarized in Table 18.6.

The calculations of 53.3 million lbs. at a 45 cent price, and 32 million lb. at 55 cents, do not provide management with the decision of whether or not to lower prices; they are merely criteria. Management must judge whether or not sales volume would reach or exceed 53.3 million lbs. if price were reduced to 45 cents per lb., or be maintained above 32 million lbs. at a 55 cent per lb. price.

Both the expected unit sales volume at 45 (55) cents per lb. and the probability that unit sales would in fact exceed 53.3 (32) million lbs., should be key inputs into the decision of whether or not to reduce (raise) prices.

Relevance of Costs

The worked examples found that for a price decrease of 10% (50 cents to 45 cents), the volume increase necessary to retain the current profit level was 32.5%. For a price increase of 10% (50 cents to 55 cents), the allowable volume decrease was 20%. These percent changes are highly dependent on the variable margin rate (VMR). Recall that VMR = VMU/SP.

At a price of 55 cents per lb., VMR = 25/55 = 45.6%

At a price of 45 cents per lb., VMR = 15/45 = 33.3%

Table 18.7 provides a simple way of calculating the percent volume increase (decrease) required (allowed) for a given percent decrease (increase) in price, regardless of the type of business.[34] The two axes on the chart are Variable Margin Rate (horizontal) and contemplated percent change in price (vertical). For a particular product with a particular cost structure, this same data can be displayed as an iso-profit line (Figure 18.9).[35]

The importance of the relative levels of fixed and variable costs is illustrated by a contemplated price change of 5%. Note that low VMRs imply high variable costs and low fixed costs; by contrast, high VMRs imply low variable costs and high fixed costs. Table 18.7 demonstrates that with a low VMR, such as VMR = 10%, the percent increase in unit sales to maintain the same profit level for a 5% price reduction is 100% (in the chart, 100 to 200). By contrast, if the VMR = 40%, the percent volume increase for maintaining the same profit level, for the same 5% price reduction, is only 14% (100 to 114).

Table 18.6 Summary of Calculations

Price	VMU	Target Volume	Target Revenues
50 cents	20 cents	40 million lbs.	$20 million
45 cents	15 cents	53.3 million lbs.	$24 million
55 cents	25 cents	32 million lbs.	$15.31 million

TABLE 18.7 Relationship between Required Volume Change and Price Change for Different Variable Margin Rates

Percent Change in Price	Current Variable Margin Rate							
	10%	15%	20%	25%	30%	35%	40%	45%
+25	29	38	45	50	55	58	61	64
+20	33	43	50	56	60	64	67	69
+15	40	50	57	63	69	70	73	75
+10	50	60	67	72	75	78	80	82
+5	67	75	80	83	86	88	89	90
0	100	100	100	100	100	100	100	100
−5	200	150	133	125	120	117	114	113
−10		300	200	187	150	140	133	129
−15			400	260	200	175	160	150
−20				500	300	233	200	180
−25					600	350	267	225

The implication of this table is clear; the firm's pricing strategy should take into consideration the product's VMR, which in turn is related to the relative levels of variable and fixed costs. In general, if the VMR is high (fixed costs high), the firm should contemplate identifying price sensitive segments such that small decreases in price might provide significant volume increases. This strategy is perhaps best exemplified by the airlines[36]; each carrier typically has a myriad of prices for each flight. By contrast, if the firm's VMR is low (fixed costs low), it should focus on raising margins by reducing costs and increasing prices.

Relatedly, the firm should carefully manage its variable/fixed cost ratio (sometimes known as operating leverage). Although this is in part determined by the technology under-

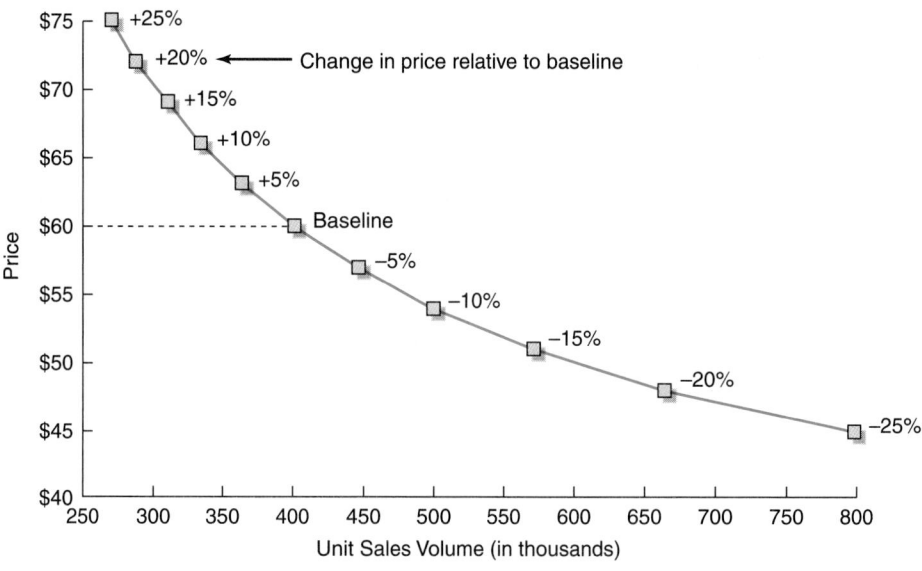

FIGURE 18.9

Illustration of the Iso-Profit Curve: Tradeoff between Price and Volume for Constant Profit

lying the firm's production system, management can have a profound influence on the ratio. Outsourcing, such as using pre-processed raw materials instead of conducting these activities internally, increases variable costs at the expense of fixed costs. A similar result is achieved by reducing the salary portion of sales force compensation and increasing the incentive portion. Actions such as these can enable better management of the financial impact of demand or price changes.

Note that many information products not only have high fixed costs and practically zero variable costs, but the fixed costs are often incurred before any product is produced. Typical examples where most costs are sunk include software, compact discs, and a variety of database offerings. For these products, not only are the VMRs exceptionally high (because the variable costs are so low), they pose difficult pricing and intellectual property/piracy issues.

TACTICAL PRICING.

The bulk of discussion thus far has focused on pricing strategy, appropriately so for a book whose primary concern is with strategy. However, it is important to recognize that most pricing decisions are tactical. This does not mean that they are unimportant. In sum, they have enormous impact upon the firm's market and financial performance. However, clear understanding of strategic principles drives good tactical pricing decisions. Figure 18.10 illustrates the variety of tactics available. These tactics constitute the means by which the firm implements its strategies and determines the actual payments it secures from customers. These elements are termed the pricing toolkit.

Elements in the Pricing Toolkit

Perhaps the most common misconception about price, second to the role played by costs and the perceived importance of cost-based pricing, is that there is (or should be) just one price or a set price for the product. The presence of a single price is almost *prima facie* evidence of lack of competition, and is rare in the real world. The pricing tool that most closely approximates this notion is the firm's **list price**. List price can serve as the basis for actual prices, but in many industries minimal business is transacted at list. List price does no more than provide the base for discounting, such as 20% off list, 30% off list. **Discounts** are the basis for departure from list. These can be based on volume (quantity discounts) firm/customer relationship, function performed (inventory, selling effort), time (buying seasonal products off-season), the requirements of a *bona fide* competitive situation, or similar criteria. Offering a discount on annual volume based on purchasing at least as much as the previous year is a creative way to repel aggressive new competitors.

Other direct and important influences on actual price levels include company policy on **allowances**, such as for advertising, selling effort or trade-ins, **returns**, and **buybacks**. In each case, policies can vary; such variations afford the advantage of lower visibility than changes in list price or discount structure. Likewise, availability and terms of **credit** (time to pay and interest rate) can be a less visible means of implementing pricing moves that are particularly potent under inflation.

Freight charges and **inventory** carrying costs are fairly obvious in their economic implications, whereas **leasing** offers variation over self-financing. Leasing is important not only because of tax implications, but also because of risk sharing. **Unbundling** refers to marketing and pricing the different elements of a complex offering separately; **bundling**

List price	Credit	Guarantees and Warranties
Discounts	Freight	Price stability
Allowances	Inventory	Acceptable currency
Returns	Leasing	Duties
Buybacks	Bundling and unbundling	Barter

FIGURE 18.10

The Pricing Toolkit

refs to treating a complex offer as a single unit. To take a simple example, most restaurants offer their products unbundled; however, for *prix fixe* meals, the offer is bundled. The separate and extended **guarantee (warranty)** offered by some automobile manufacturers provides one example of unbundling, an approach often advocated in the mature stage of a market life cycle, when customer wants are often more specific and demanding.

Finally, under inflation and fluctuating exchange rates, a willingness to assume risk in terms of **price stability** and **acceptable currency** can offer utility to the buyer and advantage to the seller. For example, a foreign seller that sets a price today for payment in 60 days in a local currency is assuming the entire risk of adverse exchange rate movements, a highly advantageous situation for the buyer. Negotiation on payment of import **duties** is another variable, but its economic consequences tend to be unambiguous. Finally, in a number of situations, it may be to both parties' advantage for payment to take the form of **barter** and **buybacks** rather than by currency transaction.

> **Examples:** The Norton company contracted with a Polish organization to erect a turnkey grinding wheel plant in Poland. In part, under a buyback provision, payment to Norton for the plant was made in products manufactured by the plant.[37] Donald Kendall, former CEO of Pepsi Inc., secured access to the Soviet Union market by agreeing to import Stolichnaya vodka. More recently, British Aerospace secured a $20 billion order for Tornado fighters, Hawk trainers, and backup services from Saudi Arabia by agreeing to be paid primarily in oil.[38] In the Altai territory in Siberia, barter comprises over half of all economic transactions, and some of the largest companies transact up to 90% of their business by barter, 10% in cash.[39]

Discussion of the pricing toolkit shows the potential complexity of actually setting prices. Although the firm may have resolved strategic pricing issues, a broad variety of alternatives is available to implement the strategy. These alternatives comprise the variety of ways the firm sets the actual price paid by customers. For example, if the firm wants to attract volume users, it can offer volume discounts; if it wants to reward specific customers, it can provide cooperative advertising allowances.

This discussion demonstrates that there are more and less obvious means of effecting price competition. In many cases, less obvious approaches are preferred, but the firm might also want to be overt and explicit, clearly telegraphing its strategy to the market. Finally, sometimes the issue of how customer value is captured by pricing is more important than how much customer value is captured.

The Pocket Price and Price Waterfall

Unfortunately, many firms do not have good systems for tracking different elements in their pricing toolkits. As a result, management does not fully understand the actual prices paid by many of their customers. Typically, list prices and invoice prices are well understood, but many pricing elements are frequently buried in a myriad of different accounts. For example, discounts for early payment typically find their way into interest expense accounts; cooperative advertising allowances are assigned to promotion and advertising accounts.

Marn and Rosiello introduced the related notions of pocket price and price waterfall to address this issue.[40] The pocket price (actual payment in the firm's pocket) is the price actually recovered by the firm. The price waterfall refers to the manner in which elements of the pricing toolkit cumulate to reduce the list price to the pocket price.

AN ILLUSTRATION OF THE PRICE WATERFALL These concepts are illustrated for an appliance manufacturer that offers a variety of discounts and other allowances to its customers (Table 18.8).[41]

In this illustration, over the years, the appliance manufacturer had developed a complex pricing structure involving 11 different pricing toolkit items. To start with, customers

TABLE 18.8
Illustration of the Price Waterfall for an Appliance Manufacturer

Dealer List Price	**$100.00**
Standard Dealer Discount	$8.10
Order Size Discount	$2.00
National Promotion Discount	$3.90
Exception Discount	$2.70
Invoice Price	**$83.30**
Cash Discount	$2.00
Co-op Advertising	$4.10
Promotional Bonus	$3.50
Product Line Rebate	$3.20
Annual Volume Bonus	$5.60
Marketing Allowance	$1.90
Freight	$2.10
Pocket Price	**$60.90**
Price Drift over the Waterfall	**$39.10**

could earn a variety of discounts for an invoice price of $83.30, $16.70 down from the $100 list price. However, in addition, seven additional elements combined to subtract an additional $22.40 from the invoice price ($83.30 – $60.90) to arrive at a $60.90 pocket price, only 60.9% of the list price and 73% of the invoice price.

Of course, not all the appliance manufacturer's customers paid this low pocket price. The prices actually paid ranged considerably as some customers received more of the pricing toolkit items than others. However, in detailed analysis of the actual pocket prices paid by customers, there was no good rationale for the actual prices paid. For example, some small customers received substantial volume discounts while some large customers did not.

MANAGEMENT RESPONSE   This illustration suggests that management should make a significant effort to fully understand the prices actually paid by their customers. This is not a simple matter, for changes in the firm's accounting system are probably necessary so that items such as interest expenses and advertising allowances can be specifically identified. Given the huge leverage that pricing decisions have for profitability, management should ensure that its prices do not drift over the pricing waterfall ($39.10 in the illustration) without it knowing.

Not only should management understand the true prices paid by customers, to the extent that its set of pocket prices do not have a good rationale, it should also attempt to understand how these prices developed as the basis for making changes. Often the best pricing deals are secured by the cleverest and most persistent customers, those that know who to contact to get an extra discount or a greater advertising allowance. Such customers know how to work the supplier's management system; the sales force, driven by unit volume or revenue objectives, tends to be a willing participant.

Example: An electronic goods manufacturer selling products through retail distribution set monthly revenue budgets for its sales force. To reach its targets, the sales force developed the habit of offering extra discounts at month's end. Over time, customers realized that better prices could be secured at the end of the month, so they held off on purchases in a self-reinforcing cycle.

Such artificial peaks and troughs create unnecessary havoc in the supply chain and should play no part in the operation of any business committed to total quality management (TQM), except under exceptional circumstances.[42]

In one case examined by Marn and Rosiello, the manufacturer took three pricing initiatives to deal with its problems. It took aggressive action to bring the over-discounted customers in line. It also targeted attractive accounts for volume increases by delivering customer specific benefits. It then brought the pricing system under control by improving the accounting system, tightening up on discounts and introducing sales force measurement systems based on the pocket price.

A final issue of concern is that not all elements of the pricing toolkit may be equally important in customers' purchase decisions. Imagine that a customer's purchasing managers were evaluated and rewarded based on reductions that they secured from sellers' invoice prices. In this situation, a $2 cash discount might be more important for securing a sale than a $2 order size discount.

ISSUES IN TACTICAL PRICING

Several issues are considered: price discretion, pricing information systems, price discrimination, gray markets, bundling or unbundling, price promotions or steady prices, psychological pricing, two-part pricing, the basis of price, set price or respond to offers, auctions, and ethical and legal issues in pricing.

Price Discretion

The degree to which management is able to take advantage of the various items in the pricing toolkit depends on both the perceived value offered to customers and the firm's relative cost position. Maximum price discretion is available to those firms with the highest perceived value and lowest cost. This position is enjoyed by many well-known companies, such as Microsoft and Procter & Gamble, in several markets where they compete.

When it has a degree of discretion, the firm can choose where it sets its prices, trading off volumes, and market share versus margins and profit. The moral is clear—improving perceived value while reducing cost puts the firm in an enviable position with respect to both pricing strategy and tactics.

Pricing Information Systems

Not only should the firm develop an accounting system that reveals its own pocket prices to its various customers, it also needs information on market prices, including the offers of individual competitors. To make good pricing decisions demands constant attention to who is offering what to whom. A good pricing information system is a most useful aid to the necessary fine-tuning that must occur in pricing decisions. In many companies, business gained and business lost reports may provide the genesis for such a system. Customers frequently provide good data to the losing salesperson, so there is usually more information value in business lost than in business won. (See Chapter 5 for issues in securing competitive data and analyzing competitors.)

Price Discrimination

Price discrimination, setting different prices to different market segments and/or customers is inherently more profitable for the seller. Since customer utility curves are idiosyncratic, this practice is consistent with pricing strategy development discussed earlier. The more customer requirements vary, and the more various non-price elements are available for the firm, the easier to implement price discrimination strategies.[43] The firm's ability to design the order, while appearing to be a costly approach, often pays profitability dividends because of the value-adding pricing flexibility it affords.

One particularly important variable in setting prices is time, especially for service products that require a high fixed investment but have fluctuating demand. Airlines, hotels, electric utilities, upscale restaurants, movie theaters, and telephone companies each fall into this category. For example, the airlines use time of day, day of the week, and time period in setting prices as a means to target offers to specific segments.[44] Another interesting example is road pricing where the toll (price) for access to central city areas varies by time of day and day of the week.[45]

However, environmental change can reduce the firm's ability to price discriminate. A particularly important change is occurring in Europe as 11 Western European countries (Austria, Belgium, Finland, France, Germany, Ireland, Italy, Luxembourg, the Netherlands, Portugal, and Spain) abandon their currencies and switch to the euro.[46] When euro bills and coins enter circulation in 2002, many firms that currently price discriminate through the medium of different national currencies will be less able to do so.

Notwithstanding the value of price discrimination, in some circumstances the firm can benefit from price inflexibility. For example, by giving salespeople only limited price discretion (or none at all), the firm mitigates aggressive customer requests for discounted prices. Furthermore, a single price can offer customers both simplicity and a perception of fairness that multiple prices do not.

> **Examples:** ATT's "One Rate" plan for long-distance telephone service has been very successful. The Saturn division of General Motors has built a single price policy into its entire market strategy.

Gray Markets

Gray markets occur when the manufacturer sells similar products to multiple geographic markets at widely different prices. The price differential allows customers to buy products in low price markets, then transship and resell them in high price markets, undercutting the manufacturer's price.[47] Manufacturers can avoid gray market problems by reducing the price dispersion.[48]

Bundling or Unbundling

Generally speaking, it is more profitable for the firm to bundle its products and set a single price than it is to unbundle and separately price individual elements. By bundling, firms can increase volume and reduce costs.[49] However, as markets mature and customers gain increasing expertise with the product and technology, they tend to become increasingly demanding. Because of the fear of poorer margins and a reluctance to make the necessary changes, market leaders are often reluctant to unbundle. As a result, they lose market share to more focused, lower-service level competitors that offer lower prices. Firms faced with weak competitors may be able to bundle longer, but, in general, firms that offer a bundled price should contingently plan for unbundling over the long run, expecting ultimately to price the different elements of a complex offer separately.[50]

One viable strategy is mixed bundling. In mixed bundling, the firm offers both individual elements and a bundled set. This can be an important approach when some items in the bundle may have little value for subgroups of customers; they can then buy individual elements. A good contemporary example is the word processor, spreadsheet, database, and presentation programs bundled in the Microsoft Office suite, but which are also available individually.

Price Promotions or Steady Prices

Many firms, especially consumer goods companies, have found that volume is sensitive to short term price promotions.[51] However, the negative effects of these promotions have come under increased scrutiny. Among the concerns are:

- Customers buying on promotion inventory products that otherwise would have been purchased at full price, especially if promotions are frequent;
- Frequent price reductions destroy the product's brand equity;
- The administrative costs of managing promotions are high—both the direct costs and related costs for distribution and inventory.

As a result, several companies, such as Procter & Gamble, have shifted from frequent price promotions to everyday low pricing, and Burger King has abandoned promotional efforts such as coupons, discounts, and direct mail.

Psychological Pricing

Although pricing tends to be viewed as the ultimate economic consideration in marketing, there are important perceptual thresholds. For many customers, the psychological distance between $9.95 and $10.00 is much greater than between $10.00 and $10.05; such issues should play a role in setting prices. Framing is also important, thus customers are more likely to buy an $8 product discounted to $7 than a $6 product carrying a $1 surcharge (also $7).[52] Furthermore, customers often think proportionately (rather than absolutely) about prices for comparable offers. For example, given the choice of buying a book in a store for $25 or walking a couple of blocks to buy the identical item for $10, many customers would walk the two blocks. However, in an identical scenario where a television was priced at $765, few customers would go a similar effort to purchase the TV for $750.[53]

Two-Part Pricing

There are at least two types of situations where firms must deal with two-part pricing decisions: complementary products and multiple use situations.

COMPLEMENTARY PRODUCTS   The classic complementary product situation is razors and razor blades: the firm must decide how and what to charge for each element. For example, should the razors be priced high and razor blades low, or should the razors be priced low (or given away) and the razor blades priced high? One problem with the latter approach is that other manufacturers may decide to offer only razor blades and, since they have no investment in razor production, charge a low price.

> **Example:** Replacement cartridges for inkjet printers are very expensive; their cost can quickly surpass the printer investment. Many printer manufacturers have embraced the razor/razor blade philosophy to make their profit on the cartridges. Because consumers are concerned about blocking their printer's jets, they demonstrate a high degree of loyalty to the printer brand in buying cartridges.

Cameras and film, automobiles and spare parts, and vacuum cleaners and vacuum cleaner bags are other examples of these complementary product pricing situations. In deciding its prices, the firm must consider demand schedules for both complementary products.

MULTIPLE USE   The firm may have to decide whether to charge a flat fee, price for usage, or some combination of the two. Credit card companies, cable TV, Internet on-line services, and telephone companies all have this pricing dilemma. Among the issues firms should consider are customers' understanding of the price they pay, easier for a fixed fee versus variable payment, and the cost of administering the pricing system, both easier for a fixed fee.

> **Example:** In 1997, America Online shifted from a fee-for-use to a flat fee pricing schedule. Its volume rose dramatically, so much so that demand outstripped capacity in the short run.

The Basis of Price

In most industries, there are accepted bases for setting prices. For example, many suppliers set prices for their products; customers may accept, reject, or bargain about these product/price combinations. However, in some product categories, the basis for price is changing. Thus, some suppliers of capital goods are "servicizing" their offerings by charging for use, for example, by the hour, rather than for the product itself. In the advertising industry, payment for developing advertising campaigns is shifting from a flat fee to payment for results. And, in Japan, rather than pay for the ordered food, the *Viking* chain of buffet restaurants charges in yen per minute! Finally, the Internet is spawning a whole set of different price bases, especially for information products (Chapter 21).

Set Price or Respond to Offers

The implicit assumption underlying the material in this chapter is that the seller sets price and buyers decide whether or not to accept the seller's offer. However, in Priceline.com's system, customers name their price for various products and services, such as plane tickets, hotel reservations, mortgages, and cars; they must accept the product Priceline identifies.[54] Such a system may have considerable potential, especially in service businesses where the product cannot be inventoried and a sale lost today is lost forever.

Auctions

Many goods, especially second-hand items, are sold at auctions. Typically, the seller sets a reserve price below which the product will be withdrawn and the auctioneer seeks the buyer willing to pay the highest price.[55] However, in a Dutch auction, the seller gradually reduces price until a buyer is secured.

> **Example:** A new online investment banking company, OpenIPO, puts out a company prospectus with no price. The price is reduced until someone bids, then is further reduced until all shares are sold. Each buyer gets the same price, but the early bidders secure better allocations.[56]

The growth of the Internet is fueling the development of auction sites not only for consumer products, but also for business-to-business exchanges where an increasing variety of services are being bought and sold. Increasingly popular are "reverse auctions" where buyers state their requirements and suppliers bid to supply. In these auctions prices go down and the lowest price secures the business.

Ethical and Legal Issues in Pricing

In many countries, pricing decisions come under legislative scrutiny and offer a variety of ways for firms to find themselves in ethical and legal trouble. In addition to setting different prices across customers for comparable offers, other potentially serious pricing actions include price fixing, predatory pricing, deceptive pricing, resale price maintenance, and bait and switch.

Price fixing refers to meeting with competitors and setting prices. Such activities are illegal in most jurisdictions as they typically lead to higher prices.

> **Example:** In May 1999, major global companies Roche Holdings and BASF agreed to pay fines of $500 million and $225 million respectively to settle a U.S. Justice Department suit for setting production quotas, global prices, and distribution for vitamin ingredients.[57]

Predatory pricing occurs when a firm uses profits from one or more operations to cross-subsidize its entry in another market. It prices below cost with the explicit intention of driving a competitor from the market. **Deceptive pricing**, where the firm does not disclose the full price or makes it difficult for customers to understand what is being charged, is regulated in many markets.[58] **Resale price maintenance (RPM),** the practice of a manufacturer fixing its resellers' prices, is illegal in many countries. **Bait and switch,** which tends to occur in retail environments, refers to the practice of advertising a low price product (bait) yet having limited availability. This product typically sells out quickly and most customers arriving at the store are offered only a higher price product (switch).[59]

SUMMARY

This chapter presented a normative approach to making pricing decisions. It emphasized the high degree of leverage that pricing decisions have on firm profitability, then focused on the importance of perceived customer value in setting prices. Critical elements of

1. What is the pricing objective? (from the market strategy)
2. What value do customers place on the firm's product/service?
3. Is there variation in the way in which customers value the firm's product? (search for segments)
4. How price sensitive are customers?
5. What is the optimal pricing structure? (e.g., discounts, bundled prices)
6. How are competitors likely to respond?
7. What actual prices does the firm receive?
8. What are customers' emotional reactions to our price?
9. Are the firm's customers profitable to serve?

FIGURE 18.11

Summary Questions for Setting Prices

---

creating, measuring and capturing that value were considered. The discussion then moved to the role of costs, competition and the firm's strategic objectives in pricing decisions and considered two special cases, introducing a new product and making price changes for an existing product.

A variety of issues in setting prices were discussed and a set of factors identified that determine the actual prices paid by customers. The notion of the price waterfall was used to show that seemingly unrelated decisions may lead the firm to realize lower prices than may have been planned.

Finally, a series of issues in tactical pricing were discussed.

Based on the discussion in the chapter, a series of questions to ask in making better pricing decisions is presented (Figure 18.11).

THE CHANGING VIEW

Old Way	New Way
Focus on costs	Focus on perceived value
Price and offer homogeneity	Price and offer heterogeneity
Customer ill-informed	Customer well-informed
Pricing complexity limited by human factors	Pricing complexity software driven
Prestige sometimes ahead of value perception	Value consciousness more pervasive among customers
Full-cost systems pervasive	Activity-based costing becoming prevalent
Destructive pricing tactics common	Growing sophistication in using the pricing toolkit
List price mentality	Varied pricing tactics
Antitrust considerations minimal	Growing enforcement in United States and European Union
Inflation permitted easy price increases	Low inflation/foreign competition hold prices down
Inefficient product markets	Efficient product markets (role of the Internet)
Perceived customer value ignored	Perceived customer value measured and tracked

QUESTIONS FOR STUDY AND DISCUSSION

1. "The purpose of price is not to recover costs, but to capture value in the mind of the customer." Discuss.

2. The section Contemplating Price Changes for an Existing Product worked through an example to determine the unit volume required to make the same profit if price were reduced from 50 cents to 45 cents. Using the same basic data

and assumptions, calculate by how much unit volume could fall such that the firm makes at least $1.4 million profit if the price were increased to 60 cents per lb.

3. In January 1998, Merck launched Propecia, a new prescription hair-growth drug that sells for about $50 per month's supply, $250 for five months. Its over-the-counter competitor, Rogaine, sells for about $30 per month's supply. The active ingredient (finasteride) in Propecia is identical to that in Merck's product, Proscar, a treatment for enlarged prostates. A bottle of Proscar tablets costs about $70. Because one Proscar tablet equals five daily doses of Propecia, some balding men are persuading doctors to write prescriptions for Proscar, then slicing the pill into five parts. In this fashion, treatment for balding costs about $14 per month's supply. Merck defends Propecia's three-four fold price premium, citing added research costs including clinical trials, estimated at $450 million. Proscar tablets are covered by most insurance policies; Propecia is not.

   Pharmacia and Upjohn, Inc., makers of Rogaine, introduced an $80 million advertising campaign for extra-strength Rogaine, a topical liquid applied twice daily. Also, on the Usenet news group alt.baldspot, a user in Italy was offering to send Proscar tablets to the U.S. for $63 per bottle, $12.60 per month's supply of Propecia.[60]
   • As Merck's director of marketing, what action would you take?
   • As the compliance director for a national HMO chain, what action would you take?
   • As Pharmacia and Upjohn's director of marketing, what action would you take?

4. Select a market with which you are familiar. Develop a customer value map. How do you interpret the map? What pricing options are available for the various competitors?

5. The text alleges that the sales force is typically volume-driven. How might this be changed? What would be the advantages and disadvantages of your proposal?

6. Why do larger competitors often choose to compete on a fixed cost basis? What alternatives would you recommend to one of their smaller competitors? Why?

7. In 1958, Kaplan, Dirlam, and Lanzillotti found that cost-plus pricing was the most commonly used pricing approach. In 1995, Shim and Sudit found that nothing had changed despite the passage of almost 40 years. The text argues that this approach is deeply flawed. How do you explain this apparent incongruity? What should marketers do about it?

8. Explain the price waterfall concept. How should management deal with waterfall problems?

9. Explain in economic terms why marketing communications should not simply be viewed as a cost.

10. Consider three products or services you have purchased in the last several days. How important was price compared with the other factors leading you to make the purchase decision? Why?

11. Bring to class three examples where the seller's ability to reduce the time, effort, and risk of purchasing its products enabled it to earn a higher selling price.

12. It can be argued that economics and accounting have paid disproportionate attention to the dollar price as opposed to the time, effort, and risk of products and services. How might societal change have affected the saliency of this argument?

13. In 1999, some parts of the world were mired in deflation. If you were the general manager of a division with profit responsibility, how might your decisions with respect to cost and price be affected?

14. Select two examples from the pricing toolkit in Figure 18.10 and describe how specific companies have used them to achieve competitive advantage.

15. Bring to class an example of what you believe to be a deceptive pricing practice. How would consumers be able to protect themselves from this practice?

16. The power of the Internet in enabling buyers to become better informed about alternatives and prices will mean that the only sustainable price differences will be based upon true differences in perceived customer value. Discuss.

17. Select a company and product with which you are familiar. How might the firm adapt Coca-Cola's plan to price its vending machine products on the basis of temperature to apply to its product?

18. What is your assessment of the future of auctions on the Internet? What sorts of products and services do you think are most appropriate for auctions?

ENDNOTES

1. In recent years, several pricing texts have attempted to remedy the lack of normative material. See, for example, K.B. Monroe, *Pricing: Making Profitable Decisions*, New York: McGraw-Hill, 1990; R.J. Dolan and H. Simon, *Power Pricing, How Managing Price Transforms the Bottom Line*, New York: The Free Press, 1996 and T.T. Nagle and R. Holden, *The Strategy and Tactics of Pricing: A Guide to Profitable Decision Making*, Prentice Hall, 1995.

2. For other important pricing work, see, for example, P.E. Green and Y. Wind, "New Way to Measure Consumers' Judgments," *Harvard Business Review*, 53 (July/Aug. 1975) pp. 107–118; A. Gabor, *Pricing: Principles and Practice*, London: Heinemann, 1977; R.J. Dolan and A.P. Jeuland, "Experience Curves and Dynamic Demand Models: Implications for Optimal Pricing Strategies," *Journal of Marketing*, 45 (Winter 1981), pp. 52–73. See also the classic pricing work, A.D.H. Kaplan, J.B. Dirlam, and R.F. Lanzillotti, *Pricing in Big Business*, Washington, DC: Brookings Institution, 1958 and J. Dean, "Pricing Policies for New Products," *Harvard Business Review*, 28 (Nov./Dec. 1950), pp. 28–36.

3. Based on 2,463 companies in the Compustat database, M.V. Marn and R.L. Rosiello, "Managing Price, Gaining Profit," *Harvard Business Review*, 70 (Sept./Oct. 1992), pp. 84–94.

4. This problem is exacerbated when salespeople are compensated on sales volume. Ford's high profits in 1999 ($7.2 billion) were in part attributable to refocusing its sales units on the most profitable vehicles and option packages, *Business Week*, April 10, 2000.

5. The exchange paradigm is central to marketing. See, for example, R.P. Bagozzi, "Marketing as an Organized Behavioral System of Exchange," *Journal of Marketing*, 38 (Oct. 1974), pp. 77–81.

6. For the time-pressured, dual-professional families of the late twentieth century, the reduction of time and effort afforded by direct marketers was a major contributor to this sector's growth.

7. Nagle and Holden, *op. cit.*, Chapter 4.

8. See B.T. Gale, *Managing Customer Value*, New York: Free Press, 1994.

9. *Market-perceived quality ratio* is Gale's term for customer perceived value.

10. Conjoint analysis copes easily with non-linear value functions.

11. This technique is known by a variety of names, sometimes industry-specific. Included are systems cost analysis, outcomes research (health care), total distribution cost analysis (logistics and transportation), and economic value.

12. See also Nagle and Holden, *op. cit.* Chapter 4.

13. In late 1999, it was reported that Coca-Cola was testing vending machines that would adjust prices upwards on hot days.

14. P.C. Browne, N. Capon, T.S. Harris, H.N. Mantel, C.A. Newland, and A.H. Walsh, *The Ratemaking Process for the United States Postal Service*, New York: Institute of Public Administration, 1991.

15. Before reading this section, students should become familiar with the material in Section 1 of the Book Appendix.

16. In a recent survey, over 80% of U.S. manufacturing firms used cost-plus pricing; for almost 70% of firms, the relevant cost base was full-allocated costs (see Book Appendix). E. Shim and E.F. Sudit, "How Manufacturers Price Products," *Management Accounting*, (February 1995), pp. 37–39.

17. Advances in Activity Based Costing (ABC) have enabled firms to gain superior knowledge of cost dynamics.

18. Selling, general, and administrative costs.

19. The hurdle rate, typically related to the firm's cost of capital, is the minimum return it will accept for a new investment.

20. See also the earlier Avon example. This target pricing method can cause difficulties if the development cycle is long.

21. To meet the required price, Ford and his brilliant Danish-born production engineer Knudsen had to invent a revolutionary moving assembly line. The rest is history.

22. The marginal cost is the cost to make and sell one extra unit.

23. In certain special cases prices below $4 might be acceptable as, for example, in cyclical situations when it is known that the product will be continued but to shut down and reopen production facilities is extremely costly.

24. *The New York Times*, November 22, 1999.

25. N. Capon, J.U. Farley, and J. Hulbert, "Pricing and Forecasting in an Oligopoly Firm," *Journal of Management Studies*, 12 (1975), pp. 133–156.

26. American Airlines' initiative comprised a combination of price increases and declines in an attempt to simplify the highly complex industry pricing system. See American Airlines (A) and (B), *Harvard Business School*, 9-594-001 and 9-594-019.

27. A.K. Rao, M.E. Bergen, and S. Davis, "How to Fight a Price War," *Harvard Business Review*, 78 (Mar./Apr. 2000), pp. 107–116.

28. A.K. Rao, M.E. Bergen, and S. Davis, *op. cit.*

29. See the discussion in Chapter 8.

30. A classic description of this strategy in action is provided by Polaroid, *The First Thirty Years, 1948–1978: A Chronology of Polaroid Photographic Products*, Cambridge, MA: Polaroid Corporation, 1979.

31. Consideraton of the time value of money has been omitted to keep the example simple.

32. Most readers have met similar concepts previously in a microeconomics or managerial accounting course. Nonetheless, the focus of this discussion on marketing likely differs from those of other disciplines. Before tackling this section, please become familiar with the material in the Book Appendix where Table 18.5 is a simplification of Appendix Table 4. Note the simplifying assumption that variable and fixed costs per unit are constant over the volume range.

33. In traditional income statements, costs are typically partitioned into cost of goods sold (COGS) and all other costs, mostly marketing and SG&A. In the income statement in Table 18.3, both variable costs and fixed costs are gathered from each of the two traditional categories. For example, variable costs comprise such items as raw materials, direct labor, electricity to power production machines and freight (from COGS) and sales commissions; fixed costs comprise indirect labor, manufacturing overhead and depreciation (from COGS) and advertising, field sales (salary, expenses), and product and marketing management.

34. Note that the chart is incomplete as the highest VMR displayed is 40%; clearly, higher VMRs are possible.

35. G.E. Smith and T.T. Nagle, "Financial Analysis for Profit-Driven Pricing," *Sloan Management Review*, (Spring 1994), pp. 71–84.

36. For a flight that is scheduled, consider the variable cost per extra passenger: extra fuel for the person plus baggage, the meal (average on domestic U.S. flights = $4.13, *The Economist*, March 13, 1999) or cookies, peanuts, and soft drinks.

37. Norton Company, *Harvard Business School*, 9-581-046.

38. *Financial Times*, February 22, 1999.

39. *U.S. News and World Report*, June 22, 1998.

40. Marn and Rosiello, *op. cit.*

41. This example assumes a list price of $100, adapted from Marn and Rosiello, *op. cit.*

42. For example, when an incumbent is attempting to fend off entry by a new competitor. A "load-em-up" strategy for the channel may contribute to a successful defense.

43. The more similar the firm's offers to different customers, the more likely it will run afoul of anti-price discrimination legislation like the Robinson-Patman Act in the United States.

44. The critical issue for these organizations is to bring supply and demand into balance. Use of time in pricing decisions is an important method of modifying demand.

45. Such systems are in place in Sweden (Trondheim, Bergen, Oslo) and Singapore, and are planned (2001) for The Netherlands (Amsterdam, Rotterdam, Utrecht and The Hague), *The Economist*, December 6, 1997.

46. The "euro" countries' population is 290 million; they account for 19.4% of world GNP (U.S., 19.6%). Britain, Denmark and Sweden have no immediate plans to join the "euro" system.

47. By contrast, black markets occur when demand is greater than supply and buyers simply resell products at higher prices. For example, in the mid-1980s, Cabbage Patch dolls, listing at under $20, sold for $100 in the black market; tickets for popular concerts and sporting events are often "scalped" at higher than list prices.

48. Sometimes laws are enacted that prohibit "gray market" products from entering a country, as in the U.S. in the late 1990s.

49. Everyday examples of bundling for volume increases are series tickets for cultural events and *prix fixe* restaurant meals.

50. See W.J. Adams and J.L. Yellen, "Commodity Bundling and the Burden of Monopoly," *Quarterly Journal of Economics*, 90 (1976), pp. 475–498.

51. A variety of price promotions may be devised, such as push—manufacturer deal to trade only; pull—manufacturer rebate to consumer only; push/pull—combination trade deal and consumer rebate, and retailer to consumer rebate.

52. For a discussion of this effect and other issues related to buyers' perceptions of price, see G.E. Smith and T.T. Nagle, "Frames of Reference and Buyers' Perception of Price and Value," *California Management Review*, 38 (1995), pp. 98–116.

53. This effect is consistent with the Weber-Fechner law of psychophysics. See R. Thaler, "Toward a Positive Theory of Consumer Choice," *Journal of Economic Theory and Organization*, 1 (1980), pp. 39–60. See also Chapter 4, pp. 98–99.

54. Priceline.com has been granted a patent on its conditional purchase offer system.

55. Several Internet companies, such as Ebay and Amazon.com, are offering online auctions.

56. *Business Week*, April 5, 1999.

57. *The New York Times*, May 21, 1999. With this agreement and four months remaining in its 1999 fiscal year, the U.S. Justice Department's antitrust division had collected $913 million in fines, substantially more than it had collected in its entire history. Landmark price fixing cases include the 1960s "phases of the moon" case in the steam turbine generator business involving Allis Chalmers, GE, and Westinghouse; this case was significant in the United States since it was the first time that company executives went to jail for this sort of offense. See R.G.M. Sultan, *Pricing in the Electrical Oligopoly*, Vols. 1 and 2, Cambridge, MA: Harvard University Press, 1974.

58. For example, advertising the price of a product as $X, without disclosing that for the product to function other critical elements must also be purchased; or, burying the extra information in the "fine print" in an impossible-to-understand format.

59. For a good overview of legal and ethical issues in pricing, see Nagle and Holden, *op. cit.*, Chapter 14.

60. D.J. Morrow, "New Baldness Drug is Older Product at a Premium Price," *The New York Times*, January 20, 1998, D1,7.

WEB RESOURCES

Alcan	www.alcan.com
Alcoa	www.alcoa.com
Allis Chalmers	www.allischalmers.com
Amazon	www.amazon.com
America On-Line	www.aol.com
American Airlines	www.americanair.com
American West	www.americawest.com
AT&T	www.att.com
Avon	www.avon.com
BASF	www.basf.com
BMW	www.bmw.com
British Aerospace	www.bae.co.uk
Burger King	www.burgerking.com
Continental	www.continental.com
Coca-Cola	www.cocacola.com
Delta	www.delta-air.com
Ebay	www.ebay.com
Ford	www.ford.com
General Electric	www.ge.com
General Motors	www.gm.com
Gillette	www.gillette.com
MCI	www.wcom.com
Merck	www.merck.de
Microsoft	www.microsoft.com
Northwest	www.nwa.com
Norton	www.nortonco.com
OpenIPO	www.openipo.com
Pepsi	www.pepsico.com
Pharmacia and Upjohn	www.pnu.com
Polaroid	www.polaroid.com
Priceline	www.priceline.com
Procter & Gamble	www.pg.com
Roche	www.roche.com
Sprint	www.sprint.com
TWA	www.twa.com
United Airlines	www.ual.com
U.S. Justice Department	www.usdoj.gov
USair	www.usair.com
Volkswagen	www.vw.com
Westinghouse	www.westinghouse.com
Xerox	www.xerox.com

CHAPTER

19

ENSURING THE MARKETING OFFER IS IMPLEMENTED AS PLANNED

LEARNING OBJECTIVES

When you have completed this chapter, you will understand

- **the challenge of creating the customer-oriented firm**
- **an overall framework that places the implementation of market strategy in the context of organizational development**
- **a set of strategic considerations for organizational development**
- **traditional and newer approaches of organizing for marketing**
- **the critical role of systems and processes, and human resource management for implementing market strategy**
- **how to maintain a customer orientation**

INTRODUCTION

In this chapter, we focus on ensuring that the various strategies and implementation programs discussed thus far in section III are actually executed as planned.[1] As Bob Joss, former managing director of Westpac, one of Australia's largest firms, has said:

> "Too often the popular conception is that strategy and vision are all that matters— 'just get the strategy right and success follows.' Nothing could be further from the truth. In business, execution is the major management challenge. Disciplined, daily, execution of a myriad of details must be done correctly to deliver a strategy."[2]

The challenge is to ensure that all functions act in concert to implement the market offer in the face of significant pressures to act otherwise. Chapter 3 explored in some depth the distinction between internal and external orientations, and showed that for firms to be successful in the increasingly difficult environments they inhabit, the job of marketing must shift from a purely functional focus to one that embraces the organization as a whole. A firm-wide shift from an internal to an external orientation was advocated, and the chapter discussed several impediments to developing an external orientation.

This issue is crucial, for although a firm may perform at a world-class level on some dimensions, "the chain is only as strong as its weakest link," and inadequate performance on one dimension may cancel out excellent performance on the others. Consider one author's experience with Dell, a company that is generally praised for its innovative direct-to-customer strategy.

Example: Dell has successfully executed a higher-education strategy that involves selling high-quality notebook computers, preconfigured to individual institutional specifications, to incoming students. The problem—a spike in demand in late summer and early fall of 1999 that Dell's manufacturing system was unprepared to handle. The result—broken delivery promises. Furthermore, information on the order status was difficult to secure, and when received, was inconsistent. Perhaps the worst feature of the entire experience was telephoning customer service and being assured by a recording that Dell was really concerned with the value of the caller's time—a little thin after hearing it for the 40th time in two 45-minute waiting periods!

Here, we develop a framework for overcoming these impediments and thinking through this shift in perspective. It is often argued that it is easier to build such an organization from scratch than to change an existing organization, especially if the current organization is large. However, the increasing environmental turbulence discussed throughout this book has taught us more about the process of organizational evolution and what may be required to create organizations that are externally orientated and customer-focused, and that seamlessly implement their market strategies. Even so, there remains an academic debate as to whether such organizations can best be created via planning or through "learning by doing."[3] Since the desired final characteristics are similar, and the debate as yet unresolved, in this chapter we focus on the outcomes.

CREATING THE CUSTOMER-ORIENTED FIRM

Chapter 3 examined several impediments to developing a truly externally oriented organization:

- Fixed investment in plant and equipment
- Rigidities in the line organization
- Short-term pressures for efficiency, cost reduction, and profit maximization
- Presence of a dominant culture
- Social fabric of institutions
- Reward systems that motivate the wrong behavior

- Generalized resistance to change
- Accounting systems do not measure customer profitability

For the entire organization to embrace the notion that customers are central to its success and to act accordingly, these and other impediments must be overcome. In the face of these challenges, the ability of the firm to satisfy and delight customers can only occur in the context of an enlightened top management that takes an holistic view of organizational development. Unfortunately, far too often top management does not pay sufficient attention to the fact that organizations are complex systems and rather approaches this task piecemeal. As a result, attempts to shift the organization to a true customer focus fail because transforming one element in the system often leads to subversion of change by the remaining elements.[4] This piecemeal thinking is reflected in the description of company re-organizations as "moving deck chairs on the Titanic."

Bringing about fundamental corporate change requires considerable skills in organizational engineering. Indeed, early attempts to implement quality management in the United States often failed because these skills were not available. Although, in recent years, organizations embracing Total Quality Management (TQM) have developed the necessary organizational skills, these abilities were never really acquired by marketers. Too many marketers believe that if they get their marketing (in the narrow sense) right, that will be enough to win. Although many organizations may have prospered in this manner in the less competitive 1970s and 1980s, competitive success in the years ahead will require harnessing of all the firm's capabilities to beat competitors in serving targeted customers.[5]

The best leaders of the change process are general managers, though not necessarily the CEO. Although change must be systemic, it does not have to embrace each business in a multibusiness organization simultaneously; in fact, change is often better started on a small scale and then extended if successful. Although still rare, learning organizations are being developed and some firms are appointing corporate knowledge managers, one of whose functions is to promote organizational best practice.[6] This movement can be harnessed to increase an external orientation and has been witnessed in several companies.

To commence the process of creating an externally focused organization, the leader has to create the desire for change on the part of organizational members by creating dissatisfaction with the *status quo*. Such dissatisfaction typically happens when a crisis occurs, but this can be an expensive eventuality. More appropriate methods that can be extremely effective in the hands of managers with leadership capability include:

- benchmarking against competitors or comparable organizations in different industries;
- raising the perceived threat level through scenario construction or even simulation;
- stirring emotions through well-crafted speeches.

A MODEL FOR BECOMING EXTERNALLY ORIENTED

The inverted pyramid model (Figure 19.1) builds on the approach taken by firms such as SAS and Nordstrom's. It places customers at the top as the most important constituent, then provides a comprehensive view of those elements that contribute to marketing becoming a true capability, rather than just a function.

For organizational transformation to succeed, all elements in the model must reflect and reinforce the commitment to change. Most transformation programs have focused on developing (or reworking) statements of vision, values, missions, or strategy. Unfortunately, they often neglect vital supporting requirements, such as organization structure, systems and processes, and human resource management. These elements both reflect and shape the firm's culture, and will defeat attempts at change that ignore them. Both strategic considerations and supporting requirements are vitally important in developing a truly externally-focused organization.

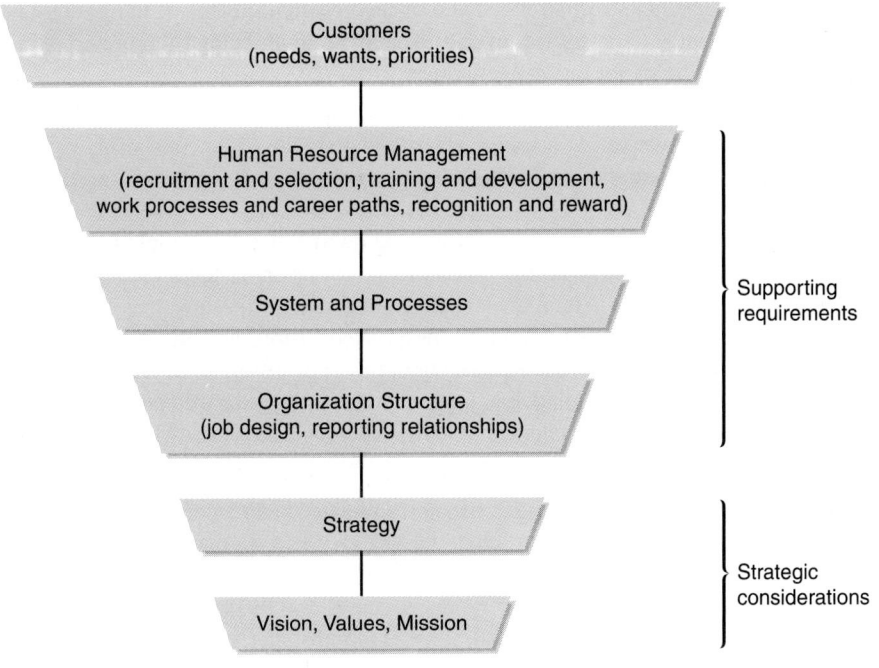

FIGURE 19.1

A Structural View for Developing Customer Focus

Strategic Considerations: Vision, Values, Mission

The leader's responsibility is to set direction for the enterprise as a whole. Vision, values, and mission are best viewed as tools for performing this responsibility. However, many important issues underlie the choices to be made, and their resolution frequently involves important marketing considerations. In particular, each concept can be used to support the growth of an external orientation.

VISION   Vision is the description of an ideal future state, a picture (in impressionistic form) of what the future should be. A corporate vision describes the future organization as a whole, but the concept is equally applicable at the business unit or even functional level. Good vision statements should not be excessively restrictive, for employees must find in the vision something to inspire them.[7] Vision statements should also not be too specific or easily achievable, for their focus is the long run.[8]

> **Example:** Incoming CEO Lou Gerstner's vision statement for IBM was simply "To lead big companies into the brave new networked world. IBM will devise their technology strategies, build and run their systems, and ultimately become the architect and repository for corporate computing, tying together not just companies, but entire industries."[9] Somewhat more succinctly, the vision of Sony MobileComm America is, "To enhance today's and create tomorrow's lifestyles."[10]

Marketing has an important role to play in formulating vision statements, for without marketing input, a vision statement may be inappropriate, or create significant marketing problems. For example, one CEO publicly announced the firm's vision of becoming its customers' most preferred supplier across all purchasing categories. This statement raised customer expectations ahead of performance thus creating significant customer dissatisfaction.

> **Example:** In summer 1997, British Airways (BA) had similar problems. BA made a public commitment to customer service as part of its vision and strategy. However, its single-minded pursuit of cost-cutting and outsourcing so alienated

its staff that the ensuing strike stranded and/or inconvenienced tens of thousands of customers. Months later, traffic levels were still running behind the previous year despite boom times for the airline industry.

In addition, the vision statement provides an important vehicle for helping the firm shift to an external perspective. At a minimum, the vision should be consistent with the concept of an external orientation and, whenever possible, actively embrace the ideals it encompasses.

For the vision to be actively embraced, it must be owned by organizational personnel. Far too often, visions are constructed by senior executives or consultants in isolation and then foisted on the organization. Although extensive involvement can slow the development process, participation not only evolves and improves the vision, but broad commitment enables other process elements to occur more smoothly. For example, at ARAMARK, a large services company based in Philadelphia, over 8,500 employees participated directly in the development of the new vision statement. On the other hand, consider what happened at Oracle, the software company.

> **Example:** In 1995, after examining Netscape Navigator and chatting with Steve Jobs (founder of Apple computer), Oracle CEO Larry Ellison mandated that all enterprise software be converted to work as Internet applications. He also ordered that the development of client-server products cease, and the sales force advise customers of product phase-out by 2000. Several months later, Ellison discovered that not only was product development not proceeding as planned, the sales force was assuring long-standing customers that client-server products would not be withdrawn.[11]

VALUES An important adjunct to vision is values, a common set of beliefs that guide the behavior of organizational members. Organizational values are often integral to company success but, with some notable exceptions, have tended to be implicit rather than explicit. More recently, environmental pressures have led executives to rethink corporate values and to make them explicit. Values can be thought of as hard (profitability, market share) and soft (integrity, respect for others, trust, and pre-eminence of customers).[12]

As with vision, values statements are only worthwhile if embraced throughout the organization. Organizational members' buy-in is typically influenced by the extent of participation in their development, and can provide the cultural glue[13] that enables some firms to thrive in times of rapid change where others struggle to survive.

Because developing a values statement gives the firm a clear opportunity to enshrine the concept of an external orientation, active marketing input is an important element in the process. The decision examples in Chapter 3 provide an excellent set of criteria against which to judge the firm's actions. Unfortunately, it is quite common to find values statements that emphasize customer importance, but behavior that does not. When management hypocrisy is evident, the effect on the morale of employees and complementers can be significant and negative.

> **Example:** In early 1998, Rupert Murdoch, CEO of News Corporation, parent of publisher HarperCollins, caused cancellation of a memoir by Chris Patten, the last British Governor of Hong Kong. The book criticized the Government of China where Murdoch was seeking growth opportunities. Murdoch came under widespread press criticism and HarperCollins faced significant author defection.[14]

Johnson & Johnson (J&J) is an excellent example of a company whose values statement both epitomizes an external orientation and drives executive behavior.[15] Its credo (Figure 19.2) was put to the test some years ago in the Tylenol cyanide scare. J&J immediately withdrew the product to protect customers from even the smallest chance that other

We believe our first responsibility is to the doctors, nurses and patients,
to mothers and all others who use our products and services,
in meeting their needs everything we do must be of high quality.
We must constantly strive to reduce our costs
in order to maintain reasonable prices.
Customers' orders must be serviced promptly and accurately.
Our suppliers and distributors must have an opportunity
to make a fair profit.
We are responsible to our employees,
the men and women who work with us throughout the world.
Everyone must be considered as an individual.
We must respect their dignity and recognize their merit.
They must have a sense of security in their jobs.
Compensation must be fair and adequate,
and working conditions clean, orderly and safe.
Employees must feel free to make suggestions and complaints.
There must be equal opportunity for employment, development
and advancement for those qualified.
We must provide competent management,
and their actions must be just and ethical.

We are responsible to the communities in which we live and work
and to the world community as well.
We must be good citizens—support good works and charities
and bear our fair share of taxes.
We must encourage civic improvements and better health and education.
We must maintain in good order
the property we are privileged to use,
protecting the environment and natural resources.

Our final responsibility is to our stockholders.
Business must make a sound profit.
We must experiment with new ideas.
Research must be carried on, innovative programs developed
and mistakes paid for.
New equipment must be purchased, new facilities provided
and new products launched.
Reserves must be created to provide for adverse times.
When we operate according to these principles,
the stockholders should realize a fair return.

FIGURE 19.2

The Johnson & Johnson Credo

capsules were affected. Other examples are Chase Bank, whose values embrace customer focus, respect for others, teamwork, quality, professionalism, and initiative. Distributor Inchape Pacific's three soft core values state:

- We care about our customers and the way in which we satisfy their needs.
- We care about our principles and the way in which we represent them.
- We care about our people and the way in which we manage them.[16]

MISSION   We now introduce the concept of mission, then discuss several bases for developing mission statements.

The Concept   Where vision and values statements embrace lofty ideals of how the enterprise will function, the role of mission is to guide, yet constrain, the firm's search for opportunity. Underlying mission is the notion that organizations can best leverage their capabilities by focusing on a limited number of areas, rather than dispersing energy in many different directions.[17] Ideally, mission codifies business domains where the firm does well or aspires to do well.[18] For firms comprising several businesses, missions should be developed at both the business and corporate levels. Of course, individual business unit missions should be encompassed by the corporate mission.[19,20] It scarcely needs stating, but the firm's definition of mission has major implications for the identity of its competitors.

Firms should proactively manage mission evolution. The impetus for mission change can come from a lack of sufficient growth opportunities (broaden), a target of opportunity (broaden), resources stretched too thin (narrow), poor financial performance (narrow), and take-over attack (narrow).[21] In addition, new leadership often sets new directions via a revised mission.[22] Capital market pressure may play an important role, even for relatively focused firms, if financial analysts believe that company break-up will release value.

> **Example:** In the late 1990s, DuPont was comprised of three types of business—chemicals, oil, and life sciences. 1997 sales (operating income) were, respectively $20 billion ($2 billion), $20 billion ($1 billion), and $2 billion (almost $1 billion loss). Although its initial response to analysts who believed DuPont should split into three firms was that synergies justified a single enterprise, it later spun off the oil operations.[23]

Mission not only influences choice of market opportunity but, via outsourcing, allows firms to rid themselves of responsibility for ancillary activities that consume management talent and investment capital but do not provide competitive advantage.

Focusing only on what the firm does well implies a strong internal focus. Choice of mission should also subsume an informed view of market opportunities. Research suggests that interrelationships among market opportunities (market relatedness) can be more important than technological competencies and synergies.[24] In recent years, hard-headed analyses revealing that current missions were unlikely to enhance shareholder value led two major U.S. organizations to abandon their historic core competencies and embrace fundamentally new directions.

> **Example:** As noted earlier, in the late 1990s, Westinghouse Electric acquired CBS, changed its name and focused exclusively on media.

> **Example:** In 1995, Corning's $5.3 billion revenues came from five major areas: healthcare services (lab testing) 39%, telecom (optical fiber) 22%, advanced materials (environmental and other) 16%, consumer (pots and pans) 13%, and information display (TV, computer screens) 10%. By 1998, Corning revenues dropped to $3.5 billion as it divested its healthcare and consumer products lines. However, return on equity increased from 16% to 24%.[25]

As late as the early 1980s, the Finnish company, Nokia, made rubber, cables, and paper. In the late 1990s, sales were increasing at 25% per annum; it enjoyed about 25% global market share in mobile telephones and had a stockmarket valuation of $70 billion.[26] Other recent mission changes include A.T. Cross, makers of high quality pens and pencils for 150 years, which increasingly defines itself as in the electronic "written communications" business. Consistent with its new mission, Cross has added pen-like styluses that write on paper pads and, using radio signals from the stylus and IBM software, can be transmitted to a computer screen.[27]

Bases for Mission Definition Mission can be developed on several "pure form" bases: three supply-side (natural resources, technology, and product/service), and two demand-side (market/market segment, and customer needs):

- **Natural resources**: These businesses maximize value from a natural resource. For example, the mission statement, "We are a forest products company," should lead the firm to consider making any product, using any technology, sold to any market, so long as it is made from wood.
- **Technology**: These businesses focus on a core technology, such as "We are a glass company," or "We are an electronics company." An electronics firm's search for opportunity would be based solely on electronics. Its products could be sold to any market and use any raw material, so long as they were based on electronics.
- **Product/service**: These businesses focus on a particular product/service, such as "We are an automobile firm." Although this mission implies a sole focus on auto-

mobiles, these may be powered by various fuels (gasoline, diesel, alcohol, LPG, natural gas) and use various technologies (steam, internal combustion, electro-mechanical, gas turbine).

- **Market/market segment**: These businesses offer selected markets/market segments a variety of different products/services made from various raw materials using various technologies. For example, consumer packaged goods firms target families, and offer various household and personal care products. Market-based definitions, often based on geographic or socio-economic segments, are most common among retail and distribution businesses.

- **Customer needs**: This mission focuses solely on customer needs. For example, a mission to serve transportation needs might lead a firm to offer bicycles, automobiles, trucks, helicopters, and airplanes.[28] Otis Elevator's mission is, "To provide any customer a means of moving people and things up, down, and sideways over short distances with higher reliability than any similar enterprise in the world."[29]

Individual pure form missions can be used separately, or combined with other bases to develop narrower mission statements. For example, Courtyard by Marriott's combines market segment and product/service "To provide economy and quality-minded frequent business travelers with a premier lodging facility, which is consistently perceived as clean, comfortable, well maintained, and attractive, staffed by friendly, attentive, and efficient people."

Although many companies today strive to state their missions in terms of a market/product scope, the importance of marketing considerations in mission statement design is not always recognized. Even more serious are those cases where executives ignore their businesses' missions and act at will, leaving underlings to dismiss the mission statement as a mere exercise in wordsmithing.

Strategic Considerations: Strategy

A strategic approach to markets (Chapters 8 through 11) is one of the most powerful drivers of an external orientation. Far too often, companies develop business and market strategies that lack any substantial insight into either their customers or their competitors. In an increasingly competitive world, it is ever-more important that firms secure real insight into customer problems and seek to identify latent, not merely expressed, needs and wants. Furthermore, although some firms have developed serviceable systems for understanding the changing requirements of target customers, fewer have developed the infrastructure for securing good insights into their competitors. In addition to deep customer knowledge, those firms that put forth the effort to really understand competitors will develop a much clearer sense of their objectives, strategies, and likely actions. They are then more likely to build market strategies based on the marketing principles of Selectivity and Concentration, Customer Value, and Differential Advantage.

Supporting Requirements: Organization Structure

Statements of vision, values, mission, and strategy represent opportunities to reinforce the message about customer centrality and the need for an external orientation. Even though these statements are arguably necessary, experience shows they are often defeated by deep-seated organizational characteristics often considered as supporting requirements.

Although organization structure can facilitate development of an integrated approach to marketing, it is more likely to impede the process. Thus despite the fact that market- and customer-based organizations have a long history in marketing, powerful internal forces have often led to organization structures formed around products, technologies, and even production facilities rather than markets, market segments, or key accounts. However, as customer power has increased, market-based organizations have gained in importance.

TRADITIONAL MARKETING ORGANIZATIONS This section illustrates several traditional organizational arrangements.

The Functional Organization   In the early stages of marketing organizations, activities such as marketing research, advertising, customer service, and new product development are often placed in an organization operating separately from the sales force. If viewed as simply supporting the sales effort, these areas may also report to the sales vice president (VP). However, if their different focus and time horizon are recognized, they may be placed under a separate marketing executive at an organizational level similar to the sales VP. The problem with this type of organization is that unresolved conflict between long-term (marketing) and short-term (sales force) perspectives can only be resolved by the firm's most senior executives. A structure in which both sales and marketing VPs report to a single executive with responsibility for all customer-related functions enables better integration of these two functions.

Purely functional organizations tend to work best with homogeneous markets and product lines. However, as these organizations become more complex, specialized responsibility for either products or markets becomes necessary. Product/ brand management and market segment organizations developed to solve this problem.

Product/Brand Management Organization   The product management organization was originally developed at Procter & Gamble. Sales and marketing activities are overlaid with a product management system in which managers are responsible for individual products and brands.[30] These managers develop marketing plans for their products/brands and work within the organization to ensure plan implementation. In successful systems, the cost of focusing on individual products is more than offset by improved financial performance.

Although widely adopted in both consumer and industrial products companies, product management systems have their problems. Although product/brand managers have product/brand responsibility, they do not have the commensurate authority and must rely heavily on persuasion. In addition, internal competition among brand managers can defeat a coherent strategy for the product group as a whole,[31] and frequent brand manager turnover can lead to excessive short-termism in developing brand strategy.

Category Management   Partly as a response to problems posed by internal competition, Procter & Gamble and many other companies subordinated the brand management system to category management. The firm's several brands in a product category are managed in a complementary manner to avoid destructive competition among company brands and brand managers.

Note that the rise of retailer power in the packaged goods industry has given a whole new meaning to category management. Sophisticated retailers now have significant data analysis capabilities at their disposal that enable them to determine profitability category by category, broken down by region, state, city and, even individual store. These retailers add new products and brands only if they help achieve goals set for the category. By contrast, the brand manager is typically only too happy to see a rival's shelf space reduced or even disappear. Currently, manufacturers hoping to extend a product line or launch a new brand are increasingly required to demonstrate that their addition will increase profits or sales for the entire category. Even then, they may be asked to pay a slotting fee.[32]

An interesting development in the United States has been the decision by some retailers to outsource the management of product categories to a manufacturer. Contracts for category captains typically run for several years and are granted based on the retailer's assessment of the manufacturer's category management capabilities, rather than on market position. Such appointments grant the category captain privileged access to retail sales data for all competitors, a clear competitive advantage.

Market Segment Organization   In this organizational form, managers are responsible for individual market segments; business-to-business marketers particularly favor geography and industry/end-use organizations. For example, a computer company's individual business sector managers may be responsible for the manufacturing, banking and financial services, transportation, and retailing industries. This system may overlay other marketing and sales functions or these, also, may be specialized by industry. The benefit of this system is that the firm is more closely aligned with its target customers, and the potential for inter-product conflict is reduced.

Combined Product/Brand Management/Market Segment Organizations The problem with the product/brand, category and market segment organizations is that each omits a crucial dimension. In the product/brand and category management organizations, no one is specifically responsible for market segments; in the market segment organization, no one is specifically responsible for individual products. Some firms have incorporated both organizations.

> **Example:** DuPont Textile Fibers has market segment managers for its various end-use markets, such as household textiles, men's apparel, women's apparel, industrial rubber goods. It also employs product managers responsible for the individual product lines, its different types of polyester, nylon, and other fibers.[33]

NEWER APPROACHES TO MARKETING ORGANIZATION This section explores newer approaches to marketing organization.

Inclusion Organizations Early in the adoption of the marketing concept, Pillsbury described how it grouped virtually all organizational activities under marketing.[34] A brute force approach to developing an external perspective, it was subsequently found unsatisfactory by Pillsbury. However, more recently, this approach to organization has been effective for British Airways (BA). Recognizing that two of customers' most important requirements, safety and schedule reliability, were controlled by operations, BA restructured to have operations report to marketing. Now that 80% of its employees are responsible to marketing, BA is close to McKenna's dictum, "Marketing is everything and everything is marketing."[35] This approach may have considerable applicability in service businesses where it is often difficult to identify where marketing starts and operations (or human resources, for that matter) ends. However, it is not appropriate for all organizations.

Organizing by Business Processes One outgrowth of the re-engineering movement is the attempt by some companies to organize around business processes.[36] The firm retains a classic functional structure, but much organizational output results from cross-functional process teams. A UK-based Unilever subsidiary reorganized on this basis (Figure 19.3). In this example, marketing's major responsibilities are innovation and brand development (strategic tasks); operational marketing, tasks such as trade promotions are conducted by the sales force.[37] A critical problem with this approach concerns recognition and reward. If this authority remains in the line organization, conflict and tension are inevitable.

Customer Management Organizations How the pressures for change in marketing practice discussed in this book will manifest themselves organizationally is not entirely clear, but an increasing number of elements will likely be focused around the customer. Whereas many industrial companies and service firms (in particular, financial service) can identify their customers by name, historically most consumer goods firms selling through distribution systems could not. However, since supplier-to-customer links are fundamental to all forms of traditional direct and Internet marketing, growth of these practices, and the increasing use of customer loyalty cards in supermarkets is making customer data more widespread.[38] The increased ability to identify customers raises the possibility of developing organizations based on customers rather than products or brands.

Although few businesses serve once-only clientele, only recently has the value of treating customers in relational rather than transactional terms been recognized. Business-to-business and service firms are perhaps further ahead in building longer-term relationships, possibly because of customer knowledge, particularly in industries with both high fixed costs and high customer acquisition costs.[39] However, for consumer goods manufacturers also, loyal customers represent substantial cash flows over time. In addition, as the pace of new product introduction increases, cash flows generated by customers can be more stable over time than those associated with the firm's individual products and brands.

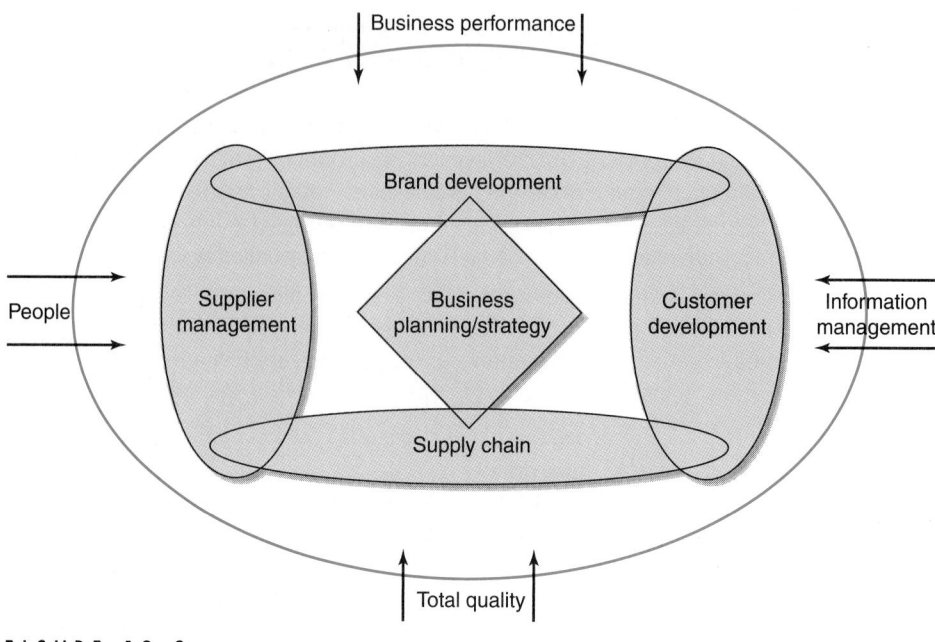

FIGURE 19.3

A Unilever Subsidiary's Process-Based Organization

Organizationally, a focus on the customer, across brands and products, can reveal significantly greater customer insight. Managers would assume responsibility and authority for a customer portfolio of some size and value.[40] Wachovia Bank, one of the most successful super-regionals in the United States, has long managed its retail customers in this manner.[41]

In essence, the product/brand management organization is turned on its side (Figure 19.4).[42] Where previously the brands ($B_1 \ldots B_4 \ldots B_n$) were the pillars of the firm and all other functional activities served the brands, in the customer-based structure, brand management is almost a staff function. The product/brand manager becomes the product/ brand expert, managing the brand asset and supporting customer portfolio managers in developing and providing products and brands to increase customer lifetime value. Customer portfolios ($CP_1 \ldots CP_4 \ldots CP_n$) become the pillars, served by the other functions and brands. This represents an enormous paradigm shift that must be supported by appropriate recruiting, selecting, developing, training, evaluating, and rewarding systems.

Significant organizational change is required to develop this organizational form.[43] However, the possibilities for true customer insight multiply as empathetic managers immerse with their customers in continuous and ongoing customer interaction, and product and brand blinders diminish.[44] Cohort matching becomes even more important, for customer contact management is an experience that must be carefully engineered.[45]

This organizational development is rare for consumer marketing but is gaining increasing strength in business-to-business marketing. Many companies now have key account programs in which key account managers are responsible for the firm's relationship with the customer at its many locations, not only in individual countries but also around the globe.[46]

Example: In 1999, faced with slow decision making, defection of talented individuals and increasingly tough competition, Microsoft redeveloped its vision and shifted to a customer-focused organization. Individual organizational units are now responsible for groups of customers—corporate customers, knowledge

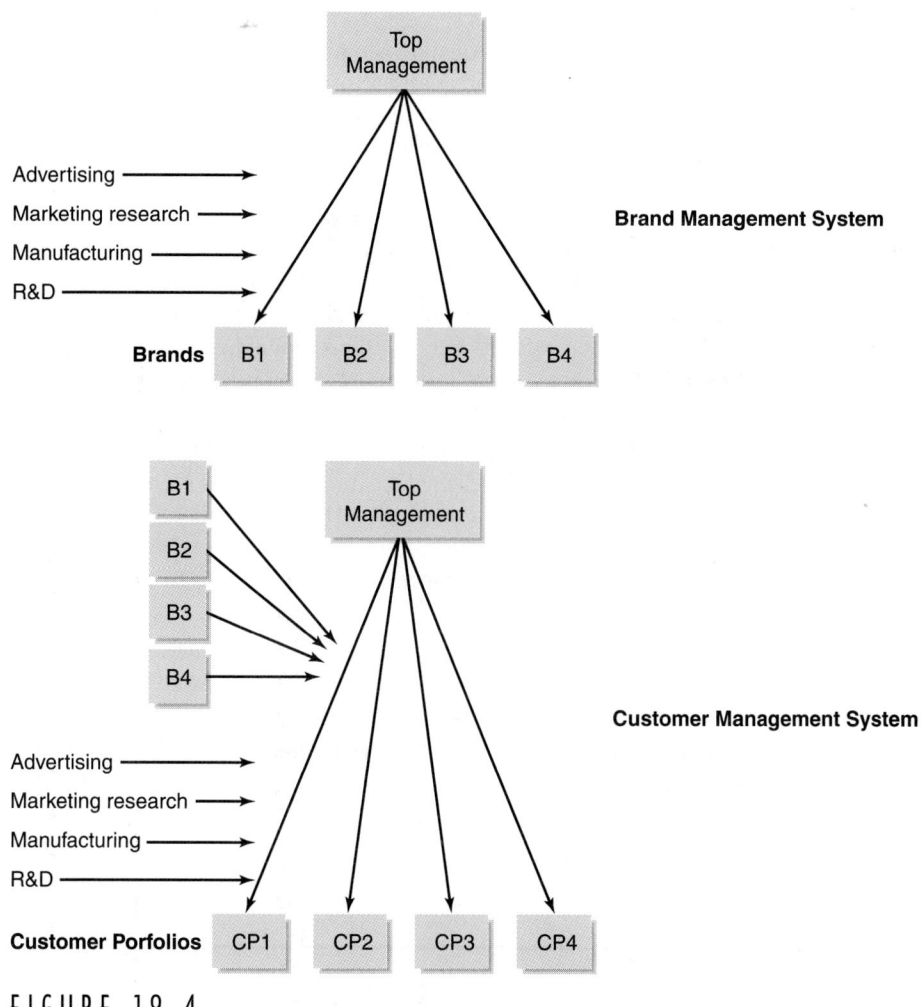

FIGURE 19.4

Transition from Brand Management to Customer Management

workers, home PC buyers, game players, software developers, web surfers, and cybershoppers. Said CEO Bill Gates, ". . . the new structure puts the customer at the center of everything we do by reorganizing our business divisions by customer segment rather than along product lines."[47]

GLOBAL ORGANIZATION FOR MARKETING   One of the more interesting marketing debates in recent years concerns the development of global markets. Levitt argues in favor of increasing homogenization of customer needs worldwide driven by greater information access via methods such as satellite TV (for example, Star TV in Asia).[48] Others have argued in favor of multiple geographic market segments based on need sets driven by cultural, nationalistic, and linguistic differences.[49]

These two separate visions of global market development lead to differing recommendations for global organization structure in general, and global marketing structure in particular. If regional differences are a critical factor, firms should consider regional organizations based on geography, such as North America, Latin America, Asia, Australasia, Europe, and Africa. Each region would enjoy significant autonomy for marketing efforts, including positioning, product design, promotion, distribution, and pricing decisions at the region and individual country level.[50]

ENSURING THE
MARKETING OFFER
IS IMPLEMENTED
AS PLANNED

Example: A major factor in McDonald's success ($35 million annual revenues), 60% of profits generated by its international division, is attributed to the degree of flexibility it allows individual countries to tailor offerings to local tastes. For example, in Vienna, McCafes offer blended coffee; in Indonesia, both french fries and rice are available; and in South Korea, customers can purchase roast pork on a bun with a garlicky soy sauce.

However, if customer needs are homogeneous, a global product management system in which the global product manager has significant authority and responsibility for positioning, product, and pricing decisions may be more appropriate. Typically, this organization is overlaid on a geographic structure in which individual country organizations have responsibility for sales, distribution efforts, and adapting standardized advertising programs for the local market, perhaps with appropriate translation and use of local spokespersons.

Example: In early 1999, Procter & Gamble (P&G) transformed four business units based on geographic regions into seven global product groups such as Baby Care, and Food and Beverage. By slimming down the organization, reducing reporting lines, and aligning executive compensation with new goals, P&G hoped to improve its product development performance and reduce the time-to-market.[51]

Whereas the debate continues in consumer marketing, homogenization of customer needs is an increasing trend in business-to-business marketing. Many multinational/global companies are demanding similar treatment from their suppliers worldwide, regardless of geography. The ability to treat customers similarly in multiple countries is severely compromised if the global organization is based on geography. The firm must develop complex evaluation and reward systems to promote the global treatment of major customers, or it must shift to a new organizational form in which geography plays a much-reduced role.

Example: Traditionally, IBM's global organization had a strong regional basis in which strong country managers reported to powerful regional executives. In the mid-1990s, IBM scrapped this system for an organization based on industry lines, such as manufacturing, financial services, and retail, each headed by an industry director. Within each industry organization, global account managers are responsible for IBM relationships with major global clients; local country salespeople report through the industry organization.[52] A geographic structure remains for government relations, corporate advertising, and the "care and feeding" of locally employed personnel, but country heads no longer have budgetary responsibility.[53]

Supporting Requirements: Systems and Processes

All organizations incorporate systems and processes to produce organizational outputs. These systems and processes can be arrayed along a continuum, from solely computer-based ("hard" systems), such as automatic teller machines (ATM), to almost exclusively manual ("soft" systems), such as retail customer service desks. In the middle are combination systems, such as those for securing telephone numbers.

"HARD" SYSTEMS   In many firms, "hard" systems are used mostly to improve operational efficiency and reduce costs, rather than increase strategic effectiveness and add value for customers. However, when used creatively, the technological power of computer-based systems can contribute enormously to making firms more externally focused, improving marketing effectiveness, and securing competitive advantage.

First, by making customer information more readily available and widely distributed, the firm can improve employees' understanding of what is important to the customer and help develop an external perspective.[54] Second, inasmuch as user-friendly, computer-based systems reduce customers' time, effort, and risk in making purchases, they enable firms to get closer to their customers. Third, by providing records of purchase history and other interactions, they allow companies with large numbers of customers to attack the soul-less anonymity of transaction-based markets. Large firms can thus emulate, if not replicate, the high-personal-service strategies of small firms, such as the local grocer who knew his customers by name and built his business on that basis.

Example: Customer loyalty programs have been established by various airlines and emulated by credit card companies, such as the Discover card and Apple Computer's Visa card. These programs are also infiltrating supermarket retailing, including UKrops and Dominics in the United States, and Tesco and Sainsbury's in Great Britain.[55]

Fourth, "hard" systems are at the core of supply chain management, offering better supply/demand matching and reduced inventory.

Example: Pioneered by American Hospital Supply[56] and practiced by such firms as Cheseborough Ponds, and Procter and Gamble, computer-based vendor-managed inventory systems offer significant advantages to both buyer and supplier.

Database systems allow firms to be more responsive to customer needs and are increasingly supporting so-called "segment-of-one" marketing.[57] Results from this approach can be dramatic.

Example: At Dell's Web site, customers can configure a computer to meet their individual requirements, and place and pay for their purchase. The product is built to order and delivered promptly. In early 2000, Dell was receiving over $10 million orders per day. Competitors Apple, IBM, and Compaq modified their production and ordering systems to emulate Dell.[58]

Personnel at companies in the vanguard of such system changes experience directly the crucial importance of firm-customer relationships.

Example: USAA is the industry-leading, best practice example in insurance; systems are an essential ingredient in its success. Not only do computer screens provide a full client record, they prompt the service associate to inquire about helping with other services. For example, a call about homeowners insurance for a new home triggers a change of address for auto insurance.

"SOFT" SYSTEMS   Soft systems can also help make firms more externally focused, improve marketing effectiveness, and secure competitive advantage. The planning system is used as an example. In many firms, this is an internally oriented, glorified budget exercise focusing predominantly on financial issues. This type of planning provides few significant benefits.[59]

By contrast, good planning is externally rather than internally driven. The planning process commences with a full environmental analysis, and significant effort is placed on understanding customers, competitors, and the environment in general. Market strategy development is a creative process that forces the firm to look externally, compared to an internal focus that erodes the quality of strategic thinking.

Good planning is also generally participative, involving all functional areas and several management levels. Whereas the functional pressures of everyday life tend to drive out an external perspective, the planning system can bring all organizational members face-to-face with external realities. Information, assumptions, and decisions are shared and critically reviewed, reducing the political gamesmanship that is characteristic of internally-oriented firms.

Outputs of the planning system set direction for the firm and also play a critical role in measurement and control. Whereas inappropriately aligned measurement and control systems can be a major impediment to implementing an external orientation, a good planning system produces measures that drive superior market performance and enhance shareholder value.

ENSURING THE
MARKETING OFFER
IS IMPLEMENTED
AS PLANNED

Supporting Requirements: Human Resource Management

The traditional tools of human resource management—recruitment and selection, training and development, work processes and career paths, and recognition and reward systems—offer many opportunities to facilitate an external orientation and enhance the probability of superior strategy implementation.

RECRUITMENT AND SELECTION Hiring personnel with the appropriate skills can have a major impact on developing an external orientation. A quarter century ago, internally-oriented firms embarked on this course of action and even today, many organizations attract marketing executives for senior positions. For example, Citibank's program to hire experienced marketing professionals from well-known marketing companies such as Procter & Gamble, General Foods, and General Mills had a major impact on developing its external perspective. And Miller Brewing's early success following its acquisition by Philip Morris had less to do with Philip Morris' understanding of the beer industry than with its cadre of consumer packaged goods professionals. Chemical Bank hired marketing professionals from American Express, and Midland Bank (UK) hired marketing expertise from non-bank companies. In each case, senior management recognized that a more external perspective was required; carefully seeding the organization with marketing professionals was one approach to achieving this goal.

More generally, recruitment and selection criteria can aid the firm's shift from an internal to external perspective. Firms as diverse as Hyatt, Singapore Airlines, Wal-Mart, L.L. Bean, and Nordstrom's go to considerable lengths to select employees they believe will be customer-responsive. Southwest Airlines makes loyal customers (frequent fliers) part of the selection team that interviews prospective customer-contact employees, and some business-to-business marketers with key account programs allow customers the final choice of key account manager among several qualified candidates. Some companies regularly recruit from their customers and, as a result, secure greater insight into customer needs.

Since they represent the firm to the customer, customer-responsive employees are especially critical for customer contact positions. However, to develop a truly external perspective, these attitudes and values must penetrate the firm as a whole.

TRAINING AND DEVELOPMENT Training and development present marvelous opportunities for attitude change as well as data and skill acquisition. These activities can help fill the gap between the knowledge, skills, and abilities (KSAs) required to perform specific jobs and the quality of the current set of human resources. If the firm is undergoing a shift from an internal to an external orientation, this gap is likely to be significant in many functions, at many levels in the organization, and some form of employee education is a facilitating precondition for change.[60]

Since the change in orientation must start at the top, in-depth marketing education for the full cadre of senior and middle management can be exceptionally beneficial. Not only can such off-site education sensitize managers to the value of an external perspective and help them learn new behaviors, team building is a valuable secondary benefit.

However, training at just the senior and middle management levels may be insufficient for many firms, especially those in service industries where many employees interact with customers. Jan Carlson, CEO of SAS, labels each employee/customer encounter as a "moment of truth," following which the customer's perception of the firm can range from very positive to very negative. Faced with research data suggesting a 1:7 positive:negative word-of-mouth ratio, SAS introduced extensive education for all employees on how to treat customers. British Airways implemented a similar program during its initial turnaround in the mid-1980s. Both airlines received critical acclaim on employee/customer-interaction performance, and subsequently, market share and profits improved.

Many companies are increasingly modifying their training courses to include greater customer participation, both as speakers and, in some cases, as participants and facilitators in the learning process. State-of-the-art companies are using various kinds of action learning to break down traditional barriers between learning and action, and between firm and customer.[61,62]

WORK PROCESSES AND CAREER PATHS   One result of the functional specialization found in most organizations is that managers responsible for critically important customer-based decisions may be organizationally far removed from the marketplace. This organizational distance can be reduced by ensuring that management in many functions, and at many levels, has consistent and regular contact with customers. Many means are available for this cultural experience. For example, bankers spend half a day per month as tellers, insurance company executives answer policyholder inquiries, and shipping personnel spend time at the customer's receiving dock.

> Example: The introduction of lunches between senior Norwegian Telecom management and customers led to a greater awareness of significant service shortfalls. A series of actions was designed to bring about greater customer awareness throughout the organization.

Periods of customer contact can be built into all career paths, preferably early in the employee's experience. For example, Avis, Disney, and many other service companies require that managers have periodic re-exposure to customers.

Going beyond the basics, companies especially creative in seeking insight into customers' lives ensure that not just marketing is involved. For example, in some Unilever companies, cross-functional teams receive simultaneous exposure to customer input. And Gessy-Lever of Brazil has experimented with ethnographic market research in which employees from multiple functions live for a several weeks in Rio de Janeiro *favellas*.

RECOGNITION AND REWARD   Just as measurement and control systems should evolve to focus on customers, so too must systems for recognition and reward. For the firm truly committed to an external perspective, real teeth can be put into its efforts by basing managerial incentive compensation on customer focused measures, and not just for the marketing and sales functions.

Managers are often skeptical about basing take-home pay on the results from survey instruments, yet many firms, such as Xerox and AT&T, report excellent results from basing managerial incentives in part on customer satisfaction measures. To the extent that the firm does a good job in survey instrument design, rigorously tests the items, and secures the services of a competent, reputable and independent research company, the more likely these methods will secure internal acceptance.

DuPont faced the challenge of improving its marketing competence. It not only trained over 20,000 (marketing and non-marketing) employees, it instituted a marketing excellence program that deliberately included extra-functional considerations, such as demonstrating intra- and interbusiness marketing excellence.

Regardless of the particular performance measure selected, it is particularly important that the required performance level be attainable. In recent years, several major companies have had to deal with severe problems because of unethical (and possibly illegal) actions of executives faced with excessively high performance targets.

> Example: In the late 1980s and early 1990s, the compensation package for Dun and Bradstreet (D&B) salespeople selling business credit reports was heavily weighted in favor of incentive compensation. Salespeople were paid a fairly low base salary, but could earn significant amounts if sales were high. However, the incentive compensation package only took effect when sales exceeded the previous year plus 15%. In many sales territories, exceeding previous year's sales plus 15% was virtually impossible, let alone increasing sales sufficiently to earn reasonable compensation. The result was that many customers received D&B reports they had never ordered. When this practice came to light, D&B paid significant

amounts to several customers, including six figure amounts to AT&T and IBM. According to one senior D&B executive, "We were a cesspool."

Example: More recently, "Chainsaw" Al Dunlap's requirements of excessively high performance while chairman of Sunbeam have been highly criticized. To retain their jobs and stock options in the face of revenue and profit targets that were "so outrageous, they were ridiculous," managers resorted to several types of aberrant behavior. They withheld commissions from independent sales reps, did not pay bills, forced vendors to accept partial payment and effectively booked future orders in the present by offering heavily discounted prices and extended credit terms.[63]

MAINTAINING A CUSTOMER ORIENTATION

While it is one thing to accomplish the change necessary to develop an externally focused organization, it is quite another to maintain a high degree of external perspective on an ongoing basis. If the firm's alignment to the environment leads to marketplace success, its actions will likely be emulated by competitors. Unfortunately, internal processes typically militate against the required continuous improvement since the very success that was the intended result of the change process often sows the seeds of complacency.

The best way to avoid this recidivism danger is to identify mechanisms that keep the firm externally oriented and ensure it becomes a learning organization.[64] These mechanisms pose a threat to tradition in those organizations that thrive on hierarchy and formalism and where traditional managers look to positional authority for their legitimacy. In these newer types of organization, control is less exercised by management, external to the individual, but is rather exercised internally. This is a sharp break with tradition but, with appropriate values and incentive systems, is arguably a more efficient and effective option for the modern organization.[65]

However, an external perspective will not long endure unless the CEO (or general manager) is committed. Senior managers must determine what is important, and provide the focal point around which to rally the firm. CEOs demonstrating such externally focused leadership include former Citibank CEO John Reed who, in the 1970s and 1980s, significantly enhanced customer satisfaction by making major investments in ATM networks. Jan Carlzon turned ailing SAS around by a single-minded devotion to serving the business customer, and James Burke of Johnson & Johnson demonstrated his company's dedication to its customers at the height of the Tylenol crisis. More recently, Lou Gerstner of IBM restored the once-proud computer giant to its former glory.

SUMMARY

The challenge addressed in this chapter was to ensure that programs to implement the market strategy are executed as planned. The starting points for the discussion were twofold. Although marketing plays the role of "architect," many other functions have roles as "builder;" the specialization inherent in most organizations frequently causes employees to optimize on sub-goals that may not enhance the firm/customer relationship.

The overarching perspective advanced in this chapter was that the chances that execution will occur as planned are greater as the firm gets closer to the external end of the internal-external axis. As a result, most of this chapter was spent on providing a model for developing a true external orientation. The structural model embraced both strategic considerations (vision, values, mission, and strategy) and supporting requirements (organizational structure, systems and processes, and human resource management). The model elements comprise an integrated whole that must be seriously addressed at every level for an external perspective truly to take root.

For long-run success the firm must create a different type of organization that is responsive yet initiating, learning but not forgetting, understanding of human resources yet demanding of high performance, customer-sensitive yet competitive, shareholder value creating yet not short-sighted. To accomplish this task, enlightened management must reconcile a formidable set of almost paradoxical demands.

THE CHANGING VIEW

Old Way	New Way
Hierarchy-based organization	Knowledge-based organization
Operational focus	Strategic focus
Structures, systems, internally oriented	Structures, systems, externally oriented
Selection, training, rewards bureaucratically driven	Selection, training, rewards strategically driven
Sales and marketing discrete	Sales and marketing merging
Rigid, inflexible structure	Flexible, adaptive structure
No customer information system	Highly developed customer information system
Customer satisfaction and loyalty low priority	Customer satisfaction and loyalty high priority
Rule-driven	Values-driven
Market share oriented	Shareholder and customer value oriented
Marketing a department	Marketing a philosophy
Neglect of human resource factors	Highlights human resource factors

QUESTIONS FOR STUDY AND DISCUSSION

1. Bring to class an example of a corporate vision statement. Do you think this statement fulfills its purpose? Why? Why not?

2. "The only values worth having are making large profits and securing a high P/E ratio; corporate values statements are worthless." Discuss.

3. Bring to class a copy of a mission statement for a corporation or a business with which you are familiar. Be prepared to argue that the mission statement is appropriate, too narrow, or too broad.

4. Many company executives describe statements of vision, values, and mission as meaningless corporate wordsmithing. Why are they skeptical about the value of these ideas?

5. What are the vision, values, and mission of your educational institution? Do these make sense to you? Why? Why not? If not, write a first draft of new vision, values, and mission statements.

6. "The true values are revealed in the behavior of organizations rather than in written statements of purpose." Tom Peters refers to the agreement between these statements and behavior as "Walking the Talk." Does your organization "Walk the Talk?" What makes you think it does? What makes you think it does not?

7. Corporate missions can be developed on several different bases. Which do you prefer? Why?

8. Brand and product management will always be the best way to organize marketing activities. Discuss.

9. The relationship paradigm mandates a shift to customer-based structures. Discuss.

10. Bring to class examples of management practices that promote internal, rather than external, orientations of the firm.

11. Human resource practices are key to successful implementation of market strategy. Discuss.

12. The material presented in Chapter 19 has no place in a graduate marketing text; it should be confined to a course in organizational behavior. Discuss.

13. Systems and structures will always lag strategies and plans, meaning that successful implementation will be rare. Discuss.

14. Contact a company with which you do business and tell them about a problem that you experienced. Be prepared to analyze and discuss your interaction with the company in class.

15. Companies too often take a piecemeal rather than a holistic approach to change and are surprised when they fail to achieve their expectations. Do you agree with this statement? Why or why not?

ENDNOTES

1. Some of the ideas in this chapter are drawn from P. Berthon, J.M. Hulbert and L.F. Pitt, "Brand Management Prognostications, *Sloan Management Review*, 40 (Winter 1999), 53-65 and from J.M. Hulbert and L.F. Pitt, "Exit Left Center Stage? The Future of Functional Marketing," *European Journal of Marketing*, 40 (February 1996), pp. 47–60.

2. *The Australian*, March 10, 1999.

3. J.C. Narver and S.F. Slater, *Becoming More Market Oriented: An Exploratory Study of the Programmatic and Market Approaches*, Boston: MA, *Marketing Science Institute*, 91–128, 1991.

4. D. Nadler and M.L. Tushman, "A Congruence Model for Diagnosing Organizational Behavior," in D. Kolb, I. Rubin, and J. McIntyre (Eds.), *Organizational Psychology*, Englewood Cliffs, NJ: Prentice-Hall, 1979.

5. J.M. Hulbert and L.F. Pitt, "Exit Left Center Stage? The Future of Functional Marketing," *European Management Journal*, 14 (February 1996), pp. 47–60.

6. I. Nonaka and H. Takeuchi, *The Knowledge-Creating Company*, New York: Oxford University Press, 1995.

7. See J.C. Collins and J.I. Porras, "Building Your Company's Vision," *Harvard Business Review*, 74 (September-October 1996), 65-77.

8. Although he does not call it a vision statement, Jan Carlzon describes exactly this problem in his book on the turnaround of SAS, *Moments of Truth*, New York: Harper & Row, 1989.

9. *Fortune*, April 14, 1997.

10. Sony MobileComm America is responsible for marketing Sony products installed in automobiles and boats, such as CD changers, amplifiers, speakers, and Sony telecommunication products.

11. *Fortune*, May 24, 1999.

12. Relatedly, in early 1998, 57% of Britain's largest companies had or were preparing a code of business ethics as opposed to 18% eleven years previously, *The Daily Telegraph*, March 2, 1998.

13. This term is attributed to Professor Lester Thomas, founder and director of the Industrial Performance Center, MIT.

14. Frank Rich, "Who's Biased Now," *The New York Times*, March 4, 1998. Rich noted that Mr. Murdoch had previously sold out the principles of an independent press to "curry favor with China," had removed BBC World News from satellite TV broadcasts to China, had HarperCollins publish a propagandist biography of Deng Xiaoping when he was in power, and invested millions of dollars in a joint venture with China's Communist Party paper, *The People's Daily*.

15. Senior Johnson & Johnson employees affirm that difficult management decisions are frequently resolved by reference to the credo.

16. See Gilman Office Automation, Bangkok, Thailand in, N. Capon and W. Van Honacker, *The Asian Marketing Case Book*: Singapore: Prentice Hall, 1999.

17. C.K. Prahalad and G. Hamel, "Core Competence of the Corporation," *Harvard Business Review*, 68 (May/June 1990); J.B. Quinn, *The Intelligent Enterprise: A New Paradigm*, New York: The Free Press, 1992.

18. Acceptance of the mission concept is contrary to the conglomerate philosophy in which many individual business units offer different products to different markets and so diversify risk. Although conglomeration has generally lost favor since the 1960s, conglomerates may still be found, such as Germany's VEBA (Germany), the U.S. General Electric, and many Far Eastern firms such as the Japanese Keiretsu, Korean Chaebol, and large family-owned businesses in smaller Asian countries.

19. Business missions may serve the function of determining organizational boundaries for the various businesses as a means of avoiding resource waste caused by multiple business units addressing the same market. Alternatively, business missions may be written more loosely under the philosophy that internal competition has positive value in ensuring that market opportunities are addressed.

20. Even if the firm has no overarching mission, as in the conglomerate case, individual business units should still have mission statements.

21. In 1986, under takeover attack from Sir James Goldsmith, Goodyear sold two operating units and refocused on rubber goods businesses.

22. In 1994, George Fisher refocused Kodak on imaging by divesting such non-core businesses as drug company Sterling Winthrop. Similarly, in 1997, incoming AT&T CEO C. Michael Armstrong divested the AT&T credit card business.

23. These analysts cited rising stock prices from chemical companies shedding mature product divisions; for example, in 1998, Monsanto's stock price was over 40 times anticipated earnings, *The New York Times*, March 3, 1998.

24. N. Capon, J.U. Farley, J. Hulbert, and L.E. Martin, "Corporate Diversity and Economic Performance: The Impact of Market Specialization," *Strategic Management Journal*, 9 (Jan./Feb. 1988), pp. 61–74.

25. *Business Week*, April 5, 1999.

26. *The Economist*, January 23, 1999.

27. *The New York Times*, March 23, 1998; *Business Week*, April 27, 1998.

28. This was the key insight underlying Ted Levitt's famous article, T. Levitt, "Marketing Myopia," *Harvard Business Review*, 53 (Sept./Oct. 1975), 26 *et seq.*

29. This is a business unit mission; Otis Elevator is a unit of United Technologies.

30. This is often described as a matrix organization as individuals charged with marketing activities, such as salespeople, execute the plans of various brand managers, yet report to their own sales organizations.

31. This is one of the reasons for the increased importance of category management.

32. Slotting fees are payments to retailers for space on the retailer's shelf, often for a limited time period. This practice originated with powerful retailers in France, but has spread to many parts of the globe. Although heartily disliked by manufacturers, they often have little choice but to pay up.

33. When an individual product is developed for a single application, the product/brand and market segment manager positions completely overlap.

34. R.J. Keith, "The Marketing Revolution," *Journal of Marketing*, 24 (January 1960), pp. 35–38.

35. R. McKenna, "Marketing is Everything," *Harvard Business Review*, 69 (Jan./Feb. 1991), pp. 65–79.

36. M. Hammer and J. Champy, *Reengineering the Corporation: A Manifesto for Business Revolution*, New York: Nicholas Brealy, 1993.

37. Hulbert and Pitt, *op. cit.*

38. R.C. Blattberg and J. Deighton, "Interactive Marketing: Exploiting the Age of Addressability," *Sloan Management Review*, 33 (Fall 1991), pp. 5–14; D. Peppers and M. Rogers, *The One-to-One Future: Building Relationships One Customer at a Time*, New York: Century Doubleday, 1993.

39. For example, Grupo Iusacell, a Mexican cell phone company, estimates it needs ten years of connection from low usage rate customers to breakeven, Grupo IUSACELL (A), N9-395-028, Harvard Business School, 1994.

40. This thinking has been influenced by the terminology of Peppers and Rogers *op. cit.* and, to a considerable extent, by Blattberg and Deighton *op. cit.*

41. N. Capon, "Wachovia Bank and Trust Company," *The Marketing of Financial Services*, Englewood Cliffs, NJ: Prentice Hall, 1992.

42. This approach is sympathetic to Tom Peters' suggestion of turning the organization on its head, T. Peters, *Thriving on Chaos*, New York: Bantam, 1987.

43. Peppers and Rogers *op. cit.*

44. J.K. Johansson and I. Nonaka, "Market Research the Japanese Way," *Harvard Business Review*, 65 (May/June 1987), pp. 16–19.

45. L.P. Carbone and S.H. Haeckel, "Engineering Customer Experience," *Marketing Management*, 3 (1994), pp. 8–19; G.A. Churchill, R.H. Collins, and W.A. Strang, "Should Retail Salespersons be Similar to Their Customers," *Journal of Retailing*, 51 (Fall 1975), pp. 29–42; A.G. Woodside and W.J. Davenport, "The Effect of Salesman Similarity and Expertise on Consumer Purchasing Behavior," *Journal of Marketing*, 11 (May 1974), pp. 198–202.

46. See N. Capon, *Key Account Management and Planning,* New York: The Free Press, forthcoming, 2001.

47. *Business Week*, May 17, 1996.

48. T. Levitt, "The Globalization of Markets," *Harvard Business Review*, 61 (May/June 1983), pp. 92–102. A more integrative view is provided by J.A. Quelch and E.J. Hoff, "Customizing Global Marketing," *Harvard Business Review*, 64 (May/June 1986), pp. 59–68.

49. S. Douglas and Y. Wind, "The Myth of Globalization," *Columbia Journal of World Business*, (Winter 1987), pp. 19–29.

50. See N. Capon, J.U. Farley, and J. Hulbert, *Corporate Strategic Planning*, New York: Columbia University Press, 1988, for empirical data concerning organization structure for international business.

51. In 1994, Ford introduced a similar organization by consolidating regional fiefdoms in engineering, design, and development into new global divisions; Motorola replaced competing decentralized businesses with three global product groups, *Business Week*, November 9, 1998. As P&G's CEO, Durk Jager, resigned in June 2000 after just 18 months on the job, the success of this move must be questioned.

52. This organization is matrixed with a brand management organization focused on IBM's products.

53. For additional insight on organizing for global account management, see N. Capon, *op. cit.*, Chapter 10.

54. V.P. Barabba and G. Zaltman, *Hearing the Voice of the Market*, Boston, MA: Harvard Business School Press, 1991.

55. F.F. Reicheld, *The Loyalty Effect,* Boston, MA: Harvard Business School Press, 1996.

56. Now Baxter Healthcare.

57. Peppers and Rogers, *op. cit.*

58. In January 2000, in an attempt to match Dell's custom-design abilities, Compaq purchased the custom-assembly operations of distributor Inacom for $370 million.

59. Capon, Farley, and Hulbert, *op. cit.*

60. Narver and Slater, *op. cit.*, pp. 6–7.

61. R.W. Revans, "Developing Effective Managers: A New Approach to Business Education," New York: Praeger, 1971.

62. See L. Fortini-Campbell, *Hitting the Sweet Spot*, Chicago, IL: The Copy Workshop, 1992, and F.J. Gouillart and F.D. Sturdivant, "A Day in the Life of Your Customers," *Harvard Business Review*, 72 (Jan./Feb. 1994), pp. 116–125.

63. J.A. Byrne, *Chainsaw: The Notorious Career of Al Dunlap in the Era of Profit-at-Any Price*, New York: HarperBusiness, 1999, excerpted in *Business Week*, October 18, 1999.

64. P.F. Drucker, "The Coming of the New Organization," *Harvard Business Review*, 76 (Jan./Feb. 1998), pp. 45–53, J.B. Quinn, *Intelligent Enterprise*, New York: The Free Press, 1992.

65. This observation is supported by implementation of Total Quality Management in many firms.

WEB RESOURCES

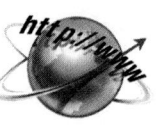

A.T. Cross	www.cross.com
American Express	www.americanexpress.com
American Hospital Supply	www.baxter.com
Apple Computer	www.apple.com
ARAMARK	www.aramark.com
AT&T	www.att.com
Avis	www.avis.com
Baxter Healthcare	www.baxter.com
British Airways	www.british-airways.com
CBS	www.cbs.com
Chase	www.chase.com
Chemical Bank	www.chemicalbankmi.com
Cheseborough Ponds	www.unilever.com
Citibank	www.citibank.com
Compaq	www.compaq.com
Corning	www.corning.com
Dell	www.dell.com
Discover Card	www.discovercard.com
Disney	www.disney.go.com
DuPont	www.dupont.com
Dun and Bradstreet	www.dnb.com
Ford	www.ford.com
General Electric	www.ge.com
General Foods	www.kraftfoods.com
General Mills	www.generalmills.com
Gessy-Lever	www.unilever.com
Goodyear	www.goodyear.com
Grupo Iusacell	www.iusacell.com.mx
HarperCollins	www.harpercollins.com
Hyatt	www.hyatt.com
IBM	www.ibm.com
Johnson & Johnson	www.jnj.com
L.L. Bean	www.llbean.com
McDonald's	www.mcdonalds.com
Microsoft	www.microsoft.com
Miller Beer	www.millerbrewing.com
Monsanto	www.monsanto.com
Motorola	www.motorola.com
Netscape	www.netscape.com
News Corporation	www.newscorp.com
Nokia	www.nokia.com
Nordstrom	www.nordstrom.com
Oracle	www.oracle.com
Philip Morris	www.philipmorris.com
Pillsbury	www.pillsbury.com
Procter & Gamble	www.pg.com
Sainsburys	www.sainsburys.co.uk
SAS	www.sas.de
Sears	www.sears.com
Singapore Airlines	www.singaporeair.com

ENSURING THE
MARKETING OFFER
IS IMPLEMENTED
AS PLANNED

WEB RESOURCES *(continued)*

Sony	www.sony.com
Tesco	www.tesco.co.uk
UKrops	www.ukrops.com
Unilever	www.unilever.com
United Technologies	www.utc.com
US Postal Service	www.usps.gov
VEBA	www.eon.com
Wachovia Bank	www.wachovia.com
Wal-Mart	www.walmart.com
Westinghouse Electric	www.westinghouse.com
Westpac	www.westpac.com
Xerox	www.xerox.com

MONITOR AND CONTROL EXECUTION AND PERFORMANCE

LEARNING OBJECTIVES

When you have completed this chapter, you will understand

- **the monitor and control function**
- **key principles of monitoring and control**
- **the different types of marketing control system**
- **how to implement marketing control systems in the corporation**

INTRODUCTION

This chapter focuses on the marketing control function. In simple terms, control is exercised by examining what the firm has done and/or the results it has achieved, and comparing these against a set of criteria. All things equal, to the extent that the firm's marketplace actions and or performance meet or exceed the criteria, the firm should reinforce the relevant behavior. On the other hand, if actions and/or performance are inferior to the criteria, management should contemplate changing behavior.

KEY PRINCIPLES OF MONITORING AND CONTROL

This chapter's approach to monitoring and control is guided by four key principles. First, although most control measures are designed with good intent, they often produce unexpected consequences.

> **Example:** Prior to publication of airline arrival performance data, U.S. airlines often competed by showing shorter flight times (even when flying identical planes on identical routes)! When arrival time performance began to be publicized, flight times lengthened as a simple way to ensure improved "on-time" performance.

Such problems are compounded when performance is sampled rather than continuously assessed. Thus, in spring 1999, a British railroad company, due to be measured for on-time performance, instructed its drivers to skip stations, leaving customers stranded, to stay on schedule. Not exactly customer-oriented! Our first principle is, therefore, to be aware of the all-too-human desire to look good and consequently to look consciously for unanticipated consequences of control measures.

The second principle is to build in redundancy. Reliance on a single measure is often quite dangerous. One of the ways to protect against unanticipated consequences is to seek multiple measures of a variable of interest. For example, in the airline case, "lengthening of schedules" is a variable that might have been measured and publicized.

The third principle is to recognize that any process is best managed by ensuring it stays within control limits rather than waiting for problems to occur and then correcting them. This proactive-versus-reactive philosophy permeates the chapter.

Finally, we approach the task of monitoring and controlling holistically, rather than piecemeal. The broad purpose of the marketing control function is to ensure that the firm achieves the best possible results for shareholders. To this end the chapter examines:

- **Performance control**: Did the firm achieve the results as planned?
- **Implementation control**: Did the firm implement the market strategy as planned?
- **Strategy control**: Is the firm's market strategy well-conceived and on target?
- **Managerial process control**: Are the firm's managerial processes the best they can be?

PERFORMANCE CONTROL: DID THE FIRM ACHIEVE THE RESULTS AS PLANNED?

The basic objective of performance control is to raise the probability that the firm will reach the objectives set out in the market strategy. Chapter 8 discussed strategic objectives—qualitative, directional, and operational objectives—quantitative, and time dependent. The examples presented are shown in Table 20.1.

In this illustration, for the upcoming operating period, the critical performance elements are the $15 million profit in 200X + 1 and 25% market share.

The critical questions now concern when the firm should measure its results, and what results should be measured.

TABLE 20.1 Illustration of Strategic and Operational Objectives

Strategic Objectives: The primary objective in the young-family-with-children segment is to increase profits from sales of ready-to-eat cereal. The secondary objective is to maintain market share.

Operational Objectives: In the young-family-with-children segment, the primary objective is to increase dollar profits from ready-to-eat cereal from $12 million in 200X: in 200X + 1 (next year) the firm intends to earn $15 million, in 200X + 2, $20 million, and in 200X + 3, $25 million. In addition, the firm plans to hold unit market share at 25% in each of the three years.

When Should the Firm Measure Its Results?

The basic approach to performance control is to measure the firm's results, then compare those results with a set of performance criteria. As a result of this comparison, the firm should either make changes to, or reinforce, current behavior. The two polar approaches to performance control—post-action control and steering control—differ on when measurement should take place.

Post-action control refers to starting the process, letting time pass, then observing whether or not the anticipated results have been achieved. In Table 20.1, this would mean waiting until the end of 200X + 1, then measuring profits and market share. This form of control does a good job of accessing the firm's success in implementing its strategy, but since the level of success is not known until the end of the period, the firm is unable to take any action to change impending unsatisfactory results.

Steering control refers to monitoring the process through time and making course corrections if results diverge from what is anticipated. Thus annual profit and market share goals should be calendarized and tracked through time. Many firms measure results against plan on a quarterly basis, but monthly measures are not uncommon. The more fine-grained, monthly measures provide greater ability for the firm to isolate seasonality differences, but run the risk that discrepancies from plan may result from random fluctuations rather than be the result of significant firm, competitor, or customer action.

What Results Should Be Measured?

A simple but useful model for linking the firm's implementation and results is shown in Figure 20.1.

Output measures are concerned with the final results that the firm wants to achieve. Intermediate measures are a set of measures that do not achieve the outputs that the firm requires, but without which desired output results would not be achieved. Input measures are concerned with actions taken by the firm. They address the question of implementation (see next section).

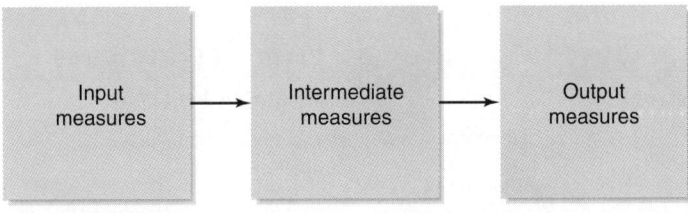

FIGURE 20.1

Implementation and Results

OUTPUT MEASURES In Table 20.1, the firm's operational objectives (output measures) concerned profit and market share. However, these are just two of a variety of measures that the firm might want to invoke. A useful classification of output measures includes four separate types—volume, market-based, profit, and "soft" measures.[1]

Volume Measures Volume measures—sales units and sales revenues (and growth rates)—focus on the ability of the firm to secure purchases from customers. These are important output measures overall, but are especially valuable for the sales force as they capture the results of their actions. However, what are perhaps more important outputs than overall measures of sales volume are those that identify the type of sales. One important sales breakdown focuses on the types of products and customers:

- old products/old customers
- old products/new customers
- new products/old customers
- new products/new customers

Depending upon the firm's strategy, sales from these different sources may be differentially more important. For example, for the firm employing a fast growth strategy, sales of new products to new customers may be more important than sales of old products to old customers.

Another important sales measure focuses on the extent to which sales are derived from existing products versus new products. In an increasing number of companies, such as diversified manufacturer 3M, general managers of business units are being evaluated on measures such as % sales revenues from products not in the product line three years previously.

The purpose of such measures is to focus attention on innovation success.

Market-Based Measures Sales volume measures suffer from the serious deficiency that they have no external referent. Thus focused just on sales volume, the firm could experience 10% per annum sales growth, blissfully unaware that the market, or a competitor's sales was growing at 20% per annum.

Market-based criteria address this problem by comparing the firm's sales performance with some external measure. The most common is market share, which compares the firm's sales performance directly with the market. Note that the market share measure in Table 20.1 was based on units; it might also be based on revenues. Either or both may be appropriate but, in any event, they are unlikely to be identical. If the firm's revenue market share exceeds its unit market share, the key implication is that the firm's prices exceed the average market price and vice versa. Other market-based measures are indicated in Table 20.2.

To understand the total performance variance, it is often useful to decompose sales volume into market share and market size variances (Figure 20.2). This decomposition separates out the source of forecasting errors (market size variance) from other sources of variance. Appropriate remedial steps are more likely to be taken with any breakdown method than with a single-minded focus on volume, units, or dollars.[2]

Profit Measures In Table 20.1, the critical operational objective, in addition to market share, was profit. Unfortunately, as discussed in the Book Appendix, bottom-line profit is not a terribly useful measure for assessing marketing effectiveness and informing future

TABLE 20.2 Market-Based Measures of Firm Performance

Measure	Calculation	Information Provided
Market share (MS)	Firm sales/sales of all competitors	Market position versus all competitors (%)
Relative market share (RMS)	Firm sales/sales of major competitor(s)	Market position versus the firm's major competitor(s) (%)
Market occupancy ratio (MOR)	Number of firm's customers/ Total number of customers	Fraction of potential customers with which the firm does business (%)

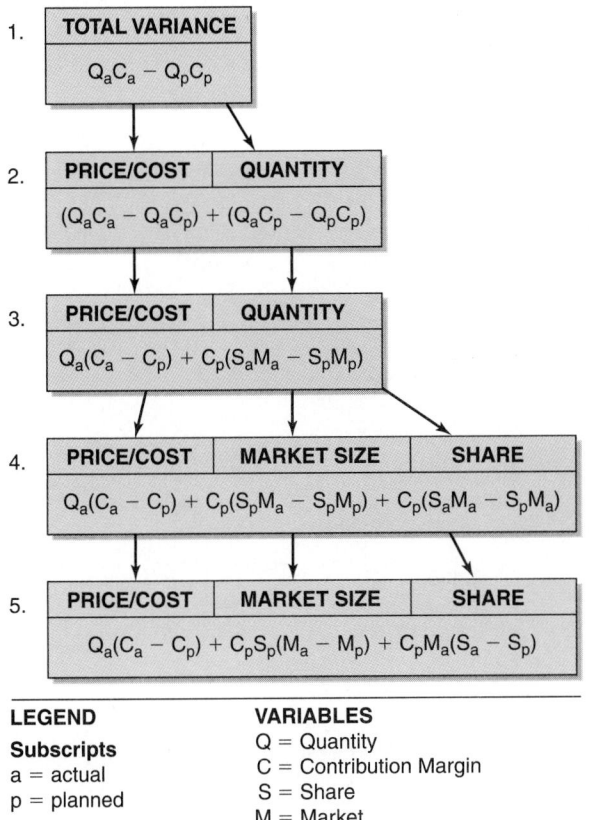

1. | TOTAL VARIANCE |
   | $Q_aC_a - Q_pC_p$ |

2. | PRICE/COST | QUANTITY |
   | $(Q_aC_a - Q_aC_p) + (Q_aC_p - Q_pC_p)$ | |

3. | PRICE/COST | QUANTITY |
   | $Q_a(C_a - C_p) + C_p(S_aM_a - S_pM_p)$ | |

4. | PRICE/COST | MARKET SIZE | SHARE |
   | $Q_a(C_a - C_p) + C_p(S_pM_a - S_pM_p) + C_p(S_aM_a - S_pM_a)$ | | |

5. | PRICE/COST | MARKET SIZE | SHARE |
   | $Q_a(C_a - C_p) + C_pS_p(M_a - M_p) + C_pM_a(S_a - S_p)$ | | |

LEGEND

Subscripts
a = actual
p = planned

VARIABLES
Q = Quantity
C = Contribution Margin
S = Share
M = Market

FIGURE 20.2

Variance Decomposition—Comparison with Plan

action. The most serious problem is that a failure to meet profit targets may be unrelated to marketing. For example, as shown in Table 20.3, a $400K increase in General and Administrative (G&A) expenses (to $1.8 million) due to an extra corporate overhead allocation would send profits plummeting from $1.4 million to $1 million. However, market performance would not have changed.[3]

Product Profitability. In general, when considering product profitability, marketing professionals prefer profit contribution measures that separate variable costs and fixed marketing costs (Table 20.4). These measures more directly isolate marketing performance. The variable (or contribution) margin measures the extent to which sales revenues exceed variable costs. The job of variable margin is to cover fixed costs and provide profit. Stated another way, profit is what is left when variable margin has paid for fixed costs.

When the various marketing expenses are subtracted from variable margin, the remaining marketing contribution has to cover other fixed costs and deliver profit. These measures provide excellent diagnostics for possible changes in firm action.

Since sales revenue is a major element in producing variable margin, the volume/price relationship is a critical marketing issue. Also, the relationship between variable margin and marketing contribution is solely a marketing issue, uncontaminated by factory overhead, and general and administrative expenses. Marketers can assess the degree to which the various marketing expenses are contributing to, or detracting from, achieving sales revenue, market share, and so forth.

Using the contribution approach just described, management can secure a good understanding of product profitability and gain valuable insight into potential future actions.

TABLE 20.3 Income Statement for Product A (000s)

Sales (40 million lbs. @ 50 cents/lb.)	$20,000
less:	
Cost of Goods Sold	12,200
Gross Margin	7,800
less:	
Advertising	800
Promotion	200
Field Sales	3,200
Product Management	50
Marketing Management	300
Product Development	300
Marketing Research	150
General and Administrative	1,400
Total Expenses	6,400
Net Profit before Taxes	1,400

Customer Profitability. Many corporations have good systems for measuring product profitability. However, the vast majority of firms are seriously deficient in the measurement of customer profitability. If customers are truly the firm's most important asset, their profitability should be measured. Conceptually, it is not difficult to make the translation from product profitability statements to customer profitability, where customers can refer to key accounts, market segments, or types of distribution channel. Product-by-product and customer-by-customer income statements are illustrated in Tables 20.5 and 20.6, respectively. The process for making this conversion using activity based costing (ABC) methods is demonstrated in the book appendix.

With this sort of information on customers, managers can make decisions concerning which customers to serve, how much and what sorts of effort to expend on each customer, and other critical resource allocation decisions.

"Soft" Measures   It is particularly important for the firm to develop systems that involve "taking the pulse" of the customer on a regular basis so that responses to firm and competitor actions can be tracked, and learning can be developed regarding the key sources of competitive advantage. For several of these measures, structured and independently administered survey instruments provide the best data. The most widely employed soft measure of firm performance is customer satisfaction. Typically, the firm develops and validates a survey instrument, then has it administered periodically to its customer base. In part to ensure anonymity, satisfaction measures are collected on several competitors so that the firm can track its satisfaction performance over time, both independently and versus competition. There is reasonably good evidence linking such measures to the "hard" out-put measures discussed previously so they might also be considered as intermediate measures.[4]

INTERMEDIATE MEASURES   Although the four types of output measures are typically the most important for firms, output objectives are only achieved after some intermediate objectives have been secured. Because, in some cases, it is difficult to demonstrate a direct link between a specific marketing action and output performance, intermediate objectives take on extra importance. To a large extent, relevant intermediate measures

TABLE 20.4 Income Statement for Product A using a Variable Budget Format ($000s)

Sales (40 million lbs. @ 50 cents/lb.)	$20,000
less:	
Total Variable Costs	11,000
Variable Margin (Profit Contribution)	9,000
less:	
Fixed Costs:	
Advertising	800
Promotion	200
Field Sales	3,200
Product Management	50
Marketing Management	300
Product Development	300
Marketing Research	150
	5,000
Marketing Contribution	4,000
Manufacturing Overhead	1,200
General and Administrative	1,400
Other Fixed Costs	2,600
Net Profit before Taxes	1,400

relate directly to the various marketing implementation programs. For example, measures relating to the effectiveness of advertising programs are different from those relating to sales force effort.

Intermediate Sales Force Measures   The specific intermediate objectives selected by the firm should reflect a model that relates actions by the sales force to sales performance. For one firm, a key issue may be securing a customer agreement to run a factory trial, for another, it may be acceptance of retail displays. Some alternative measures are indicated in Table 20.7.

Intermediate Advertising Measures   Once again, the particular advertising measures selected depend upon the firm's model of advertising effectiveness relating advertising spending to ultimate sales. A variety of models have thus far been proposed. Some of the elements that might be included are noted in Table 20.8.

TABLE 20.5 Product Income Statements ($000s)

	Product A	Product B	Product C	Total
Sales Revenues	$4,330	$6,400	$7,001	$17,731
Cost of Goods Sold	3,175	4,120	5,213	12,508
Gross Margin	1,155	2,280	1,788	5,223
Other Operating Costs				4,023
Operating Income				1,200

TABLE 20.6 Customer Income Statements ($000s)

	Account I	Account II	Account III	Total
Sales Revenues	$9,380	$4,351	$4,000	$17,731
Cost of Goods Sold	4,452	4,353	3,703	12,508
Gross Margin	4,928	(2)	297	5,223
Sales Force	425	225	225	875
Field Service	224	325	224	773
Technical Assistance	285	285	380	950
Order Processing	275	162.5	112.5	550
Delivery	437	233	205	875
Other Operating Costs	1,646	1,230.5	1,146.5	4,023
Operating Income	3,282	(1,232.5)	(849.5)	1,200

IMPLEMENTATION CONTROL: DID THE FIRM IMPLEMENT THE STRATEGY AS PLANNED?

The answer to this question gets at the heart of implementation control. Flowing out of the market strategy is a variety of implementation programs that are supportive of the core strategy or value proposition. These include the various marketing mix elements of product, promotion, price, distribution, and service, but also supporting functional programs, such as engineering, production, and technical service. Ensuring that these implementation programs are executed as planned is typically the responsibility of various functional managers. Input measures are concerned with whether the firm actually undertook the actions that it planned. As with intermediate measures, input measures are specific to the various functional areas whose actions are important for strategy implementation and should follow a steering control philosophy. For illustration, consider inputs from the sales force and product development.

Sales Force Implementation

In most organizations, sales force effort is critically important for achieving firm objectives. Companies will go to extraordinary lengths to ensure that the sales force operates as a smoothly functioning system. The items noted in Table 20.9 represent just a fraction of the input measures the firm might want to use as the basis for controlling sales force effort; generally, they relate to specific sales force objectives.

TABLE 20.7 Alternative Intermediate Sales Force Measures

Measure	Rationale
Number of factory trials agreed	Customers will not purchase the firm's products until their use has been demonstrated under factory conditions
Number of retail displays accepted	Acceptance of retail displays implies good shelf positioning
Number of acceptances to approved supplier list	Customers purchase only from suppliers that have been fully qualified
Dollar commitments to cooperative advertising	In agreeing to a cooperative advertising program, customers are placing their own resources at risk and will put out best efforts
Number of proposals accepted	Acceptance of a proposal is necessary step to winning business
Percent of targeted distribution outlets carrying the firm's products	Securing distribution is a necessary step to making sales

TABLE 20.8 Alternative Intermediate Advertising Measures

Measure	Information Provided
Awareness	Fraction of potential customers in the target market aware of the product/brand
Interest	Fraction of potential customers in the target market expressing an interest in purchasing the product/brand
Liking	Degree of positive feeling toward the product/brand
Product quality perception	Customers' perception of product/brand quality

Product Development Implementation

The examples in Table 20.10 are representative of the types of measures that might be used to monitor and control the new product development process.

STRATEGY CONTROL: IS THE FIRM'S MARKET STRATEGY WELL-CONCEIVED AND ON-TARGET?

Where a steering control approach is especially important for performance control, as it provides fast feedback on the firm's performance and encourages course corrections, a post action control approach is probably better for strategy control since the firm should not overreact to performance imbalances by changing its market strategy. Strategy is typically set for the long- (or at least) middle-run, whereas implementation tactics are, of necessity, short-term actions.

The relative roles of strategy and implementation can be seen in Figure 20.3.[5] This model is a useful diagnostic for isolating performance issues. One cell, A, suggests good performance; the remaining three cells suggest poor performance. When performance is poor, the key challenge is to isolate the cause.

- **Cell A: market strategy good/implementation good**: Assessment that the strategy was both well-developed and well-implemented should have led to good performance. The issue here is to continue to monitor the market environment, and ensure that the strategy keeps pace with emerging customer needs and competitor activity.
- **Cell B: market strategy good/implementation poor**: Performance in this cell can range across the spectrum from good to poor. If the strategy is especially robust, it can survive a variety of implementation mishaps.

  Example: Cole National targeted hardware and other small stores for sales of its package of key-making machines and key blanks. Although sales force

TABLE 20.9 Alternative Sales Force Input Measures

Measure	Purpose of Measure
Number of sales calls per day	Ensure that sales force is working hard
Fraction of sales calls on new accounts	Ensure that sales force is spending time with important target accounts
Average number of territories vacant	Ensure that sales force management is planning for sales force attrition
Implementation of sales force planning system	Ensure that sales force is planning its time appropriately
Percentage of sales force completing new product knowledge training	Ensure the sales force is competent to sell the firm's new products

TABLE 20.10 Alternative Product Development Input Measures

Measure	Purpose of Measure
Number of qualified new product ideas generated	New products will not be developed without a steady stream of high-quality ideas
Number of potential licenses/technology purchases investigated	Good new product possibilities may be generated outside the firm
Number of products completing beta tests	Thorough customer testing is critical to successful new product development
Number of new products launched	Sales are generated only when products are on the market

implementation was poor, the value offered to target customers was so strong that it succeeded in spite of poor sales force effort.

The key action for the firm is to improve implementation to defend the firm's position. More likely, however, poor implementation of good strategy will lead to inferior performance. The key issue is to highlight the implementation failures and improve implementation performance.

- **Cell C: market strategy poor/implementation good**: Rarely will excellent implementation performance overcome a poor strategy. If the firm's market offer does not provide value to customers, no matter how well other marketing elements are implemented, failure is likely. For example, the power of Frito-Lay's snack food sales force effort is legendary. Yet, although intense sales force effort secured good distribution when a cookie product was introduced several years ago, the product was ultimately unsuccessful.

- **Cell D: market strategy poor/implementation poor**: The problem here is to separate out the poor strategy from the poor implementation. With problems in both areas, the firm has a major challenge on its hands.

One of the major contributions of the framework in Figure 20.3 is that it explicitly recognizes that there may be problems with the firm's strategy. So often control systems feature an implicit assumption that the strategy or plan is basically fine, and that any deviations are due to incompetent implementation. Unfortunately, the assessment of good or poor is subjective; as a result, there is no formal process that can be followed.

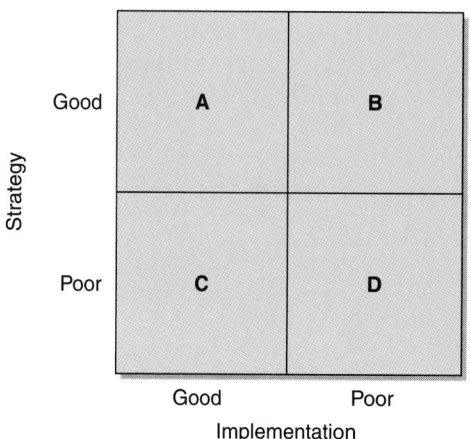

FIGURE 20.3

Strategy and Implementation

A more systematic approach necessitates an *ex post* revision of the plan based on events during the planning cycle. Based on the results of this analysis, the firm can then separate planning and performance sources of variance, and break these down further to reveal additional insights into appropriate remedial actions (Figure 20.4).[6]

Market Strategy Poor

When the control system diagnoses a poor strategy, a new strategy must be developed. As a result, the manner in which the firm approaches the marketplace must change. What management must realize is that a variety of inertial forces acts to make some changes more difficult than others. This is a special problem if the forces leading to the inappropriate strategy are fast moving. The firm's advertising strategy is among the easier areas to change; after all, most companies undertake an advertising strategy review on an annual basis. However, to shift distribution arrangements, especially if they have been in place for many years, can be difficult because of the many sets of relationships involved. With the

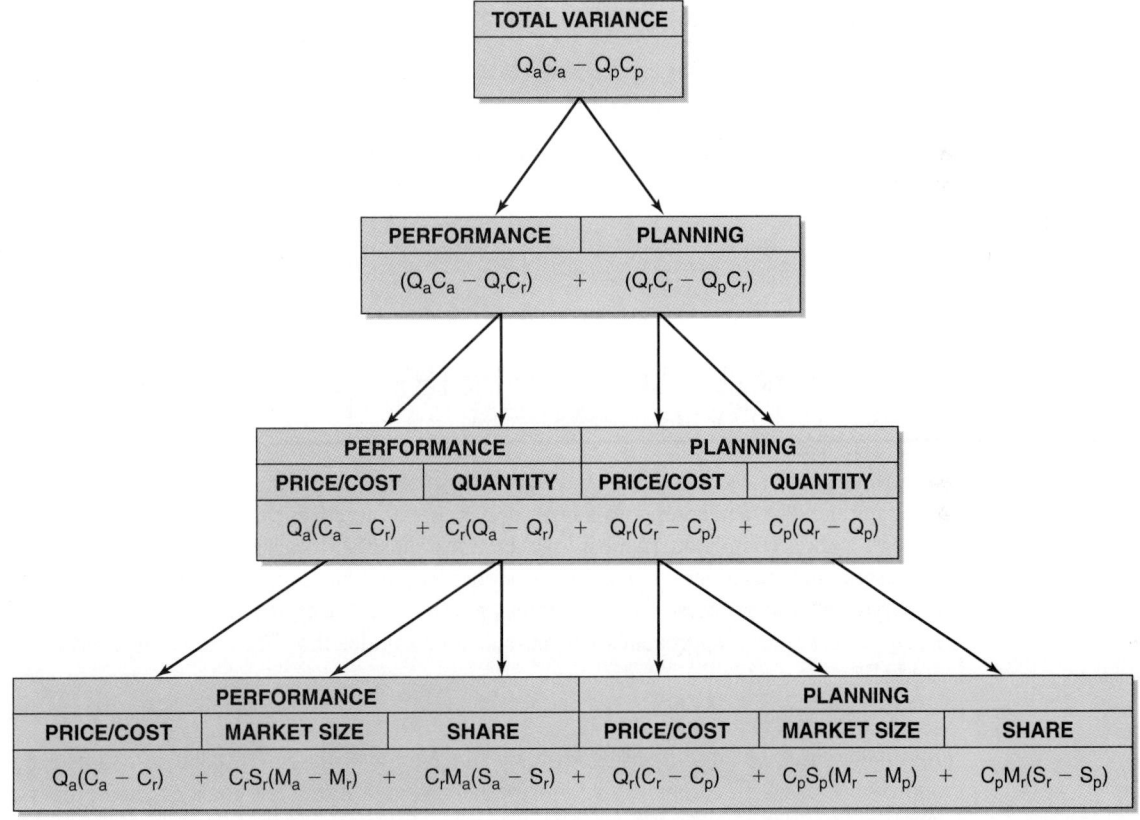

LEGEND

Subscripts
a = actual
p = planned
r = revised*

VARIABLES
Q = Quantity
C = Contribution Margins
S = Share
M = Market

FIGURE 20.4

Variance Decomposition: Use of *Ex Post* Information

*The subscript "r" indicates the standard that "should have been"; the plan as revised by *ex post* information.

FIGURE 20.5

Inertia in Marketing Implementation Variables

growth of the Internet, many firms are currently facing this distribution dilemma. Figure 20.5 suggests differential levels of inertia for different marketing implementation actions.[7]

MANAGERIAL PROCESS CONTROL: ARE THE FIRM'S MANAGERIAL PROCESSES THE BEST THEY CAN BE?

The final type of control this chapter considers relates to managerial processes. At any point in time, the firm comprises a host of managerial practices through which the organization's work is completed. In most organizations, the effectiveness and efficiency of these processes range from poor to excellent. Essentially the firm has three different approaches to improve these processes—re-engineering, best practice transfer, and benchmarking. Each of these three approaches can be subsumed under the rubric of "The Marketing Audit."

Re-engineering

Re-engineering was discussed extensively in Chapter 6. Essentially, the re-engineering approach focuses on examining various processes, identifying the goals of each process, and seeing whether or not a more effective way of conducting the process can be developed. Companies making whole-hearted commitments to process-based re-engineering include U.S. General Electric, Hallmark, Procter & Gamble, and Ford.[8]

Best Practice Transfer

Across large organizations, regardless of the particular process under consideration, it is likely that certain business units, departments, or functions are more effective than others, and have specialized expertise about particular issues. Unfortunately, it is also likely that the less effective parts of the organization have little knowledge of their more effective cousins. Although organizational barriers often make best practice sharing difficult, the firm should exercise managerial process control by developing systems for identifying superior processes and ensuring improvement to best practice levels.

Example: At Bain management consultants, each completed project is written up as a "knowledge module" to avoid reinventing the wheel.

Example: At Chevron, process masters identify and disseminate best practices; they have no formal authority, but their breadth of experience generally commands respect. In addition, Chevron's best-practices discovery team identifies groups of people sharing best practices in grassroots networks. These examples are publicized throughout the company by way of a "best practice resource map."[9]

Example: Lucent's Power Systems division, a mediocre performer, successfully used the Internet to automate clerical functions and paperwork; it also developed several internal Web sites to aid customers and the sales force. These practices are being used as an example for other Lucent divisions.[10]

Example: At BP Amoco, knowledge manager Kent Greenes and colleagues saved $20 million in their first year (1997); savings for 1998 by sharing best practices, reusing knowledge and accelerating learning were almost $700 million in such widely dispersed topics as new market entry and reducing plant downtime.[11] BP Amoco uses five basic tools:

1. **Peer assist**: People with experience in a certain area meet for a couple of days to provide insight on the focal topic.
2. **After-action review**: Four stock questions are asked after a particular activity is completed:
   - What was supposed to happen?
   - What actually happened?
   - Why is there a difference?
   - What can we learn and do from this?
3. **The retrospect**: A more elaborate postmortem than the after-action review.

These three tools are used to create a web-based folder of material on which BP Amoco has knowledge. The final two tools focus on connection among organizational members:

4. **Connect**: A voluntary Intranet "Yellow Pages" to make it easier to find expert help.
5. **Virtual teamwork**: An expensive multimedia system that allows executives located far apart to work together.

Best practices are a valuable tool for organizational learning. Unfortunately, too many firms define best practices with an internal orientation. The externally-oriented firm spends considerable effort on benchmarking (external).

Benchmarking

Xerox made an important contribution to management thinking by developing the "best in class" benchmarking concept.[12] Top management recognized that many business processes were neither firm nor industry specific, such as billing, shipping, and receiving. Xerox argued that firms learning only from their direct competitors were unlikely to gain advantage over them. However, by importing ideas from other industries, they could improve their managerial processes in ways that would be more likely to better their competitive positions.

Example: In recent years, managing global accounts has become a critical issue for many multinational firms. The Columbia Initiative in Global Account Management, housed at Columbia Business School, is comprised of several leading firms, including 3M, Citibank, Milliken, Deloitte & Touche, Hewlett Packard, Lucent Technologies, Square D-Schneider, and Saatchi and Saatchi. The forum meets bi-monthly to exchange information on global account management best practice.

The Marketing Audit

The marketing audit is a comprehensive structured process for evaluating the firm's marketing practices, including its strategy, systems, activities, and organization. The audit is best performed by an objective independent organization so that confidences can be assured and findings developed in an unbiased manner. In the process of conducting the audit, the auditors typically collect and review significant secondary data on the firm, competition and the industry, meet with firm management, customers, and industry experts, and analyze internal financial, sales, and operating information.

A MARKETING AUDIT FRAMEWORK.   One experienced organization uses a six-part auditing framework that includes[13]:

- **Marketing environment**: What changes can be identified among customers, competitors, and suppliers? What social, political, technological, and regulatory trends are impacting the industry? How are these changes and trends affecting the firm? What are the implications for firm performance?
- **Market objectives and strategy**: Are the market objectives and strategy realistic given the market environment and the firm's strengths? Are they well-understood by all managers?
- **Marketing organization**: Are the job roles and responsibilities clear? Do the measurement and reward systems motivate performance?
- **Marketing systems**: How effective and efficient are marketing systems, such as new product development, marketing research, customer satisfaction measurement, sales forecasting, sales lead generation, customer database design and update, competitor intelligence, and product pruning?
- **Marketing productivity**: How is profitability distributed across the product line? Across customers? Do some products/customers merit additional marketing effort? Should products be repriced, cost reduced, or discontinued? Should some customers be dropped? How should marketing resources be allocated across the marketing mix, such as product improvements, trade incentives, additional sales/service persons?
- **Marketing implementation**: How does the firm compare to competitors in product, price, promotion (advertising, public relations, sales force), distribution, and service? Are the various marketing mix elements mutually consistent and do they implement the market strategy?

COMMON MARKETING FAILURES   The benefits of completing a marketing audit become clear when common marketing failures are identified from a large number of marketing audits conducted across a wide variety of companies, including[14]:

- **Insufficient knowledge of customers' behavior and attitudes**: Either data on customers is collected too infrequently or, if collected frequently, is not seen by senior management and does not drive decision making.
- **Failure to segment markets effectively**: Companies tend to use geographic or demographic segmentation bases rather than probing more deeply for greater insight.
- **Cutting price rather than increasing value**: All too often management responds to sales force complaints of too-high prices by leaving insufficient margin to invest in value-adding benefits for customers.
- **Failure to invest for the future, especially in human resources**: Marketing is too often viewed as a cost rather than as an investment leading to the underfunding of marketing activities.
- **Tendency to delegate new product development to the developers**: A close marriage or integration of customer needs and technology is essential for effective new product development. Yet, far too often product development is conducted by technical people, disinclined to talk to customers in sufficient depth to understand real needs.

- **Considering marketing as the job of the marketing department**: Because customers are the firm's critical asset, marketing is everybody's business, not just the responsibility of the marketing department.

Interestingly, many of these marketing failures mirror the issues that we discussed in the first section of the book. They are reinforced in this chapter since it is so difficult for organizations to be truly marketing focused across the board. No matter how noble the firm's intentions, following through requires attention to detail and hard work. The marketing audit is a useful tool to keep the firm on track.

SUMMARY

This chapter focused on marketing Task 6, monitor and control. It was noted that the purpose of control is to improve the firm's performance by measuring its actions and performance against a set of criteria that indicate requirements for change. Four different control systems were examined—performance control, implementation control, strategy control, and managerial process control—and it was indicated how to approach these control areas.

THE CHANGING VIEW

Old Way	New Way
Measurement and control based on accounting measures of performance	Measurement and control based on marketing performance measures
Bottom-line oriented	Variety of measures
Post-action control	Steering control
Output only	Inputs and outputs considered
Accounting profit	Shareholder-value creation
Full-costing	Activity-based costing
Financial focus	Business focus
Process ignored	Process highlighted
Internally oriented	Externally oriented
Backward looking	Forward looking
Punitive philosophy	Analytic philosophy
Fact finding	Learning and improvement
Unbalanced scorecard	Balanced scorecard

QUESTIONS FOR STUDY AND DISCUSSION

1. This chapter discussed several types of output measures. Develop six other output measures that a firm might use. Discuss the specific value of each measure and identify what it adds to those output measures discussed in the chapter.

2. Identify ten intermediate measures that might have value in managing the firm's implementation programs. How might you classify these measures?

3. Identify ten input measures that might have value in managing the firm's implementation programs. How might you classify these measures?

4. Describe three control measures that you believe have had, or could have, deleterious consequences for shareholder value.

5. Many managers allege that they control by the bottom-line (profit). Explain why this may be an ineffective, even dangerous, procedure.

6. Post-action control is sometimes referred to as "Monday Morning Quarter-backing." Explain the conditions under which steering control may offer advantages and what these advantages might be.

7. Why were brand equity controls introduced in consumer goods companies? Should business-to-business marketers consider similar changes in control systems? Why or why not?

8. Many companies encourage best practice, but look only internally for examples. How would you convince senior management that this is an unwise policy?

9. Conducting a full-scale marketing audit typically involves significant political problems within the organization. How would you advocate minimizing these problems while still deriving benefit from the audit process?

10. Some business functions, accustomed to hard (or apparently hard) measures are impatient and distrustful of so-called soft measures, such as customer satisfaction. How would you convince management of the value of soft measures?

11. Input or behavioral control measures are often alleged to be superior to output measures. Why?

12. Marketers are sometimes accused of putting too much emphasis on market share as an output measure, compared with volume or profit. Do you believe these accusations have merit? Why or why not?

13. Public companies have to report income statements and balance sheets to ensure their accountability to shareholders and regulatory authorities. Do you believe these reports provide adequate information for management control purposes?

14. "The most important control measures in managing a business are those relating to achievement of the business's strategic objectives." Do you agree? Why or why not?

15. "In most businesses, credit for success rises to the top, whereas responsibility for failure always descends to lower levels." This view, while cynical, suggests that in the real world, control processes are a political rather than an analytical process. Does this conflict with the philosophy underlying an external orientation? Explain your answer.

16. The chapter alleges that appropriate diagnosis is more difficult when both strategy and implementation are poor. Do you agree? Why or why not?

17. In many companies, evaluation and compensation systems are inflexible and, at best, only weakly linked to strategic objectives. Nonetheless, too frequent changes in evaluation and reward systems can be disconcerting to employees. How might management resolve this paradox?

18. Does your professor of marketing practice principles of steering control in guiding the learning process in your class? What suggestions would you make to modify the current approach?

19. Control processes often reflect the values (implicit or explicit) of an organization. Provide three examples of relationships that you have witnessed.

ENDNOTES

1. Marketers have typically lacked the political power or technical ability to question traditional performance measures, such as sales and profits. However, fortunately, leading thinkers in accounting and finance are increasingly moving toward more appropriate measures that look outward and forward rather than inward and backwards. For example, activity-based costing is making a significant dent in traditional costing approaches; and Kaplan has made a positive contribution by calling for measures that include stock market, operations, and customer data, R.S. Kaplan and D.P. Norton, "Putting the Balanced Scorecard to Work," *Harvard Business Review*, 71 (Sept./Oct. 1993), pp. 134–142.

2. J.M. Hulbert and N.E. Toy, "A Strategic Framework for Marketing Control," *Journal of Marketing*, 41 (April 1977), pp. 12–20. Decomposition of the volume variance proceeds on the right-hand side of Figure 20.2.

3. Rappaport has noted the gulf separating accounting data from economic reality, A. Rappaport, *Creating Shareholder Value*, New York: The Free Press, 1987. Kaplan and others allege that many companies are saddled with archaic and irrelevant cost accounting systems, H.T. Johnson and R.S. Kaplan, *Relevance Lost: The Rise and Fall of Management Accounting*, Boston, MA: Harvard Business School Press, 1987.

4. E.W. Anderson, C. Fornel, and D.R. Lehmann, "Customer Satisfaction, Market Share and Profitability," *Journal of Marketing*, 58 (July 1994), pp. 53–66. Brand health checks (Chapter 11) fall into this category.

5. T.V. Bonoma, "Making Your Strategy Work," *Harvard Business Review*, 62 (March-April 1984), pp. 68–78.

6. The full analysis is developed in Hulbert and Toy, *op. cit.*

7. T.V. Bonoma, " Market Success Can Breed 'Marketing Inertia'," *Harvard Business Review*, 59 (Sept./Oct. 1981), pp. 115–121.

8. J.M. Hulbert and L.F. Pitt, "Exit Left Center Stage? The Future of Functional Marketing," *European Journal of Management,* 14 (Feb. 1998), pp. 47–60.

9. *Fortune*, September 30, 1996.

10. *Fortune*, June 7, 1999.

11. *Business Week E. Biz*, December 13, 1999.

12. R.C. Camp, *Benchmarking: The Search for Industry Best Practices that Lead to Superior Performance*, American Society for Quality, 1989.

13. W.H. Rodgers, G.A. Osborne, and P. Kotler, "Auditing the Marketing Function," in N. Capon, (Ed.), Section 7, *Marketing*, in *AMA Management Handbook* (Third Edition*)*, J. Hampton, (Ed.), AMACOM, 1994. This section is heavily based on this material. See also, P. Kotler, W.T. Gregor, and W.H. Rodgers III, "The Marketing Audit Comes of Age," *Sloan Management Review*, 49 (Winter 1989), 1977.

14. Rodgers, Osborne, and Kotler, *op. cit.*

15. Much of this chapter appendix is reproduced from Hulbert and Toy, *op. cit.* with permission of the American Marketing Association.

16. For data on the PIMS project, see Chapter 3.

WEB RESOURCES

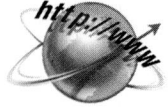

Amazon	www.amazon.com
BP Amoco	www.bp.com
Chevron	www.chevron.com
Cole National	www.colenational.com
Ford	www.ford.com
Frito-Lay	www.fritolay.com
General Electric	www.ge.com
Hallmark	www.hallmark.com
IBM	www.ibm.com
Procter & Gamble	www.pg.com
Reuters	www.reuters.com
Xerox	www.xerox.com

CHAPTER 20 APPENDIX: NUMERICAL ILLUSTRATION OF THE VARIABLE DECOMPOSITION FRAMEWORK

Table 20A.1 shows the results for Product Alpha during the preceding period.[15] The unfavorable $100,000 contribution variance could arise from two main sources:

- Differences between planned and actual contribution per unit;
- Differences between planned and actual quantities (volumes).

TABLE 20A.1 Operating Results for Product Alpha

Item	Planned	Actual	Variance
Revenues			
Sales (lbs.)	20,000,000	22,000,000	2,000,000
Price per lb. ($)	0.50	0.4773	0.227
Revenues	$10,000,000	$10,500,000	$500,000
Total Market (lbs.)	40,000,000	50,000,000	10,000,000
Share of Market	50%	44%	(6%)
Costs			
Variable cost per lb. ($)	0.30	0.30	—
Contribution			
Per lb. ($)	0.20	0.1773	0.0227
Total ($)	$4,000,000	$3,900,000	$(100,000)

Differences between planned and actual quantities can arise from differences between actual and planned market size, and actual and planned market share. Thus the potential sources of variation between planned and actual contribution are:

- Total market size;
- Market share (penetration);
- Price/cost per unit.

This approach to variance decomposition permits assignment into those categories corresponding to key strategy variables in market planning. The analysis proceeds as follows.

Price-Quantity Decomposition

To measure volume variance with the standard yardstick of planned contribution per unit, actual quantity is used to calculate the price/cost variance. (This is standard cost accounting practice.) To be more concise, the following notation can be used:

- S = market share
- M = market size (units)
- Q = quantity sold (units)
- C = contribution margin (per unit)

The subscript "a" is used to denote actual values, and "p" to denote planned values. The subscript "v" denotes variance. Thus the price/cost variance in contribution is:

Price/Cost Variance = $(C_a - C_p) \times Q_a = (.1773 - .20) \times 22,000,000 = \underline{-\$500,000}$

The volume variance in contribution is:

Volume Variance = $(Q_a - Q_p) \times C_p = (22,000,000 - 20,000,000) \times .20 = \underline{\$400,000}$

The sum of these two contribution variances yields the overall unfavorable contribution variance of $100,000, shown in Table 20A.1.

Penetration: Market Size Decomposition

The second analysis stage is the further decomposition of the volume variance in contribution into two components—the market size component and the market share (penetration) component. Figure 20A.1 is helpful in exposition of this analysis.

The differences in quantities sold ($Q_a - Q_p$), where actual and planned quantities are the product of market size and market share can be explained as:

$$Q_a = S_a \times M_a, \qquad Q_p = S_p \times M_p$$

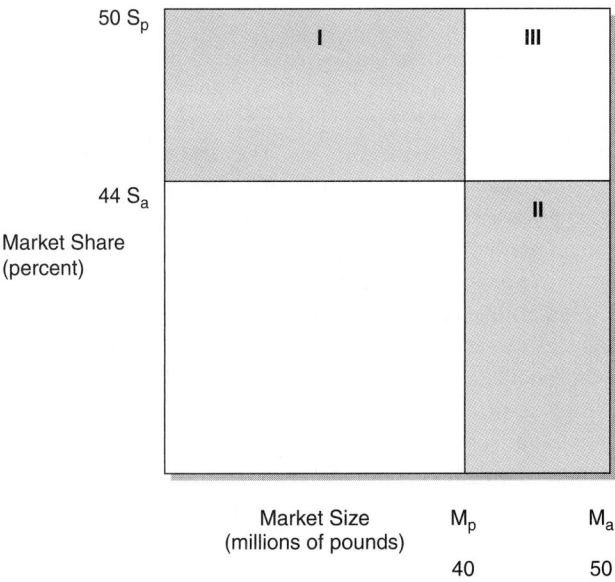

FIGURE 20A.1

Market Share and Market Size Variance

From Figure 20A.1, rectangles I and II are clearly assignable to market share and market size, respectively. However, rectangle III is conceptually more complex.

Discrepancies in forecasting market size should be evaluated using the standard yardstick of planned market share, just as the dollar value of the quantity variance is measured using the standard of planned contribution. Thus actual market size is used to calculate market share variance, where both the market share and forecast components (which together comprise the quantity variance) are measured using planned contribution. (This procedure is also consistent with recommended accounting practice.)

The market share variance in contribution is:

Market share variance =
$$(S_a - S_p) \times M_a \times C_p = (.44 - .50) \times 50,000,000 \times .2 = -\$600,000$$

and the market size variance in contribution is:

Market size variance =
$$(M_a - M_p) \times S_p \times C_p = (50,000,000 - 40,000,000) \times .5 \times .2 = \$1,000,000$$

The sum of the market size and market share variances yields the overall favorable volume variance in contribution of $400,000 derived in the previous section.

Summarizing the component variances that in total comprise the overall variance:

Planned profit contribution	$4,000,000
Volume variance	
Market share variance	−$600,000
Market size variance	$1,000,000
	$400,000
Price/cost variance	−$500,000
Total contribution variance	−$100,000
Actual profit contribution	$3,900,000

Interpretation

Variances occur because of problems in forecasting, implementation, or both. However, to use the analysis results for performance evaluation, responsibility must be assigned. For example, variances in market size are typically the responsibility of the market forecasting group. Market share (penetration) variances are more complex. They can arise from incorrect forecasts of what expected performance should be, or they may be due to poor performance itself. Apportioning responsibility clearly requires managerial judgment. However, where marketing and sales personnel participate in developing market share objectives, or when market share declines relative to previous performance, the burden of proof is more likely to fall on the operating unit rather than on a separate planning/forecasting group.

Responsibility for price variances can also be difficult to assign. For example, prices can be seriously affected by changes in market or general economic conditions beyond the control of the operating group; however, perhaps these should have been foreseen by forecasters or planners. On the other hand, prices are an integral element of the marketing mix and variances can indicate problems in implementation.

With these considerations in mind, the results of the variance analysis can be reviewed:

1. The favorable $400,000 volume variance was caused by two larger variances that partly canceled each other out. Whereas one of these variances (market size) was positive and the other (market share) negative, both are undesirable. By not achieving planned market share, the firm lost $600,000 in profit contribution.

The loss of market share may have been due to poor planning, poor execution, or both. Managerial judgment is the key factor for diagnosing the causes of this discrepancy.

2. This unfavorable market share variance seems to have been more than compensated for by the $1,000,000 positive contribution variance due to a larger than forecast market size.

This variance is unequivocally the responsibility of the forecasting group. Furthermore, this nominally favorable variance is a danger signal. The firm seriously underestimated the market size. At 50 million pounds, this was 25% greater than the forecast (40 million pounds). As the dominant competitor, the firm lost market share in a fast-growth market, the sort of error that soon leads to loss of competitive position.

The market share/market size decomposition of the volume variance emphasizes the importance of good planning, and good information for planning, in terms directly related to two crucial variables in strategy design. This form of decomposition generates considerably more useful insight into issues of marketing control than simple isolation of the volume variance.

3. The final variance component is the unfavorable $500,000 price/cost variance; again, interpretation is the job of marketing management. The accounting procedures treat price and volume variances as if they were separable yet, for the vast majority of products and services, demand is price-elastic to some degree. Thus variances in total revenue are the combined result of the interaction via the demand function of unit prices and quantities.

In this example lower price levels may have been an important factor in expanding market demand and firm sales. Nonetheless, failure to attain planned price levels led to a $500,000 decrease in actual as opposed to planned profit contribution. The reasons for this variance may lie with performance (poor implementation) or poor planning (inaccurate forecasts).

Monday Morning Quarterbacking

A crucial issue, so far unaddressed, is the appropriate criteria for performance evaluation. This basic yet nagging problem underlies the whole area of strategic control. In the foregoing analysis, it was assumed that the market plan provided an appropriate set of criteria.

Market objectives are usually derived after considerable participation, discussion, and negotiation among interested parties. As a result, they may well represent the most appropriate set of criteria that are available, at least at the beginning of the planning period.

However, in many companies, performance during the previous planning period serves as an additional set of evaluation criteria. In fact, the search for more objective performance evaluation criteria led to the PIMS project and development of the *par* criterion.[16] Thus accurate and timely industry sales statistics, combined with a flexible planning system that was able to incorporate new data into a revised plan and set of sales quotas, could preempt a problem that, by the time it is recognized, develops into a fair-sized disaster.

Of course, the marketing plan—used as the criterion in the example—is generally based upon the best available information *ex ante*. However, conditions that emerge during the planning period can be vastly different from those envisaged during plan development. In some company planning systems, these changes can be addressed by contingency planning; in others, the plan is updated when major environmental changes occur. In many other cases, the plan is not updated, at least not in any formal way.

Regardless of the comprehensiveness of systems to provide flexibility in plans, at performance review time, most marketing managers use some *ex post* information. Thus evaluation criteria, implicitly or explicitly, are generally what performance should have been under the circumstances that actually transpired. Nor is this Monday morning quarterbacking undesirable, for it is eminently more sensible than blind adherence to a plan that is clearly outdated by a violation of planning assumptions. Naturally, there are inherent dangers in such a process. Equally clearly on some occasions, unforeseen events significantly affect what target performance should actually be.

CHAPTER

21

MARKETING AND THE INTERNET

LEARNING OBJECTIVES

When you have completed this chapter,[1] you will understand

- how the Internet is changing the practice of marketing and the way business is conducted

- that the Internet age means more than adding a new customer communication channel

- how to develop an appreciation of the implications for marketing in knowledge-rich environments

- the forces fueling the Web's phenomenal growth

- the consequences for marketing and the process of management

- how cyberspace will impact the marketing mix

INTRODUCING CYBERSPACE: THE INTERNET AND THE WORLD WIDE WEB

The Net provides the means to break down bureaucracies; challenge corporate, governmental, and intellectual orthodoxies; and foster a stronger sense of community. Such developments have sparked more than one revolution. There's no reason to expect anything less this time.[2]

The Internet and the World Wide Web have the potential to radically change the nature and direction of society and business.[3] Not only are they affecting the acquisition and servicing of customers, they are transforming the structure of entire industries and their supply chains. They are also likely to change dramatically the ways in which both companies and industries are organized.[4] Both the *Financial Times* and Alan Greenspan, Chairman of the U.S. Federal Reserve Board, have ranked the information revolution, of which the Internet and World Wide Web are important components, alongside the agrarian and industrial revolutions in terms of the profundity of its implications.[5]

The information revolution comprises perhaps the greatest challenge (marketing and organizational) and opportunity of the early twenty-first century.[6] Although some argue that the Internet is first a technological medium and second a marketing medium,[7] it may constitute much more. The Internet is primarily about information—knowledge, concepts, ideas, and so forth, and the connectivity among information sources via a network. And, information behaves very differently from the traditional foundations of economic activity—capital and labor.

Knowledge-Rich Environments

Several prominent authors have described the emergence of a post-industrial economy characterized by the rise of service and information as the creators of value.[8] The critical role of knowledge at the turn of the millennium was cogently stated by T.A. Wilson, chairman of Boeing. He said that Boeing was in the knowledge business, and that airplanes were the incidental end result.[9] Drucker and others describe the "knowledge economy" for first-world nations that are becoming increasingly less materials and energy intensive.[10] As *Business Week* put it, "The traditional factors of production—capital and skilled labor—are no longer the main determinants of the power of an economy. Now economic potential is increasingly linked to the ability to control and manipulate information."[11]

The location of value is different in the knowledge-rich new economy. Traditionally value was located in the physical product, such as gold, timber, bricks, and mortar. Increasingly, the bulk of the value in market offerings is represented in their information content. For example, the (hopefully significant) value of this book is not in the paper, but in the information printed on the paper. The raw-material value of a stockmarket computer-server is relatively low compared with the value of the information used in the building process and, more importantly, with the value of information stored on the computer.

As information has become the raw material of the new commercial age, the pressing need for a global information infrastructure has become evident. The Internet is the foundation for that structure. The Internet is the informational equivalent of physical roads, railways, waterways, power lines, and airways that were the essential arteries of the industrial age. As such, it affords enormous opportunity for transforming the very structure of economies.

Knowledge-richness is also the province of marketing. From the early stages of direct marketing, the Internet not only enables marketers to address customers as individuals worldwide, but it also serves as a powerful vehicle for building knowledge about them.[12] Where database marketing is today viewed as a special form of marketing, the more precise targeting that the Internet enables affords the possibility that it will become the norm. No longer will it be necessary to trade off—knowledge richness—perviously requiring proximity and expensive dedicated channels—for knowledge reach—contact with a large number of people.[13] The Internet will create powerful opportunities to enhance company and brand positioning as broadband access and high-quality streamed video become ubiquitous.

However, perhaps the most basic question facing marketers is: How does marketing on the Internet differ from more traditional marketing? Currently, two competing models are evident—complementary and transformational. As a complementary marketing medium, the Internet enables firms to do more of what they are doing now, and possibly do it better. As a transformational medium, via reinvention and creativity, the Internet represents a radically new way of doing business.[14]

Neither model really explains the Internet phenomenon, but both are useful perspectives. Initially, traditional businesses tended to view the Internet as a complement to their marketing practices. Internet start-ups have been much more radical and innovative in inventing new business models. Thus, where automobile manufacturers such as General Motors have glossy Web sites that essentially act as online brochures (brochureware), Web start-up Priceline.com and CommerceOne have patented their Web-based auction business models. More recently, traditional businesses are partnering with Web start-ups to create powerful supply chain management tools such as the GM/Ford/Daimler-Chrysler/Nissan CommerceOne auto parts auction venture.

GetMedia, founded in 1997, provides a good example of the Internet as a complement.

Example: GetMedia creates its Internet presence through partnerships with radio networks, individual stations, and advertisers. GetMedia unites the Internet and radio to create an integrated music purchase system. When a listener enters a GetMedia-enabled radio station Web site, the album cover for the song being broadcast is automatically displayed. The album can be purchased through the Web site or by calling a toll-free number, offering concurrency unavailable from any other site.

By contrast, MP3.com illustrates the Internet as a transformational iconoclast.

Example: MP3.com is based on digital compression protocols that allow near–CD-quality music to be transmitted over the Internet at high speed. MP3.com provides samples of musicians' recordings across the music category spectrum. Artists from around the world encode and upload their music to MP3's site, which provides a chart service reflecting the number of worldwide downloads for each song. Detailed information and pictures for each artist or group are also provided, together with links to their own Web sites, publishing companies, and record labels. Listeners can purchase albums from the MP3 site or from an alternative site to which they are directed. The site's success has attracted the attention of many big-name artists. Not only can musicians bypass traditional retail distribution and sell directly to their fans, they can also eschew record companies. In the face of MP3.com's success, customers at Virgin Record Stores may make compilation CDs of MP3 songs downloaded from the Web.[15]

MARKETING AND MANAGEMENT PROCESS IN THE DIGITAL AGE: FIVE NEW FORCES

The traditional view of strategy development employed throughout this text assumes that the firm secures a good understanding of its environment then plans accordingly. This view is most acceptable when the environment changes slowly and the future is reasonably predictable. However, because today's environment is changing so swiftly, the firm's planning assumptions are often questionable. As a result, the ability to flex and adapt to change is much more important than it has been historically.[16]

Frequent dramatic changes in the environment are a relatively recent phenomenon. For example, during the Middle Ages, significant innovations appeared at a very slow rate—sometimes as infrequently as every 200 or 300 years. In the Renaissance, new technologies, such as the invention of movable type by Gutenberg appeared slightly more rapidly. During the Industrial Revolution, new inventions emerged every five or ten years, and during the twentieth century, innovations surfaced every couple of years or so.

Some innovations are not just simple improvements; they are thoroughly disruptive and have been termed killer applications, or "killer apps."[17] A true killer app does not just change a market or an industry, it changes the way society itself works and functions. Movable type was a killer app. The automobile was a killer app. The automobile didn't just replace horse-drawn carriages, it changed the way people live, shop, work, and spend leisure time. And it also changed the physical environment in most countries. In the past five to ten years, killer apps have emerged more than once a year. Currently, this rate is increasing exponentially because of spreading technologies such as the Internet. Knowledge, in its broadest sense, is now easily available and can be exchanged by people around the world.[18]

The task of strategy development is fundamentally affected by these changes. Because the relevant time frames are shortened, the typical five-year plan is less and less relevant. The annual planning cycles, almost universally linked to the fiscal year and slavishly adhered to by many firms, must be replaced by a much more dynamic, event-triggered approach to strategy development that is more opportunistic and evolutionary. Managers must accept that no matter how hard they try to forecast the future, their ability to do so will probably decrease. Organizations have to become much more flexible, adaptive, and responsive to previously unforeseen changes. These capabilities which, by and large, are not associated with most large firms are indicative of the new change agenda facing management.

Five New Forces

What, then, are the forces likely to shape the evolution of the "information economy"? We describe these as the "new" five forces, but their dynamics and potential interactions are vastly different from their forebears that assume a known industry structure,[19] diminishing returns and perfectly rational firms.[20]

MOORE'S LAW In 1965, Gordon Moore, a Fairchild Semiconductor engineer, noticed that the number of transistors on a computer chip doubled every 18 to 24 months. A corollary to that observation, or "Moore's Law" as it came to be known, is that the speed of microprocessors, at constant cost, also doubles every 18 to 24 months. Moore's Law has held up for more than 30 years. It worked in 1969 when Moore's start-up, Intel Corp., put its first processor chip—the 4-bit, 104-KHz, 2,300-transistor 4004—into a Japanese calculator. It still works today for Intel's 32-bit, 450-MHz Pentium II processor that, with 7.5 million transistors, is 233,000 times faster. Intel anticipates a 100-million-transistor chip by 2001 and a 1-billion-transistor chip in 2011. Although some observers anticipate that exponential gains in chip performance will slow eventually, most experts agree that Moore's Law will govern the industry for at least another ten years.

The major implication of Moore's Law is that computing power will become ever faster and cheaper. Not only will increasing numbers of people worldwide have access to powerful computing, but computer power can be built into devices other than computers themselves. Already, computers enable diverse products, such as vehicles, surgical equipment, and elevators, to operate more efficiently, predictably, and safely. The future may even bring computer chips to packaging as costs continue to decline.

METCALFE'S LAW The usefulness of a technology depends on the number of users of that technology and on how easily they can be interconnected. For example, a single facsimile machine is useless: no one to fax to and no one to receive faxes from. Similarly, one telephone is useless. A few telephones have limited value, but one million telephones create a vast network. Robert Metcalfe, founder of 3COM Corporation and designer of the robust Ethernet protocol for computer networks, observed that new technologies are valuable only if used by many people. Specifically, Metcalfe's Law states that the usefulness (utility) of a network equals the square of the number of users. The more people use software, a network, a particular standard, a game, or a book, the more valuable it becomes. As value increases, more users are attracted, further increasing the value and speed of its adoption by still more users. The Internet is perhaps the best illustration of Metcalfe's Law. Although dating to the 1960s, it has only gained momentum in recent years. As larger numbers of users have joined the medium, it has become increasingly useful to ever more users, thus accelerating its growth. Its potential to spread new ideas, products, and services is awesome.

> **Example:** From its early days, America Online's (AOL) strategy has been to make it simple to sign up for its service by mailing out millions of free disks. In 1998, traffic was doubling on AOL every 100 days; in 2002, the average user is expected to be online 50 minutes per day.

More recently, Kelly has pointed out that Metcalfe's Law was based on telephone or fax networks where connections are point-to-point. On the Internet, because connections can be made simultaneously with groups of people, the potential value of the network is n^n where n is the number of people connected.[21]

COASIAN ECONOMICS In 1937, Ronald Coase, later a Nobel Prize winner in economics, made a critical observation about market behavior.[22] Coase introduced the notion of "transaction costs," a set of market inefficiencies that add, or should be added, to the price of a good or service to measure market performance relative to the non-market behavior in firms. Transaction costs include those for search, contract, and enforcement. Transaction cost economics offers a method for explaining those activities a firm chooses to perform in-house (in its own hierarchy) and those for which it relies on the market. Thus transaction cost economics provides a useful way to explain firms' outsourcing decisions.

Historically, advances in communications technology led to increases in firm size. Intra-firm coordination costs were lowered so that firms could undertake many activities themselves and be able to operate as ever-larger entities. For example, multinational firms such as General Motors, Siemens, and Unilever are essentially managed from a head office. However, what is sometimes overlooked is that technologies, accelerated by Moore's Law and Metcalfe's Law, also reduce transaction costs and improve market efficiency. More efficient markets should reduce optimal firm size. (In perfectly efficient markets, firm size approaches zero.) Society may well be witnessing the first signs of this change as large firms, under the mantra of shareholder value, are increasingly willing to break up into smaller units.

> **Examples:** Both Ford and General Motors have moved to sever relationships with their in-house parts suppliers, designating them as Delphi and Visteon, respectively. Significant corporate break-ups in recent years include AT&T (twice), IT&T, and The Hanson Trust.[23]

The willingness to outsource, rather than produce in-house, is another illustration of this process. Historically widespread in the chemical industry (toll manufacturing), it has become the norm in the computer, electronics, athletic footwear, and garment industries. It is now penetrating the pharmaceutical and biotechnology industries.[24]

In a turn-of-the century interview, Coase observed that it was unclear which organizational entity was best equipped to control electronic commerce. Lower transaction costs favor a market solution but lower intra-firm coordinating costs and the potential for economies of scale and scope seemed to favor a hierarchical solution.[25]

THE FLOCK OF BIRDS PHENOMENON A key feature of the new communication technologies is that, in many cases, they do not "belong" to any single institution, nor does any particular authority control them. Some have referred to this as the "flock of birds" phenomenon.[26] When a flock of birds is observed flying in formation, or a school of fish swimming in a distinct pattern, one is tempted to speculate whether there is a bird in charge or a head fish. However, naturalists explain that flocking is a natural phenomenon and that there are no birds in charge or head fish. Rather, the network is the processor.

Humans have been conditioned to seek a controlling body or authority for most of the phenomena that they experience in life. Typically, this is a large firm, government body, or ruling institution. However, for the Internet and World Wide Web, built on open standards, no one is in charge. Not only are these great democratic mechanisms, they are also anarchic, and society may have to develop new ways to deal with these liberating effects. The flock of birds phenomenon implies equal access, most unlike traditional media. In a very real sense, no one has a better right of access, and no one, not even the largest corporation, can shout louder. The smallest player, the individual, has the right and opportunity to be seen and heard.

> **Example:** In October 1999, Steve Jobs announced that "after a good night's sleep and digesting e-mails from many upset customers," Apple Computer would rescind a retroactive price increase it had intended to impose on customers who were back-ordered.[27]

THE FISH TANK PHENOMENON   Moore's Law and Metcalfe's Law combine to give individuals inexpensive and easy access to new media, such as the Internet. Nearly anyone in the world can set up a Web site and, theoretically at least, nearly anyone can see it. As a result, many have noticed the so-called fish tank phenomenon, referring to the immense amount of junk on the Internet, such as sites showing footage from a video camera perched on top of a coffee percolator or scenes from a tropical fish tank.[28] However, in addition to Internet junk, there is also the potential for unlimited creativity. Although large organizations have the capabilities and resources to produce large, rich Web sites, they will find themselves threatened by small start-ups previously unable to gain market access. No longer will it be good enough merely to observe one's close and known competitors; in the future these competitors could be anyone from anywhere.

Managing with the Five New Forces in Mind

In the future, firms must consider the effects of these five forces—Moore's Law, Metcalfe's Law, Coasian Economics, and the Flock of Birds and Fish Tank Phenomena. The technological effects of Moore's and Metcalfe's Laws will bring hyper-accelerating change, spreading like a quickly proliferating virus. Boundaries will become blurred both within firms and across industries and markets; decision makers will have to consider a world where computer chips are not only in computers but also in many devices and articles, which in turn are part of an exponentially growing network.

Because of transaction cost economics and technological effects on firm and market efficiency, managers must constantly evaluate the optimal shape, scope, and size of the firm. These effects may drive firms to become smaller and virtual. Managers must continually consider what activities should be performed in the market and what functions should be conducted within the firm itself. For example, marketers will have to cope with the constant tussle between dis-intermediation and re-intermediation in distribution channel options.[29]

The societal effects of the Flock of Birds Phenomenon heralds communications democracy with the threat of anarchy as the Fish Tank Phenomenon brings access to all. These phenomena will require managers to work in a new environment where control and governance are less clear and less structured than they have been throughout most of history. Managing in a world where significant issues are neither under the control of a government or a government department, nor part of a large organization, will be a new and often frightening experience for most managers.

Managers can take cold comfort from identification of the five new forces. They are more ethereal than those of the 1980s; the impact on firms and industries is far less predictable. The forces are not neat and structured, nor do they provide as much comfort in terms of strategic direction as traditional tools such as portfolio analysis or discounted cash flow calculations. Decision makers will have to use them not so much as guidelines and prescriptors, but as prods to keep challenging themselves, their firms, and their markets. Much recent strategy writing emphasizes the effects of these forces and suggests that conventional management processes for strategy development will be insufficient, if not ineffective. Indeed, not knowing the source of potential competition will require constant strategy revision. When competition is well defined, or even partially defined, it can be examined and, perhaps, addressed. However, when it emanates from a computer in the bedroom of a 17-year-old in another country, life gets much more difficult.[30] In short, ensuring corporate survival in third millennium markets will become an increasingly challenging endeavor.[31]

Although there is no absolute agreement on strategy advice for the future, the five forces are likely to make their presence known in four distinct market areas[32]:

- **Business-to-Business (B2B)**: corporate procurement; examples include www.freemarkets.com and www.chemdex.com
- **Business-to-Consumer (B2C)**: retail activities on the Internet; examples include www.amazon.com and www.shoplink.com
- **Consumer to Business (C2B)**: consumers making offers to purchase products from firms; examples include www.priceline.com and www.NexTag.com
- **Consumer-to-Consumer**: consumer auctions; an example is www.ebay.com

Across the board, leading-edge authors tend to agree on certain fundamentals:[33]

- Change is too rapid for anyone anywhere to feel comfortable; more than ever, managers must beware the anesthetizing effect of success.
- It may be worthwhile for managers to continually seek ways of destroying the firm's value chain and putting it out of business. If they don't, someone else will.
- Firm capabilities are increasingly about knowledge and the ability to constantly innovate, rather than about tangible assets.
- Firms should constantly find and exploit ways for customers to do as much work as possible. Strange as it may seem, many customers want less service rather than more. Disliking dependency they want control and the power to solve their own problems.
- Increasingly, the firm-to-customer model for flows of information goods will be supplemented with customer-to-firm and customer-to-customer models. Customers will become a greater source of information to firms and become increasingly involved in the firm's product development efforts. In addition, communities of customers will form around firms, products, and experiences. Some of these communities will be ongoing; others will form for the purpose of developing buying power to drive down the prices of individual products for all members, such as zwirl.com.[34]
- As the half-life of ideas diminishes, the role of strategy will change. The traditional five-year plan will no longer be viable and the value of annual strategic planning sessions will be questioned. Perhaps strategy will become a one-page set of guidelines for action, and resource allocation decisions be less planned than incremental, revisited far more frequently. Regardless, because the Internet is information-rich, it enhances the ability of marketers to secure research data to improve and refine their market strategies and implementation programs.

Example: Fox's Eight Ball project embraces 43 million box-office and movie records, and allows it to better predict demand for its movies. As a result, distribution strategy (movie house selection) is more refined, advertising is more precisely targeted, and Fox saves on unnecessary film duplication.[35]

- Electronic commerce will significantly reduce the cost of doing business (Table 21.1).[36] In addition to cost savings, electronic commerce will provide opportunities for increased revenues, in part through better customer knowledge. See Table 21.2 for Ford's initiatives.[37]

Implications for Market Strategy

The implications of the Internet for marketers and marketing will be far-reaching. Although any predictions must necessarily be speculative, several assumptions for the advance of the information economy can be identified (Table 21.3).

TABLE 21.1 Estimated Cost Savings from B2B Electronic Commerce

Industry	Estimated Savings from Business-to-Business E-commerce*
Aerospace machining	11%
Chemicals	10%
Coal	2%
Communications	5–15%
Computing	11–20%
Electronic components	29–39%
Food ingredients	3–5%
Forest products	15–25%
Freight transport	15–20%
Health care	5%
Life sciences	12–19%
Machining (metals)	22%
Media and advertising	10–15%
MRO**	10%
Oil and gas	5–15%
Paper	10%
Steel	11%

*Analysis compared B2B techniques with traditional business methods, such as paper, telephone, fax or value-added networks.

**Maintenance, repair, and operating supplies

One perspective considers that the present is a period of economic transition. In advanced Western societies at least, the focus of the economy shifted from commodities to goods, and then to service; now it is shifting to the experiences.[38]

Example: Farmers harvesting coffee in countries such as Brazil, Kenya, and Colombia receive little more than $1 per pound, a fraction of a cent per cup of coffee. When a manufacturer, such as Nestle or Folger, grinds, packages, and sells the same beans in a grocery store, the consumer price jumps to 5 and 25 cents a cup. Fast-food outlets, such as McDonald's, sell polystyrene cups of coffee for around 99 cents. Starbucks' price for a cup of coffee is much greater. In the famous "Starbucks" scene in the movie *You've Got Mail*, the coffee price is up to $5 a cup.

Director Nora Ephron explained that she staged the scene in Starbucks because, for many Americans, the coffee chain has become a "third place."[39,40] Starbucks offers an experience more than it serves coffee—the language of the "barristas," the noise of the grinders and the espresso machines, the sights of scores of different coffee varieties and products, the feel of hot coffee in the drinker's hands, and the atmosphere permeated by the aroma of coffee. Each experience is personal and memorable.[41]

Not every organization should seek to emulate Starbucks, but the differences between extracting commodities, making products, delivering services, and staging experiences should be recognized. Experiences can be vicarious and accomplished over the Web, and

TABLE 21.2 Elements of Ford's Electonic-Commerce Strategy

What	How	Goal
Retailing	Set up BuyerConnection Web site and joined MSN CarPoint site, where consumers can order custom-assembled cars, track their progress, and apply for financing.	Reduce working capital by shrinking excess inventories and wipe out costly rebates needed to move unwanted cars off dealer lots, thus saving up to $650 per car.
Customer service	OwnerConnection Web site lets owners get online help, manage their warranty service, and check on financing.	Improve service with 24-hour access. Gather better data on customer problems. And cut costs with automated help.
Suppliers	Launched auto-exchange Web site for online purchasing and swapping of information between 30,000 suppliers and 6,900 dealers.	Save up to $8.9 billion a year in discounts and reduced transaction costs on parts, raw materials, and supplies. Speed data exchange with partners while collecting up to $3 billion a year in exchange fees.
Marketing	Teaming up with Yahoo!, TeleTech, CarPoint, iVillage, and bolt.com to monitor the interests and buying patterns of Web-surfing customers.	Improve factory efficiency by anticipating customer demand. Funnel data on customer preferences to car designers.
Digital dashboard	Equip new cars with Web access, satellite phone services, and e-mail capabilities.	Make Ford the carmaker for an Internet generation. Collect millions of dollars in fee-based services.
Financing	Shift more of the activities of Ford Credit to the Net for online financing and collections.	Cut service costs by 15% to 20%, while boosting revenues by reaching new customers.
Wired workers	Offering all 350,000 employees a computer, printer, and Net access for $5 a month.	Makes the workforce Web-savvy so it will quickly adopt the Internet initiatives, while enabling the CEO to send weekly e-mail to employees.

they can be anticipatory, such as a pre-purchase virtual simulation of the experience,[42] or real, such as a visit to the New York City ballet. However, because of differing expectations driven in part by prior experiences, a visitor from Rockford, Illinois has a very different ballet experience than a New Yorker who is a series subscriber.

Although it may be anticipated that the Web will increasingly provide new experiences for customers, some current everyday experiences will probably not find their way onto the Web. For example, the Web does not provide the social experience of shopping, the ability to "try" products, nor the same sorts of impulse purchases. In addition, except for digitized products, customers do not receive their purchases instantly. Nonetheless, the arrival of the Internet will have a profound impact on marketing activities.[43]

THE INTERNET AND THE MARKETING MIX

Customer value is delivered via the marketing mix. One framework identifies the six Cs of customer value offered through the Internet: **choice**—the variety of products and services offered by an individual on-line vendor is far greater than that available by conventional means; **customization**—the Internet offers the ability for high degrees of customization for individual customers; **consistency**—the information provided by Web sites is totally consistent in a way that other forms of corporate communication can never be; **convenience**—individuals can log on to the Internet at any time, from any place; **community**—the Internet has the ability to generate strong community affinity; change—information

TABLE 21.3 Marketing: Key Concepts and Assumptions

Concept/ Assumption	Neo-Classical Marketing	Information-Era Marketing
Space	Physical separation of customer and seller	Implosion of space: dis-intermediation and re-intermediation
Time frame	Conditioned by traditional economics (based on labor and capital)	Speeded up, determined by economics of information, knowledge and ideas
Markets	Well-defined, homogeneous markets	Fragmented markets and consumers
Competitive environment	Competition: metaphor = war	Co-option: metaphor = ecology
Customer needs/wants	Assumed pre-existing	Assumed subject to influence
Offerings	Discrete products and services, bundled and unbundled	Product/service/circumstance experiences
Decision making	Decisions must be made in a matter of months	Decisions must be made in a matter of days, hours, minutes, seconds
Focus	Focus is on selling consumer products	Focus is on attracting customers and staging consumer experiences
Senior management and company image	Monitor	Micromanage
Management style	CEO uses a hands-off style	CEO uses a more approachable management style
Company strategy sessions	Company strategy sessions held on annual cycle	CEO sets vision—continual evolution

products have the ability to provide up-to-the-minute information far more effectively than conventional means. In this section each marketing mix element is viewed through the lens of the Internet.

The Web and Product/Service Strategy

Although the Internet enables the sale of tangible products through various communication and other devices, for Internet-based products themselves, the core product is almost entirely a service. As a result, Internet products have the same characteristics as other services, such as intangibility, inseparability, variability, and perishibility (for a full discussion of these characteristics, see Chapter 17). As discussed earlier, because of these characteristics, the job of service marketers tends to be somewhat more difficult than the job of product marketers. On the other hand, product marketers have generally found it difficult to customize goods, whereas services, produced and consumed simultaneously, can more easily be tailored to individual customer needs in real time. The Internet, through its ability to mitigate some of the difficulties faces by service marketers yet also to exploit the tailoring ability, offers the ability to create sustainable differential advantage.

MANAGING INTANGIBILITY The Internet helps deal with the intangibility problems of services by tangibilizing, providing evidence, and cyberspace sampling.

Tangibilize A Web site can be used to tangibilize the intangible.

> **Example:** The Disney Web site tangibilizes a future dream. It provides graphic detail on Disney theme parks, allowing children to see and listen to their favorite characters, and to examine the rides that they might take before a visit is booked.

Provide Evidence The Web can be used to provide evidence to customers. Because customers cannot see the service, the firm can provide evidence of what they receive when they purchase.

> **Example:** The British Royal Automobile Club (RAC) enables users to enroll for membership online. Site information includes details of RAC membership benefits, the extent of assistance the club provides, service options available, and payment methods. More importantly, the site e-mails new members within a few minutes of joining, confirming all details and providing instantaneous, tangible proof of membership in the form of a membership number.

Cyberspace Sampling The best way to convince someone to purchase wine is to have him or her try a sample glass. Wine estates and fine wine stores realize this and tastings are a major element of promotional strategy. However, normally it is very difficult to sample a service.

> **Example:** Each year Harvard Business School Publishing Services generates substantial revenues from business case studies, multimedia programs, books, and the *Harvard Business Review*. Presently, approved instructors worldwide browse the Harvard Web site using powerful search facilities to find cases and other materials. When a relevant item is identified, it can be downloaded and printed for examination prior to placing an order for multiple copies. Items are watermarked indicating that the case is a sample and should not be reproduced.

MANAGING INSEPARABILITY Some features of inseparability that the Web enables services marketers to manage are customization, managing the customer as a part-time employee, and encouraging customer participation as an innovation mechanism.

Customization Because services are produced and consumed simultaneously, service providers may be able to customize their services. Because the Internet's capabilities are centered in information technology, data storage, and data processing, rather than in employees and physical location, it can customize on a scale that is impossible for traditional service providers to match.

> **Example:** Entrypoint offers an individually customized news retrieval service. Customers select personal interest categories, such as news, sports, stock quotes, or weather. Pointcast scans news providers and compiles customized offerings for each person. These offerings are updated regularly. Either the individual requests additional items, or the software learns individual preferences and searches for relevant information. Lifeminders.com offers a variety of types of information based on personal interests.

Customer as Part-time Employee In some Internet developments the customer is, in a substantial sense, a part-time employee. Not only does the customer enter the "service factory" but, in many cases, service quality is almost as dependent on the customer as it is on the service provider.

> **Example:** The international courier company Federal Express allows customers access to its system through its Web site. Customers track shipments traveling through the FedEx system by entering the package receipt number. In addition, customers can request pickups, find the nearest drop-off site, and request invoice adjustments. Previously, FedEx used a large team of service agents and a major telephone switchboard to handle customer inquiries. Now around one million tracking requests are handled on-line each month. Without the Web site, half would have used the more expensive and time-consuming telephone system.[44] Not only does this site provide greater customer satisfaction, it has also reduced FedEx's costs.

Customer Participation in Service Innovation Because customers can act as co-producers and participants in the service creation process, they afford the potential for service innovations that can create advantage in competitive markets. If the firm can create an enjoyable experience for customers willing to do some work, new products can be developed.

Example: The Firefly network creates virtual communities of customers. In each community, customers not only provide significant information about themselves, they also contribute most of the effort to create the community. Customers provide, on a continually updated basis, information about their preferences for books, music, or movies, typically in the form of ratings on scales. Firefly uses these profiles to put customers in touch with others having similar preferences and interests, and recommends new music, books, or movies. Customers also provide opinions that are fed back to other customers. Not only is this information valuable to the individuals, it is a major company asset that can be sold to film producers, record companies, or booksellers. Thus not only are customers co-creators of their own enjoyment, they also produce a valuable and salable information asset for Firefly.

Example: *Open Directory*, a catalogue of interesting destinations on the Web, is developed by 20,000 volunteers. Each volunteer collects a list of sites for a given topic. Launched in summer 1998, by end 1999, its 190,000 categories were linked to 1.2 million web sites.

MANAGING VARIABILITY   The Internet offers unique opportunities to overcome the problems occasioned by service variability.

Example: Security First Network Bank (SFNB) was one of the first financial service institutions to offer full-service banking on the Internet. SFNB, which uses a graphic metaphor (a color picture of the lobby of a traditional bank) to communicate and interact with potential and existing customers, offers an electronic inquiries desk, electronic brochures for general information, electronic security guards to ensure safety, and electronic tellers to deal with routine transactions. Compared to a traditional bank where customers can encounter variable waiting periods, great or indifferent service, warmth or rudeness, employee competence or incompetence, the service at SFNB is relevant and highly consistent. On the other hand, for the purchase of physical goods, e-commerce companies and their customers must deal with similar problems to those faced by mail-order companies—incorrect items, damaged goods, and late delivery.

MANAGING PERISHABILITY   Because products are produced before they are consumed, mis-forecasting can be handled through inventory. By contrast, since services are produced and consumed simultaneously, inventory is not an option. To minimize the effects of service perishability, astute services marketers are using Web sites to manage supply and demand.

Managing Supply   In a conventional service setting, supply is managed by focusing on all service production factors that affect customers' ability to acquire and use the service. Thus service providers must pay attention to variables such as opening and closing hours, and staffing. These issues are circumvented on the Internet as Web sites allow service marketers to provide 24-hour service to customers worldwide.

Example: United Airlines uses its Web site to provide services that, in conventional circumstances, would have been limited by people, time, and place. Customers can purchase tickets from the Web site at any time convenient to them. Frequent flyers can obtain complete, up-to-date information on membership status, including miles available for free travel.

Managing Demand   Service marketers stimulate or dampen demand by using marketing mix elements, such as promotions, pricing, and service bundling. Since high fixed costs and low variable costs characterize many service businesses it may be profitable to sell the last few hotel rooms or seats for airlines, concerts, and so forth at very low prices.

> **Example:** South African Airways (SAA) manages demand by conducting online ticket auctions on its Web site. SAA was filling about two thirds of its available capacity. By auctioning off unsold seats for imminent flights at low prices, it has been able to approach 100% capacity utilization.[45]

PRODUCT/SERVICE MANAGEMENT ISSUES The Internet has numerous interesting implications for product management and strategy. For example, traditionally, in most organizations, product management is housed separately from the warranty function and various customer service activities, such as help desks and other forms of support. This organizational separation is a weakness because information gained from these activities can be highly beneficial for modifying the firm's offer. The Internet allows all functions to be centralized on a single database, thus simplifying the communication flow from customers and allowing faster response.

> **Example:** Jeff Bezos, Amazon.com founder, received an e-mail message from a long-time customer, an elderly lady who was unable to open her book order package. In short order, the package was redesigned and made very easy to open.

Branding Product marketers have long relied on brands to differentiate their offerings from competitors. Brands facilitate consumer search through a recognition process and minimize the probability of a bad purchase via the reassurance they convey. However, although the Internet extends the brand's capability to communicate with target customers, it may render the brand less valuable from a consumer search perspective as the costs of information for products and services are lowered.[46,47]

Although some argue for marketing's indispensability in commodity markets,[48] there is no doubt that marketing efforts are most effective when markets are less than efficient. Thus as information is commoditized and markets approach efficiency, the value of brands may become increasingly problematic.[49] For example, using any of a number of search engines, a buyer can identify multiple offerings of a 35mm single lens reflex (SLR) camera with desired features. The use of search software such as "intelligent agents" will compound this capability and lessen the power of the brand. Experts predict that these agents will one day handle electronic errands, make routine consumer decisions by monitoring and learning from users' actions, make suggestions, and "even undertake consumers' handling in the marketplace."

Notwithstanding the drive to market efficiency, new brands are arising via the Internet. Search engines such as Yahoo!, Excite, and Altavista have secured significant brand equity, but so also have product providers such as Amazon.com, ebay, Etoys, and babycenter.com. The emergence of allegedly superior branded "bots" and comparison services are already being seen.[50] In addition, firms concerned about conflicts with traditional distributors may develop Internet-only brands, such as Procter & Gamble's cosmetics brand, Reflect.com.[51] The challenge for all product providers on the Internet is to develop areas of customer value that enable them to deal with downward price pressures.

> **Example:** NECX matches buyers and sellers of electronic components, computer products, and networking equipment. It was the first online retailer to post its competitors' prices, even when those prices were lower, and to provide links to competitor sites. However, by making the purchasing experience better and easier, NECX has impressive customer loyalty: 75% of orders are from repeat buyers, and half of all first-time buyers purchase again within 18 months.[52]

The importance of Web site naming to the brand building activity should not be underestimated. For example, Fidelity.com is far more user-friendly than Fidelityinvestments.com.

Digitization Many products traditionally thought of as physical have become, or are becoming, digital. Consumers do, or will, purchase the product less for its physical attributes than for the information it contains. A CD can be a product (a disk with a plastic box, cover, and sleeve information) but the music can be stored, transmitted, and played digitally; similarly for any "product" comprising words, numbers, pictures, or images, or video, for example, airline tickets, various financial services (brokerage, insurance, banking), books, and newspapers. The product implications for managers in such markets as entertainment, education, publishing, media, and art are profound. They have to rethink a range of issues, such as product design, branding, packaging, and intellectual property rights.

> **Example:** In 1999, Columbia Business School signed an agreement with Unext.com to offer certain MBA courses online. The school took an equity position in the venture and was later joined by Stanford, Chicago, Carnegie-Mellon, and the London School of Economics.[53]

Customization As noted earlier in this section, an advantage of service inseparability (simultaneous production and consumption) for services marketers has been the ability to customize offerings. Because of economies of scale provided by mass production, product marketers have generally not had this ability. However, the Internet, coupled with remarkable breakthroughs in flexible manufacturing technology, now enables customers to specify online exactly what they require. Essentially, customers are able to design their own products. This information is then downloaded to a manufacturing facility where the product is assembled. Dell's Internet model is a familiar and obvious example.[54] However, the Internet is also making it possible for smaller firms all over the world to achieve such customization.

> **Example:** GKN Sintered Metals in South Africa now uses its Web site to compete internationally in the sintered metal filters market by allowing customers to specify and design a sintered metal filter online.[55] Company software uses customer specifications to calculate the required surface area, thickness, and bead size for a specific filter. Design advice and support are available through e-mail, if required. GKN offers a price quote within a few hours of receiving the design, and anticipates that non-standard filters can be shipped within one week from the first inquiry, an important competitive advantage in a niche market.

Other examples of customization include Internet retailers like Amazon.com that use collaborative filtering to combine past customer buying history with representative survey data to make individual recommendations.

The Web and Pricing Strategy

One focus of this book is that marketing should attempt to increase the lifetime value of individual customers. By doing so, the firm increases its customer equity,[56] and maximizes the value of its customer base. A similar view is that marketing should move products and services away from the zone of commodities and towards the zone of seduction.[57]

Market forces, including competition and customer sophistication,[58] tend to work in the opposite direction. Customers become less loyal, more price sensitive and shop around. Also, essential product differences vanish leading to commoditization, and prices plunge. The forces that impel markets towards a preponderance of lower-value customers, and products and services towards commodities, occur naturally in most markets. However, they have been greatly enhanced by the growth of information technology.

Indeed the advent of the Web is already having unprecedented effects on pricing practices. For the adventurous, it opens a new world of opportunities; for the traditional, it brings overwhelming problems. For many customers, the Web will bring the freedom of the price-maker, rather than the previously entrenched servitude of the price-taker. In this section a variety of Internet pricing issues is addressed.

COMMODITIZATION AND EFFICIENT MARKETS The first goods to be bartered in electronic markets were commodities where price is the determining factor in a sale. When the commodity is perishable, such as airline seats, oranges, or electricity, the

Internet is even more compelling—suppliers must exhaust their inventory quickly, or lose the sale. However, the Internet is spawning several new technologies that greatly facilitate search.[59] As a result, commoditization can also occur with high-margin products, as even strong brand names may be insufficient to maintain premium prices. These technologies vary in terms of search effectiveness and what they achieve for the searcher. Some are well on the road to full development and implementation; others are still on drawing boards. These tools range from simple search facilitation through more advanced proactive search, to actual deal negotiation on the customer's behalf (Table 21.4).

These tools can reduce customer costs for finding potential suppliers as well as making product and price comparisons. The more sophisticated tools, such as true bots and intelligent agents, not only seek out the lowest prices, they even conduct price negotiations.

> **Example:** One of the more advanced systems, the R U Sure Shopping Agent, sits in the Windows system tray and is activated when a user visits a supported e-commerce site.[60] When the user drills down to a specific product, the agent pops onto the screen and queries 20 to 50 competitor vendor sites for the same product. R U Sure has no agreements with any vendors and site pages are not modified to accommodate the search agent. Rather, the agent is simply taught how to search each site. When the customized search is complete, the agent identifies the best price and provides a direct link to the competitor's product Web page. Categories for direct comparison will no doubt expand beyond books, toys, computer hardware, movies, and music.

CUSTOMERS MAKE, RATHER THAN TAKE, PRICES   In consumer markets, suppliers tend to make prices while customers take prices. A notable exception is auctions, but the proportion of consumer goods purchased in this way has always been small, and mainly devoted to used goods. The Internet has spawned hundreds of online auction sites where the opposite situation is occurring. Online auctions allow cybershoppers to bid not only on a vast range of products, but also for services such as airline tickets and hotel rooms. For example, the Onsale.com auction site runs seven live auctions per week where people outbid one another for computer gear and electronics equipment. Onsale buys surplus or distressed goods from companies at fire sale prices so they can weather low bids.[61] At a higher level of customer price making, Priceline.com invites customers to name their price on products and services including air tickets, hotel rooms, new cars, home mortgages, and grocery products.

In addition to these consumer focused markets, business-to-business (B2B) exchanges are fast proliferating where such diverse products as industrial chemicals, wholesale electricity, steel and metal products can be bought and sold.[62]

TABLE 21.4 Tools that Facilitate Customer Search on the Internet

Type of Tool	Functions	Examples
Search Engine	Searches by key word on the World Wide Web.	Alta Vista, Yahoo!, and hotbot
Comparison Site	Web site that enables comparisons of product/service category by attributes and price	Compare.Net (www.compare.net)
True Bot	Software that combs sites for prices each time a request is made	Bots used by search engines Lycos and Excite
Intelligent Agent	Software that will seek out prices and features, and negotiate on price for a purchase	Kasbah, a bot being developed by MIT

CUSTOMERS CONTROL TRANSACTIONS   By using a Web site to invite bids (a reverse auction), customers can take almost total control of the transaction. They make it extremely difficult for suppliers to compete on anything but price, since there is little opportunity to engage in tactical marketing actions such as product differentiation, personal selling, or adding service.

Example: Caterpillar made its first attempt at serious online purchasing on June 24, 1997 when it invited pre-approved suppliers to bid on a $2.4M order for hydraulic fittings. These fittings are simple plastic parts costing less than a dollar but can bring a $2 million bulldozer to a standstill when they fail. Twenty-three suppliers made bids via an online process at Caterpillar's Web site.[63] The initial morning bids were high, but by lunchtime nine firms were still revising offers. When the session closed at the end of the day, the low bid was 22 cents; the previous low price paid by Caterpillar was 30 cents. Caterpillar now attains a direct 6% average savings via its Web site supplier bidding system, in addition to considerable savings in negotiation time.

CROSS-SUBSIDIZATION   Several types of information products are characterized by their capability to secure revenue from two different markets. For example, print media typically secures revenue from readers for the product and from advertisers purchasing the eyes and brains of the readers. In some print media and in broadcast media, the basic product for readers/viewers/listeners is provided at zero price and revenue is earned solely from advertisers. Because the Internet functions both as a communications and selling/distribution medium, every commercial Web site has the potential for securing both types of revenue. In addition, Web sites can secure revenue by means such as memberships and selling customer information.[64] However, as with broadcast advertising, sites can decide to offer products free, or at least below cost, with the goal of securing revenue from advertisers on their high traffic sites. This sort of action adds further downward pressure on prices.

Example: Idealab's FreePC offered consumers personal computers in exchange for detailed personal information and a continuing marketing relationship.[65]

A logical extension of cross-subsidization is for the firm to set a negative price for one set of customers, in other words, pay them for being customers, then secure revenues from another group of customers.

Example: iwon.com is an Internet portal competing with Yahoo! and others. Whereas, in general, Internet portals are free to customers, iwon.com pays its customers in the form of a lottery. Each day it gives away a $10,000 prize; each month it gives away a $1 million prize; and it plans to give away a $10 million prize each year. The more an individual customer uses the iwon portal, the more entries he or she gets in the iwon sweepstakes. iwon earns its revenues from advertising.[66]

DIFFERENTIATED PRICING ALL THE TIME   The information age and the advent of computer-controlled machine tools enables consumers to have products customized inexpensively—what has been termed mass customization.[67] The Web is already an outstanding vehicle for mass customization of information products with personalized news services such as CNN and Pointcast, personalized search engines such as My Yahoo!, and the highly customized customer interaction pages of online stores such as Amazon.com. However, the Web also affords marketers the opportunity to exploit a phenomenon that service providers such as the airlines have long known: identical products and services can have different values to different customers, and hence allow different prices. For example, Friday afternoon airline seats are highly valuable to business travelers and this value is reflected in the price.

The Internet can allow the ultimate in price differentiation. By customizing both the product and the customer, prices may be so differentiated that no two customers pay the same price. Says Jerry Kaplan, founder of Onsale Inc., "The future of electronic commerce is an implicit one-to-one negotiation between buyer and seller . . . You will get an individual spot price on everything." As negotiation costs decrease, competitive bidding on a huge range of purchases becomes feasible, especially if computers bid one against each other on behalf of buyers and sellers.

OPTIMIZING PRICING BY CREATING CUSTOMER SWITCHING BARRIERS
Current technology enables sellers to collect detailed data such as customer buying habits, preferences, and even spending limits. As a result, products and prices can be better tailored to the individual buyer. Many customers like this individual recognition for it serves them better: book recommendations that match their preferences, advice on music that matches their likes, or job possibilities that match their skills. This personalization creates switching barriers for customers that competitors will find difficult to surmount by price alone. Although the customer may be able to purchase the product or service at a lower price on another Web site, if that site has not taken the time or effort to learn about the customer, it will not be able to serve the customer so well. Relatedly, Internet technology will allow for the pricing of information products by "bit," rather than for bundled information as a whole. For example, rather than setting prices for newspapers, journals, or encyclopedias, customers could be charged for those information items that they actually bring onto their screens.[68]

USE TECHNOLOGY TO DE-MENU PRICING   Most firms have menu or list pricing systems to simplify the many problems caused by attempting to keep transaction prices recorded and up-to-date. Without automation, the costs associated with changing prices, known as the "menu cost," can be significant. Because of the administrative complexity for firms with large product or service lines, it used to take months for price adjustments to filter down to distributors, retailers, and salespeople. This often led to sub-optimal pricing practices.

Whether through the Internet or extranets, network systems now make it possible to secure precise data on inventory, costs, and demand at any given moment, and to adjust prices instantly. Since menu cost and time are reduced to near zero, there is no longer any excuse for not changing prices when appropriate. However, Web merchants must be especially concerned about the accuracy of their prices since high traffic volume may lead to financial losses and other problems.

> **Example:** Buy.com began taking orders for a $588 Hitachi computer monitor, listed at $164 before discovering its mistake. It agreed to sell at $164 only what it had in stock and refused to honor other orders. This action brought on a class-action lawsuit.[69]

CUSTOMERS MAY BE WILLING TO PAY MORE THAN ORIGINALLY THOUGHT
Notwithstanding the drive to perfect markets and commoditization discussed earlier, customers will not always expect, or want, to pay less on the Web than they do in conventional channels because of the convenience and experience that web shopping offers. Indeed, managers in many industries have a long record of underestimating the value customers attach to a product or service, and therefore under-charging. This phenomenon has already been identified on the Web where some car buyers pay significantly more for used vehicles at online auctions than they would at their real-world equivalents.[70]

MAXIMIZE REVENUE, NOT PRICE   Many managers overlook a basic economic opportunity: it is often more profitable to maximize absolute revenue rather than unit price or profit margin. For example, airlines have perfected the practice of yield management.[71] These complicated pricing schemes defy customer comparison, but permit revenue maximization per flight. Many airlines now use Web sites to sell tickets on slow-to-fill or ready-to-leave flights by special purchase offers or via ticket auctions. The highly successful British Web site Lastminute.com gives marketers of such perishable offerings as theater and sports tickets, package holidays, hotel rooms, and airlines the opportunity to offload excess capacity at the last minute. Customers get great bargains, but must be flexible with regard to dates and times. Firms can maximize revenue by selling capacity that would otherwise have perished. Information technology permits the automation of such systems at relatively low cost.

The Web and Distribution Strategy

The growth of the Internet is leading to major changes in distribution. As Figure 21.1 makes clear, developments in both disintermediation and reintermediation are occurring.[72] As far as disintermediation is concerned, the information revolution has enabled manufacturers and wholesale/distributors to address consumers and end use customers directly, thus cutting out those in between, for example, travel agents and booksellers. However, Internet portals that act as shopping malls add value by bringing together many buyers.

One way of assessing the impact of the Web on distribution strategy is to consider its effects on the functions of distribution.[73] This permits the construction of the Internet Distribution Matrix, formed by combining technology impact and distribution functions that, in turn, allows for the identification of the opportunities and threats that the Web presents for distribution.

IMPACT OF TECHNOLOGY ON DISTRIBUTION   Three major effects of information technology on distribution can be identified: kill distance, homogenize time, and make location irrelevant.

The Death of Distance   Cairncross contends that "distance will no longer determine the cost of communicating electronically."[74] For the distribution of any product that can be digitized, such as pictures, video, sound, and words, distance will have no effect on costs. The same is true for many other services.

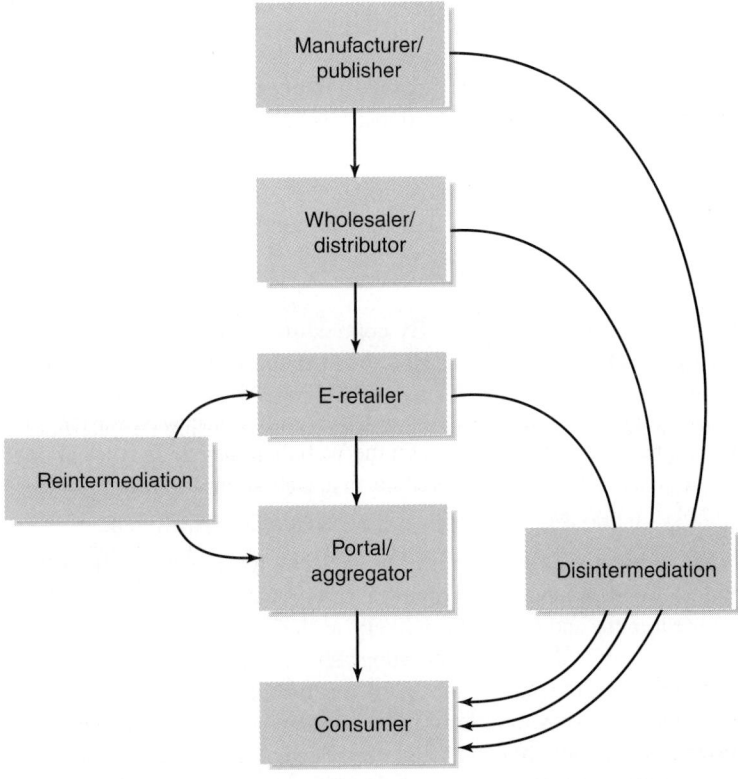

FIGURE 21.1

Rebuilding the Value Chain in Distribution

The Homogenization of Time In physical markets, time and season are critical trading variables as well as distribution variables. By contrast, the virtual marketplace is atemporal: a Web site is always open. The seller need not be awake to serve the buyer; the buyer need not be awake, or even physically present, to be served by the seller. Since the Internet is independent of time of day or season, time is homogenized—made uniformly consistent for all buyers and all sellers.[75]

The Irrelevance of Location No longer will location be key to most business decisions; the real to virtual shift is from marketplace to marketspace.[76] For example, from a marketing perspective, the location of a conventional bookstore is a critical matter (convenient location, high traffic, and pleasant surroundings). By contrast, Amazon.com's location is irrelevant, at least from a marketing perspective. It does not need to be near to its customers, and traffic and surroundings are irrelevant attributes.[77] Technology is creating many marketspace firms. Some cynics have observed that three new rules of retailing are developing—location is irrelevant, irrelevant, irrelevant.[78]

FUNCTIONS OF DISTRIBUTION Chapter 16 identified several functions of distribution—transfer of title, promotion, information provision, physical movement, inventory, finance, service, quality assurance, assorting, bulk breaking, risk, and impartiality. To illustrate the technology/functions matrix, these functions are combined to focus on three areas of distribution:

Assorting and Bulk Breaking Intermediaries support economies of scope by adjusting assortment discrepancies. Producers supply large quantities of a relatively small assortment of products/services; customers require relatively small quantities of a large assortment of products/services. Assorting and bulk breaking are critical distribution functions.

Promotion and Information Provision Different members of the system can contribute sales, advertising, public relations, and publicity efforts to enhance product movement through the channel. Various types of information, in addition to promotion, flow back and forth among channel entities. These range from data about the customer marketplace, including customer requirements and competitor activities, to operational information concerning the availability and physical location of goods, inventory levels, change in title, state of financing arrangements, and so forth.

Service Customers often require various types of service and support: pre-sale (product inspection and information about the product and its use), and post-sale (installation, repair, maintenance, warranty). In addition, various managerial and consulting services may be required.

THE INTERNET DISTRIBUTION MATRIX By contrasting the three effects of technology (vertical) with three basic functions of distribution channels (horizontal), the three-by-three Internet Distribution Matrix can be constructed (Figure 21.2).[79] This matrix can be a powerful tool for managers wanting to identify opportunities for using the Internet to improve or modify distribution strategy. It can also assist in the identification of competitive threats by enabling managers to concentrate on areas where others might use technology to perform distribution functions more effectively. Two examples are offered:

A. **The irrelevance of location/assorting and bulk breaking**. Location is typically a key element in the development of distribution systems. A major distributor function is to break bulk and offer fast delivery to the customer. Traditionally it was easier for customers to deal with local suppliers especially if lengthy face-to-face negotiations over price, quality, and specification issues were required. The Internet has shattered these assumptions and many major firms are now making major purchases through their Web sites and newly developing auction systems.

B. **The homogenization of time/promotion and information provision.** In many distribution systems, promotional activities occur sporadically. Information moves back and forth among channel members often with transmission delays and inaccuracies due to "handling" by multiple parties. These problems are exacerbated when buyer and seller operate in different time zones or at different hours of the day or week. With the Internet, these problems vanish as information can be accessed at any time.[80]

Employee recruitment, where companies search for employees and individuals search for jobs, presents a good example of these issues. In many cases, both parties rely on recruitment agencies to enter the channel as intermediaries, both to simplify the search process and to manage their time (such as when it suits the employer to interview, and the employee to be interviewed). However, the traditional recruitment agency has considerable difficulty keeping up to date with posting new jobs, removing filled jobs and, providing accurate information about available positions.

A number of enterprising recruitment sites have been set up on the Web. Among the best rated is Monster Board. It lists around 50,000 jobs from over 4,000 companies, including several blue chip employers. Job seekers are provided customized e-mail updates and potential employers can access personnel details and even resumes of suitable candidates online, anytime.

The recruitment market also provides excellent examples of "getting it wrong" and "getting it right" on the Web as a distribution medium.

Example: For many years, the *Times Higher Education Supplement* has offered the greatest selection of higher education positions in Britain and the Commonwealth. Almost all senior, and many lower level, positions in universities and tertiary institutions are advertised in the *Times Higher*. In 1996, the *Times Higher* set up a Web site where job seekers could conveniently browse through all available positions. Shortly afterwards, the *Times Higher* Web site began requiring registration and subscription, perhaps in an attempt to shore up revenues affected by circulation declines.[81]

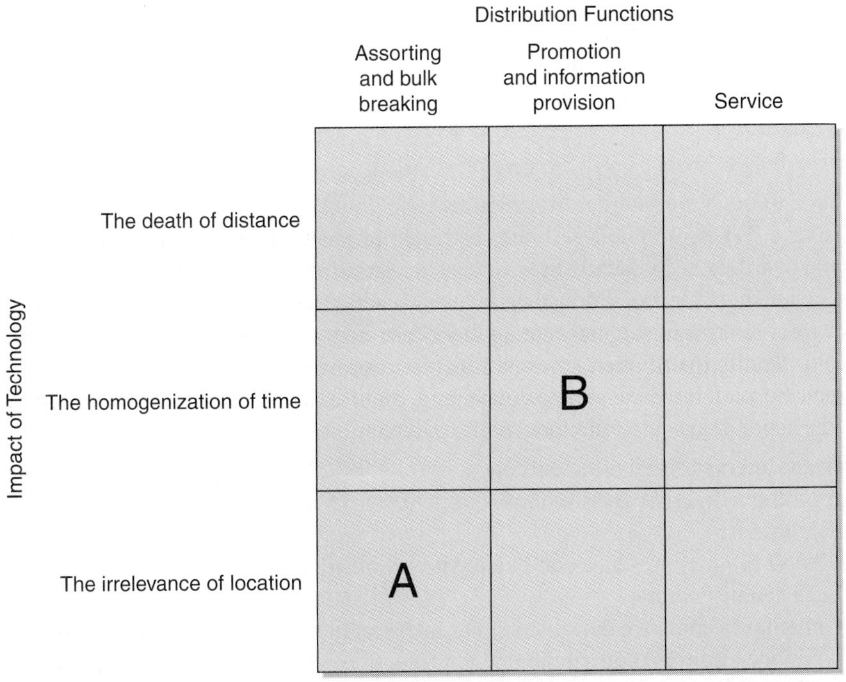

FIGURE 21.2

The Internet Distribution Matrix—Technology Impact/Distribution Functions

About the same time that the *Times Higher* was attempting to charge surfers, a university consortium set up its own Web site to which all available positions were posted. The job seeker could specify and search by criteria, and link directly to the home pages of prospective employer institutions for further information.

Where the *Times Higher* is a profit-making enterprise, the consortium site does not have to make a profit. The site reduces costs for institutions seeking employees by providing a site where job seekers come to look for positions.

COMBINING TRADITIONAL AND INTERNET DISTRIBUTION   In addition to developing alternative distribution models, Internet-based distribution systems can be combined with existing methods to produce synergy in much the same way that the Internet as a communications medium interacts with other communications media.

Example: Where many retailers are nervously watching the advance of the Internet and struggling with how to respond, The Gap, with 2600 retail stores in North America, has embraced this new technology. The Gap's Web site offers the same selection as in its stores plus additional items, and customers can return any item purchased online to a Gap store, just as with store-purchased merchandise. The Gap has also placed Web lounges in increasing numbers of retail stores for customer convenience. In addition, it offers 10% off and free shipping on customers' first online purchases, thereby developing an e-mail customer base.

Other traditional retailers have developed relationships with Internet firms in attempts to drive customers to their online stores:

Example: AOL and Wal-mart have an agreement to offer low-cost software that will provide Wal-mart customers with easy access to the Web via a joint Web site. K-Mart and Yahoo! have agreed to create a co-branded Web shopping site with Internet access.[82]

Finally, many Internet retailers are developing affiliate programs as a means of driving customers to their sites. Affiliate programs require the affiliate to include, on their site, a link to the retailer's site. In return, the affiliate earns a commission. For example, Amazon.com, which has many thousands of affiliates, might be linked to the sites operated by book clubs.[83]

DISTRIBUTION CHANNEL CONFLICT   Perhaps the most serious issue regarding distribution through the Internet for suppliers is potential conflict with traditional distribution channels. When suppliers sell and distribute products directly through the Internet, traditional distributors frequently believe they are losing sales! To a significant extent, supplier behavior should be conditioned on industry practice. For example, if sales through the Internet are widespread, suppliers can probably use Internet distribution aggressively with little fear of retaliation. Current examples include air travel and personal computers.

Conversely, if Internet sales are low and traditional distributors have significant power, the supplier has to tread more carefully. Among its options are:

- Avoid Internet distribution entirely;
- Aggressive Internet distribution—this action risks retaliation from traditional distributors;
- Modest Internet presence combined with actions to mollify traditional distributors. Such actions include:
  - attempt to convince distributors that Internet sales will not harm their business;
  - provide traditional distributors with promotion and advertising allowances (*Compaq*);
  - provide site visitors with information on convenient retail locations (*Nike*);
  - offer traditional distributors exclusive access to new products (*Nike*);
- Develop new brands solely for Internet distribution (*Procter & Gamble*—Reflect.com).

In any event, as sales through the Internet increase, firms must seriously address these issues and make difficult distribution decisions.

The Web and Marketing Communications

Marketers use various communication tools at different stages in the buying process.[84] For example, generating awareness of a new product is often achieved most effectively through broadcast advertising. Conversely, closing the sale of a complex system is best achieved face-to-face by personal selling. Although Web sites can act simply as a mass communications medium (brochureware), the Web's potential only starts to be tapped when it is used as quasi-personal communication—a mix between personal selling (engage a visitor in a dialogue) and advertising (generating awareness, explaining/demonstrating products, and providing information without interactive involvement).[85] In this mode, Web sites differ substantively from broadcast and print media as they offer customers an experience when they self-generate particular communications. Some organizations offer information value as a means to bring customers to their Web sites.

> **Example:** Infonautics offers a variety of online information and research services. To grow traffic for its Electric Library, it licensed the text of an encyclopedia then put encyclopedia.com on the Web as a free site. Many surfers who reach this site click through to the Electric Library site and become paying subscribers.

Web sites can play a cost-effective role in the communications mix. Early in the buying process they enable need recognition, development of product specifications, and supplier search. However, they can also be potent as the buying process progresses toward evaluation and choice. Sites can also be cost-effective in providing feedback on product/service performance.

Thus from a communications perspective, Web sites can be viewed as complementary to direct selling activity by industrial marketers, and as supplementary to print and broadcast advertising by consumer marketers. Some sales forces encourage customers to conduct routine tasks, such as securing information and placing orders on the Internet, freeing up time for salespeople to sell to and service customers.[86]

Although the firm's Web site may be easily identified via search engines, it can be necessary to advertise via banner advertisements on other Web sites. Banners are typically small rectangular ads that can be clicked on to access the advertiser's Web site. Alternatively, conventional communication vehicles, such as broadcast and print media, outdoor packaging, or retail store displays can be used to secure visitors.

Because site development is in its infancy, many organizations (and individuals) have yet to define communication objectives for their Web sites, let alone quantify them. Unlike broadcast advertising expenditures, or the long-term financial commitment to a sales force, establishing a simple Web site is a relatively inexpensive venture that may be developed, withdrawn, or changed with little effort. The lack of clear, quantified communication objectives, and the absence of a unified framework for performance evaluation, have compelled decision makers to rely on intuition, imitation, and advertising experience when conceptualizing, developing, designing, and implementing Web sites. Whereas Web sites are sometimes viewed as a replacement for other forms of communication such as telephone operators or on-the-road salespeople, integration of Web sites with other communication forms may be on the horizon.

> **Example:** Lands' End is exploring the potential for linking its Web site and telephone call center. In the future a telephone operator may offer advice as the consumer explores the Web site and even take control of the search process to aid the consumer.[87]

Notwithstanding the primitive state of effectiveness measures, Web site communication performance can be directly assessed using multiple indices. As a result, differing Web site objectives can be directly translated into appropriate performance measures (Figure 21.3).[88]

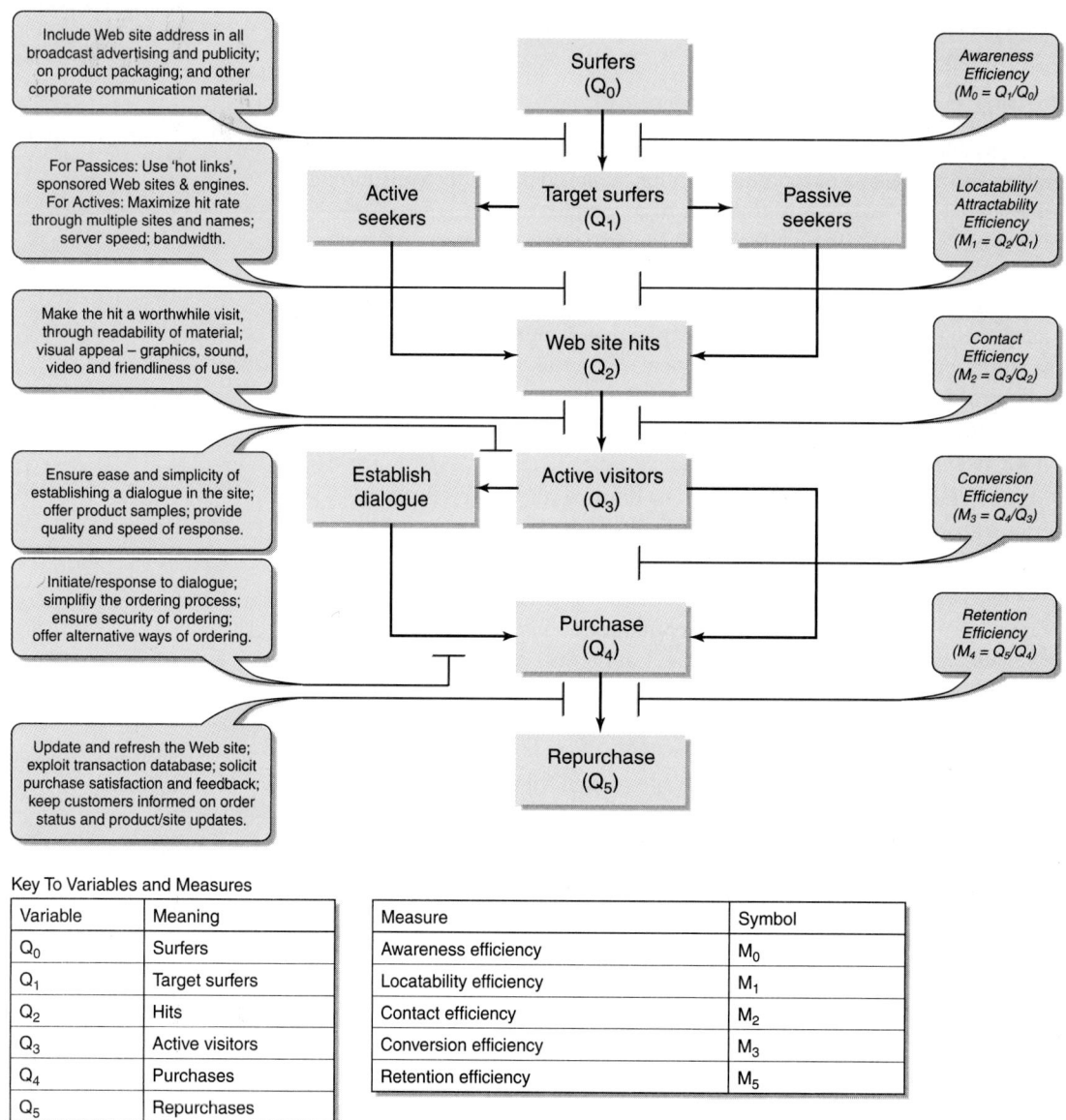

Key To Variables and Measures

Variable	Meaning
Q_0	Surfers
Q_1	Target surfers
Q_2	Hits
Q_3	Active visitors
Q_4	Purchases
Q_5	Repurchases

Measure	Symbol
Awareness efficiency	M_0
Locatability efficiency	M_1
Contact efficiency	M_2
Conversion efficiency	M_3
Retention efficiency	M_5

FIGURE 21.3

A Conversion Process and Measurement System for Web site Communication Performance

Performance measures should be linked to tactical marketing variables under the firm's control. The marketer can then relate the most likely objectives of Web site establishment to measures of performance associated with Web site traffic flow. These tactical marketing communication variables are tied to five performance measures that marketers can use to measure the communications effectiveness and performance against objectives of a Web site.

SUMMARY

This chapter considered the emergence of knowledge-rich environments and their profound implications for marketing. It explored the forces behind the rapid emergence of the Internet and the associated implications for marketing and the management process. It

TABLE 21.5 Success and Failure Issues in the New Economy

Issue	"Old Economy" Firms	"New Economy" Firms
Cannibalization	Frequently a serious concern	No problem
Channel conflict	Often considerable	No problem
Ability to finance expansions	No special advantage	High market capitalizations may make raising capital easier and cheaper
Ability to secure talented human resources	No special advantage	Stock options for talented employees have enormous value because of high market capitalizations
Physical distribution	Systems in place but not designed for e-commerce, for example, stores in high rent districts versus very large scale industrial sites	No physical plant to start, but ability to design for specific requirements
Consumer information	Aggregate in nature	Based on individual consumers
First-mover advantages	Generally not first	Often first and able to secure advantages
Profitability	Generally profitable	Generally unprofitable

examined how the Internet challenges several traditional assumptions upon which the practice of marketing is based and explored how cyberspace changes the conception of the elements of the marketing mix.

A critical issue concerns the nature of the organizations that are going to be successful in this new world. Will existing "old economy" firms be able to make the transition, or will the winners be "new economy" firms such as amazon.com? Clearly it is too early to say, but Table 21.5 highlights some of the difficult issues that "old economy" firms must confront.[89]

THE CHANGING VIEW

Old Way	New Way
Administration	Negotiation
Vertical structures	Networks
Inefficient markets	Efficient markets
Geographic location often key	Geographic location often irrelevant
Traditional competencies sufficed	New competencies mandatory
Competitive set easier to define	Competitive set extremely difficult to define, may become unstable
Order and hierarchy	Anarchistic and amorphous
Supplier-driven mix	Customer-driven mix
Customers patient	Customers want it now
Passive consumers	Active, interactive consumers
Profit based	Market share driven
Decreasing returns	Increasing returns
Richness/reach trade-off	One-to-one
Products/services	Cyberservices/experiences

QUESTIONS FOR STUDY AND DISCUSSION

1. Select a corporation with which you are familiar. Complete the following matrix focusing special attention on the Implications column:

Force	Nature	Effect	Implications
Moore's Law	Microprocessor speed doubles every 18–24 months	Processing cost reduced by half every 18–24 months	
Metcalfe's Law			
Coasian Economics			
Flock of Birds Phenomenon			
Fish Tank Phenomenon			

2. Which of the Internet businesses that today command high market values will still be in existence in five years? Explain your response.

3. "All that Internet businesses are doing is stealing volume from existing sellers." Do you agree or disagree? Why?

4. Since the rules for electronic commerce success are new and different, no conventional retail merchant will develop a successful Internet business. Do you agree or disagree? Why?

5. The Web is an overrated, overhyped phenomenon. Discuss

6. "Buyer-sponsored Web bidding sites will render marketing superfluous." Discuss.

7. "The Web reduces opportunities to create and communicate differential advantages." Do you agree or disagree? Why?

8. "The Web is the most powerful tool yet for relationship marketing." Discuss.

9. "The Internet will render traditional market segmentation obsolete." Do you agree with this statement? Why or why not?

10. It has been argued that by improving market efficiency, the Web will drive down retail margins, leading to large-scale attrition among both traditional and Web-based retailers. What is your opinion of this scenario?

11. How do you believe the role of intermediaries will be affected by the evolution of the Internet economy?

12. The addressibility of the Internet era will eliminate the distinction between marketing and sales. Discuss.

13. Figure 21.1 suggests that in the information economy, many changes are likely, not only in marketing, but also in the way firms are managed. Do you believe that the tasks and principles of marketing will be affected by these changes?

14. Your text alleged that the effect of the Internet and associated search engines might be to reduce brand value. Why might this occur?

15. Compare your Web-purchasing experience with that of your colleagues. Choose a set of criteria and contrast with traditional purchasing. (Hint: You may want to consider factors such as search time, price paid, convenience of payment system, privacy protection, and delivery delay.)

ENDNOTES

1. This chapter was initially drafted by Professors Pierre Berthon, School of Management, University of Bath, Bath, Great Britain and Leyland F. Pitt, Curtin University of Technology, Perth, Australia. It draws upon the ideas further developed in R. Watson, P. Berthon, L. Pitt, and G. Zinkhan, *Electronic Commerce: The Strategic Perspective*, New York: Dryden, 1999. See also the related Web site: www.terry.uga.edu/~rwatson/estrategy.

2. "The Internet Age," *Business Week*, October 4, 1999.

3. The Internet is a network of computers that span the globe; the World Wide Web is a set of rules governing the library of text, picture, sound, or video files stored on computers that make up the Internet. Related technologies are intranets—internal organizational communication systems, and extranets—private networks linking the firm with suppliers and customers.

4. An important issue for traditional firms venturing into electronic commerce is how to structure their Web-based businesses. Because of internal political issues that may delay or otherwise hamper response to market imperatives, some observers recommend setting up Web businesses as independent entities with total freedom to attack the firm's traditional business. See, for example, C. Christensen, *Business Week*, June 28, 1999.

5. "Survey on Information Technology," *Financial Times*, September 1, 1999.

6. J.F. Rayport and J.J. Sviokla, "Managing in the Marketspace," *Harvard Business Review*, 72 (Nov./Dec. 1994), pp. 141–150.

7. M. Bracken, "Advertising on the Web," *Internet Magazine*, (September 1997), pp. 122–126.

8. See S.M. Davis, *Future Perfect*. Reading, MA: Addison-Wesley, 1987.

9. See R.S. Achrol, "Evolution of the Marketing Organization: New Forms for Turbulent Environments," *Journal of Marketing*, 55 (Oct. 1991), pp. 77–93.

10. P. Drucker, "The New Society of Organizations," *Harvard Business Review*, 70 (Sept./Oct. 1992), pp. 95–104, S. Davis and J. Botkin, "The Coming of Knowledge-Based Business," *Harvard Business Review*, 72 (Sept./Oct. 1994) pp. 165–170 and W.C. Kim and R.A. Mauborgne "Fair Process: Managing in the Knowledge Economy," *Harvard Business Review*, 75 (July/Aug. 1997) pp. 65–75. Note, also, that in 1998 the ratio of oil and gas consumption to Gross Domestic Product in the United States was half the 1973 level (just before the first OPEC-induced oil shock), despite the fact that the inflation adjusted price of oil has changed very little. *Business Week*, Oct. 11, 1999.

11. "The Internet Economy: The World's Next Growth Engine," *Business Week*, Oct. 4, 1999; see also A.M. Webber, "What's So New About the Economy?" *Harvard Business Review*, 71 (Jan./Feb. 1993), pp. 24–52.

12. Of course, use of customer information raises important privacy issues.

13. P. Evans and T. Worster, "Strategy and the New Economy of Information." *Harvard Business Review*, 75 (Sept./Oct. 1997), pp. 71–82.

14. Note that the latter perspective positions the Internet as a disruptive technology in Christensen's terms (see Chapter 13).

15. The development of procedures by Napster and others to exchange MP3 files freely among users has the potential to severely undermine artist compensation.

16. Notwithstanding the opportunities for electronic commerce, serious operational issues must be addressed. First, sufficient access capacity must be available so that wait times for customers are minimized. Second, logistic systems must be prepared to deal with customer orders. As with all service businesses, peak times produce the biggest problems.

17. L. Downes and C. Mui, *Unleashing the Killer App*, Boston, MA: Harvard Business School Press, 1998.

18. *Business Week*, October 4, 1999, p. 72.

19. During the 1980s, Mike Porter's so-called "five forces" model was widely used as a tool of strategic analysis. See M.E. Porter, "How Competitive Forces Shape Strategy," *Harvard Business Review*, 57 (Mar./Apr. 1979), pp. 137–145, and *Competitive Strategy: Techniques for Analyzing Industries and Competitors*, New York: The Free Press, 1980. Practitioners, consultants and academics embraced the model for the insight it brought to the relationship between firms, their suppliers, customers, and competitors, direct and indirect. However, such structures have become increasingly suspect under the onslaught of technology, deregulation, and entrepreneurial activity. The blurring of "industry" boundaries is reflected in terms such as edutainment, nutraceuticals, and cosmeceuticals, as well as some of the imaginative re-positionings discussed elsewhere in the text.

20. E. Beinhocker, "Strategy in Chaos," *McKinsky Quarterly*, (1997), pp. 24–39.

21. K. Kelly, *New Rules for the New Economy: 10 Radical Strategies for a Connected World*, New York: Viking Press, 1998.

22. R.H. Coase, "The Nature of the Firm," *Economica*, 4 (1937), pp. 386–405.

23. See Chapter 6.

24. See "Increasing R&D Expenditures Drive Opportunities for Contract Research Organizations," Frost and Sullivan Report #5865-52, August 1999.

25. *The Wall Street Journal*, December 31, 1999, p. 36.

26. For example, "The Accidental Superhighway," *The Economist*, July 1, 1995.

27. "Apple Reverses a Move to Raise Some Prices," *The New York Times*, October 16, 1999.

28. "The Accidental Superhighway," *op. cit.*

29. Dis-intermediation refers to the eclipse of organizations that play an intermediary role, such as distributors; re-intermediation refers to the introduction of intermediaries into buyer/seller relationships.

30. See T.L. Friedman, "Amazon.you." *The New York Times*, February 26, 1999.

31. See *Business 2.0* for a ranking of companies taking the best advantage of electronic commerce opportunities.

32. For an excellent survey on electronic commerce, see "A Survey of E-Commerce," *The Economist*, February 26, 2000.

33. cf. K. Kelley, *op. cit.* Downes and Mui, *op. cit.*; C. Shapiro and H.R. Varian, *Information Rules: A Strategic Guide to the Network Economy*, Boston, MA: Harvard Business School Press, 1998; E. Schwartz in L. Marino (ed.), *Digital Darwinism: Seven Breakthrough Business Strategies for Surviving in the Cutthroat Web Economy*, New York: Broadway Books, 1999; C. Christensen, *The Innovator's Dilemma: When New Technologies Cause Great Firms to Fail*, Boston, MA: Harvard Business School Press, 1997.

34. C.K. Prahalad and V. Ramaswamy, "Co-opting Customer Competence," *Harvard Business Review*, 78 (Jan./Feb. 2000), pp. 79–87. Our colleague Rashi Glazer has coined what he terms the new 4 Cs of marketing—communication (dialogues with customers), customization (tailoring to customers' specific needs), collaboration (customer participation), and clairvoyance (anticipating customer needs).

35. *Fortune*, November 1, 1999.

36. Goldman Sachs, reported in *Business Week*, January 17, 2000.

37. *Business Week*, February 28, 2000.

38. B.J. Pine II and J.H. Gilmore, "Welcome to the Experience Economy," *Harvard Business Review*, 76 (Jul./Aug. 1998), pp. 97–105.

39. Director's commentary on the DVD version of *You've Got Mail*, Warner Brothers, 1998.

40. R. Oldenburg, *The Great Good Place: Cafes, Coffee Shops, Bookstores, Bars, Hair Salons and Other Hangouts at the Heart of a Community*, New York: Marlowe and Co., 1999. Oldenburg's theory is that we all need a "third place"—our homes are the first, and our places of work the second. Other frequented places become, for many, that "third place" of socialization—local pubs in England, tavernas in Greece, and sidewalk cafes in France. We might speculate that for many, the Internet is becoming that "third place," albeit a virtual place.

41. B.J. Pine II and J.H. Gilmore, *The Experience Economy*, Boston, MA: Harvard Business School Press, 1999. See also the discussion on Schmitt's work in Chapter 4.

42. L. Pitt, P. Berthon, and R. Watson, "Just When You Thought Service Marketing Was More Difficult: Cyberservice!" *Business Horizons*, 42 (Jan./Feb. 1999), pp. 11–18.

43. Because of the speed and breadth of changes, sections of this chapter may be outdated by the time you read them. Our apologies.

44. M. Walsh, "The Air Bill Joins the 8-track," *Internet World* 8 (1997), pp. 43–44.

45. Of course, the problem with such procedures is that non-auction sales may drop as customers become aware of the possibility of securing very low prices at the auction.

46. See P.R. Berthon, J. Hulbert, and L.F. Pitt, "Brand Management Prognostications," *Sloan Management Review*, 40 (Winter 1999), pp. 53–65.

47. See V. Houlder, "Fingers That Shop Around," *Financial Times*, September 24, 1996.

48. See T. Levitt, "Marketing Success Through Differentiation of Anything," *Harvard Business Review*, 58 (Jan./Feb. 1980), pp. 83–91.

49. See P. Milgrom and J. Roberts, *Economics, Organization and Management*, Englewood Cliffs, NJ: Prentice-Hall, 1992, pp. 76–77, for a classic economic perspective on this argument.

50. The next section of the chapter, The Web and pricing strategy, explains the role of "bots."

51. Reflect.com was inaugurated as a San Francisco-based, 15-employee Internet start-up, 65% owned by P&G. Initial employees received stock options, but cannot return to P&G.

52. *Business 2.0*, May 1999, p. 90.

53. See "Schools Drawn into New Webs," *Financial Times*, October 11, 1999.

54. J. Magretta, "The Power of Virtual Integration: An Interview with Dell Computer's Michael Dell," *Harvard Business Review*, 76 (Mar./Apr. 1998), pp. 73–84.

55. E. Aggenbach, *Selling Sintered Filters on the Internet*, Case Study of the Graduate School of Business, University of Cape Town, Cape Town South Africa: University of Cape Town, 1999.

56. See R.C. Blattberg and J. Deighton. "Manage Marketing by the Customer Equity Test," *Harvard Business Review*, 74 (Jul./Aug. 1996), pp. 136–144.

57. J. Deighton and K. Grayson, "Marketing and Seduction: Building Exchange Relationships by Managing Social Consensus," *Journal of Consumer Research* 21 (1995), pp. 660–676.

58. See P.R. Dickson, "Toward a General Theory of Competitive Rationality," *Journal of Marketing*, 56 (Jan. 1992), pp. 69–83.

59. J.Y. Bakos, "Reducing Buyer Search Costs: Implications for Electronic Marketplaces," *Management Science* 43 (1997), pp. 1676–1692.

60. D.I. Hopper (CNN Interactive Technology Editor), "Desktops now have power to comparison-shop," CNN Web site (www.cnn.com), October 18, 1999.

61. Onsale offers two auction formats: English—highest bidder wins available inventory at their actual bid price, and Dutch—highest bidder wins available inventory at lowest successful bidder's price.

62. See A.B. Sculley and W.W.A. Woods, *B2B Exchanges: The Killer Application in the Business-to-Business Internet Revolution*, United States: ISI*publications*, 1999. These authors identify four different trading mechanisms—fixed pricing, one-on-one negotiation, auctions, and electronic auto-execution systems as in some financial markets. Auctions may be either seller-driven or buyer-driven (reverse auctions).

63. S. Woolley, "Industrial Buyers Are Getting More Mileage out of On-Line Comparison Shopping than Individuals Are. Why? E-Muscle," *Forbes*, March 9, 1998.

64. Many Internet users are sensitive to the collection of customer data online. For example, RealNetworks was widely condemned for surreptitiously collecting data with its RealJukebox software—number of songs on the user's hard drive, which music formats, quality level of recordings, user's preferred music genre, and type of connected portable music players, if any—even though it claimed this information was not for sale, *The New York Times*, November 1, 1999. The following day, RealNetworks released a patch to its Web site to prevent ths data from being collected, *The New York Times*, November 2, 1999.

65. J. Rayport, "The Truth about Internet Business Models," *Strategy and Business*, (Q3 1999), pp. 5–7.

66. After six months in operation, iwon.com, receiving 11 million visitors per month, was the 25th most visited Web site. Other sites offering prizes in excess of $1 million were freelotto.com, extremelotto.com, and webmillion.com.

67. See Chapter 12 and B.J. Pine II, B. Victor and A. Boynton, "Making Mass Customization Work," *Harvard Business Review*, 71 (Sept./Oct. 1993), pp. 108–119.

68. We are indebted to Tom Nagle for this insight.

69. *The New York Times*, December 13, 1999.

70. P. McKeown, R.T. Watson, and G. Zinkhan, *Electronic Commerce and Pricing: The Case of Mannheim Online*, Working Paper, Terry College of Business, University of Georgia, 1998.

71. See R. Desiraju and S.M. Shugan, "Strategic Service Pricing and Yield Management," *Journal of Marketing* 63 (1999), pp. 44–56.

72. *The Economist, op. cit.*

73. For more in-depth coverage, see L. Pitt, P. Berthon, and J.P. Berthon, "Changing Channels: The Impact of the Internet on Distribution Strategy," *Business Horizons.* 42 (Mar./Apr. 1999), pp. 19–28.

74. F. Cairncross, *The Death of Distance: How the Communications Revolution Will Change Our Lives*, London: Orion Business Books, 1997.

75. This notion is akin to what McKenna called "real time" ". . . our sense of ultra-compressed time and fore-shortened horizons . . . (that) occurs when time and distance vanish, when action and response are simultaneous." R. McKenna, *Real Time: Preparing for the Age of the Never Satisfied Customer*, Boston, MA: Harvard Business School Press, 1997, pp. 4–5.

76. J.F. Rayport and J.J. Sviokla, *op. cit.*

77. Its location in Seattle, WA is not incidental, however. Seattle offers the programming skills a computer-intensive firm like Amazon.com requires (Microsoft is located there, too); the state does not levy a sales tax on books; and Ingrams, the world's largest book distributor, is only a short distance away. Other considerations for location in international business concern tariffs and local content rules.

78. In business-to-business marketing, although many elements of the supplier/customer relationship can be conducted via the Internet, physical presence of plant, inventory, and people continues to play a very important role.

79. See Pitt, Berthon, and Berthon, *op. cit.* for a similar matrix based on an alternative framework of distribution functions.

80. In a similar fashion, intranets allow salespeople to conduct activities such as checking order status and verifying price information.

81. Knowing what to charge for, and how, are issues with which most managers contemplating Web business are struggling. Surfers, perhaps conditioned to the fact that most Internet content is free, seem unwilling to pay unless the benefits are real, tangible, immediate, and direct. E.I. Schwartz, *Webonomics : Nine Essential Principles for Growing Your Business on the World Wide Web*, New York: Broadway Books, pp. 36–39.

82. *The New York Times*, December 17, 1999.

83. In late 1999, Forrester Research Inc. reported that online merchants rated affiliate programs behind e-mail, but ahead of offline advertising, sponsorships, portal deals and banner advertising as an effective marketing technique.

84. For an overview of advertising on the Internet see, "Note on Marketing and the World Wide Web," Boston, MA: Harvard Business School, 9-597-037, 1999.

85. See Chapter 14. Web sites can also be used as a promotional vehicle by offering free samples, discounts, and competitions.

86. Shifting salesperson responsibilities may lead to changes in other sales force fundamentals, such as compensation systems.

87. *The Economist, op. cit.*

88. P.R. Berthon, L.F. Pitt, and R.T. Watson, "The World Wide Web as an Advertising Medium: Towards an Understanding of Conversion Efficiency," *Journal of Advertising Research*, 36 (Jan./Feb. 1996), pp. 43–53.

89. Developed from *The Economist, op. cit.*

90. This list first appeared in *Fortune*, November 8, 1999.

91. This list first appeared in *Fortune*, July 5, 1999.

92. This list first appeared in *Fortune*, July 5, 1999.

93. Developed by Larry Chase, April 2000: http://LarryChase.com.

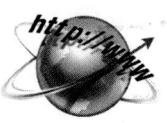

Amazon.com	www.amazon.com
America Online	www.aol.com
Babycenter.com	www.babycenter.com
British Royal Automobile Club	www.rac.co.uk
Car Point	www.carpoint.com
Commerce One	www.commerceone.com
Disney	www.disney.com
Federal Express	www.fedex.com
Firefly	www.microsoft.com
General Motors	www.gm.com
GetMedia	www.GetMedia.com
Harvard Business Review	www.hbsp.harvard.edu
Idealab	www.icp.com
Infonautics	www.infonautics.com
Ivillage	www.ivillage.com
Iwon.com	www.iwon.com
Lastminute.com	www.lastminute.com
Lifeminders.com	www.lifeminders.com
Monster Board	www.monster.com
MP3	www.MP3.com
Napster.com	www.napster.com
onsale.com	www.onsale.com
Reflect.com	www.reflect.com
Security First Network Bank	www.sfnb.com
South African Airways	www.saa.co.za
Teletech	www.teletech.com
The Gap	www.gap.com
Times Higher Education Supplement	www.THES.co.uk
Unext.com	www.unext.com
United Airlines	www.ual.com

CHAPTER 21 APPENDIX: SELECTED USEFUL INTERNET INFORMATION AND ADDRESSES

Companies that "Get It"

Petco	www.petco.com
Soutwest Airlines	www.southwest.com
Lands' End	www.landsend.com
Charles Schwab	www.schwab.com
Bertelsmann	www.bertelsmann.com
Grainger.com	www.grainger.com
ticketmaster.com	www.ticketmaster.com
Office Depot	www.officedepot.com
Fingerhut	www.fingerhut.com
United States Postal Service	www.usps.com[90]

Top 10 Job Sites

Monster Board	www.monster.com
CareerPath	www.careerpath.com
CareerMosaic	www.careermosaic.com
America's Job Bank	www.jobsearch.org
Headhunter.net	www.headhunter.net
Nationjob Network	www.nationjob.com
Hotjobs.com	www.hotjobs.com
Net-temps	www.net-temps.com
dice.com	www.dice.com
careerbuilder	www.careerbuilder.com[91]

Cool Companies 1999 (hottest tech outfits)

thirdvoice	www.thirdvoice.com
Intertrust Technologies	www.intertrust.com
Sequence Design	www.frequency.com
Financial Engines	www.financialengines.com
myCFO	www.mycfo.com
boo.com	www.boo.com
VA Linux Systems	www.valinux.com
Bidcom	www.bidcom.com
Homegrocer	www.homegrocer.com
InfoRay	www.inforay.com
Sycamore Networks	www.sycamorenet.com
Rhythms	www.rhythms.com[92]

Best Sites Web Digest For Marketers

E-COMMERCE

Circuit City	www.circuitcity.com
Kozmo.com	www.kozmo.com
BarPoint.com	www.barpoint.com
mySimon PocketShopper	www.mysimon.com/consumer_resources/Pocket_Shopper/

SMART USE OF THE NET

EFax	www.efax.com
Hot Off the Web	www.hotofftheweb.com

BRANDING

Nike Movie Maker	www.nike.com/moviemaker/index.html

RESEARCH
FACSNET   www.facsnet.org

DATABASE
Your Nation   www.your-nation.com

DIRECT MARKETING
MessageBlaster.com   www.messageblaster.com
Eletter   www.eletter.com

CUSTOMER SERVICE
Dell Support Ask Dudley   www.support.dell.com/askdudley/

PROCUREMENT
FreeMarkets   www.freemarkets.com

LEGAL
Cybersettle   www.cybersettle.com

AUTOMOTIVE
Service.Autobytel.com   service.autobytel.com

INTERNET
Topica   www.topica.com
VeloMail   www.velomail.com

PRODUCTIVITY
WebEx   www.webex.com

NEWS
Stratfor.com   www.stratfor.com

DOCUMENT MANAGEMENT
UPS Document Exchange   www.exchange.ups.com

EMPLOYMENT
Monster Talent Market   independentprofessional.monster.com

TRAVEL
UAL.com   www.ual.com

RATINGS
BizRate.com   www.bizrate.com

MARKETING
NetRatings   www.netratings.com

DIGITAL CASH
PayPal   www.paypal.com

FINANCIAL
BigCharts   www.bigcharts.com

HONORABLE MENTIONS
Palmtop Publishing   www.palmtoppublishing.com
iDecisionMaker.com   www.idecisionmaker.com
Deep Canyon   www.deepcanyon.com
Decide.com   www.decide.com
onebox.com   www.onebox.com
U.S. Department of Commerce   www.doc.gov
FreeTranslation.com   www.freetranslation.com
Domainator   www.e-gineer.com/e-gineer/domainator/index.phtml
Gizmoz   www.gizmoz.com
Jargon Scout   www.tbtf.com/jargon-scout.html[93]

POSTSCRIPT

Recently, we were talking with a senior consultant who described the coming years as the "golden age" of marketing. When we asked him what he meant, he replied that for much of its history the human race had lived in conditions of deprivation and scarcity. We were now, he alleged, entering the era of over-capacity. In a world of scarcity the producer reigned, but in a world of over-supply the customer really would be the king. With this shift of power would come an almost universal acknowledgment of marketing as a central and guiding philosophy for the firm.

We find his assessment both enlightening and alarming. Enlightening because it is consistent with the predictions of many other far-sighted individuals that stretch back to the 1950s, and it is a perspective that is, or should be, most encouraging to both existing and would-be marketers. Alarming, because if the predictions are realized, the increased competitive intensity that we see today will be mild compared with what is to come. Thus, while the importance of marketing is likely to increase, the job of marketing is likely to become ever more challenging.

These themes should not appear novel if you have read this book's 21 chapters. We have continually reinforced the view that the marketing philosophy is central to the firm's goal of creating value for shareholders. Of course, constituencies other than customers are important: without suppliers we could not generate value; without employees we could not provide service. Yet, there is, in our view, an overwhelming logic supporting the view that without customers, the efforts of our suppliers and employees come to naught. It is only when customers demonstrate a willingness to exchange their money for our products and services that the firm can truly have said to have added value.

Yet, we would argue that our consultant friend did not go far enough. While it is too early to foresee the ultimate outcome, it is clear to us that in the last few years mankind has embarked on one of its greatest-ever adventures, yet another revolution—the information revolution. This revolution is changing, and will continue to change, not only many of the processes by which we manage and conduct marketing activities, but the nature of organizations themselves. A period of turbulent change lies ahead as far as we can see. Cheap and plentiful bandwidth means easy access to information resources that will transform the efficiency of product markets on a global scale. Organizational customers are already demanding one price, in one currency, worldwide, and these pressures will increasingly impact consumer markets. Furthermore, the widespread availability of inexpensive processing power is transforming the design of products and processes by adding new functionalities at ever lower cost, even as it dramatically changes the ways companies interface with suppliers and intermediaries in the supply chain.

Changes such as these are the lifeblood of great strategic marketing, for change creates opportunity for those who truly take a strategic perspective. Unfortunately, in our experience, too many large companies are filled with marketers who see change not as an opportunity, but as a problem. These defenders of the old ways will fall by the wayside of change; unfortunately, their companies may fall alongside them!

To succeed as a 21st century manager you must have a comfortable familiarity with marketing concepts and principals. The context within which changes driven by the information revolution are worked through is likely to evolve rapidly and will impact you regardless of which department or group in the organization you happen to inhabit. Indeed, your current department or group may disappear as the organization itself evolves. As Jack Welch, chairman of General Electric has opined, "If the outside is changing faster than the inside, the only possible result is death!"

Following are several key themes for change that we believe will be important in the next few years.

THEMES FOR CHANGE

Customer Needs and Wants Connected to Marketing Activities

As we discussed earlier, scholars and practitioners alike are questioning some of marketing's fundamental suppositions. We know that technological innovation changes the world; perhaps it should be obvious that it can also change people's wants and needs. Yet, most practitioners and most marketing books proceed under the implicit or explicit assumption that customer wants are somehow exogenous to the work that marketers do. This assumption has been questioned by several scholars; as interest in, and understanding of, the process of market development and customer learning advances, it will be subject to further questioning and re-alignment.[1]

Customer Selection

Increasing competition will require continual examination of every phase of marketing activities; perhaps the best place to start is with customer selection. It is a sobering reality that, although most organizations understand product profitability, they do not have the systems in place to measure customer profitability. Firms know that they can ill afford to spend resources on unprofitable, or low-profit, customers, but for the most part they are unable to separate the two groups. In the future, management will make the crucial decisions to put in the systems infrastructure to provide this information, for they will ultimately conclude that the old saw, "if you can't measure it, you can't manage it," applies equally well to customers. When customer profitability data is revealed, we will see an increased focus on larger and/or higher profit customers and affirmative de-marketing from other customers.

Outsourcing of Non-critical Activities

Not only will firms examine every phase of their marketing activities, under intense competitive pressure they will examine *all* of their activities in a never-ending quest for lower costs and the most effective use of their resources. The growth in outsourcing, which would be impossible without sophisticated information technology, will be enhanced by the Internet and lead to networks of companies collaborating in entirely new ways. Outsourcing will continue to produce market opportunities for many product and service suppliers; for example, contract manufacture is growing rapidly in several industries and a variety of new Internet-based information services is evolving.

Trend Towards Experiential Marketing

As we might expect from scholars trained in the scientific method, research into customer behavior is overwhelmingly biased toward cognitive explanations. However, several researchers have called this assumption into question.[2] As growing prosperity drives ever more consumer purchasing into entirely volitional categories, from goods to services to "experiences," we expect that the focus on emotional and socio-psychological explanations of purchase and use behavior will increase.[3]

Two-Way Communications

Dramatic changes are occurring is in the ways in which firms and customers communicate. Traditionally, most commercial communication with consumers has been one-way, directed at mass audiences. Not only is two-way communication with customers becoming more and more common, but the Internet has enabled customers, happy or disaffected, to communicate with each other. The dynamics of this change will have profound implications for marketers.

Supply Chain Reorganizations

Under the force of the information revolution, the traditional framework and roles of supplier, producer, distributor, retailer, and customer will give way to entirely new supply chain organizations. For example, with increasing product comparability in many industries, suppliers will attempt to migrate further down the value chain to secure revenues from after-sale service activities. On the other hand, intermediary organizations with deep relationships to customers may assemble groups of suppliers to offer them extended product assortments. Finally, customers may dis-intermediate intermediaries by seeking out suppliers directly in a search for ever lower costs, either alone or in powerful buying groups. It is too early to say which of these models will become dominant or what new arrangements may be developed. Perhaps several different models will coexist, in which case those marketers that identify the best conditions for each model will secure competitive advantage.

Increased Globalization

For some time now, technological improvements in telecommunications and logistics have been key enablers for firms seeking global markets for their products and services. The Internet is a more recent technological development that is advancing the process of globalization. Internet-based systems enable organizational purchasers to scour the globe for low-cost suppliers, and such consumer-focused Internet suppliers such as Amazon.com already take orders and deliver globally. Increased globalization of both customers and suppliers places a considerable strain on traditional organizational structures and processes. These will undoubtedly be change as marketing and procurement strategies evolve.

Organizational Redesign

A particular view on evolving organizational arrangements is Jack Welch's vision at GE that organizations must become "boundaryless." Many others share this view; for example, Ray Lane, CEO of Oracle, believes that the whole vertical hierarchy of traditional organizations will disappear.[4] Certainly, evolving information technology will play a critical role in organizational redesign. Indeed, at BP, formerly a lumbering behemoth, information technology has allowed global teams to work together effectively for better, faster decision-making and turned it into one of the most admired companies in its industry.[5]

IMPLICATIONS FOR HUMAN RESOURCES

Because this book is for you, our reader, we conclude with implications for human resources. The variety and depth of change that we have discussed in the book and highlighted in this Postscript have major implications for your career and for human resources throughout the organization. We have stressed continually that customers are the critical firm assets but, beyond that assertion, increasingly, human resources are replacing balance sheet assets as the firm's critical "internal" assets. After all, the Internet is a "dumb network"; its power is in its attachments, the human resources at the periphery whose creativity uses the Internet in a never-ending quest to secure and retain customers. Indeed, the pace of change is so great that the upper reaches of the managerial hierarchy, if one exists, are increasingly unable to make the myriad of decisions necessary for organizational survival and growth, and to optimize shareholder value. Their role will evolve to one of setting broad direction, providing resources, attending to brand equity, capturing synergies and adjacencies, and overlaying skills.

In this Postscript, we have identified a few themes that will impact marketing practice in the future. Clearly, these are just a sample of the changes that we might expect, and even these may turn out to be incorrect. All we really know is that significant change will occur and this change will have important implications for you, our reader. As we noted earlier, too many executives seem fearful of change; they see only the problems it creates, rather than the opportunities it affords. To ensure that you do not become one of these managers we offer a simple piece of advice. *Don't stop now*! Learning is a lifetime commitment in a world of change. Reading a book or completing a course is like passing a crossroads along the way. In a world of change, your destination will always be receding, but with a personal external orientation, and the curiosity that marks a great marketer, you will be able to close the gap.

Perhaps there is no better way to conclude this book than to share with you a 1998 quotation from Jeff Bezos, founder and CEO of Amazon.com who, incidentally, worked with some of our Columbia colleagues before he founded Amazon:

"I constantly remind our employees to be afraid, to wake up every morning terrified. Not of our competition, but of our customers. Our customers have made our business what it is, they're the ones with whom we have a relationship, and they're the ones to whom we owe a great obligation. And we consider them loyal to us— right up until the second that someone else offers them a better service."

We hope that you will be terrified of your customers and understand that the best foundation for success is continual investment in your own learning. Thank you for sticking with our book.

ENDNOTES

1. See, for example, G. S. Carpenter, R. Glazer and K. Nakamoto, *Readings on Market-Driving Strategies*, Reading, MA: Addison-Wesley, 1997; P. Berthon, J.M. Hulbert and L. Pitt, "To Serve or Create? Strategic Orientations toward Customers and Innovation," *California Management Review*, (Fall 1999).

2. See, for example, much published work from our colleague, Morris Holbrook, and T. Ambker and T. Burne, "The Impact of Affect on Ad Memory," *Journal of Advertising Research*, 39 (Mar./Apr. 1999), pp. 25–34.

3. See B. Schmitt, *Experiential Marketing*, New York: The Free Press, 1999 and B.J Pine III and J.H. Gilmore, "Welcome to the Experience Economy," *Harvard Business Review*, 76 (Jul./Aug. 1998), pp. 97–105.

4. Interview with Ray Lane, *Financial Times*, May 5, 1999.

5. In 1995 BP equipped its staff with a desktop video conferencing system, document scanning, electronic mail and the Internet, *Financial Times*, October 11, 1998.

WEB RESOURCES

Amazon	www.amazon.com
British Petroleum	www.bp.com
General Electric	www.ge.com
Oracle	www.oracle.com

Appendix

FINANCIAL ANALYSIS FOR MARKETING DECISIONS

Introduction

The appendix presents some basic financial analysis concepts that are fundamental for making sound marketing management decisions. Although the concepts are sometimes discussed in accounting and finance courses, this material focuses on marketing-related issues.

This element is divided into four sections:

- Section 1: different ways of viewing costs and their implications for marketing decision-making;
- Section 2: various ways of viewing margins;
- Section 3: shareholder value analysis;
- Section 4: a set of problems based on the material in sections 1 and 2.
- Section 5: solutions to problems in Section 4.

Section 1: Partitioning Costs for Marketing Decision Making

For the purposes of marketing decision making, it is useful to consider three different cost classifications: variable and fixed costs; programmed and standby costs; direct and indirect costs. These different cost classifications are not independent (e.g., direct costs include variable costs and some portion of fixed costs) but each is useful.

VARIABLE COSTS AND FIXED COSTS   Variable costs are costs that vary (rise or fall) as the total volume of sales or production varies (rises or falls). They typically include items such as raw materials and components, packaging, freight, direct labor, sales commissions, and sales manager overrides.

Fixed costs stay constant (do not rise or fall) as the total volume of sales or production changes, at least over some range of operations. Real estate taxes and insurance, executive salaries, debt repayments, advertising and promotion, product development, and marketing research are typically fixed costs (Appendix Figure 1).[1]

$$\text{Variable costs} + \text{fixed costs} = \text{total costs}$$

Care must be taken in deciding whether or not a cost is variable or fixed by attempting to understand the dynamics of the cost item under consideration. For example, electrical

Appendix Figure 1: Variable and Fixed Costs

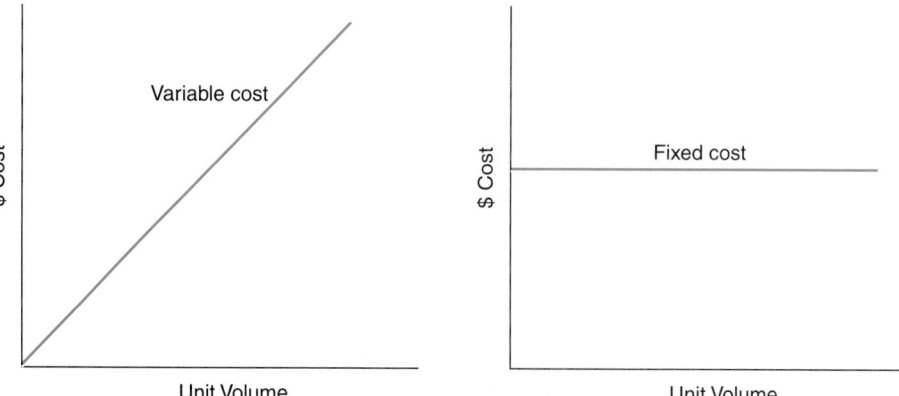

power for a factory is a cost item that is typically part of manufacturing overhead. However, electricity is used for at least two different functions: to heat and light the factory, and to provide power to the machines that produce the product. The former is a fixed cost, as it does not change with total volume; the latter is a variable cost, as it does change with total volume. In the United States, direct labor is typically considered as a variable cost. (In periods of high demand, labor is added; in periods of weak demand, labor is furloughed.) In certain European countries, for example, Germany, labor secures tenure after a short time on the job. Thus as volume of output falls, labor costs do not change. In such circumstances labor is more properly considered a fixed cost, at least downwards.

An important distinction that often causes confusion is between costs that managers choose to change and costs that vary directly with the volume of sales or production. Thus advertising and market research costs change at managerial discretion, but this does not make them variable costs. For a cost to be variable, it must change as the total volume of sales or production changes, such as raw materials, and sales commissions. A special case in which advertising can be a variable cost is in cooperative advertising where the firm provides advertising support to retailers based on the volume of retail sales.

Cost Changes with Volume

In the most simple case, variable costs (vary directly with total sales or production volume) are fixed on a unit basis. Thus suppose raw material costs $5 per unit. As the number of units manufactured increases, variable costs for raw material increase: 1 unit = $5, 10 units = $50, 100 units = $500, and so forth. This is a simplification because if production increases, the manufacturer can usually make better arrangements with suppliers. For example, if 50 or more units is purchased, raw material costs might drop to $4.50 per unit. Thus at 100 units, raw material costs would be $450, not $500. In a similar fashion, commission rates for sales people might change: 50 cents per unit for the first 500 units, 75 cents per unit above 500 units. Despite such changes, these costs vary directly with sales or production volume. It is just that the particular cost/volume relationship is not necessarily a simple linear function.

By contrast, fixed costs (that do not vary in total with sales and production volume) implicitly change on a per unit basis as sales and production increase. Suppose fixed costs for a product were $100,000. If one unit were produced and sold, the fixed cost per unit equals $100,000. If 10 units were produced and sold, the fixed cost per unit equals $10,000; if 100 units were produced and sold, the fixed cost per unit equals $1,000, and so forth. Note it is only the implicit fixed cost per unit that changes; the actual fixed costs do not change, as they remain at $100,000. Frequently, managers make the mistake of stating fixed costs on a per unit basis and then expect actual fixed costs to change as volume changes; this is an erroneous expectation. An important qualification in the fixed cost definition is "over some range of operations." As a new shift is added in the factory or a new sales region opened, new levels of fixed costs are typically established.

The manner in which variable, fixed, total, and average unit costs change with volume is illustrated in Appendix Table 1. Note that variable costs per unit are fixed over certain ranges, and fixed costs increase in step-function fashion as volume increases.

Transforming Financial Statements to a Variable Budget Format

Typically, financial statements are not organized to facilitate variable and fixed cost analysis. Thus marketing management must work with accounting and finance personnel to reconfigure these statements in a way that isolates variable and fixed costs. Appendix Table 2 is shows a typical income statement for a product; Appendix Table 3 shows the result of reclassifying costs; Appendix Table 4 shows a reconfigured income statement, often termed a variable budget format.

Although Appendix Tables 2 and 4 appear similar, there are important differences. In the typical financial income statement shown in Appendix Table 2, when cost of goods sold is subtracted from sales revenue, the result is gross margin. Gross margin has to cover

Appendix Table 1: Illustration of Changes in Variable and Fixed Costs

Unit Sales and Production	Total Fixed Costs ($)	Implicit Fixed Cost per unit ($)	Variable Cost per unit ($)	Total Variable Costs ($)	Total Costs ($)	Average Unit Cost ($)
10	100	10.00	3.0	30	130	13.00
20	100	5.00	3.0	60	160	8.00
30	100	3.33	3.0	90	190	6.33
40	130	3.25	2.5	100	230	5.75
50	130	2.60	2.5	125	255	5.10
60	130	2.17	2.8	168	298	4.97
70	150	2.14	2.8	196	346	4.94

all other expenses. After these expenses are subtracted from gross margin, any remainder is profit. In the variable budget format in Appendix Table 4, when variable costs are subtracted from sales revenue, the result is variable margin (sometimes called contribution margin). It is the job of this variable margin to cover all fixed costs. When fixed costs are subtracted from variable margin, any remainder is profit.

Variable margin is normally a much more useful concept for decision making than gross margin because it varies in a directly predictable manner with sales volume; gross margin does not. If, for example, *ceteris paribus*, the volume of product A sold was

Appendix Table 2: Income Statement for Product A ($000s)

Sales (40 million lbs. @ 50 cents/lb.)	$20,000
less:	
Materials	8,000
Direct Labor	2,000
Manufacturing Overhead	2,200
Cost of Goods Sold	12,200
Gross Margin	7,800
less:	
Advertising	800
Promotion	200
Field Sales	3,200
Product Management	50
Marketing Management	300
Product Development	300
Marketing Research	150
General and Administrative	1,400
Total Expenses	6,400
Net Profit before Taxes	1,400

Appendix Table 3: Classifying Product A Costs into Variable and Fixed ($000s)

	Cost Components		
	Total	Variable	Fixed
Materials	$8,000	8,000	—
Direct Labor	2,000	2,000	—
Manufacturing Overhead	2,200	1,000	1,200
Cost of Goods Sold	12,200	11,000	1,200
Advertising	800		800
Promotion	200		200
Field Sales	3,200	1,000	2,200
Product Management	50		50
Marketing Management	300		300
Product Development	300		300
Marketing Research	150		150
General and Administrative	1,400		1,400
Total Expenses	6,400	1,000	5,400
Total Costs	18,600	12,000	6,600

increased by 10%, it is impossible from Appendix Table 2 to determine the impact on profits. Although overall costs will increase, the statement does not indicate which costs vary with volume and which do not. Appendix Table 4, by contrast, is set up to facilitate making this kind of calculation.

If sales volume increases by 10%, variable costs must necessarily also increase by 10%. Fixed costs remain constant. Thus from Appendix Table 5, for a 10% increase in sales volume, the net profit increases by $800K ($2,200K − $1,400K). This represents a 57% profit increase: (800/1,400) × 100 = 57%. Appendix Table 5 also shows the impact of a 10% decrease in sales volume. Net profit decreases by $800K ($1,400K − $600); this represents a 57% profit decrease.

Variable (Contribution) Margin per Unit

From Appendix Table 4, it can be observed that: sales revenue (SR) less variable costs (VC) equals variable margin (VM): SR − VC = VM, or restated, SR = VC + VM.

$$20,000 - 12,000 = 8,000 \qquad 20,000 = 12,000 + 8,000$$

If these equations are divided by the number of units sold, the same equation is derived on a per unit basis:

$$SP - VCU = VMU \qquad SP = VCU + VMU, \text{ where:}$$
$$50c - 30c = 20c \qquad 50c = 30c + 20c$$

SP = Selling Price (Sales revenue divided by number of units): 20,000/40,000 = 50 cents

VCU = Variable Cost per Unit: 12,000/40,000 = 30 cents

VMU = Variable Margin per Unit (contribution margin per unit): 8,000/40,000 = 20 cents

The VMU is an extremely important concept. Because it was derived by subtracting variable costs from sales revenue, financial calculations do not have to be concerned with variable costs. The only job that the VMU has to do is to cover fixed costs; any remainder is profit.

Appendix Table 4: Reconfigured Income Statement for Product A using a Variable Budget Format ($000s)

Sales (40 million lbs. @ 50 cents/lb.)	$20,000
less:	
Variable Costs:	
Materials	8,000
Direct Labor	2,000
Manufacturing Overhead	1,000
Sales Commissions	1,000
Total Variable Costs	12,000
Variable Margin (Profit Contribution)	8,000
less:	
Fixed Costs:	
Advertising	800
Promotion	200
Field Sales	2,200
Product Management	50
Marketing Management	300
Product Development	300
Marketing Research	150
Manufacturing Overhead	1,200
General and Administrative	1,400
Total Fixed Costs	6,600
Net Profit before Taxes	1,400

Breakeven Analysis

The breakeven point (BE) is the level of sales needed to cover fixed costs. If sales volume is above the breakeven point, the product makes profit; if sales volume is below the breakeven point, the product makes a loss. Knowing the VMU makes it easy to calculate the breakeven. Since variable costs are accounted for in calculating VMU, only covering fixed costs is a concern.

Appendix Table 5: Variable Budget Format ($000s)

	Original	10% Increase	10% Decrease
Sales (@ 50 cents/lb.)	$20,000	$22,000	$18,000
less:			
Total Variable Costs	12,000	13,200	10,800
Variable Margin (Profit Contribution)	8,000	8,800	7,200
less:			
Total Fixed Costs	6,600	6,600	6,600
Net Profit before Taxes	1,400	2,200	600

In the example, the VMU is 20 cents. The number of 20 "centses" that in total sum to $6.6 million, the total fixed costs must be calculated.

BE (units) = Fixed Costs/VMU = $6.6 million/20 cents = 33 million lbs.

BE ($) = BE (units) × SP = 33 million lbs. × 50 cents = $16.5 million

Furthermore, the safety factor, the degree to which the product is operating above breakeven, can be simply calculated:

Safety Factor (%) = (Sales Volume − Breakeven Volume/Sales Volume) × 100

Safety Factor (%) = (40 − 33/40) × 100 = 17.5% or ($20 − 16.5/20) × 100 = 17.5%

Pictorially the breakeven analysis is shown in Appendix Figure 2.[2]

Variable costs are shown by line AA; as unit sales volume increases, variable costs increase in a direct relationship.

Total costs are shown by line BB. Total costs are the sum of variable and fixed costs.

Fixed costs are shown by line BB and line AA. Line BB is parallel to AA; the difference (vertical distance) between the two lines represents fixed costs.

Sales revenue is shown by the line CC. At zero sales volume, sales revenue is zero; it increases directly as sales unit volume increases.

Variable margin is shown by the distance between lines CC and AA. Variable margin is the difference between sales revenue and variable costs.

As variable margin increases from zero (at zero sales volume), it is initially less than fixed costs. The difference between the lines CC and BB (sales revenue and total costs) represents the extent to which variable margin does not cover fixed costs. This is the loss that the firm makes.

At point X, the variable margin (difference between CC and AA) equals fixed costs (difference between BB and AA). This is the breakeven point; the firm makes zero profit and zero loss. As sales volume increases above this point, variable margin is greater than fixed costs; the difference between CC and BB represents the firm's profit.

Budgeting Profit Targets

Although breakeven is a useful concept and the breakeven point an important criterion for management (shown above by the safety factor), in many cases managers set positive profit targets to attain. The key question is what sales volume must be achieved to reach a particular profit target. Suppose, for example, the profit target is $2 million.

Appendix Figure 2: Breakeven

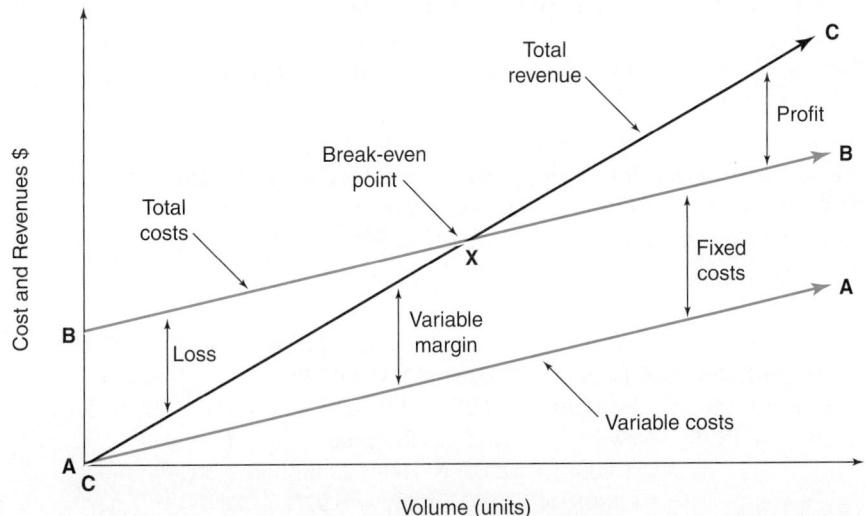

The calculation is conceptually similar to the breakeven calculation; the variable margin must be sufficient to cover fixed costs but, in addition, it must also cover the profit target. Thus:

Target to Cover = Fixed Costs + Profit Target = $6.6 million + $2 million = $8.6 million.

Calculate the number of 20 "centses" (VMU) that in total sum to $8.6 million, the total fixed costs plus profit target.

Target volume (units) = Target to Cover/VMU = $8.6 million/20 cents = 43 million lbs.

Target volume ($) = Target volume (units) × SP =
43 million lbs. × 50 cents = $21.5 million.

PROGRAMMED COSTS AND STANDBY COSTS   Programmed costs are controlled and set by management for a planning period and are controlled by a specific individual or group. Typical examples of programmed cost are advertising, marketing research, and product development.

Standby costs do not change significantly without a major change in operations, and are generally not under the control of marketing, product, or sales managers in the short run. Typical examples of standby costs are rent, depreciation, and salaries of key executives.

Both programmed costs and standby costs are fixed costs. The key distinction is that programmed costs are subject to managerial decision in the short and medium run; standby costs are not. Thus advertising and product development efforts may be increased or decreased, a marketing research study may be undertaken or canceled. By contrast, unless there is a major change in operations, the costs for rent, depreciation, and the salaries of key executives will not be canceled. Programmed costs are sometimes called decision-fixed costs; standby costs are called fixed-fixed costs.

Increases in Programmed Costs

Suppose that the firm is contemplating adding three new salespeople at a total annual fixed cost (salaries, benefits, travel, and entertainment) of $480,000. The key question is what is the minimum level of sales that they must generate to cover their annual costs.

To solve this problem, the same type of breakeven calculation is used as earlier. In this case, however, rather than being concerned about covering the new level of total fixed costs, only the extra (marginal) fixed costs for the salespeople, $480,000 are concerns. (Note that there is no concern with sales commissions (variable costs) as these are taken care of via our use of the VMU.) As previously:

Target volume (units) = Target to Cover/VMU = $480K/20 cents = 2.4 million lbs.

Target volume ($) = Target volume (units) × SP =
2.4 million lbs. × 50 cents = $1.2 million

Thus a sales increase of greater than 2.4 million lbs., $1.2 million, would improve firm profits.

Suppose that management estimated that sales would in fact increase by $1.4 million. Suppose, also, that management has two profit criteria, absolute dollar profit and return on sales (ROS). (ROS equals profit divided by sales revenue.) Before hiring the salespeople, calculate the actual profit increase and the impact on ROS.

1. At sales revenue of $1.4 million, the salespeople are selling $200K ($1.4 − $1.2 million) over their breakeven sales revenue ($1.2 million);
2. Converting into unit sales volume: $200K @ 50 cents per lb. = 400,000 lbs.;
3. Extra profit received from 400,000 lbs. @ VMU of 20 cents per lb. equals $80K;
4. For sales revenue of $1.4 million, ROS = ($80K/$1.4 million) × 100 = 5.7 %.
5. New Total ROS = New Profit/New Sales Revenue;
= ($1,400K + $80K) × 100/($20 million + $1.4 million);
= $1,480K × 100/$21,400K = 6.92%.

Management is in a quandary. If absolute dollar profit is the governing criterion, the salespeople should be added since profit would increase by $80,000. If ROS is the governing criterion, they should not be hired since the marginal ROS is 5.7% and the new total ROS is 6.92%, as opposed to the original ROS of $1,400 × 100/$20 million = 7%.

Many firms use the ROS criterion. However, it should be noted that the firm banks dollars; it does not bank ROS. The main reason to express profit as a percent is because the denominator is a scarce resource, such as return on investment, return on equity, or return on linear feet (often used by supermarkets). Sales revenue is not a scarce resource in this sense.

Reduction in Programmed Costs

Suppose that the firm is contemplating reducing advertising costs by $680,000. The key question is by what amount can sales fall such that profits are not reduced. Alternatively, the question can be stated as what level of sales would produce a variable margin of $680,000. The loss of that level of sales would exactly be canceled out by the reduction in advertising costs.

Target volume (units) = Target to Cover/VMU = $680K/20 cents = 3.4 million lbs.

Target volume ($) = Target volume (units) × SP =
3.4 million lbs. × 50 cents = $1.7 million

Unit sales volume could drop by 3.4 million lbs. or $1.7 million.

Preparing the Business Plan

Suppose the firm is contemplating making several changes in programmed fixed costs:

1. Reducing advertising costs by $680,000;
2. Reducing raw material costs by 10% at a cost of $1 million (treated as an expense to be recovered in the first year);
3. Increasing the sales force at a fixed cost of $480,000.

It is concerned about the implication of these potential changes for its breakeven volume.

As a result of these changes and at the current volume, both variable costs and fixed costs would change. Since price is not changed, the change in variable costs implies that the VMU would also change. Thus a breakeven calculation requires finding out both the new level of fixed costs and the new VMU. Changes in costs are shown in Appendix Table 6.

Note that at the current volume the variable and fixed cost changes are a wash; increases in fixed costs are totally compensated for by reductions in variable costs.

1. New Fixed Costs = $6,600K + $800K = $7,400K;
2. New Variable Costs = $12,000 − $800K = $11,200K;
3. New VCU (variable cost per lb.) = $11,200K/40 million lbs. = 28 cents per lb.;
4. New VMU (variable margin per lb.) = 50c − 28c = 22 cents per lb.;
5. BE (units) = Fixed Costs/VMU = $7,400K/22 cents = 33.6 million lbs.;
6. BE ($) = BE (units) × SP = 33.6 million lbs. × 50 cents = $16.8 million;
7. Safety Factor = (Sales − BE)/Sales = (40 − 33.6)/40 = 16.0%

Appendix Table 6: Shifting Variable and Fixed Costs ($000s)

Cost Category	Fixed	Variable
Advertising	(680)	—
Raw Materials	1,000	(800)
Sales Force	480	—
Total	800	(800)

As a result of the proposed shift between variable and fixed costs, the breakeven increases from 33 million lbs. to 33.6 million lbs. Correspondingly, the safety factor drops from 17.5% to 16.0%.

Implications of Changes in Variable and Fixed Costs

Shifting between variable and fixed costs has important managerial implications. For any business there is a range of discretion within which management can operate. Within that range, management can decide whether to operate with greater levels of fixed costs or greater levels of variable costs. For example, shifting sales force compensation towards increased commission by reducing salary levels reduces fixed costs and increases variable costs. Cutting out an early stage in the production process by purchasing higher grade raw materials similarly reduces fixed costs and increases variable costs. Conversely, increased levels of vertical integration typically result in higher levels of fixed costs and reduced variable costs.

The impact of differing levels of fixed and variable costs can be shown by reference to the previous example. Consider two cost structures: the original cost structure from Appendix Figures 2, 3 and 4, and the new cost structure worked through in Appendix Table 6. In Appendix Table 7, consider the implications of a 15% increase in sales volume; in Appendix Table 8, consider the implications of 15% decrease in sales volume.

The impact of the shifting cost structure is clearly seen. When sales increase by 15%, profits with the new cost structure are $120,000 ($2,720K − $2,600K) greater than with the original cost structure. The reason is simply that the higher levels of fixed costs in the new cost structure cause overall costs to be lower as sales volume increases.

By contrast, when sales volume decreases, profits under the new cost structure are $120,000 ($200,000 − $80,000) less than with the original cost structure. The reason is that the higher levels of fixed costs in the new cost structure cause overall costs to be higher as sales volume decreases.

DIRECT COSTS AND INDIRECT COSTS Direct costs occur because a particular product, organizational unit, or activity exists or is being contemplated. Direct costs can be identified with, or directly linked to, a product, sales territory, or function. Direct costs include all variable costs and at least some fixed costs.

Indirect costs relate to several products, organizational units, or activities. Indirect costs cannot be identified with a single product, sales territory, or activity.

The acid test of whether a cost is direct or indirect is to ask what would happen if the product, sales territory, or activity were to disappear. For example, if the product were dropped, several costs would disappear: raw materials, specific product development and support costs, sales commissions, and product manager costs. These costs are direct costs. Conversely, marketing research department costs, sales force salary (assuming a multiproduct sales force), marketing department costs, and the president's salary would continue. These costs are indirect costs.

Appendix Table 7: Shifting Variable and Fixed Costs: Sales Increase by 15% ($000s)

Category	Cost Structure	
	Existing	**New**
Sales	$23,000	$23,000
Variable Costs	13,800	12,880
Variable Margin	9,200	10,120
Fixed Costs	6,600	7,400
Net Profit	2,600	2,720

Appendix Table 8: Shifting Variable and Fixed Costs: Sales Decrease by 15% ($000s)

	Cost Structure	
Category	Existing	New
Sales	$17,000	$17,000
Variable Costs	10,200	9,520
Variable Margin	6,800	7,480
Fixed Costs	6,600	7,400
Net Profit	200	80

The distinction between direct and indirect costs is especially important when consideration is given to drop products from the product line. In Appendix Table 9, the income statement from Appendix Table 4 is expanded to indicate programmed, standby, direct, and indirect costs.

Note that advertising appears in two places: as a programmed direct cost and as a programmed indirect cost. The programmed direct cost is specific product-related advertising; the programmed indirect cost is this product's allocated share of corporate advertising expenditures.

Dropping a Product

Suppose that the average return on sales (ROS) for the firm's products is 10%. Since product A's ROS is just 7%, consideration may be given to dropping the product from the product line. The important question is what is the impact on the firm of dropping the product. Clearly, if the product is no longer in the product line, the firm will no longer receive the $1.4 million of bottom line profit. However, this understates the impact on the firm. Consider the indirect costs: $850K of programmed indirect costs and $800K of standby indirect costs, $1.65 million in total.

If the product is dropped, these costs remain. In fact, neither the $850K nor the $800K has specific meaning as an actual cost; rather, each comprises a set of allocations from some much larger set of costs. If the product is dropped, these costs will continue. For example, corporate advertising will continue, as will marketing management, product development, and marketing research.

Thus the overall impact on the firm of dropping this product is not $1.4 million. Rather, the overall impact is $1.4 million + $1.65 million; $3.05 million in total.

As noted in Chapter 12, it is not infrequent that firms make the mistake of dropping old products that are marginally profitable only to discover that overall profit drops substantially. The reason is that these old products were bearing a large share of allocated overhead. When the products were dropped, this burden fell on other products in the product line and overall profit was consequently reduced.

Allocating Overhead

The important managerial implication to draw from the previous discussion is that overhead allocations to products, businesses, sales regions, or other organizational units should be made with great care, and possibly should not be made at all. Thus in the above example, product management has no control over the $1.65 million of indirect fixed costs; neither programmed indirect costs ($850K) nor standby indirect costs ($800K). These are allocated costs.

As noted earlier, these costs do not represent any specific activity or activities. Rather, they are made up of a set of allocations from some much larger set of costs. What then is the basis upon which these cost allocations were made? As a practical matter, corporations

Appendix Table 9: Reconfigured Income Statement for Product A, Variable Budget Format ($000s)

Sales (40 million lbs. @ 50 cents/lb.)	$20,000
less:	
Variable Costs:	
Materials	8,000
Direct Labor	2,000
Manufacturing Overhead	1,000
Sales Commissions	1,000
Total Variable Costs	12,000
Variable Margin (Profit Contribution)	8,000
less:	
Fixed Costs:	
Programmed: Direct	
Advertising	500
Promotion	200
Field Sales	2,200
Product Management	50
Product Development	100
Marketing Research	100
	3,150
Programmed: Indirect	
Advertising	300
Marketing Management	300
Product Development	200
Marketing Research	50
	850
Standby: Direct	
Manufacturing Overhead	1,200
General and Administrative	600
	1,800
Standby: Indirect	
General and Administrative	800
Total Fixed Costs	6,600
Net Profit before Taxes	1,400

make cost allocations on many different bases. Costs might be allocated on the basis of sales revenue or labor hours, or capital employed, or any number of different individual methods or combinations of methods. Depending upon the allocation method used, a specific product would receive different cost allocations.

Thus in the example, a different allocation system might produce not $1.65 million in allocated costs, but $2 million, hence $1.05 million profits. A still different system might produce $1 million in allocated costs, hence $2.05 million profits. None of these profit numbers, $1.05 million, $1.4 million, $2.05 million, is any more right than the others; each is a function of the particular allocation scheme being used. The ability to generate different levels of net profit as the result of choosing different allocation systems causes firms severe problems.

It provides a misguided perspective on a product's true value to the firm. To understand the true value that a product provides to the firm it is necessary to isolate the level of contribution made by the product to indirect fixed costs. This is shown in Appendix Table 10, where the contribution to indirect fixed costs equals $3.05 million. Regardless of what allocation method the firm uses, the $3.05 million measures the value of the product to the firm.

In addition, the $3.05 million is a much more appropriate measure of managerial performance than the $1.4 million. Management has some measure of control over the sales revenues and the direct costs (variable and direct fixed costs); it has no control over the allocated indirect costs of $1.65 million which can be increased or decreased at the stoke of a pen. Thus to measure performance on the basis of the net profit is inappropriate.

Two Breakeven Points

The importance of this issue can be seen by referring to Appendix Figure 2. This figure is similar to the breakeven chart in Appendix Figure 1, but there is one important difference; the fixed costs have been partitioned into direct and indirect fixed costs. Line DD represents the dividing line. The vertical distance between DD and the variable cost line, AA, represents direct fixed costs; the vertical distance between the total cost line, BB, and DD represents indirect fixed costs. Note that the sales revenue line, CC, crosses DD at Y and BB at X.

At sales revenue less than Y, the variable margin (CC less AA) is insufficient to cover direct fixed costs and the product makes an out-of-pocket loss. At sales revenue more than X, as previously, the product produces a profit. At sales revenues between Y and X, the product makes a bottom line loss but produces some variable margin that in part covers allocated costs. At sales revenues greater than X, the product covers all direct and indirect costs.

The difficult decision for many firms is whether or not to stop producing products whose volume lies between Y and X. Of course, the firm cannot have all products in

Appendix Table 10: Short Form Income Statement showing Contribution to Indirect Fixed Costs ($000s)

Sales (40 million lbs. @ 50 cents/lb.)	$20,000
less:	
Total Variable Costs	12,000
Variable Margin (Profit Contribution)	8,000
less:	
Direct Fixed Costs:	
Programmed: Direct	3,150
Standby: Direct	1,800
Total Direct Fixed Costs:	4,950
Contribution to Indirect Costs	3,050
Programmed: Indirect	850
Standby: Indirect	800
Total Indirect Fixed Costs	1,650
Net Profit before Taxes	1,400

Appendix Figure 3: Variable and Fixed Costs

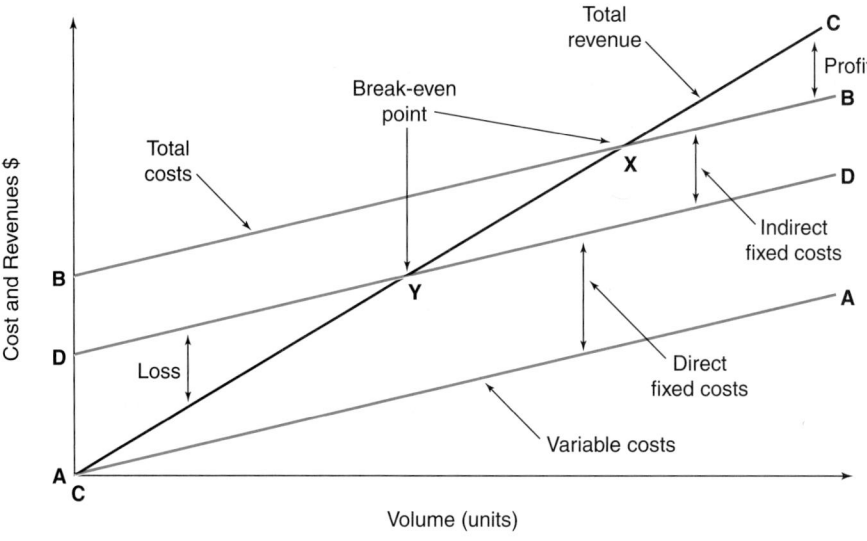

this zone, but over the short run some products in this position might provide valuable contribution to overhead costs.

CUSTOMER PROFITABILITY   The contribution measures just developed focused on product or product line and are much used by organizations with product/brand management organizations. However, as discussed throughout the book, corporations are slowly realizing that securing and retaining customers is critical to enhancing shareholder value. Not only are customer centered organizations being developed, it is critical that firms develop measures of customer profitability.

This section shows how to make the translation from product profitability to customer profitability. For simplicity, the customers are represented as key accounts. However, without loss of generality, the "customers" could be market segments or distribution channels.

Product Income Statements

Suppose the firm sells three products (A,B,C) whose income statements are in Appendix Table 11.

Assume that activity-based costing (ABC) methods have been used to arrive at appropriate cost allocations for elements of cost of goods sold in developing the various gross margins. Other operating costs include customer specific costs, such as sales force, order processing, field service, technical assistance, and delivery. In the illustration these have not been assigned to products, although companies frequently do allocate such costs on the basis of sales revenues or some other cost driver to arrive at product net incomes.

Product Revenue by Account

The revenue distribution for the three products by account is shown in Appendix Table 12.

Appendix Table 11: Product Income Statements ($000s)

	Product A	Product B	Product C	Total
Sales Revenues	$4,330	$6,400	$7,001	$17,731
Cost of Goods Sold	3,175	4,120	5,213	12,508
Gross Margin	1,155	2,280	1,788	5,223
Other Operating Costs				4,023
Operating Income				1,200

Appendix Table 12: Product Revenue Distribution by Account ($000s)

	Product A	Product B	Product C	Total
Account I	$1,030	$3,100	$5,250	$ 9,380
Account II	550	2,800	1,001	4,351
Account III	2,750	500	750	4,000
Total	4,330	6,400	7,001	17,731

Customer Income Statements—Stage 1

From the product income statements, customer income statements can be developed simply by allocating the cost of goods sold for each product by its proportion of sales revenues at each account. The result is three partial customer income statements providing gross margins per account (Appendix Table 13). In this illustration, the wide gross margin distribution occurs because of the manner in which the various factory overhead expenses are absorbed, reflecting the particular needs placed on the factory by each of the three key accounts.[3]

Customer Income Statements—Stage 2

The challenge now is to calculate the net margins per account by allocating other operating costs ($4,023,000) among the three accounts. Determine the various elements of other operating costs charged to accounts on the basis of actual activity. Suppose that these elements are sales force, order processing, field service, technical assistance, and delivery, and that the total cost of each activity is:

Sales Force	875,000
Field Service	773,000
Technical Assistance	950,000
Order Processing	550,000
Delivery	875,000
Total	4,023,000

These costs are charged to accounts as follows:

- **Sales force**: Based on actual costs for key account managers (such as compensation, T&E, assistants) and estimated time spent by the field sales force.
- **Field service**: Based on estimated time spent with the three accounts: I—29%; II—42%; III—29%.
- **Technical assistance:** Based on estimated time spent with the three accounts: I—30%; II—30%; III—40%.
- **Order processing and delivery**: Based on ABC methods. The numbers of deliveries and orders processed for the three accounts are shown in Appendix Table 14,

Appendix Table 13: Partial Customer Income Statements ($000s)

	Account I	Account II	Account III	Total
Sales Revenues	$9,380	$4,351	$4,000	$17,731
Cost of Goods Sold	4,452	4,353	3,703	12,508
Gross Margin	4,928	(2)	297	5,223
Other Operating Costs				4,023
Operating Income				1,200

Appendix Table 14: Allocating Order Processing and Delivery Costs by ABC Methods

	Account I	Account II	Account III	Total	Cost	Rate Base
Number of Orders	750	400	350	1,500	$875,000	$ 583
Number of Deliveries	110	65	45	220	$550,000	$2,500
Cost Allocations:						
Order Processing	$275,000	$162,500	$112,500	$550,000		
Delivery	$437,000	$233,000	$205,000	$875,000		

which also shows the calculation of rate base (cost per unit) (cost divided by total number) for order processing and delivery. From this rate base, the order cost and delivery cost per account are simply calculated by multiplying the number of orders/deliveries by their respective rate bases.

The final distribution of the elements of other operating costs among the three accounts is shown in Appendix Table 15.

These figures lead to the customer income statements in Appendix Table 16.

Section 2: Margins

Definitions

Unit margin as used by retailers and wholesalers is the difference between the price of a product and its cost. (This product supply cost is typically a variable cost.) Most retailers and wholesalers determine prices by a cost-plus method in which a certain percentage of the product's cost (such as invoice cost minus discounts for prompt payment plus freight charges) is added to the cost to provide a final price. Although prices are thus determined by costs, they are almost universally quoted as a percentage of selling price.

Thus a product that costs a retailer 80 cents and sells for $1 is said to carry a 20% margin:

$$\text{Margin} = ((100 - 80)/ 100) = 20\%; \text{ not } ((100 - 80)/ 80) = 25\%.$$

The difference between a product's price and its cost (20 cents in this example) is variously called margin, gross margin, markup, or markon.

The problem for the retailer is to set a price given the cost and typical percent margin. Suppose, for example, typical margins are 40% and the product's cost to the retailer is $50.

Let:

C = Cost, paid to the supplier ($)

P = Selling Price to be set ($)

M = margin (% of Selling Price, stated as a decimal)

Appendix Table 15: Other Operating Costs Allocated by Activity ($000s)

	Account I	Account II	Account III	Total
Sales Force	$ 425	$ 225	$ 225	$ 875
Field Service	224	325	224	773
Technical Assistance	285	285	380	950
Order Processing	275	162	112	550
Delivery	437	233	205	875
Total	1,646	1,230	1,146	4,023

Appendix Table 16: Customer Income Statements (Other Operating Costs Allocated by Activity)

	Account I	Account II	Account III	Total
Sales Revenues	$9,380	$4,351	$4,000	$17,731
Cost of Goods Sold	4,452	4,353	3,703	12,508
Gross Margin	4,928	(2)	297	5,223
Other Operating Costs	1,646	1,230.	1,146.	4,023
Operating Income	3,282	(1,232.)	(849.)	1,200

Then:

$$P = C + (P \times M)$$
$$P - P \times M = C$$
$$P(1 - M) = C$$
$$P = C/(1 - M)$$

Since:

$$C = \$50 \text{ and } M = 40\% \text{ or } 0.4,$$
$$P = 50/(1 - 0.4) = 50/0.6 = \$83.33.$$

Mechanically applying the 40% margin indicates the retail price should be $83.33. Frequently, a retailer would adjust the price to one more conventional in the business, perhaps $79.50 or $84.95.

Margins on Price and Margins on Cost

Percentage margin on selling price is related to percentage margin on cost. In some situations it is useful to convert from one to the other.

Let:

$$M^P = \text{Margin on price (as above)}$$
$$M^c = \text{Margin on cost}$$

Then:

$$P = C + (P \times M^P)$$
$$P - P \times M^P = C$$
$$P (1 - M^P) = C$$
$$P = C/(1 - M^P)$$

Now:

$$P = C + (C \times M^c)$$
$$P = C (1 + M^c)$$

Therefore:

$$1 + M^c = 1/(1 - M^P)$$
$$M^P = M^c/(1 + M^c)$$
$$M^c = M^P/(1 - M^P)$$

From the previous example,

$$M^P = 40\%;$$

Thus

$$M^c = 0.4/(1 - 0.4) = 0.4/ 0.6 = 0.66 \text{ or } 66\%.$$

Multiple Intermediaries

Suppose a manufacturer makes a product and sells to a wholesaler; the wholesaler resells the product to a retailer that resells it to a consumer. Each of these parties adopts the same convention, and margin is computed as a percentage of the selling price. Suppose the manufacturer's cost is $192 and its margin is $48. (The wholesaler's cost is

$192 + $48 = $240.) The wholesaler resells the item to a retailer for $300; the retailer takes a 45% margin. A number of questions can be asked of this situation.

1. What is the manufacturer's margin? From the earlier section:

$$P = C + (P \times M)$$
$$M = (P - C)/P$$
$$= (240 - 192)/240$$
$$= 48/240 = 0.2 \text{ (or 20\%)}$$

2. What is the manufacturer's markup on cost?

$$M^c = 48/192 = 0.25 \text{ (or 25\%)}$$

3. What is the wholesaler's margin? From 1 above:

$$M = (P - C)/P$$
$$= (300 - 240)/300 = 0.2 \text{ (or 20\%)}$$

4. What price does the retailer set? From the earlier section:

$$P = C/(1 - M)$$
$$= 300/(1 - 0.45) = 300/0.55 = $545$$

Note that the manufacturer's price is the wholesaler's cost; the wholesaler's price is the retailer's cost.

Target Prices

Manufacturers frequently set their prices to wholesalers in such a way to attain a target retail price. For example, suppose the manufacturer knows that the standard retail margin is 50% and the standard wholesaler margin is 25%. What price should the manufacturer set to assure a target retail price of $600?

1. What is the retailer's cost (also the wholesaler's price)? From the earlier section:

$$P = C/(1 - M) \text{ or } C = P(1 - M)$$
$$C = 600 (1 - 0.5) = 600 \times 0.5 = $300$$

2. What is the wholesaler's cost (also the manufacturer's price)? From the earlier section:

$$P = C/(1 - M) \text{ or } C = P(1 - M)$$
$$C = 300(1 - 0.25) = 300 \times 0.75 = $225$$

3. The manufacturer must set a price of $225.

Target retail prices are also important for retailers who want to maintain a price line. For example, a retailer may have a line of goods that sells at $19.95. Suppose retail margins are 50%, implying that wholesale prices are about $10. If wholesale prices increase to $12, applying the standard retail margin of 50% will lead to a retail price of $24. Rather than accept the increase, the retailer can shop around for a similar, perhaps slightly inferior product at $10, to maintain the $19.95 price line.

Inventory Turnover

In many organizations, the fundamental measure of profitability is return on investment (ROI). To calculate ROI, the concept of turnover must be added to the concept of margin. Thus a product that has a 50% margin might be far less profitable than a product with a 10% margin if far fewer of the 50% margin item are sold.

Turnover is the number of times the average inventory of a product is sold during the year. There are basically three methods of calculating turnover (or stockturn) and each gives approximately the same result:

1. Cost of Goods Sold/Average Inventory at Cost;
2. Net Sales/Average Inventory at Selling Price;
3. Sales (in units)/Average Inventory (in units).

Suppose the cost of goods sold for one year was $1.0 million. Inventory at cost at the beginning of the year was $250,000; at the end of the year it was $150,000.

$$\text{Average inventory} = (250,000 + 150,000)/2 = \$200,000$$

$$\text{Inventory turnover} = \$1,000,000/200,000 = 5$$

Turnover is an especially important control figure in retailing and wholesaling. A jeweler's turnover might be one or two times per year while the produce department of a grocery store that sells fresh fruit and vegetables might have inventory turns of forty or fifty times per year.

Inventory Turnover and Return on Investment

Return on Investment (ROI) is the fundamental measure of profitability for many businesses.

$$\text{ROI} = \text{Profit/Investment}$$

This equation can be modified by inserting sales on both the top and bottom line of the equation. Thus:

$$\text{ROI} = \text{Profit/Sales} \times \text{Sales/Investment}$$

For some businesses, such as retailing and wholesaling, inventory is a large component of total investment. If the inventory component of investment is the focus, the components of the ROI equation can be restated in more familiar terms:

$$\text{Profit/Sales} = \text{Margin; Sales/Investment} = \text{Inventory Turns;}$$

Thus:

$$\text{ROI} = \text{Margin} \times \text{Inventory Turns}$$

Consider a business (like a supermarket), where average margin is 2% and inventory turns is 25 times per year. Although the margin is extremely low (2%), the ROI is much healthier:

$$\text{ROI} = 2\% \times 25 = 50\%.$$

In considering the profitability of business with high inventory costs, both margin and inventory turns must be considered in assessing profitability.

Section 3: Shareholder Value Analysis

In many major companies, the shareholder value concept has supplemented concern with accounting profit and managers are increasing evaluated (and rewarded) on the basis of "value creation."

The acronym EVA™, standing for Economic Value Added,[4] best embodies the value creation concept. It may be simply defined as:

$$\text{EVA} = \text{Sales} - \text{Operating Expenses (incl. tax)} - $$
$$\text{Financing Expenses (cost of capital} \times \text{capital employed)}[5]$$

In simple English, no customer, product, or investment can contribute to increased shareholder wealth if its after-tax accounting profit is less than imputed cost of capital employed. Although application of the EVA concept involves several nuances, once the firm's cost of capital has been estimated,[6] its use can be illustrated quite simply.

This illustration focuses on the Income Statement for Product A in Appendix Table 9. It was determined that some of the allocated overhead (indirect fixed costs) would continue if the product were dropped. As a result, the decrease in accounting profit from dropping Product A would be $3.05 million rather than the $1.4 million reported as net profit before taxes.

If this same income was examined in shareholder value terms, a different picture emerges. Since the firm as a whole is profitable, Product A's profit is subject to tax. The rules under which profits are calculated for tax purposes are set by governments, but in general are based upon a full cost accounting philosophy. Applying a corporate tax rate of, say, 35%:

- Product A produces after-tax operating profit of: $1,400,000 − (0.35 × 1,400,000) = $910,000.

If the firm's cost of capital was estimated at 14%, and assume total capital (fixed and working) associated with producing and selling product A is $8,000,000:

- Product A's financing expense = $8,000,000 × 0.14 = $1.12 million.
- Product A appears to be value destroying: ($1,120,000 > $910,000), rather than value creating.

This simple example also illustrates some of the issues involved in using the shareholder value concept. For example, financial accounting data was used to calculate both the profit and the capital associated with product A. Thus, EVA calculations will be inaccurate if indirect fixed costs are being charged against the product.

Similarly, the net book value of assets is typically used to calculate the capital employed by the business, product or customer being analyzed. Thus assumptions about depreciation and asset replacement costs can further confound the EVA calculation. Stern Stewart and Co., a major proponent of EVA, recommends circumventing the problem of assigning book or market asset values to the asset base by focusing on year-to-year changes in EVA.[7]

More generally, the example serves to illustrate how even a well-acknowledged, meritorious concept must be subject to considerable thought and analysis before it is applied, or its use may be counter-productive. Stewart, one of EVA's major proponents, claims his firm has identified no fewer than 164 measurement issues associated with application of EVA,[8] a sufficiently large number to introduce caution into simplistic application of the shareholder value concept.

Section 4: Financial Analysis Problems in Marketing

1. A manufacturer sells an item for $100. What would be the final price to the consumer if wholesalers take a 20% markup and retailers take a 40% markup?
2. The price structure of an industry gives a 35% markup to retailers and 12% to wholesalers. The retail price is $20.00. The manufacturer's cost is $9.84.
   a) What is the wholesale price?
   b) What is the manufacturer's price?
   c) What is the manufacturer's gross margin?
   d) What is the manufacturer's gross margin percentage?
   e) What is the retailer's markup on cost?
   f) What is the wholesaler's markup on cost?
3a. What percentage markups on cost are equivalent to the following percentage markups on selling price: 20%, 37.5%, 50%, 66.6%?
3b. What percentage markups on selling price are the following percentage markups on cost: 33.3%, 20%, 40%, 50%?
4. A manufacturer of household appliances distributes its products through wholesalers and retailers. The retail selling price is $250; the manufacturing cost, $100. The retail markup is 40%, the wholesale markup, 25%. (In practice the manufacturer would price the item as: List price, $250, less 40%, 25%).
   a) What is the cost to the wholesaler? Retailer?
   b) What percentage markup does the manufacturer take?
5. Compute the stockturn rate from the following figures:

Cost of Goods Sold	$189,000
Beginning Inventory at Cost	19,600
Ending Inventory at Cost	22,400

6. Given a stockturn rate of 11 and average inventory at selling price of $34,000, find net sales.
7. Calculate the breakeven point. Estimated expenses are as follows:

General and Administrative	$120,000
Taxes	14,000
Salaries	120,000
Lease Payments	7,000
Advertising	17,000
Total	$278,000

Estimated unit variable cost is $4.11, estimated manufacturer's price is $5.09.

8. The Apex Company estimates first year fixed costs at $50,000 and variable costs at 70% of sales. Sales are expected to reach $200,000. What is the BEP? Expected profit?

9. Total fixed costs are $100,000 and total variable costs are $200,000 at an output of 10,000 units.
   a) What are the probable total fixed costs and total variable costs at an output of 20,000 units?
   b) What are the average fixed costs, average variable costs, and average costs at these two levels?

10. Compute the average inventory at cost of a firm having a stockturn rate of three times, net sales of $2,700,000, and an average gross margin of 25%.

11. What is the manufacturer's breakeven point in number of units for a type of plastic container selling at retail for $1.20 with a retail margin of 38%, and a wholesale margin of 15%. The manufacturer's variable costs per unit are $0.3124; fixed costs total $50,016.

12. A chain of nine hardware stores reports the following earnings. What is the chain's stockturn?

Gross Sales	$2,150,000
Returns and Allowances	150,000
Net Sales	2,000,000
Opening Inventory (Cost)	256,000
Billed Purchases	1,170,000
Cash Discounts	23,400
Net Purchases	1,146,600
Inbound Transport	21,400
Purchases at Net Cost Delivered	1,168,000
Total Cost of Goods Handled	1,424,000
Closing Inventory (Cost)	224,000
Cost of Goods Sold	1,200,000
Gross Operating Margin	800,000
General and Administrative Expense	660,000
Net Profit Before Tax	140,000

Section 5: Solutions to Financial Analysis Problems in Marketing

1. Wholesale price = $100/(1 − 0.20) = 100/0.8 = $125
   Retail price = $125/(1 − 0.4) = 125/0.6 = $208

2. a) Wholesale price = $20.00 × 0.65 = $13.00
   b) Manufacturer's price = $13.00 × 0.88 = $11.44
   c) Manufacturer's gross margin = $11.44 − 9.84 = $1.60
   d) Manufacturer's gross margin percentage = 1.60 × (100/9.84) = 16.3%

e) Retailer's markup on cost = $(20-13) \times 100/13 = \underline{53.8\%}$
f) Wholesaler's markup on cost = $(13-11.44) \times (100/11.44) = \underline{13.6\%}$

3. a) Percentage markups on cost = 25, 60, 100, 200
   b) Percentage markups on selling price = 25, 16.67, 28.6, 33.33
4. a) Wholesale price (price to retailer) = $250 \times (1 - 0.4) = \underline{\$150}$
   Manufacturer's price (price to wholesaler) = $150 \times (1 - 0.25) = \underline{\$112.50}$
   b) Manufacturer's percent markup = $(112.50-100) \times 100/112.50 = \underline{11\%}$
5. Beginning inventory $19,600
   Ending inventory $\underline{22,400}$
                                  42,000
   Average inventory   21,000
       Stockturn = 189,000/21,000 = $\underline{9 \text{ times}}$
6. Net sales = $34,000 \times 11 = \underline{\$374,000}$
7. BEP = $278,000/(5.09 - 4.11) = 278,000/0.98 = \underline{284,000 \text{ units}}$ (approximately)

8. Dollar BEP = $50,000/(1 - 0.7) = \underline{\$167,000}$

   Pro Forma Variable Budget

Sales	$200,000
Costs:	
Fixed	50,000
Variable	140,000
	$\underline{190,000}$
Profit	$\underline{10,000}$

9.

Output	10,000 units	20,000 units
TFC	$100,000	$100,000
TVC	$\underline{200,000}$	$\underline{400,000}$
TC	$300,000	$500,000
Average FC (per unit)	$10	$5
Average VC (per unit)	$20	$20
Average cost	$30	$25

10. Cost of goods sold = $2,700,000 \times (0.75) = \$2,025,000$
    $2,025,000/$ Average inventory at cost = Stockturns = 3
    Average inventory at cost = $\underline{\$675,000}$
11.

Retail selling price	$1.20
Retail margin (38%)	$\underline{0.456}$
Wholesale selling price	0.744
Wholesale margin (15%)	$\underline{0.112}$
Manufacturer's selling price	0.632
Manufacturer's variable cost	$\underline{0.312}$
Unit contribution	0.320

    BEP = $50,016/0.32 = \underline{156,300 \text{ units}}$
12. Cost of goods sold = $1,200,000
    Average inventory at cost = $(256,000 + 224,000)/2 = 240,000$
    Stockturn = $1,200,000/ 240,000 = \underline{5 \text{ times}}$

ENDNOTES

1. These diagrams are simplified versions of fixed and variable costs. In general, variable costs do not follow a perfect straight line relationship. Furthermore, fixed costs are generally fixed only over some volume range; they typically increase in a step-function fashion.

2. In many textbooks, breakeven charts are drawn with the fixed costs shown as a horizontal line and the variable cost line built off the fixed cost base. The preferred method of display given here shows pictorially how increasing sales provides increasing variable margin that eventually meets and exceeds fixed costs.

3. For example, product batches might be made more frequently for Accounts 2 and 3; these accounts also might order different versions of particular products that require greater processing.

4. For more detail see G.B. Stewart III, *Journal of Applied Corporate Finance*, 7 (Summer 1994), 71-84.

5. *ibid*, p.76.

6. Interested readers can pursue this topic in any contemporary finance text, such as J.C. Van Horne, *Financial Management and Policy*, Englewood Cliffs, NJ: Prentice Hall, 1995.

7. *ibid*, p.77.

8. *ibid*, p.73.

Glossary

Brand Equity   This is a two-part concept, consisting of organizational brand equity and customer brand equity. *Customer brand equity* is the value that an individual customer receives (perceives) from a branded product or service compared with the value received (perceived) from an identical unbranded (generic) product or service. *Organizational Brand Equity* is the value that an organization receives from a branded product or service compared with the value received from an identical unbranded product or service. This value can, in theory, be assessed by the discounted present value of the cash flows from the branded versus unbranded variant, and is dependent upon the customer-attracting or customer-repelling properties of the brand.

Branding   The act of associating a distinguishing name and/or symbol with an individual product (service), lines of products (services), or an organization.

Business Environment   A term used quite broadly to describe the conditions under which a firm does business. It is typically used to describe conditions not directly under the control of the firm, although in particular instances (such as influencing regulatory legislation) there may be exceptions.

Capital Market   The market for long-term financial instruments.

Complementer   Any organization (other than customers) whose activities have a positive impact on the firm's sales

Differential Advantage   A net perceived benefit or cluster of benefits, offered to a sizable group of customers, which they value and are willing to pay for, but cannot get, or believe they cannot get, elsewhere.

External Orientation   Describes a company culture that encourages looking outward to focus attention on customers, competitors, and broader environmental variables, rather than focusing internally, on products and processes.

Gaming   Initially developed by operation researchers working on problems of military strategy. Gaming is concerned with the generation and selection of strategy options, based on the firm's objectives and resources, considering the strategy options available to competitors.

Integrated Communications   Integrated communications refers to using all the various communications tools available to the firm in a coordinated and consistent manner to provide maximum impact in pursuit of the firm's goals.

Internal Orientation   See *external orientation* above.

Market Segment   A market segment comprises a group of current or potential customers that seek similar sets of benefits with similar levels of priority.

Marketing Mix   The tools traditionally viewed as available to design the marketing offer, comprising the elements of product, place, promotion and price, now typically enhanced with service. *Product benefits* are delivered to satisfy customer needs; they are designed into the product, the package, and so forth. *Place* (or *location*) benefits concern the time and place convenience of securing the product/service. *Promotion,* embracing both personal and impersonal communications, is the means by which the firm informs customers that product, service and location benefits are being offered and persuades them to buy. However, for branded products, communication adds value in and of itself because the reassurance, imagery, status, and related customer satisfaction delivered by communications is integral to what the customer buys. *Price* is the net monetary outlay that, relative to customers' perceptions of the benefits received, determines the net value they receive. *Services* included in the offer may be provided by the brand owner, an intermediary, or some combination, and may be received before or after purchase.

Monitor and Control Function   Describes the activities in which managers engage to try to ensure that the firm achieves the best possible results for shareholders. It subsumes consideration of the appropriateness of the strategy, its implementation, the results achieved, and the related managerial processes.

Principle of Selectivity and Concentration   In marketing, the two aspects embraced by the principle of selectivity and concentration are the careful and deliberate choice of target market segment (selectivity) and the focus of resources against that target (concentration).

Product Cannibalization   Refers to the sales of one product in a firm's product line leading to a reduction in the sales of another. This problem is usually most painful when the firm contemplates introducing a lower-margin product that is expected to lead to reduced sales of a higher-margin product.

Product Life Cycle   Product life cycles describe the evolution of sales (typically revenues, but sometimes units) of a product class (or category) and/or product form (or subcategory). Although individual examples may vary widely, regardless of life cycle type, graphs of product class or product form sales usually resemble classic S-shaped curves comprising:

> *Introduction:* sales volume initially low;
> *Early growth:* sales volume grows at an increasing rate;
> *Late growth:* sales volume grows at a decreasing rate;
> *Maturity:* sales volume averages close to GNP growth year-to-year; and
> *Decline:* sales volume eventually declines.

Because the life cycle concept is often used loosely, it is very important to clarify the operational definition used, whether it is at the class or form level, and whether it is defined in revenues or units.

Product Market   A term from economics, used to describe the market for goods and/or services, to be clearly distinguished from the capital market (see above).

Product Portfolio   The different product and/or service items offered to customers, for which the firm receives revenues.

Segment-of-one   A tongue-in-cheek term used to describe an individual customer. Since segments are made up of groups of customers, the term is deliberately ironic.

Segmentation Scheme   Used to describe a particular approach to segmenting a market.

Shareholder Value Philosophy   A management philosophy holding that management's job is to maximize returns (dividends and increased share price) to shareholders. It is generally contrasted with a focus on other organizational constituencies.

Strategic Pricing   Pricing decisions that involve making the fundamental price/value tradeoff for a particular product or service. Strategic pricing decisions typically arise when launching a new product, entering a new market, dealing with current or potential competitors and/or similar disruptions, and making major repositioning moves.

Tactical Pricing   Tactical pricing decisions typically deal with the implementation aspect of strategic pricing and embrace the specific pricing tools used to effect a particular pricing strategy. The term is also used to describe day-to-day individual pricing decisions that managers make, that individually may have limited financial impact, but that may be substantial in the aggregate.

Task Environment   Comprises suppliers, customers, and competitors, as distinguished from the general environment comprising governmental, economic, technological, physical, socio-cultural, and managerial process aspects of the environment.

Total Quality Management   Describes the full-fledged adoption of quality management procedures based heavily upon a customer-driven view.

Publications Cited in the Text

Academy of Management Journal—www.aom.pace.edu/amj

Academy of Management Review—www.aom.pace.edu/amr/

BusinessWeek—www.businessweek.com

California Management Review—www.haas.berkeley.edu/News/cmr

Economica—www.economica.ca

European Journal of Marketing—www.mcb.co.uk/cgi-bin/journal1/ejm

European Management Journal—http://sciserv.ub.uni-bielefeld.de/elsevier/02632373/

Financial Times—www.ft.com

Financial World—www.zagury.com

Fortune—www.fortune.com

Harvard Business Review—www.hbsp.harvard.edu/products/hbr

International Journal of Logistics Management—www.logisticssupplychain.org

International Marketing Review—www.mcb.co.uk/liblink/imr/jourhome.htm

Internet Magazine—www.internet-magazine.com

Internet World—www.internetworldnews.com

Journal of Advertising Research—http://www.arfsite.org/Webpages/JAR_pages/JAR_primary/jar_issues.htm

Journal of Applied Corporate Finance—www.sternstewart.com/journal/overview.shtml

Journal of Business Strategy—www.faulknergray.com/busstrat/jbs.html

Journal of Consumer Marketing—www.mcb.co.uk/liblink/jcm/jourhome.htm

Journal of Consumer Research—www.journals.uchicago.edu/JCR/home.html

Journal of Current Issues and Research in Advertising

Journal of Economic Theory and Organization

Journal of Economics and Management Strategy—http://netec.mcc.ac.uk/WebEc/Journal_of_Economics_and_Management_Strategy.html

Journal of Financial and Quantitative Analysis—www.depts.washington.edu/jfqa

Journal of Financial Economics—www.ssb.rochester.edu/fac/jfe/jfe.html

Journal of Law, Economics and Organization—www3.oup.co.uk/jleorg

Journal of Management Studies—http://www.blackwellpublishers.co.uk/journals/
JOMS/descript.htm

Journal of Marketing Research—www.ama.org/pubs/jmr

Journal of Marketing—www.ama.org/pubs/jm

Journal of Retailing—www.haas.berkeley.edu/jr

Journal of the Academy of Marketing Science—www.sagepub.co.uk/journals/
details/j0140.html

Management Accounting—http://www.rutgers.edu/Accounting/raw/ima/maraw.htm

Management Science—www.informs.org/Pubs/Mansci

Marketing Management—www.ama.org/pubs/mm

Marketing News—www.ama.org/pubs/mn

Marketing Science Institute—www.msi.org

Marketing Science—www.informs.org/Pubs/Marketing

Milwaukee Journal Sentinel—www.jsonline.com

New Straits Times—www.nstpi.com.my

Organizational Psychology

Psychological Review—www.apa.org/journals/rev.html

Quarterly Journal of Economics—http://www.jstor.org/journals/00335533.html

Sloan Management Review—www.mitsloan.mit.edu/smr

Strategic Management Journal—http://www.interscience.wiley.com/jpages/0143-2095/

The Australian—www.theaustralian.com.au

The Boston Herald—www.bostonherald.com

The Daily Telegraph—www.telegraph.co.uk

The Economist—www.economist.com

The McKinsey Quarterly—www.mckinseyquarterly.com

The New York Times—www.nytimes.com

The Sierra Club—www.sierraclub.org

The Times—www.the-times.co.uk

The Wall Street Journal—www.wsj.com

Time—www.time.com

U.S. News and World Report—www.usnews.com

USA Today—www.usatoday.com

Brand/Company Index

Subject Index

A

ABC. *See* Activity based costing
Acceptable currency, 504
Accounting systems, 69
Acquisitions, 38, 120, 161–163, 172
Activity based costing (ABC), 544
Adopter groups, 355
Advertisements, 387
Advertising
  budgets for, 385–386
  celebrity endorsement in, 381
  comparative, 378
  execution style, 377–378
  fear in, 381
  hierarchy-of-effects models, 376
  humor in, 378
  language of, 381–382
  media selection and timing, 382
  media strategy goals, 382–383
  message content, 377
  non-personal, 374–388
  objectives, 375–376
  setting objectives, 376–378
  spending types, 387
  strategy elements, 375
  target audience, 375
  testing levels, 387
  testing programs, 387–388
  virtual, 378–381
Age distribution, 36
Allowances, 503
Alternatives, evaluation of, 96–99
Anarchy, 565
Archetypes, innovation and customer,
  338–340
Assets, balance sheet and, 3
Assorting, 577
  irrelevance of, 578
Auctions, 509
Awareness set, 96

B

Barriers
  government-imposed, 238
  to introduction, 238–239

Barter, 504
BDT. *See* Behavioral decision theory
Behavioral decision theory (BDT), 98
Benchmarking, 551
Benefits
  choice and substantiation of, 411–412
  communicating to customers, 412
  customers as, 95–96
  dimensions of, 93–96
  economic, 93
  features *vs.,* 92
  functional, 92
  potential *vs.* actual, 94–95
  psychological, 92–93
Bernays, Edward L., 389
Boundary-spanning, 13
Brand equity. *See also* Branding;
  Brands
  associations, 286
  awareness, 286
  balanced scorecard, 287
  conjoint analysis, 287
  customer, 279–281, 286–287
  customer satisfaction, 286
  definition of, 278
  dollar metric measurement, 287
  leveraging customer, 292–295
  loyalty, 286
  measurement methods, 283–287
  measuring, 282–287
  negative, 279
  organizational, 278–279, 282–286
  organizational and customer differ-
    ence, 281
  organizational and customer relation-
    ship, 280–281
  perceived quality, 286
Branding, 571–572. *See also* Brand
  equity; Brands
  decisions, 10
  global, 296
  levels of, 274
  production and, 275
  strategies, 289–290
  successful outcomes, 277

  tree, 298
Brand(s). *See also* Brand equity;
  Branding
  associations, 291, 294
  buyers and, 276–277
  definition of, 274
  extensions, 292–295
  function of, 276–277
  global portfolios, 285
  health of, 287–288
  leading U.S., 280
  loyalty to, 278
  management issues, 288–298
  most valuable global, 284–285
  reposition of, 291
  resilience of, 278
  revitalization of, 290–295
  sellers and, 277
  signifiers of, 275
  strength of, 282
  valuation of, 282
B2B. *See* Business–to–Business
B2C. *See* Business–to–Consumer
Budgeting decisions, 60
Bulk breaking, 577
  irrelevance of, 578
Bundling, 503, 507
Business environment, 28–34
  economic influences, 29–30
  general dimensions of, 28
  governmental influences, 29
  interaction of elements, 34–35
  international, 29–30
  managerial process, 33–34
  physical effects of, 31–32
  socio-cultural, 32–33
  technological influences, 30–31
Business organization, 67
Business purpose, 337
Business strengths analysis, 195–198
Business-to-Business (B2B), 566
  electronic commerce cost savings,
    567
Business-to-Consumer (B2C), 566
Business Week, 561

Buybacks, 503, 504
Buyers, 88
  brands and, 276–277

C
Capital
  markets, 3–5
  substitution for labor, 464
Career paths, 531
Cash Management Accounts (CMAs),
    156, 238
CEO. *See* Chief executive officer
CFO. *See* Chief financial officer
Champion, 88
Change, resistance to, 68
Chief executive officer (CEO), 87
Chief financial officer (CFO), 87
Choice, evaluation of, 96–99
Clusters, characterization of, 187–188
CMAs. *See* Cash Management
    Accounts
Coase, Ronald, 564
Coasian economics, 564
COGS. *See* Cost(s), of goods sold
Commoditization, 573–574
Communication
  challenges, 364–365
  definitions of tools, 366
  democracy, 565
  effort goals, 369–370
  flows between innovation and cus-
    tomers, 338
  integration, 372–374
  non-personal, 389–392, 392–393
  non-personal advertising, 374–388
  non-personal direct marketing,
    388–389
  objectives, 370–372
  proaction in, 389–390
  product/market targets of, 367–369
  publicity for, 389–392
  public relations and, 389–392
  quasi-personal, 366–367
  responding to problems in, 391
  sales promotion in, 392–393
  strategy development in, 367–372
  targets of, 369–370
  tools of, 365
  unintended consequences of,
    391–392
  web and marketing, 580–581
  web conversion process and measure-
    ment performance, 582
  word-of-mouth, 365–366

Company-market fit, 159
Compatibility, 158
Competition. *See also* Competitors
  non-traditional, 45
  pricing strategy and, 494–499
  response to, 495–496
  spectrum of direct/indirect, 125
  supply chain of, 123–124
Competitive advantage, 16, 205–206
Competitive assessment analysis,
    129–130
Competitive data, 137
Competitive dynamics, 125–127
Competitive equivalence pricing, 499
Competitive frameworks, alternative,
    124–125
Competitive position
  follower, 244–246
  retreat, 246
  second place, 245
Competitive response, 499
Competitive scenarios, 132–133
Competitive strategic options
  business characteristics, 241
  early stage, 241–246
  late growth stage, 246–247
  leadership, 241–244
  market characteristics, 241
  market segment retreat, 243
  market exit, 243–244
  maturity stage, 258–259
  product characteristics, 241
Competitive targets, 291
Competitive threats, 126–127
Competitors, 38. *See also* Competition
  capabilities of, 127–129
  de novo start-ups, 121
  framework for describing, 128
  geographic expansion of, 121
  identifying, 118–119
  indirect, 122
  management of, 134
  new direct entrants, 121–122
  new distribution channels for,
    121–122
  ownership changes in direct, 120–121
  projection strategy of, 131–133
  response to, 496–497
  securing insight on, 135
  status quo of, 119–120
  strategic alliances with, 122
  strategic options of, 129–131
Complementarity, negative and positive,
    319

Complementers
  competitors as, 139–140
  defined, 137
  firms as, 138–139
  independent organizations as, 138
Concentration, 15
  principle of, 14–15
Concession, 15
Conflict, power and, 435–436
Conjoint analysis, 115–116
Consideration set, 96
Consumer Product Safety Commission,
    327
Consumer purchase decision process
  cognitive resources of, 102
  culture of, 99–100
  economic resources and, 102
  environmental influences and,
    99–101
  family and, 101
  individual factors in, 102–103
  personal influence and, 101
  situational factors of, 101
  social class and, 100–101
  time availability for, 102
Consumers
  indirect channels to, 441–442
  knowledge of, 36–37
  product category perceptions of, 294
  reaching, 439–441
  roles of, 89–90
Consumer-to-Business (C2B), 566
Consumer-to-Consumer (C2C), 566
Contingency planning, 41–42
Continue options, 264–265
Contract manufacturing, 275
Control
  execution of, 14
  key principles of, 540
  managerial, 550–553
Coordination, of strategies, 206–208
Cost(s)
  categories of, 94
  cutting, 54–55
  fixed, 492
  of goods sold (COGS), 325
  -plus pricing, 491–493, 498–499
  reduction of, 67–68, 165–166
  rules of, 493–494
  transaction reduction, 94
Coupons, cents-off, 392
Creativity, insufficient, 256–258
Credit extension, 66–67